ONE WAY
TICKET
TO BERLIN

ONE WAY TICKET TO BERLIN

A Day in the Life
of the Mighty Eighth

A Sequel to *Not Home for Christmas*

Collected and Compiled
by
JOHN MEURS

QUAIL RIDGE PRESS

Library of Congress Cataloging-in-Publication Data

Names: Meurs, John, compiler.
Title: One way ticket to Berlin : a day in the life of the Mighty Eighth / collected
and compiled by John Meurs.
Other titles: Day in the life of the Mighty Eighth
Description: Brandon, MS : Quail Ridge Press, 2016.
Identifiers: LCCN 2016013491 I ISBN 9781938879197
Subjects: LCSH: United States. Army Air Forces. Air Force, 8th--History. I World
War, 1939-1945—Aerial operations, American. I World War, 1939-1945—Personal
narratives, American. I World War, 1939-1945—Campaigns—Germany. I United
States. Army Air Forces--Airmen--Biography. I Bombing, Aerial—Germany—
History—20th century.
Classification: LCC D790.22 8th .O54 2016 I DDC 940.54/4973--dc23
LC record available at http://lccn.loc.gov/2016013491

ISBN: 978-1-938879-19-7

Printed in the United States of America

First printing, July 2016

Quail Ridge Press
P. O. Box 123 • Brandon, MS 39043
info@quailridge.com • www.quailridge.com
1-800-343-1583

DEDICATION

This book is dedicated to
all the brave young men of the 8th USAAF
who lost their lives over Europe
in World War II.

CONTENTS

Contents

Contents

PUBLISHER'S NOTE

In 2010, we published *Not Home for Christmas*, John Meurs' first book about a specific bombing mission over Germany by the Mighty Eight in November, 1944. This book had a personal connection for me as my brother was a crew member of one of the planes that was shot down on this mission. Raymond was killed when his plane crashed south of Hannover.

So many people, including myself, expressed appreciation for the narrative and first-person accounts that John had compiled and recorded in *Not Home for Christmas* that I was pleased to offer him publication for his new book *One Way Ticket to Berlin*.

This sequel is almost twice as large as his first book, and records more of the war-time experiences these young men faced and the courage in which they faced them. It is a honor to be able to provide a permanent written record of their patriotism, heroism and sacrifice.

Thanks again, John.

> *Barney McKee*
> *Quail Ridge Press*
> *August, 2016*

The Publisher's Note that was included in *Not Home for Christmas* is reproduced below. This will provide some background on how the series was developed.

• • •

I am the brother of one of the airmen whose tragic story is one of the many included in this book (Chapter 17). Raymond was the oldest of six in our family, and I was the youngest. He was born October 14, 1919; I was born on October 16th, eighteen years later. Our home was a small farm near Folsom, Louisiana.

I have very few memories of my brother but I distinctly remember the day my mother received the telegram bringing the news that Raymond was missing in action. Our father had died a few years earlier of a heart attack, and our family had moved to Baton Rouge. We were visiting in the country when the telegram arrived at our house in Baton Rouge. Since we were not home, our neighbor contacted my aunt who called my two sisters who worked for Esso (Exxon). They were given gas rations to travel the sixty miles to bring the sad news to our mother.

In 1948, Raymond's remains were shipped home. The initial burial had been in a cemetery in Oerie, Germany, but his remains were later reinterred in a military cemetery in Baton Rouge. This day stands out in my mind because so many relatives came to the memorial service.

Raymond and Barney McKee

It was only then that I fully realized—Raymond was not coming back.

The son my brother never knew, Raymond, Jr. was born in April of 1945. It was my nephew who John Meurs eventually located in his research, and how I became aware of this book. I was immediately impressed and appreciative of the tremendous task he had undertaken to pay tribute to the Americans who had given so much to liberate his country. John's book has enabled me to gain some understanding of what these young men experienced. Try as I might, I still cannot fathom what it was like to be in a metal cylinder at 30,000 feet with the noise, wind, and cold of an open plane while being shot at from below and all around.

Although the small publishing company I own publishes primarily regional books and cookbooks, it was an honor to offer publishing assistance to John so that *Not Home for Christmas* could be recorded and made available to the many families of the crew members.

All revenue received from the sale of this book will be used to pay the manufacturing cost plus expenses related to fulfillment and shipping. Although he has not requested any kind of royalty or other compensation, any remaining revenue will go to John for his years of dedicated effort to research and record the stories included in his book.

John and I have exchanged many emails and have come to know each other to some degree. I would like to meet him in person, but, at our advanced age, this may not happen. I, therefore, would like to take this opportunity to express my deepest gratitude and thanks to him for compiling this book, and the tribute it represents.

I'm sure I speak for the many families and friends of the other crew members as well. Thanks, John.

Barney McKee
Quail Ridge Press
May, 2009

Postscript to second edition: Actually, John and I did meet when I visited him and his wife Carien in Switzerland where he now lives. This visit was part of a trip my brother Larry and I, along with our sons Kevin and Shawn, made to Germany to view the site where our brother's plane had crashed in 1944. It was a deeply emotional and moving experience. We met two elderly men who as young boys had viewed the crash site and shared their vivid memories of the event along with actual parts of the plane they had collected over the years. We also met many other friendly and gracious German people, in particular Kim Gallop, our interpreter, and Thomas Pohl, whose family hosted us for a special lunch in Oerie.

November, 2010

INTRODUCTION

I was eight years old in the autumn of 1944, living with my mother, my brother and two sisters in a village called Apeldoorn in Nazi-occupied Holland. My parents were divorced and I was the "Benjamin" of the family. Ten years separated me from my older brother, and my two sisters were eight and nine years older.

Although the Germans were still patrolling our village, we expected that liberation was near. We were very happy when the Allied troops stormed the Normandy beaches and even more so when Paris was liberated, quickly followed by Brussels and Antwerp. We thought that liberation from the hated Germans was only a couple of days away, but the Allied advance came to a halt.

Then the British First Airborne dropped near Arnhem, a scant twenty miles south from Apeldoorn. In the days that followed we saw German armored units on their way to the front and long lines of German soldiers marching single-file along our street on their way to the Arnhem battlefield. One of them, a very young soldier, came to our door asking for a glass of water. While he was drinking my mother asked him, "Are you scared going into the battle" and he answered, "Very much so."

A couple of days later the first group of captured British para's passed in front of our house: young, healthy and cheerful guys guarded by a few old Wehrmacht soldiers. My two sisters were very attracted by their wine-red berets and offered to trade apples for these, but without success.

The Arnhem part of the Market-Garden airborne operation failed and the occupied part of Holland, north of the big rivers, entered into the most difficult phase—the "Hunger Winter"—in which thousands of civilians died of starvation. My family and I were lucky; we lived in the eastern part of the country where some food was still available, although my sisters daily rode hours on their bikes to ask farmers for food for our family. My brother, together with hundreds of thousands of other young Dutchmen, was in hiding to avoid forced labour in Germany. They were called "Onderduikers;" people living under the surface.

The Dutch resistance movement, or "Underground," was at its peak. Since uncensored news was scarce, illegal newspapers appeared all over the country. Some were professionally printed and distributed nation-wide, while others came out of hand-cranked stencil machines and served only small groups of people.

Perhaps the most important Underground activity was not only to find hiding places for the "Onderduikers," but also to provide them with ration coupons that allowed them to buy food. These coupons were either counterfeit or stolen from the food distribution offices. Some groups were experts at forging identity papers and German documents, while others were active in military espionage.

A quick look at the map shows that Holland is situated between east England, where most of the Allied bomber bases were located, and the heart of Germany. A lot of small Underground groups devoted themselves to picking up allied airmen who had bailed out over Holland, and helping them to return to England via Belgium, France, and Spain. These airmen were quickly passed on like hot potatoes along various escape routes. After D-Day, however, General Eisenhower ordered these airmen to stay put to wait for the advancing Allied troops, so more permanent hiding places had to be found.

My eldest sister Els was dating a boy named Joop Bitter, who lived alone with his widowed mother a few houses down the road from our house. He was an active member of an airmen assistance group, that numbered about ten people. You will meet Joop later in this book in connection with Bob Zercher a ball-turret gunner of the 452nd Bomb Group and Bill Moore, a pilot of the 467th.

In September 1944, two airmen were staying with Joop and his mother; the American Bob Zercher and an Englishman named Kenneth Ingram of the RAF. My sister Els saw them regularly. Bob was a sturdy, well-built man and Kenneth a small and slim guy, who looked almost like a girl.

Next to the Germans, the Dutch Underground had two other enemies: treason and indiscretion. For unknown reasons a new member of Joop's group went to the German *Sicherheits Dienst*—a security service comparable to the *Gestapo*—and handed them a list of the names and addresses of this group. The group members were quickly rounded up, but when the Germans entered Joop's house they encountered a big, unanticipated problem. Two Germans had come to arrest a young boy but were suddenly confronted by two adults they did not expect—the two airmen. In the confusion, Joop managed to escape and later returned to the house that night, but his mother had been arrested along with the Bob and Kenneth.

Two days later, on October 2, 1944, early in the morning, six Dutch members of the group and the two airmen were brought before an SS execution squad and shot. Who were these eight men?

Jan Barendsen, the eldest, was 62 years old. He had been an officer in the Royal Dutch Army and was the holder of the highest military order of the Netherlands. He had been active in various resistance groups before his capture. One of the Germans present at the execution mentioned after the war that shortly before the execution Jan opened his coat and started to sing the Dutch national anthem.

Wim Karreman, 19 years of age, was the youngest and lived with his parents. His ambition was to enter the Institute of Technology after the war.

Wim Aalders was 28 when he was executed.

Reinier van Gerrevink was 37 in 1944. He was a quiet and friendly man who certainly did not seek adventure when he joined the Underground. He was involved in intelligence, sending details of German troop movements in Holland to England via his own radio transmitter. He worked out the escape routes via Spain to England for Allied airmen, who had bailed out over Holland. His wife was also arrested by the Germans but was released after a couple of hours.

Jan Schut was 26 when he was executed. He was a member of the national police and his Underground activities started already in 1941. His father, a farmer, sheltered Jews until the end of the war and had built a hiding place for them under his cow shed. Like many members of the Dutch Underground Jan had a nickname, "Jan with the Motor Bike." As a policeman he had a motor bike that he used to transport confidential material around the country.

Hans Wijma, 27 years old, lived with his wife and a two-year-old son not far from my house. He had built a secret radio transmitter that was hidden in a concealed part of his attic.

Flight Sergeant Kenneth Ingram was 21 when he bailed over Holland from his RAF Lancaster on June 22, 1944. It was his 22nd mission over Germany. Two members of his crew died in the crash of their bomber, three were captured and three others, among them Kenneth Ingram, were taken under the wings of the Underground and found shelter in various homes in Apeldoorn. Kenneth stayed in the house of Joop Bitter until that house was raided by the Germans on September 30, 1944. When he faced his execution squad his last words were: "For King and Country."

Sergeant Robert Zercher was the ball-turret gunner on a B-17 of the 542nd Bomb Group. On Saturday, April 29, 1944, after a mission to Berlin, his damaged bomber made wheels-up landing in Holland. The whole crew walked away from their bomber and directly into the arms of the Underground, then went into hiding at various addresses in the country. They all survived the war with the exception of Bob Zercher.

Mrs. Juliana Catherina Bitter, Joop Bitter's mother, was 66 when the Germans dragged her from her house. She was sent to the Ravensbrück concentration camp for women in Germany where she died shortly before the camp was liberated by Allied troops in the Spring of 1945.

After the war a monument was unveiled at the execution site. Mrs. Bitter's name does not appear on the monument but, later a separate monument to honor her memory was added next to the main monument.

The eight people mentioned on the monument—six Dutchmen, an American, an Englishman, and a Dutch woman on the separate monument—were all comrades in arms. Because of them the people of the of the Netherlands and the other countries of western Europe have lived in peace and prosperity ever since.

Originally I wanted to write a book about these six Dutchmen and the two airmen. Later, however, as my research deepened, it became a book that told the story of all the American heavy bomber crews who, like Bob Zercher and his comrades, did not return to their bases on that fateful Saturday in April, 1944. They each had a *One Way Ticket to Berlin*.

Rüti ZH, Switzerland, 2015

***

Author John Meurs at the monument site with the granddaughter of Mrs. Bitter.

ROLL OF HONOR

Members of the 8th USAAF (heavy bombers)
Missing in Action on
Saturday, April 29, 1944

NAME	RANK	BG	BS	POS.	STATUS*	SERIAL	CHAPTER
Warren J. Adams	S/Sgt.	306	368	E	KIA	14096249	13
Robert W. Adams	2Lt.	448	715	B	POW	0-684122	49
George H. Adams	S/Sgt.	385	551	E	KIA	36267771	19
Robert W. Adams	Sgt.	388	560	BT	POW	37508772	22
Vernon B. Albares	Sgt.	95	336	WG	POW	35584971	9
Linton A. Allen	2Lt.	467	790	N	POW	0-755209	63
Henry E. Allen	S/Sgt.	467	788	BT	POW	14141180	64
William H. Allen Jr.	2Lt.	447	708	N	KIA	0-757442	40
Robert W. Allen	2Lt.	447	710	CO	POW	0-817813	44
Harry T. Ambrosini	T/Sgt.	448	715	E	KIA	19003327	52
Lawrence E. Anderson	2Lt.	448	712	CP	POW	0-806031	48
Ralph C. Andrews Jr.	S/Sgt.	384	545	RO	POW	14109029	14
Harold L. Andrews	S/Sgt.	392	578	WG	POW	17146344	31
Francis J. Andrews	2Lt.	385	551	N	POW	0-723921	19
John B. Angus	S/Sgt.	467	790	TG	POW	11007263	63
James R. Anslow	S/Sgt.	467	788	RO	EVD	15354506	64
Alfred P. Archambeau	Sgt.	392	579	WG	KIA	20101348	32
Jack Arluck	Sgt.	448	715	WG	KIA	33426161	53
Glenn A. Arndt	2Lt.	401	614	B	KIA	0-685070	34
Vernon E. Arnold	2Lt.	447	708	CP	KIA	0-818806	41
William D. Arthur	2Lt.	44	506	B	RTD	0-690535	3
Lloyd J. Arthur	Sgt.	447	708	BT	KIA	37468416	38
Norbert J. Arvin	S/Sgt.	447	708	WG	POW	15332240	37
Duane E. Atley	2Lt.	467	790	B	KIA	0-541847	63
Charles W. Avona	2Lt.	385	550	CP	KIA	0-818089	17
John R. Baas	Sgt.	452	728	RO	POW	17097724	54
Vernon M. Baize	S/Sgt.	467	790	RO	POW	16160533	63
Lester S. Baker	S/Sgt.	446	706	WG	POW	11114360	36
Robert E. Barney	1Lt.	385	550	P	POW	0-746248	16
Howard N. Barr	2Lt.	447	708	CP	KIA	0-693732	40
Clarence S. Barsuk	2Lt.	401	614	CP	EVD	0-755268	34
Thomas L. Bartley	Sgt.	44	506	WG	RTD	38274340	3
Fount B. Bartley	Sgt.	44	506	WG	RTD	38274336	3
Louis S. Beckett	2Lt.	458	752	B	INT	0-752833	59
George W. Beckner	2Lt.	385	551	CP	POW	0-163499	20
Samuel Thomas C. Bell Jr.	S/Sgt.	458	752	RO	INT	15334764	59

*KIA: Killed in Action; POW: Prisoner of War; EVD: "Evaded" (hidden by the Dutch underground); RTD: Returned to Duty; INT: Interred

Name	Rank	BG	BS	Pos.	Status	Serial	Chapter
Irving Bellitt	Sgt.	303	427	WG	KIA	32208988	12
John A. Benedict	2Lt.	447	708	CP	POW	0-1036845	39
Frank A. Bennett	Sgt.	392	577	WG	POW	33110100	29
George R. Bentley	S/Sgt.	447	708	TG	KIA	39560146	40
Emile Bianchi	S/Sgt.	91	322	R	POW	11105903	4
Kenneth G. Biedinger	Sgt.	92	326	TG	POW	39409889	6
Frank L. Billiter	2Lt.	467	790	CP	POW	0-541846	63
Lowell T. Birdwell	S/Sgt.	385	551	BT	POW	18007605	21
Robert R. Bishop	2Lt.	392	578	P	KIA	0-682775	30
Harry J. Blair Jr.	Sgt.	401	614	TG	EVD	33440210	34
Euclid F. Blanchard	S/Sgt.	44	506	RO	RTD	11083941	3
Carl J. Blom	2Lt.	447	708	P	POW	0-807979	38
Willard C. Blomberg	Sgt.	92	326	E	POW	16076934	5
James T. Blong	Sgt.	392	578	E	KIA	36296588	30
John D. Bloznelis	2Lt.	389	564	N	KIA	0-735163	25
Robert L. Bobst	2Lt.	448	715	N	EVD	0-696051	52
Vito J. Bochicchio	2Lt.	466	787	B	POW	0-682047	61
Edward J. Bode	S/Sgt.	388	562	E	POW	18192470	23
Myron F. Boerschinger	S/Sgt.	389	564	WG	POW	39826475	24
Howard J. Bohle	2Lt.	303	427	P	POW	0-753184	11
Harry L. Boisclair	S/Sgt.	389	564	WG	RTD	14084140	25
John P. Bonnassiolle	Sgt.	392	578	WG	KIA	19140409	30
James R. Boucher	S/Sgt.	467	790	RO	KIA	35544768	62
Wendell Bourguignon	Sgt.	447	711	TG	POW	11110414	46
James A. Bouvier	2Lt.	384	545	P	POW	0-813841	14
Theodore E. Bower	Sgt.	388	560	WG	POW	20759425	22
James R. Boyd	S/Sgt.	447	708	BT	KIA	14158285	40
Jack Boykoff	2Lt.	448	715	N	POW	0-750177	49
Bernard J. Boyle	F/O	401	613	N	POW	T-123920	33
Solomon W. Brackman	Sgt.	401	614	WG	KIA	12031946	34
Allan J. Brady	2Lt.	447	711	B	POW	0-757648	46
Howard G. Brannen	Sgt.	92	326	WG	POW	35602805	5
Werner G. Braun	S/Sgt.	467	788	WG	POW	unknown	64
Anatole A. Briant	T/Sgt.	385	551	RO	POW	38172299	21
Thomas B. Brigham	1Lt.	446	706	N	POW	0-752477	36
Arthur J. Brisson	2Lt.	448	715	CP	POW	0-751983	53
Kenneth Broden	2Lt.	95	412	CP	POW	0-755511	10
Earl C. Brodrick	S/Sgt.	92	326	TT	EVD	31259456	6
Reed L. Brotzman	Sgt.	401	614	WG	KIA	33464646	34
John K. Brown	2Lt.	303	427	N	POW	0-699122	11
Charles G. Browne	S/Sgt.	466	787	BT	POW	19116027	61
Francis N. Brownson	S/Sgt.	447	708	RO	KIA	39410663	41
Chester Broyles Jr.	1Lt.	389	564	B	POW	0-671276	24
Ralph S. Bryant	Capt.	389	564	P	KIA	0-477192	25
Paul P. Bunchuk	2Lt.	91	322	N	POW	0-747076	4
Charles E. Buran	S/Sgt.	447	711	RO	POW	16116609	46
Jack N. Burch	S/Sgt.	385	550	WG	POW	33539700	16
John H. Burgelin	S/Sgt.	467	790	WG	POW	32835000	62

Name	Rank	BG	BS	Pos.	Status	Serial	Chapter
Clyde A. Burnette	S/Sgt.	448	713	WG	POW	14141825	49
Norman Bussell	S/Sgt.	447	708	RO	POW	34720238	39
Donald E. Butterfoss	2Lt.	401	613	P	POW	0-810818	33
Harold G. Buzzi	2Lt.	392	576	B	KIA	0-682061	27
Sanford A. Byer	T/Sgt.	385	550	E	POW	38009220	16
Manuel S. Cabellero	S/Sgt.	448	712	E	POW	38054502	48
Jimmy L. Cahoun	S/Sgt.	446	706	TG	KIA	34395707	36
Adrien E. Caignon	2Lt.	95	336	N	POW	0-708792	9
Carl M. Carlson	F/O	448	715	B	KIA	T-1686	53
Louis S. Carusello	S/Sgt.	91	322	BT	KIA	33417904	4
Harry W. Casey	1Lt.	389	564	N	KIA	0-735171	24
Ralph F. Casey	2Lt.	448	712	N	POW	0-691953	48
John W. Cathey	2Lt.	448	715	P	POW	0-808373	53
John J. Caulfield	2Lt.	392	576	N	KIA	0-757769	28
Philip R. Cavanaugh	2Lt.	452	729	B	EVD	0-757750	55
Daniel E. Chermak	S/Sgt.	390	571	WG	POW	13116729	26
Michael A. Chiodo	Sgt.	392	578	BT	KIA	35530766	30
John L. Chisholm	Cpl.	448	712	BT	KIA	38395834	48
Kenneth L. Chism	2Lt.	94	331	P	POW	0-686540	7
Cletus C. Clark	S/Sgt.	44	506	E	RTD	17157054	3
James G. Clark	1Lt.	448	712	P	KIA	0-796780	48
Webb C. Clarke	2Lt.	92	326	B	POW	0-665995	5
William F. Clarke	Sgt.	447	710	E	POW	33586583	44
Raymond L. Cohee	2Lt.	448	714	B	POW	0-752551	50
Jesse P. Collinson	T/Sgt.	385	549	BT	POW	32761676	15
George E. Compton	2Lt.	447	710	N	POW	0-687823	43
Edward H. Condon	2Lt.	467	790	B	KIA	0-668899	62
Carl M. Connell	2Lt.	385	551	CP	POW	0-683654	21
Edward G. Connelly	2Lt.	447	711	N	POW	0-702105	47
Sandy Conti	S/Sgt.	447	708	E	KIA	31254083	41
James J. Conway	2Lt.	447	710	B	POW	0-672941	43
Frank D. Coslett	1Lt.	467	788	N	EVD	0-801361	64
Abraham Cosmer	S/Sgt.	447	711	RO	POW	36454572	47
Franklynn V. Cotner	2Lt.	466	784	P	POW	0-813568	60
John I. Coulson	2Lt.	447	711	N	POW	0-698666	46
George G. Cox	Sgt.	44	67	WG	POW	15336328	1
Joseph D. Coyner	2Lt.	388	562	P	POW	0-812950	23
Gilbert B. Creath	S/Sgt.	385	550	BT	POW	19111079	17
Henry G. Crowley	2Lt.	390	571	CP	POW	0-751273	26
Thomas R. Culpepper	T/Sgt.	448	715	E	POW	14182050	49
John A. Cumpson	Sgt.	401	615	TG	POW	33408910	35
Louis W. Curio	S/Sgt.	448	712	BT	KIA	12120419	48
William J. Cusack Jr.	S/Sgt.	390	571	BT	POW	32473966	26
Richard Danckwerth Jr.	S/Sgt.	388	560	E	POW	32605686	22
George A. Daneau	S/Sgt.	448	713	NT	KIA	unknown	49
Robert W. Danford	S/Sgt.	392	578	G	POW	16160528	31
Culmer H. Darby	T/Sgt.	448	715	BT	POW	20304517	53
William A. Davidson	2Lt.	447	711	P	POW	0-686548	46

Name	Rank	BG	BS	Pos.	Status	Serial	Chapter
Jay L. Davis	2Lt.	44	67	B	POW	0-692481	1
Dudley W. Davis	2Lt.	447	708	N	POW	0-698672	38
Max A. Davison	1Lt.	453	732	P	RTD	0-729821	57
Arthur C. Delclisur	1Lt.	389	564	B	KIA	0-688513	25
Manuel C. DeLeon	Sgt.	453	734	BT	KIA	18060438	58
Michael Dencavage	S/Sgt.	452	729	E	EVD	36175982	55
Laurin M. Derosier	2Lt.	448	715	B	EVD	0-749872	52
John A. Derschan	S/Sgt.	303	427	BT	KIA	39549202	11
Thomas Digman Jr.	2Lt.	392	578	B	KIA	0-690853	30
Albert Dilorenzo	2Lt.	448	714	N	POW	0-687932	50
Carmine G. Dimanno	Sgt.	466	787	TT	POW	31276739	61
William P. Domer	S/Sgt.	385	549	WG	POW	35382557	15
Warren D. Donahue	1Lt.	447	708	P	POW	0-803787	37
Royal V. Donihoo	2Lt.	448	714	RO	POW	38426739	50
Harold J. Donohue	Sgt.	452	728	WG	POW	32715058	54
Charles F. Doring	T/Sgt.	466	784	RO	POW	32469409	60
Thomas G. Dorrian	S/Sgt.	466	787	TG	POW	12121740	61
Charles R. Dowler	2Lt.	447	708	P	KIA	0-813870	41
George Dragich		452	729	WG	RTD	19106367	56
Edward J. Dreksler	S/Sgt.	467	790	TT	KIA	16116911	62
Charles L. Dulin	2Lt.	94	332	N	KIA	0-757474	8
Kenneth Dunaway		452	729	CP	RTD	0-755656	56
Donald K. Duncan	S/Sgt.	303	427	RO	KIA	38427372	12
Henry L. Dunning Jr.	Sgt.	385	550	WG	POW	32772545	18
Anthony Durante	Sgt.	447	709	WG	RTD	unknown	42
Robert L. Eklund	Sgt.	303	427	BT	KIA	37554963	12
Donald C. Elder	S/Sgt.	448	715	TG	POW	18333804	49
Joseph T. Elliot	1Lt.	447	709	B	RTD	unknown	42
Carroll J. Elwell	T/Sgt.	447	708	RO	POW	16087558	37
John F. Emerson	2Lt.	44	67	CP	POW	0-818847	1
Victor D. Ennis	2Lt.	95	336	CP	POW	0-815112	9
Howard Erricson	1Lt.	95	412	B	POW	0-739417	10
William H. Evans	T/Sgt.	388	562	RO	POW	16104399	23
Melvin H. Everding	2Lt.	466	784	N	POW	0-685502	60
Thomas J. Fairchild	Sgt.	385	550	BT	POW	12131581	18
Robert I. Falk	Sgt.	466	784	BT	KIA	32677413	60
Joseph G. Fanning	S/Sgt.	94	332	RO	KIA	32607405	8
Abe Farah	T/Sgt.	447	710	RO	POW	39321814	43
Edgar P. Farrell	2Lt.	447	708	P	POW	0-613683	39
Richard Ferighetto	S/Sgt.	447	708	WG	POW	33017508	38
Sammy E. Finley	S/Sgt.	385	549	WG	POW	18076079	16
William O. Fischer	T/Sgt.	91	322	E	KIA	35400877	4
Clarence E. Fishburn	2Lt.	447	711	CP	POW	0-748939	46
James H. Fisher	2Lt.	303	427	P	POW	0-753783	12
Ralph J. Fiskow	Sgt.	466	784	TG	POW	16046751	60
Dean S. Flemming	1Lt.	447	709	P	RTD	unknown	42
Everett E. Foster	Sgt.	44	506	BT	RTD	37499715	3
John M. Frangadakis	Sgt.	385	550	TG	POW	39124290	18

NAME	RANK	BG	BS	POS.	STATUS	SERIAL	CHAPTER
Douglas N. Franke	2Lt.	392	579	N	KIA	0-691739	32
George W. Franzen	F/O	303	427	CP	KIA	T-123210	12
Alfred M. Fratesi	S/Sgt.	385	551	TG	POW	2554700	20
Charles A. Frazier	Sgt.	458	752	WG	INT	37233872	59
Harold F. Freeman	T/Sgt.	389	564	TT	KIA	37135298	25
Orlando H. Friesen	S/Sgt.	392	577	E	POW	17155320	29
John B. Frisbie	Sgt.	447	711	BT	KIA	38367805	45
Waide G. Fulton	Sgt.	447	708	WG	POW	33244674	39
William B. Gaillard	2Lt.	447	708	B	POW	0-681774	37
Anthony C. Gambardella	Sgt.	94	332	TG	KIA	12192269	8
Michael G. Gannon	2Lt.	447	710	N	POW	0-702112	44
Harold F. Gantert	2Lt.	384	545	N	POW	0-703977	14
John P. Garfield	2Lt.	91	322	CP	POW	0-749223	4
Hector J. Garza	1Lt.	385	551	P	POW	0-687026	20
Dominic L. Gaudiomonte	2Lt.	94	331	CP	POW	0-819790	7
John P. Gavin	1Lt.	467	790	P	POW	0-803181	63
James E. Ghearing	Sgt.	388	562	WG	POW	35259640	23
Charles D. Gholson	S/Sgt.	92	326	WG	POW	15097711	5
Oscar F. Gibson Jr.	S/Sgt.	94	331	TG	POW	34261020	7
Edward J. Gienko	S/Sgt.	392	578	G	POW	36372955	31
Richard W. Glaser	2Lt.	385	549	N	POW	0-811623	15
William P. Glass	S/Sgt.	95	412	WG	POW	35512653	10
Eugene J. Glisynski	Sgt.	92	326	BT	POW	16080349	5
Joseph R. Gonzales Jr.	2Lt.	448	714	CP	POW	0-752196	50
Theodore F. Goobic	Sgt.	447	711	E	POW	6998040	47
Fred Gordon	2Lt.	453	734	N	KIA	0-809352	58
Marion L. Gordy	2Lt.	94	331	B	POW	0-701472	7
Frank Gorgon	Sgt.	303	427	WG	KIA	16113758	11
George Gould	Capt.	401	615	P	POW	0-900201	35
George F. Gould	S/Sgt.	401	615	E	POW	11094909	35
George E. Graham Jr.	2Lt.	392	576	CP	POW	0-794395	28
Windsor E. Graham	T/Sgt.	447	708	E	POW	14142036	38
Edwin A. Grant	1Lt.	458	752	P	INT	unknown	59
Robert J. Green	2Lt.	384	545	CP	POW	0-753877	14
Floyd H. Greene	2Lt.	44	68	CP	POW	0-812577	2
Glenn D. Gregory	Sgt.	95	336	TG	POW	35793097	9
George A. Griffin	2Lt.	458	752	CP	INT	0-812245	59
Charles A. Grinder	S/Sgt.	385	549	BT	POW	37321448	16
Eldon H. Gueck	2Lt.	448	713	CP	POW	0-805910	49
Joseph Guida	Sgt.	447	708	BT	KIA	32780718	39
Oliver R. Guillot	Sgt.	392	576	WG	POW	38428905	28
Isaac R. Guyton	S/Sgt.	447	708	WG	KIA	18083577	38
George A. Haakenson	2Lt.	452	728	P	POW	0-809947	54
William F. Hallman	T/Sgt.	448	713	RO	POW	14142190	49
Kaari M. Halvorson	S/Sgt.	448	714	RO	POW	37281150	51
George H. Hamby	Sgt.	452	728	WG	POW	33598126	54
Thomas L. Hampton	Sgt.	392	577	BT	POW	35000419	29
James J. Hanley	Sgt.	447	710	TG	POW	31325577	44

NAME	RANK	BG	BS	POS.	STATUS	SERIAL	CHAPTER
David E. Harbaugh	S/Sgt.	392	579	G	KIA	38111083	32
Albert Harmsen	2Lt.	385	551	N	POW	0-688435	20
John J. Harringer Jr.	Sgt.	392	578	WG	KIA	35541614	30
Robert W. Harrison	T/Sgt.	448	712	RO	POW	15344356	48
Francis J. Hart	1Lt.	385	551	P	POW	0-679068	21
Frank H. Hart	Sgt.	385	551	WG	KIA	12026064	19
Emmett A. Harter	S/Sgt.	385	551	WG	POW	17151658	20
Byron E. Hassett	T/Sgt.	392	579	E	KIA	36159795	32
James I. Hastings	2Lt.	385	551	N	POW	0-683131	21
Hyman J. Hatton	Sgt.	392	576	G	POW	12180670	27
Bordie S. Haynes	2Lt.	448	714	WG	POW	34490741	50
H. L. Heafner Jr.	Sgt.	466	784	WG	EVD	34472989	60
Edwin J. Heater	S/Sgt.	392	576	E	POW	12045795	28
Donald R. Heckman	2Lt.	452	728	CP	POW	0-818819	54
Albert L. Heikkila	Sgt.	448	715	TG	EVD	17155113	52
William M. Heins Jr.	S/Sgt.	453	732	WG	RTD	12204034	57
Walter R. Heldorfer	2Lt.	92	326	N	EVD	0-707050	6
Ed Helton Jr.	S/Sgt.	303	427	B	KIA	15065402	12
Charles M. Heltsley	1Lt.	390	571	B	POW	0-686152	26
William F. Henry	2Lt.	385	550	P	POW	0-682860	17
Donald W. Hess	2Lt.	392	578	N	KIA	0-814314	30
Roger Hess	S/Sgt.	447	708	WG	KIA	14187572	40
James C. Hetherington	S/Sgt.	453	732	BT	RTD	17092620	57
Joseph H. Higgins Jr.	Capt.	389	564	P	POW	0-797531	24
Charles E. Hill	S/Sgt.	446	706	E	KIA	14163634	36
John H. Hill	Sgt.	448	714	TG	KIA	36576975	51
LeRoy M. Hill	S/Sgt.	467	790	TG	KIA	18168713	62
Barley E. Hill	S/Sgt.	447	708	WG	KIA	38203503	40
Kenyon G. Hills	S/Sgt.	453	734	RO	KIA	11102662	58
Thomas H. Hines	Sgt.	448	714	WG	KIA	33560393	51
Glen L. Hinkebein	S/Sgt.	467	790	WG	KIA	17038895	63
Carl E. Hitchcock	1Lt.	466	787	P	POW	0-664597	61
Floyd E. Hobart	S/Sgt.	453	732	WG	RTD	17175501	57
John A. Hoegen Jr.	Sgt.	447	711	WG	KIA	31083077	45
Henry Hoff	S/Sgt.	303	427	WG	KIA	81039807	12
Richard M. Hoffman	F/Sgt.	385	551	E	POW	36606902	20
Joseph T. Hollamon Jr.	S/Sgt.	95	412	TG	POW	38415518	10
John W. Hortenstine	1Lt.	389	564	N	RTD	0-673077	25
Dale F. Howard	S/Sgt.	92	326	R	EVD	37410620	6
Orland T. Howard	2Lt.	448	715	P	EVD	0-808843	52
Grady V. Howell Jr.	2Lt.	448	714	E	POW	34038420	50
Russell E. Howle	S/Sgt.	448	715	E	POW	18097532	53
Richard J. Hruby	2Lt.	44	506	P	RTD	0-682866	3
Hayden T. Hughes	1Lt.	447	708	P	KIA	0-746752	40
Robert H. Hunt	2Lt.	385	551	B	POW	unknown	21
Richard L. Huntington	2Lt.	385	551	P	POW	0-754010	19
William L. Hutchins	S/Sgt.	448	715	WG	EVD	32229646	52
John E. Hutchins	S/Sgt.	385	550	RO	POW	unknown	16

NAME	RANK	BG	BS	POS.	STATUS	SERIAL	CHAPTER
James R. Hyde	2Lt.	447	711	CP	POW	0-819108	47
William H. Ingraham	S/Sgt.	446	706	WG	POW	32225861	36
Owen R. Irby	S/Sgt.	95	412	WG	POW	38444572	10
Douglas J. Irvine	Sgt.	447	711	WG	KIA	39616202	45
Louis C. Isaac	Sgt.	95	336	WG	POW	18111544	9
James J. Isherwood	S/Sgt.	447	710	BT	POW	13131743	43
Donald R. Itschner	S/Sgt.	91	322	WG	POW	39325983	4
Lloyd D. Ittel	1Lt.	447	709	CP	RTD	unknown	42
William C. Jackson	S/Sgt.	385	551	WG	POW	15063160	21
Don E. Jackson	Sgt.	452	729	WG	POW	35602808	55
Murray Jacob	2Lt.	390	571	N	POW	0-690436	26
Stanley R. Janesik	S/Sgt.	94	331	E	POW	32721556	7
John R. Jeans		452	729	N	RTD	unknown	56
Edward G. Jekel	2Lt.	447	710	B	POW	0-700106	44
Henry J. Jensen	S/Sgt.	303	427	R	KIA	39551854	11
George L. Johnson	S/Sgt.	91	322	WG	KIA	39282205	4
August H. Johnson	S/Sgt.	303	427	E	POW	17111104	12
Thomas W. Johnson	2Lt.	306	368	CP	KIA	0-815495	13
Robert L. Johnson	Sgt.	94	332	BT	KIA	15066126	8
Stacey Johnson	2Lt.	385	551	B	POW	0-750031	20
Woodrow W. Johnson	S/Sgt.	390	571	TG	POW	38444125	26
Richard H. Johnson	1Lt.	447	708	B	KIA	0-743600	40
Elmer D. Johnson	2Lt.	447	711	P	KIA	0-811210	45
Stonewall J. Johnson Jr.	Sgt.	458	752	E	INT	35499061	59
Charles R. Johnston	1Lt.	385	549	P	KIA	0-802402	15
John E. Jones	S/Sgt.	384	545	WG	POW	39205908	14
Weems D. Jones	1Lt.	446	706	P	POW	0-804674	36
Stanley. E. Jones	S/Sgt.	448	715	NT	POW	39260377	52
Johnny W. Jones	2Lt.	448	714	TG	POW	14149210	50
Osmond T. Jones	2Lt.	385	549	CP	POW	0-755570	16
William T. Kamenitsa	2Lt.	392	576	P	POW	0-671661	28
Arnold H. Kaminsky	T/Sgt.	446	706	RO	POW	12180404	36
Fred J. Kane	2Lt.	392	578	B	KIA	0-752921	31
Joseph J. Karaso	S/Sgt.	392	578	RO	KIA	33477790	30
Harold F. Kauffman	2Lt.	303	427	N	KIA	0-702444	12
Milton F. Keck	S/Sgt.	385	550	WG	POW	15337344	17
Jesse B. Kendler	2Lt.	447	710	CP	POW	0-809808	43
Roy L. Kennett	S/Sgt.	392	576	RO	POW	35610937	27
Robert C. Kerpen	2Lt.	401	613	B	POW	0-751914	33
Robert R. Kerr	2Lt.	303	427	CP	EVD	0-815165	11
Walter T. Kilgore	S/Sgt.	467	788	WG	EVD	13014321	64
Jack H. King	S/Sgt.	384	545	WG	POW	37651589	14
George R. King	Sgt.	447	708	BT	KIA	33740113	41
Alan W. Kingston	2Lt.	453	732	CP	RTD	0-755963	57
Frederick J. Kirnan	Sgt.	447	710	WG	POW	32489890	44
Gerhard W. Kirschke	2Lt.	385	550	N	POW	0-750199	17
Fred W. Kleps Jr.	1Lt.	447	708	N	KIA	0-688638	41
Edward I. Knowlden	F/O	94	332	CP	POW	T-122810	8

Name	Rank	BG	BS	Pos.	Status	Serial	Chapter
James L. Knox	2Lt.	306	368	B	KIA	0-747024	13
Harold F. Koehler	S/Sgt.	44	68	WG	KIA	15019186	2
Joseph P. Kotulak	Sgt.	447	711	E	POW	13005271	45
Eugene T. Koury	2Lt.	385	550	CP	POW	0-695265	18
Michael S. Kozak	Sgt.	388	560	TG	POW	12169514	22
George F. Kramer Jr.	2Lt.	447	708	B	KIA	0-749910	41
Jack J. Krejci	Sgt.	392	576	BT	POW	17165454	28
Robert L. Krentler	T/Sgt.	453	732	RO	RTD	16151572	57
Vitold P. Krushas	S/Sgt.	392	576	E	POW	31208307	27
Eugene J. Kuhns	T/Sgt.	467	790	E	POW	35312341	63
Joseph J. Kwederis	2Lt.	448	715	N	POW	0-814346	53
Joseph L. Kwon	1Lt.	446	706	CP	POW	0-751358	36
William C. Lake	T/Sgt.	453	732	E	RTD	35664677	57
William J. Lalley	2Lt.	92	326	CP	POW	0-705028	5
Sherwood W. Landis	F/O	447	708	N	KIA	T-123578	39
William C. Lane	2Lt.	458	752	N	INT	unknown	59
Wallace G. Lane	2Lt.	447	708	CP	POW	0-818067	38
John B. Langfeldt	2Lt.	92	326	P	POW	0-753898	6
Willard R. Larson	2Lt.	453	734	CP	KIA	0-685251	58
Earl J. Lawson	T/Sgt.	392	578	RO	POW	38123976	31
Aleck A. Lazek	Sgt.	306	368	WG	POW	6952052	13
Aaron N. Le Sieur	Sgt.	385	551	BT	POW	39415053	19
Earl L. Leaser	1Lt.	95	412	P	POW	0-798314	10
Warren A. Lee	Sgt.	401	614	BT	KIA	18007205	34
William H. Lee	Sgt.	401	613	TG	POW	18005206	33
George Le Grand		452	729	B	RTD	unknown	56
Harold A. Leighton Jr.	Sgt.	453	734	TG	KIA	32833504	58
Lynn L. Lemons	Sgt.	458	752	BT	INT	39855467	59
Dominic G. Leogrande	Sgt.	94	332	WG	KIA	13145030	8
Russell D. Leonard	T/Sgt.	448	715	RO	EVD	11044325	52
John W. Leonard	T/Sgt.	385	551	E	POW	12999957	21
John W. Levake	S/Sgt.	44	68	RO	KIA	19186283	2
James G. Levey	2Lt.	401	614	N	EVD	0-674588	34
Andrew Leydens	Sgt.	447	709	BT	RTD	unknown	42
Frank Linc	2Lt.	401	615	CP	POW	0-693383	35
Clifton W. Linnell	S/Sgt.	448	715	RO	POW	11118117	53
Frank J. Litton	Sgt.	453	734	WG	KIA	17089345	58
Alfred H. Locke	1Lt.	389	564	P	RTD	0-680460	25
Billy T. Lockman	Sgt.	447	708	BT	KIA	6945078	37
Wynne M. Longeteig	F/O	447	708	B	KIA	0-749912	39
Robert J. Longo	S/Sgt.	392	578	TT	POW	11111957	31
Robert F. Lotz	2Lt.	401	615	N	POW	0-732690	35
John L. Low	1Lt.	467	788	B	EVD	0-2043763	64
Arthur W. Luce	2Lt.	392	578	CP	KIA	0-809012	30
Alex P. Lugosi Jr.	S/Sgt.	466	787	WG	POW	36631214	61
Carl E. Lunde	S/Sgt.	385	549	TG	POW	37168579	16
David Lustgarten	2Lt.	453	732	B	RTD	0-746896	57
Warren S. Lutz	2Lt.	306	368	P	KIA	0-444564	13

NAME	RANK	BG	BS	POS.	STATUS	SERIAL	CHAPTER
Charles H. Lux	Sgt.	306	368	TG	POW	16139193	13
Harry B. Lynn	T/Sgt.	385	551	RO	POW	18190301	20
Paul B. Madori	Sgt.	452	728	E	POW	32438312	54
Joe B. Maloy	Sgt.	392	577	WG	POW	34702598	29
John J. Marabito	Sgt.	447	708	TG	KIA	13134443	41
Charles H. Marcy	1Lt.	447	710	P	POW	0-738436	43
Aram P. Margosian	F/O	92	326	N	POW	T-123986	5
William E. Marr	Sgt.	458	752	WG	INT	39192421	59
Otis E. Mason	Sgt.	447	711	TG	POW	33634500	47
William F. Mason	Sgt.	452	728	BT	POW	37472091	54
Robert S. Masten	Sgt.	385	550	WG	POW	34607014	18
Richard K. Matanle	S/Sgt.	390	571	WG	POW	12166330	26
Adger S. Matthews	2Lt.	447	711	N	KIA	0-704569	45
Francis G. Mauge	2Lt.	447	711	B	POW	0-701459	47
Henry H. Maynard	Sgt.	448	714	WG	POW	38134649	51
Howard McMahon	Sgt.	447	711	WG	POW	18034496	47
Melvin B. McArdle	2Lt.	447	708	CP	POW	0-751744	37
Joseph P. McCabe	Sgt.	94	332	WG	KIA	13167563	8
Robert L. McCalicher	T/Sgt.	392	578	E	POW	33479210	31
William C. McCarthy	2Lt.	385	549	N	POW	0-691771	16
Roger R. McCauley	S/Sgt.	401	613	R	POW	20815583	33
Joseph K. McClurkin Jr.	2Lt.	94	332	P	KIA	0-806283	8
Thomas J. McCue	S/Sgt.	466	787	RO	POW	12188732	61
Ralph L. McDonald	S/Sgt.	392	578	TG	KIA	14043603	30
James H. McGaha	Sgt.	401	615	WG	POW	18192379	35
Carl W. McGuen	1Lt.	447	709	N	RTD	unknown	42
Mauriece P. Mackey	S/Sgt.	453	734	E	KIA	18183067	58
James O. McLelland Jr.	T/Sgt.	385	549	RO	POW	39543377	15
Ralph R. McLeod	S/Sgt.	95	336	E	POW	38413175	9
Lamer McWhorter	S/Sgt.	44	68	E	KIA	34442753	2
Clarence E. Meekin	2Lt.	94	332	B	KIA	0-738712	8
Ralph W. Meeks	Sgt.	401	615	WG	POW	13133957	35
Ralph Meigs	2Lt.	448	714	WG	POW	14135725	50
Wilfred J. Miller	S/Sgt.	385	550	TG	POW	32627726	17
Gene A. Miller	2Lt.	392	576	B	KIA	0-752891	28
William F. Miller	S/Sgt.	95	412	BT	POW	13097970	10
William H. Miller	2Lt.	385	551	CP	POW	0-818916	19
George W. Milliron	2Lt.	467	790	N	KIA	0-698135	62
Roy W. Modglin	T/Sgt.	385	551	WG	POW	35371265	21
Raymond C. Moeller	1Lt.	95	412	N	POW	0-692331	10
William Moffitt	S/Sgt.	385	549	B	POW	32075641	15
Robert W. Monroe	S/Sgt.	392	579	RO	KIA	17165490	32
Harold B. Monroe	2Lt.	388	562	CP	POW	0-819143	23
Albert R. Monti	Sgt.	92	326	WG	EVD	33586813	6
Bill F. Moore	1Lt.	467	788	P	KIA	0-794442	64
Oral P. Moore	S/Sgt.	385	550	RO	POW	38341516	18
Joseph E. Moran	Sgt.	448	714	NG	KIA	15337063	51
Octavio A. Moreno	Sgt.	385	551	TG	POW	39283572	19

Name	Rank	BG	BS	Pos.	Status	Serial	Chapter
Robert W. Morgan	S/Sgt.	384	545	TG	POW	15334667	14
Lark C. Morgan	Sgt.	392	576	TG	POW	16036659	28
Marvin O. Morris	Sgt.	392	577	TG	POW	38431227	29
Dale R. Morris	2Lt.	458	752	P	INT	0-685167	59
Edward L. Mount	Sgt.	466	784	WG	POW	14140605	60
Vasilios Mpourles	Sgt.	447	708	TG	KIA	11021681	39
Paul J. Mulhearn	Sgt.	303	427	WG	KIA	31303563	11
Russell M. Munson	2Lt.	92	326	P	POW	0-687058	5
James V. Murphy	S/Sgt.	447	711	E	KIA	32725616	46
William F. Murphy Jr.	2Lt.	452	728	N	POW	0-707179	54
Michael Musashe	S/Sgt.	303	427	TG	KIA	16144401	11
William R. Muse	S/Sgt.	401	614	E	EVD	34306837	34
Charles H. Myers	S/Sgt.	448	712	WG	KIA	33257178	48
Julius V. Naber	S/Sgt.	44	68	BT	KIA	37263649	2
William Neal	S/Sgt.	384	545	BT	POW	39130152	14
John C. Neely	S/Sgt.	385	551	TG	KIA	32364402	21
Kenneth E. Neff	S/Sgt.	92	326	BT	EVD	19045952	6
Harold S. Neidig	2Lt.	448	714	N	KIA	0-684182	51
Hal J. Nelson	2Lt.	452	729	P	EVD	0-689085	55
Joseph J. Nevills	2Lt.	303	427	B	POW	0-684983	11
William Nicholas	S/Sgt.	447	710	WG	POW	32278935	43
Dennis E. Nicklin	Sgt.	94	331	WG	POW	13107228	7
Harold W. Nininger	T/Sgt.	448	715	WG	POW	39683675	53
Thomas E. Nolan	Sgt.	453	734	WG	KIA	19173010	58
Albert A. Nome	Sgt.	44	68	TG	KIA	35544549	2
Anthony J. Novelli Jr.	Sgt.	448	715	TG	POW	12158891	53
Harold G. Oakes	S/Sgt.	453	732	TG	KIA	11015918	57
John R. O'Brien	S/Sgt.	448	714	E	KIA	12187452	51
Leo E. Ofenstein	2Lt.	392	576	P	KIA	0-804718	27
Robert M. O'Hara Jr.	T/Sgt.	390	571	RO	POW	13168077	26
Joseph C. Oliver	Cpl.	447	711	BT	POW	6667036	46
Kenneth V. Olson	S/Sgt.	447	708	WG	POW	37305937	37
James F. O'Neil	Sgt.	95	336	BT	POW	31286550	9
Edward P. O'Neill	2Lt.	306	368	N	KIA	0-699234	13
Leslie E. Orr	Sgt.	447	709	TG	RTD	unknown	42
Earl W. Osborne	S/Sgt.	385	550	E	POW	34607006	18
Julius K. Otfinoski	Sgt.	447	711	WG	POW	31325992	47
Vencil Owens	S/Sgt.	385	549	WG	POW	35682557	15
Pedro S. Paez	S/Sgt.	389	564	WG	RTD	39255107	25
Harold M. Paris	2Lt.	447	710	P	POW	0-812301	44
Jack A. Parker	Sgt.	94	331	BT	POW	19112261	7
Joe D. Parker	T/Sgt.	385	549	E	KIA	18216603	15
Claud T. Patat Jr.	2Lt.	388	560	CP	POW	0-818739	22
George P. Paulk	S/Sgt.	452	729	RO	EVD	34539372	55
Robert V. Pelletier	2Lt.	385	550	N	POW	0-811730	18
Joseph S. Pennock	S/Sgt.	447	708	TG	KIA	32360546	37
Arthur D. Peper	2Lt.	447	711	P	POW	0-813772	47
Edward W. Perkins	S/Sgt.	447	710	WG	POW	20638740	43

Name	Rank	BG	BS	Pos.	Status	Serial	Chapter
Charles W. Perry	S/Sgt.	446	706	NT	POW	15333048	36
Richard C. Peters	S/Sgt.	467	790	BT	KIA	36578724	62
William R. Peters Jr.	S/Sgt.	447	708	E	POW	14159481	39
Robert Petkoff	S/Sgt.	44	506	TG	RTD	38274310	3
William H. Phillips	S/Sgt.	448	715	WG	POW	15089281	49
Charles A. Piper	S/Sgt.	389	564	TG	POW	31176906	24
Robert F. Pipes	T/Sgt.	466	784	E	EVD	20821082	60
Robert J. Pittman	2Lt.	467	790	CP	POW	0-699725	62
William D. Plascocello	Sgt.	447	709	WG	RTD	unknown	42
Lewis R. Pohll	S/Sgt.	447	710	RO	POW	39326305	44
Peter P. Pollreis Jr.	S/Sgt.	95	336	RO	POW	37461373	9
William F. Ponge	2Lt.	448	714	P	KIA	0-807869	51
Elwood G. Posey	Sgt.	385	551	WG	POW	18139021	19
Edgar J. Powell	2Lt.	467	788	TG	POW	0-692814	64
Gene C. Powell	Sgt.	94	331	WG	KIA	15065995	7
Frank P. Prokop	1Lt.	467	790	P	POW	0-687345	62
George A. Pruitt		452	729	BT	RTD	18191908	56
Thomas L. Pullen	T/Sgt.	385	550	E	POW	34357908	17
James F. Purdy Jr.	1Lt.	91	322	P	KIA	0-804503	4
David J. Purner	2Lt.	392	576	N	POW	0-808142	27
Harry H. Putnam Jr.	1Lt.	389	564	N	POW	0-747039	24
George E. Radle	S/Sgt.	446	706	BT	KIA	39011819	36
Floyd E. Ragsdale	Sgt.	452	729	TG	POW	39649424	55
Charles F. Ramlow	2Lt.	452	729	CP	EVD	0-818746	55
Dale E. Rauscher	2Lt.	44	67	N	POW	0-698774	1
Robert W. Rayburn	1Lt.	390	571	P	POW	0-803266	26
Hugh D. Reddy	S/Sgt.	401	615	RO	POW	37390073	35
John A. Reder	Sgt.	447	711	WG	POW	16081674	46
Joe D. Reed	S/Sgt.	306	368	R	KIA	38464210	13
Kenneth O. Reed	1Lt.	389	564	N	KIA	0-410197	25
John W. Reeves	Sgt.	401	613	WG	POW	34645458	33
Walter E. Reichert	Sgt.	44	67	BT	POW	19130088	1
Henry P. Reilly	Sgt.	447	11	BT	POW	31311291	47
George N. Renfro	Sgt.	44	67	WG	POW	38426809	1
Laurence W. Rice	S/Sgt.	303	427	E	POW	32712289	11
Noyes Richey	2Lt.	452	729	N	POW	0-708376	55
Gilman N. Roberts	2Lt.	44	68	B	KIA	0-688402	2
Standlee E. Roberts	2Lt.	385	551	B	POW	0-754770	19
Charles J. Roberts	Sgt.	447	711	WG	POW	3359728	46
George J. Robichau	2Lt.	448	714	BT	POW	12116192	50
Lawrence J. Rock	S/Sgt.	94	332	E	KIA	5377582	8
Gerald E. Rogers	2Lt.	392	578	P	KIA	0-806152	31
William W. Rogers	2Lt.	448	714	P	KIA	unknown	50
Sterling H. Rogers	2Lt.	385	550	B	POW	0-357924	18
Oscar S. Rogers Jr.	2Lt.	92	326	B	EVD	0-757035	6
Jack A. Roper	2Lt.	392	578	N	POW	0-695451	31
Wayne M. Rose	2Lt.	453	732	N	RTD	0-688650	57
Edwin H. Rosenberg	2Lt.	44	506	N	RTD	0-684989	3

NAME	RANK	BG	BS	POS.	STATUS	SERIAL	CHAPTER
Norman H. Roth	2Lt.	466	784	B	POW	0-686692	60
Leonard A. Rowland	S/Sgt.	44	67	RO	POW	37495062	1
Robert W. Rowlett	Sgt.	392	576	G	KIA	7388907	27
Merle L. Rumbaugh	Sgt.	447	708	WG	POW	33439025	39
Raymond T. Russell	S/Sgt.	467	790	BT	KIA	18063422	63
Patrick J. Ryan	2Lt.	392	577	N	POW	0-695455	29
Raymond A. Rybarski	S/Sgt.	91	322	TG	KIA	36630706	4
Victor A. Ryczko	T/Sgt.	452	729	WG	EVD	6976087	55
Leonard G. Sager	S/Sgt.	467	790	WG	KIA	32225485	63
Donald V. Sage	T/Sgt.	447	708	E	POW	38153527	37
Robert L. Salzarulo	Maj.	467	788	CP	POW	0-424730	64
Robert J. Sampson		452	729	WG	RTD	32381137	56
Malvin W. Samuel	2Lt.	452	728	B	POW	0-757668	54
William L. Sanders	S/Sgt.	44	67	E	POW	36634767	1
Fulton Sandler	F/O	388	562	N	POW	T-124456	23
Peter G. Sarpolus	S/Sgt.	385	551	RO	POW	16013782	19
Earl C. Savage	Sgt.	458	752	TG	INT	11038039	59
Albert F. Scerbo	S/Sgt.	385	549	B	POW	12201745	16
Oliver G. Schmelzle	Sgt.	392	576	RO	KIA	3335706	27
Harry J. Schow	Sgt.	44	67	TG	POW	36032490	1
Robert B. Schrimsher	T/Sgt.	447	710	E	POW	14182136	43
Keith C. Schuyler	2Lt.	44	67	P	POW	0-808597	1
James P. Scully	Sgt.	447	710	TG	POW	11090153	43
Robert C. Sears	Lt. Col	389	564	CP	POW	0-21906	24
Errol A. Self	1Lt.	389	564	CP	RTD	0-805988	25
Len Sexton	2Lt.	385	550	P	POW	0-809884	18
William M. Shaw	Sgt.	447	709	E	RTD	unknown	42
Fred C. Shere Jr.	2Lt.	392	577	P	KIA	0-745956	29
Kenneth U. Shimp	Sgt.	447	708	WG	POW	33558837	41
Oscar M. Siegel	Sgt.	447	710	WG	POW	33268747	44
Louis A. Silk	2Lt.	384	545	B	POW	0-754981	14
Hugh P. Simms	2Lt.	447	708	N	POW	0-811771	37
J. H. Singleton	2Lt.	401	614	P	EVD	0-747507	34
John W. Skidgell	1Lt.	453	734	B	KIA	0-663672	58
Raymond J. Small	T/Sgt.	447	708	RO	KIA	35374632	40
Thomas L. Smith	F/O	44	506	CP	RTD	T-61379	3
Arthur M. Smith	S/Sgt.	392	576	G	POW	6152284	27
David L. Smith	S/Sgt.	466	787	WG	POW	18213749	61
Walter F. Smith	S/Sgt.	385	551	WG	POW	32458651	20
Warren H. Smith	S/Sgt.	388	562	TG	POW	39464724	23
Everett H. Snowbarger	2Lt.	448	714	CP	POW	0-692835	51
John F. Sorrells	Sgt.	392	579	BT	KIA	14170070	32
Robert S. Sosa	2Lt.	389	564	N	KIA	0-752851	24
Vernon A. Sovia	Sgt.	94	331	RO	POW	16156099	7
Joseph C. Spermbaur		452	729	RO	RTD	37544660	56
Orville K. Springstead	Sgt.	447	711	RO	KIA	36559177	45
Thomas E. Sproat	Sgt.	447	711	TG	KIA	13013130	45
Everett W. Stanley	Sgt.	401	613	BT	POW	35646542	33

Name	Rank	BG	BS	Pos.	Status	Serial	Chapter
Sidney R. Stein	Sgt.	447	709	RO	RTD	unknown	42
Lawrence L. Steinhafel	Sgt.	447	708	WG	KIA	36815143	41
Robert C. Stevenson	2Lt.	447	711	CP	KIA	0-810250	45
Robert A. Strough	S/Sgt.	388	560	RO	POW	38275198	22
John B. Stuart	2Lt.	466	784	CP	POW	0-751573	60
Paul E. Suckow	2Lt.	452	729	P	RTD	unknown	56
Daniel M. Sullivan	Sgt.	92	326	WG	POW	31289068	6
Thomas E. Sumlin	S/Sgt.	389	564	RO	POW	38240180	24
Glenn H. Sweigart	2Lt.	44	68	P	POW	0-747360	2
Samuel A. Swim	Sgt.	388	560	WG	POW	18182987	22
Alfred B. Tallman Jr.	2Lt.	448	712	B	POW	0-547113	48
Marion A. Tennant	S/Sgt.	448	712	WG	KIA	35382677	48
Harold G. Tenneson	S/Sgt.	385	550	B	POW	17155122	17
Joseph J. Tercek	Sgt.	303	427	TG	KIA	19107874	12
Jack C. Terry	F/O	388	560	B	POW	T-1822	22
David J. Thomas	T/Sgt.	390	571	E	POW	13127853	26
Robert E. Thompson	Sgt.	392	579	G	KIA	17070811	32
Homer M. Tiller	Sgt.	44	68	WG	KIA	33101171	2
Robert E. Tobin	S/Sgt.	447	708	TG	KIA	35041542	38
Joseph B. Trivison	S/Sgt.	392	576	RO	KIA	15354276	28
Alfred J. Truszkowski	S/Sgt.	401	613	E	POW	32607450	33
Albert M. Tufts	2Lt.	392	579	CP	KIA	0-755611	32
Cecil A. Turner	Sgt.	388	562	BT	POW	19091209	23
John W. Turocy	2Lt.	44	68	N	POW	0-695992	2
Max E. Turpin	1Lt.	448	713	P	POW	0-675891	49
Francis R. Tye	1Lt.	453	734	P	KIA	0-737902	58
William J. Underwood	2Lt.	388	560	N	POW	0-707500	22
Dale R. VanBlair	S/Sgt.	389	564	TG	RTD	16076061	25
Edward Verbosky	2Lt.	467	788	B	POW	0-754780	64
Thomas J. Verran	F/O	448	715	CP	POW	T-122217	52
John W. Vilberg	2Lt.	95	336	P	POW	0-753825	9
Joseph J. Vistejn Jr.	S/Sgt.	401	614	RO	KIA	15377673	34
Dominick A. Vitale	Sgt.	92	326	TG	POW	20301998	5
Jay A. Wade	2Lt.	401	615	B	POW	0-694529	35
Casimer J. Wagner	S/Sgt.	384	545	E	KIA	16141960	14
Donald E. Walker	2Lt.	388	560	P	KIA	0-809899	22
Leslie E. Walker	2Lt.	447	711	B	KIA	0-749602	45
John J. Wall	2Lt.	392	576	CP	KIA	0-684087	27
Guy A. Wallace	2Lt.	92	326	CP	EVD	0-734398	6
Richard J. Wallace	T/Sgt.	389	564	RO	RTD	11040222	25
Richard J. Walsh		452	729	E	RTD	12125677	56
Owen D. Walton	2Lt.	385	549	CP	POW	0-802498	15
Roy Y. Ward	Sgt.	306	368	BT	KIA	384304343	13
Ray Y. Ward	Sgt.	306	368	WG	KIA	38430450	13
Charles R. Warlow	S/Sgt.	401	615	BT	POW	16031863	35
William E. Watkins	Sgt.	401	613	WG	EVD	39281632	33
Arthur W. Watt	T/Sgt.	447	708	RO	KIA	36719165	38
Clinton L. Watts	T/Sgt.	467	788	TT	POW	18053597	64

Name	Rank	BG	BS	Pos.	Status	Serial	Chapter
Harvey F. Watts	S/Sgt.	385	549	TG	POW	33191902	15
John E. Webb	T/Sgt.	385	550	RO	POW	16133921	17
Everett W. Wehling	S/Sgt.	92	326	R	POW	32668892	5
Alfred S. Weinberg	2Lt.	94	331	N	POW	0-694629	7
Richard A. Weir	2Lt.	392	578	CP	POW	0-811160	31
John R. Welch	2Lt.	91	322	B	POW	0-754857	4
Robert L. Westfall	2Lt.	401	613	CP	POW	0-814607	33
William V.P. Weston	2Lt.	95	336	B	POW	0-757581	9
Arnold J. Wetzel	Sgt.	448	715	WG	POW	32466992	53
Perry Wharton	1Lt.	389	564	CP	POW	0-683514	24
Ward W. Wickwar	Sgt.	452	728	TG	POW	17090301	54
Wallace J. Widen	S/Sgt.	385	551	BT	POW	38396922	20
Robert W. Wilcox	Sgt.	392	577	B	POW	12215195	29
Ralph E. Wildman	T/Sgt.	95	412	E	POW	15382594	10
Donald B. Wiley	2Lt.	388	562	B	POW	0-761345	23
Charles R. Williams Jr.	S/Sgt.	385	550	WG	KIA	18058495	17
Floyd D. Williams	S/Sgt.	467	790	WG	KIA	18042480	62
Robert E. Willson	2Lt.	466	787	N	POW	0-698245	61
Fonzy M. Wilson Jr.	S/Sgt.	392	577	RO	KIA	39690607	29
William S. Womer	S/Sgt.	392	579	NG	KIA	15074670	32
Harry E. Woodman	Sgt.	447	710	BT	POW	16008671	44
George H. Wright	T/Sgt.	95	412	RO	POW	13157961	10
Bert W. Wyatt	2Lt.	392	579	P	KIA	0-526045	32
Audrey J. Yates Jr.	S/Sgt.	388	562	WG	POW	36752917	23
David L. York	S/Sgt.	389	564	BT	POW	34472913	24
Archie B. Young	Sgt.	392	576	WG	POW	18097746	28
Lloyd G. Young	2Lt.	466	787	CP	POW	0-680791	61
Milan R. Zeman	F/O	392	577	CP	KIA	T-61361	29
Robert W. Zercher	Sgt.	452	729	BT	KIA	13092429	55
Walter J. Zesut	T/Sgt.	447	708	E	KIA	11102873	40
Dare D. Ziemer	2Lt.	447	708	B	POW	0-674825	38

BOMBERS LOST

8th USAAF losses on April 29, 1944.
Heavy bombers only

Chapter	Bomb Group	Squadron	Serial	MACR	Type	Pilot
1	44	67	42-100279	4464	B-24	Keith C. Schuyler
2		68	41-29471	4472	B-24	Glenn H. Sweigart
3		506	41-29513	xxx	B-24	Richard J. Hruby
4	91	322	42-31353	4236	B-17	James F. Purdy Jr.
5	92	326	42-3513	4260	B-17	Russell M. Munson
6		326	42-97319	4261	B-17	John B. Langfeldt
7	94	331	42-31498	4467	B-17	Kenneth L. Chism
8		332	42-102520	4468	B-17	Joseph K. McClurkin
9	95	336	42-37988	4470	B-17	John W. Vilberg
10		412	42-31320	4469	B-17	Earl L. Leaser
11	303	427	42-31241	4463	B-17	Howard J. Bohle
12		427	42-3158	4471	B-17	James H. Fisher
13	306	368	42-31556	4240	B-17	Warren S. Lutz
14	384	545	42-102448	4242	B-17	James A. Bouvier
15	385	549	42-31773	4456	B-17	Charles L. Johnston
16		549	42-97559	4459	B-17	Robert E. Barney
17		550	42-97078	4457	B-17	William F. Henry
18		550	42-107045	4460	B-17	Len Sexton
19		551	42-97226	4458	B-17	Richard L. Huntington
20		551	42-31133	4453	B-17	Hector J. Garza
21		551	42-31174	4454	B-17	Francis J. Hart
22	388	560	42-31393	4243	B-17	Donald E. Walker
23		562	42-37980	4244	B-17	Joseph D. Coyner
24	389	564	41-28676	4494	B-24	Joseph H. Higgins Jr.
25		564	41-28784	5473	B-24	Ralph S. Bryant
26	390	571	42-102526	4245	B-17	Robert W. Rayburn

Chapter	Bomb Group	Squadron	Serial	MACR	Type	Pilot
27	392	576	42-110062	4445	B-24	Leo E. Ofenstein
28		576	42-100371	4476	B-24	William T. Kamenitsa
29		577	41-28759	4462	B-24	Fred C. Shere Jr.
30		578	42-110105	4446	B-24	Robert R. Bishop
31		578	42-100100	4444	B-24	Gerald E. Rogers
32		579	42-7510	4461	B-24	Bert W. Wyatt
33	401	613	42-31226	4345	B-17	Donald E. Butterfoss
34		614	42-31116	4344	B-17	J. H. Singleton
35		615	42-31521	4346	B-17	George Gould
36	446	706	42-100360	4485	B-24	Weems D. Jones
37	447	708	42-37866	4250	B-17	Warren D. Donahue
38		708	42-37868	4251	B-17	Carl J. Blom
39		708	42-102479	4255	B-17	Edgar P. Farrell
40		708	42-31144	4247	B-17	Hayden T. Hughes
41		708	42-102421	4254	B-17	Charles R. Dowler
42		709	42-31519	N/A	B-17	Dean S. Flemming
43		710	42-97135	4252	B-17	Charles H. Marcy
44		710	42-31217	4249	B-17	Harold M. Paris
45		711	42-97501	4253	B-17	Elmer D. Johnson
46		711	42-31124	4246	B-17	William A. Davidson
47		711	42-31161	4248	B-17	Arthur D. Peper
48	448	712	42-7655	4486	B-24	James G. Clark
49		713	41-29523	4489	B-24	Max E. Turpin
50		714	42-7683	4487	B-24	William W. Rogers
51		714	42-99988	4491	B-24	William F. Ponge
52		715	41-29479	4488	B-24	Orland T. Howard
53		715	42-52435	4490	B-24	John W. Cathey
54	452	728	42-39981	4450	B-17	George H. Haakenson
55		729	42-39920	4449	B-17	Hal J. Nelson
56		729	42-31784	N/A	B-17	Paul E. Suckow
57	453	732	42-52301	4940	B-24	Max A. Davison
58		734	42-50322	4493	B-24	Francis R. Tye
59	458	752	41-28718	4451	B-24	Dale R. Morris
60	466	784	41-29399	4448	B-24	Franklynn V. Cotner
61		787	41-28754	4447	B-24	Carl E. Hitchcock
62	467	790	41-28749	4943	B-24	Frank P. Prokop
63		790	41-28730	4942	B-24	John P. Gavin
64		788	42-52506	4944	B-24	Bill F. Moore

CHAPTER 1

44ᵀᴴ BOMB GROUP
67ᵀᴴ BOMB SQUADRON

Type: B-24H • Serial: 42-100279
MACR 4464 • Air Base: Shipdham

At 14:00 hours, aircraft 42-100279 was observed straggling low and to the right of the formation. Number 2 engine was feathered but apparently under control.

Missing Air Crew Report # 4464

Pilot: 2Lt. Keith C. Schuyler, 0-808597, POW, Berwick, PA

Co-Pilot: 2Lt. John F. Emerson, 0-818847, POW, Santa Monica, CA

Navigator: 2Lt. Dale E. Rauscher, 0-698774, POW, Goodland, KS

Bombardier: 2Lt. Jay L. Davis, 0-692481, POW, Cleveland, OH

Engineer: S/Sgt. William L. Sanders, 36634767, POW, Karnak, IL

Radio: S/Sgt. Leonard A. Rowland, 37495062, POW, Portland, OR

Ball-Turret Gunner: Sgt. Walter E. Reichert, 19130088, POW, Farragut, ID

Waist-Gunner: Sgt. George N. Renfro, POW, 38426809, Handley, TX

Waist-Gunner: Sgt. George G. Cox, POW, 15336328, Louisa, KY

Tail-Gunner: Sgt. Harry J. Schow, POW, 36032490, Austin, MN

10 POW

Crash Site: Recke near Hopsten - Germany

35

44th Bomb Group, 67th Bomb Squadron (Schuyler)
(No caption available.)

Navigator 2Lt. Dale E. Rauscher recalls in his book
"The Long Year":

"For about thirty years, I have been thinking of recording for my daughter, Jane, and now also for my grandchildren, some of the things I experienced during a long, hectic year. Many things that happened, I have never talked about, even to my wife, Maxine. Events took place that I felt were mine alone and not to be shared - events I thought time would erase from memory.

"Memory is a funny thing. Some memories and events are so deeply embedded that it is impossible to forget and, so many years later, still seem to have happened only last week.

"Not wanting to rely entirely on memory, I have read several books dealing with facts as recorded by others who were in the same position and places at the same time I was. One book, "Elusive Horizons," was written by Keith Schuyler, the pilot of my crew, who recorded the events of every bombing mission on our return to base each day. His book does not record anything of the Long Year but did a lot to jog my memory. A book written by Kenneth W. Simmons, entitled "Kriegie," takes the reader in the exact footsteps that I traveled. I must have known him as it seems we were in the same places at the same time. Another book entitled "Stalag Luft 3" by Bob Neary is a book of sketches and narration of the three different prison camps I was in. Bob was in the same part of the camp as I was in. I knew him at the time but cannot remember what he looked like.

"The long year began early on the morning of April 29, 1944, and ended on the afternoon of April 29, 1945, but I am going to go back to November 12, 1943, to get into focus some of the names, places and events.

"I had finished Navigation School in Monroe, Louisiana, the 12th of November, 1943, and had been ordered to report to the air base in Casper, Wyoming on Thanksgiving Day. Maxine had been with me all the time I was in Monroe. We packed our belongings and headed by train for Goodland.

"We had a lot of luggage as Maxine had her clothes as well as mine and also all the navigation books and equipment. Also a parachute had been issued to me and that had to go along. The train was crowded as always and we had to sit on our luggage all the way to St. Louis. The train on to Kansas City was just as crowded. In Kansas City, we were unable to get tickets on the Rock Island Rocket to Goodland so we took a train to Omaha and sat up all night in the railroad station hoping someone would cancel so that we could get their reservation. About fifteen minutes before departure time, someone cancelled and we were able to get on the Union Pacific Train enroute to Denver.

"So, instead of going to Goodland, we detrained in Sterling, Colorado, called my father in Haxtun, Colorado, and he came and picked us up. My older brother, along with his new wife, was also on leave so we had a few days together. My father took us to Goodland where we were able to spend some time with Maxine's folks; then, on to Denver where we caught a train early on Thanksgiving morning enroute to Casper, Wyoming. It was a cold, snowy day.

"Casper, Wyoming - It may not be the coldest place in the country in winter but it sure comes close! It was snowing heavily when we got off the train and the air was bitter cold. We went to a hotel and got a room, hoping Maxine would be able to find other accommodations very soon as we could not afford to stay in a hotel very long. We were broke and had to borrow three hundred dollars from my father to be able to get to Casper. I could always have made it but I didn't want Maxine to hitchhike with me. Good friends from Monroe Cadet days were at the same hotel. Joyce and Duane Mitchell from Grant City, Missouri, had become good friends while we were in gunnery school in Ft. Myers, Florida. Duane now is a doctor in Mt. Ayre, Iowa, and we have remained friends over the years. We have been able to visit in their home every couple of years and they have visited us in Goodland on several occasions.

"The next morning, Duane and I, along with several others, boarded a bus for the Air Base. It was about eight miles northwest of town. It had not been too cold or windy in Casper but a regular ground blizzard was in progress at the Base. This was to be an almost daily occurrence for the approximate two months of our stay. On several occasions, we were unable to get back to town and had to stay at the quarters provided for us on the Base. In the meantime, back in Casper, Joyce and Maxine had been looking for a cheaper place to stay. They were getting to be pros in looking for lodging. Maxine's first taste of room hunting had been in

Camden, South Carolina. She was lucky enough to get a room at the home of Rev. and Mrs. Collins, pastor of the Methodist Church. They were wonderful people. After Camden, it was Ft. Myers, Florida; Monroe, Louisiana; and, now, Casper, Wyoming. They were both able to find motel rooms with cooking accommodations. It was much cheaper than living at a hotel and eating out all the time. Having been given permission to live off base, I was able to get into town most nights except when we had night flying missions.

"Casper Air Base was where crews were put together and trained for combat. It was also my first introduction to the B-24 Liberator, the first four-engine aircraft I had ever been in. I must admit, I was scared on my first flight. Here I met the nine other men with whom I was to fly for some time to come. The pilot, Keith Schuyler, was from Berwick, Penna. The co-pilot, Seymour Jarol, was from Chicago, Illinois. Jarol was taken from the crew and given his own plane and crew the day before Christmas. He was later killed in the South Pacific. Replacing Jarol as co-pilot was Jack Emerson from Santa Monica, California. Jack had just come out of twin-engine school and had no experience with a B-24. Under the tutorship of Schuyler, he became a darn good pilot and has been with United Airlines since leaving the Service. The bombardier was Larry Davis from Cleveland, Ohio. We four made up the officer compliment. The six sergeants on the crew were from several different states. Bill Sanders, engineer and top turret gunner, was from Cairo, Illinois; Harry Schow, tail gunner, was from Chicago, Illinois; Leonard Rowland, radioman, was from Portland, Oregon; Walter Reichert, belly-gunner, was from Montana; George Cox, waist-gunner, was from Louisa, Kentucky; and George Renfro, waist-gunner, was from Ft. Worth, Texas. (Renfro was the youngest of the crew —only eighteen.) I must admit, at twenty-seven, I was the old man of the crew.

"The cold was not the only enemy at Casper. The planes we were flying had seen all the combat they could take. They had been sent back to the States, patched up as much as possible and used for combat training. We had several near crashes. The first was landing with a cocked nose wheel. We had radioed in before our landing attempt. We could see all the fire trucks, crash trucks and ambulances lined up waiting for the crash we all felt was sure to come. Schuyler kept the nose up as we came in for as long as he could. As flying speed dropped, the nose came down and the nose wheel hit the runway. It jerked to the right for just a second, straightened out, and we were all okay. I really think the people lined up along the runway were sorry they had missed seeing a good crash.

"On another occasion, one engine cut out as we were on an air to ground gunnery mission, flying about twenty to fifty feet off the ground, down a small valley. Again, we were able to pull up and were safe again.

"On a night navigation training mission to Amarillo, Texas, we discovered a cap missing from the left wing gas tank and the air pressure was sucking the gas out. We were only about thirty minutes out of Casper Base so turned back, replaced the cap, filled up with gas and completed the mission.

"During the two months in Casper, we only lost one plane with all the crew. We had returned from a night flight and were watching other aircraft return to base. All at once, there was a terrific explosion as a B-24 nosed into the ground after hitting a small hill just a few hundred yards from the end of the runway. All ten men were killed in either the crash or the resulting explosion and fire. This was just the first of our friends to go.

"Finally, they decided we were combat ready. Our next stop was to be Forbes Air Base at Topeka, Kansas, where we would be given new B-24's just off the assembly line and sent on to a destination decided on by the higher-ups. We went by troop train so, again, the girls were on their own. One friend, Lt. E. Norris of Loveland, Colorado, had his car at Monroe and had driven it to Casper. They would not let him drive to Topeka but had to ride the troop train with the rest of the gang.

"We were in Topeka for about two weeks. It was a fine base where we could take our wives to the Officers' Club and the food was delicious. We knew the stay would be short. We were scheduled to leave on two occasions but were cancelled out by weather to the east. On the third day we were scheduled to leave, the weather was bad in Topeka, so I told Maxine I was sure I would be back in a couple of hours. This time the weather east was okay and we were on our way. This was the only time I ever promised Maxine I would be back in a couple of hours and didn't show up again for about sixteen months.

"Our destination this time was West Palm Beach, Florida, Morrison Field. This proved to be a very short stay. We knew we would have only one night, the next day, and would leave around ten the following night. Knowing this would be our last night in the states for some time, we all proceeded to get a little drunk.

"We didn't get much sleep and were kept busy the following day getting ready for our first over-water flight. As the navigator, I knew, for the first time, the success or failure of this night's flight depended on me. At our briefing, we were given a course to fly along with sealed orders we were not to open until two hours out. We would then know our destination and the route we would take. Maybe it was a good thing we had never heard of the Bermuda Triangle as our course took us right into it.

"Navigation, in 1943, was not what it is today. On most over-water flights, you had to rely almost entirely on celestial navigation. Accurate star shots were the secret of charting correct courses. I knew I had to do my best because the crew was depending on me and they were no more sure of my ability than I was.

"Two hours out, Schuyler opened our orders and we discovered our final destination was to be England. Our flight, for this night, was to land on the island of Trinidad, just off the coast of Venezuela. Quite a number of planes had taken off for this flight. To our knowledge, all were destined for England but, of course, all would not end up in the same group.

"It was a dark night, but at our altitude of 9,000 feet, the stars were shining brightly. On the ground, before departure, I had plotted our course to the island of Puerto Rico. We were to report, by radio, to Borenquin Field in the western part of the island, fly along the northern coast over San Juan, and then change to a more southerly course toward Trinidad. We had been told, at our briefing, that, if we got off course, be sure and get off course to the left as there were mountains as high as 11,000 ft. on the island of Haiti on the right.

"Everything went fine for a couple or three hours, then the results of my getting drunk the night before began to catch up with me. I'm sure I wasn't the only one with this problem, but I was only feeling sorry for myself. I wasn't sick but had a headache and was tired. I had taken several star shots and was sure of our position and course.

"My headache was no better and I could hardly keep my eyes open. Looking out the front of the plane, I could see the taillight of another plane en route to the same destination. I called the pilot, told him everything was under control and for him to follow the plane ahead. I decided to get a little sleep. It must have been around two or three a.m. About a half hour later, an intercom call from the pilot informed me the plane he was following appeared to be going down. This wakened me in a hurry and a quick look, along with a fast glance at my star charts, gave me information I should have realized all along. I had asked the pilot to follow the planet Venus as it was sinking into the southwestern sky. A few days later, we all looked back at this incident and laughed but, right now, it was serious business. Within five minutes, I had taken some star shots and calculated where we were. As luck would have it, Venus was sinking on a course almost exactly as our course was for Puerto Rico. No course change was needed, so, on we flew. I was wide awake now and took the business of navigation real seriously, checking and rechecking everything. All seemed okay.

"Dawn was just breaking when the pilot called, almost frantic! It appeared we were about to run into the mountains, on our right, that we had been warned of. I looked out the right side window and, sure enough, there were the mountains. I quickly gave a course change of ninety degrees to the left to get out of a possible crash into a mountain peak. After about fifteen minutes of flying scared, in the breaking dawn, the sky started to get light and those mountain peaks suddenly took on the form of high cumulus clouds. Again, I had let my eyes deceive me. You can be darn sure we were all happy to know they were clouds instead of mountains.

"As we were now within radio communication distance of Borenquin Field, I had gotten a radio bearing on the field. I had the pilot change course and flew in on the beam to Puerto Rico. We checked in, as ordered, changed course to fly east along the north coast of the island. After reaching the northeast coast, we changed course to southeast and flew southeasterly along the chain of islands known as the Lesser Antilles - St. Croix, Guadeloupe, Dominica, Martinique, St. Lucia, etc. These were all British controlled islands except Martinique, which was French.

"Sgt. Sanders, the engineer, in checking the gas reserve, felt we were a little low so the pilot radioed the landing strip on St. Lucia, requesting permission to land to take on fuel. Permission was granted so we came in in over this beautiful tropical island. The airstrip is, or was, only about a mile long. We had to come in over some coastal mountains and drop right in. The other end of the runway was a cliff, dropping into the clear, blue bay. We came in a little too high on the first pass and had to go around again. On passing over the end of the strip, we saw several planes that had gone over the end of the cliff and were a pile of junk in the water. I am sure the pilot took a double-take on this and was plenty cautious in coming in. We were all happy to get out of the aircraft and get our feet on the ground again. Before the plane had hardly stopped, a little native boy was along side with a huge bunch of the most beautiful bananas I had ever seen. I don't remember what they cost us but we took the whole bunch. I ate a couple of bananas and, as the plane was being gassed, I went over to the control tower to get weather information for the flight on to Trinidad.

"Before going back to the plane, I stopped at the Officers' Club and had a big, cold beer. It was really good and hit the spot in this hot, humid atmosphere. We were still wearing winter clothes we had taken with us when leaving Topeka. Our lighter clothing had been packed in footlockers and would reach us in England after coming by boat.

"After our short stop on St. Lucia, we were again airborne and flying almost due south toward Waller Field on the island of Trinidad. The flight would take us over several small islands, passing just to the right of the island of Tobago. We landed at Waller Field in the middle of the afternoon, were assigned quarters, briefed on our next day's flight, and went to the mess hall for something to eat. I had been sick almost from the moment we left St. Lucia. It seems the cold beer and the bananas did not mix and I had one hell of a bellyache! Our quarters were not the best but we were tired and I am sure we could have slept on a bare floor. We were assigned to tents with wooden floors. As there were tropical bugs of all kinds, each bunk was enclosed in a mosquito net. I was still sleeping soundly when we were wakened at the crack of dawn. After a good breakfast, we were off to another briefing for the day's flight.

"Today's flight would not be nearly so long but would be over some of the roughest territory in the world. We would fly over water until we reached just north of Georgetown, British Guiana, then inland over the jungles of Guiana and northern Brazil. We would cross the equator near the mouth of the Amazon River. We would go on southeasterly to Belem, just south of the equator, and near the mouth of one of the outlets of the Amazon to the Atlantic Ocean.

"At the briefing, we got another flight warning. This one concerned what is called the equatorial front. This front moves inland during the day and out over the Atlantic during the night. It was suggested, if the storm looked too bad, we fly eastward to the Atlantic and follow the coast to Belem. The thunderheads would build up so high it was impossible to get on top. I plotted a direct course for Belem with an alternate course in case we found the front too rough. We were to fly at an altitude of 11,000 ft.

"Shortly after taking off, we were over some of the most beautiful jungle you ever saw. We had seen the small jungle areas over the islands of St. Lucia and Trinidad, but this seemed to be one solid green carpet as far as you could see. Ever so often, you would see small clearings filled with grass huts. Looking through binoculars, you could barely make out natives around the huts.

"About four hours out, we began to see the huge build-up of cumulus clouds. They didn't look too bad so, with approval from all the crew, the pilot decided to continue on the direct course. All went well for awhile but soon we were into the damnedest storm you could imagine. It was impossible to go round the clouds or climb on top. I would estimate the tops of most of them to be as high as 100,000 ft. Up-drafts and downdrafts were almost constant, along with torrential rain. Water was coming in every little crack in the aircraft and there were plenty of them. The bombardier had been riding in the nose turret but had to get out because water was pouring in around the gun mounts. The men in the back of the plane had to come to the flight deck as water was coming in the open windows of the rear section. There were no windows where the guns were mounted on either side of the rear section. I watched the altimeter mounted on my desk. At times, it would read 11,000 ft., then, in a matter of seconds, we would be at 20,000 ft. Your stomach would feel as if you were in a fast moving elevator and the indicator might read 7,000 or maybe 9,000 ft. I had heard of planes dropping so fast that things would float in the air. It happened - I had to grab some of my papers in mid-air and fasten them to my desk. The movement was so fast and furious, the pilot could not handle the plane. He put it on automatic pilot, held on and we rode it out. I am sure that if we ever made this trip again, we would follow the suggestion of flying east to the Atlantic and follow the coast to Belem.

"Within an hour or so, we reached the Belem area and had to circle for about fifteen minutes until a thunderstorm moved on so we could see the airstrip. Just before reaching Belem, we crossed the mouth of the Amazon. It took us about an hour to cross the mouth of the river. We found that the B-24 was a good, sturdy aircraft. It had to be to take the beating it took in that tropical storm. We were darned glad to have solid ground under our feet as we got off the plane at the Belem airstrip. We were again assigned to tents where we were able to shave and clean up. We thought it had been hot in Trinidad the night before but, here at Belem, just a few miles south of the equator, the heat was almost unbearable. I thought back to just four days before, when we had left Topeka, where it was around zero, with lots of snow on the ground.

"The sleeping quarters and mess hall were built right on the edge of the jungle. There were signs all over warning you not to even take one step into the jungle. We were at the point where we had decided to take the advice of people in the know. We were told, and I am sure it is true, that men had simply disappeared after walking into the jungle just a few steps. As we walked into the mess hall that evening, a group of native girls were standing inside, some indicating the way to the mess line and some waiting tables. One cute little gal, black as the ace of spades, with perfect white teeth, looked at me as I came in the door. Her face broke into a big grin as she said, "Howdy, Shorty." I was sort of taken and can't remember whether I returned her howdy or not. After eating, we returned to our quarters and had a good night's sleep.

"Again, we were wakened quite early as we were to get airborne as soon as possible after eating breakfast. At the morning's briefing, we plotted our course for Natal, Brazil. Natal is right on the Atlantic coast and is one of the most easterly points on the continent of South America. This should be a fairly routine flight. We would be flying over land all the way with the coastline in sight most of the time. It was such a perfect day, as well as a perfect flight, that I left my nose compartment and joined the poker game in progress on the flight deck. It was so perfect that, at times, the pilot and co-pilot would leave the cockpit and join the game. (The plane would be on autopilot.) I even traded places with the co-pilot and took over the controls for a period of time. We had only one problem on this flight. About an hour out of Natal, the cowling from one engine was torn off. Someone in Belem, in checking the engine, had failed to fasten it properly. This gave us a one day layover in Natal as a replacement had to be flown in.

"Natal was the hopping off place for flights over the south Atlantic. Most four-engine aircraft would make non-stop flights to Africa while the single and twin-engine aircraft would stop at Ascension Island. Ascension is just a small dot of land about twelve degrees south of the equator in the middle of the south Atlantic. I was really happy we would fly nonstop rather than for the island. It would be a heck of a lot easier to find the west coast of Africa than it would Ascension Island.

"Our two-day stay in Natal was most welcome. We were not allowed off the base so spent most of the time drinking, eating and sleeping. There were hundreds of planes parked around this large base. Lots of B-24's, C-47 Transports, C-54's, B-25's, P-51's and other fighter planes. Some of the B-24 crews we had been with in Casper and Topeka were there. The Officers' Club was a beautiful thing. A long, circular constructed bar was the most popular place. Not only was it popular for the good drinks they served but, behind the bar, working as cashier, was the most beautiful girl I have ever seen. I do not know how tall she was as I saw her only sitting down. She had beautiful Spanish features, what appeared to be green eyes, and long, black hair. (I can't even describe my wife that well!) We had left Topeka a day before payday and I had only about ten bucks in my pocket when we left the States. I had gone to the military finance office on the base at Natal and was able to get an advance of fifty bucks. This had to be converted to Brazilian money to spend at the Club or PX.

"The next morning, after a good night's sleep, we wandered around the base, taking in a few sights, though not much to see except a few planes we were not familiar with. Oh yes, at night we had to provide our own guards around our own plane. The enlisted men took turns at this. At one place, we saw about fifty men

43

lined up outside a building so we had to see what we were missing. It proved to be a line waiting to buy Brazilian boots. Sure, we got in line (Schuyler, Emerson, Davis and myself) and purchased us a pair of real nice boots for five bucks. I wore them most of the time I was in England and, off and on, for several years after I got home.

"Reporting into operations in the afternoon, we were told the cowling had been received and had been placed on our aircraft. We were scheduled to leave on our south Atlantic hop to Africa at ten o'clock that night. This was about a twelve hour flight so had to leave at night to be able to reach destination at an early hour the following day. I had learned my lesson on the flight from West Palm Beach to Puerto Rico - no more following planets or mistaking cumulus clouds for mountains. Instead of going to the Officers' Club for a few drinks, off I went to quarters for a few hours sleep. I knew I would have to stay on the ball from twelve to fourteen hours. No one on the crew said anything but they couldn't help being a little leery after my boo-boo a few days ago.

"Natal is about five degrees south of the equator and Dakar, our African destination, is about fifteen degrees north of the equator. Dakar is located in what was then French West Africa, one of the most westerly points on the continent of Africa. As near as I can remember, we took off right on schedule. It was going to be a long night. Before take-off, the aircraft had been completely checked by the engineer and other crew members. The pilot and co-pilot had gone through their checklist. I had checked out my navigation instruments, paying special attention to my octant so as to be assured of correct and accurate star shots.

"My months and months of training were going to get a good test this night. I don't remember our exact course, but it must have been around seventy degrees. It was a beautiful, clear night and, according to the weather report, it would be pretty much the same for the next twelve to fifteen hours. All went smoothly. I took star shots and calculated our position about every thirty minutes. Several slight course corrections were made. About five or six hours out, after making a position check, I discovered we had a little more right of course than was safe for too long a period. We must have had quite a change in wind direction. I quickly charted our new course and called the pilot on inter-com to change to a new heading. Getting no response from the pilot, I called the co-pilot. Still getting no response, I called every man on the aircraft. I finally came to the conclusion the aircraft was on autopilot and I was the only person on board who was not asleep. Looking upward and back of my desk, I could see the pilot's legs. Among my belongings, I had a plastic rule about a meter in length. With this, I could reach through the opening and tap Schuyler on the legs. It didn't take much to awaken him have the course correction made.

"When we were about three or four hours from destination, I figured the pilot would soon be asking for an estimated time of arrival, so we had one ready when he asked. I was now able to pick up the radio beam at Dakar and had a double check as to the course in. About an hour from our ETA, we were able to sight the coastline. As we flew over the coast, we could see our landing field a couple of miles off to our left and our arrival time was within five minutes of my ETA some three hours out.

"I fastened down my instruments and went up on the flight deck for the landing. I felt darned good about the flight and felt I had redeemed myself for the earlier boo-boo. Our landing was another first - the runway was steel matting laid on a sand strip. It made a lot of noise but we were in safe from a long, over-water flight and I was pooped. After being assigned quarters and cleaning up, I slept for a couple of hours then headed for the Officers' Club for a drink. Here, we again ran into several crews who had left Topeka the same day we did - Lt. Duane Mitchell and crew being one.

"The air base was very dingy; everything seemed to be sandy and dirty. Our plane was to be checked over so we would be at Dakar this half day, that night, all the next day and again leave before mid-night the following night. We got a good night's sleep and, following breakfast the next morning, we hopped a GI truck going out to the beach. On the way, we went through the city of Dakar - a very dirty place! This was our first experience with natives running after us and begging for gum and candy. The little kids all had big smiles and did not look underfed. There were a lot of donkeys and camels in the streets. No cars except American military vehicles. On the outskirts of town, we saw a few old knotty trees with vultures sitting in them. Very filthy.

"On the beach, there were no trees, just a couple of open shelter houses. Schuyler talked a native man into taking him out into the bay to do a little fishing. Before the native would go, he wanted to play checkers. Schuyler played him a couple of games, letting him win so he could go fishing. I stayed on the beach and watched several destroyers and what appeared to be cargo ships out in the bay. After a few hours on the beach, we went back to the base and got a little more rest. It turned out we didn't leave that night but would leave before noon the next day. Our destination was to be Marrakech, in French Morocco. Most of this flight would be over the western portion of the great Sahara desert. We spent a couple of hours at the Officers' Club before turning in for another good night's sleep. I can remember it being quite hot that night but there was a breeze.

"We were up shortly after daylight the following morning and, after breakfast, went to the briefing for the day's flight. The course laid out for us was to fly northward along the coast for about two hundred miles, then northeastward over the western edge of the Sahara. Marrakech was about sixteen hundred miles. It would be mostly desert until we reached the Atlas Mountains, just south of our destination. There should be no problems on this flight as long as we did not have trouble with the aircraft. In the approximate ten hour flight, there were only two tiny landing strips where it would be possible to set the plane down. One of these was at Agmar and the other Tindouf. We had to fly far enough eastward so as to avoid flying over any part of Spanish Morocco. This was quite easy as there were a couple of mountain peaks in the Spanish territory and all we had to do was stay to the east of them. Spain was a neutral country and we were not allowed to fly over any of its territory.

"When we got to our aircraft, they were still checking it over so we decided to have a little crap game in the shade of one of the wings. One of the stupid regulations of the military was that officers and enlisted men were not allowed to do anything socially together. I guess a little friendly crap game, among crew members, was one of the things we were not supposed to do. Coming down the taxi strip, we saw a jeep coming in our direction. It was the Base Commander, a SOB, if I ever saw one. He jumped out of his jeep and proceeded to chew us out, in no dignified manner, for our little game. He said it was all right to shoot craps; but, there would have to be two games, one for the officers and one for the enlisted men. After this incident, we were all happy to climb aboard and head northward.

"It was a clear day and the aircraft was in perfect shape as we all settled down for a long day's flight. I can't remember what the country was like for the first couple of hours, but as we changed course, to a more northeasterly direction, we soon began to realize what a vast and no doubt deadly place the Sahara Desert is. For hours we flew over nothing but sandy wasteland. I had radioed in to the air strip as we passed over the village of Agmar. We could see no planes on the ground so, apparently, all other crews were doing okay. A few hours later, we passed over the airstrip at Tindouf. We could see a couple of B-24's on the ground. They, apparently, had run low on fuel or had trouble of some kind with their aircraft. I do not recall the exact altitude we were flying but we were flying too low to go over the Atlas Mountains and were supposed to fly down a valley with mountains on both sides of us. This was my main target of the flight.

"As we approached the mountain range, I could see we were about a mile or two west of the mountain pass. I suggested to the pilot he make a three hundred sixty degree turn to the left and come in a couple of miles to the east. All of us being young and foolish, we decided not to make the turn but to fly over the mountains, dodging a few peaks. Thinking back, it was really a foolish thing to do. If we had hit a downdraft, we might still be in those mountains. The pilot actually had to lift a wing now and then to avoid hitting. As we weaved around, we were climbing and, within a short time, we were past the high range.

"Marrakech is located just north of the mountains; in fact, it is almost in the northern foothills. It was late afternoon when we landed and, by the time we were assigned quarters and had gotten something to eat, we were all ready for a little sack time. As we checked in for quarters, each of us was handed five GI blankets. As it was terribly hot, we asked what we were to do with five blankets. We were told it got cold at night and before morning we would wish we had more. We were assigned tents with wooden floors in an olive grove. There were hundreds of tents. How true it was about the blankets! The winds at night, blowing in from the Mediterranean, created a bitter cold situation. The enlisted men, guarding the aircraft, had to plug in their electric suits to combat the cold. The base here at Marrakech was huge - American military aircraft of every size and description.

It had large supply and repair facilities, large hangars and shops, and lots of military personnel along with many native employees.

"I wandered into a building where, by a sign, I knew I would find a latrine. There were separations between each facility but no doors - must have been six or eight on either side of the room. Getting into position, you were facing the relief area across from you. There were no stools, just a hole in the floor, a place to put your feet, and water running down the wall to wash the waste down the hole. Shortly after assuming the position, I was surprised to discover this was a co-ed facility. Native women as well as native men came in. One woman took the stall directly across from me. All I could do was complete what I was doing and leave.

"For the first time since we left Topeka, we were given passes to go into town. There were several hundred of us ready when the trucks arrived for our transportation. Marrakech is a very old city with a population in 1944 of around 250,000. Much of the city was off-limits to us. We especially wanted to go into the old walled city but were not allowed to do so. There were MP's all over the place. We were told that, on several occasions, men had gone into the old city and were never seen again. I do not doubt the truth of this. We learned our first lesson almost as soon as we got off the truck. There were dozens of young natives with three-wheeled carts built from bicycles. Each cart would carry two people. Schuyler and I got into one, without asking what we would be charged for a short ride. A few blocks up the street, we got off and asked the price. We were asked a fantastic price, which we refused to pay. We gave the boy what we thought was fair and turned to walk off. He must have followed us for a block screaming and yelling at us; no doubt calling us every name in the book.

"After that incident, we never bought anything or used any transportation without first finding out what it would cost us. A short time later, a French refugee, about ten or twelve, speaking good English, offered his services for the afternoon. I don't remember What he charged us but it was the best investment we made all day. He took us places, told us if we were paying too much for anything, chased off the beggars and was right by our side at all times. The only thing I bought was a copper plate that I was able to send to Maxine. We still have it. I bought the plate at an outside market (most were). I remember the original asking price was about three times what I finally paid for it.

"Most of the afternoon was spent in walking around in a not-too-large area (six or eight square blocks). It was not unusual to see a car coming down the street with people all over it. As there was very little gasoline for private vehicles, the car would be pulled by donkeys or horses. It was quite a sight to see. There were sidewalk cafes all over. It was fun to just sit and watch the people. We were under strict orders as to the time we were to board the trucks and return to the airbase. The few hours had gone too fast and we were hoping we would be able to return the following day. We left our little French friend, telling him we hoped to see him at the same place tomorrow. On returning to base, we soon found out our plans for the next day would have to be changed as we were scheduled to take off around ten p.m. for the final leg of our journey to England.

"This part of the trip would be much different than any previous flight. For the first time, we would be flying over an area that could also be reached by German aircraft. Quite a number of our bombers had been attacked and some shot down on the flight from North Africa to England. Our course, from Marrakech, would take us due west for about one hundred miles, then due north along the tenth meridian west. On the north course, we would be flying fifty to seventy-five miles off the western coast of Portugal. I was given the location of two lights in Portugal that I could use for check points.

"There was to be complete radio silence at all times. We were cautioned to avoid getting too close to the Brest Peninsula as we could be picked up on German radar located there. France was still completely occupied at this time. There were German fighter bases at Brest and these we wanted to avoid. At a point about two hundred miles off Brest, we were to change course to a more northeasterly direction and fly up the St. George Channel and land near a town called Valley on Holyhead in the northern part of Wales.

"Before leaving Marrakech, we took on ammunition for all ten machine guns. For the first time, we were flying an aircraft that was capable of helping to destroy the enemy. We were hoping we would not have to use the guns this night as we would be out there all by ourselves. There were quite a number of aircraft on their way this night but it was doubtful we would see any of them.

"It was a clear night as we took off but, out over the Atlantic, it was completely overcast. We were on top of the clouds where the moon was shining brightly. It was a beautiful night! The North Star was a perfect guide for my navigation. Along with a powerful radio signal from a station in Prestwick, Scotland, I charted and kept a perfect course to our destination. I don't think anyone went to sleep during the night as we were all alert for possible enemy aircraft. The overcast continued all during the flight but was beautiful above the clouds. As the sun came up, it created rainbows on the clouds.

When my calculations indicated we were near the coast of the Republic of Ireland, I had the pilot drop below the clouds and we were all happy to see the coast of Ireland off to the left. As we dropped down to about a thousand feet, we could see signs (huge signs) along the coast, telling us to avoid landing in Ireland because, if we did, we would be interned. Ireland, like Spain, was a neutral country. I had a radio bearing on the landing field at Valley so had the pilot follow that course. My night's work was over so I put away my instruments and went up on the flight deck for the landing.

"It was nice to be on the ground again but, shortly after landing, it started to rain lightly and continued for the two days we were there. We were told to take all our personal belongings from the plane as it was to be taken over by another crew and flown to a field for immediate use in combat. When we got this nice, new aircraft in Topeka we were sure it was to be ours for use in combat. I guess it was badly needed and could not wait for us.

"After two days, we found ourselves on a troop train enroute to a staging area where we would be assigned, as replacements, to a combat group. It was a beautiful day for our first land view of Wales and England. We saw several areas that had been bombed but our first sight of devastation of war will never be forgotten. Our train route took us through the city of Coventry or, I should say, what had been, Coventry. Here we saw what concentrated heavy bombing could do. I don't think there was a building left standing - it was one huge mass of rubble. Our trip through Coventry may have been intentional so we would see what the Germans had done to English cities and we would not feel guilty about bombing German cities. If that was the intention, I'm sure it had its intended effect.

"I don't recall just how long our train ride was but we all enjoyed it as spring had come to England and the countryside was beautiful. Trees and grass were green and many flowers were in bloom. We did not know where we were going but our trip ended at the village of Stone. Stone is located in the central part of England, not too far north of Birmingham and, also, near Stratford-on-Avon, the home of Shakespeare. Stone was not an airbase but a replacement center. All crews coming here would be sent to different groups where they might be needed. We were quartered in an old convent that must have been built centuries before. The rooms were small (not over 8 x 10 feet), no heat, very poor light and very, very damp. There were several hundred of us here awaiting assignment. Again, we were not allowed off the base so most of our time was spent sleeping, drinking, playing poker or trying to beat one of the slot machines in the Officers' Club. I don't recall just how long we were there but it was just a few days and we were again put on a train and traveled to our permanent airbase in England. It was on this train ride, instead of the ride from Valley to Stone, that we went through the city of Coventry.

"Our home was to be the base of the 44th Bomb Group, the oldest B-24 group in England. The base was located in Norfolk County, near the village of Ship-dham, about eighteen miles west of the city of Norwich. The base was nestled like a hundred others amongst the pastures and wheat fields and meadows of the English farm folk. Ten new crews, of which we were a part, were assigned to the 44th. The group was composed of four squadrons - the 66th, 67th, 68th and 506th. Each squadron was composed of twelve aircraft, giving the 44th a total of forty-eight combat aircraft. I don't think it was ever at full strength as seldom a mission went by without loss of aircraft. The 44th had been in England since September of 1942 and it was now late March, 1944. All original aircraft had been lost and only a handful of the original flying personnel were still around. Some. had completed their twenty-five missions and had gone home but more had been lost over the continent, either killed or were prisoners of war.

"On August 1, 1943, the 44th had been one of several groups taking part in what was then called the greatest air assault in history; also, some history books refer to it as "the flight into hell." This was the low level air assault on the oil fields of Ploesti, Rumania. This is a story in itself and should be read by anyone who is interested in the air battles of World War II. The 44th had been badly mauled, losing, I think, eleven aircraft and crews with many wounded in the aircraft that did return. Most planes that returned were badly damaged. The 44th had flown to Libya, in North Africa, for this mission.

"Our crew was assigned to the 66th squadron. The officers were assigned to a hut (steel) with the officers of one other crew. The enlisted men were assigned to other quarters on the compound. The eight of us in our hut had been together since Casper, Wyoming, and I had gone to navigation school with the navigator at Monroe, Louisiana. I do not recall who our squadron commander was but the group commander was Colonel Frederick R. Dent. He was only there a couple of weeks when he was transferred and replaced by Colonel John H. Gibson. A former group commander of the 44th who was now Wing Commander, General Leon W. Johnson, was seen quite often at our base. He had received the Congressional Medal of Honor for his part in the raid on the Ploesti Oil Fields.

"Life on the base of the 44th was not too bad. It was strictly a combat facility - no frills. The Nisson huts we lived in were very simple; eight bunks, a pot belly stove (wood burning) in the center of the room, some lockers for storage and that was about all. The weather was very damp and cool so it was almost impossible to keep the place as warm as we would have liked it to be. The living quarters were about a mile from the flight operations area so you either had to walk or ride a jeep-pulled cart to that area. The mess halls and officers' club were several hundred yards from our area but no problem getting there.

"The first week or so with the 44th was spent in getting acquainted with the base and the surrounding area. We went on several training flights in the area. At this time, there were more crews than aircraft so we did not see any combat flying for a couple of weeks. We did get a liberty run into Norwich one afternoon. It was our first experience of being in a large city that was completely blacked out at night. You could be standing in a very busy area and not see a single light. You weren't even allowed to smoke a cigarette outside at night. We only had an hour or so before dark so did not get to see much of the city. We went to a pub and had a few beers, then went to a USO dance. There were a lot more guys than gals and I don't recall dancing once.

"After about two weeks at the base of the 44th, we were awakened bright and early on the morning of April 8, 1944, for our first mission. It seemed I had barely gotten to sleep as it was still pitch black outside. In fact, we had only been asleep about three hours. We didn't know it then but, from now on, we would be getting sleep every chance we got. After eating breakfast and going to the briefing, it was just barely getting a little light as we jumped in the trucks that were to take us to our planes.

"Our target was a military installation near Hannover. Our plane for the day had seen a lot of combat and had just come back into service after receiving one new wing. It must have taken at least an hour for all groups to get to altitude and into formation before heading eastward over the North Sea. It was quite a sight seeing hundreds of B-24's and B-17's ploughing through the skies.

"Later, we would see many of our fighters along to protect us. Schuyler began having trouble keeping the plane level almost as soon as we reached altitude. The aircraft seemed to be wing heavy on the side of the replacement wing. On several occasions, we almost crashed into aircraft on either side of us in the formation. Over Holland and still about fifteen miles from Germany, he could no longer keep formation and we turned away, from the formation and headed back for England alone. As we neared the coast of England, we circled and dropped our twelve 500 pound bombs into the sea. Four other planes had trouble and failed to make the mission. Of the forty-four planes of the 44th that had taken off, thirty-nine were able to go on. But, it turned out to be a very rough day for our group. Eleven of the thirty-nine bombers had been shot down. Of the thirty-nine, five were replacement crews who had come in with us. Out of the 110 men lost on this mission, at least twenty were personal friends. It was a little rough, especially on going back to our Nisson hut and knowing the men with whom we shared the hut had been lost that day.

"I am not going to tell you about the missions that followed as, Keith Schuyler has covered the subject very well in his book "Elusive Horizons." Keith had always planned on writing a book about our experiences so he wrote detailed notes following our return from each mission. He had a note attached requesting that they be sent to his wife, when the war was over, in the event he was unable to make it back. It took twenty-five years before he finally wrote the book but it was published in 1969.

Pilot 2Lt. Keith C. Schuyler.

April 29, 1944.

"There was a murmur through the briefing room as the pointer settled on Berlin the morning of the twenty-ninth. But the usual moan in unison was lacking as though the men could not squeeze any levity out of the situation. As a group, we were tired. Implications of the long haul, after days of bombing missions every time the weather permitted, crushed in on us, smothered us.

"Berlin was always a rough one. This was the symbol of German might. In an ideological effort, symbols are important. You protect them with your life. There were still plenty of German flyers willing to die for Berlin for ideological reasons. There were plenty more who had lost their grasp on symbols but flew and fought as exquisite machines that were manufactured out of the best parts available. Germany's best was plenty good enough. She had been hurt, badly. But like any creature that has been mortally wounded, she was still capable of fighting like hell. This we knew when the pointer settled on Berlin.

"You can expect heavy fighter opposition," we were told. "The Luftwaffe has been unusually quiet for the past week, and we expect plenty of trouble today.

You will have fighter cover much of the way, but you know they can't stick around long. Keep your formation tight so that the German fighters can't get through. We have tried to route you around the worst flak, but it will be rough over Berlin." .

"The weather would provide some clouds, but it was expected to be broken enough for good bombing. Our plane was assigned to the lead squadron. We would be flying left wing in the second element.

"Waning night was cool and starlit as we rode the truck to the dispersal area. Sanders had checked over the airplane, and his report was encouraging; "She's not quite the airplane that the last one was, but she's a good one."

"The enlisted men were always alert to my arrival at the airplane. This was one of the few disciplines I had imposed on them. In this manner, we could quickly go over the necessary inspection and reports so that all of us knew about what to expect from our airplane. They had been briefed, and we knew what we were in for together. Our crew was complete this morning. This was the way we had started on our first mission which now seemed so long ago. This was the way we wanted to end our war, win or lose.

"There was a kind of pathetic quality to the group as the men lined up in front of the airplane. They looked like half-dressed Eskimos, too small for the whale-long fuselage behind them. It was not until we were close enough in the usual half-light, and I could see their faces, that they became people. These youngsters who had started together were no longer youngsters. They were men. Even Bill Sanders' grin, which had survived the ages of our indoctrination into manhood, had a different quality. It was still genuine, but drawn, and lined with the tremendous sense of responsibility that he had discovered his job really entailed. Bill knew much of what it would take to get this B-24 to Berlin-and back.

"Cox and Reichert looked just a little old for their years, much older than they had been only twenty-one days before on our lighthearted try for our first.

"Maybe George Renfro showed it most. He was the youngest in years, and his transition to a level of manhood that we now all shared had been the greatest jump. He had been a frustrated belly gunner until he saw what came up from the ground toward this exposed part of the Liberator's navel. Then he had wanted no part of it.

"I remembered the first chance I gave him to get ready in the event that something happened to Reichert and I needed George in the ball turret. Several of us

Waist-Gunner Sgt. George Neal Renfro

were walking across the barracks area right after an announcement that we would have a day off. It was after our first rough one to Bernberg.

"This will give you a chance to practice in the belly turret," I told George, jerking my thumb toward the area where a working model had been set up for the purpose. "Give it an hour tomorrow."

"Renfro looked at me in utter disbelief, then broke out in his regular Texas grin.

"In a pig's ass, I will!" -

"We were considerably more than whispering distance apart, and George's exclamation covered quite an area. I walked closer. "George, old boy, I know just how you meant that. But if the colonel should have been walking by just then, you would have made us both look pretty bad." Poor George's face dropped to his shoe strings. "Now, you get two hours in the belly turret." He was apologetic to the point that it was my turn to be embarrassed.

"That was the closest I ever came to having to discipline any of the men. And that was a complete bust. Headquarters crossed us up and we were scheduled for the mission the following day. George never did get his time in the ball turret. Looking at him this day of the Berlin mission, I was confident that he would find a way to do whatever job was demanded of him.

"Schow was in love with his guns. He showed the strain of recent weeks, but there was a deadly earnestness in his demeanor whenever he was in the proximity of his twin fifties. He made me feel as though nothing could possibly get through Sergeant Harry J. It was a good feeling. Rowland, imperturbable as ever, was probably the least affected. Until the bad bust of two days before, he had not had to concern himself with other than his radios. Yet even he reflected the strain of the pace.

"Living together, the four of us with lieutenant's bars didn't notice the changes among ourselves as much. We lived our fears and concerns as a part, of our daily association. However, the wounds were as deep. They were just not as noticeable.

"Number ten. If we got to the action, this would give us an oak-leaf cluster on our air medals except for the two who had missed one mission. It was merely a thought in passing. It would take six clusters to buy a ticket home. And, at this point, the price seemed much too high and unattainable.

"Automatically I eased the engines into action in the knowledge that the crew chief had already made over sixty checks of the airplane. But, I watched the oil pressure move between the green lines daubed in at sixty and eighty pounds as though my first instructor was looking over my shoulder. Cylinder head temperature on each engine climbed slowly toward the max of 205°C; oil temperature moving into the proper range above 60°C; manifold pressure; fuel pressure; prop governor; magnetos; generators; vacuum pumps; de-icers; and the countless other mechanical marvels needed to get this chunk of machinery airborne and to keep her there. It's a long way to Berlin and back.

"Down the taxi strip. and a quick check of each engine individually at 1600 rpm's. Flaps down, gear locked, props in full low pitch, mixture full rich, cowl flaps closed. Turn into position for takeoff as soon as the ship ahead is airborne. Brakes full on, throttles slowly ahead until each horse had the bit in its teeth. Turn 'em loose! And you feel the power dragging at the wings with a positive pull, and you know you have another good airplane. Maybe not quite as tight as the last, but good. The airspeed needle keeps gaining on 120, mph with lots of runway left. You feel for lift, find. it, and urge her off the concrete at 120. Level a bit until you have packed more air under your wings to gain flying speed, then up toward the twin tail at few hundreds yards ahead of you.

"Strung out like a flock of pelicans, ugly and awkward on the ground but ever so graceful in the air, the formation heads out over the North Sea.

"Okay to check guns," you call, and the ship shuddered as ten 50's talk. Gradually the gaps close until the string of bombers has bunched into three tight units headed for a target over five hundred miles away. This is the way you go to Berlin; and Berlin is always a rough one.

"As we sailed in across the Zuider Zee, flak fields ahead were little more than nuisance notice of the potential trouble ahead. On each side of us there were other groups absorbing some of the flak batteries' attention, and one group at a lower altitude on the left lost a ship before we had covered much of the Dutch sky. Then we crossed the German border just north of Osnabrück. Flak was spotty - not too hard to dodge. Groups ahead helped provide a route through the stuff. And, we knew the slower B-l7's had used up some of the ground ammunition on their way in ahead of us. Some fighters overhead, friendly fellows cutting contrails back and forth in a protective web that made you feel good. Then Larry Davis cut in on the inter-phone.

"Fighters! A whole swarm of them!" I didn't see them at once. Larry pinpointed them. "Straight ahead, low at twelve o'clock!"

"Then I saw them. I took a deep breath. Coming up at us like a swarm of bees was a literal swarm of at least forty German fighters. And they were headed directly at our formation! Like specks at first, in almost an instant they materialized into wings and engines. "Give it to them," I hollered, and held tight. Trying to move in this mess would invite collision. They were packed and stacked!

"Then there was a hellish roar as everything became a confusion of sound and motion. Like entering a tunnel with the window open on a train, dust, noise, and debris became indistinguishable. Right over my windshield a German fighter came apart in a glimpse of flame and junk. That was Larry's. My impression was little more than a flash.

"From the top turret, Sanders cut the tip from the wing of a Messerschmitt 109. As it sloughed toward the ground, Schow gave it a burst. Then another 109 came into Harry's sights and he kept the triggers down. The fighter started an abrupt climb, stalled, and disappeared down out of sight.

"A B-24 that had been lagging at seven o'clock drew in close at five o'clock just as a German came through. The fighter smashed head-on into the big one right at the nose turret and both planes exploded in a ball of flame.

"Then it was over. Just like that. But back through the formations behind us the Germans barreled with reckless abandon. Airplanes were going down in every direction, the cripples staggering out of formation, clinging to life - then blowing up or fluttering down out of sight.

"We had been caught with our fighters down. But now our single-engine friends moved in for the kill. The fight drifted behind. My instruments read right. We had made it through the fighter belt on the way in. Our incendiary load still hung quietly in the racks, waiting to see if we would make it to Berlin.

"Berlin was visible long before we arrived. In the greatest daylight raid of the war to that date, German's capital city was a mass of flames and explosions as we approached. And the maelstrom of churning guts, flame, smoke, and debris extended up to the level at which we went in. Although we sat four miles above the city, we soon became a part of the picture. It wasn't pretty. The air seemed filled with bombers, but each group was taking its own heading for its own particular part in this destruction. Each course was marked by a lane of flak from the hot guns below. Somehow, we went on. And then the bombs burst out of the bays like steel confetti and scattered with the wind on their Satanic way, down, down, down.... They twinkled back at us from far below as our bomb bay doors rumbled to close the rupture in our belly. Our job was done.'

"But it was a long way home....

"Somehow, after you have dropped your bombs, you get the feeling that everything is all right. If your airplane is working as it should, it becomes more a matter of whether you have enough gasoline for the trip back. At least that is the feeling you have. After all, the Germans had their chance to stop you, and they failed. The game is over. Why should they bother with you now? You've dropped your load.

"But down deep inside you know it isn't over. This is not a game. The Germans know that you will be back with another load if you are permitted to go home. They have plans for you. They want to punish you for what you did if they can. So they try. .

"Maybe there is no other good way out. Maybe that is why the lead plane took us over Brandenburg on the way out. So the Germans get another good crack at us with their flak guns. They have had plenty of practice this day.

"The flak was heavy as we approached the outskirts of Brandenburg. We passed close to a formation of B-17's headed our way. I couldn't help thinking that these poor bastards would still be up here flying after we were on the ground. Never before had I realized the impressive difference in air speed between the B-17 and the B-24. We passed them almost as though they were standing still. That got us to the flak faster.

"Although it was heavy, we seemed to be getting by without incident. In fact, the stuff was thinning out. Then I noticed four bursts off our left wing, maybe a hundred yards out, and just below our level. Then four more, closer. Fascinated, I watched as four more burst just ahead of and below our left wing, possibly 30 yards away. I didn't see the next bursts. But I heard them. And our ship shook to the concussion. Immediately, number two prop ran away. The torque, as the propeller screamed up to over 3000 rpm, dragged at our wing, and I leaned into the rudder, then hit the feathering button. I needed time to survey the damage. We were hurt again - badly. .

"A check of the crew brought all good word from that quarter, but a hole in the cowling of number two gave visual evidence that we had caught plenty from the last volley of flak. The manifold pressure on number four was down badly. The supercharger had probably been knocked out. The engine was running smoothly, but it wouldn't do much more than carry its own weight at the over 20,000 feet we were indicating. I eased the throttles ahead a bit to take up some of the slack. Things were under control, but they weren't good. I decided to see what could be done with number two.

"Except for that hole in cowling, I could see no other damage to the engine. Propeller governors, one of the few faults with the Pratts, were apt to go haywire with a sudden change in power. Perhaps there was something left in the number two. I nudged the prop blades into the wind and fed it some power. The engine responded well, and I brought it back into cruising throttle. It pounded like a constipated threshing machine. But it was running. I suspected that a cylinder had been knocked out.

"Normally, we wouldn't have too much to worry about, but we were still a long way from home. The disruption in power had us back behind the formation. There was no chance of catching up. I personally called the lead ship.

"Red leader, we've got some problem back there. Can you slow it down a little?"

"We'll try,' the answer came back."But we can't cut it back much."

"I knew he had to maintain formation speed. And it soon became evident that we couldn't keep up. There was no point in continuing the conversation and altering any Germans listening in that we would soon be a sitting duck. We kept dropping back - slowly, inexorably... .

"If we were hit in the wings as much as I feared, there was a good chance that we would be losing gasoline from the wing tanks. I called Sanders. He climbed down from his turret to check the gas supply.

"His report confirmed my suspicions. There was a serious imbalance in the gasoline tanks to indicate that we were losing some somewhere. I asked Raucher for our estimated time of arrival in England. Some fast mental calculations convinced me that we were not going to make it home. If my figuring was right, the best we could hope for would be a ditching about halfway across the North Sea.

"The crew couldn't help but be aware that I was concerned about the gas supply. But, I said nothing to let them in on my grim secret. Rauscher could suspect, and Sanders looked worried, but at that point I was the only one who had complete information. Even to make the North Sea, we would need to use all our altitude to stretch our glide as far as possible.

"We were now so far back that I was no longer sure that we were following our own group. A short distance ahead of us another crippled Liberator was dragging toward home. And, on ahead of him there was another single B-24. I called Schow.

"Is there anything behind us?"

"No. We're all there is."

"Even today, when I think back to those times of trouble, I am amazed at the performance of the entire crew. Not once did they ask a question. As though sensing the burdens that sat with me in the pilot's seat, they never added to them by asking questions that I could not or feared to answer. Always, they kept me informed of anything they thought I should know. But they did not probe into my troubled thoughts. This was one of their greatest contributions. They stood by their guns, the charts, the radios.

"In return, I tried to keep them posted. "We are approaching the fighter belt. Keep your eyes open. If we can get past the fighters we might make it."

"I couldn't make it sound too good. Everyone could feel the vibration of the sick engine, and it was obvious that we were alone. The conversations about the gasoline supply and Rauscher's estimated time of arrival certainly did not engender much optimism. Again it was Larry who altered us to fighters.

"Off to the left. They are hitting that group off to the left."

"Well ahead, ten miles or more, we could see the action at about ten o'clock and at our level. I prayed that they wouldn't see us. But it didn't matter. Straight ahead there was another flock of fighters slicing through the group that I thought was the 44th. Bright twinkles of 20mm cannon and the smoke of machine guns were visible even at this distance.

"Directly ahead of us, the second cripple also saw them. Black blobs began to drop from the B-24. At first, I thought they were kicking loose some bombs which had become hung up. But then, the black blobs blossomed into parachutes. That crew wasn't going to stick around for the fun. I never did see what happened to the other single. Because, now all my attention was directed to the fighters.

"There were eight of them! And had they elected to come at us singly, subsequent events might have been different. But they came straight on, strung out wing to wing, like a shallow string of beads. Focke Wulf 190's they were. And under other circumstances they would have been beautiful to watch. But I had only an instant to make my decision of how to deal with them.

"Whether I was wise, foolhardy, or stupid is left to the interpretation of the individual reader. In the brief seconds left to decide, a thousand thoughts raced through my mind. One was paramount: We had come to fight. It never occurred to me to abandon the airplane, although our position was hopeless. I had a real affection for every man on that airplane, but I would not ask them to run away. Nevertheless, we were about to be blasted out of the sky. There was little chance that all of us would get out alive. I had nothing in my hands to fight with except the total airplane. So I used it.

"Get ready" I called. I, too, got ready. I did not make my move until I saw the leading edges of the FW's start to smoke and yellow balls to pop around our wings. Then I dove straight for the middle of the string of beads! Either they would get out of the way or we would take a couple of them with us. In any event, they could not all aim their airplanes at us if they scattered.

"They scattered.

"All of our machine guns seemed to be going at once as FW's scrambled out of our way in every direction. I couldn't see the action, but from shouts over the inter-phone, two of them were badly hit and on their way down.

"So were we.

"Deliberately, I held the nose of the bomber as straight down as I could manage. But, she was trimmed for level flight and wanted to come out of the dive. Jack saw my quivering arms and added his strength to keep the nose down. I wanted those fighters to think that they had us. The strategy worked on five out of the six remaining, but that one was destined to give us more trouble than all of the others combined. He didn't believe me.

"That one German peeled off' and came after us. I heard Jack shout under his oxygen mask as I felt the controls wrenched from me for an instant. Jack had seen him coming from his side and he rolled the bomber into the attack. Tracers cut by the left side of the fuselage as the tortured Liberator responded. We kept the pressure on the elevators and the nose toward the ground as I watched the air speed pass the red line. Then it touched 290 which gave us somewhere around 400 mph at our altitude. I didn't know how much of this the battered bomber could take.

"Down below I could see a solid cloud cover. It was our only refuge. But, in one of the frequent paradoxes of war, to gain them was also our undoing. Our precious altitude, needed to get us somewhere near home, whatever the consequences, was being used up in one desperate effort to escape the more obvious danger from the fighters. We would willingly have taken on this one eager beaver who stayed with us, but to change tactics would undoubtedly bring the other fighters in for the kill. We were committed.

"Twice more on the way down the one fighter came in on us. And, twice more we turned in to him as the clouds neared. Then we were enveloped in the mist, safe for the moment from our pursuer.

"In an instant, we were in serious trouble of an entirely different kind. The front surfaces of our cold airplane, dropping down from some 20,000 feet to this warm air layer of cloud at 5,000, were immediately swathed in ice. Only a tiny triangle, less than the size of a folded hand kerchief, was clear in the lower right part of my windshield. The top turret and the nose turret caught the frigid coating simultaneously. However, I was on instruments in the clouds, anyway, and my visibility was no immediate problem. My worry of the moment was with the controls. They were sticking badly. As fast as I would kick the rudders free of ice and work the elevators, they would stiffen up again. It was the first B-24 I had ever flown without de-icer boots on the wings.

"We've got to get out of this stuff to get rid of this ice, " I cautioned the gunners. "Get ready. I'm going on top."

"I poked the bomber's nose above the cloud layer and leveled of. A few minutes to let the metal of the airplane assume somewhere near the outside temperature would do it. But our little friend upstairs was waiting.

"Go down! Go down !" came from several gun positions as the 190 bored in. I thrust the wheel forward, keeping my eyes on the instruments.

"Get up! Get up!" came just as emphatically as the plea to go down,

"Puzzled, I glanced out the clear side window. We were right over a German airfield. At the altitude they could knock us down with a rock. I lifted the '24 up a little, watching out the side to make sure we were riding in the clouds. I rolled the bomber to a heading ninety degrees of our course. Maybe we could shake the fighter. After at short time, I took the original heading again, trying to keep hidden. The controls fought me back on every move. Even more serious was the loss of function in the two gun turrets. I warned the crew, then eased into the clear air on top.

"Get down! Get down!" came over the inter-phone to the shuddering stutter of machine guns.

"Well, if there was no other way, we would stay hidden and hope for the best. Anyway, the controls were beginning to work a bit more freely.

"I had time to consider our position. It wasn't good. We had given up our precious altitude just to stay alive and to keep fighting, but the end was inevitable. It was not a question of trying to save the ship; it was doomed. The one big question was just how long to continue this running battle before admitting we were licked.

"So far, I was certain that none of the men had been hurt. We were licking along at 160 indicated, at least headed for home, and at this altitude number four was doing its full share and number two was still pounding away. Siting above us was the enemy we had come to fight. If we could knock him down, our job would be done. Then we could go as far as the gasoline would allow and our war would be over. But I had no desire to engage the FW 190. None of us were likely to get home unless we could find the underground, but I couldn't see risking one life on the airplane for another crack at the fighter. I held course and altitude. Then fate took another hand.

"The cloud cover, which had parted so conveniently over Berlin to permit precision bombing, had been solid at our lower altitude for many miles. Now it started to break. At first we just hit small holes, then larger one.

"This situation was made to order for the fighter. He apparently spotted us crossing the small ponds of open air, and when we hit a big one he came in. His first attack came at 5 o'clock on the tail. Schow told me about it later: "I started firing. The tracers bounced right off him. And then, I was just pressing triggers and nothing was happening. It was an instant before I could find the extend of the damage. A 20 mm had hit us in the right elevator. It blew my hydraulic unit on the floor, clipped off my left gun, cut my mike cord about an inch and a half from my throat, and generally took my plexiglass."

"The tail gunner tried to fire his right gun manually, but it too was ruined. Schow went to the waist, where a fire had started, put on his chute, and told Sergeant Cox to relay the news to me since his mike was cut. Cox had already been on the inter-phone.

"We have a fire back here in the waist," he said calmly by way of information.

"He put no more emphasis on it than he would for a fire in an ash tray. But, it had serious implications to me. It was not uncommon for gasoline to run down inside a wing, if a tank was punctured, and spill into the bomb bay. We had evidence that we were losing gasoline; if fumes picked up that fire in the waist, we could become one big bomb!

Then I learned about Schow's trouble.

"We have another fire in the tail," the message read. The hydraulic system for the tail turret had been blown from the fuselage wall and the fluid was on fire.

"Again the clouds gave us temporary relief as the fighter maneuvered for another pass. I tried to think of an answer. It was uncomplicated and the only thing I could think of at the time.

"Put them out."

"As the gunners were working on the flames and throwing-out burning flak vests, I called to Sanders and Reichert. Our time must be getting short.

"Reichert, you take over the top turret while Bill checks the gas again."

"I sensed the exchange of positions behind me, then the clouds opened up again. Reichert had not had one chance to fire a gun. Lowering the ball turret would rob us of about five miles an hour in air speed and use up precious it gasoline. Every time we had hit fighters, we hit trouble. But, now Walt had his chance. The 190 came up off our right side, and the twin 50's followed him all the way. Then they stopped as Walt pressed empty guns.

"How is everything back there?" I questioned after the wide pass.

"Out of ammunition up here," Walt called back. "I still can't see through the frost on this turret," Davis reported from up front. I knew Schow's guns were out. Only Renfro was in business at the left waist. "Everything's okay here." But the passes were mostly from the right. I suspected that the fighter was out of 20 mm's; we hadn't seen any on the last pass. His machine guns may have been empty. That might have been why he made his last pass wide. But we had only one gun out of ten operative at the moment. There was extra ammunition, but it would take time to get it to the guns. The clouds were about all gone. Then I felt Sanders' hand on my shoulder.

"We'd better get out of here, sir. We're down to fifty gallons!"

"So – the time *had* come. You expected it, yet somehow it couldn't be you. I didn't know if the fires were out in the back; but it didn't matter now. Only fifty gallons. A B-24 burned over 200 gallons an hour when it was working *right*. Fifteen minutes of flying time left at the most. At perhaps a ground speed close to our indicated 160, this would take us forty miles. I called Rauscher. We had been flying all over the sky trying to shake the fighter, but I knew Dale would be trying to follow us on his navigation charts.

"Where are we, Rausch?"

"His answer came back quickly.

"We are just over Holland or very close to it."

"Forty miles. Enough to take us about halfway across Holland, perhaps to the Zuider Zee. Right into the flak batteries that could pick us off like we were indeed a flying boxcar at this altitude. It was time. I found another cloud, a big one.

"All right, now listen carefully. Bail out. Don't hesitate. Delay your jump below the clouds. Good luck. And God bless you. Acknowledge!"

"Roger, bombardier."

"Roger, navigator."

"Roger, waist ..."

"I grabbed Bill Sanders' hand, briefly. He had heard the order. Jack caught the movement and looked over, puzzled. Bomb doors were opening. He was on interplane frequency and hadn't heard. I jerked my thumb back. "Bail out." Our fingers caught in a fleeting farewell, and he turned to clap Rowland on the shoulder at his radio table. There was no hesitation, no question; they went. And as they went, I made my one final gesture.

"... over Holland or very close to it," Rauscher had said. The long-defeated Dutch were still our allies. A B-24 Liberator bomber could cause a lot of damage when it hit. I started a 180-degree turn. Let her blow in Germany! I took a quick glance back through the fuselage. It was empty. It was the emptiest airplane I had ever seen! In that brief second, I felt as lonely as I had ever felt in my life. I flicked on the aileron switch of the automatic pilot, always set for emergency. As I rose hurriedly from my seat, I felt something grabbing at my waist. It was the cord to my heated suit.

"Carefully I reached back and unplugged it so that the cord wouldn't break.

"Then I was on the catwalk of the bomb bays, sat down, to roll out, forward into the clouds. The wind swept my legs back. I gathered my feet under me on the catwalk and dived head first through the opening. As I tumbled below and away from our airplane, I had the sensation we once had as kids when we would dive under a high waterfall to get to the recess behind it. Then I extended my arms, as I had been. taught, to get into correct forward: position before opening my: chute. I was in no immediate hurry.

"I had told the crew to delay their chute for a number of reasons. The Kraut was still hunting for us, and he might foul a chute accidentally in the clouds. Or, as some had been in the habit of doing, he might gun the men in their chutes. The less time we hung in the sky, the less time the Germans would have to get to our landing site. And we could spare a moment or two to slow down to the terminal velocity of a falling human body of about 120 miles per hour. I almost waited *too* long...

"When in good position, I grabbed the ring on the harness of my back pack, pulled, and felt the snap. I braced for the shock, but nothing happened. I looked at my harness. The cable was still trailing from its sheath! When I pulled again, the cable came free. I clung to the ring. Somewhere I had heard that a good jumper does not lose his ring.

"I wondered why I couldn't see or hear our airplane. Years later, Renfro said he saw it blow all to hell as he was coming down in his chute. The 190 did come in on Schow. Hanging helpless, Schow just waved. The German waved back. He had his kill - chalk up one more B-24.

"Strung out behind me were the other parachutes, some still higher than mine. I reached for my leg straps, to free them so that I could take off when I hit. But the ground was coming at me. I braced with bent knees, hit, and somersaulted in approved fashion. Military chutes let you down hard. But I was okay.

"Quickly I gathered my parachute and tried to hide it from possible spotting planes. Off to my left about a hundred yards was a farmhouse, and when the German woman on the porch saw me look her way, she went inside. The sun was now shining brightly. It was about 1 P.M. I squinted toward the western horizon. There were bombers still in view sailing serenely into the west. B-17's. For an instant, I felt lonely. I thought of home. They would worry when they got the word.

"Then I suddenly realized that I was alive and well. I felt ridiculously happy. I felt a serenity completely at odds with my situation.

Navigator 2Lt. Dale E. Rauscher, second part.

"April 29, 1944 - This was to be a long and eventful day. Again, I am going to skip the mission as it is covered in Schuyler's book. I will cover things I remember from the time I heard Schuyler order us to "BAIL OUT." My first duty was to help the bombardier get out of the nose turret as it was almost impossible for him to get out without assistance. Next, I pushed the destruct button on some equipment, kicked open the bottom escape hatch, sat on the edge and dropped head first from the aircraft. We had stayed with the plane to an altitude of around 5,000 feet so could not delay too long before opening the chute. At what I thought was about 1,500 ft., I pulled the rip-cord and the chute opened with quite a jerk. I later discovered the cameo missing from a ring I was wearing. It, apparently, popped out when the chute opened.

"It was quite an experience floating through the air with the only noise being the sound of the wind going through the shroud lines. I knew we were close to the Holland border but, as it turned out, we were several miles inside Germany.

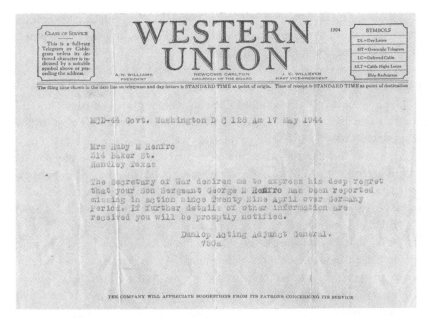

Cable to parents of Waist-Gunner Sgt. George N. Renfro

"I was coming down in open country with a river right under me. I pulled lines and landed in a ploughed field about 100 yards from a river. I came down hard, twisting my right knee a little. I managed to collapse my chute, picked it up and ran for the river. I hid my chute and flak vest under some debris and then started to run as fast as I could upstream. While running, I was looking for some place to hide. I saw a small forest and decided that would be a good place to look. I ran across a small open area to the trees but, on getting there, discovered the ground area to be clear, no place to hide. By this time, I was pretty well winded and knew I would have to find a hiding place soon.

"Beyond the wooded area was a hay field with small stacks of hay scattered at intervals. I ran for one of the stacks, dug my way in and covered myself up. My legs were weak, I as completely exhausted and, above all, I was so scared I was shaking all over. Never before had I felt so alone and helpless. I had no gun, as we had been advised not to carry our sidearms. In my position, if I had a gun and shot a civilian, I could be tried for murder. As I lay there, resting and thinking what I might do, I heard the voices of people. I dug a little hole in the hay and, looking out, I could see people coming at the haystack from all directions.

"I had been hoping I had not been seen but, after all, a chute coming down in open country would be visible for quite a distance and there were farm houses all around. As they came closer, they started to holler and I knew there could be only one person whose attention they were trying to get. I pushed the hay aside, crawled out and raised my hands over my head. There must have been at least twenty-five to thirty people closing in on me. Most carried pitchforks and clubs. I remember seeing only one man with a gun pointed at me. It appeared to be a shotgun and, looking at that barrel pointed at me, it looked as large as a stovepipe. To say I was scared is putting it mildly.

"The area in which I came down had not been bombed so the people were not as hostile as they would have been if their homes had been destroyed by our bombs. I learned later that a pilot I knew in another plane had come down in a bombed area and, after his capture, he was tied to the back of a wagon and was dragged to death.

"The man with the shotgun came over, searched me for a weapon and then they ordered me to walk toward a farmhouse. I was still dressed in my heavy flying gear and, as it was quite warm on the ground, I was soaking wet from perspiration. As we walked towards the farmhouse, all the people were still around me with clubs and pitchforks. I was allowed to wash some of the dirt from my face and hands and was then taken into a room in the house where I was told to sit while the man with the shotgun stood guard over me. A short time later, a girl about ten or twelve years old came over to me and asked if I was hurt. After telling her I was not, she turned to one of the adults and relayed that information to them in German.

"I must have sat there for a couple of hours before a German military vehicle came to the house and I was taken over by the German Luftwaffe personnel. I don't remember just how long we drove and I did not get to see anything as there was cover over the windows. I remember being told to get out of the car and was taken into a building where I was locked in a small room without windows' and no light. By this time, it was getting dark and all I could find in the room was a wooden bunk No mattress or covers, just a wooden bunk.

"I must have been in the room for at least a couple of hours when a guard came for me and I was again put in a military vehicle. After driving for an hour or two, I knew we were near an airfield as I could hear aircraft engines. Stopping in front of a building, a guard took me inside and I was locked in another room where I was happy to see most of the other members of the crew. As it turned out, We all (ten) got out of the aircraft - safely and no one was badly hurt - just a few scratches and a sprain or two. In this room, a guard sat inside with a machine gun in his lap.

"We were all happy to be together again and to find out that we all got out without serious injury. Each had to tell his own story as to what had happened after he left the plane. No one had a serious problem with either civilians or the military. We all tried to get a little sleep but it was almost impossible with the noise from aircraft taking off and we were all tense from what had happened to us plus much worried about what was in the future for us.

"It was common knowledge, back in England, that all airmen shot down would be taken to Dulag-Luft at Frankfort. This was the main interrogation center in all of Europe. Allied Intelligence regarded it as the outstanding military agency for gaining accurate and important information from allied fliers who became prisoners of war. Each prisoner was studied by psychologists in order to learn his likes, dislikes, habits and powers of resistance. The method of procedure was then determined and they, then, set out to destroy his mental resistance in the shortest possible time. If the prisoner showed signs of fright, he was threatened with all kinds of torture, some of which were carried out, and he was handled in a rough manner. Others were bribed by luxuries. They were given clean clothes, good living quarters, food and cigarettes for answering certain questions. The gullible ones were told convincing stories of why they must talk and even made to believe that resistance was futile. Those who could be neither swayed or bribed were treated with respect and were handled with care in the interrogators office but were made to suffer long, miserable hours of solitary confinement in the prison cells. Back in England, all of this information had been given to us and we knew the only information we were to give was our name, rank and serial number.

"How long we were in this room at the airfield, I don't remember for sure, but it was quite awhile after daylight when we were brought something hot to drink. It was supposed to be coffee but it was really terrible tasting. It was hot, so we drank it. We were all very hungry but we did not receive anything to eat. Some time later, we were taken from the room and, again, found ourselves in a military vehicle along with our machine gun armed guard. We were driven to the railroad station where we waited for some time for a train. While in the station, we were required to sit in a group in a corner. There were quite a few people in the station, mostly women and children. I still had my escape gear inside my shirt (the man searching me had not found it) and, knowing the guard could not see what I was doing, I decided to eat some of the concentrated food in the package. Contents of the pack included German money, compass, maps, sewing kit, food, and other things I don't recall. I ate the food, hid the maps under a bench, along with the compass, because I was sure they would find it in the next search.

"A middle-aged German woman was sitting a few feet from me and really eyed the sewing kit. Feeling sure I would have no use for it and more sure it would be taken from me, I pushed it towards her. At first, she ignored it and looked quite frightened. I paid no attention to her but, looking down at the bench a few minutes later, the sewing kit was gone so I knew she had decided to take it. I don't recall what I did with the money but I think I might have given that to her also. I never knew, for sure, the name of the small town we were in but think it was Lingen.

"After sitting in the station for some time, we heard a train coming into the station and knew we were about to depart. The train had a prison car on the back and, of course, that is where we were taken. The car was already full but we were shoved in. All seats were taken and we sat on the already crowded floor. The seats were wooden benches so I think the floor might have been just as comfortable as the seats. There must have been at least forty or fifty prisoners in the car. Most were Americans but had a few Canadians and English. There were machine gun armed guards at both ends of the car and the window shades were pulled. We were warned not to raise the blinds.

"We had had no food for over 24 hours and there was no water in the car. We were all sure we were on our way to Dulag-Luft but we were headed towards the north and Dulag was toward the south and east. As it turned out, most bridges over the Rhine River had been destroyed and we had to go north to a bridge to get to the east side of the Rhine. After crossing the river, we headed south and, after several hours, we found ourselves in the railroad station in Frankfort. As we pulled into the station, or what was left of it, the air raid sirens were wailing. As we were rushed off the train, we could see the destruction our bombs had caused. There nothing but rubble around the rails that had been cleared off and repaired.

"As we went into what had once been a beautiful station, we could see there was no roof and very little of the walls standing. A small, wooden hut had been built for the ticket agent and, as it had started to rain, he was the only person who was keeping dry. We were rushed through the debris of the station, to the steps going into the subway. I don't know how far we went down under the station but was sure glad we were under ground as the bombs from our planes started falling on the city. We must have been in the subway for at least an hour before we were taken out into the station again. Several bombs had hit near the station but there appeared to be no additional damage to the station itself.

"Later, after getting to our permanent camp, we found out that one of the fellows assigned to our room, Warren Donahue of Pueblo, Colorado, who had a broken leg, was being carried from the train on a stretcher. *(Warren Donahue, 447th BG, 708th BS, pilot of B-17, # 42-37866 – John Meurs).* When the bombs started to fall, the two guards dropped him in the rail yards and ran for the shelter. Donahue lay in the yard during the entire raid but was lucky and didn't receive a scratch. He mentioned the fact that he was scared and I'm damn sure he was.

"From the station in Frankfort, we must have walked a couple of miles to the gates of Dulag-Luft. During our walk, young people from about ten to twelve, would push us off the sidewalks, spit in our faces and call us 'names – "Luft Gangsters" is the only name I could understand. We were a little scared but our guards kept most of them away from us. It took me quite a few years to get over my hatred of the German people from this incident alone.

"After getting inside the gate of Dulag, we were taken to a huge athletic field where they had tables set up with Luftwaffe personnel sitting on chairs behind the tables. We were lined up, went by the tables and gave only our name, rank and serial number. The German officer behind the table we went to was a captain. He never looked up as he asked the questions until Harry Schow, our tail gunner, started to give his information. Harry was just in front of me and I heard the whole conversation. After getting the required name, rank and serial number, the German officer looked up at Harry and said, "Are you from Chicago?" Harry was so taken that all he could say was yes. The questions that followed were: "Do you live on such and such a street, such and such a number, your father is so and so, your mother's name is so and so, your brothers and sisters names are so and so." To all of this, Harry could only answer, "Yes," as it was all correct. The German officer looked at Harry and said, "You may not remember me but I used to work with your father at Anheuser-Busch in Chicago and I used to come over to your house for dinner when you were young. When you get home, tell your father you saw me (he gave his first name only) and he will remember who I am, I cannot give you my last name but he will know." He then said, "I'll see you later." We went and sat down on the ground and about thirty minutes later the German captain came over and talked to Harry. He didn't ask him any military information, only how his family was and if he had been hurt when the plane was shot down. As he left, he turned to all of us and said, "I want to give you a little advice - don't try to escape."

"He, no doubt, knew where we were going to be sent as we later found out that the "Great Escape" had been made from Stalaf Luft 3 in February. Over eighty men had escaped through a tunnel; only three managed to evade capture and fifty had been shot. I have never seen or talked to Harry since we got home so do not know who the man was. "There must have been at least 500 allied prisoners here this day, both British and American. We heard later that seventy bombers had been shot down and the average escaping alive was running about 50%. This would mean that 700 men had been shot down with approximately 350 escaping with their lives from the bombers alone. Along with the many fighter pilots shot down and some who had been brought in from planes flying out of Italy, plus the British, there may have been more than 500.

"With so many prisoners, it turned out that anyone below the rank of major did not receive the intense interrogation that we were so afraid of. We were taken, one by one, into rooms where they attempted to get information from us if we were willing to talk without too much prodding. I was taken into a room where I was told to sit down at a desk across from an interrogating officer. I never did see him as a strong light was shining in my face so he could see me without my being able to see him. After getting my name, rank and serial number (again), he started asking questions about my group and squadron, how long I had been in England, where my base was, what position I held on the crew, along with countless other personal questions. I refused to answer his questions but he did not seem too unhappy as I found out he knew more about my group than I did. He told me what group I was flying with, the name of the group commander, the squadron commander, where the base was located and, finally, pushed a paper towards me that was a copy of my special orders from navigation school. My name was on the list. Where all this information came from, I do not know, but their source of information was pretty good. He frankly told me that they had so many prisoners to interrogate that he was not really interested in what I might know.

After about fifteen or twenty minutes, he called a guard and I was taken from the room and taken outside. I was scared but happy that he felt I had no information that he wanted.

"It was getting towards evening when we were taken to a barb-wired enclosure where there appeared to be about ten or twelve long, low barracks. There were guard towers all around with guards at their machine guns. Here we were given some more of the terrible coffee along with two slices of black bread with margarine on the top. This was served by American prisoners who were permanently imprisoned at Dulag to help care for new prisoners. This was my first taste of the German black bread that was to become the major part of our diet except for Red Cross parcels. The bread loaf was about the size of one of our pound loafs but must have weighed five pounds. Most every bite you took, you would have to take some wood shavings out of your mouth. Before a year was over, we would be very happy to have almost anything to eat. After eating my two slices of bread, I wanted to be alone with my thoughts so went out into the wire enclosed yard and I walked around.

"A lot of other fellows were doing the same. Some were smoking cigarettes and oh how I wished I had one to smoke. I walked around the corner of a building and ran into a fellow who had both arms in slings. After bumping into him, I looked at his face and could hardly believe my eyes! It was Ward Wickwar from Goodland. I knew Ward was in the Air Force but had no idea he was in England. I had not seen him since I left Goodland in 1942.

"We later joined a large group of men sitting around telling their stories of how they got shot down. I remember one fighter pilot (P-38) telling how he and another P-38 pilot were closing in on a German fighter, when the German made a quick turn and the two P-38's crashed into each other. We had seen this happen on our way to Berlin. At the time, we saw no chutes and thought both pilots had been killed.

"Our first day at Dulag-Luft was May 1st and we stayed there until May 4th when we were again put on a train and headed eastward. The entire train was made up of prison cars. I had introduced Ward to the six sergeants of our crew and they ended up in the same camp near Kreims, Austria. Schuyler, Emerson, Davis and myself ended up in the same car of the train. The train was very crowded and we had to take turns sitting in the seats, under the seats, in the aisles and even in web luggage racks above the seats. Again, we were surrounded by armed guards and were not allowed to lift the window shades so we saw nothing of the country during our two-day trip. I don't recall too much of the two day trip from Frankfort to Sagan except that we got very little to eat or drink and were always hungry and thirsty. Of course, the crowded conditions did very little for our moral and there were short, heavy outbursts of anger between individuals at times. I'm surprised there were not more because of the very crowded conditions. I don't recall who the senior American in charge was but he did a terrific job keeping things in order. I think we sang most of the way to Sagan.

"My records show we left Frankfort on May 4th and arrived at Stalag-Luft 3 on May 6, 1944. Stalag-Luft 3 was located just outside of Sagan, which was located east of Berlin about mid-way between Berlin and Breslau.

"As we had come into the outer gates of Stalag-Luft 3, we had again been searched. We had to strip down to our under shorts, even take off our shoes. Up until this search, I had been able to conceal my GI watch and a few English coins by putting them in a small waist pocket. I thought sure I would make it into the camp with these but, this time, they found the items. The ring, with the carneo missing, was still on my finger. I turned it over on my finger so it looked like a wedding band they let me keep it. It had a diamond on each side of the missing cameo and am sure they would have taken it had they seen the diamonds.

"A few older "Kriegies" from other compounds had been transferred to the west compound so we had a few experienced people around. The senior American officer in our barracks had been transferred from the east compound. His name was John Dunn from Harnden, Connecticut. He was a Lt. Commander in the Navy. He had been flying patrol over the North Sea from an aircraft carrier and had been given a wrong course to fly back to the carrier. He ran out of gas over the coast of Norway. John had the dubious honor of being the first American taken prisoner in the European Threatre. He was about my size and, during the coming winter, he gave me his extra pair of long johns. I have always been grateful as it sure helped me keep a little warmer during that hectic winter.

"The senior American officer in the west compound was Col. Dan H. Alkire from San Diego, California. The senior American officer of all of Stalag-Luft 3 was General Vanaman. I don't know just how or when he was taken prisoner but he pretty much controlled our lives by what he could do or not do in dealing with the Germans. Prior to our entering the war, he had been assigned to a post in Berlin and knew all of the big shot Germans, including Hitler: From all I have heard during our time in prison and after coming home, he pretty much told the German officers in our camp what to do and at a time late in March, 1945, dictated where we would be moved and, also, saved us from an execution order that had been given by Hitler.

"When we first arrived in the camp, we were more or less ignored by the older Kriegies until it could be established that we were allied military personnel and not German spies planted in the camp. I was lucky because one of the first people I saw was an old friend from Johnstown, Pennsylvania, with whom I had been at pre-flight school in Montgomery, Alabama, and also at primary flying school in Camden, South Carolina. His name was Albert Radaslcy. Al had been cleared so he vouched for me and I, in turn, vouched for the other three members of my crew. Being cleared did not mean too much as I never knew if any escape plans were in progress or if any tunnels were under construction. We all knew we had radios in camp and would get the war news from The British Broadcasting Co.

"It took quite some time to get into the routine of the camp. The big thing was the hunger. All we were getting from the Germans was the black bread (one loaf per man per week), a few vegetables in season, a few potatoes, a little margarine, blood sausage and some barley soup. For several months, each man got an eleven pound Red Cross package per week. This was later cut to one package for every two men. Oh yes, the Germans allowed each man one-fourth pound ground meat every fourteen days. I am sure this was horse meat. If it were not for the food packages from the Red Gross, I am sure a lot of us would have died.

"Most days at Sagan were pretty much the same. Appel (roll call) was held early each morning. All men from each barracks were assembled as a unit and were then counted. On many occasions, someone would purposely mess up the count, and, at times, we would be assembled for an hour or more. This was fine when the weather was nice but got to be a little rough on the cold winter mornings. We were again counted in the late afternoon. On occasion, when returning to your barracks, it would be completely surrounded by armed guards and you would know the Germans were going through your barracks looking for something. While the guards were searching the barracks, all men of that barracks would be lined up, each would approach a table where he would give his prisoner number and he would be checked with his picture on his identification file card. We had this happen only twice at our barracks. On one of these occasions, a radio was found in the room of John Dunn, our senior officer. This was a NO, NO, as the radio had to be smuggled into the camp and we were not allowed to listen to anything except what we heard over the German radio. John was promptly taken to the cooler and we did not see him for a couple of weeks.

"After roll call each morning, it was back to the barracks where each man made his bed and cleaned himself up as best he could. We knew we had to keep things as clean as possible or we would soon be living like pigs. We, in our room, took turns in groups of three, to do the cooking for a week. For breakfast, we had two slices of German black bread toast with a very thin layer of jelly, along with a cup of coffee. The jelly and coffee came from Red Cross parcels. After our meager breakfast, We would scrub the room down and then try to figure out something to do the rest of the morning. It was bad to just sit or lay around and feel sorry for yourself. We had a deck of cards, from the Red Cross, and we all became quite good at bridge. The camp also had a small library provided by the YMCA of Sweden. A person never had much choice in books but took whatever was available at the time. The nine months I was at Sagan, I read eighty-one books —some were very good and others not so hot.

"At noon, our meal consisted of a soup provided by the Germans. At times, it would be nothing but boiled flour. Other times, it would be a vegetable soup made from dried vegetables. My first bowl of vegetable soup made me sick before I ate any of it. There were dozens of little white maggots floating and wiggling on the top. After a couple of days, I started picking the maggots out and eating the soup. Before the nine months at Sagan was over, the soup started to taste pretty good. One thing I never got used to was the blood sausage. It turned my stomach the first time I ate it and continued to do so all the time; but, it was food and, when you are hungry, you will eat almost anything. Our main meal was the evening meal, with the exception of potatoes provided by the Germans, the meal was prepared from contents of Red Cross packages. Meat was either Spam, corned beef or salmon.

"To keep in shape, most men walked the perimeter of the compound many times a day. I spent many an hour just walking. Most of the time I would walk by myself. I can't remember counting how many steps it was around the perimeter -1,810 steps according to what I wrote down at the time. Estimating I took a 30 inch step, it was 4,525 feet around.

"Most days were about the same except we were hot in the summer and damn near froze in the winter. I remember once during the summer when we had a very hard rain and the roof on our barracks leaked like a sieve. During the winter, it was a constant battle trying to keep warm. The little flat top stove we had in our room worked fine but we had nothing to burn. Each week we were given just so many bricks of coal. Under normal circumstances, the week's supply would not be enough for one day. We used it very sparingly in the mornings to take the chill off the room and, at the same time, toast our bread for breakfast. We could go to the cook house for hot water to make our coffee. I can't remember taking my clothes off, except for a couple of baths, from around the first of November to the middle of March.

"Each man was allowed to write three letters and four cards per month. Most of mine went to Maxine and she, in turn, would let the rest of my family know what I had written. I can't remember there being any limit on the amount of mail we could receive but I didn't receive any mail until I got a letter on September 22nd, almost five months after being shot down. Maxine was allowed to send me a personal package (small) each month and also was given a certificate each month to send to a tobacco company along with money for six cartons of cigarettes.

"The days, during the summer, at Sagan were long. The sun would come up about three in the morning and would not set until about ten at night. The latitude was about the same as the lower Hudson Bay country. It was a different story during the winter when it would not get light until about nine and be dark by three or four. Many days we would be locked in the barracks when there was an air raid in the area. On several occasions, we saw large formations of our bombers going over.

"As the days ran into months, we found ourselves getting thinner and more despondent. A letter from home would seem to cheer up every man in the room. We were getting war news from secret radios in the camp and we were able to keep track of the front as it moved closer to Germany.

"As the summer ended, things seemed to get more hectic. The Russians were advancing from the east and the Americans were advancing across France. We felt we would be home for Christmas; but, as winter approached, We gave up hope. As the bombings increased in Germany, it became almost impossible for

Red .Cross trains to get through with food and, around the first of November, our rations were cut in half. Instead of receiving a parcel per man per week, we were cut to one-half parcel.

"Winter was now upon us and the battle against the cold and hunger was difficult. The only good news was that the Russians were advancing fast in the east. As Christmas approached, there had been no mail for several weeks and a full stomach was something to dream about.

"Then - some good news! Christmas parcels from the Red Cross had gotten in and there would be a full parcel for each man besides his regular half parcel. And then, as we were assembled for roll-call on the day before Christmas, a small wagon pulled by Kregies, dressed as Santa's helpers, came into the assembly area. As they passed where the men from each barracks were assembled, they tossed out packages of mail. Mail had been held up for just this purpose, hoping each man might be lucky enough to get a letter. I was real lucky. I got three letters from Maxine including some pictures. This, along with the big bash we had the next day, made a Christmas never to be forgotten.

"As December passed and we were in the new year (1945), both the Americans and the Russians continued to advance. A few trains had been able to get through and we were put back on full parcels on January 22nd. By the 20th of January, rumors were flying thick and fast. We knew the Russians were not more than fifty miles to the east. By the 27th, we could see the flashes of the guns in the east and could hear distant rumbling that sounded like thunder.

"It had started snowing and it was bitter cold on the 27th. We were all sure we would be leaving soon and we were prepared as well as we could be. I had made a back pack from my extra shirt by sewing the front and bottom and would tie the sleeves around my neck. All food had been divided and each man would carry his share along with any personal items. At about nine o'clock p.m., we received the order to be ready to leave in an hour.

"Things then really became hectic. We decided to make a sled from one of our benches, tear and braid our mattress covers for ropes, fasten them to the bench and take turns pulling our sled with our packs on it. We were ready to leave by ten. Due to some unknown delays, we did not evacuate our barracks until a few minutes after midnight (the morning of January 28th). As we left the barracks, heavy snow was falling, with about 12 inches already on the ground. It was not too windy but it was bitter cold. I wore all the clothes I had; three pair of socks, long johns, two shirts, my GI overcoat and a head covering I had made from a scarf received from Maxine just three days before.

"We were a very sorry looking bunch as around 10,000 of us left Stalag Luft 3 that night, not knowing where we were going or what hardships that night and the following days would bring. As we passed the warehouses near the outer gates, each of us was handed a Red Cross parcel. We got these into our packs and we were on our way. As I remember, the men from the center compound led the group and our compound was second in line. As we climbed some small hills on the outskirts of Sagan, we could look down on the camp and see a lot of barracks burning. Prisoners had set the fires as they left. To the east, we could see the flashes of the guns and hear the explosions.

"So ended the nine months stay at Sagan. We felt it had been rough but the next three months would be hell in comparison.

"As we headed toward the west, the snow continued to fall and, the going was rough from the beginning. The snow was fluffy and the ground was rough underneath. Along the center of the road, it was pretty well packed by the compound ahead of us but we had to be careful slipping and falling. The sled pulled quite easily and we changed off pulling about every fifteen minutes. We would march for about an hour and then take a ten minute break. By the end of the first hour, we were already tired and weary. As the whistle blew, we would all walk to the side of the road and lay down in the snow. We walked until ten the next morning (about 30 kilometers), when we stopped in the village of Priewaldau.

"It was still bitter cold but the fluffy, falling snow had now become a regular western Kansas blizzard. We were given a few hours shelter in concentration camp buildings. There wasn't enough room to shelter all the men that were constantly arriving, so groups took turns warming themselves inside while others waited outside in the blizzard. I was inside for about two hours. Then, making way for others to get warm, our group went back outside in the blizzard. Many men were discarding any extra clothing and personal items, making as small a pack as possible for the continuation of the march. I saw men tearing up their only towel and wrapping their feet to help protect them from the cold. I had no clothing, except what I was wearing and my shoes were in pretty good shape, so had nothing to discard. You can be sure there was no food discarded. Our ill-fitting, home made packs were proving very difficult to carry.

"According to my notes, we had arrived at Friewaldau about 10:00 o'clock a.m. after leaving Sagan at about midnight - a distance of about 29 kilometers. After leaving the shelter at Friewaldau, the rest of the afternoon was spent walking around the enclosure trying to keep warm and awake. We all wanted to sleep but did not dare lay down or we might freeze to death. Several fires had been started and men were crowded about them. About 5:30 in the evening, we again prepared to leave and, by 6:00 p.m., we were again walking into the blizzard.

"The next 14 hours and approximate 45 kilometers walking has proved to be the most difficult period of my life. The snow was still coming down and walking in the darkness was really tough. We had had no sleep since leaving Sagan and everyone was completely worn out before we started walking. Many men had frozen toes and almost everyone was walking on blisters. We had walked about two hours when Bob Abrams twisted his ankle and was unable to walk. We could not carry him or leave him beside the road, so we took our packs off our sled and tied them to our backs. Then, we put Abe on the sled and pulled him about ten kilometers to a small town. It was so cold, Abe could stand only about ten minutes on the sled when we would stop and three men would get on either side of the sled and really rub and massage him to keep him from freezing to death. By the time we got to the village, Abe was in very bad shape. At his request, we found an open door to a stairway where we left him along with Clarence Pishburn. We wrapped them in their blankets, left them some food and wished them well as we again started walking.

"As we continued walking, men were dropping out of the line and laying along the side of the road. Our remaining thirteen men stayed together and helped each other as needed. I later heard that about 100 men died on the march but I could not say for sure. I only know that I saw many in very bad shape. As the hours went by, men were no longer walking but staggering, half asleep on their feet. The snow had let up a little but it was still bitter cold. By around 6:00 a.m., we were told that it was only a couple more hours to Muskau where we would be able to have shelter and get some sleep.

"An hour or so later, we were in the outskirts of the city and, in another hour, we approached a factory area. There were several large factories that were no longer being used. This particular area had not been bombed so the buildings were in pretty good shape. I think most of the west compound was put in this large, three-story building that had been a pottery plant. All the machinery had been removed so there was a lot of space. Some pottery was laying around, but the thing we really liked was all the straw in the building. We were so exhausted that most men lay down in the straw, wrapped their blankets around them and were soon asleep. I don't know how long I slept but when I awoke, I felt much better and, for the first time in two days, I was warm. I really didn't want to get out of the straw but nature called and, too, some of our group had been out trading cigarettes and soap for some vegetables, which they had used with a couple of cans of spam and had made about the most delicious stew I have ever eaten.

"Several German women were walking around the area with cans of hot water, which they gave us to make our coffee. I had received a can of instant coffee in my last parcel from Maxine and really made use of it. I then discovered there was a wash room in the building with hot water. I joined a couple of thousand others using the wash room. I shaved and felt much, much better. Then, it was back to the straw and more sleep. We had arrived at the factory at about 8:00 a.m. on January 29th and stayed until about 1:00 p.m. on January 31st. (All these dates and times I am getting from a log I kept of the march and have kept all these years.)

"Many men were in pretty rough shape, especially frozen toes and blisters. We had very little in medical supplies but our medics did all they could with what was available. We were able to trade for more vegetables and black bread and, for the first time in several months (except for Christmas), our stomachs were full. Along with the much needed sleep, we were in about as good shape as when we left Sagan.

"By the morning of January 31st, the snow had stopped falling, the sun had come out and it had warmed up a little. Colonel Spivey, of the center compound, called the block leaders together and informed them we would be leaving the nice, warm straw a little after noon, so we should prepare for our departure. We made some more stew, which we ate while it was nice and hot, repacked our backpacks and were ready to fall into formation at about 12:30 p.m. At about 1:00 p.m., we were on our way again. Much of the snow had melted and we were unable to use our sled so we discarded it and everything went on our backs. As we left Muskau, we could still hear the thunder of the guns on the eastern front. The walking was difficult, in the melting snow and slush but, as the afternoon wore on and it again began to get cold and freeze, the walking became more difficult.

"At this point, we began catching up with German civilians who were fleeing westward. It was a very sorry sight to see. Wagons and carts with their worldly possession stacked on them. There were no young people, only old men, women and children. In many cases, they had only one horse pulling on the wagon or cart and either an old man or old woman would be taking the place of another horse. In some cases, there were no horses and the people would be pulling the load. We did not feel sorry for them, at the time, but, time has gone by, I can see the tragedy of it - very pitiful.

"At about 10:00 p.m., after walking about 18 kilometers, we entered a small village and were again put up in barns filled with straw. After doing some more trading and fixing more stew, we again slept warmly in the straw. At about 3:00 p.m. on February 1st, we left the barn and walked an additional 10 kilometers to Spremberg. This proved to be the last of the walking. Here, we were up in a huge gymnasium and were given a very good soup along with a couple of slices of bread. We slept on our blankets on the hard floor but it was warm. We were in much better spirits now that we had had some fairly good food and had gotten some good sleep. Little did we know what awaited us the following day.

"Shortly before noon the next day, we were marched to the railroad yards where we were packed 53 men and a guard to a French 40-8 box car. Before entering the cars, we were given four Red Cross parcels for every five men along with a little bread and margarine from the Germans.

"These boxcars were very small and filthy dirty. We cleaned them as best we could by using our hands and feet to clear the crud. For the next two and a half days, we lived as so many pigs. Many men were still sick and were vomiting. This, along with body waste that we tried to shove out cracks in the floor, made the trip almost unbearable. There was no room to lay down so we had to either stand or sit. The nights were bitter cold and very little sleep was gotten. About midnight the first night, we pulled into the railroad station at Chemnitz. As the train stopped, the guard unlocked the door to look out. We all rushed the door and climbed down to the station platform where our car happened to be stopped. There were a lot of people on the platform, but, we paid no attention to them as almost every man pulled his pants down and relieved himself on the platform. The guards were shouting and threatening to shoot but we paid no attention. We then saw a water tank and made a dash for it. We had been given no water since we were put on the train.

"Our guards, along with soldiers stationed in the area, finally got us back on the train and we were on our way again for the rest of that night, the next day and another night. We were given water a couple of times during that period, but we were not able to get off the train again. Things were mighty bad when we pulled into the Nuremberg Station the morning of February 4th. As we got off the train, we saw that only about half the men were there. We found out later that the other train had gone further south to a prison camp at Moosburg.

"We must have been quite a sight to see - dirty, sick, some men unable to walk and being carried by their buddies. The Germans got us into some kind of a formation and we walked several miles to another prison camp. This camp was Stalag Luft 13-D. It had just been evacuated of Italian prisoners and was almost as dirty as the boxcars. At least we had a little water to try and clean the place up. There were no showers or hot water except for a little hot water to make coffee. We cleaned ourselves as best we could with cold water while standing in an old wash house.

"Here we were to spend a miserable two months existing only on what little food the Germans gave us. The rail lines had been bombed so badly that the Red Cross was unable to get food to us.

"Finally, on March 1st, we got a bath and were deloused with a powder. They also deloused the barracks, which helped quite a lot, but we never got rid of them completely. American and British air activity was heavy in this area. Hardly a day went by when we did not see our bombers and fighters overhead. On several occasions, our P-51 fighters would buzz the camp, which made us happy, knowing they knew where we were. The camp was only about three or four miles from the main railroad yards of Nuremberg, a favorite target of our bombers. We were very happy that our bombardiers had good training and could bomb the target without hitting us.

"The most awe-inspiring sight I ever saw in my life was the night of March 16, 1945. This was the most beautiful, yet terrible, display imaginable. At the sound of the sirens, we took to the slit trenches near the barracks with blankets and some wooden doors to put over us to help protect us from falling flak. There was an amplifier a short distance away that blared for the position of the bombers as they came towards Nuremberg. This was a raid by the British Royal Air Force. At first we could barely hear the engines but, suddenly, they had arrived over the city and it was a constant roar as the lead planes dumped two parallel rows of yellow flares that hung in strings forming a corridor the length of the city. These were followed by showers of red and green flares marking the center of the target. "Wave after wave of invisible bomb-laden planes then dumped their loads into the city, which erupted with explosions. It soon became a raging inferno as the bombs continued to fall. It is really impossible to describe the picture that unfolded. The earth shook from the tons of bombs and hammering anti-aircraft guns. The night was as bright as day from the flares and the burning city. Anti-aircraft shells exploding at altitude as search lights tried to spot the planes. There were many, many planes falling afire from wing tip to wing tip. It was a picture I don't think any of us, who were there, will ever forget. After about two hours, the attack ceased and the city was left to burn through the night and the next day. The following night the British were over again.

"As the days went on and we got more desperate for firewood, men began sneaking out at night and tearing the wall from the wash houses. By the time we left, only shells were standing. We also tore the ceiling from our barracks, leaving only the roof over us. You would see men walking around the camp picking up any little piece of wood, even the size of a toothpick. We made little burners from tin cans in which we would burn the small pieces of wood to heat a cup of water for coffee, if we had any. By this time, most of our clothes were getting pretty ragged and our shoes were beginning to wear out. We had not been able to wash what clothes we had so they were stiff with dirt and grime. We had managed to keep our bodies fairly clean by washing down with cold water while standing in the cold wash houses without walls. We tried to keep shaven, using cold water and very dull razor blades. There was no activity as men lay around saving what little strength they had for another expected evacuation.

"As the days went by, rumors were flying thick and fast. We knew the Americans were moving toward us from the north and west. We were also quite sure we would again be moved to keep us from being liberated. We were an awfully good insurance policy for the German High Command. During the last couple of weeks at Nuremberg, we saw thousands of American and British to prepare to walk out of the camp the following morning. So, at about 9:00 a.m. on April 4, 1945 we were again moving to someplace unknown to us. We really did not care where we went as we felt no place could be any worse than what we were leaving. Even in our weakened condition, we felt this walk would be much easier than the one before. It was a beautiful spring morning as about 30,000 of us marched out of the camp in a southerly direction. This time, as we left, we could hear the American guns in the north and American planes were over us almost constantly. Many planes buzzed our formation, cutting their motors off and on to let us know that they knew who we were.

"The first day, we walked about 20 kilometers to the town of Postbaur. Here we were put in barns again. With about 30,000 men on the move, groups were stopping in almost every village and some of the men did not leave Nuremberg until the following day so the line could be stretched out over a lot of miles. By 8:00 a.m. the next morning, we were on the move again, walking most of the day and then stopping in some woods where we rested four hours until 9:00 p.m. We then walked all night until 5:00 a.m. This was a cold, rainy walk and we were all wet and tired when we arrived at the village of Plankstettin where we were again put in barns. Guards were always placed at intervals around the towns where we stayed.

"It was the first night out of Nuremberg when Schuyler came to me and wanted me to go with him as he was going to sneak out and try to make his way to the American lines. I guess I was chicken and turned him down. I went with him to a hedge row and grasped his hand as he went over and disappeared into the darkness. Talking with him several years later, I found out that he had been captured and taken back to Nuremberg where he was liberated by American troops three or four days later. He was back in the States before we completed our walk to Moosburg.

"It was while walking on April 13, we learned of the death of President Roosevelt. When we pulled into a small village, the evening of April 13th, we again were put in barns. The back door of the barn was open so John Tyrell, Jack Emerson and myself decided we would look for a better place to sleep so sneaked out the back door into some woods a short distance away. We were not trying to escape - just get away from the crowded conditions. We decided to continue down our same road to another village just a mile or so away. We stopped at a house on the edge of the town and talked the people into letting us stay in their upstairs room. It had an outside entrance. We went up, finding old mattresses on the floor, but it was nice and clean. We dropped our packs, went back downstairs and cleaned up and shaved at an outside water pump.

"Unknown to us, a small boy of the family had gone into the village to tell some troops stationed there of us. He returned and motioned for us to follow him. We picked up our packs and followed. He turned us over to a couple of soldiers who appeared to have been drinking quite heavily. They spoke a little English and we were able to convince them we were Kriegies and had gotten behind our column. They instructed us to go on down the road and catch up with the group of prisoners who were just down the road. Not wanting to get into any trouble, we headed on down the road. About a half mile down the road, we saw a truck coming in our direction. It stopped beside us, the driver got out, went to the back of the vehicle and handed each of us a bottle of beer, then hopped back in the truck and was on his way. I think it was the best drink I ever had.

"We soon saw the group in front of us and a guard came back and picked us up, forcing us to join the group ahead. It seemed they had caught about fifteen from our group who had taken off on their own. We finally convinced the guard captain that we were ahead of our column and wanted to wait and rejoin our own group. He must have been a little afraid of what might happen when the war was over so he assigned a guard to the fifteen of us and let us stay at a farmhouse on the edge of the next village. The guard let us go looking for food, on our own, telling us not to go too far and to look out for SS troops. We were able to make some pretty good trades and came back with enough food for several days.

"At the farm was a lady and her three small daughters. The oldest daughter (about 12) could speak a little English and she told us her father was a flak gunner in Regensberg. The lady allowed us to build a fire and cook our food in the yard. It started to rain that night and continued for five days. Our group had holed up during the rain so we stayed at the farm waiting for them. About the second or third day, we again heard Red Cross trucks so we ran about a half mile to the road, stopped the truck and talked the driver into giving each of us a Red Cross parcel, also one for our guard. He was a very happy man and, apparently, went into the village and forgot about us. He did show up again in a couple of days when our column finally came and we again joined our group. We had regained a lot of our strength while at the farmhouse and felt much better for the remainder of the march.

"Two days later, on April 21, 1945, we arrived at Stalag 7-A at Moosburg. This was a huge camp and was really crowded. Prisoners had been brought here from all over Germany. We heard there were over 100,000. All the barracks were overcrowded and huge tents had been erected. We were assigned to one of these tents that held about 500 men.

"Conditions at Moosburg were really much worse than any place we had been. The very crowded conditions and the Red Cross being unable to get any supplies to us made things very difficult. One of the worst things was the lack of water. In our particular area, there was one water outlet for approximately 1,500 men. Most of us still had a little food we had accumulated by trading, while on the last walk, and, along with a little bread the Germans gave us, we were able to keep going. Morale was quite high as we could now hear the guns of the American armies and, if the Germans did not move us again, we were sure the whole thing would be over in a matter of a few days.

"By April 27th, we were all prepared to leave again. But, on the 28th, the rumor was we would stay where we were and the camp would, no doubt, be over-run by the forces of General Patton. By the night of the 28th, there was no doubt that liberation was at hand. The artillery rocked the countryside as the flashes lit up the area. We estimated the distance from us by checking the time the sound took to reach us after seeing the flash. Tiny LC-5 spotter planes with the white stars of Uncle Sam circled during the day of the 28th. They were in radio contact with our lines and, as they spotted targets, would radio back the position. Every once in awhile, they would buzz the camp and greet us by rolling from side to side.

"Sunday, April 29th, dawned and everyone was very tense and excited. The artillery was just over the hill north and northwest of the camp. Shortly before noon, bullets began to whistle through camp and the sound of machine gun and rifle fire became almost constant. During the next few hours, most of the men lay low to escape the bullets coming through camp. A few men were injured but I do not think anyone was killed during the action. Early in the afternoon, resistance ceased and Moosburg fell. General Patton came into camp and was welcomed almost tearfully by thousands of prisoners. He came into our tent and I stood within ten feet of him as a huge mob of men crowded around. He was a spectacular looking man and we were all most grateful to the 14th Armored Division of General Patton's Third Army.

"Late in the afternoon, two Red Cross trucks came into camp driven by two American girls. They were beautiful to see in their tight-fitting GI uniforms. All they had in the small trucks was chewing gum and doughnuts. The lines were long to get some of this most delicious food and, of course, we all wanted to see the girls.

"As General Patton had promised, food and medicine, along with doctors, were brought into the camp. The white bread looked and taste like angel food cake in comparison to the black bread we hoped never to see or taste again.

"It was not until the 7th of May that they were able to evacuate us from the camp and start us on our journey towards home. We were taken by truck to Landshut where hundreds of C-47 transports were lined up waiting to fly us to France.

"We were taken to an American Military Installation just outside of Le Havre, France, known as "Camp Lucky Strike." Here we were given baths and clean clothes. I think I took at least four baths that first day and got clean clothes each time. We were also given medical check-ups and cautioned not to eat too much or too fast. Our stomachs just were not in shape to take it. We were also told that, when we got back to the States, it would be a good idea to drink at least six bottles of beer each day to help stretch our stomachs. I did not like beer too well but soon came to love it and was soon drinking twelve bottles a day.

"I do not remember how long we were in "Lucky Stike" but one morning we were loaded on trucks and taken to the dock area where we were to board ships and head for the States. While walking around the area, I bumped into some of the enlisted men of our crew. They had been interned in Kriems, Austria. I did not see all of them but did find out they had all survived and all were close by. They were not going on the same ship but were supposed to ship out the same day. Later in the day, we boarded the USS Lejeune, a troop ship. Prior to the war, it had been the German Luxury Liner "Windhuk." It had been captured by the British outside the harbor of Montevideo, Uragury, at the time the German battleship "Graf Spec" was scuttled by its crew. Converted to a troop ship, it was no longer a luxury liner but it was our transportation back to the States. Leaving France, we went across the English Channel to Southampton, England, where we picked up many wounded the next day were on our way home.

"After eight or nine days, we arrived, early morning, in New York Harbor. We were the first troops coming home and really had quite a welcome. We were met by fireboats, tugs and small boats with bands. After docking on the westside of Manhattan Island, we were greeted, on the dock, by hundreds of people. I had my first Coke in over a year, candy bars, gum and milk. We were put on a ferry boat and crossed over to the New Jersey side where we boarded a train and went to Camp Kilmer, New Jersey. Here we were fed steak, given another medical examination, some clothing and prepared to board another train. We were at Kilmer for a couple of days before all preparations would be made. I was unable to call Maxine but wrote her, telling her about when I would arrive in Denver.

"Our train, leaving Camp Kilmer, was made up in three sections of approximately four pullman cars each. The first section was to be dropped in Denver, the second in Salt Lake City and the third in Sacramento, California. I think it was June 6th, when we arrived in Denver at about 2:00 a.m. I spent the next couple of hours checking out hotels to see if Maxine was registered at any of them. Our cars had been left in the station and we had a place to go back to and sleep for a few hours. About 7:00 a.m., buses from Fort Logan arrived at the station and we boarded for Logan. As I stepped off the bus, someone called my name and slapped me on the back. It was "Red" Houser from Goodland. He was in the payroll section at Ft. Logan. "Red" informed me Maxine had been unable to find a hotel room and was staying at their apartment with him and Fran.

"We were again processed, given part of our back pay and transportation to get around Denver to try and buy some much needed clothes. Before leaving Fort Logan that evening, we were given sixty day leaves. "Red" had been able to find us a hotel room so took us down town and we were together again after fifteen months. The next day, we took a train to Sterling, where my father met us and we went on to Haxton. During the next month, we spent our time in Haxtun and Goodland. Then, having to report in to Santa Monica Rest Center in another month, we left for California. We spent a couple of weeks with my brother in the San Francisco area and, while there, got a thirty day extension on my leave. We went to Los Angeles by train on the day the Japanese surrendered.

"The parents of my co-pilot, Jack Emerson, lived in Santa Monica, so spent quite a little time in their home. They gave us a key to their home so we could come and go as we pleased. After a couple of weeks at the rest center, I was sent to the air base of Santa Anna, where I was discharged around the first of November and then headed for Denver and on home by train.

"I don't think I will ever forget the many things I went through while a prisoner and would like to close this with a quote by Bob Neary in his book *Stalag Luft 3*: "I had never fully realized, before going overseas, just how wonderful this country of ours is. I had always taken for granted my complete liberty, freedom of speech and countless luxuries that I considered my heritage as an American - my year and a day of oppression and want in prison camp have changed my perspective completely. I think I have learned my lesson well and I feel that I shall never forget it - I am an American and I am grateful, Amen."

Co-Pilot 2Lt. John F. "Jack" Emerson.

Jack was born in El Paso Texas on the 4th of March 1923. His father Joseph George Emerson was an engineer. His degree was as an engineer of mines, but he turned to aeronautical engineering once he moved to Southern California (Santa Monica, on the palisades three hundred feet above the Pacific Ocean) in around 1925. He worked as such for Douglas Aircraft until his retirement in about 1955. Family lore has it that he helped design the DC 3.

His mother was Maria Theresa Droste, the daughter of a medical doctor in Grand Rapids, Michigan. She and Joe met in Washington DC, where both were in college, he at Catholic University and she at Trinity College, which was and still is for women only. Joe had previously been a student at Georgetown Preparatory School, a Jesuit boarding school founded in 1789.

Jack and his two elder brothers all attended Loyola High School in Los Angles, also run by the Jesuits. The eldest son went to the Jesuit University of the same name, the second graduated from the United States Coast Guard Academy (retiring from that force as a captain thirty years after graduation: he was also a very skilful pilot), and Jack went, after the war, to the University of Southern California. He stayed only two years, got married (in 1947) and returned to the United States Air Force, only to resign his commission (as a captain) in 1953.

Co-Pilot 2Lt. John F. Emerson

"He then joined United Airlines as a co-pilot and retired as a senior captain in 1983. He was married to Phoebe Helen Tours, the daughter of Frank Edward Tours and his wife Helen Veronica Gaylord Clark. Her father was a well known musician, and Phoebe had a degree in music and also studied at the Juilliard School of Music in New York City. They had five children together, and she sadly died in 1971. Jack married again in 1986 to Diana Allen. He had moved in the year of Phoebe's death to Pebble Beach, where he joined the Monterey Peninsula Country Club. There he played golf (he was an expert golfer into his 70's) and later bridge with his cronies. There, too, he met Diane.

Jack spoke very little about his time as a bomber pilot, and nothing at all about the actual experience of carrying out the bombings. He did speak of what happened to him after they were shot down:

He landed in a field, and, as he was taking off his parachute, he saw a farmer with a shotgun approaching over the fields. When the plane was ditched, there was some hope that they were already over Holland. But his hopes were dashed when the farmer stopping some twenty feet away, lifted his arm and declaimed: "Heil Hitler!" When my father did not return the salute, the shotgun was slowly raised and my father was led of into captivity.

He was interrogated by an SS man with a large Luger lying on the table, but nothing untoward actually happened. He was then taken East to Stalag Luft III. The famous break-out had already occurred, so nobody felt much like trying to break out. After about a year, they were marched West to escape the approaching Soviet armies. Ultimately they were liberated by units of General Patton's army.

He died on February 6, 2011 in Pebble Beach, CA. At home, surrounded my his wife and four of his children.

Tail-Gunner Sgt. Harry J. Schow as told by his son David

"Harry James "Jim" Schow was born 20 December 1920 in either Austin, Minnesota or Chicago, Illinois ... or so he was told for the first 50+ years of his life by his father, Harry W. Schow, who flew with the Cook 148 Aero Squadron during the First World War (Harry Sr. claimed to have flown Sopwith Camels; I think I still have some of his military ID).

"Jim claimed to have lied about his age to get into what was then called the Army Air Corps in 1941 - this was a popular claim among young men eager to fight - but the calendar makes him 20 or 21 at enlistment.

"He trained as a pilot on T-10s. He boxed Golden Gloves (light heavyweight) and organized baseball teams. He married his high school sweetheart, Shirley Joan Johnson, in 1940 or '41. At the time of his European missions out of Shipton Airfield in England, he was a sergeant.

"The April 27, 1944 mission was at rocket installations near Montivilliers, in France. As soon as the crew returned to base, they were turned around and sent on a second mission, to blow up the railroad yards at Chalons-sur-Marne – the first time ever that heavy bombers had attempted two missions in one day. They caught heavy flak near Paris, which tore chunks out of the plane, severed some of the hydraulic systems, and eventually killed one of the engines. Schuyler wrote; "Without knowing it, Schow had picked up a piece of flak which zipped through his flying suit and ended up against his underwear. Schuyler was forced to ditch his plane on landing, no brakes and no rudders, and the crack-up sheared off the nose wheel and warped the fuselage.

"The fatal mission of April 29, 1944, was to bomb Berlin. Just after crossing the Zuider Zee and passing the German border north of Osnabrück, the mission was swarmed by ME-109 Messerschmidt fighters. Bombs were successfully dropped in what was later called "the greatest day-time raid of the war."

"On the return flight, flak near Brandenburg took out an engine. Hits in the wing caused fuel to leak. With no gas for the trip home, Schuyler decided to ditch the plane in the North Sea. Then a second wave of fighters, Focke-Wulf 190s tore the bomber apart with 20 mm. cannon fire. Of the Fock-Wulf that came in for the kill at five o'clock, Schow later said; "I started firing and the tracers bounced right off him. And then I was just pressing triggers and nothing was happening. It was an instant before I could find the extend of the damage. A 20 mm. had hit us in the right elevator. It blew my hydraulic unit on the floor, clipped off my left gun, cut my mike cord about an inch and a half from my throat, and generally took my plexiglas." A fire bloomed in the waist of the plane. Another fire started up in the tail. The B-24 was out of ammo. As they approached Holland (and another "flak alley" that was sure to destroy them in their bomber's weakened condition) Schuyler gave the order to bail out. As he later wrote; "I wondered why I couldn't see or hear our airplane. Years later, Renfro said he saw it blow all to hell as he was coming down in his chute. The 190 came in on Schow. Hanging helplessly, Schow just waved. The German waved back. He had his kill – chalk up one more B-24."

"From May 1944 through the end of the war he was a POW at Stalag 17-B in Krems, Austria. I still have his missing-in-action telegram, sent to Shirley, who did not know he was alive for about nine months.

"When the 1950's rolled around they seriously tried to have children, but after several miscarriages and a stillbirth (a girl, buried in Chicago), they decided to adopt me – a German orphan – while living in Middlesex, England. Four years later Shirley got pregnant with my little brother, John.

"While still in the Air Force, they relocated to Fort Worth, Texas, and then Paris, Kentucky, where Jim was in charge of a radar detachment that was literally housed on the farmland of a guy named Crombie. (We went fishing there several times.) Jim retired circa 1962 or '63 at the rank of major; his discharge was signed by Curtis LeMay.

"Around late 1963, Shirley died of leukemia. I was eight years old – it was after my birthday, and after the Kennedy assassination.

"Jim remarried about a year later, after working at an auto dealership called John Fister Ford, and serving a year as Paris City Manager under mayor Buddy Case.

"About 1966 or '67, we moved cross-country to Huntington Beach, California, where Jim worked a few unfulfilling jobs (including mail delivery). He decided to attend a special school in Paramus, New Jersey, for several weeks to upgrade his skills with radar in order to work with the Defense Early Warning network (DEWLine) in the Arctic.

"The DEW Line was then-administered by ITT and its operations were classified. Jim rose from console operator to station chief to sector superintendent.

"His station chief post was in the middle of the Greenland icecap, 500 miles from nowhere, ice in every direction, including 10,000 feet straight down. He was in charge of 25 men and was the station's only "doctor," trained in first aid. The shifts were about six months each.

"While on the DEWLine, Jim met Chaplin Paul Maurer, the chaplin who famously composed the "fair weather prayer" for General Patton. I used to get Christmas cards from him.

"Jim's father died in 1971, whereupon his mother Agatha spilled the beans: Jim had been adopted, too. His birth name had been George James Siebert; they kept the "James," Jim passed the "James" onto me, and my brother – Jim's only blooded child – subsequently gave it to his son, Adan James Schow.

"After the DEWLine was turned over from ITT to the RCA Corporation – and Greenland was rendered free of Danish rule, in 1979 – Jim embarked on two assignments for ITT, both classified, both absorbing a year or more - one to assist in the installation of a secure military communications system in Spain, and another in Horsens, Denmark.

"By 1980 he had turned 60, and remained more or less retired. He had moved from Tucson to Las Vegas in the mid-1970's – collecting a third wife named Freddie M. Hewitt who lasted less than a year - and relocated to Reno shortly thereafter. He died in Reno, survived by his fourth wife, Tina (Cristina).

***

Acknowledgements;
"The Long Year" by Dale Rauscher. Widow Maxime Rauscher and the Sherman
    County Historical Society
"Elusive Horizons" by Keith C. Schyler, A.S. Barnes & Co.
David Schow, son of tail-gunner Harry J. Schow

CHAPTER 2

44ᵀᴴ BOMB GROUP
68ᵀᴴ BOMB SQUADRON

Type: B-24H • Serial: 41-29471
MACR: 4472 • Air Base: Shipdham

At 11:00 hours, aircraft 41-29471 was attacked by fighters, peeled to the left with number 3 engine on fire and spreading to the fuselage. Two men bailed out and chutes opened. Plane then went into a spin and exploded.

Missing Air Crew Report # 4472

Pilot: 2Lt. Glenn H. Sweigart, 0-747360, POW, Fort Thomas, KY

Co-Pilot: 2Lt. Floyd H. Greene, 0-812577, POW, Salt Lake city, UT

Navigator: 2Lt. John W. Turocy, 0-695992, POW, Cleveland. OH

Bombardier: 2Lt. Gilman N. Roberts. 0-688402, KIA, Brooklyn. NY

Engineer: S/Sgt. Lamer McWhorter, 34442753, KIA, La Grange, GA

Radio: S/Sgt. John W. Levake, 19186283, KIA, Walnut Creek, CA

Ball-Turret Gunner: S/Sgt. Julius V. Naber, 37263649, KIA, Marshall, MN

Waist-Gunner: S/Sgt. Harold F. Koehler, 15019186, KIA, Canton, OH

Waist-Gunner: Sgt. Homer M. Tiller, 33101171, KIA, Colorado City. TX

Tail-Gunner: Sgt. Albert A. Nome, 35544549, KIA, Mishawaka, IN

7 KIA, 3 POW

Crash Site: Bothfeld/3 miles ne Hannover - Germany
Time: 12.30

44th Bomb Group, 68th Bomb Squadron (Sweigart)
Topeka, Kansas, February 20, 1944. (No caption available.)

Pilot 2Lt. Glenn H. Sweigart recalls;

"Our call was "Smokey Blu Joe, X for X-ray." Somewhere over Germany we lost all the oil pressure on number three engine and had to drop out of formation because the prop flattened out on us. I couldn't hold altitude or air speed so we finally maintained altitude at 9500 feet and 105 mph, skidding sideways against the prop with near full rudder and still making a long arc, which we corrected occasionally by a circle. We had good cloud cover and limped along until the clouds gave way.

"Then all hell broke loose! I had told the crew that if anyone wanted to leave, they could jump at any time. I had two men I didn't know, replacing Gwin and Tony (Goodman). I told them to go if we got hit and lost intercom, cause I'd go if we got hit or went below 7500 feet. I believe that our radioman, Sgt. John LeVake, took off.

(Note: The two men that Sweigart didn't know were Julius Naber and Harold Koehler. Naber was from the 66th Squadron and had flown 22 missions previously. Koehler had joined the 68th Squadron on 31 January 1944 with the Dyer crew. He had flown 15 prior missions. —John Meurs)

"When we got hit, it took the putt-putt right out of the side of the aircraft, and split the control pedestal wide open and knocked out all controls as well as the intercom. Our bombardier, Gil Roberts, was begging for us to all to go as he would not go alone. Navigator John Turocy showed me black and blue fingerprints on his shoulder where Gil was hanging onto him when we were hit. The explosion blew Turocy out the nose wheel and Gil into the front of the airplane and killed him.

"Lamer McWhorter, my engineer, tried to get to the back of the plane to help the fellows there. He was blown off the catwalk by another hit, I think. Floyd Greene (co-pilot) then left, and I hung up my mike and earphones, looked at Greene's cigarettes and lighter – for some reasons I left them, thinking he'd be back after them.

"The aircraft crashed and burned after a long, slow, even half circle when anyone in it could have and should have bailed out. At interrogation, they kept asking me why I had only a six man crew, so I know that some of my men got out but they didn't live. Turocy, Greene and I were together. I saw who I thought was McWhorter lying in a field as I came down, and Gil Roberts was still in the plane. That makes five that I can account for. And they had pictures of Sgts. Albert Nome and Homer Tiller – that's seven.

"I bailed out without my leg straps buckled and hung myself by the neck. When I tried to take the pressure off by swinging my feet into the shrouds, I skidded back and forth across the sky. I think that's why I survived because I could hear those 88 mms going off nearby all the way to the ground and couldn't see anything else in the sky but me for a target!

"I came down in the middle of a plowed field and in the middle of about 3,000 people. I spoke enough German to get myself into the hands of a little infantry corporal, who took me to his captain and eventually to the airdrome.

Co-Pilot 1Lt. Floyd H. Greene.

Was born on February 8, 1920 to Floyd Harris Greene, Sr. and Edna Grace Smith Greene in Salt Lake City, Utah.

His father and brother were structural engineers and assumed that Floyd would choose the same profession but he went his own way into commercial art. He graduated from Woodbury College in Los Angeles, CA. During the New York World's Fair he won a silver trophy and gold medal in the 1938 national poster contest.

When the war broke out he enlisted into the Air Corps. He also married a girl named Julie. While he was in prison camp she sent him a dear John letter and married someone else.

On April 29, 1944, leaving the plane at 9,000 feet Greene fell 5,000 feet in order to escape the flak before opening his parachute. It was then that he received a near-tragic surprise. He reached for the ripcord to open the chute with his right hand, only to discover he had been hit in the right arm near the shoulder and could hardly move it. Through great exertion and pain, and by using his left hand to assist his right, he finally pulled the ripcord and felt the comforting tug of the chute when it opened.

While in Stalag Luft III, Floyd designed and made a rough draft of his characterization of the Pilot, Bombardier and Navigator and took orders from his fellow prison mates prior to being liberated. He promised to mail these from his home town of Kansas City when he returned stateside and had an opportunity to have them printed professionally. By 1946 he had accomplished this task and many veterans received their orders as promised and have had them in their studies for almost 60 years.

After returning to civilian life he resumed his career as the Art Director for Potts, Caulkin & Holden Advertising Agency in Kansas City, Missouri. He later remarried and had two children.

He was again called up during the Korean War, promoted to Captain and was stationed in Texas, then later in San Bernardino, California. He was the head of the *Flying and Safety Magazine* and one of the crew that flew the first bombers to refuel during flight. After he was released from service he and his family returned to Kansas City, Missouri.

Floyd died at age 33 while on a fishing trip when his motorcar crashed into an embankment near Iowa Falls, Iowa.

Floyd Greene at drawing table

Bombardier 2Lt. Gilman N. Roberts

A crew member reported: " It's my believe that Lt. Roberts was killed by the burst of flak that was also instrumental in throwing me up against the nose-wheel and out through the escape hatch since he was ready behind me to bail out.

Another crew member stated after the war: "John Turocy, the navigator, related to me the following story. "I was preparing to open the nose wheel emergency hatch with Roberts standing directly behind me when an explosion literally forced us forward out of the opened hatch. I don't know if Roberts got out or not but I believe the explosion got him.

Engineer S/Sgt. Lamer McWhorter

A crew member reported: "Was given orders to bail out. He was last seen on the catwalk trying to get back to the waist to let the others know of the order to bail out. I believe him to have been killed on the ground. I personally forced him out of the bomb bay then I followed. He seemed to be alright at that time."

Ball-Turret S/Sgt. Julius V. Naber

Julius Vincent Naber was born March 17th 1921 at Milford, Iowa. His family refers to him as "Pat." The family did live in several places in Iowa, including Spirit Lake, Iowa. The family were farmers, renting rather than owning land. During the depression (1929-1932), they moved to Balaton, MN. "Pat" graduated from Russell High School in 1940. After graduation, he worked on the farm, before joining the Air Corps.

Tail-Gunner Sgt. Albert A. Nome

Cris Calhoun, his niece, writes about her uncle;

"James Nome, the father, was Lebanese with a strong accent of speech and ate the middle eastern foods. Maria Yanes, mother, was from Zacatecas, Mexico. It can now never be known how James and Maria met and married, but they made their home in Michigan City, Indiana. Possibly James was trying to make his way to Detroit, Michigan, where many Lebanese and Syrians worked in the automotive industry at that time.

"It was reported by friends of their family that James and Maria expressed temperament in dramatic ways. James came to the United States as a barber and

Maria was a seamstress. She wore a long, single braid that she wrapped toward the top of her head. One day, as she sewed at her machine, having her braid unpinned and hanging down the middle of her back, James came to her while arguing, with barber shears, and snipped off that braid in one motion!

"When Maria died of tuberculosis, Mary, the last of five births, was approximately three years old. George was the oldest, approximately seven years old, and Albert was two years younger than George. Children Sammy and Annie had died as toddler and infant, respectively. James was not a nurturing man and without a wife to care for his children while he worked, he enlisted the Mishawaka Orphan's Home, Mishawaka, Indiana, to care for them. As he had no car, this was accomplished by train.

"In 1941, at the age of 14, Mary was asked to come home to live - she envisioned a loving family setting, but the truth was she was to help care for a new baby to a new wife and to clean their house and others for extra income. Her earnings were taken from her as her father had a gambling habit. The small living space the family had behind the barbershop could not accommodate the boys. They remained at the orphanage and were required to attend Mishawaka public high school. George was studious, but Albert preferred to have fun. Gifted in athletics, both played several sports and this is how they came to know the families who "fostered" them.

"The two families - The Millers and The Tritipos - also had sons in athletics who befriended George and Albert. During George's senior year of high school (1942) he and Albert were quite valuable on the football team - George quarterbacked several years running. An epidemic of mumps broke out in the orphanage and the football coach did not want George and Albert to be vulnerable to the outbreak so he asked each family if they would "foster" the Nome boys. The families readily agreed, Miller's taking Albert and Tritipos taking George. Mary was already back in Michigan City with her father and his new family. Due to some kind of illness George suffered in childhood, he lost school time and ended up in the class one year ahead of Albert, explaining why his age and graduation year never added up.

"After George graduated from high school, he enlisted in the Army and chose to be a paratrooper. Albert just had to follow his brother, and though not yet of age, he received his father's reluctant approval. This is one of many examples of Albert's lively behavior. Sadly, however, the mission this book describes is the one from which he lost his life. He had always been a curious child, rambunctious and lively. He grew to enjoy following the boxers of that time, such as Jake Lamotta of the U.S., and collected many autographed photos of them, listening intently to the radio broadcasts of the fights. Another example of Albert's feisty personality. In some ways it might be said that his death in a daring war was not to be a surprise.

***

Acknowledgements:
Deborah Green, daughter of co-pilot Floyd H. Greene
Chris Calhoun, niece of tail-gunner Albert A. Nome
"The 44th BG At War" for pilot Glenn Sweigart

44ᵀᴴ BOMB GROUP
506ᵀᴴ BOMB SQUADRON

Type: B-24H • Serial: 41-29513
No MACR • Air Base: Shipdham

---

*As this crew was picked up from the North Sea
by a Royal Navy minesweeper and quickly returned
to their airbase, no Missing Air Crew Report
had been filed.*

Pilot: 2Lt. Richard J. Hruby, 0-682866, RTD, Mt. Holly, NJ

Co-Pilot: F/O Thomas L. Smith, T-61379, RTD, Okarche, OK

Navigator: 2Lt. Edwin H. Rosenberg, 0-684989, RTD

Bombardier: 2Lt. William D. Arthur, 0-690535, RTD,

Engineer: S/Sgt. Cletus C. Clark, 17157054, RTD, Canova, SD

Radio: S/Sgt. Euclid F. Blanchard, 11083941, RTD, Belmont, NH

Ball-Turret Gunner: Sgt. Everett E. Foster, 37499715, RTD, Lowry
City, MO

Waist-Gunner: Sgt. Thomas L. Bartley, 38274340, RTD, Indiahoma, OK

Waist-Gunner: Sgt. Fount B. Bartley, 38274336, RTD, Indiahoma, OK

Tail-Gunner: S/Sgt. Robert Petkoff, 38274310, RTD, Carnegie, OK

10 RTD

Crash Site: North Sea

44th Bomb Group, 506th Bomb Squadron (Hruby), c.1944

Back row (left to right): Waist-Gunner Sgt. Thomas Bartley, Waist-Gunner Sgt. Fount B. Bartley, Pilot 2Lt. Richard Hruby, Navigator 2Lt. Edwin Rosenberg, Co-Pilot F/O Tom Smith, Tail-Gunner S/Sgt. Bob Petkoff;

Front row: Engineer S/Sgt. Cletus Clark, Ball-Turret Gunner Sgt. Everette Foster, Radio S/Sgt. Euclide Blanchard

From "the 44th BG in World War II" by Ron Mackay and Steve Adams. (A. Schiffer History Book)

"This crew was granted a reprieve from death or captivity in circumstances that were generally very unfavorable in respect of the B-24. The "art" of ditching was one that was even more incapable of being practiced than the "art" of bailing out safely. In addition to this, the ditching qualities of the B-24 were arguably much worse than any other Allied heavy bomber. The bomb-bay catwalk was really incapable of absorbing the shock of impact without collapsing, after which the fuselage was liable to split. Even if this action did not occur the "shoulder" position of the wings insured that the bulk of the fuselage was under water and liable to be swamped by the onrush of water, making the chances of getting out extremely hard.

"Pilot Richard Hruby's 506th Bomb Squadron's bomber #41-29513 had taken flak strikes over Berlin that were believed to have adversely affected the fuel tanks. In addition the No. 2 engine was suffering a power surge. Although the engineer, Cletus Clark, responded to his pilot's request for fuel status as the Dutch coast was passing by saying that the instruments gauges were almost at zero, Lt. Hruby still headed for England. Engine RPM was reduced to a minimum tolerable level and all surplus equipment thrown overboard.

"Amazingly the bomber stayed aloft until within sight of friendly soil. By the time the engines finally cut out in unison, the crew had assumed ditching positions. The pilots eased down from their height of around 6.000 feet at 125 mph and with a twenty degree flap setting.

"Radio-operator Euclid Blanchard had hardly lowered the trailing aerial preparatory to sending a distress signal when a flak jacket being thrown out chopped it off. An alternative message was hastily sent using the fixed aerial and the I.F.F. switched to the emergency band before screwing down the transmission key. (It was later established this effort proved to be in vain). The pilots donned their steel helmets, which action proved to be necessary. The bomber was levelled off in a nose-high altitude above the sea, which was displaying a slight swell.

"The touchdown was carried off so smoothly that the bomber's onrush stopped with the entire airframe intact. The impact had thrown both pilots against the windshield but their helmets absorbed the force. The cockpit rapidly filled up almost to the roof while the rear fuselage was similarly swamped. The six men up front scrambled desperately out via the cockpit hatch and all ten airmen emerged relatively unscathed to find just one of the life rafts could be partially inflated. Four men clung on to one, with a fifth inside to stabilise it, while four were similarly involved with the other raft pack. The tenth man who had swum after the emergency equipment was gradually being pulled further away from his fellow crew members who were trying to paddle in his direction.

"It was all the more fortunate that a Royal Navy minesweeper was in the vicinity, whose captain steered in the downed crew's direction and plucked them out of the water after some forty minutes. The thoroughly numbed airmen had their flight suits replaced by heavy clothing and blankets as well as a tot of rum.

Pilot 2Lt. Richard J. Hruby in a letter to the author:

"I was born in Elizabeth, NJ, on August 26, 1922. Attended high School in Springfield, NJ and was going to night school at Union College while working for Merck Chemical Company in Ranway, NJ.

"I enlisted in the U.S. Air Corps Aviation Cadet Program in early 1942. Primary pilot training in Pine Bluff, Arkansas and finally B-24 training and crew assembly at Boise, Idaho.

"Flew a replacement B-24 to the 8th Air Force via South-America and Afrika to Wales. Went to a crew replacement center in Northern Ireland and then to Shipdham Base to the 44th Bomb Group.

"On April 29, 1944, we flew a mission to Berlin in the B-24 # 41-29513.

We sustained heavy flak damage over the target. Had a damaged gas tank or gas lines and ran out of gas over the North Sea. We ditched with all the crew surviving. The plane floated about fifteen minutes, we spent another thirty minutes in the very cold water hanging to a half inflated raft. We were picked up by HMS "Cotsmuir," a mine sweeper. They cut their gear and came to our rescue. The entire crew went to the Southport Rest Home for a week or so.

Pilot Richard H. Hruby

"After having completed my combat missions I returned to the States in December 1944 and got married at the end of that month.

Daughter Christine Hruby:

"Richard Joseph Hruby grew up in several towns in northern New Jersey. Dad was going to a junior college and working part time at the chemical company, Merck, prior to enlisting in the Army.

"He came home and married my mother, Mary Elizabeth (nee Hatcher) of Mount Holly, NJ. He stayed in the Army for a short period of time and began training to become an airline pilot. Instead of doing that, he went to work for his father-in-law's textile mill in Mount Holly. He started as a weaver, at Northampton Textile Company and ended up as a salesman, credit manager and on the board. The mill ended up closing and he worked freelance as a textile salesman for several companies until he stopped working to care for his invalid wife.

Navigator 2Lt. Edwin H. Rosenberg,

By his son Bob.

"My father (I will call him Eddie, which is how he was known to most) was born May 24, 1920 in New York City and grew up on Long Island in the town of Far Rockaway. His mother was a well-established women's fashion designer, and the family was very well-to-do until the Great Depression hit and the market for high-priced dresses dried up.

"Eddie's family moved back to New York City and were very poor in the years leading up to WWII. My father recalled being embarrassed because he had to wear his brother's suit (that didn't fit him at all) at his bar mitzvah. Growing up, my father loved classical music and the big bands of the 1930s. He was very athletic and played baseball in high school. He had said that he had a chance to play professionally, but for reasons that I don't know for sure, he never did so.

He also loved golf and bird watching, both of which as it turned out, remained a big part of his entire life and that of his family.

"He finished High School in 1938. He was terrible at math but loved history. That summer he saw an advertisement that St. John's University Law School was looking for applicants. He decided to apply and was accepted. He was the first member of his family to go to college. He completed the law program and took the "Bar" exam just before the US entered the war in Europe. He was in the service when he found out that he had passed.

"When the US entered the war, Eddie decided that he wanted to join the Army Air Corps. However, how he actually got there was an interesting story that he told me shortly before he died. When he first went to the recruiting station in New York to sign up, he took the physical, but they told him he had high blood pressure and thus could not be accepted that day. They suggested that perhaps it was just nerves, and they told him to come back in a few days and try again. He did so, but it was the same thing – high blood pressure. He may have tried one more time, but to no avail. Unable to sign up for the Air Corps, he decided to go to the Army recruiting station. He assumed that they would check his blood pressure and it would again be high, and then they would give him 4-F status (medically unable to serve), and that would be the end of it.

"However, when they took his blood pressure, they said it was normal, and the next thing he knew he was in the Army! The very next day they shipped him to a camp on Long Island. To his surprise and delight, at the camp there was an Air Corps recruiting station, so he went there again to sign up (apparently, once you were actually in the Army, it was easier to transfer to the Air Corps). However,

they told him that he could not do it that day because it was the weekend, but that he could come back on Monday. But that never happened because on that Sunday they shipped him to a boot camp in Mississippi.

"He refused to give up his dream, though. He was going through basic training at the camp and had been there for a few months, when one day they were on the back of a pickup truck on the way to target practice and they passed another Air Corps recruiting station. This time he was not going to miss it – he jumped off the truck and ran inside and signed up right then and there. He was finally in the Air Corps!

Navigator Edwin Rosenberg later in life

97

"After training as a navigator, Eddie was assigned to a bomber crew that flew missions over Germany. Actually, the April 29, 1944, mission was one of his early missions and he flew dozens more after that, all with the same crew.

"After the war, having passed the Bar, he got a job at his friend Leo Salon's law firm. However, it didn't take long for him to realize that he didn't want to work for somebody else, and law took up more time and energy than he wanted to put into a career. He had so many outside interests – golf, baseball, birding among the biggest. After Leo got furious at him (rumor is that he threw a type-writer at him) for leaving work to go to Yankee Stadium to watch Joe DiMaggio during his famous 57-game hitting streak, Eddie decided to quit law and start his own business.

"He leased a small storefront on Madison Avenue in New York City and opened a hardware store in 1948 called "Edward's Housewares." The store was a great success. As it was in a very ritzy neighborhood, and Eddie was a natural with people, his customers, many of whom were very rich, loved him. Since the Carlisle Hotel was right down the street and many celebrities stayed there, they sometimes dropped into the store. Two that I remember well were actress Cicely Tyson and Jackie Kennedy Onassis. His regular customers from the neighbor-hood also included Woody Allen and director Mike Nichols. He kept the store until 1983.

"Eddie met our mom, then professional harpist Stella Seidenberg, through a mutual friend. The way my mom describes their first date, she thought she had blown it because she was so shy that she didn't say a word the entire evening. However, Eddie had been dating a girl that was really chatty, and, since he him-self loved to talk, he thought that it was great that Stella was such a good listener! They were married in 1950.

"I was born in 1951. My brothers, Ken and Gary, were born in 1954 and 1957. Both Ken and Gary are professional ornithologists. Ken is a scientist at the Cor-nell Lab of Ornithology. Gary has been a professional bird tour guide for the past 30 years and now has his own company, Avian Journeys. I am a meteorologist and a project manager at NASA. It is no accident that my two brothers became ornithologists. Eddie's favorite pastime was birding. Starting in 1961 for about 10 years, he would take off the month of August and take the family on amazing vacations. Eddie would start planning the next year's vacation in September and had it paid for by January. He funded them by saving every half-dollar that went into his cash register.

"Each vacation was centered on birding and, later, birding and golf. We vis-ited a lot of the national parks in the US and some in Canada. We went to Hawaii twice. It was a great experience for all of us. He took home movies of all the trips as well. My two brothers followed in his footsteps but took birding to the next level. Ken got his PhD and Gary his MS from Louisiana State University, both specializing in tropical birds. I was more interested in the weather in all the different places we stayed, and eventually got my degree (and ultimately my job) in meteorology. I still credit my dad for that interest since he exposed us to all the beauties of nature. So all in all, we made careers that paralleled our dad's hobbies.

"My father also loved classical music, and he immersed me in it at an early age – when I was about 3, he bought me a phonograph and classical LPs. I still remember staying up at night listening to the music. I later learned to play the piano and cello, and I played the organ in several rock bands in high school and college (I still own the Hammond B3 organ that my father bought for me in 1969).

"We all grew up in a typical suburban house in Plainview, Long Island that our dad bought in 1956. Eddie commuted 6 days/week to work in the store. We lived in Plainview until our parents moved to Florida in 1975. They went there at first so that they could help take care of Stella's aging parents, but ended up staying there for the rest of their lives.

"For their first eight years in Florida, Eddie kept the hardware store in New York City and went up to work during the month of August so that his manager could take a vacation. However, he had to sell the business in 1983 because the landlord would not renew the lease – the neighborhood was changing and a lot of the stores became boutiques and art galleries. After he sold the store, he lived on money from the sale of the business, plus social security. I guess one of his few faults was that he didn't save a lot of money, although our lives were all the richer for it because of all the great things we did and places we saw.

"So Eddie and Stella made a new life in Florida. Eddie, being younger than most of the residents in the retirement community where they lived, became active on the building board of directors. He also helped a lot of his neighbors when they became older and needed help with shopping, and rides to the doctor when they were sick or became disabled. He taught classes on birds at the local community college and became a big advocate for preservation of bird habitats in South Florida.

"In the town of Pembroke Pines, (where he lived), he got the local parks department to fence off areas for burrowing owl nests in public parks, and he convinced the city not to develop a corner lot that contained a wooded area that was an important nighttime roosting area for hundreds of herons, egrets, and other birds. After his death, the town officially named that area (the northeast corner of Palm Avenue and Taft Street) the "Eddie Rosenberg Bird Sanctuary."

"Eddie died in 2008. His mother, grandmother, brother, and sister had all died of pancreatic cancer at a relatively early age (his sister was the youngest at 42). After Eddie survived into his eighties, we all thought he had dodged that bullet, but he ended up also getting pancreatic cancer at age 87. According to his own wishes, he chose not to get any treatment. He said that he had lived a good life and accepted his fate peacefully and with no regrets (except he did admit that he was sorry he would miss the next baseball season!). He died at home in Stella's arms April 16, 2008. His ashes (and Stella's) are in Arlington National Cemetery.

"So as you can see, Eddie had a profound influence on our lives. He was always there for us – when we got into trouble as teenagers, and when we needed help or support as adults, but most importantly he was a part of our lives through all the boring stuff in between. He exposed us to immense natural beauty, which ultimately shaped our careers. He was a great story-teller and while he was known to embellish the truth a bit, we were never bored around him! He was a favorite uncle of our cousins, and a loving grandfather to all of our children. Our kids will never forget our visits to Florida, his "famous" French toast that he would cook us for breakfast, hikes through the Everglades, his great stories, and so much more.

"Eddie was also an extremely kind and compassionate person, and a very liberal thinker. Although he lived more comfortably than many around him, he never flaunted wealth and always stuck up for the "little guy." He hated racism and violence. Despite his service during World War II, he was vehemently opposed to the Vietnam war and the war in Iraq. He never really talked about his own war experiences until his very last years. He taught us to be good citizens and never take what we have for granted. How incredibly lucky we were that he survived that crash-landing in the North Sea!

lEngineer S/Sgt. Cletus C. Clark.

Daughter Debbie Cottingham wrote;

"Cletus Claud Clark was born January 8, 1924 to Arthur E. Clark and Helen Cole Clark in Vilas, South Dakota. He was the fourth of five children. On our subsequent vacations to South Dakota I heard people call him "Swede" though I don't know why since he wasn't Swedish.

"He graduated from Argonne High School in Argonne, South Dakota. He began playing on their basketball team as a freshman and was offered a scholarship to play college basketball but turned it down to join the Army Air Force. His mode of transportation to school was his horse.

"He enlisted December 3, 1942, at the age of eighteen. He was classified as an Aerial Engineer and qualified as Marksman (Rifle) on September 18, 1943. He did attend the Army Air Forces Gunnery School in Tyndall Field, Florida.

"He married my mother in Midland, Texas in July, 1945. After his discharge he and my mother moved back to Topeka, Kansas. That is where they had originally met. At that time we had a large Air Force Base that he was stationed at before going to Midland.

"He still continued flying and took subsequent flying lessons. He would fly with my mother and brother up to South Dakota for holidays. However, by the time I came along his flying days were over and he never flew on a plane after that.

"Fortunately, the only injury he received during the war was an injury his knee when they landed in the North Sea. Later they thought he might have broken his hip, but that was never confirmed."

In 1974, the whole crew came together in Oklahoma City.
Article from *The Sunday Oklahoman* of June, 16, 1974

"The crew of the shot-up, almost gasless B-24 bomber limping back toward England after a bombing run over Berlin would not have believed you if you told them that they would all be around 30 years later to laugh about their exploits. On that afternoon, April 29, 1944, the ten men's future seemed to extend no further than an imminent crash-landing in the choppy North Sea, 1000 feet below.

"You couldn't call it anything but a miracle," beamed one of the crew members Saturday.

"All nine of the men – veterans of the 8th Air Force, 506th Squadron, 44th Bomb Group flying B-24 Liberator – were together again for the first time since they went their separate ways after World War II. They rehashed their adventures during a reunion at the Habana Inn in Oklahoma City.

44th Bomb Group, 506th Bomb Squadron (Hruby), c.1974

Back row (left to right): Thomas Bartley, Fount B. BartleyRichard Hruby, Edwin Rosenberg, Tom Smith and Bob Petkoff

Front row: Cletus Clark, Everette Foster and Euclide Blanchard

101

"The men became a unit at training exercises in Boise, Idaho, in September 1943 and flew 31 combat missions over Germany, Holland, Belgium and France during their stint. Their watery induction into the "Sea Squatters Club" thirty years ago stood as the most prominent memory, overshadowing even their bombing runs over Normandy during the famous D-Day invasion.

"Over the target Berlin we got hit by a dud anti aircraft shell," recounted Bob Petkof, of Oklahoma City, the tail-gunner. "It tore a hole in the wing and we lost number 3 engine. We thought we might have enough gas to get back to England and bail out but we ran out before we got there. You don't bail out on water, you ride in," he said. "We brought it into the North Sea from about 1'000 feet with no engines," Petkof said, "That's what I call an energy crisis."

"Miraculously, he said, none of the crewmen was even seriously injured when the plane slammed into the water. "The B-24 Liberators always broke in two or fractured in the back end when they hit and then sank. It was about fifty per cent of the people who would come out alive. "Ours didn't do that," he said. "It floated for about 15 minutes. The plane carried two five-men rafts but one was so shot up during the bombing run that we couldn't use it. One man was in the other raft and the rest of us were hanging on it, riding the waves," Petkof said.

"A British minesweeper came in to their rescue 48 minutes later. The crew members said their crash was the first time a B-24 had gone down in water in the European Theatre and all crew members lived to tell about it.

***

Acknowledgements:
From "the 44th BG in World War II" by Ron Mackay and Steve Adams. A.
    Schiffer History Book.
Debbie Cottingham, daughter of engineer Cletus Clark
Christine Hruby, daughter of pilot Richard J. Hrudy

CHAPTER 4

91ˢᵀ BOMB GROUP
322ᴺᴰ BOMB SQUADRON

Type: B-17G • Serial: 42-31353 "Queenie"
MACR: 4236 • Air Base: Bassingbourne

"Aircraft B-17, 42-31353, was hit over target area at bombs away. A burst of flak hit the right wing cutting out a big section and setting the wing on fire. Aircraft peeled out of formation and one parachute came out. It then went into a spin. After dropping about one thousand feet it exploded. After the explosion three parachutes were seen floating down"

Missing Air Crew Report 4236

Pilot: 1Lt. James F. Purdy Jr., 0-804503, KIA, Little Falls, NJ

Co-Pilot: 2Lt. John P. Garfield, 0-749223, POW, Detroit, MI

Navigator: 2Lt. Paul P. Bunchuk, 0-747076, POW, Maspeth, NY

Bombardier: 2Lt. John R. Welch, 0-754857, POW, Skaneateles, NY

Engineer: T/Sgt. William O. Fischer, 35400877, KIA, Columbus, OH

Radio: S/Sgt. Emile Bianchi, 11105903, POW, Farmans, MA

Ball-Turret Gunner: S/Sgt. Louis S. Carusello, 33417904, KIA, Pottsville, PA

Right Waist-Gunner: S/Sgt. George L. Johnson, 39282205, KIA, National City, CA

Left Waist-Gunner: S/Sgt. Donald R. Itschner, 39325983, POW, Molalla, OR

Tail-Gunner: S/Sgt. Raymond A. Rybarski, 36630706, KIA, Cicero. IL

5 KIA, 5 POW

Crash Site: Berlin Kladow, Germany
Time: 11:42

Bombardier 2Lt. John R. Welch wrote in October 1946, to the War Department;

"On April 29th l944 at approximately 11:45 a.m., the aircraft in which I was flying toward the target, Berlin, was hit by flak in the number two engine. The engine burst into flames immediately and the bomber went into a spin. I was thrown out of the aircraft when the force of the spin caused the right wing, tail section, and nose section to rip off.

"I parachuted into a wooded area and was picked up by Luftwaffe soldiers immediately. They told me thc plane crashed not far away, although I didn't see it. I was told later that this was Potsdam, near Berlin.

"The last time I saw the pilot James Purdy was just after I pulled the safety pins on the bomb load, shortly after the takeoff on April 29th, 1944. I don't know which crew members were wearing parachutes when the aircraft was hit and which men were not wearing them; with the exception of the co-pilot John P. Garfield. He told me that he had to put his parachute on before he jumped.

"According to the information received from the co-pilot, James Purdy and William Fisher were still in the aircraft when he jumped at approximately 500 feet above the ground. I assume from this that they were still in the aircraft when it crashed and were killed in the crash.

Nephew Richard Welch;

"Dick was born February 16, 1920 in Newton Highlands, Massachusetts. His parents were John F. and Elise Illing Welch. They moved to Little Neck, Borough of Queens, New York City, in 1925 and Dick was raised there along with his two brothers and one sister. After high school he was admitted to Cooper Union, which provided free tuition to students who showed excellence in art, architecture, or design. He then attended Pratt Institute, a similar school, in Brooklyn.

"When the US entered the war, Dick enlisted in the Army Air Corps. He was trained as a bombardier at the bombardier school in Demming New Mexico. After he received his commission he trained at other Air Corps bases, and was sent to the 8th Army Air Force base at Bassingbourne, England. He made seventeen missions over occupied France and Germany before being shot down on April 29th, 1944.

"Following the War, he returned to Pratt, finished a degree in industrial design, and undertook work at museums as well as freelance. He then returned to Pratt and taught industrail design until his retirement in 1985. He married Gigi Ford in the early 1950s and lived in Greenwich Village, NY. However, they bought a house in Stonington, Deer Island, Maine in 1963 and spent much time there before Dick's retirement.

"Hikers find a WWII B-17 Bombardier." Bruce Pfann meets John Welch;

"On a beautiful fall day, September 2012, two 75 year old hikers, Terry and Bruce, had just finished a brisk trail walk on Deer Isle, Maine USA. They decided to get some ice cream at a tiny non-descript eatery they stumbled upon in the center of the island. The town consisted of only a small gift shop, a post office and two other old buildings. At first glance the eatery looked as if it was closed.

"As we walked into the nearly empty eatery, we noticed an elderly man sitting at a small table next to the entrance door. Terry saw that he was wearing a hat bearing the insignia of the *8th Air Army Air Force.* Both of us had been in the U.S. Army stationed in Germany in the early 1960's. We knew the horrendous story of the 8th USAAF which had made countless sacrifices during WWII with unimaginable losses of life and aircraft. Terry asked him, "Were you in the 8th Air Corps?" The man looked up and said, "Yes, I was." A few questions later we learned that he was a bombardier on a B-17 bomber shot down over Germany on April 29, 1944.

"We asked him if we could sit down at his table and he quietly said "yes." So we both sat down and leaned over the table to make sure we could hear what he had to say. His name was Dick Welch. He was trying to eat a generous serving of spaghetti and meatballs. But every time he raised the fork to his mouth, we would ask him another question. There was no way we could stop probing into this amazing story that was unfolding before us.

"There we were, in this tiny store with the two of us hanging on his every word, absolutely mesmerized at meeting a World War II hero of the *Greatest Generation.* He said that he was 92 years old. He continued saying he was on a bombing

Bombardier 2Lt. John R. Welch, 2012

run to Berlin, his 18th mission, April 29, 1944. They had just finished dropping their bomb load and were on their way home when his B-17 was blown out of the sky by flak. Of the ten crewmen in the plane, only five made it out of the ship alive. He was really lucky, because only the bombardier had a special parachute that he had to wear all the time. The other airman in the plane had to hang up their parachutes. If they needed their chutes, they had to find them, put them on and jump. Quite often it was too late. Dick said when the plane blew apart; he was blown out through the Plexiglas in the nose of the aircraft.

"After landing all five of the crewmen were eventually captured and interned in a large Prisoner Of War camp that held airmen from many countries. The German Air Force, the *Luftwaffe*, ran the camp and as Dick described, treated the captives relatively well compared to most other POW camps. Dick was in Stalag Luft III, located in Sagan (now the town of Zagan in Poland) which held many thousands of other prisoners. Stalag Luft III was immortalized in the movie *The Great Escape* about a large prison break in March 1944, just a month before Dick arrived. They were primarily British POWs; approximately seventy men got out that night.

"As we continued talking, Dick's head and shoulders became more erect and his speech was noticeably sharper and forceful. Terry and I kept questioning him for more details of his war experiences. His plate of spaghetti was now stone cold, but he continued to poke his fork into it in a meager attempt to eat. One of our questions was, "knowing that you didn't have much of a chance of living through your remaining bombing missions, how was it possible for you to get back into that B-17 day after day?" He said simply, "I just did. It was something that almost everyone accepted." He did comment that there were a number of airmen that got sick or just couldn't face another bombing mission and were hospitalized or transferred elsewhere.

"Dick mentioned that a few months after his arrival at the British base he was stationed at, he went to his squadron headquarters and asked how many of the thirty bombardiers that he came over with from the U.S. were still flying. He was told *only three of his class, including him*, were still there. The others had been either lost in combat, captured or transferred elsewhere. We were both getting quite emotional at this point. Only three out of thirty and he was still able to climb back into the plane every time, day after day.

"We had now been at his table for over an hour. Dick commented that very few people ever asked him about his experiences. He had very few friends now, as he lived alone in a small house in Stonington, located on Deer Isle and rarely left the island. He wife, Gigi, was in an institution on the island with an advanced stage of dementia. He visited her a few times a week, but it was a difficult experience for him each time he saw her.

"We discussed more about his POW experiences and how lucky he was to be interned in a Luftwaffe camp. Sometime in January 1945, the Russians were getting too close to his POW camp. Hitler didn't want all those prisoners to be rescued by the Russians. So Dick and thousands of other prisoners were forced to ride, but mostly walk, nearly 300 miles through the unusually severe brutally cold weather and deep snow to another camp. The march was later labeled the "300 Mile Death March." Many hundreds of the soldiers died along the way from starvation, sickness and the cold.

"He then started to relate how he was rescued. In an instant the story became extremely dramatic and personal to Bruce. Dick said he was liberated exactly a year after his plane was shot down. The day they were liberated from the POW camp in April 1945, he saw General George S. Patton ride up to the gates of the camp on a tank, apparently surveying the situation and organizing the release of the prisoners. It so happened that Bruce's father was General Patton's Secretary to the General Staff and was there at the same time!

"The thought that 68 years ago, this former POW sitting at the table in front of them had been freed by the actions of Patton's 3rd Army and most likely had been within yards of Bruce's father at that very moment was a staggering revelation to Bruce. The fact that this event happened nearly seven decades earlier and now brought these three people together at a small eatery in Maine, was almost too much to fathom. Bruce was temporarily overcome with emotion.

"Before the hikers left Lieutenant Welch, one of the last things the hikers asked Dick was "have you ever seen the new WWII War Memorial in Washington DC?" Dick said; "No he hadn't, but he sure would like to some day." That lit a spark in both hikers as they drove back to the house they were staying in. Upon arrival, they eagerly blurted out the story back to their eighteen classmates who were attending their annual Cornell Chi Psi Fraternity '59 reunion in Sedgwick, Maine. After telling their story to *The Group*, all of the classmates gathered there said that they were committed to sending Dick to Washington DC to visit the Washington Memorial.

"Bruce accepted the job of planning to get Lt. Welch to Washington. At first he approached "Honor Flight" which is a great organization that flies WWII veterans to Washington DC free of charge. But when Bruce inquired, the Honor Flight was booked for more than a year. Bruce discussed the situation with *The Group* and it was decided that they would totally fund the project because Lt. Welch may not be able to wait that long. The date was set to go on the 26th of October 2012.

"Bruce was also selected by the Group to escort Lt. Welch to Washington. It was agreed by all that this trip would be done "in style - first class" something that would give our new Bombardier friend a cherished memory. At 92 Dick was in pretty good physical shape at 131 pounds, although his hearing had deteriorated a bit. He still had his driver's license which was set to expire in four years. He actually drove quite a bit and was pretty good at it.

Bruce's story;

"A day before our departure on Friday October 25, I arrived at Dick's home located in Stonington, Maine, at the southern tip of Deer Isle. It was mid day and I helped him pack for the trip. Before we started packing, I presented him with a number of presents from *The Group*. To mention just a few, there was a large 3 ring binder with more than a 100 pages; inclusive of his bombardier training, details of the secret Norden Bomb Sight he operated, descriptions of his crew, pictures of his plane, his base in England, hometown newspaper clippings of him listed as missing, details of his last bomb run to Berlin when he was shot down, his POW camp; details of the "300 mile Death March," his rescue by Gen. George S. Patton at the POW camp, his time at the repatriation camp in France and so forth. It was incredible how much information was available through the Internet via US Air Force records and others.

"Several members of *The Group* had spent many hours searching and compiling the information. The binder turned out to be a formidable history of his ordeal. He also got a fancy 8th Army Air Force hat with insignia and image of a B-17G, a hooded sweatshirt with his Squadron and Group emblazoned on it and a colored picture of his B-17G named "Queenie" on the back and many other related mementos.

"This being one of the few airplane rides Dick had made since his combat days, he wasn't aware of the "newest" airline flight regulations; i.e. no liquids over 3 oz., no sharp objects, nothing that looked threatening, taking off the shoes and so forth. We got that squared away and went to dinner that night at his favorite eating establishment, *The Harbor Café*, in Stonington. Actually, at that time of year, it was about the only place in Stonington that served meals.

"Friday night happened to be "Fish Night" and Dick ordered haddock. I ordered the same. When the plates arrived, each plate contained enough fish to feed at least two people, if not three: two huge slabs of haddock, nearly a foot in length on each plate. I had rarely seen so much fish on a plate and underneath the fish was a lot of either potatoes or spaghetti. Dick cleared his plate in no time. I could barely finish mine and I was stuffed. The waitress came by and asked "can I get you some more?" I thought she was kidding. Dick immediately said "yes" and the waitress returned with his second plate just as full as the first. He polished off the entire second serving and was then ready for a large dessert which he also demolished. The reason I tell this story is that it was only a prelude to his eating three huge meals every day of his trip until we got back to Stonington. I will always remember that! And he barely weighed 131 pounds!

"The next day, Saturday, we got to the Bangor, Maine, airport ahead of time. Upon entering the terminal, they brought a wheelchair out with an attendant and we were the first through every line, just like First Class. Yes, this was the way to travel. Remember that Dick had primarily flown only in B-17s, which had no sound proofing to muffle the roar of the four huge loud engines right next to him in the very front of the plane. Most of his flights were over 20,000 + ft. and it was usually 20-40 degrees below zero exacerbated by the wind whipping through the plane because the multiple machine gun doors were wide open much of the time. Not a pleasant way to travel.

"Once we got in the airplane for the direct flight to Washington, there were constant surprises for Dick. He didn't know that the plane had taken off until he looked out the window and saw that we were high off the ground (about 20,000 ft.) because the take-off was so smooth and quiet. He couldn't get over the fact that there was almost no noise. His first jet plane ride ever. We landed at the airport in Washington and again got the special wheelchair treatment with service right to the taxi. We drove straight to the hotel in less than 10 minutes.

"Entering the hotel must have seemed to him like it was the Taj Mahal. The entrance was huge and once inside the lobby it stretched for maybe 50+ yards in length; all glass, pictures, bright colors, glass elevators shooting up and down, numerous leather coaches and chairs, a check-in counter that must have been 20 ft. long, etc. What a way to start his visit to Washington. We met Dick's nephew as we went to check in. He was a history teacher on Long Island who came to see his uncle tour the War Memorial. He was the only relative that kept in touch with Dick. It was an extra special gift to Dick. His name was also Dick Welch, so I called the Bombardier "Lieutenant" and the nephew "Dick."

"The elevator to the room was nearly all glass and it was enclosed in an all-glass shaft. At first Dick was "pasted" to the opposite side of the elevator which was only partially glass. It was obvious that he was a little apprehensive about heights and didn't want to get too near the elevator's full glass panels. The elevator was also fast which startled him. That became a comedic experience each time we got into the elevator. After a few days, Dick moved closer to the glass and finally appeared to enjoy the ride.

"We went straight to our room on the 15th floor which was large and plush. Our view from the room was looking out through a huge 15 ft. wide window at our nation's Capital Building with American flags flying all around it. What a site just five or so blocks away. He wandered into the bathroom which turned out to be about the size of his living room. Again, he was pretty quiet, but I'd have to guess he had never been in a place with such plush decor in his life time. This was first class. From the spacious living area, the large queen size beds to the 40" TV screen, it was his Valhalla. His TV at home was about 12" wide and he said it seldom worked.

"We quickly settled in and within a half an hour of arriving at the hotel, we went back to the elevator to go on a tour of the WWII Memorial. It was about 2:00 pm. We wanted to be sure to see it and not be rushed because we were going to see several museums and more in the next few days.

"We got to the WWII War Memorial and it was just as beautiful and dramatic as you can imagine. The weather was perfect. We could see the Washington Monument on one side; turn round and see the Reflecting Pool and the Lincoln Memorial on the other. What a view. We walked around with his nephew for about an hour or so, reading the signs and so forth. In one display, there were 4,000 gold stars, each star representing 100 Americans killed during the War. There was also a large cast iron plaque that showed a B-17 with the crew getting ready to board it. Dick stared at that for a long time. I can't imagine what he was thinking. We eventually went to the Vietnam Memorial and then the Marine Monument and continued to walk around. It was a beautiful and wonderful day for Dick and all of us. It couldn't have worked out better. His wish had come true.

"We returned to the hotel and went to dinner at a nearby Irish Pub. The food, the ambiance, the conversation, the noise and excitement, just everything about it was the best it could be. During dinner, Dick's nephew pulled out an object from his pocket and gave it to Dick. It turned out to be Dick's Army Air force dog tags and his German POW metal dog tags that he had worn when he was a POW. We had a short walk back to the hotel and retired to our rooms by 9:00 pm. The Capital building was all lit up with the flags flying which was a beautiful thing to see before going to bed. It was a long but eventful day and Dick didn't waste any time finding the "sand man." He was asleep within minutes of hitting the sheets.

"We got up the next morning at 6:00 am, got dressed and went down to the dining room where Dick polished off two large plates of fruits, rolls, eggs, sausage, bacon, etc. I was fortunate and had arranged a special "tour guide" which was a friend of one of the members of The Group. His name was Stephen DeVito who picked up us at the hotel and drove up directly to the National Air Museum in Chantilly, Virginia. We were extremely blessed to have Stephen as our personal guide. He lived in the vicinity and was the author of a recently published military true life history book, "*Fighting With the Filthy Thirteen.*" He had sent me his book a few weeks before which I had partially read. Dick asked to look at it during our flight to DC. He read a number of chapters before we landed and really enjoyed it.

"We were at the Museum for about three hours. To my surprise, Dick walked most of the time. I had given him a walking stick before our trip and he used that almost 100% of the time in lieu of the wheelchair. Another amazing element of the trip was Dick's stamina. The Air Museum, which is adjacent to the Dulles Airport, couldn't have had a better display of WWII aircraft and memorabilia for all of us. Dick was walking smartly and taking in everything as well as talking a lot. At one point while standing under the Enola Gay B-29 which dropped the first atomic bomb on Japan, Dick gave us a 10 minute lecture on the specifics of making a "bomb run" in a B-17. That was precious.

"After seeing most of the American, British, German and Japanese planes including numerous exhibits, we ended the tour with the Space Shuttle which was awesome. Then it was off to lunch and Stephen knew just where to take us: the Longhorn Steakhouse. The Longhorn staff was very attentive which was terrific and made us all feel very special. Dick again ordered enough for two. Then there was another special moment. Stephen DeVito brought out a copy of his new book and presented it to Dick. He had written a lengthy note to Dick with his autograph inside the cover page. He had also gotten the book signed by Jack Womer, the WWII combat Ranger the primary personality of the book.

"After a long lunch, Dick was getting a bit tired so we decided to go back to the hotel and rest. Dick's nephew said "good-bye" and caught a train back to his home on Long Island, New York. When we got back to the hotel room, Dick grabbed Stephen's book, opened it, scanned a few paragraphs or so and passed out cold on the bed for more than an hour. At around 6:00 pm Dick and I went to the Washington Train Terminal which was only a few blocks away and ate another memorable meal.

"Then we got on an Old Town Trolley and had a guided tour around the Capital viewing the various monuments, government buildings, memorials, etc. which were all bathed in lights. For me it was a nice tour, although it was starting to rain as a strong hurricane was approaching. Dick, who had been up most of the time since 6:00 am, was slowing down a little, but laughing and commenting most of the time! We finished the tour, hailed a taxi and got back to the hotel in good shape. We found out that the next day, all the transportation, tunnels, airports and government offices were closed, so we could sleep late. That was the best news Dick could have had because he really needed a reprieve from touring.

"We had planned to go to several other museums on Monday, but that was not to be. The hurricane closed all government buildings again. We slept late that Monday morning and about 9:00 am, went down and ate breakfast. To say the least, Dick enjoyed another huge buffet breakfast and again amazed the waiters at his food intake.

"The rest of the day was spent walking around the hotel, reading, watching TV, resting and marveling at the fury of the hurricane with the Capital building as a backdrop. For the two of us it provided a quiet time to get to know one another more, to discuss things about the War, our experiences in life and so forth. It was a special day for me to spend with Dick who was now a friend and person that I admired even more for the person he was and his contribution to our country. The hurricane continued in full force all day and night, but luckily it didn't shut down the hotel's kitchen, TV, electricity and water and we both enjoyed every minute of it. Dick admitted that he could stay in that environment for many more days and would relish it: me too.

"On Tuesday morning the hurricane was still in full force and everything was again shut down. We repeated the routine of the previous day. It was not hard to take. That night we spent an hour or so packing to make sure that we would not cause any delays at the airport with the security services. We had dinner at the Irish Pub again which again was great. The pub was near enough that we were able to walk to it. The wind and rain had just about ended and it was a pleasant short walk back to the hotel as we spent our last few hours in DC.

"We were up at 6:00 am and caught a taxi, planning to eat breakfast at the airport. When we got to the airport, we immediately spotted a wheelchair with an attendant and away we went. It was the First Class service again. We went right through the check in and whisked through security. To my surprise they took Dick to the front, wheeled him in with me following. They didn't bother to check my bags at all, looked at the wheelchair and waved a wand of some kind over Dick's hands and we kept on moving. The attendant took us to the restaurants, showed us the gate where we were to board, asked if we needed anything more and wished us well and departed. It couldn't have gone better. What I thought might take us at least a half hour or more to get through, took about 5-8 minutes.

"We enjoyed a nice breakfast, small by Dick's standards, got to the departure gate, were ushered to the plane in a special bus and were off the ground headed for Bangor at exactly 10:00 am, our scheduled take-off time. We landed in Bangor, were escorted off the plane, grabbed a wheelchair, recovered our bags, got to the car and headed for Stonington. We stopped for a quick lunch and got back to Dick's home about 2:00 pm where I helped him unpack and get settled. He asked me to dine with him that night which I did. He ate his usual "quantum heap of food" at the *The Harbor Café* and afterward I dropped him back at his home. I stayed in a nearby motel which I thought would be easier on him not to have to bother with having a guest in his house. It worked out well.

"The next morning I tried being upbeat, but it was an emotional departure. I finally grabbed his hand, shook it and then wrapped my arms around him while trying to tell him how wonderful this trip had been for me. But not all the words came out. I was all but speechless again. After awhile, he said softly, "This was the greatest experience I've had since I was rescued from the POW camp." I will always remember those words.

"Finally, I turned around and walked out of the house. We waved to each other. I walked slowly to my car, got in and sat there for a few minutes to collect myself and then drove away. I was overwhelmed with the events of the past six days and filled with a deep sense of gratitude to Dick for letting me into his life for those few moments. What a terrific stroke of luck it was to find such a gem of a man in a small ice cream parlor on an island in Maine. For me, a life changing event!

"That Christmas, The Group showered Dick with all sorts of gifts. He got 6+ months for free food at his favorite restaurant *The Harbor Café*, a beautiful heavy warm hooded winter coat, gloves and plush sweaters for the coming winter. Also, gasoline for his car, special flashlights, food for his cat, 5 glass vials of sand from the 5 beaches of the Normandy invasion, books on WWII planes and so forth. He probably had more presents that Christmas than he'd had for the past ten years combined. He was overwhelmed. During the Christmas season, many of The Group called him at his home and talked to him at length. He loved every minute of it.

"The Group had actually planned to see Dick the next summer of 2013 at our next reunion so he could meet the entire Group that had made his trip possible. We hired a helicopter to pick him up near his home and he was to be our guest at the reunion. He was quite excited because he had never been in a helicopter before and wanted very much to meet all his benefactors. Unfortunately, Dick had a car accident that summer and passed away soon thereafter. At our fraternity reunion that September, we had a big display about Dick's life, a large model of his B-17G, many pictures and all sorts of items that related to him and his contribution to America in those dark days of WWII.

"John R. Welch passed away on June 7, 2013.

Radio-operator S/Sgt. Emile Bianchi

Radio-Operator S/Sgt. Emile Bianchi – High School Graduation

Came to America by ship in the summer of 1929, at the age of eight, and landed in New York City, came thru Ellis Island, and went to live in Farnams, Massachusetts, where his father had previously settled and established home. Emile was educated in Adams, MA, graduating from high school in 1939. He attended technical school in Boston where he studied electronics. After completing two years to tech school he went to work for General Electric in Pittsfield, Mass.

Emile enlisted in the Army Air Corps in October, 1942, and approximately one year later (late 1943) he flew to England where he began his bombing missions over Germany. On April 29, 1944, on his 19th mission, his plane was shot down over the suburbs of Berlin. Exactly a year later he was liberated from a POW camp at Moosburg, Germany, by American forces.

He married in 1946 and moved to Pittsfield, Mass, where he worked forty years for General Electric as an electrician.

Waist-Gunner S/Sgt. Donald R. Itschner.

Cousin Stuart Hitchner wrote;

"Donald Raymond Itschner, "Ray," grew up in Oregon's Willamette Valley in the town of Molalla, a community engaged primarily in logging and farming. Looking upon Molalla in 1930, Ray, then seven years old, lived with his parents and five siblings on Third Street. The town supported a hotel, a public school, and was served by the Southern Pacific Railroad. A nearby logging railroad was also in operation. The town had the usual assortment of businesses; a meat market, drug store, pool hall, restaurant, bank, butcher shop, barber shop, hardware store, and others.

"Ray's father, Emil Itschner, was a contractor specializing in road construction. Their neighbors included a dentist, a teacher, and the proprietor of the local garage. Ray attended Molalla Union High School. Following his schooling, with World War II well under way, he joined the military. Ray became a member of the Eighth Air Force. The unit was established at Savannah Air Base in Georgia, and subsequently set up advanced training for B-17 crews in Walla, Walla, Washington.

***

"Queenie's final mission took place over Berlin on April 29, 1944. As Ray recalled the event, it was noon. He stated that they were just starting to dump chaff (strips of metal foil used to confuse enemy radar) when the right wing of the aircraft was shattered by an anti-aircraft shell. "Went right through the wing; that's what I could see." From Ray's position, the damaged wing was on the opposite side of the aircraft and forward.

Waist-Gunner S/Sgt. Donald R. "Ray" Itschner

"Following standard bail-out procedures, Ray and two others; the right waist-gunner and ball turret gunner were designated to share an escape hatch located behind the waist gun position on the right side of the aircraft. The tail gunner had his own escape hatch.

"Ray was trying to make his way to the hatch as was Johnson, the right waist gunner. Ray remembers the hatch being down, but was pinned to the floor by gravity forces, as the plane went into a dive. In his report, the post liberation casualty questionnaire, Ray stated that he did not bail out but was "blown out of the plane."

"Raymond's counterpart, **Right Waist-Gunner George Johnson** would have been one of the three crewmen whose parachutes were spotted after the plane exploded. He was captured by German forces on the ground and suffered severe injuries to his left thigh. This may have come about from the breakup of the aircraft or as Bianchi believed – as a consequence of a hard landing.

"German observers estimated the crewmen bailed out at about 500 feet, which would have required immediate deployment of parachutes. After capture, Johnson was taken to a nearby hospital and treated. According to German records, He died June 4, 1944, some 37 days later of sepsis; a form of blood poisoning, along with scarlet fever. S/Sgt. George L. Johnson was given a burial by German authorities at the Doberitz Elsgrund Cemetery, about 10 miles west of Berlin."

***

Acknowledgemens;
Bombardier 2Lt. John R. Welch: Bruce Pfann & Terrance Wilson
Radio-Operator S/Sgt. Emile Bianchi: son Bob Bianchi
Waist-Gunner S/Sgt. Donald R. Itschner: cousin Stu Hitschner & Roxie Mudder

CHAPTER 5

92ND BOMB GROUP
326TH BOMB SQUADRON

Type: B-17G • Serial: 42-3513
MACR: 4260 • Air Base: Podington

Downing of aircraft Boeing 17 F on April 29, 1944,
at Nieuw Millingen. Crew captured.

German document KU 1677

Pilot: 2Lt. Russell M. Munson, 0-687058, POW

Co-Pilot: 2Lt. William J. Lalley, 0-705028, POW

Navigator: F/O Aram P. Margosian, T-123986, POW

Bombardier: 2Lt. Webb C. Clarke, 0-665995, POW

Engineer: Sgt. Willard C. Blomberg, 16076934, POW

Radio: S/Sgt. Everett W. Wehling, 32668892, POW

Ball-Turret Gunner: Sgt. Eugene J. Glisynski, 16080349, POW

Waist-Gunner: Sgt. Howard G. Brannen, 35602805, POW

Waist-Gunner: S/Sgt. Charles D. Gholson, 15097711, POW

Tail-Gunner: Sgt. Dominick A. Vitale, 20301998, POW,

10 POW

Crash Site: Nieuw Milligen, Netherlands
Time: 14.40

Pilot 2Lt. Russell M. Munson

by his son Russell Munson:

Pilot 2Lt. Russell M. Munson

"He went to public school in Wilkes-Barre and graduated from Myers High School, probably class of 1940. When the war broke out, he enlisted in the Army National Guard and eventually was called up for basic training and active duty. It was during basic training that he learned about the Army Air Corps and signed up and the rest is history.

"As a newcomer 2nd lieutenant, he was assigned what he called a lousy plane but it successfully got him to and from targets in Germany for his first two flights. On his third, and last, flight, he lost one engine shortly after crossing the channel but was able to keep on with the mission. After bombing Berlin, he lost a second engine heading back. He was likely to make it back until he lost the 3rd engine over Holland, where he had everyone bail out before bailing out himself. He became a prisoner for the rest of the war.

"As an officer and a pilot, he was initially treated well as a Luftwaffe prisoner but this did not last long. As the war was winding down, prisoners were force-marched for miles in horrible weather with many dying along the way and others, like my father, getting significant frost bite.

"He recounted the Sagan death march were large numbers died. Food got worse as the war progressed and Red Cross supplies were diverted to the soldiers. Enlisted men were able to get some food access since they were forced to work on the local farms. Officers were not forced to work but then never had access outside of the prison.

"The senior officer in this prison building of 12 was a US Navy Colonel who reportedly was the first prisoner taken during the war. He was returning to the US from an official visit to Germany on a German ship when war broke out; the ship turned around to return to Germany and he was imprisoned.

***

"My father had life long problems with his hands due to the frost bite and life long dental problems related to poor nutrition. I believe he was about 80 kilos when he entered the prison camp and was less than 60 at liberation. My mom noted he was "skin and bones" when he returned to Wilkes-Barre.

"My parents married June 17, 1947 and certainly knew each other before the war but I do not think they became romantically involved until after the war. She was three years younger but had become a nurse and did her own war-related work here in the States. She died in 2010.

"My Dad attended Wilkes College with GI bill funding. I am not sure when he started but he only finished three out of the usual four years since my sister was born March 10, 1949. I came along December 11, 1953 and have no recollection of Wilkes-Barre early on since we moved to the Washington, DC area when I was two or three.

"He worked as a salesman for Magnus Chemical Company of New Jersey. I believe he sold industrial cleaning products to factories in the greater Washington, DC area (Maryland and Virginia), something he would do until 1963. We lived in the first, and only house my parents ever owned at 13221 Superior Street, Rockville, Maryland. I have fond memories and lasting friendships with the children from the family across the street from us.

"My Dad moved all of us to Kingston, Pennsylvania (just across the Susquehanna River from Wilkes-Barre) when he started working for his brother in his heating/cooling business. My mom took a position as a public health nurse which she kept until retirement.

"My father survived a heart attack at the age of 42 in 1964. He never smoked in high school or the army until he landed in the prison camp. He struggled with cardiac problems for years which led to early retirement in his late 50's with his cardiac disabilities.

Co-Pilot 2Lt. William J. Lalley

In his own words;

"It was 1943 and World War II was consuming all the energies of our country. I had been called up from the Air Force College Reserve Program and graduated from flight school, in January 1944. I received my wings and commission as a Second Lieutenant in the United States Air Force.

"After a short leave I joined a B-17 crew that was in final staging before going overseas. I was assigned as co-pilot with Munson as pilot, Margosian as navigator, and Clarke as bombardier. Since their training was almost complete I had very little experience with the aircraft.

"We arrived in England early April and were assigned to the 92nd Bomb Group. After a short orientation we were designated as a "spare" aircraft on a mission to Berlin on April 29th. Our responsibility was to fill in if any aircraft aborted the mission prior to reaching the channel. Being the tough target that it was, any experienced crew would turn back for the slightest reason. (Which is what they did, leaving us an "opportunity" to fill in). Being a "spare" the aircraft wasn't the most airworthy, but got us to the target where flak knocked out two of our engines.

"Limping back, we lost another engine and were forced to bail out at about

2500 feet. I landed in a tree dangling a few feet above the ground. I managed to get free, but could not free the chute. As I was crashing through the woods I startled an old farmer who was working there. I shouted to him, "parlez vous francaise" or "sprechen ze deutsch," and got nothing but a frightened stare. I ran on staying in the woods and avoiding all open areas until dusk.

"Needing some rest, I crawled under the low branches of a huge evergreen. I could see a house about 800 yards away and was pondering if someone was there who could offer some help when suddenly a man ran out of the house and began firing a gun. I thought the gig was up. I lay close to the tree until he disappeared into the house. I waited there until dark and then began walking somewhat aimlessly, since I had no idea of where we had come down since our navigator was unsure of our position before the bail out. It was dark and I wandered into a low marshy area when I heard voices that I thought sounded like Germans. I retreated and found myself on a narrow hard top road. It soon began to rain. I was able to find a haystack in the dark and burrowed in for the rest of the night.

"Daylight didn't bring any improved options. I needed some nourishment, so I wandered into the henhouse and ate a couple of raw eggs. I then decided to walk south as I felt it was the only reasonable alternative. I was on the road about twenty minutes when I saw two German soldiers approaching on bicycle. Although my heart was pounding I continued toward them and nodded as they rode by. I expected they would turn and come at me from the rear. I will never know why, but they continued on their way, and when I did look back they were well down the road. I can only surmise that they thought I was armed and did not fancy a fight with only their bayonets.

"Shortly after, I noticed a young couple ahead with their bicycles pulled to the side of the road. As I approached they motioned for me to come over. They gave me their names and told me that they would help. I followed them to their home where they hid me in a shed after some appreciated food. I assumed the older couple at the house was their parents. Just before dusk they took me into the woods and told me to hide next to a large fallen tree, and they covered me with leaves and let me know that someone would come for me.

"Just after dark I heard a low whistle and answered in kind, and was soon shaking hands with the man I was to call "Pa" for the next several months. He rode me on the cross bar of his bike for what seemed like an eternity until we arrived at his home. There I was introduced to "Moe" (mom), Edith, a Jewish girl, and Dick who had established an underground network to return Allied airmen to England. He questioned me at length to verify that I was an American airman and not a German sent to intercept his line. Apparently some members of his group were exposed and he was afraid his line would soon be rolled up. He indicated that he would not be able to help much since he planned to get back to England himself. He did warn me that going with the Dutch underground would likely result in being captured.

"I did not inquire about the name of my host since they did not volunteer it.

It was only after I returned to the States after the war that I learned that "Pa" and "Moe" Van den Top had corresponded with my family. He had manufactured bicycle parts in a small Quonset hut located behind his house prior to the German occupation. The Germans had taken over the building and were storing JU-88 aircraft engines there. The Germans were back and forth almost daily, and would get a good tongue lashing from "Moe" if they tried to come in the house. "Pa" had excavated a large area under the living room and, when the carpet was pulled back, the hinged door opened and you could view his store of wine, cigars and other "forbidden" items, including a motorcycle.

"They had two sons, Jan and Jaap who were "under-water" (hiding) to escape being sent to Germany, and visited the house only infrequently. Edith was in hiding; her mother was being sought by the Germans for being a spy. They all survived and I corresponded with them after I returned to the States.

"While I was at the house, which was in the small town of Stroe near Apeldoorn, Gene Glisynski was brought there and spent a few days. When we put our stories together I discovered that he had been on our aircraft on the 29th of April as a replacement for the regular ball turret gunner. I hadn't known him prior to that time.

"The young P-47 pilot, Connie Barr, was also brought to the house while Gene was there. I have a picture of Gene, Connie and myself taken at Van den Top's home. Connie had a harrowing experience during a strafing run on a train in a nearby village. It had been an ammunition train and blew up sending debris into his engine. He pulled up, rolled the plane over and pulled the ejection lever. On the way out his foot caught under the rudder pedal. He was pinned against the fuselage as the plane fell upside down. He finally managed to free himself and open his chute. He had torn a great gash in his heavy GI boot.

"My recollection is that Gene and Connie left together with the Dutch organization in spite of the advice that I passed on from the Englishman "Dick" that they might get caught. I believe that it was after this that Bob Bailey arrived. Bob was flying Mosquitoes for the RAF when he came down in the area of Stroe. He had been on a night mission and encountered a German ME-109 that blew up in front of him from his cannon fire. The debris fouled his engines forcing him and his navigator to bail out. The plane went into a spin as he was ejecting and he was forced against his seat half way out the door. He finally managed to free himself and open his chute. He was picked up by the underground and brought to the house looking for a place to hide.

"He was unable to stay for an extended period because of lack of room. He was extremely anxious to return home because his wife was soon to deliver their baby. When he did return, he had decided to go with the Dutch Underground. I decided to go with him, as I didn't see an end to the war in sight. We wore civilian clothes and were to pose as deaf and dumb basket makers to confirm to our identification papers.

"We left with our guides on a tandem bicycle and, after a couple of stops en-route, we arrived in Arnhem. I have pictures of Bob Bailey and myself chopping wood at one of the stops that we made. Arnhem had a busy rail station and many German soldiers were boarding and leaving the trains. Our guide took us to the second floor office of the stationmaster where we awaited our departure. We boarded the train with Bob and a guide in one compartment and I and a guide in another. Our disguise was very thin since a loud noise would have betrayed the fact that we were deaf.

"Our trip to Breda was nervous, but uneventful. My memory on our Breda stay is a little vague. Bob and I were taken to different homes and remained there for about three weeks. I don't recall where it was, but we were joined by Viv Connell, an Australian who had been shot down.

"I vividly recall being taken to a rather elegant apartment in Antwerp by two young women; Pauline Vlaming and a friend. It was a two-story flat well furnished and stocked with wine and food like we hadn't seen in other accommodations. Going up the stairs, I noticed several color photos of German aircraft - ME-l09's, F.W.'s, etc. When I asked about them, I was told that this was to give the appearance of being pro-German to deflect any suspicion that escapees where being housed there.

"We discussed further plans and it was mentioned that it might be possible to get a plane from a secret rendezvous in the Schelde Islands. There supposedly was a bridge to be negotiated at a critical spot on the route and preparations were underway to get a car or arrange some other means of getting through this obstacle.

"She returned the next day with two men who, as best I can recall, were in their 30's. There was some conversation about the plans, but I can't recall exactly what was said. It seemed that they had been unsuccessful in their efforts. We left and began walking through the city, eventually entering a rather large old building that appeared quite empty. One of the men took me into an empty office with a desk and a few chairs. He began asking me questions about where I was shot down, who I had stayed with en-route, etc. I became a little suspicious since this had not been part of the routine before. I gave him limited information about our aircraft and nothing about where I had stayed and was glad that I had not come to know the names of those that had helped me. He became a little more insistent saying that it was taking much too long to bring escapees down from Holland, and they could be handling many more if they could learn why the airmen weren't moving through the system faster. When he seemed satisfied that I wouldn't be much help we joined the others and were told that we were on our way again.

"We continued to walk through the city area, one guide in front, and the other behind. As we passed a large building and entered a foyer facing two glass doors that formed the entrance into the building, I saw men in German uniforms, and for a moment my heart sank. Instead of entering the building our guide turned up a flight of stairs at the back of the foyer, and led us into a small office on the second floor. When I expressed my anxiety about the Germans, he scoffed and said that the closer we get to them, the less suspicious they are. The two of them began questioning us again about where we had been. It didn't last long and they started out of the room saying something like, "let's go see what the Gestapo is doing." We followed down the stairs into the foyer and instead of turning out toward the street, they went through the glass door into the building.

"We'd had it!!! Their mood changed, becoming surly - pushing us around a bit, one had pulled out a gun. They chided us for being so dumb saying 'you guys would believe anything," and threatened that we would be shot as spies because we were caught in civilian clothes. I can't recall a very good description of them. One spoke especially good American English, and bragged that he had lived in Chicago for several years.

"They headed us into a car and drove us to St. Giles prison in Antwerp. We were processed in an office and assigned to a second floor cell that was about 15 x 20 feet with one window high up on the wall. Three straw mats on the floor served as our beds. We awoke in the middle of the night covered with bugs that were getting fat on our blood. The walls indicated that we were not the first escapees to occupy the cell. Red blotches with 'confirmed' and dates covered the walls indicating the previous occupants had waged an all out battle against the bugs.

"The next morning we got our first introduction to "schwarzbrot," a heavy sour bread that became the main portion of most meals. It was inedible at first, but in the later stages of captivity it brought a fair price if sold on IOUs.

"After about three weeks we were transported to Brussels where we became separated. I was placed in solitary confinement for a few days and again drilled about my activities since being shot down, still facing the threat of execution for being a spy. I was soon released and sent to Frankfurt, and became part of the Luftwaffe POW system until liberated on April 29, 1945: one year from the date that we were shot down.

"Frankfort on Main was a distribution center for all POWs in that area. Here again I was in solitary confinement and interrogated about the base, squadron, and crew members and when we had come down and where we had been and who had helped us in our escape efforts. When I refused to answer, except for name, rank, and serial number, I was returned to solitary for a few more days, then joined the other POWs in a large confined area. I learned from others that the Gennan intelligence was so good they were getting almost daily reports on activities at the American Air Bases in England.

"Red Cross representatives were at the camp interviewing and passing out parcels containing canned food, cigarettes, soup, soap, shaving gear, tooth brushes, etc'. They had forms to fill out which asked many questions the interrogators had asked that most of us had refused to answer. It struck me as ironic that the same questions were now on the questionnaire everyone filled out. We were also given a postcard that we could mail home. This was a welcome blessing since mother had heard nothing for months, except that I was missing in action.

"We were transported by train to Stalag Luft III near Breslau, about 90 miles southeast of Berlin. This was one of the better camps that Germans used when Red Cross officials would do an inspection. It consisted of an American compound, and a separate English compound. The rooms in the barracks held 12 men in triple wooden bunks with wood slats and straw-filled burlap bags for a mattress.

"For meals, the Germans provided a thin soup of turnips and rutabagas, black bread and occasionally some blood sausage. The Red Cross parcels were our main sustenance. The food was pooled in each room and meals prepared by the men. Each box contained dried milk, dried prunes, a can of meat (spam, etc.) cigarettes, soup, jam, toothpaste and other items. The POWs were ingenious in making things from the tin cans the food came in, even blowers, little cars, and track for escape tunnels.

"The Germans eventually enforced collection of all the cans. We spent the time reading, playing cards, walking the perimeter of the camps inside the high barbed wire fence, always under the watchful eye of solders in the guard towers, each equipped with rifle and machine guns.

"There had been an escape attempt shortly before I arrived. Some Canadians had tunneled under the fence, but came up short of the woods. They were caught and shot. Our senior officer discontinued any escape efforts after that. The British, some of whom had been there since Dunkirk, seemed much better organized than the Americans did. They were receiving the British Broad Casting news and would wigwag the war news into our compound and it would be spread from barracks to barracks. They also had established underground contact with some civilians and were trading soap, cigarettes and other items for eggs, bread and other food. It was not unusual to see some in full dress uniforms they had received over the years they were there.

"We had to fall out every morning for "appel" (roll call) when we were all counted. This gave the guards (ferrets) an opportunity to search our barracks and belongings for any signs of escape activities. We were locked in the barracks at night. Patrol dogs roamed through the compound to detect anyone outside the barracks.

"As the winter of '44 wore on, the Russians kept moving closer and closer to our camps, so close that in January. we began hearing their long-range artillery. There was a lot of speculation as to what the Germans would do with us. It was answered on a bitter cold, blustery night about the middle of January. The announcement came through that we would be moving out in a few hours. Everyone was scrambling around making preparations to leave. The food was divided up, we put on all the clothing we had and made a bed roll with the thin blankets. Some broke up the beds for makeshift sleds. It was the middle of the night when all the POWs were lined up on the road and marched off. I don't know how many there were from all the camps - thousands perhaps.

"Thus began what we called the 48-hour "death march." Walking in the worst winter conditions with only brief stops for rest and an over night in barns and unheated buildings. It became so bad that POWs were carrying the rifles and bicycles of our German guards. I remember hallucinating as we trudged along, seeing all sorts of odd figures and heads in the woods. I remember seeing two men leaving the column and heading into the woods through the deep snow, and I wondered if the guard dogs would thwart their escape. Many became exhausted and fell by the wayside.

"When we finally arrived in Spremberg, all were exhausted. I remember seeing a man, brought down by the weight of his backpack, falling backwards into a plate glass window. We were shuttled into a large old building that had once been a pottery factory. The dust was thick on the floors and machinery. We all sank into the dust, savoring the warming heat of the building.

"We spent about two days there. Apparently the Germans were arranging for our transportation and soon marched us to the railroad yard where we boarded on the trains. The box cars were those used in WWI. They were called Forty and Eighth, meaning they would hold forty men and eight horses. We were crammed into the cars with fifty to sixty POWs in each car. We could only move around by agreement. Many were suffering from diarrhea and found relief at infrequent stops. Most of the time they squatted outside the train in railway stations. We would jettison our tin cans from the Red Cross parcels during these stops and left a trail of crap and tin cans all the way across Germany from Spremberg to Nuremberg (Our only revenge on the Germans!)

"The prison camp at Nuremberg was in pour condition and the food situation was deteriorating rapidly. The Eastern front kept moving closer and closer. American fighter aircraft was shooting at almost anything moving on the roads and railroads. We watched the almost daily flights of our 8th Air Force bombers that were pounding German targets by day, while the British were pounding them by night. Many night raids were on the railroads marshalling yards of Nuremberg located close to our camp. In their formation the lead plane would come in, drop flares, light up the target so the bombers could make their run. I was an awesome display, somewhat frightening since a misdirected bomb could very easily have leveled our camp.

"Because of the hammering they were taking, the Germans became less and less inclined to have trucks involved in transporting Red Cross parcels from Switzerland. At a desperate stage in the food supply the Germans asked for volunteers from the POWs to drive to Switzerland and bring in the Red Cross food parcels. Fortunately there were some with truck driving experience that agreed to go. During the week or so before they returned, our food rations were stretched to starvation limits. Food remained a scarce item for several weeks until we got the word that we were moving.

"The Eastern front lines were driving ever closer to Nuremberg. Again there was much speculation as to what the Germans would do with us. It was early spring and the weather was rather good, so we were not surprised or disappointed when they informed us we were moving. There was always the hope we would be moving to better conditions. Again, these were huge columns of POWs on the road. We didn't know where we were going, but it was south. Some were guessing it was Munich where the Germans might use us as bargaining chips in a last stand battle.

"The greatest danger was from our own fighter planes that might mistake us for German troops. We had some information that our pilots generally knew the location of POW camps; however we had heard that they had mistakenly strafed a column of POWs coming out of a camp in Northern Germany.

"Being on the road was a relief from the barbed wire. The guards were rather loose in policing the columns, and we would barter Red Cross cigarettes and candy with the civilians for eggs, bread, and sometimes meat or chicken. I recall a couple of guys returning to the group pulling a small cart filled with vegetables. I think they had been gone from the formation overnight trading for food. There wasn't much point in trying to escape from our lines, as the risk was high of being shot by the Germans or our own troops.

"We did have one harrowing experience passing through a small village. A train was stopped and had been spotted by some of our P-47's. They began a strafing run and came in with guns spitting fire and the engine exploded in a cloud of steam. As they pulled up to circle, we ran into an adjacent field and spelled out POW in large block letters with blankets from our bedrolls. They must have seen the signal for they did not return for another pass at the train. It was a miracle that no one was killed or injured.

"We finally arrived at a camp in Moosburg about 30 miles northeast of Munich. It was a huge compound with thousands of POWs from other camps throughout Germany. There were Americans, British, Russians, and other national groups, including Gurka troops from India. The permanent buildings had all been filled earlier and we were assigned to large tents. Most of the cooking was done outside on tin-can stoves and wood stripped from the air raid trenches. Things were coming to an end for the Germans and they didn't seem concerned about what we did inside the camp.

"The sound of the front got louder as April wore on. Then on the 29th amid heavy firing, we saw American tanks appear on the hills far off. What a day!! Everyone was jumping up and down and hollering, when suddenly there was the rattle of small arms fire within the camp. We all dove into what was left of the air raid trenches. After a while the shooting stopped. We learned later that S.S. troops had come to the camp to get the guards to join them in fighting the Yanks. When they refused, a small war broke out between them.

"Not long after, we heard news that our tanks had entered our compound. We were FREE! The celebration erupted! After a few days they began moving groups out to Landshut, a small town nearby where C-47's were coming in to transport POWs to staging camps in France. As our column was sitting in the fields waiting, a C-47 landed and pulled up to our area. The pilot opened his window and shouted down "are you guys Russians?" Obviously we were looking pretty scruffy after the year in the camps.

"We landed in camp "Lucky Strike" outside Le Havre. POWs were being processed there for their return to the States. The first order of business was a hot shower with lots of soap and some clean clothes. Then to the mess hall where the GI grub seemed like elegant cuisine. At that point there were no restrictions on food and I loaded up on pea soup. I awoke in the middle of the night realizing the soup had been too much and barely made it to the latrine. Later we were placed on a special diet to accustom our systems to the rich food. I did hear later that when we were aboard ship and candy bars were available one returnee ate so many mars bars that he died!

"The trip home was uneventful, but seemed to take forever, as we all had to return by ship. Most of the talk was about what we would do when we got home, and when we would have our favorite meal. I eventually arrived in Chicago by plane. I was to be met by my brother Jack who was stationed at Gardner General Hospital in Chicago. As I was waiting with others who had departed the plane, he walked by and didn't even recognize me until I called out to him. Needless to say, I was not in the same shape as when he had last seen me.

"It was then on to home and a wonderful reunion with my mom. We thanked God for this day! I spent some time home on leave, then into Gardner General Hospital where all returning POWs were thoroughly checked out. I was home on leave on August 15, 1945. It was another glorious day when the Japanese surrendered. That ended any concerns about being sent to the Pacific Theater or the war.

"In November, I was faced with the question of staying in the service or getting out. Since the prospects were slim that I would be flying again and I didn't relish the other aspects of military life, I was separated from service in 1945. I never piloted a plane again, although I remained in the reserve until 1961.

"I moved to Holland, Michigan, in 1953, and among acquaintances that I met was Eddie Racks, who I discovered was the Colonel in command of the tank battalion that liberated our camp at Moosburg, Germany in April 29, 1945.

"In recent years I have been in contact with Michael LeBlanc, a Canadian whose uncle was an "escapee." He was collecting stories of pilots who had followed the same track through the underground and were captured in Antwerp. He had identified the young woman who had betrayed us. He sent pictures of her as she looked in 1944 and later in life. On the 11th of October, 1948, The Military Court of Antwerp denied Pauline Vlaming, all her rights of law, all titles, grades, and civil functions and confiscated from her, all objects that served in her offences. She was irrevocably sentenced to the death penalty. She was to be executed, at an announced place, by weapons.

"In Holland, the same charges were brought against her. On the 29th of June, 1951, she was convicted on the same evidence brought against her in the Belgian courts, and sentenced by the Bijzondere Strafkamer of the Arrondissements

Rechtbank, in Breda, to a prison term of 15 years, and her voting rights were revoked. By Belgian Royal Decree #1 101, of October the 3rd 1964, she was pardoned completely.

"He also identified the underground leader, Dick Kragt, who first questioned me. He was a British espionage agent who had been able to return many shot down pilots through his underground system in Holland and Belgium.

"I had always been curious about the fate of Bob Bailey, the English Mosquito pilot who accompanied me through the underground until we were caught in Antwerp. LeBlanc put me in touch with his wife who wrote that Bob had a successful career in the RAF, and commercial aviation before succumbing to M.S. I was sorry that I had not found him sooner and had a chance to see him again.

"I had been in contact periodically with the Van den Tops, the family that hid me in their house in Holland. They survived the occupation, but at one point had to flee their home, which was taken over by the Germans as a command post. When they returned they were surprised to find that the Germans had never found the radio that was concealed in the false ceiling in the house. We got the war news from the B.B.C. on that little set.

"Jo and I returned to the Netherlands in the spring of 1997 and visited the area where I came down and was first hidden by the underground. We later were able to locate the house in Stroe where I had been hidden for about three months. Jaap Van den Top and his wife Mini were living in the house and operating a very successful bicycle accessory factory. I revisited the bedroom where I had stayed and viewed the linen closet with the trap door where I would hide when warnings came that the Germans were searching homes in the area. We inquired about Edith (the Jewish girl who was in hiding with me) wondering if Jaap knew of her whereabouts. To our delight he told us that she lived just a 'few miles south of Stroe. He called her to see if she was home, and we were thrilled to hear that she was and would await our arrival. How excited we were to see each other again after all those years. I had taken an old letter she had written to me many years ago when she was only 13. She was so surprised and thrilled that I had saved it. She had only found out recently what had happened to her mother.

"Two years previous to the time we saw her, she had been on television doing a documentary about their experiences during the war, when a woman that lived only two blocks away called, and told her that she knew what had happened to her mother. She was picked up by the Gestapo and put on the last train to Auschwitz.

"Edith is married with a lovely family, including a daughter in the Netherlands and one in California. She and her husband Walter have visited us in Chicago after seeing their family in California, and then came to Holland, Michigan in the summer of 1999 and to Florida in the winter of 2000.

Engineer Sgt. Willard C. Blomberg

Engineer Sgt. Willard C. Blomberg was born in Moline, Illinois on January 6, 1913 and passed away on March 3, 2003. After the war he went to college on the GI bill but dropped out and went to work for Hermann Nelson, a manufacturing company specialized in heaters. He married in 1947.

His daughter describes him as "A gentle man, grateful after his experiences for a simple meal, a bed to sleep in and, in his words, "a glass of milk."

Things were tough after the war, Willard and his wife were on a waiting list for a car for at least three years. They walked everywhere, and sometimes had the use of a family vehicle. Willard gave up his place on the car waiting list to his brother, Bob, so he could get to school and get his education. Bob later became very successful in the banking industry.

"Willard lost track of his buddies, all died long before he did. They also did not want to relive their experiences. He went on to just live a life in middle management jobs. He had his daughter, and a son with cerebral palsy. He worked relentlessly just to teach him to learn how to use a bathroom. I learned all my tenacity from my dad. He had no patience with whining, or quitting what one set out to do.

Radio operator S/Sgt. Everett W. Wehling.

His daughter Connie Mackey wrote;

"He was born in Rome, NY, and grew up in a town called Verona in upstate New York. As a teenager he worked in small factories in Rome, NY, and got his first car when he was 17: a model A he paid $100 cash for. He helped my grandfather build a house on Wehling Road. That's right: the name of the road is the name that my grandmother gave it and the house is still there on Wehling Road .

"My father went into the Army Air Corps when he was 19 years old and re-tired from the military 30 years later. After he came back home after the war the military wouldn't let him stop flying because he had only just begun to fly and he didn't have enough flight hours in his logbook.

"He was very proud of the fact that he helped build the second radar tower in Japan after the war and his work training radar operators until his retirement. He was also a flight inspector for the FAA for ten years following his retirement.

"He was the smartest man I've ever known. Every time he turned around he was learning something new: reading a book on how to do it just so you could say he did.

127

"While he was a POW his head was butted with a rifle. It developed into a brain tumor which was the cause of his death when he passed away on August 16, 2010 at age 88.

Waist-Gunner S/Sgt. Charles D. Gholson
wrote to the author:

"The youngest of three children, I was born on July 11, 1921, in Paducah, Kentucky. As a result of my mother's death when I was only five years old, my father raised three boys on his own with the help of some wonderful neighbors.

"I graduated from Tilghman High School in 1940, while my father was serving as McCracken County jailer. After graduation, I began working as a bricklayer's apprentice. I enlisted into the Army Air Force in July 1942 and was called to active duty the following January. Prior to going overseas, I received military training as a top turret gunner and B-17 engineer in Gulfport, Mississippi; Burbank, California; Kingman, Arizona; and Dalhart, Texas.

"I arrived at Podington, just outside of Northamptonshire, England, on Monday, April 24, 1944 and was assigned to a crew where I was to serve as a waist gunner. I flew my first and only mission on Saturday, April 29, 1944. I was still wearing my dress uniform from the previous night's escapades into Northampton, when I boarded our B-17.

"We had flown for several hours during which time, I had been sitting on an empty ammunition box at my waist gun. The Germans were shooting at us and flak was everywhere. Our plane, as well as others in our formation, were being hit. There were holes everywhere along our fuselage.

"We were on our return flight from Berlin and desperately trying to reach the Channel, when the pilot called for me to switch the fuel tanks. As I walked over to change the tank, a shell hit and exploded the ammunition box on which I had been sitting all this time. There was no time now to switch the tanks, as the pilot announced that we were at 2000 feet and going down. It was time to bail out. Everyone made it out, but after jumping, I never saw anyone from our crew again.

"During my descent, I could hear the bullets flying by and see holes in my parachute. As I was approaching the ground, I floated six to eight feet above the coal car of a passing train. I recall being scared, as I had no control over my chute. After successfully passing over the train, my chute became tangled in utility lines just above a young German soldier who was waiting for me to descend.

"Thinking that this German soldier was young and possibly inexperienced, I decided to see if I might be able to get away. I began to run, but after glancing back, I noticed that he was raising his gun as if to fire. At that, I began to slowly retrace my steps until he lowered his weapon. We both repeated this maneuver two or three times, but I gave up after realizing that he truly had the upper hand.

"I was escorted to Amsterdam, Holland aboard a train filled with German soldiers. I did not see another American on board. It was in Amsterdam that I was entered into a transit camp and interrogated briefly by three Germans, one of whom spoke English. When questioned about what I knew, my reply brought much laughter on behalf of these Germans. "I arrived on Monday, was shot down on Saturday. I don't know anything! "

"After leaving the Dulag in Frankfurt, I was transported by train to East Prussia with other POWs. We received nothing to eat for the seven days it took to make the trip. I remained in an English prison camp in East Prussia for several months. I moved through several prison camps, but fail to recall the locations other than Nuremberg and Moosburg, in Germany.

"At one point in particular, I remember feeling sorry for myself, while being transported between POW camps in a boxcar with other prisoners. The car was so filled to capacity that we all had to remain standing. I recall it being unbearably hot inside the car. The train pulled into a station in Berlin. I was able to look through the knot holes in the boxcar to see the train directly across from us. It was filled with Russian prisoners whom were being transported horizontally in what appeared to be chicken coops.

"During a forced march of several thousand prisoners, a fellow soldier and I managed to stray from the column. My friend spoke German, so we approached a farmhouse where a lady had fresh-baked bread cooling in the window. As we were so terribly hungry, he asked if we could do chores in exchange for some bread. She put us to work cleaning her cow shed. German soldiers arrived at the house and began harassing us. The lady came to our defense, however, explaining that we were working for her. After eating, we returned to the column, as there was really no where else to go.

"I was liberated from a camp in Moosburg, Germany on April 29, 1945. We remained in camp for several days awaiting transportation. American soldiers were posted at the camp during this time for our own safety. I recall several fellow soldiers who slipped away into town, only to overeat and die.

"I returned to the United States via Boston aboard a commercial ship. I was assigned to Camp Attebury in Indiana, where by coincidence, my future father-in-law was working with the Corp of Engineers. It was here that I reconnected with my high school sweetheart, Evelyn Hunter, and we soon married.

"After leaving the service, I resumed my apprenticeship and later became a masonry contractor in my hometown of Paducah, Kentucky. I continue to reside in Paducah, along with my only son, William Winston Gholson.

Tail-Gunner Sgt. Dominick A. Vitale.

Donna, his daughter, wrote;

"My father spent his whole life—except for his wartime experiences—in Scranton, Pennsylvania. He went to Lafayette for elementary school and Scranton

Technical for secondary school.

"All his life he was a house painter and specialized in hanging wallpaper. He worked for company called West Side Painting and Decorating. He was married to my mother, Antoinette, for over 50 years.

"He had two passions (outside of my mother). One was woodcarving. His carvings are exquisite. He was especially fond of carving American Bald Eagles.

"His second passion was Boy Scouts. He was a Scout Master for many years and a Scouting District Commissioner. He was in the Order of the Arrow and received a very prestigious US Scouting award called The Silver Beaver. He liked to fish and had a little lake front lot that was his pride and joy.

Tail-Gunner Sgt. Dominick A. Vitale

"He didn't want to fly after the war. He said he had to jump out of too many burning planes. When I moved to California I finally convinced him to fly out to visit. This was when they still served food on US domestic flights. He was much surprised that he got a meal and a beer on the plane. His comment to me when he landed was "World War II was never like this"!!

"He came home with a bullet wound in the leg that had never been completed treated and had times when his leg would really be problematic. He also came home with nightmares and they would occasionally wake us up at night. He never forgot the war physically or psychologically. Prison camp made a deep scar. He would cut bread on the bread wrapper and put the crumbs in his food because he could not bear the sight of wasted food (even bread crumbs).

"Joanne and I were very fortunate to have him as a father."

***

Acknowledgements;
Russell Munson, son of pilot.
William J. Lalley, co-pilot
Connie Mackey, daughter of radio-operator.
Charles D. Cholson, waist-gunner
Donna Lupinacci & Joanne Vitale, daughter of tail-gunner

CHAPTER 6

92ND BOMB GROUP
326TH BOMB SQUADRON

Type: B-17G • Serial: 42-97319
MACR: 4261• Air Base: Podington

---

*On 29 April, 1944, at 15:30 hours, a Boeing 17G,
serial 42-97319, made a belly-landing on its
way back. The crew escaped after landing.
Two men captured.*

German document KU 1670

Pilot: 2Lt. John B. Langfeldt, 0-753898, POW, Brooklyn, NY

Co-Pilot: 2Lt. Guy A. Wallace, 0-734398, EVD, Bonners Ferry, ID

Navigator: 2Lt. Walter R. Heldorfer, 0-707050, EVD, Cleveland, OH

Bombardier: 2Lt. Oscar S. Rogers Jr., 0-757035, EVD, Henderson, TX

Top-Turret Gunner: S/Sgt. Earl C. Brodrick, 31259456, EVD, Clinton, MA

Radio: S/Sgt. Dale F. Howard, 37410620, EVD, St. Louis, MO

Ball-Turret Gunner: S/Sgt. Kenneth E. Neff, 19045952, EVD, Bell, CA

Waist-Gunner: Sgt. Albert R. Monti, 33586813, 33586813, EVD, Philadelphia, PA

Waist-Gunner: Sgt. Daniel M. Sullivan, 31289068, POW, Newport, RI

Tail-Gunner: Sgt. Kenneth G. Biedinger, 39409889, POW, Stockton, CA

3 POW, 7 EVD

Crash Site: Sailly-Saillisel, near Cambray (France)
Time: 15.30

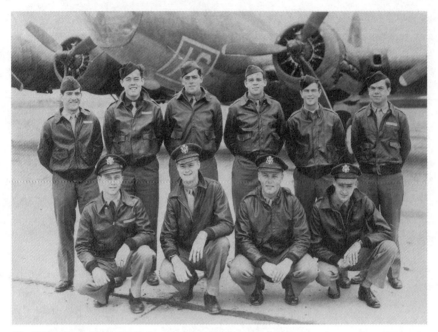

92nd Bomb Group, 326th Bomb Squadron (Langfeldt)

Back row (left to right): Radio S/Sgt. Dale F Howard, Waist-Gunner Sgt. Daniel M. Sullivan, Waist-Gunner Sgt. Albert R. Monti, Tail-Gunner Sgt. Kenneth C. Biedinger

Front row: Pilot Lt. John Langfeldt, Bombardier Lt. Oscar Scott Rogers Jr., Navigator Lt. Walter R. Heldorfer, Co-pilot Lt. Guy A. Wallace

Pilot 2Lt. John B. Langfeldt recalls;

"Our target today is Berlin," said the Operations Officer in a matter of fact tone. A groan of dismay could be heard from the assembled officers in the briefing room. Berlin - the most heavily defended city in all of Germany – was to be our target. I thought to myself "If I live through this day (April 29, 1944), I will likely never forget it." How right I was to be.

"A jeep drove us to our plane "Salvo Sally." I pre-flighted the ship and started the engines. Then came the command to take off. We rendezvoused at 12'000 feet and set our course for Berlin.

"All was peaceful as we flew over occupied Holland. No fighter attacks and only an occasional burst of flak to break the monotony. We had flown for about four hours when we sighted Berlin. Then all hell broke loose. Enemy fighters flashed down from the skies and shot up the formation. I saw several planes go down in flames. Our plane was hit, but we suffered no casualties or important damage to the plane. The attack lasted only a few minutes. We continued on to the target. Bomb-bay doors were opened. Then the voice of my bombardier "On target - bombs away." "Thank God for that – the worst is over," I said to myself.

"I had just closed the bomb-bay doors when it happened. "Bang." The big ship staggered for a moment from the force of the exploding shell. There was a fire in the number two engine right next to me. My hand shot out and closed the ignition switch, fuel supply valve, and feathering button. I knew we would blow up in a matter of seconds if that fire would go on. It seemed like an eternity, though it was perhaps twenty seconds, before the fire went out. Now with only three engines operating we couldn't keep up with our formation. We watched them disappear in the distance. We were alone.

"I calculated what our chances were of getting back to base, and concluded they were practically nil. I decided to tell the crew, for they had the right to know. I told them that the best we could hope for was to reach the English Channel. Also, they were free to parachute out if they wished. The answers came back all the same. They would stick with me and the ship.

"We had flown for about three hours, all the time gradually loosing altitude. We were just a few hundred feet over the ground, when suddenly the number one engine sputtered and stopped. I dove the plane at the ground to maintain flying speed. Just as the ground came up I pulled back on the stick as we skidded along the ground. No one was hurt in the crash.

"We quickly got out and raced to the nearby woods for cover, for we felt certain that enemy patrols were probably already on the way to pick us up. As soon as we got into the woods, I told the crew to split up in twos, as I thought they would have a better chance of escaping when they did this. I stayed with the tailgunner Kenneth Biedinger.

"We hid in the woods until dusk and then left to strike out for a village about two miles away. We had hope of contacting the French underground there. Unfortunately, there
were only open fields ahead. No cover for protection.

"We had only gone a few hundred yards when we heard in the distance the sound of a motorcar approaching. We threw ourselves on the ground, hoping they would not see us. But they had, for they drove up to where we were. An officer and five soldiers climbed out of the car carrying rifles and machine pistols. "Raus! Raus,!" they shouted. By the tone of their voices, one knew they meant "get up quickly or be shot." We surrendered. The German officer came over to me and said "Vor You Der Var Ist Over."

Daughter Linda Pedersen about her father;

"John Langfeldt grew up in the Norwegian neighborhood of Bay Ridge, Brooklyn. He had two sisters Lillian and Marion, and he had a difficult childhood as his mother died when he was only ten years old. His father came to America on one of the last sailing ships, and worked as a floor layer to support his family. His

Pilot 2Lt. John B. Langfeldt

father never remarried, and he was a "latch key" child, as his Dad was raising the children alone. Nearby relatives helped out as best they could.

"He was a very bright man, and would tell us that apparently when he was stationed in Pearl Harbor, he was told that he had the highest IQ on the base. As a teenager he was very proud of being admitted to Brooklyn Tech for his high school years. Before the war, he worked with his father in the floor laying business, and always wanted to be a pilot.

"John volunteered for the Army Air Force, and he was stationed at Pearl Harbor the day the Japanese attacked. Later he was sent to England to fly the planes he loved. He knew that it was a very dangerous assignment, but his patriotism pushed him forward to do whatever he needed do to fight the Germans. One of the days he would later talk about most often was the vision of seeing General Patton coming to liberate the POWs

"Before the war, he lived in Brooklyn, New York, and would spend some of the summers in Princeton, New Jersey, in a small summer community. It was one of the original homeowner associations, and the wives and children would have a getaway from city life. His father, and a handful of others, were the founders of the community and bought the lots and divided up the land. They named the community Norseville, as it was almost 100% Norwegians, and many relatives shared the experience together.

"The woman that he would eventually marry, Thelma Pedersen, also spent summers there, and they were friends. When he returned from the war, he started to date her, and they married one year later. Ironically, he never had a real date before this time.

"The bungalows in the summer community were converted to year round homes and the Brooklyn residents moved to New Jersey. Dad first worked at Johns Manville where he received special government training and contract experience. Several years later, he started working at Princeton University and received a faculty status position. He was very proud of his work there, and he retired from the university at 65 years old.

"All his life he told stories of his war adventures. Reporters and authors often interviewed him about his personal story, which covered Pearl Harbor, the war in Europe., and the challenges of becoming a prisoner of war In Germany.

"The war became a part of the man he had become.

Navigator 2Lt. Walter R. Heldorfer.

"These are my experiences while evading the Germans during the Second World War. After reading my story you will understand why I am so grateful to the French people. I was a navigator of a B-17 in the United States Army Air Corps, and these experiences occurred when I failed to return from a bombing mission over Germany.

"On Friday, April 28, 1944, I walked over to the Officers Club at the 92 Bombardment Group where I was stationed. I was looking at the bulletin board at the club and I noticed that my Bomb Squadron, the 326th, and myself in particular, was alerted for a bombing mission the next day. This was to be my fourth bombing raid.

"After learning that I would have to fly the next day, I left the club and went back to my barracks. From the little experience that I gained up to this time, I knew that after one was alerted he was subject to be called any time after the notice was posted. I wrote my daily letter to my wife, and called it a day about eight that evening.

"At 02:30, Saturday, April 29, 1944, I was awakened for the day's mission. Breakfast was at 03:00. After eating, we all sat around making conversation. The boys all tried to make a joke of just how many would return. They didn't seem to really get serious until station time, the time just before the airplanes take off on a mission. Also, during the lapse between breakfast and the main briefing, we all tried to figure out just where the mission for the day would take us.

"Trucks picked us up at about 03:30 and took us down to the main briefing building. There were armed guards stationed at the entrance to the briefing room, being very careful that only authorized personnel entered. The briefing room is more or less an ordinary classroom like you would see in any school. Instead of a blackboard in the front of the room, however, the wall was covered with a map of Europe. This map was then covered with newspaper. We all knew that once this newspaper was removed we could tell what the target for the day was. First the toll was taken, and after everyone was present or accounted for the newspaper was taken down. The target of the day was to be the center of Berlin. If I remember correctly we were told that that this raid was to be the biggest to date.

"The weather briefing officer told us that the sky over Berlin was overcast at the present time, but that it should break up by the time we got there. Station time was 06:25, which meant that we all were to be in our respective airplanes and in our crew positions at that time. Engines were to be started at 06:30, and take-off was to be at 07:00. Flight altitude was to be around 26,000 feet.

"The navigators were then dismissed to go over to the special navigator's briefing. Here I drew up all my course lines and measured the distances to the different rally points. After I finished my flight plan, I went to my airplane.

"We took off at 07:00 and left the English coast at 09:00. We were flying at an altitude of 26,000 feet with a solid undercast below, thus making it impos-

Navigator 2Lt. Walter R. Heldorfer

sible to see the ground. After we crossed into enemy territory an occasional burst of flak would come up, but none of it was very accurate. When we neared Berlin the undercast started to break, giving us a chance to see the target. Bombs went away at approximately 12:30 p.m. It looked to me that we hit the target right on the nose.

"As we were leaving the target, flak came flying at us from everywhere. My navigational table was cluttered with shattered glass from the nose of the airplane where flak had found its mark. About five minutes later we had to leave the formation because two of our engines had been hit by flak and we couldn't keep up with the rest of the formation running on only two engines. The pilot called me immediately and asked for a heading home. We were now at 18,000 feet and travelling alone. This was very dangerous because enemy fighters relish picking on a lone bomber, whereas they think twice before attacking an entire formation.

"A little later one of our gunners called over the intercom reporting that our tail-gunner had been badly hit by flak in his hand. The pilot was having a very difficult time flying the airplane because we were continually in the range of flak guns. Our airplane sounded as though someone had set a thousand mice loose from within – a continual ping-ping-ping. The nose of the aircraft was like a sieve, and I imagine that the rest of the ship was in the same condition. The pilot was continually changing our heading, trying to avoid flak. By this time we were flying at 12,000 feet just above an overcast. He evidently figured that it would be safer at this altitude just above the clouds; in the event of attack by fighters, we could use the clouds as concealment.

"Our intercom system was badly damaged by flak, so when we wanted to correspond with one another we had to leave our crew position. The pilot called us one at the time into the cockpit and wanted to know what we wanted to do. He said that because of the wounded tail-gunner he was going the fly the plane as long as he possibly could and then crash-land. We had the alternative of parachuting any time we wanted or to stick with him and the airplane. Every member of the crew decided to stick with the pilot. We then threw all excess equipment overboard to lighten the load on our two good engines.

"We ran out of gas and crash-landed the airplane about 03:30 in Northern France. Our orders were in the event of a crash-landing to destroy the airplane and then try to escape. After the airplane had slid along on its belly, it really started hissing and moaning. The pilot told us to stay clear of the ship. I believe that he thought it would explode any minute because of the noise it was making. At any rate, we all took off on our own and headed for the nearest wooded area. We travelled as fast as we possibly could for we knew that the Germans would be after us shortly. Luck was with us, inasmuch as we had crashed in a wooded area.

"Once in the woods I ran for about thirty minutes, and then removed my flying overalls and electric flying suit. These I hid in the woods, being very careful not to leave any trail. Just about this time I heard several dogs barking and I thought for sure that the Germans had bloodhounds searching the woods for us. I started to move faster and I came to a little stream which I thought would offer a good opportunity to evade these dogs. I waded into the creek upstream for half a mile or so. After I left the stream I was plenty wet, for in several places it was rather deep.

"I then met up with the copilot and bombardier of my crew, and the three of us set out to evade the Germans. We ran from one woods into another. In these wooded areas I noticed several things that told me that they had seen many a rough day. German helmets were laying all over, most of them punctured with bullet holes. In places the ground was literally covered with empty cartridges.

"After about an hour of running, we noticed a young man approaching the fields. At first we didn't know whether or not to chance being seen by him. He was the first sight of life that we had seen since we left the disabled airplane. We decided that the three of us could take care of him in the event that he should start trouble. We had a very hard time trying to talk to this fellow as he spoke only French and we only English.

"In our escape kits that we carried was a small compass, vitamin pills, chewing gum, first aid bandages, French money, maps, and a language translation book. This translation book certainly came in handy, and after we pointed to the French sentence saying that we were American aviators, this young fellow immediately started to cry and wanted to grab all three of us at once and kiss us. He settled for one at the time and gave each of us several kisses on each cheek, crying all the time. After we showed him the comparable French sentences he pointed out the safest route for us to follow, approximately south-east from our position. He also showed us where we were on our maps.

"We then started heading south-east, using the compasses from our escape kits. Now we were heading across open fields. Every now and then we could see people near us. We were very careful to stay clear of these people, but they gave me the sickest feeling not knowing whether they were friend or foe. We finally came to another wooded area and decided to wait there until darkness. By this time we were all very tired and hungry.

"After dark we started out again. This really was some hike, and every time we'd see a tree or hedge on the horizon we'd immediately think that it was a German and fall on our stomachs. After we fell down we would lay very still and watch the object for five or ten minutes, and if the subject wouldn't move we'd say "no German" and continue with our race-like hike. At the break of dawn we were in another wooded area and we decided to rest a bit and orient ourselves the best we could. We knew that very soon we would have to make some sort of contact or turn ourselves in to the Germans. We had not eaten since 02:45 Saturday morning and it was now 04:30 Sunday morning.

"When it became light enough to see, we saw that we were in a wooded area in the center of various open fields. We half ran until we came to the edge of a small village. We decided to wait there and make contact with the first likely prospect. We waited and watched every house in the village. This was a very small village, there were approximately twenty or twenty-four homes, and three or four stores. There wasn't any sign of life whatsoever until about two o'clock in the afternoon. We spotted a man leading two horses towards an open field, and then another man following him pushing a wheelbarrow. The man with the horses went to a rather distant field, but the man with the wheelbarrow went to a little patch of woods rather close to us.

"We decided to contact this fellow with the wheelbarrow. He seemed to be filling his wheelbarrow with twigs and carrying them into the village. On his second load we accosted him and with the aid of our translation book got it across to him that we were very thirsty and hungry. He told us to remain in the woods and that he would return with food and drinks.

"He came back with two loafs of bread and two liters of beer. This dry bread and beer tasted plenty good to us, I assure you. We tried to get it across to him that we wanted him to buy us train tickets to some point in southern France. We wanted to get as close to Spain as we possibly could, thinking that once in Spain all we'd have to do was contact the American Consul. We couldn't get him to understand this, but he told us that later on in the day his sister would come to see us and that she could speak English.

"A few hours later a girl came out with her husband and they could both speak a little English. They schoolteachers. They asked us many questions, as they wanted to be sure that we were really American aviators. These people had many experiences with Germans dressed as Americans who would try to get the French to hide them. They told us that after dark they would make arrangements to move us out of the woods, and then they left us alone again. This being alone in the woods was rather monotonous. We had nothing to do and no cigarettes to smoke.

"At about ten that evening, as it was starting to get dark we could see several people heading towards this wooded area that we were in. Among the crowd was the young man who had originally helped us, his sister and her husband. After they reached us they told us not to fear, that all these people were friends and that they would all try to help us. We again asked them about our chances of boarding a train and trying to get into Spain. We were told that at the present time this would be impossible because the Germans were watching the trains very carefully.

"A young boy from the crowd was then sent out of the woods to the center of the road that lead into this little village. He waited there a few minutes and then waved back to the rest of us in the woods. He was sent there to be a sentry, watching for any Germans who might be travelling this road.

"After he waved, Wallace, the co-pilot, and two of these people left the woods and walked across the field and down the road to the first house, all of the men carrying sticks. I don't know the reason for the sticks, but I imagine that they thought this made them look less conspicuous.

"About fifteen minutes later I followed with my French friend to the same house, and after I was inside ten or fifteen minutes our bombardier Rogers made his entry the same way. In this house I was introduced to French wine. I imagine that each of us must have drunk about a liter of wine here. They outfitted us the best they could in civilian clothes. I received a pair of knickers that reached down to my ankles (French style, I believe) the seat of these pants were plenty thin so I had to wear them over my army pants. I also received a hat, necktie and a suitcoat that was about two sizes too small about the shoulders, and about two sizes too long in the sleeves. In return we gave these people all of the insignia that we had and everything that would be evidence to the Germans that we were American aviators.

"At about eleven-thirty that night we were again moved one at a time to a house in the center of the village. Here they had a warm meal prepared for us, ready for us to sit down and eat. We stayed there for two days, upstairs in a bedroom most of the time. Our stay at this home was rather pleasant considering the circumstances. Someone was continually with us talking about this and the last war, which was of interest to us.

"The evening after these two days it was time to leave, and they made sure that we were dressed an hour before we actually left, and also packed a sack full of bread and wine to carry with us. We were told to follow two men, but that we were to stay about fifty meters behind them. We followed these men for a couple of miles and then they stopped and started talking to a couple of people on bicycles. Shortly one of the people with the bicycle came back to us with a note. We huddled together and with my cigarette lighter for illumination we read the note, which was written in English. The note read; "Follow the bicycles, be very careful and stay fifty meters behind us. If we are stopped take to the fields, but we'll expect you back on the road shortly. Burn this note immediately."

"We burned the note and started to follow the people on the bicycles. After a half hour or so we could see the headlights of an automobile coming toward us. We figured that it must be a German car so into the fields we went. After the automobile passed we continued following the bicycles. After approximately seven or eight miles we could see the people on the bicycles stop at a fork in the road, and two people came out of the darkness from the fields and took their bicycles. The people we were originally following took one road and the bicycles travelled the other road. We didn't know exactly what to do, but continued on our way to this fork.

"When we came to the fork, the people we were originally following were waiting in the darkness and mentioned for us to join them. We then learned that these people were our school teacher friends whom we hadn't since that night several days ago in the woods.

"The five of us then proceeded down the road until we came to a house on the edge of another village. After we were sure that no one was on the streets we entered this house. Here we met two new friends, an elderly couple who seemed very pleased to see us. Again the wine bottles were brought out, and we all drank to a quick victory.

"These people told us that until they could make connections we would have to stay with them. I didn't know just what they meant by "connections," but presumed that it meant other contacts to enable us to move closer to our destination, England. The three of us were then ushered out into a field behind the house, where there was a little work shed. We were told that we would have to stay in this shed because there were many Germans in this little village. In this shed we were reunited with two of the enlisted men from our crew, the engineer Earl Brodrick and the ball-turret gunner Kenneth Neff. They had travelled a different route than we had, but we were now together again.

"This shed that we were in was very, very tiny. In fact, there wasn't enough room for all of us to lie down, and one had to lay across the ankles of the other four men. During this first night we were awakened many times by the sound of trains. We were left alone all the next day – the people had told us that it would be too dangerous for them to be seen coming out of this shed. During the day we could see German trains going by as this shed was very close to the railroad tracks. The Germans were always shouting or singing, they certainly seemed to be a happy lot.

"That night our newly acquired friends brought food out to us: boiled potatoes, bread and a vegetable. This same routine continued for three days, and then on the third night we were all taken to the house in front of the shed. In this house we met two new friends, two young men who asked us several questions, such as type of airplane we were flying, the number of the crew, the airplane number, etc. Guy Wallace, the co-pilot, Oscar Rogers, the bombardier, and I were told that we would be moved to another place. These latest two friends were going to guide us. Wallace and Rogers left with one of these men and I followed with the other one about fifteen minutes later.

"This man I was with had a bicycle, but he didn't ride it. He walked at my side pushing the bicycle. This was a very dark night, I couldn't see more than a few feet in front of me, but my guide certainly knew where he was going. We travelled as far as we could down the road and then came to a wooded area. I couldn't see any entrance but my guide knew where the path through the woods was located. He told me to be very careful where I stepped. Once I stepped on a twig and it snapped, and my guide immediately stopped to make sure no one overheard the noise. After a couple of minutes we continued on our way.

"After about half an hour we neared the edge of the woods. Through the woods

I could see a road and several stores that were along this same road. Just as we got to the edge of the woods I could hear an automobile engine and voices. The guide then motioned for me to lie down. Instead of an automobile it was a truckload of German soldiers shouting at the top of their voices. The truck passed, but the guide and I continued lying there. Finally a man came out from one of the stores across the road. He stood there looking up and down the road, he didn't seem to be doing anything. After about five minutes he waved over to the woods, and the guide and I got up and went into the store. Here we met up again with Wallace and Rogers. This store was a French cafe, and we stayed there long enough to have one drink.

"Wallace, Rogers and I along with both guides then walked up the road, after the café owner had made sure the road was free. We walked a couple of blocks and entered another house. Once inside our guides left us, and we were in the company of a man and his wife. The man was a very jolly fellow, but his wife seemed very worried and was continually walking around the house every now and putting her ear against the wall to hear whether or not anyone was outside. After an hour or so this fellow gave us an old mattress and two or three blankets to carry, and the four of us left and started across the fields to an abandoned house near the railroad tracks.

"He stayed with us until we made up our bed and then before leaving told us that he would return the next day to see us. This man returned the next day with food. He told us that he had contacted an officer of the French underground, whom he called George. He told us George was going to see us. A couple of days later George came and told us that he was trying to arrange for a car to take us as near to the Pyrenees Mountains as possible. After we were in this house a couple of weeks, Brodrick and Neff were again put in with us. It seemed that they thought the Germans might search the house where they were staying.

"The next day our friend came with food, and he also brought a tiny container with a blank sheet of paper inside. He said that George had sent him a carrier pigeon and that we were to write a note that would be taken to England by this pigeon. I wrote this note and put our names on it, also indicating where we were. We were now in the little town of Peronne, which is in the northern part of France.

"A few days later all five of us were moved under the cover of darkness to a two-room hut in the center of a large swamp. Up until this time none of us were able to talk above a whisper, but at this hut we could talk in a normal tone of conversation. Before our friend left us for the night, he told us that he would return the next day with food, fishing rods, and reading material. The next day came and went but our friend did not return. He did not come back to see us until the second day. He said that the Germans had the territory under very close surveillance, evidently hunting for some crashed Allied aviators. He mentioned that it wasn't at all uncommon for the Germans to surround an entire village and search each home individually. At any rate he was with us again, and he brought plenty of food and the promised fishing rods. He brought a couple of days supply of food in case there would be any repetition of what had happened. This was very appreciated as we were all very hungry and thirsty.

"Brodrick and Rogers were quite the fishermen and they fished most of the day. I played cards, mostly solitaire, and slept a lot.

"One night when our friend visited us he told us that our pilot John Langfeldt and tail-gunner Kenneth Biedinger were prisoners of the Germans. Just how he learned this information we did not know, but later we found out that it was correct.

"One day, after about a week in this hut, Brodrick and Rogers came hurrying inside with their fishing poles. They told the rest of us that a boat was heading for the hut, and in it were two men and a little girl. We didn't know just what to do, and we all stayed inside until we could see what they would do. After a moment Rogers figured that they had seen him and Brodrick, so he went out to talk to these men. He couldn't understand them very well but he told them that there was only he and another fellow, Broderick, there. After these people left we didn't know what to do but decided that it would be best to wait for our friend to come that evening. When our friend came he told us that he knew all about the episode of that afternoon. He said that it was the owner of the hut and that we would all have to leave. This night he had brought a couple of his friends with him. One of these friends I shall call Mr. Q.

"We all got into the boat and headed towards shore. Once ashore Rogers, Brodrick, and I followed Mr. Q to the home of his mother. Here we were put in a bedroom in the attic and provided honest-to-goodness sheets and called it a night.

"The next morning Mr. Q came up to the room with our breakfast of chicory, bread and jam. He also brought his wife along and introduced her to us. During the day, after looking out the window we could see that Mr. Q lived in the house directly in front of the one we were in.

"In the next couple of days we met many people. Among them Mr. Q's son and daughter. His son was studying English and liked to talk to us. He was only eleven or twelve years old, but he could do a better job with the English language than any of us could do with French. Every evening all the people we knew would come over to visit us. We played checkers, dominos, cards or just sat around and talked.

"One day Mr. Q told us that the Germans had quartered some troops in a house very near us and that he thought it best that one of us should get up about four in the morning and stand guard. That night he took us out to the back of the house and pointed out where he thought would be a good place to hide in the event we had to leave his mother's house abruptly. We pulled straws for that first morning's guard duty and took turns then after.

"Mr. Q's mother certainly was a grand person. We all called her grandmother, and I imagine that she was about seventy years old, but she was full of ambitions. She would always get up at six-thirty and make chicory for the guard. Grandmother would take some French cognac and add several fruit juices plus the juice of some weeds to it, and called it her own special medicine. She would take a shot of this stuff every now and then throughout the day. She told us that it was for her health. One morning while on guard I unconsciously coughed, and in came grandmother with her little green bottle. She insisted that I take a shot. I drank it as I did not want to hurt her feelings, but never in my life have I ever tasted anything so horrible.

"One morning Mr. Q, his wife, son and daughter and almost everyone that we knew came in laughing and hollering. This was the 6th of June, 1944. These people certainly were happy, for this was the day they had been waiting five years for – INVASION DAY!

"On the fourth of July grandmother baked us a cake, cut an American flag out of an old magazine, and mounted this flag on a needle and stuck this needle in a cake. With this cake and a few bottles of wine we celebrated the Fourth. There were plenty of firecrackers as well, for our airplanes were bombing and dive-bombing everything around us.

"On the 13th of July, I was again moved – separately this time. Mr. Q, his wife and son were my guides. Before we left I was told that we would travel by train. I was to be accompanied by Mr. Q's wife and son, but because of the danger they would not sit with me. We went down to the train station very early, and I got on the train by myself and took a seat. Shortly afterward Mrs. Q and her son walked past my seat and dropped a ticket on the floor, then sat down two seats away from me. By this time the train was ready to pull out and several other people boarded, but luckily for me there were no German soldiers. We travelled for about two hours and then came to our destination. When Mrs. Q and her son left the train I did likewise. After we had walked for a couple of blocks past the station, Mrs. Q motioned for me to join her and her son.

"As we walked down this street we would pass a German soldier every so often, and as we did the boy would look at me and laugh and I would look down at him and wink, but all the time I was plenty scared. We entered a store in the near center of this town, which was Ham. This store was operated by Mr. Q's brother and family.

"At noon this same day a gentleman came to see me who spoke very good English. He told me that he was in the resistance movement and that he would try to place me in a tiny village a couple of miles from Ham. He also mentioned that he was a doctor and that he was very busy and might not be back until rather late.

"At eleven that evening he returned, and after he made sure that the streets were clear, he and I went out and got in his automobile. We first drove to his home which was nearby. Once inside we had a drink of wine and he gave me a cigar. The cigar was broken in the middle so he wrapped a cigarette paper around it, and apologized for doing so, saying that it was the best he had.

"When it came time to leave he told me that in the event we were stopped by the Germans he would tell them that we were on our way to my wife whom he was going to attend because she was having a baby. We no sooner left his house than a couple of German soldiers flagged us down. The doctor talked to them for a couple of minutes and then we were on our way. He told me that they asked him the direction of a certain town and that he gave them the wrong directions.

"We went to a little village called Sancourt, and down to the very last house in the street. Here I was introduced to a man I shall call Jer, and Jer's mother. They were expecting me because the wine bottles were already on the table. The doctor left and indicated that he would be back to visit me.

"The next day the doctor returned and gave me a card of identification, thus making me a full-fledged Frenchman named Paul Delaporte. This was in the event any German might happen to ask me for identification. I understand that the Germans required all Frenchmen above the age of fifteen to have these cards.

"American airplanes were constantly bombing everything that moved in France. Our airplanes were continuously in the sky. One day our planes really let go in the town of Ham. Jer asked me whether or not I'd like to go into town and see just what the bombing had done, and I replied that I would. I was given a bicycle and we went into Ham right after the all clear signal sounded. This was on or about the 15th of August, 1944.

"Our Air Force did a grand job this particular day. Strafing planes had caught a camouflaged German troop train, and just tore it to pieces. They also bombed the railroad station and everything was in turmoil. We got along the side of the shot-up train just about the same time that the Germans were returning from their shelter in the fields. They rushed about to pick up what belongings they had so hurriedly left behind.

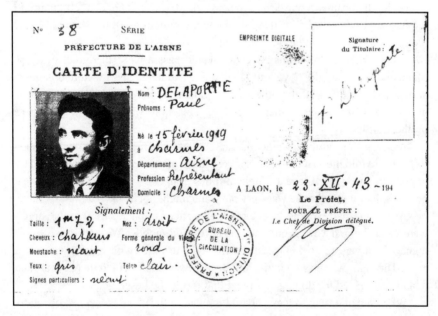

Heldorfer's French identification

"Alongside the train, Jer stopped a couple of German soldiers and offered them a cigarette. I actually lit a cigarette of one of these German soldiers with my Army issued lighter, and I had to be careful to conceal the Army Air Corps insignia on the side of the lighter in the palm of my hand. It seemed to me that these soldiers were rather old to be in an Army uniform. Jer asked them what they thought of the war and its outcome, and they said that Germany was finished and that the war would be over in a month or two.

"In town Jer and I stopped in a café for a drink. When we came in, several German officers were there sitting at a table. Jer and I went to the bar for our drinks. When we were ready to leave, the Germans had cluttered around blocking the exit. Jer pardoned himself but for some unknown reason I lagged behind, and I saw that Jer was already outside. There I was inside with four or five German officers blocking the exit. I knew that I didn't dare open my mouth, so I turned my head to one side and walked into one of the officers. He gave me the funniest look, but luckily for me he didn't say anything and let me pass. This incident was then the talk of everyone who knew who I was, for the officer that I had bumped into had been awarded the coveted German Iron Cross that very same day.

"On the way back to the farm we ran into the doctor, and he was riding a motorcycle. We asked him where his automobile was and he replied that American planes had strafed it and set it on fire, so now he only had this motorcycle.

"At noon a few days later, several Frenchmen came running down the Jer's farm. They all seemed rather excited about something. I asked Jer just what the trouble was, and he told me that the Germans were taking all of the horses and using them to haul troops and supplies. Most of their automobiles had been shot up and what they had left they didn't have enough gasoline. All of these men brought their horses down to Jer's farm and put them to graze out in the fields.

"The next day the doctor again came to visit me. This time he was walking. I asked him whether or not his motorcycle had broke down, and he replied that the Germans had taken it away from him.

"On the 28th of August, 1944, while looking out the window I noticed three German officers coming down the road. Jer told me to go upstairs and hide. I went upstairs and and climbed on top of the rafters to the roof. I could hear the Germans come inside and in no time they started up the stairs. I was in a very dark spot, thus making it possible for me to see them but they could not see me. Jer was with them and they just seemed to be looking around. After they left the farm I climbed down and went downstairs and asked Jer what was up. He said that these three officers along with seven or eight enlisted men were going to return about eight that evening and spend a few days there. These officers didn't ask whether or not they could stay, they just said that they were going to move in.

"I asked what I was going to do, and Jer replied that he was going to see the doctor right away and tell him what had happened. But before Jer returned I could see these same officers with their enlisted men coming down the road again, so back up to the rafters I went. The three officers came inside and the enlisted men went to the barn. Jer's mother fixed up a room downstairs for these officers so they didn't come upstairs.

"These Germans stayed for three days, and then left because our troops were moving up very, very fast. Just about the time they left we could begin to hear the noise of our long range guns. Shortly after this all the people in this town started living in caves that they had dug out many months before.

On the 2nd of September, 1944, the United States Army liberated the town of Ham, and the village Sancourt. I left Sancourt on the 2nd of September and was taken to Paris to be interrogated. I spent five days in Paris and then flew to London where I cabled my wife that I was safe. On the 28th of September, 1944, I boarded a plane and flew back to the States.

"Once back in the States I met up with my co-pilot and bombardier and learned that our entire crew, excepting the pilot, tail-gunner and a waist-gunner, had successfully evaded the Germans. However, in time they all safely made it back home.

"I corresponded quite frequently with my French friends. I am deeply grateful to these people and shall never forget what they did for me.

Son Ron Heldorfer wrote:

"My father was born on February 15, 1921 in Sharon, Pennsylvania, the oldest of what were to be four children. The family moved to Cleveland, Ohio in the early 1920's and settled in the near west side of the city, where my grandfather worked in the local steel mills. Cleveland was largely an industrial, blue-collar town for most of its history, although recent history has rendered a more service oriented economy, especially in health care.

"My father's mother became ill and deceased when he was 18 years old, and his late teens and early 20's were involved with helping his family, emotionally and financially. By the early 1940's he was employed at Warner & Swasey, a local company, and on September 20, 1942 he enlisted in the army.

"His goal initially was to join the Air Corps to become a pilot, but he ultimately was assigned to navigator school in San Marcos, Texas. He and my mother were wed on January 19, 1944 just prior to his being deployed overseas.

"The mission on April 29, 1944 was to be his fourth bombing raid. After he returned from France I believe he was assigned briefly to Columbus, Ohio, but he resigned his commission shortly after the end of the war. I understand that if he had stayed in the service he had been due a promotion to captain, but he resigned prior to this promotion. He worked a number of assorted jobs, including owning and operating an automobile body shop, but by the early 1950's he was employed by an engineering and contracting firm, Arthur G. McKee & Co., in Cleveland, where he worked until his retirement in the early 1980's.

"While working for McKee, he was sent for two stints to Paris, France, to work on a project, first in 1962 and again from late 1967 through the middle of

1969. He went alone for several months in 1962, and while there he made contact with some of the French people who had assisted him during the war. When he went in December 1967 the entire family relocated for the 18 month period and lived in a neighborhood just to the southwest of Paris.

"During our stay we visited on several occasions Peronne and Ham, France, the scene of where he was during the war, and met many of the people who helped him, at times in the north of France and also in Paris where some of them lived, such as Clotaire Quentin's (Mr. Q) son, Daniel. Angel Quentin, the wife of Clotaire, also visited us in Ohio following the death of Clotaire.

"My parents bought a home in Brooklyn, Ohio, a suburb of Cleveland in 1954, and they lived there until my father's death in October, 1990. My mother continued to live there until her death in April, 2007

Bombardier 2Lt. Oscar S. Rogers Jr.

From his Escape & Evasion Report;

"We were hit by flak on the 29th April, 1944 and landed our plane in a field at Templeau-le-Fosse (Somme). We split up in pairs and we all took to the woods. Two of us, Neff and Brodrick, were fed and sheltered the first night by a farmer. The rest of us spent the night in the woods. The following morning the six of us, in three pairs, left our respective hiding places, and that day made contact with friendly farmers. The farmers were in contact with the Maquis, and were in many cases active members.

"We stayed in the vicinity, the outskirts of Peronne (Somme) for about 2.5 months. Each pair stayed in a different farmhouse, and we were moved to a different house every fortnight. Mr. Albert Tillette, mailman of Flemicourt (Somme) managed our stay in Peronne. He moved us from house to house, kept us in touch with each other and secured identity cards for us. He said he was an intelligent agent, and that he sent information on targets and military movements to the British by carier pigeon and through a headquarters in Paris.

"On the 23rd July he arranged for evacuation from Peronne. We were taken by train to Ham. Three of us stayed above the wine shop owned by Maurice Quentin. The three others stayed above a café situated directly across the street from the Mayor's house. The men who sheltered us were both resistance men. Two days later we were taken by train, escorted by 30 Maquis, to Lagny (Oise).

"Wallace and Rogers stayed at the home of René Aldebert in Lagny. They had helped many airmen, their house being a sort of clearing house. They had sheltered a man for three months. While there a P-38 strafed a German truck but failed to to fire it. René rode out with Wallace and set fire to it.

"Neff and Brodrick stayed at the home of Pierre Gilot in Lagny, a very active resistance leader. He worked under the chef of Noyon. He claimed to have passed through 27 airmen, besides the 13 of us who were in that district at the time. He was a refractaire, a former railroad worker. He was an expert in railroad and power line demolition and was wanted for sabotage. A René Martin was Pierre's Aide. He worked closely with Pierre and maintained contact with the Noyon Resistance.

"Monti and Howard stayed at the home of Maurice de France in Lagny. A few days after arriving there Maurice got word that the Gestapo were on his trail so they were moved to a small farm on the outskirts of Lagny.

"A Monsieur Thibeau or Tibot, a former French army officer arranged our next move. He identified us by by asking us the difference between shack-up and sack-up. His main work was that of aiding evaders and he was in contact with an American lieutenant west of the Seine. He had received orders to assemble evaders for evacuation.

"On about the 15 August he collected the six of us, nine other Americans and three English who had been in the area and took us by truck to a woods behind a chateau owned by L. Ravel. He was a Resistance man and spoke English. He said he owned a paint factory in Connecticut. A former French captain who also spoke English and was a Resistance man stayed at the chateau and helped Ravel. We remained in the woods until the 30 August when a British unit arrived. We gathered at the chateau and Lt. Birdwell, IS-9, an American, took charge of us.

Ball-Turret S/Sgt. Kenneth E. Neff wrote the booklet "Fame's Favored Few."

"My name is Kenneth E. Neff and I entered the military from California. In September of 1940, 1 enlisted in the Army Air Corps as I had a feeling a national draft into military service was about to begin. Since I was twenty-two at the time, I knew I would be one of the first to get the draft call. I also knew I couldn't out swim a bullet so I didn't want to be in the Navy. I was pretty fast on land but not as fast as a speeding bullet so I didn't want to be a ground pounder in the infantry. Therefore, I went for the Army Air Corps. Besides, if you were on flight status, you got more pay.

"My first duty was at Moffett Field, California. The Army had just taken it over from the Navy. There were 2,700 of us stationed there and that was where we took our basic training. The Army only had one officer, one master sergeant, one technical sergeant, and five corporals assigned there to care for us. That small number of cadre couldn't keep a close eye on so many of us: therefore, we had a ball! After basic, we started training in different shops. I was sent to aircraft maintenance school in order to become a qualified crew chief.

"In December of 1940, we left Moffett Field and went to Stockton Field, California. It was a new base that was just being built and some of the buildings were just being painted. The streets were dirt, rather I should say they were mud. The engineers were starting to blacktop the dirt streets and that was even worse than the mud. At least with the mud, you could clean it off before you went into the barracks whereas the asphalt from the blacktopping went in with you. Ah yes! Those were the good old days.

"We didn't know what we were going to run into at Stockton Field. The town outside the base was an old Navy town and therefore we didn't know how the people were going to take to a bunch of young "fly-boys" moving in. I am glad to say the local folks took us to their hearts and that certainly made life much more enjoyable when we were off the base.

"I was first put to work in the base theater, and by the time it was finished I was learning to be a projectionist as well as how to do the paper work. I was promoted to private first class, a PFC as we were called, in February of 1941 and that was that. PFC Mutzenberger, my coworker, and I asked the First Sergeant if we were going to stay PFCs the rest of our hitches. The two of us assigned to the base theater were pulling KP twice a week. KP, kitchen police to you civilians, is doing menial work in the mess hall and no fun at all. The other guys in the squadron were only pulling KP once a week. Finally the theater officer went to the group commander and told him he could not run the base theater with both protectionists pulling KP twice a week.

"In November of 1941, orders came out transferring thirteen of us to another new base that was being built down in Arizona. It was to be called Williams Field and was located at Higley, now known as Chandler. Our First Stud was going down to Texas on leave so we asked him to see what kind of town Higley was. When he returned, we asked if he had checked Higley out for us. He said while driving through Arizona he had stopped at a gas station and asked directions to Higley and the attendants told him where to go. The First Stud did just what the gas station attendants had told him to do. He drove about five miles after he turned off the main road and drove another five miles and still found nothing. He drove a few more miles and then turned around and drove back to a store and gas station. He went in and asked a man working there if he could tell him where Higley was and the fellow said, "This is it." We were sure not looking forward to going to Williams Field, Arizona! The theater officer was on orders to go to Williams Field too, so he and I drove down together.

"We finally got to the new base on December fourth, three days before the surprise Japanese attack on Pearl Harbor. On Sunday morning, 7 December 1941, Japanese navy planes unexpectedly attacked Pearl Harbor and other military installations on the island of Oahu in Hawaii. The thing I remember most about December seventh was walking guard duty at the water tower carrying a broom handle in lieu of a rifle. The Army was pretty short of rifles in those days so we got broom handles instead.

"Oh, I also remember a lot of things that took place over the next year. Again there were the two of us who were still PFC's. New draftees were coming in and making corporal while the two of us stagnated as a PFC. Finally Lutz and I went to see the *Old Man* and find out what was going on. Now *Old Man* is a traditional name in the Army for any commander, regardless of how old or how young he is. In my case he was the same theater officer that I drove down to Williams Field with. We explained our position and when finished he said, "Look fellows, if I don't get something from your section putting you in for promotion, I can't do anything about it We thanked him and went back to our section. Lutz talked to his commander and told him what the CO had said. I went back to the theater, sat down, and typed a letter to the CO. I didn't say to what rank I should be promoted, only that I should be promoted. The next promotion roster that came out had both Lutz's name and mine on it as being promoted to corporal, and it was about time! Two months later when the promotion list came out, I found myself a buck sergeant. Another two months and I was promoted to a staff sergeant. I went up to the orderly room at the company and said enough is enough. It's costing me too much money having the new rank put on all my uniforms just in time to take them off for another change.

"August 1942 rolled around and it was time to move again. Orders came out for another group to go to Will Rogers Field over in Oklahoma City. Two days later we left Willie, the name we'd shortened Williams Field to. When we arrived in Oklahoma, no one seemed to know what to do with us. This was a start-up group from which a new bomber squadron was to be formed. They split us up and again they didn't know what to do with me. Finally I received an assignment and for the first time since I attended school at Moffett Field, I was able to work on an aircraft. I was now the crew chief of an A-20 attack bomber.

"One day I went up to the orderly room and requested that I be sent to gunnery school. The orderly room personnel checked into it and then informed me that since I was a staff sergeant, I was ineligible to go. I said, "OK. I'll get busted down one stripe." I'm not certain they believed me. It took me three months and three commanding officers, but I finally got it done.

"At last my orders arrived, and I went down to Laredo Army Air Field, Texas and became an aerial gunner. I graduated on 13 January 1943. From there I was sent to the aircraft armorer's school at Lowry Field in Denver, Colorado. Four months later I graduated on 15 May and was ordered to Boise, Idaho to an aircrew processing center. Here you were selected to be assigned to a particular type of aircraft. I was assigned to fly in bombers and sent to Ephrata, Washington and assigned to a B-17 squadron as a ball turret gunner. We began three months of training and ended up training at three different locations. At the end of the training cycle, the group was placed aboard a troop train and taken to Scott Field, Illinois.

"There our crew picked up our brand new B-17G, the latest model of that type bomber. We spent a lot of time and money naming that plane. We were having a lot of trouble with it and every name someone came up with was shot down. The pilot came by one morning and said, "What's wrong with this SOB today?" We all looked at him and said, "That's it!" Well, we didn't go all the way with that name. The crew did, however, have a knockout young and enticing female body painted on the fuselage but the body had an witch's head. We called the B-17 *The Miserable Bitch*. I felt really bad about never getting to fly a mission in her.

"After we'd been at Scott for two days, we found ourselves airborne for England. When we arrived at Nutscorner, Ireland, the B-17 was taken away from us for some reason unknown to us. I learned later that this happened to other crews who flew their bombers overseas besides ours.

"Our crew found ourselves assigned to the 326th Bomb Squadron, 92nd Bomb Group stationed at Podington in the southeastern part of England. It was such a small village that it didn't even appear on most maps. The nearest place of any size was Bedford, a few miles south of Podington. Here our crew was given another B-17.

"We went on our first combat mission in October of 1943 and flew up to Norway to bomb German installations there. I flew fifteen more missions between October and 31 December 1943, mostly over German occupied France and Germany but also a couple over Poland. Some of my flights weren't even with the 92nd BG but with a group known as the *Pathfinders*. I have no idea of why our crew was picked for this special assignment, but we were and we did as we were ordered. While with this *Pathfinder* group, we had moved from Podington to Alconbury which is about twenty miles northeast of Bedford.

"*Pathfinder* operations were a risky! The day of each mission, our crew would be up well before dawn in order to fly to the home base of whichever bomber organization was assigned to lead the day's attack. This usually meant flying east at the same time the Royal Air Force planes were flying west after their night attacks on the Germans. No one was flying with any lights so it was pretty risky flying like that. The RAF guys would never give way so it was always up to us to avoid a midair collision.

"Once we were back on the ground at the designated air station, we would attend the mission briefing and then roundup the deputy mission commander and put him aboard our aircraft. Our bomber had a crew of eleven men rather than the normal ten man crew. This was because the ball turret had been replaced with a radar dome that would allow bombing when the weather was so bad that you couldn't bomb on a visual bomb run. The radar operator was called a Mickey.

"Once the aircraft took off, our plane would slip into the number two slot behind the mission commander. If the weather was good, we'd stay there and drop our bomb load in the usual visual manner. If the weather precluded a visual bomb run, then our bomber would move into the lead position and we'd make a radar guided bomb run on the target and the other bombers would follow us and drop their bombs after seeing ours go out of the bomb bay. Since this radar wasn't perfect, this type of bombing was restricted to Germany or Austria as the margin of error was too much for the Eighth Air Force planners to risk using when bombing

German forces in any occupied country. After about seven Pathfinder missions, we returned to Podington.

"Late 1943 was a difficult period of time for the Eighth Air Force and the number of aircraft lost was higher than expected. On New Year's Eve of 1943, we flew a mission over Bordeaux, France. It was a bad mission, to say the least, and we got the living Hell shot out of us! The tail gunner had his little finger shot off, and the radio operator was hit in the upper part of his leg with a 7.9 mm incendiary shell that stayed burning while embedded in his leg. His pain must have been awful! During the attack by German fighters, I brought some pretty good machine gun fire on one fighter. I think the German fighter pilot did not like me shooting at him so he got back at me by blowing a hole in the glass in my ball turret that was right in front of my face. The bullet came all the way through and then broke in half I carried it around with me for a long time. I felt very lucky I didn't get seriously hurt during that attack, and I was really glad when we touched down at Podington! Someone took my picture by my shot up turret as a memento of the mission. Then we took the machine guns out of the turret, turned them in, and went through the usual post-mission debriefing. I was certainly glad when that day was over!

"For some reason after the Bordeaux raid, the crew was split up. The pilot, navigator, and bombardier were sent to other squadrons while four of us were kept together in the 326th as a lead crew. As things worked out, my seventeenth and final mission was not even with my regular crew. As fate would have it, the last mission I was to fly during World War II was with the 92nd Bomb Group on 29 April 1944, a day I shall always remember!

"It was Saturday, the 29th of April 1944. We were awakened by the Charge of Quarters around 05:00 in the morning. Our crew was due to fly this morning and for some unknown reason, this had been the first night I could not go to sleep. It wasn't because I was flying with a new crew as when I was in the Pathfinders, I had flown with many new crews. As I said before, it was for some unknown reason that I couldn't sleep.

"I went through the usual motions I always did when I was going to fly, get up in the dark, dress in the dark, and then walk half a block to brush my teeth and do all the other things you have to do when at the latrine. Following this, I walked another two blocks to the mess hall to get some chow. Getting the chow was the best part of being a gunner in the 92nd Bomb Group. The group commander said as long as he was in charge, the gunners would get the best food he could obtain for them before they went on a mission. He told the Mess Officer if he couldn't get fresh eggs for the mess to let him know four days in advance of a mission and he, the Commander, would get them.

"Some of the bomb group officers each had a shirt with staff sergeant stripes on the sleeves. These were kept in the BOO (Bachelor Officers' Quarters) so the officers could wear them to our mess hall since they always said our mess was the only place on base where you could get a good meal. The officers were supposed to eat in their own mess hall. One morning the group commander was at our mess before a mission and saw some of his officers wearing shirts with staff sergeants stripes on the sleeves. The next time we had a stand-down, he conducted an officers' meeting and made it very clear to the assembled officers that if he ever saw another one of them in the Gunner's Mess wearing a shirt with staff sergeant stripes, he would see to it that the officer was reduced to an enlisted rank which certainly would not be as high as a staff sergeant.

"After we finished eating, we had another four blocks to walk to Base Operations for our preflight briefing. After the Briefing Officer told us what we needed to know about the mission, we then went over to the Personnel Equipment Section to pick up our flight gear.

"Next we moved to the armament shack to get our guns. At that point, a truck would take us out to the hardstand where our plane was parked. Here we would dismount from the truck, install the .50 caliber machine guns in the mounts at our gun stations, and then get into our flight gear. Soon, the officers came and issued us our escape kits and our noon meal, usually a MARS candy bar. The pilot and co-pilot would check out the plane and then climb into their seats in the cockpit. Then we just sat and waited for a flare from Base Operations at which time the pilots started the engines and taxied out to get their turn on the runway for takeoff.

"The target for today is the Big B, that's what we called Berlin, the capital city deep within Nazi Germany. It is very well defended by a lot of Luftwaffe fighter planes and a whole lot of antiaircraft guns, many the dreaded 88 type. The target was not too good, lots of danger for us, but at least we had something going for us. We were flying a brand new B-17G with the nose gun turret so at least we would have a fighting chance of getting home again.

"When it was our turn to take off, Lt. Langfeldt turned the plane onto the runway, shoved the throttles forward, and down the runway we rolled, picking up speed as we went. Soon we reached airspeed and were airborne. By now it was around 07:00 in the morning. The pilot put the bomber into a steady climb and started circling in a way that he could reach his assigned position in the squadron's formation so the squadron formation could maneuver into the group's formation before heading out across the English Channel on the way to the assigned target.

"Down at Eighth Air Force Headquarters, some "BRAIN" who had done the planning decided that Dummer Lake would make a good ground check point for navigation: therefore, all flights heading into Germany were directed to fly over that lake. It didn't take the Germans long to get onto this, and they responded by covering the lake with flak barges and ringing the lake with anti-aircraft guns. Sometimes the smoke from the anti-aircraft guns was so thick you could not see the flight in front of yours and you still had another 225 miles to fly to Berlin.

"As we crossed Lake Dummer which was just west of Hannover, Germany,

153

we picked up a bit of flak in our number two engine, one of the two engines on the starboard (right) wing. That meant we had only one functioning engine on the starboard wing. The pilot should have turned around right then and there and headed for home, but no pilot wants to abort a mission when he has his crew with him for the first time he is in the number one seat. Unfortunately for all of us, Lt. Langfeldt decided to go on.

"The pilot in the lead plane of our squadron was overtaking the flight ahead of us so instead of pulling his throttles back and slowing down, he started flying what was called a Lazy S. That's a slow turn to the right and then a slow turn to the left. It might have been fine for him but for us with only three engines it was another matter. Flying a Lazy S requires the pilot to advance the throttles when going to the right and then cut the throttles back when flying to the left. This maneuver takes up a lot more gas than straight flying with the result that by the time we got to Berlin over half our gas had been used up. Not enough left to get home!

"The Eighth Air Force planners who worked on the bomb runs for that mission sure had their heads up and locked! Just west of Berlin, the 1st Air Division, of which our bomber was a part, turned and flew north for a short while, then turned east to a point and then turned south to start a north-to-south bomb run. Meanwhile the 3rd Air Division turned south, then east, then north to start a south-to-north bomb run. While all of this was going on, the 2nd Air Division flew east past Berlin and then turned around and came back on an east-to-west bomb run. The 1st and 3rd Air Divisions were at 25,000 feet while the 2nd Air Division was only at 20,000 feet which meant they were 5,000 feet under us when we dropped our bombs. Not a sensible plan at all!

"Our formation was to come out of the bombing run and head for home on the same heading we had come in on, so after the bombardier yelled, "Bombs away!" our squadron headed northwest. By this time, German flak had taken out a second engine, this time it was the number three engine on the port (left) wing. So at this stage, we had only one engine on each wing still running. We were struggling but still able to keep our spot in the formation, but suddenly another outfit in the 3rd Air Division wanted the same little spot in the sky that we were going to use.

"Somebody had to leave and our pilot decided it had better be us and quickly. Lt. Langfeldt, the pilot, could not see how close the other formation was to us but the co-pilot, Lt. Guy Wallace, apparently could and he shoved the stick forward and down we went. We were at 25,000 feet when the nose went down. As we went down and down, the nose didn't seem to want to come up again, but the two pilots struggled with the controls and finally got her to level off at about 12,000 feet. All of us were really relieved when we were back to level flight! So there we were at 12,000 feet and just west of Berlin with only two engines still running and over half our gas gone, and all by ourselves. Things didn't look too good and our chances of getting back to England seemed very slim! My early morning thoughts that this was not going to be my day were starting to come true!

154

"After the bomber leveled off, Langfeldt called Wally Heldorfer, our, navigator, on the intercom which fortunately was still working. He asked Wally to give him a heading for the shortest route home. Wally looked at his compass and maps and gave Langfeldt the heading who upon hearing it turned the plane into that heading. What no one knew at that time was that a piece of German flack had imbedded itself in our plane right next to the compass and was adversely affecting the compass readings. Instead of heading west like we thought, we were actually heading south-southwest with the result that we eventually had to crash-land in France.

"At the preflight briefing, we were told that if we had any trouble our fighters would accompany us back to England. At one time I think we had all of the Ninth Air Force fighters around us, and needless to say, they sure looked good. The pilot called the flight engineer on the intercom and told him to fire off a flare, but by the time he found the Very pistol and decided on what color shell to use, all our fighters were gone. So when we really needed help, all the fighters were gone and we were all alone, again!

"For some reason, the Germans didn't like us flying across their country at 12,000 feet and to show their displeasure, their anti-aircraft guns would pick us up as soon as they could and kept firing for as long as they could keep us in range. They were, in fact, slowly blowing us right out of the sky. You could pick a spot on the wing and before long there would be a hole right where you had been looking. Some of the blasts were so close to my gun position that I could feel them when they went off. Not a reassuring feeling to say the least! And the smoke was so thick it made visibility very difficult.

"The intercom was still working but there wasn't much chatter on it. Langfeldt said something about getting ready to bail out. I didn't wait to hear what else he had to say. I came out of the ball turret as fast as I could, snapped on my chest parachute pack, went back to the bailout door, kicked it open, and stood there ready to go out on command. I turned to see what the waist gunners were doing and found they were still at their guns and even had their flack suits on. I went up to Monti, one of the gunners, and asked him what else the pilot had said about bailing out. Monti relied, "The pilot said get ready but not to go yet."

"Sometime while we were still over Germany, Biedinger, the tail gunner crawled out of his tail turret and came forward into the waist where we were. He had about a one square inch of flesh and muscle taken out of the side of his right hand. It was a nasty looking wound as a piece of flak had taken the flesh clean out. We did not want to put a tourniquet on him because we had no idea of how long it would be before he could have the wound taken care of. Monti and I packed Biedinger's hand with a 3x3 gauze pad and then put a pressure bandage on it, and I do mean pressure. We used this technique as we both felt that a tourniquet would do more harm than good.

"At this time, we had no idea of where we were. One thing for certain, we were not on the compass heading we were supposed to be on because there was nothing showing up on the maps charts the Nav had on his desk that should have if we'd been flying on course. Of course this situation was due to the unknown piece of flak stuck near the compass. Later on, Lt. Langfeldt decided we should start throwing things out to lighten the load a bit as the remaining two engines were moaning and groaning just to keep us at 12,000 feet.

"At this time, I went back to the bailout door ready to do my part in lightening the load. The two waist gunners and the radio operator would throw stuff back to me and I would pitch it out the door. The first thing to come out of the radio room was the seat Dale sat on. That was followed by the VIIF radio. He'd pulled the bolts right out of the wood. The next item was the table the radio used to sit on. Dale had pulled it right off the wall. Next came the tuning units followed closely by the rack the tuners used to be in. The only thing Dale didn't take out was the UHF radio, and it was under the floor.

"Lt. Wallace left his seat in the cockpit and came back to the waist to see how things were going. When he arrived, he started laughing and said he'd better get out of there before he was thrown out too.

"One thing we had not thrown out was the guns and ammunition. We kept them just in case Jerry's little friends from a nearby Luftwaffe base decided to come up to see us. I took my boots, tied the shoe strings as far as part as I could. I then set them on the walkway on the right side of the aircraft near the gun. I said all I have to do when we start to leave is to put my hand down between the shoes and keep on going. I forgot just one little thing when we started to leave. Put my hand down BETWEEN the shoes.

"Lt. Langfeldt called back on the intercom and said get rid of the guns and ammunition, so they went out last.

"Finally, out in the distance we could see the English Channel. Everyone was delighted as we thought we had it made, but unfortunately about that time the number four engine on the port wing cut out due to the lack of fuel. That left us with only the number one engine on the starboard side still running and one functioning engine isn't enough to keep a B-17 airborne.

"Lt. Langfeldt came on the intercom and said we were not going to make it across the Channel and he didn't think we could get far enough out so that any British crash boats could pick us up without being blown out of the water themselves. He continued that he was going to try to get the plane as far inland as he could, so we were to get into the crash-landing position in the now vacant radio room. Except for the pilots in the cockpit, the other eight crew members headed for the radio room. The first row would sit with their knees drawn up against their chests and their backs against the bulkhead next to the bomb bay. The next row of men would sit and shove back against the first row as hard and as tight as they could.

"The pilot now had the plane in a glide looking for a clear field in which to land. From there on the floor in the radio room you couldn't see a thing. We were all hoping for the best and maybe a few prayers were offered at the same time. In a crash-landing, a light crash is when you touch down whereas in a heavy crash the nose of the aircraft digs in and you come to a screeching halt.

"All of us in the radio room felt what we thought was the initial touchdown, so everyone pushed a little harder against the one behind him. Then we felt the bomber come to a halt. Lieutenants Langfeldt and Wallace did a great job getting us safely down. We felt someone trying to open the bomb bay door so we all jumped up and there was Lt. Wallace, the copilot. He said, "We have stopped, so get the "H" out of here." The nine of us in the back made a mad dash for the door while Lt. Langfeldt went out the front hatch.

"Once out of the aircraft and safely on the ground, the ten of us took off across the field. There was a man and woman over on the side of the field digging potatoes. We had no idea of where we were let alone what country we were in. As our crew approached the couple, I was in the lead. When I was close enough, I asked them "Sprechen sie Deutsch?" just in case we might be in Germany or Holland. The man and woman merely looked at me without answering. Lt. Langfeldt was right behind me and he said, "Parlezvous francais?" The answer was, "Oui" which is the French word for yes. Now that French word may be spelled "o-u-i," but in English it sounds like "we." Lf. Langfeldt looked at the crew and said, "We are in France, fellows, so let's go!"

"Immediately the ten of us we ran into and through the woods together sounding like a herd of elephants. After a short time I dropped back to where Earl, the flight engineer, was since he was the only member of the crew who I knew because we lived in the same barracks back at the airfield in England. I told him I was leaving the group because if we stayed together like this, the Germans would be able to hear us a mile away and could move in and capture the whole crew at the same time. I asked him if he wanted to go with me and he said he would. I then said, "Let's go!" I immediately turned to the left and headed north and Earl fell in behind me. We went a little way and then turned west and went back to the edge of the woods bordering the field where the plane had crashed. Why? I just wanted to get a little space between the rest of the crew and us. After we arrived at the edge of the woods, we could see German soldiers all over the plane so we eased back into the woods and took off fast, heading east with the sun on our backs.

"As Earl and I were going through the woods, we came upon an old bunker like the ones that had been used during World War I. My curiosity got the best of me and I told him I wanted to look inside of it. Earl didn't so he crossed a small dirt road in the woods and waited while I looked inside the bunker. It wasn't long before we heard a vehicle coming and the sound prompted me to cross the road fast like. We both hid in some nearby bushes. The vehicle we heard was a German lorry with German GIs in it. Every forty feet or so, one of the Germans soldiers would drop off and head into the woods where we had just been. They were sure enough looking for us.

"Earl and I decided it was time to get out of this area as fast as we could. Once again we put the sun on our back and headed east trying to get as far from the French coast as we could.

"The first contact we made with any Frenchman, other than the man and his wife digging potatoes at our crash site, was a farmer plowing his field. Earl and I stayed in some bushes near his trailer and waited for him to come over to the trailer. As he came closer, we left the bushes and went out to talk to him. We spoke in English but he just looked at us and then started speaking in French. At that time, we took out our silk escape map and asked him where we were. To communicate with the man we took out our little English to French-French to English phrase book and pointed to the phrase we wanted to say. He would then point to another phrase to answer us. Everything seemed to be working all right until Earl pointed to the phrase. "Will you help us?"

"Back in England, the briefers had always told us never ask for help when contacting local citizens of any country we might be trying to evade capture in. If anyone is willing to help you, they will let you know without being asked. That seemed to be the rules of the evasion game. As soon as Earl pointed to the "Will you help us?" phrase, the Frenchman put his finger on the map to a town and then turned around and went back to his tractor. We figured he must have meant for us to go to the town he had pointed to, so we folded the map, went back into the woods, and headed east.

"It was late in the afternoon and it had been a long time since we ate breakfast and our MARS bars were long gone. I was really getting hungry. As we walked along, we came to a field that had some parsnips growing in it, so we each picked a parsnip and started chomping on it. I asked Earl how he was fixed for cigarettes. He looked and found something in the pocket of his flying suit. He opened the zipper and pulled out a pack of flat 50's. A lot of the tobacco companies made them up that way. It was box two cigarettes wide that would hold fifty cigarettes. That was the one thing I always sweated out, running out of cigarettes. I had taken a box of flat 50's and made it waterproof, so even if I went down in water, I would still have cigarettes that were smokable. During the last mission I was on before this one, my heated suit had developed a hot spot so when we got home, I turned it in to the Personnel Equipment Section and told them to fix it or replace it. As it turned out, they had given me a new suit, repaired the old one, and issued it to Earl. Some coincidence!

"Between 17:30 and 18:00 in the evening of the day we crash-landed, Earl and I came to a small dirt road leading off of the main road we had been following. A short way down this road was a house sitting on the corner where two roads met. It was way out in the open and you see for a long way both east and west.

"While we were there sitting and looking things over, a teenage girl came peddling down the dirt road on her bike. She spoke to us in French and because we didn't understand that language we just nodded to her. Looking around, we noticed a woman and a girl in the yard of the house on the main road so we walked up the road to the house. I told Earl not to say a thing. When we got to where they were, I asked in English if we could have a drink of water. The woman said something in French so I took my hand and motioned like I was drinking. She then turned and spoke to the girl who then went into the house and returned with a glass and a bottle of beer. We each had a glass of beer and when finished I said, "Thank you" in English to the Frenchwoman.

"We turned around and started to walk off but at that time the Frenchwoman said something to the girl and then grabbed Earl by the arm and starting pulling him toward the house. As it turned out, we went in with them and found that neither spoke English. Realizing that, we again got out our little English to French and French to English books and started communicating with them. We told them who we were and what we were doing and where we wanted to go. We never asked for help.

"All of a sudden the French started jabbering and pushing us towards a door so we figured they wanted us to go through a door and get out of this room fast. We went through the door and found it led to stairs going down to the basement. Once there, we found a place to sit down. It was a long day and in order to pass the time of day we'd take one cigarette and split it between the two of us. By now we felt certain that we had been picked up by the F.F.I., that's the abbreviation for the French Forces of the Interior which was one of several French resistance organizations. Earl and I were feeling very confident that we were now safe and on our way home, so to celebrate we each took a cigarette and lit up. It sure did taste good, but about that time one of the Frenchmen came rushing down the stairs and pointed to the cigarettes and then to his nose while uttering the word, "BOCHE." Boche was a holdover word from World War I that the French used as a derogatory term for the Germans. That was the end of our first full cigarette we had all day, and we didn't even get to finish it. War is Hell!

"A short time later the French allowed us back upstairs where we were given some food. The girl we'd seen on the bicycle earlier in the day was in the house, and we learned she could speak very good English. She had brought back a duffel bag for one of us and the people in the house got another one. They started changing the French civilian clothes in the bags for our uniforms, but they didn't have any shoes that would fit either of us so Earl and I had to keep our heated flying boots. I did, however, get a coat, a pair of pants, a shirt, and a little French beret. Earl got about the same. The French then explained to us that we would sleep in the barn and that someone would come out and wake us up so we could get to the town we were heading to before daylight.

"One of the men then took us out to the barn where we sacked out for the rest of the night. I don't know what time he came out to wake us, but a Frenchman woke us up before daylight. We walked to the house and had some coffee and French bread. When we were ready to go, we walked over to pick up our duffel bags and at that time learned the French had put some more stuff in them. We found another pair of socks, some hardboiled eggs, and more French bread plus some beer. After saying goodbye, Earl and I started down the road towards the town where the French had indicated we should go. About a mile down the road, we walked under a railroad track and heard a commotion but didn't know what it was. I told Earl, "I'll bet it's a French train.

"We were standing in the middle of the road waiting for a train to go by when we saw lights shining on the road. We knew then it wasn't a train, so Earl and I separated and headed for a ditch in which to hide. I soon saw a German truck, an army staff car, a motorcycle, and the main source of all that noise, a tank.

"The little convoy went one hundred yards past us and stopped. The vehicles sat there for a few minutes without moving. Finally the staff car and the motorcycle went straight on down the road while the truck and the tank turned right and headed south.

"After the Germans departed, I went looking for Earl but had a hard time finding him. The French cut their crops by hand and it is so short you would think you were going to get a lot of dirt with the wheat. Anyway, Earl was hiding down so low I couldn't find him for awhile, but I finally did.

"We then got back on the road and started out again. Now another problem cropped up. Just before we arrived at the spot where the German truck and tank had turned south, we saw a German soldier standing by the road. We didn't know what to do so we just kept on walking and looking at the ground. Lucky for us, the German didn't pay too much attention to us. I know one thing for sure, every step we took after we passed him was just a little faster than the one before.

"It wasn't too long before we were out of sight of the German soldier, and then we breathed a sigh of relief. Just as it started to get a little light in the east, Earl and I came to the outskirts of the town we had been heading for. It was decision time again. We couldn't make up our minds, if we wanted to go to the north or south of the town, but we were certain we didn't want to go into the town proper.

"There was a small hill to the north of town so we decided to go up the hill and find a place to hide. Being on high ground would enable us to see anyone that was coming near us. Today was Sunday, 30 April, 1944. It was going to be the first of twenty-four days we were to spend in the town of Peronne, France.

"Earl and I located a spot on the hilltop with some bushes plus a clear view of the area below and to both sides. As early as it was, I didn't think we would be seeing many people moving around below for a long time.

"We opened our escape kits to get the 30 by 30 inch silk map out as well as the English to French-French to English phrase book. Outside of those two items, we really didn't have any idea of what was in the kit. We knew there was some money, but we didn't know how much or what kind. There were fifty dollars worth of German marks and fifty dollars worth of French francs. We found two compasses. The first one looked like a button except it had a small dot painted on it. You could put it on the end of a sharp stick and the dot would always turn around to the north. The second one was a small round ball about the size of a pea. It also had a dot painted on it. When you would lay it down on just about anything except metal, the dot would turn around to the north. If you felt sure you were going to be captured, you were to insert it into a part of your body where the sun never shines.

"There was a pack of three cigarettes plus a pack of matches Other items were also in the escape kit. A signal mirror gave you something to do. Band-Aids were available if you cut yourself. A six inch long, one inch wide hacksaw blade could cut through anything you wanted cut with the exception of glass. A Thompson snare was a real handy thing to have. It was the best thing you could have for a pair of handcuffs plus if you ever dropped the loop over someone's head and gave it a jerk, that someone was not long for this world.

"Later in the afternoon of our second day in France, Earl and I saw some French women and kids coming up the hill picking flowers. We moved out of the bushes a little ways and shrugged our shoulders so they could see us. After awhile, one of the women came over to us and starting talking. We did not know what she was saying so we shrugged our shoulders again. She looked at us and said, "Vous etes anglais' The vous sounded like you and the anglais sounded something like English so we shook our heads no. Then she said, "Vous boche?" Well we knew what boche meant so again we shook our heads no. "American," I said, and her eyes got real big. She understood. She quickly turned to the other women said something in French which we didn't understand, but one of the girls did and took off down the hill. We didn't know where she was going or why. All we could do was sit, wait, and hope that things would work out.

"Approximately a half to three-quarter hour after the young girl had gone the hill, we saw two young men coming up the hill pushing their bicycles. I would say they were about the same age as Earl who was younger than 1. When they reached our location, they said something to the two French women who then left. One of the young Frenchmen could speak very good English, so that made things a lot easier. We learned his name was Paul, at least when he was dealing with any Allies on the run from the Germans. He asked us a lot of questions about where we were from in the States, what kind of plane we flew in, and when we had been shot down. While this was going on, the other young man got on his bike and rode down the hill. He was gone, I would say, maybe an hour. When he returned, he and Paul talked for a little while. I suppose they were discussing what they were going to do with Earl and me. At last Paul told us that we would all stay where we were until after dark and then go down off the hill and make contact with the FFI. The Frenchmen asked if we had any food, so we opened up our duffel bags. In them we had bread, hard-boiled eggs, and of course the wine that the French family had given us the night before. The four of us stayed there talking and munching on our food and washing it down with the wine.

"When it got dark enough, it would be time to leave. Finally Paul said it was time to go, so we got up and started down off the hill for our first meeting with the French Underground. This was another step on our way back to England. The Frenchman who spoke no English was called Eddie for some reason. He took the lead and the three of us followed him. He led us to the other side of town to what appeared to be a church. Before we got there, Eddie started walking faster so he wound up a good deal in front of us. We heard him give the identification whistle and wait for an answer. When he did not get a response, Paul told Earl and me that the Underground was supposed to have someone meet us here about midnight. Well midnight came and midnight went and no one showed up. Paul and Eddie waited but after sometime Paul said they would take us to a place to hide the next day, and they would try to make contact the next night.

"Paul took us into town to a small shack in the middle of a community garden. I would estimate the shack was about 5 feet by 5 feet. Pretty tight accommodations to say the least. Our "home" for the next day was a place to store gardening tools and us. Every time someone came to get tools, they would bring some food, wine, or beer. We certainly didn't lack for anything that day except for one thing. Someone to talk to. We couldn't talk to anyone, not even each other. We survived during the day and at last it was dark and Paul and Eddie showed up and said it was time to go. We were really glad to get out of that shack and be on our way again.

"Earl and I finally learned the town we were in was Peronne. It's a small town in the northwest part of France located about 120 kilometers from the coast and 65 kilometers south of the Belgium border. It is built on the north bank of the Somme River, a location of heavy fighting during World War I and a factor in the local population's intense dislike of Germans. While in Peronne, we never knew the names of any of the people we met or stayed with in town or any of the other places around it where we were taken care of. That was on purpose and for the protection of the people who were helping us in case the Germans ever captured us. If we really didn't know the Frenchmen's names, then we obviously couldn't tell the Germans.

"After leaving the tool shed, Paul and Eddie took Earl and me to a gin mill. It was the place in town where all the wheat and corn was ground into flour for this town. The husband and wife who ran the mill had a nice home and a real nice bed for us to sleep in. We sat at the table with them to eat our meals. In other words, we were living high on the hog, to use an old expression. There was a picture of Marshal Petain hanging on the wall. He was one of the most famous French generals during World War 1. I thought our host looked somewhat like the field marshal so I began to call him Monsieur Petain. He got a big kick out of that. The thing I could not figure out however, was why every time the woman looked at me, she would get a big grin on her face and sometimes even laugh.

"The second day we were with them I learned what caused her reactions. The pair of pants I was wearing had no seat in them as the seam had ripped out all the way down the back. The woman was nice enough to sew them up so my butt wasn't hanging out all the time.

"Earl and I stayed with this friendly couple for four days. Paul and Eddie would stop by each day and visit with us. Of course Paul did all the talking. When they arrived on the fourth day, Paul said they would be back that evening in order to take us to our new temporary home. They also told us we were now celebrities. It seems the Germans had posted the names, ranks, and serial numbers of eight of our crew on the town bulletin board with a notice about a reward for information leading to our capture. Paul told us that there were only eight names as Lt. Langfeldt our pilot and Sgt. Biedinger our tail gunner had given themselves up to the Germans in order to receive medical attention. Earl and I knew that Sgt. Biedinger was wounded because I had helped bandage his hand, but we didn't know the lieutenant had taken a hunk of flack in his leg. With those wounds, neither man could keep up well enough to avoid capture. I hope the German medics had patched them up well.

"As it turned out, all eight of us from the crew who were not wounded made it to the same town of Peronne. Here we were all to spend the next twenty-four days. Well, to be more accurate, I should say in and around the town. During this period, all the members of the crew stayed in a lot of different places, met many people, and had all kinds of food. Some of it was very good, but then some of it was like nothing we had ever eaten before.

"Anyway, that evening Paul and Eddie took us to the next place we were going to stay, but we had no idea of how long we'd be there. A nice French family lived in the house, and they cared for Earl and me for three or four days. The family gave us a nice feather bed to sleep in and like at Monsieur and Madame Petain's home, we had the run of the house.

"Earl and I said to ourselves that it won't be long now, and we will be back in England. Every day Paul and Eddie would come to visit and everyday we'd ask them when we were going to England. Their answer was always the same. "Peut-etre demain," perhaps tomorrow. That answer was getting a little old after a few days. We didn't know at the time that the United Staff Headquarters had decided that us evaders could just stay put until after the invasion and wait for the liberating forces to come through our area and recover us. It would have been much better if we had known that at the time, because Sgt. Daniel Sullivan, a waist gunner, decided he was going to leave and took off on his own. At the preflight briefings, the briefers always told us not to walk the railroad tracks because every track had many guards on it. Well, Sullivan took a calculated risk and lost. It didn't work our for him as the Germans captured him the next morning.

"As soon as they found out what his name was, the Germans knew he was one of us from Peronne. For whatever reason, he identified the French family that had been taking care of him. I suspect he told on the family because he was so frightened at being caught rather than having been subjected to torture. Anyway, it was a very unfortunate incident!

"After learning the identity of the French family who had helped Sullivan, German forces moved in and killed the entire family for aiding an American. It was to be a lesson to others who might want to help Americans. The local Frenchmen in Peronne did not trust us after that incident and you really couldn't blame them for that. For several days, the rest of our crew were under continual guard, night and day.

"About a week passed and then one evening, Paul and Eddie showed up and advised us that we were going to leave as soon as it got dark. After a while it became dark and Paul told us we could leave now. Earl and I said thank you and goodbye to the French who had been caring for us and headed out into the night.

"We four finally came to a bombed out house that was apparently our destination. We entered and found three officers from our crew; lieutenants Wallace, Heldorfer, and Rogers. They had been here since the first day they were picked up by the French Underground. Earl and I could see no furniture, no beds; nothing anywhere except a few dirty mattresses thrown on the floor for men to sleep on. If you wanted to sit, you sat on the floor and that included eating on the floor. When you wanted to go to the bathroom, you walked over to where there was a hole in the floor and stood or squatted as necessary. It certainly wasn't a very nice setup.

"We asked the officers how long they had been here and they said since the first day they'd gotten into Peronne. The officers in turn asked where we had been staying, and when Earl and I told them we had stayed at houses, eaten at tables, slept in feather beds, and had the run of the house, they couldn't believe it.

"Sometime during the day we moved into the house with the officers, Oscar, the bombardier, said, "Ken, we have been getting some meat here and I can't figure out what it is." Now Oscar was a Texas farm boy who had eaten all kinds of fur bearing animals in his life, but he had never run into this kind of meat before. Oscar continued, "Next time we have it, see if you can figure out what it is." Some Frenchmen would bring the food in each night just about dark so we could finish eating before it got too dark to see what you were doing. We couldn't have any lights on in the house. When the Frenchman came the next evening, I looked at Oscar when the covers were taken off the food. He looked at me and nodded his head in a yes motion, so I took both pieces of the leg. I worked them together so I could get some idea of the size and shape of the animal it had come from. Then I started the process of elimination. I wound up with the same opinion I think he had.

"The next evening when the Frenchmen brought the food, I asked one of them if the meat that we had the night before was cat, and he replied, "Oui. Bien oui."

and translated to English, "Yes. Well yes."

"When the Frenchmen arrived the next time, they informed us that we were leaving that night and going to a little house in the pond-pool. We could not figure out what a pond-pool was. He could see by our expressions we really didn't understand what he was saying, so he took out his little French to English-English to French book and pointed to the word lake and said, "pond-pool." The book listed both pond and pool as definitions of the word lake so he had just put the two words together and called the lake, pond-pool. So much for translations.

"Earl, the three officers, and I left the bombed out house and guided by Paul, Eddie, and another guide called Shortie walked to another place and went in. Shortie was the fellow who was in charge of the three officers. Once in the building, we were given some coffee and something to eat plus we were allowed a cigarette. That was a treat as smoking outside while we were moving around was prohibited. At last, Shortie told us to put out our cigarettes as it was time to leave again. We went outside with Paul and Eddie and started following them down the road. Guy, Oscar, and Wally took off with Shortie on a different heading. Earl and I knew we were near some water because of the smell that is only present when there is a large body of water nearby.

"Finally our little party came to a boat; well, it was actually more like a dugout. Paul instructed us to get in it with our gear, so we did. Our three officers went on further around the lake and got into a bigger boat. The individual who had to do the poling had a hard time getting through the marshland that was all around the lakeshore. After what seemed like half the night, our group came to a little shack on the shore of the pond-pool. When we got a little closer, we saw that it was not as small as we had originally thought. Upon entering the shack, we discovered two rooms. Some Frenchmen had placed a few boards across the door opening and then put a lot of straw in the back room which was to function as our bedroom. The remaining room had a table, benches, cupboards, and of all things an electric light. Now that was a surprise! Shortie had apparently rigged up the light with a rather long cord. That allowed us to hang the light on a nail in either room so if we were in the living-dining room we could hang the light in that room, and when we moved to the bedroom to get ready to go to sleep, we could move the light to a nail in that room.

"As it tuned out, the officers arrived at the shack after Earl and I got there so five of our crew were together again. The bedroom was good sized, so all five of us slept on the straw in that room. We later learned before we moved on from the pond-pool that the shack was actually a poacher's shack of which there were quite a few on the lakeshore.

"By now, the five of us had been in the shack for two or three days. Oscar and I were sitting outside fishing when out of nowhere a small boat with two Frenchmen showed up. One of the men started rattling off French to us, but since we didn't have any command of the French language we both just looked at him and

Oscar shook his head and shrugged his shoulder. We finally tried to say something to this guy and at last got across to him that we were Americans. We were somewhat surprised when he saw him get real upset after learning that there were five of us staying in the shack. He left shortly thereafter, and I might say he didn't appear in too good a mood.

"That evening, Shortie came to visit and said we were going to have to leave for another site as the guy who had come earlier in the day owned the shack and we were staying in his place. He didn't want anything to do with Americans. As it turned out, the Germans had a bigger price on his head than all five of us combined, and he knew if the German authorities caught us in his place, his life wouldn't be worth a plug nickel. Shortie went on to tell us we could remain in the shack for that night.

"What a night it turned out to be! It was almost my twenty-sixth birthday so the fellows said they were going to give me a party. The one thing we had lots of was wine. Most of it didn't have much of a kick to it at all. The guys did, however, come up with two bottles of the best wine I had yet had in France, and it had the kick of a mule. We had already drunk one of the bottles so there was still one left. My four crew buddies took the last of the two bottles of good wine and gave it to me as a birthday present. They insisted I drink the whole thing by myself. Well I did, but with some unusual results. I don't even remember going to bed that night. The next morning the others told me that after killing off the bottle and apparently collapsing on the floor, Oscar and Guy went over, picked me up, took me over to the door going into the bedroom, and threw me into bed.

"The next day went by uneventfully. As evening approached, our French guides showed up with two boats ready to escort us to our next hiding place. Oscar, Wally, and Guy went one way with Shortie while Earl and I followed Paul and Eddie. We didn't have to go very far and soon we arrived at another poacher's shack. This one was a real big place. When the Frenchman poled the boat up to the shack, the front of the boat was almost inside the building. I would say there was at most two feet of ground in the front and at most one foot on the two sides with none in the back. Inside the shack there was a full size mattress next to the door, if there had been a door which there wasn't. The opening was about two feet wide and led into a room where we did our cooking, bathing, and anything else we wanted to do. We also learned there were holes in the walls where the French could stick their guns out to shoot ducks that landed on the lake. Sometime after Paul had gotten us to the shack, Shortie arrived with our three officers, so once again we were all together.

"The day was finally drawing to a close and that evening all five of us got our things packed, and I even put on a clean pair of socks and was ready to go to my birthday party in town. We waited and waited and no one showed up and it was getting late. I said, "Well, I guess my big party was called off." Just as I said that we heard a boat coming and it was Eddie and Paul. They said we had to get out of Peronne that night. Up until then, there had not been enough Germans in town to search any given part of the town by themselves so they had to rely on the French police to help. That's like the story about the fox and the hen house. The French police were in the Underground movement, so if any of us happened to be in an area the Germans wanted searched, we would be told and moved to another part of town. That was how we'd been able to remain in Peronne for twenty-four days. But now the local German commander had brought in another German unit to help in searches, so it was time we left town.

"Paul and Eddie put Earl and me into a boat and took us ashore. We started walking and walked until we came to a house. We entered the house and found ourselves back at Shortie's home. His wife had already fixed us something to eat. We sat down and ate and drank some wine and then had a smoke. At an appointed time, Paul spoke to us and said it was time to go. Shortie gave us a wicker basket to take with us. As we got ready to leave, Shortie's wife came over and gave us a big kiss and a hug and then started crying. We figured that this was going to be the last time we would get to see Shortie and his wife, and it turned out we were correct.

"Earl and I left the house wondering where we were going next, but all we could do was to follow Paul and Eddie. We were led down the road until we reached another house. We were escorted in and found out we were back at Mr. Roberts' house. His place seemed to be the center of our hub in Peronne.

"We all sat around there for awhile, had a drink or so, smoked a cig or two, and shot the breeze some more. Finally some Frenchman said it was time to move on, so we said our good-byes to those left behind. Paul stayed with Earl and me while Eddie took off ahead of us. After we had gotten out of town for a short distance, things started to look familiar. I asked Earl, "Do you know where we are now?" Earl said, "No, I don't know either, but I have been seeing things that look familiar." Soon we passed under a railroad trestle and as we came up on the other side there was a road that turned to the north. I looked at Earl and asked, "Do you remember this place?"

"Finally we turned off the main road and started down a small side road. Paul said we would wait there while Eddie checked it out. Eddie took off down the road all by himself. We could hear him and his identification whistle, but he was getting no answer. All of a sudden, the bank above us erupted in sound and motion and two people came charging down the bank right where we were. Needless to say our hair stood on end. One of the two was a big, six foot something fellow while the other was a little short one. Paul walked over and talked to them for a little while. Then he came back to us and told Earl and me to follow them. The short one was in the lead, Earl followed him, I followed Earl, and the tall Frenchman brought up the rear.

"Finally our little group came to a small town and we stopped at a house. The little one opened the door, and we all went in. Earl and I got the shock of our lives! The little one that had walked our butts into the ground was a seventy year old grandma. The tall one was her grandson, Paul. After we got inside, Earl and I met everyone including Grandpa.

"It was a nice house having three bedrooms. Grandpa slept in one bedroom; Grandma slept in another; Paul, Earl, and I slept in the third. Outside the house was a tall fence around the back yard. The family called it an enclosed courtyard. Earl and I could go out there and walk around, do some exercises, or whatever else we wanted to do. It was a very pleasant place to while away some of our time.

"Up until this time, the French Underground hadn't made us any identity papers as they said the American photos the Army Air Force had made for us were no good. To make things difficult for the Underground, the Germans would occasionally change the type of photos they would accept on these papers. A day or so after we arrived at Grandma's, a French photographer came to take Earl's and my picture. He even brought the clothes we were to wear. Both of us got all dressed up in the French clothes and had our pictures taken for our new French identity papers, work papers, and hospital papers. All these documents were required by the Germans for all French citizens.

"That evening when we were sitting around talking, Grandma said, "The Burgermeister, the German civilian governing the town, knows you are here. He does not know you are Americans, but he knows there are two more people here today than yesterday." Earl and I wondered how she knew that bit of information so we asked her. She replied that when he grandson Paul came up from Paris to stay with them, the next day the Burgermeister brought three pigeons for them whereas before he had only brought two. Today he brought five so evidently the Germans were watching her house rather closely. The Germans killed every pigeon they saw just in case any of them might be carrier pigeons for the French Underground.

"Staying with Grandma, Grandpa, and Paul was really enjoyable for Earl and me. We had the run of the house and the courtyard. But it was not to last very long. The Germans were going to reopen the airfield five kilometers north of town and when they did, German authorities would go into all the small towns around the field and take over all the spare bedrooms in those houses. Members of the Luftwaffe would then be housed in those French homes. Grandma knew she had to contact the Underground and get us out of there rather rapidly.

"Sometime later Paul and Eddie showed up and we started back to Peronne, but we bypassed Peronne and went directly to Paul's home. Earl and I got to meet Paul's mother and his nineteen year old sister, Ginger. Both the mother and Ginger spoke English which helped things out. Paul's mother really didn't trust me at first. She said my features and eye color made me look like a typical German and therefore I was a German infiltrator trying to get into the French Underground in order to get them all killed. She was so distrustful I finally told her I would agree to volunteer to go to Paris and fight with the Liberation Forces against the Germans. That statement finally convinced her that I was telling her the truth about my status and then it didn't take too long to get her to come over to my side. Ginger was going to teach Earl and me what was on our papers- the ID paper, the work paper, and the hospital paper. Ginger was also to teach us how to respond if we were questioned. We had to learn to say things the way the French did, not the way an American might.

"Paul's family did not have a spare bedroom so Earl and I stayed out in the barn and slept in the haymow. One day while we were getting our lesson from Ginger, she said one of the German officers from the nearby base in Peronne had a crush on her. He would come out to the house and help her peel potatoes. She said, "I wonder what he would say if he knew he was peeling potatoes for Americans?" Well, it's a good thing Ginger never found out the answer to that question.

"It was imperative that we could answer German questions about our identity papers, so we studied hard with Ginger and learned what we needed to know. Earl and I finally got things down and the way to say or answer questions about our papers to Ginger's satisfaction. It was now about the first of June in 1944 when Paul said to us, "The Underground has decided it was time for you to leave the Peronne area and head south." The day before we were to leave, we learned the French were going to have a farewell party for us. On the appointed evening, we were taken to Mr. Roberts' house for the party.

"I must say it was quite a party! Everyone in Peronne who we had stayed with or with whom we had any dealings with was there. The biggest surprise was when Grandma walked in. She had told Mr. Roberts that she had made something for Earl and me and she wanted to give it to us personally. For some reason she wasn't invited to the party, but Grandma raised so much fuss that they let her come. We were certainly glad they did. Grandma had knitted both Earl and me a sweater. Mine was German gray in color and a very nice sweater that came in handy quite a few times. I liked it so much I brought it back to California with me.

"A member of the Underground briefed Earl and me about what was going to happen the next day. We were going on our first train ride. Up until now, every time we moved it was by Shank's Pony. For the reader who is unfamiliar with this term, it means plain old walking. Now that we had our French identity papers, we could ride the rails. The procedure to be followed went like this. Paul would obtain our tickets and then take us to the train depot. Here he would give Earl and me our individual tickets, and we would then climb aboard the train. Inside the passenger car there would be two seats with a magazine lying on one of them. Some Underground worker would ensure the magazine was there before we got aboard. Once we spotted the magazine, we were to pick up the magazine and sit down in those two seats. One of us was to hold the magazine until the conductor came to take our tickets at which time the magazine was to be laid down on the seat between Earl and myself. It wasn't a long train as it consisted of only the engine, one passenger car, and one car to carry all the other stuff, most of which were bikes.

"The plan worked out well and when the time came, Earl and I climbed aboard the train, found our seats, and waited. I sure wish I knew who had made the seating arrangements. Our seats were facing forward. The top front of our passenger car was open so the air could come through, but the things that came through most were hot cinders from the engine, and I do mean hot! As the train rumbled down the tracks, I looked across at two passengers sitting in the seats across from us. I whispered to Earl, "Do you know those two?" "No" was the answer. I recognized them as Dale Howard, our crew's radio operator and Albert Monti, one of the waist gunners. At that point I started glancing at the other passengers in the car and while looking across the aisle to see who was over there I saw Guy Wallace, the copilot, and Oscar Scott, the navigator. For some reason, the French Underground had sent Wally Heldorfer south ahead of the rest of us. No one ever saw Wally again while we were in France

"The little train continued chugging down the tracks taking us from Peronne south to a place we learned later was a village named Ham. I sat rather quietly and didn't act like I recognized anyone in the car, and the other crew members did the same. Since the railroad car's roof was open, it would have been nice if just the wind had been blowing through, but the cinders sort of spoiled it. The train chugged along for about two hours and then pulled into a station.

"Now when our tickets had been picked up, the magazine on our seat was also picked up, but Earl and I knew we had to keep watch for it as it was the signal that we were to follow whoever was carrying that magazine. As passengers began getting off the train, we saw a Frenchman carrying our magazine also leave the train. That was our cue, so we immediately got up, left the train, and began following the individual that had our magazine. The Frenchman we were following down the street stopped and talked to somebody he met on the street, handed him the magazine, and then each man departed in a different direction. Earl and I kept the magazine in sight and followed it into a café. The magazine was lying on the counter by itself. We went over to a nearby table and sat down. The Frenchman running the cafe came over and poured each of us a cup of coffee. The coffee was lousy, so we just kind of sipped on it. We drank enough to get the level in the cup down a bit at which time the Frenchman came over with a bottle of Cognac and filled the cups. Now the coffee tasted a little better. We continued sipping away and again the Frenchman came over and filled the cups again with Cognac. One more trip with the Cognac and the coffee was the best we had ever tasted!

"About this time, four boys came in and got some coffee. I would say their ages ran between eight and twelve years. The boys went over to the other side of the café from where Earl and I were and sat down at a table. The oldest boy was facing me from across the room. Every time I would look over at him, he was staring back at me. Finally our eyes met and we just kept looking at each other. I saw him reach down with his left hand, take his coffee cup, slide it across the table into his right hand, put his left hand back to the other side and very slowly shook his head as if saying "No." Then the boy reached over with his left hand, pulled his coffee cup back over, and took a drink. What he had been telling me was you don't drink coffee or anything else with your right hand. People on the European continent use their left hand to drink. When they are eating, they use their knife in their right hand and their fork in their left hand. The right hand is used only with a knife. Needless to say, Earl and I changed our coffee cups into our left hands. The boy knew we were not French when we made the change to our left hand. After we learned the lesson he was giving us, the boy gave us a big smile.

"As evening arrived, the Frenchman in the cafe came over and said for us to follow him. Earl and I were then taken to the back of the cafe where a bedroom was located. It was to be our bedroom to sleep in that night which we did. The next morning, the same man came and got us up and then took us back into the café and gave us breakfast. The magazine we had followed the previous day was still there on the counter. While Earl and I were eating breakfast, a Frenchman came in and picked up the magazine and after a few moments left the café. We hurriedly finished our coffee and then followed the magazine down the street. The man led us back to the train depot with a sign that read Ham. I learned later we were now south of Peronne by about thirty kilometers. We trailed the fellow to a train at the depot which was a normal train, one car for passengers and one for the bikes. Our French guide boarded the train and we followed. After we got on board we saw the magazine lying on the same seat it had been the day before. And guess what? There were Monti and Dale in seats right across from us and Guy and Oscar right across the aisle in their seats. We were all back where we had been sitting when the train arrived yesterday.

As the train pulled out of the station, our tickets and magazine were collected just as before.

"Then Earl and I started looking around the passenger car. All or most every seat was full. Away in the other end of the car were two German Gestapo men in their black uniforms. None of us were happy to see them, but then we started looking at the rest of the people between them and us and felt a little better. The passengers seemed to be all men, and they all had bumps under their coats or stiff legs when they walked. These Frenchmen were obviously bodyguards for all of us evaders on the train. We knew there were six of us from our crew aboard, but had no idea of how many more Allied fly boys there were in the car.

"The train went on down the tracks for somewhere between forty-five minutes and an hour before it came to the next stop. At this junction, two other sets of tracks met ours. A Frenchman with our magazine got off the train and headed off down the road. Someone opened up the railroad car behind us and people must have taken a dozen bikes out. Neither Earl nor I saw Monti, Dale, Guy, or Oscar get off the train, so we had no idea of where they went. We continued to follow our magazine down the road for what I would say was about three miles. The carrier of our magazine kept going until he came to a big house that sat in the middle of nowhere. Earl and I followed the man into the house and found we were in the front room where we saw a woman and a small boy around ten or twelve years old. The woman started talking to us, but we had been taught never to talk to anyone until whomever was moving us said it was all right. Earl and I just sat there and listened. We had picked up enough French by this time to know what was going on. Finally the fellow that carried the magazine into the house showed up and told us it was OK to talk to the woman.

"The woman said, "We have an American here." and Earl and I said, "You do?" The little kid that had been sitting there said, "What the Hell do you think I am?" My reply was, "I would say from your size you are a ball gunner." "That's right," he answered. We learned his name was Ogea. He had been here in this house for over a month, and he would not even try to learn French. The woman would show him an egg and say, "Euf" Ogea would say, "Earf, hell. It's an egg."

"Later in the afternoon, Earl and I were told it was time to leave so we said goodbye to the woman and Ogea. We walked to another real small town nearby called Lagny. As things turned out, we'd be there awhile.

***

"Our French helper escorted us to Lagny, a town about five miles from where we got off the train and about sixty miles north of Paris. There was a larger town down the road about five miles named Lassigny, but we didn't get to visit there for about three more months.

"The first place Earl and I were taken when we got to Lagny was a bar. The barkeeper, who was also the owner, was one of the leaders in the local Underground. We were turned over to him, and now we didn't have to follow the magazine anymore. Things were going to change a lot very soon. We arrived in Lagny on 4 June 1944 just two days before the deficit hit the oscillator down on the Normandy beaches. Now we could find out what our hosts' names were as with the pending invasion by the Allies, the Underground relaxed its policy on evaders knowing helper's names.

"Our stay in Lagny was very nice. Earl and I were taken in by Monsieur and Madame Maurice DeFrance who were a very charming couple. They had two children, Paul who lived in Paris, and Mauricette, his sister who lived at home and became the one who looked after us most of the time. She was about nineteen or so. Earl and I had the run of the place, both inside the house, out in the yard, and in the barn. It was not long before we had the run of the town. Our best pal, next to Mauricette, was the family dog, Mascot. We would often play with him in the yard. None of us ever had to worry about a German sneaking up on us as that dog could tell a German by his smell. If one were to walk down the street outside the fence, Mascot would go nuts.

"Lagny was a small farming town. It was almost two blocks long and about the same width. There were not many houses off the main street, at most I'd say two. One was the DeFrance's and one at the other end of town. Monsieur and Madame would leave the house just after the sun came up and go work in the fields. They did not have any machinery. They did all the work by hand.

"I think Mauricette was very glad Earl and I were there because she didn't have to go work in the fields. She had to stay home, so if somebody came she was there to take care of whatever came up. By this time, my French was good enough that I could hold a conversation as long the as French didn't speak too fast.

"One evening, Monsieur DeFrance said his son had a small radio, he left the room and returned with a small crystal set with antenna. The next day, I went out to the fence behind the house and put up the antenna. The radio was put in Earl's and my bedroom. We all had a private bedroom so to speak. The DeFrances slept in one bedroom, Mauricette slept in another, and Earl and I had the third bedroom. The house was two stories, but the pigs took over the top floor.

"Each evening around six o'clock, I would go into our bedroom and try to pick up the news on BBC. If I could get it, I'd listen and then go into the kitchen-living room and tell the others the news. The first time I went into the kitchen with my news report, Monsieur DeFrance and Earl were sitting at the table that had one empty chair for me. In front of each place on the table was a glass with two sugar cubes in. Madame DeFrance came over to the table with a bottle of what looked like water. Monsieur DeFrance picked up the bottle and poured enough of this clear liquid into the glass to just cover the sugar cubes. Earl and I didn't know what was going on so we watched Monsieur DeFrance to see what he was going to do. He picked up one of the sugar cubes out of the glass and placed it in his mouth and let it dissolve. Earl and I followed suit. When that sugar cube got into my mouth, I thought someone had poured liquid fire into it. That was the strongest, hottest liquid I think I ever had! When I could at last get my breath, I asked him what that liquid was. He said nonchalantly, "Calvados." We learned later that Calvados is 150 proof cider and a very common drink in that part of France. Each night after that when I went in, I would pick up the glass, dump the sugar cubes, and let him pour in the same amount of Calvados. While he and Earl were sucking on their sugar cubes, I would pick up my glass and say in French, "A votre santé" or "To your health."

"When Maurice and I would start talking about the news, we often would get into an argument about something. When he got going strong, he would switch over to German. Maurice had spent a long time in Germany and spoke German almost as well as he spoke French. Then I would tell him to get off the German and get back to French.

"For some reason, Mauricette always wanted to put more Calvados into my glass. I would always say, "No way!" One slug of that stuff was all I needed. One night while her dad and I were arguing about something on the news, she got to me. Maurice and I were going at it and when I looked down at my glass, there was Calvados in it. I was sure I had drank it before, but it was still there. I picked up my glass, made my salute, and drank it down. The next thing I knew I was waking up in bed the following morning. I asked Earl what had happened. He said, "You two were going at it when all of a sudden your mouth flew open, your eyes were glazed, and we couldn't get a thing out of you. So Maurice and I put you to bed." Those two shots of that stuff knocked me colder than a cucumber! After that when I took my slug of Calvados, I would turn my glass upside down and keep one hand on it at all times. One thing about Calvados, it's the best thing you could get if you cut yourself. Just pour a little of that stuff on the cut and it would take care of any germ. It was also the best cigarette lighter fuel you could get.

"The head of the French Underground in the area was an engineer that the Germans would have just loved to have gotten their hands on. He would come down to the house occasionally to visit. The German offered reward for his capture was about ten times what it was for ours. He stopped one day and said he had a visitor up at the bar. Monsieur Martin's place was just about a block from the DeFrance house. Earl and I walked up and found Monsieur Martin out behind the place digging up a bottle of good wine for the three of us to sit down and enjoy. When the engineer's visitor showed up, we found he was an American lieutenant and a fighter pilot who had been shot down. He had gotten into the Underground, and it was moving him south. We sat, drank wine, and shared stories for some-time and eventually killed off the bottle of wine. We told Monsieur Martin that when the engineer came back, to tell him the three of us had gone down to the DeFrance place and would wait for him there.

"After arriving back at the DeFrance house, Mauricette said she wanted to take a picture of the three of us and she did. I don't remember the fighter pilot's name or outfit, but I do remember he flew a P-47 Thunderbird, nicknamed a Jug because of its configuration. The engineer showed up a little later, and we had to say goodbye to the pilot as he took off into "the wild blue yonder."

"Every once in awhile Mascot would go on a rage. When he did, we knew there was a German nearby. If you looked out the window of the DeFrance's house, a lot of the time you could see someone walking down the road rather dejected looking. This was after the Allies had come ashore at Normandy and the German forces were being driven back. It was also the time when German soldiers first started deserting and food was hard to come by. One deserter came to the door one day begging for food. Mauricette gave him an egg. He held the egg in his hand cracked the shell, and sucked the egg into his mouth. Then he left.

"Earl and I needed something to do to pass away some time. The DeFrances had a heavy old wheelbarrow. We would take it and some rope, go up on the hill behind the town, load it up with firewood, haul it down to the house, and stack the wood up. We had to have something to do because we were going stir-crazy just sitting in the house, walking in the yard, playing cards, or out in the barn or with the dog Mascot. At least by bringing in firewood, Earl and I felt we were doing something to help out.

"Being farmers, the DeFrances did not hurt for food. They had chickens running around the yard. We had chickens to eat as well as eggs just about anytime we wanted to. The family also had a cow so we got all the milk we wanted. There was also a garden and we could go out there and pick most anything we wanted. It was a lot better deal than many of the other evaders ever had.

"We were told that two of our crew members were living on a farm near the town of Montdider which was reasonably near where we were. They were living about the same kind of life Earl and I were. Finally we learned the two were Dale, the radio operator, and Monti, a waist gunner. We heard nothing about Guy Wallace, the copilot, or Oscar Rogers, the bombardier. Earl and I hadn't seen nor heard of either of them since we got off the train just before we were brought to Lagny.

"There was an old abandoned military camp near where Monti and Dale lived. The story goes that they went over to the camp to see what was there. During World War I it had been a cavalry station. Our crewmates had found this old horse watering trough and decided it would be a good thing to take a bath in. A night or so later, they went over to the camp, stole it, and carried it back to the farm. When the Frenchman they were staying with saw it, he blew his stack! What Monti and Dale didn't know was the day they stole it, almost a thousand German troops had moved into the camp. They had walked right into the middle of an active German camp, stolen a bath tub, and carried it out without being caught. What luck!

"One day the head of the Underground came in and told Earl and me that we had to move and quick. He said that a whole bunch of Germans were coming this way, and they would probably bivouac in the open field behind the house. I said I guess I'd better take the radio antenna down. When I made that statement, the head of the Underground wanted to know what the hell we were doing with a radio. I said so we could listen to the news. At that point I left and took the antenna down and gave it and the radio back to Mauricette and told her to stash it wherever her dad kept it. Earl and I then left with the Frenchman.

"The three of us walked to the other end of town and went into a house. Inside there was a woman and two little girls, about seven and nine I would say. The woman was busy cooking and it appeared she knew we were coming and was preparing to put on a big spread for the two Americans. She was cooking a duck on an old wood burning stove and basting it with Calvados, that 150 proof cider I've told you about. The duck had to be about done. One of the little girls asked her mother something and she turned to look at the girl while she was pouring the Calvados over the duck and suddenly there was a loud Whoosh. Some of the Calvados missed the duck and hit the hot stove. The duck was now nothing but a cinder. The fire didn't last long, but it sure did a job on the duck!

"The woman took the pot with the cinder off the stove and said, "C'est la guerre." or "That's war." She went outside, caught another duck, and started all over again. She put enough food on the table to feed her family of four for two weeks. Earl's and my stomachs were smaller than theirs since we had not been eating as much as we used to. We took a little of each dish she put on the table, but she kept saying, "That is not enough." and then put more on our plates. About the time we had finished, we were ready to bust but then her neighbor came in with a cake so we both had to have a big piece of cake. I was miserable when the meal was over! I hadn't stuffed myself like that since I couldn't remember when. We stayed with the lady and her family the rest of the day. In the evening, the head of the Underground returned and escorted us back to the DeFrance house. It turned out the Germans didn't bivouac in the field after all they went right on through town.

"As I said, we had stayed in Lagny longer than any other place up until then. But all good things must come to an end. One day the head of the Underground showed up and told us we were going to move again. He said there would be a truck there the next day to move Earl and me south. The Underground had received word to form evaders into groups of twenty to twenty-five and start moving them. This was done so that when the Allied invading forces arrived, they would not have to go all over the place looking for us. After hearing this news, it was a very long evening knowing this was going to be the last one we were to spend with our new and loved French family.

"Nobody was happy the next morning. The DeFrances did not go to work in the field but stayed home with Mauricette to tell us goodbye. Earl and I tried to joke with them before we left. Even the dog, Mascot, seemed sad when the truck pulled up. The vehicle looked like a small pickup. On top of it was a large cloth bag. The driver had a fire burning in the truck and the bag gathered the smoke and fed it into the engine to make the pickup move. This system was a wartime expedient used throughout France because there was little if any gas available. The pickup was all closed in the back so it was opened for us to get in. And guess who were sitting inside? There sat our crewmates Guy, our copilot, and Oscar, the bombardier. It was good to see them again as we hadn't seem them since last May on the train down to Langny. They had been picked up first. Earl and I then said our final good-byes to the DeFrances. We had their address and they had ours. We waved farewell as the truck drove off. Another chapter of our evasion story had come to a close, and we were one step closer to getting home. At this stage, we couldn't wait!

***

"It was now late August 1944 when the pickup truck pulled away from the DeFrance house and started down the road. Oscar, Guy, Earl, and I sat in the back talking about a lot of things as we were riding along. There was a little French boy sitting on top of the cab who kept looking up in the air. By this time in the war, the Allied "Stupid Fighter Jocks" would shoot up just about anything that moved on the ground. We figured we were safe and anything as small as this truck wouldn't be considered a target to waste ammunition on. The driver was working his way south and west following mostly backcountry roads. We came down one little road to an intersection where another road turned off almost due south. This road led to where we were heading. But before we arrived at the intersection, a big German lorry, almost as big as a moving truck, came from the other way and turned onto that road. We now had to follow the German truck down the road. We were not happy about that as now it would look like a two vehicle convoy from the air. If any Allied fighter pilot saw the German lorry, we'd get caught in the aerial attack.

"About that time, the little boy on the cab roof started yelling, "Avion! Avion!" Looking up we saw a flight of American P-47 fighters flying overhead. They were quite a ways up; nevertheless, we kept an eye on them until they were out of sight. If even one of them had dropped a wing like he was coming down, there would have been six streaks off across the field, four American streaks followed by two French streaks. Better to be safe than dead!

"As we motored on, we passed three German soldiers walking down the road. The soldiers, part of the Wehrmacht, just kept trudging along, heading south to where the fighting was going on. We hadn't gone over half a mile past the soldiers when the truck quit running just as it started up a hill. Knowing the Germans on foot were coming up behind us, the French driver told the four of us to hide in the bushes. We jumped out of the pickup, took off across the field, and then hid beneath some bushes and watched the German soldiers come up. One of the soldiers asked the French driver what was wrong, and he told them he had to build the fire up some more. The soldiers said OK and moved on.

"Once the Germans were out of sight, the four of us came back to the truck and helped push it up the hill. The truck began rolling down the other side of the hill and then the engine started. We four quickly jumped in the back and were on our way again. Our driver drove into another one of those "big" towns like Lagny, all of two blocks by two blocks. How they knew we were coming I don't know, but as we drove down the street, two big doors opened up on the side of a wall. The Frenchman drove in and the doors closed right behind us. The driver opened up the back of the truck and the four of us jumped out and went into what seemed to be a kitchen area. The women there gave us some food while the men worked on the pickup truck. After the truck was repaired, the driver came in from the garage and said, "OK. I got it fixed. Let's go." We four Americans thanked the women for the food and the men for all their help and then went out and climbed back into the track. The larger doors opened, and the Frenchman drove out into the street. We were on the road one more time.

"We hadn't gone more than a half a mile when the truck broke down again. This time, it couldn't have happened in a worst place. We were right in the middle of a German bivouac area, and I mean a big bivouac area. There were German troops all around us. We could have reached outside the truck anytime and got a handful of Germans. They would come up to the truck and ask the driver what was wrong and if they could help. I laughed very quietly to myself. I was sitting in the back of the truck looking through a little peephole towards the front. A German officer asked the driver what he was carrying, and the answer was, "Pigs." The German officer was looking through the same little peephole ‹ at me as I was looking though at him. It was dark enough inside the truck that I don't think he could see me or anything else. He then walked off. The driver finally got the truck started again, and we took off down the road. We "pigs" sure were happy to get away from there!

"For an hour we drove and after that the driver suddenly pulled off the road and up a driveway into a building whose doors had been opened for us. The doors closed shut as soon as the vehicle passed through. The driver came around to the back of the truck and said, "We have arrived so everyone out." We piled out of the truck not knowing where we were or what we were going to do. The French driver came and told us to come with him. The four of us followed him down a path into the woods. It was pitch black at this time. The driver explained that we were not to get very far away or we wouldn't be able to find our way back. He sure was right. There were living quarters down there in the woods and you would never see them until you walked right into the side or back of one. The area we were in was used as a picnic area so we found a shelter with a picnic table or two. The rest of the area was a dense forest.

"As we wandered deeper into the area, we began to see some people. We found out there were twenty-two of us in this camp. Earlier there had been twenty-three, but the Underground learned that one was a German, so he wasn't there any more. The French never said what happened to him. That was pretty standard with them. Of the twenty-two men, there were seventeen Americans and five Englishmen.

"One of the American officers came over to us and asked if there any of us were officers. Lieutenants Guy Wallace and Oscar Rogers replied they were. The captain said the officer quarters were over there and the enlisted men would sleep in one shack and the officers in another. Our copilot, Lt. Wallace, said in a jovial manner, "We've put up with these low life enlisted men for almost four months now, so I think we will be able to make it through a few more days." The captain was not too happy about Guy's comment, so he left in somewhat of a huff. Then we found out that the shacks he was referring to couldn't really be called shacks as they were nothing but woven twigs and branches picked up or taken off the bushes. It was all that was available. Certainly nothing like back at the DeFrances.

"Our crew learned that the "Good" captain, the officer who didn't like our crew officers staying with us enlisted had only been in France for about a week after being shot down. He was not used to the things we had had to put up with. One evening, the French brought our tobacco and cigarette papers to us. This captain told them he didn't smoke homerolled cigarettes and to take the stuff back and bring him ready made. We decide it was time for the captain to learn a few facts of life pertaining to being an evader. He was told that the French had robbed the tobacco store so we would have something to smoke, and if he didn't know how to roll a cigarette, he was going to get an awfully thirst for one as he had right then. Not one of us would roll a cigarette for him. We all decided this was not an easy guy to get along with.

"Our crew found out later we had two in the group who were sweating out what was going to happen to them when they got back to England. One of them was a B-17 pilot who was the first to bail out of his damaged bomber. Pilots were supposed to be the last man out of a crippled bomber, not the first. It seems the bomber was hit during a mission and had to drop out of formation and on its way home ran into fog and rain, thereby getting lost. The pilot went down into the nose to see if he could help the navigator find out just where they were. He was on his way back to the cockpit when German anti-aircraft fire blew them out of the sky. The flight engineer was on his way to the escape hatch from the rear and the bombardier and navigator were on their way to the hatch from the front so the pilot kicked out the hatch and went out after it. Other members of his crew who were in the camp said he did the only thing he could have done.

"The second guy sweating out the trip home was our own "Good" captain. He had finished his combat tour and had gone home on leave. The only way you could get more than twenty-one days was to sign up for another tour in England, so he did. The captain said he had a really good leave, and it was just about over when he met and fell madly in love with a beautiful young woman. He proposed, she accepted, and they got married. He was unable to spend very long with his new bride before he had to report back to England. After returning to his squadron in England, he was shooting off his mouth about what he was going to do. The story went he would fly his fighter over France, turn it upside down bail out, get rescued and come back to England, and then get shipped home in accordance with Air Force regulations dealing with returned evaders. I doubt many took him seriously.

"Because of his rank and combat experience, the captain was made a flight leader when he returned from leave. On his first mission as a flight leader, his section was looking for something to shoot up. He spotted an airfield below the flight and told the other pilots to stay put. He was going down and check it out re was anything worthwhile, he would call them down. On his first pass he did not drop down too far and made a fairly fast pass. One the second pass he went lower and slower. On his third pass he went down on the deck and flew about as slow as she (planes are always referred to as a female) could go and still keep flying. Just about the time he got to the end of the runway he was inspecting, all hell broke loose. The end of the runway was one long string of lights which turned out to be German light anti-aircraft guns. The captain just had time to pull her up, turn her over so he could get out of the cockpit, and bail out before the fighter went down. He didn't know if any of the pilots in the flight had seen what had happened to him or not. If not, he was in a whole lot of trouble due to his boasting back at the squadron.

"While we stayed at this camp, we could hear quite a lot of artillery shells south of us. There seemed to be quite a lot of fighting going on, and it sounded like it was getting closer. One day we were sitting around in camp and suddenly saw German soldiers going through the woods near where we were. They were throwing potato mashers, the name the Allies had given German hand grenades because of their shape. These Germans were trying to kill some rabbits for food. It was a tricky attempt because if they got too close to the rabbit, they didn't get any food, just a lot of fur. We were not too happy about this because we were hiding in the same places the rabbits were. After all we had been through, we sure didn't want to get killed this way so late in the war.

"It seemed as though every time we left a place, the French wanted to give us money. Even though we did not need any money, they insisted on giving us French francs. As a result, all of us had a lot of money and nothing to do with it. While we were still out in the woods, we played a lot of poker. The idea was to have the winner give it to the girls and ladies up in the chateau who did all of the cooking for us. Have you ever tried to lose money playing cards? We tried for awhile and then gave up. We just stuffed all the French francs into a duffel bag and gave it to the women. They did a real good job cooking for us. When we got back to England, we learned we could have exchanged those notes for cash.

"I don't remember just how long our crew had been in this picnic area, but one day a Frenchman told us to come out of the woods since the Allied invading forces had passed through. We walked up to the chateau and saw a young second lieutenant from the American Ninth Air Force waiting for us. He announced he was going to take charge and get us transportation south to Normandy and then back across the Channel to England. It sounded good to all of us Americans.

"Later at the chateau, the Frenchman who was in charge gave each of us an en-velope and told us if we wanted to keep any of the papers like our forged French passports, work papers, or hospital papers plus any pictures or other things like that, we were to put them in the envelope he gave us. We were told to seal the en-velope and put our home address on it. After things returned to normal, he would send the envelopes to us. I guess things still have not gotten back to normal as the mail hasn't arrived yet. I sure would have liked to have at least my passport as a souvenir.

"As for the second lieutenant and our transportation, we would have been a lot better off if he had never showed up. The Underground had enough cars and trucks hidden out in the woods to take all of us down to Normandy. The American lieutenant said, however, that he was in charge so the French said, " OK, it's all yours." Unfortunately, this American officer wasn't even in the American sector of tactical operations where he had any authority. We all were in the English sector, so our young lieutenant had to go through the English system to try to get anything he needed. Everything he needed was heading north with the British forces pursuing the retreating Germans, so he was out of luck and so were we!

"Approximately three kilometers north of the next small town, the Germans had set up a cannon. It was up on a hill in order that the crew could see both north and south on the road below. When any British convoy would come up the road, the gunners could pick the vehicles off at their leisure. There was a road at the north end of town heading east. You could take it for just less than one kilometer, turn north on the road, and that way you could bypass the German cannon. No one, American or English, seemed capable of moving us out of the area so the members of the French Underground came to help rescue us once again.

"They could see we were not going to get out of town that day, so they took us out of the chateau and scattered us around the small town for our evening meal and a bed for the night. I don't know how they picked who was to stay with whom, but Oscar and I were selected to stay together at a nice house on the north end of town on the main street. We had a decent meal that evening with our French hosts. After eating our meals sitting on the ground in the woods for the past two weeks, it was a real treat to sit at a table for a meal. After supper our hosts took us to the front of the house right next to the main street. We were shown to our bedroom for that night which had a big feather bed, and I mean big in two ways. It was almost a king-sized bed plus it was over four feet tall. Sure must have taken a lot of chicken feathers to make that mattress. Oscar and I got ready for bed. He got on one side of the bed and I got on the other. Oscar said on the count of three we jump into bed. One, two, three. We both jumped up and forward, hit the bed, and didn't see each other until the next morning.

"The next morning Oscar and I had some coffee and more of that real good French bread we had the night before at dinner. We looked out the window and wondered what was going to happen today. While looking out the window, we saw a jeep pull up to the intersection across the street. There were two uniformed men in it and they were talking and pointing like they were trying to make up their minds on which way they were going to go. Finally I jumped up and sat in the window with my feet hanging outside. I yelled at them "Hey! If you want to get your butts blown off, go straight ahead. Jerry (a term for Germans) has a cannon sitting up on a hill about three kilometers ahead. Everyone with the exception of the first few yesterday have been taking the road east across the street and bypassing the cannon." About this time the jeep started up, drove across the street, and pulled up right to the window. The fellow sitting in the passenger's seat looked up and said, "I say, you don't sound like a Frenchman." I replied, "I'm not. I'm an American. And I still say if you want to get your butt shot off, go straight ahead."

"It was not very long until a big British lorry pulled up. Then the roof caved in as the individual in charge said they could not take any Americans, just the five Englishmen. Oscar and I jumped in the lieutenant's jeep again and made a fast trip back to the bivouac area, but when we got there, the place was as bare as Mother Hubbard's cupboards. The unit had already moved out. We were out of luck! Needless so say, the British were way up on our "Don't Like" list about that time. Dejected, we drove back to the chateau and passed out the bad news.

"While still sitting in the lieutenant's jeep near the road, another jeep pulled in with three English soldiers in it. They were getting real huffy and wanted to know what we were doing in an American jeep. We said, "We could ask you the same thing. We are Americans, but you sure are not." "You're Americans? How come you are dressed like that?" was their comment. By this time Oscar and I were fed up with all the crap we were having to put up with and looked at these guys and said, "We've been over here four months trying to fix things up so you people could come over here and take over the country." The Englishmen were not happy with us and we were not happy with them either. Things might have gotten out of hand, but since we had a Thompson submachine gun in the boot, a quaint British term for the trunk, they decided it was time to leave.

"There was still some convoys going through, and a few of them were stopping to make a spot of tea. Three or four of us from the chateau would walk up to them and just stand there and not say a word. After awhile, they would start talking about the "Damned Frogs," a derogatory name for the French used by the English. We would let them go on for awhile and then interrupt them with, "How do you damned Limeys ever expect to win a war when you stop every four hours and brew up a pot of tea?" Boy, would that open their eyes! Then usually one of them would say, "You don't sound like a bloody Frenchman." Our reply was always, "No, and we're not a bloody Limey either!" Then we'd walk away.

"One time while I was talking to a English tank crew, I heard an artillery shell coming in. The only thing I could think of was to get under the tank right now. I made a headfirst dive under the tank. When I hit the gravel, I cut my hand, but it was just a small cut. When I turned around and looked, I saw the tank crew bending over looking at me, and I felt a little foolish. One of them said, "What you doing under the tank, Yank?" I asked, "Didn't you hear that shell coming?" "Hey Yank, you don't hear them until they have passed." was his answer.

***

"Oscar and I went back to the lieutenant to see if he had any luck getting us transportation south to the American sector where we could get a flight back to England. His answer was the same as usual, "No," so we decided as a whole group to start north. It was at this point that I lost track of Earl. In fact, I never saw him again. We had been through a lot together, but I have to admit that I wasn't particularly sorry to part company with Earl as he could get on your nerves when you were around him for too long.

"The "Good" captain, who was the fighter pilot, and I ended up together on the back end of a gas truck. We went as far north as the English outfit had gotten by this time. He and I were wandering around looking for anything that was going north. The captain went into one of the buildings the English were using to see if they could tell him anything. He said he'd be right back, but if anything came up, come in and get him.

"As I said, we were looking for transportation, and at this time I was standing at a stop sign. And guess what pulled up. It was an American 3rd Armored Division water truck. I yelled at the driver, went over to his truck, and asked if he was going back to his outfit. The driver said, "Yes, as soon as I get this tank full of water." I asked if he had room for two lost American flyboys and he said, "Sure. Be right here in half an hour and we'll head north'. I went into the building the captain was in, found him, and told him what we were going to do and when at the appointed time, the captain and I were back at the stop sign waiting for the tanker driver. He stopped, and we got in and introduced ourselves.

"We traveled about five or ten miles north of where the English had stopped, turned off the main road, and came to an AP, an Air Force MP. The driver told the AP that he had two more of the lost flyboys. The AP directed the driver to take us to where the Ninth Air Force Fighter Control convoy was bedded down. The driver took off cross-country and soon came to some parked trucks. He pulled up and asked if anyone was awake. Someone came out of the tent, gave us a blanket and said, "Go over there by that tree and join the other two." We went over and to my surprise we found Monti and Dale from the crew I went down with. We sure did not need the blanket for warmth that night, but it was something to lie on.

"All of us got up early the next morning and started looking around. There was only one tent, but we saw three sleeping bags. We figured there must be a high ranking officer in the tent. There was also a jeep and a three-quarter ton truck parked by the tent. One sleeping bag that was outside the tent started to move around some and out of the bag came a lieutenant colonel. Out of the tent came a corporal. This was a little unusual so we asked the lieutenant colonel how come he was sleeping in a sleeping bag outside the tent. His answer was, "I don't want anything slowing me down in case the enemy fighters come over. I want a clear shot at that ditch." The colonel was the commanding officer of the Ninth Air Force Command assigned to the Army's 3rd Armored Division.

"The "Good" captain whose name I found out was Dick, Dale, Monti, and I talked to the colonel during breakfast. We told him all we were trying to do was find some kind of transportation south so we could catch a flight back to England. The colonel said, "This unit we are with is due in Brussels by midnight tomorrow and if we get there fast enough and before the Germans have time to blow up the airfield and docks, you could be back in England a lot faster than going south. That made sense to us, so we decided to stay with his unit.

"Within the hour after this conversation with the colonel, Captain Dick was in the jeep with the driver and the colonel. Monti and Dale were in the three-quarter ton truck, and I was in the three-quarter ton half-track with the radio operator. We were the last three vehicles in the convoy. Soon we were rolling up the highway between thirty-five and fifty-five miles per hour. I kept looking out the back and finally the radio operator said, "Hey Sarge, don't worry! We've got the infantry in front of us. We've got the tanks in front of us. And we've got the TDs in front of them and we're not going to pass them." I said, "OK." I figured he should know what he was talking about. A short time later, I saw a bunch of trucks with guys piling out of them and moving rapidly into the woods and into buildings. I turned to the radio operator and asked, "Say Sarge, isn't that the infantry we're not supposed to pass?" He answered, "Yes, but we will not pass the tanks and the TDs." I said, "Hey! I'm a fly-boy. What the Hell is a TD?" He gave me one of those "You Stupid Jerk" looks and said, "That's a tank destroyer." "OK. Now we both know," I replied.

"On up the road a short distance, I saw some tanks going into the woods and through some buildings. I asked Sarge, "Are these the tanks we were not sup-posed to pass?" and again he said, "Yes, but we won't pass the TDs." By this time the head of the convoy was-heading into the little town of Montdider. I realized that we were almost back to Lagny. None of the Allied troops had been there yet and the Germans were not too happy with us trying to run them out of town with just a few .50 caliber machine guns. The convoy did an about face real fast and started back the way we had just come.

"Our convoy went down and found a place to bivouac. It was just after noon so everyone was going to have lunch. The four of us who were just trying to get back to England went over to the colonel and told him that three of us had been here in France for over four months and we didn't want to get lolled at this late date by somebody's stupidity. We then said, "We would like to borrow your jeep and have your driver take us as far as we need to get some transportation home." The colonel, being a reasonably good guy, told his jeep driver to find out where the nearest POW camp was from where we could start working our way south with the prisoners. That is exactly what we did.

"After Captain Dick, Dale, Monti, and I had climbed into the colonel's jeep, the driver started rolling down the road. Somebody's kidney's started feeling like they were going to burst so I yelled at the driver, "Hey driver! We have to relieve ourselves. How about pulling over to the side of the road and stopping?" He turned around and looked at us and said, "You can't do that by the road. There are a lot of people around here." He was right in that there were a lot or men, women, and children walking up the road where we were traveling. We finally yelled at him again, "Just pull over to the side of the road and stop or we're going to wet down your jeep!" He did as we requested, and not a moment too soon. The four of us leaped out of the jeep and wet down the ground beside it. The driver went over to some bushes to do his thing. I'll bet you can't guess who all the French were looking at. It certainly wasn't us. They knew what we were doing, but they were wondering what the driver was doing as it wasn't the French way of doing things.

"Feeling greatly relieved, we all got back in the jeep and proceeded on down the road. At last we found an American camp for German POWs. The driver pulled up and the four of us got out of the jeep, thanked the driver, and told him to thank the colonel for us. The lieutenant in charge of the camp asked who we were and where we were going. We told him, and he said it would take about three days to get down to La Loupe, the main POW camp.

"The lieutenant asked Captain Dick and me if we would like to walk uptown and have a drink. Both of us thought that was a good idea. Monti and Dale decided they would go and try to find some place to sleep that night so they didn't go to town with us. The two officers and I walked up into town and found the local pub and went in. The lieutenant ordered three Cognacs and the gal behind the bar started in on us verbally. She had nothing good to say about the Americans or the English or the Germans. "All they know is Cognac, Cognac, Cognac. Cognac finished!" she said quite emphatically. At this point I asked her politely in French if we could have three glasses of Cognac. "Oui." was her answer. Soon there were three glasses of Cognac in front of us. I then asked her, again in French, why she would not sell it to Americans since they did pay for it. She replied; "Oui, but Cognac is hard to come by." Then I told her we were all Americans. Upon hearing this, her eyes got real big, and she said in a startled voice, "You're Americans? How come you are dressed like one of us?"

"I told her that Captain Dick was a fighter pilot and had been with the French Underground for about two weeks, and that I was a gunner on a downed bomber and had been with the Underground for over four months. The old gal let out a yell and her husband came hustling out of the back. She told him what I had just told her. The Frenchman went into the back and when he came back, he had a bag. It seems a P-47 was shot down and had crashed out behind this place. The man had gone out and gotten all of the pilot's personal effects off of him before the Germans could get there. He asked if we could get the pilot's things back to the boy's parents. Captain Dick looked at the address and said, "Yes, it's not far from where I live." Needless to say, we did not buy anymore Cognac the rest of the evening. Everything was on the house. After a very pleasant evening, the three of us strolled back to the camp.

"After arriving back at camp from the pub, Captain Dick and I learned we would leave that night with a bunch of POWs for the next camp. The drivers knew where the camps were. Our destination was a camp called La Lue. Monti and Dale showed up in time to make the trip with us. The drive was uneventful, and we arrived at the camp at one o'clock the next morning. The only ones up were the guards. Captain Dick asked one of the guards who was in charge and one of them said, "The First Sergeant." We went over the sergeant's pup tent where the captain said he would like to talk to him. The sergeant responded with, "I'm sleeping. Can't you see that?" At that smart remark, the captain moved real fast, grabbed that guy's feet, and pulled him bodily out of the tent. I'd never seen such a shocked First Sergeant in all of my military career. Then Captain Dick announced in an authoritarian tone that he was a captain in the United States Army Air Corps and then continued, "When I speak to a Noncom, I expect to be treated as an officer!"

"Then he asked who the commanding officer was and the First Sergeant provided his name. Captain Dick then asked where he was, and the First Sergeant said, "He's sleeping." The captained ordered, "Then get him up!" "No sir, I won't!" was the answer from the First Sergeant. Captain Dick gave him a hard look and said, "OK, you take me to him and I'll get him up." At that, the First Sergeant took us to the commander's tent. Along the way he apparently decided he'd better wake his boss and not have an very irate captain do it.

"After the Company Commander was awake, Captain Dick explained things to him. The commander then directed the sergeant to get us some blankets and take us down to the barn, and he would take care of us in the morning. So the First Stud did as he was ordered and gave us blankets and then escorted us down to the barn. He said, "There is hay in there for you four to sleep on." After we all got ready for bed, someone said, "Hey, there's someone else in here too!" We could hear some heavy breathing, but it didn't take long and we were also sleeping as it had been a long day. When it started to get light the next morning, we found out who had been in the barn with us. There were, I think, twelve of them, and they were all German officers of different ranks.

"The four of us got up and found the mess hall where we ate breakfast. The next leg of our journey was going to be made during the day since it was a short hop down to Camp La Loupe. It was raining that day so after we finished eating, we went down to the trucks that were going to take us on our last leg. There was a large open German lorry that the guards put the enlisted prisoners in plus an American truck fully covered for the German officers. The captain in charge of the camp told Monti, Dale, and me to get in the open lorry with the enlisted men. Captain Dick walked over to the other captain and demanded to hear again what the captain had just said. The other captain then said, "I told your enlisted men to get in the truck with the other enlisted men." After the captain was finished, Captain Dick proceeded to tell him in very precise and harsh detail what he thought of him and what a lowlife, German loving, no good he considered him to be. Dick then continued, "You have not heard the last of this!" Now Captain Dick may have been a real pain in the you know what before, but he sure was on track now and taking very good care of us. It was a very pleasant surprise for us sergeants.

"When Captain Dick was through telling the other captain off, he stepped over to the covered officer's truck and asked the German officers, "Do any of you speak English?" I think all of them said yes. "Well," said Captain Dick, "now hear this. Move it back as there are three more coming on board. "He turned to us and said, "See you in La Loupe."

"After a short haul down the road, we pulled into the POW camp. This was where all German POWs wound up. When they left there, they were shipped all over, some to camps in America, some to England, and yes, some even to Moscow.

"We were sent over to the medics, and they gave us a good going over from head to toe. The doctor that was checking me over had a hard time getting my pulse. All he had was a watch with a small second hand. I asked why he didn't get a full sweep second hand and he replied that it wasn't an issue item. I had mine that the Air Corps had given me, so I said I would give it to him. The doctor said, "You are charged with it." I came back with, "Yes, but after the past four months, I am, not charged with anything, and beside, if I go back with it, they'll take it away from me. I'll feel better if you have it to help in your work." He finally accepted the watch.

"We all got a clean bill of health. The medics said there was nothing wrong with us that some rest and three meals a day would not take care of. We thanked the doctors and started looking for the truck that was to take us to the laundry. We ambled over to the waiting truck and told the driver to take us to the laundry. The driver replied, "OK, I've been waiting for you." He drove us out into the country until we saw three trucks sitting along a stream bed. Behind one of the trucks was a bunch of wooden framing. The driver pulled up and stopped. A noncom came out and said, "Take everything out of your pockets that you don't want to get wet and put that stuff in your shoes. The rest of the stuff just leave in a pile." Then he continued, "Right around this truck are a bunch of shower heads so have at it. There is soap and everything you need." That was the first good shower we had in all of our stay in France.

"After getting under the running shower head we were not in any big rush to get out, but we finally said we'd had enough. Then we found out we didn't have any towels. One of the fellows that worked at the laundry told us to just run around the field to dry off since our clothes were not dry yet either. So the four of us ran around the field sans clothes. It must have been quite a sight! Once we and our clothes were dry, we put our clothes back on. We did not, however, have the things we had just gotten washed. The driver then took us back to La Loupe.

"After showering we were taken to an airfield near Cherbourg. We asked the driver to take us to the base operations section He located it, we got out and thanked the driver, and he was off back to La Loupe.

"Captain Dick led the way in and asked the officer behind the desk if he had anything heading back to England. The Operations Officer looked at us and asked, "What are you fellows?" We told him who we were and what our situation was. He looked and then said, "I don't have anything right now. Have you eaten yet?" Captain Dick said for all of us, "No." The Operations Officer said go and get something to eat and by the time you get back, I'll have a flight heading for England. When we asked where we could get something to eat, he said, "Come with me." We walked over to a window and he pointed toward a path that led into the woods and told us follow it. We thanked him and said we'd be back pretty soon. All of us in our little group went down and started to follow the path referred to locally as the "yellow brick road." It led to a mess hall.

"The first thing we came to was a large tent. We entered and looked at the set-up. Someone said, "This must be the Enlisted Mess Hall." We could see another tent behind this one through an opening in the back of the big tent so it was out the door and into the next tent. We looked at the setup in this tent and said, "This is the Officers' Mess." The tables were not as large as in the other tent and there was more than just one set of salt and pepper shakers on them. But we could see still another tent behind this one so we went out the door of the Officers' Mess and into the next tent. The others and I took one look at this setup and said, "This is the place where we are going to eat!" There were tables for four persons, nice soft chairs, table cloths, and silverware at each place. There were even wine and water glasses at each table setting. We each pulled up a chair and sat down. Very soon afterwards, a fellow was standing by the table asking us what we wanted to eat. Captain Dick told him the Ops Officer had sent us down to get something to eat before we took off for England. The fellow asked what we would like, and we answered by asking him what did he have. The answer was, "Just about anything you want." Each of us gave him our order for a steak. No one had eaten one for awhile, you know.

"Soon the waiter was back asking if drinks were desired, so we all ordered one. He returned shortly with our orders, so we sat and sipped our drinks till the food came. Each of us had ordered a different cut of steak and had them cooked from rare to very well done. As our waiter brought them, he inquired if wine was wanted, so we all decided that would be nice. He suggested red wine to go with the beef. The waiter had already filled up our water glasses, and we inquired where they got their water The reply was, "From England. The French water isn't fit to drink."

"When we were finished with the meal, our waiter came over and took the things off the table, and then asked if we cared for any dessert. He said they had just about any kind of dessert we could think of if I remember right, each of us ordered a different kind of dessert. After our dessert, the waiter came and inquired if he could ask us a question. We said, "Sure." I think all of us knew what it was going to be. He asked what our ranks were. Captain Dick told him he was a captain; I informed him I was a staff sergeant; and Dale and Monti said they were sergeants. After our answers, the waiter informed us that he was a staff sergeant in the Army Air Corps and then followed with, "Do you know whose mess hall this is?" We said. "No we don't, but they sure do eat good." Our waiter said, "This is the General Officers' Mess" and then informed us we had been correct about the other two tents. Our comments were, "We sure picked the right one, didn't we?" He agreed and said, "You sure did." We thanked him for the excellent service and all the good food and then got up and left.

"The four of us walked back up the path to the Operations Section, went in, and asked for the Ops Officer. When we met him, we asked if he been able to set up a flight to England for us, and he said, "Yes. See that old Gooney Bird sitting out there? Just go climb aboard. The crew is upstairs filing a flight plan and they will be out real soon." We thanked the officer for all his help and then walked out to the old Gooney Bird sitting on the ramp. I had by then and have since flown on a lot of Gooney Birds, the name given to a C-47 transport plane, but I was never in one rigged out like that one. It had plush reclining chairs plus a fully stocked and equipped bar.

"The crew arrived and came aboard. We learned that the crew chief was also the bartender. As soon as we were seated, he came and asked what we would like to drink. The crew chief took our orders, went to the bar, mixed them and brought them to us. Just about this time the pilot and copilot came and asked if we were ready to head back to England, and obviously we said we were. Both pilots went forward into the cockpit, started up the engines, taxied out to the runway, and soon we were in the air on our way back to England.

"While we were flying over the English Channel, the pilot came back and asked what it felt like to be going back to England. He said the Ops Officer had told him some of our stories. Captain Dick was the first to comment, and he said he did not have anything but the very highest praise for the job the FFI had done for him and for all the downed airmen. The three of us agreed 100% with the captain. Then we had a question for the pilot. He said, "OK, shoot." We wanted to know who this old Gooney Bird belonged to. His remarks were, "It belongs to the Army Air Corps, but if you ever hear the tail number of this airplane on the radio, just say ‹ I wonder where the Number One Man in the Army is heading now?'" That number one man was General George C. Marshal, the Army Chief of Staff.

"After nearly an hour and a half in the air, the aircraft was approaching Heathcliff, the largest airfield in England. When the pilot called in for landing instructions, all he gave was the plane's tail number and immediately the tower personnel gave us a straight in approach. As soon we the plane landed, the Follow Me truck led us right to the front door of the operations building. A very long black staff car pulled up to the door of the plane. You should have seen the look on the face of the driver when the four of us stepped out. He obviously couldn't believe what he saw, one captain and three sergeants. No doubt he was expecting a general officer. The driver recovered and asked where we would like to go, Captain Dick advised him we had been instructed to report to the United Staff (U-Staff) Headquarters on the outskirts of London. He drove us there, and we got out and went into the headquarters. Captain Dick, Monti, Dale, and I all signed in and started our debriefing. We were at last safely home from France!

***

Kenneth "Ken" E . Neff, was born May 23, 1918 in Paden City, West Virginia and joined the Army Air Corps, Aug 29th, 1940.

Ken was decorated with the Air Force's Silver Winged Boot signifying his successful Escape and Evasion. During the Korean War, he again flew with the 92nd Bomb Group as a CFC gunner on the B-29 "Peace on Earth." After Korea, he spent 12 years training crew members in the art of survival in Louisiana; Florida; Greenland; Goose Bay, Labrador and finally at Castle AFB in Atwater, CA

After retiring from the Air Force in 1966, Ken worked locally for both GE and Marakay Mills. He was an active member of the 92nd USAAF/USAF Memorial Association, Air Force Gunners Association, The Air Force Escape & Evasion Society, The Eighth Air Force Historical Society, General Doolittle Chapter, life member of Disabled American Veterans and Atwater and Winton VFW # 7792.

***

Acknowledgements;
Navigator Walter R. Haldorfer: from his book "Four Months Behind the Lines
Ron Haldorfer for his fathers biography
Ball-turret gunner Kenneth R. Neff from his book "Fame's Favored Few"

CHAPTER 7

94ᵀᴴ BOMB GROUP
331ˢᵀ BOMB SQUADRON

Type: B-17G • Serial: 42-31498 "Passionate Witch II"
MACR: 4467 • Air Base: Bury St. Edmunds

No definite information regarding the disappearance of this aircraft and crew is known. However, it is believed that this aircraft left formation shortly after leaving the target area on route out. Believed to have been damaged by flak in target area which was intense and accurate. No other information is available.

Missing Air Crew Report # 4467

Pilot: 2Lt. Kenneth L. Chism, 0-686540, POW, San Antonio, TX

Co-Pilot: 2Lt. Dominic L. Gaudiomonte, 0-819790, POW, New York, NY

Navigator: 2Lt. Alfred S. Weinberg, 0-694629, POW, Philadelphia, PA

Bombardier: 2Lt. Marion L. Gordy, 0-701472, POW, Lumpkin, GA

Engineer: S/Sgt. Stanley R. Janesik, 32721556, POW, Bronx, NY

Radio: Sgt. Vernon A. Sovia, 16156099, POW, Phillips, WI

Ball-Turret Gunner: Sgt. Jack A. Parker, 19112261, POW, Auburn, WA

Waist-Gunner: Sgt. Dennis E. Nicklin, 13107228, POW, Greenville, PA

Waist-Gunner: Sgt. Gene C. Powell, 15065995, KIA, Rossville, IN

Tail-Gunner: S/Sgt. Oscar E. Gibson Jr., 34261020, POW, Black, AL

1 KIA, 9 POW

Crash Site: Hassenberg/Coburg, Germany
Time: 11.42

Summary of the Missing Air Crew Report:

" Left the formation after bombs away probably due to flak damage. All crew bailed out at about 18,000 feet and all were captured near Herzberg/Elster, 11 miles ne of Torgau/Elbe in Germany. The B-17 flew on for about 100 miles and crashed south of Hassenberg, nine miles east of Coburg. 12 Km. w. of Kronach.

Pilot 2Lt. Kenneth L. Chism.

From Grandson Ryan Chism;

Ken Chism was born August 11, 1917 in San Antonio, Texas. He died October 13, 1983. Ken (or K.L. as he was later called in my family) grew up in Schertz-Cibalo outside of San Antonio. Ken was the descendant of Germans who immigrated to Texas in the 1850's and spoke German at home before he spoke English. He went to high school at Fort Tech in San Antonio. He was athletic, ran track, played football, and also played the trumpet. He graduated in 1934.

"In the 1930's San Antonio was a hub of military and private aviation. Somewhere in this mix, Ken learned to fly bi-wing planes and obtained a private pilot's license, flying part time as a crop duster to log more hours. Before the war he went on to work for Humble Refinery (later Exxon-Mobile) in Ingleside, Texas. He married my grandmother Betty (Baird) Chism in 1940.

***

Pilot 2Lt. Kenneth Chism receiving his Wings

"On April 29, 1944, Ken Chism and his crew were on standby and did not expect to fly the air raid on Berlin. They had off-duty passes and were preparing to go into London on an overnight trip for some relaxation. The crew was wearing their full dress uniforms, as standing by was only as a formality. However, the plane ahead of them in line apparently had engine problems and could not take off. Ken's crew was called off standby to take their place. They had to put their flight gear on over their dress uniforms and get in the air.

"During the attack on Berlin, the plane sustained very heavy damage. The crew began to bail out south of Berlin and were captured near Hassenberg. Kenneth and the co-pilot flew on in the hope that they could get closer to France and possibly avoid capture, maybe even attempting to fly over the English Channel at Calais. He very much wanted to continue participating in the war effort.

"When it soon became clear that the plane was too badly damaged, Ken parachuted out. He had never practiced a "live jump" in the air before. He had only practiced jumping from tall platforms. When he jumped, he was very scared and pulled his rip cord immediately. As a result, he had a long descent and many farmers and soldiers in the area saw him coming down and were waiting for him when he reached the ground. On the way down he ate all of his rations, knowing that he would be captured and probably not eat for a while. When Ken was captured they marched him into the town square with the other airmen. Because he spoke German he understood what the people were saying. He said that the farmers were very insulted because my grandfather and his crew were in their dress uniforms. "Look at these American sons of bitches," one said "bombing us in coats and ties and shinny shoes!"

"After capture, my grandfather was sent to Stalag Luft III in Selesia (where the Great Escape took place, but he arrived after that event). He remained there for several months and was able to write some letters to my grandmother and he even received a few back from her. He remained there until just after Christmas of 1944 when he wrote his last letter to my grandmother. There is a story that Ken's bunkmates saved up and pooled the chocolate from their Red Cross parcels in order to bake a cake. When it was complete, they spent the rest of the day showing it off until an air raid commenced on a nearby target. The men took cover and the force of the bomb blasts blew the glass out of the windows and ruined the cake. That's why later in life Ken always ate his dessert first.

"As the Russians approached from the East in 1945 he was evacuated to Stalag VII on "The March," from Selesia to Bavaria. During the march Ken made several escape attempts but was always recaptured. After the final attempt, the guards took his boots he had to continue in the snow without them, suffering bad frost bite on his toes. According to the war records Ken was at Stalag XIII-B in Nuremberg until April 12 1944 and was then moved again to Stalag VII-A in Moosburg just north of Munich.

"On April 29 1945 Ken was liberated from Stalag VII-A one year to the day after his capture. Several days afterward he was sent to France where he was treated for his frost bite. He was able to get enough money together to send a telegram to my grandmother saying that he was alive. It arrived to her a few days later, about two weeks before the official notifications arrived to her from the Army.

"Ken returned home on the Queen Elizabeth luxury liner. He kept a small journal of the ten or so days at sea in which he was very food obsessed and happy to be eating more than he occasional beans and cabbage. Unfortunately, none of the POWs were able to keep their food down because their stomachs hand shrunk and they were not accustomed to rich food because of their captivity.

"Once he returned home he and Betty bought a small farm in Fredericksburg, TX where he raised hogs for about five years. He even had a surplus P-51 fighter that he shared with friends for a few years! Ken remained in the Air Force Reserve and continued to fly out of Randolph AFB in San Antonio. There he served as the adjutant to Gen. Tex Hill, former commander of the Flying Tigers unit that helped drive the Japanese out of China during the war. My father and I actually met Gen. Hill many years later in a hunting shop when I was about 16 years old. Dad told Gen. Hill that he was Ken Chism's son. Gen Hill spent the next few minutes telling us stories and said that my grandfather was "a good pilot," which my dad took as very high praise coming from some who was played by John Wayne.

"During the 1950's my grandparents moved back to San Antonio and my grandfather opened the metal fabrication business that our family still operates today. My father, brother, mother, and I all work in the business. We joke that my grandfather was a great man, but a terrible business man. Not because he wasn't smart, but because he never worried about money. I have found this to be common among many veterans who were also POWs. If it was there, he spent it and he enjoyed himself! The business was always over-staffed in his day because he went out of his way to hire Vietnam veterans. He was very upset with how they were treated when they came home.

"I know that Ken traveled back to England and attended a large reunion of 8th Air Force veterans in the late 1970's. He passed away suddenly in 1983 at 66. Ken retired from the Air Force Reserves as a full colonel. He is buried under Major Kenneth Chism, his last rank while in active duty.

Navigator Alfred S. Weinberg.

By wife Marion.

"Al was born March 5, 1920 to Jack and Gussie Weinberg in Philly, PA. He attended University of Pennsylvania (Business and Accounting). I am not sure if he graduated. Just before the war a Philadelphia construction company gave Al a job which led to him living and working in Puerto Rico. He was there when war broke out, and then Al enlisted in the Army Air Corps.

"After he had come down over Germany he was in various camps for over a year. They used toothpaste in place of baking powder or soda to bake in the camp. Early in their marriage in Philadelphia, Al and Marion were on a TV show called the BIG PAYOFF, after which he heard from many POWs who had seen Al on TV.

"During and after the war he suffered badly from frostbite on his feet. Marion was a med tech and doctor's assistant in Philly after the war. One night Al picked her up from her work and there he was surprised to re-encounter Dr. Manny Almes who happened to have been a soldier with Patton's army. Al knew Dr. Almes because he had treated Al in Germany when Al was liberated from the POW camp. In Philadelphia Marion and Al became close friends with Dr. Almes and his wife, and they went out for dinner together frequently.

"After the war Al did accounting in Philadelphia. He moved with family to Toledo, Ohio in 1960. Worked as a metals buyer of aluminum for US Reduction Co. He was self-employed in the same field after officially retiring around 1965.

"In 1948 he married Marion Wohlman. Two sons were born in 1950 and 1952. The couple moved from Philadelphia to Toledo Ohio in 1960.

"Al had a sense of humor and rarely complained. He was very loving and patriotic and was sorry not to be able to fly for the 6-Day war in Israel. He liked to help anyone needing assistance. He loved tennis, and the Caribbean Islands. Al enjoyed Hogan's Heroes and MASH on TV, and laughed despite all he went through. He compared one of the German guards to an actual guard he encountered as a POW in Germany. He and the other POWs would play tricks on that guard.

"Marion remembers at Al's funeral in 1991 when someone said: "everyone loved Al." Later, people would tell her how much he had done for them, which she had never been aware of. Money was unimportant. He was happy to have survived his POW experience.

Waist-Gunner Sgt. Dennis E. Nicklin.

From his obituary:

"Dennis E. Nicklin, 85, of Brewster, died Wednesday, May 3, 2006, at his home. He was a 1938 graduate of St. Michael's High School in Greenville, Pa., and entered the U.S. Army Air Corps in 1942. He was a gunner in World War II on a B-17 Bomber and was shot down on April 29, 1944, over Berlin, Germany. He was held POW for 13 months in Stalag 17. He retired from Norfolk & Western Railroad and was a member of Greenville Veterans of Foreign Wars, Greenville Elks and Stalag 17 Veterans Group.

Tail-Gunner S/Sgt. Oscar E. Gibson Jr.

From Oscar's obituary;

"He was born on November 22, 1916, in Black, Alabama. Mr. Gibson moved to Chicago after graduation from business college and worked five years for Ecko Products and a brief period for Canada Dry in Los Angeles, before his enlistment into the Army in 1942. In order to see action in WWII, he later transferred to the Army Air Corps where he served as a tail-gunner on a B-17 bomber. After seven months he was shot down over Berlin and held prisoner of war at Stalag XVIII-B in Krcms, Austria for 15 months.

"After the war, Mr. Gibson returned to Chicago and Ecko Products as a sales representative, where he met and married Helen Martinek and they later had two children. He was relocated with his family to Boston and then to Dallas. His entrepreneurial adventures began in Dallas where he started Address A'Matic. He later returned to Chicago to open four donut shops with his brother-in-law Dennis Daly.

"In 1972, he and Helen moved to Fort Walton Beach and opened Sprinkler and Irrigation Supply, which they operated until their retirement in 1985.

***

Acknowledgements;
Marion Weinberg, wife of Navigator Alfred Weinberg
Ryan Chism, grandson of Pilot Kenneth L. Chism.

CHAPTER 8

94ᵀᴴ BOMB GROUP
332ᴺᴰ BOMB SQUADRON

Type: B-17G • Serial: 42-102520
MACR: 4468 • Air Base: Bury St. Edmunds

This aircraft observed to go into a shallow dive into clouds over target, apparently under control.

Missing Air Crew Report 4468

Pilot: 2Lt. Joseph K. McClurkin Jr., 0-806283, KIA, Baconton, GA

Co-Pilot: F/O Edward I. Knowlden, T-122810, POW, Lisle, NY

Navigator: 2Lt. Charles L. Dulin, 0-757474, KIA, Cedar Rapids, IA

Bombardier: 2Lt. Clarence E. Meekin, 0-738712, KIA, Avon, NY

Engineer: S/Sgt. Lawrence J. Rock, 5377582, KIA, Hubbard, OH

Radio: S/Sgt. Joseph G. Fanning, 32607405, KIA, Jersey City, NJ

Ball-Turret Gunner: Sgt. Robert L. Johnson, 15066126, KIA, Taft, CA

Left Waist-Gunner: Sgt. Joseph P. McCabe, 13167563, KIA, Pittsburgh, PA

Right Waist-Gunner: Sgt. Dominic G. Leogrande, 13145030, KIA, Brentwood, MD

Tail-Gunner: Sgt. Anthony C. Gambardella, 12192269, KIA, Bronx, NY

9 KIA, 1 POW

Crash Site: North Sea near Texel Island
Time: 14.14

From the Missing Air Crew Report:

Ball-turret gunner Robert L. Johnson and waist-gunner Dominic G. Leogrande were killed instantly by flak bursts over Berlin. German document KU 1683 reports that co-pilot Edward I. Knowlden was captured at sea at 14:45 by a rescue flying boat. In June 1944, the body of left waist-gunner Joseph P. McGabe washed ashore on the isle of Texel in the Netherlands. Also in June 1944, the body of tail-gunner Anthony C. Gambardella washed ashore and was initially buried in Den Helder, Netherlands.

The only survivor was **Co-Pilot F/O Edward I. Knowlden.**
In an interview with Margaret Hadsell on June 6, 2014;

"I was born in Granville, PA, and my parents were Robert B. and Eleanor Knowlden. Shortly after I was born my parents and an elder brother moved to Whitney Point. We were dairy farmers. I graduated from Whitney Point High School in 1939. I worked on the farm and after high school I went back to school part time to get a couple of subjects that I hadn't taken before. I worked on the Whitney Point dam which was a flood control project. I worked there all one summer up until December 1942 or 1943.

"My last job on that construction site was drilling holes in the bottom of the river where it came out of the tunnel. Then the demolition squad would come along and fill those holes with dynamite and blow it up so they could deepen the spillway. It was a job to be out on a raft in December on the river drilling holes and blowing the mud back out. You became mud encrusted. And in those days the labor rates for a jackhammer operator were 75 cents an hour but the plain labor work on the dam was 62 ½ cents an hour union labor rate.

"It was a good summer job and when that closed down in December I spent a couple months, in a shoe factory in Endicott. I think Endicott-Johnson was the sole provider of shoes for the Army during that period of time. When spring time came around, they built a new plant in Westover, just west of Johnson City, and I was timekeeper for about 120 laborers and brick layers.

"From then on I knew that the draft was soon going to pick me up because I was the right age so I decided to enlist in the Air Corps. I took tests and eventually ended up in the aviation cadet's center in San Antonio, TX. After a couple of months and after having taken all kinds of tests I actually moved for the first flight training to Muskogee, OK. There must have been twenty young guys who were flying their first time. We flew PT-19's: a single engine airplane that had two seats one behind the other with the trainer always sitting in the back seat. The only way of communication was via a speaking tube. You hold it up to your ear and you could hear what he said. Normally after eight hours of instruction they let you solo and I soloed from that time on.

"After primary flight training in Musk-ogee, OK, I was moved to Coffeyville, KS, and that is not a nice place in the summer time. It is hot and steamy and gassy. There was a stream flowing through near the barracks...you'd see little puffs coming out of the ground...and you could light them with a match. It's funny how little things like that you can remember. There we flew what I call the "Vultee Vibrator." It was a single engine plane but it had a variable pitch prop and it would rattle...it was noisy. After having finished training on that plane we were split up. Some of us continued on single engines planes while others moved on to fly two-engine planes.

Co-Pilot F/O Edward I. Knowlden

"I ended up in Altus, OK, and got some flight training there. Our crew was assembled there and I learned to fly the B-17. In the winter of '43 we went to Sioux City and after a very short time to Kearney, NE, the place where they shipped crews and planes out to go overseas. For some reason we didn't get a plane to fly over and we ended up by going by train from Sioux City to Kearney, NE ,and from there we went to the embarkation point in Fort Dix, NJ, where we got on a ship, the "Mauretania." It was a luxury British liner. The officers always ate in a dining room two meals a day. We were served by waiters in uniform with towels over their arms. The food was first class, the first time I ever had kippered herring for breakfast.

"After about four days we got off the ship there and took a train down to Stone, England. Eventually we ended up in Bury St. Edmunds, northeast of London. We were only there a few days before we went on a mission over the coast of France. It was a short flight.

***

"Saturday, April 29, 1944. I have not too clear of a feeling what happened over Berlin. We dropped out of formation and as soon as we left the battlefield over Berlin I went into the back of the plane and discovered that Robert Johnson, the ball-turret gunner and one of the waist-gunners had been killed. Over Texel Island in the Netherlands the flak hit us again and the order was given to bail out. I saw the plane hit the water – it stayed afloat a very short period of time.

"When I hit the water, I struggled to get rid of the parachute and took off my flying boots because they were pulling me down. What really saved me was my Mae West. After a few minutes I lost consciousness in the very cold North Sea. I don't know who picked me up from the sea as I only came to my senses when I was back on land. I recall laying on a stretcher with blankets over me, and electric heaters turned on me. When I was half awake they took me, one on each arm, and stood me up in a hot shower, where I recuperated a little bit.

"Later I was taken to Amsterdam where I stayed alone in a cell for one or two days. They sort of semi-interrogated me, but they knew more about me than I knew about myself. It's marvelous what their intelligence force knew. From Amsterdam I was taken to the Frankfurt interrogation center and a few days later from there to Stalag Luft III in Sagan. I don't really know who or where the communications came from ,cause we had a briefing every week on how the war was going.

"We spent the summer and part of the winter in Stalag Luft III until the 29th of January 1945 when they moved the whole camp back towards Berlin because the Russian forces were coming in from the east. We walked for a couple of days and were then packed in box cars and shipped to Nuremberg. That wasn't a nice place to be for anybody because the British Royal Air Force came over at night time and bombed the Nuremberg rail yards, and our camp was relatively close to these yards.

"When General Patton was coming in from the west they decided to move us all again, down towards Munich. We ended up in Moosburg were we were liberated by Patton's troops. The next day Patton actually showed up in the camp. He came in his little fortified jeep, made a little speech and disappeared. We were left on our own on a small grass airfield and had no food for about three days. Then DC3's came and flew us to Nice in France. We then went by train to Camp Lucky Strike near Le Havre on the French west coast and by ship to Southampton in England from where we boarded ship destination the States.

"After arrival in Boston we went to Fort Dix by train. I took another train to Albany and changed trains and went to Syracuse and I picked up a Greyhound bus in Syracuse and down old Route 11 to my Aunt's house.

"I only weighed 140 pounds when I got out of the POW camp. It took me a couple of months to get back to about 160 which was a good weight for me.

"I was the first electrical apprentice in the City of Binghamton under the GI Bill. I then read about the Bliss Electrical School, in Maryland just outside the district in Washington and I looked it up and this was a well-known electrical school. I went there five days a week, eight hours a day, for many months. After I had finished I immediately got a job in Syracuse with GE. That didn't work out quite well so I got another job with Westinghouse in east Pittsburgh where they made motors and generators. I worked there for several months but the union was very strong there, in fact I call it pink, and one day they decided to close the plant down so I said heck that would be a good time to go home and that's what I did.

"I had put an application with IBM. They were starting up a new program at the time and they wanted about fifteen or sixteen local men, they didn't mention women at that time, and it was a training program that lasted about a year. We worked half time in the factory where they built the machine and we spent the other half day in a classroom. We were well-trained Customer Engineers at the time.

"I ended up at Washington, DC where I met my wife Juanita. We met in the laundry room of the apartment building that we were in and she was working as a secretary to one of the American railroads. She came actually

F/O Edward Knowlden later in life

from Johnson City so we went there and got married. Some time later the twins were born.

"I was pensioned after 30 years with IBM. I bought a little beat up cottage up on Oneida Lake and had a fairly good sized boat with it.

Edward's daughter, Judy Wilbur, recalls:

"Dad was able to visit me when my ex-husband and I lived in Germany. During the visit we and my parents traveled to the Netherlands. Standing near the ocean my Dad announced that he was rescued near where we were – I never knew he was shot down over the North Sea until then.

Ball-Turret Sgt. Robert L. Johnson

was a replacement for George Schneider who had been with the crew since their training days in Texas. George recalled in an interview;

"The crew was assigned to the 94th Bomb Group and arrived in Great Britain in April 1944, just two months before the invasion of Normandy. The pilot, Joseph McClurkin, who was nicknamed "Mac," led his crew on several training missions.

"We were on our last training mission and I started to feel sick. I told Mac on the intercom that I was feeling pretty bad. A couple of the fellows pulled me out of the turret and put me in the radio room and Mac headed back to the base.

"Schneider had the flu. The flight surgeon grounded him the next day when his crew flew their first combat mission in a factory-fresh B-17 so new they hadn't had time to give it a name. "They knew it wouldn't be much of a mission, so they didn't even replace me on the crew," Schneider said during a post war interview.

"Although he was still sick the next day - April 29 - when the second mission was planned, Schneider went to the crew briefing. The flight surgeon refused to let him fly and the crew received a replacement for Schneider – a spare gunner who had only a few more missions to fly before he could go home. "His name was Robert Johnson, and I went out to the plane with him," Schneider said. "He was really glad to be going because he was in a hurry to get back to the States."

"The plane took off with the rest of the group. Schneider found out later in the morning that their destination was Berlin in a raid that was the greatest air in battle of the war at that time.

"They didn't come back," George said. "Some fellows from intelligence came by later to tell me that they had been shot down and that everyone had been killed." .

"When Schneider recovered from the flu, he tried to join other crews as a replacement. He had no luck, he believes, because the tide of the air war against Germany was changing as an ever-increasing number of fresh crews and aircraft arrived from the United States.

"He also was depressed. He had trouble putting the memory of his crew out of his mind. "You don't train with men that long without becoming close to them," he said. "I had a hard time dealing with it."

"He finally wound up on a ground crew where he put his size - 5-foot-6 - to use climbing into tight spaces to repair battle-damaged bombers. He never flew a combat mission.

***

Acknowledgements;
Edward J. Knowlden, veteran
Judy Wilbur, daughter of Edward Knowlden
Bob Knowlden, son of Edward Knowlden
Margaret Hadsel, interview with Edward Knowlden.

CHAPTER 9

95ᵀᴴ BOMB GROUP
336ᵀᴴ BOMB SQUADRON

Type: B-17G • Serial: 42-37988 "Flagship"
MACR: 4470 • Air Base: Horham

B-17, # 42-37988, piloted by 2Lt. John W. Vilberg, was seen to leave the formation on way back from attacking Berlin, Germany. When last observed the aircraft was under control and no attempt was made to abandon this ship.

Missing Air Crew Report 4470

Pilot: 2Lt. John W. Vilberg, 0-753825, POW, Mt. Horeb, WI

Co-Pilot: 2Lt. Victor D. Ennis, 0-815112, POW, Wilmington, DE

Navigator: 2Lt. Adrien E. Caignon, 0-708792, POW, Woodside, NY

Bombardier: 2Lt. William V.P. Weston, 0-757581, POW, Philadelphia, PA

Engineer: S/Sgt. Ralph R. McLeod, 38413175, POW, Hannibal, MO

Radio: S/Sgt. Peter P. Pollreis Jr., 37461373, POW, Omaha, NE

Ball-Turret Gunner: Sgt. James F. O'Neil, 31286550, POW, Springfield, MO

Left Waist-Gunner: Sgt. Vernon W. Albares, 35584971, POW, Minneapolis, MN

Right Waist-Gunner: Sgt. Louis C. Isaac, 18111544, POW, Monongahela, PA

Tail-Gunner: Sgt. Glenn D. Gregory, 35793097, POW, Cincinnati, OH

10 POW

Crash Site: 13 miles w. of the Steinhuder See, Germany
Time: 11.00

95th Bomb Group, 336th Bomb Squadron (Vilberg)

Back row (left to right): Pilot 2Lt. John W. Vilberg, Co-pilot 2Lt. Victor D. Ennis, Bombardier 2Lt. William V.P. Weston, Navigator 2Lt. Adrien E. Caignon

Front row: Radio S/Sgt. Peter P. Pollreis Jr., Tail-Gunner Sgt. Glenn D. Gregory, Engineer S/Sgt. Ralph R. McLeod, Ball-Turret Gunner Sgt. James F. O.Neil, Right Waist-Gunner Sgt. Louis C. Isaac, Left Waist-Gunner Sgt. Vernon W. Albares

Pilot 2Lt. John W. Vilberg.

"I was born in a little town, Mt. Horeb, about 20 miles from the Capital city of Wisconsin, Madison. My parents were from Norway. Wisconsin became a state in 1848 so was being settled by emigrants around that time. My father came under an agreement to work on a farm which he did but then shifted to other occupations. He married and they had two sons and one daughter, who died in her infancy. His wife died and he married my mother, who was younger than he, and had three sons, me being the youngest. Interestingly, my oldest half-brother served in Europe in the first war and me in the second. My two half-brothers also had one son each that served in the second war and were both killed in the Japan action.

"Back to me, I graduated from the University of Wisconsin in 1937, went to work for a pubic accounting firm in New York City. They transferred me to their Milwaukee office after a year where I stayed until about three years later when

I took a job in the auditing operations of the Detroit Ordinance District of the War Department. From there I signed up under an aviation cadet program that the Army had and spent three years in the Air Corps, of which the last was in a POW camp.

"After I got married we moved back to Mt. Horeb to assist in taking care of my ailing parents and eventually went to work for the State of Wisconsin Insurance Department first on regulating Welfare and Retirement Funds but after the Federal government took over that function and prohibited the states from doing so I was then in charge of the Consumer Complaint section of the Insurance Department and eventually retired from that job.

"My wife was employed by the University for many years but decided she would like to have a embroidery store in our little town of Mt. Horeb specializing in counted stitchery which was beginning to be very popular in the US and had always been a type of stitchery in the Scandinavian countries. I should mention that Mt. Horeb, where I grew up was primarily populated by families of Norwegian blood. As a matter of fact the church which I grew up in, Lutheran, had services in the Norwegian and English languages during my youth. We made many trips to Europe, particularly to the Scandinavian countries, to both visit with my relatives there and also to purchase merchandise for my wife's store.

"My father came from a farm near the Oslo airport while my Mother came from a town in the way north of Norway. We made many visits to both areas. We also went to Nuremberg, Germany, a few times as I was especially interested in what happened to the city I had watched, from a POW camp, the British bombing at night and the US by day continuously with the whole place apparently on fire.

"We sold the store and eventually our house in Mt. Horeb and bought a Condo in Miami where our oldest son lived. We weren't fond of Miami: particularly the hot, humid summer temperatures so in the summer joined our middle son and his family who lived in Pennsylvania at that time. Both he, Tom, and his wife worked so we took care of their two daughters and general housekeeping.

"We eventually sold our condo in Miami, bought a cabin near Clarion, PA where my son teaches at the University and, at the time, his wife also worked there. My wife's health failed and she died in 1999 and I eventually moved to an apartment in Clarion. Then my back gave out but after rehabilitation efforts I am in pretty good shape for a 98 year old guy. I'm at an assisted living place, Highland Oaks, which has about 35 residents many of which have a dementia condition but not all of us have that problem - at least not yet. So that's me."

Co-Pilot 2Lt. Victor D. Ennis

Victor entered the Air Corps in 1943, earning his wings at Columbus, MS, in November 1943, and took advanced training at Avon, FL, going overseas in March of 1944. He was shot down on his second mission, April 29, 1944 and became a prisoner of war in Germany for a year, being freed by Patton's army on April 29, 1945, at Moosburg, Germany.

In 1947 he graduated from the Ford Merchandising School a Detroit, Michigan. He passed away on February 25, 1955.

Right Waist-Gunner Sgt. Louis C. Isaac.

His son Jim Isaac wrote;

"My dad – who went by his middle name Cal - was born in Monongahela, PA on February 11, 1924. His parents were Aaron Reese and Ethel G. Isaac. Reese was a WWI veteran - having served in France. Prior to WWI Reese also served in the campaign against Pancho Villa on the U.S.-Mexico border.

"Dad graduated from Monongahela (Mon City) High School, class of 1942. He did some training at Boeing in Seattle…also in Kingman, AZ…before heading over to England.

"My dad never talked much about his time as a POW…except to say that the German Sgt. in his prison camp was a lot like the character Sgt. Schultz from the 60's TV show "Hogan's Heroes." He said the Germans were not inhumane…but that certainly the conditions were not comfortable by any stretch. Another Mon City buddy of his, Al Bartoe, also was a POW in Dad's prison camp.

"After the war my dad came back home for a while…and a few years later re-enlisted and was sent to Korea as part of the CID.

"After Korea he came back home for good. Cal got his college degree at Indiana University of Pennsylvania and worked as a bank branch manager for Western Pennsylvania National Bank (WPNB) – later known as Equibank. He married Gay Smith and had four children. Cal was a member of Toastmaster's International and the Finleyville Lion's Club.

"Dad was diagnosed with leukemia when he was only 44. He also suffered from asthma and his physical activities were limited for that reason. He enjoyed watching my brothers and me play Little League baseball…and he liked watching the local softball teams as well.

"Dad was just a straight up, stand up kind of guy. He was much respected, well-liked, solid through and through. He taught us values, respect, right from wrong, and to be responsible for our actions.

***

Acknowledgements;
Veteran John W. Vilberg
Jim Isaac for right waist-gunner Louis C. Isaac

CHAPTER 10

95TH BOMB GROUP
412TH BOMB SQUADRON

Type: B-17G • Serial: 42-31320 "I'll Be Around"
MACR: 4469 • Air Base: Horham

The B-17, # 42-31320, piloted by 1st Lt. Earl L. Leaser, was seen to be hit by flak in the Dummer Lake region en route out from an attack on Berlin, Germany. The # 2 engine was feathered and the aircraft peeled off to left and followed behind. This engine was started again but aircraft continued to drag back under control. There was no fire or smoke. The ship was last seen near Lingen, Germany still coming home. No chutes were seen to leave aircraft.

Missing Air Crew Report # 4469

Pilot: 1Lt. Earl L. Leaser, 0-798314, POW

Co-Pilot: 2Lt. Kenneth Broden, 0-755511, POW

Navigator: 1Lt. Raymond C. Moeller, 0-692331, POW

Bombardier: 1Lt. Howard Erricson, 0-739417, POW

Engineer: T/Sgt. Ralph E. Wildman, 15382594, POW

Radio: T/Sgt. George H. Wright, 13157961, POW

Ball-Turret Gunner: S/Sgt. William F. Miller, 13097970, POW

Left Waist-Gunner: S/Sgt. William P. Glass, 35512653, POW

Right Waist-Gunner: S/Sgt. Owen R. Irby, 38444572, POW

Tail-Gunner: S/Sgt. Joseph T. Hollamon Jr., 3841558, POW

10 POW

Crash Site: North Sea west of Haamstede, Holland
Time: 14.41

95th Bomb Group, 412th Bomb Squadron (Leaser)

Back row (left to right): Waist-Gunner S/Sgt. Bill Glass, Bombardier 1Lt. Howard Erricson, Ball-Turret Gunner S/Sgt. Bill Miller, Engineer T/Sgt. Ralph Wildman, Tail-Gunner S/Sgt. Tex Hollamon, Radio T/Sgt. George Wright

Front row: Right Waist-Gunner S/Sgt. Owen Irby, Pilot 1Lt. Earl R. Leaser, Co-Pilot 2Lt. Ken Broden, Navigator 1Lt. Ray Mueller

Pilot 1Lt. Earl L. Leaser.

An interview by David Venditta of *The Morning Call*, November 11, 1999.

"I was born and raised in Greenawalds, PA, and graduated from South Whitehall High School in 1938. I had a job in Allentown when America entered WWII. I worked at Arbogast & Bastian and became very familiar with an individual names Charlie Mack. He evidently wanted to fly ever since he was 3 feet high, so he talked me into going down to Philadelphia to try to get into the Naval Air Corps. We went down there but found out it would be impossible to do, because you needed two years of college. Neither of us had that, so we checked on the Army Air Force, and they wanted two years of college or the equivalent. So we boned up and went to night school, and after going there we took the test, and we both passed. The traveling physical board came down to 5th and Hamilton Streets, and would you believe it? I passed the physical and he didn't. That really hurt him. The thing he couldn't pass was the depth-perception test. That's what washed him out

"After getting my commission and pilot's wings, I asked to be in twin-engine light bombers, and I got it. I lucked out, because you don't often get what you ask for. So I flew the A-20 Douglas and had just cracked 50 hours in it when a wire came in, saying all twin-engine pilots with 50 or more hours will go to four engines. I started sweating out what type of an airplane I was going to get, a B-17 or B-24. I wanted the B-17. I had heard stories about the punishment it could take. The B-17 is what I got. I went through the training and got over to England in 1944. I was with the 412th Bomb Squadron, 95th bomb Group.

"My 19th mission came on the 29th of April, and it was a big one over Berlin. We weren't even supposed to fly on that particular mission, but there was a crew that had gone through more fighter attacks and flak than we had, and they were not in the kind of condition that we were, so the squadron commander asked if we would fly that day. The plane we took was called "I'll Be Around."

"We got all the way in over Berlin and dropped our bombs, but is wasn't thirty seconds later going to get back that we got a direct hit in engines No. 1 and 2 on the left side. It knocked them both out. We could still fly, but at about 28,000 feet, we couldn't hold our altitude with two engines. We were dropping down. There was no problem, though, because there were escort fighters out there, P-47 "Thunderbolts," and a couple of them stayed with us. There wasn't too much talk on the intercom, but there was no doubt in our mind that we were getting back to England. The thing was, would be get back to our base or have to land at another base?

"We started to throw things out of the airplane to lighten the load as much as possible. The gas was going down on the right side, so we decided to transfer fuel from the left to the right. As the fuel transfer started, we watched but nothing was happening to the fuel instruments. The level remained the same for the left and didn't increase for the right. We tried everything, with the exception of going out and hauling it across with a bucket. Evidently it was a lucky hit. It must have gotten the fuel transfer line as well as the engines.

"It became apparent that we were not going to get back to England. We just kept flying the airplane until we were completely out of fuel, and then we ditched just about where the North Sea and the Channel merge.

"It's amazing as to what happened in the ditching. We had read about it in a book, and everything that was in the book happened. They told you that when you hit the water, it's as if you've gone underneath the water, then all of a sudden, you're back out of the water and you skip, and then you have another bounce, and then the airplane kind of settles in. It worked just that way.

"Also, you practised getting out of the airplane after every mission. It was an orderly procedure, because sometimes there were three or four people who went out of one exit. The airplane could have gone down in two minutes and we all would have been out. But it stayed floating eighteen minutes.

"The only casualty was the radio-operator, who panicked. He couldn't swim, and he wanted to get out before it was his turn. Somebody pushed him down and stepped on his nose and it hurt him pretty much, but that was the only injury.

"We had two dinghies and life preservers that we wore. With all the flak we took, there were holes in one of the dinghies, so we put four crewmen in that one and six in the other and connected the dinghies with a rope. We weren't in the water more than 45 minutes when a couple of P-47's buzzed us. They left after a while, and a twin-engine Lockheed Hudson with a boat on the bottom arrived.

"The procedure was they would make a run and drop a smoke pot to check the wind drift. They would drop the boat from upwind, and it would float in to you. After dropping the smoke pot, the Hudson made a wide sweep and came across again, so we figured, now the boat is coming. But no boat. The next thing, they left. This was in the afternoon. We went through the night.

"In the morning, P-51 Mustangs buzzed us. We had drifted in close to the shore, and the German shore batteries were firing at the P-51's, so the planes didn't stay out too long. Later we saw a boat coming towards us and as it got closer, we saw it was German, similar to a Coast Guard cutter. We had been in the water about 24 hours, and I had almost frozen feet and couldn't walk.

"The Germans took us through Holland to an interrogation center called Dulag Luft near Frankfurt in Germany. They separated me and the three other officers from the six airmen. I was interrogated by a German first lieutenant who probably spoke better English than I did. He had been a pilot flying at the Russian front, was knocked down and hurt, so they made an interrogator out of him. I was interrogated three different times. They always told what they could do to you. If you didn't talk – they would shoot you – but at that time it was name, rank and serial number.

"The first two times he opened his drawer and there were Chesterfields, Lucky Strikes, Camels, and he blew smoke in my face continuously. I just told him it didn't bother me, because I wasn't smoking then. What he was trying to do was, if I was a smoker, this would get me to want cigarettes, and maybe I'd do almost anything for one. And then he said, "Well, if you're not talking to me, let me show you something." He reached behind me and got a big book out and started paging through it, and he came to the 95th Bomb Group and went a few pages past it, and he said, "I missed your outfit, didn't I?" So he paged back to the 95th Bomb Group. It almost knocked my socks off. They had the squadron commanders' names. They had a picture of the airfield, where the airplanes were parked, and they actually had tail numbers.

"The interrogator told me. "It's too bad the Americans and Germans can't get together and take on the Russians. There's no doubt in my mind who's going to win the war." And he pointed to me, "The United States will win, and England. You're going to fight the Russians."

"I was taken to a camp near Berlin, Stalag Luft 3. I never had any physical mistreatment. The only thing I went through was lack of food, the same thing most everybody went through.

"Starting off, there were American, British and Canadian Red Cross Parcels. You were supposed to get a parcel a week, then it was a parcel every two weeks, then a parcel a month. Finally we didn't get any more parcels.

"At first, trying to escape was a big sport. The Germans considered it a big sport, too. Then it got to the point where it said, "If you try to escape and we catch you, we're going to shoot you."

"The first night of the Battle of the Bulge, the Hauptmann of the camp started screaming throughout the compound, "Now the Allies have had it! Germany is on the march!" And that was a low point. But I don't think there was any doubt who was going to win the war, and morale was so high that even though you were there, you thought you'd get out, that you'd make it.

"When they moved us out, it was December and we were heading towards Nuremberg. We marched most of the way and were in boxcars part of the way. It was cold, we were tired. I vowed then that I would never, ever complain about the heat – and I never have. That month I turned 24. We were liberated on April 29, 1945, exactly a year after we ditched "I'l Be Around."

***

Earl Leaser returned to the States, got married and made the Air Force his career, including a stint as commander of Travis Air Force Base in California. After he was in the service 25 years, Lockheed – the maker of the plane that somehow failed to rescue him and his crew – offered him a job. But he turned the company down to work in the Pentagon as chief of the airlift division. He passed away on June 8, 2010 age 89, in Whitehall. His obituary reads; "During his tenure, he also served during the Korean War and the Vietnam War. He was a graduate of the Naval War College in Newport, RI. His last assignment was Director of Air Lift operations at the Pentagon, retiring in 1972."

Engineer T/Sgt. Ralph E. Wildman

By daughter Joyce (Wildman) Robbins.

"These are Ralph Edward Wildman's notes that he wrote when the doctors told him that he had bone cancer and needed to go home and get his affairs in order. He was encouraged by his wife, Betty Marie, to write about the good memories of his life. As his daughter, Joyce Ellen (Wildman) Robbins, I will try to translate some of the details that he put into print.

"Ralph Edward Wildman was born July 30, 1923, when they lived on a farm one mile south of Newtown, Indiana. He was the son of Fenton and Pauline (Greve) Wildman. There were many good memories on this farm. At four or five years old, everything seemed big and beautiful. Dad would stand on the barnyard gate and watch his dad come in from the fields each day. Grandpa had a team of big white horses and Dad liked watching the dust fly up in big clouds from their feet hitting the ground.

"Grandma taught the five girls good housekeeping and how to cook. Grandpa taught the five boys how to farm and fix any of the machinery, as well as good livestock breeding. In a few years the farm was the second highest producing farm in Fountain County. Dad said that when they were working with the mules in the field and the fire siren at Newtown blew at noon, the old mules would stop and not go another round; the boys had to go in for lunch.

"The summer that dad was sixteen, he sold his dairy cow and bought a 1929 four-door Ford. He was the only one to have a car, in his class, that year. The summer between dad's junior and senior year, he had an ice route. Grandpa helped him set up his ice route, like the one grandpa had a few years before. After the electric refrigerators came out, grandpa bought grandma one. Then they stored a lot of their tools in the old ice box.

"December 1942, dad enlisted in the Air Corps and basic training was at Miami Beach, Florida. After basic training dad was shipped to Amarillo, Texas, where he took airplane mechanic school training. He was grateful that his dad had showed him this kind of work on the farm. After graduating he was told that he had a choice of gunnery school or cook school. He knew how to slop hogs, but didn't want to cook, so he got to fly after all. He took his first phase flying at Moses Lake, Washington and this is where they picked up the crew that he would spend the rest of his Air Force time with.

"Moses Lake is where he picked up his nickname; "Daddy." He got up each morning at 6:00 a.m. on the farm and this habit carried over and he didn't need an alarm clock. There was only one time it was hard to get one of the boys up. It was cold and as he passed this guy's cot, dad took all of his bed covers with him.

"My mother's birthday was in October and he didn't know if they were going to get to go on a furlough, so dad sent her money so she could buy herself a cedar hope chest. They did get the furlough and he gave her an engagement ring while home.

"Mother said that she would try to come out to see dad before he went overseas. He told her that if she did, she would not go home single. They were married December 23, 1943, in Soux City, Iowa. Dad's radio man, George Wright and his wife from Pennsylvania, stood up with them. George and Jo had just gotten married the week before.

"Christmas morning, two days after the wedding, the crew had to pick up two planes in Nebraska. They didn't get to have Christmas dinner with their wives. They would put five men on each plane. After picking up the planes, they headed for Goose Bay, Labador. After a couple days there, they took off for England. After taking off, one of the generators regulators quit working. Dad had to ground the plane, because all things had to work before they could cross the water. They were ready to leave for England again, but was held back, because someone with a childhood disease, brought a quarantine; another week.

"They took off and landed at Nuts Corner, Ireland, 8 ½ hours later. The next day they went by boat from Belfast to Liverpool, England. They then took a train to their base at Horham, England.

"March the 4th was the real first daylight raid over Berlin in 1944. Dad said, "How well he could remember. That was his first mission. That was also his mother's birthday and she was 44."

***

"Berlin, Saturday, April 29, 1944. The day they went down a shell had gone through the number 2 engine, taking the left landing gear with it. With only two engines, the pilot was having a hard time holding the plane at 6,000 feet. Dad told the crew to throw out all the guns, flack suits, and ammunition to make the plane lighter. The pilots handled the plane very well as it hit the water at 90 miles per hour. All but the pilots set on the floor in the radio room, with their backs to the bomb bay door. Dad was last in line, which put him over the camera hatch. Being the lead plane, they had the camera with them. When they hit the water, the water came through the hatch and dad went up in the air and came down on the radio table. When he got up he pulled the two levers that inflated a rubber raft on each wing.

"The raft that the officers were in had a few flak holes in it. It turned over and dumped them into the very cold North Sea. Dad said that he didn't think he would get his breath back. The pilot was the last to get back into the raft, froze his feet and they had to help Leaser walk for two days.

"The S.O.S. had been picked up and two P-51s circled over them and relayed their location to the rescue group in England. The Germans fired at the P 51s and one got hit, but it didn't bring it down. The Germans came out and picked them up off the coast of Holland. Dad said that there were acres and acres of beautiful tulips in bloom.

"Dad weighed 180 pounds the day they were shot down and he weighted 111 pounds when liberated. He was a tall 6 foot man, I can't even imagine how gaunt he must have looked. He received his discharge October 15, 1945. The folks lived a mile south of Newtown, where dad had lived from 8 years old until he went to the service. Their first child, Joyce Ellen, was born while living there.

"Mother had saved up her allotment checks and Dad's back pay for the year in POW camp, so they were able to start up farming on a small scale. They bought the farm at Smartsburg, Indiana, that belonged to my grandparents.

"Joyce was their only daughter and Fredrick Karl (German spelling) was their only son. He was born in Crawfordsville September 22, 1947. When they moved to Crawfordsville, giving up farming, mother's dad, Grandpa Dawson, gave dad his first job; Dawson and Sons Roofing and Building. Dad later went to R.R.

Donnelly Printing until he broke out with ink allergies. Dad had worked in grain mills, but most of his life was in construction; remodeling old homes and building new ones.

"When he bought a new 1969 Grand Prix Pontaic, he cut the top of the steering wheel off, so it would look like the ones they had on their B-17 Flying Fortress.

"After we kids were gone from home the folks traveled a lot. They went to San Francisco. At noon one day they met Diane Leaser (Dad's pilot's daughter) for lunch. She took them to a quaint Italian restaurant. By this time Earl and Gerry Leaser had been transferred to Washington D.C. Another trip was out east where they visited Earl and Gerry Leaser. Earl was still stationed in the Pentagon. They took the folks on a tour of the Pentagon and they got to sit in Earl's big chair in his office. Before Earl went to Washington D.C., he was commander of Travis Air Force base in California.

"August 16, 1989, is the end of dad's notes and the last paragraph says: "Here is wishing everybody many more beautiful days like today. May all of our grandchildren raise their children the way God would have them to be."

"Ralph Edward Wildman died September 17, 1994 and Betty Marie (Dawson) Wildman followed him in death on September 27, 1998. They are buried together in the new Crown Hill Cemetery south of Crawfordsville, Indiana U.S.A

Left Waist-Gunner S/Sgt. William P. Glass.

By daughter Kay Gunsolly.

"William "Bill" Glass was born November 30, 1920 in Frazeysburg, Ohio, to Robert and Frances (Orr) Glass. His father worked in the oil fields pumping wells in Central Ohio. Bill entered the Air Corps on September 23, 1942 and met Lily Pedersen while stationed at the base in Sioux City, Iowa prior to being deployed to war.

"After being discharged from the Service October 27, 1945, Bill returned to Ohio and sent for Lily and they were married. They returned to a small town near Sioux City, Iowa called Lawton where he farmed land owned by his wife's father. They had two children together Daniel and Kay.

Left Waist-Gunner S/Sgt. William P. Glass and wife Lily

"After farming for four years, Bill and his family moved to Bladensburg, Ohio where Bill worked in the oil fields pumping wells until the couple divorced 13 years later. He then married his 2nd wife, Betty.

"The couple moved to Las Vegas, Nevada where Bill worked on a government project at a test facility in the desert. After that, he worked as head of security at the Stardust Casino. After his 2nd wife passed, he moved back to Bladensburg, Ohio until his death on September 23, 2009. Bill was an avid fisherman and hunter. He had a cabin on Lake Mead until the Hoover Dam acquired the land and it had to be demolished. He went horseback riding with friends in the mountains in Pennsylvania to hunt for moose.

"Bill's children remembered their Dad bringing home animals to skin that he had hunted – turtles, deer, frogs, fish, etc. His daughter asked him several years later about his experiences in the war, but he refused to talk about them as was the case when he was asked by other family members. Basically, all he shared was the hunger the POWs experienced.

***

Acknowledgements:
Pilot Earl L. Leaser; An interview by David Venditta Of The Morning Call,
Joyce Robbins, daughter of engineer Ralph Wildman,
Kay Gunsolly, daughter of waist-gunner William Glass

CHAPTER 11

303ᴿᴰ BOMB GROUP
427ᵀᴴ BOMB SQUADRON

Type: B-17G • Serial: 42-31241 "Spirit of Wanette"
MACR: 4463 • Air Base: Molesworth

Howard J. Bohle, received a direct flak hit in the Nos. 3 and 4 gas tanks.
The tanks were punctured and considerable gas was lost. The aircraft
skidded out of formation, jettisoned its bombs and feathered the No. 3
prop. 2Lt. Bohle tried to get back into formation, but turned away when
he realized that his B-17 had a gas leak. Lt. Robert Kerr, copilot, later
recounted that the crew decided to head for neutral Sweden.

From Mission Report 144 of the 303rd Bomb Group

Pilot: 2Lt. Howard J. Bohle, 0-753184, POW

Co-Pilot: 2Lt. Robert R. Kerr, 0-815165, EVD, Chicago, IL

Navigator: 2Lt. John K. Brown, 0-699122, POW

Bombardier: 2Lt. Joseph J. Nevills, 0-684983, POW, St. Louis, MO

Engineer: S/Sgt. Laurence W. Rice, 32712289, POW, Jackson Heights, NY

Radio: S/Sgt. Henry J. Jensen, KIA, 39551854, Mcfarland, CA

Ball-Turret Gunner: S/Sgt. John A. Derschan, 39549202, KIA, Los Angeles, CA

Waist-Gunner: Sgt. Frank Gorgon, 16113758, KIA, Detroit, MI

Waist-Gunner: Sgt. Paul J. Mulhearn, 31303563, KIA, Milton, MA

Tail-Gunner: S/Sgt. Michael, Musashe, 16144401, KIA, Chicago. IL

5 KIA, 4 POW, 1 EVD

Crash Site: Oedegard, Denmark
Time: 13.29

303rd Bomb Group, 427th Bomb Squadron (Bohle)

Back row (left to right): Radio S/Sgt. Henry Jensen, Engineer S/Sgt. Laurence Rice, Tail-Gunner S/Sgt. Charley Brock, Right Waist-Gunner Sgt. Paul Mulhearn, Ball-Turret Gunner Sgt. John Derschan

Front row: Pilot 2Lt. Howard Bohle, Co-pilot 2Lt. Robert Kerr, Navigator 2Lt. John Brown, Bombbardier 2Lt. Joseph Nevills

From Mission Report 144

Howard J. Bohle, received a direct flak hit in the Nos. 3 and 4 gas tanks. The tanks were punctured and considerable gas was lost. The aircraft skidded out of formation, jettisoned its bombs and feathered the No. 3 prop. 2Lt. Bohle tried to get back into formation, but turned away when he realized that his B-17 had a gas leak. Lt. Robert Kerr, copilot, later recounted that the crew decided to head for neutral Sweden.

Pilot Howard Bohle tried to reach Sweden but as flak at the coast damaged the control cables and the no. 2 engine emitted black smoke the pilot ordered the crew to bail out. Unfortunately some crew members came down in the Baltic Sea and drowned. The tail-gunner was killed by flak and went down with the aircraft. Four bodies were recovered from the Baltic Sea on various dates.

On May 2 the body of radio-operator Henry Jensen was found in Grønsund Sound between the islands of Bogø and Møn. The body was handed over to the Wehrmacht. On May 8, 1944, Jensen was buried in the Svino cemetery. On May 18, 1944, the body of waist-gunner Paul Mulhearn was found in the Storstrømmen still with his parachute attached. The body was taken to the chapel of Gyldenbjerg church at Orehoved. He was buried by the Germans in the Svino cemetery. The body of ball-turret gunner John Derschan washed ashore in the Valse

Ball-Turret Gunner Sgt. John A. Derschan

Vig Bay. He was also buried in the Svino cemetery. On June 8, the body of waist-gunner Frank was found on Eno beach near Karrebaksminde and initially laid to rest in Svino.

The remains of Mulhearn, Derschan, Jensen and Gorgon were disinterred on May, 8, 1948 and were evacuated to the American cemetery at Neuville en Condron in Belgium by the US military where Gorgon still rests. His comrades have been brought back to USA.

Co-Pilot 2Lt. Robert R. Kerr.

Evaded capture by the Germans.

On May 13, 1944, he was interviewed by the US Military Air Attaché in Stockholm in neutral Sweden.

"This is the personal narrative of 2nd Lt. Robert R. Kerr, Co-Pilot, 0-815165, 303rd Bomb Group, 427th Bomb Squadron, B-17G, # 481. Departed England 07:00 hours, 29 April, 1944, to bomb the target Berlin, Germany.

"Heavy flak was encountered over the target area. A concentrated burst knocked out # 4 engine, and caused a severe gas leak in # 3 feeder tank. The pilot, 2nd Lt. Howard J. Bohle, feathered the engine, but the gas remaining was insufficient to return to England. He asked the navigator, 2nd Lt. John K. Brown for a heading to Sweden.

"The ship crossed the Baltic Sea and through a hole in the clouds land was seen. At the same time a ME 210 attacked the plane, but was shot down by the tail gunner. However, the German pilot evidently had radioed the ship's position to the ground flak batteries, for a barrage of flak was shot up. It was very accurate, hitting the plane square, jammed the stick in a fixed position, knocked out # 2 engine: the pilot could not recover control, so he ordered the crew to bail out. It was 13:00 hours, April 29, 1944.

"Before I left the ship I noticed the altimeter read 15,000 feet, so I waited about forty-five seconds before pulling the ripcord. I was directly over water, but drifting towards land and was able to aid my direction of descent by manipulating the shroud lines. Landed in an open field, about fifty yards from a farm house, where a young boy was watching my actions. Immediately after touching the ground I released the chute harness, gathered the equipment, placed my Mae West in the folds of the silk, and hid them in nearby bushes. I learned from the boy that I was in Denmark and that the Germans were close.

"I started to walk towards the wooded area, but before I reached it, a man on a bicycle approached, removed his hat and made signs of friendship. I told him that I was an American flyer. Speaking broken English he said that he would help me. I followed him by a back road to his home where I was given a a good meal and a bottle of beer. After the meal he told me to hide in the woods until dark, then he would return and do all possible to aid in my escape. His wife furnished me with candy, sandwiches and beer. I proceeded to the wooden area he indicated and hid. During the late afternoon I could hear the Germans searching, but they did not come near my hiding place. There were several German planes flying low in search also.

"The man and his wife returned at dusk with food, civilian clothing, and a bicycle. He rode with me to a nearby town, where we were met by another man on a bicycle. They escorted me to the village of Eskildstrup, to the home of a school teacher, where I stayed until Monday night. There was the question as to the best way for me to reach Sweden. At first the plans were to put be aboard a boat at Stubbekjobing, bribing the fisherman 4000 crowns. The money was obtained, and all arrangements made when word was received from Copenhagen to wait.

"Monday afternoon, May 1, 1944, a lady arrived from Copenhagen to accompany me there. I left all me flying clothing, escape kit, and equipment with the school teacher to be destroyed. We left that night and arrived at Copenhagen at 23:00 hours, making the trip without incident. Two men met us at the station, and took us to one of their homes, where I stayed until the night of May 9, receiving excellent treatment. I was in a position to observe many interesting things, and met influential people in the Danish underground.

"Tuesday morning, 9 May 1944, a man called and escorted me to the home of a friend, where I stayed until 02:00 hours, 10 May 1944, at which time we took a taxi to a rendezvous point at a harbor near the city. Here we were joined by nine Danes, six men and three women, who were also escaping. We boarded a small fishing boat, hid in various spots, then waited until daylight. At 06;20 hours the engines were started, and we proceeded cautiously from the harbor, avoiding German patrol boats and planes which were in the vicinity. At 10:00 hours we were in international waters, within sight of Malmo. We waited for the arrival of a Swedish fishing boat, which drew alongside at 11:00 hours. We transferred, arriving at Malmo 22:00 hours, 10 May 1944.

"We were taken to the police station, where I was separated from the Danes, interrogated, given a medical examination, and ration coupons. I was then taken to the American Consulate office.

"I departed Molmo for Stockholm Wednesday night, arriving there 07:58 hours, 11 May 1944. Lt. Herman F. Allen, of the Military Air Attaché office, met me at the station.

Bombardier 2Lt. Joseph J. Nevills.

By his daughter Judy Fiedler.

"My Dad, Joseph J. Nevills, Jr. was on his third mission. In the attempt to reach neutral Sweden his bomber came down over Denmark. Half the crew survived and half perished. My father sprained his ankles as he was wearing an ill-fitting parachute, which did not allow him to see his feet when he landed. The Germans captured him and three other crew members.

"After their capture, the men were sent by rail to their POW camp. My Dad spent the next year in two of these camps. Over the years, my father would tell some stories about his time behind barbed wires. He was not required to de physical labor, but starvation and boredom were with him daily. The prisoners received Red Cross parcels and my father would tell about how he would take one small M&M chocolate, bite it in half and save the other half for another day.

"During the winter of 1944-1945, he went on a forced march to another POW camp as the Russians were approaching from the East. This was extremely difficult and many prisoners perished because of the harsh weather and their poor health. He was liberated one year to the day that he was interned; April 29, 1945. General Patton arrived in their camp with sirens blaring from his jeep.

"Looking back, I think it was his spirit of independence and positive attitude that helped him endure the hardship and deprivation of this harrowing time.

***

He and my mother Helen had married shortly before he went into officer training and then overseas to battle. When he was shot down, my mother was pregnant with my sister Nancy. In fact, they chose the name Nancy because my dad had flown a mission over Nantes, France.

"When he returned to his home in St. Louis, he and my mother had to live with my Mom's family. With so many returning GI's, affordable housing was scarce. My Mom and dad and sister slept in the hallway of that home for a while.

"My father's first job was with one of the St. Louis newspapers in the advertising department. After working at the paper, he went on to build a very successful career in advertising sales, working for at least two advertising agencies. He traveled extensively throughout the Midwest and became a top salesman for both companies. In the meantime, he and my mom moved to the suburbs of St. Louis and raised a family of three children; my sister, Nancy, my brother Joe and me.

"In the mid 1960's my father started his own advertising agency. He continued to run this small business and renew customer accounts until he suffered a stroke in 1991.

"In 1977 my mother passed away, and a few years later my father met and married Jackie Potter from Rolla, Missouri. He was married to her for ten years, and after she passed, my father moved back to St. Louis where he lived with my sister Nancy and her husband, David.

"In his later years, my father continued to run his business and have an active social life – he met another woman, Rosemary Forchee, and his friendship with her lasted for another ten years. Although they did not get married, they were great companions and often enjoyed a night out dancing. My father was a great dancer – I think that kept him young at heart.

"In 2005, my father started another business venture with my husband Charles Fiedler. The company is the 303rd Engineering Group, named after his bombing group. The company is still in business today. Unfortunately, in 2009, at the age of 91, he suffered a stroke, which caused him to aphasia and partial paralysis. The aphasia made speech very difficult for my father who was always very verbal and had a way with words. Still he persevered and worked very hard to get his point across. Due to the effects of the stroke, he moved to a senior facility in St. Louis, and he lived there in his own apartment until he passed away in July 2013 at the age of 95. Up until the end – even despite the debilitating effects of the stroke – my father remained independent and maintained a very positive outlook.

***

Acknowledgements;
Judy Fiedler, daughter of 2Lt. Joseph J Nevills, bombardier

CHAPTER 12

303ᴿᴰ BOMB GROUP
427ᵀᴴ BOMB SQUADRON

Type: B-17F • Serial: 42-3158 "Max"
MACR: 4471 • Air Base: Molesworth

In the target area this bomber was straggling and enemy fighters attacked it. Aircraft # 42-3158 exploded in the air, and one parachute came out. This happened just before bombs away.

Missing Air Crew Report # 4471

Pilot: 2Lt. James H. Fisher, 0-753783, POW, Lindsey, CA

Co-Pilot: F/O George W. Franzen, T-123210, KIA, Jamestown, NY

Navigator: 2Lt. Harold F. Kauffman, 0-702444, KIA, Louisville. OH

Bombardier: S/Sgt. Ed Helton Jr., 15065402, KIA, Whitley City, KY

Engineer: S/Sgt. August H. Johnson, 17111104, POW, Lake Crystal, MN

Radio: S/Sgt. Donald K. Duncan, 38427372, KIA, Dallas. TX

Ball-Turret Gunner: Sgt. Robert L. Eklund, 37554963, KIA, Duluth, MN

Waist-Gunner: S/Sgt. Henry Hoff, 81039807, KIA, Holyoke, MA

Waist-Gunner: Sgt. Irving Bellitt, 32208988, KIA, Bronx, NY

Tail-Gunner: Sgt. Joseph J. Tercek, 19107874, KIA, Portland. OR

8 KIA, 2 POW

Crash Site: Schwielowsee near Caputh, Germany.

303rd Bomb Group, 427th Bomb Squadron (Fisher)

Back row (left to right): Engineer S/Sgt. August H. Johnson, Monfort (not on final crew), Radio S/Sgt. Donald K. Duncan, Tail-Gunner Sgt. Joseph Tercek, Waist-Gunner Sgt. Irving Bellit, unknown

Front row: Pilot 2Lt. James Fisher, Co-Pilot F/O George Franzen, Navigator 2Lt. Harold Kaufmann, Parker (not on final crew) "

Summary of the MACR;

"The bomber left the formation before reaching the target and was attacked by German fighters scoring hits between no, 3 and 4 engines. The plane exploded in mid-air and crashed in the Schwielowsee, west of Caputh, due sw of Berlin/ Potsdam. It is reported that all ten crew members bailed out. However, only two were taken prisoner.

"The body of Ed Helton was recovered from the lake 1100 yards nw of Caputh on May 20, 1944 and was buried in the cemetery of Caputh together with George Franzen and Donald Duncan. A German officer informed James Fisher that Franzen, Kauffman and Duncan were beaten to death by hostile civilians. All were later reinterred in the Ardennes cemetery and four are still buried there. Kauffman was returned to Ohio and Duncan to Texas. Robert Eklund and Robert Tercek could be individually identified and received a group burial in Custer Battlefield National Cemetery, Montana.

Pilot 2Lt. James H. Fisher.

"After flying three milk run missions, our fourth mission was to Berlin on April 29, 1944. We were hit by flak between no. 3 and 4 engines and had to feather no. 4. We were unable to keep up with the formation but did continue over the target and dropped our bombs.

"Shortly after leaving the target we were attacked by ME-109s. After being literally shot to pieces I gave the order to bail out. Only two of us survived. I must assume that the rest of the crew members were killed by the withering fire from the ME 109s. I was wounded; probably from fragments from the instrument panel after machine gun bullets shattered the panel. I was roughed up by civilians on the ground before German soldiers rescued me.

"After a short stop at Dulag Luft near Frankfurt, I went to Stalag Luft III near Sagan and remained there until the night of January 28, 1945 when we were marched out around midnight. After five days of marching in the snow and freezing weather, we reached Spremburg; there we were loaded onto "40 and 8" boxcars for a trip to Neremberg, arriving at February 5, 1944 where we were interned in Stalag XVIII D.

"I celebrated my wife's birthday on April 22, 1945 by crawling out from under a railroad trestle somewhere in the western part of Germany, and surrendering to a scout party of the US Army 45th Infantry Division. And "surrender" is exactly the word I mean, too.

"My companion in the adventure, John Maksymic and I were the first allied prisoners of war these American troops had encountered and they were taken no chances. They were all too aware of the kind of deadly tricks they would encounter from a desperate and resourceful enemy.

"The story of how we got to that railroad trestle began when Stalag Luft III was evacuated in January, 1945. The group I marched out with eventually wound up at an abandoned Italian prison camp in Nuremberg. This camp was a far cry from Stalag Luft III; it had open bay sheds for barracks, filthy and loaded with bed bugs and every kind of vermin known to mankind.

"While we were there we had front seats of the most spectacular sights I have ever seen. For fourteen straight days the Americans bombed during the day and the British bombed at night. From our vantage point about two miles from the rail yards, we could see it all, and it was spectacular.

"We felt relatively safe because the

Pilot 2Lt. James H. Fisher

224

bomber crews knew where we were and we also had some concrete slit trenches that had been made for outdoor latrines but had never been used. Admittedly we were a little apprehensive during the first American daylight raid through a thick overcast – we had never heard of radar-controlled bombing.

"We had been at Nuremberg about two months when the rumor started that the Gestapo was going to hold all officer personnel as hostages to be used to bargain with when the time came for them to surrender, which everyone knew was not too far off. The rumor got more believable when we saw some of the men in their long black leather coats in the Vorlager (outer camp) of the camp.

"Mac and I decided it was time to go, reasoning that we would rather die trying to to escape than to take our chances with the Gestapo. We picked a night when the British were bombing because on these nights all lights were out, including the sweeping searchlights on the guard towers. On the night of April 1 or thereabouts we managed to climb over the fences using a piece of siding from one of the latrines to walk over the coiled barbed wire between the fences.

"It was after about three weeks of walking at night and sleeping during the day that we arrived at the point under the railroad trestle.

"During this 21-day trek we were recaptured once. We walked right into a German scout post. I guess the Germans were as surprised as we were, and for reasons known only to God, they didn't shoot us. We were being marched back towards the interior by two German GI's, sleeping in barns at night and stopping for food along the way at farm houses in the country and at little home cooking cafes in the villages. It was while we were in one of these little cafes that Mac and I thought that our time had come. There was a sudden loud explosion and the building started collapsing around us. Needless to say, the Germans went one way and Mac and I went the other.

"After we got out of the building we ran to a wooded area just outside of town and from there watched two P-51 fighters strafe the little town with .50 caliber machine guns. The town was a motor pool and truck depot for the Germans, which they were out to destroy. And that they did, believe me!! It's only by the Grace of God that I am alive to-day. A few nights later we holed up under the railroad trestle and that was our ticket home.

"The American scouting party we surrendered to marched us back to their headquarters with our hands held high and there we stayed in the custody of the Military Police while they checked out our stories. In my case they contacted the 303rd Bomb Group in Molesworth, England who verified that Lt. James H. Fisher, serial number 0-753783, a B-17 pilot, had been shot down on April 29, 1944, was reported captured by the Germans and held at Stalag Luft III. When Mac's story checked out too, they treated us royally.

"After dining in their field kitchen on pork chops and cherry cobbler, we were given a little car that had been "field requisitioned" from a German civilian and were allowed to make our own way back. We were given directions to a field hospital where we were given a cursory physical.

"While waiting at the hospital, we met two pilots of some kind of small airplane that could handle short-field landings and take-offs. Their job was to pick up and return crew members of downed aircraft. They took us to Bruxelles where they had a building with four apartments all to themselves. They had found the the basement stacked with Deagram's 7-Crown, apparently left when the Germans evacuated. Three drinks and I passed out. While I was there I had my first ice-cream in more that a year.

"After we spent a day sightseeing in Bruxelles, the flew us to Paris, where we checked in with the American Command at Allied Headquarters. After we received $300 pay advance and a new outfit of clothing at the PX, we were allowed two days of sightseeing and entertainment, including the Follies. Then we proceeded to Camp Lucky Strike for the boat ride home.

Biography by daughter Linda Fisher:

"James Howard Fisher was born October 1, 1916, in Shawnee, Oklahoma. When he was seven they moved to Lindsay, California in a search for work for Harold, his father, a mechanic.

"When James Howard was 14 his father died, a victim of TB. His mother Rose worked in the Lindsay Ripe Olive Cannery for, I think, 40 years. My mother Doris Lundgren Fisher was staying with her when I was born because Daddy was already in basic training. Rose died in the late 60's, but her address was always listed as our "home."

"After high school Daddy went to college in Oregon or Washington for about six weeks and then quit. He then lived in Los Angeles driving a truck, doing a little boxing, playing on one of the big oil company's baseball teams, etc. Doris left the farm in North Dakota as soon as she turned 21 and went straight to L.A. where she was waitressing in a place Daddy frequented... 6 weeks later they were married in Las Vegas on the long 4th of July weekend, a match meant to be!

"After the war, Daddy got out and tried not very successfully to start a trucking company, and then my brother James Harold was born making us now a family of four. So, even though he never liked flying, Daddy went back into what was by then the United States Air Force for another, I think, 25 years. He flew nearly every bomber from B-17s to B-52s, and we were stationed all over the U.S. but never overseas. (In fact, until I was in graduate school, no one in our family was ever even up in a plane except obviously Daddy, although my brother joined the paratroopers so as not to be drafted and sent to Vietnam.)

"As Austin was the last place we were stationed (Bergstrom Air Force Base is now Bergstrom Airport.) and my brother stayed, our parents retired there. They were very active in their church, and they took trips to Europe, Israel, etc. and to almost every place I opened a new show (I am a costume designer.)... until Mamma started showing signs of Alzheimer's. She died in 2005, although she was gone to us many years before her heart actually stopped. Since then Daddy just waited until he could join her, never understanding why he didn't die right after her.

Bombardier S/Sgt. Ed Helton, Jr.

Ed Helton, Jr. was born September 1, 1923 in McCreary County, Kentucky. He went to high school in Berea, Ky. and joined the service right out of school. He was one of five brothers who served in WWII: Hoyt, Luther and Kenneth were in the Army, Stanley was in the Navy and Ed in the Air Force.

From Robert G. Stephens' "A Lost Heritage for a Changing People"

"Ed Helton Jr. enlisted in the Air Corps on January 13, 1941. He trained at Maxwell Field, Alabama and from there went to the Panama Canal. Then he was transfered to Trinidad, South America where he completed a flying course. He was then sent to Dutch Guiana, Surinam, South America. He passed the examination as a flyer. His name was on a list for those recommended to go to Officer's Candidate School.

"When his South American tour ended, Ed Helton, now a sergeant, came home on leave after three years in the Army. His next assignment was to the 317th Bomb Squadron in Walla Walla, Washington. He was assigned to a crew as a bombardier. The members of his crew were next found in England and all, including Edward Helton, Jr. received the "Air Medal" and "Oak Leave Clusters" awards. Ed, Jr. stated that his crew had successfully completed seventeen missions over Germany. He was the tail-gunner on his bomber, which was one of the most critical and dangerous positions to defend the plane.

"Mr. And Mrs. Ed Helton received a message from the War Department prior to 27 June 1944 that Ed Helton, Jr. was missing in action over Germany. The War Department wrote the crew of another bomber on the same mission had seen the bomber, on which Sgt. Helton was the tail-gunner, disabled and that they observed only one of the crew bailing out.

"Then on 29 August 1944 word was received from the International Red Cross in Germany that Sgt. Edward Helton, Jr. was officially dead. The German government confirmed his death, while in action over their homeland. There had been messages from parents of other crew members, stating that their sons were prisoner of war. Sgt. Helton was flying his twenty-ninth mission over enemy territory and would have had one mission to go before returning to the United States. He was regularly a gunner but on his last mission was a bombardier.

"He had flown five missions over Berlin. He was on some of the longest and toughest missions the Eighth Air Force ever made, including Marienberg, in Poland, Augsburg and Regensburg in South Germany. He had been awarded the Air Medal and three Oak Leave Clusters and had been recommended for the Distinguished Flying Cross. Edward Helton, Jr. was a true patriot. He volunteered many times for the hazardous mission that others found reason to ignore. His enthusiasm and spirit that flashed for a brief time in the sky over Germany, France and Poland has carried even to this day the generations of soldiers that have followed. He was a true hero of our times.

Ball-Turret Gunner Sgt. Robert L. Eklund

Memorial announcement in the *Duluth Herald*, June 29, 1945:

"Memorial services for Sgt. Robert Eklund, son of Mr. and Mrs. Oscar Eklund, missing in action over Germany in April, 1944, and later reported dead, will be held at 4 p.m. Sunday in Trinity English Lutheran church. The sergeant was the husband of Mrs. Jeanne Eklund."

Engineer S/Sgt. August H. Johnson.

From daughter Jeanne Sumnicht

"August Johnson was born on the family farm in Blue Earth County, Minnesota, on February 1, 1922. Augie went to the country school, a one room school house, until he completed 8th grade. He then went to work on the farm full time. His sister, Almeda, went to the high school in Lake Crystal, where she became best friends with Alice Jenkins. It was Almeda who introduced her big brother, Augie, to her best friend, Alice. My parents were married on October 27, 1943. Augie had joined the Army Air Corps after war was declared by President Roosevelt. (His brother, Arlo, served in the Navy at Pearl Harbor.) August and Alice were married while he was on leave. After the wedding, Alice went with her new husband to Ardmore, Oklahoma, where he received more flight training. When Augie was shipped to England, Alice returned to Minnesota where she worked in munitions plants throughout the war.

"When my father's plane was shot down over Berlin, he was able to parachute out, along with the pilot. His parachute stuck in a tree, and he hung there all night. That was probably fortunate, for he was captured by German soldiers and not civilians.

"Daddy was sent first to Nuremberg. He didn't arrive in Stalag 17B in Krems, Austria until late in the summer. Because he was the only soldier arriving at the camp at that time, with no other crew to vouch for him, the prisoners were very suspicious. It was when they found another soldier in the barracks who was from Mankato, Minnesota, only fifteen miles from Lake Crystal, that Augie was able to convince them that he was an American and not a spy planted by the Germans. This soldier was Harry Rudberg. Augie and Harry became very dear friends. After the war, Harry came to visit Augie. He later married Almeda, my father's baby sister, and my mother's best friend. Our two families remained very close.

"Life in the prison camp was hard, but my father said that he could not fault the soldiers who were asked to guard them, because they were serving their country, just as he was serving his. He also said that the war had one good outcome, giving him the best brother in law ever. When the war in Europe was ending, the Germans shut down the camp and marched the POWs across Austria to Germany.

"When they crossed into Germany I believe they were liberated by French soldiers. The POWs were put on a ship and sent back to the U.S. Daddy said they had food available 24 hours a day. The men were all extremely thin - my six foot father weighed 120 pounds - and they tried to fatten them up. Because he had no visible wounds, he was given a two week leave to visit my mom. He was on his way to California to serve in the Pacific Theater, when the bombs were dropped on Japan and the war was over.

"After the war, Augie returned to Lake Crystal. His father had sold the farm, since he had no sons to help him run it (the three oldest were married with families and Daddy and his brother were serving in the war.) So, Augie went to work in the grain elevator, the hardware store, the post office and the local power plant. Augie and Alice had three daughters, Judy, Jeanne, and Diane. In 1956 he moved the family to Albert Lea, Minnesota, where he worked as a government meat inspector with the United States Department of Agriculture until his retirement.

"My dad was a very dear man. Everyone loved him, because he loved everybody. I think that the experience of being a prisoner of war helped him appreciate the importance of friends and family more than anything. He loved being surrounded by people, and went out of his way to be with family almost every weekend after we moved away from Lake Crystal. I was always impressed that he could go through so much and not harbor any anger.

"At the age of 86 he fell and suffered a severe brain injury. We were in St. Mary's Hospital in Rochester, Minnesota when Daddy requested that Mother bring his album about the prison camp to the hospital so he could show it to the medical staff. I believe he knew at the time that he was not going to live much longer. But before he died, he could say one more time; "Look what I went through! And I survived." He died on August 20, 2008. Members of the American Legion and the Veterans of Foreign Wars filled the two front pews of the church, and he was given a 21 gun salute at the cemetery.

***

Acknowledgments:
Summary of the MACR – Jan Hey of he Netherlands
Pilot James H. Fisher, Story - American Ex-Prisoners of War.
Linda Fisher, daughter of pilot James H. Fisher,
Jeanne Sumnich, daughter of engineer August H. Johnson
Bombardier Ed Helton,from Robert G. Stephens' "A Lost Heritage for a Changing People"

CHAPTER 13

306ᵀᴴ BOMB GROUP
368ᵀᴴ BOMB SQUADRON

Type: B-17G • Serial: 42-31556
MACR: 4240 • Air Base: Thurleigh

At approximately 12:25 hours, near Magdenburg, Germany, Lt. Lutz was hit by flak. The cover of the right wing seemed to be stripped off. He peeled up over the lead, rolled over, and went down straight enveloped in flames. No chutes were observed.

Missing Air Crew Report # 4240

Pilot: 2Lt. Warren S. Lutz, 0-444564, KIA, Southampton, NY

Co-Pilot: 2Lt. Thomas W. Johnson, 0-815495, KIA, Deerfield, MA

Navigator: 2Lt. Edward P. O'Neill, 0-699234, KIA, Peoria, IL

Bombardier: 2Lt. James L. Knox, 0-747024, KIA, New Albany, MS

Engineer: S/Sgt. Warren J. Adams, 14096249, KIA, New Orleans, LA

Radio: S/Sgt. Joe D. Reed, 38464210, KIA, Okmulgee, OK

Ball-Turret Gunner: Sgt. Roy Y. Ward, 384304343, KIA, Fort Worth, TX

Waist-Gunner: Sgt. Aleck A. Lazek, 6952052, POW, Cameron, TX

Waist-Gunner: Sgt. Ray Y. Ward, 38430450, KIA, Fort Worth, TX

Tail-Gunner: Sgt. Charles H. Lux, 16139193, POW, Chicago Heights, IL

8 KIA , 2 POW

Crash Site: Hecklingen/Stassfurt, Germany
Time: 12.30

Waist-Gunner Sgt. Aleck A. Lazek.

"I was born on May 20, 1923 as Elias Kasper Lasek but Elias became Elick, pronounced like Aleck (as in Ellis). The sisters in the orphan home in Galveston gave me the name Aleck Andrew.

"Was born in the Marak community north-west of Cameron. Parents separated (never remarried) in 1925. The girls Edna and Molly Mae went to live with the Marak grandparents and the boys, Fred (7) and Aleck (2) went to live with the Lazek grandparents – all in the town of Cameron, all attending the same school and the same church there.

"Fred and I were rascallions, and Grandpa and Grandma Lazek could not control them 24 hours per day although "Dad" was home when not working. In August 1928 after a series of "incidents" the boys were placed in St. Mary Orphan Home in Galveston – a Providential move.

"The orphanage, all in all, was a very happy place in regard to spiritual, educational, recreational, sports and social activities. The boys had a class division system in boxing regulated by the big boys with fair, true sportsmanlike rules for all: little boys, middle-size boys and big boys. The years spent with the Sisters in Galveston were more than a spiritual blessing; the time there had a profound influence on the rest of my life. However, I would be amiss if I didn't mention the fact that I received an average of one spanking a week my entire stay there

"The idea of becoming a priest was becoming firmly implanted in my mind about this time. I was about a B to A student, participating in sports, fairly good in football, track. Fairly fast, did broadjump 21 feet.

"Grandfather was a great spiritual influence on me; every day morning and evening he would kneel down and recite his daily prayers. Here was a fellow who was a rough and tough cobbler and soldier in Balkan wars from the old country who came to America with Grandma and four children, cleared and farmed land and retired in 1925.

"I graduated from High School in 1939. After a short stint at Texas E & M entered the Air Corps. Randolph Field, Texas, played football there. Chanute Field IL (also instrument tutoring): then maintenance personnel at Ellington Texas: then instrument personnel at Midland AFB and San Angelo AFB (both bomber training schools). Then pilot training at Kelley Field Texas and Vernon, Texas. Dismissed. Laredo Gunnery School at Salt Lake City. Overseas training. Kearny, overseas departure. Prestwick, Scotland and finally 8th Air force, England.

"April 29, 1944, shot down coming back to England about ninety miles from Berlin after dropping bombs on that city. Upon landing after parachuting out of a B-17 I lifted my eyes up to heaven and thanked God! Obviously God had other plans for me; the priesthood, but I kept saying "No."

"Ended up at Stalag VII at Krens, Austria, practically on the Danube river. The morale was exceptionally good there. Activity as much as permitted; sports, card-playing, entertainment (music, plays, etc.) There were about 4000 GI's and about 60.000 Russian POWs there, but no fraternization with the Soviets allowed in April 1945. Since the Russian Army was only about sixty miles away - artillery flashed let us know - we went on a 150-mile march, ending up nearly in Innsbruck.

***

"The day of my Ordination and the day of my first Mass - were the two happiest days in my life. On the day of my Ordination, my mother and dad came together to be the first ones to receive my first Priestly Blessing, and the next day at my first Mass. The were the first ones to come up together again to receive Holy Communion. Remember; they had been separated thirty-five years!

Ball-Turret Sgt. Roy Y. Ward and Waist-Gunner: Sgt. Ray Y. Ward.

By cousin Janice Randolph.

Ball-Turret Sgt. Roy Y. Ward   *Waist-Gunner Sgt. Ray Y. Ward*

"The twin brothers were born on August 11, 1923, in Mansfield, Texas. Their parents were Newton Benjamin Ward and Nora Etta Ward. The twins were part of a family of 13 children (6 boys, 7 girls). They were number 11/12. Both graduated in 1941 from Polytechnic High School in Fort Worth, Texas.

"After graduation Ray worked in the warehouse of the National Biscuit Company and Roy as an apprentice pharmacist at Renfro Drug Store. Roy was smaller physically, but was the decision maker of the pair. Ray was the listener, and followed Roy's lead. The twins enlisted together in February 1943. Tests showed they had very high IQs so they were assigned to Air Corps. One of their older brothers, John Smithee Ward, was a Tech Sergeant in the 36th Infantry Division, 5th Army. This division was with the first troops that landed on European soil - Salerno, Italy on Sept. 9, 1943.

"The two brothers underwent training at Keesler Field, Mississippi, Lowry Field, Colorado, Kingman, Arizona, Salt Lake City, Utah, Sioux City, Iowa and Kearney, Nebraska. They arrived in England in the spring of 1944 and on April 29, 1944 – their third mission – they were killed over Germany.

"When their brother John learned of the death of his twin brothers, his captain called him in and offered to send him to a non-combat zone. He added that he considered John to be a key non-commissioned officer and if he would stay with his unit, he would give John the first furlough back to the States. John stayed with his unit until he was sent home.

"After the war one of the two sole survivors of the crew – probably Aleck Lazek - came to visit Nora and Benjamin. He told them that Roy the ball turret gunner took a direct hit. When the crew was told to abandon ship, Ray - after being told that Roy was gone - insisted on checking on him and also lost his life.

"Their older sister Lucille received a letter from Catholic Father John Heuschen dated July 23, 1946 informing the family that Roy was buried at Margraten, but that Ray was not. Roy's grave had been adopted by a Dutch family.

"Ray's and Roy's bodies were returned to Mansfield, Texas, USA for reburial in December 1948, just months after their father died. Dr. J.M. Price performed the funeral and told members of the family decades later that he saw Nora standing between the two caskets with the bodies of her boys - one hand on each casket - and pray, thanking God for giving her the gift of their lives for almost 20 years.

***

Acknowledgements;
Dennis Lazek, nephew of waist-gunner Aleck A. Lazek
Janice Randolph, cousin of gunners Roy and Ray Ward

CHAPTER 14

384TH BOMB GROUP
545TH BOMB SQUADRON

Type: B-17G • Serial: 42-102448
MACR: 4242 • Air Base: Grafton Underwood

April 29th, was a rare April morning in England in that the heavens were clear and the stars were shining brightly. As I was checking out my gun, I was whistling the song, "O What a Beautiful Morning." The thought occurred to me at that time, "why are you whistling, you may not come back from this mission."

Radio S/Sgt. Ralph C. Andrews Jr.

Pilot: 2Lt. James A. Bouvier, 0-813841, POW, Bristol, VT

Co-Pilot: 2Lt. Robert J. Green, POW, 0-753877, Irvington, NJ

Navigator: 2Lt. Harold F. Gantert, 0-703977, POW, Newark, NJ

Bombardier: 2Lt. Louis A. Silk, 0-754981, POW, New York, NY

Engineer: S/Sgt. Casimer J. Wagner, 16141960, KIA, Chicago, IL

Radio: S/Sgt. Ralph C. Andrews Jr., 14109029, POW, Atlanta, GA

Ball-Turret Gunner: S/Sgt. William Neal, 39130152, POW, Kentfield, CA

Waist-Gunner: S/Sgt. Jack H. King, 37651589, POW, Ottumwa, IA

Waist-Gunner: S/Sgt. John E. Jones, 39205908, POW, Bremerton, WA

Tail-Gunner: S/Sgt. Robert W. Morgan, 15334667, POW, Smithfield, KY

1 KIA , 9 POW

Crash Site: Stackelitz sw of Berlin, Germany.
Time 12.25

384th Bomb Group, 545th Bomb Squadron (Bouvier)

Back row (left to right): Engineer S/Sgt.Casey Wagner, Waist-Gunner S/Sgt. Jack King, Radio S/Sgt. Ralph Andrews Jr., Ball-Turret Gunner S/Sgt. William Neal, Waist-Gunner S/Sgt. John Jones, Tail-Gunner S/Sgt. Robert Morgan

Front row: Co-Pilot 2Lt. Robert Green, Co-Pilot LT Olson (not on final crew, Navigator LT Wacker (not on final crew, Bombardier: 2Lt. Silk

Pilot 2Lt. James A. Bouvier.

Lt. James Bouvier was assigned to the crew after they arrived at Graton Underwood. This was done to provide the crew with an experienced combat pilot. This change moved the previous pilot, Robert Green, to co-pilot, and the original co-pilot, Lt. Olsen to another crew.

Daughter Connie LaRose;

"My father was born in Starksboro, Vermont - a very small town about eight miles from Bristol. In those days, most births were home births. He was the third born of seven children, although the oldest died very young. The oldest son, Lawrence (Toot) Bouvier enlisted in the Army Air Corps at the same time as my father, and wanted to fly bigger planes, but he ended up flying small aircraft that were used for what I believe was "information gathering missions." I remember my mother once saying that the instructors had felt Toot was too reckless with his flying to be entrusted with a large plane.

"Dad graduated from Bristol High School. All stories I have ever heard indicate that my dad was an excellent student with a brilliant math mind. He wanted to go to college, but his family did not have the money to send him. I have heard many stories about his friends coming home from college on weekends to have my father help them with their trigonometry, calculus and other math work.

"I believe during the years of at least World War II, a man wanting to become an officer and pilot needed to have a college degree, but that requirement was waived during war time due to the need for so many additional pilots. The officer candidates, I believe, had to pass some entrance exams to qualify for enrollment in pilot training.

"After the war my Dad returned to Bristol, Vermont. It is a wonderful, small community to grow up in and raise a family. Most people still leave the keys in the car overnight in their driveways, and don't ever lock the doors of their homes. Bristol now has perhaps 3,200 residents, although up until about 15 years ago, that number was closer to 2,200. We have a volunteer fire department in town, and my father served in that for many years. All six of his sons serve or have served in the Bristol Fire Department. The oldest, Mark, was the Chief for many years. Six of his grandsons presently serve in the fire department. He was also a leader of our Bristol Recreation Club, and a proud member of American Legion Post #19.

"We were all raised Catholic, attending St. Ambrose Parish, and we never missed Sunday Mass. There was never much extra money for anything after paying bills and buying groceries for 11 people, but I fondly recall my parents taking us on picnics. We would all pile in the family station wagon, my mother would bring along some hamburger, a loaf of bread, and maybe some Kool-Aid to drink, and her big cast-iron skillet. Dad would build a small fire and mom would cook the burgers. We would never go farther than five - ten miles from home for our big adventure, but we all thought it was a great thing.

"At Christmas time - this would be after we were all grown and out of college and my parents began to have some extra money - my dad would always make a large donation to the area food shelf. He always told us that he knew what it was like to be hungry, and no one should ever have to feel that way.

Pilot 2Lt. James A. Bouvier

Navigator 2Lt. Harold F. Gantert

Daughter Debbie Ganter:

"My Dad was born in Newark, New Jersey on January 1, 1922. His early years were spent in Vermont, where I believe Walter, his father was from. His father died when my Dad was 10 years old and they moved back to New Jersey. He graduated from East Side High School in Newark in 1940. He took Home Economics and Secretarial courses. He often told me that he was the only boy in those classes, but felt that everyone needed to have those skills, men and women.

Navigator 2Lt. Harold F. Gantert

"He wanted to go to college, but did not have the money, so on Christmas Eve 1943 he joined the Air Corps. I often wondered why he choose Christmas Eve to join, but I never really asked.

Harold's story by Reverend Jeff Edwards and Sandra Bostwick

"On April 7th, 1944, Lt. Harold Gantert, a 22 year old United States Air Corps navigator from Newark, New Jersey arrived by plane at the air base in Grafton - Underwood, England, anticipating his first combat action in the allied fight against Nazi Germany. Four years earlier, German armies had invaded France, establishing military bases there. From these bases Germany routinely sent bombers across the English Channel to make strikes on England. Harold would be a part of the ongoing counter attack of the allied forces.

"A year earlier, Harold had kissed his mother goodbye at their home in Newark. Up until this point Harold had never traveled more than fifty miles from home; in the coming months he would be stationed at bases in Louisiana, Florida and Iowa where he would undergo the intensive training required to become a navigator. The final six weeks were spent in Grand Island, Nebraska, where Harold was assigned to a bomber crew consisting of ten men. On a bombing mission five crew members would be located in the front of the plane: pilot, co-pilot, bombardier, radio man, and navigator. The other five -- an engineer and four gunners – would be located in the rear.

"Within three weeks of their arrival Harold's crew embarked on their first mission, flying off in the early morning as part of a squadron of fifteen planes making strikes on German forces in France, returning to the base by noon. Up until this point in the war a single mission would have completed a crew's work for the day. The Allied counterattack, however, was just beginning a dramatic escalation. Harold's crew refueled and reloaded their plane, and promptly set out for a second, successful mission into France that very afternoon.

"Harold's second day of flight as a navigator involved a test ride on a new bomber. Apparently, the plane was not ready for action; the plane crashed on the runway, engulfed in flames. Fortunately, Harold and his two fellow crew members managed to escape the plane without injury.

"The very next day, however, Harold was awoken early and ordered to report for duty. A crew was about to depart on a bombing mission, and their navigator was unable to accompany them. Harold was needed to take his place. And so it came to pass that on April 29th, 1944 Harold took off with nine men he had never before met. Ironically, the navigator whom Harold substituted for that day would be killed two weeks later on another mission.

"The crew flew all the way to Berlin, Germany to attack a railroad station in order to disrupt the Germans' capacity to transport supplies to their armies at the front.

"Having dropped their load of bombs, the plane turned back towards England. At mid-day, flying at an altitude of 15,000 feet, Harold suddenly heard an ear rattling explosion. Under fire by both flak as well as by a German fighter plane approaching from behind, Harold's plane had been struck. Although Harold was unscathed, several of the crew members were injured from the flak, though none mortally. The plane was going down. The bombardier, having been hit, seemed dazed, so Harold helped him position himself to follow the two pilots and radio man in jumping from the front of the plane, while the other five crew members evacuated from the rear. Harold said a little prayer asking God to take care of him. Feeling strangely calm and at peace, Harold followed the others, leaping from the plane into space.

"From his previous experience of parachuting from a plane, Harold knew that normally there would be a sudden jolt as the parachute opened. This time, however, Harold was surprised to feel no such jolt. The only sound was the swoosh of air rushing by. Shortly afterwards the plane exploded. Harold drifted peacefully down into a forest, landing in a tree, where he got stuck about fifteen feet above the ground. After attempting without success to swing to the trunk of the tree, Harold dropped to the ground below, where pine needles helped softened his landing.

"With no sign of the other crew members, Harold found himself all alone in the forest. He began making his way westward, walking at night by cover of darkness beneath the stars in the sky. It was cold and damp, and Harold got a touch of frost bite on his feet, but he felt oddly free, enjoying the quiet countryside and the tranquility of the forest. Harold doubted he would be able to make it all the way out of Germany, but he thought he might as well give it a try. Keeping himself hid from sight, Harold slept during the day on a bed he made from straw he had found in a barn. His only food consisted of a solitary chocolate bar issued to him by the Air Force in his emergency kit.

"While it was still light in the early evening of the fourth day, Harold knelt down to drink from a stream beside a road. A man in a uniform came by riding a bicycle. Harold tried to hide, but it was too late - the man had seen him. The man called out to Harold in German, not unpleasantly. Quite hungry by this point, Harold decided to go with the man in the hope of a meal.

"The man took Harold to a house in a nearby town, which turned out to be the home of the burgomaster, the local mayor. Unlike the man on the bicycle, the tone of the burgomaster's words was harsh as he pulled out a gun and placed it under Harold's nose. Soldiers were called, and Harold was taken across the street to a fire house where he was locked up alone over night.

"In the morning two German officers who spoke English arrived and questioned Harold, but Harold had little information to offer, and an unwillingness to share what little he did have. Repeatedly, one of the officers asked, sarcastically, "Ah, just shut up and keep smiling, is that it?" Harold found this amusing, which made him smile all the more. All of the American soldiers had been instructed to do exactly that should they find themselves prisoners of war, and so Harold figured the German officer was getting pretty tired of it.

"A friendly German soldier who spoke English was assigned to accompany Harold on a several hour train ride to Oberursel near Frankfurt where captured airmen would undergo further interrogation. The train was loaded with soldiers as well as with other prisoners. At one point the soldier briefly left Harold alone, leaving his gun on the seat for Harold's taking. Harold briefly considered this possibility, but realized that with the train full of German soldiers, this would be a very foolish thing to do. He wasn't the Hollywood type.

"Harold spent three days at the interrogation center where once more he was questioned, but again he had little to say. During the time there Harold was permitted to exchange his light uniform for one made of heavier material. Because of his small frame, an American uniform could not be found to fit Harold, and so to his amusement, Harold ended up wearing a uniform of the British Royal Air Force.

"Harold was loaded onto a second train crowded with prisoners and guards. The ride took three full days during which it was difficult to sleep. At last the train arrived at Stalag Luft #3, the prison camp in which Harold would spend the better part of the coming year. Entering the heavily barbed-wired compound, Harold and the other prisoners of war passed under a huge sign that warned, "Escape Is No Longer a Sport." Less than two months earlier, seventy-six prisoners had attempted to escape the prison through tunnels they had secretly dug underneath the barbed wire fences. After a massive manhunt, all but three of the escapees were recaptured. Fifty of the captured escapees were promptly executed.

"Immediately upon their arrival, the prisoners were required to pose to have their picture taken for their prisoner of war identification cards. The photographer tried to compel Harold to "smile like the others," but defiantly he refused. The picture shows a young man quietly confident, in need of a shave, his head tilted jauntily to the side; his eyes staring calmly into the camera.

"Harold was escorted to the small room that would provide the sleeping quarters for him and fourteen other prisoners. Inside there were five triple-decker bunks with wooden slate frames containing mattresses filled with wood chips. There was a single, small window that was shuttered closed at night, and a metal heating stove for burning coal or trees stumps dug up by the prisoners' bare hands. Not far from their sleeping quarters stood a small building referred to as "the cooler," serving as a cell for the solitary confinement of rule breakers.

"Mail from prisoners-of-wars traveled slowly back home to the United States. It was not until August 31st that Mrs. Gantert received her first two letters from Harold:

What follows is Harold's own diary of the final weeks of the war.

"Evacuation of Stalag Luft #3. The Adjutant's call sounded at about 8:15 pm on January 27, 1945, calling all Kriegies to report to their respective blocks where we received orders to be ready to move out by 9:30 p.m. All men who were unable to walk were to report to the gate immediately.

"We all packed our few possessions in record time and on the order we fell out onto the road. After waiting there for a while, we were told to return to our block and build a sled. We made a mad rush for our room and started ripping things up and put together a sled that should have had a horse in front of it instead of men. All of us discarded some things from our packs to reduce the weight and make them easier to carry. At 12:10 am we move out collecting one Red Cross parcel per man as we passed the gate. It was fairly warm and we soon felt pretty tired under the weight of our packs and the sled. We pushed on until it was too difficult to pull the sled any longer, so we ditched it by the roadside and proceeded with only our back packs and blankets.

"We had only a few rest stops and at 11 a.m. on January 28, we arrived at a detention lager in Friewalden. Everyone was extremely fatigued, but there were accommodations for only a few men so we spent two hours indoors with the balance of the time outdoors where it was wet and cold with snow and sleet falling continuously. Several of the men escaped from here, but were later picked up and shipped to the new camp. The town was flooded with refugees and the roads were pretty well clogged with their wagons. At 5:20 pm, after six hours and no sleep we left Friewalden.

"A man in our group had some pain in his groin and was unable to carry his back pack. Rather than leave it behind, I put it in a Red Cross suitcase and dragged it along behind me. That night there was heavy snow and sleet falling and the roads were very icy. Consequently, before long our feet were soaked and very cold. After several kilometers of marching, several of our men were unable to proceed any further and were left at Pribus.

"We were informed that our next stop would be Muskau, about twelve kilometer away, so we figured we could make it okay. The column moved on and after about four hours we were feeling just about dead, but no Muskau and the guards seemed to be lost. Many of the men could hardly walk and many times I slipped and fell. It was extremely difficult to get up with the heavy back pack. The guards told us it was only three more kilometers and an hour later it was the same story and the next hour the same again. By this time, a couple of the men had collapsed; one went blind and had to be led. Many of the men were hysterical, but still continued on.

"Finally, after seven hours we reached Muskau at 7 am. The streets were jammed with men everywhere, lying where they had collapsed from exhaustion. Some were out of their minds; some just stood still, unable to move any further. I nearly collapsed when we stopped but managed to control myself after a few seconds. We had marched about forty-two kilometers instead of thirty-six because of the roundabout route. Instead of marching twenty kilometers in a day we had traveled seventy-two (45 miles) in thirty hours, having not slept for forty-eight hours and with constant exposure to snow sleet and frigid temperatures.

"After some delay, the men were quartered in churches and factories. Our group drew a paper mill and stayed there for two days. We received some soup and once in while some bread and margarine. We traded some cigarettes with French workers. I was able to get two pocket knives and some marks, which I used later. We also built another sled and some Red Cross girls supplied us with some hot water.

"At 12 noon on January 31 we marched on. A large number of men were left behind because they were badly crippled form the previous march. This time we marched only eighteen kilometers to Schonheide where we were housed in barns; fifty men in each barn. The people here supplied us with spuds and onions which some guys cooked up into a stew for the rest of us. The weather warmed up and the ice melted so that we had to abandon our sleds.

"At 4 pm on February 1st, we left for Spremburg and arrived there at about 9 pm. We slept on straw in a Wehrmacht garrison and were given some soup to eat. At about 8 am we were given four parcels for five men which included some bread, margarine and blood sausage. Our train cars were of World War I vintage, "40 and 8's" (room for 40 men and 8 horses) and there were 54 men in each of them. It was so crowded in the cars that it was difficult to breathe, so some of the men borrowed a bayonette from a guard and cut holes in the side of the cars to let a little air in. We were in the train for two days, and at one stop (Chemnitz) I bought some beer with my marks that I had obtained from a French worker. At 4 pm on February 4th we arrived at Nuremburg and our new home: Stalag 13D, where we spent two months with fleas, filth and short rations, not to mention sleepless nights when we sweated out the air raids by RAF in the night and daytime raids by the USAAF.

"Our stay at Stalag 13D was not exactly pleasant. We were housed in large barrack-like buildings. Instead of individual rooms, each group was assigned a partitioned-off section with bunk beds, straw mattresses, a stove and table. The rations of coal bricks were very scant, so we slipped out at night and ripped wooden siding off the communal wash room to use as fuel. Our food consisted of some scant German rations, supplemented by an occasional Red Cross parcel. Most of our cooking was done on our stove in home made tin utensils fashioned from the tin containers in our parcels. There were no organized activities, but we kept occupied with whatever we could conjure up for ourselves. We survived this way until the end of March and our departure from Stalag 13D.

"On March 28 we were alerted for our second evacuation and march. At about 4 pm on April 3rd we were informed that we would move out at 9 am on April 4th. We actually left Nuremburg at 11 am. We marched eight kilometers to Feucht, four kilometers to Ochenburck, twelve kilometers to Pfiefferhutte, five kilometers to Oberfersfeld and two more to Doftbauer, arriving at 6 pm. We spent the night in a barn. In the morning the weather was good so we didn't mind the walking. We left Dofbauer at 8:30 am April 5th marching six kilometers to Polling, where we arrived at 10 am and spent an hour and twenty minutes enduring an air raid.

"We left there and arrived at Newmarkt at 1:45 pm where we received some rations and stopped in some woods until 9 pm., at which point we marched out for twenty-one kilometers, arriving at Burching at 4 am on April 6th. It was rain-ing, but we spent four hours sleeping in the rain. We departed Burching at 8 am and arrived at Plankstettin at 9:45 am. While there were received one half of a British parcel.

"On April 7th at 11 pm. We again started on a night march, traveling twenty kilometers, arriving at Pondorf at about 5:30 am on April 8th. We spent the rest of the day at Pondorf, leaving there at 11 am on April 9th for Schampten, then to Sandersdorf, Mindelstetten, Foreheim and Marching, where, after marching twenty kilometers we arrived at 3:30 pm on April 9th and were issued one half of a Belgium parcel.

"At 11 am on April 10th we departed for Neustadt, then Muelhausen arriving at 2 pm. Here we were issued one third of an American food parcel. We spent three days in Mulhausen during which time Artik, Simms and myself made con-tact with a German family who let us stay in their barn They were very kind to us and even provided us with some home cooked food. The family's name was Loibl and I had the opportunity of visiting them after the war. We finally moved out of Mulhausen at 11 am on April 13th, traveling to Seigen, Neiderumelforf and Oberemeldorf until 4:20 pm when we stopped in some barns.

"While staying in the barns some of us did some foraging and managed to trade some cigarettes with French workers for some eggs and ham, which we cooked in the barnyard, much to the dismay of the German guards. I was told that ten men were caught and beaten for their efforts. Fortunately we were not bothered. We left the barns at 11:30 am and marched ten kilometers through Ludmannsdorf, Pfefferhausen and Holzhausen. We stayed there until 11 am on April 19th. Leaving there for Obersussbach and Obermunchen, about ten kilometers away. On April 20th at 11:30 am we left Obermuchen and traveled through Amelsdorf, Willetsdorf and Schwarzdersdorf. The final day of our excursion started at 9 am and carried us through Durnseilboldedorf and Pfettrach to our final destination of Moosburg, arriving there at 12 noon on April 21st. We had marched a total of 145 kilometers.

"At Moosburg we were housed in large tents, sleeping on cots and preparing our food outside with homemade utensils. General Patton and his men were approaching the area and we often had to dodge bullets whenever there was an attack against the local town. Finally, on April 29th, 1945, exactly one year after I was shot down, Patton and his men arrived at our camp and we were liberated.

***

Daughter Debbie Ganter continues;

"Sometime between 1948 and 1950, he was stationed in El Paso Texas, where he met my Mother in 1951 through one of her sisters.

"He stayed in Texas until 1960, when he was grounded. He told me it was because of a small health problem. It was also easier for him to get promoted. Upon being grounded, he was stationed in Madrid, Spain, where he became in charge of supply and was promoted to major. He was there until summer of 1963, when he was transferred to Lompoc California and was promoted to Lt. Colonel, Commander of Supply. He retired on May 31, 1965.

"My Dad never liked to remain idle, while he was in Texas, he enrolled in The University of Maryland Correspondence Program and eventually in the mid 1970's got his College and Masters Degree of Business Administration from Fairleigh Dickinson University in Madison, New Jersey. When we were in Spain, every Christmas, he would gather his buddies and bring gifts to an orphanage. In Rota, Spain there was a Air Force and Naval Camp called Camp Columbus, which they turned into a facility for families to vacation. The barracks were used for housing. My Dad built a play ground with swings for the kids. When he moved back to NJ, he was on The Board of Education and head of The Adult School for several years as well as the Kiwanis.

He rarely talked about his time during the war until recently. The only thing he ever said about it was that it closed his emotions up. It was hard for him to feel things sometimes.

Radio S/Sgt. Ralph C. Andrews Jr.

"On Sunday, December 7, 1941, our Grant Park football team was playing football at Piedmont Park in Atlanta where we usually played each Sunday in the fall of the year. My girlfriend Lanore Setzer accompanied me in my 1936 Pontiac and was a spectator at the games. I usually had a couple of other Grant Park players riding in my car. Jackie Osburn, Lanore's best friend would go along to keep her company.

"When the game was over, we got into the car and turned on the radio and we heard the news that Japan had attacked Pearl Harbor. Needless to say, this shook us all up; we knew we would be entering the service to fight a war because we were the age to be drafted and most of us had already graduated from high school. I was working at J.E. Hanger, Inc. manufacturing limbs. I could not see where that would contribute much to the war effort. Immediately applied for a position with the U.S. Government as a junior draftsman and was accepted.

"After Christmas, December 29, 1941, I reported to the Charleston, South Carolina, Navy Base. The base was expanding personnel so fast that they had no drawing table available for me; I just stood around with nothing to do. On one occasion, I did assist a senior engineer on board a British corvette. I held the end of a tape measure while he took various measurements. I was assigned to a male bachelor dormitory on the base. The room contained a double-deck bunk, one small desk and a straight chair at the desk; that was going to be a Spartan existence. I had to eat my meals off base at a boarding house.

"At about 1:00 am, January 1, 1942, I packed my one suit case and got into my car (actually my father's 1935 Chevrolet; which we traded for me to make this trip because his car was in better mechanical condition) and started back to Atlanta. Somewhere in a small town in Georgia the fan belt broke. I spent the rest of the night in the car parked in a service station waiting for the station to open. I had a new fan belt put on the car and continued the trip. I arrived in Atlanta before lunch on New Year's Day and called Lanore. Before going to Charleston, I had asked Mrs. Setzer (her mother) to teach Lanore how to make biscuits. Her first words to me were, "You did not give me time to teach Lanore anything."

"I went back to my old job and in May, 1942 I took the Air Corps Cadet examination in Atlanta and passed it. I enlisted in the Air Corps as a cadet on May 19, 1942, but was not called into active duty until October 28, 1942. I left Atlanta on a railway car filled with potential Air Corps cadets. At the Classification Center in Nashville we were subjected to extensive physical and written examinations. I failed the eye examination due to a astigmatism; this eliminated me as a pilot or bombardier. My mathematical achievement was not high enough to qualify as a navigator. My eyes would not even qualify me to be an aerial gunner. The only way I was going to be a "fly boy" was to attend radio school.

"During my brief stay in Nashville, my Mom and Pop brought Lanore up for a weekend visit. After 36 days at Nashville, I was shipped out by train along with other "washouts" to Keesler Field, Mississippi.

"We arrived at Keesler Field, Mississippi on December 6, 1942. We were billeted in the tent city. At night it was cold and damp and the next morning at 5:00 am you put on cold and damp clothes (there was no heat in the tents). We took calisthenics before breakfast and drilled the rest of the day. We cadets had a month of drilling behind us so the drill sergeant had us assisting him with some of the new recruits that could not determine their left foot from their right foot.

"On December 22, 1942, we shipped out of Keesler Field. Prior to boarding the train we had to stand in a pouring rain for about three hours. The GI raincoat acted like a sponge after a while. Most all of the cadet washouts were scheduled to go to a radio school so when we shipped out we were hoping to be sent to the Boca Raton, Florida Radio School. The train headed east to Mobile, Alabama, but then turned north and ended up in Sioux Falls, South Dakota. on December 25, 1942 (Christmas Day). That was not where a Georgia boy wanted to be in the winter.

"The barracks were single-story wooden structures covered with black asphalt paper. They were heated with coal burning space heaters. There were about 50 men to each barrack. The latrines were outside of the barracks; which made for an uncomfortable morning shave, shower and constitutional.

"That winter a large number of us came down with severe colds or pneumonia. I never went on sick call because I was afraid they would put me in the hospital. The rumor was that people were dying in the hospital. I treated myself with aspirin and Vick's Vapor Rub.

"The Post Commander permitted you to work out in the gym rather than take calisthenics if you participated in the gym program. I opted for the gym program. I participated in weight lifting, gymnastics, boxing and wrestling. The Post held boxing and wrestling exhibitions and tournaments each week in downtown Sioux Falls in front of civilian and military spectators. I represented our squadron as a novice welter weight boxer and held the Post title until just before I shipped out. I also wrestled for our squadron when we were short of wrestlers. I really enjoyed that part of my stay in Sioux Falls.

"The radio course consisted of theory, maintenance, operation and code. I did well on all phases accept code. The code was monotonous and difficult for me. I spent hour after hour with headset on typing to develop sending and receiving speed. On one occasion, our squadron had to stand retreat in subfreezing cold for about an hour until the Commanding Officer arrived. I thought my nose was going to drop off. On Sundays only one mess hall was open and all the squadrons used it. This meant long periods of waiting on the outside in the cold before you got to eat. On Sunday nights the Army only fed you cold cuts.

"I completed Radio School May 22, 1943. The Army Air Corps "in its infinite wisdom" shipped me off to Laredo, Texas on May 29, 1943 to spend the summer.

"I arrived at Laredo, Texas June 1, 1943. There was not much to Laredo, but a lot of Hispanics and they all seemed to live at the poverty level. There was a nice hotel downtown and we tried to eat lunch there each Sunday, which was my day off. They had a new YMCA which was used as the USO. After lunch we went to the USO and hung around or went swimming in the USO pool. I also did a lot of swimming at the Air Base pool. You put your clothes into a basket and checked them into an attendant at the USO for security reasons; however, that was not a very secure procedure, since my high school ring was stolen and later my billfold and watch were stolen while I was swimming.

"Gunnery training was conducted in the classroom, on the ground, and in the air. You learned to assemble and disassemble the .50 caliber machine gun while blindfolded. We also had hours of aircraft identification classes. Silhouettes of aircraft were flashed on a screen and you had to identify the aircraft. An enjoyable phase of gunnery training was skeet shooting. That was the only time I ever fired a shotgun. We not only participated in regular skeet shooting, but we rode around on the back of a pickup truck firing a shotgun at skeet as they were released from the trap house.

"We started out the aerial gunnery training in an AT-6. You stood in the back cockpit and fired a 30 caliber machine gun at a sleeve target being towed by another AT-6. You fired tracer bullets so you could see if you were hitting the target. When you finished firing, you held up your arm to signal the pilot and he would bank away sharply and leave you hanging by your check strap. The pilots thought that was fun.

"After the AT-6, you advanced to turret training in AT-11 and AT-18 which were twin engine planes. Again you fired at a sleeve target but from a turret. On one occasion, after I had finished firing, the pilot invited me to sit in the co-pilot's seat of an AT-11. He then gave me a few instructions on how to fly the plane and turned it over to me. I flew it back to the field; of course, the pilot landed it. When we landed, the other students in the back of the plane complained about the pilot's rough flying.

"When a GI was strolling the streets of Laredo, he was frequently accosted by young Mexican boys who were soliciting for their sisters; at least they said they were their sisters. While at Laredo each trainee was allowed to cross the border once to Nuevo Laredo, Mexico. We looked forward to that occasion. The Air Corps withheld pay from us prior to our visit across the border so that we could not "blow" our paycheck in Mexico. I went into Nuevo Laredo with only $4.00. I spent $2.00 on a hand embroidered blouse for Lanore. The first time she washed it; the embroidery thread ran and ruined the blouse.

"Each GI had heard so many stories about the houses of ill repute in Mexico so they felt they had to visit one. I accompanied several of my buddies into one as a sightseer. They had an armed guard at the door and it resembled a regular night club downstairs with a bar. One of my buddies urged one of the "ladies" to try to seduce me, but I was able to withstand her advances without succumbing to her temptation.

"We had been warned not to eat or drink anything in Mexico unless the drink was bottled. Since I did not drink alcoholic beverages, that left nothing for me to drink across the border. Tequila was the prevalent Mexican alcoholic beverage in Laredo. The drinking GI found it difficult to handle. One night I was on the bus headed back to the Air Base when a lieutenant vomited all over the floor of the bus as the result of drinking too much of that stuff. On another occasion, the guy in the bunk above me came in after a night on the town and got sick in the bunk and leaned out over the edge of the upper bunk and vomited into my shoes. Looking back on my stay at Laredo, I guess the gunnery training was more fun than the visits to town. I completed the training as an aerial gunner on July 7, 1943.

"On August 11, 1943, a large detachment of us packed our bags and loaded the bags onto a baggage car. The troop train did not arrive until three days later. We shipped out on August 14, 1943. Any troop movement entailed several blocks of walking with your own baggage. At that time my baggage included a barrack bag, a footlocker and a flight bag. The flight bag was carried on your back like a knapsack. You carried the foot locker by its handle in one hand and the barrack bag in the other hand. That was quite a heavy load for a 148 pound man to carry any distance.

"While I was at Laredo, Lanore graduated from Commercial High School on June 7, 1943. She then went to work for the Fourth Service Command (Army) in July 1943 as a Clerk Stenographer making $1440 per annum. As a senior in high school, she worked in the afternoon as a stenographer for Retail Credit Company making 50¢ per hour. As soon as she graduated and I could get a furlough we were planning to get married.

"From Laredo we shipped via rail to Salt Lake City, Utah Air Base and arrived August 17, 1943. We were on day coaches about three days. They were of the 1890's vintage. The seats and backs were made of cane. We had to sleep on the benches or floor. To stay comfortable, we kept the windows open so the coal smoke from the train engine came into the cars. After three days on the train, plus three days at Laredo with the same clothes on, our khaki clothing was filthy. On troop movements like that, the train would stop at prearranged points for you to eat. Food would be brought to the rail depot and you would eat from mess kits beside the train. Hot coffee would be served from big galvanized garbage cans. The coffee would turn the cans green. The trip from Laredo to Salt Lake City went by way of the Royal Gorge in Colorado (through the Rocky Mountains); that was a spectacular trip.

"We were housed in permanent buildings at the Salt Lake City fairgrounds which was adjacent to the airfield. We were at Salt Lake City only to await assignment to an operational phase training air base. I spent three months there just waiting, although radio operators did have to continue to practice sending and receiving code.

"On one occasion, I was assigned to washing pots and pans while on KP. After shying greasy pots and pans all day, I became nauseated and could not eat dinner that night. Those pots were big enough to get into. The State Fair was held while I was stationed at the air base. It was adjacent to our housing area. After the fair was over, our area was infested with swarms of flies as a result of the animal droppings. When you ate you had to pick the flies from your food.

"Again I was exposed to the Army's "make work ethic." I was assigned to a detail that disassembled double deck wooden bunks. When we completed the task in one of the buildings, we were instructed to start reassembling the bunks. At that point, I started "goofing off" and almost missed my furlough papers, because I was hiding out behind a building. I did not mind work that was necessary, but did not see any need for the "make work ethic."

"In October 1943, I was issued an eleven-day furlough and Lanore arranged for our wedding in Atlanta on October 12, 1943. It was a beautiful wedding and was attended mostly by relatives. My father was best man and Unetta (Lanore's older sister) was maid of honor. There were very few males at the wedding because they were all away in the service. My brother, Nat, was in the Army, and Lanore's brothers Frank and Johnny were in the Army and Navy respectfully. We had a five-day honeymoon at the Henry Grady Hotel in Atlanta. The other six days were consumed by the train trip from Salt Lake City to Atlanta and back. One night we ate at the Ship Ahoy Restaurant which was Atlanta's best seafood restaurant at that time. Being a country girl at heart, Lanore ordered fried chicken and I ordered fried shrimp. Lanore had not been exposed to shrimp before; she asked if they were good and I said "try one." She reached over and took one of the tails that I had disposed of on the edge of my plate. She chewed on it for a few moments and said, "I don't see what is so good about shrimp." We both had a good laugh when I told her what she had tried to eat.

"On my return to Salt Lake City, I got back into the routine of roller skating and bowling in town at night. On November 22, 1943, I was sent by train to Alexandria, Louisiana for operational phase training.

"On Thanksgiving Day, November 25, 1943, at 8:00 pm, I arrived at Alexandria Air Force Base and at 10:00 pm sat down to a Thanksgiving dinner of cold cuts at the base mess hall.

"At Alexandria I was assigned to an air crew to start combat training in a B-17. The crew consisted of: Lieutenant R.J. (Bob) Green, pilot; Lt. Olsen, co-pilot; Lt. Wacker, navigator; Lt. Silks, bombardier; Sargent (Sgt.) Casey Wagner, engineer; Sgt. Robert Morgan, tail gunner; Sgt. Jack King and Sgt. John Jones, waist gunners; Sgt. William Neal, ball turret gunner; and myself, radio operator. The enlisted men were assigned to the same barracks so we got to know each other quite well.

"Phase training consisted of constant flying both day and night for the four officers and the engineer and radio operator. We spent hours upon hours formation flying and "shooting" landing and takeoffs. On one occasion during bad weather we got separated from our formation hundreds of miles from the base. Lt. Green started talking about having to land at some strange field, but fortunately we eventually found our way back to Alexandria.

"While I was at Alexandria, one of the B-17's had engine trouble and the crew had to bail out, but two of the enlisted men "froze' and refused to jump and went down with the plane. I resolved that I would use the parachute if it ever became necessary.

"When we flew at lower altitudes the air over Louisiana could be rough and many of the men got air sick but it never bothered me. We frequently flew over New Orleans at night and I would listen to the music from the civilian radio stations on my plane radio. The other crew members did not have that privilege. The lights of New Orleans reflected off Lake Pontchartrain at night; it was really beautiful.

"Alexandria had a civilian population of about 25,000 people. In addition to the Air Base, Camps Beauregard, Claiborne, Livingston and Polk were in the vicinity. The small city was inundated with soldiers which made it difficult to find rooms or apartments for wives and practically impossible for a wife to find a job other than waiting tables.

"As soon as I arrived in Alexandria, I started seeking a room for Lanore so she could join me, but it was difficult to find one. I finally located a room in a widow's home that rented for $10.00 per week. The room was off the front porch and you had to go through her living and dining room to get to the one bathroom.

"Lanore came down from Atlanta about a week before Christmas to join me. When she arrived at the railway station she had a detachment of Marines escorting her. She had a sailor help her make the train transfer in New Orleans. That was her first train trip.

"The landlady locked up the house about 10:30 pm each night which posed a problem for us. I was flying different hours throughout the day and night, so when I got back to the room at night, Lanore would open the window for me to slip into the room. Needless to say, the lady did not approve of that and told us so.

"In a short period of time, we were able to locate a rooming house that was full of soldiers and their wives. There we had to share the bathroom with every couple on our floor. Since our income was limited, Lanore had to eat her meals at a little diner not far away. Practically every night we ate oyster stew in that diner. We did eat Christmas dinner at the hotel in Alexandria. We bowled a few times and went to a few movies, but it was a Spartan existence for her. We celebrated New Year's Eve, 1944, by lying in bed listening to WSB radio in Atlanta. The room had only one uncomfortable chair in it.

"On February 20, 1944, I was informed that we would be restricted to the base the next day because we would ship out. That night I took Lanore to the railway station for her trip back to Atlanta, but we could not get a ticket that night because service men had priority and the train was full. I had to leave her at the YWCA for the night because I had to be back on the base by 11:00 pm. We had to say our goodbyes at the YWCA which was the last time we were together until I returned from overseas. She did manage to get a ticket and seat on the train the next day. I was really worried about her safety when I left her, but I had no choice. When I got to my next destination, I immediately called her to see that she got home safely. She said she had a miserable and uneventful trip.

"The crew left Alexandria on February 21, 1944, via train, and arrived at Grand Island, Nebraska Air Field on February 23, 1944. That air base had the best service club I saw during my stay in the Air Force. It had walls covered with life-size paintings of pinup girls. We were assigned to a new B-17G; the officers named her the "Mexican Hayride" after a Broadway show which was playing at the time. The cast members of the show promised to send autograph copies of pictures to us; if they did, they never reached us. On March 10, 1944, we flew that plane out of Grand Island headed for England.

"We did not fly a direct route to Presque Isle, Maine as we were instructed. Lt. Green decided to fly over Casey Wagner's mother's apartment in Chicago. We buzzed the apartment and I looked out the side window and saw church steeples. We then flew over Lt. Green's home in New Jersey and flew low over it. Over New England he "wagged" the tail of the plane for the "hell of it" and broke the energizer loose and did some minor interior damage to the waist of the plane. Before reaching Presque Isle, we started running low on fuel. The pilot told us to put on our parachutes and said he said he was going to ride the plane down if he could find an open field. I was going to jump rather than ride a plane down in a crash-landing. Fortunately, we found the airfield before we ran out of fuel and landed safely. While we were at Presque Isle another B-17 landed and one wheel locked while taxing and ran into a hanger; the bombardier and navigator were killed.

"We were in Presque Isle for several days while maintenance tried to determine why the plane used so much fuel on the flight. They were never told of the extra miles flown on the trip. Maintenance was told that we ran into rough air which caused the damage to the waist of the plane. Needless to say, it was cold in Presque Isle in March.

"From Presque Isle we flew to Goose Bay Labrador. I had never seen so much snow. The walkways between buildings, as well as the runways, were clear of snow, otherwise, the snow was shoulder deep. We were there only one night, but I did take a 30-minute hot shower. That was the only time I was warm on the trip across to England.

"We then flew across Greenland to Iceland and spent a day or two at Reykjavik Air Base. When we approached the airfield, a snow storm was in progress. B-17's and B-24's were stacked up over the area trying to get permission to land. I was listening to my radio and monitoring the conversations between the control tower and different planes. It was a critical situation because some of the planes were running out of fuel. As I listened, one plane did crash-land without tower permission. We finally landed without any difficulty on March 18, 1944.

"From Iceland we flew the "Mexican Hayride" to Prestwick, Scotland. The crew was then transported by train to an Air Force facility about 20 miles outside of London where we stayed a few days awaiting assignment to a bomb group.

"On March 20, 1944, we were shipped by train to the 384th Bomb Group. The airbase was in the midsection of England near a small village by the name of Graton Underwood; the closest town was Kettering.

"Our enlisted crew was housed in a Quonset hut with several other enlisted men whom I never got to know. We were assigned to the 545th Squadron. The squadron leader's radio operator was in our Quonset hut. He and his pilot had completed six combat missions and had more missions than anyone else in the squadron when we arrived.

"The base covered a large area and it became apparent that I needed a bicycle to get about more quickly and with less effort. I purchased an old beat-up English bike for four pounds and 10 shillings ($26.00); it was worth about $3.00 in the States. In the short period of time that I used it, it had two flat tires, a broken front axle and a broken sprocket; however, I was able to get parts for it and repair it. I also had it slide out from under me once on a curve and bent a pedal. Someone appropriated by bike when I did not return from a mission and probably sold it again to a new combat crew member.

"Casey Wagner and I went into Kettering on a Sunday and ate lunch in a small hotel. That was when I realized the British people did not have much to eat. The meal consisted of a piece of lettuce, a thin slice of beef roast and a small potato; I ate at the base thereafter. Earlier I had tried to buy an English candy bar at a railway station and was informed I had to have a ration ticket to purchase it. Even at the base Post Exchange (PX) we were limited to two candy bars, two packs of gum and seven packs of cigarettes per week. The English people were wearing clothing that was five years old and the girls could not even get makeup.

"Morgan and I went into the village of Grafton Underwood once and visited the town pub. Since I didn't drink beer, it was a waste of time, but I did get to experience the atmosphere in the pub. Most of the customers were middle-age English people. While at the pub I needed to make a "pit stop." I was directed to the back of the pub which was a stable area dating back to the middle ages. I had to wait behind a peasant-type older woman, who in turn was waiting for her female friend in the privy. The privy was emitting a running water sound and the woman turned to me and said, "She sounds like a cow, don't she?" That earthy comment from a strange older woman really shocked me. I recall only going off base those two times. I had no reason to since there was nothing for me to do in town.

"As stated earlier, the squadron leader and his radio operator had only completed six combat missions. We had to complete 30 missions before we could rotate back to the States. It didn't take a genius to see that the probability of accomplishing that was not likely. I wrote Lanore and discretely tried to tell her that if she received a missing-in-action notice that I would be a POW.

"At the 384th Bomb Group, Lt. Olsen was assigned to another crew and plane which had a crew that had experienced some combat. I believe Lt. Olsen completed his 30 missions. Our crew and plane got an experienced combat pilot (Lt. James Bouvier) who had completed about nine combat missions. Lt. Green was moved over to the co-pilot's seat.

"Before I flew my first combat flight, I flew with an experienced radio operator over England and practiced the routines that was expected of a B-17 radio operator in combat. The officer heading up the base radio unit was from the Grant Park area and we attended junior high school together.

***

"Our first combat mission was April 24, 1944. We were awakened early in the morning around 4:00 am and ate breakfast and then went to the briefing room along with all the other crews that were to fly that mission. The briefing room was blacked out with all windows and doors closed. Most of the men lit up cigarettes and in a short while the smoke was dense; for a non-smoker like me that was rough. We then checked out our parachutes and the radio men got necessary information and codes for the day. At the plane the gunners checked out their 50-caliber machine guns to see that they were working all right.

"Our first mission was deep into Germany to to bomb an aircraft factory north om Munich. Our group had 30 planes in the air on that mission. We flew over French and then German air space. I observed the Eiffel Tower in Paris from the plane that day even though it was many miles away. Over France we encountered sporadic flak.

"The first fighter plane we saw appeared to be a ME-110 and all guns were ready to fire at it as it approached, but as it got closer it banked so that we could see that it was a P-38. When we reached German air space, FW-190's started attacking our formation. They made frontal attacks through the group. Every gun on our plane seemed to be firing at the bogies. I was spraying the air from my position in the hope one of the bogies would run into one of my slugs. Actually, the radio man's gun had only limited firing arc; a bogie would seldom attack from that angle. We were flying "Tail End Charlie" for our squadron of six planes on that mission, which meant the planes ahead of us were more likely to get hit on the frontal attacks. We had P-51 escorts part of the way into the target. I will never forget watching one FW-190 going by my window with a P-51 on his tail. That FW-190 never pulled out of his dive.

"We encountered heavy flak over the target. After releasing our bombs and leaving the flak area, FW-190's resumed the attack and again P-51's assisted in fighting them off. Morgan, our tail gunner, claimed one bogie went down as the result of our guns. The net result of the mission was the loss of three of our six planes in our squadron and seven out of 30 planes in our group. Our squadron commander's plane went down that day. He and his radio operator went down on their seventh mission. The radio operator was in our hut. That evening other enlisted men came into the hut and divided up his personal belongings. Their callousness bothered me at the time. It was a way of life in a combat environment.

"After our first mission, I caught a cold and was grounded for about a week to protect my ears. My crew went on a "milk run" over France to bomb a railway marshalling yard while I was grounded. The group lost no planes on that mission.

***

"On April 29, 1944, we were awakened in the early morning hours and told to get ready for a mission. After breakfast at the briefing room, the map on the wall was uncovered. That string stretched all the way into Germany to Berlin. My first mission was an eight-hour mission and the second was going to be about that long.

"The B-17 flew between 20,000 and 23,000 feet over Germany and at that altitude it could be 40°F to 60°F below zero. The flying attire got to be uncomfortable after several hours. Normal flying attire consisted of ·long underwear and wool socks, regular wool olive drab (O.D.) trousers and shirt, electrically heated suit, fleece-lined leather trousers, jacket, boots, gloves and helmet. Your face was covered with goggles and an oxygen mask which was attached by hose to the plane's oxygen system. The electrical suit was plugged into the plane's electrical system.

"Over all that you wore a parachute harness that had to be snugly strapped to prevent injury if you had to bail out. If you had to move about in the plane you had to detach and then reattach the equipment. A portable oxygen bottle was used to go from one position to another. On long flights it was usually necessary to make a pit stop in the bomb bay into a special tube. It was very difficult to make a pit stop under such conditions.

"April 29th, was a rare April morning in England in that the heavens were clear and the stars were shining brightly. As I was checking out my gun, I was whistling the song, "O What a Beautiful Morning." The thought occurred to me at that time, "why are you whistling, you may not come back from this mission." Lt. Wacker was sick that day and in his place as navigator was Lt. Harold Gantert.

"The flight to Berlin, as I recall, was uneventful for our group in that we experienced only sporadic light flak and no enemy fighters. Over Berlin flak became extremely heavy; as we would say, "it was heavy enough to walk on." On the bomb run with bomb bay doors open, we took a flak hit, but held our position in the squadron long enough for bombs away. The flak knocked out both engines on the same side and knocked out the intercom system. Each crew member wore headsets and a throat mike to communicate with one another. Suddenly I felt all alone when I could not hear any other crew members. I could only see the two waist gunners. I did not know what was going on in the front of the plane or in the tail of the plane. With two engines out, the pilots could not maintain our position with the group.

"We dropped away seeking cloud cover. Casey (the engineer) came back into the waist and helped get Neal out of the ball turret. They then proceeded to try to release the ball turret in order to reduce weight and wind resistance. We also were instructed to start throwing out excess 50-caliber ammunition.

"About 80 km from Berlin, I glanced out of the window just in time to see a ME-109 go by. It attacked from the tail. Morgan (tail-gunner) was throwing out ammunition and never did see the bogie until it was too late. Neither did the waist gunners, because they were working with the ball turret. The ME-109 sprayed our plane with 20mm shells.

"Morgan received multiple minor shell fragments in his legs. King received a few minor shell fragments in his legs and I took one large piece of shrapnel through my right thigh. A 20mm shell exploded under the radio room floor. It knocked me off my feet and I struck my head on the bulkhead. As I lay on the floor looking at that hole in the floor, Casey went by me through the bomb bay to get his parachute. I stood up and got my parachute and hooked it onto my harness (we all used chest type parachutes) and proceeded to the waist door. One or two of the men in the waist had already jumped. When I looked out into all that open space, I stepped back and checked every snap on the harness and chute connections to make sure everything was in order. I said a quick prayer and dived out.

"We had been instructed to pull a delayed jump if we had to "hit the silk." You took a free fall until about 5,000 feet and then pulled the rip cord. When I could see the tree tops, I pulled the rip cord and again started desperately praying that the chute would open. It did not open fast enough to suit me and I started trying to help pull it from the pack. When it finally did open, the jolt temporarily caused me to black out. Moments later, I landed in a pine tree and was hanging about 10 or 15 feet from the ground. I was wearing a British-type harness, so all I had to do was slap the release on my chest and slide down the tree trunk to German soil.

Due to the wound in my leg, I had no thought of trying to escape, but rather to surrender to the first German I came across. I hobbled out into an open space in the pine forest and came across Lt. Bouvier (the pilot) and asked him the direction to take to find a village. At that moment he shouted, "watch out," as the ME-109 came at us and strafed us. I heard one 20mm shell explode about 25 yards away. I suspect he was just trying to pinpoint our location to ground personnel. Even so, I hid behind the trunk of a pine tree that was no more than six inches in diameter and sucked in my gut as he circled overhead. Lt. Bouvier disappeared into the forest.

"In short order I came across a German in a green uniform (probably a game warden) wearing a side arm. I hobbled toward him with arms raised. He could speak English and one of the first things he asked was, "are you married?" I suppose I looked too young to him to be married. In a few minutes, King was brought up to join me. King mentioned that he had seen a body surrounded by Germans, but he didn't know who it was. We were put on the back of an old wagon drawn by a tractor and taken to a German Air Force base.

"The "Mexican Hayride" and its crew went down at 12:25 PM at Stackelitz, which was 15- km North-Northwest of Coswig. At the air base we were put into a room and before the day was over all members of the crew were there, except Casey, for a reunion. It must have been Casey's body that King saw. When I last saw Casey in the plane, he appeared to be all right. Whether he was strafed, chute failed to open or German civilians killed him on the ground, we never knew.

"I was given first aid for my leg and it was wrapped with paper wrapping. That night, I was put into the base hospital in a room by myself. It was staffed by slave labor orderlies; they wore blue and white vertical striped clothing. I was brought a meal consisting of cottage cheese and unseasoned boiled potatoes and a hot tea-like substance. I could not eat the meal, so I offered it to one of the orderlies and he wolfed it down. The next morning we were shipped out by train to Dulag Luft. The Eighth Air Force lost 66 heavy bombers and 11 fighters on April 29, 1944. The 384th Bomb Group lost 20 planes during April, 1944. That was almost twice as many as the group lost in any other month of operation. As fate would have it that was the month I became a part of that group.

***

"Dulag Luft (German Interrogation Center) was near Frankfurt at Oberursel. Our rail car spent the night in the Frankfurt railway station. There was much evidence that the station had been bombed many times before. I prayed that would not be the night that the RAF would make a return visit. The next day, May 1, 1944, we were transported to Oberursel and then had to walk quite a distance (seemed like a mile) to the camp. By then, my leg was throbbing with pain. The Germans immediately took me, via truck, to Lazarette Holemarke (POW hospital). I arrived there on May 1, 1944. They put me into a nice clean room and held me in isolation for several days. I was interrogated each day, but all they got from me was name, rank and serial number. The interrogator did not put too much pressure on me, probably because I was wounded.

"I was then moved into a ward room upstairs. It was difficult to sleep in that room because of one British turret gunner. His turret took a direct hit and a flash fire resulted from hydraulic fluid which severely burned his face and hands. He would cry and moan during the night while he thought we were sleep; during the day he never whimpered. I finally got adequate first aid on my leg by a British medic. He squeezed about a cup of pus from the wound.

"At Hohemarke, I was first introduced to some German cheeses. I was given cheese which was covered with mold and it smelled awful and at that early stage of internment, I would not eat it; later I would eat anything.

"I had the opportunity to talk to a full colonel at Hohemarke. He was being held at the hospital, even though he was not wounded, because the quarters were so much nicer. He had commanded a P-47 fighter group before being shot down. The Germans had even taken him up in one of their planes because they thought they could get him to talk. On May 5, 1944, I was shipped out of Hohemarke via train.

"I arrived at Lazarette Obermasfeld (POW hospital) on May 9, 1944. During the first week in the hospital an American doctor, who was also a POW, operated on my leg and removed several pieces of shrapnel. While I was at this hospital, an American lieutenant died of wounds; a military funeral was held for him. One day I was lying in my bunk putting together a jigsaw puzzle when a German officer came by on inspection and stopped and attempted to find a piece that would fit in the puzzle. The doctors kept me off my feet while I was at that hospital.

"On June 27, 1944, I was transferred about 10 km to Lazarette Meiningen (recuperation hospital). It appeared to be an old opera house which was surrounded by a wire fence. The stage and the auditorium floor were covered with cots. I would estimate that about 200 men were housed there at any one time.

"The men were recuperating from all manner of injuries, although broken legs were the prevalent injury. Most of the legs were broken when the men hit the ground after their parachute jump. One man had been severely burned as a result of a flash fire in his B-24 turret. His nose, eyelids and ears were burned off. Another man had his legs amputated at the hip. One fighter pilot had been a professional baseball player; his leg had been amputated as a result of a crash-landing. He had been shooting up a train in his P-38 and the train's antiaircraft guns got him. I will never forget watching one fellow playing ragtime music on a piano. He had a cast on his torso because of a broken back, but the piano was up on an old wagon and he was standing on the side of the wagon; he was having a ball.

"I was always hungry at the hospitals although things got worse later. Breakfast consisted of a slice of hard-black bread and sometimes there might be margarine and jelly on it (depending on the arrival of the Red Cross parcels). We would also get a cup of ersatz coffee or instant coffee, when available. At lunch and supper we could expect either barley cereal, boiled potatoes, or an occasional meat stew. Now and then we might be given some German cheese. Each man received the equivalent of one-half Red Cross food parcel per week. We were supposed to receive one full parcel per week. The Red Cross food parcels were paid for by the American or British Governments. The Red Cross was the agency which was responsible for getting the parcels into Germany. We actually didn't see the parcels because the contents were taken and used in the kitchen to prepare our meals. I used my allocation of cigarettes from the parcels to trade for food.

"I was on crutches during my stay at Meiningen and became quite adept in the use of crutches; I could even run with them. Meiningen's rail facilities were shot up by American fighters one day while I was there in the hospital, which caused some concern at the time. On September 20, 1944, I was shipped out with a number of other men to a permanent POW camp.

***

"We left Meiningen via train and rode eastward and crossed the Oder River at Frankfurt on the Oder. That was the first time I knew that Germany had two cities named Frankfurt. We ended up on September 22, 1944, at Stalag Luft IV, which was about 3 km from the small village of Kiefheide and 10 km from Belgrad. The camp was situated close to the Baltic Sea and between Danzig and Stettin and about 120 km from the latter.

"From the train station our group of twenty to thirty men had to walk several miles to the camp. We were surrounded by armed guards and German police dogs. They were marching us at a good pace and some of the men were having difficulty keeping up because of their injured legs. A few of us asked the guards to slow the pace down and they did. I later learned that some of the preceding POWs were forced to double time to the camp and those that lagged behind were cut with bayonets.

"Stalag Luft IV had been activated in May 1944, so it was a relatively new camp. We were taken into the Vorlager (outer camp) to be processed. There we were fingerprinted, photographed and strip searched. They searched our meager belongings and clothes we were wearing. They confiscated a needlepoint belt I had made and a statue of a gunner I had carved at the hospital. I sat down to redress and was immediately informed, in no uncertain words, that I had to stand while redressing. The Germans had a giant of a man that helped process us; he was called "Big Stoop" by the Kriegies (German for POWs). He did not appear to be too bright, but his purpose was to intimidate the Kriegies. I later was told at Camp Lucky Strike, France, that he had been killed by liberated POWs. I was also told that his head had been split open with an axe.

"After processing, we were marched to Lager C and put into Barrack #1, Room #2. There were 10 barracks per lager and 10 rooms per barrack. Each room was about 15' x 23'. Each barrack had a wash room and pit latrine (for night use only). Five barracks and a pit latrine were on each side of the lager. An administration-type building was at the end of the lager, which contained the kitchen and library. In the center of the lager, between the barracks, was the athletic area or parade ground.

"Around the perimeter of the lager was a walkway; but outside the walkway was the trip wire. Between the trip wire and barbed wire fence was no-man's land. If you went into that area you could be shot by the guards manning machine guns in the watch towers.

"Each room was designed to house 16 men, but we had 24 men in each of the rooms. The room contained double-deck bunks with three men sleeping side by side at each level. I managed to get an upper bunk and on the outside. The mattress was filled with wood shavings and supported by wooden planks. Each of us had a U.S. Army GI blanket to cover us. There was a table and benches in the center of the room, but only about eight men could sit at the table at any one time. There was a small charcoal burning stove in each room, which was used to take the chill off the room and heat water. The charcoal was rationed to each room.

"We were always hungry and food became the all important thing in our lives. Breakfast consisted of hot water for ersatz coffee or an occasional cup of instant coffee (from Red Cross parcel) and a thin slice of hard black German bread. Lunch could be any of the following: barley soup, cabbage soup, boiled kohl-rabies or dehydrated vegetables (weeds). Supper was usually boiled potatoes or potato stew with an occasional meat (of uncertain source) in it. The meals were brought to each room from the lager kitchen in a 10-quart pail and ladled out into each man's bowl.

"The German ration was augmented by food from the Red Cross food parcels; but rather than the one parcel per week per man, we received only about one-fourth of a parcel per week in the camp. The dehydrated vegetable stew did contain some protein in the form of little white worms about 3/8 inches long. At first I picked the worms out, but after about a week I ignored them and ate them because it was impossible to pick them all out. On one occasion our pail of meat and potato stew had an eyeball floating in it and a jawbone of some type of creature.

"The hard black bread was brought into the lager on a horse-drawn wagon. The loaves of bread were stacked onto the boards of the wagon with no effort made to protect the bread from germs or dirt. Those same wagons were used to haul all types of other goods. Septic tank wagons came into the lager periodically and pumped out the pit latrines. On one occasion, one blew up to the delight of the Kriegies.

"At night the barrack doors were barred, window shutters closed and lights turned off at about 9:00 pm. Twice a day, in the morning and at dusk, we had to stand "appel" or roll call in front of each barrack. We would have to stand in formation as the Germans counted us to ascertain that no one had escaped.

"There were no showers so you had to take a bath using a wash basin and cold water in the wash room. Sometimes you could heat enough water on the room stove to take the chill off the water. Your clothes were also washed the same way. Under those conditions, you only bathed about once per week. I shaved every other day with cold water and bath soap. We had one man in our room who was depressed and would not take part in any activity and would not bathe. After a couple of months, some of the men took him bodily to the washroom and forced him to bathe and wash his clothes.

"To keep from going stir crazy I read a number of books from the library. I played two-handed touch football for our barrack team in the lager tournament. I played bridge and other card games in our room every day. All leisure activity equipment was supplied by the YMCA. I also walked around the lager on the walkway to stay in shape.

"Since I did not smoke cigarettes, I traded the Red Cross parcel cigarettes with other Kriegies for extra food. Some of them had rather smoke than eat. The Red Cross Christmas (1944) parcel contained a pipe and a can of smoking tobacco. I smoked that package of tobacco in that pipe; this was the first time I ever smoked anything.

"We could write two letters and four postcards per month from the POW camp. Lanore actually received 13 letters and three postcards from Germany. I don't recall receiving but three letters in Germany, but one of the letters from Lanore contained a couple of photographs, which helped improve my morale. Lanore and Morn also sent me some personal parcels, but I never received them.

"The latter part of January, 1945, we began to get the word that the Russian Army was approaching our camp and we might have to evacuate the camp on foot. I got a new pair of GI shoes, but they were one size too narrow. I started increasing my walking to break in the new shoes and to build up my stamina.

***

"On February 6, 1945, our lager of over 2,000 men marched out of Stalag Luft IV and headed west away from the approaching Russian Army. We each had made a knapsack out of a brown Army towel. In the knapsack we carried our meager toilet articles and eating utensils and one Red Cross food parcel. We also had a change of underwear and socks and a GI blanket. I wore wool trousers, shirt, jacket, overcoat, knit cap and high-top shoes. All of the clothing was American Army GI issue, which came by way of the Red Cross.

"I teamed up with Floyd Owens, a Kansas wheat farmer. For the rest of the march we shared equally in our food and experiences. The German armed guards that accompanied us were battle weary and not fit for combat duty.

"The first three days of the march we covered about 68 km and on the fourth day we had a layover and rested. Each night we were locked up in barns and we slept on hay. Throughout that sightseeing trip we slept in barns at night, with a few exceptions, with the doors closed and locked. We slept in all manner of barns, large and small. That fourth day my feet were so swollen I had to borrow Floyd's shoes to go outside in the mud to eat and take care of necessities.

"Throughout the march we could expect a couple of unpeeled boiled potatoes at night. We were given a partial loaf of hard black bread about twice per week, which worked out to be a slice a day. We were given a cup of stew or barley soup a couple of times per week. Occasionally, we received a partial Red Cross food parcel. I also traded cigarettes for food with the German civilians whenever possible.

"After the layover on February 9, 1945, we marched for another four days and covered about 100 km. On that fourth day, we marched 40 km and that night slept on the ground under a blanket in the rain near Pritter. The next day we marched another 20 km and crossed the Oder River at Sweinemunde. I saw some German naval vessels there; Swienemunde was a naval base. Somewhere during that phase of the march, some slave farm laborers put a 10-gallon can of milk out on the dirt road for us, but as I was about to fill up my cup with milk a German guard kicked it over and the milk spilled out on the road.

"After we crossed the Oder River, the German guards seemed to think we were safely away from the Russians for the time being and our pace slowed down some although we covered another 65 km in the next three days followed by a two-day layover. We marched another 22 km in three days followed with an eight-day layover on a farm.

"It was relatively warm those eight days and we enjoyed the rest. There was a seed potato mound on the farm and after I saw a couple of other Kriegies digging into the mound to steal some potatoes, I followed their example and did the same thing. That could have been hazardous to my health since the German guards were instructed to shoot if they saw such activity.

"The next eleven days we covered about 164 km followed by a six-day layover. At this time I noticed I had guests. I had lice on me. Those were bothersome little creatures. They set up housekeeping in the most inappropriate places. At night you felt them crawling around. The next morning you took off your clothing and tried to pick them off without much success.

"By now all of us were experiencing dysentery or diarrhea. We had no medication, but someone said that eating charcoal would help alleviate the problem. We were building little fires with dead tree branches during the layovers to heat water or boil potatoes. We started eating the charred wood from the fires and I believe it helped. I had been a relatively modest individual before taking the scenic tour of Germany, but after the experience with dysentery I lost some of my inhibitions. Nature calls had to be taken along the road as we marched whether civilians were in sight or not.

"During the next nine days we marched 131 km, but three of those days we had layovers. It had long since became apparent that our German guards did not know where to go or what to do with us. On one of those layover days it was warm so I took my first wash basin bath (cold water) of the march. I also washed my clothes that day. I had gone 48 days without a bath; but I did shave about twice per week.

"During that nine-day period (March 21, 1945) we crossed the Elbe River at Domitz. On March 28, 1945 at Ebstorf the Germans packed us into small boxcars (about 50 men per car). These were of the same type used in World War I and probably had the same hay on the floor. We stayed in those boxcars for 33 hours before the train pulled out. They would let us out of the cars to eat and take care of necessities. It was impossible for you to stretch out on the floor in comfort. We had to entwine ourselves over each other to rest and sleep. That boxcar was an unpleasant experience. When the train did start, we rode only about 50 km to Fallingbostel and were interned at Stalag XIB. Imagine, we were held three days in that boxcar and traveled only 50 km.

"Stalag XIB was an old POW camp which housed many nationalities, mostly French and Russian. They put us up in two-man tents sleeping on the ground covered with straw. We were segregated from the other nationalities, but I did go over into the Russian compound and into one of their barracks. They were a pathetic looking group. They had to sleep on bunks with no type of mattress; they had to sleep on boards. They wore striped uniforms and their heads were shaved and they were gaunt looking. They looked at you with an expressionless stare. They looked like the living dead. That was a depressing sight, so I didn't tarry in that barrack too long.

"We reached Stalag XIB on March 30, 1945, and April 3rd we got a hot shower and were deloused with a powder spray. I did receive 1/2 of a Red Cross food parcel there and a half a loaf of bread. On April 6, 1945, we American Kriegies marched out of Stalag XIB and headed north. We could hear heavy gun fire from the south toward Hannover, which was about 50 km away.

"A night or two after we left Stalag XIB we spent the night in a barn as usual. The next morning we fell out and the German guards took a count of us and discovered several of our group missing. The guards figured that the missing men had dug down into the hay and were trying to hide out so they could escape back to the Allied fighting forces who were getting close. The guards shot into the hay a number of times, but apparently they didn't hit anyone and did not find the missing men.

"In the next 12 days we marched about 148 km and crossed the Elbe River again at Bleckede. During that period we frequently had Allied fighters and bombers flying over us. We held our ranks and waved at them to keep them from strafing us. We later heard that one group of marching POWs had left the road and sought cover in the trees and as a result got strafed. I should mention that the Germans kept us off the main roads. During the whole march we were walking on country dirt roads, except when we crossed rivers. On March 13, 1945, one of our men collapsed on the side of the road and I was told he died there.

"As mentioned previously, we usually were locked up in barns at several old palatial estates; they looked like castles. During layovers we watched farm laborers go about their chores. Wagons were usually pulled by horses; I even saw one old wagon being pulled by one horse and one cow. On one occasion, I observed a cow being serviced by a bull; two farm hands were in attendance. At one of the big farms I saw a very pretty girl of about 18 years old standing outside the kitchen. She was very sad looking; she was a household slave laborer from one of the Eastern European countries that Germany had overrun. At one of the estates

I saw a fancy carriage being pulled by two beautiful dapple grey horses. The Germans had rounded up all the good horses in Europe.

"About half way through our march we were issued one half of a loaf of bread for both Floyd and me. That night Floyd put it under him in the hay. During the night one of our fellow Kriegies stole that bread. That was at least a three-day ration for us. My morale reached its lowest point then.

"Another time, I attempted to milk a cow in one of the barns while Floyd stood as a lookout. That cow recognized a city boy's fingers and would not cooperate. On another occasion, we had a layover at a big farm that had a hen house. The guard was walking back and forth and as he went by with his back turned, I slipped into the hen house and quickly felt in each of the nests. I felt an egg and put it into my pocket. When the guard passed by again I slipped back out of the hen house and examined my egg; it was a glass egg (glass eggs were put in the nest to entice hens to lay). I slipped back into the hen house and returned the egg. At that same farm I observed one of the Kriegies catch a chicken by the neck and slide it under his overcoat. He had chicken stew that night.

"In the next 14 days and after crossing the Elbe River for the second time, we only marched about 70 km and ended up at Gudow on April 30, 1945. During those 14 days we only marched four days and laid over the other 10 days. The war was winding down and the German guards did not appear to know what to do.

"Finally, on May 2, 1945, the German sergeant who was in command of our group arranged to surrender us and his troops to a British reconnaissance patrol. While we were waiting for the British, I traded a Red Cross parcel chocolate bar to one of the guards for his side arm (Walther 7.65 mm Automatic).

"After 369 days of captivity, I was a free man at last. There was no great celebration or showing of emotion among any of the men in my group that day. The ordeal was over and we could now go back to the States and join our loved ones; my prayers had been answered. I kept a log on the trip and recorded the towns and km shown on the road signs between towns. As stated earlier, we were on dirt roads most of the time and we probably followed a twisting and turning route. According to my recordings (based on road signs) we marched 787 km on our tour of Northern Germany. We traveled in the German states of Unter Mecklenburg and Niedersachsen and in the last few days into the state of Schlesweig-Holstein.

***

"We were liberated by the British near Buchen. The British directed us back toward Lauenburg on the Elbe River. Floyd and I stopped to watch the British soldiers as they were rounding up hundreds of German soldiers at a village and putting them behind barbed wire. As I was standing there a pretty young woman in black slacks turned to me and in perfect English asked, "What will they do with me?" She then added that her husband was behind that barbed wire fence. I often wondered how she fared for the next few weeks while Germany was in such turmoil.

"Floyd and I casually walked back toward Lauenburg and came across a German village that was void of inhabitants. The tile roofs had been shot up and each house was open. Apparently, the Germans had put up some resistance in that town. The British had piled up a stack of civilian shotguns and other type hunting rifles; each gun's stock had been broken off. We went into one or two of the houses to see how they were furnished and could have taken home fine china and porcelain, but we chose not to.

"As we approached Lauenburg, we joined some other ex-Kriegies and got on the back of a German flatbed truck that was loaded with German supplies. I found a box of cigars and passed them around; that was the first cigar I had ever smoked. The driver of the truck started down the hill in Lauenburg toward the Elbe River bridge. He shouted, "This truck has no brakes;" he then ran the truck into a wall to stop it.

"We walked on across the bridge, and on the other side of the bridge a British MP asked if we wanted a car, and we said we did. He then stopped a green 1939 Ford occupied by four German officers and made them get out. I was the first one into the car and headed for the back seat to liberate a pair of military field glasses behind the back seat. The other ex-Kriegies liberated some bottles of Schnapps in the car. Five of us got into that car and drove off to Lüneburg.

"At Lüneburg, we ex-Kriegies were given the opportunity to take a hot shower and clean up; we were sprayed with DDT to kill the lice. A German barber reluctantly gave us haircuts. This temporary assembly area was a permanent German Army facility. We spent two nights there and .the .next day, May 5, 1945, a British truck convoy drove us about 75 km to an airfield near Soltau. We stayed in tents awaiting planes for three days. On May 6, 1945, we heard on the radio that Berlin had fallen to the Russians. I talked one of the British soldiers out of his Army-issue pocket knife.

"On May 8, 1945, we took off in a British Dakota (C-47) plane. That plane must have been used during the complete war, because it shook and rattled like it was going to fall apart. The pilot had on board a BMW motorcycle that had been liberated from the Germans and he was taking it back to England.

"On May 8, 1945, we landed at in Brussels, Belgium. That afternoon Floyd, Claude Brown and I walked the streets of Brussels and helped the Belgium people celebrate VE Day. On May 9, 1945, we were shipped via train to Namur, Belgium. We spent three days at Namur. We were processed, deloused again with DDT and given new GI clothes.

"On May 12, 1945, we boarded a train for Camp Lucky Strike, France and arrived May 14, 1945. This camp was close to Le Havre, France. It consisted of one huge tent city. All of the ex-POWs were being brought into that camp. They gave you physical examinations and fed you well. I quickly put on a few pounds. For recreation you could go to movies; I saw my only USO show at camp Lucky Strike.

"I came across a number of old buddies at the camp. Robert Morgan, our tail gunner, and Lt. Silk, our bombardier, were there. I also met Captain Jimmy Noble; we went to Tech High School in Atlanta together. We went to Nashville as cadets in 1942 on the same train. As mentioned earlier, Claude Brown (a buddy from gunnery school) joined me in Brussels. I told Claude that I went down on my second mission; he said, "You should complain, I went down on my first mission and not by enemy action - our plane just quit flying and we had to bail out.

"While at Camp Lucky Strike, we were offered a pass to go to Paris, but I refused to go because I was afraid I would miss my boat back to the States. I could have gone to Paris several times because I didn't ship out until June 12, 1945.

"We left Le Havre on the U.S.S. General Butner. It was a fast troop ship which was built during the war. As always, I got the top berth (hammock); I was so close to the ceiling I could barely turn over. The Navy apparently believed we had been fed too well at Camp Lucky Strike, because they fed us only two meals per day while we were on the ship.

***

"On June 20, 1945, the "U.S.S. General Butner" docked at Newport News, Virginia. I spent a day or two there. We did note that German POWs were the KP's in the mess hall at Newport News; we resented the fact that they were being fed well and we had not. A large group of us were put on a train and shipped out to Atlanta. We arrived at Fort McPherson and Lanore, Mom and Pop met me there.

"I was issued a 60-day recuperation furlough. Lanore quit her government job and we started a 60-day honeymoon; we bowled, swam and just had fun. Pop had sold my 1936 Pontiac for me so we had to purchase a car. Lanore had saved all of her $50.00 per month allotment checks and I had received about $1,880.00 for the time I was a POW, so we had the money to purchase a car. There had been no civilian automobile production during the war, so cars were in short supply. I finally located a black 1940 Studebaker coupe which we purchased for about $650.00. That was as much as the car cost new, but we had a set of wheels.

"Since the war in the Pacific was going so well, I was given a 30-day extension on my furlough. Pop and I celebrated VJ Day by working on my Studebaker.

"After the 90-day furlough was up, I was sent to San Antonio, Texas. There I waited around for the Air Force to determine what was next for me. I was then sent to Greensboro, N.C. At Greensboro, I was given a pass for a few days to go back to Atlanta; I got Lanore and the car and we returned to Greensboro. We rented an upstairs bedroom in a nice home in Greensboro which had an outside entrance. The only problem was the room had twin beds, so we slept on one of the twin beds, which made for real togetherness.

"On November 20, 1945, I received my discharge at Greensboro and for us the war was over. We drove up to Boone, NC for breakfast and casually drove down the Blue Ridge Parkway to Asheville, NC and then to Atlanta. It was a memorable trip, which we both enjoyed.

***

"During my stay in Germany I had many hours to think about my future. I realized that one needed a college education to better succeed in life. Congress had passed the GI Bill and I decided that was too good of an opportunity to let pass. I applied to Georgia Tech and was accepted, but I could not start until January, 1946. Congress had also authorized a program for returning GI's which would pay $20.00 per week for 52 weeks, or until the returning GI could get a job; it was known as the 52/20 Club. I joined that club until I could start to Georgia Tech.

"The Bell Bomber Plant apartments in Marietta, Georgia were made available to married Georgia Tech students. We bought some basic furniture and moved into one of the apartments. Lanore got a job with the Veterans Administration as a secretary in Marietta, Georgia, and I became a full-time student at Georgia Tech.

***

Son Steve Andrews about his father's post-war years;

"Tech Sergeant Ralph Cash Andrews, Jr. was discharged on November 20, 1945 in Greensboro, North Carolina. He liked to tell the story when he was out processing from the US Army Air Force. He was asked what he did before the war and he responded that he made artificial limbs. He was told that it was best that the Army remain unaware of this skill, or they might change their mind about discharging him.

"Bobby (or Bob), as he was called by family and friends, returned to Atlanta, where his wife Lanore, and both their families lived. While a POW, he had plenty of time to reflect on his future and realized that he needed a college education to better succeed in life. Fortunately, Lanore had saved his pay while he was a POW. She continued her work as a secretary for the US Army at Fort MacPherson, Georgia, which enabled him to start classes at the Georgia Institute of Technology (Georgia Tech). During his senior year, Lanore gave birth to their daughter, Diana. Bob graduated with a Bachelor of Science degree in Textile Engineering in Spring, 1950.

"Upon graduation, he initially went to work as an engineer in Decatur, Alabama, but soon returned to Atlanta working at Fulton Bag and Cotton Mills. This helped them to buy their first home, in the Atlanta suburb of College Park. Bob moved when better opportunities presented themselves with other companies, but he always made sure that he only took positions that were not too far away from family in Atlanta. Including Atlanta and Decatur, his career took his family to Rock Hill, South Carolina; Athens, Georgia; and Easley, South Carolina. While living in Rock Hill, Lanore gave birth to their son, Steven.

"By the time Bob and Lanore moved to Easley, they were empty-nesters. Diana had gone to college, married, and was raising a family of her own. Steven followed his father's footsteps by attending Georgia Tech, and received a commission in the US Army after graduation. Bob and Lanore lived happily in Easley and were active in their church, Bethesda United Methodist Church. Bob's favorite hobbies were boating, water-skiing, fishing, and wood-working. He always said that he was most at peace when fishing on his boat. After retirement, Bob reconnected with the other surviving crewmen from his plane, recorded his memoirs of the War, and became very passionate about family genealogy.

"In June 2010, Bob had a heart attack. He survived, but he and Lanore had to leave their home of 33 years, and move to an assisted-living facility in Greenville, South Carolina. He quickly made new friends, and on the few occasions he was not with Lanore he was most comfortable with his new buddies who also happened to be World War II veterans. Bob passed away on November 6, 2012. He was buried with full Air Force honors on Veterans Day, November 11, in the Robinson Memorial Gardens Cemetery in Easley, South Carolina. He was followed in death by his wife, Lanore, on February 15, 2015.

Waist-Gunner S/Sgt. John E. Jones.

"It was April 1943 - I was eighteen years old. I had just graduated from High School. Bremerton, Washington. What did the future hold for my classmates and me? The war made things look very grim. We had already seen the impact of the war in our military town, soldiers sailors, barrage balloons, blackouts, anti-aircraft emplacements all through out the county, with sub-marine nets in Puget Sound to keep the Jap subs from getting at the Navy ship yard and ships.

"I like many others of my class signed to enter the service to do our part! I was sworn into the military service, April 6, 1943 at the Federal Building in Seattle, WA. The group of us were put immediately on a bus and off to the Army Base at Fort Lewis, Washington. Several of us were assigned to the Army Air Corps, which had been my choice. We received our Serial Number, GI clothes, hair cut and the complete military indoctrination. This is it, no turning back now; you are in the Army Mr. Jones! -

"They sent us by troop train to Fresno, CA for our basic training. Then to Denver, CO, and to Las Vegas, NV for three months aerial gunnery school. My next stop was Alexandria, Louisiana for extensive B-17 combat training. With training complete, on to Salt Lake City, Utah.

"Here I was assigned to a ten man crew along with a new B-17. We named her "Mexican Hayride." At this point we were eager and ready for our overseas duty!

We flew from Salt Lake to Kearney, Nebraska, to Gander, Maine, to Iceland and on to England where we were assigned to the 384th Bomb Group, 545th Squadron, with the 8th Air Corps, based in Grafton-Underwood, England air base.

"It made you stop and think when you discovered, your crew was part of the 100% replacement for the 545th Squadron. This made me realize just how expendable our crew was in this war!

"My position was left waist gunner, which I had trained for and was assigned. Just before our first mission I "just" happened to see a fine supply of flak jackets. Three of them some how found their way into our plane. I stood on one, the other two I attached under my .50 machine gun for protection from flak, as the thin skin of the plane (aluminum) would not stop 20mm or flak shrapnel!

"The flak jackets proved their worth on our second raid, as we were hit by fighters from 9 o'clock, the flak jackets took the 20/mm impact from the fighter attack, instead of my midsection. You can bet that I quickly found two more lying around!

***

"On our fourth mission, April 29,1944, we were briefed the target would be "Berlin." This was the big one everyone had waited for! (The British only bombed at night, they felt they encountered fewer German fighters and less flak than during the day.) The Americans felt that day light raids were much more accurate and precise. There were a thousand allied bombers that took part in this Berlin raid.

"After we crossed the English Channel, we were met with very heavy flak and German fighters all the way to Berlin. Just after we dropped our bomb load our plane took two direct hits from anti-aircraft fire between number one and two engines, disabling both of them. We were unable to feather the props (turn them into the wind to-stop the drag) of the two engines, which caused an extreme vibration on the wing. We could not maintain our altitude or speed: that made us fall out of the formation. We threw out any equipment that was not bolted down to lighten our plane.

"By now we were alone, without our group or fighter escort for protection, just a sitting duck! The enemy fighters really go after a damaged crippled aircraft. During the attacks every one of us enlisted men had been wounded from shrapnel from the exploding 20 mm shells. Most of our electrical system was shot out during the attacks. Our intercom, the alarm to bail out was out. We were on fire, in a dive and at less than one thousand feet; it was time to bailout!

"My parachute had flipped over on to my back while the plane was taking evasive action during the fighter attacks. I did not notice it was not snapped on, and I did not have the time to secure it on the front properly. At this time I was the last to leave the plane. My parachute opened with a severe jerk in the slipstream of the plunging plane. It really injured my back and dislocated my right shoulder.

I was bleeding a great deal from my wounds - three in my right leg, one over my right eye and one in my chest.

"I got out of my chute in time to get behind a log as the ME-l09 strafed my chute, or I would be history today! With my arm dislocated, I found a tree branch that I backed up to. It fit under my right armpit so that twisting to the right I was lucky, it slipped back into the socket.

"I had landed in a wooded area and was unable to walk with my leg wounds, but was able to use a fallen limb for a crutch. A short time later James Bouvier, our pilot, Robert Green, co-pilot and Louis Silk, bombardier found me. They tore up my undershirt to bandage my wounds. Louis still had the ring and rip cord from his chute. Since I did not have any boots on, the ring fit over my foot, with the cord still attached to the ring I could lift my foot and limp slowly on. I had tied my GI boots to my parachute harness, but the force of the chute snapping open sent them flying.

"I told the officers to move out while it was still light and gave them my escape kit, as I knew I could not travel very far in my condition. I did not want to hold back their chances to get as far away from the area as they could.

"After they left, using the parachute ring and ripcord I made my way west. Two German soldiers captured me a little over an hour later. I was put in a flat bed trailer with two of the crew members from our plane. We were driven through several towns, going very slowly, giving the civilians the opportunity to spit, hit with clubs and stone us.

"We were taken to a Luftwaffe base. They attempted to tend our wounds, but without much medical care. They used a pair of forceps and pulled the shrapnel from the calf of my leg. When removing it much of the muscle came out with it. They just stuffed it back in my leg and wrapped it with crepe paper. My wounds were not attended to until I arrived in prison camp at Stalag 17-B in Krems, Austria.

"From the Air Base we were sent by train to their main interrogation center near Frankfurt, Germany. We were put in solitary confinement for six or seven days. Each day we were questioned, but gave only our name, rank and serial number! When not answering their questions or filling out their papers they would backhand you along side of the head, threaten you with death. I was hit so hard along the side of my head my ear would bleed. Still, only name, rank and serial number! They would brag they knew all about us, town, family, schools. Their underground in the USA would send the news paper items on through Northern Ireland and into Germany. They were sure they could break our spirits, but no way!

"We were taken from the interrogation center to the Frankfurt railroad-marshaling yard, crammed into their small boxcars, so crowded that you could only sit with your knees under your chin. It was impossible to move around. The smell of the men was unbelievable! The wounded, burnt, pitiful unkempt! To look at them, they were a beaten, degraded group of soldiers; we were a sad lot. We sat in the marshaling yards for two nights, and both nights the British bombed the yards. I still dream of being locked in that pitch black boxcar during the air raid; I shook with fear like a trapped animal! I cannot to this day be confined, locked in or limit my area of movement or I will blow!

"The next day we left for our permanent prison camp, five days later we arrived in Krems, Austria on the Danube. Two and a half miles north, we arrived at Stalag 17-B, our new home. To quote Military Intelligence war reports, Stalag I7-B was one of the worst prison camps next to 2-B! Our camp contained 29,800 prisoners of various nationalities. That is including 4,000 American POWs, all Air Corps personnel.

"When we arrived, I was put in the Revier (camp infirmary) to spend the next month or so. My leg and wounds were in need of medical attention. Both tendons in the back of my right knee had been hit with shrapnel, and had started to heal with my leg bent back at a 40-degree angle so that I could not straighten my leg. They even had to sit on my knee to break the tendons loose.

"After my wounds healed I was assigned to barracks 29-A. I received the last bunk in the barracks. The camp had fleas, lice, and vermin during that time and never was cleaned when they assigned the first Americans to use the barracks in the POW camp. The barracks were 2x4 construction with only boards on the outside with paper over that. The tarpaper we had torn off for fuel, so it didn't keep much wind and snow out.

"Built to accommodate 240 men, we had 400, 200 to each end. A wash room in the center with six basins with one faucet for each basin. All were cold water Bunks were triple decks, two men per deck or six men per bunk. A single stove in the middle of the barracks, 54 lbs of coal a week - less than a bucket a day for warmth. German issues for blankets were two cotton ones, table cloth weight! The men slept two to a bunk to keep warm. The water supply was turned on two hours in the morning and two in the afternoon. We kept our tin cups filled at all times, but the nights were so cold the water would freeze. It was Europe's coldest winter in 45 years.

"The latrines were open pit out-house type. Built to accommodate 48 men, our compound had close to 1600 in it. From 9 pm to 6 am you could not leave your barracks, or you would be shot! The wash room had a one hole for night use. With no hot water to wash clothes or blankets, the fleas, lice, vermin just multiplied. You would see blankets on the barb wire fence and you could see the fleas, lice, etc. moving, crawling all over them!

"Approximately 150 men went on sick call each day with skin problems, upper respiratory infections and stomach ailments. About 30% of sick calls were for skin problems that were from living conditions, no hot water, the filth, and over crowded conditions. Another problem was, frozen feet and hands; both of my feet were swollen, black, split and bleeding. l could not even get my shoes on. They finally gave me over size clogs with wooden soles so I could get to the roll calls with something on my feet.

"Our food was very poor in quantity and especially poor quality! The daily ration was six to nine men to a loaf of their black bread weighing approximately 3 pounds (75% saw dust) and 1/2 pint of very thin soup and a couple of small potatoes. If and when we received Red Cross parcels, the Germans cut the issues of food by 50%. The parcels when available were shared with two to five men.

"I had only two showers during my internment. On arrival in camp, they showered and deloused us and shaved our heads. The second came six months later when they heard the Protecting Powers were to inspect our camp. Great, we just put our same infested clothes back on!

"The first part of April, there were rumors the war was winding down. Then we heard the Russians had surrounded Vienna, 60 to 70 miles to the east of our camp. The German camp commander gave orders to prepare to evacuate the camp.

"On April 8, 1945 we POWs left camp in groups of 500, with 20 to 30 guards and two police dogs. We headed west through the mountain foothills in Austria, about 18 to 20 kilometers our 1st day. The country was beautiful, with small towns snuggled in the mountains, also the beauty of the many shrines along the back roads. It was an uplift we all needed. The weather was cold and we had to bivouac in open fields. Most men had only one blanket and if you had a German issue, it was cotton, a thin one. To keep warm we teamed up, five men in a group. You started on one side and moved across each night. That gave you two nights on the outside and three in the center for warmth. You would wake up to frost, then later freezing rains. The heat on the march were the bonfires at night - trying to dry our wet clothes and shoes, and socks.

"It did not take long for you to have blisters on your feet, which made walking sheer agony. They only gave us four short breaks during a day, which averaged 8 to 14+ miles a day. The daily ration of food was a very small cup of sour barley soup and a small loaf of black bread for 10 to 12 men. Not much nourishment to maintain our strength. The lack of proper food made the days long and the nights way to short.

"Some of the thirty guards were Volksturm (older home guard) German soldiers. We decided it was time to shake up the guards, so every day around 1:00 we stepped up our cadence to the tunes from basic training. This really had the guards worried, not knowing what was up so it made them more alert than normal. They became as tired as we were but we pushed that much harder, until one of the Volksturm Guards had a severe heart attack and died.

"The forced march was taking its toll on every one of us, young and old! The rugged terrain was making it tougher each day. My hunger by this time, if we stopped near a farmhouse, I would dig through the manure piles for any discarded food of any kind. I would clean the rot off of the old potatoes, and put them in the coals of our campfire. I ate the charcoal along with the potato to help check the ongoing dysentery problem. I picked sour grass and dandelion leaves by day, and would boil them in the fire at night for food. Water for drinking and washing, came from mountain streams.

"April 13 our Guards informed us President Roosevelt had died, we hoped this would not hinder our peace efforts!

"We finally came down off the mountains and followed the Danube River. The valley was much easier walking. We went through the City of Linz just as the town was being bombed, great! The flak shrapnel would rain-on us like hail. What more do we need?

"The food was getting a little better, and then we heard the Protecting Powers from Geneva were in the area. The Protecting Powers promised us Red Cross parcels in a few days. We could only hope at this point, as we were all ready to drop from hunger. The Protecting Powers departed and it was back to the old starvation and abuse!

"The weather was getting warm now, felt good. Still receiving a small cup of watery soup with our proteins, swimming in it. We are coming into the hilly country again. I find it strange, with the bombs destroying almost everything along the countryside, not one of the shrines had been hit or destroyed. As we would pass some of the older women on the road, they would look at us with tears in their eyes. We must have been a sad bedraggled looking group of human beings!

"In the distant hills we could see, to our surprise, trucks with Red Cross on them. FOOD! The parcels were British and French. The British parcel contained oatmeal, biscuits and other good food. My luck, I received the French parcel, cupcakes, candy and other sweets, which did not help our dysentery problems. I, like the rest could not keep away from them and many were quite sick. What we needed at this point was Moms cooking!

"We passed a group of Jew's being marched in the opposite direction. I thought we looked bad, they were walking skeletons! We shared everything we had with them. If they would stumble and fall the Jerries guarding them, shot them on the spot. It was hard to look at this beaten, starved mass of tortured humans, it made each one of us want to cry! We all knew then and now, why we were in this war! I

"They told us we would reach our new camp in two days. We could not be happier; we will end our 18 days, 291-mile march. It was located southwest of Brenau, Austria (Hitler's hometown). We were told this is it, and can you believe, there was nothing but trees No camp, no barracks, no hospital, and no water! The water was a mile to the river. The German Commander said this is it, make your shelters from the pine trees and pine boughs. I'll tell you now, pine boughs do not keep rain out. We had campfires going all the time to keep warm and dry out our blankets and clothes.

"We knew when we went to the river for water American troops were near as

271

we could hear the heavy gunfire. About May first, one of our POWs decided to swim the river about 3 :00 am to see how close our troops were. He saw them on the other side of the river with guns raised. They finally understood his shouting that he was an American. They told him he was lucky they didn't shoot, and if he had not swam over to them, they were going to shell the woods as they had no idea who was bivouacked in the woods with all the camp fires.

"May 3, 1945, the 13th Armored Division liberated our camp in the woods. They easily captured the remaining 205 guards. We were evacuated around May l0, taken out by C-47s to Le Havre, France, Camp Lucky Strike. There we were put on troop ships - on to the good old USA - what a great feeling!

"When our ship pulled into the New York harbor, we passed by our country's greatest symbol of freedom, the Statue of Liberty. You could not find one dry eye aboard ship. Statue of Liberty stands for our love of our country~our flag and our family. You could see in each of the men's eyes what brought them through the months and years of mistreatment in Prison Camp; Patriotism, Honor and Pride.

Tail-Gunner S/Sgt. Robert W. Morgan.

Tail-Gunner S/Sgt. Robert W. Morgan

"They tell me I was born out on Sunnyside Road at a big white house on Dwight Raymer's farm and across from Bob Banta's farm on December 8, 1921. I don't remember this great event, because I was small at this time as you well know. Since that time the old house has been torn down.

"My father and mother moved to Middletown, Ohio to look for work. We lived up there a couple of years and then they moved back to Smithfield, KY and lived with my grandparents for a while. My family then rented a house, which was the 3rd house west of the Smithfield Mill and we lived there for several years.

"I started school when I was five years old and I remember that I really liked it. I remember my first whipping by my dad. I like to play marbles and I would stop at the L 85 N Railroad Depot and play Keeps. My parents told me to come on home after school, but I stopped off and played marbles until nearly dark and Dad paddled my rear end. I still have some of my marbles until this day. I have two agates that my half uncle Oscar Wilson gave me.

"I went to my first 8 years of school at Smithfield. Then I went to New Castle 4 years of high school. While in high school and I turned 16 and I got my driver's license. My father had a Model A Ford. I thought I was a great driver and couldn't have a wreck. One day while going out Sunnyside Road with my daddy in the front seat on our way to go fishing, I ran off the road and into the culvert. So when my children come in telling me they had a wreck, I know how that happens. My boys had a lot of this trouble.

"I remember the Flood of 1937 when most of Louisville was under water. During my senior year, I remember when Adolf Hitler was starting his conquest of Europe.

"After I graduated in 1939, my Uncle Olen Miller came to Smithfield on a visit to his mother (my grandmother). He lived in Los Angeles, California. When he went back, I went with him to work on roof work back in Los Angeles. While there, we went deep sea fishing, and to San Francisco to the World's fair. I stayed out there 3 months, but I got home sick for family and friends and my girlfriend. Unfortunately, when I got back home, my girlfriend had found another boy to fill my place.

"I came back and went to work in construction at Fort Knox, Kentucky, since the war effort was getting underway. I worked there over a year and then I went to work for the DuPont Powder Plant in construction in Charlestown, Indiana. I then went to work for the Goodyear Bag Plant which made bags of powder for the big guns in the Army and Navy.

"The United States went to war with Japan, Germany and Italy after Japan bombed Pearl Harbor on December 7, 1941. I remember I was in Smithfield washing my car when this happened. It was a nice warm Sunday afternoon.

"I decided to sign up. I enlisted in the U. S. Army Air Corps on October 31, 1942. I first tried to get in our Air Force as a pilot, but I was turned down for high blood pressure. I then tried to get in the Air Force as a mechanic and I took the entrance exam. They told me I was fine. I had a high aptitude in mechanics and so I enlisted. I went to Bowman Field for Basic training for three months.

"After training, I was put on a train and I didn't know where I was going. I wound up in Fort Logan, Colorado in clerical school. They said I had high aptitude and I should be in clerical work, so they taught me typing and bookkeeping. When I finished school, they sent me to a service squadron in Montana, who repaired planes, but I worked in the office. They then sent me to Nashville to take more tests. When I arrived, they said I was qualified to be a pilot or navigator training, so I chose to go to pilot training.

"They then sent me to San Antonio, Texas for pre-flight training. This was officer training such as they do at West Point. When I finished, I was sent to Cuero, Texas for Primary training for the PT 19 Fairchild. On my first solo, I landed and put the wing of my plane in the ground, so I took off and went back into the air. I came back around the field and landed my plane. After this, I was checked out by the Check Pilot and was washed out of pilot training. They said that I was dangerous to my life, as well as others. My flight instructor washed out all five of his students.

"All of the students that had been washed out were put into a group and were sent back to Shepherd Field, Texas to be reassigned to other parts of the Air Force. While at Shepherd Field, we were all reclassified. I asked for them to send me back to work in the office, because I was qualified to do that, but they said I had all of this flying training, so they sent me to Las Vegas, Nevada to gunnery school to become an aerial gunner. We fired guns on the ground and also had air to air gunnery practice.

"After I finished gunnery school, they sent me to Grand Island, Nebraska to be formed into bomber crews to receive more training. The crew that I was put into was sent to Alexandria Army Air Base near Alexandria, Louisiana. One day while at the bus station, I was asked by a girl if I would buy a chance on a bale of cotton. I said I would if she would give me a date. She agreed to this and I got to know Rose Maria Spears. I visited her several times while I was stationed there. She later became my wife after I finished my overseas tour of duty. I was in Louisiana about 4 months.

"We left Alexandria on February 21, 1944. We then went to Grand Island, Nebraska and while there, they gave us a new B-17 pane to fly over seas to combat. We left Grand Island, Nebraska near March 9, 1944. As we flew over Chicago, Illinois, we dropped down over our engineer's home and flew so close to the ground that we could see church steeples out our plane's windows.

"From there we flew up over the Great Lakes on into New. York and up over Boston, which was our navigator's home city. When we got to Maine, we got lost over the state in a snowstorm and when we finally got to Presque Isle, Maine Air Field, we were nearly out of gas. We stayed there a couple of days and we left on March 17th and went to Newfoundland, Canada. We left there after only one day and flew up over Greenland and on to Iceland. We stayed there a few days and while we were there, we went into Keflure, Iceland and saw how they dried fish on trays all around the town and the smell was horrible.

"We left Iceland March 19th and flew to Scotland and stayed through March 21st and then flew on to our Air Force base where we flew combat into Germany. Our base was close to Ketering, England. While we were there, I bought a bicycle to ride around the base on into town. The old people and young alike would pass me like I was sitting still, since they were used to riding bikes. I was in England only a short time. We flew five missions and two spares in only about two weeks.

"On our first mission we went into Germany just across the Channel. We flew one mission down into the southern part of Germany down near Switzerland. This raid was to try to draw up the Luftwaffe and try to get rid of most of the German fighter planes before the invasion of England.

***

"On April 29, 1944, we were on a Berlin mission. We were carrying incinerator, phosphorus incinerator bombs and had left out after daybreak. This was our 5th mission and even though we had some fighter cover, we were still hit with flak over the city. We had two engines shot out, so we had to drop out of formation and our plane began to lose altitude. We did have a call for fighter escort and did have P-38s come in and they did stay with us for a short time.

"While we were throwing out everything that we could to try and keep altitude, a German fighter came in, came down to the side of our plane and turned around and came into my tail position. I didn't know he was as near as he was, because our intercom had been shot out. When I finally got to my firing position, the fighter plane's guns were already firing into my position.

"The pilot put our plane into a dive to get out of the fighter plane's guns. (I prayed to God to be with my mother at this time.) When the plane leveled out, we were instructed to bail out. Of the ten man crew, nine got out of the plane safely. We had one crew member, our engineer, who was killed, but we aren't sure if he was hit while in the plane, in the air or on the ground.

"It was at this time that I received about a hundred pieces of shell, aluminum, and Plexiglas in my body. When my parachute opened and I fell, I was in a large tree. We came down in a wooded area approximately fifty miles from Berlin. When the air went out of my parachute, I landed on the ground. I disengaged myself and began to walk the short distance out of the forest. l was losing so much blood that I was becoming weaker by the minute. I had multiple wounds in my arms, legs, chest, back and hands and needed help.

"I made it over to a road and two Polish prisoners of war came along on a bicycle. I didn't try to evade my captors. They picked me up, placed me on the bike and took me to their cabin. They were prisoners whose responsibility was to take care of the forests. They offered me coffee, D-bars, and what they had received from the Red Cross parcels that they had received. The Germans came to their home in a bus and took me to a German Luftwaffe Hospital. The doctors and nurses gave me fairly good care and they picked out metal from my wounds and then bandaged me. They didn't have but very little cloth at this time, so they had to bandage me with a lot paper bandages.

"The Germans put several prisoners on a train and we arrived at Dulag Luft in Oberursel on May 1, 1944, where we were to be interrogated. All Americans were there about one week in interrogation. I was told that that they didn't know whether I was a flyer or not, or that I could be a spy. I didn't have any dog tags on me due to them being shot off, or just lost when we bailed out.

"They tried to get information out of me, but I had only been in the group for a short time. The Germans on the whole knew more about our group than I did, so I couldn't tell them anything new.

"We were there about a week and then sent to Obermassfeld (Allied Staffed Hospital) where they took care of my wounds. The doctors who took care of me here were British and Australian doctors who had been captured on the front. My arm at this time was paralyzed and remained this way for about 6 months.

"On June 6, 1944, the invasion of France took place at 1:00 am on that day. We heard about it about 8:00 am. that morning when the doctor came to the ward to make his examination of us. I was at this hospital for about a month. When they thought I was able to be moved, they put several prisoners on a train with several guards and took us through Berlin to Stalag Luft 4 Prisoner of War Camp, which was over in Gross Tychon, East Germany near Poland. This was around July 7, 1944.

"My family didn't know whether I was killed or a POW. It was in July of that year that my mother was notified by the German propaganda radio station Axis Sally that I had been captured and that I was a prisoner of war.

"When you first arrive at the camp, rank was important. If you were an American airman and shot down, you would automatically become staff sergeant. By the Geneva Convention; staff sergeants didn't have to work. So in this way, most airmen didn't have to work while they were prisoners of war.

"We didn't get too much to eat while in prison. We had kohlrabies, Irish potatoes, cabbage, carrots and turnips. We also had brown bread to eat with the vegetables. When we were first shot down, you could hardly eat the bread, but we got hungry and you could eat about anything. At the beginning, our meals were subsidized by Red Cross packages once a week, but later on in our stay, we then had to share a parcel with 3 other prisoners. We didn't have any problem with anyone being overweight, so when people say that they can't lose weight, I know how to correct that problem.

***

"The British did more when it came to escaping than the Americans, because they could speak more than one language and were more familiar with the country and the people. There was one guy who escaped out of camp and stopped at a small barn. He took a cow, put a rope around} its neck and marched it completely out of Germany, pretending to be a German.

***

"Toward the end of the war our food supply was shorter. The Germans heard that the Russians were getting closer and the soldiers who were taking care of the prisoners at our camp did not want to be taken prisoner by the Russians, so they pulled out and left our camp and let the Russians take over.

"The Germans left us on our own with Colonel Zemke commanding on April 30th at 10:30 pm. We also received word that Mussolini was killed by Patriots on April 30th. We were liberated by the Russians on May 1, 1945 about 10:15 pm. And there was a great celebration and at 10:32 we received word that Hitler was dead. .

"On May 2nd at about 1 pm, we were allowed to tear down the barbed wire and go into Barth. On the way, we passed a camp where prisoners of Russia, Poland and other countries were kept by Germans. A lot of them starved to death and those who were left were skin and bones. I also saw an elderly lady and her baby who had been shot. The baby was still in the baby buggy. There were also dead bodies on a flat car. The Russians killed a lot of the Germans, just as the Germans had done with the Russian people, as they had gone through Russia.

"When we got to town there was a great celebration. Some of the boys got drunk for the first time in months. Many of the Germans claimed that they like the Americans and the British and hated the Russians, but this was because we were the victors and not the POWS. I went to the flak school and got a few German souvenirs.

"On May 5 we had a big day. First General Aristoff, Maj. General Sakovich, Field Marshal Rofososky and General Borisoff, who was the well-known veteran of Stalingrad, arrived. While Colonel Zemke and the Russian generals were in conference, a major, two captains and a sergeant drove into camp in a jeep. They were the first Americans to arrive. The following day, Sunday I went into Barth and I got a pair of German flying boots. I went to church and later had a meal of fried spuds and fish at 1400 - 2 pm. At 6:00 pm, I had a meal of fish and fried spuds.

"May 8th. The war was over. It was a great celebration, but not as great as the day we were liberated. I went out to the airfield and looked it over. The Germans didn't destroy so much equipment. The field was ready for allied planes to land and take us out. The Russians offered Zemke one thousand hogs, but he only accepted a few of these because we still had a few Red Cross parcels left.

"May 9th — We received word today that we would be out of here in four more days. - Hope so. We told the Russians that we needed food, so they drove a large herd of Holstein cows into camp. Some of our prisoners killed them for meat. One of the prisoners in our room was from Wisconsin, so he decided to get one of the cows and tied her close to our barracks and proceeded to milk her. He wanted fresh milk, but after a couple of days, she made so much noise, he turned her loose. We were also given Red Cross parcels that the Germans had locked in storage. This was the first day that I had beefsteak since I had left the USA.

"On May 13th - We marched over to the airfield and we were loaded into a B-17 and were on our way. We passed over the German towns of Hamm, Munster, Essen, Cologne, Dusseldorf and could see Frankfurt off to the left. The cities were all in ruins. We could see what our bombing had done to help win the war. We landed in Lyon, France. From there we caught a truck and went to Reims and stayed there all night.

"The next day we took a shower and got all new clothes. We went out to the airfield and caught a C-47 and rode to La Havre, France. In route, we passed over the large city of Bayonne, France. At Le Havre, we caught a truck and came to the US army base named Camp Lucky Strike. I visited most of the Red Cross Clubs and looked the camp over. We received new clothing, got hot baths and plenty of food.

"On May 16th - we roamed around the camp all day and that night. That night we went to a show and saw "Bowery to Broadway." That was an awfully good show, the first American show that I had seen since I became a guest of the Germany Reich.

"June 11th – we got on the "U. S. General Buckner" and came back to Fort Dix, New Jersey. While on the ship, we ate, slept, played cards or shot craps. I won $800 shooting craps and used it to take a great honeymoon in New Orleans later on.

***

"I got home to Smithfield, Kentucky about the first day of July, 1945. I went to Eminence on the 4th of July to a picnic. After this I got a bus ticket to Lettsworth, Louisiana to check on my girlfriend Rose. I was there about a week before Rose accepted my offer of marriage. I asked her daddy if I could have his daughter for my wife. He said I could have her, but he didn't want her back. He said he wasn't an Indian giver.

"Rose's brother Biggy and his wife took Rose and me to New Roads, Louisiana and we were married by a Justice of the Peace. We went to New Orleans on a honeymoon for a few days and then came back to Lettsworth for a few days. We then got on a train and went to Smithfield, Kentucky for a few days to visit my family. We then caught another train and went to Miami Beach, Florida for a 30 day leave.

"After my leave, the Air Force sent me to Camp Atterbury, Indiana to work in the office until I had enough points to get out of the Army. (Rose and I lived in Franklin, Indiana at this time.) I was discharged from the Air Force on November 2, 1945.

***

Acknowledgements:
Parsippany Community News by By Reverend Jeff Edwards for Navigator Harold Gantert.
Steve Andrews, son of radio-operator Ralph Andrews
Connie LaRose, daughter of pilot James Bouvier
Debbie Gantert, daughter of navigator Harold Gantert
Jack Jones, son of waist-gunner John Jones
Mechelle Flowers, daughter of tail-gunner Robert Morgan.

CHAPTER 15

385TH BOMB GROUP
549TH BOMB SQUADRON

Type: B-17G • Serial: 42-31773
MACR: 4456 • Air Base: Great Ashfield

This aircraft had a damaged tail section and was out of control at this time. The ship was reported by another crew as having a damaged left wing, a result of fighter attacks. It left the formation rolling completely over, ultimately going into a dive. Prior to this two chutes were seen to leave the aircraft, one of these believed to have been the tail-gunner as it was seen to come from that section of the aircraft.

Missing Air Crew Report # 4456

Pilot: 1Lt. Charles R. Johnston, 0-802402, KIA

Co-Pilot: 2Lt. Owen D. Walton, 0-802498, POW

Navigator: 2Lt. Richard W. Glaser, 0-811623, POW

Bombardier/Tog: S/Sgt. William Moffitt, 32075641, POW

Engineer: T/Sgt. Joe D. Parker, 18216603, KIA

Radio: T/Sgt. James O. McLelland Jr., 39543377, POW

Ball-Turret Gunner: T/Sgt. Jesse P. Collinson, 32761676, POW

Left Waist-Gunner: S/Sgt. William P. Domer, 35382557, POW

Right Waist-Gunner: S/Sgt. Vencil Owens, 35682557, POW

Tail-Gunner: S/Sgt. Harvey F. Watts, 33191902, POW

2 KIA, 8 POW

Crash Site: Fallersleben, Germany, on the Volkswagen factory.
Time: 11.10

The complete crew bailed out before bomber exploded after attacks by German fighters. According to other members of this crew engineer Joe D. Parker was killed by civilians. Pilot Charles Johnston was seriously wounded and died the same day in the hospital of Wolfenbuttel, Germany.

***

385TH BOMB GROUP
549TH BOMB SQUADRON

Type: B-17G • Serial: 42-97559
MACR: 4459 • Air Base: Great Ashfield

---

*Aircraft 42-97559 left the formation after the final
attack by enemy fighters. It circled to the right away
from this Group's formation with no. 4 prop windmilling
and no. 1 engine smoking. This aircraft was last seen
slowly spiralling downward. Apparently under control.
No chutes were seen leaving this aircraft.*

Missing Air Crew Report # 4459

Pilot: 1Lt. Robert E. Barney, 0-746248, POW, Parsa, MO

Co-Pilot: 2Lt. Osmond T. Jones, 0-755570, POW, Houston, TX

Navigator: 2Lt. William C. McCarthy, 0-691771, POW, Bristol, CT

Bombardier/Tog.: S/Sgt. Albert F. Scerbo, 12201745, POW, Fulton, NY

Engineer: T/Sgt. Sanford A. Byer, 38009220, POW, Meaderville, MT

Radio: S/Sgt. John E. Hutchins, KIA, Glenn, MI

Ball-Turret Gunner: S/Sgt. Charles A. Grinder, 3732144, POW, Salinas, CA

Left Waist-Gunner: S/Sgt. Jack N. Burch, 33539700, POW, Covington, VA

Right Waist-Gunner: S/Sgt. Sammy E. Finley, 18076079, POW, Plainview, TX

Tail-Gunner: S/Sgt. Carl E. Lunde, 37168579, POW, Milwaukee, WI

1 KIA, 9 POW

Crash Site: 1.5 Km. north of Grasleben/Helmstedt, Germany
Time: 11.30

Pilot 1Lt. Robert E. Barney.

From Robert's book "Bulletproof."

"On April 29, 1944, we awakened at 3:00 p.m. for an obvious Maximum Effort raid. This would be another strike deep within enemy territory. The day ahead looked grueling.

"Breakfast did not appeal to me. I sleepwalked to the briefing room early and sat with the impending deep penetration target, probably Berlin, Big B, foremost in my mind. The early awakening, coupled with the extended string and curtain to the target, presented sufficient indication that a rough day lay ahead. Smiles were noticeably absent.

"The briefing officer indicated that a Pathfinder (PFF) operator would be assigned to our group since overcast was expected in the target area. PFF was primitive

Pilot 1Lt. Robert E. Barney with wife

American type radar known as Mickey, that made it possible to bomb through clouds. Since our group had no Mickey operator, one was assigned to us for this particular mission.

"A low ceiling and light rain did not deter us. Thankfully we were able to view the center white runway line during take-off. Upon breaking out on top at about 12,000 feet, we lunged a very heavy aircraft into our assigned position.

"We considered it favorable news that the Eighth Air Force put up a vast number of aircraft that day. Comfort in numbers diminished our feelings of being singled out by the Luftwaffe.

"At some point along the way, enemy fighters fiercely approached, attacking our formation from all directions. Crewmember voices, loud and excited, yelled through the inter-phone, "Fighters at three o'clock;" Fighters at 6 o'clock;" "Fighters at 9 o'clock;" "Fighters queuing up at 1 o'clock high for a head-on attack." Machine gun fire from the top turret was deafening. A tremendous crash shook the aircraft as we took a direct hit. It seemed as though a building had toppled onto the right wing. Perhaps flak hit us, or a rocket from a ME 110. We accessed our condition to find number one and four engines smoking, with the latter hanging loosely from the wing.

"We fell from the formation, and I ordered bomb release. I tried to turn the aircraft away from the flight path, but it would do nothing except hang sluggishly in a near stalled position. Rudder was the only available control, as we had lost control of both the aileron and elevator. The plane banked steeply toward the the number four engine, and a spin seemed inevitable. I had cranked in full trim, and there was no aileron control. Woefully, the engine broke into sheets of flame.

"Escape looked hopeless. I chopped the throttles of the two left engines to the extent that the aircraft returned to a near-level position. Sgt. Sanford Byer, the flight engineer, left his turret position behind the flight deck, grabbed a walk-around oxygen bottle and shouted, "Fire in the bomb bay." I noticed that he was wearing his chest pack.

"I pushed the throttle and super-charger forward on number three engine until the manifold pressure indicators were in the red, but the aircraft failed to respond. We were floundering like a fish out of water. With maximum power and no controls, the plane stuttered a warning of a power-on stall. A stall under those conditions, without elevator and aileron controls, would result in a spin and likely death of the entire crew. With a smoking left engine, fire in the right engine, we expected explosion at any moment.

"The ball-turret gunner, Charles Grinder, called on the inter-phone to advise that Charles Hutchins, the radio-operator, had been struck by enemy fire. It was later revealed that Hutchins had left his position to manually free Grinder, the ball-turret operator. I was too occupied trying to control the aircraft to consider the details, for the fate of the entire crew loomed at stake.

"A forward glimpse quickly revealed several German yellow noses queuing up for the kill. In a matter of seconds they would split and come at us in a savage head-on attack, claiming us as their victim. We flew alone, and presented an easy and inviting target. I was fighting to steady the aircraft in order to evacuate the crew. We were out of time and there was nothing left to do. I hit the alarm switch three short rings, followed by one long, which was an unconditional order for all crew members to immediately depart the aircraft. At the same time I called over the inter-phone, "Hit the silk."

"I had been too busy to talk to Lt. Osmond Jones, my co-pilot, but upon glancing his way I noticed that he appeared to be frozen in his seat. Once I sounded the bail-out signal, he evacuated in a flash with William McCarthy, our navigator, close behind.

"Momentarily I felt the loneliness of being the sole occupant of the aircraft. However, the sight of yellow noses scattered about the sky in great numbers, with three of them breaking for a head-on pass, prompted me to react.

"As I scrambled from my seat and bent down to reach for my chest pack, an indescribable noise of metal against metal and the shattering of glass deafened me. I rose to a slight crouch and saw that the windshield had burst, and blood spurted from my face. My aircraft was falling apart at the seams, and I needed to execute a speedy exit. The top turret had become a mass of twisted metal and it was impossible to pass through to my primary exit, the bomb bay. The nose hatch remained the only escape route. Generally it was considered too small for a safe exit but in the impending situation, my adrenaline easily propelled me headfirst through the diminutive opening.

"Relieved to be out of the aircraft, I concentrated on deploying my parachute. Counting to three, I pulled the ripcord and held onto the chest pack to keep the chute from opening. An explosion occurred almost directly overhead, which was surely our bomber. The tragedy of losing the aircraft, Hutchins, and other crew members, flashed through my mind, but my instincts kept me focused on survival. Freefalling in an effort to avoid being shot up by German fighters or ground fire, and plunging wildly towards a landing in Germany, overshadowed all else. Spinning out of control, I attempted to use one arm as an airfoil to slow the rotations. My other arm gripped the parachute. When changing arms, spinning in the other direction commenced.

"The bailout had been initiated at an altitude of about 22,000 feet. I stayed in that dizzying free fall until I noticed the ground rushing upward, which would indicate an altitude of about 3,000 feet. When I finally released the chest pack, the chute gently opened and the spinning ceased. But there was something horribly wrong. Both arms were pinioned above my head, and the harness chest strap from the chute stretched across my face. My hands were rendered useless, and I could not assume any directional control. With some difficulty, I peered down and caught the sight of my leg strps swinging freely. I had neglected to fasten them after using the urine relief tube! To this day, I marvel at how I beat the odds and remained in that harness. I suspect that the parachute harness somehow lodged to the oral inflation tube of my Mae West, for it occupied a position even with the parachute chest strap.

"When nearing the ground, I observed that the landing would place me in a residential area with a welcoming committee of citizens. Would they be bloodthirsty after all the bombings?

"I impacted heavily into a crowded street, heels first and then bounced backward. A mild wind added to my harsh landing and my head collided with the pavement, knocking me nearly unconscious. As my head began to clear, I tried to stay calm but teetered on the brink of panic. It seemed that I was soon destined to be a statistic, for the neighborhood group, mostly women and children, kicked and whacked me with whatever crude weapons available. One woman flailed me wickedly with a poker. A profusely bleeding face may have contributed to my survival. The blood had congealed in the cold air during the fall, but the warmer surface temperature and the mauling made quite a mess of my appearance.

"Fate was again on my side as a middle-aged woman took charge in a commanding matter. She brought a halt to the assault as she grabbed my arm, helped me to my feet and led me to her home. Although in near shock from fear and the fall, I recognized her as an ally. In broken English she bade me to take a seat, fetched a glass of water, and washed the blood from my face. After attempting to make me comfortable, she showed me a picture of her son and told me that he was a Kriegsgevangene (POW) in New Mexico, USA. The treatment he was receiving as a prisoner in the U.S. pleased her, and I surmised that she extended me the kindness in reciprocation.

"Nevertheless, the Gestapo was summoned, and within a brief time I was dumped unceremoniously into the slammer. I had hoped that she would call the Luftwaffe. We believed at that stage of the war that any guest of the German Gestapo would likely face execution.

"I found no way to relieve my mind of an overwhelming sense of apparent doom. Our intelligence had indicated that German civilians, in all probability, would execute captured airmen. However, capture by the military presumably meant safety. In either case, death appeared imminent if armed at time of capture. Fortunately, I carried no weapons.

"It was a pleasant surprise when a guard appeared at my cell and asked me in English to play checkers. I happily consented, and he opened the cell door wide, spreading the board on the threshold floor. Instead of checkers, he pulled out a small bag containing an assortment of buttons that we awkwardly used as pieces.

"His friendliness put me somewhat at ease. In just a few moves, I knew that I had the upper hand in the game. I wrestled with the idea of whether or not it would be wise to trounce him. The question mattered little, for another guard, seemingly the senior one on duty, walked up and with a kick of his knee-high boot littered the hallway with the makeshift checkers. He severely berated the young guard and then nodded me into the cell, slamming and locking the door. My heart beat like a drum.

"Later in the afternoon, I caught the voice of another prisoner as he entered a nearby cell. He also heard me and recognized my voice. Within a few moments, he called my name, and I delighted in finding that Jack Burch, one of the two waist-gunners on our crew had survived the bailout. However, he confirmed my grim fear that Hutchins, our radio operator, lost his life by enemy fire before my order to evacuate. Jack had pulled the rip cord on Hutchin's parachute and thrown him from the aircraft.

"Burch also informed me that when departing the aircraft, he spotted Sgt. Lunde, the tail-gunner, hanging with his parachute shrouds snagged to the tail of the aircraft. With that news, I held little hope that Lundy had survived. The plane had been ablaze and exploded within seconds following my departure. As he brought me up to date, a guard advanced and put a quick stop to our chatter.

"Looking forward to finding peace in sleep, I fashioned my shoes and trousers for a pillow, and bedded down for the night. However, my thoughts kept returning to Hutch, Lunde, and the other crew members. I relived the horrible moments before bailout, trying to reassure myself that most of the crew escaped the burning aircraft. Seeing Burch bolstered my morale, but my mind remained restless. The wooden bed, minus bedding, added physical discomfort to mental anguish, and tortured sleep.

"The Luftwaffe arrived and escorted me away the following morning, leaving Burch behind, which created additional mental anguish. The guards placed me in an outdoor enclosure, termed the Bull Pen, with perhaps a dozen or so other officers who shared my experience of parachuting into enemy territory and subsequent capture. Through a discussion with German officers, I learned that we awaited transportation to Dulag Luft, the prime interrogation center in Germany at Frankfurt, located on the Main River near Wiesbaden.

"The German officers spoke English and displayed a fair amount of congeniality. They made it abundantly clear that they idolized Adolf Hitler, and recounted in detail some of the important work he had accomplished for the "Fatherland."Their friendliness relaxed us for the moment, but we dared not speak out against Herr Hitler for obvious reasons.

"After four hours in the bullpen, our course was set for Dulag Luft, which entailed a two-day train ride in a small partitioned section of a passenger train car. The crowded conditions made it necessary to sleep in sitting positions. When passing through a German city, we let our defenses down and made the foolish mistake of pointing and laughing at some bomb-gutted buildings. Our behavior enraged our guards and they quickly subdued us with rifle butts.

"Another peculiar incident occurred during a short stop. We were ordered to detrain and stretch our legs. A squat middle-aged German officer, looking much like a bulldog, walked by accompanied by a Frau or Fraulein, whose beauty gained our immediate attention. With unbecoming manners, we emitted a few wolf calls and whistles. Officer Bulldog halted, and with blazing, bulging eyes, gave us a severe tongue-lashing in German. He terminated his tirade by vehemently uttering, "American Pigs." One could hear a pin drop as he rested his right hand on his pistol holster. The woman touched his arm, prompting him to board the train. She seemed to wear a slight smirk, and I suspect that she was less bothered by our crass behavior than her escort.

"In mid morning the second day of travel, we arrived at the interrogation center and the guards escorted us to individual cells. The impending interrogation weighed heavily on my mind. I prayed that I would have the courage to give only name, rank and serial number, as required by the Geneva Convention. Of course, the possibility of abuse lingered foremost in my mind.

"In the afternoon, my cell door opened, and a courteous guard mentioned me to follow. He spoke excellent English, and asked me about the comfort of my accommodations. I simply nodded, not wanting to offer anything except name, rank and serial number. We climbed a flight of stairs and walked down a hallway, entering an office where a dapper officer greeted me with a wide smile. The surreal experience made me feel as though I was watching myself play a role in a movie. In perfect English, he addressed me as Lt. Barney, politely bade me to take a seat, and offered me a cigarette. I readily accepted without much thought. In those days, smoking was an accepted habit. Allowing the craving to control my actions in the presence of the enemy irritated me.

"After lighting my cigarette, the officer congratulated me on commanding an aircraft. It proved a mystery to me how he had gained that knowledge. He talked smoothly, suggesting regrets that Germany and the United States were adversaries when they should be united against England and Russia. The next topic of discussion shocked me as he displayed knowledge of major league baseball in the states, particularly the St. Louis Cardinals, my favorite team since childhood.

"The officer mentioned having attended college at George Washington University, and added that he enjoyed his time spent in the United States. He again displayed regret over the United States and Germany's involvement in wartime activities against one another. Following a bit more idle chatter, to which I occasionally nodded, he asked me an apparent insignificant question. My reply was; "Sorry sir, I can only give you name, rank and serial number." He cheerfully clapped his hands, the guard appeared, and back to my cell I went.

"As I contemplated the worldwide scope of the war, I wondered if I would still be alive at its termination. How many years would it last, or would it go on indefinitely? Gloom and doom set in. Moroseness prevailed, and I could hardly lift my chin. As despair reared its ugly head, my energy and optimism vanished.

"Eventually, I reasoned that I had already survived some dangerous activities, and could continue to handle whatever would come my way. Strangely enough, after regrouping a bit, I looked forward to another visit with my acquaintance upstairs. Undergoing a variety of wildly fluctuating emotions, I knew that improving my frame of mind was essential to survival.

"That afternoon a guard came to escort me to another meeting. The same gregarious fellow greeted me with a bright "Hello." He again displayed excessive hospitality offering me a comfortable chair and a cigarette. To my surprise, he produced a bottle of wine and tempted me with a glass. Before succumbing, I shook off the distraction and put a hold on what sanity remained. Boldly and proudly, I emitted the word "Nein," and added "Danke," meaning, thanks. I feared that a few sips of alcohol might cause me to loosen up and become chatty. Unbeknownst to me, if I had accepted his offer, it would have appeared on my German POW record, which, at the end of the war, became the property of the U.S. government.

"My interrogator inquired as to how many missions I had flown. I refused to answer and he began a monologue that jolted me to the core. He knew the commander's name that led the bombing mission on which I was shot down. My military and personal life history spewed from his mouth, including the name of my group commander, my home base, the hard stand on which our plane was parked, the particulars of my Air Corps class, and my birthplace. He knew that I played both baseball and basket ball in high school, and stated emphatically that he possessed all pertinent details of my life, but would not waste his breath.

"I wanted to ask if he was through with me, but dared not be arrogant lest he keep me additional time to "pick my brain." The British intelligence had certainly been correct in stating that they Germans had amassed amazingly detailed personal file of their enemies through an intelligence service second to none.

"My interrogator summoned the guard to return me to my cell, and I could not resist uttering the German words "Guten Tag" (Good day) to which he smiled. Grateful to having stuck to my guns in offering only name, rank and serial number, I welcomed the confines of my cell.

"On the following morning, worry set in about facing my slick, amiable inquisitor. I intended to be hard-nosed and refrain from uttering a word in English or German. By unyielding, perhaps I would be moved to a POW Camp, as images of spending the rest of my life in a cell panicked me.

"Common sense comes and goes under such stressful circumstances. One has to experience those kind of situations to understand how despondency suddenly takes hold. It is crushingly disheartening to be a prisoner completely under the control of an enemy. I bolstered myself, determined to find a method of escape. Moreover, attempted escape fell within our military duty.

My reflection was interrupted as a group of us were assembled and hustled into a truck. A short ride deposited us at a train depot where the guards herded us in to a crowded boxcar for a miserable two-day ride to an unknown destination. It turned out to be POW Camp Stalag Luft III.

***

Ackonwledgements;
Patti Gattari, daughter of pilot Robert Barney

CHAPTER 17

385TH BOMB GROUP
550TH BOMB SQUADRON

Type: B-17G • Serial: 42-97078
MACR: 4457 • Air Base: Great Ashfield

Aircraft no. 42-97078 was reported to have been hit by enemy aircraft fire between 11:15 and 11:22 hours in the Magdeburg, Germany, area....Suddenly, it went into a dive out of control and started to burn. Five to six chutes were seen leaving the ship at this time.

Missing Air Crew Report # 4457

Pilot: 2Lt. William F. Henry, 0-682860, POW, Canton, KS

Co-Pilot: 2Lt. Charles W. Avona, 0-818089, KIA, Shelter Island, NY

Navigator: 2Lt. Gerhard W. Kirschke, 0-750199, POW, Saginaw, MI

Bombardier/Tog.: S/Sgt. Harold G. Tenneson, 17155122, POW, Makinock, ND

Engineer: T/Sgt. Thomas L. Pullen, 34357908, POW, Grand Isle, NE

Radio: T/Sgt. John E. Webb, 16133921, POW, Green Bay, WI

Ball-Turret Gunner: S/Sgt. Gilbert B. Creath, 19111079, POW, San Diego, CA

Left Waist-Gunner: S/Sgt. Milton F. Keck, 15337344, POW, Clearwater, FL

Right Waist-Gunner: S/Sgt. Charles R. Williams Jr., 18058495, KIA, Edcouch, TX

Tail-Gunner: S/Sgt. Wilfred J. Miller, 32627726, POW, Middle Village, NY

2 KIA, 8 POW

Crash Site: Zerbst/Helmstedt - Germany

Pilot 2Lt. William F. Henry

From the author to son David Henry

"When I received "An American Love Story" I had the intention to transcribe only the part devoted to your Dad's wartime experiences. However, after reading the booklet, I came more and more to the conclusion that it describes a person I had more or less neglected until now; the wives of the airmen who stayed behind when their husbands went to war. These ladies heavily contributed to the American war effort by working in the industry while worrying about the fate of their husbands. They became independent personalities, working for their daily bread while coping alone with the thousand-and-one inconveniences of a country at war.

Pilot 2Lt. William F. Henry

"An American Love Story"

"Captain of the Hamilton High School football team, Bill (Henry) had grown up with his two brothers and two sisters in a variety of oil fields where his father worked before settling down in the oil-field community of Seely. A lot of oil companies were supporting the education of their employees' children if they majored in petroleum engineering. Bill's intention when he enrolled at El Dorado Junior College in the fall of 1939 was to earn his two-year degree with good enough grades to gain financial aid from Darby Oil to study at a four-year college.

"El Dorado Juco was the only school he could afford because it charged no tuition. Kansas school districts paid a minimal tuition for each graduate who attended El Dorado, leaving the student responsible only for books, room and board.

"Bill joined the football team and earned 25¢ an hour through the National Youth Assistance program as a school janitor. His training in the oil fields made him a whiz at repairing all sorts of machinery.

"And that's how he met Gaila Selvy. Like Bill, she came from a much-traveled farm family that moved - not from oil field to oil field, but from farm to farm. Gaila was born into a family of six girls and two boys on a farm outside Burns. Each of the eight kids attended college, although they had to work to do it. When Gaila joined the 300 El Dorado Juco students in the fall of 1939 to study education, she brought with her a $10 bill, three dresses and a suit made from one of her dad's. She worked as a school secretary, a job she handled with ease ...

except for the mimeograph machine, which broke down regularly.

"It was one of those breakdowns on an autumn day in 1939 that sent her scurrying down three flights of stairs to see if anyone in the janitor's office could help. Bill didn't make much of a first impression. "I was awful busy having a good time that first year," she recalls. "I was working long hours and going out with boys. I was never going to get married, and I just wouldn't let any man impress me." But he walked up three flights of stairs and fixed the mimeograph machine. And he made that trek many more times that year … sometimes when the machine wasn't broken.

"She bowled me over. I was impressed," he says. "She was a beautiful young lady with an excellent personality. She wasn't timid, and I liked that in a lady. I was taken by her."

"When he got up the nerve to ask her out, they went to a movie at the El Dorado Theater, and Gaila found she enjoyed being with him, even though he was quieter and more soft-spoken than the young men she usually dated. By their sophomore year, they were sharing classes and lunches and going out together more and more. They saw movies like "Cabin in the Sky" and "Gone With The Wind." But because they walked most places, they almost never went dancing in roadhouses, which were too expensive anyway.

"The more time she spent with Bill, the more Gaila realized that, while she was physically attracted to him, she was also attracted to his quiet strength, voracious reading and deeply held beliefs. She was surprised to find the excitement she had previously sought in parties, travel and adventure by simply sitting opposite Bill as they played Rook, Hearts or Old Maid.

"And then, there was the evening at the college when she saw him at the bottom of the stairs staring up at her. Suddenly, she felt weak, and something inside her said, "Oh-oh." Gaila was in love.

"Bill spent most of January 1941 attending an aircraft tooling school in Wichita. On Jan. 22, following his teacher's instructions, he took his graduation certificate to the personnel director of Boeing, where a job was supposed to be waiting. But at Boeing, a guard told him to stand in line with hundreds of other job applicants. "This is a little different," Bilt told him. "I'm supposed to report to this fellow to go to work."

"No," the guard said, "you're gonna go stand in line."

"No," Bill replied. "I'm not gonna go stand in line."

"He walked out of the Boeing's offices and drove downtown to do what he had really wanted to do all along: enlist in the Army and take the written examination for pilot training.

"But while there were 200 enlistees taking the test, there were only 50 openings for pilot training. So the recruiting sergeant said that only the first 50 to turn in their papers with passing scores would be admitted. Determined not to blow his big chance, Bill rushed through the test … and blew his big chance. He came up one point shy of making muster. But his score was high enough that the sergeant asked him what army job he wanted to train for when he was inducted. Bill replied that he wanted to take that pilot training test again and was assured he would get that opportunity.

"It was a rocky start, but at least he was on his way to getting what he wanted in the Air Corps. Now, there was the matter of getting something he wanted even more.

"A few days after he enlisted, Bill took Gaila to dinner in El Dorado. He drove her home through heavy snow and subfreezing temperatures. Bill pulled the car off the road and parked. Haltingly, he gave the toughest speech he'd ever made. He told her he wanted to spend the rest of his life with her, but that he wouldn't ask her to marry him until he could support her and have her with him. "So will you wait for me? And then will you marry me? She said yes.

"Bill retook and passed his flying-cadet exam at Lubbock Army Flying School in Texas and waited for assignment to cadet training class. Gaila wanted to join one of the newly formed women's corps — the WACs or WAVES - but Bill, who always wanted to know that she was safe, asked her not to. And, uncharacteristically, she acquiesced. But though she stayed home, she characteristically couldn't stay away from the action. So when the school year ended, she took a job in Boeing Master Control typing up orders and routing them to the proper departments.

"She was one of thousands of young women who had been drawn to Wichita aircraft plants by steady work at good pay ever since the boom began in 1934. That's when the first Army contracts had come in for Stearman Kaydet trainers. Boeing began delivering them in 1936; by the time the war ended, the company had manufactured more than 10,000 in Wichita.

"Bill went to Sikeston, Mo., for primary training and waited until Gaila was able to visit him January 16, 1943, before giving her her Christmas present. It was a diamond ring and a proposal to marry when he earned his wings and second lieutenant's commissions six months later. She returned home full of plans and happiness. But she hadn't planned on her parents' reaction to the news.

"You can't get married during wartime!" they said. "What if you had a baby, and Bill would be overseas and … anything could happen to him." They didn't understand. They didn't understand at all. Gaila interrupted all the logical arguments. '

"This is a decision we've made, Bill and me. I'd like to do it with my family in a church. But I'm gonna do it." They never discussed it again.

"June 26, 1942, Gaila rode to Altus with Bill's parents and her wedding gown. If Bill didn't get a long enough leave for a wedding in Burns, they'd find a preacher in Altus. But Bill - who ranked second in his class of 400 in the final physical efficiency test - got his silver wings, second lieutenant's commission and a 10-day leave.

"And so, three days later, they were married in front of fifty guests in the Burns Methodist Church. Bill was late to the wedding because he had to stop twice on the way from Canton to patch flat tires on his brother-in-laws 1937 Ford. But there were no flats on the drive to the Hotel in El Dorado, where the honeymooning Henrys were a million miles away from the war in a world that nothing ugly or hateful could invade.

"Well … almost nothing. The second day of their honeymoon, Bill sat Gaila down and told her that the Army figured he had a 40 percent chance of coming home alive. Then he read from the Officer's Manual just what steps she should take to get help and benefits if he did not.

"No, Bill" she cried. "l can't listen to this! I can't!"

"Honey, you've got to," he said.

"Less than a year later - as friends who had lost their husbands wondered what to do, and as she herself waited to find out whether Bill was dead or alive - Gaila would recall that day and those words. And she would remember them as yet another measure of Bill's love.

"A time for couples to say good-bye. A week after their June 29 wedding, Bill and Gaila Henry said good-bye again. She moved in with her parents and waited for him to complete B-17 flight training with his newly formed crew - training so intense that wives weren't allowed on base or in the nearby town of Pyote, in West Texas. But even though they were separated again, Bill and Gaila had a couple of reasons to be optimistic about the future. For one thing, American industry had, by mid-1943, supplied the war machine with the weapons it needed to turn the tide. "The Axis powers knew that they must win the war in 1942 or eventually lose everything," President Roosevelt told the country. "l do not need to tell you that our enemies did not win this war in 1942… . I can report to you that with genuine pride on what has been accomplished in 1942. We produced 48,000 military planes - more than the airplane production of Germany, Italy and Japan put together."

"After a month at Pyote, Bill would be sent to a different base for final pilot training. And Gaila would go with him. So in the six weeks before he went overseas, they would live together as husband and wife.

"They went to Dalhart. Because Bill didn't get leave between assignments, Gaila had to meet him there. Climbing off the train at 11 p.m. on a hot August night, she dragged her suitcases to the hotel where he had made a reservation for her… only to learn the hotel had given out all the rooms on a first-come, first-served basis.

"In the lobby packed with tired and angry people, Gaila tried repeatedly to phone Bill at the base. But when she finally got through, no one knew anything about the newly arrived Lt. Henry. She left messages for him, but he never called. Finally - like everyone else in the lobby - she gave up, curled up in a chair and snatched a couple of hours' sleep.

"The next morning, she called the YMCA in search of a room and was told they were full. So she set out for the only other place she could think of where she might get some help: the Methodist church. She walked until she found it and told the secretary who answered her knock that she needed a place to stay until she could find Bill. Fortunately for Gaila, the church was renting out tiny places to service couples, and one - a basement apartment with water pipes running through it and a shower down the hall - had just become vacant.

"Gaila moved in and continued her search for Bill. Meanwhile, her frantic husband had been calling the hotel all night and morning. Told she hadn't checked in, he left messages for her, but she never called. He couldn't leave the base to search for her, and he didn't know where to look anyway. He didn't even know if she arrived in Dalhart.

"Later that day, a young woman who rented a room in the Methodist minister's home heard of Gaila's predicament and called her husband who was stationed at the air base. He was able to track down Bill and told him that his wife was not only in town but had already rent an apartment. Their tiny place was palatial compared to many. Other couples rented chicken coops and dirt floor garages divided into rooms by nothing more than curtains.

"She hadn't thought she could ever miss that ratty little basement apartment. But it had been their first home for six weeks. And six weeks had never passed so quickly. Now, on a blistering hot September morning, he was putting her on a train for Wichita.

"Bill was excited about what lay ahead. He would report to Grand Island, Nebraska, for staging, and then he and his crew would be somewhere in the middle of the war for which they had trained for more than a year. "Our training had been good," he recalls. "I felt I had nothing to worry about. We all tried to instill in ourselves the thought that it just won't happen to me, and I'm not gonna worry about it. I was 100 percent sure I was coming back. There was no question in my mind."

"But Gaila kept remembering that the Air Corps had told him he had only a 40 percent chance of coming home alive. She had thought she was prepared for this moment. But she wasn't. She never would be. The world she re-entered seemed strangely alien. She didn't belong here. She belonged with Bill. But the war was taking him away.

***

"Bill Henry had arrived at a base near Ipswich, England, northeast of London, late November 1943... and celebrated Thanksgiving with Spam sandwiches and K-rations. A co-pilot, he was anxious to become a pilot with his own crew and craft. He had to fly 25 missions before he could go home to await a new assignment, and - despite the overcast skies that postponed missions and the bone-weary exhaustion that accompanied them - he was anxious to get those 25 flights logged as quickly as possible.

"Bill and his crewmates conducted their bombing runs in a Boeing B-17. Sometimes they would fly five or six days in a row. Then, there would be two or three days when cloud cover over England or the Continent kept them grounded. When they flew, they dropped their bombs deep inside occupied Europe, often on Berlin and sometimes even deeper into Germany. They always encountered anti-aircraft fire, often were attacked by fighter planes and always suffered losses. But with each mission flown, Bill was able to count off one more day until he could see Gaila again.

"Gaila was as busy as Bill, working to stave off loneliness and worry. She was back at Boeing. But while the Wichita plant continued to build B-17s, she was working on a secret giant bomber, the B-29, the existence of which would not be revealed to the public until a squadron of them raided Japan in June 1944.

"Wichita's population in 1943 was 189,000; 29,795 people worked at Boeing, and half of them were women. The company had a golf course, baseball league, bowling alleys, private lake, shopping centers and a housing development.

"The whole city was on a wartime production schedule. Cessna built Boeing bomber sub-assemblies, gliders, cargo planes and 5,000 twin-engine trainers, which it turned out at the rate of 10 a day. Beech built wing assemblies for the A-26 attack bomber and AT-10 (plywood) and AT-11 (metal) versions of its Model 18 aircraft. Coleman had more than $1 million in defense contracts for such crucial supplies as portable stoves and lanterns, which became such staples that during the Battle of the Bulge, one Allied password was "Coleman," and the countersign was "lamp."

"Bill liked the British people and admired their courage in the face of daily air raids. And although neither England's capital city nor its restaurants suited his tastes, he spent most of his three-day passes in London. He visited all the historic sites and saw as many different stage shows as he could. He stood in long lines to see one movie twice — "For Whom the Bell Tolls," in which Gary Cooper played a Montana schoolteacher who fights against the fascists in the Spanish Civil War. He shopped for material he could have fashioned into the current rage - an Eisenhower jacket.

"And he slept. On one visit, he awoke at 10 a.m. in the Red Cross Club barracks to find he was the only one there. As he dressed, he noticed broken glass all over the floor. When he walked into the room next door, he learned that he had slept through a bombing raid that had destroyed the building across the street and blown out all the windows of the barracks in which he had been sleeping.

"Just as his cadet class distinguished itself in training, Bill's crew so distinguished itself on the "landscaping missions" that their plane was made a squadron leader and their pilot, Dick Rowe, was promoted to captain. Bill wrote Gaila that he was proud to have the lead spot in the formation, even though it meant extra work. By March, he had flown 18 bombing runs. Seven more and he'd be home.

"When he had only six more missions to fly, Bill was promoted to pilot and flew his first mission the very next day in the lead aircraft.

***

"Nine days later, on April 29, 1944, he was offered the final mission ... No. 29. It was offered to him because of a military custom that gave pilot and crew a choice - right after the early-morning briefing - of accepting the final mission in their tour of duty or waiting for the next assignment. Bill was in no mood to stay. Nor were the four crew members for whom - like him - this was the last mission. And, because the five new crew members had no vote, that settled it. They'd take the mission ... even though it was to Berlin.

"Berlin was the most heavily fortified city in Germany, ringed with anti-aircraft guns on the ground and Luftwaffe fighters in the air. Still, this crew had fought its way through those defenses to bomb Berlin twice before. They'd simply do it one one more time.

"So at 6 a.m., Bill took the pilot's seat, met his new co-pilot for the first time, started up the engines, lifted the Flying Fortress into cloudy skies and headed out over the English Channel. The skies were hazy, visibility poor. They had trouble getting the group together, and even more trouble getting into formation. Later, an investigation would lead to the court-martial and demotion of the squadron's lead navigator for mistakes that took the planes across the channel 100 miles south of their planned course - the corridor American fighter escorts patrolled all morning for bombers that never arrived.

"Lost deep in Germany, without fighter escorts, the bombers were attacked by Luftwaffe fighters. The fighting was fierce and constant, and both sides lost massive numbers of planes. Bill's plane was devastated by 20mm cannon fire from the fighters. Reports of good hits and bad damage came from every part of the airplane. Incendiary bombs, broken open in the bomb bay, had started a fire that now raged throughout the plane.

"He had no report on casualties - didn't even realize he had been wounded - but, with fighters still attacking, Bill knew his final mission had come to an end.

"He peeled away from the besieged group, set the automatic pilot and gave the order to bail out. Then, as he turned away from the controls, he saw that the oxygen supply beneath the catwalk was burning the length of the airplane. Anyone who didn't get out now would probably burn to death before the plane crashed.

He turned back to the controls, and his world went black, apparently from lack of oxygen. When he came to - he had no idea how much later - he was struggling beneath the shot-out windshield to carry his co-pilot out of the diving plane. But when he pulled the man off the control panel and stared down at his face, Bill saw that he was dead. That was the last thing he saw before the world went black again.

***

"Gaila awoke suddenly and sat bolt upright in bed. For several minutes she couldn't do anything but sit there in the dark trying to breath, trying to stop shaking. The next morning, her friend Glenna found her in the adjoining sitting room, staring at an open book on her lap.

"What are you doing in here?" Glenna asked.

Gaila closed the book she had been trying to read.

"Something happened to Bill last night," she said.

"Gaila, Don't say that"

"He's alive, but he's in trouble."

"You're imagining it"

She shook her head slowly. "I'm not imagining it. Bill's in terrible trouble."

***

"Bill awoke paralyzed and in pain. The last thing he remembered was ordering his crew to bail out of the burning B-17 and trying to drag his co-pilot out of the cockpit, only to find him dead. Then he had blacked out. More than a year later, he would piece together some of it, when his top-turret gunner, John Webb, told of finding him slumped over the steering column, overriding the automatic pilot and causing the plane to dive. Webb said he pulled Bill off the controls, decided he was dead, and followed the rest of the crew out of the airplane. Co-pilot Charles Avona and gunner Wilfred Miller died in the aircraft. And - his crew believed - so did pilot Bill Henry.

"But somehow, he ended up in a hospital in Zerbst, Germany, that treated Poles, Russians, and Frenchmen who were forced to work on area farms. The doctors assessed his injuries under a fluoroscope: every rib broken and shoved beneath his sternum, two ribs broken off his spine, his lungs punctured and bleeding, a bullet wound in his left forearm and several flak wounds.

"They didn't treat him or even administer a painkiller. Instead, they wrapped him in tape from navel to armpits and sent him back to bed, where, over the next three weeks, he regained use of his limbs. The pain subsided enough that he could think clearly again, and he essentially healed himself.

"From the hospital, Bill was taken to an interrogation center in Frankfurt, where he was kept in solitary confinement for 10 days and interrogated by a German officer who asked questions about his base and the men in his squadron. After each question, Bill replied: "l can't answer that. I can only give you my name, rank and serial number."

"Well, it doesn't matter," the officer finally snapped. He whipped a thick folder from a cabinet and read a detailed report on staff, weapons and activities at Bill's base, down to the nickname of each squadron commander. It made Bill angry that the base security had been so seriously compromised. It also made him feel helpless.

***

Western Union
Washing DC
Mr. Virgil F. Henry
Canton, Kansas
THE SECRETARY OF WAR DESIRES ME TO EXPRESS HIS DEEP REGRET
THAT YOUR SON 2ND LIEUTENANT WILLIAM F. HENRY HAS BEEN RE-
PORTED MISSING IN ACTION SINCE 29TH OF APRIL OVER GERMANY. IF
FURTHER DETAILS ARE RECEIVED YOU WILL BE PROMPTLY NOTIFIED.
Dunlap
Act. Adj. General

"Bill and Gaila Henry had decided a year earlier that Bill would list his dad as next of kin because Gaila's address would change when he went overseas. And so it was that Virgil and Grace Henry drove to Wichita to find Gaila.

"Bill's letters had stopped arriving a week after she had awakened in the middle of the night with the certainty that he was in trouble. Through the next 12 days, Gaila had suppressed her emotions, stolidly going to work in the morning and coming home to check for mail at night … longing for word, but dreading the words.

"Now, a woman hurried up to her at Boeing and said, "Gaila, they want to see you in the central office."

"She knew what that meant. The central office was a mile away. "l can't walk over there," Gaila told herself. "l'll never make it." But she did - every head turning to follow her - and found Bill's parents waiting there with news of what she already knew.

"l hope he's not out in the cold," she said. "And l hope he's not hurt too bad."

"But she never let herself think the he might be dead.

***

"Stalag Luft 3 was one of several prison camps in Germany for Allied airmen. This one, 100 miles southeast of Berlin in Sagan, held 10,000 prisoners. Bill was assigned to the West Camp — 17 ill-constructed barracks, a cook house, shower building, laundry building and theater. The prisoners were crowded, cold and hungry, but Bill thought they probably didn't fare any worse than the average German soldier in the final year of the war.

"He discussed homesteading in Alaska with fellow prisoner LeFloy Adams, a B-17 navigator. And he discussed food with everyone. Because they were always hungry, it was their principal topic of conversation. They entertained themselves. by recalling recipes from home, which Bill carefully copied down and bound in a book fashioned from a tobacco tin. The pages were unwrapped cigarette packs

— Flaleighs, Camels, Wings… . He still has that book today. And in the back of it are detailed plans for the house he would build 35 years later.

"As U.S. troops moved into Germany from the west, Russian forces advanced from the east, heading directly toward Stalag Luft 3. At noon Jan. 27, the prisoners were told to prepare to evacuate the camp. Rather than give up those 10,000 prisoners, the Germans were going to move them … on foot.

"Bill and three others tore their bunk beds apart and fashioned them into a sled on which they loaded their meager possessions and Red Cross rations. Thirty minutes past midnight, the entire population of the prison camp began walking southwest in a blizzard. They could hear the Russian artillery just 30 miles behind them. Bill's group took turns pulling the sled in two-man teams, as the blizzard worsened. Snow fell steadily for four days in near-zero temperatures. Prisoners collapsed with frozen hands and feet.

"The first day, they walked 18 miles in 11 hours. Then, at 6 p.m., they began again. By the early morning hours of Jan. 29, they were stumbling through 6 inches of snow. But when they walked out of the snow on Feb. 1, things were no better, because they could no longer pull their sleds. They transferred their belongings to improvised backpacks and kept moving.

"When Jake Powell, a fighter pilot, tried to carry too much in his pack, he pulled a leg muscle. Bill and others took turns carrying Jake and his pack for the next two days.

"Each night, they would be marched into a village. Occasionally, the Germans would bring in a wagonload of boiled potatoes, but for the most part, the prisoners were left to their own devices to find food and places to sleep. Bill often traded Red Cross chocolate, cigarettes and instant coffee with German civilians for bread and eggs.

"Six days and 62 miles from Stalag Luff 3, Bill and his fellow prisoners were packed into railroad box cars so tightly there was barely room to stand. They rode like that for three days, to a camp in Frankfurt, where the only food they received was marked "unfit for human consumption." Two weeks later, they were moved to Moosburg, near Munich.

"At Moosburg, they lived in tents, slept on wood shavings and seldom ate. What food they occasionally received was a slice of bread one-sixteenth of an inch thick made from sawdust and ground potato peels. It was dark and heavy and it tasted terrible. Bill ate it because he was determined to survive.

***

"Gaila had been ill with the mumps in February and depressed in March. Now, in April, she struggled to close out the school year. And she waited … for the war to end, for Bill to come home, for the world to give her life back.

"Then a large package containing Bill's personal effects arrived from England. And there was money in the package from Bill's fellow officers, who had gone through his things, taken what they wanted and sent Gaila money to pay for it.

"The silver service and Scotch plaid he had bought for her and the forest green material he had bought for the Eisenhower jacket he so wanted made were all gone, bought and paid for by those who, it seemed, considered him dead. Fighting to control her emotions, she bent to work unpacking his neatly folded clothing and hanging it beside her dresses in the tiny closet. His shoes were brightly polished, with shoe trees inserted. "He's so neat," she thought. And that's when the dam of self-control she had maintained all these months broke. She began to cry. She couldn't stop, and she didn't try. Much later, when there were no tears left, she carefully put the rest of his clothing away.

***

"They had been in the prison camp at Moosburg only nine days when the faint sound of artillery fire told them American troops were closing in. Bill and his fellow prisoners prepared their backpacks for another forced march to yet another camp. But no order of any kind came down from the war-weary guards, even though the artillery grew louder each day until it finally shook the ground on which they stood.

"But as the possibility of freedom grew stronger, Bill grew weaker and became violently ill from food poisoning, the flu or some other infection. Finally, he no longer had the strength to leave his bed. His buddies brought him news of German Panzer divisions retreating to the camp and trying to force the guards to join them in making a last-ditch stand. When the guards refused, the Panzers tried to take over the prison and shot several guards. But they failed to get inside the gates and continued their retreat.

"The gunfire was constant now and seemed to be just over the hill from the camp. Overhead, two tiny spotter planes circled, spotting German forces for U.S. artillery. When they flew over the camp, they buzzed down low and waggled from side to side in a form of greeting.

"Then - a week to the day after the prisoners had first heard the artillery fire - the 90th Division of Gen. George Patton's 3rd Army came rolling into camp. The guards laid down their arms. Patton arrived and was cheered by the men. It was over. Moosburg had fallen. April 29, 1945 - two years from the day he was married, and one year from the day his plane was short down - Bill Henry was free. And on May 8 - Harry Truman's 61 st birthday - the president announced that Germany had unconditionally surrendered.

***

With the European war over, and everyone's someone either home or en route, Gaila still had heard nothing about Bill ... not from him and not from the U.S. government. It was maddening, but - as Bill had been over the course of this insane year — she was determined not to be beaten. She would survive and prevail. But as she stared into the darkness in the early-morning hours, she admitted to herself that she didn't think she could do it without Bill.

"Then on the last day of school – when she came home exhausted and wondering what she could do for a summer job – she received in quick succession ... . a telegram:

Western Union – New York – June 5, 1945
Dearest Gaila. arrived this afternoon. Will be in Leavenworth, June 9. Will wire you from there so you will know when to expect me in Wichita. All my love. Bill

"... . .and a phone call; "Gaila, this is Bill."

"She hadn't heard his voice in nineteen months. And she had so much to say to him that she couldn't say a thing. Just, "It's soo good to hear your voice, Bill! I'm so glad you're back!" over and over again.

"Around 10 p.m., the train pulled in from Kansas City, its whistle echoing off the walls, steam rising from the tracks, as the engine slowed and the brakes squealed. Bill rushed from the window to the rear of the car and peered out the doorway into the crowd.

"Then he saw Gaila. The pain that still wracked his body was suddenly forgotten. Just the sight of her drove it away. His nerves may have been shot, and his confidence at its lowest ebb, but as he stared down at her he knew he'd make it through all the problems and perils that lay ahead. Because she would be with him.

"He clambered down the steps toward her. She stood in a brand-new dress and scanned the faces above the uniforms until she caught a glimpse of Bill. He looked great. But she felt so strange. It was as if she were meeting a stranger. She knew the man who had gone to war. Yet she didn't really know the man who had come home. They were starting over again, she realized. "What will happen now?" she asked herself.

***

"He was moving through the crowd toward her. She ran into his arms, and they kissed ... for a long, long time. After the thousands of words in the thousands of letters that had kept their dreams alive, there should have been words for this moment. There were none. But that night on that train platform in Wichita, Bill and Gaila Henry were neither ending a chapter in their lives nor starting a new one. Rather, they were continuing a love story that transcends beginnings and endings.

"So there were no words. And —for the first time since Dec. 7, 1941 — there was no war to come between them. While the people and the trains and the world spun about them, Gaila and Bill were finally back where they belonged. Together.

**

"At home, life moves one step at a time. Like thousands of young couples after the war, they faced a staggering number of loose ends and new beginnings. They couldn't blithely pick up where they'd left off. Finding a future wouldn't be easy. But then, nothing ever had been for their generation.

"So, Bill and Gaila Henry set out to meet this brave new world head-on. Bill was scheduled for three weeks' rest and rehabilitation in Miami Beach. So they bought an old Pontiac and drove there, taking their time, stopping along the way to visit his grandparents in Missouri.

"In Florida, they got to know each other all over again, and Gaila came to understand something of the deprivation he had suffered. He couldn't step inside an elevator without experiencing the claustrophobia of three days packed in a boxcar somewhere in Germany. There were dozens of foods, such as cabbage and brussels sprouts he could no longer eat without flashing back to the subsistence prison camp diet. He was constantly shaking his head in appreciation over such seemingly ordinary wonders as tablecloths, hot baths, sheets on the bed... .

"After Miami, they were stationed at Lockburn Army Air Force Base in Columbus, Ohio. But there was nothing for Bill to do. In fact, his only duties were to call in each morning and to fly four to six hours a month to qualify for flight pay.

"This wasn't the Henrys' idea of getting on with their lives. So after his four

Enjoying a night out after the war (left to right): Gaila and William Henry, Donna and LeRoy Adams. LeRoy was a fellow POW of William Henry.

years' duty were up, Bill became a civilian, they found an apartment in Wichita, he was hired at Beech and they began again. But in 1947, the aircraft industry went into a tailspin, and Bill was laid off a week before their first child was born.

"He was accepted to study petroleum engineering at the University of Tulsa and to work for Phillips Petroleum in Bartlesvllle. But neither city had a place for the couple to live. And he refused to ever again live without Gaila beside him.

"Bill worked as a housepainter for a year and took other jobs just to get by. Then, in 1954, he went to work as a sales representative for Associated Industries. And in 1970, he and partner Bob Clark acquired all the stock in the company, of which Bill remains president today. Associated Industries distributes a variety of raw material for airplane parts to companies such as Beech, Cessna, Boeing, Learjet and McDonnell Douglas.

"Gaila taught for eight years in the Derby schools as a reading specialist. Since 1976, she's kept characteristically busy volunteering at nearby schools, the Childrens Museum, League of Women Voters and Pleasant Valley United Methodist Church. She also drives cancer patients to and from chemo therapy as part of the national project of her sorority, Phi Beta Psi.

"But most of their time is spent together, traveling (most recently to the Panama Canal), taking classes (most recently, stained glass), attending concerts and Music Theatre performances, cooking, entertaining friends and doting on their four children — David, Gaila Lynn, Mark and Marlys — and nine grandkids.

"Besides the physical attraction," Gaila says, "we've always been mentally attracted. We'll read poetry together, go boating together and one night we spent hours finding out who led the Charge of the Light Brigade."

"For years after he came home, Bill's back would occasionally fester, and a dark and jagged piece of shrapnel would work its way out of his body... a reminder of the nightmare he carried with him.

"But then, the beautiful home he and Gaila built on the bank of the Arkansas River in northwest Wichita bears a striking resemblance to the house he designed on the insides of unfolded cigarette and food packs in Stalag Luft 3. That, too, is something he carried with him through the darkest time of his life ... a dream he made a reality.

Bombardier/Toggler S/Sgt. Harold G. Tenneson.

By widow Corinne Tenneson.

"Harold Gunnar Tenneson (he was always called Gunnar by family and friends) was the eldest son of Alfred and Marie Tenneson. He was born on December 22, 1920 in Antler, North Dakota. The family moved to Mekinock, North Dakota, where he attended elementary school and helped on the farm.

"On November 3, 1942 Gunnar enlisted in the U. S. Army Air Corps. He received his discharge from the Army on December 27, 1945. After his discharge he returned to farming for a short time. He then moved to California where he attended Santa Monica City College, and from there to the University of Southern California. He earned a degree in civil engineering in June of 1955. In June of 1954 he married Corinne Moen.

Bombardier S/Sgt. Harold G. Tenneson

"Gunnar spent most of his working years employed by the Federal Aviation Agency. On June 29, 1979 he retired. He then worked as an independent airport consultant. In 1988 he and Corinne moved to Idaho, built a retirement home, and spent his time working in the wood shop and hunting and fishing. In April of 1995 he passed away from a heart attack.

"Ironically, Gunnar was severly injured in a small plane crash in 1975 at the Quincy, California airport, on a business trip. In this incident, the pilot was killed, and Gunnar and the other passenger were severely injured.

Radio T/Sgt. John E. Webb.

By daughter Amy Unrath

"Though his birth name was John, he was called Jack by all who knew him. He was born on November 4, 1923, the second child and oldest son of John and Naomi Webb. His father had been exposed to nerve gas during WWI and suffered physical and mental problems as a result. When Jack was only five, his dad was sent to a VA hospital in Chicago and he never saw him again, leaving him with few memories. John senior died when Jack was thirteen. His mother grew to depend on him as the "little man around the house" and his brother and two sisters as well. He adored his mother and they had a special bond. In her eyes he could do no wrong even though he was a fun loving little boy and young adult and got into plenty of mischief.

"He attended Catholic grade and high school where he was an average student who preferred hanging out with his friends, playing sports (he became a state champion wrestler), driving fast cars, and partying to doing school work. Shortly after graduating from high school, he joined the Air Corps as it was the thing that all able bodied young men his age were doing at that time.

By grandson Jake Darrow

"My grandfather and the right waist-gunner Milton Keck had each completed 28 missions. They took another mission with William Henry's crew (their original CP) as they had before on April 20. They would have had all their missions done, but they had both missed one. By this time, only 7 of the original 36 men in their barracks had not been shot down.

"On April 29, 1944, they decided to get their last mission over with and joined a mission with men from another barracks.

"One of the biggest dangers to a bomber in the European theatre was updrafts, which were especially strong in the spring. The lead bomber was equipped with new radar to detect these updrafts. In order to avoid these, the lead navigator led them nearly 50 miles off course, thus missing their fighter escorts.

"There were 27 bombers in formation flying at 20,000 feet, with no protection against 150-200 German fighters. The German fighters continuously attacked the bombers with caliber machine gun fire, 10-15 planes at a time.

"The co-pilot Carles W. Avona and the right waist-gunner, Charles R. Williams were killed in the plane during these attacks. Two of the engines were knocked out and one was on fire as the remaining pilot fought for control by feathering the engine to give his men time to bail out. Seven of the ten men made it out of the plane and parachuted into the heart of Germany. The plane rocked left and right while losing altitude and speed. Then suddenly it began to dive out of control, started to burn and exploded before even reaching the ground.

"My grandfather said it seemed like forever until he reached the ground. He was not thinking about himself, but worried about his mother. His father had died when he was young, so he knew his capture would be very hard on his mother.

"He reached the ground and saw German civilians beating up another airman who was shot down and feared he'd be next. The German police captured him, after being on the ground for only 60 minutes. It was actually a good thing to be captured by the police or by German soldiers. If caught by civilians, they would beat you to death, rather than turning you in to be a prisoner of war.

Daughter Amy continues;

"After he was discharged from the service, he returned to Green Bay where he spent a year recovering from the war using his mustering out pay to get by. This

Radio T/Sgt. John E. Webb

was a wild time for him just catching up with old friends, partying and generally enjoying life until he met my mother, Mary Ann who was to become the love of his life. She was a deeply intelligent woman who helped him focus and convinced him to use the GI Bill to go on to college. They were married on June 1, 1946 and moved to Madison, WI so that Jack could attend the University of Wisconsin. He would eventually graduate as a landscape architect. In June of 1947, there first child was born a daughter named Amy. They would go on the have five more children.

"After college, he worked for a short time for a local landscape firm but quickly realized that if he was going to be able to support his quickly growing family he would need to go into business for himself. Webb Landscaping, Inc. was formed and was a successful operation for close to 35 years when he sold it and retired. Many of the major buildings in Green Bay are surrounded by a beautiful landscape that he designed.

"The years of the 50's and 60's were a time of raising his children and building his business. He always maintained a certain childlike spirit of fun and his children and their friends enjoyed being around him. Along with his brother and sisters, he built a cottage along the shores of Green Bay where the summertimes were filled with water sports, ball games, and other fun with aunts, uncles, cousins and grandma Naomi.

"Jack became a successful father, husband and business man despite suffering the lingering effects of prison camp and war in general. He dealt with anxiety and occasional bouts of depression. His basic fun-loving spirit and sense of carrying on no matter what life dealt you got him through. He was not a deeply introspective man or overly verbose. He would often use quips to communicate and one of his favorites was: "I moaned and groaned because I had no shoes until I met a man who had no feet." He would use this whenever we would go to him whining about some mishap in our lives but it also tells you about the way he lived his life, without regrets and with a let's just get on with it attitude. He died in February of 2003 ostensibly of complications from surgery but his wife had died two weeks earlier and his children believe that he died of a broken heart unwilling to go on without her.

***

Acknowledgements:
David Henry, son of pilot 2Lt. William F. Henry
Corinne Tenneson, widow of bombardier S/Sgt. Harold G. Tenneson
Amy Unrath, daughter of radio-operator T/Sgt. John E. Webb
Jake Darrow, grandson of radio-operator T/Sgt. John E. Webb

CHAPTER 18

385ᵀᴴ BOMB GROUP
550ᵀᴴ BOMB SQUADRON

Type: B-17G • Serial: 42-107045
MACR: 4460 • Air Base: Great Ashfield

Aircraft 42-107045 was hit in the right wing by a 20 mm. shell from an enemy aircraft. The ship immediately left the formation and was last seen going down through the overcast, out of control in the vicinity of Maagdeburg, Germany.

Missing Air Crew Report # 4460

Pilot: 2Lt. Len Sexton, 0-809884, POW

Co-Pilot: 2Lt. Eugene T. Koury, 0-695265, POW

Navigator: 2Lt. Robert V. Pelletier, 0-811730, POW

Bombardier: 2Lt. Sterling H. Rogers, 0-357924, POW

Engineer: S/Sgt. Earl W. Osborne, 34607006, POW

Radio: S/Sgt. Oral P. Moore, 38341516, POW

Ball-Turret Gunner: Sgt. Thomas J. Fairchild, 12131581, POW

Left Waist-Gunner: Sgt. Henry L. Dunning Jr., 32772545, POW

Right Waist-Gunner: Sgt. Robert S. Masten, 34607014, POW

Tail-Gunner: Sgt. John M. Frangadakis, 39124290, POW

10 POW

Crash Site: Schleibnitz/Magdeburg, Germany
Time: 11.45

385th Bomb Group, 550th Bomb Squadron (Sexton)

Back row (left to right):Pilot 2Lt. Len Sexton, Navigator Livingstone Hearne (not in final crew), Bombardier 2Lt. Sterling Rogers

Front row: Engineer S/Sgt. Earl Osborn, Right Waist-Gunner Sgt. Robert Maston, Radio S/Sgt. Oral Moore, Left Waist-Gunner Sgt. Henry Dunning, Ball-Turret Gunner Sgt. Tom Fairchild, Tail-Gunner Sgt. John Frangadakis

Not pictured: 2Lt. Gene Koury, who was assigned as co-pilot after this photo was taken, and 2Lt. Robert Pelletier who replaced Hearne as navigator on April 29th. (Hearne was sick with a cold.)

Navigator 2Lt. Robert V. Pelletier.

"I was born in Minneapolis, Minnesota, USA, on March 21, 1920. I graduated from North High in Minneapolis; attended the University of Minnesota in Minneapolis, majoring in mechanical engineering. I was also taking civilian pilot training and had already passed my pilot exam when the war broke out. I immediately enlisted in hopes that I would be accepted, but my eyes failed the physical exam. It was a big disappointment.

"I was sent to Navigation School in Selma Field, Monroe, Louisiana. At this time I received word that my father was dying, and was granted permission to visit him. Fortunately, I made it in time and when I visited him at the Veterans Hospital his first words were "I see you got your wings!" With that he closed his eyes and smiled.

"I returned to Navigation School in time to graduate and receive a Commission in the U S Army as a Lieutenant.

***

"On April 29, 1944, I was on my 15th mission. We were flying at 26,000 when we were shot down over Germany. We were on a mission to bomb Berlin, and we had a few encounters with flak. We got shot up and lost control of the plane and the pilot said, ‹We're not going to get home today, boys. Bail out! Bail out! Bail out!'

"My escape hatch was frozen stuck and I couldn't open it. On the floor we had sheets of metal for protection against flak. I picked up one of the metal pieces and banged it and finally broke open the door. Then, the bombardier hadn't tied his chute properly, so I helped him. I took off my oxygen equipment and jumped.

"I came down between a high tension line and a railroad track. I wasn't able to control my chute. I was trying to hide my chute so the Germans couldn't find it, but farmers gathered around me. We were on the edge of a field. They had pitchforks and clubs and they were all getting around me to hit me. One of the fellows hit me in the face and knocked me off my feet and a boy about twelve years old waved a pistol at me but. They took me and put me in a dungeon. I had cash for purposes of escape, and they took all that and everything I carried, like my flight boots, my watch and my jackknife. Later some uniformed Germans came and ultimately I ended up in Stalag III.

"When the Russian troops advanced in the spring of 1945 we went on a forced march in a blizzard for 75 hours straight without sleeping or eating. One night, we cut into a haystack to keep warm, but I got frozen feet and I couldn't feel anything. I started to walk with a limp. We kept marching. We came into a town and managed to get some onions and received Red Cross parcels. After a few months, we marched to another camp.

"We were liberated by General George S. Patton's troops and by George Patton himself. I had been a prisoner of war for a whole year and lost 25 pounds.

***

"After the war I attended a University in Omaha, Nebraska and earned a degree in Engineering, receiving Honors and a write up in the local newspaper. I was sent to a base in Sacramento, California, where I was questioned about my background in math, including Calculus, at the University of Minnesota. I was assigned to training in Nuclear Weapons.

"In 1947 I began receiving Weaponaire Training at Sandia Base, New Mexico. In 1949, I was assigned to Castle Air Force base as Wing Weaponaire Officer.

I made major in 1957, and authored the Continuity of Operations in World War Plans which was signed by General Benjamin Davis. Later, in 1957, I was sent back to Castle Air Force Base in California for additional training as a Navigator on a tanker aircraft used for Air Refueling (KC-135). In 1961, I participated in project Crome Dome, refueling B-52s off of the coast of Spain for 5 to 6 weeks. After a 30-year career in the Air Force I retired as Lt. Colonel.

Bombardier 2Lt. Sterling H. Rogers.

Bombardier 2Lt. Sterling H. Rogers and his wife

Sterling Rogers was born on a West Texas dry-land farm in 1924. His childhood and adolescent years were profoundly influenced by the Great Depression. When others fled the Dust Bowl, his parents chose to stay and tough it out. The resulting years of hard-scrabble living set a pattern which stood him in good stead for his privation to follow in World War II.

His formal education ended with graduation from high school in Colorado City in 1941. He could not afford the cost of college, and the military soon claimed his service in any case. He joined the Air Corps in 1942 as a private, being assigned to aircraft maintenance duty and skipping basic training entirely. He was soon persuaded, however, to enter the aviation cadet program where he refused pilot training, preferring bombardier training instead.

Stirling Rogers in his own words;

"Our departure in the morning of Saturday, April 29, 1944, was not particularly unusual. The crew navigator had a cold so we had been assigned a spare from another crew. Our briefings had gone well and we were full of the confidence and self-assurance of youth. Our plane had checked out with no obvious faults – the bomb load, which was my special province, was loaded and safe-tied to my complete satisfaction.

"Of course we experienced some misgivings: at a time like this every man gives some thought to the fact that he may not survive. But our misgivings were only vaguely felt and totally unexpressed. We were much too busy with the details of readying ourselves and our equipment for the next six hours or so of flight. I recall going back a second time to check the safety wires on the bomb fuses because I had the experience one time of having one work free, leaving a live bomb armed and ready to detonate in the bomb rack.

"That business of the spare navigator, Robert Pelletier, did cause some minor concern because he was a stranger to us all, but he seemed so competent in checking out his guns that we dismissed our doubts quickly. After all, he had seen a lot more missions over Germany than the rest of us had.

"We climbed through the overcast and joined the swarm that was forming for the flight eastward. The early morning skies were streaked with the flairs of lead ships calling their flights together: two red and one green for us, the opposite for our sister outfit. We found our place almost immediately then circled endlessly with the rest of the formation while the stragglers labored through the cloud-deck and struggled upward into their assigned places. I used the time to get my bomb-sight set up with all of the previously calculated data. If I should be allowed to use it those last-minute corrections would only take a few seconds and the time on the bomb run could be shortened accordingly.

"If I should be allowed to use it. I carried a bombsight but I was not the lead bombardier. Because we practiced pattern bombing it was standard procedure for all other bombardiers to toggle out their bombs on cue from the lead bombardier. This made for a highly destructive pattern of explosions on the target, but it also gave ulcers to bombardiers who had to sit through the interminable period of someone else's sight synchronization, What took me ten seconds to do seemed to take forever when someone else was doing it. Those sudden, fire-shot balls of smoke just beyond the plexiglass added urgency to the task. I could see them, but the lead bombardier could see only that little circle in his telescope.

"If I should be allowed. But I didn't want that either because it would mean that the lead plane had gone down. We were flying the number-two-slot and so were prepared to take the lead if necessary, but we hoped it wouldn't be. Somehow you always set out with the idea that today would be a milk run and were a little surprised and upset when it didn't turn out that way.

"After one final sweep above the Wash to gather the last straggling Fortresses into the formation we climbed eastward over the North Sea. Our target was Berlin so we could not afford to make very many deviations from the direct route there. Besides, we counted on our numbers and our immense firepower to protect us more than our evasiveness. Our altitude made anti-aircraft guns almost useless except for a barrage effect, and what fighter pilot in his right mind would face that imposing array of armament?

"In mid-climb we picked up a mixed escort of P-51's and P-47's. They idled along high above us like a pack of bird dogs, trotting first one way and then another, trying for the scent of the quarry. They seemed impatient with the idle pace, sometimes racing ahead and than turning to coax us on.

"We expected flak from the coastal batteries and from the flak barges on Zuider See and we sure not disappointed. They did their best to lay a carpet of explosions but the deadly nap of it lay far below us. Those few explosions which reached our altitude burst so far ahead of us that it was obvious that the gunners had been misinformed in their expectations. They would correct their error before the second wave of planes came, but we were gone before they realized their loss.

"We were gone deep into the heartland of Germany. We swept eastward majestically, a flying wedge aimed toward Berlin. Jerry was hard-pressed in those days to supply his fighter force with enough gasoline to defend against all the attacks but we had expected more opposition than we had met so far. Intelligence had predicted continuous fighter attacks from the Zuider Zee on and, so far we had none. So we bored on, drawing a little closer together as we went, feeling a little distrustful of the inactivity and wondering when it would be shattered, as surely it must.

"Air battles in movies are things of violent sound and motion, causing the focus of the eye and of the ear to blur with the force of it all. But that is not the way it really happens. The classic description of such things would have the Jerry burst upon us suddenly with a rattle of gunfire and a blase of action. Countless movies over the years have built these scenes to a crescendo of tenseness until it is sometimes difficult to remember that it wasn't that way at all.

"We saw them first as tiny black dots far off to our right climbing toward our level. Tiny, impersonal black dots that moved ever so slowly and silently upward. The escort inexplicably peeled off to the left and began to diminish into the distance. Then I saw that there were little black dots there too. In every direction the little black dots were climbing and struggling upward, moving always in the same direction that we were. Moving silently and menacingly. Moving to get ahead of and above the formation so that they could cut back through like a scythe. There was no sound save the drumming of the engines and the crackle of static in my earphones. The dots were there, moving ever so slowly upward and ahead of us, but they came no closer. We tracked them with our guns end fidgited impatiently, but there was nothing more we could do. They were far out of range and pulling away.

"Those next few minutes were an eternity that, strangely and in retrospect, seems to consist of vignettes and still shots and ghastly silence. I do not see in my mind's eye the swirls of motion and flashes of color that must necessarily compose such a battle. The ear of my memory retains no trace of the clatter and rattle of machine guns nor the drone of engines. Instead, I see the snout of a Fucke-Wulf suspended in perfect quarterings of the cross-hairs of a gunsight. I see the Fourth of July effect of an anti-aircraft shell exploding dead ahead: not the violent motion of the explosion but the still photoplate of the outward thrust of thousands of bits of shrapnel. I feel again the jolting physical blows to the diaphragm when the ship was hit by explosions, that instant response by the human body to the overpowering resonance of TNT.

"A burst of flame is captured in my memory, but oddly not in color, as it streamed outward from an engine. Again a vignette, without any sense of motion, the flame and cowl flap in sharp focus, rapidly diffusing into a background of nothingness. There is the view of an engine oddly canted on its mounts in that instant before it dropped clear of the wing.

"The feeling through my gloves of the bomb-bay switches and the sudden lift of the plane as the bombs fell away. The little hole in the bulkhead behind me still stands clear in my mind, its tipsy L shape clearly seen in spite of the years. I did not know then, and thirty years later I still do not know how that particular bit of shrapnel managed to travel from its point of origin in the explosion just beneath our bomb racks through the maze of cables and controls and bulkheads and instruments and pilots to leave that drunken L in the bulkhead and to fall spent on the floor beside me. And the wonder of it is that nothing seemed to be damaged by it. Its companion shards had made a sieve of the bomb bay, but I did not know that then, so that my memory is of that little hole.

"The bombs were gone from the bomb bay when that flak-burst came. Otherwise we would have been blown into oblivion by it. When the number four engine dropped off its mounts I opened the bomb bay and jettisoned the load. I wanted desperately to drop them through the doors and be done with it but I didn't dare. A trailing door would reduce our speed still further and make us more vulnerable. And we needed every bit of speed we could muster. With the bombs gone we took the flak burst without any vital damage. It came before the doors had completely closed, but it did not stop their closing.

"I remember thinking sometime during those minutes of heaviest attack that, if we should all be killed, I would have to write letters of condolence to all those wives and mothers. The incongruity of such a thought escaped me at the moment. The possibility of my own death was considered only in the general "we" of the whole crew in which I could function as a part of the total organism while simultaneously maintaining my own existence as an individual. Thus if we the crew should die it did not necessarily follow that I the individual would be free of the obligation to condolence. It scared me because I did not know how to comfort the bereft.

"Somehow during the flight we found ourselves fighting for survival. There was no single occurrence which stood out as the turning point, no event which proclaimed "you have gone too far." There was only an osmosis of knowledge upward from the gut that time had run out. And with it came the steel set of mind that we would not go without leaving a good account of ourselves. I really believe that a well-trained crew has a being of its own, that it is an organism, and that the individual members respond to the needs of the whole without discernable communication. At least we seem to have reacted that way. We became an animal at bay, waiting with taut muscles for the last possible moment to strike, inflicting the maximum damage while conserving our own resources as much as we could.

"But the time came inexorably. In a flying sieve with a gaping hole where an engine should be and another prop acting as a drag because it would not feather properly, with an upper turret warped from its track and the tail-gunner unable to use his guns because they were trailing in mid-air air, clinging to the rest of the ship by imagination and a wisp of metal. In these conditions and with half the control cables shot away, it became obvious that we would have to abandon ship. We were alone now, the rest of the formation having long ago disappeared ahead of us, and even the enemy fighters had left us for more dangerous game. Only the flak guns kept up their steady barrage.

"When the order came to bail out I suppose that I reacted as quickly as anyone else, but my memory is of immense, deliberate concentration. I had been drilled so often in my responsibilities in case of emergency that my only thoughts were of the destruction of the bombsight and Mickey set. I felt the hard, sharp tug of the chute pack being snapped onto my harness but I did not see the navigator do it, for I was concentrating on the placement of the magnesium bombs and could not spare the time to adjust the chute. I took the consequences later in an uncontrolled parachute fall, but for the moment all of my concentration was centered on insuring that we would leave no secrets to be unearthed in triumph by the Germans.

"I was aware of the opening of the escape hatch, more a sensing of the changed atmosphere than a literal knowledge of the act, and I saw shadowy forms in the tunnel while I struggled to set the last of the magnesiums on the Mickey set, but the idea of using the escape hatch myself did not occur to me. I was an automation going from task to task, making mental marks on an internal check-list.

"When all my tasks were done and 1 could think of myself again, I realized that one parachute strap dangled unfastened and that the whole harness hung loosely on my frame. If I jumped in that condition I would slide through the harness and become a living bomb, arching through space on a trajectory that would bring me at terminal velocity to: I sat in the tunnel and began pulling each strap into adjustment.

"My progress was slowed by the erratic spinning and buffeting of the aircraft. I was slammed against the bulkhead by centrifugal force one moment and suspended in mid-air the next. I did not know that the wild gyrations were manifestations of a life-or-death battle between the pilot and an airplane hell-bent on self-destruction. I thought I was alone so I struggled to get that harness adjusted before I gave it the final test.

"It seemed to be half an hour later, but was no more than a minute at the most, that the plane leveled out and stopped its pitching and bucking. I marvelled to myself that it could have set itself so to rights, and wasted no time while trying to finish my harness adjusting. But I could not get that dangling leg strap fastened. As I fought it I felt a hand on my shoulder and knew that I was not alone. I went out the hatch into the blast of frigid air.

"I had always feared that escape hatch. It was so small that I found it necessary to turn my shoulders corner-to-corner in order to pull myself in through it. (It was the normal entry to the nose compartment.) And I always pushed my chute pack in first because I could not fit my frame in through the hole otherwise. I worried that, if I should have to use it in an emergency, I would not be able to get out through it with my chute on. But when the time came in earnest I went through that hatch with square yards to spare.

"That a slice of time so small can contain so many currents of thought and sensations has always been a marvel to me. The elapsed time from my leaving the hatchway to being completely clear of the ship is infinitesimal, yet my mind was a drum-roll of do's and don'ts overlaid with worry that the belly guns might have been left down, and that in turn was overlaid by the thought that my chute might not open. And there was an accompaniment of mental checks of the things I had done. All of this was going on simultaneously in my mind, each thought occurring at it's own level without interfering with any other thought, and all progressing at their own speed.

"I saw the bulk of the airplane pass over me and was dimly aware of another human form beneath it and knew that we were both safely out. Holding my left arm tightly across the chute pack on my chest I pulled hard on the ripcord with my right hand and felt the pressure of the drogue against my arm. Now my chute would open when I relaxed the pressure. If I should faint from lack of oxygen (I had abandoned my mask when the order came to bail out) at least I would not plummet into the earth without opening my chute. The flak guns might get me but I would have to run that risk. But before I could work up a good worry over that I passed out.

"Seconds later my mind cleared and my grip relaxed as my lungs screamed for air. As the drogue chute leaped out from the pack I turned to fall head down. I wanted to take the shock of the opening chute on my shoulders, thinking to avoid any possibility of slipping through the harness. I hadn't considered the whiplash effect this would have. When the canopy caught the air and snapped to its full-open spread I was instantly reversed and the force of the reversal cracked every joint in my body. Now I know the persuasiveness of the medieval rack. To be suspended in midair with only a silken canopy to support you is a sensation that defies description. You hang, not uncomfortably, with no sensation of movement or or wind. The sounds of the earth beneath you seem distant but have a clarity that is startling. The sound of guns is somehow intermingled with the trilling of a bird, the frightened squawk of a chicken with the sputter of a motor-cycle. You are motionless, yet the earth beneath you moves gently to and fro.

"The sound of guns. Suddenly I became aware that guns were still firing be-low me and that there were wicked black puffs above. I was in the line of fire, or maybe I was the target. I didn't know which and I didn't wait to find out. I grabbed the shroud lines with both hands and pulled hard. The forward edge of the chute collapsed and my harness went slack for a moment. Then the chute refilled. But in the process I had come noticeably nearer the ground.

"It had worked so well that I did it again. There was the sudden sense of weightlessness as I fell free, and then the tightening of the harness as the chute again bit into the air. Feeling rather pleased with myself I looked up at the cano-py, only to find that I was looking down instead!

"Down! I was swinging through an arc that took me, at ist peak, dangerously near to falling back into my own chute. One more tug on the shrouds and I would fall to earth in a flutter of silk. I tried to stop the wild gyrations but my efforts only served to add a spin to what was already a sickening oscillation. The unfas-tened leg strap made it impossible to control the chute, so I gave up and waited for my fate or for the motion to subside, whichever came first.

"And I wasn't sure which I wanted to come first. The violent motion had made me sick. Viscerally, desperately sick in a way that air sickness had never affected me. I wanted to vomit, to empty my stomach of everything in it, but nothing would come up. I hung limp in my chute and wished that I could die to be done with it. And I swung inexorably back and forth and around and around as I slowly dropped nearer the ground.

"I was still swinging when I hit the ground. Those last few moments saw the sense of motion, which had seemed suspended when I first opened my chute, suddenly spring to life so that the earth rushed up at me like a train coming head-on. Every thing was blurred by my motion and I could not see precisely where I would land. And I was aware that I was being carried along, too, by spanking breeze that was going to make it hard to dump that chute.

"Then I hit. Hard. It was new-plowed ground, bedded for the spring planting. Not only did I land cross-wind, but cross-furrow too. I took the shock of it on one leg and collapsed, trying to roll toward my chute. But the force of the landing took the breath out of me, and the plowed ground made it hard to spill the air. Gasping for breath I was being dragged over the furrows like a cotton-picker's sack at day's end.

"I had not seen her there although she must have been working in the field from the start. But suddenly she was there and her strong hands gathered in the silk as she strode over the furrows toward me. As she released the pressure on the shrouds I unsnapped my harness and shrugged it off, trying to stand up. My knees buckled and I was saved from falling by her quick grab of my arm. We stood there, my weight half supported by her sturdy grip, while a uniformed German rode his motorcycle over the bumps toward us.

"Brrr-umpphf! Brrr-umpphf! Brrr—umpphf!" The motorcycle alternately purred and grunted as he forced it diagonally across the furrows toward us. As he bumped to a stop in front of us she held out the bundle of silk and cord wordlessly. She had said nothing to me and she said nothing to him now. She just held out the parachute in a gesture that acknowledged his authority. He rapped out some guttural command to her that I did not understand and motioned for me to mount the motorcycle behind him. Whatever it was that he said stirred her to speech too, for she erupted into verbal fireworks. Then I understood her help to me. It was more than just compassion, for the stream of invective that she poured on his unmindful head was all in French! As we rode through the hedge and onto the road she was still clutching the parachute and shouting imprecations at my captor.

"As the motorcycle puttered through the silence of countryside I took stock of my situation. I was deep inside Germany not sure of my precise location, and, judging from the pain beginning to make itself felt in my left leg, not in too good condition either. But I was alive, and my captor seemed to be trying to make it easy for me to stay that way. He was armed, but his pistol was holstered on his hip beneath my hand and the knife he carried could be slipped out of its sheath before he could act to stop me. At any secluded spot along the road he could be mine.

"But he knew more than I gave him credit for. At no point in our ride were we ever out of sight of others. Always there was the crew of an anti-aircraft gun, or a detachment of Home Guards, or some other armed group within easy hailing distance.

"At one point where the road cut through a small woods we were stopped by a troop of Hitler Jugend.. They were a strapping lot of teen-aged kids in lederhosen, showing their new-found masculinity in boisterous activity, cradling their rifles self-consciously. Their leader, a little older perhaps than their twelve and thirteen years, and certainly bigger than the others, bounded down the embankment to discuss the situation with my captor. His HJ shirt, with all its decorations and shoulder patches, was a bit too small for his shoulders and his lederhosen, obviously having served several older brothers before him, were ready to be passed on to the next. They were so tight in the crotch that he seemed to walk with a wince as if in a state of constant sexual excitement.

"He and my captor exchanged a few comments, the one showing the bravado of youth and the other an amused tolerance. I didn't understand any of it, but I did not miss the hard cold hatred in the eyes of the blond youth when he looked at me. Nor did I fail to see, as we pulled away, the gesture as he spat contemptuously in our direction. I shuddered to think what my fate might have been when and his crew of adolescent thugs got to me first.

"As I said, we were never alone. For quite some distance we puttered along with a small military convoy until it came to a stop near a gun emplacement. And other traffic came and went, never giving me that one chance I needed. If I had got it I don't know what I would have done. I had no real knowledge of my location except that I was somewhere west of Berlin and east of the Rhine. And my chances of making my way back out of an occupied Europe were just a dream.

"I had not yet learned to recognize the different German uniforms, but I have been eternally grateful since that my captor represented the Luftwaffe. I was to find that there was a sort of chivalry which required that one airman treat another with respect even when they were on opposing sides. And that fact operated to my advantage when he deposited me at the city jail in Burg. I could not understand his conversation with the jailer, but he repeated "Luftwaffe, erst Luftwaffe" several times and I took it to mean that I was to be released only to the Luftwaffe. And, as it turned out, that was exactly the intention.

"Much later I learned of men who fell into the hands of civil authorities and were held for months before they were permitted even to leave their cells. Others who were captured by less humane captors than mine were given over to the Gestapo for non-stop questioning for days on end. It was that point in the war when the German economy was being beaten to its knees and the natural reaction was for them to strike back at any symbol that came to hand. at any symbol of the Allied air raids which were a constant reminder of their predicament.

"He had been my captor, my escort, and, in a sense, my security on the long ride into the town. And I felt a sense of loss at seeing him go. I remembered the Hitler Jugend in the woods and wondered if I had got past one bad situation only to fall into another.

***

Following the end of World War II Stirling Rogers served a short stint as a squadron commander in the Air Force, but chose to revert to enlisted status. He served in the Berlin Airlift, the Korean Conflict, and the early stages of the build-up in Vietnam before retiring as a Senior Master Sergeant.

In civilian life he became a computer programmer and analyst, working for many years for one of the major computer manufacturers. He retired for good in 1988 and has devoted his time since to art and to writing.

Engineer S/Sgt. Earl W. Osborne.

"I was born in Halifax, Va. June 19, 1923. My family and I moved to Greensboro, N.C. when I was 2 years old in 1925. I attended grade school and high school in Greensboro and in my early years, I worked for O'Connor's Florist on the street selling flowers at the age of 8 years old. Later I rode a bike delivering telegraphs for the Western Union Company after school hours.

"Sometime after my 16th birthday, I worked for Burlington Industries at

Greensboro Weaving, working from 12 midnight to 8 a.m. five days a week. At age 18 I left this job as I was drafted into the Army. When drafted, I was placed in the Army Air Corps where I attended various schools for training. I attended Gunner School, was trained as an Army Aircraft mechanic, met my crew and attended Flight Engineering School. Came out as a top-turret gunner/flight engineer as well as Crew Chief. Wound up in the 385th Bomb Group.

Engineer S/Sgt. Earl W. Osborne

***

"We took off early in the morning of April 29th in our B-17 Flying Fortress, gaining altitude to reach our assigned height of 29,500 feet. Over the coast of Holland, we received our first hit with a shell going through somewhere in the intake of our external super charger on the number one engine. We continued the flight and we were attacked periodically by German fighter planes.

"We reached our target and lost our number four engine and then shortly, the number three engine. We still continued and held our altitude but shortly after, a shell from flak exploded just under our bomb bay. This force knocked my top turret up out of the control socket and my head hit the top turret. I fell out between the pilot and co-pilot. I got back into position but the turret would not operate properly. The pilot gave the order to bail out and we all followed orders.

"I bailed out, pulled the rip cord – chute opened – and all of sudden, I realized I was thousands of miles from home with no visible means of return. I landed in a plowed field, surrounded by a group of German citizens armed with pitchforks, etc. I was scared and they were afraid of me. They were standing back and all of sudden; I realized there were two German soldiers running across the field. They were hollering at the civilians holding them back.

"The soldiers took me to the road and a command car came up, put me in the back seat with armed soldiers on each side, turning on a siren and red lights taking me to a city jail. Here they kept me overnight. The next morning, I was put on a trolley or bus standing up at the front with guards. They took me to a train station taking me to an interrogation center.

"After being interrogated, I was sent with the rest of our crew of enlisted men to Stalag XVII B at Krems, Austria. Early in April 1945, we were marched out under guards for a reported approximate 280 mile march. We went through German lines early in the morning and about three days later; we ended up in a patch of small pine woods, on top of a hill near the Inns River. There were roughly 4,000 Americans, as well as British & Russian prisoners,

"Early in the morning, an American captain and three or four soldiers in a tank came up – made the guards stack their guns – the captain radioed back to his outfit and gave them our location, Shortly after this, American fighter planes were buzzing by us, waving their wings.

"Later on, we were taken to Le Havre, France – after being deloused, we remained there a few days and were fed very well – gained weight – then put on a liberty ship returning to New Jersey. I was home in Greensboro, NC on June 15th, 1945. Thank God the ordeal was over.

***

"Back home in Greensboro, NC. I married my girlfriend who had waited for me all these years in May 1946. We have been happily married for 66 years. We have 4 children, 7 grandchildren, 1 great grandchild and one on the way.

"Regarding my work history following the war, I went to work for International Harvester Co. in Greensboro, NC in 1948 where I worked for one year then transferred to Charlotte, NC. In Charlotte, I was placed into management and worked with International Harvester for 33 ½ years. I retired at 58 years old. After about 6 months of retirement, a neighbor and I started an insurance business selling business insurance. We did quite well for about 4 years and I then sold my half interest to him and retired again.

***

CHAPTER 19

385ᵀᴴ BOMB GROUP
551ˢᵀ BOMB SQUADRON

Type: B-17G • Serial: 42-97226
MACR: 4458 • Air Base: Great Ashfield

Aircraft 42-97226 received violent attacks by German fighters in the Magdeburg area.
This aircraft was last seen as it left the formation, on fire, about 16 miles West of Magdeburg.

Missing Air Cew Report # 4458

Pilot: 2Lt. Richard L. Huntington, POW, St. Paul, MN

Co-Pilot: 2Lt. William H. Miller, POW, Glendale, CA

Navigator: 2Lt. Francis J. Andrews, POW, Swampscott, MA

Bombardier: 2Lt. Standlee E. Roberts, 0-754770, POW, Overton, TX

Engineer: S/Sgt. George H. Adams, KIA, Ocante, WI

Radio: S/Sgt. Peter G. Sarpolus, 16013782, POW, St. Clair, MI

Ball-Turret Gunner: Sgt. Aaron N. Le Sieur, POW, Sacramento, CA

Left Waist-Gunner: Sgt. Elwood G. Posey, 18139021, POW, Winnsboro, LA

Right Waist-Gunner: Sgt. Frank H. Hart, KIA, Brooklyn, NY

Tail-Gunner: Sgt. Octavio A. Moreno, POW, Los Angeles, CA

2 KIA , 8 POW

Crash Site: Helmstedt, Germany

Co-Pilot 2Lt. William H. Miller.

By wife Patricia and sons.

"William H. Miller (Bill) was born in Stockton California on March 9, 1924. His family moved to Glendale California when he was 12 years old. He attended Glendale High School and graduated in 1942. He was attending Glendale College when he was drafted into the Army in 1943.

"He returned from the war on August 1, 1945. He attended USC and in 1950 moved to Lubbock Texas with his wife and sons. He went to work in the insurance business with Great Southern Life Insurance. He became a manager and moved his family back to California in 1959 when Great Southern Life opened a Los Angeles office.

"After retirement in 1992, He and his wife moved to Palm Springs, CA. He played golf and volunteered at the Palm Springs Air Museum touring people through the B-17 that was on display there. He was also active in the POW group where he met Tom Gibbons who was with Patton's 3rd Army which liberated Bill at the close of the war. Bill passed away on March 4, 2012.

Navigator 2Lt. Francis J. Andrews.

Francis Joseph Andrews was born in Lynn, Massachusetts on March 10, 1917. He spent two years in Lynn and then moved to Swampscott, Massachusetts. He spent his childhood there and graduated from Swampscott High in 1934. He played baseball and basketball in High School, and true to his modest personality, he admits to not playing very well. He had a life long passion for sports, particularly baseball, and had a steel trap memory for all things Red Sox, the Boston Massachusetts home team.

In October 1934 he joined the CCC Civilian Conservation Corps. He was stationed in Oregon from 1935-1937. Performance records indicated that he was an excellent worker. He left the CCC in the Spring of 1939 to work for the Federal Government cleaning wooded areas that were destroyed during the "No Name" hurricane of 1938. He left that job and worked in a paper mill making napkins for a short time.

In 1940 Frank moved to Hartford, CT to work for Pratt & Whitney Aircraft, machining parts for aircraft engines.

Frank joined the Army Air Corps in March 1943 as an aviation cadet. He was commissioned a 2nd lieutenant in December 1943 as a navigator. He was assigned to Sioux City, Iowa where crews were assigned.

Their 1st mission was in France and was uneventful. The 2nd mission was to Frankfort, Germany. Anti aircraft killed one engine and they limped back without further problems.

322

***

His third and final mission was on April 29, 1944. They were headed to Berlin and were shot down many miles from their destination. Apparently Frank was hit with shrapnel and knocked out. The bombardier woke him up and told him that they had to jump. They did jump, but two of the ten crew members went down with the plane.

They were captured by the Germans and sent to prison camp. The other three officers were sent to the same camp as Frank. The four enlisted men were sent to a different camp and he never saw them again.

Frank Andrews was discharged from the Army Air Corps in November, 1945. Following his discharge, he lived with his mother, Isabel Andrews in Swampscott, Massachusetts and he worked for a company in Lynn, Massachusetts that made shoes. (Lynn was noted for its shoe industry.) In 1946, Frank, along with his brother Bob, purchased a three family home on Sydney Ave. in Lynn. Bob and his wife moved into the first floor and Frank and his mother into the third floor.

In 1947 both Frank and Bob took advantage of the GI Bill and enrolled in Boston University in Boston, Massachusetts. Around that time, he met and fell in love with Nora Geaney, and they were wed on May 22, 1948. They soon moved into the vacant 2nd floor apartment of their home on Sydney Ave. Both Frank and Bob graduated from Boston University in 1950 and they both accepted jobs with General Electric. Frank worked in the Jet Engine Division as a planner, and retired from General Electric in 1979 after nearly 30 years of service.

Those thirty years brought many changes into Frank's life. On January 8th, 1950, a son, Francis Junior was born, and on Friday the 13th of July, 1951, a daughter, Carol. A year later, on September 1, 1952, another daughter, Ellen, was welcomed into the family. In 1953 Frank and Nora moved their growing family into the home where he remained the rest of his life, on Short Road, in Lynn, Massachusetts. Another son, Robert was born on February 1st, 1957.

Frank was a true family man. His schedule was always predictable. He returned home from work every day at 4:45 and Nora would have dinner on the table by 5:00. This gave Frank just enough time to clean up and put records on the record player. He loved music. His children's childhood was filled with the sounds of many genres of music, including classical, popular, big bands, and musicals to name a few. He kept a written record of what was played each night so he would be sure to hear it all.

Frank always enjoyed watching sports, especially baseball. And, he was a coach for his sons' baseball teams for many years. Frank Jr. felt at times it was a disadvantage, because his Dad did not favor him at all! After Frank passed away, his children found an autographed baseball card of the beloved baseball star Babe Ruth tucked away in a desk drawer. His children considered it a parting gift from their Dad.

The only sport Frank actively engaged in was bowling. His children would ask how he did on his score and he would say something like: "I had a total of 300 for 3 strings of play. I had an 87, and a 102." It would be up to the children to figure out what the third score was. He felt very strongly about the benefits of a good education and he was an active participant in his children's education. He checked their homework nightly and if he found a math mistake, the child had to make up five similar problems and complete them correctly. Likewise, if there was a grammar mistake, several similar sentences were expected to be composed. Needless to say, his children tried hard not to make mistakes! Frank's son, Frank Jr. recalls having trouble with his phonetics. His dad made flash cards and reviewed them with him every night until he mastered them.

Frank also made sure that his children had good table manners. It was not uncommon to hear reminders like: "No elbows on the table" or, "no singing at the table." He also enforced very strict rules about making sure his children ate all the food on their plates. In retrospect, his children suspect that his adherence to this rule may have stemmed from his experience in the POW Camp in Germany.

And, Frank was very honest. He would never take as much as a paper clip that did not belong to him. He was very proud of his daughter when he got a call from a gentleman. She had skidded on ice in a parking lot and dented his car, and left a note on the car with contact information. His daughter had hardly given it a thought. She had been taught to always do the right thing.

The entire Andrews family suffered a huge loss when the youngest child, Robert, was diagnosed with leukemia in 1979 and died 11 months later at the age of 23. Frank had been retired only one month before his son got sick.

Frank was a quiet, unassuming man, who showed his affection more by his actions that by his words. Lung disease claimed his life on Jan 22nd, 1996.

Bombardier 2Lt. Standlee E. Roberts.

By son Carl Roberts.

"My father graduated from bombardier school in Victorville, California. After training in Sioux City, Iowa, they transferred to Nebraska where they received their new Boeing B-17. Then they started their trip to the European Theatre of operations. They flew from Nebraska to New York State, refueled, and flew to Iceland.

"The entire crew was extremely proud of their new shiny silver B-17. They had all I thought that when they reached England it would be the bomber they would be flying into the heart of Hitler's Third Reich. But that would not be the case. They arrived at Great Ashfield on April 5, 1944. The home of the 385th Bomb Group and his crew was assigned to the 551st Squadron. After their arrival at Great Ashfield, they found out that the B-17 they ferried over from the US would be assigned to a seasoned crew.

"They were assigned to their barracks, went through several briefings and I believe they were given a few days leave and went by train to London. After leave they were told that they would fly their first missions with the seasoned crews. Their crew was broken up and assigned to crews that needed replacements. My father's first mission was on April 22nd, to Hamm, Germany, to bomb the marshalling yards. He could not remember his pilots name and thought there were no casualties. His second mission was on April 24th, to Fredrichshafen, bombing a ball bearing factory. There were no casualties.

Bombardier 2Lt. Standlee E. Roberts

***

"My father's third and last mission was on April 29, 1944. Two crew members were killed in action and my father was hit in the back by three pieces of shrapnel. Three days before the 29th, my father became sick, similar to the flu. He went to the infirmary and checked himself out on the afternoon of the 28th, because he feared they may keep him, and he did not want to miss his first mission with his own crew.

"On the morning of the 29th at the briefing, he found out that his crew would be flying in the lower squadron, number 3 plane, tail end Charlie. My father was flying in the third division so their division was last to embark on the mission to Berlin. They departed into the clouds. According to Bob Barney's book, "Bullet Proof," they broke through the clouds around 12,000 feet. Climbing through the clouds after takeoff was the only thing that scared my father. After that they headed for the rally point, and then flew over the North Sea heading for Germany. At some point, once over Germany, the navigator Francis Andrews and my father knew something was wrong because they had not yet rallied with their fighter escort yet. They must have been off course. Their bombardment group was assigned a Mickey operator from another group and my father would find out later that they were at least 40 miles off course on one leg of their mission.

"At some point over German airspace, my father looked out the port side of his bomber and saw between 200 and 300 German fighters lining up parallel with them. It appeared to him that the fighters went forever. One of the things that stuck in his mind was a fighter with a yellow nose cone and a black spiraling stripe near the front of the line of fighters, was doing a barrel roll showing off as well as trying to be intimidating. He said the next thing he knew, several other fighters behind him started doing the same or different maneuvers. He said he was impressed and worried at the same time. He was trying to figure out what they were up to. A few minutes later they accelerated and disappeared. Several minutes later he found out exactly what they were up to. They attacked the division from the front at approximately 11:05 am. My father said fighters were coming from everywhere. He could hear Octavio Moreno, the tail gunner, saying one or two fighters were set up behind the squadron directing traffic. First fighters passed under the squadron and then flew up through the squadron. He thought it was a dumb move in his opinion because they were more vulnerable from this angle. One of the fighters, a FW-190, flew right up the front of their B-17, one of only two fighters to pass their plane. He fired his .50 caliber at him and a flap flew off the fighter.

"Then all the squadrons started breaking formation and it turned into extreme chaos. Then he saw an amazing yet horrible sight. One of the first fighters flying up through the lower squadron misjudged his angle of entry and hit a B-17 head on.

"After the fighters had made their first pass from the front, two German fighters approached from behind their bomber. The next thing my father knew he felt a large impact to the bomber and he flew over the top of his bomb sight. Initially he thought the navigator Francis Andrews had fallen into him knocking him over his bomb sight. When he pulled himself up off the bombsight he saw Andrews lying on the floor by his seat unconscious or semi unconscious. He immediately dragged Andrews towards the bail out hatch and returned to his position and his .50 caliber when he heard over the intercom to bail out. He met co-pilot William Miller at the bail out hatch and Miller helped my father out of the hatch and he assumed Miller followed.

"Almost immediately after deploying his parachute, three ME 109's approached him and one broke away from the group and did a 360 degree turn around him. On the last quarter radius they could see eye to eye. My father said what the hell and he smiled as he waved to the German pilot. The German pilot game him a short hand wave, nodded and turned away and flew off. My father said he was really worried because he had heard stories of German pilots flying around airmen floating down then thrusting their engines causing the parachute to collapse, sending them to their demise.

"When he got closer to the ground he heard a whizzing noise go by him followed by a cracking sound and he thought what the hell was that. A few seconds later he heard the same noises again. At this point he realized that he was being shot at from the ground. He heard one more shot before hitting the ground near a set of railroad tracks. He discarded his parachute and walked over to a tree and sat down. At that point, he realized he was wounded when he coughed up blood. It wasn't severe, but enough to worry him. He figured he would be dead as soon as the person that was shooting at him arrived. He pulled out a cigarette and a pack of matches. His hands were shaking so bad he couldn't light the cigarette.

"While he was sitting next to the tree he heard a noise like hail hitting the ground. He then realized that it was .50 caliber shell casings raining down from the battle above. He thought wouldn't that be a hell of a note to have just gone through all he had to get hit by a shower of shell casings and killed.

"After about twenty minutes, an old man in his late 80's, obviously the one shooting at him on his way down, walked up pointing a side by side double barrel rifle with firing hammers. My father said he was as scared as the old man because the gun he was aiming at him had to have been made in the 1800's. He was most afraid of the old man's hands shaking and the hammers were shaking as much. He was afraid that the gun was so old it might accidently go off. After a few minutes they both calmed down and my dad tried to light his cigarette again, but couldn't because his hands were still shaking. At that point the old German man reached out and took the matches and lit the cigarette for him. After that the old man signaled for my father to start walking.

"They came near a village where a group of men came and took my father away from the old man and marched him about 500 yards to a large barn. That's when he met up with Peter Sarpolus, the radio-operator. They both realized that they were about to be hung on the side of the barn. They put ropes around their necks and began to string them up when out of the blue the old man that had originally captured my dad showed up with three Luftwaffe soldiers. They fired a shot in the air and the hanging came to an immediate halt. My father was very happy to see the old man, but at the same time he was mad and cussing the group of men that tried to hang him.

"They were marched to another barn a few miles away where they were consolidating POWs. When he entered the barn, there were about 30 to 50 wounded POWs. A group of about 30 were separated from the group and were in horrible condition. He only talked to me about two of the severely wounded. One was a P-38 pilot whose plane had been hit and the cockpit burst into flames before he could bail out. His entire face was burnt off. My father said it hurt you to look at him and see the pain he was in.

"They were detained in the barn for a day or two and then loaded into trucks to be transported to Dulag Luft near Frankfurt. While in the barn, he befriended an airman whose arms and face were burned black and he had hundreds of pink cracks on his black flesh from every time he moved. When my father got back to the states and was married they both went to Miami, Florida for discharge. One evening my mother and father were walking down the street going to dinner when at an intersection they heard someone yelling "Hey Lieutenant!" And because the city was filled with servicemen, my fathered didn't realize the man was yelling at him until the man yelled "Hey asshole, stop!" That got my father's attention and he stopped and turned around to see a facially disfigured man run right up to him and said "Lieutenant you probably don't recognize me." My father looked at him and said no, I'm sorry, I don't. The man saw my father's name tag on his uniform and said "Lt. Roberts, I've tried to remember your name since prison camp." He said "I was the burned soldier you befriended on the day we got shot down." They ended up going to dinner together. My father and that soldier kept in touch for several years.

***

"After my father was liberated he got tired of waiting to be flown back to France. He met a group of Army engineers with the 28th Infantry Division nicknamed the "Bloody Bucket" moving thru Moosburg Germany. My father and another POW named Eddie Allen from Houston, Texas asked them if they found a car down the road please bring it back and they would drive themselves back to France. To their surprise the next day one of the sergeants came back and told them that they had found a car and hidden it in a barn, gassed up and ready to go. The guys from the 28th had painted it up for them with "Texas Bound" on the back and stars all over so they wouldn't get shot by US fighters still roaming the sky's. They drove across Germany to Camp Lucky Strike in France.

"My father began his trip from Moosburg with Eddie Allen on the second night after liberation. A U.S. guard at one of the gates at Stalag 7A was a younger brother of a good friend of my father's from San Angelo, Texas. He let them out, gave them a small automatic pistol and wished them good luck. When they found the car, in the trunk of the car they found several German Luftwaffe officer's uniforms, dress daggers and pistols. They also found a couple of cameras and film. They started the car and began their journey to France.

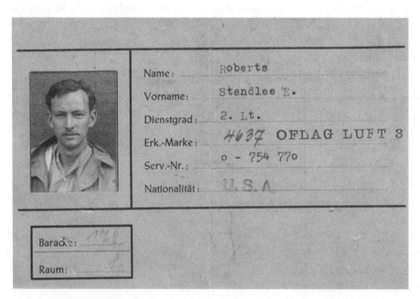

Stanley Roberts' German ID

"They went west from Moosburg and ran into part of the Autobahn. Some-where between Moosburg and the Autobahn, they ran into an eight man German patrol retreating south from the US Army. My father and Eddie did not realize that Patton had surged ahead of all the divisions west of his 14th armored. My father said that when they saw the German Wehrmacht soldiers, Eddie reached down to grab the little .25 or .32 caliber pistol. My father immediately said no, hide it, we wouldn't have a chance with 5-7 shots left in the pistol. Later in life he said that was one of the smartest things he did in the whole war. They would have been annihilated in seconds. Every German had an automatic rifle. My father stopped the car and the German soldier could see they were POWs although my father and Eddie were wearing German coats and hats from WWI.

"When they stopped the car, a German Oberfeldwebel cautiously approached them and in broken English, asked who they were and where they were going. He appeared to be the oldest in the group at around forty years old. It was hard to tell his age because the war had taken its toll on the soldier. My father replied that they were POWs and were going home, but they were lost. He asked my father where they had come from and was the US Army there. My father said Moosburg and yes a lot of them. My father asked him what direction they should go to get as far away from the war as they could. The Oberfeldwebel grinned and pointed north. He then swung his arm in that direction and said go now. My father did not hesitate.

"As they were pulling away, my father looked in the rear view mirror and saw a young soldier pointing his machine gun at the rear of their car. My dad thought that's it, we're dead and at that moment the German soldier just shook the gun acting like he was shooting. My dad always figured that the German soldier ver-bally made a shooting noise and probably said something like "Easy pickings." That was the last they saw of them. They knew the war was lost. My father hit the Autobahn and headed north running into a US patrol who told them to get the hell off the Autobahn, that the German's had blown up at the overpasses and they had mined it preparing for the invasion They were given a map by the patrol and told to keep heading north until they hit US troops. The route they took was from Moosburg to Pfaffenhen, to Inglestadt, to Frankfurt, to Mainz, to Bingen and then into France.

***

"Once home he married went to Texas A&I University in Kingsville Texas. Worked on the King Ranch to help pay for college and a home. After graduation he went to work for Shell Oil Co. and in 1952 he was called back to active duty for Korea. He trained for a little over a year and then was discharged because he had been a POW.

"At that time my parents had three children. He went to work for a plumb-ing supply in Dallas, Texas. Three years later he was hired by Tyler Pipe and

Foundry, Tyler, Texas. He moved to Houston in 1957 and because Houston was growing so fast, plus NASA and the Rio Grande Valley, not to mention Austin, and San Antonio, as well, he became the number one salesman in the US, for the largest soil pipe foundry at that time. He remained number one until 1970 when he started his own business. Stan Roberts & Assoc. Inc. A Manufacturers's Representation Agency, selling pipe valves and fittings.

"My father worked until 2007, but still stopped by the business weekly until 2009. He passed away on April 25, 2010. Two weeks before he died he said he was going to try and make it to the 29th. He always called that his true birthday because he was shot down on the 29th and liberated on April 29.

"His older brother was a company commander in the 11th Armored division. He was killed in action 70 miles southeast of Stalag 7A on April 30, 1945. One day after my dad was liberated.

***

Acknowledgements;
Wife Patricia for 2Lt. William H. Miller, co-pilot
Carl Roberts, son of Bombardier 2Lt. Standlee E. Roberts.

CHAPTER 20

385ᵀᴴ BOMB GROUP
551ˢᵀ BOMB SQUADRON

Type: B-17G • Serial: 42-31133
MACR: 4453 • Air Base: Great Ashfield

Aircraft 42-3133 suffered hits from enemy aircraft fire in the vicinity of Magdeburg, Germany at about 10.55 hours. No. 3 and no. 4 engines were on fire. This aircraft then left the formation, making a steep turn but losing altitude rapidly. It was last seen about 16 miles West of Magdeburg, where from 4 to 7 chutes were seen leaving the aircraft.

Missing Air Crew Report # 4453

Pilot: 1Lt. Hector J. Garza, 0-687026, POW

Co-Pilot: 2Lt. George W. Beckner, 0-163499, POW

Navigator: 2Lt. Albert Harmsen, 0-688435, POW

Bombardier: 2Lt. Stacy Johnson, 0-750031, POW

Engineer: F/Sgt. Richard M. Hoffman, 36606902, POW

Radio: T/Sgt. Harry B. Lynn, 18190301, POW

Ball-Turret Gunner: S/Sgt. Wallace J. Widen, 38396922, POW

Left Waist-Gunner: S/Sgt. Walter F. Smith, 32458651, POW

Right Waist-Gunner: S/Sgt. Emmett A. Harter, 17151658, POW

Tail-Gunner: S/Sgt. Alfred M. Fratesi, 32554700, POW

10 POW

Target: Berlin Friedrichstrasse Railway Station

Crash Site: Hessen/Halberstadt, Germany
Time: 11.40

385th Bomb Group, 551st Bomb Squadron (Garza)
Official Photo USAAF, AAB Grand Island, Nebraska

Back row (left to right): Radio T/Sgt. H.B. Lynn, Sgt. Joe Posser*, Tail-Gunner S/Sgt. Al Fratesi, Ball-Turret Gunner S/Sgt. Wallace Widen, Left Waist-Gunner S/Sgt. Walter. Smith, Engineer F/Sgt. Richard Hoffman

Front row: Navigator2Lt. Albert Harmsen, Bombardier 2Lt. Stacy Johnson, Pilot 1Lt. Hector Garza, Pilot E.E. Powers*

*Joe Posser and E.E. Powers were not aboard on April 29,1944

Co-Pilot 2Lt. George W. Beckner.

By son Richard Beckner.

"George was born on September 25, 1918 in Miamisburg, Ohio. His father, George Beckner, was the Assistant Clerk of Courts for Dayton and Montgomery County. His mother, lda Mae, stayed at home to care for George and his sister.

"George fondly remembers frequenting the local swimming pond and riding the street car from Miamisburg to Dayton with his neighborhood friends. While attending Miamisburg High School, George was the center on his school's football team that went undefeated for three consecutive years.

"After graduating in 1936, he continued his education at Miami University and completed two years there before going to work for he National Cash

Register Company. He was drafted into the Army Signal Corps in 1942. He and one of his friends were the first boys on his street to be drafted.

"George met the love of his life, Jeanne Baker, at a high school dance. They were married on March 18, 1942 while he was stationed in Texas.

"George didn't stay long in the Signal Corps because the Air Corps were looking for pilots and George volunteered. After he completed his training and became a B-17 pilot, he was sent to England on the Queen Mary.

"While in England, George flew four missions before being shot down on April 29, 1944 over Magdeburg, Germany on his fifth mission. After a successful parachute landing,

Co-Pilot 2Lt. George W. Beckner on his wedding day

he was hospitalized in Obermastfeld for a gunshot wound to his arm and was later transferred to Stalag Luft III, a prisoner of war camp near Zagan, Poland. The movie "The Great Escape" was based on the escape attempts at this prisoner of war camp.

"As the Russians moved closer, George and the other prisoners were moved west to Stalag Vll-A near Moosburg, Germany, where they were liberated on April 29, 1945 by General Patton.

"Upon his return home to the United States, he had the bullet removed from his arm. He was discharged in 1947 after his rehabilitation. George worked at his family's miniature golf course and driving range until his son Richard was about five years old. He then worked for the United States Post Office as a letter carrier for a few years before going to work for the Defense Electronic Supply Center in Dayton, Ohio. He retired from there in the late 1970's. George was an avid golfer and played into his nineties.

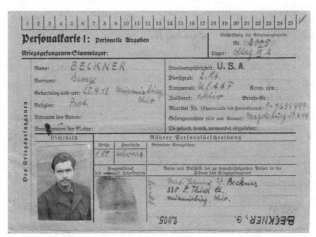
2Lt. George Beckner's POW ID Card

Navigator 2Lt. Albert Harmsen.

By nephew Edward Biehl

"For years I have been interested in the World War II experiences of Uncle Albert Harmsen, husband of Aunt Betty, father of Bruce and Debbie. I was a pallbearer at his funeral in 1995 and again I was struck by the photo of Uncle Al in his Army Air Corps uniform together with Aunt Betty. I had never asked him about his experiences in combat. That was not considered in good taste at the time, something I sadly regret.

"The 385th was located at Great Ashfield (a former RAF base), 90 miles southeast of London, 10 miles east of Bury St. Edmonds in Suffolk. It was designated Station 155; 20 miles from the English Channel. interestingly, the 549th Squadron was located near a farm that raised sugar beets and used human waste from the base for fertilizer. When the wind was just right the fertilizer stench was god-awful for the 549th.

"Based on photographs from other bases the buildings look much the same as they did in the movie "12 O'Clock High," and despite the difference in materials they're all very similar. Today the airbase has been reduced to one landing strip for light aircraft and all but a few buildings, including the tower, are gone. The remainder of the base is now farmland.

"At Great Ashfield, a number of neighbors have heard a "Ghostly B-17" landing there at night. Suspecting smugglers, the police responded immediately; they never found an aircraft there. As a result, a lot of the British now call Great Ashfield the "Haunted Airbase."

"The 385th Bomb Group flew some incredible missions and was twice awarded the Presidential Distinguished Unit Citation, once for a very dangerous raid on a fighter factory at Regensburg and the second for a raid on Zwickau, Germany.

"The 385th's first mission was flown on July 17, 1943; its last mission was flown on April 20, 1945. The Group flew 296 combat missions, 8264 sorties, and lost 129 B-17s in action.

"Often, flying conditions were absolutely horrible. At altitudes of 25,000 feet, or more, with no pressurization and no heat, conditions within the B-17 were 55-60 degrees below zero in the cold clear skies high over Europe and the wind through the waist guns apertures was 150-160 miles per hour. The crew wore heavy, electrically warmed suits, goggles and face masks. Despite these precautions there was a great deal of frostbite, some of it severe. Missions lasted approximately 7-9 hours and sometimes 11 hours for missions far into Germany. And then there was the incredible amount of flak and the multitude of Luftwaffe fighters whose single mission was to destroy the entire 8th Air Force, and they tried very hard to do it.

"With the cold, the fighters and the flak, the hammering of your own guns in your ear, the navigators did things that were almost magical – finding the target, and bringing the ship home. Kind of different today when you push a button and your GPS tells you exactly where you are. Uncle Al and his fellow navigators did it another way... with charts, protractor and dividers, correcting the course by citing towns, lakes, rivers and cities, memorizing the position of 50 stars at night, using the octagon to "shoot the stars" and spherical trigonometry to plot their aircraft's position on a dark night.

"Members of the 8th Air Force used the F-word a lot, with totally different meanings. To them the F-Word meant any or all of the following together: "Flak, Fire, Fog, Frost, Fear, Flame, Fatigue, Fock-Wulfs," and above all what they realistically called the "Five Fickle Fingers of Fate."

"On April 29, 1944, The 385th and 447th were blown far to the south, more than 122 miles west- southwest of Berlin without any American fighter cover. Then, at Braunschweig, they were attacked for 30 minutes by an extremely determined and aggressive force of 125 German fighters which inflicted heavy damage on the bombers.

"The "lost" and badly damaged 4A Wing then attacked Magdeburg, an important city on the Elbe river as a target of opportunity. The German fighters continued their action through the target area and the first few minutes of the withdrawal.

Right Waist-Gunner S/Sgt. Emmett A. Harter.

From a newspaper article.

"This is a story of a young airman who faced death over the skies of Nazi Germany in World War II. His story resonates with adventure, terror, determination, courage, and in every sense of the word, heroism. It would be very hard to make up a story like this one. But, it is also a story that could be mirrored in thousands of tales from those who faced combat defending our freedom. Many of you have 'heroes' in your family tree. So this story is for those of you who haven't had the opportunity to hear the tales from your hero including those who won WWII. Please take a moment to remember and thank those who saved you from being a member of Hitler's Youth Corps or a worshiper of a Japanese Emperor.

"On an April morning in 1944, one more bombing run to Hitler's Third Reich was planned. Wake up time was at 3 AM on a dark, damp, overcast, cold English morning. Bud couldn't find his 'lucky' shirt. It wasn't where it had been every for the last five months! The thought of going on another mission was bad enough, but going without THE lucky shirt could be mind chilling. Some SOB in one of the two new crews probably had it. Bud hoped the sleeves reached the thief's knees. As the right waist-gunner in a B-17 bomber, Bud was a little taller than the rest of the crew.

"Bud was scheduled for his 23rd bomb run over Nazi Europe that morning.

Usually, after twenty-five runs, an airman was "through" and could return to America. But, this limit was changed to 29 in 1944 because of higher than expected losses. Fortunately, the limit for anyone already having over twenty runs was frozen at 25. Staff Sergeant Bud was a very experienced airman with only three more runs to make. And like most seasoned airmen, Bud knew staying alive required a fair dose of luck. Lucky charms became part of the ritual of preparing your mind to face another mission. The loss of a lucky charm could prey on the minds of these young airmen far from home and in harms way.

"Bud's plane was named "The Spirit of Chicago" with nose art depicting Chicago's colorful reputation. The nose had a whiskey jug labeled XXX with a ghost spirit, floating out of the jug holding a violin case slightly opened to show a machine gun. So far that ghost had been very lucky. And "Spirit" had sprayed bullets and bombs all over Germany as part of the 385th Bomb Group.

"Bud's troubles continued when he found that his heated shoes were out for repair. The only shoes available were two sizes too big. And that made the search for some fur lined boots time consuming. Two beat up, mismatched boots were finally found, but Bud was now behind schedule. Then a new major stopped him and demanded to know where the major's plane was parked. After being shown to his plane, the major refused to drive Bud back to his own plane; the major claimed he couldn't find his way back. So Bud walked a mile across the muddy field, carrying his parachute and duffel bag, shoes flopping, and almost missing his flight. He had to put on his flight clothes in the plane, in the dark. A bad start for a dangerous mission.

"The weather man predicted poor visibility and he was right. The haze was so bad that the Group was late forming up in the air and heading out over the English Channel. Bud fired his waist-gun to check its operation, and each of the ten men reported to the pilot every ten minutes for the rest of the mission. With the cold and lack of oxygen at 25'000 feet, everyone needed to keep in touch and be alert.

"On April 29th, 1944, the 8th was scheduled to visit Berlin with Maagdenburg as an alternate target if Berlin could not be bombed for any reason. Berlin was heavily defended as the Luftwaffe was to save their leader Reich Marshall Hermann Göring from Hitler's wrath. Goring had boasted that no Allied plane would ever be seen over German skies. Now they were as plentiful as clouds! Allied experts were divided on why Berlin was a "good" target. It contained several important factories and was the capital of Nazi Germany.

"Just as important, the Luftwaffe was determined to to protect Berlin and so could be coaxed into coming up for a fight on every mission instead of waiting for opportune conditions to attack American planes. This caused the Luftwaffe to lose more planes and pilots than it could replace. Some believed bombing Berlin would soon kill the Luftwaffe and give the Allies uncontested air superiority. So Berlin became a magnet for repeated bombing attacks. This "grand strategy" seemed to justify the cost of these repeated attacks that was paid in American airmen who never returned.

"Precision bombing from five miles high was difficult and, in 1944, primitive radar called Micky, was being employed on lead aircraft to get each Group to its assigned spot on time even if the weather didn't cooperate. The "Spirit" flew above a solid under-cast following its lead aircraft with a new, inexperienced, mickey operator.

"Unfortunately, the 385th got a "bad" mickey operator. Over Germany, the Group discovered that is was alone in the sky. The Mickey operator had strayed about forty miles away from the main Bomber Stream. Bub was about to get a Mickey Finn! If only he had found that lucky shirt.

"All of a sudden the "Spirit" ran into flak. Shells ripped into the right wing, shooting off the flap and wing tip. Fuel started to leak out of one fuel tank. Then the lead plane saw a landmark, changed direction, and decided to hit the alternative target Maagdenburg, as it was too late to reach their assigned spot over Berlin on time.

"As the Group started its bomb run on Maagdenburg, with open bomb bay doors, Bud's bombardier called out, "Flak at 12 o'clock! Oh shit, that ain't flak, it's German fighters! There are hundreds of them!" In fact, the 385th had probably run into the rendezvous point of many of the Nazi fighters defending Berlin. A best guess was a mix of at least 200 Focke Wulf 190's (the Nazi's best fighter) and Messerschmidt 109's. Bud started to cuss out the unknown SOB who had taken his lucky shirt. The odds against the 385th were the same as Custer faced at Little Big Horn! It looked like luck had finally run out.

"One hell of a collision was about to occur. Thirty B-17 in a box formation three city blocks high, three blocks long and seven blocks wide equaled 63 cubic city blocks of metal, guns, bombs and flesh. Two hundred Nazi fighters were going to try to fly through this occupied space at full speed, in a head-on attack with all guns blazing. Considering that the American bombers would be firing all their guns while taken evasive actions, what might be empty space one moment would be filled the next. Well, 200 fighters don't go into 30 bombers safely, so many men are going to die in a short time period.

"To the watching Americans, the attack seem to develop slowly. The Nazis moved in closer, flying parallel to the B-17's, weaving back and forth, bouncing up and down like they were trying to psych themselves for the attack. The B-17's started to "dance" up and down, side to side, tasting the maneuver room available. There wasn't much as the bombers were trained to fly "cover" for each other, requiring they maintain positions close to one another so all guns could support a united defense.

"At least that was the theory. There wasn't an atheist in the 385th as the German fighters pulled slowly forward and climbed to 12 o'clock high to start their attack. Everyone was praying, mostly for help in controlling the fear washing over them. No one wants to die young and most of these American airmen were young. The B-17's could not turn around and quit the fight. Strapped into their positions, the men could only sit and watch death approaching. Then the lead bomber came on the radio, "Okay boys. On your toes. This is it." And the Nazi fighters turned into the bomber formation.

"The enemy attack was deadly, terrifying, and yet dramatically beautiful as it flowed against the 385th. The lead Nazi had a yellow nose and, as he fired, he rolled upside down to expose his armored belly and and dived below the Group instead of trying to penetrate. He knew how to survive. But the followers weren't as fortunate as they continued straight in to the bomber formation in rows of ten fighters, five rows at a time. BOOM! One fighter collided with a B-17 and they exploded instantly into a giant, flaming, red fireball. Debris was flung out in all directions; engines, metal, bodies, propellers, and unidentified pieces. And it was spectacular, colorful, frightening, and happening way too fast.

"The first pass had hurt the 385th badly. The formation was strung out from evasive maneuvers and had lost altitude. Several B-17's were "gone," along with their ten men crews. Bombers were jockeying to reassemble the Group and re-establish cover fire. The Nazi fighters were also strung out and had to regroup but quickly swung into a second attack. The noise of the fifty caliber guns of the B-17's was deafening. Spent shell casings spewed from other planes and inside each plane. With all the exploding shells, the air looked like a lit Christmas tree.

"Then Bud's plane shuddered as German bullets tore into the bomber. The *Spirit*'s chin turret was shot away and a 20 mm. shell exploded, knocking the oxygen regulator off the wall beside Bud and knocking his goggles off. But Bud got a solid hit on a FW-190 as it streaked by. Then the *Spirit* was hit again: it shuddered as through hitting a wall and four engines were knocked out.

"With its engines shot up, wing and tail control services to pieces, Bud's *Spirit* immediately pitched nose up. Then it slid off towards the right wing and headed down. It went into a deadly spin, pinning everyone where they were. Death was rushing to claim the crew when a miracle happened. The *Spirit* somehow stopped spinning and flattened out for just a moment. It could have been the pilots desperately fighting the controls or more probably the weight of the still loaded bombs that helped stopp the spin. Or it could have been the *Spirit*'s ghost helping a hand.

"The pilot was repeating, "Bail Out. Bail out!" Bud leaped off the waist wall where he had been pinned, grabbed a parachute, snapped it into place, kicked out a small emergency door in the waist of the bomber, and jumped out before the spin could re-start. Everything was still happening too fast, but training aided his survival instincts.

"As soon as he was in the clear, Bud pulled the ripcord and the chute opened. But he was still too high and too near the continuing attack on the 385th. He wished he would have waited until he lost some more altitude. But there hadn't been time to think about anything but survival. German fighters flashed by and

and wreckage rained down around him. Bud saw several smoking fighters go by and one was burning. Two B-17's were spinning down as the sun reflected off their unpainted metal wings. Another B-17 exploded above Bud.

"Remarkably nothing came too close. Maybe, just maybe the *Spirit*'s ghost was helping Bud this morning. Bud drifted slowly away, down through the clouds towards Nazi Germany, where most citizens already knew of at least one relative or neighbor killed by an Allied bomb. Bud had lost his luck this morning, but he was going to have to get some back quickly if he intended to stay alive down there!

"He drifted slowly towards a small German town and landed in a plowed field. Unfortunately he was not alone. Townspeople had seen the parachute and were pounding towards the field in a mob. With pitch forks and old shotguns they faced the dazed airman. Bud couldn't raise his arms to unlatch the chute harness. He had such a death grip hanging on to the chute risers it took a get enough blood into his hands to let go the ropes and get out of the parachute.

"Deutscher?" asked one. Bud shook his head no. "Englander?" Again no. "Amerikanisch?" screamed the man with his voice getting higher. Bud didn't have to answer as it was obvious he was an American. Another man speaking English said; "So you are an American gangster! You are sent to murder our people and, Gott dammit, we hang murderers!" with lots of shouts and arms waving, the townspeople marched Bud and his floppy boots back into the town square.

"In the square was an old horse trough with a long post in the middle. As Bud was marched up to the lamp post, he noticed that someone had found a long rope. A solid citizen started to tie the rope into a noose, and they urged Bud to get up on the rim of the horse trough. A good old fashioned town hanging was in full progress to the delight of the mob. As they were trying to get the rope around the top of the lamp post, a Nazi officer walked into the town square. The SS major started to lecture the crowd. But the crowd started yelling back, finally, the major pulled his Luger pistol and aimed it at the loudest citizen. All became quiet. The noose was taken off Bud's neck and the major pulled him down the street.

"Bud was taken to a nearby building, strip searched, and thrown into a solitary cell. After he ate a meal of potato soup, black bread, and ginger ale, a couple of Luftwaffe soldiers came and put him into a truck. For the first time that morning, Bud thought he might be alive to see the next sunrise. The truck also collected the *Spirit's* left waist-gunner, Smitty, and the tail-gunner, the Greek, among others. Bud was busted alongside the head with a rifle butt while helping a man with broken ribs into the truck.

"For the next three weeks, Bud spent time in and out of solitary confinement. The Germans wanted to know about Bud's past flight history but he would tell them only name, rank and serial number. Twice a day prisoners got a potato and a slice of bread. One day Bud's questioner said he didn't need any information as they already had everything they needed. The officer proceeded to tell Bud about his military history, including home address and next of kin. But there was a one month gap. And the officer wanted to know where Bud was during that time. Bud didn't dare say. During that time he had been assigned to a Mickey unit which was a secret to Germans would love to hear more about. Eventually, the Nazis gave up, allowed Bud to wash up for the first time since he was captured, and transported him to a Luftwaffe prison camp in East Prussia (Lithuania), Stalag Luft 6, the last part of May.

***

Acknowledgements;
Richard Beckner, son of co-pilot 2Lt. George W. Beckner
Edward Biehl, nephew of navigator 2Lt. Albert Harmsen
Waist-Gunner S/Sgt. Emmett A. Harter, The story entitled "Death Stalks Airman Over Nazi Skies" was published in three installments in a weekly local newspaper called "Newstime."

CHAPTER 21

385ᵀᴴ BOMB GROUP
551ˢᵀ BOMB SQUADRON

Type: B-17G • Serial: 42-31174
MACR: 4454 • Air Base: Great Ashfield

Aircraft 42-31174 was attacked by enemy fighters in the area of Magdeburg, Germany. Both wings of this aircraft caught fire and the ship ultimately exploded. No chutes were seen to leave this aircraft. Due to the rapidity and continuity of the enemy aircrafts, few details surrounding the loss of this aircraft and other aircrafts lost by the Group on this date are very few.

Missing Air Crew Report # 4454

Pilot: 1Lt. Francis J. Hart, 0-679068, POW

Co-Pilot: 2Lt. Carl M. Connell, 0-683654, POW

Navigator: 2Lt. James I. Hastings, 0-683131, POW

Bombardier: 2Lt. Robert H. Hunt, POW

Engineer: T/Sgt. John W. Leonard, 12999957, POW

Radio: T/Sgt. Anatole A. Briant, 38172299, POW

Ball-Turret Gunner: S/Sgt. Lowell T. Birdwell, 18007605, POW

Left Waist-Gunner: T/Sgt. Roy W. Modglin, 35371265, POW

Right Waist-Gunner: S/Sgt. William C. Jackson, 15063160, POW

Tail-Gunner: S/Sgt. John C. Neely, 32364402, KIA

1 KIA, 9 POW

Crash Site: Eckertal/Bad Harzburg - Germany
Time: 11.30

Pilot 1Lt. Francis J. Hart

Col Joe" is of the Greatest Generation. He grew up in a single parent family with two brothers and four sisters living in Chicago, struggled thru the great depression, never knowing what welfare was. His brothers and sisters went to work after the tenth grade; only by agreeing to do the necessary tasks in the home was he allowed to continue his education until graduation from high school. Spending money was earned working on the weekends. His first job with Illinois Bell Telephone was operating a cafeteria automatic dishwasher. He had just transferred to a decent paying job at the Western Electric Co. plant in Cicero, Ill, when the Japanese bombed Pearl Harbor. Twenty days after Pearl he raised his hand and repeated the Oath to defend the United States from all enemies. He enlisted in the Army Air Corps and was accepted for Aviation Mechanics School. After processing at Camp Grant, Illinois, he was shipped to Sheppard AAF Base, Wichita Falls, Texas, for training.

After completion of mechanics training, he successfully passed tests for pilot training and was transferred to Kelly AAF Base as an aviation cadet. After training at bases in Texas, Oklahoma and Kansas he received his silver wings and gold bars of a second lieutenant. He was transferred to a B-17 Flying Fortress provisional training group as a co-pilot on a crew. After the second phase of crew training, he was pulled from the crew, assigned his own crew, repeated first and second phase combat training. After receiving overseas orientation in Nebraska; he traveled to the New York Port of Embarkation, and boarded the Queen Mary. He was assigned to the 551st Squadron, 385th Bomb Group, 3rd Air Division, and 8th Air Force, based at Great Ashfield, England.

Colonel Joe flew his first combat mission, December 13, 1943, a 7 1/2 hour round trip to the German seaport of Kiel. Col Joe remembers it well. Kiel was very heavily defended with flak guns as it was a major port for the German navy. The most memorable missions, beside the final trip on April 29, 1944, were during the month of February when the Eighth Air Force challenged the German Air Force for control of the air. In 6 days he flew 4 missions, 3 of the 4 were 10-hour missions. One mission to Regensberg was when for the first time he saw fighter support all the way to the target and back. They were P-51s, "little buddies."

Not all memories are pleasant however. On the same mission, two aircraft in his three-plane element took direct hits from anti-aircraft flak on the bomb run to the target. Both ships went down. The mission on April 29th 1944, No. 29 his last required mission before rotation to the States, is the most memorable.

Francis J. Hart - My 29th and last mission

"This may not appease anyone but myself – this is written for my benefit only. "Mission Day" as I shall choose to call April 29th started at 2.30 in the morning – which is a mean time especially after four previous missions. It was a hell of a day out there, as we started down for breakfast, which comprised, fruit juice, cereal, fried eggs, toast, coffee and a smoke.

"The weather was still holding bad as we piled in our truck and headed for the briefing room. There were many a "bitch" too about being up so damned early and everyone knew it was going to be a long one. It didn't bother me too much as I was getting close to the end. I was worrying about our ship. It just had a wing change and I thought it might not be ready to go.

"We piled into the briefing room and waited for the screen to get up and show our job for the day. I noticed on the board that that I was to fly number 5 spot in a squadron that was to fly with another Group.

"Finally the screen was raised to show that our target were factories in the Berlin area. This was to be my seventh trip there. We listened to the usual instructions on take-off and assembly.

"As usual after briefing we went over to the locker room to dress. That was when Jim went into his act of being sick. I razzed him about being scared and now wished I hadn't as he would probably have been grounded and wouldn't be a POW to-day. But it seemed at that time damned necessary to me so I razzed him into going. Robert Hunt was riding with me that day as bombardier and Jim as navigator. Then there was Mike, Leonard, Micky, Neely, Birdwell and two waist-gunners whose names I don't remember.

"Things went as usual out at the ship. We weren't to diligent in checking it as we figured that it was sure the mission to be scrubbed. I remember my crew chief remarking that the ship had been on the ground for quite a while and as yet hadn't been checked out and that if things didn't go right to bring it back.

"We waited around and finally it came time to start engines and as yet the mission was still on. So we climbed on board and started engines and taxied out in our turn. At the head of the runway Robish blew a tire and had to pull off in the grass. That left the squadron lead up to "Pat."

"We started off and began our climb through the overcast which began around 2'000 feet and ended somewhere around 13,000. Well we never did meet the other two squadrons so we went back to our group and circled above them until we went along the Wing assembly line. It was there that I spotted Drobeyh and I immediately tacked on to his right wing.

"That went alright until some "baby" came up crying for his "spot" and cried so damn much that the boss "Mac" called up and told me to get out. Well. I couldn't go to my assigned position as somebody else had already grabbed it, so I just tagged along behind the high squadron. By the time the Wing was on course across the North Sea heading for big "B" I noticed that the high squadron in the lead Group had only six ships so I decided to fly along as number seven. Still no semblance of wing formation. Then damn if the no. 5 & 6 men of the Low Squadron didn't abort and then no. 4 man started yelling like hell for the ships in the High Squadron to fill in.

"Finally after about half an hour Masters called me by name so down I went. I had just gotten down there when the flak came up and boy it was damn close. We were still not in any decent formation, and then we started climbing; we were at about 12,000 feet then. We went along for a while when we started having trouble with the no. 2 supercharger surging. It was then that I learned over the VHF that we were twelve minutes late and five miles south of course.

"It was then that I first saw the Luftwaffe. They looked like a big swarm of bees. It was later said that there were 200 plus. They comprised 109's – 190's and a few JU-88's. They were off at one o'clock to our formation. I called the boys over inter-phone and let them know and immediately after; the first attacking wave came in head on. We were in very poor formation at the time. The Low and High Groups were out of sight and our Lead Squadron was 700 feet higher and 200 or 300 feet ahead of us. Each Squadron had its hands full as they picked on them separately. All I could do was to watch my element leader although I did see seven FW's coming head on to us.

"Right after, all hell broke loose in the Low Squadron. There were 20 mm exploding all the way through. We suffered a lot of holes in the left wing; no serious damage as yet. The top-turret suffered a direct 20 mm hit seriously wounding my engineer in the face and around the eyes. Also the top windows of the cockpit were blown out. The right side of the fuselage suffered quite a few hits – one hit taking the right dinghy and a good portion of the fuselage with it. I looked around and noticed the engineer holding his face in his hands with blood oozing from between his fingers. The second wave of FW's hit us damned hard. It practically tore the nose out of our ship. The bombardier was hit in the face, hands and legs with 20 mm. Jim also was hit in the hand; later he told me a 20 mm took the barrel off his gun.

"The rest of the ship was torn to hell. Number 2 tank was leaking – it was luck we didn't have a fire. No. 1 engine must have taken a direct hit because the bottom cylinders were missing. Also caught our oxygen system and hydraulic liners and the inter-phone system went out.

"One of the strangest sensations I've had in my life happened then. Evidently fragments cut the rudder controls because both pedals disappeared and my legs shot straight out along the rudder slides; having on the heavy boots and in the excitement I thought my feet were gone. It took me a few seconds to get up nerve enough to look down to see if I still had them.

"Things started happening pretty fast about then. I nosed the ship down to lose altitude and never bothered about pulling the throttles back. Mike jabbed me and pointed to the oil pressure gauges. They were down to zero – but I noticed all the other instruments were hay-wire but the engine temp and they seemed normal so we let them go. Jim and Hunt were trying to get back into the radio room and Hunt's face was a bloody mess. Leonard thinking they were trying to bail out and not being able to see went out the bomb bay. Parts of the nose were blowing back under the cockpit floor and the oxygen bottles were going off with a bang.

"Noticed we were at 10,000 feet so started to ease out of dive, glanced at I.A.S. and noticed it over 300 m.p.h. so eased back on stick with care. Reached forward to punch V.H.F. fighter button and the damn set was gone. We were heading about 300° for some low clouds in the distance. I sent Mike back to tell the boys to hang on for a minute to see how we'd make out. Noticed the hydraulic motor burning and smoking and also some smoke from up front in the nose. Also the R/T set above our heads was all shattered. There was a big hole on Mike's side – big enough for a man to crawl through. Looked out to see how the left wing was doing and noticed that the airelon was pretty badly torn up, tested it and found out there was no control over it.

Mike came back about then and said Mickey was injured and the radio room pretty badly torn up. Also that the ball-turret was all shot up and that Tex was salvoing it. About that time I noticed three fighters off at three o'clock from us, and thought at first they might have been escort. But I was soon assured they weren't when the first boy peeled off and came head on to us. His shots went high and to the left of us. I noticed that when it went under us it was a peppermint striped FW. Figured we didn't have much chance with just waist and tail guns so I sent Mike back to tell the boys to bail out. I turned towards the other two fighter boys figuring to cause them to overshoot, but the dirty bastards did a barrel roll and were up the same distance away.

"Leveled ship up and started adjusting A.F.C.E... – looked back into the bomb bay and noticed Mike and Jim taking off, started to get up out of seat to go back to bail out and damn if the chute did not catch between the seats. Finally managed to get loose and started crawling through turret to bomb bay, stepped into the catwalk and gripes the place was a mess, one door was gone and the sides were peppered. Noticed the ship turning so I swung one leg over the turret and let go.

"After I jumped and dropped free I was snatched and thrown around like a feather - all the time remembering a lecture about protecting one's …against the shock of the chute opening. I held off until I finally went into a cloud and frantically pulled the ring and damn I started floating through the cloud. I could hear the fighters buzzing and finally came out the base. I looked down and I was heading right for virgin forest. I waited until I figured about a minute more. Then I crossed my legs, put my arms over my face and blam!! I went crashing down through the trees, branches snagging my coveralls , legs, jacket, and arms; finally with a jolt I stopped and as soon as possible opened my eyes and there I was about ten feet above the air suspended by my chute. I squirmed around and got my scout knife out. Starting to swing I finally reached the trunk of the tree and wrapped my legs around it. Reached up and cut the shrud lines. Bracing myself and let go and put two feet on terra firma.

"After dropping to the ground I got rid of my harness and mae west and took off. I walked for fifteen or twenty minutes and stopped to rest and take a few bearings. After resting I decided to get rid of some of my flying clothes, so the first thing I did was to rid myself of my boots and next my coveralls. I was in doubt as to my jacket so I turned it inside out and decided it would be okay as it might get cold. I scraped aside some branched and leaves and dug a small hole. In it I placed the boots, and coveralls, and all the papers I had in my wallet and pockets after I had torn them as fine as possible, covering all with the dirt, leaves and branches.

"I decided to see how much distance I could get between myself and my parachute. Taking out my compass I set out to the north – presently I came to a wagon trail that seemed to be heading my way. At first I hesitated to follow it – but on looking closer I noticed the ground was wet and didn't see any fresh track so I started hiking up the road.

"Walking along I was really surprised at the clean and fresh appearance of the forest around and it was quiet as a morgue. Tall, stately pines closely spaced and in rows, and I thought of the poem "Trees," no doubt the prayers were in order. It was all strange and coinciding with the violent battle of death that I had just emerged from. I noticed my legs in the crotch were tightening up, and started to wonder how bad they were from the parachute shock.

"Here and there there were sections where the trees had been cut and split and were piled on the opening. Rounding a little turn in the lane I saw another road up ahead. I ducked off the lane into the side brush and thought I'd better wait and see if there was any traffic on the road ahead. After sitting about 20 minutes I hadn't heard a sound so I left the brush and walked to the road ahead. There I found the road a little wider but apparently used little as there was only one set of tracks and those of a wagon. Being anxious to get out of the area as quickly as possible I thought I'd travel as far along the road as I could.

"I must have walked about two or three miles I came to a small stream and a set of narrow gauged rail road tracks. I stopped at the stream and drank a little of the water. It was cold and tasted damn good. I washed my face a little and decided to take a look at my legs. I opened up my belt and lowered my trousers. My legs were a little read up close to my "stomach" and a small swelling. I remembered how Mum used to put cold knives on bumps on our heads to keep them from swelling. I took out my hanky in dipped it into the water and bathed my legs.

"Not wanting to waste time I dressed and started walking again. After walking a while I heard a faint knocking. I stopped to listen. I couldn't tell where it came from as it came from as it seemed all around. I walked a little further and knew it was coming from somewhere up ahead. The little railroad I noticed was off to the right. I decided to follow it and crossed over to it. I traveled about two more miles and noticed smoke and too much activity and got off to the side into the edge of the woods. Finding a few boulders I dropped behind them and decided to wait for dark to keep on moving.

"As I sat there I recalled what had taken place when I sent Mike back to have them jump. Why was Micky still there when I first started into the bomb bay. And then, after my frantic waving and going back into the cockpit to read just the A:F:C:E:, and returning back to the bomb bay why was Micky still standing there, gaping. I figured if after Jim and Mike jumping out the bomb bay and Hunt out the waist door, and the three or minutes time interval between then and my appearance they still would hesitate. I figured the reason was because I was still there and, as they always said, they would stay as long as I would. I uttered a prayer to God that the A.F.C.E. would have lasted a a few minutes more and the fighters seeing the chutes would hold off – I figured I must go or they would still stay.

"All of a sudden I was snapped out of my dreams by a rock which was bouncing by me. Cautiously I peeked from around the boulder and holy Mac Kabel there were German civilians with shotguns aimed at me, and a whole mass of kids spread to the right and left of them. I took one look at the ends of thes guns pointed at me, and slowly got to my feet and raised my hands above my head, with anger in my heart, and a lump in my throat. My escape was over!

"Not knowing what to do and not being able to understand what they were talking about I stood still. Two of the older men came up to me and asked for "pistol" and I shook my head "no." They then came up and searched me and took all my belongings including my rosary beads. Then these two old birds started marching me off down the road. Presently we came to the source of the knocking; a group of Russian POWs were working in the forest. When they came up to join us they gave me the "V" sign and winked at me, being sure not to let the guards see them.

"We continued down the road for about a mile and presently came to a cross road where two more boys came up and searched me again. It was then that I heard my first word of English. One asked me something about "Chicago" and I just shook my head "no." With the new guards and my belongings minus my rosary, knife, and money we started walking again.

"Presently we came to a small town. There was a big turn out and the boys seemed to walk me up and down just to show me off I guess. I remember one old boy he really must have been tear-assed cause he took a cut at me with a black whip he used on his horses. After our parading around they marched me into a small two story house – into a side room and sat me down. Then it started. A couple of young girls (who weren't bad) came into the room and looked me over. Then came the rest of the town, young, old, and both sexes.

"It was then that I had my big surprise. One came kind of close said a few words in German then banged me with the back of his hand and almost knocked me off my stool. After 15 or 20 minutes they marched me into another room and there sat Jim. I noticed he had his head bandaged but he assured me it was nothing.

"About half an hour later they marched Mike G. in. He was jabbering like a chatter box and he too was hit. He had practically to undress to look at his wounds. He had them in his shoulders, ass, back and leg. Well, we shot the baloney between the three of us for about half an hour when the local constable came in and marched us off to the train station where we waited for an officer of the Luftwaffe. Well our boy took us in tow and we got in a train and rode for quite a while finally reaching our destination Halberstadt. We waited around in the Red Cross room for a car the hotrock had called for.

"When it arrived we piled in and drove to an airdrome. A nice cell awaited me there. Small with one little window and with a hard plank for a bed. After a few questions were asked about my rank and what not I was locked up and left to my self.

"Early the next morning we were taken out and also was Joe Garza and Allen and began our trip to Dulag-Luft. Went through a number of towns that I think were heavily hit, but then it all changed when I saw Frankfurt.

"When we arrived at Dalag-Luft I first saw Leonard but the poor kid couln't see me. We were brought inside and seperated. I was put downstairs and boy it was cold. More fellows came in and then after a while they started taking us out, me last. What went on after that I'll have to trust to memory. I was bad enough that I was sent back down to my cooler in solitude.

"The next morning we went across the road to our first American cigarette and coffee since the morning before take-off. We spent three days here and then made up a shipment for Sagan. Eight of us in one compartment. It was here that the nervousness and anxiety for my crew started easing off due to my companions Ace – Stretch – Ike – Rabbit – Allen – Kendler – Mike. What a trip – spent half the night along with Ace up in the baggage rack. The other half on the bottom of six men and two seats.

"On the morning of the third day we arrived outside of Stalag-Luft and marched from the train up to the gate.

***

For the next year he was a guest of the German Air Force as a prisoner-of-war and was a inmate at three POW camps. After a week of solitary confinement and interrogation, he was transferred to Stalag Luft III, where he along with 10,000 other prisoners struggled to survive. January 1945, the camp was evacuated because of the Russian Army's drive to Berlin. After 36 hours on the road in temperatures that reached -35 degrees and a train trip his group arrived at Nuremburg. Two months later they were marched to a camp called Moosburg Stalag 7A.

April 29, 1945, exactly one year later, tanks from General Patton's Army liberated the camp. During a short, volunteered, stay, Col Joe, in a team of armed GI's scoured the countryside looking for and returning to US control, Allied prisoners who had been put to work on farms and in small factories. Col Joe's weight had dropped from 200 pounds to 135 pounds.

***

After 90 days on official leave back home in Chicago, he decided to continue a military career. There followed a number of assignments including military schools. After completion of an Aircraft Maintenance Officers Course at Chanute AF Base, Rantoul, Ill., he was assigned as the base aircraft maintenance officer, Elemendorf AF Base, Anchorage, Alaska. When he returned from Alaska he was assigned to the Airforce Plant Representative Office, Boeing Airplane Co. plant, Wichita, Kansas as a Flight Test and Acceptance Pilot.

The Boeing Airplane Co. was manufacturing and assembling the new six jet-engine heavy bomber, the B-47 Stratojet, which was in development. Col Joe recorded his first pilot time in the B-47, January 1951. He was assigned as the Chief of Flight Test, Air Force Plant Representative, Douglas Aircraft Co., Tulsa, OK in the B-47 program. He then completed an Advance Management Course, in the Air Force Institute of Technology at the Graduate School of Business, University of Pittsburgh.

Col Joe was then transferred back to Germany and was assigned to the U.S. Consulate in West-Berlin as a Procurement Liaison Officer for U.S. Air Force units stationed in Europe. His mission was to assist in rebuilding the economy of West Berlin by placing all procurements possible with West Berlin vendors. He was awarded the Air Force Commendation Medal for his service during this assignment.

Upon his return to the States, he was assigned to the Site Activation Task Force (SATAF), McConnell AF Base, Wichita, Kansas as Commander of the Contract Support Detachment. He was responsible for the administration of all Air Force contracts assigned to the SATAF for activation of the Titan ICBM site. He was awarded the Air Force Commendation Medal for his service during this period. He was next assigned as the Air Force Plant Representative, Thiokol Chemical Co., Brigham City, Utah, and GE Co., Syracuse, New York. He retired with the rank of Lt. Colonel on December 1, 1967 after 26 years of service.

Following his retirement he moved to Denver, Colorado, to work for the Denver Division of the Martin Marietta Corp. For 18 years he was employed in the Quality Control Department. The last 13 years he was Manager of the Quality Assurance Program of the Titan family of missiles including the current Titan IV. During this period he worked with a program called Mission Success which became a very important part of his life since his retirement from Martin, June, 1986. Six months prior to his retirement he had to make a very tough decision to put a 6 lb Toy Poodle to sleep because it's kidneys were being destroyed by a poison. He became very upset when expert Veterinarian Drs. would not treat the poodle without knowing exactly what poison was damaging the kidney.

After the event, in a terse conversation with one of the "experts," he was told there is one poison very damaging to renal tissue (kidney), called *Oxalates*, a word he had never heard. At that time he made a vow he would find out what killed the poodle named "Turk." He did find out what killed Turk. It was *Oxalates*, and it was he who provided the poison. He unknowingly fed it to Turk. What you have read gives credit for his qualifications to conduct the scientific research that has resulted in the Notice of Allowance by the US Patent Office of his "Claims for Oxalic Acid or Oxalate Composition and Methods of Treatment dated February 15, 2000. What is most significant is that the compositions and methods of treatment can be accomplished by a diet procedure.

Ball-Turret S/Sgt. Lowell T. Birdwell.

By daughter Phyllis Luce.

"Lowell Birdwell was the middle child of three born to a tenant farm family in Henderson TX. His family was very poor and life was hard. He took on the family farm from his father at the age of 16 and continued until age 21 when he graduated from high school in June of 1940. He required longer than others to finish school as he was unable to attend during the farm season.

"He enlisted in the U.S. Army Air Corps in November 1940 at the age of 21. Basic training at Barksdale AFB; 6 months of training at Jefferson Barracks, St Louis MO; Attended clerk-typist school at Fort Logan CO; in August 1941 he was transported by troopship from Fort Slocum NY to Base Headquarters in Barinquin, Puerto Rico where he was assigned as clerk-typist. He completed a 6 week radio operator school there.

"April 1942 he volunteered for aerial gunner training and completed first in his class. June 1943 assigned to B-17 combat crew as radio operator and gunner. July 1943 attended Phase I of B-17 training.

"In September 1943 he embarked on the "Queen Elizabeth" for Liverpool, England. October 1943 he was assigned to 385th Bomb Group, 551st Bomb Squadron at Stow Market, England. His first aircraft commander was killed on the second mission and the crew split up.

"Birdwell was assigned as temporary waist gunner and flew four missions with new crew. In Nov '43 he was assigned as radio operator on another crew. "Birdie" flew three missions as radio operator and was then reassigned as B-17 ball turret gunner. Shot fighter down on his first mission.

***

"April 29, 1944 at 11:15 a.m. on his 30th mission, his plane was hit while he was reloading his weapon. Three engines were knocked out, part of the ball turret and Vickers unit were shot away and "Birdie" received powder burns in and around his right eye, shrapnel in his wrist and groin, before parachuting from the disabled plane. They were shot down 10 miles west of Berlin. Crew parachuted to safety except one, the tail-gunner John Neely. Birdwell bailed out at 32000 feet, opening his chute at 1000 feet, he landed in a tree and dropped out of his chute.

"His B-17 cleared the mountain he landed on and crashed into the next. He could hear Germans coming up the mountain. He discarded his equipment, leaving a false trail for them to follow. He evaded capture by the Germans for 8 days. He approached a woman hanging clothes on the clothes line and asked for something to eat. She willingly took him in. When she went to get food, she notified the police.

"On May 8, 1944 he was transported to Frankfurt on Main Dulag for interrogation. After seven days he was put on a train with four guards to East Prussia Stalag Luft 6 on the eastern end of the Baltic Sea. On his arrival there were 2000 POWs at this camp.

"In August 1944, he and other POWs were marched to dock and loaded into a coal ship. Vessel had a V-shaped hull with one ladder going down into hull, no ventilation. Men were stacked up the walls of the hold. A bucket was lowered each day and filled with urine and excrement. No food during the four days in the hold. Approximately 25 men died due to overcrowding, heat, and lack of oxygen.

"Four days later the coal ship docked and the POWs were packed in a standing position in a cattle car with no room to sit or stoop. They traveled for four days without food or water. Approximately fifty POWs died on cattle cars. They were unloaded on the fourth day and marched in four columns, forced to stand for three hours until the next train arrived with a company of the Hitler Youth. Marched POWs down the road in columns of four commanding loudly, "Los, los, los" (hurry, hurry, hurry). POWs were forced to run while the Germans turned attack dogs loose and bayoneted those who could not maintain and fell out of ranks.

"He and other POWs were forced into a holding compound at Varlegar where POWs spent the night in the open. The next day, 200 POWs were jailed in the barracks designed for 50 men. Jailed at Varlegar for 6 months, their diet consisted of coffee for breakfast, a potato for lunch, a potato for dinner and possibly horse meat and water. Red Cross parcels that were intended once a week per prisoner, were shared by 4 men once a month. POWs had no medical attention.

"February 1945 they were marched from Camp West to the Oder River, then south, evading the Russian advances. "Birdie" was locked in a barn at night with other POWs. All of them developed dysentery from the filth. On other occasions during this forced march, they had to sleep in the open, snow covered fields. "Birdie" attempted to escape seven times during the thirteen months he was held as a POW and the last time the German soldiers smashed his feet with their gun butts.

"On May 6, 1945, after 93 days on a death march, they were surrounded by the 106 Infantry Division and the German captors laid down their weapons. He was liberated at Bitter Field, Germany. He and 8000 ex-POWs were airlifted to Camp Lucky Strike, near Le Havre, France. His normal body weight was 138 and he weighed 84 pounds when he was liberated. June 1945 he was transported to Camp Kelmere, NY via a hospital ship and then by train to San Antonio TX.

"Birdie" re-enlisted in May of 1946 as an aircraft mechanic based at Johnson Field, Japan. He flew 54 B-26 missions in Korea, before being transferred back to the US where he was assigned to Strategic Air Command as a flight Engineer Training and served on a KC-97 tanker until his retirement as Master Sergeant at Malstrom Air Force Base, Great Falls, Montana in 1961.

Left Waist-Gunner T/Sgt. Roy W. Modglin.

By daughter Abby Skilling.

"Roy was born March 26, 1918 in Salem, Illinois, to Ruth and Roy Modglin. He married Marion L. White in 1940. The had two children and died of heart failure at home in Lancaster, Ohio on January 31, 1990.

"He attended Ben Davis High School, Indianapolis, Indiana, and went to work for the International Harvester Company, a maker of farm machinery. He entered the military service Sept 28, 1942 and trained as a gunner on B-17's. He went to England in September 1943.

"Roy flew with the 385th Bomb Wing in B-17s from the airbase at Great Ashfield, 18 miles northwest of Ipswich on the east coast of England. On April 28, 1944, he wrote to Marion that after three more missions he would get a home leave. He was shot down the next day, west of Magdeburg, Germany, which is about 80 miles southwest of Berlin.

"Like many WWII veterans, Roy didn't talk much about his wartime experiences, at least until later in life, when his son and daughter were able to coax some stories from him. He liked to recall that he parachuted right into a group of German soldiers taking a break! No chance of a run for it! He also recalled that in January 1945, the Russians were approaching his POW camp, Stalag Luft IV, from the east. No one wanted any-

Left Waist-Gunner T/Sgt. Roy W. Modglin

thing to do with the Russians – not the Germans, not the POWs. Thus began an infamous starving, freezing, exhausting forced march away from the Russians which lasted almost three months. Finally, Roy was liberated on April 26 by the US Army 104th Division.

"Roy came home through the port at Newport News, Virginia, and he vividly remembered walking through an archway there set up just for the returnees as they disembarked.

"He returned to civilian life and rejoined International Harvester. Not exciting enough for him, he rejoined the Air Force in 1948. During the Berlin Air Lift he was a flight engineer on C-54's flying to Berlin out of the airfield at Celle, south of Hamburg, in the British zone.

"From there he went into the aircraft maintenance profession, still in the Air Force. He was stationed at Atterbury Field, near Columbus, Indiana. In 1952 he was transferred to Tachikawa Airbase, near Tokyo, Japan, at first "unaccompanied," and then joined by his family for the last two years. In 1955 he transferred to Goodfellow Air Force Base at San Angelo, Texas, then in 1958 to Webb AFB, Big Spring, TX. In late 1961 he went "unaccompanied" to RAF Bentwaters, 12 miles northeast of Ipswich, on the east coast of England. In 1963 he returned to Webb Air Force Base. Subsequent assignments were to Vietnam, back to Webb, then Thailand, where he served as the enlisted head of maintenance for the HH-43 "Huskie" fire fighting and rescue helicopters which were stationed at each U.S. base, but belonged to central squadrons.

"He retired from the Air Force from Thailand in 1973 as a senior master sergeant, and moved to Terre Haute, Indiana, where he worked for the Air National

Guard as a civilian employee. After retiring a second time, he moved to Lancaster, Ohio for the rest of his life.

***

Acknowledgements;
Pat Hart, daughter of pilot Francis J. Hart
Phyllis Luce, daughter of ball-turret gunner Lowell T. Birdwell
Abby Skilling, daughter of waist-gunner Roy Modglin

CHAPTER 22

388ᵀᴴ BOMB GROUP
560ᵀᴴ BOMB SQUADRON

Type: B-17G • Serial: 42-31393 "Snafu"
MACR: 4243 • Air Base: Knettishall

Left formation about 25 minutes before reaching Berlin, due to flak damage. After fighter attacks the B-17 went into a dive with the bomb bay on fire but pilot regained control and the whole crew bailed out. Pilot Donald Walker bailed out without a parachute.

Summary of Missing Air Crew Report # 4243

Pilot: 2Lt. Donald E. Walker, 0-809899, KIA, Springfield, MA

Co-Pilot: 2Lt. Claud T. Patat Jr., 0-818739, POW, Outherst, GA

Navigator: 2Lt. William J. Underwood, 0-707500, POW, Houston, TX

Bombardier: F/O Jack C. Terry, T-1822, POW, Independence, MO

Engineer: S/Sgt. Richard Danckwerth Jr., 32605686, POW, Bloomfield, NJ

Radio: S/Sgt. Robert A. Strough, 38275198, POW, Davenport, OK

Ball-Turret Gunner: Sgt. Robert W. Adams, 37508772, POW, Independence, MO

Left Waist-Gunner: Sgt. Samuel A. Swim, 18182987, POW, Roaring Springs, TX

Right Waist-Gunner: Sgt. Theodore E. Bower, 20759425, POW, Topeka, KS

Tail-Gunner: Sgt. Michael S. Kozak, 12169514, POW, Blasdell, NY

I KIA, 9 POW

Crash Site: Parsau, 17 miles n. of Helmstedt Airfield, Germany
Time: 11.30

388th Bomb Group, 560th Bomb Squadron (Walker)

Back row (left to right): Pilot 2Lt. Donald Walker, Co-Pilot 2Lt. Claude Patat Jr., Navigator 2Lt. William J. Underwood, Bombardier F/O Jack Terry

Front row:.Engineer S/Sgt. Richard Danckwerth, Left Waist-Gunner Sgt. Samuel Swim, Radio S/Sgt. Robert Strough, Right Waist-Gunner Sgt. Theodore Bower, Ball-Turret Gunner Sgt. Robert Adams, Tail-Gunner Sgt. Michael Kozak

Ball-Turret Gunner Sgt. Robert W. Adams.

By son Mike Adams;

"They called the bomber *Snafu,* and it had flown more missions than their crew. They were a replacement crew and it was their second mission.

"They took several flak hits, including on one of the engines and the pilot put the plane in a dive to extinguish the engine fire. The dive was successful, the fire went out. It was a standard procedure aimed at using the fast air flow to "blow out" the fire. My Dad mentioned the engine fire extinguisher as either not working - probably due to damage - or not being sufficient. After the fire was out, they couldn't feather the prop: it was "wind-milling" and shaking the plane badly. The crew was worried the engine would fall off and take out part of the wing. This also robbed them of speed over and above that which resulted from the loss of the engine.

"Before the dive; the pilot ordered the ball turret gunner out so he would have a chance of escape if they had to bail out as it takes some time to exit the ball turret and there is no room for a parachute in the ball turret. My Dad then went to the radio compartment to help render aid to a wounded crew member.

"The dive had taken them out of the formation and they couldn't maintain enough airspeed to catch up. At that point they new they were running out of time for two reasons. The wind-milling propeller essentially doomed the plane, making it unlikely they would get back to England. Dad said they also knew the German fighters would go after any stragglers, so they would have to be lucky not to be detected.

"At some point he went to the waist area to help one of the gunners clear a jam. I remember hearing him say that he shot at the incoming fighters with one of the waist guns and that he could see one of the pilots as he flew past. They were attacked by several Bf-109's. They made one or maybe two passes and were coming in as a group rather than one at a time. My Dad was wounded for a second time at this point by shell fragments from the German 20mm cannon and also pieces from the plane. The Bf-109 cannon usually fired high explosive or high explosive incendiary shells. I say wounded twice because my recollection is that he said he was also hit by flak, which was before the fighter attack.

"After the pilot gave the order to bail out, my Dad went out through the waist door. He landed in a wooded area and crossed his legs and put his arms over his face when he came down through the trees. He was caught in a tree, but not far off the ground, released his harness and dropped to the ground. He tried to hide and ran through a creek to cover his trail. After some time, he found Underwood the navigator who was in pretty bad shape and bleeding from a wound in his groin. At that point, Dad put a bandage on Underwood and then took him out of the woods to seek the Germans and get treatment for Underwood. I don't remember him saying much about the events around his capture except that he got "cold-cocked with a pipe."

"I asked Dad about the story that the pilot bailed out without a parachute. Dad didn't actually see anything, he just said "that's what they said" and I could tell he didn't want to discuss it any further. Dad was in the back of the plane and the pilot was in the front, so he would not have had any opportunity to see what was going on in that portion of the plane. I always wondered about why the pilot would forget his parachute. It seemed to me that the stories Dad related depicted a pilot who was in control of events and doing the right things, so I always wondered why he "forgot" his chute. Perhaps the Germans found his body without a parachute and that was the basis of the report. Walker was probably the last man out of the plane so it is not surprising that nobody saw what happened. Finding a body without a parachute does not really prove he bailed out without one as parachute silk was valuable and anyone could have taken it off the body.

Left Waist-Gunner Sgt. Samuel A. Swim.

By his son James Swim.

Left Waist-Gunner Sgt. Samuel A. Swim

"Samuel Alderson Swim was born in Tolbert, Wilbarger County, Texas, USA, on August 4, 1923 to Jessie Thomas Swim Sr. and Minnie Russell Alderson Swim. His friends called him S.A. His birth certificate shows his birthday as being on August 3, 1923. However, his mother stated that he was born on the 4th of August and this was the date he always used and celebrated. Tolbert was a small farming community in 1923 which was located about ten miles northwest of Vernon, Texas.

"Jessie sold out his interests in the Tolbert area and moved his family to Roaring Springs, Motley County, Texas, in 1928. The family lived on the farm where they raised cattle, farmed cotton and raised a family garden. Samuel's chores consisted in helping feed the cattle, milking the family cows and doing other work about the farm. His mother, Minnie, said she knew it was time to get up and start breakfast when she heard S.A. leaving the house to milk the cows early each morning.

"S.A. attended the Roaring Springs schools from the first grade through twelfth grade. His family always related how S.A. was a "scrapper" during school. With two older brothers attending ahead of him, he was always being pitted against other students by his brothers to fight other boys. He would take on anyone and usually was the one who won the conflict.

"As he grew older he participated in the school sport programs. Being a small school the boys usually played in a number of different sports such as football, basketball, track and baseball. He was a qualified lifeguard. This skill allowed him to do some lifeguard duty while training in the Air Corps.

"World War II started for the United States on December 7, 1941, when the Japanese bombed Pearl Harbor. This happened during S.A.'s senior year of high school. He stayed in school and graduated from Roaring Springs High School May 28, 1942. During the summer of 1942 S. A. moved to Corpus Christi, Texas, where he found employment with the U.S. Navy Department working on PBY patrol planes. His job title was skin-man. The job entailed the removal, repair and/or replacement of damaged wing parts such as the leading edges, wing struts, fairings and tail assemblies. He was trained in blueprint reading by the Navy for his job.

"He enlisted into the Army Air Corps on October 30, 1942, in Lubbock,

Texas. After he completed six weeks of basic training he reported to Amarillo, Texas, for Airplane Mechanics School. The men attending this school studied maintenance of the B-17 Flying Fortress type aircraft, its structure control cables, engines, electrical and hydraulic systems, ignition and carburation. He spent sixteen weeks attending this school to qualify for doing mechanical work on aircraft. Amarillo is about 140 miles north of Roaring Springs, Texas. This relatively short distance allowed him to visit home on those occasions when he had a leave from base.

"One of the duties at the Amarillo base was pulling guard duty. S.A. liked to relate how he was relieved of doing any guard duty. One night while on duty, the duty officer was making his rounds. When the duty officer approached S.A.'s position, S.A. shouted out asking for the day's password. When a password was not forthcoming from the duty officer, he shot in the direction of the duty officer. That was the last night S.A. had to do guard duty.

"After the Amarillo training, he was assigned to Aerial Gunnery School in Las Vegas, Nevada. He spent six weeks at this school learning how to fire and maintain .30 and .50 caliber machine guns. The men in this school studied the operation and maintenance of these machine guns, the Sperry turrets and gun sights. After this training he was assigned to a flight crew. The flight crew spent time flying a B-17 Flying Fortress and becoming acquainted with one another. As a Flight Maintenance Gunner, his duties included the transfer of fuel, checking instruments and dealing with engine performance. He kept the flight log while in flight and during combat fired the .50 caliber machine gun at the waist position.

"The crew was in Utah when they received orders to report to the European Theater of Operations. S.A. wrote to his parents on March 31, 1944, that he was shipping out and provided them with his temporary address. The crew flew a new B-17 Flying Fortress to England where it was parked with a group of other planes.

"The crew arrived in England on April 10, 1944. The crew was assigned to the 560th Bomb Squadron, 388th Bomb Group, 8th Air Force. The crew was stationed in Knettishall, England. They used older B-17s which had seen a number of previous missions for previous crews and had not been assigned a permanent plane. S.A. related that they made seven bombing runs but were only given credit for two because the targets were not hit. The crews received the same attention from German gunners and fighters as they did on the two credited combat missions.

"On April 29, 1944, Don Walker and crew along were assigned the mission to bomb Berlin, Germany. Lt. Walker and crew flew B-17 42-31393, "Snafu." Snafu had flown 25 previous missions. According to Ed Huntzinger in "The 388th At War": the 388th provided 21 aircraft for the low group and seven aircraft for the high group. All planes were airborne and assembled by 06:53 hours. The bombers followed the briefed route to Berlin and dropped bombs visually. The primary target was not hit, but bombs did fall on the southeast area of the city at the Tempelhof Airdrome, Potsdamer and Anhalter Railway Stations. The flak was heavy and accurate over Berlin and Magdeburg. All aircraft had battle damage upon return to base.

"Lieutenant Walker's plane was hit by flak over the target and was shot down by fighters over Parsau, Germany. This sortie was the second official combat mission for S.A. and this crew. S. A. and eight other crew members were able to bailout of the plane. The pilot, Don E. Walker, went down with the plane and was killed. The Army Air Corp lost 64 bombers and fourteen fighters on this mission.

"S. A. bailed out along with eight other crew members. As he was parachuting to the ground, he was shot at by fighters and attempts were made to collapse his parachute. He was captured when he landed and was escorted to a holding cell. He had several wounds from flak but was in good shape otherwise. He was interrogated after about ten days. He had a scar on his forehead which he received when a German woman hit him over the head with an umbrella as he was being walked to the jail.

"His first letter home after being captured was from Stalag Luft III in Sagan, Poland and was dated May 12, 1944. He was transported to Stalag Luft III by train. He related how the food rations were very meager. He was responsible for cutting the bread loafs for his barracks. He always got what was left over after everyone else had chosen their bread slice. They would receive a weak soup with some potatoes for meals. The daily activities were confined to exercise and some sports. A lot of visiting took place and with the cards furnished in the Red Cross parcels they played cards. He did not smoke and used his cigarettes to trade for items.

"He taught himself how to knit while a prisoner. He had watched his mother knit when he was younger. He traded for old sweaters which he unraveled and then reused the yarn to make hats which had a bill and ear flaps with a chin strap tie. He made several of these for other prisoners.

"He eventually was moved to Stalag Luft IV in the far eastern part of Poland. As the Russians began to march westward, the men of this camp were moved west towards the German heartland. He talked about the walking they had to do on this occasion and related how the men who fell out had the dogs turned loose on them. S. A. estimates he walked nine hundred miles during this time and before he was liberated. The men would steal potatoes from farmers during the march in order to have something to eat.

"S. A. was located in Stalag 357 at Fallingbostel, Germany after the march from Stalag Luft IV and was liberated on April 16, 1945 by British troops from B Squadron 11th Hussars and the Reconnaissance Troop of the 8th Hussars. He wrote home on April 19, 1945 informing his parents he was alright. He lost over fifty pounds during his time as a prisoner.

***

"Upon returning to the States, he had an extended furlough after which he reported to Florida for medical evaluation and treatment. He would continue to have nightmares and flash backs for several years after returning home. The doctors of the time told him he would be luck to live past fifty years of age.

"After his separation from the Army Air Corps in October, 1945, he returned to Roaring Springs, Texas. He married Darnelle Rae Morrison on November 13, 1945. He farmed cotton after his marriage in the Roaring Springs area and they had their first child in March of 1948. He moved his family to California in 1950 where he worked on a dairy farm milking cows and later worked on a General Motors assembly line.

"In early 1952 the family moved to Wilburton, Oklahoma. He ranched there for two to three years and operated a cattle spraying truck. In 1954 the family moved to the Fort Worth, Texas area. He worked for the Manor Bread Company and at various other jobs until he was hired by the St. Louis Southwestern Railway Company in 1956. He worked as a clerk for the railroad until he retired due to poor health in 1980.

"S. A. always enjoyed the out of doors. His main hobby was working with horses. His ideal job would have been a ranch hand. However, he realized he could not support a family working for someone else on a ranch. He always kept a few head of horse on hand. He was a farrier and earned some spending money for his horse hobby plying this trade. S. A. and his wife moved to Bella Vista, Arkansas in 1984. A few years later they started to travel with a RV and eventually sold their home and became full time RV-ers. S. A. died on April 29, 2002, in Medina, Texas where the RV was parked.

Right Waist-GunnerSgt. Theodore E. Bower.

From son Thomas Bower and daughter Janet.

"Theodore "Ted" Edward Bower Jr. was born in McPherson, Kansas on 30 August 1918. At that time, his father was a sales rep for Colgate Palmolive. His mother, Merle Decatur, was from Joplin, Missouri. While Ted was young, the family moved to Topeka where his father got a Real Estate License and began selling real estate.

"Ted graduated from Topeka High School in 1936. During this time and some after, he worked for a downtown drug store. He attended Washburn University in Topeka and the University of Kansas in Lawrence. He was a student when the war broke out. The war interrupted his college plans and he never returned to school.

"Around 1940, he met Lorinda Somers at a church function at Grace Cathedral. They dated and planned to be married at Christmas time in 1942. Ted was in the National Guard unit that was activated after Pearl Harbor. He had been shipped to Little Rock, AR, so they got married on December 15, 1941. Both sets of parents and Ted's brother Gene took the train to Little Rock for the hastily arranged ceremony.

"The guard unit was Cavalry but Ted was offered an opportunity to transfer to the Army Air Corp to learn to fly. I remember seeing him as a child with his Cavalry boots and pants on. He had various assignments for flight training and gunnery training. He was an instructor on the .50 calibre machine gun before being shipped to England with the 8th Air Force. They were forming crews for B-17s and training them before being sent out. He was made a waist-gunner since he was pretty accurate with the .50 calibre.

"Ted's plane went down on their second mission. He and the bombardier helped get the crew, many of whom were wounded, out the bomb bay doors as the ship was going down. He said he thought all got out but the pilot, who did not bring his chute so he went down with the plane.

"Dad was captured right after landing. He had a flak wound on his right hand. The Germans eventually took him to a POW camp in western Poland. It was a regular POW camp with the usual minimal accommodations. Since it was 1944, the Russians were moving toward Poland forcing the camp to go on a couple of forced marches west.

"During this time, little word came back regarding his crew. Initially the report was "missing, presuned dead." The local paper ran an obituary. Some time later, the Red Cross got word to his wife that he was a POW.

"He was liberated after the war ended and was sent to the States aboard a liberty ship. He spent some time in rehab camps before being sent home. He was well under 100 lbs. and had the usual deseases, including what he called "yellow jaundice." He was known to say he looked like a "scarecrow."..all skin and bones.

"Upon his return from the military, Dad and Mom like everyone else, started to grow a family and bought a house. Dad's father had an established real estate firm and Dad worked with him for a few years, got a license and a brokers license.

"During the mid fifties, Ted Sr decided to sell out and later moved to California. At this time, Dad took over the company. It was Ted E. Bower Real Estate Company for many years. Dad had a pattern of buying a house, moving the family in, letting our mother refurbish or redecorate and then selling it. We moved six times while living in Topeka. He claimed he never lost money on these transactions. He continued the tradition after moving to Florida.

"Dad would seldom talk about the war or his experiences. They were the source of some psychological issues that surfaced through his life. There were some foods he refused to eat. He claimed that white rice looked too much like the maggots that thrived in the bread they were given and he could not abide anything made with turnips because in POW camp, that is all they had to eat. In his later years, he joined a group therapy at the VA hospital. There he shared his experiences and learned the importance of setting some demons free. He would at that point talk more about his experiences. He joined an Ex-POW group and they helped him greatly in getting the disability classification of 100%. By this time, he was in his mid seventies but still working some.

"Dad was very well known and respected in Topeka and was involved in the civic goings on. He established the Multiple Listing Service for the area and served as a president of the Kansas Board of Realtors. His office was in several locations, he had a sales force of about six. I seldom saw much of him during this period. I would often tag along on Saturdays to look at houses and stay with him on Sunday Open Houses. If he was not doing an Open House, the family would strike out after church and check out all the new listings and new house construction.

"The business grew and life was pretty good for us. The stresses of it all took a toll on Dad and in 1962, the folks decided to sell out and move to Florida. He often said that Florida was where the pot of gold was at the end of the rainbow. There, Dad was a sales agent for several Real Estate companies, maintained his brokers license, went to work for the Corps of Engineers appraising properties for condemnation for a large dam project.

"After that he worked as an appraiser and eventually worked for both the Federal Housing Administration and the VA. He was an excellent appraiser and trained many future appraisers. He retired from full time appraising about 1980 but he was still doing VA appraisals on a part time basis throughout parts of the 90's.

"The folks did some traveling and enjoyed life. They were very involved with their church; The Episcopal Church of the Good Shepard in Dunedin, FL. They went to England twice to visit my mother's extended family (her mother had been a WW1 war bride) and see the sights. He had no desire to visit Germany or most of the rest of Europe.

"Dad had fairly good health until later in life. His coronary artery disease was later determined to be partly as a result of the "binge eating" he and his fellow POWs did to keep the German prison guards from confiscating the food contents of the Red Cross "care packages" they received. He had two bypass operations, 1981 and 1990. He was very patriotic so it was important that he had a flag pole where he lived. When he died in 1998, I arranged for the American Legion to provide military honors at the graveside.

***

Acknowledgements:
Mike Adams, son of Sgt. Robert W. Adams, ball-turret gunner.
James Swim, son of Sgt. Samuel A. Swim, left waist-gunner.
Thomas Bower & Janet Spaldin, son and daughter of Sgt. Theodore E. Bower, right waist-gunner.

CHAPTER 23

388ᵀᴴ BOMB GROUP
562ᴺᴰ BOMB SQUADRON

Type: B-17G • Serial: 42-37980 "Bessie"
MACR: 4244 • Air Base: Knettishall

"We were flying about 500 feet, trying to stay below the flak. Two German fighters closed in and started firing. I was transferring gas from the dead engine at that time. They hit us in cockpit section, injuring the pilot, Joe Coyner, Waist Gunner Yates, and me. We lowered our flaps and the planes left us. We were on fire and belly landed in a terraced field near Ypern, Belgium."

Sgt. Edward J. Bode, top-turret gunner

Pilot: 2Lt. Joseph D. Coyner, 0-812950, POW

Co-Pilot: 2Lt. Harold B. Monroe, 0-819143, POW, Syracuse, NY

Navigator: F/O Fulton Sandler, T-124456, POW, Long Island, NY

Bombardier: 2Lt. Donald B. Wiley, 0-761345, POW, Atlanta, GA

Engineer: S/Sgt. Edward J. Bode, 18192470, POW

Radio: T/Sgt. William H. Evans, 16104399, POW, Columbia, MO

Ball-Turret Gunner: Sgt. Cecil A. Turner, 19091209, POW, Riverside, CA

Left Waist-Gunner: Sgt. James E. Ghearing, 35259640, POW

Right Waist-Gunner: S/Sgt. Audrey J. Yates Jr., 36752917, POW, Hurst, IL

Tail-Gunner: S/Sgt. Warren H. Smith, 39464724, POW, Spokane, WA

10 POW

Crash Site: Watou, 12 miles w. of Ypres, Belgium
Time: 15.05

388th Bomb Group, 562nd Bomb Squadron (Coyner)

Back row (left to right): Bombardier 2Lt. Donald B. Wiley, Pilot 2Lt. Joseph D. Coyner, Co-Pilot 2Lt. Harold B. Monroe, Navigator F/O Fulton Sandler,

Front row: Ball-Turret Gunner Sgt. Cecil A. Turner, Engineer S/Sgt. Edward J. Bode, Left Waist-Gunner Sgt. James E. Ghearing, Radio T/Sgt. William H. Evans, Tail-Gunner S/Sgt. Warren H. Smith, Right Waist-Gunner S/Sgt. Audrey J. Yates Jr.,

Pilot 2Lt. Joseph D. Coyner.

By his children Mike, Beverly and Nancy.

"Joseph Diller Coyner was born in Waynesboro, VA on April 14, 1917 to David Joseph Coyner and Booker Brown Coyner. He was the 2nd child of 5, and the only son. David Joseph Coyner was a farmer. The farm was lost during the depression and Joseph Diller Coyner worked on various farms to help the family. He used to tell us stories of walking to school in the snow with an apple butter sandwich. Later, the family moved into a house in Fishersville, VA where Booker Brown Coyner lived until her death.

"After finishing high school, Joe went to Virginia Polytechnic Institute (then called Virginia Polytechnic Institute and State University) – now more commonly called VA Tech in Blacksburg, VA. He left school after two years and began work at Dupont in Wayneboro, VA.

"Martin Harris and Joe were close friends – and Martin later became Joe's brother-in-law when he married Nellie. Martin and Joe went to a dance where Joe met Frances Rebecca Michael (Becky). Joe & Becky eloped in October, 1942. Becky went with Joe to some of his training facilities prior to his shipping out to Europe.

"Becky lived in Staunton and worked as a hair dresser while Joe was in the Army Air Corps. After he was shot down, she received several telegrams – one stat-

Pilot 2Lt. Joseph D. Coyner and his wife

ing that he was missing in action; one that he was missing presumed dead and on that he was captured. Thankfully, the one that stated missing presumed dead arrived late – after she had received the one stating that he was a POW.

***

"My father's most frequent comments about his life as a POW were about being hungry. I don't think he ever quite got over that. He loved to eat. He gave credit to the Red Cross for keeping them alive because they sent them food and that was the organization that he donated to afterwards. If we picked at our food at the table, he would tell us we didn't know what hunger was and that he ate worms because he had been so hungry. There was another prisoner who had a broken jaw so he couldn't chew food. This man caught a rat that ran thru the camp even though he couldn't eat it. That man gave the rat to his fellow prisoners to eat. He talked about how whenever they would get bread, he would ration it out so it would last instead of gobbling it down all at once.

"He also said that his German guards were regular men, just like them and hungry too. He was thankful that the SS didn't have control of his camp...he thought the camp would have been much different if they had.

"He talked a little bit about the march that last winter of the war as the Allies were coming. I don't remember him talking about the march itself, but that they shared their food with their guards. General Patton was Daddy's hero as that is who freed them.

***

"When Joe was on his way home, he sent Becky a telegram to meet him at the station without lipstick. Billy Harris (Martin & Nellie's oldest son) tells of the family all being at the station to welcome Joe home and that no one could get to Joe because Becky was sitting on his lap.

"Becky and Joe lived in Staunton, VA, after he returned from the war. They had four children – Joseph Michael, Samuel Glenn, Nancy Kemper and Beverly Jeanne. Mike was born 9 months and a few days after Joe returned from the war. Mike and Sam were born in Staunton. In 1948, Joe was transferred to Chattanooga, TN when Dupont opened a plant there. Nancy & Beverly were born in Chattanooga. Joe worked at the Chattanooga plant until he retired at age 62.

"Every summer after school ended for the year, Joe would pack up the car and take Becky and the four children to Staunton for the summer. One of the things he loved to do was to drive around the country showing us the various farms where he worked; old home places; churches that the family attended; the cemetery where the first German ancestor that moved to the states is buried. The German family name is Keinadt. There are various spellings of Coyner – Coiner and Koiner are more common. Joe's grandfather changed the spelling of our last name from Coiner to Coyner. At the end of summer, he would take his two weeks of vacation to visit with family and then travel back to Chattanooga for us to attend school.

"Joe enjoyed golf until his health prevented him from continuing to play. He also enjoyed meeting a group of retired Dupont employees and other men every morning for coffee. He was active in the Lions Club for many years. One of the club's projects that he worked on for many years was the annual Christmas tree sale.

"He loved listening to music and would spend much time sitting outside with his radio while he enjoyed nature. He enjoyed woodworking, and made many things for family members – tables; bluebird houses; potato bins; trash cans. We still have bluebird houses that he made.

"Joe Coyner was a good man, husband, son, brother, father, and grandfather. He provided for his family and taught us the values and beliefs that we hold to this day. Not only did he talk the talk, but he walked the walk. Daddy was not one to talk just to talk. We learned that going to work was the expected behavior of an employee as he never missed work, even when he was sick. Graduating from college was expected. So, we had to take college prep courses in high school. My brothers were taught that they must have a profession that would provide for a family. He would tell us that if we couldn't say something nice, don't say anything at all. I remember him going through the house singing "Oh how I love Jesus." He was typical of the men of our greatest generation of the United States of America. He was open about his experience as a POW. I believe that he talked about memories if they were prompted by a comment or situation. I learned after he died that he had PTSD. I was shocked to learn that. The chronic pain that he experienced as he grew older made it more difficult to close off those feelings so he started having nightmares. I wish I had known.

Daughter Nancy Hennessee visit to the crash site;

"In May, 2015, my husband and I made a trip to Watou, Belgium, to visit the site where my father crash-landed on April 29, 1944. We had the privilege of meeting Wilfried Busschaert, his wife and grandson. His grandson acted as translator for our visit.

"Wilfried and his family lived across the road from the field where my father crash-landed. He and his family continue to live in the area. Wilfried was 7 years old at the time, and told us he is the last surviving eye witness to the crash. His father had told him to hide anytime he heard shots. There was a millstone in the yard that he got behind when he heard the shots the day daddy crash-landed.

"He witnessed the plane descending with two Messerschmitt 109's firing on it as it crash-landed. The plane came to a stop about 100 meters from a tree that is still standing in the field. I told him that daddy had told us of girls who gave him and his crew milk to drink – it was Wilfried's sisters that did that.

"Wilfried showed us two silk maps that came from my father's plane. He also had a picture dated June 4, 1944 that had his sisters standing on what was left of the tail of the plane. We walked the field to the spot where the plane stopped. He pointed out the area from which the German's came to arrest the crew.

"It was an amazing experience to stand at the very spot where daddy had crash-landed 71 years before. And a awesome experience to visit with a gentleman who had witnessed it all and was willing to share his memories with us. Before we left that day, Wilfried's wife gave me the original picture of Wilfried's sisters standing at daddy's plane.

"After all these years, we experienced the gratitude of local people who willingly opened their hearts and home to us and made us feel welcomed and loved.

Engineer S/Sgt. Edward J. Bode

Daughter Susan Bode;

"Edward Joseph Bode was born January 6, 1923 on a farm three miles west from Okeene, Oklahoma. He was the youngest of eight children. At birth he weighed only 2 pound and 7 ounces. As he was born at home, he was placed in a shoe box and placed in a warm oven – a makeshift incubator in that day.

"He attended a one-room school west of Okeene, and often told his daughters about his trek of several miles to school and back each day. He then attended St. Mary's Catholic School in Okeene and graduated in 1941.

"Following the war he returned home to Okeene, Oklahoma. On May 30, 1948 he married Peggy Ann McFadden from Fairview, Oklahoma. Four daughters were born in this union.

"He was employed at United States Gypsum Plant in Southard, Oklahoma. He also owned and farmed 120 acres, seven miles west from Okeene, where he raised wheat and cattle. He worked at U.S. Gypsum for over 32 years and retired in 1984. He continued farming until 1995.

"Ed passed away following a short illness on Sunday, September 14, 1997 at 74 years of age.

Edward Bode's story, dictated to his wife a few years prior to his demise;

"After I enlisted in the Air Force and went through the required training, I was sent to Knettishall, England to be attached to the 8th Air Force, 562 Squadron and the 388th Bomb Group. I was a Top-Turrett Gunner/Engineer on a B-17.

Engineer S/Sgt. Edward J. Bode

"On April 29, 1944, in aircraft # 42-37980, we set out on our mission, to bomb Berlin. We were hit by flak before we reached the target. The #3 engine was shot out and the prop wouldn't feather, but we went on to target and dropped our bombs. We thought we might head for Sweden but decided to stay in the formation.

"Two of our fighter came to escort us, but soon had to leave us as their gas was running low. We were then flying about 500 feet, trying to stay below the flak. Two German fighters closed in and started firing. I was transferring gas from the dead engine at that time. They hit us in cockpit section, injuring the pilot, Joe Coyner, Waist Gunner Yates, and me. We lowered our flaps and the planes left us.

"We were on fire and belly-landed in a terraced field near Ypern, Belgium. A woman came out with a bucket of milk for us to drink. The German soldiers began descending on us with pitch forks, clubs, and other assorted weapons. They kicked Coyner in the back many times. They then took us to a dungeon or cave. Later that night they took me and Yates to a small hospital, where I was given a large white pill to swallow. When I came to, I was on an examining table. They then took us back to the dungeon.

"The next morning they loaded us up in a truck. Yates and I were sent to a jail somewhere in Belgium while the rest of the crew was taken to interrogation in Frankfurt. Our jail food consisted of one bowl of soup per day. We were taken from our jail cell on the tenth day. We were examined by a German doctor who was very upset about the poor medical treatment we had received from the first doctors.

"We were then taken to a large hospital, which I thought was in Brussels. I was there about two weeks. Yates was still there when I left for Frankfurt for interrogation. There I met up with some on my crew. The cells in interrogation were about 4 x 8. We had to take our shoes off and leave them outside the cell. In interrogations, they knew all about me. They knew that my mother was of German descent, where my pilot got his wings, and much more personal information. When I refused to give them only my name, rank and serial number, they beat me with a rubber hose across my back and neck.

"After interrogation, 64 of us were loaded into a box car. We had to take turn sitting down because we were so crowded. Several times our train was fired on by our planes. The Germans would abandon us until the air raid was over. When we arrived we marched 2 miles to our new home, Stalag 4. We were the first "guests" and were in Lager A. More prisoners arrived weekly. When the mess hall opened I worked in it along with Mess Sgt. Neil West, Rex Silver, Bill Finklin and a guy we called "Big George." Food was in short supply and consisted mostly of boiled potatoes. Occasionally we would receive a Red Cross Parcel.

"On February 6, 1945, they marched us out to get away from the Russians, who were closing in on us. There was ice and snow on the ground and it was bitter cold. Each of us had one blanket. At night, Bill, Rex, and I would lay one blanket on the ground and covered up with two. The bottom blanket would be frozen to the ground in the morning. The first three weeks were the hardest. We walked every day. Later, we did get some shelter in barns and we didn't march every day - just enough to keep away from the Russians.

"One day I stole a can of beef from a German guard wagon. They knew it was in my side of the barn so I slipped it to Rex Silvers who was on the other side in the next barn. We got separated again and Rex carried the can of beef for about two weeks before we got together and could eat it.

"One night Rex and I were in a barn and spotted a chicken. We caught it and choked it and picked it dry. The farmer found the feathers the next day and reported it to the German guards. They threatened to kill five men if the guilty party didn't step forward. No one admitted to stealing the chicken and the five men were not killed. We carried the chicken about ten days, wrapped up in a blanket. Since the weather was cold, it stayed frozen. Later we cooked the chicken with potatoes on our little burner that we had made out of a can. Sure was good.

"We marched for about three months and were then liberated by the British and Canadians.

***

Acknowledgements;
Nancy Hennessee, daughter of pilot 2Lt. Joseph D. Coyner.
Susan Bode, daughter of engineer /Sgt. Edward J. Bode

CHAPTER 24

389ᵀᴴ BOMB GROUP
564ᵀᴴ BOMB SQUADRON

Type: B-24H • Serial: 41-28676
MACR: 4494 • Air Base: Hethel

Two dead. Villiage Cemetery of Päpsen.
3. May buried.

German Document KU 1709

Cmd. Plot: Lt. Col. Robert C. Sears (453 BG/735 BS), 0-21906, POW, Atlanta, GA

Pilot: Capt. Joseph H. Higgins Jr., POW, Hartford, CT

Co-Pilot: 1Lt. Perry Wharton, 0-683514, POW, San Antonio, TX

Navigator: 2Lt. Robert S. Sosa. 0-752851, KIA, Douglas, AZ

Navigator: 1Lt. Harry H. Putnam Jr., 0-747039, POW, Walnut Creek, CA

Navigator: 1Lt. Harry W. Casey, KIA, Philadelphia, PA

Bombardier: 1Lt. Chester Broyles Jr., POW, Chico, CA

Radio: S/Sgt. Thomas E. Sumlin, 38240180, POW, Simsboro. LA

Ball-Turret Gunner: S/Sgt. David L. York, 34472913, POW, Corinth, MS

Waist-Gunner: S/Sgt. Myron F. Boerschinger, POW, Dallas, TX

Tail-Gunner: S/Sgt. Charles A. Piper, 31176906, POW, Derry, NH

2 KIA, 9 POW

Crash Site: Päpsen, Germany
Time: 13.25

Command Pilot Lt. Col. Robert C. Sears

From Newspaper Clipping.

"An aerial thriller was the experience of 27-year-old Lt. Colonel Robert Carver Sears, son of a Portland army officer who recently returned to the United States after being held a prisoner in Germany. In a letter received by the Air Force officer's brother, David Sears of Carvallis, Col. Sears related a remarkable escape from his plane over Germany.

"Col. Sears was leading an Air Division in a 1200 plane raid on Berlin when Nazi fighters shot off six feet of the plane's left wing, shot out half of the control cables and set a gasoline fire in the bomb bay. Both Sears and the pilot exerted all their strength to keep the ship level and to prevent it from going into a spin from which no one could escape.

"With the left wing off, the plane tended to roll over to the left in spite of the fact that the steering wheel was twisted all the way to the right," he wrote. "I tried to keep it level by gunning the left outboard engine, but it ran away. About the time the pilot started to leave, I thought that if I could dive a little and pick up speed, I might be able to maintain better control while he jumped. However, it did't do any good. When the pilot got to the top escape hatch (escape through the bomb bay was impossible because of the fire) the plane suddenly lurched and rolled over on its back, which was a lucky break for him as it threw him clear from the tail.

"I left my seat then, after covering my face and hands with helmet, goggles, oxygen mask and gloves to protect me from the fire. By this time our altitude was 16,000 feet (we started at 22,000). I got to the top escape hatch okay and got out, except for my legs. The terrific centrifugal force of the spin pinned my legs up against the roof of the plane and made it impossible to move. At about 5,000 feet everything loosened up and I went sailing out into space. I was on my back in the air.

"I wanted to see the ground so I could tell when to open my chute, since a delayed opening is considered desirable. Above me I saw the plane circling towards me and I thought it was going to hit me. I figured if I opened my chute I would slow down enough so the plane would go under me. It did but only misseed me by a few feet. I could feel the vibration from the prop that came closest to me. Immediately after passing me the plane blew up. I could't see it but I heard the explosion."

"My chute opened about 200 feet above the ground. I made a good landing and tried to get away but was captured almost immediately. My goggles and oygen masks were very badly burned, but these afforded perfect protection for my face."

"Col. Sears later escaped from the Nazis during a march from one prison camp to another and hid in a barn for three weeks with a very limited supply of food, until Allied troops rescued him.

"The airman is the son of Colonel Robert Sears, who was a Portland athlete in his youthful days. A West-Point graduate of 1909, the elder Sears, although over age for troop duty, got a combat assignment in Italy in WWII and later commanded the 137th Regiment of the 35th Division through the Normandy campaign.

"Lt. Col. Sears also is a Westpointer, graduating in 1939. His mother, the former Miss Marguerite Hume of Portland, has been engaged in Red Cross work in San Francisco during the war.

Navigator 2Lt. Robert S. Sosa.

Navigator 2Lt. Robert S. Sosa

After the war bombardier Chester Broyles reported that Lt. Sosa refused to bail out due to extreme fear and could not be thrown out as he fought to resist it. The he, Broyles, bailed out leaving Sosa behind.

Robert Sosa's biography.

"Robert S. Sosa was born July 30, 1919 in Douglas, Arizona, to Alonzo P. and Matilda (Campas) Sosa. His name on his birth certificate is Roberto. The S. stands for Silva. It was not a given name, but he liked it because it was a maternal family name on his father's side and so he incorporated it into his name.

"Alonzo worked in the Calumet & Arizona Smelter, which was the smaller of the two copper smelters in Douglas. He and Matilda had six children, two boys and four girls. Robert was the younger boy. Mary was the oldest girl and to her fell many household chores, including ironing her brothers' shirts. Alonzo Jr. always wore white shirts, she said, while Robert favored prints.

"Robert attended Douglas schools and graduated from Douglas High School in 1938. He was a multi-sport letterman and earned the school's all-around athlete award his senior year. He went to Arizona State Teachers College in Tempe, Ariz., on a basketball scholarship and graduated with a Bachelor of Education degree in 1942. He immediately entered the Army and selected the Air Corps.

"He was married by then to Jane Collar. She had Douglas relatives. The couple had a daughter, Rebecca, born two months after Robert went overseas.

"His sister Mary says that surviving members of the crew told the family that Robert was trapped below the main deck where the bombs were when trouble came.

Bombardier 1Lt. Chester Broyles, Jr.

From "An Experience to Remember"

Bombardier 1Lt. Chester Broyles, Jr. and his wife

"On the morning of April 29, 1944, I was awakened from a cosy sack and informed that I was to have the pleasure of making a round-trip tour to Berlin by air. At that time little did I realize the trip would only be half by air and the rest by land. Nevertheless I took off that bright frosty morning with great visions in mind, for I was leading the Second Division which is a great honour to bestow on a lowly first lieutenant.

"We formed our Division over England, and headed out to sea. All was well as we had a mighty armada of planes. The enemy coast came into view and passed with little event to our plane. All was still going well and the weather was so that I might do visual bombing.

"All was changed when we were within seventy-five miles of Berlin. Our Micky equipment became in-operative either from flak or some unknown reason. We were then forced to turn the lead over to our deputy and continue on in their position.

"We went on the bombing run over Berlin and I witnessed the bombs striking in the built-up area around the marshalling yards. After we had passed I could look back and see other groups, B-24's and B-17's hitting other areas in Berlin proper. It was a visual fact that Berlin took one of its worst poundings of the war on that day.

"I might mention the flak over the target but it need no mentioning, as it is a known fact that it is a mighty unhealthy area for any Allied airman. Anyone flying through it will not soon forget the great billows of smoke left by bursting flak. We were fortunate enough to bypass the area with little damage to our plane and were continuing on our way home with a great deal more confidence of obtaining a large drink of whisky when we got home than we were a few minutes previous.

"Our career of Allied airmen in the European Theatre of Operations was soon brought to a close. We were in the vicinity of Drummer Lake, when the Jerries decided to put us at ease for the duration. There was some dispute as to the number of enemies attacking us because estimates ranged from thirty to fifty grouped in a wolf pack. They attacked head-on but kept themselves unobserved behind a cloud formation until they were well upon us. They surprised the entire group so none had a chance to return much accurate fire. It was later heard that they downed five planes in one pass. We being the first to go.

"We received several direct hits, how many we were unable to tell. Some exploded in the waist and one injured Charles Piper the tail-gunner in the shoulder and anus region. The bursts doing the real damage were hits on our number one and two engines and one in the bomb bay which started a fire.

"The plane at once became uncontrollable, and started down. I then first realized I would have to jump but dreaded the idea of having to pay a visit of undetermined length in Germany. My mind was soon made up for me as our top-turret gunner came to the nose with his hair singed off from the fire in the bomb bay and said, "Jump." I needed no more encouragement and so I immediately jumped and was followed by the rest of the crew that were able to get out.

"The ride down in the chute is one I will long remember. The very stillness of the air around me and looking up I could see the many planes still on their homeward journey. Many times before I had seen other chutes floating down but until then I didn't realize their lost feeling.

"I was unfortunate on my landing and hit a fence post which sprained my knee and ankle so it was impossible to try to escape. It was just as well for it wasn't long before I was surrounded by German soldiers and taken prisoner.

"I was taken to a nearby small town and put in a workshop along with other members of my crew to await a coming train. We were then taken to a Gestapo headquarters but were not kept there long. A truck was brought up and we were taken to a French prison camp near Hannover and put in solitary for two days. We were then taken to Dulag-Luft near Frankfort which is the interrogation center for all Allied airmen. Again I was put in solitary and stayed there for eight days during which I was interrogated four times. This prison is the last before going to the American prison camp. They endeavor to obtain all information possible from you.

"Upon release from solitary I was sent outside to a barracks area where I got a square meal. The first since being shot down. It was a half can of corned beef, a Canadian cracker and a cup of coffee. Which I might add was one of the beat meals I ever had. Two days later I was sent to Stalag Luft 3 where I met other officers of my crew and where I am now residing.

Radio S/Sgt. Thomas E. Sumlin.

"The War Story" as told by T. E. Sumlin

"We had ten men on each plane. When we had done our twelfth mission, we were the only original crew on the base: all of the others had been shot down.

"Then we were transferred to the Pathfinder crew so that we could lead the formations for others. They could use our radar instead of having to put radar in all the planes, because this was a new invention, and they didn't have enough of it to go around. The British developed radar for the RAF and shared some with us. Our plane had the command pilot, and we had the radar. All the other planes watched us and dropped their bombs, when we did.

"There were six Pathfinder crews in the whole 8th Air Force. On all the missions we went on, we suffered enemy fire. It knocked holes in our plane on every mission except two. An important mission was to the Ruhr Valley, to Frankfurt on the Mainz River. The target was the I. G. Farbe Chemical Industry. This factory complex, which employed over 25,000 workers, was set on fire from one end to the other before we even left the target.

"We took many pictures. When the plane landed, a man in a jeep would chase the plane before it stopped and would grab the pictures and rush to headquarters. Then another jeep would carry the men back to headquarters. They were all given a shot of whiskey and the officer would question them about the target, where they encountered anti aircraft guns, how many fighters they saw shot down, how many of our own planes down, how much damage to our own plane, how many wounded aboard and especially about the actual target. They would run the film showing the pictures taken. The officers always made the men feel important and were praised for having done a good job.

"Bombs used were incendiary bombs. They were small magnesium bombs used for the purpose of setting fire to everything they touched. They were stored in the plane in bundles with a belt around them, but as soon as they were dropped, the binding came loose and they were scattered over a wide area (each one was no more than 30" long and 2" in diameter). There were about 100 to a bundle with many bundles in the plane.

"We had bombed Berlin and were heading back when we were attacked by German fighters. Our plane caught fire, and the pilot ordered everybody to bail out. When I landed, I was about six feet off of the ground because my parachute was caught in the top of that tree.

"Germans came and I borrowed a knife from them to cut the shrouds on the chute so I could drop to the ground. They took me to a headquarters in a town nearby. There were German officers inside. They kept saying "Heil Hitler" every time they answered the telephone. One of them wore an iron cross, which was a very high decoration.

"All of our crew survived except two. Our navigator was killed, and one other man who was flying with the command pilot. We had picked up a command pilot because we were a pathfinder crew.

"A few days later, we went to a train station after we had been in jail a while. It was a huge, huge, railroad station, covered over with glass panes like a hothouse. Most of the panes were broken and shattered from bombings. An agitator tried to get people to hurt the prisoners as they stood there waiting at the station, and we were really frightened to think what they might try to do to us

"We finally wound up at Krems, Austria, where we were in a prison camp for one year and one week At the end of that time, the Russians were marching toward the West, and so the Germans knew that they would be at our place in a few days. They moved us out in a forced march across the length of Austria.

"We came to a place in the woods. There weren't any houses or anything; they just had guard towers and wire fences around a cleared area. There was a heavy snow on the ground. We had plenty of wood from the forest where we could make fires.

"After we had been there a while, the snow melted. General Patton's Third Army was coming from the West. Patton sent a jeep with three soldiers to accept the surrender of about fifiy German guards, who gave up their guns to these three. They disarmed them one by one as they went by; they made them throw their guns in a pile. They couldn't give us any food or anything.

"Six of us went out in the countryside. We had two German rifles with some bullets. People would run out of their houses and beg us to stay there because they preferred Americans stay there than the Russians. We came to one place and we asked where the Burgermeisters house was. We were going to run him out and stay there, but when we went there, they had turned it into a kind of hospital and had a bunch of wounded people.

"We went a little further and came to a kindergarten. The lady in charge begged us to stay there, so we did. While we were there, two Yugoslavs came with our engineer. They had met somewhere earlier taking some prisoners to a town. They came in and talked to us. They were very courteous, saluted us and knocked their heels together. They seemed very interested in me because I knew about Michaelovich and Tito. They asked if they could take one of our guns, and we said "Yes, go ahead." We didn't know what they wanted. We heard a shot fired, and I felt real bad. I thought they had killed somebody. A few minutes later, they came in with a big hog they had killed. They dressed the hog and cooked it. It fed everybody really well.

"We were all happy and rejoicing! After a few events like this, we got word that the Americans were going to gather somewhere, so we went to this place in trucks. We got on an airplane and flew to a place in France called Camp Lucky Strike. We stayed there a while and came home on a ship called *The Sea Robin*. We came into New York Harbor past the Statue of Liberty. We walked along the city streets of New York and caught a train to New Jersey. They cooked "the biggest steak you ever had" And that was just about it, I guess.

The Crash, seen through German eyes. By Jens Schaper, local researcher:

"This is the story of the Higgins Crew, whose plane, as well as two other B-24s crashed on April 29, 1944 in the area west of Nienburg, Germany. They were part of the 8th US Air Force and were on their return to England from their raid on Berlin.

377

"Various factors led to delays on the return flight which resulted in the absence of allied fighter plane protection in the area of Hannover-Diepholz. German fighters took advantage of this situation, tore the B-24 formations apart, and shot down or damaged many of the bombers. The B-24 with the Higgins crew was a "Pathfinder" with an eleven man crew, leading a formation of sixteen B-24s.

"At about 13:20 hours, in an area north of Nienburg, a German fighter fired on the plane, hitting both left engines. The plane started to lose altitude while maintaining a westerly course over Heemsen, Blenhorst and Wietzen. The flight ended at about 13:25 when the plane crashed in Päpsen near Siedenburg, killing two of the three navigators. Nine crew members bailed out safely.

"The story which follows is the result of the author's four month research effort in the summer of 2007. It is the story of the Higgins crew and their American B-24 bomber which crashed on this day of war near the residence of the author. With the help of the Internet, contact with important US archive information was quickly obtained. As part of this process, the author came in contact with an American lady in Virginia, Annette Tison, whose uncle died on the same day and at the same time in Lohne-Dinklage in another US bomber.

"Tail-gunner Charles Piper informed the author in August 2007 by telephone that the flight to Berlin was without major problems, other than from some anti-aircraft fire. Some of this might have damaged a radar antenna because bombardier Chester Broyles noted in his journal that 75 miles from Berlin his high frequency radar H2X, which was necessary for the bomb drop, was no longer functioning, so he had to turn over the lead of the 2nd Air Division to someone else, as an accurate bomb drop through the clouds could no longer be assured. According to Piper, escorting fighters could be seen during the entire outbound flight and also for a short part of the return flight.

"At 12:50 the last of Allied fighters of this Group left the Nienburg area because of fuel shortage after some had been circling the Steinhuder Lake for as long as an hour. A window of about an hour was thus created and was taken advantage of by the German Air Force.

"As the Higgins crew with its formation of 16 B-24 bombers reached the Lichtenmoor area they were surprised by 30 to 50 FW-190 fighters which belonged to the First Squadron of Fighter Group 11 of the German Air Force. Their B-24 was quickly hit on engines 1 and 2, both on the left hand side of the bomber. The complete electrical system as well as the on-board communications system and the hydraulic-driven top turret were no longer functioning.

"The situation was now becoming more dramatic as ball-turret gunner David York approached the flight deck by way of the catwalk, His hair was singed and he hollered, "Jump, jump." Broyles immediately ordered everyone to get ready to jump. Sosa was so terrified he refused to put on his parachute. As Broyles attempted to use force, Sosa resisted physically. Thereupon, Broyles let Sosa go, opened the escape hatch, and jumped—the first one to leave the front portion of the B-24.

***

"Heinz Wilkens was nine years old. As the air raid alarm had sounded that day, there was no school. He was observing the events from the south side of his parents' cabinet-making workshop. Belgian POWs, who were making ammunition boxes by order of the Armed Forces, directed him to get behind a concrete post as the smoking B-24 drew near and gradually losing altitude continued flying in the direction of Päpsen. Beyond the Hägermann-Meyer farm, the plane began to rotate around its lengthwise axis and after that did several tail spins before it disappeared from his view.

"Further left, in a southerly direction, Heinz saw two or three parachutes descending. At first they were small, but as they lost altitude they appeared larger. They were blown toward the south by the wind. One parachute landed just a few hundred meters south of him but he was afraid to go there as he feared that the airmen could be armed.

"Heinrich Ruge, then 11 years old, remembers this day especially well because he was spending time in the Harbergen train station restaurant with his friend Günther Bockhop. On this day, like almost every day, there was an air raid alarm. On such days, if the weather was bad, the children could go home, but if the weather was good, lessons would continue in the forest on tree trunks. On this afternoon the children were doing homework together.

"Heinrich remembers. "In the mornings we would see the bomber formations flying away to the east and in the afternoons coming back to the west, but no longer then in a larger formation. They were in smaller groups and even single planes. We were angry, of course, that the enemy was bombing all the German cities and we were glad to see that on the return flight some were shot down by German fighters."

"We were sitting on the south side of the station embankment and had a clear view of the fields in the direction of Holte. From there we could see approaching from east to west the already lightly burning machine. It was clearly not under control. It was flying slowly, smoking, and losing altitude. We saw how one person with a parachute jumped out of the plane. The parachute was being blown toward Holte and I remember that we asked each other, "Why don't more jump out?" A German fighter coming from the north hit the plane with a few machine gun bursts, without receiving any return fire. It would certainly have crashed even without those shots. The view toward the west was limited because of station buildings and sheds; the plane disappeared from our sight behind them. But before they disappeared, we saw two more parachutes."

"After a while, after everything had quieted down, we rode on our bicycles toward Staffhorst. At this time German troops were in the woods around Harbergen and were also billeted in the larger farms. I remember that we encountered armed German soldiers with a group of captured Americans in Staffhorst near the farm of Grasmeyer-Wilkens. I believe there were three or four of them. We rode our bicycles over there and looked on. I also remember that there was a hand cart there on which one was sitting. While we were approaching the Americans, we thought to ourselves, "So this is what our enemy looks like, people like us, who attack and destroy our beautiful German cities every day, whereby thousands of innocent civilians are incinerated and die."

"Gerhard Hillmann, then 11 years old, from the Langeln section of Wietzen stated that from his family farm he saw a parachute being blown over his house in a westerly direction which then landed in the area of Steinheide. This was confirmed by the later mayor of Staffhorst Werner Holle who saw this American in his parents' house in what is now the Guesthouse Weigel. The American was thirsty and asked for water before he was trucked away by an Army unit toward Nienburg by way of Wietzen.

"World War I veteran Bobrink came out of his house with his rifle 98 to capture Sears. Heinrich Ostermann, and six year-old Udo Ahl, son of the teacher, joined him. Quoting Ostermann: "Bobrink and we youngsters saw that the American packed up his parachute quickly and tried to hide in a shed. Gesticulating, Bobrink ordered Sears in slang German to 'come out now' which of course Sears didn't understand. Bobrink's warning shot through the roof of the shed persuaded Sears to surrender. Then Bobrink took his prisoner away on foot down Päpsen Street in the direction of Siedenburg."

***

Acknowledgements;
Bombardier 1Lt. Chester Broyles, Jr., from "An Experience to Remember"
Radio S/Sgt. Thomas E. Sumlin, from "The War Story" as told by T. E. Sumlin
Jens Schaper, German local researcher.

CHAPTER 25

389ᵀᴴ BOMB GROUP
564ᵀᴴ BOMB SQUADRON

Type: B-24H • Serial: 41-28784
MACR: 5473 • Air Base: Hethel

"Generator trouble developed soon after take-off. The entire electrical system was impaired. Over the target an engine was knocked out by flak. The ship led the formation over the target, but dropped out during the return trip. A fuel reading revealed that fuel was low, so orders for ditching were carried out. The plane was ditched about 30 miles from the English coast."

1Lt. John W. Hortenstine, navigator, Missing Air Crew Report # 5473

Air Com.: Capt. Ralph S. Bryant, 0-477192, KIA, Marion, SC

Pilot: 1Lt. Alfred H. Locke, 0-680460, RTD

Co-Pilot: 1Lt. Errol A. Self, 0-805988, RTD, Oklahoma City, OK,

Navigator: 1Lt. Kenneth O. Reed, 0-410197, KIA

Navigator: 2Lt. John D. Bloznelis, 0-735163, KIA

Navigator: 1Lt. John W. Hortenstine, 0-673077, RTD

Bombardier: 1Lt. Arthur C. Delclisur, 0-688513, KIA

Radio: T/Sgt. Richard J. Wallace, 11040222, RTD, Claremont, NH

Top-Turret Gunner: T/Sgt. Harold F. Freeman, 3713298, KIA, Hannibal, MO

Waist-Gunner: S/Sgt. Pedro S. Paez, 39255107, RTD

Waist-Gunner: S/Sgt. Harry L. Boisclair, 14084140, RTD, Leesburg, FL

Tail-Gunner: S/Sgt. Dale R. VanBlair, 16076061, RTD, Quincy, IL

5 KIA, 7 RTD

Crash Site: North Sea
Time: 15.00

Pilot 1Lt. Alfred H. Locke.

From a letter from Alfred to his wife.

"On the morning of April 29th we were assigned as deputy lead of the 466th group which was leading the 46th Combat Wing on a mission to Berlin. As we taxied our on the runway for takeoff, Capt. England, assigned as lead ship, sent word that, due to a dangerous bomb release, they would take off late and join us in the air. We then took off, formed the wing, and formed the division, on course and on time. Shortly afterwards, the engineer Sgt. Freeman, reported that two generators were out. I asked him if the others were alright- he replied that they were, but that two generators wouldn't last long with the extreme load of our equipment. The Command Pilot Ralph Briant decided to keep the lead, since there were no others - he thought - able to replace us.

"We continued on course as lead, since the other lead ship didn't show up. I later found out they had further mechanical difficulty. Since we were draining excessive current I turned off the automatic pilot and all other electric source we could get along without so as to give full current to our special equipment for navigation purposes, there being a 6/10 to 8/10 cloud cover at the time.

"When we arrived at the mission Initial Point I informed Captain Bryant that we would have to bomb by PFF, though the conditions bordered on visual, since a checkup showed we had not enough current to operate the bombsight. After entering the city, we obtained a direct hit on no. 3 engine by an 88mm shell which did not explode but tore through the wing leaving a gaping hole. This however didn't interfere with the bomb run, as we got bombs away about two minutes later, on the center of the city.

"On leaving Berlin I feathered number 3 engine and the inter-phone and electrical system failed soon later. Captain Byant suggested that we take a course for home, since we were off course to the south. But since we were with the division I suggested that we stay with the other wings, fighter support being completely lacking and he agreed.

"Coming back on course again fighters harassed us from the Magdeburg area to the Zuider Zee. At two different times I saw about 30 nazi fighters "gang up" abreast and attack elements of our wing.

"After progressing all the way across Germany, it became apparent that we were unable to lead the wing because of our slow airspeed and fluctuating power. It was a continual fight to keep the manifold pressure under control on two of the remaining three engines.

"We left the combat wing lead and came up to the rear of the formation, and almost immediately our plane was attacked by enemy fighters, who were driven off by the gunners, operating their turrets manually. The attacks were repeated in about 15 minutes by other fighters, again without success.

Here ends the letter abruptly.

In the fall of 1945, Al resumed his studies at the University of Oklahoma in Norman. In 1946, he was appointed as a first lieutenant in the Air Reserves. He graduated from OU in June 1950 with a BS in Electrical Engineering. In 1953 he was designated as a standby reservist with the 14th Air Force at Robins Air Force Base, Georgia.

Al worked for the Oklahoma Gas and Electric Company in Oklahoma City from 1950 until his death in 1972. He published several research articles and served as a representative on a national committee planning the transition to the metric system by the electrical engineering profession. At the time of his death, Al was supervisor, Department of Transmission and Distribution.

Al and his wife Patsy had three children. After the kids had all graduated from high school, Patsy went back to college and earned her degree in elementary education. She completed her MA in Library Science in 1977, and taught school in the Putnam City school district in Warr Acres OK until she retired in 1987.

Navigator 1Lt. John W. Hortenstine

wrote on May 14, 1944 to his mother about the ditching;

"I am residing at a "rest home" at the present time and will be here for a few weeks. It is located in southern England on a big estate: probably some lord's home before the war.

"The reason for my being here, however, is for a recuperative rest. We had a little accident coming home from Berlin last week: we had to crash in the North Sea due to having a couple of engines shot out and lack of gas.

"When we hit the water, I got out, some way, and then my "Mae west" didn't inflate. This was quite a quandary as it's pretty hard to stay afloat for more than a few minutes due to the heavy clothing. In fact, the navigator sank in about four minutes. He was right beside me.

"But due to the fact that I had just bought a quart of Scotch the day before and had it waiting on me back at the base, I had a great incentive to stay up; and I did for about 15 minutes. As I was just about ready to go down, an oxygen bottle that had torn loose form the plane came to the surface about 20 feet from me, and naturally I grabbed it. This kept me afloat until the boat came.

"Three men went down with the plane and two died when they were on the rescue boat. Locke and I got out without a scratch. The others that got out had big cuts and there were two with fractured skulls, etc. The bombardier died.

"I won't be flying for quite a while; maybe not any more over here. This place is very nice. They have horses, tennis, golf, and boating. The food is wonderful. It is located on a big river. There are some of the boys from my old group (448), so I'm enjoying it a lot. I repeat, I don't have a scratch."

Tail-Gunner Dale VanBlair wrote about John Hartenstine;

"After the ditching, he served for about three months in Intelligence, then got to thinking that, according to regulations, if he went back to flying he could collect flying pay for the previous three months. When we got together at a 448th reunion in 1992, he told me, "I got greedy and requested assignment to flying duty." He served as an instructor for crews taking PFF training and also flew eight night missions scattering propaganda leaflets behind the German lines.

"After the war, John, who remained in the Air Force Reserves, went back to Virginia Tech, where he was enrolled when he enlisted, and graduated in 1946 with a degree in chemical engineering. He worked at various engineering jobs until he was recalled to active duty during the Korean War. After flying sixty-one missions in a B-26, he returned to the States, then was sent to England for a four-month tour. He was stationed at Alconbury, which is in the same area as Seething and Hethel, where we were based during WWII. In his first letter to me in February, 1986, he wrote, "I even looked up some of my old English girl friends." John was discharged in 1952, but remained in the Reserves in the Air Transport Command until he retired as a lieutenant colonel at age 60.

"After being released from active duty, John resumed his career as an engineer in Abingdon, Virginia, and later got involved in real estate. When we began corresponding in 1986, he had quit his engineering practice but was still doing a "little real estate work," as he put it, and then added, "I have a farm or two to keep me busy"

From son John Hortenstine.

"I can tell you what a great man my father was. I have always looked up to him since early childhood. On an entrance "Questionnaire" upon starting college, one of the questions was "Who is your hero?" I simply put "My father." I meant it. He nor my mother know about that. I've kept that just for me I suppose.

"At his funeral every aspect of society was present; judges, State Senators, work peers, fellow farmers, all down to tenants that leased from him. Farmers that worked his land.

"He was a quiet man. Didn't talk for no reason. Could be extremely funny. Dry sometimes, but very witty and funny. A pleasure to be around. A gentleman that worked for dad for many years on his survey crew once told me my father was one of the smartest man he had ever met.

"He was very generous to others but very frugal for himself. Looking at him on any given day, you wouldn't have thought he was worth a dime. He drove a tiny pickup truck to work. Two wheel drive, no air-conditioning, no radio. A four speed straight. We lived on a hill in a very modest home as I was getting older. He drifted off the hill, down Church Street and all the way to Valley saving money on gas.

"He had four brothers. All of them went to WWII and all five of them made it home. My grandmother surely thought there was no way all of her boys would make it home in one piece. They did.

Navigator 1Lt. Kenneth O. Reed.

Official statement by Navigator John Hortenstine immediately after WWII:

"After the plane had settled I went out through the escape hatch on the flight deck. After being in the water about 10 minutes I noticed Lt. Kenneth Reed in the water about fifteen yards from me and he was making no attempt to stay afloat, and his head was under water. I swam to him in an effort to help him. His Mae West was not inflated and I attempted to inflate it but could not. I was then forced to leave him as my Mae West was also not inflated either. I swam and caught an oxygen bottle and then returned to Lt. Reed using the oxygen bottle as a means to stay afloat. I raised Lt. Reed's head from the water and tried to bring him to consciousness, but was unable. I presumed him dead and as I could not hold him up any longer so released him. I did not see Lt. Reed after this but I am quite sure that he would not be otherwise than dead.

Tail-Gunner Dale VanBlair wrote;

"I began corresponding with Mrs. Henrietta Reed, Ken Reed's mother, following my return to the U.S, in November, 1944, and continued to do so until she was taken by cancer about twenty years later. The first excerpt, however, is from a letter that she wrote to our co-pilot, Errol Self, a copy of which I have. The second is from a letter that she wrote to me on March 1, 1945. These excerpts are a tribute not only to Ken but also to the spirit of American mothers like Mrs. Reed.

'I am glad that Ken was brave and good and kind. He was always that way when he was with us - quiet and patient. Even as a child, he had dignity and courage. He was a good boy. Both his life and his death were good. I shall never forget him, dear Errol. He is with me even more than before he went away. Yes, Ken will be with you too when you need him, whether you fly again or not. You must not feel bad about Ken and the others who have gone away. God took them and left the rest of you. It was in His hands. Those of you who still have the gift of life on this dear earth will live lives that will bet he fulfillment of our mighty

struggle

"*Someday we will understand the entire scheme of things when the Great Adventure comes to us, too. And I know that will mean happiness for you and all the fine boys who have gone ahead. And as for Ken, I understand that both John Hortenstine and Errol Self tried to keep him up. This knowledge is of superlative comfort to us. It was just one of those things, Dale. And we are so very grateful that seven of that splendid twelve are still here. We have looked the facts in the face from the beginning. I firmly believe that the five are all right. Why wouldn't they be, Dale? They were fine fellows, and they with all of you that day, were doing their duty, a duty of great difficulty and a duty essential to the welfare of our fine country.*"

Tail-Gunner S/Sgt. Dale R. VanBlair.

By Dale. August 2015.

"I was born on June 17, 1921, in Quincy, Illinois, by the Mississippi River. My parents were Cecil and Lora VanBlair. Dad was a machinist – he operated a turret lathe - and he was responsible for my becoming a machinist - after I graduated from Quincy High School in 1939 - at the company for which he worked. It was the tail end of the Great Depression, and jobs were hard to come by in Quincy, so I was thankful for Dad's help. I went to work at the Rock Island Arsenal in Rock Island, Illinois, in January, 1942. I could possibly have continued to receive a deferment throughout the war, but I decided to enlist in the U.S. Army Air Corps and was sworn in on Nov. 3, 1942. In March, 1943,

Tail-Gunner S/Sgt. Dale R. VanBlair

two friends and I volunteered for aerial gunnery school. I joined the Alfred H. Locke crew, which was assigned to the 448th B.G. and which had just begun training. The 448th arrived in England in early December, 1943, and my crew flew its first mission on Christmas Eve day.

"In February, 1944 our officers, engineer and radio operator were transferred to another base for a month of training preparatory to our becoming a lead crew. We four gunners remained with the 448th and were subject to being used to fill in on other crews for wounded or sick gunners. During that month I went on five missions, including the first major daytime raid on Berlin on March 6. In late March our officers and radio operator (our engineer had developed bronchitis and been returned to the U.S.) completed their training, and we were transferred to the 564th Squadron, 389th Bomb Group.

"On the morning of April 29 we were briefed for our fifth mission as a lead crew. We were to be deputy lead for the 466th Group leading the 2nd Combat Wing to Berlin. Not counting the mission of April 18, when we flew over the outskirts of Berlin, it would be my third time over the heart of the city, the first for the rest of the crew. Our target was the Friedrichstrasse rail station in the middle of Berlin, the center of the main rail and underground system networks.

"On arriving at our plane, I was introduced to Lt. John Bloznelis, who had been added to our crew as dead reckoning navigator. Lt. John Hortenstine would continue as the Mickey (radar) navigator; Lt. Kenneth Reed, as instrument navigator. We had two substitutes: Sgt. Harold Freeman as engineer and Sgt. Richard Wallace as radio operator. Also flying with us as Command Pilot was Captain Ralph Bryant, operations officer for the 786th Squadron of the 466th.

"This was the thirteenth mission for the other six members of our original crew; and as we stood around on the hardstand awaiting taxi time, though not superstitious, I joked with them about my having to sweat out two "unlucky thirteenth" missions: mine on March 16 and theirs. I should have known better.

"The mission began ominously, for shortly after we became airborne, our plane developed generator problems. Normally we would have returned to our base; but the lead plane had run into problems. In doing research on this mission, I corresponded with the Command Pilot on the lead plane, B. E. Steadman, who I believe was C.O. of the 466th. He explained what happened. Their problems began with a fire at the radio operator's station as they were waiting for clearance to take off. After they had taken off in a replacement plane, two or three of the smoke bomb markers began smoking heavily and had to be salvoed into the North Sea. The lead crew returned to the 389th base and took off in a third PFF plane. As they were attempting to overtake our formation, two generators went out. At that point Col. Steadman radioed us that he was aborting and that we should take over the lead. Thus, even though we also had generator problems, we had no choice but to continue, with Captain Bryant now becoming the Command Pilot.

"After the 466th formed behind us, we crossed the North Sea and Holland. Shortly before we entered Germany, our formation was attacked by FW-190s that were driven off by our fighter escort after about ten minutes. About twenty minutes later we were again hit by 190s, but again our escort of P-51s discouraged them, destroying one that I saw go down. We had come through two fighter attacks without undergoing an attack on our plane. I hoped our luck would hold out. Those two encounters left me on edge and encouraged me to keep an especially vigilant lookout for enemy planes. I kept my eyes and head moving, up and down and from one side to the other.

"As we approached Berlin, Lt. Delclisur reported that not enough power was being generated to operate the bomb sight properly and that we would have to bomb by radar, even though there was not enough undercast to interfere with the more accurate visual bombing. Immediately upon entering the bomb run we ran into intense flak. One shell scored a direct hit but, fortunately, was a dud or had been set to explode at a higher altitude. Instead of exploding on contact, it put our #3 engine out of commission and exited through the top of the wing, leaving a gaping hole. If the shell had exploded, the wing would have buckled and our plane would have gone down. I've often wondered if some slave laborer had sabotaged that shell. In the few minutes we were over Berlin, our plane was hit several other times, but none of our crew was wounded. Luck was still with us.

"Our luck ran out, however. The disabled engine was leaking gasoline, which could result in our running out before getting back to England. Then, just after Lt. Delclisur released the flare that signaled the other planes to drop their bombs, our generators went completely out, leaving us with no power for gun turrets, radio, intercom, and other electrical equipment.

"Not long after turning away from the target, we were again attacked by a group of FW-190s and a few ME-109s. Since we were caught without fighter support, the Germans were free to give us their undivided attention. One flew by so close to me going from front to rear that I thought I might recognize the pilot if we ever met again. The loss of intercom and my limited view from my tail turret kept me ignorant of the engine problems and leaking gas; however, I knew we must have problems besides the loss of electrical power when I saw that we had dropped back to the rear of the formation.

"The loss of power for turrets was a major concern to me. After going through the simple procedure for converting to hand cranks and foot firing pedals, I practiced maneuvering the guns and turret. As I already knew, the emergency system was a far cry from the hand control that activated the hydraulic system. Using the hand cranks, I could not turn the turret and raise or lower the pair of fifties nearly fast enough to track any German plane that came into my view. The German that had attacked from the front and flown by so close to me had zoomed out of range long before I could do anything. Had my turret been operating normally, I'd have had a good chance of downing him. Fortunately, none of the enemy made a direct attack on our plane from the tail except for one FW-190 that started my direction but swerved when I fired. I triggered a burst occasionally, primarily in the hope that the Germans would think my turret was functioning properly and stay clear. The front and top turret gunners were also operating their turrets manually and doing their best, along with the waist gunners, to fend off the Germans, most of whom were attacking from the front.

"I watched as one of our planes slowly dropped further and further behind our formation. I knew what was going to happen. If a plane that had been hit could keep up with the formation, it had a fair chance of getting back to its base because of the protection it received from the guns on nearby planes; the Germans, however, were almost certain to gang up on one that fell behind. Sure enough, as soon as the bomber was out of range of the guns of the planes at the back of the formation, three FW-190s attacked it and quickly sent it down in flames. Then another B-24 began lagging behind and met the same fate. Since they were 466th planes, there was no chance of my knowing any of the men who went down with them. I was thankful for that but still grieved for them and their families. Twice more within fifteen minutes I watched the same tragic drama played out. I saw not a single chute come out of any of the four. That's us if we can not stay with the group, I thought, and anxiously kept an eye on the nearest *Liberator* to see if we were dropping behind. After a few minutes, I was much relieved to note that we had maintained our position. Twenty to thirty minutes later, however, I discovered that I could see no other planes. We were no longer with the formation. I had seen no Germans for a few minutes, though, so perhaps we would make it. It wasn't to be. Because of my limited field of vision, I didn't know that two German fighters which had attacked from the front had punctured a gas tank and knocked out another engine before being driven off by three P-47s.

"When I at last saw the North Sea below us, I began to relax, for we had never been attacked after leaving the continent behind us. We had it made now. In forty-five minutes to an hour, we should be landing. I sat in my turret and watched enemy territory drop away. Then I felt a tap on my back. It was Hank. "We're going to ditch," he shouted above the noise of the wind and the engines. "We don't have enough gas to get back." After a brief moment of disbelief, I thought of Shorty and hoped I would fare better. Shorty, who had been our ball turret gunner and was like a brother to me, had been lost in a ditching when he had to sub on March 8 with another crew. I saw a bit of irony in the fact that the receipt for his fiancee's bracelet, which I had kept as a remembrance, was still in my billfold. Then I thought of my parents and was glad that they couldn't know what was going on.

"I learned later from Lt. Locke that had it not been for Capt. Bryant we might have made it back to Hethel. After we lost Virgil, our engineer, from our crew, Cappy had been assigned the responsibility of seeing that we used up the gas in the wing-tip tanks first when starting on a mission and then flipping the switch to the main tanks. With Cappy missing, the routine was upset, and Harold Freeman, our replacement engineer for the mission, forgot to use the auxiliary wing-tip tanks first before switching to the main tanks until we were out over the North Sea headed for the continent. At that time Harold started to get out of his top turret position to switch to those tanks, but Capt. Bryant ordered him back to the turret to watch for fighters. It would only have taken Harold a few seconds to switch to the wing-tip tanks and then, when that gas was about used up, another few seconds to switch back to the main tanks. No fighters could have sneaked up on us in that length of time; besides, the waist gunners could see almost all the sky covered by the top turret. Following the loss of our generators, no power was available to switch to the wing-tip tanks when we ran low on gas. I don't doubt that Capt. Bryant, in his own mind, felt justified in what he did, but had he not interfered, we would probably have had enough gas left in the main tanks to get us back to England. As Command Pilot, Bryant was commander of the formation, but not of our plane, which was Lt. Locke's responsibility. Bryant had no business interfering with Harold.

"After Hank brought me the bad news, I went back to the waist section to help throw all removable equipment -waist guns, ammunition belts, parachute packs, etc.- out the waist windows. With no power for the radio, we could send no SOS; however, firing up flares calling for fighter support brought two P-47s to us. Using hand signals, we tried to convey that we had to ditch and that our radio was out. They signaled that they understood and flew with us until the time came to hit the water.

"The waist was considered the least desirable ditching position because of the B-24's tendency to break behind the bomb bay. Because there was not enough room, however, for all of us on the command deck, the area just behind the pilot's and co-pilot's seats, four of us remained in the waist: Lt. Self, Pete, Hank and me. We stretched the ditching belt and fastened it on each side of the fuselage. We then sat facing aft with our backs against the ditching belt and our hands with fingers locked behind our heads. As we waited for Lt. Locke to set the plane down, I prayed that we might get through the ditching safely and be rescued.

"In view of the small place that I had given God in my life since entering service, I knew that I had no right to expect Him to answer my prayer; nevertheless, I prayed. I was aware that the *Liberator* was a difficult plane to ditch successfully and the rate of survival for crew members was rather low; however, even though I dreaded the prospect of ditching in the frigid North Sea, I believed I would survive. I was still an optimist.

"When Lt. Locke dragged the tail of the plane in the water to slow it prior to setting the plane down, the escape hatch flew open and icy water sprayed us. It was unbelievably cold. Lt. Self jumped up from where we were sitting on the floor between the two waist windows and tried unsuccessfully to slam the hatch shut with his foot, then sat down again. Seconds later when Lt. Locke attempted to set the plane down, a large wave caught the nose. It was like slamming into a concrete wall. The plane broke behind the rear bomb bay, and I found myself instantaneously submerged in the frigid water without even having time to take a deep breath.

"As I fought to get back to the surface, my forehead slammed against a metal object so hard that I thought I might be seriously injured. My lungs were demanding air, and I thought, I'm going to drown - what is it going to feel like? I even remembered reading somewhere that drowning was not such an unpleasant way to die and hoped it was true. I felt that I could not hold my breath one more second, yet somehow I did. At that moment my head broke above the surface, and I gratefully gulped in air. It was almost like being brought back from the dead - one moment after I had faced an imminent death, life was handed back to me, at least for the moment. I still had a chance of surviving.

"I was still inside the waist section, which had not broken completely free of the forward section. If it had, I would have gone down with it. Seeing that the right waist window was completely blocked, I turned to the other window, where Pete was struggling to get through the half of it that was not covered by wreckage. For a few seconds I tried unsuccessfully to force my way through a narrow gap in the tangle of aluminum, then dropped back into the water. I thought about pulling the compressed air cylinder cords to inflate my Mae West, but stopped on thinking that I might have to dive beneath the surface in order to get out. In retrospect, I am surprised that I could swim with all the clothes I had on, which included heavy flight boots, but I do not recall having any problem. Fearing the waist section would break loose any second and sink, I frantically looked for a way out. Spotting a small opening in the side of the fuselage at the water's surface, I paddled over to it. I thankfully discovered that the fuselage had been completely ripped away beneath the water and left me plenty of room to pull myself through.

"As I was about to exit through the opening, someone screamed, "Help!" I turned around but saw no one. The last thing I wanted to do was to spend any more time inside the battered plane, but I could not leave if someone needed help. Hoping that the waist section would not break loose and that the entire plane would not suddenly go under, I swam back a few feet and scanned the water, but saw no one. Pete was gone from the window. Not hearing another call for help, I swam back to the opening and pulled myself through. Once outside, I reached down to pull the cord that would cause the compressed air cylinder on the right side to be punctured, which would inflate that side of my Mae West. As I did so, I thought, what if it doesn't work? I yanked on the cord and was relieved to see that side puff up. A pull on the other cord inflated the left side, and I began paddling away from the wreckage. I feared that if the plane sank, the suction would pull me under, but it continued to float.

"Hoping that someone had released a life raft, I looked around. No raft. I thought about attempting to climb up onto the wing to pull the raft release handle but was doubtful that the plane could continue to float long enough. I spotted four men in the water, but the only one close to me was Lt. Delclisur, who had a large gash over one eye with blood streaming from it. He called, "Let's stay together." I tried to swim to him but could make no progress against the waves. My arms soon felt like lead, and I reluctantly gave up. The waves washed me away from him, and I lost sight of everyone. Surprisingly, the plane was still floating, and I regretfully thought that I would have had ample time after exiting the waist section to swim to the wing, climb up on it, and release the life raft. I did not see our plane sink, so do not know how long it remained afloat.

"I continued to paddle around dog fashion on top of my Mae West, finding it

more and more difficult to hold my head up out of the water. I was now completely exhausted, but I feared that if I turned over onto my back, the waves would
wash over my head. Finally I could hold my head up no longer, rolled over, and
gratefully discovered that the Mae West held my head above the water and rode
me up over each wave with no effort on my part. Someone should have told
us about that during our training, I thought. Having had no experience with life
preservers, I didn't know that they were designed to float a person on his back.

"I kept watching the horizon for a rescue boat, but none appeared. Never before had I felt so completely alone. Since my watch had stopped at 3:06 when we
ditched, I had no idea how long I had been in the water, but it seemed like hours.
One thing I was sure of: I was very, very cold, and I knew my chances of surviving were not good. I didn't give up nor panic, but I kept thinking, I don't want
to die out here where my body might not ever be found. I thought of my parents
and how grieved they would be to receive a telegram notifying them of my death.

"Hearing the sound of an aircraft, I looked up and saw a B-24 approaching. It
flew over very low with its bomb bay doors open, and I saw a man standing on
the catwalk. I thought he was going to drop a life raft; however, the plane circled
twice and flew off. Why didn't they do something? I was angry.

"I debated whether to take off the heavy flying boots that weighted down my
feet but, since the Mae West was supporting me satisfactorily, decided against
removing them. If the B-24 should return and drop a raft, the boots might help
retain some warmth in my feet even though they were wet. The Mae West continued to carry me up and over one wave after the other. How long, I wondered,
would this ordeal go on. I suddenly realized that I no longer felt so cold and
wondered why. The reason was probably hypothermia.

"Then, off in the distance, I saw the most beautiful object that I had ever laid
eyes on in my 22+ years: a boat heading in my direction. I later learned that Royal Marine Launch 498 had been contacted by the P-47s and given our position.
As it came closer, I waved and saw someone wave back, then watched the boat
pick up two of our crew. That was the last I remembered except for having, at one
point, a vague sensation of someone trying to pour a bitter liquid down my throat.

"Regaining consciousness was a strange experience. I was lying in a large,
black tunnel. Remembering the ditching experience, I began to wonder if I were
alive or dead, for there was no recollection of having been picked up. If I am
dead, I thought, I must not be in hell because I do not feel either hot or tortured,
but I was afraid to open my eyes. When I finally summoned the courage to do so,
I found myself lying in a bunk with Lt. Locke looking at me from the bunk above.
I was alive and I was safe! What a flood of relief I felt.

"Am I glad to see you! I exclaimed.

"He grinned. "How're you feeling? I was worried about you."

"Cold, but otherwise okay, I guess. How about you?"

"He told me he was all right and that we were docked at Great Yarmouth and would soon be taken to a hospital. I had been unconscious for however long it had taken the boat to finish picking up our crew and then cover the thirty miles from our ditching site to Great Yarmouth. I had been in the water for about an hour and was the last of our crew to be picked up. My memory of someone trying to pour something down my throat was the result of a crew member's trying to get me to drink some scotch after I was rescued. Since I had heard that twenty to thirty minutes was about as long as a person was supposed to survive immersed in the cold water, I was fortunate to be alive.

"Lt. Locke filled me in on what had happened to the others as we waited to be taken to the hospital. Capt. Bryant and Lt. Delclisur died of injuries and shock after being picked up. Lt. Hortenstine saw Lt. Reed with his head hanging into the water and tried to hold onto him, but became exhausted. Kenneth slipped away from him and was not seen again. Lt. Bloznelis and Sgt. Freeman were never sighted, hence probably were killed in the ditching. What made Harold Freeman's death especially tragic was that he had completed his missions and was awaiting orders to return to the States when he was assigned to fill in on our crew. He had almost certainly written his parents about completing his tour, so that the word of his death would come as an even greater shock than if they thought he was still under the required number. He should not have been forced to fly with us. A few weeks later, Mother wrote me that Harold's parents, who lived about thirty miles away in Hannibal, Missouri, had contacted her to see if she could supply information about the ditching.

"Lt. Self suffered a broken back and chipped shoulder bone. He later received the Soldier's Medal for freeing Pete, who had got caught on wreckage while trying to get through the waist window. It was probably Pete whom I had heard calling for help. Lt. Self had come up outside the waist window and, in spite of his injury, immediately pulled Pete loose after the one call for help. I have never figured out, however, why I did not see them when I exited through the opening in the fuselage, which was only ten to fifteen feet behind the waist window. Perhaps I remained inside longer than I realized after hearing the call for help, thus giving them time to swim away.

"The other survivors had escaped uninjured or with relatively minor injuries. Lt. Hortenstine, who had been in the compartment behind the cockpit for the ditching, had covered himself with flak jackets, which had prevented his being injured when the top turret broke loose and fell on him. He was able to push the turret off and escape through the top hatch. Hank came up outside of the waist section on the opposite side from which I escaped. He lost about a half-inch from the upper left ear lobe.

"Lt. Locke was knocked out by the force of the impact. When he came to, he was under the water and still strapped to his seat. After releasing himself, he escaped through a hole in the side of the cockpit and pulled the cords to inflate his Mae West, only to find that the jacket was split and would not hold air. Fortunately, an oxygen bottle floated by, which he grabbed and held on to until being picked up.

"Locke later received the Distinguished Flying Cross for keeping the plane up in the formation with one engine out and for bringing it back as far as he did with two engines out. As he later said to me, "Even if we had got back, those two engines (meaning the good ones) would never have been used again. They'd have been burned out." The last sentence of his citation, a copy of which I have, reads, "The superior flying skill and sound judgment displayed by Lieutenant Locke reflect the highest credit upon himself and the armed forces of the United States." If ever an award was deserved, that one was.

"Like Harold Freeman, Dick Wallace had also completed his missions and was awaiting return to the States when summoned to fly with us as radio operator. Dick, however, escaped with no injuries.

"From the Air-Sea Rescue launch we were taken to a WREN hospital in Great Yarmouth. WRENs were British women serving in the navy. The one bright spot in the whole miserable experience was being taken care of by young, pretty nurses who gave us lots of attention. The thought occurred to me that Yarmouth might be a good place to spend a two-day pass, but I found out later, much to my disappointment, that it was off limits to American military personnel.

"I have no idea what my body temperature had dropped to when I was pulled from the North Sea. Although I was not told so, I assume I was suffering from hypothermia, for I shivered and shivered and shivered. The nurses put hot water bottles around me and piled blankets on me, but I continued to shake. The nurses came in throughout the night to replace the cooled-off hot water bottles with warm ones. It was nearly dawn before I finally warmed up and went to sleep.

"About the middle of the morning a nurse came in to tell us that our transportation to the 389th base had arrived. We had to remove the pajamas that the WREN hospital had provided and wrap ourselves in blankets brought from our base for the trip back to Hethel. We were stark naked beneath our blankets. We thought the English could at least have loaned us the pajamas for the trip home with the understanding they would be returned, but apparently their regulations forbade that. Such is the nature of red tape. The clothing we were wearing when picked up should have had time to dry, but we never saw it again. Perhaps it was returned to our supply, however.

"I expected to see an ambulance waiting for us outside the hospital, but instead there sat a truck, of all things. Lt. Self was the only one transported in an ambulance. That was the longest thirty-mile ride I have ever taken. I was so weak that even sitting up in that rough-riding truck was almost more than I could manage; each time we went around a curve, I had to cling with both hands to the slatted seat to keep from falling off. I was ready to collapse by the time we arrived at Hethel.

"I was put in the base hospital to recuperate, where I remained for three days.

During the first day I began having a rather severe headache which aspirin did not relieve. Thinking teeth might be the problem, the flight surgeon sent me to the dentist the second day. The dentist found six cavities, which he filled, but the headache persisted. Some time during the third day I became aware of a kind of grating in the side of my head when I turned onto my left side and mentioned it to the doctor. At that point I was transported to the 231st Station Hospital on May 2, where x-rays revealed a skull fracture. The blow that I had received on the forehead had been so severe that it caused the skull to bulge enough to cause a minor fracture on the left side. In view of the sizable abrasion on my forehead, I could not understand why the doctor did not immediately suspect a skull fracture when the headache began instead of shipping me off to the dentist. The teeth needed to be filled, but that was not the most opportune time for me to have to undergo that ordeal.

"Since a truck taxi ran daily between Hethel and the hospital, less than an hour's drive, men from my hut visited me and brought my mail three or four times during my stay. After two or three days the headaches completely disappeared, and I began enjoying being a recuperating patient - no duties and nurses to give me a back rub each evening before the lights were dimmed. The day before I was released, though, I was brought back down to earth with a thud by being assigned K.P. duty in the ward's small kitchen. All it involved was running the dishes through the dishwasher, but I thought that as a staff sergeant I was forever free of that undignified labor.

"On learning that Lt. Self was in the ward next to me, I went to visit him. He had two broken vertebra and was in an uncomfortable body cast, which would not be removed for about three months. He was expected to make a complete recovery.

"After ten days in the division hospital, I returned to Hethel on May 11. When I entered our Nissen hut, first one man then another came bringing various items of my belongings to me, which I had rather expected to happen. When a crew was lost, the accepted practice was for other men in the hut to appropriate any items of equipment other than personal things before Supply came to take everything away. It may sound cold-blooded but really was a very practical understanding among us - we preferred for someone we knew to have an item than for it to go back to Supply. Sometimes two of us would make an agreement. For example, the man who bunked next to me, Sgt. Ziglinski, and I had an understanding that if I were lost, he got my sheets; if he were lost, I got his leather A-2 jacket. At any rate, every item that belonged to me was returned without any prompting by me. In lieu of my A-2 jacket, which had gone down with our plane, Supply issued me an English-made wool jacket that I liked very much, especially since no one else I knew had one like it. I still regretted losing my A-2, however.

"The watch that I had purchased in Brazil was a casualty of the ditching. I normally wore my old watch at all times because I preferred to save the new one for post-service days, but on a whim I put on the new one the morning of the mission. By the time the personal belongings that accompanied me on the mission were returned and I was able to take the watch to a Norwich watch repair shop, the watch's works were so damaged by the salt water as to be beyond repair.

"Three weeks after the ditching I developed spinal meningitis, a result of the time I spent in the water. The hospital fortunately had an adequate supply of penicillin, and I recovered except for complete loss of hearing in the right ear. As a result I was grounded and made squadron gunnery sergeant, a position I held until returning to the U.S. in October, 1944. I then worked in an office at Lowry Field near Denver, Colorado, until my discharge October 4, 1945.

"I enrolled at Quincy College (now Quincy University) in September, 1946, and graduated in June, 1949, with an English major and qualified to teach. After seven years of teaching English at Vandalia, then Champaign, both in Illinois, I was hired to teach for District 201 (a high school district) in Belleville, where I remained until retiring in 1982. For sixteen years prior to retirement, I was English Department chairman for from 35 to 40 teachers (the number fluctuated according to student enrollment). I obtained my Master's degree in English at Drake University, Des Moines, Iowa, and later completed an additional 45 semester hours at Southern Illinois University in Edwardsville, Illinois.

"I met my future wife, Mary, in June, 1946, and we were married in April, 1949. We adopted two infant girls, Deborah and Karen, in 1954 and 1958, respectively. I lost Mary to cancer in 2002. Debbi, who never married, now lives with me, while Karen and husband Doug are about a 35-minute drive from my home. Their daughter, Elizabeth, completed the course work for a doctorate in math and is now proof-reading and editing math textbooks for a publisher in California.

***.

Acknowledgements;
Tail-Gunner S/Sgt. Dale R. VanBlair.

bombers, but there are no newer records in his archive until November 24, 1943, when he arrived in England. He was soon assigned to the 571st Bomb Squadron, based at Framlingham, Suffolk. He was shot down on April 29, 1944, liberated on April 29, 1945, first arrived back in the USA on June 12, 1945, and, officially separated from active duty November 24, 1945.

"In all, he flew 27 combat missions as co-pilot and pilot of a B-17. He logged over 200 combat hours, and 8 active months as a B-17 co-pilot.

***

"April 29, 1944. The normal plane for this crew was the "Dorothy Dee." That B-l7 was on the ground for extensive repair, having been badly shot up on the previous mission - the "Dorothy Dee" finished the war, flying more missions than any other B-17. The replacement plane they crewed that day was flying in lead position for the group during this bomb run over Berlin.

"Flak struck the plane, damaged two engines, and knocked out the electrical system. So as the plane lost altitude, the rest of the formation followed. They tried to wave the formation off, having lost their radio when the electrical system was knocked out, but the other planes in the formation did not realize that the plane was damaged until the crew started to bail out. In fact, even the crew members toward the back of the plane didn't realize how damaged the plane actually was. When they were ordered to bail out, one crew member was remembered to have said "Is he really serious?"; another was alleged to have said "Do you know where we are?."

"They finally left the plane in a rush after the radio station was blown, perhaps thinking that the plane had just been hit. I believe all this occurred before the bombs away, somewhere near Berlin.

"Henry related that as he was approaching ground after parachuting from the plane, he saw a small band of people rushing towards where he was about to make landfall. Also he saw what looked like a small squad of military troops approaching his landing spot. He focused on a woods not too far from where he would land, and decided that heading for the woods would be better than being caught by either of the groups he saw - apparently during pre-flight briefings, crews were warned to avoid civilian groups in Germany if at all possible.

"Once he shed his chute, he started running for the trees. His mind was soon changed as the military group fired at him and yelled "Halt." He stopped, put up his hands, and surrendered.

"Much of the captured crew was assembled and stood around a fountain in the middle of the nearby town before being transported to the authorities responsible for captured prisoners of war. He spent one year to the day as a guest of the German government. He tells few tales of that year, but does relate that when first placed into a POW camp, he and other new arrivals took the hard biscuits that they were given as food, and threw them into the rafters of their huts in disgust.

He also said that a couple days later, these same new arrivals were all climbing up into the rafters to retrieve the biscuits that they had turned their noses up to when they first arrived. He became a voracious reader during captivity and he remained so for the rest of his life. He also became the camp librarian during his time in the camps. His only injury during captivity was a very bad case of frostbite in both feet.

Navigator 2Lt. Murray Jacob.

By his son Bill Jacob.

Navigator 2Lt. Murray Jacob

"My father, Murray Jacob, was born in May of 1919, in the Bronx, New York. His father, Harry Jacob worked for the Post Office in Manhattan. He had one older brother, Jules Jacob, who moved to Hollywood in the 1930's and became a musician. My father played the trumpet, but not professionally. One summer he took a job on a freight ship and traveled to South America. He went to City College in New York, where he studied account-ing. When the war broke out he enlisted in the Army.

"He was initially stationed in Washington D.C. in the coast artillery, however, wanting to see action he volunteered for the Army Air Corps. He went to officer training school in Hondo Texas, where he said it was so hot and humid that he had to place his dress pants under his mattress at night to press them, otherwise they would be wrinkled in the morning. Also, as a new recruit, he was issued overalls made of denim, however, not wanting to seem like a new recruit, he and the new other men washed them many times in order to fade them like the soldiers that had been there for a while. He went through a testing process to de-termine his skills. It was determined that he would be best suited as a navigator.

***

"He was stationed in Framlingham, England. His plane was named the *"Dor-othy Dee."* Typically when the planes flew over the English Channel they would test fire their guns. On one mission the Plexiglas nose of his plane was hit by spent shell casings from another plane and they had to fly the mission with a hole in the nose, making the conditions even worse than normal. When he started, the limit was 25 missions before you were "rotated out," however, just before he completed his 25th mission, the Air Corps increased the minimum number of missions you needed to complete.

"He was shot down on his 26th mission on April 29, 1944. Unlike easy missions which were called "milk runs," this mission was headed to Berlin, which was heavily guarded and therefore everyone knew it would be tough. They were not on the *Dorothy Dee* on that mission as it was being repaired. They had dropped their bombs and were returning to England when the plane was hit by flak. They lost one engine and dropped out of formation. The decision was made to feather the engine, or cut power, then to bail out. He went out through the open bomb bay doors. On crew member, called "horizontal" by the other men since he liked to lie down much of the time, spilled his chute in the plane because he was afraid it wouldn't open. He then gathered it up and jumped.

"My father came down and got caught in a tree. He could see a German soldier riding a bicycle through a field coming to get him, so he sat down and lit a cigarette. Since he was in the middle of a field in Germany there was nowhere to hide. He was brought to a town, where he saw other members of the crew tied up to a fountain in the Town Square. The soldiers had to protect the airmen from the German townspeople, who wanted to kill them. He was then interrogated by a Luftwaffe Officer, but first the German soldiers took his leather flying boots and leather flying jacket. He was asked his name, to which he replied, Murray Jacob. He was then asked his father's name, to which he replied, Harry Jacob. The German officer then stated, "...so you are a true son of Jacob" (making a biblical reference to the fact he was Jewish). The Luftwaffe officer then went on to say "...even though our races are at war, and you Air Gangsters have bombed my home town and killed members of my family, since you are an American Officer

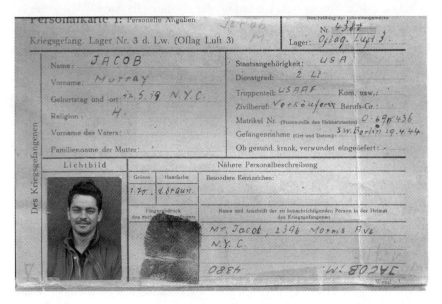

Lt. Murray Jacob, German ID Card

and we observe the Geneva convention, you will not be killed."

"He spent one year, to the day, in prison camp, first in Oflag Luft 3 - which was the camp the 1960's movie "The Great Escape" was made about - then, towards the end of the war, was marched into Bavaria to Stalag 7A. The Germans were consolidating the prisoners ahead of the American forces. On the march, every time an allied plane flew over, the men were forced to dive off the road into the shoulders in order to hide. While in POW camp he could get Red Cross packages, including chocolate bars and cigarettes. He traded a guard some chocolate for a bone handled knife which I still have.

"On the last day, April 29, 1945, they woke up to find all the guards gone. They could see a Bavarian town off in the distance and saw the Swastika come down and the American Flag go up. Then General Patton's 3rd Army came and liberated them. He was given white bread, which he said tasted like cake, compared to the blood sausage and bread made with saw dust that they were forced to eat. He was then sent to Atlantic City to recuperate.

***

"After the war, my father returned to New York, where he got a job in the garment industry. He met my mother at work and they were married shortly thereafter. They initially lived in Greenwich Village in New York, then moved to Red Bank, New Jersey where they ran a clothing factory. They then moved back to the Bronx, where I was born. In the early 60's we moved to Long Island. My father continued working in the garment industry, first in sales, then in management, until he retired in his mid 70's. When my mother passed away in 2002, he moved to Massachusetts to live with me and my family, however, shortly thereafter he had a stroke and passed away in 2004, at the age of 85.

Radio T/Sgt. Robert M. O'Hara Jr.

By Nancy Belack; sister.

"Bobby, as our family called him, was born in Pittsburgh, Pennsylvania on July 14, 1924. He was the second child of Robert Michael O'Hara Sr. and Ruth Lowery O'Hara and the only boy of five children. When he was seventeen, Bobby graduated from Carrick High School, a year earlier than his classmates and then attended Connelly Trade School, a technical and industrial training school. Because of circumstances in our family, Bobby stepped up and took over many situations, looking out for our mother and his four sisters. Even after he came back from overseas, he continued in this role.

"When war was declared in December 1941, it became difficult to find employment as potential employers knew he would be eligible for the draft at age 18. Fortunately he found a gas station job earning 25 cents an hour. While the pay was minimal, our family really needed the money. When my older sisters found jobs and were able to help the family financially, Bobby enlisted in the U.S. Air Corps in November of 1942. The reason he selected the U.S. Air Corps was because he would be away from the ground fighting and safer than the "boots on the ground guys."

"My brother did not have to join the services because he was an only son and the United States government exempted all such boys from the draft since they were the ones to carry on the family line. Many, many years later when I asked him why he joined, he answered "because it was the right thing to do."

Radio T/Sgt. Robert M. O'Hara Jr.

"By age nineteen, my brother had flown over twenty-five combat missions. On April 29, 1944, during his 27th mission, his B-17 plane took a direct flak hit and the crew was ordered to bail out. A 1964 letter from a former crew member who was fortunately not be on this mission stated: "they told me your ground crew chief wept when you guys got shot down – said you went down with all props turning practically over the middle of Berlin."

"On bailout, Bobby sustained a back injury when his parachute opened - he experienced significant pain in his lower back and legs the rest of his life. Barely conscious when he hit the ground, Bobby vaguely remembered a female farmer standing over him with a pitchfork until German soldiers arrived. He was in and out of consciousness for the next two weeks.

"Bobby and his crew were sent to Stalag 17(B) in Krems Austria where he was a prisoner of war for the next 1 year and 5 days. POWs were permitted to send postcards home, but these cards were highly censored. These cards always painted a rosy picture of otherwise horrific living conditions.

"On April 8, 1945 with the Russian Army advancing, Stalag 17 POWs were forced to march 181 miles towards the Austrian western border without proper clothing, food or shelter. They were liberated by General George Patton's 1st Army on April 25 at the junction the Inns and Salzach Rivers outside of Braunau, Austria, (Hilter's birthplace).

"When Bobby returned home, jobs were still hard to find. He worked for Trans World Airlines (TWA) and then applied for a position with the United States Postal Service. Bobby became a postman and met his future wife, Grace Hoge, while delivering the mail. They were married 52 years and had 2 daughters, Patricia and Sheila. He retired in 1980 and kept in touch with his former crew and POWs often attending reunions every few years. He died of pneumonia on March 11. 2006 and received a military burial at the National Cemetery of the Alleghenies. For his service, he received the Distinguished Flying Cross with Four Oak Leaf clusters, the Bronze Star and Purple Heart.

"My brother was like so many others who fought in the war in that he did not talk about his experiences– said nobody would believe what they saw and went through. In his gracious manner, he always credited his fellow soldiers as doing most of the work while he was in the POW camp.

Left Waist-Gunner S/Sgt. Daniel E. Chermack.

From Daniel's wartime diary

Raid # 27 Berlin

"We received a direct hit from flak between no's 3 & 4 engine. We were hit be-tween the I.P. and the target. No's 3 & 4 went dead and we started to lose altitude and being the lead ship in the low squadron the rest of the squadron started to follow us down thinking we were running on four engines because the shot out engines wouldn't feather.

"The pilot tried to to call the rest of the squadron to get them back into the formation, but couldn't contact them. German fighters were seen and reported in the area and he was forced to overboost No.'s 1 and 2 engines as a last resort to get them (the squadron) into formation. He succeeded but one engine started to bopping cylinders.

"After we had brought the squadron back into the formation, we had one en-gine left, and were forced to drop out, and lost altitude rapidly. The bail-out bell sounded the warning, and the pilot said stand-by to abandon ship, and as soon he was positive we were clear of danger, he gave the bail-out order as planned in training.

"We bailed out at 18,500 feet. After we bailed out German fighters shot down the ship, and we heard it blow up. Due to the quick and sensible thinking of the pilot, the squadron was probably saved.

Right Waist-Gunner S/Sgt. Richard K. Matanle.

Richard enlisted not long after graduation from the Thomas A. Edison High School in Elmira Heights, NY. He worked briefly at the Eclipse Machine Company in Elmira before enlisting.

"Mission 27 – 3 More and We Go Home" by R. Keith Matanle

"April 29, 1944, 12:55 p.m. We were the lead B-17 for the 390th Bomb Group, Eighth Air Force out of England. The target, "Big B" - Berlin. We had been there four times before, and I had a feeling our luck was running out. Our intelligence officers told us at an early morning briefing that the Germans had doubled the number of heavy anti-aircraft guns in and around the city.

"About 13 miles from the target the flak was so thick you could walk on it. Suddenly We took a direct hit in the starboard wing and lost both engines and a big wing section. I was flying as the right waist-gunner, and the bailout call came quickly. All ten crew members were able to get out of the burning, spinning plane, which was in itself a miracle.

"We were all captured within a few hours by German soldiers and taken to Frankfurt to Dulag Luft for interrogation. We were kept in small, damp, smelly solitary cells. They constantly took airmen out, threatening to shoot them if we didn't tell them more than name, rank, and serial number. They were particularly tough on anyone who had an H (Hebrew) on his dog tag.

"After six days of this grilling, we were loaded and locked in box cars. We were taken to Krems, Austria, where we were held in Stalag 17B. I had seen better cattle barns than the so-called barracks we found at 17. They were rough wooden barracks with one stove inside. The Germans gave us very little wood and occasionally a few pieces of coal to burn. We ended up tearing boards off the wall and taking two slats out of our bunk beds for fuel.

"We were supposed to receive one Red Cross food parcel per man per month. We soon learned we would receive one parcel for every two or three men per month or two months. The parcels consisted of four packages of cigarettes, can of instant coffee, chocolate D bars, can of powdered milk, small can of margarine, can of liver paste, can of corned beef, and one can of Spam. We formed "combines" of three or four men to share the food, cigarettes, etc. Many of us used our cigarettes to trade with the guards for onions, bread, and eggs. American cigarettes were worth $40 a pack in trading for some essential items. The guards would have been shot if caught trading with prisoners.

"The Germans furnished black bread, one loaf for three men, once a week. They also occasionally gave us potato or barley soup, which was always wormy. If you waited until it cooled, the worms came to the top. We picked them out and warmed the soup when we had fuel. Any meat we received was horse meat, which the German guards were also eating at this time. With this diet, needless to say, everyone lost considerable weight and had many health problems.

"We organized the camp with an elected commander, barracks chiefs, security force, and escape committee. We had a grievance committee to meet with the German commandant and attempt to upgrade our miserable living conditions.

"While tunneling was being done under a barracks in one compound, the other compounds would perform all sorts of diversions - fake fights, loud yelling, softball games, or everyone walking in a large circle in each compound. This usually made the commandant and guards nervous and caused us to stand a lot of roll calls, which we managed to prolong. By men standing in columns of five we could goof up the count. When the weather was good we could make a roll call last three to four hours.

"Our bunk beds consisted of six slats, two of which we burned for heat, and a straw-filled, long burlap bag, which we shared with the fleas. We were fortunate, as we had all had typhus shots. However, the Poles and Russians were not as fortunate. They had not had shots, and many died of typhus. We all experienced stomach upsets, dysentery, and severe colds. Many suffered from back and leg pains as a result of the parachuting and poor sleeping conditions.

"Any mail we received was censored to the point that it was difficult to understand what the writer was saying. Our mail going out could consist only of saying we were fine, everything was OK, or it would be destroyed by the Germans. We cooperated only so our loved ones would know we were alive.

"On April 10, 1945, the Russians were approaching Vienna, which was 60 miles from our camp. The Germans were petrified of the Russians and decided to take us on a forced march toward American lines. We marched all day and slept in fields at night. Food and water were very scarce. Everyone was suffering from blisters, dysentery, and malnutrition.

"We were 4,200 sad POWs when we reached Branau, Germany about April 26, 1945. We were forced to live in pine forest outside of Branau. The Germans got some axes and saws, and we made shelters out of pine branches.

"Three or four nights later, the Americans were on the other side of the Inn River and began shelling Branau. The Germans blew up the bridge about midnight. The German guards had disappeared during the night, we discovered. Many of us had pieces of a homemade American flag, which we pinned together with safety pins we'd saved from Red Cross parcels. We hung the flag from two trees facing the river in hopes the American troops would see it and not shell our area. Two days later we heard American tanks approaching.

"When the American troops arrived, they took us to a factory which had escaped shelling. We were kept there two or three days while receiving medical attention. We were then taken to Le Havre, France, to an American camp for liberated POWs. We were extremely disappointed when we found our stomachs had shrunk to the point where we couldn't eat a whole hamburger or drink a whole milk shake. We had dreamed about this type of food for a long time. It took several weeks before we could eat a decent meal.

"Eventually we were returned to the good old U.S.A. You don't really understand the value and benefits of living in a free country until you lose that freedom. Freedom is precious and often taken for granted. We should do whatever is necessary to preserve it.

***

After the war Richard was employed by the Marine Midland Trust Company (later Marine Midland Bank, subsequently acquired by

HSBC). He was promoted to Vice President, the position that he held when he retired. His obituary referenced his community service (Director of the Water Board, Chairman, Planning Board/Zoning Board). He enjoyed his membership in the local skeet shooting club (Fur, Fin & Feather), commenting that his shooting skills were attributable to his training in the Army Air Corps. He died on January 29, 2010 in Owing Mills, Maryland.

***

Acknowledgements;
Tim Crowley, son of co-pilot 2Lt. Henry G. Crowley.
Bill Jacob, son of navigator 2Lt. Murray Jacob.
Nancy Belack, sister of radio-operator T/Sgt. Robert M. O'Hara Jr.

CHAPTER 27

392ND BOMB GROUP 576TH BOMB SQUADRON

Type: B-24J • Serial: 42-110062
MACR: 4445 • Air Base: Wendling

On April 29, 1944, at 11:20 hours, Liberator was shot down and crashed 3 km. south of Marklendorf, district of Fallingbostel, serial no. 2110062.

German document KU 1674.

Pilot: 2Lt. Leo E. Ofenstein, 0-804718, KIA, Washington, DC

Co-Pilot: 2Lt. John J. Wall, 0-684087, KIA, Bridgeport, IL

Navigator: 2Lt. David J. Purner, 0-808142, POW, Johnson City, TN

Bombardier: 2Lt. Harold G. Buzzi, 0-682061, KIA, Garfield, NJ

Radio: S/Sgt. Roy L. Kennett, 35610937, POW, Dayton, OH

Engineer: S/Sgt. Vitold P. Krushas, 31208307, POW, Brockton, MA

Ball-Turret Gunner: S/Sgt. Arthur M. Smith, 6152284, POW, Roxbury, MA

Left Waist-Gunner: Sgt. Oliver G. Schmelzle, 3335706, KIA, Ogdensburg, PA

Right Waist-Gunner: Sgt. Hyman J. Hatton, 12180670, POW, Jamaica, NY

Tail-Gunner: Sgt. Robert W. Rowlett, 7388907, KIA, Sikeston, MO

5 KIA, 5 POW

Crash Site: Marklendorf/Hannover - Germany
Time: 11.30

Pilot 2Lt. Leo E. Ofenstein.

By his son Leo E. Ofenstein.

"My dad's father was Clarence Leo Ofenstein. It's kind of interesting to note that he was the first person in the United States to get a degree in aeronautical engineering. He was the first civilian chief of what later became the FAA. Just before the depression; he quit his very secure government position. In September of 1929, he set out to establish his own aircraft company... now this is not good timing! He no sooner got it set up, and then the great crash put the kibosh on that. He ended up working as an aircraft engineer for other people. In fact, he worked for North American-Northrop in San Diego and was the principle designer of a rather bizarre aircraft

Pilot Leo E. Ofenstein's headstone

called "*the flying wing.*" It was the grandfather of the stealth bomber of today. I think it was kind of a flop at the time; the main reason was that they didn't have computers to fly aircraft, like they do now. Anyway, my dad had a pretty solid background in aviation.

"When war broke out my father tried to enlist but was rejected. First of all, he wasn't draftable because the height limit was 6'4 and he was taller. There was another thing; he had scarlet fever as a youngster and had a heart murmur as a result. That same thing kept him out of West Point. He ended up at Virginia Military Institute instead, in aeronautics.

"When they rejected him from the service, he went around from one enlistment center to another. Finally, he found one with a doctor who didn't listen to carefully to his heartbeat. Needless to say, my mother was not thrilled by this at all...not even slightly happy about it. From that point on, both of their lives changed track dramatically. I guess a lot of people's personal dreams got put on hold "for the duration."

"One of the reasons he got involved in this whole thing was, that he was in college in the middle 30's and had to drop out. His dad couldn't afford to send all of the kids to college so, he decided make it on his own. He wanted his younger sister to go. His parents had told her that since Leo and Charles were in college, she couldn't go. So he said, "Okay, fine. I'll quit and now she can go!"

"Probably, he wanted to prove something in the field of aviation. I have a feeling it was all a part of the reason why he put himself to so much trouble to get assigned to a combat crew. Perhaps his long range plans included getting in there and having a good War; then continuing on as a commercial pilot or something of that sort. Maybe, he was planning a military career...although I kind of doubt it.

"He was apparently a hell of a good pilot. Our family has been blessed with good physical skills. One of the stories that goes around, is that my dad was just a basically good natural pilot. When the Army figured that out, he was promptly turned into an instructor. He had to do quite a bit of fast-talking and finagling to go out and get assigned to a combat crew. I know he wanted to be a fighter pilot, but his size might have gone against him there. I'm sure the combat assignment didn't sit well with my mother.

"Somewhere along the line, my father got transferred to San Antonio, Texas in conjunction with his flight training. That's where the name of the plane might have originated. I know my parents got married in Austin. He was twenty five and she was nineteen. I suppose it wasn't so unusual back then for a guy out of college to marry a girl out of high school. It's amazing to think that these people were all so young. My mother was only twenty three at the end of the war.

"I've spent a good deal of time growing up associated with the military in one way or another. After the war my mother was a civilian army employee, doing accounting. We spent several years of my youth in Europe. At one point, we moved to England and actually lived in Kings Lynn, right in the middle of the territory used by the Eighth Air Force. That part of England was full of abandoned airfields. We kids used to travel around and look at all the sights in the area, and you couldn't miss those old flat concrete strips.

"It's amazing to think the crew only lasted five weeks over there. I've heard that from late 1943 until just before D day, the life expectancy of an Eighth Air Force bomber crew was about sixty days. Something like fifty percent of them were gone in sixty days. I remember talking with a fellow from my dad's group who told me that people were just coming and going constantly...some of them didn't even get to unpack their bags. They'd come in at night, sleep, and the next day have to go out on a mission and maybe never come back. He told me it got to the point where the "old timers" didn't want to know these new people. They didn't want to grieve for anyone anymore, so maybe they just didn't get close to anyone. There has always been the image of great camaraderie, which you might have in a platoon in the infantry. There you have a whole lot of people together for a long time; but these guys weren't together for a long time!

"My dad is just pictures to me. I was just a baby; a year old when he left. I've got pictures where I'm in there with him...just a little guy all swaddled up.

Navigator 2Lt. David J. Purner

"I was a flier during WWII, stationed in England with the 8th Air Force, assigned to the 392nd Bomb Group, the 576th Bomb Squadron, flying combat missions over enemy-occupied Europe and using B-24 Consolidated Liberator bombers.

I was the navigator on my crew. During its tenure in England the 392nd BG dropped 16,000 tons of TNT on German targets while flying 285 missions. In this process my group lost 281 B-24 bombers, each with a crew of 10 men.

"On Saturday, April 29, 1944 they woke us up at 3:00 a.m. We had breakfast and went to our briefing sessions. When they unveiled the war map and we followed that ribbon up to our target for the day, we saw that it was Berlin, "Big B." Now we knew this was going to be a rough mission, and we knew, too, that many of our bombers would not be returning. Actually we were to lose 64 bombers and 14 supporting fighters, 700 men on this one mission.

"Many of you I'm sure have had the opportunity in recent years to travel in Europe and visit Germany; and I'm certain you enjoyed the beautiful German countryside under tranquil blue skies. Now imagine with me for just a moment those tranquil blue skies filled with about a thousand 4-engine bombers flying in formation in the middle of the day converging on Berlin. Now add to that another thousand friendly fighter escort, and now fill the sky with everything the German Luftwaffe could coax into the air in defense of Berlin, not to mention those deadly black puffs of ack-ack (anti-aircraft fire) that nearly blanketed the sky. That was quite a show and it taxes the imagination to paint that mental picture.

"For this all-out effort the 392nd BG put up sixteen B-24 bombers. We crossed the English Channel, flew over the Low Countries, crossed the German border, and flew past Hannover and beyond. Just as we were turning on our final leg into the target, the German Luftwaffe decided to hit the 392nd BG. They came at us out of the sun, 11 o'clock high, 50 Focke-Wolfe fighters in block formation. Each of those fighters fired machine guns out the wings and a 20-mm cannon out the nose; so that formation of 50 presented an awesome firepower as they roared directly through my group - with the result - eight of our sixteen B-24s were on their way down at the same time.

"My ship was hit hard. We had two engines out and a third on fire. The tail assembly had been nearly shot away. My crew reported fires throughout the aircraft. The bomb bay with its full load of bombs was a roaring inferno. We immediately fell out of formation, losing altitude rapidly in a flat spin. The pilot dropped the landing gear as a sign of our surrender. He would attempt to straighten the aircraft and bail the crew out or try for a crash-landing. We were hit at 20,000 feet and when we had dropped to about 15,000 the plane suddenly jerked into a tight spin and began to wind up like a 2-story house. At that same time the co-pilot hit the bailout bell.

"My escape hatch was the nose wheel door, but since the pilot had dropped the landing gear, that nose wheel was now in my way. That was the only way out, so out I went. I wound up straddle that nose wheel, sitting on a mud guard directly above the wheel with my head and shoulders still in the aircraft. Immediately and with tremendous force the slipstream ripped the boots off both my feet. I remember this as a frightening experience and a bit painful. I had been wounded in the air battle and I now had shrapnel in my left leg and foot. My foot was broken. I knew all I had to do was lay back, fall off that wheel, and pull the ripcord on my chest pack parachute. I simply couldn't do it. Oh, I tried, but the slipstream was still working against me and now with the ship spinning, the centrifugal force had me pinned against the side of the ship and I couldn't move a muscle. Every time the plane went around I could see the trees getting closer and closer. I gave up.

"I knew I was going to crash with that aircraft. There just wasn't anything I could do about it. But then at something under 1000 feet the aircraft exploded and I was blown free. I began to scratch frantically for my ripcord, couldn't find it and began to panic until I glanced up and saw my chute was already open and swinging wildly, all but spilling among all the flying debris and billowing smoke. Without first seeing it I hit the ground in my socked feet and I hit it hard. I saw German troops scouring the landscape, looking for downed parachutists like myself. I dropped to the ground and wiggled out to the center of a large field and lay there afraid to move, afraid to breathe. I was scared to death.

"In just a few minutes I spotted Arthur Smith, the tail-gunner from my crew. I called to Smitty and he wiggled out to where I was and we lay there together. In a short while we watched the mighty 8th AF flying in formation back to England. Not a very pretty picture! Almost immediately my wounds became a big concern. They didn't look good. They were painful and I didn't have any medication with which to treat them. I found some chlorine pills in my escape kit and purified some water from an irrigation ditch in that field. Having been in retailing before the war, I knew there was a white lining in the collar and cuffs of my officer's shirt. I ripped these out and washed and bound my wounds as best I could, but that foot would swell to three times its size and turn every color in the rainbow. It was a source of worry and I was fearful of the possibility of losing my foot or leg.

"Sgt. Smith and I had to have a plan. We couldn't lie in that field for the rest of the war, so after some discussion we decided to head north and try to reach the Baltic. I was a navigator and knew precisely where we were. Reaching the Baltic we would look for a ship flying the Swedish flag, steal aboard, stow away and sail off to neutral Sweden. For the next three days Sgt. Smith and I managed to evade capture, traveling at night and hiding during the days.

"On the third day we were hiding in a little wooded area waiting for it to get dark, but about dusk some German children from nearby houses came into the woods to play. A little girl hid behind a tree directly above my head and it wasn't long before she spotted me and ran off screaming the alarm. Smitty and I got out of there and tried to hide again in a nearby wooded plot, but by this time the entire German populace was out looking for us. They crisscrossed that woods and it wasn't long before they flushed us out. Now we are faced with a large crowd of about two hundred German civilians, very angry and very vocal. They were armed with everything. They had guns, pitchforks, clubs, dogs, rocks, spit; you name it, they had it.

"Smitty and I were beaten, hit with clubs, rocks, spit on, cursed. We were resigned to the fact that we were going to be hung. They had a rope. It was around my neck and they were pushing us toward a tree when two older men armed with Lugers finally persuaded the young hotheads in charge of that mob that we should be held for military interrogation. They saved our lives. We were pushed down a road into town and thrown into a barn-like structure that was obviously their town hall. Here we were beaten and questioned repeatedly. They were trying to find the rest of our crew and they thought we could help them. This went on until about 2:00 a.m., when we were turned over to some Luftwaffe personnel. They took us to a nearby slave labor camp and we spent our first night there.

"The men in this camp had been brought in from the Low Countries as slave laborers to work the surrounding fields. The next morning as we prepared to leave, these men lined up to bed us goodbye and one of them pressed a pair of felt house shoes in my hands. He had noticed I was wounded and in my sock feet. Under the circumstances, that man gave me a fortune and I have always regretted that I was never able to properly thank him. Then we were placed aboard a German troop train under guard. Smitty and I stood between the feet of three German troops on either side of that little train compartment. These troops were in full field pack and heading for the western front, anticipating the coming invasion. They weren't absolutely thrilled with their assignment; we all knew it was going to be bloody and they weren't at all pleased to have Smitty and I standing between their feet. This made for a very long train ride from Celle south to Frankfort.

"As we reached the outskirts of Frankfort, I was exposed for the first time to the complete devastation of aerial bombardment. I recall looking out the window of that train trying to pick out a whole building. I saw rubble. I saw walls, but I could never spot a complete building. Frankfort had been bombed repeatedly. On the edge of Frankfort was a German POW camp called Dulag Luft. Its primary function was for the military interrogation of captured allied fliers. At Dulag Luft I was placed in solitary confinement. My cell was very small, very confining. It had no window, no running water, and one naked light bulb. It was furnished with a single uncomfortable cot, period. The door was solid steel, and that made it all the more confining.

"Each morning I was given a slice of bread and a glass of water and then plenty of time to think and to worry and ponder my fate. I was concerned about my wife. I knew she would be receiving a telegram that I was missing in action and I knew she would be worried. I was concerned, too, about my crew. At this time I was not sure what had happened to them, and I was very concerned about myself. What was to be my fate? As the days dragged by, the walls of that little cell began to close in and the silence became a deafening roar. I craved to hear a human voice, even my own, so I began to talk out loud just to hear my voice. I recited everything I had ever learned in school or Sunday school; The Lord's Prayer, the twenty-third Psalm, over and over just to hear my voice.

"Then I found a small piece of brown paper on the floor and I tore it into 52 pieces the size of my thumbnail. I broke a piece of lead wire off the cot and, using that as a pencil, I created a deck of playing cards and I played solitaire, game after game of solitaire just to keep my mind occupied and keep from going nuts. Let me say this about solitary confinement: It can be a very dehumanizing, traumatic experience. You feel very much alone and surrounded by well-trained experts who know very well how to apply the psychological pressure. But I survived that and was informed that I was being sent to a permanent POW camp, Stalag Luft III located in Silesia, clear across Germany. It would require a four-day train trip.

"When I was being admitted to Dulag Luft, all of my belongings were taken from me; but as I was leaving, a young German clerk pressed my wedding band into my hand…an act of compassion for which I have been forever grateful.

"This time we were placed in small box cars made to hold 48 men, but they crammed up to 150 in a car. We were packed in so tightly we couldn't all sit at the same time. We took turns standing and sitting. We were locked in those cars without food, without water, and with no toilet facility. Many men were sick and began to vomit. My wounds had not been treated and were showing signs of infection; I was quite concerned about that. With no toilet facility and under these conditions, that four-day train trip became a real traumatic nightmare.

"When we arrived at Stalag Luft III, I was placed in a so-called hospital. It actually was a POW barracks used for that purpose and staffed by doctors who were themselves POWs, having been picked up in North Africa, Dunkirk, or wherever. They were using very meager Red Cross supplies and doing the very best they could; no wonder drugs. Here my wounds were probed to remove foreign matter behind my tendons. Then my leg was elevated and for seven weeks saline compresses were applied. Salt water is very healing and after seven weeks my wounds had healed sufficiently that I could be transferred to the regular camp.

"Here I was placed in an eight-man cooking combine. At this point in the war we were very fortunate to have a small supply of Red Cross food parcels. A food parcel was very small, about 12 inches square and 6 inches deep. They were doled out very carefully, 1/8 parcel per man per week, so that eight of us could control one complete parcel. Using water to make soups and stews, we would attempt to stretch that food and make it last a week. It was tough to do.

"Once this supply of parcels was depleted, we would see no more for the duration of the war, and that was when things really got rough. That was when the starvation diet really set in. I remember eating something called barley soup with little black specks floating on top. When a new "Kriegie" would join a cooking combine, he might start to pick the black specks out, but the older Kriegies would jump on him like a bird on a June bug and yell, "Don't pick 'em out! If you don't like 'em, don't eat 'em, but don't pick 'em out!" You see, the little black specks were actually little black heads on little white worms. I've been told that, once cooked, that made for good protein, but I wouldn't recommend it. Before the end of the war we got down to grass soup. Sometimes it had horse bones in it. There was never any meat on those bones, but we cut cards for the bones so the lucky man could break the bones and eat the marrow in an effort to survive.

"Now that became the name of the game: Survival! When you first are captured, a feeling of utter helplessness and hopelessness engulfs you, but that gives way to extreme anger at your situation, and then this motivating desire to survive sets in. You begin to tell yourself over and over, I will survive. I don't know if it's for one year, five years or ten, but I will survive. I'll eat anything. I'll do anything, but I will survive. Without that motivating desire under certain circumstances, there could be no survival.

"As the war dragged on we knew the Russians were approaching from the east and we had high hopes they would reach our camp and liberate us. But Adolph Hitler had issued a decree and kept promising the Germans that the Allied flyers who had bombed German cities unmercifully would never be allowed to leave the POW camps. We expected at some time an attempt at annihilation. So when the Russians got close enough for us to hear gunfire, Hitler's decree held and we were placed on the road in a forced march in the middle of the night and in the middle of the coldest winter in Germany in 100 years, with snow and ice on the ground at 20 degrees below zero.

"For the first 72 hours we marched, running from the Russians without food, water, or shelter. Our casualties were high. Frozen extremities were commonplace. I survived that march using some lump sugar, some dried prunes, and one concentrated chocolate D bar that I had saved when we had the food parcels for just such an occasion. I drank snow.

"We arrived at our second camp Stalag XIII D at Nuremberg. A real hell hole. The filth of this camp is indescribable. We had no soap; very little water. We cleaned the floor and table of our barracks using brick and sand. We shaved the hair from our bodies in an attempt to keep clean, but we became vermin infested. I had bedbugs. I had fleas and body lice. At night when you would try to sleep, the vermin would eat. My hips, wrists, and ankles were eaten raw, and I carried sores from that for a long time after coming home.

"At night we were locked in our barracks, and our toilet facility was a G.I. garbage can with a board across the top. Most nights were spent standing in line for a turn at the barrel, which inevitably overflowed. Most of us were sick with dysentery and jaundice. At Nuremberg we were on the receiving end of bombardment when the allies bombed Nuremberg 15 days in a row; the British at night and the Americans during the day. It was nerve wracking sine the camp was located one-half mile from the railroad marshalling yards. Four barracks in the camp had been wiped out.

"But once again our morale was high. These were our people approaching Nuremberg and this time we would be liberated. Hitler's decree held and we were put on the road in a second forced march. This time we were in no condition to make a march. We had been on a prolonged starvation diet. We had no medical or dental care. If you got a toothache, you toughed it out; if you got sick, you prayed. My body weight had dropped to 95 pounds. But we made that march, and this time our column was strafed on three separate occasions by our own fighters.

They couldn't tell from the air that we were POWs and they had orders to shoot anything that moved. Fortunately, only three POWs were killed, but several were wounded.

"We arrived at our third POW camp, Stalag VII A at Moosburg. This camp was designed to hold 10,000 POWs, but upon our arrival they had crammed over 100,000 into that camp. It was chaotic. Food and water were all but nonexistent, as was shelter. We slept on the ground. Fortunately in just a few days, General Patton and his 3rd Army with their beautiful tanks overtook us at Moosburg and, after a pitched battle with fanatical SS troops, he liberated our camp.

"Liberation Day! That has to be the highlight of my 78 years. I remember standing in that camp looking toward the town. There was a little white church in the immediate distance and G.I.s had raised Old Glory of that little church. I had been separated from my flag and all she stands for, the protection she gives, for over a year. As I watched, the breeze caught her and she fluttered beautifully, and I began to cry. I cried like a baby, unashamed. Today when Old Glory passes me in a parade, oftentimes I cry.

"In closing, let me say it is never my intention to glorify war, God forbid. But I do feel an obligation to reach out, especially to young people, and remind them that their American freedoms were not free.

"For more than 50 years I have lived knowing full well that on April 29, 1944, at precisely 11:30 a.m., the Lord saved me. He pulled me from a spinning aircraft and opened my parachute. Some people have a hard time with that. Some people find that hard to believe, but I know; I never pulled my ripcord. But that has left me with a terrible guild complex. He saved me, but my pilot, my co-pilot, my bombardier, my ball-turret gunner, and my little 18-year-old gunner were all killed in that crash. He saved me; why me?

Engineer S/Sgt. Vitold P. Krushas.

From "Staring at the Sky"

"April 29, 1944: Their B-24 crossed the English Channel on a daylight run, their eighth mission, although only five were actually recorded in the Bomber Command books. Mechanical problems had sent Vit and crew home on three missions without dropping their bombs; tough luck, fellas, no bombs, no credit. Thirty-one complete missions bought a ticket home, a long-shot outcome at this stage of the war.

Vit was a top-turret gunner - dream job for a kid who loved guns and planes - and on this day he was one of thousands of gunners in 751 bombers thundering toward the Friedrichstrasse Railroad Station in Berlin. The flak was pretty thick - you had to fly right through it - when 50 German fighter planes came in rows of ten out of the sun. "Like a flock of blackbirds," says Vit.

"Now if you want a primer on how to operate a machine gun, how the bullets come out of the muzzle and hit walls of streaming air, how to gauge angles and firing radiuses and what deflection shooting means, then Vit's your man. He had trained for months, he was top-class. But on that day it did not matter, and it still bothers Vit, the crack rifle-club shot, the kid who could spatter a squirrel at 40 yards, that he could not protect the plane. In seconds his right 50mm and its elevation motor were shot up. He could see the German pilots just off the wing tips. There was nothing he could do.

"The plane burned wing tip to wing tip, says Vit, "aluminum peeling off like wax paper," and below him the fuel tanks - "they looked like coffins"—burst afire. Vit knew they were going to their deaths, and the only way out was through the open bomb-bay doors. Vit slapped on his parachute but the damn thing was upside down and covered with burning fuel, and he struggled to get it latched right. Then he leaned forward, 25,000 feet over Germany, and fell.

"His float down seemed to take ages, a lifetime between sky and earth, and at one point a Me-109 fighter appeared. Vit hung loose, as if dead. The plane swerved away. Finally, approaching fast, he saw "a golden field, yellow from early spring" and he landed in a tree with one of the chute cords wrapped like a noose around his neck. He blacked out. That was it.

"Lucky for Vit, a German cut him down from the tree. He awoke to a new world. His savior wore a civil-defense hat and let Vit lean on his bicycle as they moved along. He took the American flier home to show his family - his wife had a sister in Boston - and Vit wondered if this wasn't his lucky day. Maybe they would hide him. Maybe he had found the underground. Then the military arrived, very business like, and several days later Vit stepped off a boxcar and walked into Stalag 17B, a prison for noncommissioned officers and less-than-human Russians.

"All his life, Vit says, he lived on hot dogs, hot dogs, hot dogs. Oh boy, those jumbo dogs from Howard Johnson's restaurant, he would bike an hour for one of those! At Stalag 17B it was rutabaga or potato soup for lunch, with maggots like grains of rice. For breakfast and dinner, hot water. Red Cross parcels were infrequent. During his year of captivity, Vit withered from 165 to 100 pounds, and come winter the fragile, shivering POWs burned tar paper from the barracks walls for heat. Roll calls were constant, day or night, sun or sleet, and the camp was surrounded with two barbed-wire fences charged with electricity. A deadline wire had been strung inside the fences; step over the line, you're dead.

"But still, it was not always awful. They had their moments. At night the POWs played poker, the games lit by socks filled with butter they acquired from trading cigarettes with the guards. POWs had the better cigarettes - Avalons, Wings, and Red Dogs for poker or trading with other prisoners. Old Golds and Camels for greasing the palms of Germans. A batch of Camels fetched radio parts, and for awhile the POWs even managed a tunnel between the American and Russian compounds.

"In early April 1945, the POWs were marched out of 17B in groups of 500, as Russian artillery sounded from the east. Vit had kept active in the camp, even as he starved, so the daily 20-mile march was not excruciating for him. The big problem was scrounging for food, scraps, anything to fill your stomach. As the days passed Vit could not help marveling at the beauty of the Austrian countryside, and the deer bounding across clearings reminded him of the Green Mountains of Vermont where he had hunted. At the same time, men were dying of illness and starvation all around him, and some POWs who ran from the column were killed by civilians or German patrols.

"One day, as they tromped uphill, the POWs were directed to look at the house where Adolf Hitler was born. There was nothing special about it. A house like all the rest. Another day, as the column moved into Breneau Woods, Vit encountered a little Bavarian boy in front of an Alpine house. The boy carried a "beautiful engraved knife," he remembers, inlaid with a swastika. In the steel were carved the Words "Blut und Ehre." Blood and Honor, the SS motto.

"The American flag saved them once, says Vit. On a straight road, just out of the mountains, a P-47 roared down and strafed the column. POWs and guards jumped into the brush; several men were hit. On the second pass, a couple of POWs unfurled the American flag and used it to signal the plane. It veered away, tipping its wings.

"It's a hell of a lot more than a symbol," states Vit, and with startling anger he criticizes a girl at a local high school who turned her back on the flag during an assembly, her way of protesting the war in Iraq. He is reluctant to admit that it may have taken some courage for the girl to do such a thing. What would she and Vit, who glimpsed hell, say to each other if they sat down together?

"The march ended at a prison camp north of Breneau, Austria, and the POWs built lean-tos from pine logs. It was cold and snowing, but still Vit noticed the buds showing on the tips of tree limbs, the buds so fragile and dusted white in the first days of May. And he spied, days later as he scooped water from a river, white-starred tanks in the distance. "Patton's here!" he cried, "Patton's here!"

***

"While Vit's wife Anna stayed in the hospital for the last time, volunteers from their church renovated the Krusha's living room. So now the walls are painted soft green and the moldings and baseboards are cut sharp and snug. A pyramid of logs, constructed by Vit to burn for hours, glows in the new granite fireplace. Anna loved fireplaces, but did not live to see the final product. "We never imagined we wouldn't get her home," he says.

"In the critical care unit Vit got in the habit of staring at his wife's heart monitor. He would watch the line go up and down, up and down, and he thought about how he had suffered from a "runaway heart" as a young man with a family to support on a machinist's salary, and how he had learned to calm his heart by holding his breath, by keeping the frantic present and ugly past out of himself. So Vit tried that sometimes, at her bedside, holding his breath so Anna's heart would calm. The nurses had to turn off the heart monitor because it was upsetting him too much.

"There is too much space, not enough furniture in this renovated room. Not enough stuff collecting ages of dust. It has been, like he says, a hell of a year. So many loved ones gone and no energy to shovel snow or dig in the garden. Skinny as a sapling, Vit folds into his chair. He smokes a pipe and tells his war stories. All the while a black-and-white cat they adopted years ago, named Kitty, comes and goes as she pleases.

"Vit Krushas continued to lose weight over the next 13 months. He died of a stroke in January 2005 and now his ashes have been placed next to Anna's.

Gunner S/Sgt. Roy L. Kennett.

From the website stalagluft4.org.

"I was kind of worried about jumping before I did it – I didn't know if I could do it, but in our case, there I was standing in the bomb bay with fire all around me. I didn't think twice about it. I said to myself "Gee, mothers going to worry now!" Well, finally I landed - I ran - tried to get away and they caught me - they took me to a little town that was close by there and threw me into a stable. I was in there overnight and the next day a policeman came and took me to a Gestapo headquarters. They kept me there overnight in a cell.

"The following day I went by train to the camp Dulag Luft near Frankfort. It was the interrogation center and they put me there for several days. I was alone in a cell; they gave me a piece of bread every day and some water - that's all. Then they took me out, put me in a room with an interrogator and he's got this questionnaire. He asks me my name, rank and serial number and then these other questions. I tell him: "I'm sorry; I can't give you that information." He keeps asking me these other questions and I keep telling him, "My name is Roy L. Kennett - staff sergeant - Army serial number ----- "

"Well, he starts to yell and scream at me." Dis is for de ret chross! Don't you vant you mutt er and fatter to know ver you are? If you anser dees kvestions, you can go out ant play wis zee boys!" You can see out the window, there are guys in the stockade throwing a baseball around. So after a while he says; "We already know the answers to all this anyway; we know who your pilot was and your bombardier." He tells me what kind of a plane we flew and where we were stationed and the whole thing.

"Then they take me out and who should come walking down the hallway, but Hymie Hatton, one of our gunners! And that's when we met for the first time after the crash. We grabbed each other and hugged each other...and they took us both out to the stockade.

"I had been in solitary and hadn't seen anybody (since the crash) until I came out of interrogation. Hymie was standing down the end of the hall, waiting. There were 4 or 5 of us waiting. After we went into the stockade, we spoke to Krushas. He was really despondent and didn't want to talk. It was a rough time for all of us.

"After several days they took us on a truck or train up to the Baltic Sea. At Memel, we went first class on a regular passenger train, though I can't remember the route. We had a compartment, but they didn't let us look out of the windows. It was a civilized journey, that particular ride and it was the only one! Hydekrug was our camp (Stalag Luft VI) in East Prussia on the border of Lithuania.

"I remember a boy from camp got a letter from his mother, which said they had a German prisoner who was working on their farm. They gave him the guys' room and hoped the German people were being as nice to him as they were being to the German boy! They'd take the kid to the movies on Friday night and take good care of him. Well, our boy reads the letter, goes over to the wall in the barracks and starts beating his head on the wall! We said, "Wait a minute what are you doing?" He says," Read that goddamn letter - that friggin krout! Yah know? "

"Right at the end of the war, they marched us down to Nuremberg -which is where our final camp was. It was right outside of that stadium where they had the Olympic games. They moved some of the prisoners from Luft 3 into our compound. That's when we saw Dave Purner, our navigator, again.

"When we first got to Nuremberg, the Senior American Officer, named Spivey, came into our enlisted men's compound. He said he wanted 25 orderlies to come over to the officers' side to sweep out the officers' rooms. Well - nobody would go and he threatened us. People were yelling things at him from the ranks and he said "He is going to have us court marshaled." "Who said that" and so forth. Well, he finally left and never came back; but can you imagine that. That big blow hard guy believed that officers were God and enlisted men were servants; and we'd better hop to or else he'd make trouble for us. Everybody was yelling obscenities at him from the ranks. He kept on trying to find out who was saying that to him!

"Some of the officers came over to our compound, when they first came in to Nuremberg. After they got things straightened out they put all the officers into a separate camp. I remember one of the guys had a bad case of diarrhea. I had a few extra rolls of toilet paper and I gave him some, because he was in such bad shape. We cut up cigarette packages to make playing cards and toilet paper. If you rubbed them between your palms a whole lot, then straightened them out, you could make them real soft. I had a whole stack which I made (along with some regular toilet tissue from the Red Cross package). I figured the guy needed them more than I did.

"Hymie Hatton was with me up at Luft IV, but Smitty was there in Nuremberg. That Smitty was something else; always ready to mix it up. We used to play a lot of bridge to kill time. One day, I was playing with Verdie and Smitty was partners with some other guy. Smitty's sitting there and he puts up the Ace of Clubs; the King is gone. I've got the Queen in my hand and a couple of little Clubs. I reach into my hand to take out the Deuce of Clubs, and throw it down. Instead it's the Queen, so I say "Whoa - I didn't mean to play the Queen." Well Smitty comes back with "A card laid is a card played!"

"About that time the table went flying and Smitty hit me, so I hit him; and we went round and round. We had a hell of a fight! There was a heavy little pot bellied stove with Klim cans tied together to make a pipe, and that whole thing came crashing down. All 26 guys in the room were trying to grab us before we could get at each other!

"It's a funny thing, but the Germans gave us stoves without stove pipes. We took Klim cans and cut slices in them on the edges. Then we'd save those metal strips you get when you open the can with a key; they would be clinched all around the outside of the joints. You would stack them up on top of the stove and put it out through the chimney. That way we could use our stoves.

"On April 4, 1945, they decided to move us to Munich, Germany and we moved out of Nuremberg. When we left on that April fourth march, Smitty and I talked it over. We said: "Now this will probably be a good time to escape." We don't know how soon the war's going to be over or anything. Smitty says: "Yeah, I think you're right." I said, "If we see a chance, let's go!" So he says, "OK, I'll stay behind you. If we see a chance and you think its ok, then I'll be right behind you!" I said, "Oh-Kay!"

"So we're walking down the road and these P-47's come over us and do an Immelmann. They start strafing us from the back and are coming towards us. Well - everybody starts jumping into the ditch - POWs are running up and down this road. There's no guards, so I say, "Now's my chance!" I take off through the woods like a scared ape and I get way up on the side of a hill. I turn around and say, "We made it Smitty!"

"Well, by God, Smitty's no where around! He's lying down there in the ditch and I'm all by myself. So I get up there on the side of that hill and watch, while they reform the column. The planes are gone and they march away. I just set up there and watched them leave.

"I was free for about seven or eight days, trying to work my way back to the front lines. I followed the sun and the stars (I kept them in line - just kept walking and when the sun came up, I knew which way was east. I could just keep it behind me and then I'd tried to hide during the day. At night I'd go out again.

"That was a story unto itself, because so many things happened to me during those seven days. I met one of those guys who flew the P-47's over us on that march. He told me, that their orders were to "fly over Germany and **shoot anything that moves**." They didn't know that we were prisoners of war; they just thought that we were German troops going towards the front. When I was sitting up there on the side of the hill, I could see guys hooking towels together - anything that was white! They went out into the field and made a big "POW" sign.

"This pilot ended up being my boss, a few years after I got out of college and we got to be buddies. One day we started to talk about our war experiences and it turned out that he was a fighter pilot. I was telling him about our being strafed by P-47's and he said "Hey that was me! I remember that ... there was a long string of guys down there and four of us. We just flew over you, then rolled over and started shooting at you guys. Our orders were to shoot anything that moved! "Well," I said to him, "you dirty so and so" - He replied, "Heck, we didn't know!" Well, we both had a laugh over it.

"Smitty told me later, that, he had the best time as a prisoner after that strafing business. The column moved on and farmers were coming out, trading for eggs and bread. The guards got pretty lax. When I came back home on the ship I met some of the guys who had gone down to Munich and they had been liberated too. Well, they said that it was really a mistake for me to have run off like that, because it was the easiest time they had ever had as prisoners. They were trading cigarettes to farmers. They were getting fresh eggs and cooking them down along side the road. They were just having a picnic. The German guards knew the war was over and they didn't care.

"I had a little something to eat. I carried with me the crackers and grape jam in those short cans that come in the Red Cross packages. The guards hadn't punched ours with a bayonet, the way they usually did. I also had a D-Bar and two boxes of Domino sugar. That sugar kept me going for quite a while.

"I stopped one night and dug out some potatoes that were in a farmer's field. They buried them over there, under big mounds, and I could dig down and get some.

"That night I had an interesting experience. It scared the hell out of me. I was walking down this road, and I was hungry. I spied one of those mounds and I thought this must be full of potatoes. I went over to it and started digging down, when all of a sudden dogs started barking. It seemed like there were dogs all over Germany. I though: "Oh my God! They're after me!" So I got up and started running down this road to get away from them. Just then, these sirens started going off. I thought: "They've seen me and they're blowing the sirens! Pretty soon they'll be after me with cars and motorcycles and trucks!" I saw these other big dirt mounds - maybe four or five of them alongside the road. I ran over to them, but they were pretty high, so I laid down right along the edge of one of them.

"Soon, a bunch of Germans came running out of a building - maybe fifty yards away. They were coming right towards me! I'm thinking: "Oh .... They got me!" Well, they come up and start to climb those mounds and get down inside (up at the top). I laid there as they went along this little path right by me. It was pitch black and I could see them against the sky as I looked up, but nobody saw me.

"They were all up in the mounds, but I couldn't figure out what they were doing. I laid there for ten or fifteen minutes and listened as they talked to each other. I was afraid I would sneeze or breathe too loudly. Finally the siren went off again - it was the "all clear" signal. The Germans all came down off those mounds and headed for their barracks. I crawled up there when they were gone to look: Do you know what I was in? I was right in the middle of a flak battery. They had those great big guns up there and I was lying right in the middle of all that crap. If they would have caught me, they would have killed me for sure. They'd have figured I was trying to sabotage their guns! Boy, I sure cleared out of there fast.

It was getting daylight and people were starting to move about. A German guard from the Volksturm was standing on a bridge. He was a policeman with a long green coat and a hat with the spike on top. A milkman with a tricycle type of milk cart was selling stuff to the people walking by me. They were saying "morgen" and I'd say "morgen" under my breath.

"I've got a knit hat on, that I'd made out of the sleeves of a Canadian blue sweater and it had "USA" written across the top. I had a U.S. Army overcoat with British shoes, okay. So there I was, sticking out all over and I say "morgen" and keep right on walking. I'm thinking: "The only chance I have, is to get across that river and into the woods over there. But there's a guard on the bridge!"

"I kept on walking and I got pretty close to the bridge. I bent over, with my head down and my arms tucked in, and I let spit drip down onto my chin and started to breathe heavy. I went: "Hughh .... ahhh ... hughhh ... ahhh ... hughhh..." You know, I walked right by that guard, right across the bridge and straight into the woods. He never stopped me; he just stood there looking, shaking his head.

"I was out in the middle of woods with no place to hide. A big patch of brambles was all there was. So I tunneled into it and unrolled the British blanket I had on my back. t was daylight when I finally pulled the blanket up over my head.

"After some time, I awoke and heard people out in the woods, having a picnic. It was a bunch of frolicking boys and girls. I thought, "Oh damn it, couldn't they find someplace else to have their picnic?"

"A guy and a girl came walking down towards my bramble bush and saw me in there (my head was only a foot inside the bush). They crawled under, stuck their hands up and pulled back the blanket to see what was under it. I looked up, saw them, and then pulled the blanket back over my head. "Nichts," I said real loud. The girl looked at me and said, "Ohh - Schlafen gutt." They left me alone and never turned me in.

"I went through a little village while they were evacuating it.I knew I was getting close to the frontlines. There was a wagon and people climbing on it. Meanwhile, I was doing my act, limping and so forth. This feldwebel (that's sergeant in German) says to me "Blah blah blah - blah." I said back to him, "jawohl" and kept on walking. He comes over to me, grabs me by the shoulder and spins me around. He points to the wagon and tells me again in German, "Boo lagga da blaggada blah blah!" You know ... so I say to him "Yawohl" and just keep on walking: He shrugs his shoulders and says "Humphh" as if to say "Get on the wagon - we'll give you a ride away from here." And I'm walking forwards to the front lines. I guess he was saying "To hell with you - go on ahead!" He let me go - boy that was something!

"Later that night, the Germans were marching troops up to the front lines. They were really old guys and I watched from the woods as they sat around smoking their pipes. Big fat guys, they were, with big old mustaches.

"Now I thought, "What better way, then to just follow them!" So I'm following along and I think: "This is crazy, me fighting through the woods - when I could be out there on the road walking right along with them." These old guys were talking with each other as they marched and pretty soon someone said "Take five (or whatever they say in German) ". Well, they all sat down and lit their pipes up, so I sat down right close to them. When their sergeant hollered for them to get up again, I just fell in and marched right along with them all night! With U.S.A. on the front of my cap! It was dark and they weren't allowed to have any lights.

"When it started to get daylight, I skidded off into the woods and found a place to hide. I knew I was real close now, because I could hear the small arms fire. Eventually I got into a little town with a river and I knew the front lines were right across there. I figured to get across and find some place to hide, because I thought the Germans would be defending the river. I thought: "If I can get across one more river, get in about half a mile and get low... I can wait for our troops to go by, stand up and surrender. I will have successfully escaped."

"I went into the town, but I don't want to go into the river. It had rained on the 5th or 6th of April and I had just gotten dry. Walking all night in the rain gets you soaking wet and I'd had enough of that - no, I wasn't going to swim across that river.

"I found a doorway overlooking this little bridge and just watched and waited. First two people crossed over, and then someone went by on a bicycle. A couple of ladies were going out towards the woods to gather firewood and they came back with bundles under their arms. Those woods over there were always so darn clean because of this. Time passed on and I thought, "Well, there's nobody around."

"It was quiet. I imagine the time was around 3:30 or 4:00 in the morning, so I walked away from the doorway and out towards the bridge. Boldly, I walked across ... there was nobody about and I tried to act like I was a regular citizen just going about my business.

"Well ... I got half way over that bridge when every German in the world jumped out and said, "Halt - halt." They had guns and everything. They wanted my "pistole" but of course, I wasn't armed.

"My hands up in the air, they marched me across and took me to a little room somewhere. I figure they were a home guard watching that bridge for anything suspicious. They saw me in the doorway and just waited for me to make my move. Then they grabbed me. I never will understand why all of a sudden they paid so much attention to me. I didn't hear or see anyone and I don't even know where they came from!

"After I was recaptured, they put me in jail overnight in Nuremberg. It was the same jail where they would hold prisoners for the Nuremberg trials...they put me in a cell there with a couple of Aussies...I think there were three and the Aussies wanted some water. The Germans wouldn't give us any - well they had tin cups and they went up to the bars and yelling "Vasser-Vasser" and the guards came running down there and told em to be quiet .Pointed their guns at 'em and everything - well - they just kept it up !! I thought any minute they were going to fire right into the cells and just do away with all of us. They didn't fire, but those Aussies were crazy...they'd do anything.

"Anyway, they caught me and took me and right back to the camp that they had first moved us out of. A couple of weeks later, Patton's 7th Army came in there and liberated us.

"We had to stay there (after liberation) for a couple of days. Trucks were going through all the time carrying German prisoners. I bummed a ride with one of those guys and it took me back to the rear lines. We just had to find our way back by ourselves. Those front line troops who came in there and liberated us - they took the Germans ,made them prisoners, sent them back, and then they went on up to the lines. They didn't have time to fool with us!

"We got back, one way or another, to the rear echelon. There they organized us, took our names, did all that kind of stuff. But you had to get back pretty much on your own, because those guys that were fighting' had other things to do. They couldn't be fooling around with us.

When I got to Nancy or Evian, France, I got in with a group of guys who came from my area of Ohio. They had a bunch of German prisoners there - they had a compound for the prisoners and they asked me if I'd like to see the German prisoners quarters. Well, I said "yeah." They had Simmons mattresses on their beds; they had sheets and pillows with pillowcases. I couldn't believe it!!! I couldn't believe that the Americans were treating them so good. I bet they didn't even have it so good in their own army! The Americans really took the Geneva Convention seriously.

***

"When I got to Camp Attleboro, Indiana they gave us all new clothes. I go in the mess hall, and there's German prisoners behind the mess line - they were working back in the kitchen. Americans were passing out the food. I go along there and two Germans were sitting back at a table in back of the kitchen area.

"This German gets up and comes over to the food line with his tray. He just starts dipping in there, throwing food up on his tray - and this guy who was working in the mess line says nothing. I tell him I want some more potatoes or something so he says, " Eat what you have - come back if you want some more."

"All of us were prisoners who'd just gotten back and that didn't sit well with us. - Well...I was the first one over the steam table after that guy and then the rest of the guys stormed over -- all, this clatter and noise brings the mess officer running out, wanting to know what was going on .The guys told him, you know, so he says "ok-ok. Everything is alright now - just get back over on the other side of the line. You give these guys whatever they want!"

Tail-Gunner Sgt. Robert W. Rowlett.

From the *Sikeston Standard* of May, 19, 1944.

"Sgt. Robert "Wayne" Rowlett, 20, who could knock a sparrow out with a BB-gun when he was a kid in Sikeston was reported missing last May 15. Wayne was a gunner on a flying fort and had been in England since three weeks before Christmas.

"He is the grandson of Mr. and Mrs. Robert Gunter of Sikeston and has made his home with his grandparents almost all his life. Wayne had a premonition that things might not go right but he was not depressed. In his last letter to his grandparents, received two weeks ago, he said; "I don't care much about flying over there and have the Germans shoot at me. They are getting pretty good with their flak guns."

"Wayne attended school in Sikeston and worked at the Star Restaurant until he enlisted over a year ago. He has a brother, Pvc. Warren Rowlett, also of Sikeston, who is in North Africa with the Signal corps. Both boys enlisted at the same time.

"The grandfather, Robert Gunter, a mild soft spoken man said they hope for the best. "Maybe Wayne is in one of these prison camps. Mother and I pray so, anyway. All that, as long as it was going to happen, I'm glad it happened over Germany; cause Wayne always said the he would never surrender to a Jap." He said; Grandpa, I got a .45 and it is fully loaded and if I go down where the Japs can get me I'm going to fight until all bullets are gone." And he meant it too.

"Wayne's last letter, addresses to his Grandmother he called "Mother" follows; " Dear Mother. I hope this letter finds you all well. I am still up and going. I think I am going to London on a three day pass in the next few days. I hope so. If Marshall is at home now, have him write to me sometime. I haven't heard from him for ages. Well, I have in three of my missions now. I'll sure be glad when I have them all in."

"This letter was followed in two weeks by the Government's telegram informing the Grandparents that Wayne was missing in action.

***

Acknowledgements;
Leo E. Ofenstein, son of Pilot 2Lt. Leo E. Ofenstein
Engineer S/Sgt. Vitold P. Krushas's story appeared in "Journey Out of Darkness"

CHAPTER 28

392ᴺᴰ BOMB GROUP
576ᵀᴴ BOMB SQUADRON

Type: B-24J • Serial: 41-100371
MACR: 4476 • Air Base: Wendling

Bomber 42-110062 piloted by 2nd Lt. Ofenstein was attacked by fighters, veered sharply and collided with 41-100371, pilot Kamenitsa. The latter lost part of its tail and this a/c part of its left wing. Belly landed about 11.00 hours one mile east of Meitze, 14 miles north of Hannover. After examining 371 the Germans estimated the damage was only 30%. Three men were killed in the landing and Lt. Kamentsa was unconscious for thirty minutes.

Summary of Missing Air Crew Report # 4476

Pilot: 2Lt. William T. Kamenitsa, 0-671661, POW, Youngstown, OH

Co-Pilot: 2Lt. George E. Graham Jr., 0-794395, POW, Ozone Park, NY

Navigator: 2Lt. John J. Caulfield, 0-757769, KIA, Chicago, IL

Bombardier: 2Lt. Gene A. Miller, 0-752891, KIA, Omaha, NE

Engineer: S/Sgt. Edwin J. Heater, 12045795, POW, Gouldsboro, PA

Radio: S/Sgt. Joseph B. Trivison, 15354276, KIA, Cleveland, OH

Ball-Turret Gunner: Sgt. Archie B. Young, 18097746, POW, Flint, TX

Left Waist-Gunner: Sgt. Oliver R. Guillot, 38428905, POW, Brookston, TX

Right Waist-Gunner: Sgt. Jack J. Krejci, POW, 17165454, Omaha, NE

Tail-Gunner: Sgt. Lark C. Morgan, 16036659, POW, Chicago, IL

3 KIA, 7 POW

Crash Site: Meitze/Hannover, Germany
Time: 11.00

392nd Bomb Group, 576th Bomb Squadron (Kamenitsa)

Back row (left to right): Foss (not on final crew), Navigator 2Lt. John Caulfield, Bombardier 2Lt. Gene Miller, Engineer S/Sgt. Edwin Heater, Right Waist-Gunner Sgt. Jack Krejci

Front row: Left Waist-Gunner Sgt. Oliver Guillot, Pilot 2Lt. William Kamenitsa, Ball-Turret Gunner Sgt. Archie B. Young, Tail-Gunner Sgt. Lark C. Morgan, Radio S/Sgt. Joseph B. Trivison

Pilot 2Lt. William T. Kamenitsa.

"When the war started, I was in the infantry at Camp Walters. I knew I was going overseas and I knew right away that I had to get out. At that time, the only way out of the army was up, and that meant the Air Corps. I had an officer friend who owed me a favor and he assisted me in getting transferred to pilot training. I went through Randolf Field, the Gulf Coast Command and got my wings.

"My love story was really with the A-20, even though I ended up a B-24 pilot. We trained in B-17's, B-24's, and the A-20. Now, that was an airplane. You flew it, you didn't just drive it. Frankly, I was unhappy with both the B-17's and the B-24's. I remember well, the first time I ever saw a B-24 liberator; it was so ugly you'd wonder how in the hell it ever flew. We used to say it was the box that the B-17 came in...they were "flying coffins" or the "flying boxcar."

"The advantages that Liberators had, were speed and bomb load. When we got into combat, the Air Force in its wisdom, combined us in their attacks with the B-17's; that couldn't allow us to get to our maximum cruising speed. We'd

428

fly about 10 miles per hour slower than the ship was designed for; with the load factor we had, we were on the edge of stalling out, maybe sixty percent of the time. That's why some guys never learned to fly the B-24.

"I had a co-pilot who flew with us through training until we got to England and he never made a take off or landing. I didn't have the time to teach him and he was happy to just be in the right seat. The co-pilot would normally be second in command and take care of the crew. Gene Miller, our bombardier, handled the job well and he took that job over. He was the buffer between the enlisted men and myself. I had the final say, but he was the guy they would go to with their gripes and bitches ... then he would come to me.

"We first put our crew together in Colorado and I think we went into Topeka, Kansas, on the 25th of January. We were probably about four weeks behind Ofenstein's crew and didn't cross his path until training in Ireland.

"We picked up our B-24 in Kansas and we had a full compliment of people. With the exception of the co-pilot, we had the same crew from training through combat. What started out as a well balanced but young team of strangers grew into a disciplined flying unit. Even so, there wasn't a lot of time for us to get real close; the events of April 29th bonded those of us who survived.

"There was this major at Topeka and at one of our briefings; he gets up and says: "Boys, I wish I were going in your place!" I said: "You can have my place!" That went over like a ton of bricks, but I hated that guy! I was the beginning of my long career as a second lieutenant.

"We got our orders and flew the southern route to England: Morrison Field, Florida; Trinidad; Belem, Brazil; Fortaleza; then over the ocean to Dakar and Marrakesch. When we got into Marrakesch, it was late and they weren't going to feed us. I should have known there was trouble in store because there were actually buzzards sitting on top of the mess hall. Well, I raised hell! The guy comes out and says: "Don't you know, there's a war on!."..I said: "Where in the hell do you think I am going, moron!."..He says: "Lieutenant, you can't talk to me like that!."..I said: "I just did!."..He says: "I'm going to get my commanding officer!" Sure enough, the C.O. comes out and what do you think he says?: "Feed these men!."..and I quietly said: "Thank you."

Pilot 2Lt. William T. Kamenitsa with his wife

"We were sent up to Ireland, theoretically for training. Trouble was, when we got there, they didn't have any ships flying. As soon as the opportunity presented itself, I went over to the sergeant in charge of operations and told him: "Sergeant, I will check in every morning and you let me know if there's any ships available. If there are, we'll come back. We're going down to Belfast (it was just up the road from us) and I'll have the crew check in with me every morning."

"I called in about three days later and the sergeant said: "Get your butt down here! The inspector general is here!" When we got back to the base, they said: "I want to see you and your crew in the office, in full class A uniforms! On the double!.".I said: "Yes, sir!.".. we got in there and this captain chews us out: "I'm going to court marshal you and send you back to the States!" I thought to myself... "Hell, yeah! - right now! Send me back." Then he says:"I've got a better idea - instead of doing that, I am sending you and your crew into combat immediately! We're not going to train you!"

"Well, he was full of crap and we knew it! Hell, there weren't any planes for us to train in. We were there a week and didn't take-off or shoot a weapon. And how was he going to send us back to the States in disgrace, when they're killing guys right and left over in Germany! They needed our bodies to sit in an airplane and they had ten of them right there. Sure enough, they shipped us out in a couple of days and off we went into combat.

"Wendling, England was cold and wet. I was never warm a minute of the time I was there. The only time, was when I came down after a flight and drew a hot tub of water in a cement tub. I'd just sit in it up to my neck. You'd steal anything that would burn just to keep those huts warm.. .I was always shivering. Those Quonset huts were sometimes cut up into little rooms and others were just open. We had two or three crews in ours, in one open bay. Base personnel, who were there all the time, had divided their's off into little rooms. We never had the time to fix up our quarters. We were a lot of "ships passing in the night" and I really only knew two other pilots while I was there...Lieut. Rogers and Lieut. Offen-stein. Our three crews all came into Wendling about the same time and we were in the same squadron.

"We always had a good ground crew, back at the 392nd. They would have the planes ready, out on the line, and worked hard to keep us flying. I told that guy who took care of us: "The only thing I want of you is, that if I want you to go up for a ride.. .you put on a chute and go." He said: "That's good enough for me!" and so that was it.

"We called the cockpit, "The Front Office." When I got to Wendling, I had the great good fortune to get a new man on the crew, George Graham. He'd flown hundreds of hours on sub-patrol and had been in the squadron since Dec. of 1943. Our first mission with him as a co-pilot was his thirteenth, but of course he never told us that.

"Now, there are not many flight instruments in the cockpit... only the airspeed indicator, needle and ball, altimeter, and climb indicator. The rest are engine in-struments. Before take off the co-pilot, engineer, and pilot coordinate everything.

The pilot sets all the throttles and fuel mixtures the same, the co-pilot would check the magnetos and then energize the start-up motor. This was a heavy duty thing that would rev up to high speed and then engage the engine. It would turn the props over like a starter on your car and it made that special high pitched whining sound as the engine engaged. *It was the sound of World War Two for many of us.*

"You'd go down the line from one engine to another and then throttle back until every thing was in tune. Next we'd run up the engine, pull off to the side, and run the props through to see if they are working. You'd taxi out for take-off and you were ready to go to work.

"You have these moments when you remember how intensely scared you were; how frightened you were when you saw the first aircraft go down...and the first time you get shot at. It's something you can never tell anybody about until you've been there yourself. Somebody's trying to kill you and mother isn't there!

"There was a mission where we went up over the North sea and we turned right and headed into Germany itself. We got hit by fighters and I never actually saw them, it happened so fast. I saw sparkles and I said: "Oh... What?? That's pretty." I didn't realize at the time, it was 20 mm! I looked out my window and there were two B-24's going down. I swear , I do not know how this could happen, but they were tumbling wing over wing! I'm up on the rudder pedals and my feet were pumping away like it was a bicycle. My hands were on the control column rocking it left and right, and George was in the co-pilot's seat looking at me. I didn't have any more control over that aircraft than if I was a five year old. I was scared to death.

"I wasn't the only one on the plane who was impressed by combat. Gene Miller, the bombardier, was down in the nose of the aircraft, all cramped up. His bladder released and he learned first hand about some of the unique problems presented by those electrically heated flying suits we had. The wires were always breaking or they'd burn you in one spot and freeze you in another. His shorted out that day and he called up to me: "Kamy, it's cold up here" (we were at altitude). I said: "I know it's cold, but what do you want me to do? I can't leave the formation." When we got back over the English coast, I made a dive, but that was the last Miller had a problem. From then on he made sure to take a can along with him.

"We were emotionally drained after our fights. We came down, went through debriefings and that was it. Our crew flew its first mission on the ninth of April (Tutow) and we flew 10 damn missions before the 29th of April when we got shot down. You figure it out...we were pretty busy! Man, you don't know how many crews were getting shot down, we were just numbers. They shot 65 crews the day we went down! Until recently, our wives and families were in the dark about a lot of this stuff because we had a shell around us. I've had my son tell me: "Well, you never told me any of those things" ... I just buried it all.

431

"One time, we had our own private little war. There were three planes from the Luftwaffe that were shooting at us. We had three planes and they had three planes. We got about two miles from each other and shot guns; they would shoot and we would shoot. Then they'd break away and come back around at us, but nobody got hurt or anything. None of us could hit the broadside of a barn that day and we all came home alive. Another mission I remember fondly was the day we took off and were flying blind from the time our wheels started to roll. George was watching the right side of the runway ad I was watching the left side. When we hit take off speed, I was on instruments. Operations had said: "Clean sailing above 4,000 feet" Well, we broke out about 16,000 feet and we're headed towards France. There was still nothing but clouds around us. Everybody was aborting and ships were falling off all the time. We started out in the third vic, way back in the pack, and were flying the right wing of the lead before we ended up.

"Just as we broke out over the target, an airfield, they nailed #4 engine with flak. I said: "That's enough of this garbage." So we went home. When they called us over to Intelligence, they asked me: "What did it look like over there?" I said: "It looked like hell.

"We had #3 and #4 engines out, four different times. On the 24th of April the target was Leipheim and, we actually ran out of gas; we ended up landing at the 44th across a hot runway. We were on our way home from the mission and I told the engineer, Heater, to go back and check the fuel level. Back in the mid-wing section, behind the bulkhead they had these glass test tubes that they called fuel gages. It was fifteen cents worth of glass in a $425,000 bomber. Heater said: "We've about 200 gallons, skipper," which was plenty for the sixty to ninety minutes we had left. We were "letting down" and were about 12,000 feet then. It seemed to me we were burning up a lot of fuel and I made the decision to land at Shipdam. The 44th bomb group was our sister group. They flew the same missions, had the same targets, and came back at the same time.

"We were turning in on our final approach....that's when you line up with the runway and make your landing. We were in the turn and George says: "# engine just quit!.".. I said: "Feather it.".and we went through our ritual for feathering a prop. We hadn't even got through our routine when #3 engine went out. I said: "Hell, we're going in!" I don't know if I told the guys in the waist to come forward into their crash positions, but we were so busy by that time, I couldn't check. It must have been obvious we were in trouble! I knew I had to get around and get flat, if I wanted to make the landing. I got flat, and just in front of us was a hill. So, we go down and pop over the hill, and there was a taxi-way strip. That is not made for landings...No way, Jose...we hit the front of the taxi-strip and I yelled: "Get on the brakes" George and I stood on them! We finally got that rascal stopped and it was just inches from the end of the grass. We had landed across what should have been a very "hot" runway, but when we finally looked up, we realized there wasn't any aircraft coming in behind us. I went into the operations office and they said: "We can't help you right now, we're looking for a ship that went down." I said: "Hey, that's us."

"I looked around...everything was too quiet to be the end of a mission, "What's going on here?" He explained, "Well, last night we had chocolate pudding and everybody got food poisoning. We weren't able to put a single aircraft in the air!" A whole Group out of action.

It was late in the afternoon when we came in there and later yet when we got back to Wendling. Don't you know, all our stuff was locked up and they were ready to ship it out. Some of our guys had a hell of a time retrieving all their personal items. They had to go to several other Quonset huts before they rounded up all their clothes and effects.

"Now, this wasn't the end of it for us. I was mad as hell that they had risked ten lives by not taking care of our fuel situation! I went down the next day to engineering and looked for the C.O. I wanted to know how we could run out of gas. We flew good, tight formation in our Group, we had good navigation and the fuel sets were proper." He invited me into his office and shuffled through some papers. Finally, he said: "We changed plugs in your aircraft and we put a new type of plug in both your #3 and #4 engines. I guess they're burning more gas than they're supposed to use."

"I was steamed up. "Hell, you send us out in an airplane that you haven't tested yet! We're on a bomb run while you sit on your big... " It was plain to see I'd never get any more silver bars on my uniform. Truthfully, I was drafted and I never quite got used to the army way of doing things.

"For example, I tried to get more ammunition for my gunners. It seemed to me impossible that anybody could trace an incoming aircraft... especially from the waist. I maintained the position that we were closing in at 500 mph (250 and 250 indicated the airspeed at altitude) and the best thing a gunner could do would be to just tie down the trigger and put out a hail of bullets. I asked if we could get more ammo and the response was: "Oh, we can't do that." I asked: "Why not?."... "Well, we can't do that. It isn't done that way. Fire a burst of ten and let up."

My guess is that most gunners just held down the trigger anyway. In fact, unknown to me, my guys brought extra ammo on board and even another gun barrel. Come to think of it, with that load of iron in the back, maybe that's why we ran out of gas!

The bomb loads we carried varied according to the targets, but I really use to sweat those cluster fragmentation bombs and the incendiaries. It was volatile stuff and a very unforgiving load. The forward squadrons carried the heavy demolition bombs and they'd put us idiots in the back end. We would go down with time delay butterfly bombs and incendiaries. Those butterfly or frag bombs were put in there ,so they would kill the people who came out to put out the fires. First we'd bomb them, then burn them and then kill them when they'd try to put out

433

the fires. It sounds gruesome, but we weren't over there on a Cook's tour.

"The raid on Hamm (on the twenty-second of April) was something we all remembered. We were approaching the target and Ollie Guillot, in the waist, called out:"Skipper, there's another group at the same level and they're heading for us!" The 392nd was coming into the target fast and I told George to check right, so we could get the hell out if we had to: "Keep an eye on them and the second we drop our bombs, we'll vacate." So, we keep checking, checking, checking... we were still clear, so we dropped our bombs and formed up with this guy from the other squadron, Lt. Hammond.

"He had flown 25 missions.... One of the few. They said: "We'll send you back home for 60 days and give you a promotion if you fly 5 more missions." They were short on experienced pilots. So, the guy said: "It's a piece of cake. I'll fly the five missions!" Well, this was his 26th mission.

"We joined up with him after the target and were flying in the slot behind him. The Germans were lining up, high on our left. We had some P-47's over in the back of us and some P-38's on our right. These crazy Germans are up there bee hiving... so they start down through the formation. Boy, there's nothing like this happened before; .tracers are all over the place. Then our fighters peeled off and they came down right through our formation. This guy, Hammond got #2 engine hit, so he's puffing smoke out of there. About eight minutes later, chutes start coming out. We counted five or six of them. Well, he is still up there with that thing smoking and burning...just plugging along...toot, toot, toot.

"I told George: "We better drop back, because this guy is going to blow!" We loosened up the formation and stayed with him until Belgium or Holland. Hammond was behind us by then. The ship finally blew. Guess who was the first person we saw, when we walked through the gates of Stalag Luft 3? It was Lt. Hammond!

"It was not often you could control your own destiny, but we gave it a good try. Once we were flying the inside of a vic and the idiot leading us just kept getting further and further behind the rest of the group. I told the co-pilot: "Watch this" I picked up my microphone and said: "Hey, you dumb-ass back there in the far corner. Are you trying to get yourself killed? Get those 3 ships back up here in formation!" Then I hung up the mike. Boy, you could see the black smoke pour out of those engines. Man, they moved right into the formation...pronto. They did not know who was talking to them, but they weren't taken any chances!

***

"The 29th of April started early, like any other mission and I probably wasn't any happier to get up and get going than on any other mission. We put up eighteen ships that day and lost eight of them; it was one of the heaviest losses for the group.

"Just after the fighters attacked, my waist gunner informed me that part of our wing was missing. George and I were up front and weren't able to see behind us; we didn't know what was happening back there. We jettisoned our bombs immediately and started to go back to England. I think that's when I informed the crew that I would try to get back into the cloud cover.

"The window started to ice up, so Heater came down out of the top turret. He started scratching the windshield with his fingernails. I'm looking out of the left-side window see a field down below. We were dropping fast and there's no time to make a choice.

"I never have figured out, why we were not shot down by those ME-109's circling us. We had dropped our wheels as a sign of surrender. Of course, I was yelling back to my gunners: "Cease fire!" and hoping we did not shoot one of them down! I think we were doing at least 150 miles per hour, but the faces of our instruments were all iced over, so we couldn't tell. George was in his right seat destroying the orders of the day; that was standard operating procedure. Heater was still standing between our two seats, trying to give me some forward visibility. The field was in such a position that we actually had to skim over some treetops, just before we hit the field.

"We set the plane down and must have rolled a few hundred yards before we hit a culvert. The dust was flying over the top of the aircraft in great clouds and then, the top turret failed. It came crashing down on our backs; the seats came in on us and it was absolutely black in the cockpit. I figured: "Well, this is it" All of sudden,.we stopped. The ship settled down at a steep angle. The nose opened up in front of us and Heater went flying right out. He took off and got about five feet from us, then I yelled some sweet words at him He had a foot in the air and I remember distinctly, he did a 180 turn in mid-air. He grabbed George and myself and helped us down out of the aircraft. I hit the ground and passed out.

***

"It took four weeks for my folks to find out I was a POW!. The army told them I was MIA about the second week in May; two weeks later, they got a personal message that I was alive. The Germans would broadcast a list of captured airmen, every night. People on the east coast would listen and then mail cards to families all over the country. My mom and dad got about a dozen of them saying: "*your son, William T. Kamenitsa, is being held by the Germans. He's alive and a POW.*" It took a while for the federal government to catch up with the hams.

"George, my co-pilot, and I were sent to Stalag Luft 3. Three other crewmen (Heater, Krejci and Guillot) all went over to Stalag 17B. There was only 150 miles between us, but it was if we were all on different islands; it was 45 years before we'd see each other again.

435

Crashed B-24, # 41-100371

Bombardier 2Lt. Gene A. Miller.

Letter from Gene's mother to mother of Bud Guillot dated July 20, 1944

"My Dear Mrs. Guillot,

"I was indeed happy to receive your letter today. I wish I had news for you concerning your son, but I only can tell you that I don't know a great deal about the crew only that my son and the navigator John Caulfield have been reported Killed in Action and the rest of the crew as prisoners of war.

"I had a letter from Lt. Kamenitsy's mother yesterday and she wrote that they had received a card from their son written in his own handwriting and that he was well and safe, a prisoner of Germany.

"I hope you will soon hear from Oliver and that every thing will be alright with him and that you will be able to rest easier and not worry like you have these past months. I only hope and pray that it is a mistake about Gene but realize there is very little I can do - only wait.

"Gene was just 21 years old April 13th. He loved being alive and had many plans for after the war. I can't hardly bear the thought that they may never be realized by him.

"If you have a snapshot of your boy that you could spare to me I would love to have one. I want to have one of each member of the crew. It will help me to know what the other boys looked like that were with Gene.

"I received the first telegram from the War Department May 15th that Gene was missing in action over Germany April 29th. Then June 6th I received the second telegram saying he had been killed on that same date as he had previously been reported missing. That is all the information I have received to date.

"I have one other son, Roy, who is just 18. But I need Gene so badly too. I just have the two boys. I have been a widow for over 15 years. It's very hard to give him up and just yet I can't do it. I have much consolation from the fact that I think Gene enjoyed flying and the friendship of his crew members. He wouldn't want me to feel too badly - but it hurts dreadfully.

"I am sending you a snapshot of Gene taken at Christmas time in Colorado Springs. Keep it and give it to your boy when he gets home. God be willing that he does. If I should hear any further news I will surely let you know. Please do write me again.

"I send my best wishes to you and my thoughts go to you over the miles.
<blockquote>
Sincerely,
Mrs. Virginia Miller
</blockquote>

Radio Operator S/Sgt. Joseph B. Trivison.

From his niece Gwen Cartulla.

"Sorry it has taken so long to respond to your request for information about my Uncle Joe Trivison. I was five years old in 1944. There isn't too much that I remember about him,but I will tell you what I do remember. The last time I saw him, was on the sidewalk in front of the house where we lived. His fiance Irene lived downstairs of this house, address 14623 St. Clair Ave. Cleveland, Ohio.

"Even at that young age, l knew how handsome a man in uniform was. I was so proud he was my uncle. l remember asking him if he would take me for a walk, down the street. He said; "Honey I can't. I have to go because I have a job to do." My poor little heart was crushed, and so he left,and I never saw him again

"There was this little trick he used to show me as we laid on the front room floor. He got a ash tray and a book of matches. He would peel apart the paper matches and place them one after another, then light the first match and they would all take turns burning. That was one of the things he did to amuse me.

"He was an all star basketball player at Collinwood High School. Now in the front of the high school there is a plaque on a rock with names of the boys that were killed in the war. His being the last; Joseph R. Trivison.

"My Dad, Louis Trivison, his brother loved to play golf. So did Uncle Joe. I have pictures of them two laughing at me, at maybe four years old, trying to swing a golf club.

"There isn.t too much more that I remember, except the day they received the telegram telling them that Uncle Joe was killed in action. It was a horrible day. I remember Irene reading the telegram, and fainting right in the middle of the frontroom floor. My Grandma lived with us at the time, and I loved her dearly. I remember going into her bedroom and crying my eyes out. Grandma stroking my hair, and talking to me in Italian, which I didn't understand, but I know it were words of comfort.

"We moved away from that house, and lost touch with Irene. It was years later, that maybe I was ten years old, she came to visit us. During that visit she gave me the engagement ring that Uncle Joe gave her. She also gave me his wings from his uniform.

"Now after all these years of wondering how he died and where he is buried, I finally got answers from people like Bud Guillot and Annette Tison. God bless them, I can finally put my wonderings to rest...Uncle was a radio operator, I was a police dispatcher and then a police officer....Loved the radio, and loved the uniform...must be in the genes Cartulla

Engineer S/Sgt. Edwin J. Heater.

By his son Jim Heater.

"Edwin James Heater was born November 3, 1917 in Gouldsboro, Pennsylvania to Annie Englert Heater, a German-born housewife, and William S. Heater, a railroad brakeman for the Erie Lackawanna railway. Ed was the last of eleven children. He attended elementary school in Gouldsboro and graduated from high school in Tobyhanna, Pa. in 1935. Ed was very interested in mechanics and tinkered with cars with friends. He worked with his brother Ray, an electrician, helping to build a beautiful big lodge and several houses. Later he worked with his brother Bill for a trucking company in Johnson City, NY.

"As the war drew near, Ed enlisted in the Army Air Corps in Binghamton, NY. He was trained at Keesler field Mississippi as an airplane mechanic, and Tyndall field, Florida in aerial gunnery, making his military occupational specialty a flight maintenance gunner.

"Ed's plane, a B-24 Liberator went down on April 29, 1944 while on a mission over Berlin. They were flying toward their target in Berlin when they started taking flak. One of the planes near them was hit, came up, and took off part of their wing. The plane could not stay airborne, so the crew was given the choice of bailing out or riding the plane down.

"As the plane made its rapid descent, from his position behind the pilot, Ed used his bare hands to scrape ice off the windshield so the pilot, Captain Bill Kamenitsa, could see where he was going. Incredibly, "Kami" brought the plane down in an open field into a smooth landing until they hit a ditch between fields. The plane slammed forward on its nose.

"Ed was not strapped in at the time and a pipe pierced his leg. He jumped out of the plane and backed away from it thinking an explosion was imminent, but he heard Kamenitsa calling for him to come back and help him get out of the plane. He ran back and only with his hands he clawed at the impacted dirt that pinned Kamenitsa in the wreckage. As he frantically dug, Kami was better able to breathe, and finally Ed pulled him from the wreckage.

"After everyone exited the plane, a German farmer held them at gunpoint until troops arrived and took them prisoner. Officers were separated from enlisted men and were taken to POW camp Luft 4, northeast of Berlin. Ed and the other enlisted men were transported to Stalag 17B, near Krems, Austria.

"Food at the camp kept them alive, but not much more. The prisoners were fed a lot of raw potato peelings, especially toward the end of the war. Cigarettes in Red Cross packages were bartered with guards for items, usually extra food if there was any to be had. Someone made a radio so the POWs were able to keep up with the progress of the war but we can only speculate if any of the components came from the guards.

"For the rest of his life Ed was always a very light sleeper. When awake he wanted to stay busy all the time, probably to limit memories of his imprisonment from flooding his mind. After the war, Ed rarely talked about what he had experienced, but opened up more after meeting with the crew years later.

"Ed was imprisoned for approximately a year in Stalag 17 and was liberated by General Patton's forces. The freed POWs made their way to France where they were shipped to the USA.

"He was separated from the service on October 11, 1945 in Rome, NY with a payment of $105.55, part of a $300 sum for mustering out pay. He traveled to New York City where he bought a custom made Army Air Corps uniform to replace the only garments he owned; the ragged clothing he was wearing when his plane was shot down.

"After about a year spent recovering from the physical and mental toll of prison camp, Ed went to the Binghamton, NY area to look for work. He received three job offers - General Electric, Bell Telephone, and IBM. He selected IBM.

"Once he had a job, Ed felt that he could get married. Ed and Jean Catherine Westcott were wed on July 30, 1946. They first lived in Johnson City, NY, and then had a house built in Vestal, NY where they lived many happy years. Ed and Jean had one child, James Westcott Heater, born in Endicott, NY on October 29, 1954.

"Ed retired from IBM on April 30, 1981 after a 35 year career. During that time, he had worked as a machinist, a manager, and a quality assurance specialist.

"He enjoyed fishing and hunting, and spending time at their summer home on nearby Stanley Lake in Pennsylvania. Ed was a skilled cabinet maker, building furniture and grandfather clocks. He busied himself with home improvements, finishing off the basement, adding a bathroom, remodeling the kitchen, and working on cars with Jim and his friends.

"Ed and Jean moved to North Carolina in 1984, following their son, who had married and found work at IBM in Charlotte. After they settled in, they made several trips around the southeast. A grandson, Daniel Westcott Heater, was born on February 27, 1985. Danny has fond memories of watching baseball games on TV with his Grampa.

"A couple of years later, Captain Bill Kamenitsa located Ed through some relatives in Gouldsboro. Crew reunions were held in Texas, Florida, California, and at Ed and Jean's home in Harrisburg, NC. Ed passed away on December 1, 1994 from complications of emphysema.

Right-Waist Gunner Sgt. Jack J. Krejci.

As told by Bud Guillot:

"I knew Jack had a girlfriend in Omaha that he had gone to school with and he was very much in love with and wanted to marry when the war was over. A couple of years ago Loretta told me that she was Catholic and Jack was not and she told Jack that she loved him very much but could never marry anyone except a Catholic. For the year and five days we were in Stalag 17B there was also a Captain Cain, Catholic Priest, in Stalag 17B who had been captured by the Germans during the African campaign.

"Unbeknownst to the rest of our crew Jack went to Captain Cane and said he wanted to become a Catholic. Over the following months Jack met with Captain Cain almost daily until he completed all the requirements to become a Catholic and Father Cain documented that Jack was a Catholic.

"After the war and Jack's first day back in Omaha Jack proposed to Loretta. Loretta told Jack that she loved him but could not marry him until he became a Catholic. Jack says let's get married tomorrow then; because I am a Catholic. Loretta could not believe this was legal in the eyes of the church and insisted on seeing her bishop. The bishop could not believe Jack had completed all the requirements to become a Catholic while in a German POW even though Jack had papers from Father Cain. Jack had the Bishop phone Father Cain. After the telephone conversation the bishop says; "I can marry you two any day you choose." That marriage lasted to Jack Krejci's death.

Right-Waist Gunner Sgt. Oliver "Bud" R. Guillot.

From Bud, March 17, 2013.

"I was born on a cotton farm in Shiloh, Texas, in the Red River Valley on April 16, 1922. Now don't get all excited and grab your Texas map to "look up" where Shiloh, Texas, is located, because it's not on any map. It never was. Most people will say, "the little town I am from was just a wide spot in the road." The old one lane dirt road that went from Paris, Texas, through Shiloh and headed due west to Bonham and places west, didn't even widen out where it went through Shiloh.

"Shiloh consisted of one wooden framed store about 15 by 20 feet. The store carried some of the basics a farming community needed, canned goods, flour, sugar, coffee, salt and pepper. The store sold no fresh foods or vegetables. The farmers grew their own vegetables. The store carried no meats. There was no electric-

Bud G. Veterans 2014

Waist-Gunner Sgt. Oliver Guillot on Veterans Day, 2014

ity and no ice to keep meat fresh. My grandfather, W. E. (Bill) Oliver owned the store.

"There was a two-room wood framed schoolhouse. The school had two teachers and usually about 35 students. The school taught classes from first through tenth grade. The school had a well for drinking water and a potbellied wood burning stove in each room for warmth during the cold winter days. There were no lights at the school.

"Shiloh had a small one room wooden church. Residents of Shiloh did not have: electricity, radio, phones, refrigerator, TV, running water, washing machine, water heater, natural gas, just to mention a few. We used wood that we chopped for cooking and heating. We used kerosene lamps for light. Kerosene was 5 cents a gallon. Gas was 10 cents a gallon. I can never remember my father ordering more that 10 cents worth of gas at one time. I had never flipped a light switch until I graduated from high school and left home.

"The great depression did not affect us on the farm very much. We grew almost everything we needed to eat. Sugar, coffee, flour, salt, pepper and clothing were about the only things we needed to purchase. We had nothing before the depression and we had nothing after the depression, it had no effect on my family. If you think this is going to be a whining story about my deprived and rough childhood you are wrong. It was a great life, wonderful friends and great learning experience. It toughened and prepared me to where in later years; some of the hardships for some of my buddies were a "piece of cake" for me.

"There was no government agency telling us we were poor and needed help so we didn't realize we were poor. If an agency had offered us help my parents would have been insulted and would have turned it down. I can always remember my mother saying how well off we were because our pinto bean soup was thicker than our neighbors. I always went through life thinking my bean bowl was never half empty but always half full.

"It was great growing up in a crime free area. The 18 years I lived in Shiloh I never heard of a crime any more serious than stealing a chicken. There are several reasons why it was a crime free area. Every household had at a minimum, a pistol, shot gun and rifle. Each family member, over the age of seven, knew how to load and fire each weapon. Each household had two or three large mixed breed dogs. These dogs were friendly and loving to everyone who approached the home when the occupants were home but if a stranger approached the home when the family was gone they better keep the engine running and the windows rolled up. We never once locked our doors, night or day, whether at home or away. What if one of our neighbors needed to borrow something, came over, and found our doors locked? I never lived in a house with a lock on the door until I was about 26 years old.

"After I graduated from high school I moved to Houston Texas and went to work at an insurance company. After working in Houston for about seven months; a young man I had befriended, Fred Pierce and his wife Janet, were going to California seeking a job in the aircraft industry. Fred needed money to pay for the gas to drive to California and offered to take me to California for $10. It took us four days and three nights plus eleven flat tires to get to Inglewood California. Within days Fred went to work at North American Aviation in Inglewood and I went to work at Douglas Aircraft Co. in Santa Monica.

"I had Sunday December 7, 1941 off and had taken a long drive up the coast, no radio in my car. Did not know of the Japanese attack on Pearl Harbor until about 5:00 PM when I got back to where I was living and everyone was gathered around the radio. On February 26, 1943 I went into the Army Air Force.

My Longest Day - April 29, 1944 – The Berlin Mission
By Oliver (Bud) Guillot

"After basic training I went to Armament School and then Aerial Gunnery School. I was then assigned as left hand waist gunner and armorer on Lt Bill Kamenitsa's 10 man crew. I was lucky to be assigned to Kamy's crew. Kamy was about 5 years older than the other new pilots and wiser. Kamy did not drink any kind of alcohol beverages and he did not smoke. It was comforting knowing you were flying with a sober pilot with lots of stick time. Kamy had enlisted in the Army and had spent two years as a foot soldier. When war broke out Kamy said he realized that he was too short and stocky to walk through mud and ice all day and sleep in a foxhole on cold wet nights, so he signed up for pilot training, passed the tests and was accepted. After basic flight school Kamy was assigned to fly A 20, two engine attack airplane and loved flying the fast maneuverable A 20 at tree top level.

"The Air Force High Command determined they needed more heavy bomber pilots to neutralize the mighty German war machine industry before an invasion could be successfully conducted. Kamy and a cadre of newly graduated A 20 pilots were reassigned to heavy bomber pilot training.

"Our co-pilot was John Foss but when we got to the 392 Bomb Group John was replaced by George Graham and George flew all our combat missions as our copilot. George stayed in the Air Force after the war and worked to the rank of Lt Colonel and Base Commander.

"On March 18, 1944 the 392nd Bomb Group of the 8th Air Force, stationed in Wendling, England was briefed for a bombing mission to Friedrichshafen, Germany. The 392nd briefed 28 crews for this mission and the 28 planes started taking off at 10:00 a.m. Four planes aborted for mechanical difficulties and returned to base. The remaining 24 planes proceeded to the target. Heavy antiaircraft fire and fierce enemy fighter attacks were devastating to the group, 15 of the 24 airplanes were lost with 154 casualties. Enemy fighters and antiaircraft fire had damaged all 9 returning planes. Our crew, the Roger crew and other new crews were sent to the 392nd to replace their losses.

"The enlisted men from the Kamenitsa and the Roger crews were assigned to a small Quonset hut. The hut was set up to house twelve people. There were no partitions, just one large room. When we entered the hut it was cold and empty except for metal cots and two-inch pads for each of us. There was a cast-iron potbelly coal burning stove in the center of the room for warmth from the cold, damp, English nights. What really made cold chills run down our backs was when we looked at the walls and saw all the maps of Europe. Each map had a crew's name on it to keep track of their bombing missions. For each combat mission completed, a red line was drawn from our base in England to the target in Germany. Some would have only one or two red lines drawn on their map, but none on our walls showed more than twelve. At that time of the war the heavy bomber crews were required to complete 35 missions before they could be rotated back to the states. You could read each crew's combat history on those many maps and quickly assess our chances of completing 35 missions.

"On our first night there, a small black and white mixed breed cocker spaniel entered the airlock to our hut and quietly crawled into a box that had been placed there for her. It was obvious that she had been a mascot and friend to one of the crews whose uncompleted map was on our wall. Her crew had probably brought her to England on their B-24. Because of the heavy turnover of crews we could not find anyone who knew the history of the dog. For lack of knowing her real name we started calling her Duchess.

"Duchess would not make up to us. She would tolerate us but rather we leave her alone. She would only shiver and pull away when we would try to pat her. Before sunup the following morning she was out of the hut and headed for the runway. The airplane parking pads were dispersed around the runway with sufficient distance between parked airplanes to minimize damage to aircraft during German bombing raids on our airbase. We noticed that Duchess was sitting at the same airplane parking pad each day from before sunup until after dark. Each time a B-24 airplane came in to land; Duchess would stand up and start wagging her tail. When the airplane taxied past her parking pad she would sit down and continue her vigil. It was obvious she was waiting for her lost crew to return from their mission. We would steal food from the mess hall and bring it back to the hut for her. She always had a good meal and fresh water waiting for her when she returned at night from her day-long vigil. She did not like us and only tolerated us because we were supplying her with food.

"We flew our first mission on the morning of April 8, 1944. The target was an aircraft factory at Brunswick Germany. By April 29, 1944 we had flown 10 missions deep into the heart of Germany. In the evening of April 28 I check the squadron bulletin board and see that Kamenitsa's crew is scheduled to fly a mission on April 29, 1944.

"On the morning of April 29, 1944, we were awakened at 5:00 AM by the squadron orderly. The first sequence of events before going on a mission was going to breakfast. Duchess jumped out of her box and followed us to the mess hall and ran past the mess sergeant and stood by our feet as we ate. She had never done this before. We went to the dressing room to pick up all of our flight gear and parachutes and get dressed for our mission. Duchess followed us there. We closed the door to keep her out, but the next person that opened the door she squeezed by and came in to see us. Next was the briefing auditorium where all the crews flying a mission that day were briefed on the mission. Duchess slipped into the auditorium and jumped up on the bench beside us. We began to feel uneasy about Duchess' strange behavior. Why was she acting this way today?

"When the briefing officer pulled the curtain and exposed the large map of Europe there was a long red line stretching from our base in England to Berlin. The room became deathly quiet then there was a deep groan by everyone in the room. We knew the Germans would be defending their capital with everything they had and it was going to be a brutal and costly day for both sides. Duchess was sitting on the bench looking at the map and not moving a hair during the briefing.

"After the briefing we went to the armament room to get our .50 caliber machine guns and a jeep and driver to take us to our B 24 on its parking pad. Duchess tried to get into the jeep with us but we threw her out and the driver took off with Duchess in hot pursuit. She got to the airplane shortly after we did. As we were putting machine guns, parachutes, and other flight gear into the bomber, she kept trying to jump into the plane. On that cold foggy morning while our airplane was picking up speed to take off on our bombing mission to Berlin, we could see Duchess standing on our parking pad watching us depart for Berlin.

"There were lots of airplanes in the sky above England that morning shifting position and trying to get in their assigned position behind their lead airplane.

The lead airplane had to find his assigned place in his division. Each of the three divisions worked to their assigned flight plan. These plans were set up so no two divisions were over the target at the same time. When it was time for a division to head toward the target, they started in that direction on time whether everyone was in position or not. Those not in position; had to fill in some place in the back of the formation. Our flight plan called for an easterly, slightly zigzag course to avoid as much antiaircraft fire as possible. At a designated point east of Hannover we were to make a right turn and we would then be on a course straight to our target, Berlin.

"We started picking up heavy anti-aircraft fire as soon as we hit the occupied Netherlands coast. We continued to have heavy pockets of flak ntil we were past Hannover. We made our right turn and were flying straight at Berlin. Even though we were many miles from Berlin, it was a clear day and I could see all the heavy bombers over Berlin and the sky was black with anti-aircraft fire. The 8th Air Force Division I saw over Berlin was scheduled to be there, drop their bombs and depart before we arrived. The planes over Berlin were so far away they looked like little miniatures but I could see they were sure taking a beating from the intense flak barrage. I knew we would be in that same position over Berlin in less than ten minutes and all that upcoming flak would be concentrated on us.

Someone in the front of our airplane called out over the intercom: "Bogies (German fighters) 12 o'clock high – a hell of a bunch of them." It was later estimated by the returning crews, there were 55 German fighter planes in that first group that came barreling through our formation with all guns blazing. We took out some of them and they took out lots of us. The fighters pulled around for another pass at us. Leo Ofenstein's crew was flying on our left side and behind our left wing in his assigned position. That first wave of fighters ripped his aircraft badly. Over the intercom I yelled to Kamy: "Left wing man going to hit us." His airplane nosed up slightly, moved forward over our wing. His left wing went down at a 35 degree angle; they dropped and took 10 feet off our left wing. They headed down at a very steep angle with black smoke coming from their airplane. From my left-hand window I could see this entire scene happening. It happened so quick there was nothing that could be done.

"The crash knocked us out of the formation and we started going down. With ten feet of our left-hand wing missing, we were in a tight circle to the left and going down. Kamy gives both engines on the left side full throttle and backed off the power on the right side. This allowed him to lift the left wing and partially stabilized the plane. Kamy says: "I am going to try to make it down to those clouds below us and if I can, we will fly in them back to England, hiding from the German fighters."

"We were almost to the clouds when three German fighters spotted us and dived down to finish us off. We made it to the clouds but the airplane did not have enough wing surface to hold altitude. We went right on through the cloud cover.

Kamy says: "I see a field down there and I intend to land there. You can bail out or ride it in with me. The choice is yours."

"We had been descending so fast the windshield was covered with ice. The entire instrument panels were frozen over and the pilots could not see any of their instruments. Heater climbed down from the upper turret, was standing behind Kamy, and scraping ice from the windshield with his fingernails. Heater could only provide Kamy with a six-inch circle of clear windshield to look through. It is very difficult to land a big awkward airplane under those conditions. They cannot read any of their instruments but their "gut feeling" told them they were traveling at twice the speed they normally land.

"The pursuing German fighters have come through the clouds and spotted us. We skim along the top of a pine tree forest for about 200 feet. Pine needles and small branches are flying through the airplane. At the edge of this forest is the farmer's plowed field Kamy had picked as his landing site. He sets the airplane down in the field and we are having a good roll out. In front of us was a small raised dirt road separating two fields. Our nose wheel hits that raised road and folds back under the airplane. We are still moving at a fast speed when the nose of the airplane hits the ground and our forward momentum tears the complete front section of the airplane off and rolls it up under the airplane. There is no part of the airplane in front of the pilots. We are still moving forward and dirt piles up to the necks of the pilot and copilot before the plane comes to rest. The plane came to rest in a 45 degree tail up position. The bomb bay is full of dirt and my only exit is to jump out the rear hatch which was 30 feet above the ground.

"Heater just walks out through the front of the airplane and starts digging out the pilot and copilot. One of my jobs was to burn the airplane if we ever crashed in enemy territory. I quickly counted heads and only came up with seven. Three men were missing. The farmers were running toward us from all directions, with shotguns and pitchforks and the three German fighter planes were circling us to keep us from running for the woods. I had but a fraction of a minute left to torch the plane, but I could not do it. I did not know if the three men had bailed out earlier or were they trapped somewhere in the wreckage and still alive.

"Some of the German farmers wanted to kill us but several army people came and took control of us, and the civilians calmed down a bit. We were later told by the Germans that bombardier Lt Miller, navigator Lt Caulfield and radio operator Sgt. Trivison were killed and their bodies were found in the wreckage.

"We were taken into the village of Meitze and held in a military building. Later more captured Americans who had been shot down were brought in and placed with us. Later that evening we were trucked to Hannover, Germany and we arrive in Hannover after dark. The building we are in looks like an ancient prison. It is constructed of rough-cut stones. We are all in one big room. The German guards keep bringing in American prisoners they had captured that day. The room is getting packed with people. The guards start taking people out of the room and moving them to another place.

"A guard comes over and motions for me to follow him. He leads me down a dark narrow stairway to a basement. This was obviously an old prison. On each side of the narrow hall are rows of heavy wooden doors with hand hammered metal hinges and latches. Each door has a small sliding window in the upper part of each door. The guard opens one of these doors and shoves me in and I can hear the door being locked. The cell has a 25 watt light bulb in the ceiling and a six-foot wooden bench built into the wall on each side. The room is damp, musty and cold. It is made of solid stone. I look around and the only modern thing in the room is a new electric heater mounted in the back wall. This heater is four feet long and one foot high. I am alone in this dark damp room. No food since early morning breakfast.

"They took my watch and in a place like that you soon do not know how long you have been there. You begin to wonder, have I been here for days and they forgot about locking me up in here. I had probably been seeing too many Hollywood war movies. I thought about that big heater in a small room. I began to wonder, is this place is where they sweat information out of prisoners. I decided they were not going to use that heater to sweat information out of me. I pull a metal button off my trousers and use it as a screwdriver. I unscrew the mounting screws for the heater and pull it out from the wall just enough to reach the electric wires. I first start to disconnect the two wires then I reasoned, they could just come in and hook them up again. I decided to jerk on the wires and separate them somewhere way up in the conduits. I start jerking one of the electric wires until it either breaks or comes loose from its connection. I then jerk on the other electric wire until it separates. I then remount the stone frame.

"I then heard the door open and the guard shoves Lt. Jack Roper, the navigator from Rogers's crew, into the room. At least I have someone I know to talk to. The room is getting colder we are both damp, cold and our teeth are chattering. Roper has burns on his hands and forehead and he is sure suffering from the cold. I hear the little slide window being opened. The guard sticks his head to the window and in broken English says: "Is it cold in there? I will turn on the heat." I then hear a switch being flipped. Roper cheers up a little and says: "It's going to be nice to get a little heat in this damn room." I don't dare tell Roper I don't think the heater is going to work. Roper is the only one in the room cursing the damn Germans all night because it is cold.

"About 5:00 am on Sunday April 30, 1944 we are roused and put on trucks and ferried to the train station in Hannover. On the trip to the train station we witnessed the war damage in Hannover. The buildings are mere shells. The railway station and right of ways look unusable. The civilians are very hostile and threatening to us, shouting and calling us names. I am sure glad I don't understand German and we have lots of German guards with guns with bayonets.

"We are on the train all-day. We arrive at a small town outside Frankfurt about

5:00 pm. We have to march under many guards for about one mile to the Frankfurt Dulag-Luft prison. Dulag-Luft is a temporary prisoner of war camp where you are questioned for military information. We are each put in a small room with a single cot, sawdust mattress and one very thin warn-out blanket that was probably used during WWI. I see no other Americans for the three days they question me. There is almost 18 hours a day questioning. I am always alone when I am being questioned. Sometimes there are two interrogators in the room and sometimes only one. I got hoarse standing at attention and giving them my name, rank and serial number.

"Each day, for the remainder of the war, I wondered if Duchess was sitting on our parking pad, in the cold and rain, waiting for us to return – jumping up and waging her tail each time a B 24 lands and sitting down and continuing her vigil when it taxies past our parking pad. I am not superstitious. Not in the least. No one can foresee the future. But - why the sudden change on that day??? Did that damn dog know something the US Air Force Intelligence Corp and 8th Air Force High Commend didn't?

***

"From within the triple barbed wire fences that surrounded Stalag 17B in Krems Austria I could hear the distant thunder from the Russian artillery advancing on Vienna some 50 miles east of our prisoner of war camp. It was late March in 1945. In early April 1945 our German guards got orders to start a forced march of all American Prisoners at Stalag 17B westerly along the Danube Rived in front of the advancing Russian army.

"After marching for 30 days and sleeping on the cold damp ground each night; one morning on May 5, 1945 I woke up to the most beautiful sight I had ever seen; Two jeeps with four of General George Patton's 3rd Army soldiers coming down the dirt road. They quickly disarmed our German guards, liberated us and reversed the balance of power. A few hours later General Patton and his jeep driver came to the area we were in. General Patton stood in his jeep and gave a short speech. He said he had a battle ahead and could not help us with rations but help would be arriving in a few days. General Patton says. "That town down the road is yours. Move in, scrounge for food and find a warm place to sleep."

"I found an abandoned manufacturing building with a luxury office and a nice large couch to sleep on and made that office my home. In about two days K rations were brought in, by the Army, and were distributed. In about five days the army flew in DC3s and moved us to Camp Lucky Strike in France. We were issued new uniforms, shoes, underwear and toiletry. The mess hall and ice cream stand were open 24 hours a day. The food was gourmet to us. The Army did not want our parents to see us so under nourished. The new clothing they issued to us was at least two sizes too large. They knew they were going to fatten us into them before they sent us home for a long awaited visit.

"One day Sgt. Archie Young, our ball turret gunner, and I walked into town which was about three or four miles outside Camp Lucky Strike. The quaint little town had several small bakeries and the smell of the fresh baked bread was irresistible. Archie and I went to one of the bakeries and with hand language we each purchased a fresh baked loaf of French bread. We had no idea bread was rationed and it was against the law for them to sell it to us.

"As Archie and I were walking down the street each eating his loaf of bread; a jeep with two Military Police pulled up and told us it was against the law for us to buy bread and it was against the law for the baker to sell it to us. We were not worried about them arresting us and putting us in jail we knew the jail would seem like a room at the Hilton compared to what we were used to. We were concerned about the baker that sold us the bread. The MPs questioned us about where we purchased the bread and we just said back there some place. The MPs told us to get in the back seat and show them where we got the bread. They drove us to a dozen bakeries and some of them twice and Archie and I still eating our fresh baked bread and both kept saying. "That's not it; there is another bakery you are missing." We got a wonderful personal guided tour of that beautiful little French town courtesy of the US Military Police. The MPs finally gave up on us and told us to get out of their jeep and never buy bread in that town again. We talked the two MPs into drive us back to Camp Lucky Strike; which they agreed to do if we would finish eating our loafs of bread before we got to the guard gate.

"After about one week at Camp Lucky Strike we were loaded on a troop ship and sailed to New York. The food on the ship was excellent and abundant. In New York we were segregated by state and sent to Army Air Force Bases in our respective state for reassignment and a two week furlough to visit our loved ones. Six of our original ten man crew that flew to England returned to the US. Co Pilot Lt John Foss, Navigator Lt Joe Caulfield, Bombardier Lt. Gene Miller and Radio Operator Joe Trivison were killed in action in the skies over Germany.(Note Lt. John Foss had been reassigned to another crew and was killed on a later bombing mission to Berlin).

"We six surviving crew mates, buddies, friends who had been so close and a well-knit team for so long; shook hands, wished each other good luck and departed for our respective next assignment. I got two weeks' vacation with my parents in Paris, Texas, and then reported to Ellington Field in Houston, Texas to await an assignment to the Pacific Theater of Operation.

"President Truman made the ultimate decision to quickly end the war in the Pacific and save a million+ lives, Japanese and American, by dropping the atomic bomb on two cities in Japan. The war ended on August 15, 1945. I was discharged from the Army Air Force on November 5, 1945. I took a train back to California. On my first day back in Inglewood California I went to the Douglas Aircraft Company where I had worked before going into the Army Air Force. The personal officer told me my pay would start as of 8:00 that morning and for me to take the rest of the day off and report to work the following morning. Manufacturing at Douglas Aircraft had changed. Company pride and work ethics were deplorable. Manufacturing had been unionized.

"After three months I refused to work in a unionized shop. One lunch period I walked across the street to North American Aviation who did not have a union and hired in at North American Aviation. I worked a NAA until 1983. Over the years at NAA I progressively moved up the ladder from the manufacturing assembly line to Manager of Scheduling, Change Control, Project Coordination & Work Sequence Engineering. Some of the most interesting projects I worked on were: P-82 Twin Mustang, F-100 Fighter, B-70 Bomber, Apollo and the B1 bomber.

"I met my wife Vi at a young people's recreation center and we were married in 1949 and have two children and one grandson. I always worked longer hours than was expected of me but I never let that interfere with all my hobbies which are too numerous to mention but I will try; painting: both oils and water colors, dirt motorcycle riding, jewelry making, gardening, spelunking, backpacking, mountain climbing, prospecting, construction, square dancing, line dancing, photography, cross country sightseeing trips. I never saw a dirt side road leading out across the desert that I didn't wander where it led to. I took most of them with Vi saying. "Not again. I am not walking back to the main highway if the road gets so bad you can't find a place to turn around or get stuck."

***

Acknowledgements;
Gwen Cartulla, niece of radio-operator S/Sgt. Joseph B. Trivison.
Jim Heater son of engineer S/Sgt. Edwin J. Heater.
Right-Waist Gunner Sgt. Oliver "Bud" R. Guillot.

CHAPTER 29

392ND BOMB GROUP 577TH BOMB SQUADRON

Type: B-24H • Serial: 41-28759
MACR: 4462 • Air Base: Wendling

"...He [Pilot 2Lt. Fred C. Shere Jr.], kept that ship up 'til everyone else was out. He wasn't looking out for himself, he was looking out for nine other men...he still lives with us as a hero. If there ever was a man that deserves credit, he does."

From a letter of Engineer Orlando Friesen
to the widow of Pilot Fred Shere

Pilot: 2Lt. Fred C. Shere Jr., 0-745956, KIA, Denver City, TX

Co-Pilot: F/O Milan R. Zeman, T-61361, KIA, Avalon, PA

Navigator: 2Lt. Patrick J. Ryan, 0-695455, POW, Green Bay, WI

Bombardier: Sgt. Robert W. Wilcox, 12215195, POW, Corning, NY

Engineer: S/Sgt. Orlando H. Friesen, 17155320, POW, Fairmont, MN

Radio: S/Sgt. Fonzy M. Wilson Jr., 39690607, KIA, Los Angeles, CA

Ball-Turret Gunner: Sgt. Thomas L. Hampton, 35000419, POW, Mt. Vernon, OH

Waist-Gunner: Sgt. Joe B. Maloy, 34702598, POW, Montgomery, AL

Waist-Gunner: Sgt. Frank A. Bennett, 33110100, POW, Brownsville, PA

Tail-Gunner: Sgt. Marvin O. Morris, 38431227, POW, Fort Worth, TX

3 KIA, 7 POW

Crash Site: Nortrup/Osnabrück, Germany
Time: 13.30

392nd Bomb Group, 577th Bomb Squadron (Shere)

Back row (left to right): Pilot 2Lt Fred Shere, Co-Pilot 2Lt Milan Zeman, Bombardier 2Lt Robert Wilcox (KIA 8-12-44), Navigator 2Lt Patrick Ryan.

Front row: Radio S/Sgt Fonzy M. Wilson, Tail-Gunner Sgt Marvin Morris, Waist-Gunner Sgt Joe Maloy, Waist-Gunner Sgt Frank Bennett, Ball-Turret Gunner Sgt Thomas Hampton, Engineer S/Sgt Orlando Friesen.

(Photo courtesy of Joe Maloy)

Pilot 2Lt. Fred C. Shere Jr..

From the, July 7, 1945, letter of engineer Orlando Friesen to the widow of Pilot Fred Shere;

"I can't tell you too much about what happened to Lt. Shere, but will do the best I can. I will start in the morning before the mission and go on through until we were taken prisoner.

"We were awakened on the morning of April 29, 1944, at about 03:00 hours. We went down, had breakfast and went to the briefing room where we were given the details of our mission. We were told that our target was Berlin and to expect plenty of fighters and flak.

"At 07:05 we shoved the throttles forward as we rolled down the runway. Everything went well until we got to the target where we ran into extremely heavy flak and we were hit, but not seriously. After we had dropped our bombs we started for home and were getting along very nicely, but when we hit Drummer Lake, there again was very heavy flak but we received no more hits. Drummer Lake is about 100 miles west of Berlin.

"Shortly after that, we spotted enemy fighters and that is when the trouble began. We were hit several times and the inter-phone went out. So from that time we had no contact with the rest of the crew.

"My turret was shot out of commission on the second pass that the fighters made. After my turret was out, I began to throw all unusable equipment overboard to make the plane lighter. From what I could gather from the rest of the boys, it was on the second pass the fighters made that the boys were wounded.

"After the second pass we were pretty well shot up, but neither Lt. Shere nor F/O Zeman were hurt to my knowledge. Lt. Shere gave the orders to prepare to bail out to the radio-operator S/Sgt. Robert Wilson who relayed the message to me. He went to the back of the plane to tell them to bail out. That is the last I saw of him. I then began to open the bomb bay doors to make an escape hatch for Lt. Shere and F/O Zeman. I had a lot of trouble with the doors because they were pretty well torn up and when I did get them open, I realized we were very close to the ground and knew that I must see that they got out.

"I motioned to them that the doors were open and to get out. Lt. Shere motioned for me to get out and fast. It wasn't until then that I realized how close I was to the ground. My chute just opened long enough to break the fall and I hit awfully hard and was knocked unconscious.

"There are two things that could have happened after I left. The plane could have blown up in mid-air or they realized they were too close to the ground and tried to make a crash-landing, or they were too close to the ground and their chutes didn't open.

"This information is true to the best of my knowledge. It isn't exactly what you wanted, but I am sorry to say I can't help much on anything else because I don't know.

"One thing I will say, he kept that ship up 'til everyone else was out. He wasn't looking out for himself, he was looking out for nine other men, and even though he is dead he still lives with us as a hero. If there ever was a man that deserves credit, he does. That is about all I know. If there is anything I missed and you think I may be able to tell you, be sure and ask.

Love and my deepest regrets and sympathy,
S/Sgt. ORLANDO H. FRIESEN
Flight Engineer

Navigator 2Lt. Patrick J. Ryan

In his story "Mooning Frankfurt" Patrick remembers:

"Early on the morning of the 29th of April 1944, we were part of a four plane B-24 element of the 392nd Bomb Group that took off from Wendling, East Anglia, England. We were on loan to the 44th Bomb Group and the target was Big B; Berlin.

"The weather at take-off was bad and we had some difficulties forming up. It seemed to me that we were in multi-layers of clouds and visibility was the main problem. It was planned that we would have fighter escort almost into the target, drop our bombs and pick up fighter escort again on the way out. Going into the target everything seemed to go well and we dropped our bombs as planned. Then, still in the Berlin area, we were hit by flak but were not too seriously damaged. One engine was feathered but we were able to go under the formation for protection and still keep up.

"A little later a flight of German fighters came down through the formation and knocked out two planes above us and badly damaged our plane too. Now we had one other engine out and windmilling. We could not maintain altitude or position and were in a long gradual descent headed generally in the direction of England and hopefully home. Our nose-turret was out, and since it was hydraulic, that probably meant that all turrets would only work on manuel. We had a sort of bicycle arrangement to turn the turret and elevate the guns. The chanche of bringing the guns to bear on a target was remote at best.

"No one was telling us anything on intercom so I don't know how things were on the flight deck. I would get up in the astrodome to try and see into the flight deck but it didn't work because of glare. I felt however, that we still might make it to Holland and the coast. To myself I wondered if anyone was flying the airplane or if it was on autopilot – unattended. The flight deck seemed to have taken the most damage.

"About that time along came a lone M-109 that had evidently used up all his canon shells. He must have known we were ineffective because he set up a figure eight pattern over us and laced us with the small caliber stuff until we were done. Someone hit the bail-out bell and we all went out. The nose-gunner, Robert Wilcox, was not too eager to bail out so I went first. I later learnt that engineer Friesen had sounded the bailout bell, so everyone else on the flight deck must have been dead.

"After bailing out I had delayed pulling my ripcord almost too long and my chute opened very close to the ground. Even so, I had a relatively easy landing except that I got draped over a fence and got some scratches and bumps from that. The terrain was a combination of forest and fields. Waist-gunner Joe Maloy saw my chute from above and came hot-footing it across the field just as I was hiding my chute in a bush. There were a lot of people chasing him and by the time he got to me, he was gasping and wheezing, blood was streaming down his face, and I thought he must be seriously wounded. In the minute or so it took to convince me that his wounds were slight, the German people were on us. There were German soldiers stationed at the corners of the path that went around each field so we never would have been able to evade capture.

"We were surrounded by people from a nearby village. A young boy was acting as interpreter. The first question he asked was ‹Do you want to go to Berlin?' We said, "Hell, no, we just came from there.' That probably was not a good thing to say because they immediately shook a few pitch forks at us. We were taken to the little village jail.

"Hampton, Bennett and Wilcox were already there. Hampton had an abdominal wound that didn't seem too serious. Morris was brought in later with a leg wound that looked very bad. A direct hit in the tail turret ammunition cans caused several .50 caliber rounds to explode and go through his leg. (In 1992, Joe Maloy told me that Morris got patched up very well and had no bad effects from his wounds). One of the first things I did was fall asleep, but when I woke up, reality had set in. I was so nervous, and my hands shook so badly, I needed help to light my cigarette.

"From the village jail we were taken to a bigger jail, probably in a town called Bippen. There I was given my first piece of German bread. I couldn't eat it. It tasted moldy and I threw it out of my cell. The German guard chew me out for that, picked it up and ate it. Little did I know that this bread would become the "Staff of Life." In the jail in Bippen I learned that Friesen was also captured, but I never saw him again. He had fallen upside down in his chute, landed on his head and was knocked out.

"Next we were taken to some military base, possibly Oldenburg. Here I was told that Fred Shere, Milan Zeman and Fonzy Wilson were killed in the crash. The Germans took all my government issue items leaving me only in my long-john underwear, socks and a ring given to me by my future (and still) wife June. I considered it my engagement ring.

"From this military base we were taken by train, with other prisoners, to Frankfurt. The buttons on the back flap of my longjohns were missing so when they marched us through the city of Frankfurt to the interrogation center in Oberusal, I mooned the whole city. Although this was not an intentional act, it could have expressed my attitude completely, but all I felt was the draft.

"Oberursel was the location of the infamous Dulag Luft interrogation center. By then we were a large group. The interrogators were not much interested in what a nervous, young 2nd lieutenant, on his second mission, might know. So, I was never really questioned. They had too many others to work on. My pride was a little hurt but not much.

"After a few days we were split up and sent to our respective prison camps. The crew went to Stalag Luft VII B. As the only remaining officer of the crew I was sent to Stalag Luft III at Sagan, an officer's camp.

"We were liberated exactly one year after I was shot down – April 29, 1945. During that year we did a lot of things to make time pass, but it was still a long haul. Some things that happened were good, a lot were bad. We were marched, starved and frozen. We were herded like cattle, strafed by our own aircraft and went through numerous bomb raids. But we survived.

"The friendships I made while a prisoner I will treasure forever. Now some of my happiest times are at the Stalag Luft III reunions where I see my old friends and make many new friends since we all had so much in common. The slogan of the 1995 reunion was;"Stay alive ,till ,95."

Engineer S/Sgt. Orlando H. Friesen.

By daughter Pat Salazar.

"Orlando Harold Friesen was born August 29, 1923 in Mountain Lake Township, Cottonwood County, Minnesota to Dietrich Ernst Friesen and Agatha Balzer. He was the second child of this marriage. The Friesen family farmed in southeastern Minnesota. Orlando was born with red hair and later had a red beard hence his name that everyone knew him by as "Red."

"Growing up in Minnesota he attended Amber Lake District 21 school near Fairmont, MN from September 1929 until June 1937 (a one room school house). He and sister walked to school even in the coldest of weather. As he got older he was allowed to take a .22 rifle with him so that

Engineer S/Sgt. Orlando H. Friesen

he could trap and hunt and thus provide food for the table. He attended school through the 8th grade at which time it was necessary for him to begin working. As part of a farming family, Red was responsible at an early age for the Percheron draft horse team that they used to plow and harvest the fields. His great affinity with animals was evident throughout his life.

"From June 1937 until November 1942 he worked as a truck driver, farmhand, mechanic, welder and equipment operator in the Fairmont area.

The following was written by Friesen documenting his military service:

"I, Orlando Harold Friesen, enlisted in the Army November 4, 1942 at Fort Snelling near St. Paul, Minnesota. A week of evaluation got me assigned to the Anny

Air Corps and I was sent to St. Petersburg, Florida for basic training. During six weeks of Basic I learned how to swear like the instructor and which foot was my left foot. My next stop was at Sheppard Air base in Texas. I went to Aircraft Mechanics School, then Aircraft Engine School in Baltimore, Md., and then on to Gunnery School at Tyndal Air Base in Florida.

"I was then sent to Gowen Air Base in Idaho where our aircrew was assembled. My job was the Engineer and Top Turret. We did most of our flight crew training flying out of Gowen Air Base. After 8 weeks of flying as a crew we were considered to be combat ready. We were issued a new airplane in Florida, and instructed to fly it to England. Our route was Miami to Belem, Brazil, then to Dakar, Africa; next stop was Marrakech in North Africa, then on to England.

"We were assigned to the 392nd. Bomb Group. We were now in the war zone. The Germans were bombing targets in England almost every night. After a few days of final instruction we were sent on our first mission in an older combat weary plane that had patches on patches from bullet holes and flak. Flak is the product of exploding anti aircraft shells that explode in the air much like fireworks. The first mission was uneventful as we encountered little flak and no enemy aircraft.

"Mission number two was on April 29, 1944. It was a very long mission to bomb Berlin. This was the fifth time the Americans had bombed that city. The Germans were waiting for us. The flak was so thick it was impossible to fly through it without being hit by an exploding shell. We were on our bomb run when we took a direct hit on our number four engine. As soon as we got rid of the bomb load we were much lighter and were able to get back in formation for the trip back to England, but that was not to be. Sometime later German fighters attacked our formation and took out two planes that were helping to protect us as well as knocking out our number three engine.

"Now we were in real trouble, a long way from home and all alone. At this point we had no injuries on board. Later in the afternoon a lone German ME-109 Fighter came into view out of range of our guns. I am sure he saw we were crippled so decided to finish us off. He came at us from the front and below with his guns blazing and did a lot of damage. Our radio, electrical system and hydraulics were all inoperable. The turret I was in was jammed in a position that made it very hard to get out. I had to remove my parachute to get out then put my parachute back on. The pilot was injured; the co-pilot and the radio operator were dead. I could not help any of them - It was time to bail out!

"My avenue of escape was through the bomb bay doors. They were open because of the failed hydraulic system. We were very close to the ground and I pulled the ripcord as I went headfirst out of the plane. As the chute opened it snapped me into an upright position and my feet were tangled in the parachute shroud lines. I hit the ground in that position. I only remember three things in the next 8 days. #1 A German soldier put a wet rag on my face, #2 A room with very bright lights, and #3 Being in a railroad cattle car with other American soldiers.

"Eight days after I bailed out I was coherent enough to realize I was a POW in Stalag XVII B near, Krems, Austria. You may remember from your childhood history lessons reading about King Arthur's Castle on the Danube River. Stalag 17B was across the Danube River from the castle, and on a clear day we could see the outline of the Castle.

"Life in 17B was not quite like it was portrayed on TV: The perimeter of the camp had two fences approximately 10 feet apart and 10 feet tall. At the corner of each compound there was a guard tower. A guard was in each tower and guards walked between the fences 24 hours a day. The camp consisted of several compounds with six double barracks set end to end with a wash room between them. Each barracks housed 200+ POWs. The wash room was for washing and drinking water only. There was no hot water and no showers here. Once a month we were marched to a communal shower for a two-minute shower. Toilets were outdoor type; six holes each, two to a compound. They were equipped with a terrible odor, lots of flies in the warm months and very cold in the winter months.

"Sleeping bunks were four high made of rough cut lumber with a burlap pallet filled with straw that was host to a multitude of creepy crawlers. The Germans furnished a blanket to each prisoner. The bunks had a six-foot space between them. The eight men in the two bunks formed a small commune to help each other and to share our food rations, etc.

"Food: The Germans cooked the food in a central kitchen and it was delivered to each barracks half by a detail of men assigned from each barracks. It was delivered in a wooden tub about the size of a half-barrel. The ration per man was about the size of a #2 vegetable can once a day five days a week. Two days a week we had two meals a day. On the days when we had two meals there was a meat ration for one meal. The last six months of the war meat became very scarce. One meal was always vegetables. It might be potato today and cabbage tomorrow or spinach or whatever was available.

"Early in my confinement we received a half loaf of German black bread per week. As the war went on even that became a scarce item and the ration went to a loaf for six men then to eight and sometimes none.

"Sometime after WW1 the International Red Cross signed many nations to a "Treaty for the Basic Care of Prisoners of War" called "The Geneva Convention." The rules allowed the home country to send food and mail to be given to the POWs, with the Red Cross supervising the distribution. Each POW was supposed to get a 10-pound food parcel per week. I was never fortunate enough to more than once a month and they completely disappeared near the end of the war. The food parcels contained a can of dried milk, a small can of cocoa, a can of Spam, two packs of cigarettes, a package of soda crackers, a can of liver pate and a Hershey Bar.

"The Russians did not sign the Red Cross agreement and therefore any Russian POWs were at the mercy of the Germans. Part of the Geneva Rules specified that noncommissioned officers could not be forced to work. All of the American POWs in 17B were noncoms. A large Russian compound was next to the compound that I was in and the Germans used the Russians, not being a part of the Geneva rules, for slave labor.

"The Russians were treated very badly. They were given less food than we were and forced to work. Many of them died. We could only watch in horror as a burial detail left the camp nearly every morning with those that had died in the previous 24 hours.

"In March 1945 the Russian army began their siege of Vienna, Austria. Vienna was 50 kilometers east of 17B and at night we could see and hear shells exploding. The sky was a large red glow over the city. The Germans were getting very nervous and did not want to be captured by the Russians. A short time later we were to begin a forced march away from the invading Russian troops.

"The trip was to take 22 days. We arrived at a forest where the trees had been cut down in a large square with trees left standing in the middle. It was called the Branau Woods. This was to be our home until we were liberated by the US 13th Armored Division.

"The twenty-two day march was pure hell. The weather was cold and wet. Food was very scarce not only for the POWs, but also for the German guards. Most of us were wearing the clothes we wore when we were shot down. We were in poor physical condition, cold, hungry, and many were sick. Some days the Germans would bring in some field rations. Drinking water was where we could find it, not very sanitary to say the least, and a source of diarrhea. There were casualties nearly every day.

"When the 13th Armored arrived they disarmed the German guards and they became POWs. Our POW camp leaders sent details of men out into the county side to look for food. The farms in the area had little to offer as the Germans had taken most of the food products away from the farmers already.

"On the third day after we were liberated a small US army detachment arrived and we were to move again. We were taken to Branau, Austria nearby. The town had a large aluminum factory and this was the first time we were inside a building in more than a month, and it was dry. The next day an airlift began and we were transported by air to Camp Lucky Strike near Le Havre, France. The C-46 planes could only transport about 40 men per trip. This camp and others like it were set up to take care of us POWs. There was food, shelter, medical attention, hot showers, and new uniforms. After some medical evaluation we were to start our trip back to the USA.

"Approximately 900 ex-POWs were put on the USS "Le June," a converted troop ship. I began to get seasick as I walked up the gangplank and continued to be sick the entire nine days it took to get to the US. We docked at Trenton, New Jersey and were taken to a nearby army base. I was given a 30-day furlough. My parents and the girl that was to become my wife were waiting for me when I got off of the bus. That was the most pleasant sight I had seen in a long time...

"I used those thirty days to reorganize my life. Jackie and I were married July 15, 1945 while I was on leave. Jackie was a big boost to my morale and she is still the light of my life. At the end of my furlough I went to Miami, Florida, to a recuperation hospital for some serious medical attention. I was in the hospital on VJ day. What a relief that was, we would not have to go fight the Japanese.

"When I was released from the hospital I was sent to Truax Field near Madison, Wisconsin. I finished my three-year enlistment and chose not to reenlist. I was discharged October 31, 1945, 2 years 11 months, and 27 days after enlistment. That was enough for me!

"This is a true account of my life in the US Air Force more than a half century ago. I have purposely omitted some of the most gruesome details and the memories still made me shed some tears, and caused some sleepless nights."

In 1994 he was contacted by one of his crew members and gave the following account of his post war life:

"Now a little about my life since our Kreigi days: I could not get back to the girl I loved fast enough and I married on July 15, 1945. We had dated since she was 14 years old. We have had a very good life together and enjoy each other's company every day.

"I worked in Minnesota short time after being discharged in November 1945. At the time it seemed there should be something better than mosquitoes in summer and snow and cold in winter. I spent the rest of my career life working for three heavy construction companies. The most recent job lasted 30 years. I retired in 1986.

"I went to auction school, and formed Colorado Auction Service that we operated for 7 years. We still have a storage business that is as demanding as a herd of milk cows.

"Jackie is an exceptional artist and thru the years has been in the antique business, my secretary, bookkeeper, business manager, auction clerk and loving wife. Without her I would not have been as successful.

"My hobbies lie in the antique farm tractors and antique cars that I buy, sell, trade and restore..."

Radio Fonzy M. Wilson Jr.

From niece Jan Post.

"Fonzy Madison Wilson Jr. was born in Long Beach, California, on August 14th 1922. His Dad had heard that there was an "Utopia" in Mexico and he decided to take his family and go there. From Wallowa County, Oregon to Mexico;

hundreds of miles. They had a touring car and a truck loaded with all their household items. Grandpa hired a man and his son to drive the truck. They camped out in the open every night. It must have been terribly hard on my Grandmother. Pregnant with 4 little kids, my mother being the youngest, age 3. Grandpa had a sister in Long Beach so they stopped there, and grandma had Fonzy Jr in the hospital there. I don't know how long it was after he was born that they did go into Mexico, but found no Utopia. They had no money left, so they wired home to the great-grandparents for money to get home.

Radio Fonzy M. Wilson Jr.

"They lived in Wallowa County, Oregon for a few years and then moved to Elgin, Union County, Oregon. Fonzy went to school in a one room country school, until high school, then went to Elgin, High school in town. They lived about 6 miles out in the country. After graduation jobs were scarce so he and at least two friends decided to go to California to work in the aircraft factory.

"While there he met and married his wife Billie, an only child. We can't remember her last name. Then the fellows decided to join the Air Corps, which later became the Army Air Force. He was stationed at Gowan Air Base in Mountain Home, Idaho. He had sent for his wife and was able to spend some time with her as well as the rest of his family. She was pregnant with their only child at that time. The child was a boy, but never got to see his Dad, nor did Fonzy ever know he had a son. The boy was named Michael.

"Billie and Michael lived with her mother Honney. As you can expect Billie went through a very rough time dealing with the grief. Billie and Honey doted on Michael. She always sent us pictures of him and she would send us gifts at Christmas. He grew into a very handsome man. Looked a little like Parnell Roberts the American movie actor. He married and learned wood working. He was very good at it. Made spinning wheels and wooden music stands for orchestras among other things. He also was an accomplished Chef.

"But Michael had a drinking problem. It worsened over the years and he lost his wife. He was living in Ohio at the time he called my aunt. They went and got him and got him settled in a house and set up his wood working shop. He would be sober for awhile and then he would be drinking again. So he entered a rehabilitation facility here in Pendleton. He was suppose to stay there a year. But he only stayed a few months and decided he was leaving. So he went back home, and it wasn't long before he died from drinking.

Ball-Turret Gunner Sgt. Thomas L. Hampton.

By daughter Mary Lou Hampton Doup.

"Tom was born July 20, 1914 in Baywood, Virginia. He attended school there until he quit to help on the family farm. He moved to Akron, Ohio about 1930, where his older sister lived. He and my mother, Coreta, were married in 1936, I was born June 21, 1937. Unfortunately, they were divorced.

"Tom went to work on the Mohican Dam in late 1937, he was injured when the truck he was driving went over an embankment. He was in the hospital in Mansfield, Ohio and Grandma Ella went to stay by his side until he was out of danger.

"He enlisted in the Army on November 16, 1940. Photographs indicate he was at Fort Benjamin Harrison in Indiana 1941 through 1942.

Ball-Turret Gunner Sgt. Thomas L. Hampton

"At the age of 26, he was too old to become a pilot, which was his first choice. He began training at a Florida Army Base and became a tail-gunner, later became a waist-gunner.

"On April 29, 1944, he was reported missing in action. In August, 1944, word was received by the family that he was a German prisoner. He was in Stalag 4 Prison Camp. His plane had been shot down and he was wounded in the leg while parachuting from the plane.

"He married Iona in December, 1945. They had been away from home on March 8, 1948. Tom dropped Iona off at her parents home and went to the Hampton farm to do the chores. On his return from the farm, his car caught fire, forcing through a fence on the Grace Doup farm, where it came to rest in a creek. I was 11 years old when this happened.

Newspaper article of March 9, 1948.

"Thomas Lee Hampton, 34, Amity, a Purple Heart veteran of the Army Air Corps who was a prisoner in Germany for a year, was cremated as his auto caught fire and burned on rout 3 a mile north of Amity at 6:30 p.m. Monday. He was married and father of two children.

"He was on his way to Mount Vernon at the time to be initiated into Dan C.

Stone Jr. post of the American Legion.

"State highway patrolmen said Hampton was driving a 1929 Ford coupe with the gas tank in front of the dashboard, and the gas tank exploded. The blast occurred in front of the Harry Kuhlman gas station, and state patrolmen were summoned from there.

"Patrolman and other persons carried water from the station and succeeded in putting the fire out, but not until Hampton had burned to death. Dr. C.L. Harmer, the coroner, gave a verdict of accidental death.

"Patrolmen said the interior of the coupe was probably filled with fire, immediately trapping Hampton and causing him to lose control of the car, which swerved from the road and into a ditch.

"His father, William Hampton, said the gas tank on the car had been leaking, according to patrolmen who were still continuing their investigation this forenoon.

"He was one of the first men inducted from Knox county in World War II, entering the army in October, 1940. He went overseas as a sergeant, waist-gunner on a B-24, in March 1944, and two months later was taken prisoner when his plane was shot down over Germany. He was liberated a year later, on May 3, 1945, and was awarded a Purple Heart medal for wounds.

Waist-Gunner Sgt. Joe Maloy

From his handwritten notes.

"As we crossed into the Netherlands, we caught some heavy flak. Some of it was 105mm. rather than the usual 88mm. stuff. I knew what to expect; the bright red explosions, three to four at the time, the dirty smoke ball that seemed to whip by, the force of the concussion against the plane's thin aluminium skin. As we made our way into Germany, fighters were spotted but were chased off by our P-51 Mustang escorts. So far, so good.

"When we were about an hour away from our target, I lowered the turret. Everybody was sure that we would get heavy resistance. I was barely settled in when two things happened almost simultaneously. Two planes in our Group collided and both went down. While I was looking at this, almost in hypnotic, unbelieving trance, they came like a swarm of birds, spread out across the sky and coming directly at me.

"Fighters, 12 o'clock level! Fighters twelve o'clock high" came over the intercom from Bob and "Swede."

"God, there must be hundreds of them," I heard myself saying but actually there were fifty. I squeezed the gun sight reticles closed with the foot pedal control, trying to get one between the vertical posts. I latched on to one but before I could fire, he rolled, dove beneath us and headed out for another run. Their standard tactic when attacking formations. They had learned early on that it was too costly to attack from the rear. The closing time was too slow. While it gave the fighter pilot more time to aim it also gave the gunners more time to shoot back – the target plane and other planes in the formation could put up a deadly stream of .50 calibre bullets. So they devised the "head on" tactic. They came in waves with a closing speed in excess of 500 miles per hour. The German pilot would line up on a target plane, get the range with his .40 calibre machine guns, open up with his 20 mm. cannon, roll over, dive beneath the formation (heavy armor on underside of the fuselage), pull up, get ahead of the bombers and come back until he exhausted his ammunition.

"I heard the "Swish, swish" of planes going past me and the loud popping noises of 20 mm. shells exploding. As I scanned the sky looking for more planes, I saw one plane in our four plane squadron falling away, trailing smoke and fire. Suddenly it exploded, leaving a big smoke ball and long streamers of of smoke and fire reaching for the ground.

"Here they come," shouted "Swede." This time I was able to get a FW-190 in my sights. Time seemed to slow to a crawl. I saw him boring in, saw the winking flashes of his machine guns and the larger flashes from his cannons. Heard myself instructing my thumbs "to fire short bursts, short bursts" and watched with heart pounding joy as he exploded. As we hurtled past the debris I heard the sound of my own voice talking to "Pappy"; "One down, ninety-one to go."

"This "eyeball to eyeball" confrontation was the fulfillment of our "Hero stories" – knights jousting, duelists facing each other, gun fighters on a dusty cow town street. No place to hide, just you and me!

"FW's and ME-109's kept coming through our formation, wave after wave. They were barreling in close, making a desperate effort to scatter the tight bomber formation so that they could pick off lone planes. As we fired back, the plane would vibrate as many .50 calibre guns opened up and I was vaguely aware of the popping sound of exploding 20 mm. shells.

"I was not conscious of being afraid. It almost seemed that I was directing someone else as I tracked and fired. Sometimes seeing obvious damage, sometimes not. However, when I got a short respite, I became aware that my heart was pounding and I was freezing. Even a heated suit won't keep you warm when your body is soaked with sweat, not at 40° below zero. I knew that we knocked down several planes but we also lost several more.

"This running gun fight had lasted for about forty-five minutes. The fighters broke off just as we reached the perimeter of the "famous" Berlin flak. During this time the formation would have to fly a straight and level course so that the bombs could be accurately aimed. The only feeble defence against this massive array of radar controlled anti-aircraft batteries was a "radar fooling" device first tried in 1943. At the first sign of flak, the waist-gunners threw out small bundles on tin foil strips (chaff). The light weight metallic material dropping from the bomber formation floated down slowly creating a phantom formation below the real one. Radar picked up the phantom and fired into it. Generally, the Germans caught on and changed to conventional methods (sometimes had a captured American plane fly along beside the formation to relay speed and altitude). They also put up box barrages , i.e. simply fire into a zone over the target that was defined by width, length and depth.

"I could see that in addition to the pounding that we were getting that a "box" barrage was waiting for us over the target. Technically our target was the railway station at the intersection of Wilhelmstrasse and Frederickshavenstrasse. What I think is that our target was anything in Berlin and our objective was to destroy planes and pilots. There is even some evidence that targets were "leaked" to encourage the Luftwaffe to take the bait.

"I saw what appeared to be thousands of dirty, black smoke balls whizzing past and then we were in it. The shells burst like a string of giant fire crackers with bright orange-red centers. The "Whump - whump - whump" was continuous. Below me a plane got a direct hit, the right wing disappeared as the plane fell away spurting flame from the stump of the lost wing. I saw two nearby planes with feathered props (if possible the propeller blades of a disabled engine were rotated to zero pitch, otherwise they would "windmill" and create extra drag). There were two more within my view that were several damaged. The pilots were making an all out effort to close up the gap and keep the formation tight for the bomb run.

"It seemed an eternity before Bob called out; "Bombs Away."

"As the bombs fell and the bomb bay doors closed, I felt the plane surge ahead but at the same time I saw that we were peeling away as the Group heeled away from the target.

"Here they come!"

"I saw them hit a Group ahead of us. It was awesome to watch the pyrotechnic display of hundreds of .50 calibre guns converging their fire at the attacking planes. Now they were after us. I locked on to one, fired but didn't see any damage. I picked another, he rolled and dived below us, one veered off, out of range. During this time I could hear the "Swish" passing through out of my field of vision and the "popping" of shells was distinct.

"During a respite I looked for damage and was relieved to see nothing serious. However, my anxiety level went up a little as I heard others calling in to report some large holes and some damage to the control surfaces. The worst news was that the number one engine was showing low oil pressure – an ominous sign!

"We were in a loose formation but I wanted to believe that the worst was over and that we'd just follow that "Red Yarn" back to home. I knew that we had been in the lion's mouth and I knew, even with my short experience, that we'd been in a hell of a fight of course. I didn't know that historians would dub this April 29th air battle as the fiercest of the war. We destroyed eighty-eight German planes and lost seventy-seven of our own but in the words of their commanding general this was the beginning of the end of the Luftwaffe. Only two planes appeared over the Normandy beaches on June, 6th, 1944.

"They were gone. I started to feel better about our situation but I didn't see any of our escort. "Where were they?" Probably many of them had to get rid of their drop tanks when we got the first sightings and then couldn't make it to the target. As I scanned the sky for any sign that the Jerries were back.

"I thought about the people on the ground who had observed the great battle. What they saw was the vast, blue, almost violet, sky "canvas" cut horizontally by 4'000, pure white condensation trails from the half-mile wide, 100 mile long formation of a thousand four-engined bombers flying over to five miles above them. Off to the sides and above and below single con trails from the fighters were etched on the "canvas" in long spirals and curves.

"As the FW-190's and ME-109's approached another set of trails appeared. This "canvas" quickly took on the appearance of a child's fingerpainting as the swirling, looping fighter trails intermingled with with the straight line bomber trails; the effect of the Luftwaffe attack and the escort's counter attack. Overlapping the scene was the fireworks of many machine guns firing from the bomber formations. Intermittently, this artist's rendition was dotted by fire and smoke from burning and exploding aircraft, falling planes, debris from explosions, bodies falling and parachutes. If they were watching near the target they saw this juggernaut fly straight and level into a maelstrom of fireballs and their fingerprints – dirty black smoke balls. They saw planes disappear in a flash, wounded planes falling away out of control.

"It was like flying into a meat grinder but no one flinched, "Ours but to do or die." The world will never see such a sight again but how will it be remembered? By the time the survivors were landing in England the con trails were gone, debris and bodies of airmen both dead and alive had found their way to earth. The "canvas" returned to its virgin state like the magic printers the children enjoy. The dark images made so clear by marking upon the plastic cover with a stylus are gone at a twinkling of the eye when the sheet is lifted, no sign that anything was ever there! As with the toy pad, the scene is blank. The only evidence of this historic battle is in the memories of those who survived and in time that also shall be gone, forever. There are no stone or bronze monuments in the sky.

"Without any warning the waist section of the plane was filled with bright green and orange fireballs. I saw Hamp double over and through his waist window I spotted three ME-109's turning to come back to us. The plane was shaking violently and black oil was pouring from number two engine. Once the prop was feathered the vibration stopped. Now my earphones were crackling with a jumble of excited calls of fighters. I got one in my sights and observed pieces flying from it as he fell away. There were three and the other two got hits. Our number one engine, hit over the target, was now giving off smoke. My mind told me that we'd never make it with two engines out on the same side.

"Morris was calling for help. He had two .40 calibre bullets through his right leg. "Hamp" had a 20 mm. shrapnel wound in the groin but was still on his feet.

"We were far behind our formation and slowly losing altitude. I anticipated "Pappy's" instructions and retracted the turret. He and Pat were talking about the shortest route to the North Sea. Once out of my turret, I went back to check on Morris. He was hurting but not bleeding much because of the extreme cold. He wanted to stay in the turret. I went back to "Hamp" and got him to sit down. I took his gun.

"Damn!" The two remaining ME109's were back. They got hits, more basket-ball size flashes in the fuselage and now black oil was pouring from number one.

"When they made their next pass, they made a mistake by coming in from 8 o'clock high. We could get on them from the tail-turret, the top turret and my waist-gun. I tracked one in (this is when quail hunting and skeet paid of). As cannon shells burst around me, missed. Now I was on his companion who skidded right into my tracers. I could see his goggled face as the 109 began to disintegrate and at the same time I had the sensation of being hit hard in several places. (I had 20 mm. shrapnel wounds in the head, arm, shoulders and back). They were gone but I instinctively knew that "we'd had it."

"We had been clobbered and were about to become statistics. I called to "Pappy," got no response, jerked my connections loose, opened the bulkhead door and looked through the bomb racks toward the flight deck. I saw "Swede" trying to help Fonzy – he was dead. "Swede" saw me and signaled us to bail out. At that instant the bail out bell sounded. I motioned to the others, grabbed my chute and attached it to my harness but forgot my shoes!. Bennett and I got Morris out of the tail turret, put his chute on him and pulled him up to the hatch. I was responsible for clearing the waist so with Bennett's help we rolled Morris out of the hatch and then helped "Hamp" out. We shook hands at the hatch, he rolled up and tumbled out head first, and I followed.

"There was a sudden blast of air as I hit the slipstream, then I was on my back, suspended in space with no sensation of falling at all. I knew that we had lost altitude so I was torn between my desire to delay opening my chute and my fear of waiting too long. The longer I waited, the better my chances for escaping and avoiding being shot at from the ground.

"While this was going through my mind, I removed my helmet and goggles and my gloves. I was amazed, they just floated along beside me! I was surprised by the amount of blood inside the helmet (it turned out that none of my wounds were deadly but there was a lot of blood and I picked buckshot sized shrapnel out of the wounds for the next couple of weeks.

"I decided that is was time, so I moved my arms around, got myself positioned at about 60°, head down and pulled the ripcord. With great relief, I saw that the small pilot chute fly out, dragging the main canopy behind. The chute popped with such force that I was jerked upright while my fleece lined boots ripped away, headed for the ground. I was left with my "bedside shoe" type heated boots. I would rue the day that I forgot my G.I. shoes.

"I looked around, saw a clear field, a tiny village and a patch of woods. I wanted to get close to the trees but not in them, so I pulled on my shroudlines to partially collapse one side. This allowed me to slide in the direction of the collapsed side. As I pulled on the lines, I looked up and my breath stopped – the canopy was badly damaged, long rips and cut cords. It had been hit by flak or 20 mm. shrapnel and I thought for a split second that that it was going to collapse. I didn't but I decided not to guide myself anymore.

"In any case, the ground suddenly jumped up to meet me. I landed with a thud. Landing with an intact twenty-eight foot chute was about the same as jumping from a twenty foot high wall. "Son of a bitch." A pain shot through my right knee. I rolled over, unhooked my harness, bundled the chute and harness and took off toward a barbed wire fence bordering the woods. I had seen a chute there just before I hit the ground.

"I had only gone a few steps before I realized that I couldn't run, the pain in my leg was too much. I limped along, favoring the injured leg, knowing that this was going to be a serious problem."Bloody, awful luck!" I thought it was a sprain but x-rays after I was liberated showed evidence of a hairline fracture of the tebia.

"As I approached the fence, I saw that Pat and his chute were tangled in the wire. I helped him get loose. He looked as if he had been in the middle of a cat fight. We were about to head into the woods when we saw an old man running towards us. Pat thought that we were in Holland and the man looked harmless so we waited.

"Are you Dutch," I asked. "Ja, Dutch," he answered, or so we thought. We didn't know that what he was actually saying was "Deutsch"; German. He pointed towards the woods as he glanced furtively back toward the village. We thought he was trying to help us, so we headed into the woods. We heard a few shouts and a couple of shots. We wanted to find a gully and cover ourselves with leaves until darkness. A young man had about "zero" chance of going undetected if he tried to move around Germany or occupied Europe during daylight hours.

"We found a good spot and began to dig out leaves as fast as we could. We must have sensed them because we looked up at the same time to see a German officer and about eight to ten soldiers with rifles standing on the bluff above us.

"Ve see you zere, come out wit hand op or you vil be shot"; he shouted.

"I looked at Pat, an officer after all. He was looking at me. They would have killed us both before we could have drawn our pistols. We put our hands up and walked up the bank...... Here the document ends abruptly.

From his obituary.

"Joe B. Maloy, Jr., age 82, died January 30th, 2006. He was born in Montgomery,

Alabama, the son of Joe B. Maloy Sr. and Lucretia Boothe Maloy. After graduation from Sidney Lanier High School in 1942, he was drafted into the Army and volunteered for the Army Air Corps. He was originally assigned for pilot training. However, he was afraid WWII would end before he finished that lengthy training and asked to transfer to gunnery school.

"He became a ball-turret gunner on a B-24 with the 392nd Bomb Group, 577th Squadron stationed at Wendling, England. His bomber was shot down by German fighters during a 1000 plane raid on Berlin, Germany. Maloy and six other survivors of the ten man crew were taken as POWs. He was sent to Stalag 17 in Krems, Austria, where he stayed until April 8, 1945. Maloy and his fellow POWs were liberated on May 3, 1945.

" After the war he returned to Montgomery and married Ida Merle Weston in 1947. He received both a Bachelor and a Masters degree in engineering from the University of Alabama. He worked for short periods for both St. Regis Paper Company and Dupont before going to work for Kimberly-Clark Corporation.

"During his 33 years with Kimberley-Clark he held various engineering and management positions. He was a Registered Professional Engineer for 33 years. For twenty years Maloy taught mathematics, engineering, and management courses (evening classes) for Pensacola Junior College, the University of Tennessee and Augusta College.

"Upon retirement, Joe and Ida moved to Peachtree City. Joe had become an avid runner and the golf cart paths offered the perfect track. He ran every day until he was in his late seventies. He was an active member of the Peach Tree City Running Club and treasured his 10'000 mile jacket.

"He was a voracious reader and student of the southern vernacular. He and the late Atlanta Journal Constitution columnist Celestine Sibley corresponded for years over the origine of southernisms like "I'm bounden to" and "I'm fixing to go."

"On July 17th, 1996, he carried the Olympic torch in Peachtree City, Georgia. He was selected by the coca-Cola company to represent veterans and former POWs of WWII. His run was shown on national television. He carried the torch with the names of his air crew comrades clenched in the fist carrying the torch.

***

Acknowledgements:
Pat Salazar, daughter of engineer Orlando H. Friesen.
Jan Post, niece of radio-operator Fonzy M. Wilson Jr.
Mary Lou Hampton Doup, daughter of ball-turret gunner Sgt. Thomas L.
    Hampton;

CHAPTER 30

392ND BOMB GROUP 578TH BOMB SQUADRON

Type: B-24J • Serial: 42-110105
MACR: 4446 • Air Base: Wendling

Sixty years after riding a B-24 Liberator on a bombing mission over Berlin, John P. Bonnassiolle is finally home. The plane carrying Sergeant Bonnassille, age 20, and nine other crewmen in April 1944 never returned, but on Tuesday his remains were buried in the family's cemetery plot. "We have closure," said Andrew Kelley, 88, who, like his younger brother John, flew bombers in the war.

New York Times, August 10, 2010

Pilot: 2Lt. Robert R. Bishop, 0-682775, KIA, El Reno, OK

Co-Pilot: 2Lt. Arthur W. Luce, 0-809012, KIA, Fort Bragg, CA

Navigator: 2Lt. Donald W. Hess, 0-814314, KIA, Sioux City, IA

Bombardier: 2Lt. Thomas Digman Jr., 0-690853, KIA, Pittsburg, PA

Engineer: Sgt. James T. Blong, 36296588, KIA, Port Washington, WI

Radio: S/Sgt. Joseph J. Karaso, 33477790, KIA, Philadelphia, PA

Ball-Turret Gunner: Sgt. Michael A. Chiodo, 35530766, KIA, Cleveland, OH

Left Waist-Gunner: Sgt. John P. Bonnassiolle, 19140409, KIA, Colma, CA

Right Waist-Gunner: Sgt. John J. Harringer Jr., 35541614, KIA, South Bend, IN

Tail-Gunner: S/Sgt. Ralph L. McDonald, 14043603, KIA, East Point, GA

10 KIA

Crash Site: D-Meitze
Time: 11.10

392nd Bomb Group, 578th Bomb Squadron (Bishop)

(Left to right): Left Waist-Gunner Sgt. John Bonnassiolle, Radio S/Sgt. Joseph Karaso, Ball-Turret Gunner Sgt. Michael Chiodo, Baxler, engineer (not on final crew), Pilot 2Lt. Robert Bishop, Right Waist-Gunner Sgt. John Harringer Jr., Bombardier 2Lt. Thomas Digman Jr., Co-Pilot 2Lt. Arthur Luce, Navigator 2Lt. Donald Hess

Researcher Annette Tisson:

"The Bishop crew took off at 07:39. Around 11:03, after the first fighter attack, the Sabourin crew saw them pull away from the formation, reporting that it "looked like the right elevator was shot up badly. No chutes."

"Sgt. Guillot, Kamenitsa's left waist gunner, remembers that when his airplane came to rest after the crash and the dust had settled, he could see a huge fire and black smoke near a farm house or barn a few hundred yards away. He was sure it was a bomber from his own Group, perhaps Ofenstein's, since their two planes had collided and left the formation at the same time.

" As it turned out, the plane was actually Bishop's. German witnesses remember seeing the dogfight between the fighters and the bombers in the sky over the farm, and then the B-24 spiraling down toward the horse pasture below. They confirmed that everyone was killed in the crash. About an hour after the impact, a bomb exploded in the wreckage, destroying much of what remained of the plane and sending debris far and wide through the little town.

***

In 2003, a German national located the site of the crash and recovered human remains, which were turned over to US officials. In 2005, a joint POW/MIA Accounting Command Team (JPAC) excavated the crash site and gathered additional human remains, military equipment, and metal identification tags for Bishop, Blong, Bonnassiolle, and Harringer. The team also recovered a class ring with the initials AWL, presumably belonging to co-pilot Luce. In 2007, a JPAC eam completed the site excavation and found additional evidence that helped to confirm the identity of the crew.

Navigator 2Lt. Donald W. Hess.

Lt. Donald W. Hess, 28, was born in Sioux City. He was a graduate of Central High School, University of Iowa, and the school of Southern Methodist University of Dallas, Texas.

According to a story in the Sioux City Journal's archives, he was a graduate of Sioux City Central High School, and after completing law school, he practiced with his father, A. G. Hess, in the firm of Hess and Hess in Sioux City. Donald Hess served as an assistant Woodbury County attorney for about 5 months in 1942. A gravestone in his honor stands in the Ida Grove, Iowa, cemetery where his parents ar buried.

In the summer of 1942, he enlisted in the Air Corps. He was called for service in February, 1943, and received his commission in October of that year. He went overseas in February. 1944 as navigator of a B-24 Liberator. He was reported Missing in Action over Germany on April 29, 1944, His plane crashed near East Meitze, Germany, and Donald was killed on that date.

According to a POW/Missing Personnel Office news release, German forces buried the remains of three of the men from that plane around the time of the crash. In 1946, those remains were exhumed and reburied in a U.S. military ceremony in Belgium. A German citizen in 2003 located the crash site and recovered human remains. In 2005, an American recovery team excavated the sight and gathered additional remains, military equipment and metal identification tags for four of the crew members. The team completed the excavation in 2007 and found additional evidence that helped confirm the crew's identity. Forensic identification tools and other evidence were used to identify the remains.

Waist-Gunner Sgt. John P. Bonnassiolle.

By Paulette Gooch, sister.

Waist-Gunner Sgt. John P. Bonnassiolle

"Last Spring, driving the 300 miles home from a wonderful party for my mother's 101st birthday, I reminisced about a sister who had passed away much too early and my brother, John Bonnassiolle, that I had lost when I was a small child. Fortunately my sister left a family that I can enjoy and she is with me through them. Then I thought about all the years my brother and I could have shared and the family he might have had. Yes, there were definitely missing plates at the festive table the night before.

"Through the years my mother was reluctant to talk about my brother's death (we called him Jack). I respected that though I wondered if there were papers somewhere that would give me some information. I only knew that he died in World War Two, somewhere in Germany.

"I decided to try the Internet to see if I could find out anything about him and his crew. I really wasn't very hopeful about it. His short life seemed like a blip on the family screen and he was fading away very fast. My hope was that I could leave a history for the rest of the family and a place for him in their memories. The first interesting site that I found was that of the National Cemeteries in Europe. I discovered that there is a memorial site in the Netherlands with his name, and the names of most of his crew, on a memorial wall. Wow, what a rush that was but I had no idea of what was to come. Because I had gleaned the airplane's identification number and his unit description from the cemetery site I posted a note on a B-24 site asking for more information.

"I quickly received an e-mail from a man named Jim Marsteler who is deeply involved in B-24 history and he thought that I would be interested in talking to a man in Germany by the name of Enrico-Rene Schwartz. I sure was! I soon was speaking to Enrico on the phone and via e-mail. Soon Enrico and the MAARCT team began looking for my brother's airplane. He was amazed that we had connected too. His phone calls were thrilling and the search totally fascinating. Our correspondence went on all Spring and Summer as the team spent all their spare time excavating the site and doing much more in the way of obtaining permits from a variety of government agencies – no easy task. Mother's age gave them a special purpose in finding Jack and the crew. However, Enrico told me that everything was going exceptionally well and he thought it was because Mother was waiting for the news about her son and even the government agencies seemed to

473

respond to her need.

"The Gudehus family that owns the farm where the plane crashed opened their hearts and their gates to MAACRT and later to me and my son Shawn. The present day owner, Willy Gudehus, was a seven year old boy on the day of the crash and he vividly remembers the dog fight in the air overhead. The German fighter planes attacking and the large B-24 bomber spiraling down to the horse pasture below. Just before impact he ran for cover to the family bomb shelter. He remembers that about an hour after the impact a bomb detonated in the wreckage sending debris far and wide through the little town. Only a minute separated that crash and the crash of another B-24 that came down on the same farm. One of the survivors, Bud Guillot, is now a friend and willing to share his memories of that day.

"Although, the MAACRT crew worked diligently through the summer they didn't locate a definite identification of the airplane and were feeling frustrated. One Sunday as Enrico was returning home to Bremen from a business trip, he felt the impulse to get off his train in Meitze and try once more. He told me he didn't hold out much hope. However, he began sifting dirt through the screen that the team constructed. During this time he spotted some fuzzy object in the dig that he thought should be relegated to the refuse pile and he picked it up. He tossed it to an area with other debris, it looked like it might have been the lining of a gunner's jacket. When he tossed it the construction of the material seemed different – like it was wadded up. So, he picked it up again and began gently pulling it apart. Then, he saw a strip of leather in the middle of the fuzz and a letter... J... then a B..and the rest of the letters... onnassiolle - my brother's name. He got goose bumps and tears finding it. I have goose bumps and tears whenever I think of it and right now typing this story. Later, the same day he found two engine identification numbers that definitely identified the airplane.

"Later, In October, my son and I went to Germany to visit the crash site and to say goodbye to my brother before the U.S. Army took over the site and the excavation was filled in. Most of the little town of Meitze came to the crash site to be with us. A wonderful minister, Reverend Stern, blessed the crew and the site and gave us much comfort. Following the ceremony the Gudehus family gave us a reception in their charming historic home. The present day Gudehus family is the sixth generation to occupy the home and farm the land. I feel blessed that the crew and their plane came to rest with this generous and caring family.

"Later that day we went to another spot on the farm where the plane of Bud Guillot crashed. Bud had called me the day before I left for Germany and asked me to look for a piece of his airplane. The plane didn't come apart as the Bishop plane had and we didn't know if there would be anything to find after almost 60 years. However, my son with his logical engineer's mind and his experience in surveying figured out from the picture of the crash and the road nearby and just where the plane landed, and there at his feet was a piece of the cowling. The only piece left of the airplane. I was put in charge of bringing it home. I packed it in my hand, I packed it in my purse, I changed its location a dozen times. With a sense of great relief I did return home with it and mailed it to Bud.

Ball-Turret Gunner Sgt. Michael A. Chiodo.

By cousin Joyce Wittal.

"Michael A. Chiodo was born 18 June 1921 in Cuyahoga County, Ohio. He was the eleventh of twelve children. His parents and the two eldest children were born in Catanzaro, Calabria, Italy. Michael graduated from Collinwood High in Cleveland and worked as a drill press operator at the Breckenridge Machine Company before entering the Army Air Corps in January 1943.

"Two of his brothers, Adolph and Frank - also enlisted in the Army and his sister Rose Ann enlisted in the Women's Army Corps during the war. His brothers were wounded, but survived the war. Michael was not so fortunate.

Ball-Turret Gunner Sgt. Michael A. Chiodo

"Michael's niece, Mrs. Joyce Wittal remembers; "The family grieved inconsolably for their baby boy. Although I've never met him – I know him through all the stories from my aunts and uncles. Michael's sister, when asked what she thought of her brother and his crew being honored in Arlington Cemetery stated: "Yes, that is where heroes go.""

Tail-Gunner S/Sgt. Ralph L. McDonald.

Staff Sergeant Ralph McDonald was born on July 11, 1921 to a family in rural Georgia who found another child was too many to care for. Ralph was adopted by Robie and Mary Baldwin McDonald who had been married for eight years and did not have children of their own. Both were living in Georgia but were natives of Alabama. The family moved back to Alabama during the Great Depression, closer to their extended families.

Ralph's schooling ended at sixth grade and as a teenager he moved to find work in Atlanta, Georgia. He worked as a driver of various vehicles from taxi cabs to buses and trucks. On January 24, 1941, Ralph visited the enlistment office at fort McPherson in Atlanta and joined the US Army Air Corps. He was trained as a tail-gunner and was a member of the 392nd Bomb Group of the 8th USAAF.

On April 29, 1944, Ralph and his crew was dispatched to bomb Berlin. The aircraft was shot down just north of Hannover, and the entire crew lost their lives. His remains were recovered more than 65 years later and was buried on March 25, 2011 next to his mother's final resting place.

***

Acknowledgements;
Paulette Gooch, sister of waist-gunner Sgt. John P. Bonnassiolle.
Joyce Wittal, cousin of gunner Sgt. Michael A. Chiodo.

Bishop's crew honored in Arlington Cemetery

CHAPTER 31

392ND BOMB GROUP 578TH BOMB SQUADRON

Type: B-24H • Serial: 42-100100 "Double Trouble"
MACR: 4444 • Air Base: Wendling

"On the April 29, 1944, mission over Berlin, they were assigned a different B-24 bomber as the "Bad Penny" was grounded.... On that mission, my father's plane was attacked by Messersmitt 109's. He managed to parachute out of the burning plan, but before jumping he realized he had forgotten to destroy the radar set. He went back to push the button but was badly burned because of this."

Laurie and Jamie Roper, daughters of Navigator 2Lt. Jack A. Roper

---

Pilot: 2Lt. Gerald E. Rogers, 0-806152, KIA, Hayward, CA

Co-Pilot: 2Lt. Richard A. Weir, 0-811160, POW, Worcester, MA

Navigator: 2Lt. Jack A. Roper, 0-695451, POW, New York, NY

Bombardier: 2Lt. Fred J. Kane, 0-752921, KIA, Wichita, KS

Engineer: T/Sgt. Robert L. McCalicher, 33479210, POW, Pottstown, PA

Radio: T/Sgt. Earl J. Lawson, 38123976, POW, Hobbs, NM

Top-Turret Gunner: S/Sgt. Robert J. Longo, 11111957, POW, Westerly, RI

Waist-Gunner: S/Sgt. Robert W. Danford, 16160528, POW, Detroit, MI

Waist-Gunner: S/Sgt. Harold L. Andrews, 17146344, POW, Akron, CO

Tail-Gunner: S/Sgt. Edward J, Gienko, 36372955, POW, Chicago, IL

2 KIA, 8 POW

Crash Site: Fuhrberg/Hannover, Germany
Time: 11.06

Pilot 2Lt. Gerald E. Rogers.

By son Dennis Rogers

"Gerald. E. (Buck) Rogers was born in Burley, Idaho in 1917 and moved to Salinas, California area when he was young. He attended the city college in Salinas and was then employed locally as a accountant for a mining firm.

"He was driven to enlist, as were many, many young men at thc outbreak of Pearl Harbor bombing. I understand he had a unquenchable desire to fly and did so as a young man, flying crop dusters in the central valley of California. He enlisted in the Army Air Corps with the intent of being a bomber pilot.

"His deployment came around fall of 1943. He went to Ireland after crossing the pond via the southern route. He and his crew were called to Wendling, England around the end of March 1944 and his first mission was the infamous bombing run that found Switzerland rather than Germany on April 1st. Not a good April fools joke on the Swiss. He flew 12 more missions before the April 29th mission to Big B (Berlin). His demise was just eleven days after I was born so I'm pretty sure he didn't know I was here.

"His remains were found over three years after the mission and imposed great hardships for my mother. I don't think she ever recovered from this and was in some sort of depression thereafter until her early demise at 53 years old. I really didn't have much connection to my fathers relatives as I think it was painful for my mother who tried to forget this man and hopefully move on. That is the silent tragedy of the war orphans and their families.

This is a thumb nail sketch of Lt. Gerald Rogers. His nickname of Buck Rogers was taken from the comic book hero. His navigator was Kane, and was nicknamed Killer Kane. These two comic book characters were the only two that didn't survive that mission. Kane was killed on board during the attack of the German fighters that set the plane on fire and resulted in the bailout somewhere over Hannover/Celle area.

Co-Pilot 2Lt. Richard A. Weir.

By son Richard A. Weir Jr.

"My father grew up in Worchester, MA, and Graduated from Commerce High School. He worked odd jobs, and played recreational football. He was spotted by a college recruiter, and given a football scholarship to Holy Cross College in Worchester, MA. He graduated in 1940, with a Bachelor of Science in Economics.

"He wanted to fly, but was too tall for the Navy. Once war broke out he went to Boston and enlisted in the Army Air Corps. He met my mom before leaving to train in Colorado and Idaho. After being shot down, he spent a year in Stalag Luft III, they got frostbite on march to a new camp near end of the war. One day they awoke to find all guards gone. They walked until meeting General Patton, who was chasing the Germans. Upon returning home, he resumed seeing my mom, Margaret Case, and proposed 1-2 months later.

"They had four boys while stationed in Ohio, Massachusetts, Rhode Island, Florida, Brazil and Maryland. He was a Lieutenant Colonel in the Air Force Systems Command at Andrews Air Force Base when he retired at age 54. He then sold real estate and was a substitute teacher. They celebrated their 50th anniversary in 1995 at the Andrews Officers Club. He died of blood cancer in 2000 at 85 years old.

Co-Pilot 2Lt. Richard A. Weir in New York

"He never said much about his crew, only that one of his biggest regrets in life was that he didn't do more for them. He received a small piece of scrapnel through his lip into the roof of his mouth after parachuting out of the B-24.

Navigator 2Lt. Jack A. Roper.

From daughters Laurie and Jamie Roper.

"My father, Jack Roper was born in the Bronx, NY in Oct. 1915. His mother was Anna Roper and father Aaron. Aaron died when my father was very young so he and his brother Burt, who also became a lawyer, were raised by his mother.

"He attended The New School of Social Research in New York City and St. John's University for his undergraduate degree. We aren't sure what he majored in.

"Dad joined the Air Corps just before his 26th Birthday. He had hoped to be a pilot but due to inner ear infections, he was not able to attain this goal but instead became a navigator.

"My father had to fly 25 missions over different areas of the Fatherland before the crew was to be shipped back to the States. He told me that no one believed they would meet that goal as in the early months of 1944, the Allies were losing bombers at a deadly rate. On one mission to Frankfurt, his bomber "Bad Penny" took poundings from anti-aircraft guns and managed to limp back with only two working engines.

"But on the April 29, 1944, mission over Berlin, they were assigned a different B-24 bomber as the "Bad Penny" was grounded. The crew was convinced their luck would not continue. On that mission, my father's plane was attacked by Messersmitt 109's. He managed to parachute out of the burning plan, but before jumping he realized he had forgotten to destroy the radar set. He went back to push the button but was badly burned because of this.

"He landed in a tree in a forest. Released from the tree, he became a prisoner of war. His face and hands were burnt and he had a piece of flak in his leg, but he was alive. And he fortunately remembered to throw away his dog tags stamped with his religion.

"While confined temporarily in a prison cell he overheard guards who spoke a smattering of English say that the American flyers were Chicago gangsters who were hired by the US Military to bomb German cities and kill the civilians.

"He was taken to Stalag Luft III on April 29th and released one year later to the day. Stalag Luft III was where the Great Escape took place just weeks prior to my father's arrival. The men were still mourning the deaths of their British comrades and talking about their 13 months of labor building the tunnels Tom, Dick and Harry.

"Many stories were relayed in the barrack where 15 American pilots and navigators shared their capture experiences late into the nights. One stood out; a B-17 navigator with the 15th Air Force in Italy was on a mission to bomb the Ploesti oil fields in Romania. As the plane was cruising about 16,000 feet high over the Austrian Alps, it was hit by anti-aircraft fire and exploded. My father's roommate wasn't wearing his parachute. He went hurtling through the air and plunged into the side of a snow capped mountain and tumbled down the slope. Upon waking up, he only saw white and cried out, "There really is a heaven!" He felt his body, learned he was in one piece and started walking. Still convinced he was in heaven, he eventually came to a house. Rushing to knock on the door and, there stood a German officer.

"He graduated from New York Law School Summa Cum Laude after the war and was asked to teach there which he did in the evenings while holding a job as Asistent Chief Attorney and then Chief Attorney of the Veteran's Administration in New York City.

"He married my mother, Ruth Mervis in 1946. He retired to Miami, Fla. at age 60 with my mother. He suffered from anxiety attacks and claustrophobia for the rest of his life. We believe it was due to the stresses of the war so we were elated for him when he took an early retirement. Dad went into a coma after celebrating his 98th birthday and died one week later.

***

Acknowledgements;
Dennis Rogers, son of pilot 2Lt. Gerald E. Rogers
Richard Weir, son of co-pilot 2Lt. Richard A. Weir
Laurie and Jamie Roper, daughters of navigator 2Lt. Jack A. Roper

392ᴺᴰ BOMB GROUP
579ᵀᴴ BOMB SQUADRON

Type: B-24H • Serial: 42-7510 "El Lobo"
MACR: 4461 • Air Base: Wendling

German eyewitnesses report hearing the sound of gunfire in the clouds and then seeing this B-24 descend through the clouds. Neither right engine was working and thick black smoke was coming from the forward part of the fuselage. The plane impacted in a forest on the outskirts of Dinklage in Germany.

From the 392nd Bomb Group Web-Site

Pilot: 2Lt. Bert W. Wyatt, 0-526045, KIA, Pittsburg, PA

Co-Pilot: 2Lt. Albert M. Tufts, 0-755611, KIA, Brownsville Junction, ME

Navigator: 2Lt. Douglas N. Franke, 0-691739, KIA, Anoka, MN

Engineer: T/Sgt. Byron E. Hassett, 36159795, KIA, Chicago, IL

Radio: S/Sgt. Robert W. Monroe, 17165490, KIA, Jewell, KS

Nose-Turret Gunner: S/Sgt. William S. Womer, 15074670, KIA, Cochocton, OH

Ball-Turret Gunner: Sgt. John F. Sorrells, 14170070, KIA, Hartford. AL

Left Waist-Gunner: Sgt. Robert E. Thompson, 17070811, KIA, Clare, IA

Right Waist-Gunner: Sgt. Alfred P. Archambeau, 20101348, KIA, Cambridge, MA

Tail-Gunner: S/Sgt. David E. Harbaugh, 38111083, KIA, Corpus Christi, TX

10 KIA

Crash Site: Dinklage/Quackenbrück - Germany
Time: 13.45

Pilot 2Lt. Bert W. Wyatt

Bert was born September 6, 1923 and raised in Greenfield, Illinois. His parents were divorced; perhaps as a result, he was very close to his mother. He found odd jobs and worked whenever he could help to mother, brother, and two sisters.

His niece Betty remembers him as a "tall, handsome man with twinkling eyes." He was an exceptional ahlete and played football all four years in high school; he was also an excellent boxer. He was the valedictorian for his graduating class. His brother Tom remembers that he had a beautiful tenor voice.

He was commissioned as a 2nd Lt. and received his pilot's wings on June 26, 1943. He was the only married man on the crew, having met his wife while he was undergoing pilot training in Massachusetts. Their son was born in September 1944.

Navigator 2Lt. Douglas N. Franke.

By Annette Tison, whose father was Navigator Franke's brother.

"Both his paternal grandfather and great-grandfather were born near Berlin; his grandfather immigrated to Minneapolis, Minnesota, in 1881when he was in his late teens. His father was born in Minneapolis but his mother had emigrated from Sweden when she was 6.

"Doug was born February 1, 1923 and grew up in the small town of Coon Rapids, Minnesota. He became an Eagle Scout in 1940. In 1941, he was admitted to the University of Minnesota and enrolled in both chemical engineering and Navy ROTC classes.

"He enlisted in the Army Air Corps Reserve on June 23, 1942 and was later ordered to report for duty no later than Jan 4, 1943. He proceeded by train to the Air Corps Classification Center in San Antonio, TX. Soon after, he had completing preliminary testing and wrote, "Congratulate me, I'm in! Today I signed the official papers classifying me as a navigator, exactly the job I picked when I stated my preferences."

"In Feb 1943, he was transferred to Ellington Field, near Houston, TX, for pre-flight training. In May 1943, he transferred to Advanced Navigation School at San Marcos, TX.

"He was absolutely thrilled to be in the Army Air Corps and especially to be trained as a navigator. It wasn't all bookwork, though, and it wasn't all safe. While in navigator school, he wrote his parents on July 11, 1943: "The last week or two, the field has had quite a bit of tough luck, ten men killed in three days and another plane forced down in Mexico. The first crash was in the daytime. The plane was above an overcast and the navigators, five of them, didn't know where they were. When they thought they were over destination, they descended thru the overcast and banged head-first into a mountain. The second crash was a group of fellows on a celestial mission. The same thing occurred, and they were found still strapped in their seats the next morning. But the percentage is so small that it isn't anything to worry out. If the navigators know what they are doing," Doug assured his family, "everything works perfectly." He was excited about upcoming celestial navigation. "Is that ever going to be fun, flying all night with just the stars to guide us. But before we fly those missions we have some interception, search, and radius of action flights to get out of the way. So far everything is rosy, and I have high hopes toward getting through this course O.K."

"He was commissioned as a 2nd Lt, navigator, on September 16, 1943 to continue in force "during the pleasure of the President of the United States for the time being, and for the duration of the war and six months thereafter unless sooner terminated." Granted ten days leave, he traveled to the University of Kansas where his youngest brother Bob (my father) was in military training. My Dad told me how proud he was of his brother and how impressive he looked in his sharp pinks and greens and shiny Second Lieutenant bars. September 17, 1943, was my dad's 18th birthday and the last time he would ever see his brother Doug.

"It took until the new year, but the Wyatt crew was finally on their way overseas. In a letter from Topeka, KS, dated Feb 2, 1944, Doug said, "The Air Corps finally kicked thru with a little present for us, transferring us back into heavy bombardment... As to when and where we are going, of course I can't say. But if you don't hear from me for quite a while, you will know I'm 'on the way,' and for heaven's sake don't worry about me. I'll probably wind up in some paradise with nothing to do but a native wave a fan over my face."

"The Wyatt crew flew via the southern route to England. After thirteen days travel time and 53 hours in the air, Doug's crew finally arrived in Great Britain on Mar. 3, 1944. His first communication home was in a V-mail dated March 9, 1944, postmarked 17 March;

"England. Dear Folks, Have a little more time tonight, consequently I will endeavor to tell you a little of what has happened so far. The trip over wasn't as nerve racking as I thought it would be; of course it was really magnificent out there with nothing around but the blue-gray ocean. At times the clouds would form an impenetrable blanket beneath us, much like giant puffballs they were so beautiful. First impressions of England. The country itself is probably as diverse as one could find anywhere, ranging from jagged mountains to fertile valleys where they grow an abundance of foodstuffs. Nevertheless England is primarily a manufacturing country converted, as everyone knows, to the production of war material. Upon first conversation with one of the British, one can hardly notice

the steely resistance they were called upon to use in the Battle for Britain. Yet, from the matter-of-fact manner in which they talk of their homes and industries being bombed, one catches a fleeting glimpse of the courage and fortitude that are two inherent characteristics of the race. Outwardly, they are polite, reserved, and extremely hospitable. On the whole, my first acquaintance with Britain is highly favorable...So long, Doug"

A V-Mail dated 20 March, told that they were in Ireland as;

"Before flying any bombing missions, we have to undergo some specialized training; consequently it will be a little while yet before we actually win the war for the allies. Hell, if they keep shifting us around very much longer, the war will be over before we even fire a shot."

A few days later, he wrote,

"Our training here is just beginning, but all in all it will only be about a month until we see the action we are prepared for. Gosh, it sure seems funny that after over a year of training in the states, there is more vital information we must know before we take the bit in our teeth. Be that as it may, anything they can teach me that will help in future operations will be gratefully received and duly credited.'

Finally, orders dated April 10, 1944 transferred the Wyatt crew to the 392nd Bomb Group. His last letter home was written April 19, 1944.

"Well, here I go again, still alive and kicking about everything in general. Outside of a poker game, the club is quite quiet today. Quite a few of the boys have been on a rampage in the continent and are hitting the sack. It sure is swell to be finally settled. Around here the chow is wonderful. Towards the last of our stay in Ireland, it was terrible, about every other night, my bombardier and I would go into town for a real feed. The field is so spread out here that I had to buy a bike the other day. Seven pounds it set me back, the equivalent of $28 in our money. The monetary values over here are all screwed up, of course, but time and a good poker game teach its use in a hurry.... Guess that's about all.... Be sure to write when you have time because I sure miss you all around the old homestead. So long, Doug."

"At this point, Uncle Doug had been briefed for, started, or completed missions for eight consecutive days. On April 28, the entire 14th Combat Wing was stood down. The next day, April 29, was the mission to Berlin.

"Uncle Doug's remains were returned to the US aboard USAT *Haiti Victory*. Also on this ship were the remains of Sgt. Thompson and Sgt. Archambeau. He was buried in Hillside Cemetery, Minneapolis, MN, on June 27, 1949.

Radio-operator S/Sgt. Robert W. Monroe.

Was born 7 Jan 1924. According to the 1930 census, both his father's parents were born in Germany. He entered the service from Kansas.

After the crash, he was identified by the Germans and buried in a marked grave. He is buried in the Ardennes American Cemetery, Plot C, Row 4, Grave 42.

As radio operator, S/Sgt. Monroe sat at a table on the flight deck directly behind the copilot. All radio operators were graduates of both gunnery school and radio school. There, he learned electronics, mechanics, Morse code, and how a radio worked. He studied the radio inside and out and probably was required to disassemble and then reassemble a radio while blindfolded. He had the least glamorous job on the plane, listening to static over his earphones for hours on end and giving position reports every thirty minutes. And yet, he was the vital link between his plane and the rest of the formation.

Nose-Turret Gunner S/Sgt. William S. Womer.

He was born March 22, 1922 and grew up in the small town of Coshocton, Ohio. He was named William Stacy Womer after his father and everyone called him "Junior." (His niece even called him "Uncle Junior.") This niece remembers that he liked the outdoors and when she was five or six years old, he would play hide-and-seek with her.

He enlisted on January 24, 1942 for the "duration of war plus 6 months." He stated on his Enlistment Record that he had completed two years of high school and been a pottery worker for a year (salary $25 per week).

He was originally a member of 2Lt Dallas Books' crew. William Womer suffered severe frostbite on a mission and was convalescing when the Books crew was shot down during the Friedrichshafen mission on March 18, 1944, with only one survivor. After his crew was lost, he apparently became a permanent substitute, filling in with whatever crew needed him:

He is buried in the Ardennes American Cemetery, Plot A, Row 26, Grave 20.

Ball-turret Gunner S/Sgt. David Elton Harbaugh.

He was the oldest on the crew, born May 10, 1914. According to his younger brother Wayne, he was an excellent gunner. Wayne visited him while Elton (as he was called by his family) was at gunnery school in Harlingen, TX. Elton told him that he had made the highest score of anyone who had ever been through that school. And when Wayne visited him in Meridian, MS, Elton's friends asked him how much skeet shooting Elton had done, because they were amazed at his prowess. Wayne attributes Elton's skill to the fact that he hunted when he was young, and "could hit a quail through the head with a .22."

Wayne was in the Army at Ft. Jackson, SC, when got the word about the crash. In a letter to Annette Tison dated 26 Feb 2004, he wrote, "A Battalion runner came to my C.O. while we were involved in a field exercise. I saw him approach and talk to the C.O. He then came over to me - I told him before he spoke 'It's my brother, Elton.' He replied 'David E. is missing in action.' I looked for my brother as we liberated prison camps in Germany and questioned released prisoners." According to Wayne, the family had always "heard" that the crew had successfully bailed out of their plane near Magdeburg but were killed by an angry mob upon landing. He had also been told that their bodies were buried in a mass grave about 10 km away from where they landed. He was relieved to learn that his brother did not die as the result of mob violence.

On 27 June 1946, his mother wrote the government, "We ... want our son brought home. I am proud he gave his life for his country and want him to rest here, not on foreign soil." He was buried in Rose Hill Cemetery, Corpus Christi, Texas, soon after his body was returned there on July 30, 1949.

Annette Tison visit to the crash site in 2004. Her narrative;

"Dinklage is a small village (population 11,600) that has been in existence since the 1200s. The crash site is on property owned by the Vila Vita Burghotel, which is just 1.5 km east of the center of Dinklage.

"To get to the crash site, we walked out of the hotel and turned left onto a paved road. If we kept walking on this paved road, we would come to what is now a Benedictine abbey. We turned left onto a dirt path and came to a small, circular crater filled with rain water. Just beyond it is a larger, more irregularly shaped crater. The plane crashed here, and the craters are where her bombs exploded a few days later.

"Here is what we think happened to El Lobo and her crew on April 29, 1944. The Wyatt crew took off at 7:35 a.m., joined the 44th BG in the air, and headed to Berlin. Captain Robert Copp, command pilot for the 392nd BG, wrote Dad that he saw El Lobo over the target. That is the last time El Lobo was positively identified by any American.

"April 29, 1944 was a Saturday. One German told us that he was always happy when the weather was good during the week because that usually meant the bombers would be passing overhead about 9:30 or 10:00 in the morning and he would be dismissed from school for the day. This precaution was for the safety of the children. If there were bombers in the air, there was the definite possibility of dogfights with German fighter planes. Even if there were no crashes, spent machine gun bullets, pieces of 20 mm cannon shells, or even fragments of damaged planes falling from 20,000 feet would kill anyone on the ground that they hit.

"There is obviously no way to know how badly damaged the plane was or if anyone in the crew had been wounded or killed in the dogfight. One eyewitness remembers that a crewman jumped out without his parachute, sure proof that things were desperate inside the plane. It seems he knew the plane was going to crash and he decided to jump out and hope for a miracle. The witness remembered that the crewman had reddish hair and a rosary in his pocket. Sgt. Alfred Archambeau, the tail gunner, had reddish-brown hair and was a Catholic, so I suspect he was this desperate man.

"Another eyewitness, who was then 13-year old, could see thick smoke coming from the forward part of the fuselage. As he watched, the plane went into a flat spin, and then went behind the trees. He heard only one sound, the sound of impact. He then saw a cloud of dust emerge from the treetops. By the time he got to the crash site, it was obscured by smoke and flames. Apparently, just before the plane hit, another man bailed out. He was found dead, dangling from his partially-opened parachute that had been caught in a tall tree. After looking at a photo of the crew, the witness thinks this man was my uncle, 2Lt Douglas Franke, the navigator.

"The wreckage remained on fire for many hours after the crash; the flames caused machine gun bullets inside the plane to explode and kept people from getting too close. Most of the fire was put out and the bodies removed that same day.

"As the bodies were taken from the plane they were then moved to the nearby town of Vechta, put in individual coffins, and buried the next day in individual graves in the Waldfriedhof, or "Forest Cemetery." During our trip I learned that seventy percent of the residents of the county of Vechta are Catholic and the number might have been even larger in the 1940s. I was told that "these people worshipped God, not Adolph Hitler," so I am absolutely convinced that the bodies were treated with respect and dignity by the townspeople.

"In late April 1946, the U.S. Army Graves Registration Service came to the area. All ten bodies were removed from the cemetery at Vechta and taken to a temporary US military cemetery near Neupre in Belgium. Ultimately, next of kin for five of the men requested that their remains be buried overseas in an American military cemetery. They were eventually reburied in what is now known as the Ardennes American Cemetery.

"On April 29, 2004, I went to the crash site early in the morning. Birds were singing, the sun was shining, and it was as peaceful as any place could be. I said each man's name aloud and told them their families still missed them.

***

Acknowledgements;
Annette Tisson for her excellent research of the losses of the 392nd Bomb
   Group on Saturday, April 29, 1944.

CHAPTER 33

401ˢᵀ BOMB GROUP 613ᵀᴴ BOMB SQUADRON

Type: B-17G • Serial: 42-31226
"The Saint and The Ten Sinners"
MACR: 4345 • Air Base: Deenethorpe

Damaged by flak over Berlin and dropped behind formation with # 1 prop feathered. Number 2 engine also went out thirty miles wsw of Berlin. Crew abandoned the bomber over Holland.

Missing Air Crew Report # 4344

Pilot: 2Lt. Donald E. Butterfoss, 0-810818, POW, Flemington, NJ

Co-Pilot: 2Lt. Robert L. Westfall, 0-814607, POW, Newport, KY

Navigator: F/O Bernard J. Boyle, T-123920, POW, Chicago. IL

Bombardier: 2Lt. Robert C. Kerpen, 0-751914, POW, Flushing. NY

Engineer: S/Sgt. Alfred J. Truszkowski, 32607450, POW, Bayonne, NJ

Radio: S/Sgt. Roger R. McCauley, 20815583, POW, Marshall, TX

Ball-Turret Gunner: Sgt. Everett W. Stanley, 35646542, POW, Gassaway, WV

Left Waist-Gunner: Sgt. William E. Watkins, 39281632, EVD, Fullerton, CA

Right Waist-Gunner Sgt. John W. Reeves, 34645458, POW, Charleston, SC

Tail-Gunner: Sgt. William H. Lee, 18005206, POW, Lone Oak, TX

9 POW, 1 EVD

Crash Site: Lieren w. of Beekbergen, Netherlands
Time: 15.15

489

401st Bomb Group, 613th Bomb Squadron (Butterfoss)

Back row(left to right): Engineer S/Sgt. Alfred Truszkowski, Ball-Turret Gunner Sgt. Everett Stanley, Radio S/Sgt. Roger McCauley, Right Waist-Gunner Sgt. John Reeves, Left Waist-Gunner Sgt. William Watkins, Tail-Gunner Sgt. William H. Lee

Front row. Pilot 2Lt. Donald Butterfoss, Co-Pilot 2Lt. Robert Westfall, 2Lt. Roy Lang (not on final crew), Bombardier 2Lt. Robert Kerpen

Pilot 2Lt. Donald E. Butterfoss

By daughter Jill Bateman.

"Donald Earl Butterfoss was born on March 26, 1922, in Flemington, New Jersey. The sleepy little town was ringed by fertile farms, some cleared of trees by Don's Dutch, English, and German ancestors in the late 1600s.

"Donald's parents were a bit of a mis-match. Florence graduated from Syracuse University with a B.A. degree in Latin. Earl often joked that his "college" was the one-room Stone Hill School he attended through 8th grade. He managed a local grocery store, while Florence enjoyed playing bridge.

"For a kid, living on Main Street was never boring. People were in and out of the Post Office just down from the Butterfoss family's drafty Victorian house. The next building - the public library - Don avoided like the plague. But, if he dodged Model-T's chugging down Maple Avenue and scooted past the Methodist

Church, Grandfather Cooley's drug store would pull him in like a magnet. Don was quite sure that the store's soda fountain was the biggest and fanciest one to be found anywhere. Little sister Betty agreed with him.

"Being the county seat of Hunterdon County, Flemington's white-pillared courthouse was often busy. But in January of 1935, it felt as though the whole world had squeezed into town. The trial of Bruno Hauptmann, alleged kidnapper and killer of pilot Charles Lindbergh's baby son, had world-famous reporters and radiomen filling Union Hotel and every spare room in town. Miles of new telegraph and telephone wires stretched the length of Main Street. 12-year-old Don and his friends balked at going to school those six cold weeks, for fear of missing any of the drama.

"Football, basketball, baseball, and good friends helped Don, called "Butter" by his friends, graduate from high school in 1939. A year at Fishburne Military School in Waynesboro, Virginia, finished his formal education. Once again, football and baseball helped him survive the academics.

"Unfortunately, war in Europe was an unsettling presence in everyone's mind on graduation day. Four years later, Butter celebrated his twenty-second birthday by jumping from a truck, shouldering his kit bag, and reporting for duty at Air Station 128 just outside the village of Deenethorpe, England. 2nd Lieutenant D. E. Butterfoss was now first pilot of a B-17 replacement crew assigned to the 8th Air Force's 401st Bombardment Group (Heavy), 613th Bomb Squadron.

"Butter's crew flew its first mission to Brunswick, Germany, on April 26, 1944. Bombing the city's industrial section was a success - a "milk run" with no flak, no enemy fighters.

"Butter's second mission was far from being a "milk run." Anti-aircraft guns guarding Berlin were ready for Butter's plane, *The Saint and Ten Sinners*, as it approached its target on April 29, 1944.

2Lt. Donald E. Butterfoss' speech at Flemington Rotary Club.
From the *Flemington County Democrat* of July 5, 1945.

"Lt. Butterfoss said flak ripped off part of the tail of his ship, put one motor completely out of commission, crippled another and tore a great hole in one of the wings. This sent the Fortress behind the formation and presented the crew with difficulties when time came to drop their bomb load, and they found the mechanism for operating the bomb bay had been damaged.

"After the bombs were finally released, they limped away from the target in an effort to get home, meanwhile encountering successive waves of flak as well as German fighter opposition. Two attacking fighters were destroyed by his aerial gunners before the great ship, its progress impeded by motor trouble, got protection of clouds, the airman said. The ship emerged from the clouds, still operating against head winds on two and a half engines, as it passed into Holland, making less than a hundred miles an hour.

"At this point more trouble was encountered - trouble which finally sealed the fate of the plane and its crew. When an attempt was made to draw gasoline from tanks supplying the out-of-service and crippled engines over to the other engines, it was found this apparatus was also out of order. It was impossible under the circumstances to get back to England or even make the Channel.

"At this point the pilot and co-pilot noted a German airfield below and planes taking off. Lt. Butterfoss issued the order to "hit the silk" the men bailed out. It later proved that every man in the crew landed without a scratch.

"Lt. Butterfoss had determined that the plane was probably over Dutch soil and this proved to be the case. He landed in a pine woods, his parachute being caught in the upper branches of a tree so his toes barely touched the ground. Releasing himself, he ran across open fields and finally sat down, exhausted, and ate two chocolate bars he carried. This was his first food since 1 a.m., when the crew had been ordered out. It was then approaching nightfall.

"Lt. Butterfoss observed that he was near a small village. He decided to hid near the roadside and wait until dark, then go to the village and rap on the door of a home and trust he might meet friendly people.

"At dusk he saw a young man and woman out for a stroll on the road. He followed, finally hailed them, and asked for help. They were Dutch. The young man could speak English slightly. He sent the young woman back to the village for help, waiting with Butterfoss until she returned. Another young woman accompanied her.

"Lt. Butterfoss put on the young man's topcoat and hat and the four walked into the village, each couple arm in arm, and through the streets to a large house. Here Lt. Butterfoss was given soap, water and some food, then taken to the top floor of the big dwelling. There he was presented to two Jews, who had occupied the chamber for about one years, hiding from Nazis. They conversed in English and he retired early in the morning, after 24 hours of uninterrupted excitement.

"The following morning, his host said they would send for a friend, a representative of the Dutch underground. The man came. He spoke excellent English. While the underground representative said it was possible to escape to the Channel and get across, he would not recommend attempting it under existing conditions because the Germans had everything guarded, because of the impending invasion.

"Lt. Butterfoss said he had little choice but to accept the advice of the Dutch agent. This was to surrender to the German officer in command of a local school for training troops. Soldiers came in a car and drove Butterfoss to the German post. The officer was considerate, and it was not long after he had been ushered to his quarters that he encountered the bombardier and navigator from his own crew. They were all taken to nearby Arnhem, where the tail gunner and co-pilot later joined them.

"Then they went to Amsterdam where they were put into solitary confinement and later questioned by German intelligence officers. The questioning was accompanied by threats on their lives, all of which they had been told before taking off would be the Nazi routine. At Amsterdam other members of the crew joined them, making eight out of the ten accounted for.

From Amsterdam the airmen, with a couple of carloads of other Americans, were put on a train and shipped into Germany. They passed through bombed Cologne and other Rhine cities, where they peeked under the curtained car windows to observe the havoc wrought by Allied bombing. At another city the group stood on a station platform an hour and experienced the cursing and jibes of civilians whose hatred for Allied airmen had been aroused by months of bombing.

"Who could blame them?" said Butterfoss, "after the beating they had taken."

"Arriving at the prison which was to be their home the men were placed into barracks, which Lieut. Butterfoss said were not so bad, considering what many American prisoners of war suffered. They had some recreational facilities and while the food was poor, they were sustained by Red Cross packages, which arrived at irregular intervals.

"Early in January, news announced that the Russians were approaching. Finally they could hear the booming of guns on the front, some 40 miles away.

"Orders came one cold night to prepare to march, and the men, weakened by scant rations and a long period of comparative inactivity, were given one hour to get their belongings together and form in line in the snow. Nearly 2,000 men marched out. The next days and nights were bitter cold, and the men were kept marching a good deal of the time. About 800 of their number fell out by the wayside. Others kept going and finally arrived at a prison camp near Nuremberg. Here they witnessed the nearby city blasted from the air and many days and nights they feared for their own lives from bombs dropped by the Allied planes. It seemed that air raid sirens sounded continually.

After a period of imprisonment at this place, they were marched again to the outskirts of Moosburg, where conditions were the worst they encountered. Fleas and filth were everywhere. Here they witnessed fighting between German soldiers who were assigned to guard them and SS troopers who were trying to force the guards to fight the Americans.

Climax of the months of imprisonment came when they saw the Nazi flag hauled down from a nearby military post and the American flag raised. Soon after the doughboys arrived in force. General Patton later visited the prison compound and addressed the Americans.

"Lieut. Butterfoss said at no time did his fellow prisoners lose their sense of humor, even when conditions were at their worst or the treatment almost unbearable. "You'll never get me back to Germany --- never," said Lieut. Butterfoss, in closing his talk.

Daughter Jill Bateman continues:

"Three weeks after stepping off a train at the Flemington Station, Butter married

493

his fiancee, Marine Corporal Helen Best ("the prettiest potato peeler in the whole Corps"). He talked to the Flemington Rotary Club about his war experience soon after. But that was all. Butter was done talking about the war. He believed in never looking back. Snacks, though, were always at hand and his kids had a father who cooked more than most did in the '50s.

"First Jill, then Bob arrived to keep Butter and Helen busy. Hard as the war had been, the true heartbreak in their lives was that their youngest child David was born with Downs Syndrome.

"Butter traveled each workday, selling bricks. Golf was a welcomed change on summer weekends. He grilled hot dogs for the Kiwanis Club, served as a town councilman, and whenever the fire siren wailed in the night, he threw on clothes and headed cross town to jump on a waiting firetruck.

"Family, friends, trains, one of the first home computers in town, square-dancing, high school football games, and the Mets. Add in more than a few visits to Disney World on the auto-train and an occasional hour, or two, maybe even three, playing casino video poker, and Donald Earl Butterfoss was a contented man.

"Cancer forced Butter to pull up roots and move closer to his children. He and Helen built a home in Elizabethtown, Pennsylvania. He died at home several years later, on Palm Sunday, April 16, 2000.

Bombardier 2 Lt. Robert C. Kerpen

By son Jack Kerpen U.S.N.

Bombardier 2 Lt. Robert C. Kerpen

"Robert Kerpen was born on September 27, 1919 in Jersey City, New Jersey. The family had green houses and owned a florist/landscaping business in Jersey City. He and his family moved to Rockville Center, Long Island, N.Y. where he resided with his parents, Frank F. Kerpen II and Elizabeth Meyer Kerpen. His father continued to own and operate the florist business, his mother was a house wife. He had two older siblings, a brother and a sister. His brother also joined the Air Corps and retired after thirty years of service as a lieutenant-colonel.

"Robert graduated from South Side High School in Rockville Center, N.Y. in 1937. He worked for his father's company in Rockville Center after high school. He was employed by McGraw-Hill Publishing before enlisting in the U.S. Army Air Corp. He was very artistic and began a career in advertising. Robert attended Pratt School of Art for some time.

"Robert married his one and only wife, Elizabeth C. Thiergartner in 1943 in San Bernardino, CA. They were married for 56 years until his wife passed away in 1999.

"Robert was stationed at a number of bases stateside while he continued his training. He left from Alexander, LA for England in 1943. He was a bombardier on a B-17, "The Saint and the Ten Sinners." His plane was hit by flak on his third mission and the crew was ordered to bail out. He was captured by the Germans and became a POW for one day short of a full year.. He spent that year in Oflag Luft 3 in Germany. He was liberated on April 29, 1945

"After the war, he and his wife lived in Flushing, New York. They had two sons. He reenlisted in the Air Force Reserves where he reached the rank of Major. He retired on September 27, 1979.

"Robert was employed with the J.T.Graff Company in Manhattan, N.Y., an advertising company and became Vice President of that company. The company moved its headquarters to Guilford, CT in 1957. Robert and his family followed the company and took up residence in Madison, CT. Robert always said that Madison, Ct was "God's country." The company closed its doors in the 1970's or so.

"My Dad then was hired by the Electric Boat Co. in Groton, CT where he was a technical writer for the submarine builder. In 1974 he and his wife moved to Deep River, CT where he retired in the 1980's. During his time in CT he became very active in the Cub and Boy Scouts of America, from Pack Leader to "Mountain Man" to a member of the local counsel as a commissioner. He enjoyed gardening, his church, sailing, fishing, camping, good times, jokes, friends and his family. He lived alone (1999-2001) after his wife passed away, in Deep River, CT. There he fell and broke his hip. The hip replacement was on the mend but he passed away in 2001 from a bout with pneumonia. Robert had a good life with many family and friends across the country. His wit and sense of humor followed him his whole life. He had an eye for art and dabbled in drawing and art work, being a writer, he loved the use of words in ways that made people reach for a dictionary.

Son Jack came across the following unfinished draft letter written by Robert to navigator Bernard Boyle's widow. It details the account of April 29, 1944, the day they bailed out of "The Saint and The Ten Sinners."

"Upon landing after parachuting, we were quite a distance apart and out of eyeshot. I ran from my landing place in a forest toward the west, away from Germany. After a half hour, I was out of the forest and into a field, with a grove of trees ahead of me. Bernie was in the grove and reading his map for orientation. I recognized him and cautiously approached the grove. When within earshot of Bernie, I called out "Halten Sie"! But it didn't scare Bernie as I had planned.

"We decided to stay together and try to make our way south to Spain. Including sleeping in evergreens under leaves and rain. While walking around, which happened to border a German camp, a young Germen soldier approached from the opposite direction. We could hear his hob nail boots with each step but kept our eyes fastened to the road as we walked. His footsteps slowed, we passed each other and his footsteps quickened again. We thought we had convinced the German that we were merely two Dutchmen out for a stroll. But a few minutes later we heard his footsteps approaching from behind. As he passed us, his pace quickened, then he turned into the entrance to the camp. When we reached the entrance, he and two German camp guards stopped us.

"As I had a smattering of the German language, I told Bernie I'd try to convince the Germans that he was deaf and dumb and he couldn't speak. To no avail. We were taken to the camp Commandant, who interrogated us through a young interpreter. They asked if we were hungry. We replied that we were and were seated at a mess hall table. Shortly two bowls of hot brown soup were placed before us, which we devoured. Then a plate of hot meat was brought out. The delicious soup was actually gravy for the meat.

Here the draft letter abruptly ends.

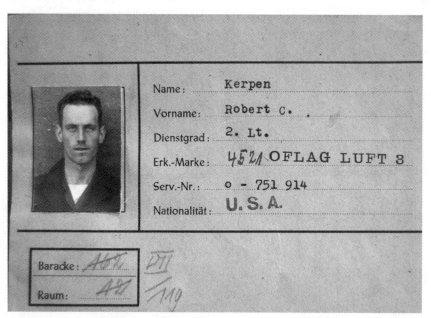

2Lt. Jack C. Kerpen, German ID card

Ball-Turret Sgt. Everett W. Stanley.

By grandson Wayne Roberts.

"Everett W. Stanley was born September 13, 1922 in Gassaway, West Virginia, where spent his entire childhood. While attending Gassaway High School, he was the captain of the football team. He graduated in 1941. Everett met my grandmother, Alice at a drugstore in Gassaway just prior to enlisting in the Army Air Corps.

"After he completed training, he was deployed to England with the Eighth Air Force. His first combat mission was flown on April 26, 1944. The target of this mission was the industrial section of Braunsweig. The group did not encounter any enemy fighters and flak was moderate over the target.

"His second and final mission was flown on April 29, 1944. The crew flew in "The Saint and Ten Sinners." Flak was extremely heavy going in and out of the target. The group also encountered numerous enemy fighters.

"My grandfather's plane was hit several times by flak. The plane received heavy damage and at one point was flying on only two engines. The crew was able to drop their bomb load over the target and attempted to return to England despite the damage that the aircraft had received. The pilot was able to nurse the aircraft out of German airspace into occupied Holland.

"At this point, the damage to the aircraft was too severe to make it safely to England. The pilot decided to order the crew to bail out over Holland. All crew members made it safely out of the aircraft and landed near the Dutch city of Arnhem.

"My grandfather met up with one of his crew, the engineer Sgt. Truskowski once they were on the ground. Both men were later captured attempting to cross the Arnhem-Apeldoorn Road near Terlet. The rest of the crew was captured within the next few days with the exception of Sgt. Watkins.

"Sgt. Watkins received assistance from the Dutch Resistance and eventually made his way back to Allied units after the D-Day invasion. He returned to the United States and I believe that he was not involved in any other combat for the rest of the war.

"The captured crew members were transported to Dulag Luft near Frankfort which was the interrogation and assignment center that all POWs were sent to just after capture. All of the officers were eventually sent to Stalag Luft 3. This was the same camp the "Great Escape" took place. That famous escape took place about a month prior the arrival of the Butterfoss officers. My grandfather and the other enlisted crewmen were sent to Stalag Luft 4. This was a relatively new camp that was located in the eastern part of Germany that is part of present day Poland.

"My grandfather never really talked about his experience during the war. My mother said that she would ask him questions as a child and that was the only time he would ever talk about it. My grandfather told her that the train ride to the camp was inside a cattle type car. He said that they crammed a lot of POWs in each car and there was not a lot of room to move around.

"In 1945, my grandfather said that the Russians started to get closer to the camp and the Germans decided to march the prisoners toward the interior of Germany. The march began in the middle of the winter. The temperature was below zero and there was heavy snow on the ground. They were only allowed to take things that they could carry and did not have any winter clothing. Some of the POWs made small sleds in an attempt to carry additional food.

"My grandfather said that a lot of the POWs became sick and had a hard time keeping up with the others. Most of the nights, the POWs had to sleep outside on the ground. Food was very scarce. On one occasion he and some other prisoners had to dig up some potatoes at a farm and then ate them uncooked. At some point during the march, my grandfather injured his leg. It became very difficult for him the walk but two of his fellow prisoners helped him to continue.

"This march lasted for a couple of months and covered around 800 miles. They finally arrived at another POW camp that he described as worse than Stalag Luft 4. There was little food and lots of lice. My grandfather told my mother that at the end of his captivity, the German guards simply left the camp one day. He said that he left the camp with a lot of the other prisoners and started walking down the road. A short time later they were liberated by British soldiers.

He was taken to Camp Lucky Strike near Le Havre in France and was eventually sent back to the United States where he was discharged from the Army Air Corps. He was awarded the Purple Heart for the wound he received during the forced march from Stalag Luft 4.

***

"My grandfather married my grandmother in Baltimore Maryland in 1946. They moved to Charleston West Virginia in 1947 after the birth of my mother. During this time while in Charleston, my grandfather enlisted in the National Guard. It is not known what other job he held during this time.

"In 1952, my grandfather enlisted in the newly formed United States Air Force. He specialized in aircraft ordinance (bombs). His first station was in Madison Wisconsin. In 1955, my grandfather was transferred to Spangdahlem Air Force Base in western Germany, where he was stationed for three years. My mother has very fond memories of Germany and thought it was a very beautiful country.

"In 1958, my grandfather was transferred to Langley Air Force base in Hampton, Virginia. He remained at this base until his retirement. He served a tour in South East Asia during the Vietnam War in 1966.

"In 1972, my grandfather retired from the Air Force at the rank of Chief Master Sergeant, which is the highest enlisted rank. After retirement, he worked as a car salesman for a time and then worked for a contractor that maintained the wind tunnels at NASA in Langley. Those tunnels can be seen in one of the scenes in the movie "The Right Stuff." He remained at this job until his death.

"On August 12, 1993, my grandfather died after a battle with cancer.

Waist-Gunner Sgt. William E. Watkins

By daughter Nancy (Watkins) Huggins.

"Dad was born on November 19, 1923 in the city of Anaheim, Orange County, California. His father, Cecil Fay Watkins, born in Oklahoma in 1899, was an oil worker at the time of Dad's birth. He was of Welsh descent. Grandpa died of pneumonia after over exposure to the sun and heat while on a fishing trip with his brothers. Dad was 16. Carrie (Caroline) Cecelia Corona, born in California in 1899, was a housewife at the time. Later she worked at the orange packing plant. She died at the age of 80. Grandma was of Spanish descent.

"Growing up, Dad was not great with academics but, had a love for sports and airplanes. One of his cousins mentioned that Dad had model airplanes suspended from the

Waist-Gunner Sgt. William E. Watkins

ceiling of his bedroom. This is a tradition that was carried on by my brothers and then my sons.

"At the age of fourteen he was an Eagle Scout with the Boy Scouts of America. He had earned ribbons for track and field events, and certificates for being a "Safety Officer" with the Fullerton Junior Traffic control, 1938 – 1940. With his parents, Dad enjoyed camping in Yosemite and visiting his uncle who had a sheep ranch in North Orange County, the San Bernardino area. There he was able to roam and explore the great outdoors and learned how to roast lamb in a pit, Basque style.

"Dad left high school at the completion of the 10th grade. This is about the time of Grandpa Cecil's death. The exact reasons for leaving school are unknown to me. Before Dad went into the Army Air Corps, both Dad and Grandma Carrie worked at the Douglas Long Beach plant. He worked on the B-17 line, she was a drill press operator. This may have contributed to his desire to join the Air Corps rather than regular Army.

"Dad and Mom met in the alley between their homes in Fullerton, California. Mom, Merilyn Lee Johnson, was born in Bakersfield, California, October

13, 1925. Of Dad, Mom's mother would say, "He's too good lookin' to be any good!" She was so wrong!

"Some of the activities they enjoyed were, spending time at the beach, soap box racing down the highest hill of Huntington Beach, California, and flying remote controlled planes. They married September 1, 1943, a few months later, Dad went off to the War. (Mom took an office job at March Air force Base so she could be close to information about Dad and his crew's well-being and where-abouts.) They remained faithfully married until Dad's death in April 1990. They had five children, 3 girls and 2 boys, 13 grandchildren and 26 great-grandchil-dren.

"As a family, we enjoyed camping trips on the then remote beaches of South-ern California and Mexico. We made trips to Disneyland, Knott's Berry Farm and of course, often visiting with grandparents and cousins. On many occasions our outings were with them as well. Mom and Dad taught us to be honest and considerate of others, patriotism and to have faith in God.

"There was one occasion when I discovered Dad's war chest. In his old foot-locker he held the many memories of the days he was in the Army Air Corps. There were letters and telegrams which I set aside. Medals, silk maps, an odd roll of foreign money, his uniform jacket still adorned with patches, and many other trinkets that he held dear.

"One of the items I pulled from the treasure was an identification card. I read the name: Petrus Wilhelmus Cox. This was such a funny name to me, being in junior high at the time. When I asked, "who is Petrus Wilhelmus Cox?" He ex-claimed, "That's me!" Then he told me of his story of being hidden by a Dutch family. He had to pretend to be a deaf mute and lived as a member of their family. I guess his blue eyes from his Welsh background helped out here! He said in the winter the family stored potatoes and other foods under the snow near their barn.

"As a newly married bride, Mom gave me an old cardboard and cloth suit case full of photos and letters. She wanted me to keep what ever I fancied. While rummaging through the old photos I came upon those letters and telegrams I had seen several years before. This time I read them. I cried and cried that day as I realized the pain my mother must have felt as a new bride, the love of her life had gone to war and was missing! As the months carried on with no word of Dad's whereabouts he was to be declared dead! The thrill I felt as I read the final telegram, "Well and safe. Hope to see you soon." I was elated! It is funny how our emotions go. I had Dad my entire life and now I was so very grateful to have had that privilege.

Escape and Evasion Report of William E. Watkins.
Saturday, April 29, 1944

"On April 29, 1944, we were on our way back from bombing Berlin. Over Arn-hem, Holland, we were hit by flak, and the pilot ordered us to bail out. I was the first to jump. While I was dropping I saw four other chutes. I jumped at 10,000 feet and opened my chute at 5,000. I landed in some trees and got out of my chute quickly. I hid it under some trees and then observed my location. I started going East leaving a false trail of equipment. I went about two and half miles in that direction, then three miles South and then four miles West. Here I climbed a tree and saw a farmhouse about a mile and a half away.

"I descended the tree and approached the farmhouse with caution. I came to the back of it and noticed there were no wires to it. Soon an old man of sixty rode up on a bicycle and entered the house. Then I went to a haystack where I stayed until 8 o'clock p.m., when the old man came out. I whistled to him to approach. I told him I was a parachuted airman and wanted food and help from the underground, and gave him a cigarette. He called to his wife who came and I repeated my story to her. She told me she knew no one in the underground.

"I left going North and contacted a farmer near Apeldoorn. He fed me and let me sleep in the house that night. The next morning I met a couple who spoke English. They said that they were members of the underground and that they had helped a lot of Jews. For that reason they could not help me and wanted to turn me over to the Germans. I couldn't agree to this. I asked about routes North or South. To Sweden or Spain. They said I would find no help to the North, but going South would be easier. That night at 23.00 hours I started out in the latter direction.

"At five o'clock the next morning I took shelter in a haystack near a house. During the day I observed the house and saw no wires to it and no Germans arrived. At night I knocked at the door and asked the man who opened it for food. I spent the night with them. The following day I was taken by bicycle to a small village East of Arnhem, where I met a member of the underground who spoke English. He gave me civilian clothes. Then a Dutch policeman arrived with a car and I was driven into Arnhem. This was May 8.

"I stayed in the policeman's house for three days. They were making arrangements to move me South. On May 11 I went by police car to Nijmegen. There another man appeared who took me by train to a station between Venlo and Roermond called Swalmen. From there we went into the woods and met the man with whom I was going to stay in Malbroek, four kms. East of Roermond. I stayed with him until January 1, 1945.

"During those months I lived very quietly, going out only at night. When the Allied armies came near us I wanted to try to get through the lines to them, but the man said this was too dangerous and it would be better to wait until we were overrun. In the middle on November and the middle of December, the Germans conscripted Dutch labor. During these periods we lived in the woods and his wife brought us food. During the December period the man went back to his house after three days and stayed there. His wife continued to bring me food until January 1, 1945, when she told me that I couldn't come back to the house, that her husband couldn't come out, and that she could no longer bring me food. She told me I should try to make my way through the lines and pointed out the best route.

"That night I started out to the South-West. As I went along I noticed trenches, foxholes, tank traps, and gun emplacements concealed both in thickets and haystacks. I walked all night and then took shelter in a haystack. Later in the morning I came to a house where a man took me for a Belgian and gave me food. After watching him for a while I felt that he was a patriot and I told him that I was an American and wanted to cross the River Maas. He arranged to have me taken across at Vlodrop in a cart filled with hay. From the West bank of the river I proceeded on West for the rest of the day and then slept in a haystack.

"The next day I went on until I came to a farmhouse near Putsbroek where I asked for food. There was an English speaking man in the house who asked me from where and when I had left England and what my mission was. Then someone gave me a haircut. Afterwards the English speaker told me that he was a member of the Royal Australian Air Force. He said that there was no way to get through the lines and that we should wait. I stayed in that house for three weeks. On January 22, we were overrun by a British unit, the 11th Hussars. We were sent back to the British interrogation center, and from there I came to Paris.

Waist-Gunner Sgt. John W. Reeves.

He was born November 20, 1922 and died October 16, 2007. His obituary, which appeared October 18, 2007 in the *Charleston Post and Courier* newspaper, said;

" John W. Reeves, age 84, of North Charleston SC died Tuesday, October 16th, 2007 at a local hospital. He was born in Charleston, SC on November 20th, 1922 to the late Wallace Reeves and Lila Walters Reeves. He was a wonderful husband, father, … He was of the Baptist Faith. He served his country during World War II in the Army Air Force and was a POW in Germany. He retired from Southern Lumber and Millwork Corp. as Vice President and supervisor of millwork after 44 years service. He enjoyed hunting and fishing and was a member of American Legion Post #0179.

On May 10, 2012 Oliver Guillot (392 Bomb Group – pilot Kamenitsa) phoned John Reeves's widow:

"I phoned Laverne Reeves, John Reeves widow. I talked to Laverne and their daughter. John Passed away in 2007. They both said John would never talk to anyone about the war. He would only say. "it was terrible" and clam up. He documented nothing and passed on nothing. I asked Laverne what POW camp he was in and she said. "I think #4 something" Laverne said John was very frail and skinny when he returned after the war. They married after John was discharged.

***

Acknowledgements:
Jill Bateman, daughter of 2Lt. Donald E. Butterfoss
Jack Kerpen, son of 2Lt. Robert C. Kerpen
Wayne Roberts, grandson of Sgt. Everett W. Stanley.
Nancy (Watkins) Huggins, daughter of Sgt. William E. Watkins
Marianne Cawley, Charleston County Public Library for Sgt. John W. Reeves.

CHAPTER 34

401ST BOMB GROUP
614TH BOMB SQUADRON

Type: B-17G • Serial: 42-31116 *"Cawn't Miss"*
MACR: 4344 • Air Base: Deenethorpe

Left formation near Hannover after being hit by flak in the tail area. With two engines, controls and intercom knocked out after an attack by six FW190s, the bomber spun in from 6000 feet. Pilot sounded the alarm bell to bail out but those crew in the rear of the aircraft did not respond or were already dead or wounded during the fighter attacks.

Missing Air Crew Report 4344

Pilot: 2Lt. J. H. Singleton, 0-747507, EVD, Lake Wales, FL

Co-Pilot: 2Lt. Clarence S. Barsuk, 0-755268, EVD, Philadelphia, PA

Navigator: 2Lt. James G. Levey, 0-674588, EVD, Bronx, NY

Bombardier: 2Lt. Glenn A. Arndt, 0-685070, KIA, Skokie, IL

Engineer: S/Sgt. William R. Muse, 34306837, EVD, Laurinburg, NC

Radio: S/Sgt. Joseph J. Vistejn Jr., 15377673, KIA, Conneaut, OH

Ball-Turret Gunner: Sgt. Warren A. Lee, 18007205, KIA, West Columbia, TX

Waist-Gunner: Sgt. Reed L. Brotzman, 33464646, KIA, Port Ann, NY

Waist-Gunner: Sgt. Solomon W. Brackman, 12031946, KIA, Brooklyn, NY

Tail-Gunner: Sgt. Harry J. Blair Jr., 33440210, EVD, Dormont, PA

5 KIA, 5 EVD

Crash Site: Leers s.e. of Roubaix, France
Time: 13.31

Going Back to England – this photo, purported to be made at Patton's Third Army HQ, shows several downed allied airmen being repatriated back to England using the personal aircraft of Vice Air Marshall Tedder of the RAF. Tedder is on the far right just in front of the plane's door. Four 'evaded' members of the "Cawn't Miss" are J. H. Singleton (6th to the left of Tedder in the leather flight jacket, then to the right are in order, Levey, Muse and Blair.

Pilot 2Lt. J. H. Singleton.

By daughter Nancy Wheeler.

"J H Singleton - also known as "John" or "Johnny" - was born at home in Calhoun County, Florida; the birth was registered at the county seat at Blountsville, FL. John was the sixth of nine children born to John Henry Singleton and Janie Chafin

"Most of his growing-up years were spent in Lake Wales, Florida on land that the world-famous Bok Tower now occupies. He left home at sixteen and went to Miami where he found work parking cars.

"In June of 1941 he joined the Army. While stationed at Chanute Field in central Illinois he met his future wife, Norma Jones, from nearby Danville, Illinois. After the beginning of WW2, he applied for Officer Candidate School and flight training and was transferred to California to begin training as a B-17 pilot. Norma travelled to California and they were married on November 14, 1942.

His training sites included Marfa, Texas and Ephrata, Washington (incidentally the 'home' of the 401st Bomb Group).

"The eldest daughter, Nancy, was born in Danville, Illinois on December 16, 1943.

***

"In March of 1944 John flew a brand-new B-17 to Deenthorpe, England via Iceland and Ireland. While in transit, he was grounded for two weeks in Reykjavic due to fog and had to keep the engines running the entire time just in case the fog should lift. Also, his navigator missed a critical beacon in Ireland. John knew that they must have overshot the beacon,

Pilot 2Lt. John Singleton at home, Fall 1944.

turned around and found it. He always did his own navigating from then on, including his post-war flying in B-47's and B-52's.

"Arriving in Deenthorpe with the 410st Bomb Group in April. His first two missions were 'milk runs' over the coast of France. His third mission, April 29, 1944 to Berlin, ended with his plane severely hit by flak just outside of Berlin. He then took his plane out of formation and headed back to England. He estimated he was within five minutes of the English Channel when fighters from JG 26 jumped him and shot him out of the sky. At that time, flying on only the two starboard engines, he had jettisoned all extra weight including all armament and, at only 5000 feet elevation, was helpless to fend off the fighters.

"They were hit with 20mm cannon fire, setting the plane on fire and killing four of the crew (Visteju, Lee, Brotzman and Breckman). Six were able to bail out, but Arndt's chute opened too late and he was killed on impact. John's chest-pack chute initially failed to open and he ripped it open with his bare hands, feeding out the chute. It opened just in time but he did severely injured his back upon landing. His walking gait was never quite the same. The other four survivors landed okay.

***

"Upon repatriation back to the States, he continued his service, first at Ft. Meyers, Florida, then Clark Field in the Philippines and then Guam. During his tour in the Philippines, Norma took both Nancy and Linda (second daughter, born November 24, 1945) to join John in 1946 at Clark Field in civilian accommodations on a troopship from San Francisco.

"We returned to the States in 1948 to McChord Field, Washington. He was transferred to recruiting duty at Altoona, Pennsylvania during 1949-1950. In 1950 he was transferred to McConnell Air Force Base, Wichita, Kansas to train as an instructor pilot in the Air Force's new jet-powered B-47. After completed his B-47 training, he was transferred to Pinecastle Air Force Base (now Orlando International Airport) to train new B-47 pilots. We were at Pinecastle from 1952 through 1958 where John rose to Squadron Commander of the A & E (Armaments and Electronics) Squadron as a Major. While at Pinecastle, he became best friends with his wing commander of the 321st Bomb Wing, Colonel Michael N. W. McCoy. Colonel McCoy and the entire crew were killed in a B-47 crash during a bombing competition with the English RAF on October 9, 1957. John went to the national military cemetery at Arlington, Virginia to make the burial arrangements and was one of the pall bearers. As an aside, John was initially scheduled to fly at copilot with McCoy on the fatal flight but was bumped by a higher ranking English officer.

"In the summer of 1956, John suffered his own crash at Pinecastle. Four minutes after takeoff on their way to North Africa, smoke filled the cockpit. John turned around, notified the tower they were coming back for an emergency landing. Fire trucks were sent to the south end of the 2-mile long runway while John actually landed at the north end. The drogue chute failed upon landing. All crew got out, ran for the ditch alongside the runway, turned around and saw the plane exploding. They were carrying unarmed nuclear weapons. No one was injured.

"Also, the youngest child of John and Norma, John Michael (born in 1954) was named after McCoy. Pinecastle was renamed McCoy Air Force Base in 1958, hence the airline designation MCO for Orlando International Airport. The

2Lt. J.H. Singleton's false Belgian ID

507

base was deactivated in 1975 and given to the City of Orlando.

"In 1958 we were transferred to Bergstrom Air Force Base outside of Austin, Texas. John flew B-52's as part of the Strategic Air Command (SAC). At that time, John's eyesight had begun to deteriorate and he was taken off flying status. He was sent to Lakeland Air Force Base, San Antonio, Texas to get a diagnosis of his eye problem. He was found to have a very rare, slow-growing cancer with no treatment options. This was the beginning of eventual loss of his sight due to macular degeneration. He was declared legally blind in 2007.

"Once it was determined he could no longer fly he retired from the Air Force in 1961 as a Lieutenant Colonel after twenty years service and moved back to Orlando, Florida. After his retirement, he worked in the space program at Brown Engineering and Boeing at Cape Canaveral (now Cape Kennedy Space Center), Florida. John passed away in April of 2013 at the age of 92.

J.H. Singleton's Escape and Evasion Report.

"Pilot J.H. Singleton (initials only), navigator James G. Levey, tail-gunner Harry J. Blair and engineer William R. Muse came down on April 29, 1944. Singleton landed in Leers, France, on the border between France and Belgium (the location and dispositon of co-pilot Clarence Barsuk, the last man out of the crippled airplane, was unknown although he did survive and was returned to the US). A member of the Belgian White Army called Albert picked up Singleton at once and took him to his mother's house in Leers where he gave him civilian clothing. He then took Singleton to his own house in Leers Nord (Belgium). After a couple of hours a small man, 24 years old, who lives with his wife and baby in Leers Nord, came in and led Singleton to a church in Nechin where a priest and doctor took his escape kit and interrogated him. "The commandant of the police in Templeuve then took him by bicycle to the house of Angel van Leuerck, a police man in Templeuve, who lives next door to the commandant. There Singleton found William Muse, his engineer.

"Muse had also landed in Leers. There a member of the White Army had taken him home, given his clothes, and had hidden him in a ditch. An hour later a priest came and told him that another man would soon take him away. This other man arrived and led him to the church of Nechin from where the priest took him to a house in town where he turned in his escape kit. The commandant of the police of Templeuve then arrived and took him by bicycle to the house of an Englishwoman in Templeuve, but could not leave him there, for there happened to be a stranger visiting the woman at the time. He then took Muse to Van Leuerck's house whither a few hours later Singleton was brought.

"Singleton and Muse stayed with Van Leuerck for the night. The following day, he and the commandant led them to Blandain to the house of a man named Walter. They remained there for half an hour and then moved into the house of

Edmond de Wolf where they remained for three weeks. Thereafter they moved to the house of Mr. Daniel (family name unknown) in Blandain for five days and then were taken back to Templeuve to the house of Edgard Gilbert Merchez. Here they lived from May 26 to August 1. During this time Walter in Blandain got identity cards for them and said that plans were being made to send them to Switzerland whence they could return by air to England. He finally told them that someone would come to get them in a car and before they left gave Singleton a message to be delivered to the British Intelligence in the U.K. This message Singleton managed to swallow when he was captured by the Germans.

"On August 1, 1944 an automobile appeared. In it was a woman in her early thirties, blond hair and dark eyebrows, well dressed and heavily perfumed, who spoke English fairly well (it was later learned from Mme. Denille that this woman was the wife of Dr. Watteau of Tournai); and a man called "the mad Russian." They gave the password "La cérise est une drogue," and were admitted to the house. They then wanted to take the dog tags from Singleton and Muse; but the Americans pretended they had only one apiece, and so succeeded in retaining one. Singleton and Muse were then in the automobile to pick up F/O Leon Panzer (RCAF), Sgt. Roy Brown (RCAF) and Lt. Levey, the navigator aboard Sigleton's bomber.. The whole party then motored to Brussels.

"James Levey had also landed in Leers. The whole town was out to meet him; but the Germans were near, and he ran away from his admirers and hid in a ditch. Presently a young man named Jean, who wore under the lapel of his jacket a tin badge inscribed "Deputy Sheriff, Texas" a souvenir from a "cracker Jack" box, found him, led him through the woods to another young man who gave Levey a coat, and then took him to a road where two men with bicycles were waiting. Then began a mad ride along roads and paths, dodging Germans, and passed from house to house until Levey found himself in a house in a unknown village where four members of a B-24 were staying,

"Ultimately all four, in early August of 1944 and along with other allied airmen, were compromised, turned over to and interogated by Luftwaffe Intelligence and then transfered to St. Gilles prison in Brussels.

"On September 2, 1944, the British Second Army was in the process of liberating Brussels. In the early hours of this same day, some 1,370 Belgian political prisoners and Jews - and 41 allied airmen from St. Gilles prison were loaded onto 32 ,freight wagons' for transport to Germany. Due to heroic machinations by members of the Belgian Underground and the train crew, the train never got very far and ultimately had to return to Brussels on September 3rd. There, the German soldiers accompanying the train fled in the face of the rapidly advancing British forces. The four escaped from the goods wagon and made there way to the center of Brussels at the Hotel Metropole where an English Captain, Dunn, gave them orders and arranged their transportation back to the U.K. on September 9, 1944.

Co-Pilot 2Lt. Clarence S. Barsuk.

From his Escape & Evasion Report dated August 30, 1944.

"Our target on 29th April 1944 was Berlin. Our plane never reached the target, as we developed engine trouble and had to drop out of formation. As we broke out of the overcast, we were hit by flak and the controls and the auto-pilot were shot away. We dropped our bombs on a German town, and the plane went out of control and we had to bail out.

"When I came out of the ship, I saw four chutes above me. I believe, however, that all the men got out safely. I was the last to go out, and it's sure that no one was in the plane at that time.

"I landed about two hundred yards off a main highway in a field. My chute caught in a tree, but I wriggled out of it and started on the run to get away from the plane. I found a culvert under the highway and hid in this until it became dark. After dark I began walking. When I had gone about ten miles, I came to a railway track and jumped onto a train that passed me going very slow – about five miles per hour. I rode on this train until it became daylight and then jumped off and hid in underbrush all that day. I noticed a sign board which indicated that I was two hundred kilometers from Hannover.

"I really didn't know where I was, but I figured that I was some place in Germany. When it got dark, I began walking again and crossed the Belgian border about fifty kilometers from Liège. This was the first time I was really oriented about my location.

"By this time I was really hungry, so I stopped at a Belgium farmhouse and told the farmer who I was. He let me sleep at his home and gave me food and civilian clothes. I put the clothes over my uniform and took off again for Brussels, by way of Liège, after staying at the home of the farmer until about May 13th.

"From May 13th to May 19th I walked almost day and night towards Brussels, getting food from friendly Belgians. When I arrived in Brussels, I saw a German soldier park his bicycle against a café. I stole this and traveled in style out of Brussels to Ninova, from there to Renaix and then to Asq in France. In Asq I stayed four days with a farmer.

"I left Asq then and went on down to Dourges, where I found out that my bicycle was completely worn out. So I began walking again towards Amiens. I circled around Arras, and arrived in Baume on May 26. At Baume I stayed with a French family until June 9 when I began walking again, making my way south to Albert and from Albert through Amiens. Near Amiens I stole a bicycle again and made my way to Fouqiercer where I stayed with another French family for three days. On the second day I was there some Frenchman came to see me , and they arranged my journey to Paris, where I stayed until American troops entered the city.

Bombardier 2Lt. Glenn A. Arndt.

By cousin Sue Carey.

"Glenn Albert Arndt was born October 30, 1923 in Downers Grove, Illinois. He attended elementary school in both Downers Grove and Skokie, and the high school division of Concordia Teachers College at River Forest, Illinois. In September 1938 he was enrolled at Niles Township High School and graduated with the class of 1940.

"Glenn joined the Army Air Corps on November 12, 1942. He was trained at Ellington Field, Houston, Texas; at the Bombardier School, Midland, Texas; and at Langley Field, Virginia. Lieutenant Arndt then shipped overseas to serve as bombardier with the Eighth Air Force, based in England.

"On April 29, 1944 Glenn was returning from a mass mission over Berlin in a Flying Fortress which had been severely damaged by flak. Two engines were knocked out of commission and it had been impossible to keep up with the formation. All equipment including guns and ammunition had been cast overboard to permit maintenance of flying speed. On the outskirts of Lille, France, after heavy loss of altitude, the helpless bomber was attacked by six enemy fighters. The cabin caught fire, the tail was shot off, and the ship went into a nose dive. Disregarding an order to bail out, Glenn engaged in a fruitless effort to assist four badly wounded crew mates. By the time he jumped, the plane was a scant hundred feet from the ground – too low for his parachute to open.

"My uncle Glenn was originally buried in the Southern Cemetery in Lille, France. After the war he was moved to a cemetery in Skokie, IL where he is buried with his parents and my mother. He was survived by his parents, the Reverence and Mrs. Otto F. Arndt, and one sister, my mother Maralyn, all living in Skokie at the time.

"Though he passed at the age of 21, his high school years found him to be full of life and a bit of a prankster. Being a "Pastor's Kid" he was under the microscope of church members, but he was said to be quite the charmer and considered rather good looking.

Engineer S/Sgt. William R. Muse.

By his mother Jennie Muse, shortly before she died.

"On September 14, 1920, a pretty little red cheeked boy came in time for supper. We had ordered a girl *(to keep the symmetry of two boys and two girls),* but the order, evidently was misread and we received the boy. We were very well pleased and decided to keep him. We named him William Rowe, after his great grandfather, who was a Methodist minister.

"I think our children had fairly happy childhood lives. They did not have many toys like the children of today, but they enjoyed their make believe lives. They played Cowboy and Indians, mostly with homemade guns and homemade bows and arrows.

"One time their daddy brought an old carriage. It was a beautiful thing in its time, but he wanted only the springs and running part to make an easy carriage for his dewberries, which had to be shipped with greatest of care. So he left the body of the coach in the back yard so our children could play in it. They liked playing stage coach and robbers.

"Billie was always such an active child, so full of energy he did not have time to try to read. He heard the other three children reading and memorized enough to take his book and read as loud as any of them. He would read stories that were not in that particular book, which would last about two minutes and then he had business elsewhere.

"He did very well during elementary grades but let go in high school. We finally sent him to Edwards Military School his senior year. He settled down there with nearly all A grades. We enrolled him in college the next fall but he went about six weeks and came home. He wanted to go to Georgia Tech, but we did not have the money to send him there.

"In the fall of 1942, he and a friend went to Canada to get in the Canadian Air Force. Because of a busted ear drum, Billie did not pass the rigid pilot's examination and came home. After the bombing of Pearl Harbor, he enlisted in the Air Corps.

William R. Muse in his own words.

"I played one of the deadliest games of hide and seek in the world with the Belgian Underground against the infamous German Gestapo and came out the winner.

"For four suspenseful and fearful months, my life and the lives of four of my fellow soldiers lay bare in the hands of a small group of Belgian patriots, whom I will never cease to regard as the bravest, most loyal, and most self-sacrificing people on earth.

"On maps the Rhur Valley is a wide strip of thickly populated land snaking across the middle of Germany. To those of us who flew over it at the height of World War ll, it was "flak alley" - the most dreaded run a bomber could make.

Engineer S/Sgt. William R. Muse

From one end to the other, German anti-aircraft guns spewed a steady stream of leaden death at any Allied plane that came within their sights. Many a good pilot and crewman crashed to a fiery death somewhere along its twisting path.

"I was a nervous 23 year old with only three bombing missions when the Rhur threw a pair of loaded dice in my face and would have claimed the life of Sergeant William Muse had it not been for the Belgians, who hated the Germans with an intensity impossible to describe.

"It all started on a typical English morning in 1944. The date was April 29th. We took off from Deenethorpte in central England at 6 a.m. sharp. Lieutenant Johnny Singleton, a husky resident of Lake Wales, Florida, was piloting the "CAWN'T MISS" and our target was Berlin.

"As a sergeant, l was the engineer in the crew of ten aboard the B-17, a small cog in the 614 Bomb Squadron of the 401st Bomb Group. We carried six 500-pound demolition and six 500-pound incendiary bombs and hoped to put them to good use within a few hours. We were flying "tail-end Charlie" in a formation of 36 bombers and were listed as a spare - to go in on target if one of the lead planes was unable to make it.

"It took about an hour of circling to make up the formation. It was around 7 a.m. before we were over the Channel. The coast of Holland, the morning sun sparkling on it like a precious jewel, was in sight 45 minutes later.

"Still at the tail end of the formation we sighted Hannover, Germany, at approximately 8:30. Altitude was 27,000 feet and we were climbing rapidly when flak knocked out the number two engine. Singleton, a veteran pilot and one of the best, feathered it. We were still in good shape after jettisoning our 3,000 pounds of incendiary bombs.

"We dropped back to join the Triangle J group and took position again as "tail-end Charlie." Thirty minutes out of Berlin, the "CAWN'T MISS" was rolling along on three engines at a height of 29,000 feet when, bang, the German gunners scored another hit.

"This time our number one engine went out of commission and we were in serious trouble. I dropped flares and in a matter of minutes five Thunderbolt fighters had shown up to escort us back to England. Every man breathed easier with the comforting sight of the P-47's on both sides, but our good fortune was short lived. There was a heavy overcast and we lost the Thunderbolts at 22,000 feet.

"We entered the Rhur Valley at 10:45, flying 115 mph at 5,500 feet, and must have looked like a sitting duck to every gunner in the German Army. No aircraft was ever more appropriately named for the occasion than the "CAWN'T MISS." The Germans couldn't miss and kept up a steady stream of fire while we frantically tried to dump out every piece of moveable equipment. All ammunition, guns, escape hatches, and everything else we could tear loose went over the side, while the terrific pounding from the ground continued.

"Nobody had to be told that our position was absolutely hopeless and we all knew it was just a matter of time. I had inched my way forward to the pilot's compartment when the killing punch was delivered. Five FW190's came knifing in from 3 o'clock, while a single ME109 poured machine gun slugs into our belly from underneath. They made two passes and it was all over - all controls were out and the plane was on fire.

"The deadly hail from the German fighters had claimed the lives of our bombardier, ball turret gunner, both waist gunners, and radio operator, leaving the pilot, co-pilot, navigator, tail gunner, and myself to bail out.

"As soon as the order was given, I jerked open the bomb bay doors and jumped. Unfortunately, a strap of my chest chute caught on the door handle and there I was dangling almost head downward somewhere over Belgium. Summoning all my strength, I managed to get one foot braced on the bomb bay cat walk and the other on the foot rest and draw myself up enough to untangle the strap. I pulled the rip cord as soon as I was free of the plane. The shock of the parachute opening swung my body high in the air like a pendulum.

"We had been shot down near the French city of Lille, which was German headquarters for that area and only a few miles from the Belgian border. Every man, woman, and child in the neighborhood must have been watching the fight from the ground. I was hardly out of my chute harness before a little Belgian boy - the border was less than half a mile away and our plane actually crashed in Belgium territory - came running up. I couldn't understand a word he said, but I knew the best thing I could do was get away from the area as quickly as possible.

"The German fighters were still circling overhead to mark the spot for ground patrols. I didn't know what had happened to the other four men who had bailed out and at the moment didn't have time to consider their fate.

"This Belgium boy, who couldn't have been more than six years old, took off towards the village like a scared jackrabbit with me right at his heels. I had time to get a glimpse of a squad of German soldiers heading on the double for the crash scene before we ducked behind a row of houses.

"Thank heaven the Germans didn't see us. We ran about 500 yards when a boy about 17 years old met us. He gave me a bicycle and trotted alongside to guide me to a house on the out-skirts of the village. There I was given a change of clothing, some food and wine, and managed to take a bath.

"I stayed there about an hour, leaving just in time. I later learned the Germans arrived five minutes afterwards to search the premises. I was led across a grain field and through some woods to another tiny village. Here I met a priest who hid me in a ditch and told me to wait until a man showed up to lead me into town. I waited in the ditch, scarcely daring to breathe, for what seemed like an eternity. Actually it was only about an hour before I heard a low whistle.

"Just as I climbed out to follow the man, I saw two German squad cars passing along a road a short distance away. Holding my breath, I pretended to look at some cows grazing in the field, and they passed by. I was led down a series of back streets and finally into the back room of a bar. After staying long enough to gulp down a badly needed shot of brandy, I was directed to a church across the street where the priest I had met earlier was waiting. He took me to his house and called the local doctor to examine the slight flesh wounds in one hand and leg that I had received somewhere along "Flak Alley."

"While I was at the priest's home, members of the underground took all the maps out of my escape kit, but left the money - about 2,000 francs. I finally went to sleep, the first time in almost 24 hours, and did not awaken until the chief of police from a small Belgian village showed up. He gave me a bicycle and we pedaled about four miles to the town of Templeuve.

"I ate supper and went to bed, but was roused about 11 o'clock by someone climbing the stairs. Not knowing what to expect, I was set to jump out the second story window when the door opened and in walked my pilot, Johnny Singleton.

"He had escaped in about the same fashion as I had, and we spent the remainder of the night briefing each other on events, and musing on the fate of the other fellows. The next night Singleton and I were moved to another Belgian town, Blondoin, and quartered with the Raoul Dewulf family. He was a railroad worker and took great delight in telling us stories about underground sabotage in which he was involved. One of his favorite tales concerned the misrouting of a carload of ammunition which he had helped dump in a nearby river. Dewulf and one of his two sons were later imprisoned for reading Allied propaganda leaflets, and the boy died in a concentration camp.

"We stayed with the Dewulf family for two weeks while the Underground investigated us thoroughly, just lounging around the room and reading a few old English magazines that our host had. Time literally dragged and we were restless to be on the move but were assured by the Underground that we would be moved as soon as practical. Finally, we were transferred to another house in the same village and here I made a near fatal mistake. I stepped out into the courtyard one morning and was seen by a man working on a nearby rooftop. He turned out to be a collaborator and we were hustled out of there and back to the town of Templeuve that same night.

"While at the Dewulfs we had learned that our navigator, Lt. Jim Levey of Parkchester, New York, was alive and being hidden in the same area. On our return to Templeuve we were quartered with Mamma and Pappa Guilbeit and their two daughters, and were fortunate enough to send and receive notes from Levey on several occasions.

"Gestapo headquarters was only four doors from the Guilbert house and we could hear the Germans marching back and forth at all hours of the day and night. Our host owned a huge German Shepherd dog that had been trained to growl every time a German came within smelling distance and he kept us pretty well posted on the goings and comings of the Nazis.

"We stayed with the Guilbets until after the Allies invaded France. During this time I was unlucky enough to come down with a severe case of yellow jaundice which required medical treatment on several occasions.

"Late in July we learned that Black Maria, an Allied air unit assisting with espionage work, was scheduled to make a pickup around August lst somewhere north of Brussels. Arrangements were made for Singleton, Levey, myself, and two Canadians to rendezvous with this group. My Belgian passport issued to a French laborer by the name of Jean Bienvenaun was exchanged for a forged Turkish document. We were ready for the 60 mile journey to Belgium's largest city.

"We made the trip in an auto driven by an unidentified Underground worker whom we called the "Mad Russian." He and his wife dropped the five of us at a house in the heart of Brussels. Our luck, fantastically good up to this point, was fast running out. We learned the Black Maria pickup had been canceled and that we would now be guided to a point near the Swiss border from where we could walk across into neutral territory.

"We were moved to another house and scheduled to leave for Switzerland that night. Just to kill time and feeling pretty cocky with freedom just around the corner, we decided to take a look outside. We stuck our heads out the door and right into the middle of half a dozen German soldiers, calmly waiting with enough machine guns to capture an army.

"Somewhere, somebody along the Underground line had sold us out. We learned later that the first house at which we stopped in Brussels was actually operated by the Gestapo and that we had been in German hands from the time the "Mad Russian" and his wife dropped us off.

"We were five chagrined men as the Germans hustled us to gloomy St. Giles prison where we were thoroughly interrogated and placed in solitary cells. I remained alone for two days and was questioned on three different occasions. The Germans wanted to know who had helped us escape, but I refused to answer. The questioning periods were mainly a waiting game and occasionally they slapped me around when I tried to give a smart answer.

"A Belgian woman, with a voice like a hog caller, lived right across the street from the prison and each day she shouted the latest news at the top of her lungs. Although she spoke French, some of the boys were able to translate and pass the word along. I learned of the liberation of Paris in this manner. We thoroughly enjoyed the increased signs of nervousness among our captors as each day passed.

"Although there were 43 Allied prisoners at St. Giles at the time, the Germans kept us well separated. We were allowed to exercise 30 minutes a day in a small open circle within the prison walls. That was about the only activity to break the monotony, but on the meager diet of watery soup, eratz coffee, and stale bread we were fed, it was enough.

"During one of the exercise periods, l accidentally bumped into Sergeant Harry Blair, the tail gunner from our ship. I learned he had been captured about the same time and in the same fashion we had. He and I worked out a system of code communication using steam pipes that ran through the cells and were able to talk back and forth almost at will.

"We had been in prison exactly one month when we were herded into the marshalling yard and loaded on a train for transfer to Germany. There were 43 of us in an old baggage car. The Germans had grown so panicky as Allied forces moved closer and closer that they dropped off all political prisoners.

"We stayed in the baggage car on a siding just outside Brussels for about 24 hours before the train got underway. During this time Levey and I got the bright idea of trying to escape.

"There were four guards, two at each end of the car. The only door was in the middle, and we figured if we could get it open we could drop off and run for it while we were still close to Brussels. The fellows in the car cooperated by crowding around to block the vision of the guards while we worked the door open. Then, just as the train rounded a sharp curve, Levey and I jumped. We hit the ground and rolled under a line of stationary box cars on an adjoining track. Evidently we caught the guards by surprise because there was only sporadic gunfire and none of it in our immediate direction.

"It was almost noon as we hurried back across the marshalling yard and finally located a deep canal. We followed it, wading to throw the dogs off our trail, for perhaps two miles back into Brussels. Neither of us had any plans or ideas of what we would do other than try to keep out of sight of the Germans. We decided to take a chance on contacting the first likely-looking Belgian we saw and hope for the best.

"Our canal led us to a fair-sized brewery where we saw three men standing on a loading platform. One of them saw us and motioned for us to stay where we were. He came out in a few minutes and took us to the boiler room, directing us to hide in one of the boilers. He showed us a German Luger, which was supposed to be the Underground insignia, but, having been betrayed once, we were taking no chances and hid on a raised platform until we could see whether he would return alone.

"Our latest friend, whose name was Serge Dewerpe, came back a short time later with dry clothes, wine, food, and blankets. He had cookies, eggs, cheese, and bread. We ate like pigs because it was the first decent food we had seen since our capture a month before. We told Dewerpe about the train and how we had escaped. He informed us that the car in which we had been riding had been derailed a short time after our escape and had been abandoned by the Germans. This meant that all our buddies had gained freedom almost as quickly as we had and without near the trouble.

"We awoke the next morning to the most joyful news I ever hope to hear – Brussels had been liberated. We lost no time in reporting to Allied Headquarters at the Hotel Metropole. Before we let Belgium we took two days off to return and thank the brave men, women and children who had done so much for us.

"By September 12th we were back with our old outfit in England. There we learned that the fifth man who had bailed out of the "Cawn't Miss," co-pilot Clarence Barsuck, had made it to Paris without ever falling into German hands and had been liberated several weeks ahead of us. It was a grand and glorious reunion when the five surviving crew members of the gallant "Cawn't Miss" sat down together, but before we started our celebration, we each offered a silent prayer of thanks to the gallant Underground, at least two of whom, we learned, paid with their lives for aiding American flyers in distress.

Tail-Gunner Sgt. Harry J. Blair Jr.

By daughter Elizabeth Blair Vuono

"Harry J. Blair Jr. was born in Pittsburgh PA January 1, 1926, on his father's birthday. He was the only child of Harry J Blair Sr. and Anne Idela Delcamp Blair. My Grandfather attended Bucknell University and my Grandmother attended The University of Pennsylvania. My grandfather was an accountant and became the owner of The Pittsburgh Garter Company. My Grandmother was degree nurse.

My Dad, enlisted in the Army Air Corp in March 1943, apparently at that time if you signed up before you turned 18 years of age you could choose what service you wanted to go into and Dad wanted to fly. After completing his training in the U.S., Dad was sent to Langley Field where he was trained on the first group of B-17's with radar, so the Air Corps could bomb through the clouds. Previously pilots had to visually see the targets before they could release bombs. But due to heavy cloud coverage in Europe the radar was a tremendous asset.

"To get to Europe the pilot, navigator, engineer and radio operator flew the plane over. My dad, the tail gunner and the other crew members went by ship, the *Aquitania* to Scotland and then to Bath England.

"Dad was reassigned to a different crew to replace a tail gunner who had a sinus infection, making him not able to fly. Dad flew a total of 4 missions. His second and third mission was flown on the same day, setting a record of missions by an American crew.

***

"On April 29, 1944 Dad flew his last mission. Their bomber, as he stated was "in bad shape. We had a lot of problems." One engine was shot out, another was on fire, flak shells had penetrated the plane. Dad had obtain shrapnel in his back side and hip.

"On the return flight the pilot had to crash-land in in Leers, Belgium. Dad was picked up by a man from the underground who hid him till the night. He learned that the plan had landed in a back yard of a very nice chateau. The five men, who had been killed during the fighter attack, were still on board.

"At night fall they crossed the border into France, right passed the German guards. This man then hides him in his house until he passed him off to a friend until after D-day. Eventually he was captured by the Gestapo and was transported to Saint Giles Prison in Brussels, where he found his pilot, navigator and engineer.

"On September 3, 1944 they were put on a train to Germany. They managed to escape from the train, found a church where a priest told them that Brussels had been liberated. Later they encountered British troops who took them to the Belgian capital where they stayed the night. The next day they returned to England.

***

"Dad went to the University of Pittsburgh where he was enrolled in Pre Law School. There he met my mother, Mary Lou Fitzsimmons, who was also attending The University of Pittsburgh, where she earned her degree as a teacher. Dad graduated from the University of Pittsburgh, but never obtained his Law Degree. My parents married in 1951, as we say in the family in '51 the fun begun. My parents got nine children, three boys and six girls. My father passed away a few years ago. At that time I was the only child that attended the funeral, as my father was estranged from the family.

"After my parents married my dad went to work for the Pittsburgh Garter Company and became President. Later my father founded Bethel Sewing and then Park Industries, whereas children we all worked as a family, to develop the business. We grew up in a very nice section of Pittsburgh, Pennsylvania called Mt. Lebanon. I am still in the Pittsburgh area but moved out of Mt. Lebanon area about 15 years ago.

"Dad had many interests, but his primary interest was his family. My dad and mother were always together. Beach vacations were the best, Dad took us to Long Beach Island in NJ and then to Carolina Beach in NC. Mom and Dad were history buffs and exposed their children to many historical places and events. In the 70's, when my oldest brother Harry J. Blair III, attended Annapolis Naval Academy my parents took up sailing. Frequently on weekends we would go as a family and take the sailboat out for the weekend.

"My Father passed away in 2008, at age 83.

***

Acknowledgements;
Reid Wheeler, son-in-law of pilot J.H. Singleton
Sue Carey, cousin of bombardier Glenn A. Arndt.
Elizabeth Blair Vuono, daughter of tail-gunner Sgt. Harry J. Blair Jr.

519

CHAPTER 35

401ˢᵀ BOMB GROUP 615ᵀᴴ BOMB SQUADRON

Type: B-17G • Serial: 42-31521
MACR: 4346 • Air Base: Deenethorpe

"Our B-17 was crippled by enemy ground fire, and we lost two engines. We became separated from our formation, and then the German fighters closed in and further damaged our aircraft, including loss of power on our third engine."

Co-Pilot Frank Linc

Pilot: Capt. George Gould, 0-900201, POW, Hollis, OK

Co-Pilot: 2Lt. Frank Linc, 0-693383, POW

Navigator: 2Lt. Robert F. Lotz, 0-732690, POW, Cleveland Heights, OH

Bombardier: 2Lt. Jay A. Wade, 0-694529, POW, Champaign, IL

Engineer: S/Sgt. George F. Gould, 11094909, POW, Cleveland Heights, OH

Radio: S/Sgt. Hugh D. Reddy, 37390073, POW, St. Louis, MO

Ball-Turret Gunner: S/Sgt. Charles R. Warlow, 16031863, POW, Roberts, IL

Waist-Gunner: Sgt. James H. McGaha, 18192379, POW, Ada, OK

Waist-Gunner: Sgt. Ralph W. Meeks, 13133957, POW, Sharon, PA

Tail-Gunner: Sgt. John A. Cumpson, 33408910, POW, St. Thomas, Canada

10 POW

Crash Site: Platendorf/Gifhorn, Germany
Time: 13.00

Pilot Capt. George Gould

By sister Mildred (Gould) Wild;

"The Gould family moved to Hollis, Oklahoma, in January 1932. My dad, L. F. A Gould, worked for the Katy Railroad. My mother, Mrs. May Gould, did alterations for Collins Cleaners.

"George and I were juniors in high school. We graduated from high school in May 1933, the same year the Keys quadruplets graduated. There were four other sets of brothers and sisters in the class.

"The next two years 1 attended Cameron Junior College in Lawton, Oklahoma. George worked for the Frederick Press, and in 1935 he received an appointment to the Naval Academy at Annapolis, Maryland. He graduated as an ensign in 1939 and served on the battleship Nevada at Pearl Harbor for two years.

"ln July 1941 George was sent to Bangor, Maine, and attended the Navy's first radar school. December 1, 1941, George resigned his commission in the Navy and the same day was sworn into the US. Army Air Corps. He became a B-17 pilot and on April 29, 1944, was shot down over Germany in a 2,000-plane raid over Berlin. He was a prisoner of war for 14 months and returned home in May 1946.

"George was married and had three children. He retired from the US. Air Force as a full colonel and died in April 1989. George is buried at Arlington Cemetery, Washington, D.C.

Co-Pilot 2Lt. Frank Linc

From the 8th Air Force Historical Society, MN, website.

"I was working for Vega Aircraft in L.A. at the time of Pearl Harbor, and I remember the close-down. I worked in the aircraft company inside the fuselage of a bomber and all of a sudden all the lights went out. They were out for two hours because of Pearl Harbor." Frank started as a Vega Aircraft riveter on twin engine airplanes being built for Britain and he moved up the company ladder with two other jobs before going into the service. This aviation background probably helped him to get into the aviation cadets.

"On his first mission he was flying as co-pilot, and the pilot had a psychological breakdown and stopped functioning during the bomb run. He had to take over flying the plane on the mission.

"Frank said his crew wanted to get through their missions quickly so at one point they flew six missions in seven days. They went to bed at around 11 and got up at around 4 so it was quite exhausting, but they were young.

"Our April 29, 1944 and 12th combat mission over Germany was a "maximum effort" with over 800 heavy bombers participating. The 800 bombers flew in tight formation and covered the sky: an impressive and sobering sight regardless of your vantage point: from the ground seeing the contrails or from the cockpit seeing your neighboring aircraft.

"Our B-17 was crippled by enemy ground fire, and we lost two engines. We became separated from our formation, and then the German fighters closed in and further damaged our aircraft, including loss of power on our third engine. We dove into the heavy cloud cover, out of sight of the German fighters. Knowing that the fighters would be waiting for us above and below the clouds, and that we could not get far with only one engine, we had to bail out at 20,000 feet under the protection of the clouds."

"I was captured and interned as a POW in Germany for one year: experiencing minimal food, living in barracks and tents without heat, one blanket, and sleeping on wood shavings. I lost 45 pounds, suffered from frostbite, and back injuries.

"On May 15, 1944, my wife was notified by the War Department that I was missing in action. Two weeks later she received a telegram informing her that I was a prisoner of war. I can only imagine the anxiety felt by my wife and family."

"After nine months of captivity, the sound of Russian artillery was heard, sounding ever closer as the Russian front advanced. It was a cold night on January 27, 1945 when we were alerted that the Germans were evacuating the prison camp, and we had thirty minutes. We quickly made packs from extra shirts and other material for carrying our meager possessions and extra food, which we had been conserving for emergency use, in case we were left without sustenance.

"The march to a new location began about 10:00 pm. The call to "fall out" was given. The blocks assembled and marched out of the gate of Stalag Luft III. Our south compound was first to leave on that Saturday night."

"Twelve thousand Allied airmen were on the march, many out from barbed wire imprisonment for the first time in one to five years. Other camps too were on the march from the East Front to the interior of Germany. The snow lay deep and it was bitterly cold. Guards were on all sides: some with dogs, all with ready weapons to prevent escapes.

"As the march progressed, the roadside became cluttered with discarded articles. We soon found that the decadent life of a prison camp had left us unfit for the endurance of a long forced march with full pack. Packs were lightened at each halt. Halts were five minutes every two hours. We marched for 48 hours with a short break at daylight."

"The march was hindered by German refugees, who were also running from the Soviets. A scene imprinted on my mind forever is that of one family stalled on a slope of a country road, their horses too tired to pull their wagon on the icy slope, children and women huddled in the wagon were wrapped in blankets to ward off the wind and cold. The father approached us and showed us his frostbitten fingers and asked for our gloves. We all understandably refused, not knowing what lay before us in the next few weeks. Nevertheless, I still hold a guilt feeling since that day and often wonder what became of that family."

"On the evening of the second day - we still had not slept – there suddenly was a series of gunfire from the German guards. Everyone thought was to be a massacre of POWs in the woods by the German guards or the Russian Army overtaking us. As a consequence, every prisoner broke ranks and attempted to bury themselves in the snow. We lay there for about an hour, wondering if we would ever see our families again, when our senior officer walked along the road assuring us all was well' and we should return to the road. A German guard had accidentally discharged his rifle. This caused all of us to assume the worst. The remaining guards, expecting a mass escape, set off a volley of rifle fire in the air, so as to control us."

"It began to snow harder and harder. The wind strengthened and chilled us to the bone. The line crawled, for now many were lame and blistered. Lightened packs were still further lightened, and some men began to fall back, and back to the end of the column to become stragglers. The first few men to drop by the wayside were put on the one German wagon accompanying the column, but it could only hold five or six, and soon these were only the unconscious and paralyzed.

"Now complete packs were being thrown away. The whole line straggled, strung out for miles. POWs were helping their buddies until it was all they could do to help themselves. Men seemed to be walking in their sleep; and men were dropping to the road, being urged to keep on, for they would freeze to death where they fell, if allowed to remain there. I often wonder how many POWs had fallen by the wayside and perished."

"On that evening of the second day, my right foot felt very cold, and upon inspection I discovered the sole of my shoe had detached itself and just hung at the heel. I was literally walking on my stocking foot. Luckily We arrived at the small German village of Moskuo, after two days without sleep, about 10:00 pm, and a large group of us were sheltered in the basement of a pottery factory for the remainder of the night. The factory was warm, and the men slept on the floors and on benches. I slept well that night atop a stack of firewood near the ceiling, with my feet against a steam pipe."

"The next morning, after a meager meal of barley soup provided by the factory kitchen, I was contemplating how to provide sufficient protection for my foot when one of the POWs who was bedding down at the other end of the building approached us. He said he had heard that someone needed a pair of shoes. I showed him my shoe. He had carried an extra pair of shoes and said, 'if they fit they were mine.' They fit.

"Imagine the probability of the two of us meeting under those circumstances - of the more than 10,000 POWs - he with the only pair of shoes and my being the only "lost sole. I have remembered that day for the past 64 years, and I know God was watching over me."

"The march did not end at the village of Moskuo. After a night's rest, those who were capable marched one more day to Spremburg, the end of the march, where we were put up in a warehouse on a Wehrmacht military post. Sleep that night was intermittent. There was no heat and the cold, hard concrete floor made it necessary to repeatedly turn over. This was the end of our wintry march."

"The next day we were packed into railroad boxcars, 70 men to a boxcar, in preparation for transportation to a prison camp on the outskirts of Nuremberg, Germany. We provided space on the boxcar floor for six men to lay, for those who were too ill to stand. The remainder of us stood for nearly three days, shoulder to shoulder. Every bone in my body ached. This standing for three days in a moving cattle car was physically the worst part of his POW experience. The Germans didn't check up on their welfare either."

"We remained in Nuremberg for one month at an old deserted, flea-infested, bombed out, forced labor compound. There were many British night raids on the city and we could hear the tumbling sound of the falling block-buster bombs and felt the ground shake upon impact."

"After one month we were marched for two weeks to our next destination: Moosburg, Germany. It was now spring in southern Germany and the outdoors were a godsend, free from the cold and fleas and lice."

"Due to the breakdown of the German transportation system, supplying the long column of POWs and German guards with food was very difficult. The overnight stops at small villages allowed us, as well as the guards, to go door-to-door requesting food. It was interesting to note that the people in the villages were very accommodating, and seemed to have a dislike for the Hitler regime." ,

"One day we knocked on the door of a small farmhouse occupied by an elderly lady. We asked for food and she invited us in. While she was slicing some bread, there was a hard knock at the door. The lady was frightened. It was one of the German guards, and ignoring us he demanded food. The lady gave him a slice of bread with lard. He took the bread without thanking her and left. She then proceeded to give us each a slice of bread with jam."

"Years later we were informed that Moosburg was only 30 miles from Dachau, a concentration camp where thousands of political prisoners were put to death. The camp at Moosburg was also an old bombed-out camp where we lived in tents among bomb craters.

"After one month, the American Third Army, led by General Patton, liberated us on the morning of April 29, 1945, one year after I was first captured. I will never forget the scene of General Patton entering the camp, standing in his jeep, hands on hips, and wearing two ivory-handled pistols, while the American flag was being raised. There was not one dry eye."

"After one year as a POW-captive of the Nazi, thank God I was once a again a free man, less 45 pounds and much more appreciative of what it truly means to be free."

Ball-Turret Gunner S/Sgt. Charles R. Warlow.

By his widow Shirley Warlow;

"He was born on a farm in Stanford, Illinois, on December 23, 1923. He attended a country school in Covel, IL. Through the 8th grade. He attended high School in Stanford, Il.

"After the war he went to an accounting school in Peoria, IL. He then opened his own accounting office in Gibson City, Il. Some years later he he moved his business to Robert, Il. He remained in business until 2005. He was married and has two sons; Kevin and Eric. He died of bone cancer on September, 24, 2010.

"WWII as Remembered."
By Charles for his two sons.

Ball-Turret Gunner S/Sgt. Charles R. Warlow

"I learned about Pearl Harbor on December 7, 1941 from the radio at the age of 17. My parents had moved to Roberts, Illinois in 1940. My dad had purchased a tavern there called "Dick's Place." I stayed in Stanford, Illinois to finish my senior year. I lived with Mrs. Imig in exchange for doing chores and other odd jobs for her. I had a Model A car. Roberts was about 50 miles away and I had been to Peoria once (70 miles).

"As a farm boy I had never been away from home. I worked for $1.00 per day and dinner, 6 to 6. At one time I worked for a neighbor who had a contract with the state highway department mowing. For this I received $2.00 per day and finally reduced to $1.00 as times were tough. I drove tractor and truck for this man.

"After graduation in the spring of 1942, I moved to Roberts and got a job as a painter for $0.35 per hour. While still in school our teacher had told us that we should enlist and become pilots as the future was where the air was. On December 1, 1942 I went to Rantaul, Illinois and enlisted in the Air Corps. My parents dropped me off and in I went.

"The next day l was shipped to St. Louis by train. Here I was given my uniform, IQ test (139) and rated as air craft mechanic. After a few days I was sent to St. Petersburg, Florida for basic training. This took eight weeks. We were stationed in an old hotel and it rained most every day in the afternoon. Here I learned to march in step, how to carry a rifle while marching and a lot of calisthenics. I was here about two months, then sent to Sheppard Field in Wichita Falls, Texas. Here I learned mechanics on light bombers. There were no trips to

Wichita Falls as this was off limits to us. Here we found out that we could volunteer for gunnery school and come out as a buck sergeant (three stripes). This was a big incentive as we finished mechanics school as private first class and sergeant ordinarily was two to three years on the date. We left here by train to go to Panama Beach, FL. Again off limits and no passes to town.

"Here we learned to shoot various weapons, rifles, pistols, machine guns and learned to assemble them. We had ground to ground, ground to air, air to air, also skeet and trap shooting. We traveled in the back of a truck and shot skeet birds as thrown from cover to sides, front and rear. We had to be alert for this. As a farm boy I was already familiar with rifles and shot guns. I excelled on the ranges.

"Next we flew in AT-6 (double open cockpit) with single machine gun in rear and shot at target pulled behind another plane. All of this was done out over the Gulf. After completing the course we received our "wings" and Buck Sergeant rating and were then sent to Oregon.

"In Oregon I was assigned to a crew of ten and a B-17 heavy bomber. As I was the smallest, I drew the ball turret and was then designated as 2nd Flight Engineer.

"We flew cross country several times. I was then acting as flight engineer. Our crew for these flights were me, radio-operator (we were the only two enlisted men), pilot, co-pilot, bombardier and navigator. We were the only ones on these practice flights or missions and landed at many other air bases throughout the U. S.

"These flights were to train navigator, pilots and radio man. I had now traveled thru or stopped at all U. S. states except a few in the northeast (I had been to Maine though). After 30 days of this training, I was shipped to Port of Debarcation in New York. Our pilot had screwed up so we went by boat and did not get to fly a plane to England. We were sent as replacements to the 401 Bomb Group.

"We were on a troop ship going across the North Atlantic and very rough. I spent most of my time on deck watching waves because quite a few below were sick and this was not fun to watch. The northern route was safer from sub attack, however we had two alerts but no sightings. I played some poker and did not lose but I had to loan the tail gunner money because he did and it still has not been paid back.

"This was a big convoy with destroyers, troop ships and supporting vessels. The crossing took about 2 1/2 weeks. We landed in southern England. My back pay was increased 29% for overseas service, 50% for hazardous (flying) service, something like 180$ per month total.

"We were assigned to an airbase in southern England at a town called Deenethorpe, which was about thirty miles south of London. Heavy Bombardment Group 401, Squadron 615. All B-17's, better know as flying fortress. We spent a week flying practice missions around England and the North Sea. Part of Deenethorpe had been destroyed by a bomber that crashed on take off and blew up with full bomb load.

"After about 5 missions, I was promoted to Staff Sergeant (4 stripes) and remained as such until I was discharged.

"After 10 to 12 missions we were given a two day pass and the radio operator and me went to Nottingham. We stayed overnight and came back the next day. We could hear bombing and rocket explosions in London.

"When we started flying actual missions to Germany and a few to France, we desired France because of fighter cover. In Germany they only flew part way because of fuel range. Anti-air craft guns were heavy fire at all allocations.

"Our missions started at 3.00 a.m. Breakfast, briefing on where the target was and what enemy resistance would be expected. We then would pick up our equipment, check guns, etc. Missions were twelve to fourteen hours long. Those to France were short, six or seven hours. If weather was bad and we couldn't see target, we would drop our bombs over "Northern Germany" or "Northern France." We didn't want to land with a load of bombs.

"On our 10th mission, I claimed one aircraft shot down. I didn't get to see it explode but the tail gunner did. On this mission we received much plane damage from flak and fighters and thought we would have to ditch in the English Channel. However, we were able to get to a base in southern England. We got extra air time by dumping overboard extra amino, guns, and gear. We were then able to get to land. We impressed the new arrivals with all the damage to our plane. These planes cost about $ 250.000 which was a staggering amount to me.

"Our fifth mission was to Berlin. This was by way longest and toughest of all other targets. Our fighters could not go this far. They would meet us over France and give us cover part of the way in and again on part of the way back. Anti aircraft fire was extremely heavy there. Our normal load was 2000 lbs. and we flew over the target at 25,000 to 30,000 feet and sometimes it was 80 degrees below zero. All but the pilot and co-pilot manned guns when fighter planes appeared. I would enter the ball turret after we were in the air by pointing guns straight down. This was also my position over the targets so that I could report on the damage that I could see.

"After our 16th mission, we were on a "stand down" day. Anther ball turret gunner and myself spent most of the day figuring out how to get a chest chute into the ball with us when on a mission. We normally would wear a back chute left above in the waist-section of the plane. In a spin it would be impossible to get up into the area above to put on the chute and crawl back to the waist door to exit at the rear of the plane. I learned later that my buddy the other ball turret gunner did not get to use his chute as his plane blew up over the target by a direct hit by flak.

***

"On Saturday, April 29, 1944 on our 17th mission, target Berlin, we were the lead group over the target and assistant operations officer was our pilot. Our regular pilot (a Boston Blue Blood) was in a flak house (nerves) after five missions.

"Over Berlin we were hit several times by flak and lost two engines, which dropped us from our formation and made us easy prey for fighters. As we were hit by fighters on return, I thought I had shot one down and saw him crash. The temperature at 30,000 feet was often 80 degrees below zero but we had electric suits on to keep warm

"After fighters shot out our #3 engine, the #4 started to runaway and the pilot called to us to bail out. We were in a spin and I couldn't go up because of centrifugal force. Then I opened the door behind me and pushed out. My left leg caught on the gun sight and I had to pull myself back into the turret, loosen my foot and then push out again at about 10,000 feet.

"I saw our plane in a spin far below and crash as I was floating downward. It was very quiet and peaceful in the air going down. Some of the crew had been machined gunned down by fighters or by people on the ground. This did not happen to me, thank goodness. As I was enjoying the ride down, the ground suddenly came at me in a hurry. I was landing in a forest but did not hit a tree. My left leg hit something and again re-injured it. It was black and blue for over four months.

"When I landed I said a short prayer of thanks. I looked down a row of trees, row upon row, and all were trimmed 20 to 25' up and no place to hide. I stumbled across a road and hid in some plants. However, somebody saw me cross the road. I was rousted out by pitch forks, clubs and guns. They already had our bombardier and I joined him. Our waist gunners had bailed out long before into the mountains and were severely frost bitten. My captors were ready to take me to town. They were Home Guards and only two were in uniform. I was beaten with a rifle but and didn't know why until the bombardier told me that they wanted me to go and I did, bad leg and all. As a flier I thought I didn't need the calisthenics or exercise to keep in shape. Wrong. I wished I had been in better shape and tried to hide.

"We were then marched or paraded through the streets of Hannover. We were taunted, things thrown at us, etc. Finally taken to a jail where we were turned over to military. In a few days I was taken to an interrogation center.

"At the center I was in solitary for four or five days. I only gave name, rank and serial number, but they knew about us pretty well. I told them this was my first mission, hoping to get off easier. I was threatened with death each time but we had been told this would happen to a prisoner at our briefings. So I didn't worry much. There were so many planes shot down that they couldn't handle all of us at once, so they didn't spend as much time on us as they would have liked to.

"We were then shipped by cattle cars to a POW camp at Kriens, Austria, about 38 miles from Vienna. Hitler had a hide-out there. The train was so crowded, we had to stand up for eight to ten hours. Once or twice a day they stopped for us to urinate or defecate in the open, in freight yards as people watched. At night we would be stopped, still in the freight car, in a freight marshalling yard. This was the usual target of the British bombers at night. If we were killed on the way to prison camp, it would not be their fault.

"We wound up at Kriens 17B Stalag. Our group filled up the remaining empty barracks. They held about a total of 4500 Americans. Our bunks were two stories high, two long and two wide as I remember them. Burlap bags with a small amount of straw and sawdust served as our mattress. We were issued a blanket that was not too heavy.

"After three months, I was finally given a pair of pants. I had spent all this time I was in long underwear. My original issue was taken at capture because the electric suit did not qualify as a uniform.

"I never went to sick bay as I was afraid I would never be allowed to leave. We formed a Combine (partnership) the waist gunner and I to cook together and share food. When we received Red Cross packages; we would divide them up and make them last twice as long. We were supposed to get a Red Cross Parcel every week, but they were usually six to eight weeks apart. Our daily ration was a bowl of very thin cabbage or potato soup and a slice of dark bread which was half sawdust and a cup of hot water for breakfast.

"We were next to the Russian Compound. They were as close to animals as I had ever seen. They had no education. They would kill for a slice of bread or a package of cigarettes.

"There was a small stove in our half of the barracks with a few pieces of coal per day. A lot of the wood was taken from our building and bed slats for burning. We had cold water about two hours each day to drink, clean up with, wash clothes, etc. This washroom was in the center of the barracks. Every two or three months we would be taken to a shower house with warm water for delousing and clean up.

"Roll call in the morning was an ordeal of one, two or more hours. We were standing in mud and water and their temperature was about the same as ours here. The Germans had trouble counting us, so we had to be counted over and over. The camp Commander would tell us about all new and old rules and regulations at this time. If anyone crossed warning lines they would be shot. These wires were about 36 feet from a tall electrified fence.

"Guard posts were at each corner of each compound. Our compound was about one city block square. In the center was the outhouse with barracks on one side and the balance of the area was used to walk in, which I did. Toilets were like old time outhouses but with forty holes which were sometimes full before cleaning out by the Russians and it did ever smell. Because of food allowance, we only needed to go about every 3 days.

"Our pastime was spent playing the card game of bridge. Ralph Meeks, my combine partner, and I were partners. We played for cigarettes. Mistakes and errors were subject to much criticism. Cigarettes were the legal tender in camp. One pack worth about $40.00 in Vienna and .30 cents in the States.

"I continually had boils or carbuncles on my neck and/or hip: no doubt due to lack of cleanliness.

"In April of 1945, we were taken on a forced march. We were marched back to Germany away from the Russian front. This was about 280 miles at twenty miles per day. I saw the Blue Danube River as we walked along side of it. At night we slept in barns (if lucky) or outside. Escape would have been easy but would have been a death sentence if caught.

"We met Jews being marched in the opposed direction. The tall and strong were in front leading the others and herded by SS troops. They were marching double time or so it seemed. You could smell and feel the fear from the group. The weak ones dropped out behind. When they could no longer keep up the pace, they were shot and thrown along the road. A rack wagon followed and picked up the dead. About every 200 yards another Jew lay dead. This was my first knowledge of the treatment of the Jewish population. We later were marched past a death camp but did not get to see inside. If we had we probably would not have gotten out.

"After being on the road our rations were mostly what we carried with us. After the first day we discarded almost everything except food, cigarettes and coats in order to be able to walk and keep up. We were fortunate that most of the guards were old and not SS troops, so we were route step and stretched out for miles. Our final spot of internment was in a woods. My boyhood upbringing helped us to make a lean to and branches of pines for beds. We were here about three weeks.

"One day a US soldier from Patton's advance guard came and accepted surrender from the guards and we were told that the U. S. would be there the next day. Most of the guards had slipped away at night before the troops arrived the next day. In two or three days we were moved to a factory building where it was dry and safe. We must have been fed something but I don't remember that we were.

"Then we were placed on air planes and flown to France where we were staging to go home. There we lived in tents. We were given new clothing and shoes. After a time we were taken to a ship to be returned to the U. S. The ride back was uneventful.

"At the time I was shot down, I weighed over 155 pounds due to the Air Forces good food. I went into service weighing 135 pounds. When I got out of prison camp I weighed 110 to 115 pounds and could not eat a full meal for several months.

"In the U. S. again we were sent to Miami, Fl. where I got a red sunburn swimming in the ocean. Then we got a train ride home for a sixty day leave. After sixty days we were sent to Fort Logan, Colorado where we were given a medical discharge and sent home September 1945.

"My brother Paul was in the 1st Marines as an artillery spotter. He would go ahead and call back instructions to move the shelling side to side, front or rear. He participated in several invasions and also in the occupation of Japan. So my parents still had a lot to worry about even though I had returned.

"I didn't do much when I returned home. I finally applied for a job in Bloomington as a janitor. On the way home I decided that this was not what I wanted to do with the rest of my life, so I went to school on the GI bill.

Waist-Gunner Sgt. James A. McGaha

By his son Mike and grandson Matt McGaha.

"James Houston McGaha was born on Sept 15, 1923 in Ada, Oklahoma. Ada is a town of 16,000 in southeastern Oklahoma. He was one of six children. His father was a custodian at the local small college. He attended Horace Mann High School where he played on the basketball team. After graduation he worked for local auto parts shop and took classes at East Central Oklahoma State College. In 1942 he married Joan Long.

"After volunteering for military service he was trained as an aircraft mechanic. One day an officer walked into his duty station and said, "you, you, and you come with me." From then on he was assigned to a B-17 heavy bomber.

Waist-Gunner Sgt. James A. McGaha

"On April 29 of 1944 my father was on mission number ten. They were assigned to go to the heavily fortified capitol city of Berlin. Over the target area they lost two of their engines to anti aircraft fire. This caused them to lag behind the the formation on their way back. Then they lost a third engine to German fighter aircraft.

"My father was the first one to bail out of the plane since he was standing next to the door. When his parachute deployed, it jerked him so hard that one of his flight boots flew off. He had an extra pair of boots but they were not insulated. After a few days on the ground he took off those walking boots and discovered that his feet were turning black. He had to seek help immediately.

"This presented two major problems. He had to be captured without being shot and he had to hope for proper medical treatment. He accomplished goal number one with the help of a German farmer who was out in a field cutting hay. This man took him to his home and then went and notified the local military authorities. While sitting on the farmers front porch, the local people from the area gathered in the front yard to stare at him and then venture up to touch his uniform. He accomplished goal number two when the Germans allowed a captured Australian doctor to amputate all of his toes. The operation was performed using raw ether and it took place inside of a dairy barn.

"About a year later he was allowed to be part of a wounded prisoner exchange that took place through the neutral country of Switzerland. In early 1945 against many odds he miraculously and joyously returned home. He received the Air Combat Medal, Purple Heart, and the Prisoner of War Medal.

"He never said one critical or harsh word about his German captors. After the war he worked at jobs in the auto parts business. Most of these jobs required him to be on his feet all day. He was never a complainer or a shirker. In 1975 he was elected as Pontotoc County Clerk in his first bid for elective office. He retired from that position in 1986. He passed away on April 25, 2013. His funeral was conducted on April 29, the same day as the fateful bombing mission to Berlin. He was the epitome of the term "Quiet Hero."

***

Acknowledgements;
Mildred (Gould) Wild, sister of Pilot Capt. George Gould
Co-pilot 2Lt. Frank Linc; from the 8th AFHS MN website
Shirley Warlow, widow of ball-turret gunner S/Sgt. Charles R. Warlow.
Mike and Matt McGaha, son and grandson of waist-gunner Sgt. James A.
    McGaha

CHAPTER 36

446TH BOMB GROUP
706TH BOMB SQUADRON

Type: B-24J • Serial: 42-100360 "Luck and Stuff"
MACR: 4485 • Air Base: Bungay

"Communication between the waist of airplane and the cockpit was not possible due to the raging fire that threatened the lives of everyone and blocked the passage in the bomb bay. We encountered a tail attack by enemy aircraft: bullets were penetrating the aircraft."

Statement by co-pilot Joseph L. Kwon.

Pilot: 1Lt. Weems D. Jones, 0-804674, POW

Co-Pilot: 1Lt. Joseph L. Kwon, 0-751358, POW

Navigator: 1Lt. Thomas B. Brigham, 0-752477, POW

Nose-Turret Gunner: S/Sgt. Charles W. Perry, 15333048, POW

Engineer: S/Sgt. Charles E. Hill, 14163634, KIA, Etowah County, AL

Radio: T/Sgt. Arnold H. Kaminsky, 12180404 POW

Ball-Turret Gunner: S/Sgt. George E. Radle, 39011819, KIA, Ramsey County, NM

Waist-Gunner: S/Sgt. William H. Ingraham, 32225861, POW

Waist-Gunner: S/Sgt. Lester S. Baker, 11114360, POW

Tail-Gunner: S/Sgt. Jimmy L. Cahoun, 34395707, KIA

3 KIA, 7 POW

Crash Site: Helmstedt, Germany
Time: 13.00

Pilot 1Lt. Weems D. Jones.

"We were No. 3 on the Squadron formation when we left the formation. I bailed out as other crew members of my crew through the nose wheel door and the ones in the rear through the side windows. Sgt. Baker had a hand injury (thumb), Sgt. Kaminsky had a leg injury and Lt. Brigham was OK, when I saw them at time of capture. S/Sgt. Calhoun was injured, according to Sgt. Baker, a waist gunner, Sgt. Calhoun was hit by bullets from fighters.

"Due to the bomb bay fire and lack of communication I was unable to check Sgt. Calhoun. I have seen no one who saw Sgt. Calhoun, believe he did not leave the ship. S/Sgt. Radle bailed out at the same point as the other crew members, he was injured and was last seen at capture. Sgt. Radle was seen by Sgt. Kaminsky, who said that Sgt. Radle had a foot blown off and was dead. S/Sgt. Hill was seen when he left the turret to repair the supercharger control, he may have gone to the rear to warn the crew of the fire before it was too bad. I am positive he was not in the pilot or nose section when I left the ship."

Navigator 1Lt. Thomas B. Brigham.

Born September 3, 1919 in New York and passed away on February 14, 1993.

"We lost one engine over Berlin and were straggling. Three ME-I09 fighters attacked us from the rear, set the plane on fire and injured seven crew members. We left the formation about the rally point twenty minutes from the target. Pilot Jones, radio-operator Kaminsky, nose gunner Perry and myself went out thru the nose wheel escape hatch. Co-pilot Kwon crawled thru the one foot opening of the bomb bay doors. Waist gunners Ingraham and Baker went out the waist windows. We landed near Helmstedt, Germany.

"S/Sgt. Radle was hit in the knee by heavy caliber machine gunfire. He bailed out but was found dead on the ground by the radio-operator Kaminsky. He helped

Navigator 1Lt. Thomas B. Brigham

carry Radle away from the spot where he landed. He said that they figured that Radle had died on the way down. I didn't see Kaminsky until reaching a small village outside Helmstedt, this village was the first place were we were taken, so Radle must be buried someplace nearby.

"Tail-gunner S/Sgt. Calhoun was injured and I believe unable to leave the plane. He was probably injured by fighter attack from the tail. The last contact we had was that Calhoun reported fighters in the distance. When the enemy fighters appeared in the distance Calhoun put his parachute on and closed the turret doors again. I expect that Calhoun was injured by the fighters and never left the ship. The bomb bay was on fire and at least three of the men in the tail were injured so it seems highly probable that Calhoun was also injured. When the surviving crew members got together at the prison camp none of us had any more information about Calhoun or about Hill.

From nephew Stephen Volkamer:

"I never met my great uncle Tom personally but I have heard a bit about him and regard him as one of the more interesting people in my family tree. My grandmother Shirley remembers her brother Tom as being very kind. The Brigham family lived in Rochester, New York. The children of that family were raised Catholic. My grandmother said that even though he was a very young man at the time, Tom helped pay for her Catholic girl's schooling as the family was not wealthy. Before enlisting with the US Army Air Corps he had tried to gain a commission to the prestigious West Point military academy. He ended up being offered the commission but it was too late as he'd already enlisted with the Air Corps.

"I know that he was intelligent, and following the war he went to the Wharton School of Finance at the University of Pennsylvania. He became a businessman and lived in Ohio. He and his wife had eleven children. Sometime during the 1970s he became mentally ill and began wandering around the country, much to the heartbreak of his family. In the fall of 1984 he was accused of a train station bombing in Montreal, Canada, and was subsequently held for a number of years in an institution.

"His first two trials were overturned and he was awaiting his third trial, when he died in Quebec, Canada on 14 February 1994. His family believes that he was innocent, and that he being mentally ill had been framed for the bombing by others.

"Thomas B. Brigham Sr.'s younger brother was 2nd Lieutenant Richard Francis Brigham. Richard was also a navigator in the US Army Air Corps but flew with B-17s in the 388th bombardment squadron based out of Knettishall, England. He ended up flying 5 missions before being shot down on the last one and killed in action. The B-17 was hit by flak, exploded, and much of the debris and the bodies landed in Rheidt, Germany.

"The story about Richard and Thomas was that they had arranged to meet at a theater in London sometime in February-March 1944. Thomas went to the rendezvous but his brother Richard didn't show up as planned, and that's when Thomas knew that his brother had been killed.

Nose-Turret Gunner S/Sgt. Charles W. Perry.

"I received my training with the 446th Bomb Group in Denver, Colorado and flew over with them in the original Group and landed at our base in England a few days before Thanksgiving 1943. I flew all my missions with McKeny's crew with the exception of the last two. I flew nose turret gunner on my final mission with 1Lt. Weems Jones, replacing a Lt Hoover who was assigned to our lead ship. The mission was to Berlin on 29 April, 1944.

"We were 'Stood down' for two hours waiting on the weather to clear up over the target. Finally we were given order to take off. I begged Jimmy Calhoun, tail gunner, who was killed on the first fighters pass, to let me operate the tail position but he would not agree to this. So off we went for Berlin.

"Forming was uneventful and we fell into the bomber stream for Berlin. It was a beautiful day up there with about 8/10 cloud cover most of the way to the target. P-51 escorts flew over us on the way to their assigned area, mostly silvery colored, as I remember. Some gunners ahead of us got a little nervous, I guess and started shooting at the P-51's who simply wheeled out of range and proceeded on their way. I can imagine what they were saying.

"A German fighter poked his nose through the clouds at 12 o'clock low and was quickly jumped by a flight of P-38's and reduced to an orange ball of flame. Too far away to tell if the pilot got out in time or not.

"Nearing the target area flak was fairly heavy and on the bomb run we apparently caught it in No. 2 engine and began to loose our oil which prompted the feathering of that engine. Coming off the target Lt Jones asked that I re-toggle the bomb switch as we were still carrying two 500 pound bombs that refused to release, nothing happened and the bomb bay doors were closed and we headed home with them still in the racks.

"We cut across to the Rally Point to slide underneath our Group but could not keep up and thus became a straggler. No escorts were to be seen as head winds had delayed their contact with our wing.

"Approaching the Braunschweig area a decision was made to call for escort and we got them anyway in the form of FW-190s. They set fire to No. 3 and No. 4 engines and fire broke out on the half deck where Sgt. Hill was transferring fuel. The navigator, Lt Brigham, banged on the nose turret doors informing me that we were going down and I would have to get out. After untangling all the wires about my feet, I tumbled out of the nose turret to face Lt Brigham, who was holding my chest pack for me. I snapped it on and followed him out the nosewheel door, entered the slip stream into another world.

"I freefelled to just above the clouds before opening my chute. "Luck and Stuff" had blown prior to this. A FW-190 circled me as I neared the ground, radioing my position, no doubt. Landing in young timber, with very little shock of contact with the ground, I was surrounded by about 300 civilians, armed with various weapons such as hoes, axes, clubs etc. and two young Wehrmacht soldiers. I at once set off in their direction. They gave me the protection that I needed. From here I was marched to a small town's police station, detained over night and moved to Dulag Luft near Frankfurt and then by train to Stalag Luft VI in East Prussia. The nearest town of any size that I came down near would be Helmstedt, Germany.

"According to information I received from S/Sgt. Lester Baker at Stalag Luft IV, S/Sgt. Hill evidently burned to death on the half deck, S/Sgt. Calhoun was shot on the first pass of the fighters and S/Sgt. George Radle took a 20mm shell in the knee and bled to death in his chute before reaching the ground.

Waist-Gunner S/Sgt. Lester S. Baker.

"A Tale of Two Brothers" from a newspaper article

"S/Sgt. Lester Baker and S/Sgt. Studley Baker came home from the European Theatre together, following many months as German prisoners. Both were members of the Army Air Corps and both flew several missions over continental Europe before they were captured. Studley was captured March 6, 1944 and Lester, April 29, 1944.

"Lester and Studley went into service with the Army Air Corps within a few months of eat other. Studley enlisted January 5, 1942 and Lester enlisted October 29, 1942. Studley became an aerial gunner and Lester a waist-gunner. Only once during their training in the Sates did the brothers meet, in Arizona, where Lester met the members of his brothers' crew, whom he was to meet again much later in Germany.

"The young flyers met in England by chance following their transfer there. They had both flown over, Lester arrived November 16, 1943 and Studley 21, 1943, but it was not until February they met in England and then by chance.

"On Saturday, April 29, 1944, Lester bailed out over Germany. After having passed through the interrogation center near Frankfurt he spent three months in a German hospital before being sent to Satlag Luft 4 where he met his brother Studley.

"Lester explained that he did not know where Studley was, but that he met two of the men of Studley's crew he had met the only time in the States he had been with Studley in Arizona. They told him Studley was in the next compound.

"We asked the Kommandant," Lester recalls, "for permission to stay together and after four weeks our request was granted.

Waist-Gunner S/Sgt. William H. Ingram recalls;

"Communication between the waist of the airplane and cockpit was not possible due to the raging fire that threatened the lives of everyone and blocked passage in the bomb bay.

"We encountered a tail attack by enemy aircraft and those in the waists were subjected to more danger of death than those in the nose. Bullets were penetrating the aircraft and the chances of being hit fatally was very possible. I remained about four minutes in the burning plane after signal to abandon ship was given. This means that the aircraft did not explode for at least four minutes after the signal was given to abandon ship, and there was sufficient time for everyone to get out, unless fatally wounded.

"Fire was raging from bomb bay to waist making it difficult to help or see who was injured. According to Sgt. Baker, S/Sgt. Radle bailed out and was found dead upon touching the ground due to loss of blood caused by bullet wounds. He had no other information as to what was done to the body. I believe he either died as told or possibly in a German hospital.

"The right waist gunner said he thought he saw Sgt. Calhoun stumble outside of the tail turret, possibly due to bullet wounds. No assistance could be given due to the intensive heat created by developing flames and the graveness of the situation. Believe he was wounded fatally and that his body could not be found due to possible explosion that ensued after S/Sgt. Hill was ordered to make a fuel transfer. Believe he was fatally wounded either in the catwalk or possibly in the waist. Visibility was zero in the bomb bay due to the fire. No one saw him either bail out or taken prisoner.

***

Acknowledgements;
Stephen Volkamer, nephew of navigator 1Lt. Thomas B. Brigham

CHAPTER 37

447TH BOMB GROUP
708TH BOMB SQUADRON

Type: B-17G • Serial: 42-37866 "Bloated Body"
MACR: 4250 • Air Base: Rattlesden

With the tail section badly damaged by fighter attacks the crew bailed out when the aircraft caught fire. Two of the crew were killed in the aircraft.

Missing Air Crew Report # 4250

Pilot: 1Lt. Warren D. Donahue, 0-803787, POW, Pueblo, CO

Co-Pilot: 2Lt. Melvin B. McArdle, 0-751744, POW, Chicago, IL

Navigator: 2Lt. Hugh P. Simms, 0-811771, POW. Chicago, IL

Bombardier: 2Lt. William B. Gaillard, 0-681774, POW, New York, NY

Engineer: T/Sgt. Don V. Sage, 38153527, POW, Oklahoma City, OK

Radio: T/Sgt. Carroll J. Elwell, 16087558, POW, Climax, MI

Ball-Turret Gunner: Sgt. Billy T. Lockman, 6945078, KIA, Wilkes-Barre, PA

Left Waist-Gunner: S/Sgt. Kenneth V. Olson, 37305937, POW, Hemming, MN

Right Waist-Gunner: S/Sgt. Norbert J. Arvin, 15333240, POW, Montgomery, ID

Tail-Gunner: S/Sgt. Joseph S. Pennock, 32360546, KIA, Mt. Holy, NJ

2 KIA, 8 POW

Crash Site: 9 miles e. of Brunswick, Germany
Time: 11.15

B-17 Serial #42-37866 "Bloated Body"

Pilot 1Lt. Warren D. Donahue.

By his son Pat.

"My dad, Warren Drysdale Donahue, was born in Pueblo, Colorado, August 23, 1920 the first child of Ben and Nina Donahue. Two years later, Jack their second and last child was born."

"Ben worked in the machine maintenance and repair shop at Colorado Fuel and Iron Corp, at the time the largest steel mill in the United States West of the Mississippi River. During the Great depression to make ends meet the family moved in with Ben's mother, dad's grandmother. I only knew her as Great Grandma Donahue, but I know she had the most significant and positive influence on my dad during his growing up."

"After high school he went to Greeley, Colorado to attend Colorado College of Education, what is now University of Northern Colorado. He met Helen Hannen, his wife and my mother to be, in the first chemistry class of the term."

"Before completing school my dad joined the Army Air Force in early 1943 and he and my mother were married in June 1943 before he left for England. As I was born Feb 1944, I was obviously conceived before his departure as well."

***

"His last mission. The only thing dad ever talked about was parachuting from the plane just west of Berlin, and breaking his leg on hitting the ground. He said his foot was twisted all the way around to where it was pointing forward again. That leg ended up a little shorter than the other but fortunately didn't bother him in later life, in fact I was eight or nine years old before he told that, there was no visible evidence."

"After some time in solitary confinement, he was sent to Stalag 3 at Sagan. Later he was moved (marched) to a Stalag at Spremberg, and then moved to Sta-

540

lag 13D in Nuremberg and finally to Stalag 7 A at Moosburg."

"Dad told us how during one of the marches, he carried a fellow prisoner who was still in bad shape from injuries."

***

"After returning home Dad went back to school on the G.I. bill. Before being shot down, he had planned on staying in aviation, but after losing some of his crew, he said that he didn't want to ever again have the responsibility of other people's lives in a plane. He was truly bothered by being the pilot of a plane in which some of his crew lost their lives."

"He graduated with a teacher's degree when I was four years old and taught for one year in a small four room school in Valley View, Colorado, near Greeley, Colorado. In 1950, we moved to Yakima, Washington where he taught at Yakima Valley College, the Dean there was a fellow prisoner of war with my dad and talked him into coming to Yakima. We only stayed one year and returned to Greeley and a year later moved to Longmont, Colorado where he taught grade 6 math, I actually had my dad for a teacher in grade 6."

"In 1957 we moved back to Yakima and he taught again at Yakima Valley. Then in 1959 we moved to Vista, California where he taught math at Palomar State College, ultimately becoming head of the Math Dept., and remained there until he retired in 1986 and he and my mother moved back to Colorado to stay for the rest of their lives."

From an interview in the *Estes Park Trail – Gazette*:

"Memorial Day: WWII Veteran Warren Donahue recalls his time as a German POW."

"Warren Donahue was twenty-three years old in 1943, and flew a B-17 Flying Fortress on bombing missions over Nazi Germany. His young wife, Helen, was living in Greeley. On his third bombing mission to Berlin, his 28th overall mission, he was shot down.

"We didn't have any parachute training at all," he explained. 'They just said, 'Here's your parachute, and pull the handle.' So when I bailed out of the plane and landed, I broke my ankle on both sides, and the small bone in my leg. I crawled through the forest the rest of the day and that night I got picked up by Polish prisoners of war who were farm workers. They turned me in to the town Burgomaster,

Pilot 1Lt. Warren D. Donahue

and he turned me over to the German Luftwaffe."

"Donahue was now a prisoner of war in Nazi Germany. The bomber crews were referred to as "terrorfliegers" (flyers of terror), in Germany. 'The first thing they did was put me into solitary confinement for about 12 days," he recalled. 'The prisoners that had been there before me had made marks on the walls, seven or nine or twelve slashes on the wall. I wondered what happened to the guy in there before me on that thirteenth day. Then they took me into interrogation, and the interrogating officer was dressed in civilian clothes. He offered me a cigarette, but I didnt smoke, so I didn't take it. He started asking me questions.

"You're taught to tell them nothing but your name, rank, and serial number, and he said, 'Let me show you something.' He went over to a bookcase on the wall that looked like it had a set of encyclopedias in it. He said, 'Let's see...you were in the 447th Bomb Group,' and he pulled down a folder. He opened it up and said, 'What would you like to know? Here is your cook, here are your barracks, and here are your planes. We knew what your target was before they woke you up that morning.' He knew more than I did, so how could I answer any questions?" Donahue continued.

"I think that they probably treated all Air Force personnel the same way," he said. 'There was quite a camaraderie between flyers. We would shoot down fighters, but when the pilot bailed out, you didn't shoot at him uinder his parachute. The Germans did the same thing; they didn't shoot at us as we parachuted out of our planes. I was a prisoner of the German Air Force," he explained, 'Because I was in the Air Force.

"Part of surviving in a situation such as that requires keeping a sense of humor, and there were many instances that the POWs had fun at their keeper's expense. "Twice a day we would fall out to be counted in formation in the camp," said Donahue. "And one night a week they would do a bed count after the lights went out at midnight. Two guards, that we called 'goons' would come through with flashlights and count us. There were fifteen of us in this room, and a fellow named Bob Abrams from St. Louis slept in one of the top bunks. Well, Bob picked up German pretty fast, and he would add a couple of numbers to their count. In the silence he would throw a couple of extra numbers in there and that would add to that total so there would be 17 or 18 men in the room instead of the 15. Two hours later they would come back and count again, and they made a lot of noise, banging the door, and their boots would make a lot of noise. But if you felt like it, you'd get up, fold up your mattress, and get in a locker so that you're not there, and this time, they'd have 13 or 14 instead of 15. They wouldn't get it straight until the morning appel (roll call). They were doing their damndest to get the right number," he chuckled.

"The Red Cross received word that Donahue and his colleagues were being held. They notified his wife, and started sending Red Cross parcels containing raisins, a can of corned beef, vitamin C, Lucky Strike cigarettes, and whole powdered milk. Everyone would keep the cigarettes and the vitamin C, but would give the food to two men who designated themselves as the cooks. When everyone shared, everyone got a little more than they would have on their own.

"You had to make a paste out of the powdered milk," recollected Donahue. 'Otherwise you'd never get it fixed because of the fat content. And from the paste then keep adding water.' The POWs were moved that winter as the Russians pressed forward into Germany.

"When the Russians crossed the Oder River, we walked with civilians, old people, children, and women carrying babies with old wagons and wheelbarrows and carts full of their belongings. We were just ahead of the front lines, in the snow, and I thought, 'Boy, they are worse off than we are. Most of our guards at the camp were WWI veterans, they were my parent's age, and even though we were POWs, we were in better shape than they were to be on a forced march. One guard I met and talked with a little bit had lost two sons in the Russian fighting, and his wife and one or two daughters had been killed in the bombings. He had nobody to live for, and he was not angry with us. He saw the futility of war. He had nothing to live for, but he was still pleasant. Bombing is not accurate. They don't tell you when you go out on a mission that you are going to bomb the city center, they say you are bombing marshalling yards, railroad yards, but all those cities in Europe, there's a railroad yard right next to the city or right inside it.

"Well, an interesting story about human nature," began Donahue. "There were fifteen men in our room and we got a loaf of bread each week per man. When we got notice that we were going to have to march because the Russians were moving in, it was bread ration day, and some of our fellows were already out in line to get counted. My buddy Glenn and I grabbed enough bread for us all, found our roommates and gave them their bread. I remember it had a lot of rye in it.

"We were out on the march for about 40 hours when we got to a stopping place. We were in the snow and the cold, and Glenn and I would pull out our loaves of bread and slice them up and share them with our roommates. We got to a wood pulp factory and were there for about three days or so when Glenn and I ran out of bread. So we turned to our roommates and said, 'alright let's slice up yours," remembered Donahue. His 'friends,' his 'family' that had been through so much together already, refused to share their own bread with them. "We didn't get a single slice of bread from one of those guys," he said. 'After sitting at a table and eating, and reading letters from home, and reading together and playing cards together, that's what we got. So I turned to Glenn and said, 'Glenn, we're going home together, or we're not going home at all,' and he said, 'it's a deal.' which was the pledge of our lives to each other. I've always wondered how a psychiatrist would interpret that kind of reaction. So in my opinion, if you have one good, loyal friend in your life, you're lucky.

"Nuremberg. 'We were there for two months," continued Donahue. 'The barracks were really full. The bunks were three high and four wide, with twelve men on each side of the room and the bedbugs and lice would just eat you alive. We didn't have any Red Cross packages for nearly the entire time we were there."

The men were fed soup that they called 'The Green Death." 'Do you know what insulate is? On farms when they grind up corn and grains, and grasses, they dump it in a silo and it somewhat ferments. They feed it to cattle in the winter. That soup looked like they had taken insulates and boiled it and served it to us. Sometimes we would get potatoes with manure stuck to them because they would dig these trenches, put the potatoes in them, and cover them with straw and manure so they wouldn't freeze during the winter. They'd bring these potatoes in and throw them in the stew without washing them off. So there was a lot of dysentery."

"To pass the time, the POWs would play bridge and share books, they would read aloud letters they got from home, and pass around pictures. "We were a family," said Donahue. They even became chummy with some of their guards. One guard at the camp had been a bartender in New York City. and spoke English. "His name was Fisher, and he would come in to the barracks and say, 'Now don't believe all the B.S. you are hearing on the loudspeakers. You guys are winning the war and will be home before Christmas.' Well, we didn't make it home that Christmas. But we were home for the next one.

"We would get compressed coal to burn in the stove to stay warm, and we would only get so many per man a week. Fischer would come and march us out to get the coal, and we would carry it in cardboard boxes. Well, we'd give Fisher a pack of cigarettes and he would say, 'I'm going to go over here and have a smoke, but remember, only six coals per man,' which really meant, 'help yourself.' He'd never count. Then when we would get back to the gate, he would clear us with the guard on the gate and we'd go in and have extra coal to burn.'

"When we got to Moosburg we went to a field and were stripped naked. We got deloused, and I don't know if it was DDT or what the stuff was, but it looked like we'd fallen into a flour barrel. It clung to you and there were no showers," he said. "Then you went into a building and they had your number and picture and your pack and stuff. They would go through your stuff and you would get a sock at a time or a shoe or underwear and whatever you had in the pack.

"General Patton liberated us," said Donahue. "His tank outfit. He had been in contact with the British and they were in contact with him before he got there. Patton said, 'We'll be there at about ten o'clock in the morning.'"

"Next to our camp there were some forced labor camps where people worked on farms. They were Polish and Czech. But every once in awhile we would trade with them. We'd throw cigarettes over the barbed wire for things. So my buddy traded three or four packs of cigarettes for a fish. They'd caught a bass or something and threw it over to us. He baked the fish the night and we ate too much." Their bodies were not accustomed to the protein beyond the occasional corned beef, and it made him sick. 'I was too sick to get up to see Patton come through the gate, but I wish I would have dragged myself out there."

"But the Germans didn't surrender without a struggle. "There were about 10,000 prisoners in that last camp in Moosburg," explained Donahue. "It was down near Hitler's hangout. And we thought maybe we were going to be held for hostages. Why were they concentrating us all down there?

"Moosburg wanted to resist the Allies, but the town was declared an open city and our German guards in the towers were being shot by the SS troops. They were shooting at their own guards. Then it got silent after a lot of machine gunfire. And then somebody said, 'The tanks are here.'

"I got out of the tent long enough to see the German flag come down and the American flag go up. No one gave the Pledge of Allegiance, no one saluted the flag, nobody sang 'The Star Spangled Banner," but everybody knew what that flag stood for. There wasn't any question about it. We were going home."

"There were so many prisoners at the camp that the senior officers assigned to each barracks had to cut a deck of cards to determine who would go home when. The senior officer assigned to Donahue's barracks drew the King of Spades, and they were on their way out of Germany by the third or fourth day.

"They trucked us to an airfield and we flew to Paris," he said. "The French USO girls were there with coffee and donuts for us, two donuts to each prisoner. Well, I hadn't had a donut in well over a year, and we wanted a third one. They said no. That the day before one of the POWs had died from eating three of four donuts. So we didn't argue with them after that," he laughed. 'My buddy and I could have got a pass to go to Paris, but they said that when the ship sails, it sails, and if not, you were going to have to wait for the next one. My buddy and I decided that we would just go to wait on the ship. We were there for two or three days before we sailed."

***

"Donahue's ship landed north of Boston. While he was a prisoner, his wife had given birth to a son, Pat, who was 15 months old by the time Donahue returned to the States. "Don't think I got down and kissed the ground, or anything like that," said Donahue. "The greatest part was meeting my wife and son in a park in Denver. I came in on a troop train and called her. She didn't want to drive in downtown Denver, so I told her to meet me at the east edge of city park, and that I'd find her. So she and my son came down. Of course I'd never seen him, and he was the kind of kid that didn't really liked to be picked up by strangers. He'd really study you if he didn't know you. I walked up to the car, and he was sitting on the driver's side, playing with the steering wheel, and my wife was sitting on the passenger seat. I walked over to the driver's side window, looked in and said, 'Hi, Pat.' He looked up at me for just a few seconds, and held up his arms to be held. That was the best part."

***

Acknowledgements;
Pat Donahue, son of pilot 1Lt. Warren D. Donahue

CHAPTER 38

447ᵀᴴ BOMB GROUP
708ᵀᴴ BOMB SQUADRON

Type: B-17G • Serial: 42-37868 • "Due Back"
MACR: 4251 • Air Base: Rattlesden

Aircraft was hit by enemy fighters and was knocked out of formation. Last seen going down, apparently under control but with engine #3 afire. Four chutes observed.

Missing Air Crew Report # 4251

Pilot: 2Lt. Carl J. Blom, 0-807979, POW, Portland, ME

Co-Pilot: 2Lt. Wallace G. Lane, 0-818067, POW, Yonkers, NY

Navigator: 2Lt. Dudley W. Davis, 0-698672, POW, Raleigh, TN

Bombardier: 2Lt. Dare D. Ziemer, 0-674825, POW, Ulica, KS

Engineer: T/Sgt. Windsor E. Graham, 14142036, POW, Lithonia, GA

Radio: T/Sgt. Arthur W. Watt, 36719165, KIA, Elwo Isle, IL

Ball-Turret Gunner: Sgt. Lloyd J. Arthur, 37438476, KIA, North Bend, NE

Left Waist-Gunner: S/Sgt. Isaac R. Guyton, 1808577, KIA, Fort Worth, TX

Right Waist-Gunner: S/Sgt. Richard Ferighetto, 33017508, POW, Colver, PA

Tail-Gunner: S/Sgt. Robert E. Tobin, 35041542, KIA, Union City, IN

4 KIA, 6 POW

Crash Site: Six miles n. of Helmstedt, Germany
Time: 11.30

Navigator 2Lt. Dudley W. Davis stated after his return to the States;

"The co-pilot Wallace Lane, after turning on the bail-out bell and giving the bail-out command over the inter-phone, tried to right the plane both physically and with the use of the automatic pilot unsuccessfully. He bailed out through the front hatch immediately after I did. Engineer Windsor Graham was on the cat walk when I bailed out and immediately followed the co-pilot out.

"The above took place within two minutes. Waist-gunner Sgt. Richard Ferighetto stated that he bailed out when the plane was in the steep spiral, after the bail-out command. All these men landed on or near the airfield at Helmstedt, Germany, and were confined in the hard cooler at the airfield.

"I personally never heard the bail-out command or the bell, probably due to the fact that I was slightly wounded when the plane was hit and the intercom was in- operative. I had no inter-phone connection during the last five minutes of the flight, due to flak and 20 mm damage.

Engineer T/Sgt. Windsor E. Graham reported after the war;

Engineer T/Sgt. Windsor E. Graham and his wife

"The last intercom report I was able to hear said everyone was okay. This was just as we were attacked by enemy planes. In the second attack by the German fighters I was knocked from my turret position by a 20 mm. shell from a FW 190, one of five enemy fighters attacking our plane from the rear. This shell struck the flak helmet I was wearing just over my left eye, also breaking the oxygen line and the oxygen fastening straps connected to the flak helmet. It also disconnected the plane intercom headset so I was unable to hear anything over the intercom system.

"The exploding shell had put me out for a short time and when I recovered we were descending rapidly. I then tried to go through the bomb bay into the rear section of the plane but was unable to do so because of the plane being out of control and tossing around like a fallen leaf.

Daughter Virginia Harper wrote;

"Daddy was born October 14, 1924 in Stone Mountain, GA. His address was Lithonia, GA but he grew up in Stone Mountain. He went to school until the ninth grade and then went to work in a saw mill. He later went back to school to get his GED. His parents were Offie Jones Graham and Arthur Windsor Graham. He was an only child.

"He was in Stalag Luft 3A or 4A from April 29, 1944 to April 29, 1945. When he came home he and my mom were married on Sept. 1, 1945. They spent their honeymoon in Miami, FL in a rehab center.

"Daddy worked at several jobs through the years but retired in 1982 from General Services Administration with the Federal Government.

***

Achnowledgements
Engineer T/Sgt. Windsor E. Graham, by daughter Virginia Harper.

CHAPTER 39

447TH BOMB GROUP
708TH BOMB SQUADRON

Type: B-17G • Serial: 42-102479 "Mississippi Lady"
MACR: 4255 • Air Base: Rattlesden

---

*"Target time was approx. 11.45. About ten minutes before
reaching target as plane was turning into the bomb run at an
altitude of 18,000 feet, the plane was hit by anti-aircraft fire which
exploded the oxygen bottles in the waist section. Immediately
following this the plane was hit by fire from enemy fighters which
set fire to the left wing just behind the gas tanks. At this time Lt.
Farrell gave the order to bail out over the intercom system and he
also rang the alarm bell."*

Official Statement made by Pilot Edgar Farrel

Pilot: 2Lt. Edgar P. Farrell, 0-613683, POW, Atlanta, GA

Co-Pilot: 2Lt. John A. Benedict, 0-1036845, POW, Glendale, CA

Navigator: F/O Sherwood W. Landis, T-123578, KIA, Pittsburgh, PA

Bombardier: F/O Wynne M. Longeteig, 0-749912, KIA, St. Paul, NE

Engineer: S/Sgt. William R. Peters Jr., 14159481, POW, Cosburn, VA

Radio: S/Sgt. Norman Bussel, 34720238, POW, Memphis, TN

Ball-Turret Gunner: Sgt. Joseph Guida, 32780718, KIA, New York, NY

Left Waist-Gunner: Sgt. Merle L. Rumbaugh, 33439025, POW,
McDonald, PA

Right Waist-Gunner: Sgt. Waide G. Fulton, 33244674, POW, Oxford, PA

Tail-Gunner: Sgt. Vasilios Mpourles, 11021681, KIA, Lowell, MA

4 KIA, 6 POW

Crash Site: Eickendorf, Germany, 15 miles sw of Gardelegen
Time of crash: 11.35

Pilot 2Lt. Edgar P. Farrell.

On September 14, 1945, Edgar Farrell was interrogated officially about the death of navigator F/O Sherwood W. Landis.

"Lt. Farrel was first pilot on B-17 plane, 29 April 1944, on a mission to bomb Berlin. Target time was approx. 11.45. About ten minutes before reaching target as plane was turning into the bomb run at an altitude of 18.000 feet, the plane was hit by anti-aircraft fire which exploded the oxygen bottles in the waist section. Immediately following this the plane was hit by fire from enemy fighters which set fire to the left wing just behind the gas tanks. At this time Lt. Farrell gave the order to bail out over the intercom system and he also rang the alarm bell. Just prior to giving the bail out order, the bombardier had notified Lt. Farrell over the intercom system that the navigator , F/O Landis, had been hit but did not describe Landis's injuries. The co-pilot told the bombardier to take care of Landis. It later developed that the bombardier was seriously injured by sudden flak burst immediately following the intercom conversation with Lt. Farrell.

2Lt. Edgar P. Farrell, pilot, with wife

"The co-pilot went to the top turret position to assist the top turret gunner who had been injured. Lt. Farrell then held the plane as level as he could until believed that all personnel was out and he then went to the nose hatch where he found F/O Landis leaving the plane also by the nose hatch. Lt. Farrell states that he spoke to Landis before Landis jumped and asked him if he had his parachute in good order and although Farrell believes that Landis did not understand what he said, he did receive acknowledge from Landis and Landis then jumped. Lt. Farrell states that Landis did not at that time appear to be seriously injured or handicapped. Farrell noted that Landis had pulled his chute ripcord and was holding it against his chest and it appeared to be hooked on. Lt. Farrell followed Landis a few seconds later and after Farrell's chute opened he noticed another chute about one-half mile distant and considerably below him, but he was unable to identify the chute. Lt. Farrell landed at a point which he estimates to be about 20 miles west of Berlin and about three miles distant from a small village, name unknown.

"Lt. Farrell started in the direction of the other parachute that he had seen but after he had traveled about ¼ mile he was captured by German civilians and a soldier. He was immediately taken to the village mentioned above where he was turned over to the burgomeister. He was joined there by the co-pilot, Benedict, and later that day the nose turret gunner, Peters, and right waist gunner , Fulton, were brought in. Late that afternoon they were picked up by the Luftwaffe soldiers who took them by truck towards a flying school about 50 miles away. En route to this school the party picked up Lt. Farrell's radio-operator, Bussel.

"At this flying school Lt. Farrell and the other members of his crew met de left waist-gunner , Rumbaugh, who stated that he had been delivered to the school earlier in the day. Farrell and his crew stayed at this school for three days and were then delivered to Dulag Luft, Frankfurt. While at Dulag Luft the copilot was advised by the interrogating officer that Lt. Longsteig, bombardier, Sgt. Guida, ball-turret gunner, and Sgt. Mpourles, tail gunner, had been found dead in the plane. No mention was made up to this time of F/O Landis. Lt. Farrell was then sent to Stalag Luft III and he did not hear any more concerning the crash.

"Lt. Farrell does not know whether or not F/O Landis is living or dead but it is his opinion that if Landis did not survive the jump the only plausible reason he could advance would be that he may not have had his parachute attached, or if attached it was not properly attached. He states that the civilians in this area did not appear to be hostile or angry and made no attempt to set upon him when he landed.

My memories of Pop by son Bill;

"Pop had a very difficult childhood being raised in the middle of a large ten member family ravaged by the depression. A solution was to give at least three of the older kids up for adoption. Dan Farrell, a wealthy businessman, adopted Pop and an older brother and sister. Their teenage years were very pleasant, I am sure, but Dan did not fare the depression well and lost everything. I am sure this was very unsettling for Pop, but he weathered the storm, and left college to join the Army Air Corps. I am certain all this stress made him the sensitive man he became, ready to do his duty. He was a very good father to me, giving me the philosophies of life that I try live by to this day.

"Pop was older than most of the fellows in his crew and was shot down by a fighter by a frontal attack and one of Pop's crew, Norman Bussel, said it was a flak hit that ignited the oxygen tanks. I understand three of the crew were killed and Pop was injured by shrapnel, hitting his leg (fanny). He parachuted, landing in the only tree of a large open field. He was "captured" by a farmer and his son.

"Pop said he was treated decently by the Germans and only the food was lacking, as it was for the Germans at this time. This changed during a forced winter march to a new camp where many were shot for they gave up and refused to continue. Pop and his friends were surprised in that most of these men were younger, but decided that they must not have had anyone waiting for them at home. I am sure his strong faith (Irish Catholic) helped him cope with the stress of internment.

"As a child I was touched when every Christmas, the mother of one of the crew who was killed, would call. This would upset Pop terribly and he would always cry. I did not understand as a child, but now I know it was an expression of his sensitivity and loss. This continued until her death. I hoped it helped her, for the cost to Pop was high at this time of joy.

From grandson William Farrell,

"I was 17 when I drove from university in North Carolina to Atlanta for the funeral. I hadn't had time to process what had happened, at least emotionally. We were going through the motions of the funeral. I was holding strong, until we started to sing, as a family - Amazing Grace. I couldn't hold in the emotions any longer. We were all there, the golden angels of the family, the bad boy uncles, everyone was there, and … Pop was too, but he was looking down. I had a good cry and found the loving arms of my father softly hugging me. Fathers are important. So powerful, especially when they are gentle, kind and compassionate like my father Bill and of course like Pop.

"I remember Pop mostly from family get-togethers, birthdays, Christmas, weddings. Pop had a deep voice. He was a handsome man and he was strong. My father, Billy used to tell me about Pop's strength. Pop could do multiple one-arm pull-ups. Perhaps this was the norm for the American boys in uniform, but as an accomplished rock climber, who trained for a solid decade, I can tell you that multiple one-arm pull-ups are hard. Pop used to throw the youngsters around like pillows, picking us up effortlessly, like big guys do. He laughed deeply, his breadth with a slight hint of Scotch.

"More importantly was Pops infectious smile, deep laugh and warm eyes. He used to sit in his chair, a bit like Santa Claus, everyone gathered around.

From daughter Linda Shippey.

"My father, Edgar Patrick Farrell, was born on March 25, 1916, in Atlanta, Georgia. He came from a very large Catholic family and, because it was the depression, his parents adopted out their three oldest children, one of them being my father. Sadly, they were adopted out to an aunt and uncle – and his aunt was very mean to him. This breaks my heart because my father was such a sweet and loving man. He was very close to his brother and sister, both of which he lost at fairly young ages. His brother, Will, was killed in a terrible car accident with his wife. So, so sad – I had never seen my dad cry so hard.

"My father – who we called Pop when he started having grandchildren, went to Boy's High and the Marist School in Atlanta. It is a Catholic school and, back then, wore uniforms and was very influenced by the military. As far as college goes, we think he went to Emory for about a year.

"After my father came home from the war, he married my mother – Margaret Manning. My mother had been married to William Jacobs who was killed in the war. They had a three year old son – Billy – who my father adopted immediately.

"My father and mother had four more children – three girls and another son. He worked very hard and started the mortgage loan department at Adair Realty, which was a very prominent real estate company in Atlanta. He worked very hard to keep five children in school, clothes etc. At the height of my mothers illness, Adair Realty decided to weed out the older generation and bring in young executives to replace them. It was a terrible time in my fathers life. He had worked for that company for 36 devoted years. He had medical bills that were overwhelming for my mothers illness. He managed to pull himself up somehow, which I attribute a lot to his faith. He was a very devout Catholic his entire life, never missing church on Sunday, and never letting his children miss Mass. He was a fun dad and loved us all very much. He always loved big family gatherings with all the kids and his grandchildren.

"My mother had a very long and expensive illness and my father took such good care of her – but finally, after 7 months in the hospital, she died at the age of 48. This nearly broke my sweet father both emotionally and financially. My father was heartbroken, but he did remarry and was married to my step mother – Lillian Massey – for many years. Lillian died a couple of years ago which, unfortunately, was the last hold we had with that generation. She and her first husband and my father and mother were very good friends so I learned some things from her – but not as much as I would have liked.

Radio-Operator S/Sgt. Norman Bussel.

From his memoirs.

"I was falling through the sky feet-first now, and I watched the fragments of my B-17 until they disappeared from view. It was hard to believe that the "Mississippi Lady" was no more, her graceful wings torn asunder, her throbbing, powerful engines silent forever, violated by the long, probing anti-aircraft guns that sent flak tearing through her fuselage, ripping her apart.

"When I jerked the pull-ring on my chute, the unbuckled left side flew up and hit me under the chin, knocking me out. When I came to, I was surrounded by a thick white mist. There was no feeling of motion, and I figured I was dead. I pondered the horrible boredom of going through eternity enveloped in this moist white fluff.

"As I began to pray aloud, I recoiled in surprise at what I first believed to be the booming voice of someone else. Then, I realized that the shouting was coming from my own throat. The sudden change from being on a burning plane, with its engines roaring as it tore through the sky, to the ethereal quiet of this new, white, white world in which I now floated was so shocking, so breathtaking, that I was completely frozen.

"Then my face began to sting where I had suffered powder burns from my exploding ammo. I touched my face and it hurt like hell. I didn't have to be a scientist to realize that the dead feel no pain. When I burst out into the open and saw land beneath me, I remembered that at our briefing that morning, we were told to expect cumulus clouds at 14,000 feet over the target. I was floating 14,000 feet over Berlin, but I was alive!

"For the past several days, I had been having nightmares about being shot down and captured by the Germans. In keeping with my plan for survival, I reached up and pulled my dog tags from my neck, the newly issued tags with the telltale "H" pressed into them. The "H" was the United States Armed Services designation for Hebrew, which meant that I was Jewish. I felt that disclosing my religion to the Nazis could be suicidal, so I threw the tags as far away as I could. Wounded and defenseless, I drifted toward the ground, toward a welcoming committee of hate-filled civilians who were hell-bent on killing me.

"Flying has always been a surreal experience for me. As a plane rolls swiftly down the runway on takeoff, your speed is visible. You look through the windows and see objects on the ground flashing past: people, vehicles, trees, and houses. But once you're airborne, once you're far-above the earth, there is no visual movement to relate to and you feel as if you are literally hanging in space. There is no sense of motion.

"It is a similar sensation coming down to earth in a parachute. I had bailed out of my burning plane from a height of 28,000 feet, but since there was nothing close by to give me a feeling of speed, I felt as if I was simply floating. Intellectually, I knew that I was moving rapidly toward the earth, but my senses were incapable of confirming this.

"Then, as I came closer to the ground, my perceptions quickly began to change. I could see that I was moving toward a stand of trees and, recalling my brief instruction in guiding a parachute, I reached out with both hands and pulled on one of the cords attached to my chute. This did indeed move me in an opposite direction from the trees, but I felt a sudden acceleration and, looking up at my chute, I saw that half of it had collapsed, so I immediately released my hold on the cords. The chute re-inflated, but I was descending much faster than before. Then, suddenly, I was no longer moving and floating toward the earth. The earth was flying up to meet me, and I slammed into it with such a crushing impact that I felt as if I had been swallowed by it.

"Momentarily unconscious, I was quickly brought back to reality by many hands jerking me to my feet. Had I not been supported, I would not have been able to stand. I had landed first on my right knee, where I had taken a piece of shrapnel. I was bleeding from wounds in my arm, body, and face, which was also burning from the explosion of the shells in my gun.

"Looking around, I realized that I had landed in the backyard of a large house. I was surrounded by three women and two men armed with garden hoes and rakes, and they began beating me about the head and back with the wooden handles. They were angrily shouting at me in German, but their words came out in torrents and, with my meager knowledge of the language, I was able to understand little of what they said.

"Then one of the men broke away, ran over to a toolshed, and returned with a length of rope, which -he tied tightly around my neck. He threw the loose end of the rope over a tree limb, and then they all took hold and began to pull. Frantically grasping the rope just above the noose with both hands, I was standing on tiptoe when I heard the sound of a motorcycle and saw a soldier roar into the yard and jump off his bike. "Nein," he shouted as he rushed over and snatched the rope from their hands.

"My captors were still hell-bent on hanging me, however, and began to argue loudly with him. The soldier spoke slowly and more distinctly than my would-be executioners, and I was able to understand when he told them that first he would search me, and if he found a gun, they could hang me as a spy. Otherwise, he would have to take me in for interrogation. He quickly determined that I was unarmed, then, seating me behind him on the motorcycle, he gunned the machine and spirited me away. He didn't bother to bind my hands, and I held on to him tightly to keep from falling off. Having just saved me from a lynching, he apparently felt that I was eager to put distance between myself and the civilian mob and, since I was obviously weakened by my wounds, he appeared to have no fear of my attacking him.

"We drove for about fifteen minutes, until we arrived at a small command post in an old house in the suburbs of the city. Taken inside, l was ushered into the office of a German major who appeared to be in his sixties. He had probably been a reserve officer who had been called back into service and stationed at this outpost, which was a processing point for POWs.

"He seemed really eager to converse with me, but I tried to make it clear thatl spoke no German. "Can you speak in German?" he asked.

"No," I answered. "Only English."

"French?"

"I speak some Spanish," I said.

"Nein," he said in disappointment.

"Then an orderly entered and, from what I could gather, suggested bringing in someone who had lived in Milwaukee before the war. The major agreed and dispatched the soldier to fetch the person.

"Meanwhile, he continued trying to converse with me. He obviously considered the English and Americans to be worthy foes, and was trying to impart that the Russians were subhuman. Seated behind his desk, he raised his index finger and inclined his head forward to assure my attention. There was a cup on his desk, and an empty plate with a fork lying beside it. Picking up the fork, he pretended to take food from the plate; bring it to his lips; take it into his mouth; then slowly chew and swallow. Again, he pointed his index finger at me. "Americanish essen so," he said.

"Then he reached for the cup and carefully picked it up between thumb and forefinger, curling his pinkie as he brought it to his mouth and delicately sipped. "Englander essen so."

"I almost jumped out of my chair when he leaped up, rushed around to the front of his desk shouting, "Rooskie! Rooskie!" Then the major got down on all fours, placed his face close to the floor, began snorting like a pig, and said, "Rooskie essen so. Nicht mann. Animal! Animal!"

"Before he could continue, the door opened and the orderly brought in an old man who appeared to be in his eighties. Now the major became even more excited. He shook hands with the old man and turned to me, saying, "Milwaukee. Milwaukee."

"The old man, smiling broadly, came over to me, saying "Hallo, meester." Pointing to himself, he continued, "Me Milwaukee. United State."

"Hello," I answered. "When were you in Milwaukee?"

The major beamed. We were conversing. He ordered the "interpreter" to ask me my name. The old man nodded and said, "Was ist deine namen?"

"I made believe I didn't understand. The major was getting annoyed. Now he shouted at the old man to ask me my name in English, not German. I guess he hadn't spent as much time in Milwaukee as he'd led people to believe, because he now turned back to me and, with a nervous tic at one side of his mouth, said, "Hallo, meester. Was ist deine namen?"

"I shrugged my shoulders and looked confused. This was too much for the major, who began shouting imprecations at the "interpreter," grabbed his arm, and escorted him to the door. He then had a heated conversation with one of his aides and dispatched him on a mission, the purpose of which I could not understand, other than that he wanted something to take place and he wanted it to happen fast: "Schnell!"

"Then he took a German/English dictionary from a shelf, sat down at his desk, and began leafing through it. Occasionally he would glance over at me as if he were about to speak, then he thought better of it and went back to his browsing. Soon a soldier came into the office carrying a medic's kit and began to examine my badly burned face. Then he opened the case, took out a jar containing some kind of white powder, and began to dust it onto my face by tapping the jar with his forefinger. My face stung as the powder adhered to my weeping flesh. Although bloody holes in my uniform clearly indicated that I had been injured and I had visible shrapnel wounds to my jaw and temple, the medic made no attempt to give me further treatment.

"Shortly after he left, there was a knock at the door and the dispatched aide returned, beaming, with an officious-looking lieutenant in tow. The officer clicked his heels and saluted the major smartly. They had a brief conversation, and then the lieutenant came over to me and said: "Stand." He stared into my eyes with obvious contempt. "For you der Var iss ofer."

"Then he handed me a pad and ordered me to write down my name, rank, and serial number. According to the rules of the Geneva Convention, which the U.S. and Germany had both signed in 1929 and which entered into force in 1931, this was the only information I was legally obligated to disclose, so I did as l was told. The major then began to dictate questions for the lieutenant to ask me.

"Why do you come to bomb our glorious Berlin?"

"I didn't come to bomb Berlin."

"What did you come to bomb?"

"I did not respond to this question.

"You come to bomb untersea boats?"

"Submarines sounded like a good target. "Yes," I responded.

"Where are your dog tags?" I

"Of course I had jerked my dog tags from around my neck as I descended in my chute and thrown them away. I hoped they had fallen where they would never be found.

"I don't have any," I said. "The chain broke and I lost them when I bailed out of my plane."

"Hah! Without identification, we can shoot you for a spy."

"I'm sure you can," I replied, "but I'm not a spy."

"Then he unbuttoned the jacket to my heated suit and found the inside pocket that held my escape kit. The kit contained maps, a compass, and counterfeit German money. This was obviously the first time he had seen an American escape kit. He put the maps and compass on the desk. Then, when he pulled out the currency, he and the major both began to laugh.

"Zis money is worth nossing. You hear? Nossing. You could not spend it in Germany. It iss only paper."

"Then, his fingers discovered the wires that ran through my flight suit, like an electric blanket, to conduct heat to my body. He had a serious discussion about these wires with the major and then asked me to remove my jacket and pants. Using a penknife, he exposed some of the wires, then grasped them tightly in his hands and pulled. The wires tore loose, taking with them large pieces of cloth, some of which had already been burned, and shredding my suit.

"After he'd ripped out all of the wires, satisfied that there was no more contraband, he handed my clothing back to me. I got dressed, but my insulated suit had been reduced to rags. When I bailed out, the last thing on my mind was the shoes I wore, and this is something that I lived to regret for many months to come. In my confusion, I forgot my durable GI shoes as I jumped from the burning plane, and though my fleece-lined flying boots were warm and cozy on the plane, they were not designed for walking. The boots were covered with the thinnest sliver of flexible leather, and within three weeks they disintegrated and I was barefoot.

"I hadn't really had time to think of my fellow crew members until the Germans finally completed their body search and interrogation, then more or less ignored me. The major and the lieutenant had apparently gone to lunch, and my single guard spoke no English and seemed disinclined to try to converse with me. Left to my own thoughts, it suddenly dawned on me that I was probably the sole survivor from my crew. I thought I couldn't feel more miserable about my situation, but this sad realization made my despair deeper than before.

"Soon, a sergeant I had not seen before appeared and growled, "Raus," a contraction of "Heraus," meaning "Out." This was a command that I would soon become very familiar with. My right knee had become very swollen from the piece of shrapnel that had penetrated my patella, and when I stood up I found that I could put very little weight on that leg. I struggled painfully to keep up with the sergeant as he made his way outside the command post.

"As we walked up the road, I could see several German guards coming toward us, escorting a group of five men who appeared to be American soldiers. When they came closer, I was overjoyed to recognize them as part of my crew.

"Red was the first to yell a greeting. "Norm! I thought you were dead. You're so damned slow, I just knew you never made it out of the plane." Red was supporting Rum, whose legs were so rubbery they were practically useless. The front of Rum's flying suit was soaked in blood and he looked ghastly. I later learned that he had taken a 20-millimeter shell in his shoulder. That is a very large caliber bullet, and I was surprised that he had survived such a severe injury at all.

"I didn't know what to say to Rum and was afraid to touch him anywhere, so I just reached out and gently ran my hand across his head. It was shocking to see the face I remembered as always being wreathed in a smile, now twisted into a mask of excruciating pain. I thought about the medical kit that burned up on the plane and how the morphine it contained would have brought some relief to him. The Germans had given him no medical treatment at all.

"Waide had a piece of cloth covering both his eyes and was being led along by Daddy. I was shocked, assuming that he had been completely blinded. Fortunately, he had lost only one eye from a fragment of flak that had ricocheted off his machine gun. I didn't ask why both eyes had been covered by the makeshift bandage; I was just grateful that he was still sighted.

"Daddy grinned broadly and squeezed my hand. "I was really worried about you, Norm. The rest of us came down fairly close together and we couldn't figure out what happened to you. We lost Landis and Longteig. Rum believes that Bill and Joe were wounded and never made it off the plane."

"I asked Waide how he was doing, and he said, "Not so good." In my imagination, I often envisioned how we might be wounded in combat, but in my mind I had never even thought of the peril of blindness. Waide was a very lucky guy.

"A military truck pulled up beside us, and our guards herded us aboard. We were driven for less than an hour over some very bumpy roads. The truck had no seats, and the hard floorboards conducted every jolt right up to my knee. I could only imagine what this terrible ride was doing to Rum and Waide.

"Finally, we turned off into a small airport and drove around it until we came to a one-story building from which German soldiers were coming and going. The truck pulled up in front, and we made our way inside. A sergeant, sitting at a desk, was handed a sheaf of papers by one of our guards and called out our names. Then we were led down a tile-floored hallway with four barred cells on the left and windows on the right. At the end of the hallway there was a latrine with a single commode. Each cell contained a wooden cot, fashioned at a permanently reclining twenty-degree angle. They were constructed of very rough wood and had no mattress or cover.

"Rum and Waide were each put into a cell, but the doors were left open. We were able to go into their cells and give them water, which was all we had to offer them. At least we could sit on the edge of the cot and talk with them. Daddy and Red had on jackets, which they removed and balled into "pillows," forming at least some cushion against the hard wood.

"A guard, stationed at the entrance to the hallway, spoke a little English, and we asked him about getting medical aid for our wounded crew members, pointing out the gravity of their condition. He said that 'Rum and Waide would be going to a military hospital in the morning. I began to wonder if Rum was going to make it through the night, he had lost so much blood. He was intermittently moaning from the pain.

"Waide began to yell for the guard, who turned and called to the sergeant at the desk. The sergeant went into Waide's cell, and we were all startled to hear Waide berate him because he had received no medical help. "According to the Geneva Convention, which the United States and Germany have both signed, you are obligated to give us medical attention, and I demand to see a doctor right now."

"The sergeant understood most of this, because he said, "Yah, Morgen in Krankenhaus. Morgen." Then he left. The guard translated, "Tomorrow, you will see doctor in hospital." Waide was far from appeased, but his further complaints fell on deaf ears.

"It was now late afternoon, and we wondered if they were ever going to give us any food. None of us had eaten since about five a.m. What they eventually brought in was not what we were expecting. Each of us was given a cup of what they called "Kaffee." It was ersatz, of course, and tasted like no coffee I had ever drunk before. I called it Black, Burned, and Bewildered, because of its color, its flavor, and my inability to even remotely compare it to anything had ever consumed before. We were also given one slice of black bread each. I've been a lover of pumpernickel bread all my life, but I wouldn't give you a nickel for a whole loaf of this pump.

"Contrary to the coffee we drank, which was at least a hot liquid, this bread had no taste at all. It was dark and heavy, coarse-textured, and had not the slightest flavor of wheat. We later learned that one of the main ingredients was sawdust and that it couldn't be eaten for twenty-four hours after baking, because it was poisonous until then.

"We each took a small bite out of our slice, then laughed at this ridiculous excuse for bread, and placed the remainder on the windowsill. We didn't know that a single slice of bread would become our morning and evening meal, along with a cup of imitation coffee or tea, and that we would soon wait eagerly for it.

"Daddy, Benshit, Red, and I were ordered to sleep on the tile floor in front of the cells. I lay down beside Red and, surprisingly, I quickly fell into a deep sleep filled with the ghastly events of that morning, only this time it was like an out-of-body experience and I had a view from above the entire air battle. Many planes were on fire and twirling out of control in death dives, others were exploding in mid-air; crews were bailing out, many with their chutes ablaze, while German fighters sprayed them with machine-gun fire. Some of our group were dropping their bombs on other B-17's below them. It was a horrible nightmare, but I don't recall waking up once during the night.

"The next morning I woke up slowly, trying to remember where I was. I tried to open my eyes, but they remained shut. I had sometimes experienced terrifying dreams when I felt as though I was awake but couldn't open my eyes or move my limbs, and I thought this was one of those. Then I heard German soldiers talking outside, and I moved my hands and feet. Now I knew that I was wide awake … and I panicked. I was totally blind!

"Reaching out, I felt Red's arm and latched on to it with a death grip. "Red!" I screamed. "Red, I'm blind! I'm blind!"

"Shut up, fool. You ain't no such thing. Matter's got your eyes sealed shut. Let go my arm so I can get some water."

"I felt a wet cloth being gently wiped across my eyelid. At first, nothing happened. Then I saw a tiny glimmer of light as a part of my eyelid became unsealed. "Red, I can see. I can see light now."

"I told you it was just matter. Now, lay still so I can get your other eye open."

"To my delight, both eyes were now unstuck. My facial burns had caused a drainage of fluid during the night that sealed my eyes shut. I was immensely relieved to know that my sight was not impaired. Even looking through the grimy windows of the jail, the sky and the sunshine were wonderful'.

"The guards brought us each a cup of hot liquid that they preposterously called "tea." It wasn't Lipton's, that's for sure. It was some sort of mint-flavored water, and it burned as it went down your throat. They also gave each of us another slice of the black bread. Suddenly, the bread was not nearly as bad we had thought. Not only did we eat every morsel of the mornings ration of bread, we also gobbled up every crumb from the slices we had made fun of the day before.

"Rum and Waide had gone through a rough night. Rum was in a lot of pain and would periodically groan. His eyes were glassy and he seemed to be running a fever. He refused anything except a little water. Waide drank some of the tea but wouldn't eat any of the bread.

"He complained about the discomfort of the wooden cot and said that every bone in his body was aching. He wanted to go to the latrine, and I led him down the hallway. I was glad that he didn't mention his blindness, because I wouldn't have known how to handle the subject.

"Shortly after I brought Waide back to his cell, a guard told us we would soon be leaving for an interrogation center in Frankfurt am Main. We asked about medical treatment for Rum and Waide and were told that transportation was on its way to take them to a hospital. We all went in to say good-bye to them. It was hard to leave them so grievously wounded, but we had no choice. We wished them well and told them that we'd all be together again soon.

"As it turned out, Rum's injuries were so severe that he was ultimately repatriated to the U.S. in exchange for a German POW who was also gravely hurt and held by the American military. Waide, after his eye was removed and he was released from the hospital, actually ended up in the same POW camp as Red and me, but he was in a different compound and we were not aware of this until we returned to the U.S.

"When a large truck pulled up in front of the jail, the guards motioned us out of the building. When Daddy, Benshit, Red, and I climbed on the truck, we saw that there were already about twenty American POWs on board. They were all Air Force, but none from our bomb group. All had been shot down on the Berlin raid the day before.

"We were driven to a train station and remained on the truck until the train pulled in and all passengers had disembarked. The guards seemed jittery as they formed a phalanx around the truck and ordered us to board the last car. We wondered if they were afraid that we might try to escape, but their real concern was that we might be recognized as American airmen and attacked by the civilians on the platform.

Because the U.S. Air Force had no dress code for combat crews, we were a pretty nondescript bunch, but some German civilians on the platform did recognize us and the word spread quickly through the crowd. Our guards hustled us on board the train, shouting, "Schnell! Mach Schnell," and slammed the doors shut against the rising roar of the enraged throng. The train slowly pulled out of the station, and it was none too soon for us, because the mob began pelting the windows with rocks, garbage, and any other objects they could lay their hands on.

***

Returning home, Norman Russell attended Memphis State University on the GI Bill and then joined the family supermarket business. In 1965, he entered the publishing field, becoming an Editor at *Progressive Grocer Magazine* and was later promoted to Profit Center Manager. Later, he joined Supermarket Business magazine as Research Director. In 1980, he and his wife, Melanie, founded Melnor Publishing, Inc., providing the drug store industry with marketing information. Now retired, he has been active for more than 20 years in the Hudson Valley Chapter of American Ex-Prisoners of War (AXPOW) serving as Trustee, Adjutant and Commander. He has served in the N.Y. State Department of AX-POW as member of the Finance Committee and as delegate to national conventions. He also has held positions in the National organization as Public Relations Director and as committee member. Elected as a Director on the board of the AXPOW Service Foundation in March 2000, he was named Vice President in September 2000 and elected President in 2003. He was also Editor of the *Foundation TIMES* newspaper. He retired from the Foundation in 2007 to concentrate on his writing.

"In April, 2009, Norm Bussel was called to testify before the House Veterans' Affairs Subcommittee on Disability Assistance and Memorial Affairs regarding legislation affecting veterans who served in combat areas.

"In August 2008, Norman was elected Vice President of the 447th Bomb Group Memorial Association; his wife Melanie was elected secretary. In April, 2010, Norm Bussel was appointed to the National POW Advisory Commission, which makes recommendations on POW issues directly to the Secretary of Veterans' Affairs.

Left Waist-Gunner Sgt. Merle L. Rumbaugh.

By daughter Susan Rumbaugh-Gilbert

"My father was born on December 30, 1923. He was raised in a rural part of Pennsylvania in a village called Venice. His father was a coal miner. He had one younger brother Edgar. He had lots of family in the area, grandmother, aunts, uncles and many many cousins. He had a very strong sense of family bonds. He actually met my mom at his cousin's farm just a few miles from his home. They all lived within miles of each other.

"My dad loved farm life, especially horses and ponies. When he was just a little boy, before school age, he'd run out - without his mom knowing - and hop on the milk wagon with the milkman. Back then it was horse drawn and I am sure that's when he learned to drive a team of horses.

"He loved baseball and was a really good pitcher in his younger days. Back then every little town and some companies had a baseball league. That was the major past time and communities would turn out to watch the games. I remember reading in one of my dad's journals during basic training and his mention of who was winning the baseball world series in 1943.

"After getting out of school and before entering the service he worked the local oil fields. My dad was adventurous and life was never dull when he was around.

"When he entered military service on February 27, 1943 he had just turned twenty about two months before. In his handwritten journal he said he landed in Miami Beach Florida on Friday March 12, 1943. He did his basic training for the Army Air Corps at the 402nd Training Group, Flight S-21 in Miami Beach, Florida. He said Miami was a swell place. I'm sure for a small town boy that had never been far from home it was a beautiful place to start this new adventure.

"From there he went to airplane mechanical school in Lincoln, Nebraska. He wrote in his journal that he made good marks all through the schooling and he really enjoyed going as it was something he always wanted to do. He said if he came out of this war he hoped to make use of this knowledge. I can attest to the fact he made very good use of the knowledge from that school as I can't think of anything mechanical my dad couldn't repair.

"After completion of airplane mechanic school he decided to become an aerial gunner. Graduated from Aerial Gunnery School November of 1943 and was promoted to Sergeant. He was assigned to the 88th Bomb Group at Avon Park, Florida.

***

"From here on I can only relate what I remember being told by my mom mostly as dad virtually never spoke of his wartime experience. On April 29, 1944, he flew his first and last bombing mission. Their plane, the "Mississippi Lady", was hit by fighters over Brunswick, Germany. Dad was hit by fragments of a 20 millimeter shell and was one of the last to bail out. His parachute brought him down into an enemy patrol waiting for him on the ground. He and the other members of the crew were captured and held overnight before being sent onto a POW camp and in my dad's case what passed as a medical facility. In later years his brother crew member, Norman Bussel, stated they didn't know how my dad made it to the next morning with such severe wounds and loss of blood.

"Most of his nine month internment was spent in hospitals where he was taken care of by English doctors who were also POWs. He also mentioned that an Austrian doctor helped save his arm. His body fought infection and pain for weeks on end.

***

"He returned home on the ship Gripsholm. On January 29, 1945 the War Department notified his parents he would arrive in Staten Island, NY, by the next week and he would contact them.

"After spending a few days with his parents and family he entered Deshon General Hospital in Butler, PA, for more surgery on his shoulder. I remember my mom saying the doctors wanted to amputate his arm but his dad would not allow it. It took months for his shoulder to heal and he lived with limited use of his arm the rest of his life. He ended his time in the Army Air Corp as Staff Sergeant with the 708th Bomb Sq. (H) 447th Bomb Group and received an Honorable Discharged October 25, 1945. He then was 21 years old. What a life he lived in that one year.

"After dad was discharged from the Army Air Corps he lived at home with his parents – still healing from his surgeries - although he had his arm on a board and cast for months it didn't stop him from working. He was never able to raise his hand higher than his chest.

"He got a job working as a millwright in a steel mill. He bought a house in Midway, rural Pennsylvania. He married my mom, Ruth Sickles, on November 21, 1947. They lived in the Midway house on Massey Road the rest of their life. They had four children, John, Richard, Susan and Brian - they were the perfect parents who raised us with love and values. Dad and mom instilled in us a love for God, family and country. Their love extended to the lights of their lives, their eight children.

"Dad had a great sense of humor. His laughter and energy is something anyone who knew him never forgot. He also was a man to lend a hand when ever and where ever needed without question. He enjoyed working on my mom's family farm. He could fix anything from cars to houses as well as training bird dogs to hunt and the ponies to pull the little red cart he bought for his grandchildren.

"As a millwright his job was to keep the blast furnaces running: no easy feat. When there was a problem it was my dad they called out to make the repairs.

"After almost forty years in the mill when my dad was sixty years old he suffered from a collapsed lung, due in part from the heat from the furnaces. He then contracted pneumonia on top of that. My dad passed away August 27, 1984 when he was 60 years old. My mom was only 57 years old when dad passed. She lived by herself in the Midway house that dad bought her until her passing December 13, 2002. Our families all lived close to home so we enjoyed many years of wonderful unforgettable times with mom and dad. .. we still miss them every day.

Right Waist-Gunner Sgt. Waide G. Fulton.

By daughter Sandra Day.

"Staff Sergeant Waide G. Fulton, son of Andrew C. and Eva Belle Sprout Ful-

564

ton, was born at home, November 23, 1916, in Pilot, Maryland. Waide and his mother survived the influenza pandemic of 1918. Waide attended grades 1 through 8 in a one room schoolhouse in Pilot. As a boy growing up near the Susquehanna River, he enjoyed fishing and hunting arrowheads. He graduated from Rising Sun High School, Rising Sun, Maryland, Class of 1934 where Waide continued his education after his family moved to Pennsylvania. The family lived in the small village of Union in Lancaster County.

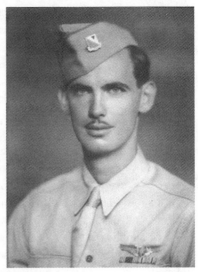

Right Waist-Gunner Sgt. Waide G. Fulton

"Before entering the military, Waide worked as a timekeeper at the Sun Shipyard in Chester, PA and at the Oxford Cabinet Company, Oxford, PA. His first paying job may have been gathering glass bottles as a child for which he was given five cents per bottle by the bootleggers. He recalled seeing government agents going off across the land, hearing a loud boom (as they blew up the illegal stills hidden in the woods) and then seeing the agents return carrying away salvageable parts of the stills.

"Waide entered the Army Air Corps November 1942 at Fort Meade, Maryland. He was 26 years old. After travelling almost forty hours by train, he arrived at Basic Training Center #4 in Miami Beach, Florida, on November 30, 1942, where he was given the choice to go to Officer Training School, but chose instead to train as an armored gunner. He was transferred to 768th Technical School Squadron, Buckley Field, Denver, Colorado, December 19th for nine weeks of school for .50 and .30 caliber machine guns, 37mm cannons, 20mm cannons, ammunitions and explosions, sights, cameras. A measles outbreak at the camp resulted in daily examinations for most of January of 1943.

"He graduated from Air Force Technical School as a Fighter Aircraft Armorer - February 27, 1943. He was assigned to Army Air Corps Gunnery School, Tyndall Field, Panama City, Florida —March 12, 1943 for 6 weeks. While there he completed the altitude training course. Waide was promoted to Sergeant and received his wings upon successful completion of the course — May 4, 1943.

"Upon arriving in England, March 31, 1944, as replacement crew, Waide attended an orientation course designed to help newly arrived Air Corps soldiers prepare for life in a combat theatre. Waide was assigned to the 708th Squadron, 447m Bomb Group, Rattlesden Station 126, one of the many stations in East Anglia. In his first letter home, written April 10, 1944, Waide described the English countryside as "very pretty, like home in the springtime."

"On his third mission, Waide's plane, the "Mississippi Lady," a B-17G Flying Fortress was shot down over Germany. It took only minutes for the plane to explode. Of the ten man crew, six survived.

"After bailing out, Waide's parachute went over a pine tree. "I could just barely touch the ground with my toes." Prisoners of the Germans got to him and helped him out of his harness. A German soldier arrived and he was taken prisoner. He was taken to a jail where the rest of the crew was being held.

"After a day or two, Waide was taken to Bremen to a hospital. He suffered severe burns and a badly injured eye. "I was operated on in the hospital. They brought in four men who were prisoners and held my feet and arms and they removed my eye with no anesthetic or anything —just held me down and did it. I didn't know what they did for a long time. I had a lot of pain when they finally gave me a tablet to take and that eased up. I was in that hospital for a few days after that and then we went from there to Frankfurt am Main. There was not really a hospital there, but a building had been set up and staffed by English doctors and medics. That's where I finally found out I had lost my eye."

"From Frankfurt am Main, Waide was taken to Obermassfeld to a clinic for treatment of his severe burns.

"Waide arrived at Stalag Luft IV near the Baltic, in September of 1944. Prisoners stayed in tents until a new section of barracks were built. They then slept on pallets on straw on the floor. Approximately twenty prisoners were assigned to each barracks, ten to a room. A small stove in the center was used to heat the barracks. The prisoners received two slices of bread a day and soup at lunchtime that "looked like they mowed the road banks and used that to make the soup." They also received some potatoes and a few items from Red Cross parcels.

"They did not have changes of clothing, just whatever they were wearing when they arrived at the camp. Waide's clothing and boots had been nearly burned off his body when his B-17 had been hit. The clothing he wore in the prison camp had been given to him by the English at the medical clinic.

"Twice daily the prisoners reported outside to be counted. The Germans would lose count and would re-count again and again leaving the prisoners standing in the cold for long periods of time. After six and a half months, three letters from home finally arrived in time to celebrate Waide's twenty-eighth birthday.

"Waide was held at Stalag Luft IV until sometime near the end of January/beginning of February of 1945, when the Germans took the prisoners out of the camp to get away from the approaching Russians. During what became known as The Death March, prisoners walked 81 days covering a distance of over 500 miles. "We walked all day in the rain, slept in fields at night in the rain... We didn't have lice in the camps, but we got them after we got out on the road sleeping in barns and things like that."

"Upon reaching the Elbe River, "the Germans let us go through the German ranks and we crawled across the Elbe River on a blowed up bridge and went to meet the American 104th Infantry Timberwolves. That was our liberation." Waide had been a Prisoner of War three days short of a year.

"A few days later, Waide was flown to Rheims, France, and from there went by truck to Camp Lucky Strike which was a collection camp for ex-prisoners. Waide's letter home dated May 7, 1945, reads, "Dear Mom & Daddy, Well what do you know? I am a free man again."

"Waide left Le Harve, France, and came back to the United States on a Navy ship in June of 1945. He was hospitalized at Fort Dix, New Jersey, before being admitted July 1, 1945, to Valley Forge General Hospital in Phoenixville, Pennsylvania. He received a prosthetic eye while at Valley Forge where doctors perfected the process in the newly formed "Artificial Eye Laboratory."

"He also had surgery to reduce the keloid from the burns on his neck. He was a patient at Valley Forge from July, 1945 until January of 1946. He was awarded the Purple Heart for his injuries. Waide was honorably discharged as a S/Sgt. from the Army Air Corps after serving thirty-seven months. .

***

"Waide went to work for the U.S. Postal Service in Bainbridge, Maryland. He worked there until the base at the Naval Training Center Bainbridge was closed in 1947. He transferred to Oxford, Pennsylvania, working as a mail carrier for several years and later retiring as the Assistant Postmaster in 1972.

"A romance which started when the bride was a nurse and the bridegroom a patient at Valley Forge General Hospital culminated in marriage when Waide married 1st. Lt. Virginia Hughes, Army Nurse Corps in 1946. The marriage ended in divorce thirteen years later.

"Waide was very active in the Gray-Nichols Post 1779 Veteran of Foreign Wars serving as Commander for many, many years. He worked diligently assisting veterans to understand and obtain benefits and services provided by the Veterans Administration. He belonged to several Veterans organizations including American Ex-POWs and Eighth Air Force Historical Society.

"Waide was a lifelong fisherman, collector of arrowheads and avid reader. He worked outside nearly every day in his numerous gardens, having a natural green thumb. He raised orchids and was also a terrific cook! He and his second wife Lucille had an antiques business for many years.

"Waide and Lucille travelled extensively throughout the United States and all over the world enjoying new sights and making new friends along the way. Waide, Lucille, daughters and their families returned numerous times to England for Waide's 447th Bomb Group Association reunion activities at Rattlesden. Daughter Sandra and grandson Michael continue to attend the reunions as often as possible drawn by the shared respect and admiration for the men of the 447th Bomb Group as well as the warm friendships forged over 20 years with the members of the 447th BG UK.

Waide and Norman Bussel— maintained a 60+ years bond of friendship, connecting each April remembering that fateful day in 1944 until Waide's death, March 26, 2011.

***

Daughter Sandra Day continues

"On my first trip to England for a 447th Reunion, we met an English couple, Daphne and James Mott, in Lavenham, England. Her family farm backed up to the airfield at Rattlesden. She told us each morning she and her sister would run upstairs and throw the windows open when they would hear the B-17s start up their engines. The two of them would count the planes as they took off. Later in the evening, they would run back upstairs to count the planes as they returned home. She said they were always so glad when they could count them "all home." She remembered the day my father's plane was shot down because so many did not return. We continue to maintain a 20+ year friendship, correspondence and visiting through the reunions over the years.

Tail-Gunner Sgt. Vasilios Mpourles.

From Nephew George M. Burliss.

"Bill (the English translation for Vasilios) was born and educated in Lowell, Massachusetts in 1918. His father, Costas, came to America in the early 1900s was a mill worker in the textile factories of Lowell. His mother, Stella died in 1928 at about 32 years of age during a surgical procedure and left behind her husband and 4 young sons. My Uncle Jim states he thinks that Bill graduated from Lowell Trade School but is not certain. Bill, as well as the other three brothers, worked at one of the first department stores in Lowell called the "Giant Store." All of them worked at the lunch counter. Right before leaving for the service he was engaged to be married and left behind a heartbroken fiancée.

"He lies buried in the Saint-Avold Cemetery in France.

***

Acknowledgements;
Bill Farrell son, William Farrell grandson and Linda Shippey, daughter of pilot 2Lt. Edgar P. Farrell.
Radio-operator S/Sgt. Norman Bussel. His memoir, *MY PRIVATE WAR–Liberated Body, Captive Mind, a World War II POW's Journey,* was published by Pegasus Books.
Susan Rumbaugh-Gilbert, daughter of waist-gunner Sgt. Merle L. Rumbaugh.
Sandra Day, daughter of waist-gunner Sgt. Waide G. Fulton
George M. Burliss, nephew of tail-gunner Sgt. Vasilios Mpourles.

CHAPTER 40

447TH BOMB GROUP 708TH BOMB SQUADRON

Type: B-17G • Serial: 42-31144 "Rowdy Rebel"
MACR: 4247 • Air Base: Rattlesden

Was hit by fighters and knocked out of formation. Aircraft was last seen diving into clouds but still under control. There was only one survivor; Roger Hess was admitted to the German Air Force Hospital in Braunschweig.

Missing Air Crew Report # 4247

Pilot: 1Lt. Hayden T. Hughes, 0-746752, KIA, Washington, IA

Co-Pilot: 2Lt. Howard N. Barr, 0-693732, KIA, New York, NY

Navigator: 2Lt. William H. Allen Jr., 0-757442, KIA, Leedey, OK

Bombardier: 1Lt. Richard H. Johnson, 0-743600, KIA, Minneapolis, MN

Engineer: T/Sgt. Walter J. Zesut, 11102873, KIA, Glastonbury, CT

Radio: T/Sgt. Raymond J. Small, 35374632, KIA, Hobart, IN

Ball-Turret Gunner: S/Sgt. James R. Boyd, 14158285, KIA, Chattanooga, TN

Left Waist-Gunner: S/Sgt. Roger Hess, 14187572, POW, Durham, NC

Right Waist-Gunner: S/Sgt. Barley E. Hill, 38203503, KIA, Montgomery, TX

Tail-Gunner: S/Sgt. George R. Bentley, 39560146, KIA, Long Beach, CA

9 KIA , 1 POW

Crash Site: Destedt, 7 miles east of Braunschweig, Germany
Time: 11.05

Pilot 1Lt. Hayden T. Hughes.

While the 447th was training at Harvard, Nebraska there was a horrific mid air collision involving 3 B-17s on August 28, 1943. 14 men were killed, only 3 survived. Hayden Hughes was a student pilot on one of those B-17s, he survived by bailing out at 600 feet.

Co-Pilot 2Lt. Howard N. Barr.

Daughter Kathy Barr wrote:

"My father was born in New York on March 19, 1917. He was 27 when his plane went down. I was born almost exactly two months later. His family life was centered around music. His father and brother were both professional musicians. My father played the viola, and his mother played the piano. He graduated from New York University and had studied to be an accountant. He wrote to my mother almost every day in a steady hand, even after harrowing missions, and I have a collection of wonderful letters which include the one below.

Co-Pilot 2Lt. Howard N. Barr.

Howard Barr had a harrowing mission to Berlin on March 6, 1944. In a letter to his wife he wrote:

"We were just over the target ready to drop our bombs and the flak was very heavy. Suddenly, there was a terrific crash and we were thrown up about 100 feet right out of our place in formation. We both worked on the controls as they were very stiff and difficult to move. We later found that the control pulleys were damaged by a piece of flak. Well, we also had a fire in #3 engine which we got out and slowly worked our way back in formation and then tried to see the mess and what shape we were in.

"A heavy shell had hit us direct in the bomb bay, came up through the radio room and exploded there. Result: we could see there was nothing left of the bomb bay except one bomb which was jammed in the rack, bomb bay doors were blown off and also the catwalk in the bay was blown out. The radio room which is in the back of the bomb bay was completely blown out - floor, sides and all equipment in it - never saw our radio operator again. Someone in another ship said they saw a parachute open after the explosion and I hope he was in it. Our inter-phone and radio system was all wrecked and with the floor blown out in the bay and the radio room we had no way of telling how the boys were in the back.

"Well, we dropped out of formation as the strain was too much on the engines and straggled back across Germany alone. The left wing and main spar were in very bad shape from the explosion but the ship flew and so we decided to get it back as the boys in the back might be in bad shape and couldn't bail out so all we had to worry about now was getting tapped by German fighters, how long the ship would hold together, and the live bomb still in the bay which we couldn't pry loose.

"Hylton climbed into the bay and safe-tied the bomb while I held his harness as there was no catwalk and the doors were off.

"Suddenly three twin engine fighters came in from nowhere and I began to say my prayers - and the lord answered it - they were P-38's and they escorted us all the way back across the channel. We picked up a few P-47's also on the way. They protected us like a hen takes care of a crippled chick.

"We reached our field and circled it once and shot off a flare meaning wounded aboard and made a crash-landing. We had no brakes and the ship practically shook apart when we rolled down the runway. The boys were all watching and said that so many pieces of junk were coming off our ship as we rolled down the runway it looked like a garbage truck. We also had a flat tire. Art really made a masterful landing - the finest crash-landing I've ever seen.

"The meat-wagon was waiting for us and it was then that we rushed out and looked at the back to see who was left. The tail gunner and the waist gunner were both wounded - each had a piece of flak through their thigh - one got it almost square in the behind. Our engineer had a cut leg. But the other gunners were unhurt and had been taking good care of the wounded men. You don't know any of the enlisted men so I won't go into names. They are all fine and out of the hospital now.

"We were congratulated by the colonel and he gave us all that seven day leave the next day. The ship was not our own ship. Ours was being repaired and we had been flying another crew's ship - *Dottie Jane*. It was such a mess that it was junked - but I came out safe and sound and so there must be meaning to it. The Lord is always on my side. Maybe it's because I try to be a good husband and love my wife with such devotion. I know that you will be worried when you read this but you are bound to find out anyway as articles appeared in many papers around March 10th-15th.

"When we were interviewed by reporters I asked them to exclude my name because of you but they said it would only get into the Midwest papers and not New York papers - the liars, it was printed all over. I'm sorry to cause you all the worry, darling. I realize now that I shouldn't have become a flyer because to have you worry hurts me more than anything else. But I know that you understand what I'm doing it for and who I'm doing it for…

Navigator 2Lt. William H. Allen Jr.

By first cousin Eben W. Allen

"My name is Eben W Allen and I am a first cousin of William Jr. I am 81 and knew him well. My dad, Eben Allen and his dad, William Allen were brothers. We both were the only child of our parents. His wife was Lucille and her maiden name was Moore. I was about 12 years of age when I saw him last, he and his parents and also his wife spent the Sunday with us on the farm of my parents which had also been his grandparents farm. He spent a lot of time there when he grew up. He was a very good looking guy, also his wife was a beautiful lady. He was on leave and shipped over to England very shortly after this day. He had gone to Oklahoma University and received his education.

"He went into to the Army Air Corps and became a navigator. If he had completed this mission he would have been rotated back to the States. His wife had already rented an apartment in Leedey for this period of time. I remember the phone call we received about noon. My uncle, Mark Allen, lived with us and he took the call. it was a very sad day. Bill was missing in action and then it was not very many days until we received another call that he was killed, tears flowed freely at our home and also at his parents home in Leedey.

"When I was in the service during the Korean Conflict I was stationed in Germany. I made a special trip to Holland to a cemetery where Bill Jr as he was commonly called is buried. It is US Military Cemetery in Margraten Holland and over 8,000 American boys are buried there. I went to the directory and found his grave and spent some time there. As far as I know I am the only relative to ever visit his grave. His grave is plainly marked with his name, rank, squadron, and date he was killed. I spent the night with a family who visited his grave and corresponded with my aunt. This was some time in 1953.

Radio T/Sgt. Raymond J. Small.

Raymond was born on July 9, 1921 in Hobart, Indiana. His parents were George E. Small and Nannette Small. He graduated from Hobart High School and prior to enlistment worked for Gernsey Food Service, Pool-Arnoldt & Company (both in Hobart) and Inland Steel Company in East Chicago, Indiana. He married Doris C. Schnabel on March 28, 1942. They had one daughter, Sharon, born on April 28, 1944 one day before Raymond lost his life over Germany. He joined the Army Air Corps in October 1942.

Newspaper Notice;

"Word was received this week by Mrs. Doris Small of Hobart, that the body of her husband, Tech. Sgt. Raymond J. Small, is being returned from overseas for re-burial. The body will arrive in Hobart within the next two weeks and will be taken to Calumet Park Cemetery near Crown Point, for final burial. He has been temporarily buried in the Military Cemetery at Margraten, Holland.

"He served in the 8th Air Force as a radio operator on a B-17 and was stationed in England for six months before his death. He was killed while on a bombing raid over Germany. This was his 29th mission, having one more mission to complete before he would have been entitled to return to the States."

Radio T/Sgt. Raymond J. Small

Right Waist-Gunner S/Sgt. Barley E. Hill.

By sister Ms. Mary Gibbons.

"Barley (nichnamed "Snookie") was born October 9, 1921. He was the fourth child of ten born to a farm family Barley W. and Carrie Hill. Barley attended public school until he was fifteen years old, finishing nine years at Montgomery school. He dropped out of school to help on the farm and worked on the farm unil drafted.

"Barley was a real Texas boy. He wore cowboy boots and a western hat. He loved horses and was very good at training them. He loved country western music and dance.

"Barley was a generous person, a loving son and brother. He was 23 years old when he died.

***

Acknowldgements;
Kathy Barr, daughter of co-pilot 2Lt. Howard N. Barr.
Eben W. Allen, cousin of navigator 2Lt. William H. Allen Jr.
*Ms. Mary Gibbons, sister of w*aist-gunner S/Sgt. Barley E. Hill

573

CHAPTER 41

447ᵀᴴ BOMB GROUP 708ᵀᴴ BOMB SQUADRON

Type: B-17G • Serial: 42-102421
MACR: 4254 • Air Base: Rattlesden

"About ten minutes from the target, our plane was attacked by enemy fighters."

Waist-Gunner Kenneth U. Shimp, sole survivor

Pilot: 2Lt. Charles R. Dowler, 0-813870, KIA, Iowa Park, TX

Co-Pilot: 2Lt. Vernon E. Arnold, 0-818806, KIA, Clear, IN

Navigator: 1Lt. Fred W. Kleps Jr., 0-688638, KIA, Amherst. OH

Bombardier: 2Lt. George F. Kramer Jr., 0-749910, KIA, Freeland, PA

Engineer: S/Sgt. Sandy Conti, 31254083, KIA, Websterville, VT

Radio: S/Sgt. Francis N. Brownson, 39410663, KIA, Del Paso Heights, CA

Ball-Turret Gunner: Sgt. George R. King, 33740113, KIA, Washington, DC

Left Waist-Gunner: Sgt. Lawrence L. Steinhafel, 36815143, KIA, Tomahawk, WI

Right Waist-Gunner: Sgt. Kenneth U. Shimp, 33558837, POW, Baltimore MD

Tail-Gunner: Sgt. John J. Marabito, 13134443, KIA, Erie, PA

9 KIA, 1 POW

Crash Site: 2 miles nw of Weferlingen, Germany
Time: 11.35

Bombardier 2Lt. George F. Kramer Jr.

By Ruth Reimschissel, niece

"George Franklin Kramer, Jr was born June 12, 1921 in Freeland, Pennsylvania. Only son in a family that had delivered six girls previous to and two girls after George. My mother, the youngest surviving, spoke many times of how the whole family adored George. I can certainly imagine this with his being the only boy.

"He graduated from Freeland High School and was employed by Copperweld Steel Company in Warren, Ohio.

"He enlisted as an aviation cadet in July 1942, trained at Santa Ana, California; Beming, New Mexico; Lake Charles, Louisiana; and Avon Park, Florida, before going overseas. He was commissioned in June 1943.

Bombardier 2Lt. George F. Kramer Jr.

Right Waist-Gunner Sgt. Kenneth U. Shimp, the sole survivor of this crew stated officially after the war:

"About ten minutes from the target, our plane was attacked by enemy fighters. The left waist-gunner was hit in the forehead by a 20 mm shell and fell to the floor. Then I was hit by flak and I think the plane was hit in the right wing at the same time. When I came to, I was sitting on the floor of the plane putting on my parachute. Then I passed out again or must have been semi-conscious and when I came to again I was in a German car riding down a road with four German guards around me. I don't remember anything that happened between then and have no knowledge what happened to the rest of the crew. I was taken to a jail in Helmstedt."

To the families of the other crew members he wrote in July, 1945:

"I returned to the States about two weeks ago and I am now home on a thirty day furlough from Walter Reed Hospital in Washington. I will then report back to have a few small pieces of flak removed from my body, and then get a sixty day furlough. It certainly is well to be back home again except that I miss the other fellows in our crew as we always had such a fine time together.

"On March 31, 1944, we boarded the Queen Elizabeth in New York City and had a nice time getting over. It took us five days. We docked near Glasgow,

Schotland and then went by train to an Air Force Replacement Center near Stone, England. We had about twenty days of ground school and practice missions over England before we became operational as a crew. As a rule they would send one or two fellows from the new crew on their first missions with an experienced crew. We were assigned to a new plane. It's name was "Little Rock Blonde II" and I think the last three numbers were 421.

"My first mission was on April 27, target was an airfield in France. Lt. Dowler was the pilot and the rest of the crew except for Dowler and myself had eighteen missions in. On the 28th of April we went on a practice mission over England. We used another plane called "Trouble Maker" and when we landed the wheels collapsed and we sled along the runway on the belly but no one was injured.

"On the 29th of April we were awakened at 3:00 a.m. for breakfast, had briefing and got our plane ready for the mission. We took off at 7:30 a.m. for the underground railroads in Berlin. We were to have a fighter escort to and from the target, but our Group was about ten minutes late in the take off and the escort didn't wait for us.

"Everything was going along just fine until we got to the Initial Point which was about fifteen minutes from the target, and we made a ninety degree turn to the left, then the German fighters ME 109's and FW 190's started to attack our formation and the sky was full of them. We were also receiving plenty of flak 88 mm. and 105 mm. anti aircraft fire from the ground. Larry Steinhafel was shot in the face with the 20 mm. shell from a German fighter and fell on the floor. I tried to give him first aid but I was hit in the forehead with a few fragments of flak. I then fell to the ground unconscious.

"When I came to again, I was trying to get my parachute on but I was groggy from the lack of oxygen. The plane had been hit in number three engine, the right wing was on fire and the plane was going down fast. Then I passed out again, and when I came to I was riding down a road in an old open car with four German soldiers guarding me. I must have been semi-conscious and had gotten out of the plane and pulled the ripcord but don't remember a thing about it.

"I was then taken to a German prison in Helmstedt, Germany, where I was held for about four days. There were eleven planes shot down that day including about six planes out of our squadron of eight planes. In the prison I talked with a few of the pilots in our squadron and they said that they had seen our plane get hit, start to burn and leave the formation and head to the ground. The pilot who was flying along side our ship said that he saw one parachute leave our plane and there were two other chutes nearby but they could have been of another plane that was shot down at the same time that ours was. Then he said our plane exploded.

"All this happened about five minutes from the target and we hadn't dropped the bombs as yet. I always kept looking for the other fellows of the crew when I would be sent to another POW camp, and I talked with a few fellows from our crew we trained with in Florida, and they were in different hospitals and camps in Germany, but none had run across any of the other fellows.

"There isn't much that I actually know myself, about what happened. About all I know is from the other crews that were shot down with us. I am still in hopes that the other fellows are still alive and are around somewhere as I can't believe that they were all killed either."

Navigator 1Lt. Fred W. Kleps Jr

Fred was born in Vermilion Ohio on Jan. 17, 1921. He went to school in Lorain, Ohio, then graduated from Oberlin High School - Oberlin, Ohio. He was a postal carrier in Oberlin until he enlisted into artillery school at the age of 21. He was also an accomplished accordian player. He completed his artillery training at Fort Sill, Oklahoma. He then transferred to the Army Air Corps where he became a Navigator. He was killed in action on April 29,1944 at the age of 23.

Tail-Gunner Sgt. John J. Marabito.

By cousin Denise Stiffler;

"My uncle Johnny was the 7th child out of eight born into and Italian American immigrant family. He was born on November 15th, 1916 in Clarksburg, West Virginia, a coal mining area of the United States. The family relocated to Erie, Pennsylvania and John went to a public high school. He was a well liked young man. He did well in school and played American football. He was very good looking and polite. After high school he got a job in a factory, The Ruberoid (a company that manufactured roofing materials), as a receiving clerk.

***

Acknowledgements;
Ruth Reimschissel, niece of bombardier 2Lt. George F. Kramer Jr.
Denise Stiffler, cousin of tail-gunner Sgt. John J. Marabito.

CHAPTER 42

447TH BOMB GROUP
709TH BOMB SQUADRON

Type: B-17G • Serial: 42-31519
MACR: NA • Air Base: Rattlesden

"The Air/Sea Rescue boat pulled alongside on the left and we paddled away from the plane in our dinghies and were immediately picked up. The aircraft floated for 35 minutes."

Pilot Dean Fleming

Pilot: 1Lt. Dean S. Flemming, RTD

Co-Pilot: 1Lt. Lloyd D. Ittel, RTD

Navigator: 1Lt. Carl W. McGuen, RTD

Bombardier: Lt. Joseph T. Elliot, RTD

Engineer: Sgt. William M. Shaw, RTD

Radio: Sgt. Sidney R. Stein, RTD

Ball-Turret Gunner: Sgt. Andrew Leydens, RTD

Left Waist-Gunner: Sgt. Anthony Durante, RTD

Right Waist-Gunner: Sgt. William D. Plascocello, RTD

Tail-Gunner: Sgt. Leslie E. Orr, RTD

10 RTD

Crash Site: ditched in the North Sea.
Time: 11.30

who would become his wife and our mother.

"Pop's assignment at Westover was to transition B-17 pilots who were returning from Europe into B-24 Liberators for redeployment to the Pacific Theater. Libs had longer range and could carry a larger load, so they were better suited for the Pacific Theater. Pop himself was also being transitioned into Douglas A-26 Invaders, also for deployment to the Pacific. However, one day when he had taken his morning training flight, upon landing he reported to the control tower, and as he did, the officer there informed him that his stint in the war had ended and that he would not fly that afternoon and that he should muster out and go home to Maine. This was important because the afternoon flight would have qualified him for his monthly flight pay, and he lost out on it.

"Dad returned to Skowhegan where he took a Post Office job carrying a mail bag door to door. He had been given the opportunity to begin a career in a bank, and to this day questions whether it would have been more lucrative. He and my mother started a family at this point.

"When I was five years old, Dad was transferred to the Albany, New York region, where he assumed ever increasing positions of responsibility in the postal service. From that time on, we would move about every fours years as he assumed new positions. He retired from the postal service in 1978. He was, at that time, responsible for the second largest postal district in the United States; that being Maryland, West Virginia, northern Virginia, and Washington, DC. The only larger district is Los Angeles. After retiring, he remained in Maryland until 1983 at which time he and my mother moved to Stratham, NH.

"My father lived his life with a strong faith in the Lord. He never missed church on Sunday and always insisted his family joined him. My brother, Dean and I were allowed to miss only if we were away on Boy Scout camp-outs. He served in numerous positions within the local churches he attended. His family was expected to be home at dinner-time; it was important to him that we eat together. He was as honest as any man could be. I can recall several occasions when I was young when I would ask to borrow a pen to do my homework, only to be told that it was against regulations to use government pens that were imprinted with ‹Penalty for Private Use'.

Engineer Sgt. William M. Shaw.

By his son Bill.

"Dad spoke often of being in the "Gold Fish" club. He said that McGuen broke his leg because he was not where he was supposed to be when they landed in the water. Dana Flemming indicated that as they were dropping in altitude quickly, my dad had leaned down and asked Flemming in a respectful way, didn't he think it was time to land this thing in the water. I do not know if that is what happened but Dana said that it did. I know that earlier in this year on Memorial Day dad and I were sitting in his garage talking about the landing when Dean Flemming called to say hi. He told me that he would probably not be here today if it was not for my dad telling him that he needed to think about ditching. Dad said he would not be here if Dean had not landed the plane so well in 5 foot waves. My dad's eyes got real waterey and he said, "Dean Flemming saved all our lives." I started crying and I don't think I ever loved my Dad as much as at that moment.

Radio-Operator Sgt. Sidney R. Stein.

From a newspaper article;

"On April 29, 1944, 20-year-old Sidney R. Stein sat in the radio room of his crippled B-17 bomber as it began its descent into the north Sea, hoping the SOS signals he'd sent out would bring help soon. "Four hundred feet," Mr. Stein said to the men clinging to one another at the far wall bracing for impact. "Three hundred feet."

"The "Flying Fortress," leaking gas and running on the last of its four engines, had been hit hard during a raid on Berlin, where dozens of enemy fighters had seized on a weak American formation. "Two hundred feet, "Mr. Stein said, scrambling to lock down his radio before heading over to his comrades.

"Ten seconds later, the tail of the 27-ton, bullet-riddled plane hit the North Sea at about ninety miles per hour: a good crash-landing, but one that still left him dazed. "When I come to, I see all this blood," Mr. Stein remembers 70 years later, retelling the moment in a calm, steady voice. "Turns out it wasn't me - one of the gunners hit his head."

"After pulling themselves out of the ill-fated plane, the ten crew members - one with a broken leg, another with a gash in his head, all alive - piled into lifeboats and began paddling. "What do we see coming at us?" Mr. Stein asks, a smile stealing over his face. "A nice little yacht."

"The speedy rescue is a point of great pride for the decorated 91-year-old veteran and 50-year Worcester resident. It didn't happen by accident. Twice when the plane was limping home, Mr. Stein made contact with British radiomen, getting a heading for both his own navigator and the men who would eventually send the boat to their rescue.

"When it became clear the plane would come down, his SOS signals found the mark, aiding rescuers in pinpointing his location. "You have to be calm," Mr. Stein said, "This is all morse code, not free language. You can't be so excited. You have to get the information and decode it."

"Mr. Stein said he's very proud of the work he did that day because it helped save lives. But he doesn't have any illusions that his crew was better or more special than the many crews that never made it back. "You have to be good. You have to learn to do things. You also have to be lucky," he said. Sometimes the flak hits the plane to the right of you. It could have very well have been you.

"Inside a meticulously arranged scrapbook he assembled long ago lies a piece of paper illustrating the point. "On this 13th day of May 1944, the fickle hand of fate finds it expedient to trace on the roll of the Lucky Bastards Club the name of Sidney R. Stein," the certificate reads. The citation goes on to laud the radio operator and gunner "for having this day achieved the remarkable record of sallying forth and returning no less than 30 times, for having braved the hazards of Hun flak, for bringing to Hitler and his cronies tons of bombs, for bending the Luftwafe back."

"Though he has numerous awards and medals - including the Distinguished Flying Cross with four oak clusters - the certificate is significant because it commemorates his survival. For too many of Mr. Stein's friends and comrades, the 30th mission was one they never saw. Mr. Steins 447th Bomb Group lost 21 planes in April 1944 alone, the second-worst single-month tally of any bomb group. Of the 27 planes in his group that flew to Berlin on April 29 - deemed the "Berlin Massacre" by those who lived it - 11 were knocked out of the sky. "These are the guys that got shot down," Mr. Stein said, his wrinkled fingers tracing the page of a book about the 447th that include the names of the downed pilots.

"Lost four new fellows in barracks on their first hop (mission)," Mr. Stein scrawled in his service diary two days before the Berlin flight. "No damage to us."

"Mr. Stein's 447th Bomb Group helped pave the way for the invasion of Normandy, attacking submarine pens, naval installations, and cities in Germany along with airfields and other German targets in France.

"1,000 U.S. ‹Heavies' blast Berlin," The New York Times headlined a front-page article appearing the day after the Berlin strike, proclaiming that the Americans "gave the Reich capital today a blasting comparable to any ever before delivered." Looking back on his time in the Air Corps, Mr. Stein said he was amazed at how little training he received before being thrust 15,000 feet in the air in a massive warplane.

"The son of Russian Jewish immigrants, Mr. Stein grew up the oldest of five children in Milford. His father delivered pastry and rye bread from Worcester to earn a living, and Mr. Stein wanted to be a dentist when the war came on in 1941. He enlisted in 1942 at age 18, figuring he would soon be drafted and deciding he preferred the Air Corps to the luck of the draw. At 5-foot-7 and 135 pounds, Mr. Stein wasn't a large man, but said he also wasn't one to shrink from a tall task.

"After more training and a few more flights, he had three stripes. "Now I am a radio-operator and a gunnery specialist, and I didn't know anything," he said. I'd flown four times in a plane. Though he went through more training in Washington and Nebraska, he ended up getting his most handy instructions on the job. "you learned a little bit every time," Mr. Stein said, "and if you were lucky, you were afforded the chance to use that knowledge to stay alive.

His memory still sharp, Mr. Stein goes about describing his flight-day regimen like a man who had just completed one last week. On a mission day, wake up was 2 a.m., followed by breakfast and briefing, Mr. Stein said, recalling the exact time he was expected to report for each task. "Getting dressed was an elaborate deal," he said, "as the temperature at 15'000-plus feet in the air reached 20 below zero. In addition to extremely heavy socks and undergarments, each man wore several jackets, a heated suit and heated shoes and gloves.

"It's really a drag," Mr. Stein recalled of the lengthy pre-flight ritual. "You've been up seven hours already and you haven't left England yet.

"Though its binding is well worn, Mr. Stein still has the service diary he filled out after coming back from every mission. "Remember, the value of this record lies in the future, the time to create that value is now," the Army presciently wrote in the opening pages of the diary. "Make this book a treasure trove of rich memories.

"Written in big block letters in black ink, Mr. Stein's entries describe in plain and humble detail the missions that would earn him the Distinguished Flying Cross. "In addition to warding off many enemy attacks from his gun position, Sgt. Stein distinguished himself by calm and skillful handling of his radio during aerial combat," the Army noted on his medal citation.

"Mr. Stein's entries are those of a man cool under pressure and not given to hyperbole. They do not express fear or excessive emotion. "Mission rough on all. Had sixty flak holes," Mr. Stein recounted simply of a mission in which two planes were shot down around him. "Looked as if we were going down but we made it back," he wrote of mission number 22. "Came all the way back alone and again would have been (sitting) ducks for fighters."

"Though he had his share of "milk runs" - missions that went silky smooth - Mr. Stein's crew also had its share of run-ins, including one mission where his pilot had to make a tricky "Deadstick" landing in a field.

"In his most excitable moments, the 20-year-old Mr. Stein was prone to using an abundance of exclamation points. "No. 30!!!!!!!!!!!!" He wrote on May 13, 1944, his final mission, going on to list how many more missions his friends still had left. "Hope to hell they all make it," reads his last sentence, written in bold capital letters.

"After the war, Mr. Stein studied engineering, but eventually settled into the furniture business in Worcester with his brother Edward I. Stein, who still owns Eddy's Carpet and Warehouse Outlet.

" Mr. Stein met his wife Sarah in 1950 on a blind date. "We met in April, got engaged in May and got married in October, and it only lasted 61 years," Mr. Stein said with a laugh. The two spent many a winter together at a condo in Florida. "You hear about the millionaires and their social seasons. Well, we had the same thing without the money," he joked.

"Mrs. Stein died in 2012, and Mr. Stein for the past few years has been living at the Bet Shalom Apartments after nearly five decades at the family home on Sussex Lane. Pictures from his children's weddings adorn his apartment walls, and group pictures of his family's many generations are placed in just about every nook and cranny.

"If something went different on one of those flights and he got shot down, (we all) wouldn't be here," said Mr. Stein's 39-year-old grandson, Rick Stein, who still watches his grandfather speak with a look of reverence and awe.

Mr. Stein said he was honored to have been able to serve the country whose flag he grew up saluting every morning in school. "We ran into a lot of things in Europe," he said simply, "and we took care of them

Tail-Gunner Sgt. Leslie E. Orr.

"Back after Thirty Bombing Trips." A newspaper article.

"After ten months of overseas combat service as a tail-gunner on a Flying Fortress, based in England, wearer of the Air Medal with five Oak Leave Clusters, along with the Distinguished Service Cross, and officially credited with the shooting down of a Nazi FW-190 fighter plane, Technical Sergeant Leslie E. Orr, is home on a furlough.

"This young air warrior, native of Bartlesville but reared in Ramona, through grade schools and graduate of the high school class of 1937, switched from the vocation of steel worker back in February, 1943, while he was employed near Bedford City, Indiana. He got his silver wings and gunnery rating and then joined his bomber crew and took his immediate oversear training at Harvard, Nebraska, but went by ship across the Atlantic to Scotland in November, 1943.

Tail-Gunner Sgt. Leslie E. Orr

"Despite the thrill of shooting down an enemy plane, he thinks that the highlight of the thirty missions he made over Europe came the early morning in the cold of December, 1943, that he crawled back into the cramped quarters of his Flying Fortress as his pilot headed the ship on a round trip of nine hours, to Ludwigshafen, Germany, to drop bombs on a synthetic oil refinery. This mission was accomplished, he said as were all of the other 29 with unusual good fortune, the ship being shot up at times but with none of the airmen wounded nor the Fortress greatly damaged.

"I never could get quite used to riding backwards," said Leslie, "and, like most all the rest of us, I never became calloused or without excitement as I prepared for new adventures over the enemy territory. We all have that sense of nervousness and tenseness before each mission. Something such like football player, no matter how many years he had played, feels just before the start of a new game. Once, however, we are upstairs and on our way, all that nervousness disappears as by magic.

"Other raids include bombings of Berlin, Brunswig, Frankfort, München, Augsburg and many other missions of relative less importance such a bombings of railways, trains, and bridges in France and crackdowns on the buzzbomb coast.

"But as for the successful encounter with the German plane, Orr relates that it was on a raid to Bordeaux, France last January. Not long after the return flight had started, eight FW's took in after the squadron, one, eventually coming straight on the tail of Orr's plane.

"There wasn't much to it," he said, modestly. "I just got him in the sights of my .50 calibre machine guns and when he was about 800 yards away, I let him have it. As the German plane went out of control, I saw the pilot bail out, and the parachute open."

"Orr said that he had completed his 30 missions, had received the rotation orders to return to the states, and was grounded when the invasion of Normandy took place.

***

By sons Leslie and Gene.

"My Dad, Leslie E. "Gene" Orr, grew up in the area around Bartlesville, Oklahoma, and graduated from a small rural school in the village of Ramona. He was very athletic, and as with most kids in the USA during the '30s, was active in most sports offered in the schools. He earned 16 varsity letters while in high school, four each in football, basketball, track and field, and baseball. I also found in my archives a program from a play put on by his high school senior class, and Dad had a role in it. He was Loyd Hamilton – a wealthy young man – in the play "You're Telling Me," performed April 23, 1937 in the Ramona high School auditorium.

"Once he graduated from High School, he must have found work on various construction projects around the Midwest. In early 1941 he was working for Massman construction Co, in Kansas City, Missouri and in 1942 he was working for Maxon construction Co. in Burns City, Indiana. During this stint with Maxon he met my mother, Catherine.

"Dad's dates of service were from February 8, 1943 (Induction) until September 19, 1945 (Honorable discharge). He flew his first combat mission on December 30, 1943 and his last on May 20, 1944. He logged over 200 hours on 30 missions. In addition to being granted membership in the "Goldfish Club" for the

April 29, 1944 mission, he was also in the "Lucky Bastards" Club, seemingly a special club within the 447th Bomb Group. The citation reads "For having this day achieved the remarkable record of sallying forth and returning no less than thirty times, for having braved the hazards of the Hun flack, for bringing Hitler and his cronies tons of bombs, for bending the Luftwaffe's back, all through the courtesty of the VIII AAF who sponsors these programs in the interest of liberty-loving people everywhere." The citation also specifies that Dad was the tail gunner of the Flying Fortress *Wolf Pack*, which must be the one he and the crew were assigned to after the plane they ditched on April 29, 1944.

"After the war Dad returned to Bartlesville, Oklahoma and we lived there a few years, right behind his mother's house. We then moved to Indiana and lived in three different towns: Bedford, Crane, and Bloomington. Dad had a Civil Service job working for the U.S. Naval Department as a construction superintendent. He also pursued correspondence courses and in 1956 earned a diploma in structural engineering. Then we moved to North Dakota and by this time he was an ironworker and was helping to build a big dam there. He must have been as good a man then as he was later because a friend of the family decided to follow my Dad around the country and continue working for him. That man, Morris Endris, eventually married a hometown girl and settled down and we are friends to this day! From North Dakota we moved all the way to Louisiana, to a couple of suburbs of Baton Rouge. During these early years, his favorite pasttime was playing in city softball leagues, and he and my Mother began to participate in bowling leagues.

"From there we moved to California. I think Dad was working for the same company in several locations, and eventually moved up to being a superintendent of the ironworkers. However, something happened in California and the company went bankrupt and the employees were not paid for several months. My parents left California and swore to never return! We moved from there to Cheyenne, Wyoming, then to New Mexico where we lived in two towns: Aztec and Bloomfield , then back to Cheyenne for a few months. We then moved to Lincoln, Nebraska. While in Cheyenne and Lincoln, he worked on missile silos that housed part of the U.S. ICBM arsenal.

"My Father had said all along that when I reached high school, he would get out of construction so we could settle in one place for high school. That's how we ended up in Golden, Colorado, where I attended tenth, eleventh, and twelfth grade. My brother, who is three years younger, was thus able to attend both junior high and high school in Golden.

"When we first got to the Denver, Colorado, in 1961, Dad was working on the first skyscraper ever in Denver, called Brooks Towers. After he finished that job, my Father took some courses and became a motel/mobile home park manager. My Mother often worked with him in the office. They managed the mobile home park we lived in for several years, then a motel in Denver for a year or so, then a mobile home park in Kissemmee, Florida and Tallahassee, Florida, then retired to Oklahoma City, eventually buying the house across the street from my Aunt Kay, Dad's youngest sister. These later years found my parents quite active in bowling leagues, but they also enjoyed such card games as bridge and pinochle.

While they lived in Tallahassee, I graduated from college. I hoped to work in agricultural research - to help better/increase crops in third world countries - but was ahead of my time and couldn't find work. There were only about 50 small companies in the entire USA doing that work at this time (1978) and none of them were hiring. So I followed my folks to Tallahassee and after a year or so there joined the Air Force.

"While in Tallahassee, my Father made a rare visit to the doctor to complain of pain in his left arm. They did surgery to biopsy the lump they found in the arm, but just closed the wound back up.............the oncologist said it was cancer and the arm would have to be amputated. My Dad said no way, particularly since he was left-handed. One of his sisters lived in Houston, Texas, where the famous M.D. Anderson Cancer Hospital is located. So we all went to Houston and stayed with sister Phyllis while my Dad underwent well over two weeks of additional tests. It turned out to be a different type of cancer and was treatable. He underwent chemotherapy there and a few additional treatments at home, and was eventually cured. By the time they moved to Oklahoma City, he was diagnosed with some heart problems, made worse by his life-long smoking. He underwent cardiac artery surgery and was in the hospital ten days, but when he got out he continued to sneak a cigarette now and then.

"During this same time frame, I was reassigned from Nellis Air Force Base, Nevada, to Germany. I was nervous because my parents were getting elderly, but excited to live in and tour Europe. However, my Mother was sliding into Alzheimer's. While living in Germany, we talked on the phone every Sunday. But by the end of my three years in Germany, Mother wasn't even talking on the phone calls, just listening.

"I returned to Keesler Air Force Base in Biloxi, Mississippi, for some additional training. During this time, my Father asked my brother and I to come to Oklahoma and help him decide on a nursing home for my Mother. He said he had cared for her day and night for several years, and couldn't do it any more. This was finalized and we moved my Mother. This was very difficult on my Dad and in addition, she would run away from the nursing home, looking for him, causing more stress and anxiety. Twenty-eight days after her admission, he died at home. The neighbor doctor who went into the house to check on him said he had died peacefully lying on his bed: he did not have a look of agony on his face, nor was he stretched out as if reaching for his nitroglycerine pills. This was comforting to us.

"My Aunt Kay checked on my Mother occasionally, and some time the next year, my brother and I were able to fly her out to the Denver area where I was by now living. I had gotten off active duty and into the reserves to take care of my stepchildren, and we had all moved to Colorado. However, my Mother's medical needs were too great for me to care for her at home, so she lived in several nursing homes until the end.

***

Acknowledgements.
Dale Flemming, son of pilot 1Lt. Dean S. Flemming.
Bill shaw, son of engineer Sgt. William M. Shaw.
Leslie and Gene Orr, sons of tail-gunner Sgt. Leslie E. Orr.

CHAPTER 43

447TH BOMB GROUP
710TH BOMB SQUADRON

Type: B-17G • Serial: 42-97135 "Hey Mabel!"
MACR: 4252 • Air Base: Rattlesden

"When attacked by fighters, the plane was hit, caught fire and left the formation. Because of the fire in the nose and flight deck, the radio-operator, tail-gunner, and both waist-gunners bailed out just after the plane was hit. This was in the Magdenburg and Halle area."

Co-Pilot Jesse B. Kendler

Pilot: 1Lt. Charles H. Marcy, 0-738436, POW, Conneaut, OH

Co-Pilot: 2Lt. Jesse B. Kendler, 0-809808, POW, New York, NY

Navigator: 2Lt. George E. Compton, 0-687823, POW, Williamsport, PA

Bombardier: 2Lt. James J. Conway, 0-672941, POW, Springfield, MA

Engineer: T/Sgt. Robert B. Schrimsher, 14182136, POW, Gadsden, AL

Radio: T/Sgt. Abe Farah, 39321814, POW, Portland, OR

Ball-Turret Gunner: S/Sgt. James J. Isherwood, 13131743, POW, Pittsburg, PA

Left Waist-Gunner: S/Sgt. Edward W. Perkins, 20638740, POW, Detroit, MI

Right Waist-Gunner: S/Sgt. William Nicholas, 32278935, POW, Newark, NJ

Tail-Gunner: Sgt. James P. Scully, 11090153, POW, Cambridge, MA

10 POW

Target: Berlin Friedrichstrasse Railway Station

Crash Site: Zermütsel, 3 miles n. of Neuruppin, Germany
Time: 12.30

Newspaper article

"Suicidal Onslaught Takes Out Eleven 447th Forts."

"At 11:00 hours, the formation was subjected to heavy fighter attacks. A force of 100-120 single engine fighters, mostly 109's attacked with ferocity and persistence. They came head on through the formation taking three bombers in their first pass. The attack continued for 35-40 minutes with intense flak at the same time, our formation became scattered. The enemy fighters came on diving through their own flak in near suicidal attempts to further break up the shattered formation.

"*Hey Mabel!* had its radio room and tail wheel blown out by Fock Wulf cannon fire. Another burst of cannon shells exploded throughout the cockpit starting a fire and destroying instruments and hydraulics. Having suffered a flak wound earlier that day, the cannon fire struck pilot Charles Marcey in the right hand, arm, and chest amputating two fingers and opening a deep wound from his wrist to his elbow. He also suffered burns to the face. His flak suit protected him from more serious injury.

"Charles Marcy slid the plane out the formation and went into an almost vertical dive with a column of flame and smoke streaming back from the two engines and the left wing close to the fuselage. At about 15,000 feet he leveled off and chutes began to pop out from below the plane.

"Because of the fire in the nose and flight deck, Charles had ordered the radio man, ball gunner, tail gunner and both waist gunners to bail out just after the plane was hit. The remaining crew extinguished the fire and Lt. Marcy turned towards the Baltic coast to attempt to reach Sweden when the ship was again attacked by the fighters.

"Suffering from shock, pain, loss of blood and with use of only one arm, Lt. Marcy dove the big ship into a bank of clouds to evade the fighters and dodged from cloud bank to cloud bank only to break out at 7000 ft over Berlin. Caught in an intense flak barrage, the *Hey Mabel!* was hit several more times and Charles Marcy was wounded yet again.

"The bomber seemed to be disintegrating after a huge explosion in the waist section either from a direct hit or from exploding oxygen tanks. Lt. Marcy ordered the remaining crew to bail out and held the crippled bomber in level flight while they made good of their escape. He then set the auto pilot, destroyed the IFF equipment, bailed out and lost consciousness. Lt. Marcy was promptly captured and imprisoned. He then was 23 years old.

"All of the crew of the *Hey Mabel!* survived and became POWs for exactly one year until being liberated on April 29th 1945 by elements of the 3rd Army near Moosburg Germany.

"The crew remained in contact with Charles Marcy long after the war and still today several of them maintain close contact with their pilot and leader. Charles

Marcy has counted every day since April 29th 1944 as a gift, for it would seem that was the day God was asking for his last full measure. Allowed to live, he was and is a wonderful son, brother, husband, father, grandfather, great grandfather, patriot and friend.

Pilot 1Lt. Charles H. Marcy.

Scott and Hugh Marcy, sons:

"Chuck Marcy was born in Conneaut, Ohio, on 22 August 1920 to Mabel (Horn) Marcy and Hugh Marcy. Mable graduated from Ohio University and was a triage nurse in France during WWI and Hugh, educated at the Oberlin Conservatory of Music, was an ambulance driver. Both were in the Lakeside Hospital Unit of the Red Cross from Cleveland Ohio, the first American unit in Europe during WWI.

"Hugh Marcy was in the family funeral business, started in 1868. He founded the Cowle Post of the American Legion is Conneaut and was the first Post Commander. Mable was a nurse. Hugh died suddenly in 1940. Mable went on to

Pilot 1Lt. Charles H. Marcy

become Post Commander during WWII. She lived a long, productive life and passed on in 1980. Their daughter Mary Jane is a nurse and, as well as being an Army nurse during WWII, she has practiced in Bahrain and many cities in the US.

"Chuck grew up in Conneaut, with his sister Mary Jane, who was 18 months younger. Chuck showed early singing talent, which he has practiced throughout his life. He was also a good athlete. Chuck received a scholarship offer from the New York Conservatory of Music, but when he discovered they didn't play football, he turned down the scholarship and attended the College of Wooster in Ohio for two years beginning in 1938. He played football and sang! By this time it was becoming clear that this handsome, fit talented musician and athlete had a lot going in his favor. He later learned too that he had acute long-range vision to which he partially attributes the long survival of his crew in action; being able to spot fighters 15-20 seconds sooner than one with normal vision made a difference in aerial combat.

"Upon the death of his father, Chuck left Wooster to begin his apprenticeship while studying embalming in Cleveland OH to become a funeral director, assuming his father's share as a partner in the family business.

"When the US installations in Hawaii were attacked on 7 December 1941, Chuck, 21 years old, along with thousands upon thousands of others, went to sign up. He intended to go into the Navy and drive PT Boats because he grew up with boats on Lake Erie. The line was too long and he was impatient so he found a shorter line, which happened to be the US Army Air Corps.

"Chuck boarded a train in Conneaut bound for California to begin his training as an air cadet at Santa Ana, CA for basic and primary. After earning his wings he was selected for multi-engine training at Stockton, CA where he was the only graduate held there as in instructor for the incoming class. He took four cadets through their multi-engine qualification and was then selected for four engine transition ultimately to assemble his B-17 crew in Moses Lake, WA.

"They trained as a crew there, then in New Mexico and finally combat qualifications at Harvard NE where the 447th Heavy Bombardment Group was formed. When finished there they went by train to another field where dozens of new B-17s sat on the apron. Chuck's crew went to their assigned ship, preflighted it and flew to Goose Bay Labrador to top off with fuel, get a thorough maintenance check, rest and fly solo to Nuts Corners, Ireland; from there they went on to Rattlesden England for the duration of the war. All but two of the 27 odd ships of the 447th made it to the UK. One crashed on takeoff killing all aboard and the other was lost with all hands in the Atlantic. All the remaining ships and crews of the original cadre were killed or captured within 9 months.

***

"When Chuck returned from the War, he took a refresher course in embalming, married Ruth Colson, a high school classmate and sweetheart, and resumed his position in the Marcy Funeral Home business. He soon grew frustrated with family politics, left the business and bought a roofing and heating company. He and Ruth ran Marcy's Heating and Roofing until 1986, when they sold it. Chuck worked for the new owner for a couple of years and helped out at the Funeral Home.

"Chuck was an active citizen of Conneaut. He was the first Legion Post Commander after WWII, he was very active in Rotary, the First United Methodist Church and the local music and theater scene. He was also very active in the Chamber of Commerce and true spokesman for the town of Conneaut.

"He is a strong believer in giving back, being involved in the community and giving service to the Country. If he had a mantra, it would simply be "Do your job!"

"Chuck was quite special. When a situation called for leadership, selflessness and courage, he could be counted on to step forward and take charge. This shown through clearly in what could be considered the most dangerous job there was in the ETO – flying a bomber for the 8th AF. But it was there too when responding to the not infrequent tragedies and emergencies in our small town of 12,000. The funeral home also ran the ambulance service so railroad and dock company accidents called for quick thinking, decision making and issuing instructions in conditions where people are frozen by fear, shock and horror. His leadership was not limited to emergent situations, as a community, church, and family leader he was recognized as exceptionally reliable, stable and trustworthy. He was a great role model for many young men in our home town.

Navigator 2Lt. George E. Compton.

By George himself.

"I was born in Middleburg, PA, on 4 February 1921. We moved to Williamsport, PA, when I was five and I grew up there and was schooled there. My family consisted of three girls and three boys, I was the youngest boy. I graduated from high school in 1938, but my family could not afford to send me to college. Found a job and also started in night school to further my education. The war in Europe started and soon there was talk of our entering it.

"My older brother Kenny enlisted in the Navy and since there was a draft law I realized that I had to make a decision as to what I wanted. I was very good at math so I applied to the Army Air Force cadet program to go to navigation school. I was accepted and flown to Texas for training when I was 20.

"I graduated the following August as a 2nd Lt in the Army Air Force. After a two week leave I reported to Moses Lake, Washington. There I was assigned to a crew and we were given a B-17 bomber. We were sent to Harvard, Nebraska for training prior to flying to Europe. While there we went on a navigational flight to Cheyenne, Wyoming to Denver, Colorado then back to our base. There was a dense overcast and while letting down for our landing we bounced off the ground while our altimeter was reading 800 feet. Chuck managed to stop the plane and his face hit the dash and I went flying through the nose and ended up with cracked ribs. We were given a new bomber - no. 2. The squadron then flew to Northern Canada for the flight to England.

"We started taking off after midnight and set a course for England. This flight was no picnic for us. After three hours Chuck called and said we were icing up and needed to fly at a lower altitude until the ice melted. We did and slowly regained our flying altitude. A while later when we started to see some daylight, Chuck called and said there was a large fire on the ocean. Since German subs were hunting transport ships he asked for a heading south away from the fire. However as we did, it rose out of the water. We then realized it was the sun rising and went back on course.

"Things quieted down and we proceeded on course. We were flying on top of a solid overcast, when Chuck called and said we were low on gas how was our position? My Estimated Time of Arrival was almost up and a hole appeared in the overcast below and we decide to go down thru it. The overcast went almost to the ground when we leveled off, we saw a tip of land and the huge letters E R I E and realized we were over South Ireland. Being low on gas Chuck had to hedge-hop to make it to an alternate base in North Ireland. We arrived at Nutts Corner and Chuck had no time to ask for landing instructions but landed and we ran out of gas on the runway. We coasted to a stop at the end of the runway and had to be towed to a parking plase. Very close call.

"After two days we flew to our base at Rattlesden, Sussex, England. We spent December training and getting used to the weather. My first mission was to Ludwigshafen on December 30th and it lasted 9 ½ hours. We flew four missions in January, four missions in February, seven missions in March plus an abort. Shortly after getting over France we lost an engine and had to turn around go back to England. We chose to dump our bombs in the ocean and fly around till our gas was very low. When we started to land one of the wheels stuck and we were forced to belly land. The landing was safe for all but me. We were given bomber no. 3. The next morning I awoke with my testicles swollen to twice their size, there-by losing my ability to be a father.

"I spent most of April in the base hospital and my first mission was the 29th of April to Berlin. This was my 21st mission. We made it up thru a heavy overcast, over the channel, across the Zuider Sea. We turned on our bombing run and the sky became a mass of planes, bombs dropping like rain and exploding flak shells.

"Just after we dropped our bombs we were hit in our left wing and lost an engine and our place in the formation, I was firing my machine gun when a shell from a fighter entered the plane that passed by my face and up thru the dashboard and hit Chuck in the chest area and he lost two fingers from his right hand. The fragments hit my face and ripped out my right eye and blinded my left eye. For a while it was very quiet, I pried open my left eye and looked at my altimeter and it was spinning around. I grabbed the engineer's leg and pointed to Chuck. It turned out the co-pilot was frozen on the controls and Chuck was unconscious. Somehow he was able to awaken Chuck and we leveled off around 8,000 feet and headed north toward Sweden.

"However we were again shot at by fighters, we soon were down to one engine and Chuck gave the bail out call. Since I could not see they attached a line to my chute and threw me out. This line opened my chute and I floated amid whistling flak shells as we were still over Berlin. After a long while I heard voices and I hit the ground on my right side and felt my right leg break. Hands grabbed me and took the cigarettes from my pockets and my insignias. They put me in a stretcher and carried me into a building and unto a bed. It turned out I landed on a hospital lawn outside the Northwest sector of Berlin.

"The next morning I was taken to another room where they sewed the mouth area and put a cast on my leg. I was taken to another room where I could hear

American voices and I felt safer even though I could not open my mouth (I was fed thru a tube). About a week later the nurse came and removed the tube and I had some solid food, I thanked her and Chuck called out is that you, and I said yes.

"The building turned out to be the Herman Goering Luftwaffe Hospital. We were on the top floor and ducked under our beds when air raids occurred. After 21 days there we were bused to a railroad station and taken to Frankfort and to an interrogation center. After several hours there we were taken to prison. The cell was completely bare with a bare light that never went off. The door was flush with a metal rod you could bang to get attention. There was a metal cot with a cover, no mattress.

"After a day I was taken to a train and taken to a large house staffed with British medics and the next day they removed what was left of my right eye and very slowly my eye sight in my left started coming back. The security was handled by a German sergeant. He was from Detroit, Michigan. He came to Germany as he saw opportunity to benefit from the war. He spoke five or six languages and liked to talk with me.

"One day he asked me to collect some cigarettes, chocolate bars and powered coffee from our Red Cross parcels. I was able to and let him know. He then said to be at the front gate the next morning. I was and here he comes and waved to the guards to open up and we walked out and down to the railroad station. We boarded the train and he cleared out a compartment for us and said the excuse for the trip was to have a glass eye made for me and to give him some time to womanize. Half way we had to get off for the night. He put me in a building where the officers from the Russian front came for R and R. I was settled down on bunk bed and he said he would be back. In the middle of the night all the lights came on and there was the sergeant and two buddies all beered up. He pointed out my eye socket and the cast on my leg. After a long discussion, they left.

"The sergeant arrived the next morning and off to the train we went. By evening we were at the end of the line up in the mountains. He took me to a house and met the owner. He turned out to be a dentist who was blowing glass eyes for the German military. After we gave him the items I brought, I was taken to a real bedroom and spent the night. The next morning he gave me some food and starting forming my glass eye. Later in the day the sergeant came and we walked around the village visiting other places where other glass items were being blown. Most of the workers were from WWI and I shared my cigarettes with them and had conversations. Back to my room while the sergeant sought women. The next day the dentist took colored glass and added the pupil and veins. I was picked up by the sergeant and off to the train. This time we arrived back at the hospital safely.

"Shortly after that I was moved to another house set-up as a hospital. There my leg and ankle were re-broken and set in a new cast. When healed the cast was removed and I could walk normally. When I was strong enough I was sent to Stalag Luft 111 at Sagan, Germany. I was placed in the British sector as my name is very English. The next day I walked from the camp into the American sector. There were forty men per room with four high bunk beds. The only one left was the one at the ceiling. However I was able to attach a piece of bright tin to the ceiling and could lay in bed and practice moving my eyes and practice blinking. Besides conversations, I served as a cook and played a lot of bridge.

"The camp was in the path of the Russian offensive and we soon could see the flashes from their cannons. The Germans had all POWs who could walk well enough start on a walk south towards the American sector. The rest of us stayed put a few more days and then loaded into freight cars and headed south into the American sector. The train only moved at night and during daylight we were off loaded and could exercise talk. We were off loaded about two days walk from Moosburg where a large POW camp was. On our 1st day one of our fighter planes started to fire on us and soon pulled up. From then on we always had a plane checking our progress.

"When we arrived at the camp it still had German guards. However when General Patton's tanks were due the next day, they gave up their guns. At daybreak, a car with four black-shirted Germans arrived at the gate. When they saw the guards had no guns, they shot them and sped away. Later that day General Patton's tank force arrived with the General riding the lead tank.

"It was on 27 April 1945 and for us POWs the war was over. Finally on the 5th of June we were flown back into France the evening of the day the peace treaty was signed. We boarded a train and ended up at Camp Lucky Strike near Le Havre. There we were cleaned up and given new uniforms and medical check-ups. Sometime later we went aboard an ocean liner and sailed back to The US. We were able to go home right away and see our families.

"When I arrived home, I met with everybody and related all my experiences and answered all their questions. Then I said I would never discuss these things again as I want to put them in the back of my mind as I wanted to concentrate on living a life. They agreed and I held out until I was 50 and retired.

"I married in January 1946 and entered Penn State University that fall and earned my BS in mechanical engineering in 1951 and accepted a position with the Naval Ordnance Laboratory. After a few years I joined the team that was developing the Polaris Missile. When that was completed, I went into the non-destructive testing field until my retirement in 1971. My wife had died in 1967 and this time I married a widow with three children and finally had a family I could not have on my own.

Bombardier 2Lt. James J. Conway.

"At the age of 20 I enlisted in the Army Air Corps as an Aviation Cadet. I still remember the tears in my father's eyes as he drove me to the station, the only time I ever saw him cry. My official enlistment date was March 18, 1942.

"I was excited upon arriving in San Antonio, Texas at Kelly Field, where I endured the hazing, drill, etc. before shipping off to Fort Worth, Texas, for Primary Flight training.

"That didn't last long as I was not destined apparently to become a pilot and upon wash-out I was sent to Bombardier School in Big Spring, Texas, where I successfully completed the training and was commissioned a 2nd Lt. on February 18, 1943. (Many years later I was proud to pin the wings of an Air Force Pilot on the uniform of my son Daniel in Lubbock, Texas.)

Bombardier 2Lt. James J. Conway and his wife in 2000

"Certain members of the graduation class of bombardiers who were considered more proficient in math were selected to train as Navigators and I, being one of them, was sent to San Marcos, Texas Navigation School, and therefore I could now function in more than one capacity.

"In the summer of 1943 I was transferred to Moses Lake, Washington and became a member of the 447th Heavy Bombardment Group, and was assigned as bombardier to a ten man B-17, 4 engine bomber crew in the 710th Squadron.

"Moses Lake was the most desolate area in Washington so we used to go to Spokane or Seattle on weekends. On one occasion, while hitchhiking off the base, I was given a ride by an elderly lawyer who advised me to buy land here as it would greatly appreciate in value. Of course I paid no attention to him but many years later I read in Collier's Magazine that property values had skyrocketed here.

"We used to fly over Lake Chelan, 50 feet above the water, buzzing pleasure boats with 50 calibre machine guns, with live ammunition, trained on the occupants. But no itchy trigger fingers activated the guns. I've often wondered what those people thought. .

"After training in the State of Washington, we shipped out to Nebraska for more practice in formation flying and other preparations for overseas duty. We used to hunt pheasants in the corn fields of Nebraska, using shot guns fiom the back of a moving convertible car. Our co-pilot Tom Radle's wife used to make the best pheasant dinners. Tom was the oldest and only married crew member.

"One night, Chuck Marcy took our plane, named "Hey Mabel" after his mother, on a training flight with only a skeleton crew. I was not present due to other duties. Nebraska is flat as a pancake but there was one small hill near the base. The weather this night turned to soup and Chuck was unlucky enough to hit this small hill in the cornfields and he and others were injured in the crash, though not seriously. My bombardier's position in the nose was so completely destroyed that crew members walked through the huge opening to evacuate the plane. In this whole history I recall how many times I was so lucky as to never get a scratch.

"Eventually in late 1943, we received orders to proceed overseas. On our way to Labrador, Chuck flew over his home town on Conneaut, Ohio. He took full advantage of the opportunity to let the hometown folks know we were on our way by buzzing the town ten times. He flew so low we could read the lettering on the water tower only by looking up. It was great fun!

"Our overseas flight, on November 23, 1943, from Goose Bay, Labrador at night heading across the Atlantic for Scotland, proceeded with bombers taking off, at one-minute intervals. One bomber blew up ahead of us on take-off, but of course we continued on. Several hours out our pilot was startled to see what he thought was an explosion of an aircraft ahead and he tried to fly around it. But it turned out to be only the moon on the horizon appearing suddenly out of the clouds in a manner that gave the appearance of a great explosion.

"In the early morning daylight we were starting to get very concerned about fuel as there was no sign of land yet. George Compton, our navigator, could no longer use celestial navigation with no stars out, and even the figures for sun shots were not tabulated for that hour in the very early morning. When our radio operator, Abe Farah, made SOS calls we received an answer from somewhere - could be Germans below in neutral Ireland - telling us what heading to fly. We were suspicious of this as it later proved out to be apparently an enemy trick, which, had we followed this bearing, would have landed us in occupied France. On occasion German fighter planes intercepted and shot down bomber crews, tired and sleepy, after a long ocean crossing.

"So from 20,000 feet, we descended on a very low altitude and suddenly saw, below the edge of some clouds, white stones on a beach spelling out EIRE. Then we flew the whole length of Ireland about 400 feet above the green farms and villages, and landed at an airport near Belfast, Northern Ireland, called Nutts Corner, missing our destination by one whole country. There we ran out of gas on the runway. That night we went to a dance, stayed out very late, and were locked out of our hotel. At the dance I met a very pretty girl, but was cut out by a major who pulled rank on me.

"After practicing formation flying and other skills at our base in Rattlesden, England, near Ipswich, about 50 miles north of London, we embarked on our first combat mission on December 30, 1943. Altogether I flew 29 combat missions, the last one April 29, 1944, over Berlin, Germany. The tour requirement had been 25 missions, but approximately halfway through, the total number of missions was raised to 30, so I missed coming back to the States and therefore spent a year as a prisoner of war in German camps.

"On one mission we flew flying over England all day after dropping my bombs in the English Channel. This was due to one engine malfunction, but also because of the inability to lower one wheel. We were ordered to burn up almost all our gasoline and to prepare for a belly landing on a special grassy airfield. We tried to dislodge the belly turret to facilitate the landing but it wouldn't budge and even the wrenches in our tool kit fractured in the effort. So we played poker and listened to music on the radio all day and finally Chuck and Tom made a perfect belly landing. Since this was the first bombing mission to Berlin all the news media were present to record the "heroes" back from Berlin. It did make Pathe News in the movie theaters.

"On another mission to Germany we flew up over the North Sea. However the cloud formations grew to over 30,000 feet exceeding the ceiling of the B-17. Each group on a mission consisted ideally of a total of 21 aircraft. The commander of the group ahead of us, due to the high clouds, without any warning to our people, turned his 21 planes back 180 degrees and 42 planes flew thru each others air space. There were immediately five midair collisions, involving ten B-17s and a hundred men were instantly blown apart. Out pilots were lucky enough to avoid collision by wracking our ship all over the sky, but a good friend of mine who was in formation immediately behind us died in the collision.

"When bombers were victims of enemy action and crews bailed out we always tried to count the number of parachutes. I'll always remember the poor fellow who successfully left his burning aircraft, but whose clothes were on fire. Even though his chute opened the fire eventually consumed everything and he fell to his death as we all watched his descent. However Chuck Marcy couldn't look and did not wish to be told about it.

"On another occasion, while taking off from England, and climbing up through the usual overcast in winter, for 10 to 20 thousand feet, the pilots got disoriented and asked for my help. The aircraft were equipped in those days with an instrument we called a "G" Box. All 21 aircraft took off for a mission at approximately one minute intervals. They flew a rectangular pattern, over and over, so many minutes on each leg of the 4 headings, climbing all the time. However there were many, many groups taking off all at the same time, and all from this small part of England, from airfields close to each other. Consequently there was always the danger, especially when you could see nothing in the midst of the soup, of mid-air collisions, which happened quite frequently. With fully loaded gas tanks and bomb bays carrying usually 10-500 pounds bombs, or on occasion incendiaries, there wouldn't be much left if a collision occurred. The scariest time to me always was this time when you had to sweat out the climb and felt so helpless. Many times our aircraft would exhibit turbulence due to propwash from another airplane which meant we just missed colliding with it. In any event on this occasion with my use of the "G" Box, I was able to give the proper headings to our pilots, and finally we did breakout into the blue, and there immediately in front of, and slightly to our left, was another B-17 at our exact elevation!

"On returning from a mission we usually let down crossing the English Channel, often in sunshine, and then approached cloud covered England. We ducked under the low overcast and flew to our base at very low altitudes. With the thousands of allied aircraft flying at all times over England it was very common to have friendly aircraft fly head on through our formation, somewhat disconcerting.

"As dangerous as combat conditions were still there were those who would tempt the gods. Just for kicks, Tom Radle would, upon returning from Germany, leave his position as co-pilot, to occupy the belly turret to see how it was landing on the runway. This was strictly forbidden, of course, because if the wheel undercarriage failed he could be squashed like a bug, as did happen to some poor fellow trapped in this position during a belly landing.

"After a number of missions the process of letting down thru thousands of feet of solid cloud, caused our pilot, Chuck Marcy, to be inflicted with a phobia against this. So the commander ordered him to practice taking off and climbing up through the "soup" over England and letting down through it over and over again until he overcame his phobia.

"Our crew was given credit for shooting down thirteen enemy aircraft. This, to me, was the most exciting part of combat, and it was like a football game, where fear went out the window and the adrenaline took over. I shot at a lot of fighters but can't honestly say I got one - but things happened so fast one never knew in many cases. I do credit the German fighter pilots with great skill and bravery. To take on a group of B-17 Bombers, each with thirteen .50 caliber machine guns, by flying head on through the group, took a lot of guts. Once an empty .50 caliber shell hit me in the chest. It came from a B-17 above our aircraft and broke through the plexiglass in front of me. I hollered "I'm hit" but no harm was done.

"I remember very vividly, one German fighter plane, with all guns blazing, flying straight at me. I returned fire with my twin 50 caliber machine guns right at him and I was so sure I hit him that I hollered on the radio, "I got that S.O.B." But he avoided last minute head on collision by pulling the stick back and flying over my right shoulder through our group. When he did this he exposed his underside and I got in some more fire but whether he was hit or not I'll never know.

"Another problem was oxygen. The rule was to put on oxygen masks at 10,000 feet altitude. Lack of oxygen above this altitude leads to the equivalent of drunkenness. On one mission the lead plane in another group suffered an oxygen leak in the nose area where the navigator and bombardier were. This led to a fist fight between these two lead individuals and contributed to some problems completing their mission to say the least.

"Out of our 710th Squadron complement of 17 original crews 14 were shot down, about half killed and half becoming prisoners. Some also were drowned in the English Channel where the winter sea water temperature meant almost instant death, if rescue wasn't immediate by Air Sea Rescue Crews, usually British.

"Between series of missions we were given leave and most of us went to London, which was a great liberty town. We used to leave a pub with beer glasses in hand and go out in the street when the Germans were bombing another part of the city, just to see the action, which, of course, was very foolhardy. I also spent one three day pass on a visit to Scotland with one of our crew members. I didn't care for Glasgow, an industrial type city, so continued on to Edinburg, which was much nicer I thought. I noticed all the Scotch girls here drank boilermakers, a shot and a beer, very unusual.

"In London we went to the theaters in Picadilly to see live shows where smoking was permitted in the theater, and, at intermission, tea was served.

"Money had no real meaning. We used to play poker gambling with 20 pound notes (about $100) in those days. I remember taking about $400 on leave in London on one occasion. This, I suppose, would be at least $6000 today.

"General Jimmy Doolittle, who was placed in command of the 8th Air Force, and who had a terrific record for years of daring and bravery, and of course the flight off a Navy carrier deck of a squadron of B-25 bombers to bomb Japan, was not well thought of by many flying personnel in England. One gripe was that he was great at organizing and starting a mission towards Europe, but would fly his plane back to base and say the equivalent of "Go get 'em, boys!" All other commanders would never do this, but would take the same risks as everyone else. The more important gripe was that Doolittle, in a war of attrition, sacrificed many crews by sending them out on missions, in very foul weather, knowing the losses would be high. The strategy was successful, of course, as the goal of no significant German air fighting capacity by D-Day, June 6, 1944, was accomplished.

***

"Around noon on April 29, 1944, south of the city of Berlin, our aircraft was hit by a burst of 20 mm machine gum fire thru the instrument panel, from a German ME 109 fighter plane. Chuck Marcy, our pilot, had two fingers shot off, plus chest and leg injuries, and was knocked unconscious. Our navigator, George Compton, had an eye shot out and was semi-conscious.

"Our co-pilot, Tom Radle, was assigned to other duties this day, and a substitute was flying co-pilot on his first mission. He froze in panic and the plane went into a dive from around 29,000 ft. To around 6,000 it. The pilot recovered consciousness and together with our top turret gunner, engineer Bob Schrimsher, only 19 years old, the control of the plane was accomplished and recovery from the dive took place. Again I didn't get a scratch.

"The group had gotten off course and we were south of Berlin instead of north of the city. We had lost two engines out of the four so decided to try for Sweden, a neutral country, where we could sit out the war and have fun with the blonde Swedish girls. So we proceeded on a new course I gave our pilots.

"No such luck! We came over the city of Berlin, from south to north, at about 6,000 feet. The anti aircraft gunners, who were very good at 25,000 to 30,000 feet, had us in their sights at an altitude now, that it was like shooting fish in a barrel. The shrapnel hitting the plane sounded like a hail storm.

"Next the plane caught on fire so Chuck ordered Bob Schrimsher to tell the crew members in the back to bail out. Our intercom had been shot out. When Bob went to the rear of the plane no one was there. The rest of the crew didn't have to wait to be told to jump.

"So we all bailed out of the front hatch and Bob and I pushed George Compton out using a static line to open his chute. This exit hatch was very dangerous as the bomb bay door were open and they could cut a body in half, which had happened to others.

"I enjoyed drifting down in the parachute. It was very quiet except for the anti-aircraft guns still firing. When I was close to the ground I could see below me a group of people that consisted of Hitler youth under the leadership of what we might compare to a scoutmaster. This was in the suburbs of Berlin. I decided to throw away my Lucky Strike cigarettes because I didn't want any damn Nazi to enjoy my American smokes.

"There was a strong ground wind blowing and when I hit the ground it threw me flat on my back, knocking the wind out of me. The German official in charge of the young men, an officer, hit me on the top of my head, and getting no negative reaction told me I was ok. Of course the Germans took my parachute. (They say German girls made petticoats out of them.) Then they took my flying coveralls from me. Underneath I was wearing a bright blue electric heated suit.

"They had an old tank, World War I vintage, with the turret missing. They placed me in this turret opening standing up in the bright blue suit, and took me through the streets of the suburbs (like a conquering hero!) Eventually I was transferred to an open touring car and driven to an office in Berlin where a girl typed up my name, rank and serial number and nothing else. I wasn't wearing any dog tags for some reason, so they threw me in a lousy solitary jail cell, with threats and name calling such as "schweinhund." Of course with no dog tags, and now no uniform, the thought of being considered a spy went through my mind.

"Eventually we were taken to the train station in the City of Frankfort to be transferred to a POW Camp, namely Stalag Luft III, run by the German Air Force. At the Frankfort station we were guarded by soldiers to prevent civilians from attacking us. We saw a prosperous looking German business man, while shaking his fist at us, stumble and trip on the curb and fall flat on his face. No one dared laugh!

"On one occasion as we were being transported in a German army truck, guarded by very young German soldiers, actually teenagers, who could speak some English, an argument broke out about who was going to win the war. The young Germans, completely indoctrinated with propaganda to the effect that the invincible German military machine would win out, were adamant in their support of Hitler and victory. The American flyers finally shut them up with the statement that their great general Rommel had been kicked out of Africa, an ignominious defeat for the Germans, and this would eventually be their fate as well.

"I did not see Chuck Marcy, our pilot, or George Compton, our navigator, for a long time. They were both in a hospital in Berlin. When air raids threatened the hospital, the German staff let all the POW patients to fend for themselves and they went to the air raid shelter, namely the hospital boiler room, actually no great shelter. George was later taken to a small German village where he was fitted with a glass eye.

***

"At Stalug Lufl III, about 100 miles Southeast of Berlin, we lived for about nine months in a barracks, with double loaded corridor. We had in our very small room three triple bunks to accommodate nine men and a small stove, which burned a very limited amount of coal bricks. There was one kitchen stove for the whole barracks for men to take turns cooking on. Rations consisted of a limited amount of a German type of bread with a consistency of sawdust, and a few potatoes, plus large garbage type barrels of so called soup. One we called the "Green Death," and the other was a white gruel with white worms in it, which provided protein. We also ate spoiled cheese, and just cut out the rot. Thank God for the Red Cross parcels which supplemented the above!

"The camp was surrounded by two high fences about ten feet apart, with guard towers at frequent intervals, manned by armed sharp-shooters. There was a third fence, only about a foot high, about 20 feet inside the double-high fences. In between was no-man's land. On one occasion, while chasing a soccer ball that had gone over the low rail fence, I jumped over it to get the ball. Fellow prisoners immediately hollered, "Look out!" Upon seeing the nearest guard tower soldier aiming his rifle at me, I quickly hopped back over the low rail. The hell with the ball!

"In prison camp, we were able to listen to a German radio loudspeaker and read German newspapers. However, some prisoners were able to make secret radios from parts bribed from guards and they could get the BBC News, especially as it pertained to the war. So for example, from German sources, the results of an American air raid might be expressed as say, 62 heavy bombers shot down. The BBC figures might report that allied forces admitted to losing perhaps 38 bombers. The true figure might be somewhere in the middle. Propaganda existed on both sides.

"An interesting feature of the prison camp was the use of a small room called a map room, in a central building that also contained a theater. On one wall was a very large map upon which Americans kept track of the battle lines using red strings, both on the eastern and western fronts. The position of the red strings, changed daily, were per the German news sources, obviously. Every day the German guards, who also visited this map room, would observe the changing battle lines expressed by the red strings. They would exit the building shaking their heads in frustration as the status of the German forces deteriorated, especially after D-Day. Of course we all knew that the true position was even worse for the Germans because of our BBC information.

"A new jet fighter ME-262 was developed by the Germans which, in speed, greatly exceeded any allied aircraft. We saw these planes occasionally, and sometimes they would fly over the camp at very high speed and low altitudes, to perhaps rub it into the flyers grounded below.

"Around the bend" was an expression used by POWs to describe anyone who was losing it mentally. They were a few cases but most men in the Air Corps, the cream of the crop, came through both physically and mentally in good shape. Part of this was due to strict discipline of the American officer chain-of-comrnand. Saturday inspections were the norm by senior American officers and rules of behavior and appearance were mandatory, such as no beards, clean-shaven, bunks made, rooms kept up neatly, and other disciplines. Chain-of-command included a senior officer in each barrack in charge, and each room had the ranking member in command, whom we called "Fuhrer."

"We had arrived at this POW camp just one month after the Germans had executed 50 out of 76 British airmen who had escaped through a tunnel they had patiently dug for months. The German military had a no nonsense approach to guarding POWs and required all prisoner personnel to fall out in military formation twice a day for a head count, which could last for hours until every single man was accounted for. In cold rainy or snowy weather this was a miserable experience.

"In the January winter of 1945, one night all prisoners were told to get ready to evacuate the camp and carry whatever food they could and dress as warm as possible. This took place about midnight and this was due to the Russian advance from the East. We could hear the guns in the distance. So at midnight thousands of men left the barracks and marched through back roads for about thirty hours with breaks every hour. Any men who could not keep up were picked up by the Germans and placed on horse-drawn wagons. Some had frost bite, some dysentery, and some not enough willpower to keep going. One reason it took so long was that the dammed German captain lost his way.

"We were allowed to sleep in barns and in one factory that made pottery, so tired men just fell asleep on the floor. One enterprising prisoner here made arrangements with a German housewife to swap some coffee for a pot of boiled potatoes. After an hour or so the exchange was made by throwing the items over a fence. But first the American removed all the coffee from the small can, filled it with sand, and covered the sand with a quarter inch layer of coffee. The red-faced German housewife came back shortly after, screaming at the American, and if she could have gotten through the fence she would have killed him. It was a dirty trick but funny at the same time.

"We were then placed on a train, pulling the old World War I freight cars that were designed for 40 men or eight horses. However, the Germans crowded in more than 60 men, such that there wasn't enough room to lay down to sleep. So some men made hammocks out of overcoats to create room for those below. Sanitary conditions were horrible, and we were in these freight cars for four days until we arrived outside the large city of Nuremberg. Here we were placed in filthy barracks, with hardly anything to eat and no heat. So men burned anything they could to stay warm, even the latrines.

"In April the American troop advance caused the Germans to move us once again to a camp near a small town called Moosburg, not far from the large city of Munich. This march was a breeze, as the weather was mild, it was a beautiful part of Germany, and the guards knew the war was about over. We could leave the line of march at will to sleep in German houses or barns and trade for food. The German women had no trouble with Americans sleeping in their homes but were terrified of the Russian troops, and with good reason.

"Another fellow and I traded cigarettes for eggs - one for one - we scrambled up about two dozen over a small fire and the two of us ate the whole batch. We always asked civilians for food. Sometimes the people did help us. One man threw a half loaf of bread to a prisoner, who must have been an excellent outfielder as he made a beautiful catch. Another time I asked a woman, who appeared to be very fat, for food. She wasn't fat but trudging along a rural path heading for the hospital to have a baby all by herself.

"In the Moosburg camps there were tens of thousands of prisoners, besides the American and British. There were French, Greek, Italian, Russian, etc. I toured the site in 1992 in the company of a German citizen who had an interest in American ex-POWs in particular, and when I visited his home he showed me American POW magazines and articles that were surprising to me. When I asked him if he had served in the war he said as a boy of 16 he was a member of an anti-aircraft gun battery trying to shoot down American bombers.

"Eventually on April 29, 1945, General Patton's Third Anny tanks began shelling the town and the German guards disappeared. So we left the prison campgrounds and congregated around the tank crews joyfully where we were treated to food and wine in abundance. I remember General Patton himself, standing a few feet from me, in a bull session with the freed POWs.

"The Russian prisoners of war were treated horribly. Their camps were full of disease including tuberculosis. Russia was not a signatory to the Geneva Convention and the Germans took full advantage of their ability to avoid humanitarian treatment of these men. Many of the people in the multitude of nations within the Soviet Union were men with a Mongolian cast to their features. Such a group I observed, alter the guards abandoned us at Moosburg, enjoying a feast of stolen chickens. They made a large campfire and threw the chickens, feathers and all, onto the flames. Then they pulled the hot chickens, half cooked, from the fire and tore the flesh off with their dirty bare hands.

"After a day or two we were all flown in C47 s to France to Camp Lucky Strike for new uniforms, delousing, medical check-ups, record keeping, etc.

"Finally we were shipped out to the States on a large vessel and came to New York City by way of Trinidad. Here my cousin Helen Hackett met me and took me to her home in Brooklyn. After this I had two weeks R&R in Atlantic City staying in a Boardwalk Hotel. Discharge was not until November 21, 1945.

All in all, good and bad, the four years in the Air Force, as a single man, were the best years of my life and I wouldn't trade them for anything.

***

By daughter Kathy McKee.

"After his return from the war my Dad was a civil engineer with a company in Holyoke, MA. He married my mother when he was 29 and she was 22. The had met at a bus stop in New York and pretended he was lost and didn't know which bus to take. He was a student at Rensselaer Polytechnic Institute in Troy, New York. My mother was a nurse. They dated for two years and got engaged on St. Patrick's Day. They were married in 1950. They moved to Massachussetts, where my father eventually got a job with a constuction company which built many area bridges, schools and hospitals. He loved his work and became the chief engineer. My parents had 13 children, 9 girls and 4 boys.

"We moved many times over the years. We lived in California for three years and moved back to Massachessetts. When my Dad retired, he went back to school and finished his original degree in engineering, and earned two more degrees in Liberal Arts and History.

"My parents traveled frequently to Ireland, they went to Germany for a reunion and to England for another reunion with some of his friends in the military.

"My Dad was truly my inspiration. He taught me to work hard, have strong morals and to always put family first. He was funny, had great sense of humor and wit.

"When I was younger, he talked only a little bit about the war. But then as I grew older he began to talk more about it. He eventually re-united with the men from his crew. He learned to use a computer and was able to find all of them and they had many happy reunions and we were able to meet them and hear first hand of their war experiences.

607

Engineer T/Sgt. Robert B. Schrimsher.

"My Grandfather Is a War Hero." High School Paper written by granddaughter Lindsay Stone Schrimsher.

"On April 3, 1924 a hero was born in Decatur, Alabama. Robert Bibb Schrimsher, my grandfather on my father's side, became a prisoner of war in Germany in 1944. His heroic deeds did not start there, but began way back in the beginning of his training in Fort Benning, GA 1942.

Engineer T/Sgt. Robert B. Schrimsher

"I had always heard the story that my grandpa was a prisoner of war in Germany during World War II. This class assignment to write an article was the perfect opportunity for me to call him in Texas to find out more about his experiences. I am very amazed at what I learned. He asked me to e-mail this paper to him so he could check for accuracy before I turn it in.

"My grandfather will be 79 years old in a couple of months; yet when I called him to ask about his war experience, his memory was as good as if it all happened last year. He sent me some memorabilia and newspaper clippings of his reunions that he has had over the years with other crew members of his downed plane. Here is the story he shared with me last week on the phone.

"Bob was 18 years old when he volunteered to join the Army Air Corps in November of 1942. He said, "That was just the right thing to do." He traveled more in the next two years than anyone in his family had traveled in a life-time. First he was sent to Fort Benning, GA for induction, then to Miami, FL for shots and more induction, then to Amarillo, TX for Air Craft Mechanic School for a few months. His next stop was Harlingen, TX for Gunner School where he said he had to learn to take a big 50 caliber air craft gun apart and put it back together—blindfolded!

"He was then sent to Moses Lake, WA for more training and for his crew assignment. He had requested the 'top turret gunner' assignment and was amazed when he got it. He said that usually when someone made a specific request they got kitchen duty instead. In Washington he met his crew of ten for the B-17 bomber he was to serve on. The pilot was Charles Marcy, the bombardier was Jim Conway (he also operated the chin turret) and the navigator was George Compton.

"Four of the ten crewmen were officers: the pilot, co-pilot, navigator and bombardier. The other six were enlisted men like my grandfather. He was called the flight engineer and his rank was Tech Sargeant. The four officers were up front in the B-17 bomber along with the top turret gunner (Grandpa), and the other five were in the back of the plane at the other guns - the waist gun, the tail gun, the ball turret gun. The ten crew members were moved together to Harvard, NE where they got their first B-17 to train on. It carried ten 500 pound bombs and had thirteen 50 caliber guns.

"They practiced many of the mission maneuvers there and in Kearny, NE also. During one of those practice missions their altimeter went out, and they accidentally crash-landed the plane – "flew it into the ground." They were all OK. So they got a new plane. The pilot always got to name the plane he flew, so he named it after his mother. It was called *'Hey, Mabel!'*. (Grandpa said they belly landed another plane at an English airstrip in early 1944 because the wheels would not come down on about his 14th mission out of England; and when they got a new one it was also named *'Hey, Mabel!'*.

"In September of 1943 they loaded their plane in Nebraska and Grandpa says they "headed overseas." They went to Fort Wayne, IN then on to Goose Bay, Labrador. Their next stop was Ireland, then on to their base in Rattlesden, England which is south of London.

"His first mission was quite eventful. It was Christmas Eve 1943 and his crew was going on their first bombing run. But for some reason he was told to go for more gunner training which would have made him miss the first mission with his crew. He did not like this plan, so he bribed the top turret gunner that was to go with his crew that night. The bribe was a carton of cigarettes, and he then sneaked onto the mission which bombed a chemical plant. When the officers who planned the missions found out, he was in trouble and got 'busted' down in rank. But then they let him go on the second mission with his crew and continue on to fly with them.

"He said his first missions did not make it all the way to Germany because they did not have fighter escorts. They flew over France and shot at "anything that did not have four engines." During this time, the Army realized that they needed to teach several more of the crew members to fly the plane in case of an emergency landing. They taught some of the crew members up front— the flight engineer, the navigator, the bombardier— to fly and land a B-17, including my Grandpa.

"He flew 27 missions over the next 6 months. On a mission day they would get up at 3:00 or 4:00 a.m. and be fed fresh eggs and milk, get their briefing, then fly out at about 7:00 or 8:00 a.m. If they were given powdered eggs and powdered milk, that mean they were not going into battle over Germany. They flew in such tight formation that you could "count the rivets on the plane next to you."

"Later in the phone conversation, Grandma got on the phone and started telling the story of the second time Grandpa got in trouble with the commanding officer. His crew had gone out on a bombing mission and things started going wrong. It was foggy and the pilot, Marcy, was having a problem. He turned the plane around and returned to the air base. When the crew got off the plane and lined up, they were confronted by the commanding officer. He yelled "Why are you not up there on your mission?" Marcy said it was foggy, he got vertigo and he lost his nerve! He said it did not feel right to risk the lives of all his crew with a pilot who lost his nerve.

"The officer ordered Grandpa and the others to form up and join another pilot on another mission leaving right then. Grandpa refused! He said, "By God, I'm not going up there to risk my life up there with anyone but my pilot." The officer threatened to put them in the brig. Grandpa said it would be much safer (with Marcy having a problem today) to be in the brig than if they were up in the air being shot at by Germans. He said more words were exchanged and the result was that the officer backed off; and Marcy went back up with a skeleton crew (only the front 5 including Grandpa) and just flew around for a while to get Marcy's nerve back. After this event Grandpa was busted down from Tech Sargeant to Private, but then they quickly put him back up to Staff Sargeant - just one rank lower than Tech.

"On April 29, 1944 during his 27th mission they were flying a brand new plane - it had only been on three missions. On their bombing run over southern Berlin, a German fighter, a Messerschmitt ME 109, hit them straight on from the front with 20 mm gun fire. The pilot, Marcy, was hit in the hand and lost two fingers; he was also hit in the leg and was knocked out of his seat. The navigator, Compton, was hit in the eye (he lost it) and in the leg and was unconscious. Since the five gunners in the back could not raise the cockpit on the intercom and they saw all the smoke, they immediately bailed out over southern Berlin.

"Bob (remember, he is barely 20 years old) jumped down from his gun to help lift the pilot back into his seat. They were hit at 29,000 feet and began a dive. The co-pilot froze in fear and just grabbed on to the control column. Bob helped the pilot, Marcy, pull out of the dive by using all his force to pull back on the control column with the injured pilot. They leveled out at about 6,000 feet; oxygen tank were burning and so was the plane. The co-pilot was still frozen with fear - this was his first mission! While Grandpa wrapped the pilot's bleeding hand, the navigator, Compton, regained consciousness for a moment just in time to see the situation (with his one good eye). Compton yelled at Bob to hit the co-pilot with a wrench to knock him out and get him out of the way. But the pilot, Marcy, had a better idea - he gave the co-pilot an order. Marcy ordered the co-pilot to take the top turret gunner position in Bob's place, and he ordered Bob to be the co-pilot. The co-pilot obeyed the order and got out of the way.

"As they continued flying north over Berlin, they were hit by ground fire - flak from what Grandpa called an 88 mm 'ack ack gun'. With their wing on fire, they had nothing left to do but bail out. Since Compton was unconscious again,

Bob hooked him up to the static line and threw him out of the plane. The static line is attached to his parachute and makes it open automatically. Then all the rest of them bailed out - Marcy, the pilot; Conway, the bombardier; the co-pilot; and Grandpa. He found out later that all ten survived the bail out and were made prisoners of war. Compton landed in the courtyard of a hospital and was taken into surgery immediately! They gave him a false eye over the next year and fixed his leg. Grandpa just saw Compton and Conway, the bombardier in Florida this month. Conway came home from the war to raise a family of 13 kids!

"There were 62 B-17 Bombers that were shot down that day over Germany. That makes 620 possible prisoners of war, not including the fighter escorts. The Germans had an organized system of processing prisoners of war. Bob was taken on a train kept in the basement of the penitentiary in Berlin where the 'Unter Officer' asked him in perfect English, "Are you hurt!" Grandpa was covered in blood and hydraulic fluid and really looked bad. He said he was OK and the officer asked again, "Are you sure?"

"He was interrogated over the next several days as to the kind of plane they were flying and the mission target. All he was taught to say was his name, rank and serial number. He could not say that the mission target was the marshalling yard where new trains were coupled together and sent off. The Germans sent him by train to Frankfort, Germany for more interrogation and then by train to Stalag XVII-B in barracks number 29. Yes, just like the old TV show, Stalag 17! It was in Krems, Austria.

"He spent the next year in this POW camp at the base of the Alps. He said the American POWs were not allowed out of the compound, but the Russians, Italians, French and other nationality POWs were allowed to go out to work in the fields. This was a privilege since those who worked in the fields got much better food than those who were forced to stay in the camp compound. The compound held about 2000 Americans and a lot more prisoners of other nationalities. Grandpa said they were all confined within a very small space - "maybe a couple of acres."

"Due to the fact that the Americans had the reputation for escaping, the Germans would not let them outside the camp. Grandpa said that the Germans knew that the Russians, Italians, French and others were content to sit the war out in a prison camp, but the Americans wanted to fight. Inside the camp the Americans arranged an escape committee. If a person had an escape idea they had to come to the committee first to see if it would be allowed. They all had to report to roll call outside the barracks everyday, even in the deep snow.

"They would do little things like mess up the roll call so the Germans would not have an accurate count. They also stole a bike. Grandpa said the guards were not monsters; they were old men. But Grandpa said you would be shot to death if you tried to go through the barbed wire fence and escape. On very cold days, they would huddle all day under a blanket in the one bunk that four men occupied. He said that the Geneva Convention (which Germany had signed) saved him from the kind of horrible, unspeakably torturous experience that the Americans had in the Japanese POW camps. His main trials were not enough food and the cold.

"He was a Prisoner of War for about one year in Stalag XVII-B until he was liberated on May 8, 1945 by part of the Third Army, 13th Armored Division led by General George Patton. The Germans knew that the war was ending and that the Russians were coming at them from the east while the Allies were moving in fast from the west. They did not want to just sit there, so for the last 18 days of Grandpa's imprisonment, the Germans marched them along the Danube back toward Germany. They would march all day and sleep on the ground at night. Remember, it is still cold in late April in the shadow of the Alps. They were in the woods just outside Braunau, Austria when the Germans realized time had run out. Grandpa said, "The Germans left us there and the Americans came, liberated us and took us into Braunau, where they put us up in a mill that produced aluminum."

"The liberating soldiers had D-bars which were rich chocolate bars that they gave to the POWs. Since the men had been eating thin soup and maggot filled potatoes for a year, the rich food made them very sick. After the liberation, three men died from eating too many donuts. It may sound funny now, but all the POWs were then put on strict diets that allowed them to eat only certain portions of certain foods.

"The freed POWs were taken to Le Havre, France where they stayed in a tent camp called Lucky Strike. After having his name pulled out of a hat, he caught a flight on a C47 to a French port and then traveled on a hospital ship, the USS Argentina, to Boston's Camp Miles Standish. I was surprised to learn that he was not discharged immediately; he went to Georgia and Florida and worked briefly as an MP and in supply. Finally they let him go back to his Mom (we all called her Momma Dot years later when I was a baby) and his two sisters in Alabama. He remembers that they gave him $300 when he got to the States, and part of that money was supposed to get him home.

"During the last few minutes of our conversation over the phone, my grandmother had to get on the phone and finish the story. She said this was the most he had ever talked about his war experience. He didn't want to keep talking so long and said, "I don't dwell on it." Grandpa's reunion in Florida early this year was the first time he had seen Compton since Grandpa had to throw him out of the plane over Berlin - unconscious and injured. Grandpa had made contact with Marcy on April 29, 1976 (the anniversary of being shot down in 1944) and made contact with Conway some time later. He keeps up with all three of them now. Speaking of anniversary dates, when Grandpa returned from the war, he married Louise and they had my father on April 29, 1951. So April 29 has both good and bad connotations in our family.

"Sometimes it is hard for me to understand why it would be so difficult for someone to talk about a very big and important experience. But after the talk with my grandfather, I now have a better understanding. There are some things you just do not want to keep remembering over and over.

Radio T/Sgt. Abe Farah.

By son David Farah:

"My father was born July 6 1920 in his child hood home on 63rd Ave. In S.E. Portland. He and his siblings attended Arleta grade school (as did my brother and myself) and went on to graduate from Franklin High School.

"His father owned a small shoe repair shop. Dad chose not to work there, but did odd jobs to help out the family, he was very devoted to his mother and helped her as much as he could.

"He worked as a grocery clerk at a national food chain. in his spare he liked to lift weights. They were so poor , he had to go down to the local car wrecking yard

Radio T/Sgt. Abe Farah

yard and get old car axles w/wheels in place of regular gym weights. When the car axles no longer worked he obtained truck axles, he also did some amateur boxing and won many Golden Gloves competitions.

***

Transcripts from Abe's war diary;

"First mission, December 30, 1943. Ludwigshafen, Germany. This was the factory of IG Farben Chemical Works, Dyes, etc. 9 hour flight. Heavy flak. Friendly fighters escort were P-51's, P-47 and P-38"

"March 3, 1944. To-day our target was to be Berlin. We were woken very early this morning for this raid. We took off in the very early hours and it was very cold outside. We took out over the Channel and headed for the Holland coast for our course to Berlin. As we got a little way over the coastline, something happened that was worse than a nightmare.

"I still don't know the reason for it but every bomber in the sky started turning around and also our own formation. There were at least 800 planes turning around at the same time and crossing over and under us. Bombers were colliding with each other and two bombers hit head on just in the back of our ship which shook us violently. They blew up and pieces were flying all over the sky. *"Hey! Mabel"* was really in the middle of things and twice nearly was run into. God was with us that day and brought us home safely. Two crews of our squadron are missing. Planes were crashing in the North Sea and men were bailing out by the dozens. The worst part of this ordeal was that many men bailed out into the water and in the North Sea a guy freezes to death in less than five minutes. Three of our guys were picked up in a dinghy and were found frozen to death. It was 54° below zero to-day and brother that's cold. They counted this as a mission even though we did not go to our objective. What happened to-day was worse than any mission I've been on yet."

"March 9, 1944. To-day's flight wasn't counted as a mission because we had to abort in the middle of the Channel. We took off at 9:00 a.m. this morning and the weather was bad. We took off through the low clouds and flew up to 12,000 feet and the overcast was really thick. We finally got into formation and followed our Group half way across the Channel and then our no. 3 engine went out and so we turned around and headed for home.

When we got over the field only one wheel would go down half way. We called the tower and they advised us to go back over the Channel and drop our ten 500 # bombs and return to the field for further instructions. We dropped our bombs and came back over the field. The tower advised us to go to Honnington and to crash-land our ship. We flew over to this field and circled for two hours waiting for instructions.

"At 3:30 p.m. we were given the clear signal to come in. Eight of us braced ourselves in the radio room and waited for the crash. We were given a chance to bail out but we preferred to ride the ship in. We were all tense and I thought of many things during those few seconds before the crash. The ship finally hit and the whole ship shook violently and came to an abrupt stop. We didn't waste any time in getting out and run like hell. The ship didn't catch fire, thank God. Fire trucks, ambulances photographers were on hand waiting for any trouble that might have come.

"After all the excitement had passed we got our things off the ship and put them in another ship and flew back to our own base. Our ship *"Hey! Mabel"* was wrecked completely and will never fly again. She has fourteen missions to her credit and was a good ship. God brought us down safe and sound without anybody getting hurt. Our crew now has to wait for another ship. This makes our second crash-landing; once in Harvard and once here. I hope this don't become a habit."

The last entry in the diary was dated April 27, 1944. Two days before Abe was shot down over Germany and became an prisoner of war.

"Rocket gun installations in France. To-day we got up at 4:30 a.m. and had our usual breakfast and then to the briefing room. Our target was to be fifteen miles into the coast of France to knock out rocket gun emplacements. We flew around England for two hours getting into formation and then headed over the coast line toward our objective. As we entered over the enemy coast we were met by heavy flak. We flew over the target but didn't drop our bombs because we couldn't see the target. All this time the flak was terrific and we made another run on the target and also this time we didn't drop our bombs. We continued on our way out over the coast toward England and dropped our bombs in the Channel. This mission was plenty rough even though we didn't go very far into enemy territory. Flak is my greatest fear and we had plenty of it to-day, believe me. We lost one ship from our Group and it was their first mission. We got back to the base at 12:30 p.m. God surely is watching over us. I now have six missions to go."

***

Saturday, April 29, 1944. By Abe Farah as told to Richard Nelson. *The Walad Arab* magazine, August 1956.

"They talk about the luck of the Irish, but take it from a former GI named Farah, the Irishers don't have a corner on the market. Luck and the kindness of the good Lord are the only reasons I'm still around today.

"It started back in November of 1942. I was twenty-two years old then, and plenty ripe for some kind of military service. It was a pretty grim time for America, as you'll remember, and like most other guys my age, I wanted to do my part. I had tried to enlist in the Navy and Coast Guard, but I was turned down by both these services. High blood pressure, they wrote on my medical report. It looked like I was going to spend the war fighting the battle of the shipyards. Then I got notice to appear for an army physical. To tell the truth I wasn't very anxious to get drafted into the infantry, but I didn't worry much about it, because of my high blood pressure.

"That's where I got fooled. Imagine my surprise when the medic finished my exam, gave me a big grin, and said, "Sound as a dollar, son. You're in the Army, now." Well, it wasn't quite that quick, of course, but it did seem like no time at all before I was getting my basic training as a radio-gunner in the U. S. Army Air Corps.

"After basic training came final training, and assignment to a fighting unit. I was sent to Harvard, Nebraska, where I joined a crew manning B-17's ... the famous Flying Fortresses.

"Now, this is where the Farah luck got its first workout. One night we were on a training flight in a B-17, flying about 8,000 feet over the Nebraska farm lands. I was in the radio room, trying to stay awake, with that throbbing roar of the four big engines lulling me to sleep. Suddenly the plane seemed to lurch in flight. There was a peculiar, grinding screech, and the roar of our engines audibly

615

changed pitch. In my ear-phones, I heard our pilot, Chuck Marcy, yell something like "Hang on!" and I did, hard. Then there was another crash, the real thing this time, and I was thrown face-first against my radio. That was the end of my fine Arab profile. It was also the end of our training ship.

"Later, in the hospital, I found out what had happened. Three thousand feet is normally a safe altitude when you're flying over the Nebraska prairie lands. But it seems that there are one or two Nebraska hills that reach up a bit higher. One of these managed to get in our way, and we hit it. Or, to be more accurate, we grazed it … bounced off the top of it, losing one of our engines, and then we came down a mile away in a corn field.

"The plane was a total wreck. Fortunately, my nose could be salvaged. We spent a week in the hospital for observation, but as it turned out, no one was any more seriously hurt than I'd been. After being released for active duty, our crew was assigned to Squadron 710 of the 447th Bomb Group, stationed at Rattlesden, England.

"Before we left the United States, we were given our combat bomber, another B-17, which we named *"Hey Mabel,"* in honor of our pilot's mother. *"Hey Mabel"* was a sweet ship. We had a chance to get well acquainted with her on our flight from the United States to England. That ferrying flight managed to give us several bad minutes, but our troubles had nothing to do with the ship itself. Somehow or other, we got lost.

"We had taken off from Goose Bay, Labrador, with enough fuel for eleven and a half hours of flight. When ten hours and forty-five minutes had passed we could still see nothing but sky and the Atlantic Ocean. Nobody could figure out where we were. According to our navigator, we should have flown over Ireland several minutes ago. But all we could see in any direction was that slate-gray ocean, reaching out to the edges of the sky.

"I don't know what the other guys in our crew were thinking then, but I was remembering what I'd heard about the temperature of that North Atlantic ocean. It was so cold that you could only live about five minutes in the water. Believe me, I wasn't looking forward to ditching.

"Several more minutes slipped by, with our four big engines gulping fuel at a frightening rate. And just when it seemed that there was nothing left for us but a forced landing in the water, our navigator caught a glimmer of green against the gray of the eastern horizon. It was Ireland, and not a minute too soon.

"We made a bee-line for the nearest landing field, which was in the vicinity of Belfast. We dropped our flaps and landing gear and came in without so much as a waggie of our wings, and it was well we did. When the pilot switched off his engines after landing, there was just fifteen gallons of fuel left in the tanks-enough for less than one minute of flying time. If we'd tried to circle the field even once before landing, we wouldn't have made it.

"The hop from Belfast to our new base at Rattlesden was uneventful, and in a short time we were up to our necks in war... flying daylight precision bombing raids against German-occupied territory, and into the heart of Germany itself.

"We were on our way to Berlin one clear March morning in 1944. Our squadron was part of a flight of between 600 and 700 bombers, all cruising at about 20,000 feet. We had just cleared the English Channel, and the occupied French city of Le Havre was below us. The Nazis had their ack-ack tuned up to concert pitch that morning, and the smoke from flak bursts was like a layer of cloud formation just beneath us. "Polack," our feisty little tail-gunner from Chicago, was giving us a running commentary on the action that was going on behind us. "The Krauts are really pourin' it on," his voice told us over the inter-com. "There's a Fort from the Hundredth Squadron goin' down ..." There was silence for a moment, then: "Eight chutes opening ... guess two of ‹em -won't make it ..." More silence, while we thought about the two men out of that crew of ten who would never see home again . . "Couple more turnin' back to England Polack reported ... "One of 'em's makin' smoke ..."

"He was interrupted by a jolt that rocked the whole ship. I was nearly thrown off balance, but caught hold of a bulkhead and held on. "We just took one someplace," our pilot was saying. "Anybody hurt?" Rapidly, the crew reported over the intercom. No one was injured, but we still had troubles.

"Hey, I feel woozy," complained our waist-gunner, a guy we called Nick the Greek. As soon as he said it, I noticed a fuzziness in my own brain, and my breath was coming fast and heavy.

"Damage to the oxygen system," our engineer chimed in. I heard Chuck 'Marcy, the pilot, swearing under his breath. "That's the end of this mission, then," he told us. "Let's go home."

"Abruptly, the *"Hey Mabel"* pulled up, out of formation, and turned west, to England. Soon the Channel was beneath us again, and we all began to breath easier. That is, we breathed easier until our co-pilot tried to lower our landing gear. That's when we found out just. how much damage the flak had done. Our left wheel dropped about halfway into landing position, and stuck. The right wheel didn't even budge.

"Over our base at Rattlesden, we reported our damage and received our instructions. We were to fly out over the Channel again, dump our bomb load into the water, and then head for an emergency landing field which had a strip of soft turf especially for crash-landings of the type we would have to make. But when we arrived over the emergency landing field, they wouldn't let us come in. Our plane was loaded with gas for the long flight to Berlin, and we had to circle the field until most of it was gone. That took from ten in the morning until 4:30 in the afternoon. It was a long six and a half hours, believe me.

"Finally our fuel tanks were almost empty, and we bellied in. Chuck did a beautiful job, the *"Hey Mabel"* settled into the turf as smooth as a mallard into a duck-pond. We were all braced and in the safest parts of the ship, so no one was injured. But our biggest fear was fire. The ship had barely ground to a halt when we were piling out of the escape hatches and running in all directions. There was no fire, though … our luck hadn't let us down.

"Although we'd come through the crash-landing safely, the "Hey Mabel" had taken too much, and never flew again. And so our crew enjoyed a week's rest, until a replace ment ship was ferried from America. The new ship was a real beauty, a B-17-G, the newest heavy bomber in the air, and were we ever proud of her. We named her "Hey Mabel II," and there we were, back in business again.

"By this time I was counting my missions, looking forward to the time when I'd be ready to return to the States. Bomb crews had to fly 30 missions before they were eligible for non-combat duty. We all dreamed of getting back home soon, and as the missions were flown and checked off, it began to look as though we'd make it with no more trouble. Our missions were rough, but we always came through.

***

"Then came our 25th mission. We were flying against Berlin again, in one of the biggest raids of the war. I felt uneasy as we droned over Germany toward our target. On previous raids, we had always run into the stiffest German resistance over Berlin. The flak was always the thickest there, and the Luftwaffe intercep-tors were almost fanatical in their attempts to protect the capital city. Often they would fly through their own flak in their attempts to get at us, and more than once German planes were shot down by German anti-aircraft fire.

"We were nearly over Berlin when the reports started crackling over the ra-dio;. "Bandits above us." "Hundreds of 'em." "Looks like the whole blasted Luft-waffe!" The enemy interceptors were already formed and waiting for us, several thousand feet above our flight level. They looked like swarms of angry bees, waiting to pounce from above and below hundreds of puffs of dirty-white smoke were breaking like kernels of exploding popcorn … The Nazi flak was tuning up to welcome us.

"I manned my fifty-caliber machine gun and waited for the bandits to jump us. Ahead of us, I saw group after group of the German planes peel off and dive on the lead formations of our bombers. Planes began going down all over the sky … some burning, some pinwheeling out of control, some disintegrating in a furious explosion when enemy fire penetrated their bomb-bays.

"Then we were settling into our bomb-run … the bombardier's voice droned over the inter-com, directing the pilot's line of flight. We never finished that run.

"Customers!" our tail-gunner yelled, and I looked up to see them swarming down on us, guns winking fire as they came. All over our ship, the big fifties started chattering. One big Junkers 88, a twin engine attack bomber, suddenly filled my gunsights and I swiveled to keep my tracers pouring into him. He was starting to smoke when he dropped out of my line of sight. I pulled the guns up again, firing burst after burst as the bandits hurtled in on us. Then our ship was shuddering as the enemy fire chewed into us, and abruptly our two port engines were burning.

"Party's over, guys!" the pilot yelled, "hit the silk!" I didn't have to be told twice. I ripped off my oxygen mask, squirmed down out of my gun turret and bolted out of the radio room, bound for the nearest escape hatch. A crash behind me made me glance around to see the radio room demolished by a flak burst ... a hit that would have been fatal for me if I'd still been in there.

"Then I was at the escape hatch, fumbling for my parachute rip cord, and when I had it firmly in one hand, I leaned out into space. Never having jumped before, I felt a momentary panic that every first-timer probably feels: "Will the chute open?"

"I was pretty sure this one would. It was brand, spanking new. In fact I had just been issued this chute in trade for an old battered one that had been kicked around the radio shack for weeks. The slipstream had hit me like a truck when I leaned out. I felt momentarily dazed, then I was remembering what they'd told me about parachuting from a crippled plane. "Count to ten, slowly," the instructor had said ... "Then yank the ripcord."

"That might be all right at a lower altitude, but I bailed out at 29,000 feet. I knew that if I took time to count to ten, I'd be sound asleep from lack of oxygen before I could pull the cord. I didn't relish that thought, so I just leaped into space and yanked the cord, practically in one coordinated motion.

"There was a stunning jolt as the parachute smacked open above me. Then I was floating, with no sensation of moving downward at all. I was really feeling the lack of oxygen, now. I remember twisting in my chute harness, trying to watch the rest of that huge air battle over the city, and then I lapsed into unconsciousness.

"When I came to, I had dropped about fourteen or fifteen thousand feet. The ground seemed much closer, and I could see that I was going to come down in a suburb of Berlin ... an area with several small homes and farms.

"At about 10,000 feet, the pilot of a German Focke-Wulfe 190 fighter plane spotted me and began circling slowly around me. He waved at me and 1 waved back, almost glad of his company. He was so close at times that I could see his lips moving, and I realized that he was radioing his headquarters to tell them approximately where l'd come down. Then he waggled his wings and banked away from me and was gone. I was sorry to see him go. A parachute jump is a mighty lonely experience.

"I wasn't really scared, during my descent. All I could think of was my mother, back home in Portland, Oregon. I could see her puttering around in her kitchen and I wanted more than anything on earth to be able to talk to her now. But then the earth was rushing up to meet me, and I saw that I was going to land in a plowed field. At one corner of the field I could see a group of about ten civilians, holding what looked like rifles. One of them was watching me intently through binoculars. I got so interested in them that I forgot to roll into the dirt when I hit the gound. I hit pretty hard and one ankle buckled under me. That was my second and final injury of the war … a painfully sprained ankle.

"While I struggled out of my chute harness, the group of civilians advanced on me cautiously, holding their assorted weapons ready. I knew there wasn't a chance for me to get away from them, so I decided to ignore them.

"That didn't work for long, though. In a few minutes they were surrounding me, and when I got a look at the expressions on their faces, I decided that maybe I'd better not ignore them, after all. One of them, a big, beefy character, stuck his rifle in my middle and demanded, "Habes du Pistole?"

"I don't speak German, but I caught the word "pistole" and shook my head, indicating I wasn't armed. Then they all began yammering at me. One of them, a woman, was crying angrily and I got the impression that someone close to her, one of her children, perhaps, had been killed in the bombing recently. The big character said a lot of things, most of which sounded like "Amerikanischer Schwein," and then, after he'd worked himself up a bit, he gave me a nasty back-hand across the face. Almost simultaneously somebody kicked my behind, and I began to wish very hard that I was somewhere else.

"The worst was yet to come, though. After they were through showing me how sore they were at me and every other American flyer, one of them came forward with a long length of rope, one end of which was tied in a makeshift noose. When I saw that noose, I was really scared. I began trying to reason with them in English and Arabic and everything else I could think of, but that only made them madder. And then they put the noose over my head and began dragging me determinedly toward a grove of trees at one corner of the field.

"Well, I thought it was all over right there. And I guess it would have been, except for that blessed luck of mine. I was pulling one way on the rope and the ten of them were pulling the other way, and I wasn't making much headway, believe me.

"Then, out of the corner of one eye I saw a German Luftwaffe private, in full battle dress, come pumping along the country road on a bicycle. I was never so glad to see anybody in my life. At any other time, that Nazi on a bicycle would have looked sort of ridiculous, with his rifle slung over his shoulder, and his gas mask and hand grenades dangling from his belt, but right then, he looked like Lawrence of Arabia.

"Quick as lightening he was off his bicycle and charging across the field, waving his rifle at us. There followed a long, heated discussion between the civilians, who insisted they were going to hang me, and the Luftwaffe private, who insisted they weren't. 1 guess it was a good thing for me that Hitler had taught his people to respect a uniform, because eventually that one lone private won out. The last I saw of those civilians, they were still standing in the field, all waving their fists at me as we rounded a bend in the road.

"After that, I had a long, painful walk of about nine miles to the nearest Luftwaffe airbase. There, the *Lieutnant* in charge dutifully noted my name, rank and serial number, and turned me over to a black-shirted Gestapo man who proceeded to search me roughly and thoroughly. I had no idea what he was looking for, and I don't think he did either. At any rate, he finally let me go and I was herded out of his office and into a big storeroom where about 75 other American prisoners were already assembled.

"We spent our first night in Germany in that room. The Germans assigned one little soldier who looked like he was no more than 12 years old to stand guard over us all night, and when morning came, that poor youngster was practically hysterical. We had a lot of fun, keeping him scared and on edge all night, but we didn't really enjoy ourselves. A few of our men had been badly hurt and the skimpy medical attention they had received from the Germans wasn't enough to make them comfortable.

"When morning came, we were all packed into a bus and driven to a railway station, where they put us on a train for Frankfurt. After an uneventful ride, we arrived in Frankfurt and were taken directly to the *Luftwaffe* interrogation center there. At the center, we were split up into groups of a dozen each and shut into tiny underground cells. Those cells weren't built to hold a dozen men and we had to take turns sitting down.

"Then, after a wait of about an hour or so, a guard appeared at our cell door and took one of our men. They disappeared down a long, dimly lit corridor. About thirty minutes later, the guard returned alone, took out another man and took him away as he had the first. It was a cute psychological trick and it made all of us plenty nervous. We had no idea what was happening to the men who were taken one by one from our cell and our imaginations were sure working overtime.

"But finally it was my turn. I followed the guard down the corridor and up to the ground floor, where he ushered me into a small office which held a German in civilian clothing. Apparently he was with the Intelligence Service. He wanted to know all about my squadron, where we were based, how many planes we had, and on and on. But I was feeling stubborn and told him nothing but my name, rank and serial number. He pleaded, threatened, and finally dismissed me.

"Then I was taken to another cell, where I spent the rest of that day and night. For supper, I had a chunk of stale bread and a cup of ersatz tea. I was beginning to feel very much like a Prisoner of War. In the morning, I was taken to an assembly base and placed in a group of five other Army Air Corps sergeants. The Germans marched us under heavy guard to the railway station and there we were loaded into boxcars. Twenty-five Americans were put in each boxcar. We were placed in one end of the car, then barbed wire was strung across the center of the car and seven Germans with rifles and a mounted machine gun occupied the other end of the car. Those guards were with us from the time we pulled out of Hannover until we arrived at Stalag 17, four days and three nights later.

"It was a rough trip. We couldn't move around much, and constantly staring into the muzzle of that machine gun got plenty nerve-racking. On the second night of our trip, we were side-tracked for several hours in the railroad yards of a large German city. That night the British came over on a raid and for two hours bombs fell all around us. The freight car shook like jelly when those big block-busters went off nearby. Luckily for us, the British weren't too accurate, that night, and the yards weren't hit. When the raid was over, we pulled out and were on our way again.

"Finally we arrived at the small Austrian town of Kreins. Here we were ordered out of the boxcars and formed into squads for marching. It was about three in the morning, and raining with a grim, steady drizzle. We slogged for two miles up a muddy road, and then, just as the first light of false dawn was breaking in the east, we arrived at the barbed wire gates of Stalag 17. I took one look at those squat, ugly buildings, the desolate mountains lurking above us in the faint, cold morning light, and my heart sank. So this was Stalag 17, the place where I was going to spend the rest of the war … they can shoot me right now, I said to myself. This place must be pure hell.

Abe's post war bio;

Abe Farah was released from the service in 1946 and returned to his home of birth, with his mother, father and siblings. He stayed close to home until his mother passed away in 1949. Abe met his future bride Luella in 1950. They dated for three years and married on June 28th, 1953 at St Marks Lutheran Church in Portland, Oregon. Abe became a deputy sheriff for the county of Multnomah, city of Portland in 1952.

They had their first son, David in 1954 and second son Douglas in 1956. Abe had an outstanding record as a police officer for 25 years. He retired at age 55. Abe enjoyed family activities, was an avid reader and loved to play poker and go to Las Vegas … he favored blackjack.

***

Acknowledgements:
Scott and Hugh Marcy, sons of pilot 1Lt. Charles H. Marcy
Kathy McKee, daughter of bombardier 2Lt. James J. Conway
Lindsay Stone Schrimsher, granddaughter of engineer T/Sgt. Robert B. Schrimsher,
David Farah , son of radio-operator T/Sgt. Abe Farah

CHAPTER 44

447TH BOMB GROUP
710TH BOMB SQUADRON

Type: B-17G • Serial: 42-31217
MACR: 4249 • Air Base: Rattlesden

Aircraft flying # 4 lead squadron was hit by enemy fighters and fire started in left wing. Aircraft remained under control for about 45 seconds and then exploded in mid-air.

Missing Air Crew Report # 4249

Pilot: 2Lt. Harold M. Paris, 0-812301, POW, Hapeville, GA

Co-Pilot: 2Lt. Robert W. Allen, 0-817813, POW, Patchogue, NY

Navigator: 2Lt. Michael G. Gannon, 0-702112, POW, Long Island City, NY

Bombardier: 2Lt. Edward G. Jekel, 0-700106, POW, St. Louis, MO

Engineer: Sgt. William F. Clarke, 33586583, POW, Philadelphia, PA

Radio: S/Sgt. Lewis R. Pohll, 39326305, POW, Cildquia, OR

Ball-Turret Gunner: Sgt. Harry E. Woodman, 16008671, POW, Elkhorn, WI

Left Waist-Gunner: Sgt. Oscar M. Siegel, 33268747, POW, Curtisville, PA

Right Waist-Gunner: Sgt. Frederick J. Kirnan, 32489890, POW, Quebec, Canada

Tail-Gunner: Sgt. James J. Hanley, 31325577, POW, Hartford, CT

10 POW

Crash Site: east of Eggenstedt, 16 kms w. of Magdeburg – Germany
Time: 11.30

Pilot 2Lt. Harold M. Paris.

"I was born on December 13, 1921 in a three room tenant house to a 17 year old mother, Mary Ina Jones Paris and a 25 year old father, Harold Lawrence Paris, who farmed for a living in old Milton County, Georgia, between the towns of Ocee and Alpharetta. I am told the doctor came to deliver me at the house and charged $ 10.00. Twenty-one months later the same doctor returned to deliver my sister, Myrtle Cleo Paris, but this time charged $12 due to the "inside plumbing."

"I started school at Harris Street Elementary school in East Point, Georgia, after my dad began working in a furniture store in Atlanta, Georgia. In the fifth grade we moved back to Ocee, Georgia where I attended Ocee Elementary School until I went to Milton High School in Alpharetta. During my senior year at Milton, my parents once again relocated to East Point so in order to finish high school I alternated staying with both sets of grandparents who lived in Alpharetta. I graduated from Milton High School in May, 1939. I attended Green Leaf Business School for eight months and was hired as a shipping clerk for Berkeley Pump Co. until I decided to enlist.

"I had asked for airplane mechanic school, but was sent to radio school and later to Florida for radar training. I then decided to apply for pilot training. When I went to take my

physical, I was too tall and too skinny, but the sergeant giving me the exam added five pounds to my weight and took 1 inch off my height. This was in Boca Raton, Florida. For preflight training I was sent to Montgomery Alabama. For primary training I went to Arkansas.

***

"The mission of April 29, 1944, our second mission, was an all out bombing mission to Berlin. It was foggy when we took off and we flew around a while to get into formation before crossing the Channel. By the time we crossed into Germany we ran into heavy flak and German fighter planes were everywhere. I lost three engines and had to drop my bombs to try to keep up with the formation. It was then that my right waist gunner called to say that the inside right engine was on fire. As this was our last engine, I proceeded to order my entire crew out. My tail gunner was barely able to squeeze through the escape door because he was shot through the shoulder and leg. He was the only one badly hurt, but was able to return home thanks to some good German doctors who tended to him. I was the last to jump out.

"As I was coming down in my parachute I saw a police motorcycle coming down the road in my direction. When I landed and disentangled myself from my chute, a German policeman was standing nearby pointing a gun at me. My crew was scattered across the German countryside and we were all taken prisoner.

"I ended up in Stalag Luft 3 which was a camp for pilots and aviators run by the Luftwaffe. Airmen were treated better than most POWs but not treated well by any means. The "Great Escape" had occurred about a month before at this camp and so things were tight! I was finally liberated exactly one year later on April 29, 1945.

***

"After my return to the States I attended the High Museum of Art, got married for the first time and started teaching art at Campbell High School. I attended the University of Georgia in Athens and received a Bachelor of Fine Arts degree. Later I received a Master's degree in Art Education and became Assistant Director of Art Education for Fulton County Schools, Atlanta, Georgia. I Retired after 34 years as Director of Art Education for Fulton County Schools. I am blessed with two children, six grand-children, seven great-grand- children with one more on the way (in June 2015)!

Co-Pilot 2Lt. Robert W. Allen.

By his son Joel Allen.

"Dad was born an orphan in 1918, he believes in Jamaica, NY (a few miles east of New York City on Long Island) although we don't know for sure it was Jamaica and we don't have any birth certificate. We don't know who his biological parents were either; I tried to learn the details of his adoption but the records are basically sealed. We do know his adoptive parents were Joel Nott and Fanny Walton Allen. Mr. Allen was a trained artist and portrait painter, a fairly well known one in New York

Co-Pilot 2Lt. Robert W. Allen, with his wife

City circles and at the height of his career painted portraits of some of the most well known citizens of the city. When the depression hit in 1929 I got the feeling that much of his business dried up and they moved out to Patchogue, NY – a small village about 50 miles east of New York on the south shore of Long Island. That is where Dad went to high school, met his future wife Louise, married and started to raise his family after the war. Dad's adoptive parents were caring and kind people and brought up Dad as if he were their own. He never had anything but nice things to say about them."

625

"Dad graduated from Patchogue High School in 1937 and soon after went to work for Patchogue Electric Light - a small local utility. He went to high school with some of my Mom's brothers and that is how he met Mom. He worked at the utility until the war started and at some point joined the USAAF, was commissioned as a second lieutenant and began his training as a pilot in Texas. He trained at Foster Field (near Victoria, Texas) on the AT-6D aircraft and later in Avon Park, Florida on the B-17F version – all in 1943. He earned his wings at the end of 1943, and was sent over to fight the war. And as Dad liked to say, the sum total of his combat experience was ½ a mission – over but not back."

***

2 Lt. Robert Walton Allen shared his WWII memories with family on Jan 1, 1996.

"Saturday, April 29, 1944. The mission started at about 6 o'clock in the morning. We were queued up to takeoff. We had a good breakfast with bacon and eggs and then got into our airplanes and all lined up. It was dark, but blue indicator lights were on, so we could see the airplanes in front of us and those around us."

"We were all concerned about the possibility of actually getting off the ground with the bomb load that we had. When I arrived at the base on about April the 6th I was sound asleep in bed when I heard a tremendous blast. I grabbed some pants and rushed outside and asked what had happened. They said a plane hit a tree at the end of the runway and exploded and that was the end of that plane, the crew and everything else. Then again, later in that month, but before April 29th, they were loading bombs on to one of the B-17s on the hardstand, which was like a parking spot for a B-17. They dropped a bomb; it went off, and the whole airplane went up and a couple of maintenance people were lost."

"But anyway, we taxied out. When the B-17 in front of us got off the end of the runway and we could see that he was going to clear everything, we gave it all four throttles and we took off. We got to 200 feet and we looked around and we couldn't see anything. We were in a solid overcast. We had a certain pattern to fly: so much time in this direction, so much time in that direction, climbing at around 500 feet a minute."

"So round and round we go, climbing at the same time and finally we got together in a formation, a group which consisted of four squadrons - each squadron putting out seven planes. In our particular squadron we were number seven, which made us "tail end Charlie" for our squadron."

"We were approaching Germany and pretty soon we started hearing and seeing flak; not a real heavy barrage that you would get if you were over a target area. I heard a loud crack like a live firecracker had been fired. I looked out my side window - I was the co-pilot, and there was a big black clump of smoke, where the flak had exploded. A flak shell when it explodes, lets loose 1500 small pieces of steel. If they hit an aircraft, or are close enough to it, they can inflict a tremendous amount of damage. We did take some hits but nothing serious."

"Then Bill, up in the top turret said, "We got bogies at 12 o'clock and 1 o'clock and 2 o'clock." He had really good eyes and pretty soon I looked around and I noticed them out our cockpit window. They came up and got in front of us and six of them peeled off. They were about 2000 feet above us and came down through our formation, kept on going right down through it and disappeared out of our sight, go down, do a loop, come back up, roll and shoot from beneath. One of them seemed to have our plane picked out as the one that he wanted to get."

"Now the tactics by the 8th Air Force were to fly a "tight box"- and that meant there were 10 machine guns in every aircraft and if you got all your airplanes in close and you had 21 airplanes with 10 machine guns, you had 210 fifty caliber machine guns spitting out eight or nine hundred rounds per minute and anybody who wanted to fly through that really had a lot of guts. That was the theory, but the theory didn't work too well, because we didn't fly as good a formation as we should and we didn't have a good airplane. The number of missions a bomber had flown was indicated by a bomb painted on the side of the cockpit. Now this plane had bombs on it, from here to New York!"

"Now to get back to the German Messerschmitt. He had zeroed in on us. I could see him and I felt at the time, "Gosh I wish I had something to shoot. I haven't got a darn thing to shoot." And here comes this Messerschmitt diving in on us. He's got a 20 millimeter canon in his nose shooting through the prop and it's going wink, wink, wink, and all of the sudden there is a big flash in front of my nose – and one of the "explode on contact" shells had hit the astrodome. The astrodome was a plastic dome and it was used for the purpose of celestial navigation. That shell exploded and the German fighter by that time is going past us. We were flying probably 250 MPH and he was probably flying close to 400 MPH so we had a closure rate of over 600 MPH. So you didn't have a long time to look at him. It was whoosh, and he was gone. This guy lifted his left wing and went over the top of our right wing and when he went by, he turned around in his aircraft and he looked at us and I'm looking at him. It was a millisecond that it happened, but I distinctly saw the pilot in the Messerschmitt."

"It wasn't long after that, that I heard a sound that sounded like some gas was escaping. I called on the inter phone to Bill in the top turret. I said, "Bill would you come down and check the deck. I hear something leaking down here and I don't know what it is." He came out of the top turret with his walk-around bottle of oxygen, looked around but didn't see anything. Just about this time now, as he's down amongst us, a shell hits our top turret. It wiped it out. It broke up all the glass, the frame and it destroyed the gun. I think for that reason Bill's been sending me a Christmas card every year since."

"The further we went the worse it got. At the time of the attack, we were

60 miles off course from the main stream of planes who were 60 miles north of us. And the German radar controllers down on the ground, must have said, "Achtung! Look at those crazy Americans! There are 21 "ships" out here all by themselves!" So they feasted on us. They got 12 of the 21 airplanes. I don't know if it was flak or fire from the fighters, but they set our tires on the undercarriage on fire. We got that under control by just lowering the wheels. Lowering the wheels slowed the plane up by about 40 MPH and that didn't help. Then we got the wheels back up again and then I noticed that the oil pressure and the number 4 engine was going down. So I shut that down and we feathered the prop, and then the number 3 was going down, and we shut that down, also feathered the prop."

"We finally got to the point where we had only one working engine left and the bail out order came. We heard that the tail gunner was shot through the neck and he was out, unconscious. The two waist gunners had gone back because they couldn't hear him on the inter-phone when the pilot had called everyone to check in. They found him and dropped him out first. We then were at 20,000 feet."

"The bombardier and the navigator went out and then it came our turn. Pilot Harold Paris said; "Come on, go, go, go." To get to the escape hatch, you had to go back off the flight deck and go down three or four little steps. You are then in a cramped space and the door is open and you sit down on the edge of it and swing your legs and then when you are ready, you give a little push on the sides and out you go. So I got down there and I was just about to push off when I looked down and saw that the straps around my legs were not clipped in. When you jump in that condition and the chute opens you pop out of the chute harness like a banana out of a banana peel. So I hooked them on and jumped."

"My chute opened. You hear lots of stories about getting yanked and banged around but my chute opened up gently. After all the noise that you are subjected to in a not insulated bomber with four big engines I was just floating down in death-like silence - just like in a graveyard."

"I came down in farm country; great big areas of green fields. This was April and in Germany the farmers had got everything planted. I got down to about a thousand feet when I heard voices and saw an old farmer with two kids running across the field. Then I heard a "putter, putter, putter" and there was a black Model A Ford – a two door sedan - coming down a little road right next to the little field I was going to land in. The Ford stops and at least an admiral or a brigadier general gets out, because he's got the most gorgeous uniform you ever saw. He had a Sam brown belt, a pistol and a rakish hat."

"He gets out, and also started running across the field. He got to me a few steps ahead of the farmer and his kids. He was threatening with his pistol and I didn't know whether he was going to use it on me or use it on them. He stopped and the farmer backed off. Then he came over, undid my harness, got me up to a walking position and walked me back to the car. Of course the farmers latched on to the parachute - pretty nice silk. "

"We got back to this little Model A Ford and he put me in the back seat. In the front seat, on the right hand side was a civilian in a black coat and black Hamburg. It turned out that he was the mayor of this little town near where I was shot down. Both of them couldn't speak English and I didn't speak any German so we didn't have any long conversations. All I could say to them, was 'Luftwaffe, Luftwaffe', because we'd been told that if we were ever captured by any civilians you should let them know that you wanted to be taken to a Luftwaffe base as there was a certain amount of respect shown between the German Air Force and the British and the American airmen."

"They kept me in 'jail' for that one night and called the Luftwaffe base in a nearby town. The next day a sergeant came out from there and escorted me into Eggenstedt, 16 km. west of Magdenburg. We took a streetcar along with the civilian population. We rode on that through town and people got on and people got off. I sure as hell wasn't going to run anywhere and everybody knew that, because you just stuck out like a "sore thumb" in your flying clothes. I was taken to a cell in a jail in Eggenstedt. The other officers from my plane were there as well as airmen from other planes that were shot down, though I didn't know it at the time."

"The next day a couple of German airmen with wings on and wearing the Iron Cross came into my cell and one of them said, 'I am the pilot who shot your aircraft down,' he might have been telling that to everybody. He noticed I had a G.I. issue watch on. He said; 'That's not your watch, that's your government's watch, so I'd appreciate it if you would take it off your wrist.' So I took it off and gave it to him."

"A few days went by until they had assembled enough prisoners for a train load. They put us on a train and took us to Oberursel a small suburb Frankfurt; the site of the German air intelligence, where they interrogated captured airman. We got on this train that was also carrying a bunch of German soldiers on R & R coming back from the Eastern front. They'd been fighting the Ruskies and now they were coming home to their beloved city, and their wives and their daughters, and all the rest of that good stuff. A friend of mine Jesse Kendler could speak pretty fluent German and he started talking with one of these people and they seemed to be getting along pretty well. We got to the outskirts of the city of Frankfurt. And if you have ever seen pictures of a city that has been leveled - Hiroshima for example - this is what Frankfurt looked like: just bare chimneys sticking up with smoke and rubble all over the place. These soldiers came home and now they could hardly find their street, much less their address on the street."

"I looked over my shoulder and one of these soldiers was looking out of the window – his nose almost touching the glass - and his face was getting redder by the moment and tears were pouring down his cheeks, and I really felt sorry for him. I don't remember whether he was armed or not, but I was getting ready to dive under a seat, because the logical reaction to what he was seeing and being on a train with a bunch of guys that have committed this crime was; I'm going to get those bastards right now and shoot them"

"Frankfurt on Main station was a great big steel structure with glass on the top of it all, which provided a lot of light. It had many different tracks. We pulled in there and they had to set up a line of guards to keep us separated from the civilian population that was also using the Frankfurt station. There were a lot of civilians there and they clearly didn't like us at all!"

"We were marched us up to Oberursel for interrogation. We didn't know if they were going to use other than ordinary means to get us to give them information. When they finally called me and my turn came, I went into a room and was told to sit down in front of a table, behind which sat three officers. We had been told of course, that according to the Geneva Convention, the only information that you had to provide was your name, rank and serial number. So we went through that procedure and then he started asking me questions, like 'Were you with the 447th Bomb group?' and I refused to answer. And 'Were you flying at 23,000 feet?' and again I didn't say anything. After more of this, finally one of them said, 'Lt. Allen we know everything we need to know about you. For starters your home town is Patchogue, New York – you went to Patchogue High School there.' He went on to tell me I was flying tail end Charlie on the 710th Squadron of the 447th Bomb Group and that we'd taken off at such and such a time, at such and such an altitude, our radio call sign was Chairleg and information about our bomb load 5,000 pounds per aircraft. They knew the whole schedule of our particular mission."

"The German intelligence system was very thorough, very complete and the American society is an open society. It's not a society that hides things. If anybody wanted to know where any place is in this country today, all they have to do is get a road map – and all the cities and population districts are all there. Everything is available. The German intelligence community had no problem obtaining American newspapers. These would cover graduations, (whether high school or flight school) and it would say, 'Graduating Robert Allen of 8 Wiggins Ave. Patchogue, received his Air Force wings in Albany, GA on Dec. 22, 1943' and even such little bits of information, however insignificant, were filed away. Of course the information about the actual mission itself, namely flight times, and altitudes - that sort of stuff - was picked up by listening to our radio transmission and by use of radar. The altitude we were flying at on that day was also available. The German fighter pilot that went right by us would have reported, 'I hit these guys at 21,000 feet' so that's no big deal. Our bombers had identification numbers and if you were to look at our aircraft, it had on the tail a big square box with a K on it, and they knew that the K signified that the plane was from the 447th Bomb group. The planes could all be identified by squadron and by group."

"The thing that they would like to know, of course was, "How far advanced are you guys in getting a jet fighter operational? We wouldn't have known that, not at our level. When I got in a POW camp, one day in summer, we saw an airplane up at 10,000 feet going like crazy (fast) and we couldn't see any means of propulsion. We had never seen or heard of a jet. But it was a German Messerschmitt 262."

"About a day later they put us on a train and shipped us northeast to a town called Sagan, about forty miles from the Polish border and the same distance from Breslow, Poland. This was a brand new camp, because they had shot down so many American airmen. There were four compounds in the camp and in the compound I was in there were around 2500 American airmen - officers only. All in all, they had 10,000 airmen in this one camp."

"Our breakfast would consist of some ersatz coffee which tasted like it was made from rubber bands, some toast with a little margarine. Then at noontime they would come into the barracks with a big bucket for each room that contained barley soup. At night we would take what they'd given us - potatoes for example - and we'd take some of the things from what we got in our Red Cross parcels and we would make a meal with that."

"The Red Cross parcels - we got one parcel every two weeks - contained food and five packages of cigarettes and these constituted the 'currency' of the camp. Some enterprising boys had set up the 'food exchange.' If you wanted to sell something, you would take it over there and put a price on it based on the number of cigarettes you thought it was worth."

"The camp was pretty nice in the summer time. The Germans provided us with athletic equipment. They had also provided us with musical instruments and we formed a band and did concerts. But then when the cold weather came, we were allotted just so many briquettes a day to keep the room warm and there wasn't enough. So we were walking around with probably 6-7 layers of clothes just to keep warm. We had been moved into a barrack that was made out of "green" wood. When you looked down you saw the ground through the cracks in the floor. So one enterprising guy says, 'Hey look, there's one thing we don't have any shortage of: we've don't have any shortage of G.I. soap. We can take this fairly soft soap, pack it in, fill up all the cracks and no more cold air will come blowing up through the floor.' We said 'great idea'."

"We went over to the boiler room, where the soap was stored and we brought it back. We didn't tell everyone else what we were doing, just our particular room. We packed it in there, and sure enough, it did a good job. But then we would get rainy days, and we'd go out and walk around, or have to go to a "john" and come back with dirt on our feet and wet boots. Pretty soon the soap began to get awful, slimy all over the floor. It was a mess, black and slimy, and if you weren't hanging on to something and took a big step, you'd probably wind up sitting in it."

"We had a high ranking officer of the US Army in our compound who had flown a mission as an observer and was shot down. He was a West Point man and when he got into our camp and looked around at his fearless aviators, he was appalled at their appearance - unshaven, dirt under fingernails, smelly because they hadn't had a bath in months."

"He called an inspection and went room to room in our barracks. When he got to our room, he asked, 'What the hell is that?' and someone answered, 'Sir that is soap'. He said he wanted it cleaned and would be back in a couple of hours to inspect. He also said, 'I want to see that floor scrubbed, immaculately clean. I never want to see anything like this, in this room or any other room in the camp.' So we went and got scrubbing brushes, and a bucket and tried to scrape it up with a knife. Well, the more we put water on it and tried to scrub it, the more suds we got. So now we had suds 4-5 inches up off the floor. We then looked for rags and towels and to make a long story short, we finally got it all cleaned up, and passed the inspection."

"About the beginning of January, at Stalag Luft III at Sagan, the Germans were always conscious of the fact that the Russians were getting closer and closer. We had a band and we would go to the boiler room because there would be steam and heat and we would practice with our instruments there. A German guard came in one time and we had about eighteen musicians blowing their brass instruments loudly, and he came in and said, 'You guys have to stop playing so damn loud or the Russians will be able to hear you.' I didn't know whether he was half serious or just joking."

"Later in April the Germans decided once again that the Russians were getting too close to Nuremberg, and the 10,000 prisoners they had there were bargaining chips they could use, if it came to a point of surrender. So they put us on the road. We marched from Nuremberg south to a place called Moosburg. We walked 18 or 20 miles or so, and when we would come to a small town and our German guards would say, 'You can sleep in that barn over there, or sleep over here or whatever, but whatever you do; if you see any German troops get out of the area as fast as you can.' They were, more or less, just 'babysitting' us rather than actually keeping us under tight control. We wound up in Moosburg which was a camp designed for maybe 3000 prisoners, but now we had prisoners coming to this camp from all over! All the barracks were taken and they put us in tents."

"On April 29th, we heard small arms fire, and we didn't know where it was coming from. But we looked out and we could not see a German guard anywhere - no goons in the towers, or anywhere around. This camp had the usual camp configuration with barbed wire all around it, with goon towers on the corners and maybe if a side was a long run there was a goon tower in the middle. But there were no guards. Even the German Nazi flag that had flown from the administration building was gone. And the next thing you know, a Sherman tank knocked down the gate and in come these guys from the 14th Armored Division and we were pretty glad to see them! That was the day that we were liberated."

"We stayed around Moosburg for about a week while the army organized transportation to take us to a city called Regensburg and from Regensburg we were put on DC-3s and flown out to Le Havre, France and the camp there called Camp Lucky Strike. When we got there the doctors looked us over and we began to eat some decent food. My weight went from 160 pounds down to just 120 pounds during my POW days. One guy was so enthralled with eating good American food that he managed to put away 40 doughnuts."

"Then after a week of that, they put us on a liberty ship and took us back to New York. It took us about ten or eleven days to get across. Coming home on a liberty ship was a lot different than going over on the Queen Elizabeth. One time, down in the bowels of the ship, I'm sleeping in a hammock, and a destroyer, not too far away set off a couple of depth charges. Of course sound travels through water really well, and we heard the loud 'boom' and so we thought we had been torpedoed. So everybody is jumping out of their hammocks landing one on top of the other in a melee on the floor and then running for the companion ways and up the ladders to get up on deck and see what's going on. The sailors were really enjoying this: all these intrepid airmen, fearless guys that had done this, that and the other thing, and here somebody sets off a little depth charge and they are ready to man the life boats. But outside of that incident the trip home was pleasant. It was in the middle of May and it was sunny; we had good weather."

Son Joel recalls;

"Dad then returned to Patchogue, got his old job back at Patchogue Electric Light and convinced Mom to quit college (she had completed 3 years in route to becoming a teacher) and come back to Patchogue where they got married in June of 1946. And as was the custom in those days for many in our country, they almost immediately started a family and I came along in August of 1947. They lived in a very small apartment in the center of town and then moved into my Grandma's (on Mom's side) house so they could save a little money while they built their own house. They had someone dig a big hole, pour the foundation and frame the house and then Mom and Dad did pretty much the rest of the house. Both were very handy – particularly Dad who was a fine carpenter and woodworker."

"Three sisters came along and Dad worked while Mom stayed at home and took care of the house and us. At his peak Dad was making about $6,000 a year at the utility and eventually realized that he wouldn't be able to provide for his family in a manner that suited him and thus at the end of 1959 he packed us up and moved us down to New Orleans, La. He had obtained a traveling sales position (wire and cable) with Anaconda – at that time one of the larger and more reputable companies in the United States. To me it was a bold move; on the map New

Orleans is 1,400 miles from Patchogue; in reality it was a million miles away in terms of culture, ethnic makeup, services, schools, politics, etc. It was also a time when our country was going through the painful and sometimes violent process of racial integration and the deep south was the epicenter of that battle."

"When I look back on it I realize that Mom and Dad were both brought up during our country's long and deep depression of the 30's, were used to dealing with problems and I believe that those experiences helped them take on the challenge in the first place and then handle the transition well. They had a vision for the family, made the move and it paid off. They had another son in 1961."

"Dad prospered in his career and with Mom's help managed to get us all through college and marry us all off. They retired to a beautiful home out in the country north of New Orleans and lived there until 2005 when they were effectively evicted by the disaster known as Hurricane Katrina. They then moved up to Maryville, Tennessee to be near sister Cindy and that is where they passed away: Mom from Parkinson's disease at age 83 in 2007 and Dad at age 92 in 2011. They are buried side by side in the veteran's section of the Grandview Cemetery in Maryville."

"From my experience both my parents were, in their own way, remarkable people. Mom was athletic (an all Suffolk County, NY soccer player in high school), feisty at times, competitive, tough-minded, patient when needed, impulsive at times, kind and very resourceful. She took care of me better than any nurse could after I was seriously injured in an auto accident and laid up in plaster for six months. She had her own way of thinking, a way that I could never understand, but she was right as much as anyone. I remember she was dead set against the Vietnam War at a time in our country when her view was not popular. She also liked to go to the races, bet on the horses and play the stock market; she was always pretty much up for anything. The last four or five years of her life she suffered the horrible ravages of Parkinson's disease and faced it with an equanimity and courage that I will never forget."

"Dad was more an engineer type; he took his time, planned his actions carefully and was pretty much a perfectionist at everything he was good at. And he was good at a lot of things; he was an excellent carpenter, photographer, tennis player and musician. I still have his trombone, given to him by his father at the height of the depression and costing about $50 bucks - at the time a veritable king's ransom. It is a classic King Liberty model (the one Dad said was played by America's most famous Trombonist – Tommy Dorsey) and still sounds great. Dad was very patient with me, taught me the game of tennis, how to play the baritone and trombone (which I still do), took me on many of his sales trips throughout Mississippi and Louisiana and got me through college. The latter was a Herculean task as I was a goof-off as a student and I'm sure that with my poor grades he was tempted to cast me adrift; money was tight and he had four children lined up after me for their turn."

"He didn't though and for that I am forever indebted to him; eventually a light bulb turned on somewhere in my head and I made it through. We used to team up as doubles partners in our local tennis leagues in New Orleans, played many matches together and had some memorable victories. He also took me to my first baseball game at the most famous ballpark in our country - Yankee Stadium. I have been a baseball nut ever since and my wife Lidia and I have traveled our great country from stem to stern visiting ballparks and the communities in which they reside. So our parents, (Lidia's as well) although long gone, are still alive in our hearts and are still providing us with joy and great memories."

Navigator 2Lt. Michael G. Gannon.

By daughter Rosemary Gannon.

"My father was born in New York on June 23, 1923. He attended grade school, graduated from Bishop Loughlin High School and enlisted in the Army Air Corps in January 1942. He graduated from the Air Force Advanced Navigation School of Ellington Field, Texas on December 4, 1943. He served in the 477th Bomber Group flying strategic bombardment mission out of Rallesden, Suffolk England. Michael along with the crew of the B-17 were shot down over Germany on April 29, 1944 and held as Prisoners of War. He was liberated on April 29, 1945. His military service continued until 1968, when he retired from the U.S. Air Force Reserve with the rank of major.

Navigator 2Lt. Michael G. Gannon

"In 1946, Michael started a career in law enforcement with the New York City Police Department. He retired as a Lieutenant from the NYPD in 1966 and joined the Scottsdale Police Department, retiring as Chief of Police in 1988. He was married in 1949 to Anna May Lennon and together they raised six children. Michael was a Rotarian and active in several veterans and military associations through out his life.

"My father valued education, and while military service followed his high school graduation; he ultimately continued his education and graduated from St Mary's College of California with a Bachelor of Arts in Public Management in May 30, 1977.

"He was inducted in th Arizona Veterans Hall of Fame Society in 2005."

Engineer Sgt. William F. Clarke.

From the Eighth Air Force Historical Society – Chapter Philadelphia

"Shot down during a bombing mission on Berlin, Germany, 29 April 1944. Though wounded himself after bailing out, he carried one of his crewmembers that had a broken leg and was severely wounded until they were surrounded by enemy soldiers and captured. After being captured, Mr. Clarke continued to protect his wounded comrade. While loaded on a train headed to Frankfurt Germany for interrogation, German soldiers boarded the train, rifle butts first, striking everyone they could. Clarke put his crew member in the over head luggage compartment to prevent further injuries.

"Was interrogated in Frankfurt and sent to Stalag 17B where he was a POW for a year. Toward the end of the war the Russians were advancing south and so the Germans evacuated the camp and headed south. Some 200 sick stayed behind at the camp and were liberated by Soviet forces on 9 May 1945. Some 75 men attempted escape from the March columns, but were recaptured and returned to the camp. On the forced march south under German Guards, the rest of the camps 4000 enlisted men marched 18 days, 280 miles to a wooded area outside Braunau, Austria. While camped outside in the woods, Mr. Clarke and some other men went down to the Inns River on water detail under German Guard. When he thought the time was right, Clarke made his move and dove into the icy cold water.

"After making his way across the river he waited till dark and moved along the rivers edge until he came across some men of the 13th Armor Division, 3rd Army, building a pontoon bridge. He listened for a while till he recognized them as Americans. Mr. Clarke says, "You can always tell an American GI by the way they talk." Mr. Clarke told these American soldiers that he was an escaped American POW. He was interrogated by a Msgt. Bill McCarthy the First Sergeant of the 13th. They're where no officers present at the time of this interrogation because they had been killed the day before. The 13th Armored was and is known as the "Black Cats."

"Clarke told Msgt. Carthy that there were some 4000 POWs in the woods across the river. The 13th was planning a river crossing and was unaware of the POWs there. Prior to any crossing the area would be shelled, but because of this new information the shelling did not take place. A day later the crossing took place. The camp in the woods was liberated on the 3rd of May 1945.

"Mr. Clarke and a few men from the 13th Armor went into the village and overran some German troops there. They took a small bus, loaded it with food, (meat and bread) and took it back to the POWs that were camped in the woods. The POWs were starving.

"He then did not hang around to be repatriated, but headed north and met up with the 300th Infantry and was with them when Salzburg was taken. He made it all the way back to his unit in England where he was interrogated by the CIC and made to sign a statement never to discuss his escape. Then he was sent back to the States where he showed up on his mothers' doorstep in Philadelphia PA., wearing the same clothes he had worn for a year as a POW, escaping, making his way across Europe to England an ocean crossing, and hitchhiking a ride from New Jersey to his mother's home in Philadelphia.

"After being honorably discharged from service, William went to work as a civilian for the government at McGuire AFB, New Jersey, for 35 years where he held several positions including X-Ray Technician, Quality Control Inspector and Weight & Balance Authority. Mr. Clarke along with his wife of 62 years are original owners in Levitton where they raised five children.

Radio S/Sgt. Lewis R. Pohll.

Undated account by Lewis Pohll

"Shot down on mission to Berlin, Germany, April 29, 1944. Held in detention and interrogation camp, Frankfurt, for nine days. Transported, with large group of other prisoners, in closed box car. Arrived in Kriens, Austria, and marched to Stalag 17B. Poor clothing, eating and sleeping conditions. Experienced quite a few occasions of being woke up with a bayonet and forced out of barracks.

"We went on a forced march in April of 1945 from Stalag 17B to the north. The group I was in was forced against the Danube river south of Lenz, Austria, and held under rifle and machine gun pressure when a large group of Jewish men, women and children were pushed south by German Soldiers who shot or bayonetted any of the people who fell down and could not get on their feet or be carried by any of these people. I saw over a hundred bodies when we were marched out of there.

These two things I have been reliving more within the last three years. It bothers me and my wife considerably when I will wake up in the middle of the night – yelling and shaking. I am getting more nervous and reacting by losing my temper too much. Especially against my wife. It is hurting our marriage and I hate that I am getting more depressed and remote because of it. It seems as if I cannot do anything right anymore. I have a hard time remembering things I should do and when I am to do them. Memory of names is very hard.

From Brother Bill Pohll

"When Lewis returned from the war he decided to locate in Seattle, Washington. He started to work for the Seattle Transient systems. Two weeks after his return he met and married a young lady, he had quite a bit of money but when the money ran out so did his wife. He married for the second time and had one daughter from this marriage that ended after about one and a half years. Lewis then moved to Klamath falls and went to work in the saw mills.

"He was an avid hunter and fisherman. He married for the third time but this also ended in divorce after about 2 years. Lewis was a very troubled man. He came from a family of six and had very devoted parents. The family tried to help him as much as they could. He married again for the fourth time to Dolly Lewis who was the love of his life.

"Lewis suffered nightmares at night and Dolly was a great comfort to him. They were very happy together. It was very humorous to see the two of them, in their seventies, both suffering from emphysema, wearing their oxygen tanks, on a train to go see the sites in New York. Lewis was in a very happy marriage. Dolly passed on and Lewis again became troubled. He lived about three years after she died and when he became ill I put him in an assisted living home and the last day of his life I had visited him and brought him ice cream and fed it to him. I left for a while and then received a call that he had passed on.

"He was buried from the church he and Dolly attended for years and was laid to rest beside his beloved wife.

Right Waist-Gunner Sgt. Frederick J. Kirnan.

By daughter Sandy.

"Fred Kirnan was born in Parishville, New York on March 26, 1921. As a child, the family home caught ablaze and burned to the ground. After this tragic incident, the family decided to move over the border to Canada, specifically Huntingdon, Quebec. Fred attended St. Joseph's Catholic School in Huntingdon. Before entering the military he worked at the Huntingdon Woolen Mill, which was one of the largest employers in town. While working at the mill he met his wife, Jeannette Lalonde.

"Fred tried to enlist in the Canadian Army but was denied due to issues with his feet (while escaping the fire that claimed his childhood home, his feet had become badly frost bitten). This didn't deter Fred, as he was later accepted into the American Army Air Corps.

"After the war, Fred returned to Huntingdon and resumed working at the mill. He decided to move to Syracuse, New York around 1947 after some friends had moved there. After relocating to Syracuse, Fred began working as a buffer at Fisher Body Division, which was part of General Motors. At the time working conditions were very poor, and Fred decided to join the United Auto Workers (UAW) Union. He became chairman of the union and was able to negotiate many changes that benefitted the workers, including better pay and safer working conditions. Fred was Chairman for years, and was later honored by having the plants' snack shop named "Kirnan's Corner." He retired from the plant in 1977 and devoted all his time to the business that he had started years earlier in 1958, Kirnan Real Estate, Inc.

"Fred also helped many people obtain homes who otherwise were denied this opportunity. He joined the local Board of Realtors as well as the Town of Salina Assessment Department. He had a desire to help everyone, including those who were struggling as well as the affluent. He made a great impact in the Syracuse, New York area and touched many people's lives.

Frederick J. Kirnan recalls;

"I was shot down on a bombing raid over Berlin, Germany on April 29, 1944 at noon time. Our B-17 Bomber was hit by ground fire shortly after we had dropped our bombs We had heavy fires burning in the bomb bay area and the radio room. Due to the damage we were required to fall out of formation and had no protection from our group. We were immediately attacked by German fighters. We fought a 12 or 15 minute battle with these fighters. They inflicted heavy damage on us. They knocked out 2 of our 4 engines and also did extensive damage to our gun turrets. We fought them until all our ammunition was used up.

"I was ordered to bail out. I did and German Folk Wolf 196 fighter machine gunned me on the way down. He did not hit me but he put alot of holes in my parachute. I landed real hard on top of a building and my parachute pulled me across the roof injuring my knees. I removed by parachute and placed it behind one of the chimneys so it would not be seen. I concealed myself and waited, hoping I wasn't seen and I would wait for darkness but unfortunately within minutes crowds of people started forming around the building and calling me "Flieger Gangster" (Flying Gangster).

"After approximate fifteen minutes they were calling me from the ground demanding that I stand up with my hands up in plain view. The person addressing me spoke perfect English. I did not move or answer him. Shortly thereafter approximately 12 civilian men came on the roof. They were all armed with shot guns and rifles. I put my hands up and they attacked me with the stocks of their guns. They beat me unconscious. They smashed my face and busted my nose real bad. I had to have plastic surgery years later to reconstruct my nose.

"When I came to I was lying on the ground by a stone wall approximately 150 feet from the building I had landed on. The only clothes I had on was my electric suit and socks. The electrical suit is like a pair of long johns with electrical wires. They had stripped me of all my clothes, including leather pants and jacket, shoes, wrist watch and ring.

"The group that attacked me on the roof was standing approximately 25 feet from me and behind them there was a very large crowd of people. The group that beat me ordered me to stand back against the wall and face them. I complied with their orders. I stood up with my back to the stone wall and faced them. They started shooting at me. it was firing squad style but none of the bullets hit me. I knew there was something wrong because their range of fire was so close that they couldn't miss me unless they wanted to.

"During this episode the regular German Army and three armored vehicles arrived and pushed their way through the crowd and took control. They placed me in an armored car and headed out of the area. I was told by the regular German army later that this group that did the shooting at me took pictures to show off to their girl friends and wives, they did not try to hit me.

"I was taken to the Burgermaster's house, something like our Mayor or the Justice of the Peace here. I think the name of the City was Brandenburg. The Burgermaster cursed me calling me an American flying gangster and after cussing me out he ordered me out of the house. The military took me to jail. I think the name of the city was Magdenburg. When I got to the jail there was a large crowd of people, they were screaming American gangster. The military forced a road through the crowd and took me into the jail.

"The jail was under the control of the Luftwaffe. I stayed there for two days. On the third day a German air force officer came to my cell and informed me that I would be removed from the jail and taken to a train after dark and I was not to speak to anyone: I was to remain silent on the trip. He also informed me that all the prisoners received the same orders. Anyone disobeying an order will be shot on the spot.

"We were moved that night. Twelve prisoners were moved, both American and British. I did not know any of the prisoners. We were taken to a railroad station and put on a train, it was a passenger train with all the windows in our car painted black. I was told in the car that the painted windows was for the protection of the prisoners.

We were taken to Frankfort on the train for interrogation. When we arrived at Frankfort we were marched on the street towards the interrogation center. During the march we were attacked by Hitler Youth and civilians. The German Air Force guards lost control but managed to get us into a church until the military came to our aid to take us to Dulag Luft, the interrogation center. I was interrogated several times. The interrogators were very intelligent and professional. They spoke perfect English. I was never threatened or abused at this Center. I gave my name, rank and serial number only.

"After approximately one week I was removed from the interrogation center and taken by train to Kriens, Austria. I spent approximately ten days and nights on the train, it was a freight train with no toilet facilities. We were under the guard of the German Army. They had almost as many guards as they had prisoners.

"I spent a year at Stalag 17-8, Kriens, Austria. I never received any medical treatment from the Germans. I injured my neck, shoulders and back during my confinement at Stalag 17-B POW Camp during an American bombing Raid. I suffered a lot of pain with my knees in the camp and also after I returned home.

"This is the first statement I have written on my experience on being shot down. it's over 51 years ago now and my mind will not let me forget it.

***

Acknowledgements;
Joel Allen, son of co-pilot 2Lt. Robert W. Allen.
Rosemary Gannon, daughter of navigator 2Lt. Michael G. Gannon.
Bill Pohl, brother of radio-operator S/Sgt. Lewis R. Pohll.
Sandy Kirnan, daughter of right waist-gunner Sgt. Frederick J. Kirnan.

CHAPTER 45

447ᵀᴴ BOMB GROUP
711ᵀᴴ BOMB SQUADRON

Type: B-17G • Serial: 42-97501
MACR: 4253 • Air Base: Rattlesden

"Aircraft blew up immediately after I bailed out.
Fire throughout the cockpit uncontrollable."

Engineer Sgt. Joseph Kotulak, Missing Air Crew Report # 4253

Pilot: 2Lt. Elmer. D. Johnson, 0-811210, KIA

Co-Pilot: 2Lt. Robert C. Stevenson, 0-810250, KIA

Navigator: 2Lt. Adger S. Matthews, 0-704569, KIA

Bombardier: 2Lt. Leslie E. Walker, 0-749602, KIA

Engineer: S/Sgt. Joseph P. Kotulak, 13005271, POW

Radio: S/Sgt. Orville K. Springstead, 36559177, KIA

Ball-Turret Gunner: S/Sgt. John B. Frisbie, 38367805, KIA

Left Waist-Gunner: Sgt. John A. Hoegen Jr., 31083077, KIA

Right Waist-Gunner: Sgt. Douglas J. Irvine, 39616202, KIA

Tail-Gunner: Sgt. Thomas E. Sproat, 13013130, KIA

9 KIA, 1 POW

Crash Site: 6 miles ne. Of Helmstedt, Germany
Time: 11.30

Engineer S/Sgt. Joseph P. Kotulak.

Letter from Joseph Kotulak to mother of radio-operator Orville Springstead dated July 21, 1945.

"Dear Mrs. Springstead,

"Hardly know where to begin, as you already realized it is very hard for me to write knowing it will sadden you, but I fully realize it may also give you some very slight satisfaction knowing just what did occur on our last flight. I had hoped and planned on paying all of the families a visit, but now I know I'm not quite up to it physically as well as mentally, perhaps though in the future sometime it may be possible.

"Our last flight was our tenth raid, up until then we had had no casualties, although we did come back badly shot up on some occasions. The flight itself was a normal scheduled mission, up at three a.m., breakfast and then down to the briefing room for full particulars of the flight.

"We were all a little apprehensive when we discovered the raid was to be on Berlin, but our crew had an unusual gift for horse play, so our spirits were soon back to normal. Take-off, flight across the Channel, testing of guns and a constant flow of talk over the inter-phones was all routine. Although the remarks over the inter-phones were just a little wittier than usual. The tail-gunner Sgt. Sproat, said he felt like a "G. man," because he felt as he were always following us around.

"And so it went, we had a good fighter plane coverage so we expected very little opposition from German fighter planes. Over Berlin we flew through the thickest concentration of flak, we had ever run into. We broke thru after awhile and headed for home, just about then our fighter cover, was called away to help another squadron. At the same time we were hit by about 130 German fighter planes. We weathered the first attack, but Sgt. Thomas Sproat was killed, he never knew what hit him. I felt myself getting warm, so I turned the control knob on my heated suit to a cooler position. Your son, O.K., checked in, saying, "everything O.K."

"On the second and third attacks we lost an engine, shot completely off by the Jerry, planes of both types, ours and Jerry's were going down on all sides, all of the action took place in split seconds. On the fourth attack, I found myself getting unbearable warm. I looked down and found I was standing in a pool of flame, my clothes were all a fire. I bent into the flames for my chute, and burned my face a little, the covering of my chute was afire.

"I looked back at Lts. Johnson and Stevenson, they were getting ready to leave also. I waved by hand, and fell out of the bomb bay, immediately on leaving the plane blew up. Nobody got out, and their deaths were accomplished in the blinking of an eyelash. We all prayed, if our time had come and we had to die, we prayed it would come that way.

"This may all sound harsh and cold to you, but believe me, it was just as hard, in my own way, as it was to you in your way. We were all very close, not because of our experiences, but because we were friends. Everything we did, work or play was done as a crew. Our lives was one constant horse-play, with reprisals and counter-reprisals and the following hilarity. Our work was closely coordinated, we worked as one. I'll always by thankful for their companionship, and I hope it gives you some satisfaction in knowing your son's death was quick without suffering or pain.

"Our first trip to London had been anticipated for weeks before. The day finally came, after a rather hard mission. We all went together as we always had. We joked and laughed on the train, and we talked about what we would do. On arriving we were impressed as we knew we would be, by the sights and subjects we were familiar with at school. We got our rooms, and a tour of the "pubs," and then a sightseeing tour of the town. All the time there was this constant flow of talk. We were all like a bunch of kids on a picnic. I'm afraid I just can't write anymore. So, I hope this finds you in good health, and might I salute a Mother, who had such a fine son.

***

Joseph Kotulak died April 21, 1964, while on active duty at Patrick Air Force Base at the base hospital. One day after of his 44th birthday. He is buried at Arlington in section 35, grave 1362.

Radio S/Sgt. Orville K. Springstead.

From nephew John Springstead.

"When Orville was drafted into the Army in 1942, my father Ivan Springstead Jr., who was two years older than Orville went to Naval Flight School in Oxford, Ohio for flight training and aeronautics. At the time Orville was in training in Utah to be a gunner and radio man. My father became a pilot and captained a lighter than air blimp in the Pacific till the end of the war.

"Ivan Sr. had been in the Army infantry in WWI and was gassed with mustard gas by the Germans in the battle of the Argon Forest. He suffered from lingering effects of the gas throughout his life as well as the

S/Sgt. Orville K. Springstead's grandson at Orville's grave

mental carnage that he had witnessed. When he returned home he became a vegetarian as he could not stomach the image of any creature being slaughtered. He was quite distraught when both his sons entered the war.

"My Grandparents had not heard from Orville while stationed in England for quite awhile. A friend called and said they had been to the movies and during a newsreal prior to the main movie they had seen Orville. My grandparents rushed down to the next showing and in the newsreal as the camera panned down a row on bunks in the barracks they saw Orville.

***

Acknowledgements:
John Springstead, nephew of radio-operator S/Sgt. Orville K. Springstead

CHAPTER 46

447ᵀᴴ BOMB GROUP
711ᵀᴴ BOMB SQUADRON

Type: B-17G • Serial: 42-31124 "Lady Lilian"
MACR: 4246 • Air Base: Rattlesden

---

*"My plane got hit by fighters and flak and we got knocked out
of the formation with several other planes. We tried to reform
to give each other protection from the fighters. One B-17
pulled along side and I could see the waist gunner. Suddenly
all that remained of the plane was a huge orange ball and
pieces of the plane were scattering about. I saw no chutes."*

Tail-Gunner Sgt. Wendell Bourguignon

Pilot: 2Lt. William A. Davidson, 0-686548, POW, Teague, TX

Co-Pilot: 2Lt. Clarence E. Fishburn, 0-748939, POW, Phoenix, AZ

Navigator: 2Lt. John I. Coulson, 0-698666, POW, Arlington, NJ

Bombardier: 2Lt. Allan J. Brady, 0-757648, POW, Detroit. MI

Engineer: S/Sgt. James V. Murphy, 32725616, KIA, Rosedale, NY

Radio: S/Sgt. Charles E. Buran, 16116609, POW, Racine, WI

Ball-Turret Gunner: Cpl. Joseph C. Oliver, 6667036, POW, Cincinnati, OH

Left Waist-Gunner: Sgt. Charles J. Roberts Jr, 3359728, POW, Philadelphia,PA

Right Waist-Gunner: Sgt. John A. Reder, 16081674, POW, Chicago, IL

Tail-Gunner: Sgt. Wendell Bourguignon, 11110414, POW, Providence, RI

1 KIA , 9 POW

Crash Site: Eickendorf, Germany
Time: 11.30

447th Bomb Group, 711th Bomb Squadron (Davidson)
(No caption available.)

Right Waist-Gunner Sgt. John A. Reder.

By daughter Joanne Besonen.

"My Dad was born August 17, 1921 in Chicago. His parents were Albert and Marie Reder. He grew up in the Lakeview neighborhood of Chicago where he lived at 2613 Lawrence Ave in a 2-flat. He was a star athlete at Lakeview High School, excelling in Track and Field, Football and Crew (a rowing sport done on the Chicago River). He graduated in 1939 and went to work at the Hudson Screw Machine Products Company in Chicago as a machine operator. He also played semi-professional football in a league in Chicago. My dad, like so many his age, enlisted in the Air Corps. He went through his basic training in Texas, and was soon shipped overseas. His plane was shot down during a bombing mission and he spent about a year in a series of German prison camps as a POW.

"After the war my dad's life picked up where it had left off. When he got home, there was a big party for him. That is where he met my mom. They knew each other in High School and both families attended the same Catholic church. My mom went to his welcome home party with another man as her date. By the end of the evening, she had broken it off with the "other" guy. Both my mom and dad said it was love at first sight. His parents did not want him to be with my mom. She was an Irish girl, and they thought she was not good enough for him. Those were the attitudes towards the Irish at that time. They had to sneak around for a while, until his parents finally accepted the fact that they were in love.

"He returned to his old place of employment. He and my mom got married within a year. Like many young couples, they started their married life living with the in-laws to save money, and soon after the babies started coming. They quickly outgrew the flat in Chicago and bought a home in the suburbs, where he lived for

Right Waist-Gunner Sgt. John A. Reder

the rest of his life. Although my dad never went to college, he was very successful in his career, rising to a senior management position. He was a self-taught metallurgical engineer.

"We had a large family. My mom and dad had seven children in eleven years. While we were growing up we were never rich but we had a lot more than others. Our hectic house was filled with love.

"When he could afford it, my dad bought land on a beautiful lake in Northern Wisconsin called Twin Lake. That was my parent's paradise. He built a small cabin which was a work in progress right up until he died. All of us kids loved to go up north to the cabin. Many of my best childhood memories are from our summers there. After retirement, my parents were able to live up north for many years from April-October; returning to Illinois for the winters. He loved to fish, and was happiest in a boat out on the lake. He taught all of us kids to love and respect nature. I could bait a hook and take a fish off the hook by the time I was five. My dad started a lake association to preserve his paradise for future generations.

"My dad was just a regular guy who worked hard to raise his large family. He was highly intelligent and had a razor sharp wit. He loved classical music and the TV show MASH. My dad loved to play practical jokes at work and at home. He loved to laugh. My dad had integrity. He provided us kids with strong convictions about right and wrong. He judged people for what was inside them and taught us to be non-prejudicial. He was a fair and honest man whom everyone respected. My dad had many friends who he would give the shirt of his back and was liked by everyone he met.

"My dad seldom talked about the war. I never even knew there was a box of his letters, uniform, pictures and diary until after his death. I think like many POWs he tried to forget. One funny story we were told was of a train ride after being deployed. All the soldiers got drunk on rum. They were hanging off the train and several fell off. Another story was much darker. It was when he escaped a prison camp with another POW. They had to eat a raw chicken in order to survive. They were caught, and his friend was killed. He would never eat chicken again.

Some parts from his diary;

"Shot down over Berlin, Germany, on April 29th at 11:16. Bailed out at 29,500 feet. Evaded for a few hours but finally discovered by dogs. Taken to Helmstedt and interrogated at Dulag Luft. In the cooler for three days. Krauts are clever in trying to get info. Week in hospital at Frankfurt, five air raids. Shipped to Luft 6 at Heydekrug. Fifty men to a car.

"Uncle Joe on the move so we left on July 14, trains to Stettin and prison ship to Schweinemunde. Turned over to Kriegsmarine and put in chains. Another train ride and then a 3 kilometer run in 12 minutes, still in chains and encouraged by bayonettes and dogs. Arrived at Luft 4 on July 12.

"Uncle Joe again, so we start walking on February 8. Walked until May 3 when we took off at Ludow.

Tail-Gunner Sgt. Wendell Bourguignon.

"I enlisted in the Army Air Force because at the time everyone I knew was trying to enlist to help in the war effort. I first tried the Marines, the Navy and then took the exam for the Aviation Cadets. The Marines would not take me because of my little toes. They said I couldn't march. The Navy said I had a hernia. I didn't wait for the Aviation Cadets to call me and I went into the Army Air Force and was sent to Ft. Devens, MA with my two buddies, Hanley and Rooney. Ft. Devens was like a madhouse with people coming in at all hours.

"Prior to my enlistment I had worked as a sheet metal apprentice at Davisville Air Station and I remember one summer I worked for the railroad - painting bridges. What a

Tail-Gunner Sgt. Wendell Bourguignon

hot, smelly job that was. I remember that my mother was working at the Swiss Laundry as a clerk at the time and my father was a salesman for Narragansett Brewery. They were divorced by the time of my enlistment in 1942. I remember my Mother taking me to the bus station for departure to Ft. Devens.

***

"My career as a member of "The Wild Blue Yonder" was short lived - it ended on April 29, 1944 on a trip to "Big B." This was my fourth combat mission.

"My plane got hit by fighters and flak and we got knocked out of the formation with several other planes. We tried to reform to give each other protection from the fighters. One B-17 pulled along side and I could see the waist gunner. Suddenly all that remained of the plane was a huge orange ball and pieces of the plane were scattering about. I saw no chutes.

"So with engines on fire and fire in the bomb bay our pilot ordered the crew to bail out. My assigned exit for bailout was a small hatch near my station in the tail. Next to the hatch were my shoes. During the flights we wore fur lined boots and electrical slippers and when they worked, they kept your feet warm. Europe was cold and at flying altitudes the cold was intensified. We had no heaters and open waist windows - the cold was almost unbearable. In my haste to get out of the plane, I forgot to tie the shoes to my chute. On my exit one boot flew off, so the penalty for forgetting – I limped around for a day with only one boot.

"My heavy flying equipment saved me from serious injury but I injured my back upon landing and could not get up. German citizens were surrounding me, kicking me and hitting me with large poles. A group of German soldiers arrived and took me to a farm house where they searched me and forced me to remove my clothes. Me, standing naked and them taking turns punching me. Fortunately I was able to duck most of the blows. There were also some women present but I didn't have time to be embarassed.

"On our way to a police station a very young American lieutenant was loaded on our truck. He was in terrible shape as he had been shot four or five times and was in shock and shaking as if he was cold. I removed my heavy flying jacket and put it over him. Shortly thereafter we left the truck and the lieutenant. What happened to him is something I frequently wonder about, did he die or did he finally receive some sort of medical attention. All we could do under the circumstances was to try and make him comfortable and hope the Germans would give him medical attention.

"At the police station I saw a waist gunner from my crew. Many other Americans were also being brought into the station. I was told to stand against a rear wall and in this position I was able to see soldiers arriving with some more American flyers. When they would first enter the room the soldiers would be facing me, they would snap to attention and raise their arms and shout "Heil Hilter." I was afraid to laugh - I thought "Jesus, they can't be doing that for me." Later, when we were leaving I noticed a picture of the 'great one' was hanging just above where I'd been standing.

"During transfer from the police station to the railroad station we were placed in the basement so the German civilians could not get us. I believe the railroad station we passed thru was Frankfurt on the Main which is a large complex. The roof was constructed with many panes of glass or I should say used to have many panes. The Air Force bombing days and the RAF at night was really demolishing the cities and towns - everything was in rubble. All you could see was half of houses, piles of debris everywhere.

"We were transported to Dulag Luft, were jammed into cells and then taken out one by one for individual interrogation. We were never provided any food nor water during any of this time.

"Once again we were put into boxcars, standing room only. We spent one night in a marshalling yard as the British bombed all around us. The freight cars really vibrated from the concussions.

"We were then transported to Krems, Austria and Stalag XVII-B. With pieces of flak still in my legs we were deloused, checked for body lice and crabs, and our heads were shaved. Before we hit the shower a POW from some other country would examine us for body lice, and crabs. He sat on a stool and when we stood in front of him he would use a stick and prod around the pubic hair. We were then put into a shower and marched to the main camp. We received no medical care.

"I remember being so cold during the winter. My feet were frozen at times and we wore the same clothes that we had been captured in for the entire time we were at Stalag XVII-B. We slept eight men to a bunk which had slats of wood for the base and straw encased in burlap bags as mattresses. There were plenty of bedbugs, lice, and fleas. Prisoners from other countries were allowed to work outside the camp but not the Americans. The Americans NCOs were separated from the rest of the POW population. I remember that the Russians would throw onions over the fence and we would push and shove each other and dive into the mud just to get them.

"During my entire confinement I was cold, hungry and miserable. I remember standing - freezing - during the many roll calls. When I recall the cold, I can't help thinking of my frozen feet. Did they hurt, especially when they were thawing out. The toes were black and swollen. They would split open. It was hell trying to get around, shoes were out of the question, I could only wear clogs. Fortunately the weather was warming so my feet healed in time for the march.

"I also remember eating watery barley soup loaded with maggots - as we said, we needed proteins. Well, we got plenty. We were also given black bread - filled with wood chips and sawdust and, of course, rotten potatoes which we always had to share within our little groups. I might add that we became very lean and mean. When we received our rations of the bread we would cut it on paper so as not to lose the crumbs. We used to get 1/8th of a kilo and had to divide that between eight men.

"I recall an incident with a Sgt. Frank Grey who was brought into our camp in handcuffs. He was being transported to a civilian prison for causing problems and destroying property. The Germans brought him into the camp, removed his handcuffs and left him for the night, planning on picking him up the next day and continuing on. When morning came the Germans could not find him. We had roll call after roll call. They brought in the dogs but still could not find him. I forget how long this went on, but they finally gave up thinking that somehow he escaped from the camp. I later learned that he had climbed down in the outhouse until things slowed down. He was then moved around the compound and hidden in a hole under one of the barracks. They never found him. I met Frank again in 1949 when we were both in the 307th Bomb Group in Tampa at McDill AFB.

"On April 7th we were notified that we would soon leave Stalag XVII-B. At this time we could see flashes of rocket fire and hear the sounds of heavy bombardment as the Russians assaulted Vienna.

"Prior to the march, discipline became quite lax in the camp. It brings to mind that just before our departure the frenzy of trading and bartering that was going on with the Russian prisoners. My barracks, number 29, was located next to the Russian compound, separated by the guard walkway and warning wire. At first we would throw whatever over the fences, eventually cigarettes, etc. some of which would land short of the mark inside the warning wire. When the guards were not apparently in sight, some brave or extremely desperate Russians crossed the warning wire and made a dash to the fences, grabbed whatever and ran back to safety. After a few more dashes with no retaliation by the guards the whole group charged the fence.

"We traded for knives, cigarette lighters and onions from the Russians. We traded whatever we could. I still remember an instance of one Russian laying on the ground with his head and one arm between the barb wire. He finally reached a pack of cigarettes and was trying to ease away from the wire when some Russian stepped on the wire which was around the guy's throat and was demanding the cigarettes. The one on the ground refused to give them up and his neck started to bleed profoundly when the other guy started jumping up and down on the barb wire slicing into the his neck. He gave up and relinquished his prize. Hunger and greed entices people to do strange things.

"These Russians were a sad looking lot. Dirty, worn clothes. As far as their government was concerned they were expendable and the Germans did not want them. The Russian government refused to recognize their own soldiers. They had no use for them.

"April 8, 1945 we were informed that we would be leaving Stalag XVII-B and would take the scenic route thru Austria on foot. When we left the camp we passed thru Krems and travelled on a narrow road. Two young ladies with their kids said "Roosevelt Kaput." It took some time for that to sink in - the President was dead.

"Further along, somewhere along the Danube, we met up with some young German troops. They looked as if they were in their late teens. They were tired and hot from carrying their equipment and scared. The officer was also young looking. Guess they had a right to be scared - they were on their way to fight the Russians. This was a light infantry squad. Later, as we passed thru a small village, we saw old men preparing to fight. They had armed themselves with all kinds of vintage weapons. When the Americans did come they met with no opposition from these people.

"As the war neared its end the POWs of Stalag XVll-B were forced and expected to march 25 miles per day. At night we slept in fields and, on occasion, in barns. We were told not to try to escape as the civilians would kill us. Some tried and were never heard from. SS troops were everywhere.

"The infirmed stayed behind in the camp but that is another story. There was much rain and it was extremely cold. We tried building some type of shelter but could not escape that cold rain. We were soaked and cold. It was one of their coldest winters.

"Once on a farm I caught a chicken but not until after I chased it so it couldn't run anymore. Being a city boy I was told to twist his neck. I carried him around and thinking him dead I put him down, he let out a squeal and took off. Somehow I did him in (maybe a heart attack) and cleaned off the feathers and stuck him in a pot and boiled him.

"POW William ‹Count' Clarke swam across the Enns River to alert the 13th Armored Division that we were on the other side. This was quite a heroic feat, considering his physical condition and the icy waters. It is amazing that he made it. The Armored Division had no idea we were in these woods and they indicated that they would usually shell a wooded area before moving on.

"At the Stalag XVll-B reunion in May 1997, Sgt. Clark was presented with a plaque expressing our gratitude and admiration for this unselfish act.

"C-47s then came in and flew us to France - Camp Lucky Strike. After a few days hanging around I took off for Paris and found a Finance Office who would give me a supplemental pay. So I stayed in Paris until I spent what money I had and then returned to Camp Lucky Strike. Apparently nobody missed me. While standing in a chow line with our mess kits General Eisenhower came thru the camp. While speaking with several of the former prisoners he told us not to complain to the politicians if we had to sleep on the decks of the ships. A few days later we boarded a ship at La Harve, France bound for New York and 60 days leave.

"Upon completion of the leave I reported to Atlantic City, NJ and I stayed there until it started to get cold. Atlantic City was special - we were billeted in luxury hotels on the boardwalk. It was really great! About all we did was go to some lectures, one I remember was some guy giving us some sort of test for duty on B-29s in the Pacific. I told him what he could do with the paper, I told him I'd already been to war, now he could go.

"Needless to say, I did not take the test. After being there I also observed that when you finished attending the different briefings you were re-assigned, usually to a base near your home. I just sat back and decided they could win the war without me, so only went to a few of the briefings and enjoyed whatever pleasures I could find on the boardwalk. I suddenly realized I was the only one left in my room - everybody else had shipped out. But the weather was still nice, so I did not make any attempt to complete the briefings. When the boardwalk started to empty of people and it started to get cold, I completed whatever it was and was assigned to Grenier Field, NH to some job in operations. I then went thru the motions until my discharge in September 1945.

***

Acknowledgements:
Joanne Besonen, daughter of waist-gunner Sgt. John A. Reder.
Donna Lilley, granddaughter of tail-gunner Sgt. Wendell Bourguignon.

CHAPTER 47

447ᵀᴴ BOMB GROUP
711ᵀᴴ BOMB SQUADRON

Type: B-17G • Serial: 42-31161
MACR: 4248 • Air Base: Rattlesden

---

*"I remember when I was young, he (Sgt. Theodore F. Goobic)
always wore a back brace. One day I asked him why he had
to wear it and he said, because German civilians stuck a pitch
fork in his back several times when he hit the ground."*

Granddaughter Jennifer Nociasta

Pilot: 2Lt. Arthur D. Peper, 0-813772, POW, Spring Valley, NY

Co-Pilot: 2Lt. James R. Hyde, 0-819108, POW, Allendale, NJ

Navigator: 2Lt. Edward G. Connelly, 0-702105, POW, Waldwick, NJ

Bombardier: 2Lt. Francis G. Mauge, 0-701459, POW, Chicago, IL

Engineer: Sgt. Theodore F. Goobic, 6998040, POW, Wilkes-Barre, PA

Radio: S/Sgt. Abraham Cosmer, 36454572, POW, Chicago, Il

Ball-Turret Gunner: Sgt. Henry P. Reilly, 31311291, POW, Lawrence, MA

Left Waist-Gunner: Sgt. Howard McMahon, 18034496, POW, Bremond, TX

Right Waist-Gunner: Sgt. Julius K. Otfinoski, 31325992, POW, Middletown, CT

Tail-Gunner: Sgt. Otis E. Mason, 33634500, POW, Beaufort, NC

10 POW

Crash Site: Gollbogen, four miles n.e. of Zerbst, Germany.
Time: 11.30

Engineer Sgt. Theodore F. Goobic.

By his granddaughter Jennifer Nociasta.

Engineer Sgt. Theodore F. Goobic

"Theodore Francis Goobic was born to Theodore and Anna Goobic on February 24, 1921 in Hudson Pennsylvania. Hudson at that time was also referred to as "Irishtown." He graduated from Plains High School in 1939 and immediately enlisted in the United States Air Corps.

"When he returned home he became a mechanic at the garage that his uncle owned and operated. He became acquainted with my grandmother because she was very good friends with his niece. On Feb.1, 1947 Ted and Heather Bell were married and bought a small home on Bald Mountain in Wilkes Barre Pa. (My Grandma still resides there to this day.) They had their first child, a daughter Bonnie Lynn Goobic on Jan. 26, 1948. It wasn't until six years later my mother June Heather Goobic was born on the same exact day Jan. 26, 1954. They lived a modest but happy life. He later became employed with the Tobyhanna Army Depot and worked there until his retirement.

"I remember when I was young he always wore a back brace. One day I asked him why he had to wear it and he said, because German civilians stuck a pitch fork in his back several times when he hit the ground.

"My Grandpa was the greatest man I ever knew. He was the bravest, humble, patient, considerate, kind, and God fearing man you could ever have had the pleasure of knowing. He loved baseball and gardening and his favorite team was the Philadelphia Phillies. On any given day he could be found sitting peacefully in his favorite chair listening to a baseball game on his black transistor radio. Sadly, at the age of seventy-five he became stricken with Alzheimer's disease and battled that disease for ten long years.

"My Grandma took great care of him for seven long years until it became to much for her to handle. With much anguish the family made the decision that he live out the rest of his days in the Department of Veteran Affairs Medical Center in Plains Township. It broke everyone's heart to watch him slowly slip away. My Grandma would spend everyday with him at the VA. Everyone in my family would take one day out of the week to be with him. The only time he was left alone was when he was sleeping. We were all there the night before he passed holding hands praying around his bed telling him it was okay to go home. He died on March 6, 2006.

Right Waist-Gunner Sgt. Julius K. Otfinoski.

Daughter Pamela Shalvoy recalls;

"My father was born May 28, 1923 to Stephen and Sophie (Rajtar) Otfinoski. Both of his parents came from Poland. When his parents arrived in America, they settled in Middletown, CT, since they knew people there. My father was the third oldest of eight children. Middletown at that time was still fairly rural, and he had a normal childhood filled with school and chores. He was a paperboy.

"He went to public elementary school until grade six. In seventh grade, he went to the school associated with our church, St. Mary's School. Classes were taught in both English and Polish. Julius then went to Woodrow Wilson High School, where he was a good student, particularly in math.

Right Waist-Gunner Sgt. Julius K. Otfinoski

"At the time my grandparents lived in Poland, the country was divided. They lived under the Austrian emperor. Consequently, my grandmother knew how to speak German. In America, she did fancy ironing work for a German man in Middletown. They listened to Hitler on the shortwave radio, and realized the horrors he was preaching. My grandmother, much to my father's objection, made him take German for two years in high school. She said a war was coming and he had to know how to speak it.

"Later, he said his German saved his life. When he parachuted out of the plane, he was stunned when he hit the ground. Older German men in the fields would come for these men with pitchforks. My father was able to speak to them and they allowed him his life. He was captured by German soldiers and put into the famed Stalag 17B POW camp for 13 months until the war ended. Again, his German came in handy as he was able to negotiate with Nazi guards for items or privileges.

***

"After the war, he returned to Middletown and to his job as a machinist for Pratt & Whitney Aircraft. He worked for them his whole life, advancing through the ranks, and taking classes, to become an industrial engineer. He once told me if he had been able to go to college, he would have liked to have been an accountant.

"He married my mother, Elizabeth (Bette) Bonvino in June 1949. They were happily married until his death in October 1978.

"My father was an amazing man; kind, patient, smart, funny. To this day, people will tell me what a good relationship they had with him. He always listened and gave good advice, and made each person feel special. He was a man of character and integrity.

"He had a good life after the war, filled with friends, family, and activities. He was active in our church, St. Mary's, in numerous capacities. He helped form the local chapter of the Catholic War Veterans, and was extremely active in that. He bowled and enjoyed all sports; especially the New York Yankees.

"He was diagnosed with lung cancer when he was 45 and needed to have one lung removed as well as part of the other. He met this adversity with a lack of complaint and a will to get better. And he did. Two years later, he and I went on a long bike ride with a stop at a castle for lunch!

"Unfortunately, he passed away at the age of 55, from angiogram complications after a heart attack suffered a few months earlier.

***

Acknowledgements;
Jennifer Nociasta, granddaughter of engineer Sgt. Theodore F. Goobic.
Right Waist-Gunner Sgt. Julius K. Otfinoski. daughter Pamela Shalvoy

CHAPTER 48

448TH BOMB GROUP
712TH BOMB SQUADRON

Type: B-24H • Serial: 42-7655
MACR: 4486 • Air Base: Seething

---

*"The men left by nose hatch door
as bomb bay doors were not able to be opened
because of battle damage."*

Missing Air Crew Report # 4486

Pilot: 1Lt. James G. Clark, O-796780, KIA, Holyoke, MA

Co-Pilot: 2Lt. Lawrence E. Anderson, O-806031, POW, Chicago, IL

Navigator: 2Lt. Ralph F. Casey, O-691953, POW, Kirkwood, MO

Bombardier: 2Lt. Alfred B. Tallman Jr., O-547113, POW, Hamburg, NY

Engineer: S/Sgt. Manuel S. Cabellero, 38054502, POW, Galveston, TX

Radio: T/Sgt. Robert W. Harrison, 15344356, POW, Tiffin, OH

Ball-Turret Gunner: S/Sgt. Louis W. Curio, 12120419, KIA, Yonkers, NY

Left Waist-Gunner: S/Sgt. Charles H. Myers, 33257178, KIA, Tyrone, PA

Right Waist-Gunner: S/Sgt. Marion A. Tennant, 35382677, KIA, Fairmont, WV

Tail-Gunner: Cpl. John L. Chisholm, 38395834, KIA, Tishomingo, OK

5 KIA, 5 POW

Crash Site: Wildeshausen/Pestrup, 20 miles sw of Bremen, Germany
Time: 13.58

Co-Pilot 2Lt. Lawrence E. Anderson.

From "Budd" Anderson's memoirs.

"From Langley Air Force Base we were sent to the New York area and picked up a brand-new B- 24. It only had eleven hours of flying time on it. From there, we flew it to Palm Beach, Florida to receive our overseas assignment. Upon receiving those orders, we were told to open the envelope one hour after flying due south. We knew it would be either the Eighth Air Force in England or the Fifteenth Air Force in Italy. We had hoped it would be the Eighth and it was.

"Our first stop in South America was in Georgetown, British Guiana. We had one day there and then went to Belen in Brazil. Before leaving there we took a low-level flight down the Amazon. It was a scenic flight to see how the tribesmen lived in that area. After a day in Belen we took off on a twelve hour flight to Dakar, Africa. We wanted to check out our navigator on this ocean flight by giving us directions from celestial navigation only. Of course we had the radio range signals to check with, but the navigator brought us to within five miles.of the base, so we knew we had a good qualified navigator.

"After a rest stop there we flew to Marakesh, Morocco It was sure a scenic town to visit. Our next stop was in England, but we had to fly over the ocean and bypass Portugal, even though they were a neutral country. We were alerted to the possible strong radio range signals that the Germans use from the Brest area in France. They had the same radio range signals that were sent out of England. We understand that a few of our aircraft accidentally followed the wrong signal and landed in Brest.

"So, we made sure we were on the right range and landed near Lakenheath, England. There they took our new B- 24 and sent us by train to Stanaviera, Scotland and then by boat to Belfast, North Ireland. From there we went by bus to an Air Force base about 58 to 60 miles from Belfast. The RAF headquarters was there, beyond German bombers. We got to the town there on Saint Patrick's Day, March 17, and boy did they ever celebrate. By noon you hardly saw a sober man. I must say we didn't help them to celebrate that way. We were just glad that we got that far on our trip to Europe.

"We had three weeks of ground training on what aircraft bombing was doing over France and Germany. Then by boat from Ireland to England and to the 448th Bomb Group. Our first night at the bomb group we were bombed by a German Junker 87 dive bomber. Evidently, the German pilot knew the color of the day and shot three colored flares. This normally meant that a British aircraft was in trouble and needed to make any emergency landing. So the runway lights were turned on. After the first bomb was dropped the guys were all in the fox holes. After the plane left we all got back in our tents, (four men to a tent) and we discussed what a way to be welcomed to England for our first time. His target was evidently the ammunition storage dump but he missed it, thank goodness, for no damage appeared in our living area.

"Now my combat missions start. My first three missions were successfully flown as five to eight hour missions. Then, on Saturday, April 29, 1944 I was called for an unscheduled mission at 3:15 am to fill in as a co-pilot with another crew. Their co-pilot was sick so in the last minute I was called in to fill his place. For that crew it was their 21st mission and fourth mission to Berlin. I was scheduled to fly with crew members I had never met before.

"We were briefed by 6:00; the Berlin railroad yards were the targets. That was a twelve-hour mission. Practically, more than eleven hours of it was over enemy territory. This meant our flying time was tense since take-off.

"Our pilot, James Clark, had already had four missions over Berlin. This was to be his 21st mission. This flight was to give me experience on a long mission. Some of the flying time for me was watching our panel board instruments and helping to fly when we had close wing formation. There was a large number of aircraft that were in our entire formation group. Approximately 1,200 aircraft, bombers and fighters were on this mission

"During our first hours of flying, nothing serious seemed to show up.- but then we seemed to come into black anti aircraft fire from the ground. Some flak pieces hit our aircraft then - but nothing serious. We did manage to drop our bombs but then evidently some flak hit our #4 engine and that called for shutting that engine down and drifting back from our group.

"Shortly thereafter a ME 109 shot at us from behind and underneath. Bullets flew through the aircraft - most damage was in the bomb bay area, but we also lost our hydraulic system and trim tab controls so we dove down into the clouds from 22,000 ft. to about 7,000 ft. and directed the flight to go toward England. During that time the German fighters shot at us and a lot of damage was done. but we were still able to fly. Fortunately no crew members were injured.

"After about three-and-a-half hours, ice formed on the wings and we had to go down to about 3800 feet. When we dropped below the clouds we received some local gunfire and all the members were told to bail out from the aircraft.

"When the emergency sign went off we started our bail out. Our navigator thought we might be over Belgium by that time. No one could use the bomb bay doors because they were shot up and could not be opened. Those of us up front had to use the nose wheel door area and five of us got out from there. I was the last one out of the nose wheel door and the plane stalled out and spun in. The pilot was crawling out behind me in the crawl space in the nose but he didn't make it down the emergency shaft. Later, I found out that only five of us survived.

"As I bailed out, the aircraft headed straight to the ground - from about 2000 ft. While falling in my chute I didn't see others so I was not aware of who did or didn't make it. While descending, I saw the B 24 spin into the ground on its nose and it folded up like an accordion. We were one of the 64 planes lost that day. When I landed, no other crewmen were in sight.

"After a safe parachute landing I was sitting on a plowed farmland area. I then noticed a man in a long black over coat carrying the German Luger. It was pointed at me so I stood up and spoke first. I said, " Is this Belgium," he replied, "Nien, das es Deutchland and for you da var es over." His next words were unbelievable. He said, "How's de beer in St. Louis these days." My wife and I lived there for about nine years.

"His parents had died and he acquired their property. But then the war broke out and Hitler wouldn't let him out because he was a property owner. He put his pistol in his back pocket and said "I won't need this." In a few minutes four soldiers came with their fire arms, but they didn't startle me. They told me follow them to town, about a half a mile away, and there they locked me in solitary confinement for five days in the local jail. I couldn't tell if there were any other crew members there or not.

"The few civilians that we passed showed no signs of me being an enemy but they did take my parachute, probably to make silk dresses. No warfare had taken place around that small town because it was before D day and no bombs had been dropped by that town. That area was about sixty miles. southeast of Bremen.

"Normally all prisoners were taken to the Interrogation Center at Frankfurt, but we were not interrogated because of the great number of airmen men being interviewed. Instead we were kept in private jails in solitary confinement for about three days. There they fed us twice a day by sliding some food under the iron gate. There were names scratched or penciled on the wall of the small rooms so I knew previous airmen had been in there before. When I was searched my flight suit pockets were emptied. They even took my wrist watch because it was a military issued watch. When the guard found the little New Testament I kept zipped in my flight suit he said, "OK, you keep dat."

"From that area we were shipped by rail and spent two days crossing Germany to Sagan, Germany, Stalag Luft III. Incidentally the glass windows were all covered with steel guards plus a guard with a rifle to make sure that no one could escape.

"Our main concern on that trip was when the train spent hours at night time in railroad yards: favorite targets for British night bombers. But we ended up OK at Sagan. The men in our group were taken into the west compound Stalag Luft III. That was the newest section because they already had a north, south, east, and center compound and they were loaded.

"That camp had primarily pilots, navigators and bombardiers. Military prison camps were supposedly controlled by the rules established by the Geneva Convention so we were not treated like civilian prisoners in concentration camps. According to the Geneva Convention of War, officers were not allowed to work.

"It was on May 5th, (the day our son was born) that I arrived at Stalag Luft III. Arriving there gave me a feeling of satisfaction that I had arrived in a good physical condition and was hoping that some day I would make it home.

Budd's biography by son Robert Anderson.

Lawrence E. 'Bud' Anderson was born March 1917 in Chicago, Illinois, the oldest of 5 siblings. His grandparents emigrated from Sweden in the 1880's, and his father was a ship's engineer on the Great Lakes. During the Great Depression, Bud dropped out of high school, taking whatever work he could find to help his family. He later graduated from night school. Bud was musically talented, playing organ and piano for his church and later trombone in a military band.

When the US entered WWII he was in an Illinois National Guard artillery battalion but transferred to the Air Corps. He married, Ellen, his wife of 69 years in August 1942 during pilot training.

He spent just over a year as a prisoner of war first in Stalag Luft III, which was abandoned as the Red Army approached. After a winter march and rides packed in railroad cars he arrived at Stalag Luft 11A and finally 7A. One of his memories was standing next to General Patton who visited Stalag 7A shortly after it was liberated.

He was a career US Air Force officer (Major) followed by ten years of Civil Service. He lived in many places around the country and the world. During an assignment to Japan, he taught jet fighter ground school to the Japanese Air Self Defense Force. Many of his students had been Japanese fighter pilots during WWII. He retired to Spokane, WA in 1991. He passed away, April 2012.

Navigator 2Lt. Ralph F. Casey.

He was born in St. Louis, Mo. in 1915. As a young man, he served his country in WWII as a navigator on a B-17 in England. Bill was shot down in Germany and was taken as a prisoner in Germany for a year to the day.

Returning to the states at the end of the war, he married Georgia Wooley and they had three children, Douglas, William and Jane. Bill was the founder of Associated Equipment Corporation manufacturing battery service equipment.

He was widowed and in 1973, he married Jeanne Rassieur Carter. They worked together for many years and retired to Green Valley in 1991. Bill died Sunday, August 28, 2011.

***

Acknowledgements:
Robert Anderson, son of co-pilot 2Lt. Lawrence E. Anderson.
Bill Casey, son of Navigator 2Lt. Ralph F. Casey.

CHAPTER 49

448ᵀᴴ BOMB GROUP
713ᵀᴴ BOMB SQUADRON

Type: B-24H • Serial: 41-29523
MACR: 4489 • Air Base: Seething

Liberator was shot down on 29 April 1944, at 14:30 hours near Penningsehl. Crew: presumably 10, 9 captured, 1 dead.

German document KU 1703, captured and translated after the war.

Pilot: 1Lt. Max E. Turpin, 0-675891, POW, Ashland, KY

Co-Pilot: 2Lt. Eldon H. Gueck, 0-805910, POW, Scottsbluff, NE

Navigator: 2Lt. Jack Boykoff, 0-750177, POW, Brooklyn, NY

Bombardier: 2Lt. Robert W. Adams, 0-684122, POW, Rawlins, WY

Nose-Turret Gunner: S/Sgt. George A. Daneau, KIA, Amesbury, MA

Engineer: T/Sgt. Thomas R. Culpepper, 14182050, POW, Natasul, AL

Radio: T/Sgt. William F. Hallman, 14142190, POW, Atlanta, GA

Left Waist-Gunner: S/Sgt. Clyde A. Burnette, 14141825, POW, Newnan, GA

Right Waist-Gunner: S/Sgt. William H. Phillips, 15089281, POW, Red Lake Falls, MN

Tail-Gunner: S/Sgt. Donald C. Elder, 18333804, POW, Indianapolis, IN

1 KIA, 9 POW

Crash Site: Penningsehl/Nienburg/Weser - Germany
Time: 13.40

Co-Pilot 2Lt. Eldon H. Gueck.

By daughter Joan Koehler.

Co-Pilot 2Lt. Eldon H. Gueck

"My father, Eldon Gueck, was born on November 16th 1921 in Scottsbluff, Nebraska, to Florence Firme Gueck and Harry E. Gueck. He was their only child. In high school Eldon was a very good athlete. He played football, basketball and ran the hurdles in track. He played the trombone in the high school band and that became useful when he became a prisoner of war and a band was formed at the Stalag. He attended college for two years at Scottsbluff Junior College studying business. His father was a cattle rancher and also owned the sale barn in Scottsbluff, Nebraska. He grew up in a nice home with loving parents but the Great Depression was very hard on the ranching business and money was scarce, life was hard. Before WWII started, my father was planning on taking over the family business but the war changed his plans.

"He chose to enlist in the US Army Air Corps because he did not want to be in the infantry and some college was necessary to become a pilot, so that is what he chose. He was sent to Biloxi, Mississippi, for flight school. His yearbook from his time there contains a very happy and innocent picture of him and pictures of all of the other soon to be graduates. Little did they know what the next few years had in store for them.

"Eldon was stationed in South-East England and was flying over Germany on his 13th mission when his plane went down. One member of the crew was killed on the plane when it was attacked, the rest of the crew parachuted out of the damaged plane. It wasn't until after the war at "Camp Lucky Strike" in France, where liberated prisoners had been taken, that he heard his name being called by another member of the crew and found out that all of the rest of the crew had survived the war at another POW camp for enlisted men.

"While in the POW camp, the prisoners formed a band with instruments donated by the Red Cross and they gave concerts for other POWs. They learned how to cook with limited supplies such as canned milk and they also learned to made tools and games out of the empty cans. In the fall of 1944 my Grandmother sent my father a package with mittens and the ingredients for his birthday cake and the Red Cross actually delivered the box unopened! My father and the other prisoners made a cake and many men enjoyed a little taste of home. My grand-mother always said that the worst thing for her was "not knowing" if my father was dead, injured or had been taken prisoner. It was several months before she was informed that he was in a POW camp. She tried to keep in touch with him and some letters got through but getting a package to him with food in it when most of Germany was starving was amazing.

"My father was a prisoner for exactly one year. General Patton and his Army liberated him. One month before being freed, the whole camp was forced to march over 100 miles farther into Germany during the very bad winter of 1945. Many of the men had trouble marching in their weakened condition. The prisoners tried to help each other but most everyone was weak and had lost a lot of weight on the meager food rations at the Stalag. The snow was very deep, it was very cold and the men didn't have the proper clothes for that kind of weather, but Eldon survived.

***

"After the war my father returned to Nebraska and went into the ranching business with my grandfather. He met my mother, Sue, on a blind date (she was a nurse) and they were married in 1949. My grandfather died one month before the wedding. My grandmother lived to be 100 and died in 1991. Eldon and Sue had six children, four girls and two boys.

"We never lived on our ranch. We lived in town in a beautiful home. My father drove the eighteen miles to and from work everyday. The ranch was a little over 9,000 acres and we also had a farm/feedlot a little closer to town. My father was a very successful rancher and when he died in 1967 at the age of 45, it was a very big news story in Scottsbluff, on TV and the front page of the newspaper. He came from a prominent family who were some of the first people to settle in Scottsbluff in the early 1900's. Unlike the eastern US, many places in the western US, the prairies and high plains were just being settled then. Today, everything is modern just like the rest of the country. We still have cowboys and cattle but most of the time the work is done using pickup trucks with GPS and we use horses just for round-ups on the more rugged parts of the ranch.

"My father was played classical piano. I remember one of his favorite pieces to play was "Clair de Lune" by Debussy. He also liked to listen to big band music on the radio. He liked to bowl, play cards with his buddies, play basketball with his kids and watch American football on TV. One of his favorite things to do was to go to airports and watch all planes take off and land. When I was a little girl he would get us all into the car and drive to our local airport in the evenings and we would have a contest to see who could spot the lights of the airplanes coming in from Denver and Omaha.

"After the war my father always said that he would never be hungry again and he would never eat brown or black bread again. Since he was a rancher we always had a big freezer full of beef; steaks, roasts and hamburger. As a kid I got very tired of all of that red meat and wanted chicken, pork and fish, not just beef, beef and beef. My father never did go hungry again.

"After his death, among his belongings I found a letter that he had written while living in England, just before his plane was shot down. He had never mailed it and the letter had never even been folded. It is written in his very distinctive printing style and signed by him. In the letter he describes the previous bombing mission that was aborted somewhere over France because the cloud cover was too thick. They had to turn around mid-flight and fly back to England and then try to land in the fog without being able to see anything. His plane made it, but the next day he describes how many other planes and crews didn't make it because they couldn't find the runway or they flew into trees and crashed. One line in the letter states that "this war will take 20 years off of everyone's life because of the stress." He died at the young age of 45, well before he should have, just liked he predicted in his letter.

Bombardier 2Lt. Robert W. Adams.

By son John Adams.

"My father was born in Superior, Wisconsin on October 8, 1917 to Bill and Maude Adams. He died at the age of 64 years old about two weeks before his 65th birthday from a heart attack caused by a congenital heart valve malfunction. He led a very interesting life. He was born poor, on a dairy farm near Superior. He attended school in Wisconsin and took up boxing as his favorite sport. He was not big, about 5 foot 6 inches and weighed around 150 pounds.

"When he was 19 years old, the family moved to Rawlins, Wyoming, to find work in a dairy. He said they arrived in a 1935 Ford with $750. My grandpa Bill managed a dairy, which

Bombardier 2Lt. Robert W. Adams

they eventually bought and renamed the Adams Dairy. It was a family business and quite successful. My grandpa, my dad, and his brother Joe, ran the dairy and delivered milk all over the State of Wyoming. My grandma and his sister Elva, ran a coffee shop and lunch counter where the buses stopped.

"When the Americans became involved in WWII, my dad joined the Air Corps. He intended to be a pilot but his eyes were not good enough so he settled for bombardier. It was on his 16th or 17th mission over Germany that he was shot down. I believe if you lived through twenty missions, they sent you home. I guess the odds were not with them on that day.

"When he reached the ground, he landed in a tree and was met by an angry group of farmers with pitchforks who he thought would kill him right there. Luckily, soldiers arrived and took him to prison.

"My dad spent just over a year in the prison camp named Stalag Luft 3. He told me it was the same camp where "The Great Escape" occurred when 50 some men escaped at one time. As a result of this escape, the Nazis made the unwritten rule that if you escaped with more than three people, you would be turned over to the Gestapo and shot.

From the very beginning my father planned to escape and he used to run everyday around the camp to keep in shape so he could run across Germany. As the war progressed, it became clear that the Nazis were losing because the camp was moved a couple of times further back into Germany. My father feared the Nazis might line everyone up and shoot them. At that time, the guards were made up of old men and young boys because all able bodied men were at the front. It was on one of these marches when they moved the camp that he escaped. As they were being marched deeper into Germany, they jumped out of line and hid in a ditch. It was my dad and three others.

"Escaping was the easy part. Now they had to find the US troops. They hid during the day and ran at night towards the "guns" which I believe were over 100 miles away. They feared they would go the wrong way and be shot by the Russians who were advancing also. My dad and his friends lives were saved by a German farm family. It seems they were hidden for a few days and given food by this family. My dad said they even got drunk with them one night.

"The rest of the story about how they finally got to the US lines is a little sketchy but they made it. My dad returned to Germany in the 1970's and looked up this family. He helped them out with a "loan" of $25,000. He knew he would never get repaid but he really did not care. A small payment for saving his life.

***

After the war my dad started the Adams Restaurant and Flame room. It was "the" spot in Rawlins. He told me when he was in prison camp he used to dream about food. He would dream about eating a whole head of lettuce.

"He became a very successful businessman in Rawlins. In addition to the restaurant and dairy, we owned a motel, a liquor store, a candy store and three drive in movies around the state.

"In the mid 50's, uranium was discovered in the desert north of Rawlins. My dad had a small airplane and equipped it with a geiger counter and began to fly around looking for uranium deposits. He would land in the desert, stake a claim and fly away to the next claim. So began his new career in the mining business. He became one of the founders of the US uranium industry, started a public company called Western Nuclear, and built the first uranium mill in the Wyoming. His career spanned thirty years in the uranium and coal business until his untimely death in 1982.

"During that time we owned the largest coal mine in Colorado located near my home in Steamboat Springs Colorado. The company was known as Energy Fuels Corp and produced over 4 million tons of coal a year. We also were the largest producers of uranium in the US throughout the 80's and early 90's. Our main partners were three Swiss utilities who funded much of the uranium mining in exchange for fuel for their nuclear plants.

"He was my idol and the most amazing man I have ever met.

From Robert's obituary

"Bob Adams was a giant of a man. His shadow of concern touched the lives of all of those who surrounded him. He was benefactor, preservationist, protector and, above all, citizen concerned with his world. He was a "get things done" man who spared neither time nor his personal fortune in seeing projects completed, considering not their size but rather their importance for the future.

"He died, as he had lived, with flare. Bob Adams was in New York City on business when death came. He passed away in the Essex House of a massive heart attack at 11:15 pm. on Thursday Sept. 23, 1982. He was 64.

"In tribute to his love affair with Routt County, his family has created, in a irrevocable trust, a wildlife preserve of the 240-acre tract which includes Fish Creek Falls, picnic area and surrounding property. Adams had been in the final stages of a land trade with the Routt Forest which would turn the Fish Creek site over to the USFS in return for certain other properties in South Routt County. According to Bob's son, John, the land will be held "in perpetuity" by the family. It can never be developed, subdivided or sold, John said.

"Interment was held on Adams' property in Routt County on Tuesday afternoon. Only the immediate family was present. "Dad loved Steamboat Springs and Routt County," his son said. "He wanted to be buried there, in the Yampa Valley, where he had found so much joy.'

"Bob Adams is dead. His thoughtful generosity will live on as long as Fish Creek flows and the grain ripens on the reclaimed slopes of South Routt County from which his company had taken coal.

Nose-Turret Gunner S/Sgt. George A. Daneau.

By nephew Frank Daneau.

Nose-Turret Gunner S/Sgt. George A. Daneau

"I had a female cousin in her teens, Althea Brown, on my mother's side of the family, from Fryburg, Maine. Her family was rather poor, so during the summer months as my parents had a small business, they would pick her up and bring her to stay with us and help out. I believe she was about a year younger than George as he had just graduated from high school - he was an excellent scholar as well as an athlete - and she had one year remaining. My parents brought them together one day and to say it was love at first sight would be an understatement as they fell madly in love and carried on practically unseparated throughout that summer of 1941.

"When Althea returned to Maine at the end of the summer to complete her high school education it was a very sad day indeed due to their upcoming separation made even more so for George had decided to join the Army Air Corps because he was going to be drafted anyway and felt that he would have a better chance at something he wanted to do by volunteering. They had however, made plans for a future life together after the war and his commitment was complete.

"When he left, it didn't seem to be much of a big deal, after all it was kind of a way of life. Everybody did it. It was kind of what you did at this stage of your life, part of the plan, so to speak. After all, three of his older brothers were already in the army and two of them on duty. One had been seriously wounded in battle and was recovering.

"The rest is kind of history. However, I do remember my grandparents receiving telegrams pertaining to the dreaded news announcing "wounded," "MIA," or "KIA," all of which they received, and the sadness associated with the devastating news. However, my being so young at the time, I don't think, looking back that I fully understood the meaning of it all. It seemed that all family's in our small town were experiencing some measure of hardship, grief or disaster due to the war. It also seemed that most houses displayed in their windows a sort of banner with stars on it representing how many sons or daughters were serving the war effort.

From a newspaper article:

"Staff Sgt. George Andrew Daneau, 21, son of Mr. and Mrs. Arthur Daneau, a turret gunner on a Liberator bomber, is missing in action over Germany, according to advices received by his parents from the War department last evening.

"We are sorry to advise you," read the telegram, "That your son, Staff Sgt. George A. Daneau is reported missing in action over Germany on April 29. Additional details will be forwarded to you as soon as received."

Staff Sgt. Daneau who is one of four brothers to join the armed services, enrolled in the Air Corps 14 months ago. He became attached to the ground crew and received his basic training at Roosevelt Filed, New York. He developed and interest in mechanics and soon began to concentrate on the motors of planes and shipped overseas as a motor engineer in the Air Corps.

When in England he received additional training as a gunner and his particular assignment on the bomber to which he was attached was that of the first engineer.

Mr. and Mrs. Daneau have three other sons, Edgar, Richard, and Paul all of whom are serving in the Army. The son who is reported missing is the only one so far reported to have gone overseas.

The Daneaus recently received from their son (George) Andrew, an air medal which he had received from combat duty over Germany. Although his parents are not certain, it is their belief that the flight on which he is reported missing was his 22nd mission over Germany."

Left Waist-Gunner S/Sgt. Clyde A. Burnette.

The April 29, 1944, mission was his 17th. He had his 20th birthday that month. Four FW-190's attacked his bomber from 2 o'clock high. Shells hit engine No. 3 and the fuel tanks in that area killing George Danau, the nose-turret gunner. The plane quickly caught fire and waist-gunner Clyde Burnette was hit at his head by a part flying around, presumable from an exploded oxygen bottle. He was under shock but when he regained perception he knew that it was time to bail out, there was no command for that. He looked for his shoes, bailed out and opened his chute at an altitude of approx. 3000 feet.

When he approached the ground he saw the soldiers from the air who captured him later. Next day he was taken to the Luftwaffe Interrogation Center near Frankfurt and later to the Kriens Stalag POW camp.

***

Acknowledgements;
Joan Koehler, daughter of co-pilot 2Lt. Eldon H. Gueck.
John Adams, son of bombardier 2Lt. Robert W. Adams.
Frank Daneau, nephew of nose-turret Gunner S/Sgt. George A. Daneau.

CHAPTER 50

448ᵀᴴ BOMB GROUP 714ᵀᴴ BOMB SQUADRON

Type: B-24H • Serial: 42-7683
MACR: 4487 • Air Base: Seething

"Our plane was shot down over Germany on April 30 (sic) 1944. They can say what they want about the Germans, but their doctors are really good and full of patience. They really did everything they could for me."

Letter from Waist-Gunner Ralph Meigs as a POW – August 1944

Pilot: 2Lt. William W. Rogers, KIA, Collinsville, IL

Co-Pilot: 2Lt. Joseph R. Gonzales Jr., 0-752196, POW, Oakland, CA

Navigator: 2Lt. Albert Dilorenzo, 0-687932, POW, Weymouth, MA

Bombardier: 2Lt. Raymond L. Cohee, 0-752551, POW, Long Beach, CA

Engineer: T/Sgt. Grady V. Howell Jr., 34038420, POW, Waynesville, NC

Radio: T/Sgt. Royal V. Donihoo, 38426739, POW, Dallas, TX

Ball-Turret Gunner: S/Sgt. George J. Robichau, 12116192, POW, Quincy, MA

Left Waist-Gunner: S/Sgt. Ralph Meigs, 14135725, POW, Macon, GA

Right Waist-Gunner: S/Sgt. Bordie S. Haynes, 34490741, POW, Kingsport. TN

Tail-Gunner: S/Sgt. Johnny W. Jones, 14149210, POW, Leetonia, OH

1 KIA, 9 POW

Crash Site: Dreiecksmoor/Goldenstedt, Germany
Time: 13.48

Pilot 2Lt. William W. Rogers.

William's father died when he was three years old. A year later he was taken into the home of Mr. and Mrs. Harvey Rogers, where he resided until he was about nineteen years old. He was inducted at Rockford, Illinois. He was commissioned as lieutenant in the Air Corps in August, 1943.

Served with the 8th USAAF in England serving as a pilot. He had a brother with the Armed Forces in India. T/Sgt. Grady Howell, a crew member, stated in a letter that when he bailed out of the plane, Lt. Rogers was standing on the catwalk in the bomb bay ready to come out after him;

"On April 29, 1944, I was a waist-gunner in a B-24 bomber. We were returning from a mission over Berlin. At or near Vechta in Germany, we were under attack from several FW 190's and the fight continued for ten to twenty minutes. I did not see Lt. Rogers at that time. To the best of my knowledge, this took place during the early part of the afternoon. A 20 mm. shell hit our plane about one foot from me. I was wounded and knocked unconscious. When I came to the plane was going down. The only crew members I saw at that time were those in the waist.

Navigator 2Lt. Albert Dilorenzo

Born in Weymouth, MA. While at Weymouth high School he was a member of the wrestling team and won the state scholastic championship in the 155-pound class. After graduating he attended Tufts College, but left there in 1943 to enlist in the Army Air Corps.

He received his training at New York, Sioux City, Iowa and graduated from the Army Air Corps Navigation School, San Marcos, Texas, in August 1943.

Engineer T/Sgt. Grady V. Howell Jr

By son Seaton Howell

"My father was born on December 9, 1921 in a small cross roads community named Bethel which is in Haywood County, North Carolina. He was the son of Grady and Winiford Howell. He became Grady Vincent Howell Jr. My father's family later moved to the other side of the county to an area called Jonathan Creek.

"He was the oldest of 3 children. After graduating from high school, he went on to attend NC State University for a time before winding up in the Army Air Corps.

"Grady became engineer on a B-24 bomber named "Sweet Sioux" - one of many by that name. He was on his next to last flight when they were shot down over Germany. He said he was the last person out of the plane before it crashed. When he landed he saw the Germans coming for him, so he hurriedly buried his service revolver in the field. I wonder if it is still there.

"After they arrested him, he was transferred to Stalag 17B. They made a movie about that Stalag after the war, but he said the movie was nothing like the real life in there. They received Red Cross parcels containing also chocolate and cigarettes. He claimed to be very rich while there as he would horde the cigarettes as he did not smoke and then sell them to other prisoners.

"He was incarcerated for 14 months. When he returned to the states after the war, he reenlisted and became a recruiter for the Army Air Corps. It was along then that he met my mother in Greenville, NC and they were married. After his term as a recruiter was up, he started working for an auto finance company and later he started a truck rental and auto sales business. He died in 1996.

Ball-Turret S/Sgt. George J. Robichau.

By niece Debra Bennett.

"George was one of three children. His parents were Margaret Messier and Charles Robichau. He was born on March 24, 1924 in Quincy, MA and passed away on October 3, 2007.

"Moved to Quincy when he was around age 15 and lived in the Hough's Neck section. He went to Central Junior High School, Went to Quincy High School and enlisted at 17 years old (1943) after Pearl Harbor.

"After WWII George worked in a neighborhood mom & pop grocery store in either Hough's Neck or Dorchester with his father. Went to college (Bentley College) after the service, got degree in accounting, worked at AT&T (American Telephone & Telegraph Company) with computers and retired in 1980 at 55.

"His wife Barbara was working at the phone company when she met George. They married at St. Ann's Church in Wollaston, MA on Oct. 9, 1948.

"Barbara got pregnant with daughter Janice but pregnancy was difficult and they weren't able to have more children so they adopted son Jimmy at about 18 months; early family years were spent in Holbrook, MA until they moved to 162 Elmwood Avenue in Wollaston, MA.

"George used to like to go fishing; golfing and bowled with the Knights of Columbus. When the children were little, the family used to do day trips to NH, Nantasket Beach, Santa's Village, Edaville Railroad. They always had cats: Mingo, a Burmese cat that lived to be 21 years. old and "Taz," Tasmanian Devil, a short-haired Oriental, that lived to be 17 years old. He liked boats and used to have a 14 ft. boat with an 18 horse power motor. He loved to take boat out into Boston Harbor and go to George's Island.

Right Waist-Gunner Bordie S. Haynes.

By stepson Kenneth R. Cox.

Right Waist-Gunner Bordie S. Haynes

"Bordie married my mother a couple of years after the war. He was in Stalag 17 for a year and a day. He was wounded in the head and leg with shrapnel that remained in his body to the day he died.

"Bordie was a very intelligent person. He was valedictorian of his class. He got a job a Tennessee Eastman, (a division of Kodak Eastman at the time), where he worked until he got bladder cancer. He was always very nervous and never able to drive a car. Mama always drove. One time when Eastman sent him to New York for a seminar, we had to talk to him for weeks to get him on a plane. Probably the first time on a plane since the war. Our doctor gave him something to settle him down during the flight. I believe his experience in the war plagued him all his life.

"Before he died, the shrapnel in his leg started bothering him and I drove him to the VA center to get it checked out and to see about partial disability, but I believe he got cancer before it cleared the red tape. He died in 1970 from cancer. It's a shame one of our heroes had to die of cancer so young.

Left Waist-Gunner S/Sgt. Ralph Meigs.

As a POW he wrote in August 1944;

"Out plane was shot down over Germany on April 30 (sic) 1944. They can say what they want about the Germans, but their doctors are really good and ful of patience. They really did everything they could for me.

"After I bailed out of the plane I landed near a farmhouse. The farmer could not understand English but called the German Air Raid Guards and they carried me to a first aid station. After a little delay, only a few minutes I was brought on here in the hospital.

***

Acknowledgements;
Seaton Howell, son of engineer T/Sgt. Grady V. Howell Jr
Debra Bennett, niece of ball-turret S/Sgt. George J. Robichau.
Kenneth R. Cox, stepson of waist-gunner Bordie S. Haynes.

CHAPTER 51

448ᵀᴴ BOMB GROUP
714ᵀᴴ BOMB SQUADRON

Type: B-24H • Serial: 42-99988
MACR: 4491 • Air Base: Seething

On the return trip from the target, I saw two ships go down.
One was piloted by Lt. Ponge and the other by Lt. Rogers.
One ship what I believe to be Lt. Ponge was attacked by
fighters and shortly thereafter 8 chutes were seen to open.
Aircraft was in steep vertical dive when last seen.

From Missing Air Craft Report # 4491

Pilot: 2Lt. William F. Ponge, 0-807869, KIA, Hollis, NY

Co-Pilot: 2Lt. Everett H. Snowbarger, 0-692835, POW

Navigator: 2Lt. Harold S. Neidig, 0-684182, KIA, Lebanon, PA

Nose-Turret Gunner: Sgt. Joseph E. Moran, 15337063, KIA, Hamilton, OH

Engineer: S/Sgt. John R. O'Brien, 12187452, KIA, Brewster, NY

Radio: S/Sgt. Kaari M. Halvorson, 37281150, POW, Portland, OR

Left Waist-Gunner: Sgt. Thomas H. Hines, 33560393, KIA, Baltimore, MD

Right Waist-Gunner: Sgt. Henry H. Maynard, 38134649, POW, Caddo, TX

Tail-Gunner: Sgt. John H. Hill, 36576975, KIA, Detroit, MI

6 KIA, 3 POW

Crash Site: Pennigsehl/Nienburg/Weser, Germany
Time: 13.35

Co-Pilot 2Lt. Everett H. Snowbarger.

By son Richard Snowbarger.

"Dad was born March 18, 1919 on a farm outside Sylvia, Kansas, a small farming community. He lived there until 17 years old when he graduated from high school then moved thirty miles to Hutchinson, Kansas to live with his sister while going to Jr. College. At that time he started working for Dillons Food Stores, a local grocery store. He returned to this company after the war. The company grew and eventually was the largest supermarket chain in the 3-state area of Kansas, Missouri and Oklahoma. He was eventually made President of this company.

Co-Pilot 2Lt. Everett H. Snowbarger

Interview by Dean Hinnen

"When Everett Snowbarger's phone rings at 4 a.m., he usually expects bad news. Like a robbery or a fire at a Dillon store somewhere. Snowbarger, president of Dillon Stores Division, got an early morning call, but the only bad news was some that was more than thirty years old and with the passage of time the news was almost pleasant.

"The call was from an American Broadcasting Company newsman in Portland, 0regon, who was a radio man on an American B-24 that was shot down over Germany on April 29, 1944. Snowbarger was co-pilot on that plane and was one of three surviving members of the plane's nine man crew.

"I hadn't seen or heard from him since the day we got shot down," Snowbarger said Friday. The radio operator was Cory Halvorson, the same age as Snowbarger, and an ABC news employe. He told Snowbarger that he got off work at midnight Thursday and decided he would take a "shot in the dark," and call Snowbarger, whom he knew lived in Hutchinson before the war.

"Snowbarger said he barely knew Halvorson, who filled in as radio man after the plane's regular crew member wounded his hand with a pistol. But it was obvious that Halvorson knew about Snowbarger.

"He told me, "You may not remember me, because I hadn't been with your crew very long, but I was your substitute radio man. I watched you jump out of the plane," Snowbarger said. The more Halvorson talked, the more Snowbarger learned about an event that had happened to him nearly 32 years ago. "He told me a lot of things that jelled with what I had been told before, but he also confirmed a lot of things I wasn't sure of and told me some things I didn't know," Snowbarger said.

"There was no doubt in Snowbarger's mind that Halvorson was on the plane when he told about watching Snowbarger hesitate before parachuting from the burning B-24. "There was a catwalk back to the bomb bay," explained Snowbarger. "I remember sitting down and putting one foot down and feeling the jet stream. I pulled my foot back up and had about a two-second conversation with myself, and told myself I didn't have any choice. Then I jumped."

"Snowbarger landed in a field, hurt a knee in the landing, and ran as best he could to a nearby hedge row where he hid out until nightfall. Then he walked until he found a farm shack where he spent the night. The next morning he began walking, found a railroad track and followed it to the northwest.

"But with the injured knee and without survival clothing and equipment, Snowbarger turned himself over to an elderly couple and a young German civilian later that day. They walked him to a nearby village where he was turned over to the military authorities.

"After two weeks of interrogation in Oberursel near Frankfort, he was sent to a prisoner of war camp. He was liberated April 29, 1945 – one year to the day from the time his plane was shot down. Among the new information Snowbarger learned from Halvorson was the fact that the plane's first pilot, Lt. William F. Ponge, did parachute from the burning bomber. Ponge was one of three of the plane's crew members whose fate was never known.

"Of the nine-man crew on board that day, Snowbarger, Halvorson and Sgt. Henry Maynard, the plane's waist gunner, survived and became POWs. Three men were confirmed killed and Ponge and two others were listed as missing in action and never accounted for by either the Americans or the Germans.

"Halvorson told Snowbarger that Ponge had left the plane shortly before Snowbarger. Halvorson said he was the last to jump out of the aircraft.

"The bombers flew at 23,000 feet, and were above a thick cloud cover. Neither Snowbarger nor Halvorson knew where they were when they jumped from the plane. "There was flak, parachutes and planes going down everywhere," said Snowbarger. News accounts said 77 American planes were lost in that day's raid over Berlin.

"He thought he was over the North Sea and I thought I was over the English Channel," Snowbarger said. The bombers were stationed in Britain and had made their attack on Berlin - only the third air attack on the German capital at that time - from the north, coming in over the North Sea to get to Germany. It was the crew's sixth mission, but its first over Berlin.

"We took a flak hit over Berlin and were lagging in formation and a fighter finished us off," Snowbarger said. "I don't know where we were hit by the flak. but it effected the way the aircraft flew and we were trying to keep up with the formation when the fighter got us." '

"Although both Snowbarger and Halvorson were taken to Frankfurt for inter-rogation, they never saw each other. Halvorson remained at Frankfurt for only three days. Snowbarger was there two weeks.

"The radio operator was an enlisted man and was sent to a different POW camp than was Snowbarger, who was a second lieutenant.

"Snowbarger was first taken to a camp known as Stalag Luit 3 at Sagan, Ger-many. Most of the prisoners at the camp were American officers, although there were some British prisoners there too. He later was moved to a camp near Mose-burg when Russian troops began approaching the area of the first camp. General George Patton's 3rd Army liberated the Moseburg POW camp April 29, 1945!

"The paths of all three surviving crew members crisscrossed at Lucky Strike, a camp near Le Havre, France, where American POWs were taken before being returned to the United States, but they never saw one another.

"Halvorson told Snowbarger he saw the Hutchinson man's name on a list at Camp Lucky Strike. Snowbarger said he had not seen Halvorson's name there, but did see Maynard's. Snowbarger and Maynard later wrote to each other, but had since not communicated for several years. And Snowbarger and Halvorson had not communicated with each other since the fateful flight.

Radio S/Sgt. Kaari M. Halvorson made the following official state-ment immediately after WWII:

"On April 29, 1944, we embarked on a bombardment mission; the target being Berlin, Germany. We bombed the target and upon returning we received a direct 20 mm, shell hit under the cockpit of the B-24, causing a fire on the flight deck and setting at least one engine on fire.

"I saw the pilot, 2Lt. Ponge bail out, however, I never saw him after that time and there was apparently no fire on his clothing and he did not appear to be injured. He bailed out at 23 to 24 thousand feet. I did not see his chute open and I have never seen him since that time.

"The bombardier 2Lt. Niedig, and the nose-gunner Sgt. Joe Moran were both in the nose section where the 20 mm hit was received. As this was an explosive shell it is very possible that they were both killed or seri-ously injured preventing them to bail out.

"Waist-gunner Sgt. Maynard told me that due to the dive of the plane and the fact that the plane was out of control, the only method by which he was able to clear the ship was by opening his chute on the inside and throwing it out the escape hatch, thereby the chute pulled him out. He stated that at the time he went out

Nose-Gunner Sgt. Joe Moran

one of the waist-gunners and the tail-gunner were trapped on the floor and it was his opinion that they were unable to get out prior to the crash.

"The engineer, John O'Brien was standing in the front portion of the bomb bay ready to bail out when I started to jump. Due to the plane being out of control he hung up in the bomb bay while bailing out and although I did not see him jump it was my impression that he did so. At the time I bailed out he was not in any way injured and his clothing was not on fire.

By son Gory Halvorson:

"He was born in Norway and the family moved to a farm in North Dakota when he was two or three years old. I know times were tough and I know he entered the CCC's at some point. We have a picture of him and he looks to be very young and maybe in some sort of kitchen uniform. I think he may have done this to help support the family.

"Before the war he was living in Burbank, CA and I think he worked at some sort of aircraft factory. I know he said the weather was like being in heaven compared to the cold in North Dakota.

***

Acknowledgements
Richard Snowbarger, son of co-pilot 2Lt. Everett H. Snowbarger.
Gory Halvorson, son of radio-operator S/Sgt. Kaari M. Halvorson

CHAPTER 52

448ᵀᴴ BOMB GROUP
715ᵀᴴ BOMB SQUADRON

Type: B-24H • Serial: 41-29479 "Gypsy Queen"
MACR: 4488 • Air Base: Seething

Bomber left the formation after bomb run. Three engines, nose and the right stabilizer had been damaged by flak. All of the crew bailed out over the Danish island of Bornholm in the Baltic Sea before the bomber crashed on the southern tip of the island.

Missing Air Crew Report # 4488

Pilot: 2Lt. Orland T. Howard, 0-808843, EVD, Billings, NE

Co-Pilot: F/O Thomas J. Verran, T-122217, POW, Newport, MI

Navigator: 2Lt. Robert L. Bobst, 0-696051, EVD, St. Charles, IA

Bombardier: 2Lt. Laurin M. Derosier, 0-749872, EVD, Yuma, AZ

Nose-Turret Gunner: S/Sgt. Stanley E. Jones, 39260377, POW, Venice, CA

Engineer: T/Sgt. Harry T. Ambrosini, 19003327, KIA, Fresno, CA

Radio: T/Sgt. Russell D. Leonard, 11044325, EVD, Taunton, MA

Left Waist-Gunner: T/Sgt. Harold W. Nininger, 39683675, POW, Topeka, KS

Right Waist-Gunner: S/Sgt. William L. Hutchins, 32229646, EVD, Jamaica, NY

Tail-Gunner: Sgt. Albert L. Heikkila, 17155113, EVD, Coleraine, MN

1 KIA, 3 POW, 6 EVD

Crash Site: Bornholm, Denmark
Time: 14.30

448th Bomb Group, 715th Bomb Squadron (Howard)
(No caption available.)

Pilot 2Lt. Orland T. Howard reported after his arrival in Sweden;

"Over the industrial district nw of Berlin, we turned into our bomb run and were hit by flak over the city. We were losing about 200 feet of altitude a minute and were down to 17000 feet, still above the cloud deck, but icing heavily. Just east of Lübeck we cut through the clouds at about 14,000 feet. About half way over the sea at 11,000 feet we were flying on one engine and going down fast. We prepared to ditch and sent out a SOS. Since the intercom was cut, I told the co-pilot to pass on the order to bail out as soon as we were over land.

"The first man went out at about 3400 feet. No one was in the plane when I left at 2400 feet. I blacked out momentarily and landed with a jolt in an open field. I hid my equipment in a mud hole in a clump of trees and headed for a larger group of trees about a hundred yards away. I had on my green flying suit, an excellent thing for hiding. I went into some sort of evergreen underbrush. At about 17.00 hours A German soldier passed within 30 feet of the place where I was hiding but did not see me.

"At around 22.00 hours I started walking north, intending to get to the northern part of the island and find a fishing boat in which to go to Sweden. I walked until 03.00, took a benzadrine tablet, continued an hour and then lay down under a tree and went to sleep. I got up early and continued north, walking through woods until noon.

"About noon I saw a farmer's house and watched it for about three hours. Then I showed myself to the farmer. When he came over I indicated that I was hungry. He brought me sandwiches and beer and said something which I thought meant that he would come for me later, but then he seemed to ask me what I was going to do. I decided he was not going to help me. He brought more sandwiches and beer so that by then I began to feel pretty good. I walked on, reaching the coast about midnight. It looked like rain, so I got in an old marble quarry and tried to sleep under a wheelbarrow.

"The next morning was foggy and overcast. I walked ten or fifteen miles in the morning continuing nw. At noon I began to feel pretty low, found a haystack, and climbed in. My felt boots were soaked. I stayed there all afternoon and night during a continual drizzle.

"The next morning I started walking what I thought was north-east. At last the sun broke through. I ran into a farmer and, since I was getting kind of disgusted with the whole affair, I did not wait before I called him over and tried to explain my predicament to him. He took me in and gave me some coffee and sandwiches. About 09.00 he took me right into a town and walked down the street to a store where he expected to find a man who could speak English. When he could not find his man there he took me to the edge of town to find another man. This man could not be found either. The farmer saw that he could not help me and left.

"I started walking on the main road. Two farmers came, took me off the road, and explained that the Huns used it. They told me to go to the house of a certain farmer who they thought had a boat. I went, told the man who I was and what I wanted, and was hidden in the hay loft. He brought me some food and beer.

"That evening I was taken to a place from which my journey was arranged. I asked the people who helped me why they did it, realizing that if I was captured I would be taken POW while they would be shot. They tried to explain that we were fighting the war one way and that they were fighting the war in the only way they could fight it at the time. All that they wanted was to be able to help us and for us to keep absolutely quiet about what they did for us. They did not want us even to mention them to our intelligence at American headquarters. They were angry about all the publicity which had come out in connection with previous Americans coming out of Denmark. The wanted us to say absolutely nothing even in Sweden about our experiences.

Co-Pilot F/O Thomas J. Verran.

"These pages are written, as insurance against time erasing from my memory those vivid days as a prisoner of war. Time is the only commodity that we have an abundance of. In taking advantage of this time, I have attempted within these pages, to put down my experiences and the impressions I have during this required stay within the barbed wire walls of Stalag Luft 3 in Sagan, Poland.

"Now my thoughts and dreams are centered on the future. Some day these dreams will be a reality and once again I will take luxury and safety for granted. Maybe, as I go through these pages in the time to come, I will not forget how much I have to thankful for, how little I have to complain about and how much I owe to the Red Cross.

Co-Pilot F/O Thomas J. Verran

***

"We left Ditchingham Air Force Base in England on April 29, 1944 at seven o'clock in the morning. I was the co-pilot on a B-24 bomber. The plane we were flying was named "The Gypsy Queen." Our target was Berlin, Germany. Our mission was to soften up the Germans before the D-day invasion.

"At 1200 hours, over Berlin at 24,000 feet, we were hit by heavy flak on our first bombing run. After our bombs were away, our number two and four engines were shot out. We had to break away from formation and head north towards Sweden, hopefully a possible quick landing. We also found that our radio was out, as well as our intercom system.

"We quickly started to lose altitude, approximately 300 ft. a minute. We started to make our plane lighter by throwing overboard our machine guns, our gun mounts, and every other thing that was not nailed down, but than our number three engine started to act up. Our pilot, Lt. Orland Howard, decided to head for the nearest land, which was the Denmark island of Bornholm in the Baltic Sea, just north of Germany. At 3,000 Ft. over Bornholm, we lost our number one engine, and started to fall fast.

"I gave the command to bail out. I was riding with the original crew that I flew over to England with. The wind that day was very high, approximately 40 miles an hour, which made it very rough for a parachute jump. I jumped out the bomb bay doors at approximately 2,500 Ft. I had a hard time opening my chute at 1,000 Ft. The chute spilled most of the way down. Everything seemed so still and quiet after leaving the plane.

"As my chute opened, I saw my ship hit the ground and burst into flames. Then I hit a tree at a terrific rate and ruptured a couple of arteries in my back. I cut my way out of the chute and half walked and half crawled to a nearby farm house. The people at the house were kind to me and gave me coffee and bread. I left my gun and most of my flying cloths at the house and headed for the woods since this island was full of German soldiers.

"After the war, the people, that helped me, the Gaarde Jer O. Roford family, wrote me and ask me how I was. They also said that two other fliers came to the house after I left, and they gave them food and sent them on their way. They also said that they were questioned several times by the German police and the Gestapo, but were able to get rid of them without any problems.

"I stole a bicycle and started making my way to the northern tip of the island, which was only about 40 miles from Sweden, where I would be safe. I traveled by night and slept by day in barns and in the woods. I made it to the sea at the northern part of the island, but I could not find a boat to get to Sweden. I escaped several German patrols, and later I found out this island was a rest camp for German officers.

"By this time I was getting pretty weak from my wounds, so I gave myself up to the Germans on May 1, 1944, and I was taken to a hospital. There I found out that Stanley Jones and Harold Ninninger my waist and ball gunners respectively were also in the hospital. I also learned that my engineer, Harry Ambrosin, had been killed upon hitting a tree after bailing out.

"On May 4, we were taken to Kopenhagen, Denmark's capital. It was a four hour trip in a torpedo boat. We were housed in a hospital for six days, where we were treated fairly well except for being kept in solitary confinement. On May 10, we were taken to Frankfurt, Germany, Dulag Luft, for interrogation, where I was kept in solitary confinement for four days. On May 16, I was taken to an officer's prison camp, Stalag Luft 3 in Zagan, Poland. There I met several of my old flying buddies.

"Six months after D-Day, our troops were getting closer as was the end of the war. On January 27, 1945 around mid-night the German guards marched us out of Zagan. After two days of marching, we arrived at Muskau. The march was hard, and the weather was freezing cold. Another way we could tell that the end of the war was near, was that our guards were old men and young boys. The regular guards were needed up on the front lines.

"We stayed in a pottery factory for two days. We then marched to Spremberg, where we stayed in a barn. Then 52 of us were put in a train boxcar and were sent to Nuremberg. To my delight this is where I met my old friend Chuck Shafer. Our next march out, Chuck and I led the column. We took cover once, when we were bombed by our own planes. We marched into Newmark, where we were given some soup and bread. Then we marched all night and arrived at Plankstetten, Germany early in the morning. The people there were very good to us, putting us up in their barn and feeding us potatoes, soup, and bread.

"On April 6, 1945, Chuck and I decided to escape by hiding under the hay in the barn, when the guards marched the others out in the morning. It worked; we were free the next morning. To our surprise a few other men were also left behind. Some of the men hid as we did, while others we too ill to move on. The Germany villagers were good to us. We traded with the villagers for eggs, milk, bread, and potatoes. We had good reserves, enough to live on for about two weeks. In the barn up in the loft we dug a little room in the straw and put all our supplies and blankets in it. The villagers told us that we had to be careful, because their sons were soldiers, and if they found out that they were helping us, they would turn us all in, and we all would be executed.

April 8, there were still a few ill men around. Chuck and I decided to go into town, and do some trading for bread and eggs. Strangely enough, we met an American girl that was married to a German. She helped us out a great deal. Did some more trading for supplies, and by April 10, all the other men in the barn were gone. Chuck and I were all alone now. In the days to follow we went into town for supplies.

"April 10, we came out of our hiding place and found out four other fellows were doing the same thing that we were doing. One day latter we just about got caught coming out of our hiding place. A farmer turned his dogs out to look for us. We got to a Polish family's house, and we were safe. These people filled our water bottles. We also got some exercise and went back into hiding in our barn.

"The next night, we went to our Polish friend's house. We found out that a German garrison was supposed to move in and possibly into our barn. We then moved our things out of the barn, and then decided to move it all back again, thinking we could hold out even if the German were there. The German troops moved in, but we still could get out at night when the Germans slept. The next day we contacted a German friend who supplied us with bread, water, and news of the German's movements. He had good news for us. He expected the American troops to advance into town within a week. Bad news, we found out President Roosevelt was dead.

"On April 15, one of our friends brought us news that the American soldiers were two miles from the town. We also started to hear gun fire from our troops. Lots of people are starting to leave the town now, because of the gun fire. We also found a new way out of the barn so we could get supplies without getting caught. The next day when a friend brought us some eggs and meat, the barn started to shake indicating that the fighting and our troops were very close.

"The next morning, we had a little good news. It won't be long now. From the sounds of things our troops are getting very close. Had a hard time getting out of the barn because of the presence of a few German soldiers, but we got out and got some exercise and some food from our Polish friends. The next day we kept very quiet all day in the barn. The Germans were pulling out. By 9:00 AM, they were gone. Boy what a relief! Went out that night and celebrated with our Polish friends. Feel a lot freer now.

"April 19, saw our Polish friends. The firing sounds a lot nearer now. Got some eggs and potatoes. We went into town that night to see our English speaking girl for what news that we could get. When we got home, we found that German troops had moved back into our barn. Boy, what a day! To top that off, it had been raining all day. The next day, the Germans were still in our barn. So we had to stay out and visited some friends and got some food.

"The next day, April 22, we sneaked back into our barn, while there were still soldiers and horses in the main part of the barn. The Germans did not turn on the barn lights until we were in our hiding place. So, we were safe again. The next day it was still raining hard. Boy, it was good to be back in our barn, where our food and blankets are! Bad news, the Germans are still living with us, and we almost got caught. The next day, they left the barn, and put a large gun into service, about a half mile north of us.

"On April 24, we heard mortar gun fire over the hill, and looked out of the barn and saw American tanks coming over the ridge. Boy, what a sight! We were liberated! We made contact with the major in charge. He put us in a half track, and took us to the headquarters of the 14th Tank Division, 448th Tank Battalion at Hilpoltstien, Germany. On the next day, we left on an Army supply truck for Nestsdt. Then we went to the airfield. On April 26, we were flown to La Havre, France, and got on a bus and taken to Camp Lucky Strike. We filled out some papers, and we were on our way home.

Navigator 2Lt. Robert L. Bobst.

By Printha Fox, daughter.

"Robert Bobst was born April 6, 1921, in Alexander, Iowa. His parents were Fred A. and Kathryn Bobst. When Robert was young, the family moved to a farm in southern Madison County, Iowa north of the town of St. Charles. He attended Ebenezer Elementary school and Patterson Public School. To get to school at Patterson, he walked almost two miles to meet a bus. At one place along the way, he would cross the Middle River. He didn't do sports or after school activities partly because of the distance he would have to walk after practice. He was 16 when he graduated in 1937.

"Electronics had always interested Robert. He built his own crystal radio when he was at home. He had completed 3 quarters (1 year) studying electronic engineering at Iowa State College of Agriculture and Mechanic Arts (now Iowa State University), at Ames, Iowa, when he enlisted in the Army Air Corps.

"Meanwhile, his future wife, Sheryl J. Junkin, was working at the draft board for Madison County. She got the job through her father who was on the Madison County Selective Service Board at the time. He resigned afterward to avoid conflict of interest.

"Sometime while Sheryl was working in Winterset, Robert and Sheryl met and became friends. They didn't date for very long before they decided to marry. Robert proposed at Sheryl's family's home near Earlham, Iowa. Sheryl's father told her to be sure to be willing to marry half of the man as well as the whole man. She was.

"They were married in San Marcos, Texas on October 2, 1943, while Robert was in training. Sheryl came back to Winterset to work during that time. He trained at Boise, Idaho - the crew was assembled there - and at Topeka, Kansas and Sheryl would take trips to visit him. In Boise, Sheryl stayed in the former governor's house.

"Robert's parents also went to Topeka to see him. There they met other members of the crew; among them co-pilot Jack Verran. Robert wanted to show his father his plane, but security would not allow them near it.

"The last time Sheryl saw Robert was in Topeka. She stayed there until he left for overseas. Then she went back to work at the draft board.

"On February 27, 1944, the crew left for overseas via the southern route. They were to go to Brazil, but had to stop in Puerto Rico because they were late taking off. On February, 28 they arrived in Belem, Brazil and flew the next day to Natal, Brazil, their taking off point to cross the Atlantic. The plane made it safely to Dakar, Senegal, in West-Africa. Verran mentions in his diary that Bobst made a good navigator. Next they flew to Marrakech in Morocco in Africa, where they stayed in an old French Foreign Legion fort. According to Verran, they had very nice quarters. On March 8, the crew landed in England at Valley in Wales.

"Robert didn't mention much to Sheryl about life for the people of England except to say that at one social event he attended, a woman opened a coat she was wearing to reveal that she was wearing only a coat.

"The crew had combat training in Ireland and traveled there via Scotland. By March 28 they were back in England. On April 10, 1944, the crew went on their first mission; to Southern France. There was some flak as they passed over the French coast. On April 11 Verran writes; "went on my second mission today. The target was a JU88 factory near Berlin. We lost three ships. We ran into heavy flak and German fighters. The 8th Air Force lost 64 bombers and 14 fighters today."

"On April 12 the base was bombed but missed the crew members "by about 600 feet." Verran's April 20 entry: "We did not fly today. I lost some good buddies yesterday, when Davis's crew went down. That's what really hurts. There are now four empty beds in our B.O.Q."

"On April 22 the crew went on another mission to the Ham's Marshaling Yards, then the largest yard Europa, but had to turn back just over the enemy's coast. The rest of the group came back an hour later followed by enemy fighters. Verran recalls; "They shot three of our bombers down over our field. It was a mess, bullets and flak everywhere. Scaggs brought his ship in on fire. It blew up later."

"April 25. Verran wrote: "Today our mission was in S.W. Germany. We did not get to drop our bombs on the primary target. Our electrical system went out, our number two engine was shot out, and our oxygen was running low. We just made it back to the English coast and set her down. They sent another ship down to pick us up. It was a long day, from 0200 to 2200 hours. I was sure ready to spend the duration in Switzerland. The next day, we slept all morning and flew a practice mission in the afternoon."

"April 27. Co-pilot Verran: "Well, we had an early start today, 0300 hour. We bombed targets just over the French coast. We're getting ready for the second front, the invasion of Europe, D-Day. We were hit by flak twice, but made it back OK. We were all set to go on the second mission of the day, but our ship was out of commission.""

***

"Bobst's account after his arrival in neutral Sweden; "When I followed Sgt. Leonard out the bomb-bay the co-pilot was standing on the cat-walk. I tried to make a delayed jump, and I imagine it was almost 500 feet before my parachute opened. About five seconds later I hit the ground hard and was knocked out. When I recovered consciousness, two men were helping me. One rolled up my parachute, and both pointed to the woods. One told me to hide and pointed East, remarking, "Deutsch." "

""In the woods I threw my parachute, harness, and Mae West under some ferns and my mike and headphones into a clump of bushes. I hit for higher ground, feeling pretty groggy. Soon I passed out and must have been unconscious for a couple of hours. When I came to, two men were pointing to two parachutes in the trees. They brought me some coffee, a girl who spoke a bit of English, and a Danish-English book. I explained that I was going to head NE at sundown. These men seemed to have no definite instructions for me and gave me only some food." '

"At sundown, I started off up a small road. I saw some men on bicycles about 100 yards away. They approached, and one called "American," pointing North West, and indicated that there were 20 "Deutsch" that way. I tried to say "Danke" and followed a stream in a generally northern direction, heading for the NE edge of the island as I recalled it from the air. I ran into a railroad, followed it a bit, by-passing the stations, and continued North. About 22.00 I dug into a haystack and stayed there until late afternoon the next day, sleeping when I was not shivering."

"At daybreak I got up and went down to the sea, and in a gully ran into Sgt. Leonard. I discovered that he had some arrangements, so I waited for his friends to turn up. While we were waiting we carefully hid from a couple of men who were searching in the area - only to discover that they were Hutchins, the right waist-gunner and Albert Heikkila, our tail-gunner."

***

"In Winterset there was a soldiers' wives club, and a bowling alley and a skating rink. Sheryl would usually spend her evenings with friends at Tim's café in Winterset, but the evening of April 29 (the date of Robert's plane being shot down) she said she just couldn't go. She said she just felt something compelled her to stay home.

"When Robert's parents and Sheryl learned about Robert being MIA, Sheryl and her mother went to see the Bobsts at St. Charles. It was a cold day and when they got there, Mrs. Bobst had baby chicks in the dining room in a box next to the heater.

"At home in St. Charles was Robert's little brother, Paul, who was about 6 years' old. He knew something important was happening when Robert's mother placed a flag in the window that marked the home as an MIA home. He remembers the flag being a red flag with a white center with a blue star. There was a gold tassel at the bottom and a dowel at the top.

***

"Robert's family and Sheryl didn't know that Robert was back in the States when he called his parents to tell them to be at the "Y" south of Bevington in an hour. They got in the car. When Robert stepped off of the bus, Paul learned that the person they were meeting was his brother - he didn't know he had one. Paul still has the thumbnail-sized compass and the $25 war bond his brother gave him.

"Later, Robert was given a pin that had a boot and a propeller he wore under his lapel that signified he had walked out of Germany. He was not allowed to show it. Sometime many years later he was upset that he had lost it. According to Michael, Bobst's son, It's one of the few times that Bobst ever mentioned the war.

"After spending time with his mom and dad and brother, Robert went to Winterset to surprise Sheryl. She had been spending the weekend with her parents on the farm near Earlham. Leona Duncan, the lady in whose house in Winterset Sheryl was living, told Robert that he shouldn't surprise her with such big news. He called Sheryl at her parents' house. Sheryl remembers running up the 1/2 mile lane to meet his car.

"When the war in Europe was over, he served as an instructor. On training flights, the 3-man crew would fly everywhere in the U.S., sometimes delivering soldiers who were on leave. On one training flight, Bobst flew from Walla Walla, Washington, to Des Moines, Iowa, but he couldn't land in Des Moines because the landing gear wouldn't operate. They flew to St. Louis and back before the landing gear would work and then they landed.

"He was allowed to make the trip to Iowa because his grandfather had passed away. He was to stay three days, but somehow he got to stay three weeks. Meanwhile, Sheryl was in Walla Walla, pregnant with their first child. She was upset that Robert chose to stay away so long. To ease things over when Robert was to return to Walla Walla, his mother sent along two chickens for Sheryl. Kathryn worried about the chickens staying fresh for the trip. Bobst told her not to worry. The plane would be flying high enough for most of the return trip to freeze the chickens. Robert and Sheryl didn't share the chickens with anyone.

"In the winter of 1960, Robert's family went to California. There they visited the family of Harry Ambrosini, the engineer who was killed. The family had a vineyard in Fresno. The Bobst family visited nose-gunner Stanley Jones in Mercedes/Venice, and Orland and Borgie Howard in San Francisco. Mr. Howard was still in the service stationed just north of San Francisco.

"As a civilian, Robert along with Sheryl, made a good life for his family. At the end of the war, Robert and Sheryl and their 6 month-old son lived with Robert's parents. Through the Gl Bill he was given $90 per month until they could make a living farming. In 1947 they moved to a farm south of Earlham. Printha and Chris, their daughters were born there. In 1959 they lived in Panora, Iowa on another farm and moved back to Earlham in 1961. Robert and Sheryl worked together in the farm implement business, "Bobst Implement," where they managed the selling and repair of International Harvester and Ford tractors and equipment.

"Bobst changed jobs in 1968 to work as an engineer at Iowa Public Television. He retired in the fall of 1986. He was an avid Ham Radio operator -signal KOSGE. Bobst's other hobbies included polishing rocks and doing silversmithing to make jewelry. He also always had a vegetable garden.

"He passed away in January of 1987. Sheryl was going to retire with him, but at that time she was working for the Iowa Federation of Women's Clubs as their state bookkeeper. She decided to continue working there and she did until she retired in 1996.

Engineer T/Sgt. Harry T. Ambrosini.

Harry T. Ambrosini was born in Fresno, California on January 27, 1920. His enlistment records states he had completed 4 years of high school and was employed as a farm hand when he enlisted as a private in the Army Air Corps on October 8, 1941.

After basic training, he was selected to attend mechanics school, and soon underwent the necessary training to become a flight engineer. He also graduated from the aerial gunnery course of instruction. He also received intensive training as a combat crew member on the B-24 type aircraft.

In late 1943, the combat crew to which he was assigned was deployed to England as a replacement crew. The crew was assigned to the 448th Bomb Group at Seething RAF Station 146, and later was sent to the 715th Bomb Squadron there.

On April 29, 1944, while on a mission to bomb German war facilities in Berlin, Germany, his B-24 received several hits from flak on the bomb run. Three engines were knocked out, the nose turret was put out of commission, and the tail assembly badly damaged. The pilot was determined to see if he could make the return trip, but began losing altitude rapidly. The bomb bay doors were cranked open by hand as they were damaged, the pilot alerted the crew for bail out over the Danish island of Bornholm, and all crew members left the aircraft.

Sgt. Ambrosini's parachute did not open, and he was killed upon impacting the ground.

Right Waist-Gunner S/Sgt. William L. Hutchins.

From the Escape & Evasion Report, dated May 6, 1944, at the Legation of the United States of America, Stockholm, Sweden.

"This is the personal narrative of S/Sgt. William L. Hutchins, top-turret gunner, 3222646, 448th Bomb Group, 715th Bomb Squadron, B-24H, # 479. Departed England 0730 hours, 29 April, 1944, to attack the target Berlin, Germany.

"Heavy flak was encountered over the Drummer Lake region, the target, and southeast of Hannover. Number one, two, and four engines were knocked out. As the formation crossed the German coast, somewhere north of Stettin, where engine # 1 failed, the plane lost altitude so rapidly that the pilot headed for the nearest land.

"Lt. Orland T. Howard, the pilot, issued orders for the crew to bail out as they crossed the southern tip of Bornholm Island, Denmark.

"Bailed out of the ship at 13.45 hours over the southern coast of Bornholm island. I landed near a farm house where the people helped me dispose of my equipment, given food and civilian clothes, and told by a doctor who was there to proceed due north, to stay off the roads, keep under cover or travel in the woods as much as possible."

"I started walking at 14.15 hours, and decided to stop and rest until morning. At 06.00 hours, 30 April 1944, I started out again, but only walked about a mile when I approached a farmer who spoke English. He gave me a place to stay, food and water. By 22.00 hours I was again on the move, travelling North across the country. At 02.00, 1 May 1944, I came to a haystack and slept until 06.00 hours."

"After leaving the haystack I headed in the direction of Listed on the coast, arrived there and received shelter and food from a farmer, after explaining to him my situation. He went for a man who could help me to leave the island. This man came and and told me that I would have to stay where I was until he could make the proper arrangements. He told me that he already had four other Americans hiding, waiting for the same opportunity to escape."

"At 16.00 hours, 1 May 1944, he took me to another house in the neighbourhood where I met Lt. Robert L. Bobst, T/Sgt. Russell D. Leonard, and Sgt. Albert L. Heikkila, and later Lt. Laurin M. Derosier. At dusk we set out by car for the

692

fishing village of Tjen, where we boarded a fishing boat at 01.00 hours, 2 May 1944, and set sail at 02.15 hours.

"We arrived at Ystad, Sweden, at 07.15 hours, 2 May 1944, and turned over to the Swedish police. About 13.00 we were taken by train to Malmo, arrived at the police headquarters where we were interrogated and records made. The only information they received was our rank, name, serial number, and that we were American airmen who had escaped from Denmark. The American Consul came for us at 18.00 hours."

"We arrived in Stockholm at 20.15 hours and were met at the station by Lt. H.F. Allen, of the Military Air Attache office.

Tail-Gunner Sgt. Albert L. Heikkila.

By daughter Sharon Kleinendorst.

"Albert was born on August 10, 1923 in Grand Rapids, Minnesota. He was raised, along with an older brother and a younger sister in Coleraine, Minnesota, where he graduated from Greenway High School in 1941. After graduation he worked as a Shop Maintenance Mechanic at Coleraine Airport.

"He enlisted in the Army Air Corps on November 2, 1942. After his discharge from the service on November 6, 1945 he worked for United States Steel as an automotive mechanic/foreman until his retirement 1982.

"He passed away on January 9, 1996, in Grand Rapids, Minnesota.

Tail-Gunner Sgt. Albert L. Heikkila

***

Acknowledgements;
Printha Fox, daughter of Navigator 2Lt. Robert L. Bobst
Sharon Kleinendorst, daughter of Tail-Gunner Sgt. Albert L. Heikkila

CHAPTER 53

448TH BOMB GROUP
715TH BOMB SQUADRON

Type: B-24H • Serial: 42-52435
MACR: 4490 • Air Base: Seething

"Shortly after being captured I was taken down a dirt road in the woods where there was a group of soldiers standing in the center of the road and as I approached they stepped aside and on the road laying on the ground was our bombardier. He had been shot in the back and was grievously wounded. I was allowed to help in any way that I could but it was quite ineffectual. There was nothing I could really do and he died in my arms perhaps an hour or so after I first found him."

Co-Pilot Joseph Kwederis after his return to the States

Pilot: 2Lt. John W. Cathey, 0-808373, POW, Nashville, TN

Co-Pilot: 2Lt. Arthur J. Brisson, 0-751983, POW, St. Paul, MN

Navigator: 2Lt. Joseph J. Kwederis, 0-814346, POW, Brooklyn, NY

Bombardier: F/O Carl M. Carlson, T-1686, KIA, Salt Lake City, UT

Engineer: S/Sgt. Russell E. Howle, 18097532, POW, Yantis, TX

Radio: S/Sgt. Clifton W. Linnell, 11118117, POW, Hyannis, MA

Ball-Turret Gunner: T/Sgt. Culmer H. Darby, 20304517, POW, Sarasota, Fl

Left Waist-Gunner: Sgt. Jack Arluck, 33426161, KIA, Pittsburgh, PA

Right Waist-Gunner: Sgt. Arnold J. Wetzel, 32466992, POW, Maplewood, NJ

Tail-Gunner: Sgt. Anthony J. Novelli Jr., 12158891, POW, Brooklyn, NY

2 KIA, 8 POW

Crash Site: Elbergen/County Lingen, Germany
Time: 13.56

694

Pilot 2Lt. John W. Cathey.

By Roger C. Cathey, son.

"John William Cathey, was born on March 23, 1922 in Chapel Hill, TN. His parents were John M. Cathey and Mary Elizabeth Early. John graduated from East High School, Nashville, TN and met his wife Eulalia at a local roller skating rink. The two married in 1942. John then worked at Stephen's Market, a local grocery store at the time.

"John remained in the Air Force after WWII and made a career of the military. He was stationed for a while at Tinker AFB in Oklahoma before coming back to Nashville. Later in 1949 he was trans- *Pilot 2Lt. John W. Cathey.* ferred to the Island of Bermuda, taking his wife and children with him. He was stationed there for approximately three years. Back home to Nashville, TN, again where he trained pilots at Seward AFB in Smyrna, TN (just outside of Nashville) for the Korean War.

"In 1953, he was transferred to McClellan AFB in Sacramento, CA, followed by Whittier Air Force Depot in Whittier, CA, where he stayed for approximately 3 years. Next transfer was to Norton AFB in San Bernardino, CA, for another 3 years. In 1958, John was transferred to Arlington, VA, and was stationed at the Pentagon, where he remained until he retired in 1967 as a Lt. Colonel.

"After retiring from the Air Force, he started his second career at Lockheed Aircraft Company in Ontario, CA. He remaining at Lockheed for 15 years before retiring again. He passed away in California, on March 14, 1996.

Co-Pilot 2Lt .Arthur J. Brisson

told his story in a series of conversations during the 1970s with work colleagues. They recorded his account and transcribed it. In Arthur's words:

"It was about the end of January, 1944, when I received orders to report to Mitchell Field, New York, with the crew I'd been assigned to, and we arrived at Mitchell Field sometime probably in the early part of February. At about that time I managed to get a quick trip home before leaving for overseas, which was a rather unexpected windfall. I did get home to St. Paul to visit with my family, then went back to New York.

"In New York we had been assigned a brand new B-24 airplane. We took off from Mitchell Field on the first leg of our overseas trip and flew to West Palm Beach, Florida. We landed at West Palm Beach, got some further instructions, then from West Palm Beach we flew to Trinidad. It was a very interesting flight. I had never flown over the Caribbean before, and flying over Cuba and the other islands was beautiful. It was a perfect day, visibility absolutely unlimited. I never saw such a beautiful sight as those islands. Viewed from the air under those conditions they just looked like emerald gems in that sea of blue.

"We landed at Trinidad Island. Nothing unusual happened, strictly routine flight. We spent a day or two on the island

Co-Pilot 2Lt .Arthur J. Brisson

of Trinidad getting ready for the next leg of our flight, which was to be to Belem, Brazil. We took off from Trinidad early one morning and flew in a southeasterly direction. We flew over the mouth of the Amazon River and through that shoulder of South America and landed at Belem, another uneventful flight.

"The next leg of our overseas flight was from Belen to Natal (Brazil). That proved a rather interesting flight because we encountered tropical storms. I have never seen it rain so hard in my life. It was sort of like flying through a waterfall – torrential rains, just unbelievable. It was rather frightening in a way because cylinder head temperatures on the engines dropped considerably below normal operating temperature. However, we were warned that such a thing could happen.

"The interesting thing is as we were approaching the landing field, which was totally obscured by rain and so on, without any warning we broke out of the rain storms into brilliantly shining sunlight and into a traffic pattern that was cluttered with every kind of an airplane I guess the United States had in the air. There were PBYs, C-47s, C-46s, C-54s, everything imaginable – all trying to land, all flying at different air speeds. After the tense flight, running into this situation was somewhat nerve-wracking. However, we were successful in making a landing and spent two or three days at Natal.

"The next leg of our overseas flight was something of a question. I don't remember exactly how many nautical miles it is from Natal to Dakar (in western Africa), but at the rate we had been consuming fuel the B-24 airplane we were flying just would not have that much range. I spoke to the Engineering Officer at Natal and he kind of smiled and thought we were pulling his leg or some such thing, and I didn't get a great deal of consideration from him. So we took the crew and redistributed the weight in the airplane. It seemed to allow the airplane to fly better.

"So at about three o'clock one morning we had been gassed up and we were all set to go. We started the south Atlantic crossing. It was quite a thrill because as a young boy I had dreamed of doing just that. We had been weather briefed of course. We were told that there would be an equatorial front, and after we had flown the required number of miles sure enough there was the equatorial front. This is a weather characteristic along the equator of the Atlantic Ocean and is just about absolutely predictable.

"After flying through the equatorial front I continued on course and landed at Dakar sometime in the neighborhood of three o'clock in the afternoon. The landing was rather exciting because we had never landed on a metal landing strip before. When the wheels touched this landing strip there was an awful racket and it was rather a surprise after having landed on concrete runways and asphalt runways up to this time. We were taking the airplane over to a parking spot and on getting out of the airplane we discovered that Africa can really be hot. It was just unbelievable. The date now would probably be around February 11th or thereabouts.

"We were furnished transportation from the flight line to the living quarters of the base and eventually ended up at the Officers Club. I was very surprised to find a great number of my friends from cadet days and from different stations all en route to some station in Europe.

"We spent probably two days in Dakar and prepared for the next leg of our flight, which was from Dakar to Marrakech. This was a rather interesting flight: We flew over the Sahara Desert. It's just as big as they said it was. We landed at Marrakech and spent a day or two there and were lucky enough to go into the city. We went to the casino area, which was supposedly off limits I guess, but anyway this was our first look at an African city of any size and it was very interesting, colorful – something that you read about.

"The next step on our flight was from Marrakech to Prestwick, Scotland. This is a rather long flight. It was undertaken around midnight, I believe. We flew northwest over the Atlas Mountains, out over the coast of Africa, and up along the Atlantic seaboard west of the coast of Spain, made landfall on the southern tip of Ireland, turned up into the Irish Sea, and proceeded into Prestwick.

"There is a rather interesting little note at this point because the English seemed to have a rather peculiar sense of humor. Across the beginning of the runway they wrote the word *Achtung,* which of course you know is German for attention.

"My memory gets a little fuzzy at this point. From Prestwick, Scotland, we boarded a train and went down to London. I don't exactly remember what the point of this particular trip was. Anyway we knocked around the city for a while and we were next sent to a base in Northern Ireland just out of Belfast. We were sent to this Irish base with the understanding that we were supposed to be taught

U.K. procedure, short for United Kingdom radio communications procedure. During the entire time that we were in Belfast or near Belfast we received no instruction whatsoever. However, the Officers Club was quite a place. There was a perpetual craps game going and a friend of mine and I were rather fortunate. We made quite a bit of money playing craps there.

"From Belfast I was assigned to my regular combat group, which was called the 448th Heavy Bombardment Group, Third Wing, 8th Air Force. We were stationed just south of Norwich in a small town by the name of Seething. This is close to the North Sea. It was the first field coming in from Germany as you crossed the North Sea and entered England at the point south of the Great Yarmouth.

"It took a bit of time to become operational with this combat group. We had to learn the area, learn the necessary procedures for that area, and become indoctrinated into the group's policies. As it was the first airfield in the from the coast, the Germans had a rather unpleasant knack of running intruder airplanes into bombing this particular base. They were considered nuisance raids, but they made it a little difficult trying to get some rest on those nights.

"On April 29th, 1944, we were scheduled for a raid on Berlin. On that particular flight our group was the last wave. This was called the tail-end-Charlie group. In that group we were flying in the high right position. That happens to be the most vulnerable position, being exposed to enemy fighter attack from the high right.

"This particular mission proceeded as normal until we got over Berlin. By the time we got there the sky was black with flak and smoke. There were quite a few airplanes that had been hit. This was a maximum effort mission, which meant that 800-plus airplanes – B-24s, B-17s – were on that mission.

"While we were over Berlin we took a direct flak hit on the number one engine, and by the time we came out of the flak area and headed 270 degrees for home we were losing speed and altitude. We were hobbling along someplace near 29,000 feet, losing altitude. We were able to hook onto a couple of groups passing by beneath us and we managed to fight our way back to near the Dutch-German border. It was about that time that five enemy 109s ganged up on us. They took turns making passes on our tail and they finally got us shot down.

"At that particular time during the war the Air Force did not have fighter airplanes that could provide fighter escort all the way in on the deep penetration missions. They would protect us in a way that then we would be on our own, then on the way home they would pick us up. This particular day on our way back home we just did not get picked up by friendly fighters. Tragically, while we were in the process of being shot down our waist-gunner Jack Arleck was hit and killed in the air.

"As we were going down we lost all power and all engines – remaining engines, that is – and the signal was given to bail out. To the best of my knowledge everybody got the message and everybody got out, including the man who had been killed. We all hit the silk and we were all captured on the ground as we had come down in a military maneuver area.

"Shortly after being captured I was taken down a dirt road in the woods where there was a group of soldiers standing in the center of the road, and as I approached they stepped aside and on the road lying on the ground was our bombardier. He had been shot in the back and was grievously wounded. I was allowed to help in any way that I could, but it was quite ineffectual. There was nothing I could really do and he died in my arms perhaps an hour or so after I first found him.

"After that we were taken by our captors to a small town, probably three or four kilometers from where we had been picked up. It was at this point where we were put into the hands of people who were really professionals at handling prisoners.

"We were transported from this small town through various truck and train rides to Frankfurt, Germany, which at that time was a primary interrogation center for captured Allied fliers. At Frankfurt the POW camp was called Dulag Luft, and that was the first point where we were questioned and interrogated. After interrogation we were put into a holding pen and held for several days while a prisoner group of adequate size was being made up to ship to to a permanent POW camp.

"By the time our group had been assembled to an adequate size we were put on a POW train. That meant that the coach windows and doors were all barred and there were guards throughout the train. This trip was from Frankfurt to east Germany. Along the route we had the unpleasant experience of being bombed. I can remember a bombing raid at Chemnitz. We were left in the railroad yard with bombs flying all over, locked into our train coaches. Another bad time I believe was at Leipzig. I think we were probably bombed about three times en route to our permanent camp, which was at a place called Sagan.

"Sagan is a small German town located on a line southeast of Berlin by probably 100 to 150 miles or so. Actually the prison camp at Sagan wasn't too bad: It was a new place, the barracks were pretty good, and we were being fed somewhat decently. We were getting Red Cross parcels. That was an eleven-pound parcel of food. Each man got one package per week, so things were going pretty good. But the time that this lasted was pretty brief because shortly thereafter it became two men to a package per week and then as time wore on it got to be practically non-existent. It was an event when we got a Red Cross parcel.

"Time in the POW camp at Sagan passed rather well because the conditions weren't too bad. The weather was nice through the summer and there were a lot of my friends there. We were playing softball and volleyball and things like that as long as we had the equipment. Things were going rather well, but as time went on through the months of September and October we knew that the Russians were approaching from the east because we could now hear the sound of heavy artillery.

"And that continued up to December 28th, when about nine-thirty at night we were roused and told immediately to prepare to march out of the camp. We gathered our possessions as best we could and strapped them on our backs, in bags, or whatever. We made sleds out of tables and the like and we left the camp. It was now snowing and starting to turn cold. We marched all of that first night and part of the next day. Now the weather had become severe. It was as cold as it had ever gotten in that part of Germany at that time of the year. We walked for two, three, or four days in these very severe conditions, and finally we were brought to a railroad yard where we were put in boxcars.

"There were 55 men to a car, and there really isn't that much space in a European boxcar. It was determined that if half of us sat down and half stood and we alternated, we could manage to get a little rest. We were locked in these boxcars for four or five days and eventually we were taken out of them at the city of Nuremberg. The weather had moderated somewhat by this time, though it was raining. We were marched from the railroad yard in Nuremberg to a prison camp that had been occupied by Italians. This camp was absolutely horrible. It was filthy dirty, everything was broken, there were no facilities to speak of. I believe it was around the first few days of February that we arrived there. It was also at this time that the Allies – both the Americans and the English – were bombing railroad yards throughout Germany. And unfortunately this prison camp was located just two miles east of the marshaling yard at Nuremberg, so during the day we were bombed by the 8th Air Force and during the night we were bombed by the British.

"These British night shows were something because the racket would be unbelievable, with the ground fire from the German 88-millimeter guns and the bombs falling and the shooting back and forth between the airplanes. It was a real bedlam and the sky would be lighted with flares and the fires – it was really Dante's Inferno.

"It was at this time that food was practically non-existent. We were literally starving on our feet. It was at this time that perhaps I became most disgusted. I really didn't think that we would be able to survive too much longer under the conditions in which we were living. However, we got a break because on Easter Sunday a long line of Red Cross trucks was seen coming down the road toward the camp. They were allowed to enter the camp. Parcels were handed out and we had what was known as a "kriegie" bash. (Kriegie is short for the German word *kriegsgefangener*, meaning POW.) Everybody had something to eat. What a time!

"It was shortly after this good fortune that the Americans and the British were coming down toward Nuremberg from the north and the west and we were again told to pack our belongings. We were marched south out of Nuremberg on a march that probably would have taken four or five days. During this time I managed to escape on five different occasions but was recaptured each time. The final time I was taken to the town of Moosburg and put in a POW camp there where my friends had been brought from Nuremberg. And I was there about two days when finally the Allies came and the camp was liberated.

"After being liberated we organized our groups of POWs and we were furnished air transport out of the city of Regensburg and flown from there to Reims, France, for processing back into the Armed Forces. From Reims we were sent to a place near Le Havre. It was called Camp Lucky Strike. It was a tent city that housed probably 20,000 to 25,000 men. It was strictly chaos because they had expected to retrieve POWs at the rate of about 10,000 a day and actually what happened was they were getting 100,000 a day for the first few days. This number might be a little strong but anyway things were totally disorganized.

"However, after a certain length of time we were put on shipping lists and as our names came to the top we were taken by truck down to Le Havre, where we were put on ships to be transported back to the U.S. The ship that I came home on was a brand new 22,000-ton Coast Guard vessel. It was her maiden trip carrying troops and it was a really very nice ship. We made it from Le Havre to Boston in five days, and upon docking in Boston there were trains waiting for us. We were taken to Camp Miles Standish, where we were given clothes and the like and then separated out into groups for the different parts of the country. Being from Minnesota, I was put in a group on a train scheduled to go into the north central states: Illinois, Missouri, Minnesota, Iowa, North and South Dakota. Things happened so fast that I wasn't even able to telephone my folks that I was back in the U.S.

"When we arrived it was about nine o'clock at night, and a friend of mine who had been on the train called his sister who would come and drive us to our homes. I knew that I just couldn't come walking into the house when my folks thought I was still in Europe, so as we were going through the downtown district of St. Paul we stopped the car and I picked up a phone and called my folks. They were absolutely flabbergasted. It was ten minutes later that I was walking into my own home. There's not much more to tell: I was given leave, rest and recuperation for sixty days at home, at the end of which time I reported to Miami Beach, Florida, for further R&R. From there I asked for and got a transfer to San Antonio, Texas, and was up for reclassification or separation. In the interview it was determined that I could remain in the service, but there would be no guarantee for the time after June 30, 1946. So, facing that sort of proposition, I elected to separate from the service.

By daughter Mary Brisson;

"Upon leaving the Air Force Arthur dreamed of having a family and living in California, where he had spent his early days in the service and had trained to fly.

"In 1956 he married Betty Galloway, who shared his wish for children, his talent for dancing, and his love of travel. Together they built a home in North St. Paul, Minnesota, and within a few years had a daughter and a son.

"The family took the first of many road trips to the West when the children were small. Art was proud to show them the National Parks, and he passed along his love of the spectacular Western landscape.

"While working for the United States Postal Data Center in Minneapolis in 1966, Art won a job transfer to California and the family moved to Sunnyvale, a city on the San Francisco peninsula. Art soon became an administrator in the medical research department of the Veterans Administration hospital in Palo Alto. His business skill and personal warmth made him much admired by the medical staff there and at Stanford University as he facilitated programs on which the two institutions collaborated.

"During the Sunnyvale years, Art played a little golf, drove the family all around the West on summer vacations, and made sure his kids stayed on track to college.

"After he retired from the VA in 1978, he and Betty moved first to the Sierra foothills and eventually to Arizona. They had fun entertaining friends, playing golf together, and traveling widely in the United States and Canada by recreational vehicle. They also made trips around Europe and to New Zealand, always driving on their own itineraries.

"In Germany once they visited some of the places where Art had been held as a POW. He had often spoken of the kindness of the German families who risked their own safety to help him in the last days of the war as he repeatedly broke from the forced POW march and tried to make his own way. He harbored no grudges, though the effects of constant danger and near starvation remained with him throughout his life. His war stories were of the heroism and resourcefulness of his fellow airmen and POWs. He mourned his lost crew members and cherished his lifelong friendship with Joe Kwederis.

"Art and Betty had moved to the Seattle area and were in their fifty-fifth year of devoted marriage when Betty passed away in 2011. Art followed the next year, at the age of 95. Until his latest days, at the sight of a family member or the memory of piloting an airplane, his face would light up with joy.

Navigator 2Lt. Joseph J. Kwederis.

From his obituary.

"Joe was born in West-Point, New York on January 13, 1922. He was educated and enjoyed his childhood surrounded by a large and loving family in highland Falls, NY. After graduating high school he moved with his family to Brooklyn, NY where he met, courted and married the love of his life, Elaine.

"At the time they were married, he was enlisted and commissioned as a Second Lt. in the US Army Air Corps where he served as a B-24 navigator. In January 1944, he was sent off to Europe to fight in WWII.

"On April 29, 1944, after several successful bombing missions over Germany, his mission ended with the downing of his aircraft. He and his surviving crew of the B-24 "Liberator" were captured. He spent the next year as a POW in a German camp. He was repatriated in May, 1945 and returned home to recover from his injuries. He was honorably discharged in October, 1945.

"Joe began his civilian life working and going to college at night. Soon after the birth of their first son Joseph in 1946 they moved from brooklyn, NY to their first home in Fair Lawn, NJ. Joe earned his Bachelor of Industrial Engineering degree in July of 1954 from New York University. With their family now numbering four – three boys and a girl – they purchased their second home in Oakland, NJ, where he remained until his death.

"Joe had a long career in sales and marketing for various manufacturing companies. After retiring, he started his own company, Ramapo Hill Associates. "There was no way of stopping Joe," as Elaine would say.

Bombardier F/O Carl M. Carlson.

Bombardier Carl Carlson was shot in the stomach at point blank range by a German guard when the airmen were ordered to pack their chutes properly. He was taken to the Gaststätte Klüsener Inn at Elbergen and died on the table in the inn. Buried in the New Cemetery in Lingen, Germany.

Navigator Joseph Kwederis stated after the war:

"The following explanation of the fate of Flight Officer Carl M. Carlson, T-1686, is absolute fact, eyewitnessed by myself and seven other crew members. F/O Carlsen bailed out of the B-24 in excellent condition. He was definitely **not** wounded at the time of the jump. He was however found by us crew members about half-an-hour later in the company of German Whermacht soldiers. At this time we discovered that he had been shot at close range, in the abdomen. The size of the wound was extremely large and he was nearly unconscious and losing much blood. In talking to Lt. Arthur J. Brisson, co-pilot of the crew, F/O Carlson told him that he had been shot by a German soldier for no apparent reason. However, it is believed that Carlson was trying to evade the enemy that caused his death. I should strongly urge that he be awarded the Bronze Star for this heroism.

Engineer S/Sgt. Russell E. Howle.

By his widow Virginia Howle:

"Russell E. Howle was born March 31, 1922 to Governor (Gove) and Martha Ellis (Banks) Howle at Gamblin, Texas. He was the twelfth child and the eighth boy born into this family. He grew up in the family farm with these brothers and four sisters and worked very hard as most kids of this time did. He attended

Gamblin elementary school near his home until high school. He was the only one of the boys who actually went to school; the others quit and worked.

"To finish high school, Russell had to walk or ride a horse about six or eight miles to Alba High School. He played basketball and often after a ballgame, he would sleep in the woods between school and home. He was too proud to allow friends to take him home! He finished high school in 1941 and worked odd jobs until Pearl Harbor. He then enlisted in the Air Corps on September 3, 1942.

"This was a whole new world for this farm boy who had never been more than a hundred miles from home. He trained at bases in Texas, New Mexico, Utah and finally some on the East Coast. He shipped out of Langley Field,

Engineer S/Sgt. Russell E. Howle

Virginia on February 22, 1944, went to Brazil, Africa, Scotland, Ireland and finally England.

"The war really began for him at this time. He flew missions almost every day. He said that taking off with a load of bombs and fuel was bad, but having to abort a mission and having to land with this load was worse! He said that on the day they were shot down he was very edgy but most of the men were very calm.

"When he landed, the civilians got him and almost killed him before the German soldiers arrived and saved him. When the Germans marched the men out of Stalag XVII-B ahead of the Russians, it was bad for them because they had no idea where they would land. The march was a long torturous ordeal. Most of the men were so poor and weak that walking was difficult. The men who were in better shape helped the ones who needed help. In fact, Russell carried one of his buddies (a little, thin guy) bodily a lot of the time. Russell was not very well himself. He had to stay at Camp Lucky Strike two weeks longer than the others. The doctors told him that he had the worst case of malnutrition they had ever seen. This scared the young farm boy very badly because he didn't know what malnutrition was. He would tell this on himself to show how "dumb" he was.

"After he came home and got out of service on November 4, 1945, he worked for his brother at a gasoline service station. I met him soon after this and helped persuade him to attend college on the GI bill, which he did. He became a teacher and was in education for nearly forty years, helping so many kids along the way. His Post Traumatic Syndrome finally hit him and he had to give up education. He really did suffer from this!

"During the teaching and education period we attended nearly all the National POW Conventions. This way we kept up with buddies and made so many wonderful friends. Also, after he retired, he became a National Service Officer for the VA and helped the guys and their widows get the financial aid they were due.

"He had a wonderfully productive life and was never bitter toward the Germans. He and I had been married 62 1/2 years!

Waist-Gunner Sgt. Jack Arluck.

Jack Arluck enlisted in the Army from Pittsburgh, on 13 February 1943 as a private. He attended four years of High School and worked as a semi-skilled routeman.

Fighters heavily damaged # 42-52435, piloted by John Cathey. They left the formation near Osnabrück on the way back. They bailed out at 13.56 and the plane crashed four kilometers west of Eibergen, Germany. Sgt. Arluck perished in the crash. He was probably unconscious due to lack of oxygen or wounded or killed during the fighter attack. He was probably still in the bomber when it crashed. He was initially buried in the Neuer Friedhof in Lingen and after the war re-interred in Margraten, Netherlands.

The crash of the bomber.
By German researcher Reinhard Bojer.

"Shortly after nine o'clock a.m. on Saturday, April 29, 1944, the air raid warning was sounded over Lingen and surroundings. A bit later, a seemingly endless stream of aircraft passed overhead in the direction of Berlin.

"Around two o'clock p.m. bomber formations appeared again over the Ems area on their return flight to England. The people on the ground were still waiting for the "all clear" signal when all of a sudden a B-24 with roaring engines flew slowly and at a low altitude over the southern part of Darme. The bomber carried the serial number 42-53435 and belonged to the 448th Bomb Group.

"The people of Darme and neighboring villages witnessed a vicious air battle. Two German fighters appeared at full speed and attacked the bomber with blazing canons. The altitude of the bomber then was only few hundred meters and it was obvious that she would crash. The fighters attacked again and again, flying around the bomber like insects. The pilot of the bomber, John Cathey, still managed to bring the stricken bomber across the Ems River.

"The crew waited to bail out until the very last moment, they just had enough time to open their chutes before they reached the ground. While descending they must have seen their bomber crash on the Elbergener Field. Debris of the bomber was spread out over a length of 800 meters. At the end of the crash site the heaviest components of the bomber, the four engines, penetrated two meters into the sandy heather soil. Smoke was rising above what remained of the proud aircraft.

"Due to the delayed bail out and the low altitude of the bomber the crew members made a hard landing but nobody was seriously injured. The left-waist gunner Jack Arluck was killed in the crash of the bomber. He was buried the following day in the civil cemetery of Lingen and was after the war reinterred in an American-Belgian cemetery in Neuville-en-Codroz in the Belgian Ardennes.

"As always, quite a few people ran to the site of the crash, among them a German soldier on home leave. He carried his gun and wanted to capture one of the American "terror fliers."

A memorial erected at the crash site of B-24 #42-52435, dedicated to the two arimen killed in action: Arluck and Carlson

Quite a distance away from the wreck of the bomber he found himself confronted with one of the airmen; the bombardier Carl M. Carlson. What then happened is unclear but the fact remains that he shot the airman at close quarters in the belly.

"Two airmen helped to bring the badly wounded Carlson to the town of Eibergen, about three miles away. Having arrived there they waited for help that never came. He died an extremely painful death on a table in a local pub that lasted three hours. His screams could be heard all over the center of the village. He was also initially interred in Lingen.

"Carlson's murderer was never brought to justice but people who knew him said that for the rest of his life he suffered under the remorse of this deed.

***

Acknowledgements;
Roger C. Cathey, son of 2Lt. John W. Cathey
Mary Brisson, daughter of 2Lt. Arthur J. Brisson.
Glenn Kwederis, son of 2Lt. Joseph J. Kwederis
Virginia Howle, wdow of S/Sgt. Russell E. Howle
Reinhard Bojer, Germany.

CHAPTER 54

452ND BOMB GROUP
728TH BOMB SQUADRON

Type: B-17 • Serial: 42-39981 "Rugged but Right"
MACR: 4450 • Air Base: Deopham Green

Aircraft B-17G 42-39981 was damaged by flak over the target area, straggling behind the formation under control along with aircraft B-17G 42-39920 also missing, and flying low just above undercast.

Missing Air Crew Report # 4450

Pilot: 2Lt. George A. Haakenson, 0-809947, POW

Co-Pilot: 2Lt. Donald R. Heckman, 0-818819, POW

Navigator: 2Lt. William F. Murphy Jr., 0-707179, POW

Bombardier: 2Lt. Malvin W. Samuel, 0-757668, POW

Engineer: Sgt. Paul B. Madori, 32438312, POW

Radio: Sgt. John R. Baas, 17097724, POW

Ball-Turret Gunner: Sgt. William F. Mason, 37472091, POW

Left Waist-Gunner: Sgt. Harold J. Donohue, 32715058, POW

Right Waist-Gunner: Sgt. George H. Hamby, 33598126, POW

Tail-Gunner: Sgt. Ward W. Wickwar, 17090301, POW

10 POW

Crash Site: 15 miles n. of Magdeburg, Germany
Time: 12.20

452nd Bomb Group, 728th Bomb Squadron (Haakenson)

Back row (left to right): Pilot 2Lt. *George Haakenson,* Co-Pilot 2Lt. *Donald Heckman, Unknown,* Bombardier 2Lt. *Malvin Samuel*

Middle: Ball-Turret Gunner Sgt. *William Mason,* Right Waist-Gunner Sgt. *George Hamby,* Engineer Sgt. *Paul Madori,* Left Waist-Gunner Sgt. *Harold Donahue*

Front: Radio Sgt. *John Baas,* Tail-Gunner Sgt. *Ward Wickwar*

Navigator 2Lt. William F. Murphy Jr.

By the family of William Murphy, Jr.

"William (Bill) was the older of two children born to William F. Murphy, Sr. and Mary Hickey Murphy. William Jr. was born July 29, 1916 in Chicago, IL. His father was a professional painter and his mother was a homemaker. The Murphy family was Irish Catholic with both sons attending St. Anselmn and St. Ambrose Catholic grade schools. Bill graduated from Tilden High School. Bill married Rose Bonde on July 10, 1943, after a seven-year engagement.

"Before military service, Bill worked both as an elevator operator and bellhop in the prestigious Palmer House Hotel in downtown Chicago. He was inducted into the Army at Camp Grant, Rockford, IL and then transferred to Camp Polk, Louisiana for basic training. He then served as company clerk at Fort Knox, Kentucky before being assigned to Camp Cooke, Lompoc, CA for armored training.

"After a requested assignment transfer to the Army Air Corps, Bill graduated as a navigator in 1944 in San Marcos, TX. From there combat crew training was conducted at Dyersburg Army Air Base, TN. Bill and his crew flew their B-17 to England and were based at the RAF airbase Deopham Green in Norfolk.

"On May 19, 1944, Bill's pregnant wife Rose received a Western Union telegram stating that William F. Murphy Jr. was missing in action. After two weeks of tears and prayers, a second telegram arrived declaring William F. Murphy Jr. as a prisoner of war. Rose lost their first child, Rosemary, to a full-term stillbirth during Bill's internment. Rose tried to shield her husband from the tragic news but eventually had to inform Bill via a letter. Both Bill and Rose were

Navigator 2Lt. William F. Murphy Jr

devastated by the loss of their first child, but remained strong out of their concern for each other.

Navigator William F. Murphy remembers;

"On April 29, 1944, we took off from our English base on our first deep penetration mission. We were on our way to bomb Berlin in the heart of Germany. We flew at 30,000 feet after crossing the coast of Holland and didn't encounter any anti-aircraft fire until just as we started our bomb run on Berlin.

"The flak was so thick you could walk on it. As we were dropping our bombs, we were hit by flak and an engine was damaged. This slowed us down and as we left the bombing area, we started to fall behind our formation and lose altitude.

"Pretty soon we were all alone in the sky. However, we were quickly joined by German fighter planes who began peppering away at us. By this time, we lost another engine and could just lumber along trying to evade the fighter's gunfire. Our plane was losing altitude fast and the pilot couldn't control it with only two engines so he gave the order to bail out and we all did.

"As l jumped out of the plane, I remembered that we had been instructed to fall as far as possible before pulling the ring on the chute. This was to avoid being a target for the fighter planes that were in the area. When l jumped out, we were at about 28,000 feet, so the ground was a long way down.

"As I left the plane, l heard a loud swish and then almost complete silence and it seemed as though l was floating. The ground was a long distance away so l just relaxed and kept floating even though I was falling fast, it didn't seem so because I had no reference point to judge my speed of falling. It didn't take too long, though. All of a sudden the ground appeared to be coming at me like a huge wall with the speed of an express train.

"I reached for the parachute ring to pull it and it wasn't there. My heart was in my mouth and I became panicky searching for the ring. In falling, I turned over and over and I was using my left hand to find the ring; I had forgotten the ring was on my right side. Of course, I had never jumped before and didn't know any better. All the while the ground is rushing toward me or I'm rushing toward the ground, I could almost see myself when we met. I remember talking to myself and saying not to lose your head. I remembered the story of a flyer whose chute had not opened an how they found him. His flight jacket,shirt and skin were all clawed through as he had kept trying to find the ring.

"I said to myself, 'Murphy, why don't you try the other hand?' I can remember, very deliberately I took my left hand with my right hand and removed it from the front of the chute. I then placed my right hand on the right side of the chute and there was the ring. I pulled and the chute opened. By this time, I was less than 1,000 feet above the ground and even with the chute open, I was falling fast. I relaxed a little so that I would not land stiff legged and break a leg and about that time I hit the ground. I rolled over and pulled on the lines of the chute so that I could unbuckle the harness. I got the harness off, stood up and saw my pilot and engineer about 50 yards away from me.

"A lot of German soldiers were running toward us with guns. I went over to the pilot and engineer and we waited till the Germans came up to take us as prisoners. We had no place to run as we had landed in a large open field. It was about 12 o'clock noon.

"The German soldiers pointed their guns at us and motioned with them to move. We did. We came to a road where a German officer was standing beside a car. He said, 'Welcome to Germany. For you the war is over." I couldn't think of anything to say so I took out a cigarette and said "Do you have a match?" One of the soldiers took out a match and gave me a light.

"They put us on a truck and took us into the town where we were put in a jail in which we stayed overnight. The next morning, we were put on a train and taken to an interrogation center near Frankfort, Germany. We stayed there about a week while the Germans asked us a lot of questions and processed us for shipment to a permanent prisoner of war camp.

"We arrived at Stalag Luft III near Sagan, Germany in the second week of May, 1944. The first news we got was that this was the camp where the English flyers were kept and they just had an escape attempt and many of them were killed in the attempt. We were told that there was no way to escape and not to try it under penalty of death. We were issued a straw mattress, straw pillow, two blankets, one sheet, one pillowcase and eating utensils. Then we were assigned to large barracks that were divided into rooms about 20" x 24" with wood bunk beds, 10 men to a room.

"The whole camp was inside a wire fence with guard towers all around it.

Further away was another camp in which the English prisoners of war were kept, too far away for us to talk to them. My bombardier and pilot were with me but the enlisted men were sent to an enlisted men camp and we never saw them again while we were imprisoned. Our co-pilot wasn't captured until the end of June, 1944, when he was sent to our camp.

"Our camp was operated by the German Wehrmacht or Regular Army. They patrolled the grounds all the time and at night they had German dogs with them. No one ventured outside after dark as the dogs were extremely vicious. We could play ball or walk around the campground during the day, but had to stay away from the fence. We got Red Cross parcels each week, one per man, plus a daily ration of German bread and potatoes. Sometimes we got hot soup. at noon. When the Germans gave us meat, it was usually blood sausage. I ate it once, but never again.

"Each week we were supposed to assign two men from our room to be the cooks for our room. After the first two or three assignments, the two fellows who were better at cooking what we had were elected to be the permanent cooks. The rest of us cleaned up the room and washed dishes. It worked out better that way.

"By September, 1944, the number of prisoners had increased so that we had twenty-one men in our room. instead of double bunk beds, there were now three high. It wasn't so bad as we stayed out of the room during the day. We would walk, talk, play ball or go to the library. The Red Cross had sent in books and we had one building for a library and dispensary. Mostly the dispensary had aspirin and baking soda pills. You just didn't get sick or you'd go to the German hospital. It probably was all right but no one wanted to try it.

"Somehow we managed to have a secret radio receiver hidden in the camp and fellows assigned as Intelligence Officers handled the news from the British Broadcasting Co. They would get the news at specified times and then send word to each barracks as to what time someone would be around to brief us on the news. We had to make sure no German guards were near and when the time came for each barracks to assemble in one room, we posted watchers outside the barracks at the doors and all four corners of the barracks to warn of any guards approaching while the new report was being given. The Germans had a radio up at the soup kitchen and they broadcasted daily at different times. Their news always told how they were winning even when we knew Patton was on the move and inside Germany.

"Time was our worst enemy and you had to do something in order to get through each day. We'd play cards for hours. We would have bridge tournaments and I became a pretty good bridge player during my year in prison, even though I don't play at all now. We celebrated all the holidays and fellows birthdays just to have something different going on. We had band instruments from the Red Cross and gave a band concert once a month along with an amateur night. One of our guys had a trumpet and we would have our own sing-a-longs in our room at night when we felt like it. Naturally, I was the Bing Crosby of our room. "Prisoner of

Love" was our theme song.

"Christmas of 1944, we had a party and some of the fellows dressed up as girls, including me, and we had a ball. Just like the movie only we didn't have any beer or liquor.

"Right after New Year's, we got orders to move out as the Russians were advancing on the Eastern front. We were told we would walk to wherever we were going and had to carry our own gear. Everybody started out with lots of food parcels but after one night's walk, it was below zero, they began unloading stuff. It was miserably cold. We would camp alongside the road and at night we might get to sleep in a farmer's .barn or yard.

"After walking about a week, the Germans decided to put us on trains and send us to Nuremberg, where they had a large prison camp. We were scared to death because the American fighter planes were shooting up all the trains that were running. We were sure they would get us, too, as it worked out, we traveled at night and made it. _

"When we came to the camp, it was only a mile or so outside the city Nuremberg that had become a primary target for bombing raids by the Americans during the day and the British at night. We had air raid warnings all the time and could see the planes over the city dropping the bombs. One night, we saw two or three planes hit by German flak and catch fire. The crew members bailed out but some of them were on fire and the parachute of some caught fire. They never made it. We could see because when the air raid warning went off, we all had to leave our barracks and get into foxholes outside the barracks. After that one night, l never went out, l stayed inside and figured if a bomb dropped close to our barracks it would hit the foxhole, too so I had nothing to lose. One night a bomb did hit about 100 yards outside our camp. lt shattered all the windows in our barracks and the barracks around us. The noise almost deafened us and we were sure the next one would get us, but that was the only one. We guessed it was a bombardier kicking out a bomb that had hung up over the target and he had to get rid of it fast.

"We stayed for about five or six weeks and had to move again. This time no trains. We were to march south but we didn't know how far or where we were going. Our food was short and the Red Cross could not get any food parcels to us because the trains were all being shot up or bombed. We really got hungry.

"After about two days march, the Red Cross trucks came in with the parcels and we got to eat again. On this march, the guards weren't so tough or trigger happy. If you fell behind they didn't pay too much attention and you could be on your own. l guess they knew Patton was right behind us somewhere. Another fellow and I would detour off the road during the day and go begging at the farmhouse we were passing. We asked for eggs or bread or coffee. Instead of giving us something, the farmers would invite us into eat. We were leery, but because we were hungry, we went in. It was. pretty good for us.

"One afternoon, we went to four different farmhouses and had to eat at all four. We stopped that day because we couldn't eat anymore and it would look bad to ask for food and not eat it. We were lucky being alone that we never met any SS soldiers. We heard at one of the stops on the march that the SS had shot a couple of prisoners who were off on their own like us. You'd think that we would stay with the march after that but we didn't. We just followed them close enough to join them when they stopped at night.

"I can't remember how many days we were on the road, but one day American fighter planes flew over and started shooting at us. They could just see a long column of men and assumed we were German soldiers. We all scattered into the woods and hugged the ground while they made a few more passes at us. No one was hit, but we were all shaking in our shoes. We waited a long time before we would get back on the road, even the German guards.

"One day, we arrived in Moosburg and it seemed as though all the American and British prisoners of war were there. There was no place to put us all. Large and small tents were all over the place. We were put in a tent that was as big as a circus tent. Each man had enough room to put down a blanket and space on the side to stand up. There were five or six aisles the long way in the tent so you could get in and out. We didn't know what the score was because we had no news from the BBC for several weeks. We did learn from the prisoners there ahead of us that Patton's Army was getting close. We loafed around for some days. It was a little warmer as it was April, 1945 and we waited for the end of the war.

"On the night of April 28, 1945, we got word that Patton and his tanks were just over the hill and he was going to attack the next morning. The German commander of the camp sent word to Patton that if he did, all the prisoners would be shot. The story is Patton told him he was coming in anyway and all the Germans would be shot. The German commander agreed to surrender the next morning.

"At 12 o'clock noon, tanks were in the town of Moosburg and the American flag was hoisted in the square All the German guards were taking off for the woods, and left us to ourselves. It was a great day.

Daughter Judith Murphy continues

"On April 29, 1945, a year to the day of Bill's capture, General George S. Patton liberated William F. Murphy Jr. and the other prisoners of war at Moosburg. Bill returned home to Chicago and Rose after the war. He went to college at Northwestern University at night to earn his accounting degree. He worked as a bookkeeper/accountant at the University of Chicago.

"They bought their first home in Homewood, IL, in 1952. Bill served as Treasurer for Enterprise Wire Co. for approximately 15 years, and then became an accountant for General Electric, followed by twenty years of federal service as an auditor for the Internal Revenue Service in Chicago until retirement at age seventy-one.

"He thoroughly enjoyed retirement socializing with friends, family, and reading two to three mystery and spy novels per week. In celebration of his 90th birthday, Bill took a commemorative flight in a B-17 in the Chicago area, the only flight in a B-17 after his parachute jump from their aircraft on that fateful day. As he walked around the aircraft he was amazed at how small the aircraft appeared.

"Bill passed away in December 2007.

Radio Sgt. John R. Baas.

"I was born in Beemer, Nebraska, on December 25, 1921 and attended and graduated from West Point, Nebraska public school in 1940. I worked as a clerk in a man's clothing store until my enlistment in the U.S. Army Air Corp in 1942.

***

"At breakfast on April 29, 1944 I sensed this mission would be a lot bigger than the one I made the previous day (my first) over sub-pens on the coast of France. This became more evident after takeoff when I saw the size of the group of aircraft being assembled.

"As we progressed deeper into the continent we picked up P-51 escorts which were a welcome sight. I don't remember how or when we learned the target was Berlin, but the day was sunny and bright and I remember seeing the red tile roofs of the city as the bombs were released.

"The flak was heavy and close. I was busy throwing out chaff to detract radar when I noticed we were falling behind. Then the fighters came and I manned my gun. Shortly thereafter the ball-turret gunner Harold Donohue came out of his turret and showed me he had taken a hit in his hand and was bleeding profusely. I attempted to apply a tourniquet but the airplane started to spin and he was thrust away from me.

"I immediately began to put on my parachute but every time I had about succeeded the force of the aircraft spin pulled the chute away from the buckle. Obviously I finally succeeded. It became apparent that it was time to bail out. As I worked my way back through the waist I saw the gunners had already bailed. When I got to the escape hatch the door was open. I attempted to exit but was temporarily suspended half in and half out of the door because of the spin of the airplane.

"I finally exited and as I neared the ground I saw uniformed and armed people awaiting my arrival. I was captured together with the engineer and tail gunner and taken to a nearby airbase. I was locked in a solitary confinement cell and began my life as a POW.

"The next day we were escorted via public transportation to Frankfort for interrogation and subsequent internment in Stalag 17B at Krems, Austria.

***

"After the war I attended the University of Nebraska on the G. I. Bill and graduated in 1948 with a Bachelor of Sciences in Business Administration. I worked for the General Electric Company from that date until my retirement in 1984.

Ball-Turret Gunner Sgt. William F. Mason.

By widow Margaret Mason.

"William Franklin Mason was born in Ashland, Nebraska, on November 12, 1918. He attended Ashland High School and graduated in 1938. He played football, track and basketball. After graduation Bill attended Boyle Aircraft School in Burbank, California. He was then employed by Lockheed Aircraft Factory and worked on the first P-38 fighter aircraft that distinguished itself later in the war by tracking Admiral Yamamoto and destroyed his aircraft.

"Bill and his wife Margaret Bachman were married in Quarzite, Arizona, August 31, 1941. They lived in Glendale, California until December 1941 when they returned to Ashland. Bill taught at Frey Aircraft and South High School until he enlisted in the Army Air Corps. In 1943, he was assigned to Amarillo, Texas, for training as a flight engineer and gunner on a B-17 bomber.

"After training Bill was stationed in Attlebury, England with the 8th Air Force. Bill participated on thirteen missions and was shot down on the last one by anti-aircraft fire over Berlin on April 29, 1944. He was awarded a Silver Star for bravery uncommon amongst men, for helping a wounded crew member who had lost his hand. Bill harnessed himself into his parachute and holding the wounded man he jumped out of the aircraft. Bill then pulled the man's ripcord, then, free falling away, he pulled his own cord. Being wounded in the process, Bill was also awarded a purple heart. Bill was subsequently catured by the Germans and was a prisoner of war at Stalag Luft 5 and 6.

"He was held fourteen months and seven days and was liberated by Russian troops in Annaburg, Germany. His return to Ashland was in August of 1945. He was discharged on November 30, 1945 in Lincoln

"Bill's career then turned to electrical power station construction which resulted in a move to Colorado and then back home to Ashland. He then was employed by the O.P.P.D. and later by the Civil Service Commission and worked in both Lincoln and Omaha where he was an electrical foreman.

"Since retirement began, Bill became very interested in golf. That resulted in three rounds a day many times. The American Legion was a favorite activity and Bill participated in many Legion events. Bill was a Past Commander and and a lifetime member of Post 129 in Ashland. Bill passed away January 27, 1987 at Clarkson Hospital in Omaka, Nebraska.

Left Waist-Gunner Sgt. Harold J. Donohue.

By widow Doris Donohue

"Harold Joseph Donohue grew up in Westbury on Long Island, NY, during the "Great Depression." He was the fourth child (three boys, one girl) of John Donohue and Ingeborg Iverson Donohue.

"Inge had been brave enough to come from Norway to America while still very young because her aunt, who had taught her to sow, had emigrated and had established a successful sewing business in Bay Ridge, NY. She therefor had immediate employment. She was truly passionate about learning to speak English with absolute no accent and becoming a "real American." She was also determinate to master the most challenging sewing projects (such as tailoring men's 3-piece suits) in an era when clothes were still made to order and men's suits were a major investment.

"In time, she met and married John Donohue and moved to Westbury, where she lived with her husband's Irish family. Westbury and most of the land around it was owned by a few of the wealthiest families in America, who lived in large, elaborate, self-sufficient estates and who employed many people. Those living in and near Westbury either worked on or for the estates or in businesses that were in large part dependant upon the estates. (And odd as it may seem, Westbury with all its wealthy families, was without electricity).

"When Hal was still very young the depression hit. A few years later his father died. Inge went to one of the estates and applied for work as a dressmaker. In a while she was mending and altering things on a temporary basis, but her superior skill was apparent, and she was soon given the difficult work and a permanent position in the big household. This meant she she did not see much of her children but it was necessary and she counted herself lucky to have any job when so many were destitute.

"One day she went to a local tailor shop with a men's suit to be dry cleaned. Another customer began to closely examine the suit she had placed on the counter. He asked if this tailor had made the suit and commented that he had never seen such perfect work. When he learned it was Inge's work, he immediately offered her a job. He was the designer of the spectacular Radio City Music Hall's costumes (for shows with hundreds of performers).

"This meant that Inge had to commute by railroad to the city, but she sailed through the depression with steady employment, a regular salary, and exciting work.

"Things were still very difficult, but Inge was a disciplined and determined person. By saving every penny she possibly could, she was able to rent a house for her family. All the children had to help out. Hal and his brothers fished constantly for food. Their sister kept house. Some farmers allowed children to pick produce and to keep a small amount in payment. Inge had them bury the fish cleanings and vegetable scraps in the yard where they started a garden. It soon yielded abundantly and fed them. During most of the year, they bought only a few cans of evaporated milk; in winter they bought a wooden barrel of salt cod and an occasional turkey (the cheapest meat available). Inge made all their clothes on an old treadle machine.

"There was a man in the area who owned a very large nursery business, orchards and and a good deal of farmland, and who took a compassionate interest in the many fatherless boys during those difficult depression years. He gave them work so that they could help their families, tried to keep them out of trouble, and was like a father to many of them. His name was Henry Hicks. Hal was one of his boys. Since Inge had to be gone all day, she was very grateful for this help.

"Inge finally saved enough to buy the house she was renting. She mastered the the English language with absolutely no hint of an accent. She persued her own self-education until she died, a living demonstration of the value she placed on developing one's mind. She taught a kind of grateful patriotism and pride in being American.

"Henry Hicks instilled in Hal the habit of viewing a situation as through the eyes of the other participants, the value of helping others, and of giving without accepting rewards. He taught Hal much about horticulture and many practical skills. He was later largely responsible for Hal's recovery, education and success when he returned from the war.

"These two people, Inge and Henry Hicks, were so influential in shaping Hall's thinking and character that I would say they prepared him to survive the physical, mental and spiritual challenge, he was to face. They were accomplishers, people of extreme determination and integrity. They taught him never to give up, never to complain, never to waste anything. They taught him patriotism and the value of education.

"Hal attended grades in Westbury and graduated from the local high school. He and his brothers were fascinated by planes and flight. They spent every spare moment at nearby Mitchell Field, which was like a magnet for excitement because it had been the site of the take-off for Lindberg's famous flight and of all the preparations for it, and it continued to draw pilots, builders of "flying machines," investors, daredevils and boys with dreams. I was an exciting atmosphere, and all the boys dreamt of being pilots.

***

"Then suddenly we were at war. Hal's older brothers left for the service, but he was still to young. He took a job in an aircraft factory and continued to work there until he entered the Air Corps.

"He spoke very seldom about the time he spent in the service, and I did not question him. It was only gradually that I put together bits and pieces of his last mission and the events that which followed, usually as a result of a nightmare or of conversations while visiting with the two buddies that came out of prison camp with him.

"Before they took off, Hal had a dream which some of the crew members remembered. One of them told me it was "spooky." He said; "If we go on this next mission, we'll be hit and have to bail out. We'll be separated, but we'll all be captured and I am going to lose my right hand." He lost his left hand but the rest was true.

"Ball-turret gunner William Mason was the man to whom Hal owed his life. Because Hal was unconscious, the courageous Mason took the time to secure Hal's parachute, drag him over and throw him out of the plane. After the war, Hal spent some time with the Masons.

"Hal and others came down in a field, and some men ran out and grabbed them. They had pitch forks and were about to use them to dispatch the airmen. However, a German officer on a motorcycle intervened. He took the prisoners to a railway station, and while he was reporting for further instructions, the crowd tried to hang them. Another officer appeared on the scene, rescued the prisoners, and they were separated and taken away for questioning.

"Hall was taken to a place where German officers went for R & R. The German officer who had crippled their plane came to see him. After he had spent time in America; he had gone to school here. He inquired about Hal's injured hand and apologized for having caused such misery, saying that although each of them might lament the war, he must do his duty to his respective country. Hall agreed; he always expressed respect for this officer.

"Then came the questioning. He was told many times that if he would just answer the questions, he would be given medical attention. But since he would not give the information that was wanted, he was denied medical treatment and placed in solitary confinement repeatedly, where he developed a raging infection that caused him to be very ill and eventually be sent to a hospital for amputation of his hand. While being readied on the operation table the nurse struck him in the face causing him to fall on the floor while she told him about airmen and the horror they caused by bombing innocent children, women and old people.

"This incident had a profound effect on him. He always made excuses for her action, and what she had said stuck with him all his life. And he spent much of that life trying to make up for the suffering he had caused, and studying various wars, their causes and effects, the building of abusive governments, the climb to power of ambitious politicians, reasons behind the making of wars.

"Hal went from the hospital to a prisoners of war facility for a time. His arm was swollen and painful, and he was getting sicker.

"His mother was notified by the government that he was missing in action. Of course, she did not know if he was alive. Some months went by before a ham radio operator located information that enabled him to notify her that Hal was a prisoner of war, but alive and in a Berlin hospital.

"Later, he was made part of a group that was being marched north to Ober-masfeldt at the Baltic. He was unable to remember where and when he joined this group. By the time they arrived at their destination, he was being dragged by his buddies who were so exhausted that they all dropped to the ground just inside the gates of their new camp. A Canadian doctor came out. He took one look and just sat on Hal and pushed the infected mass out of the arm. This, of course, was what enabled him to survive. Later, he made a number of attempts to find this Canadian doctor to thank him, but was unsuccessful each time until just a few years before he died.

"Conditions were poor in the camp. The climate was harsh. There was very little to eat, but Hal said that the Germans did not have much to eat either. Early each day the prisoners each received two very small unpeeled potatoes, or one potatoe and a piece of turnip, which had been boiled in a large drum of water. Later in the day, they were given a cup of "soup" which was actually the water in which the vegetables had been boiled.

"Hal was amazed to see that although they were all very hungry, many would actually pull off the potato skins and throw them away. He remembered life with Inge during the depression years when she said that the fruit and vegetable skins must never be wasted because they contained the greatest concentration of nutri-ents. When he mentioned this, most of the men stopped throwing anything away, but even then a few could not bring themselves to eat the skins. He offered to trade one of his daily potatoes for two discarded skins. He said he thought that helped him pull through in spite of the continued infection. When Red Cross par-cels arrived, they were cause for celebration. But the climate and the lack of food took their toll. Some died, some developed tuberculosis, many had abscessed teeth, all were emaciated.

"Then came the notice that those prisoners whose condition was such that they would never be able to fight again would be traded for German prisoners of war held by the Allies whose condition was similar. Amputees, of course, were among those who would be traded, as were others who were permanently disabled. They were paired up to help each other on the journey; one who was blind was paired with one who could see, and one who couldn't walk with one who could., etc. Hal was paired with a buddy who had lost his leg. They were joined shortly by one who had lost part of his hand and who could not get along with his assigned buddy. (Later; when all three had healed, had re-entered civil-ian life, had found a career and had married, we three couples remained closely connected for life).

Those prisoners who were being traded were loaded into box cars, the roofs of which were painted with large red cross. This was to keep our Allied bombers from targeting them. However, knowing that the enemy sometimes loaded cars that were so marked with munitions, we sometimes bombed them anyway, which was not comforting to the prisoners being transported. They had to reach Switzerland to be in comparative safety. Because the Swiss were neutral, they would escort prisoners from any country to transportation that would take them home. Ours were headed for a ship waiting for them in the Mediterranean. On the way in Germany, when the train would stop, volunteer Red Cross ladies would be on the platforms with fires going under great drums of "soup" like what they had been existing on during captivity. They said it was full of maggots, but because they were so terribly hungry they remembered it as being the most delicious soup they had ever tasted.

"When our three prisoners finally reached the Mediterranean they boarded a hospital ship, the "Shipsholm." She could not leave the Mediterranean because in order to cross the Atlantic it would have to join a convoy for protection from German U-boats. While waiting for convoy, the injured and sick men could at least rest in freedom, enjoy the sunny weather, have enough to eat and gather some strength. The wait was long. The Norwegian captain and Hal became good friends. Hal, who had been raised by his Norwegian mother, always laughingly joked that he was the only Norwegian Donohue in the world. They would pass the time on deck playing cards or just chatting. Finally there was a convoy. They crossed the Atlantic without incident.

"Just as privately owned passenger ships were used by the military during the war, so were buildings such as college dorms, apartment houses, and hotels. One of these was Hotel Haddox Hall in Atlantic City, New Jersey, a seaside resort on the northeast coast. The hotel became England Military Hospital for the many returning wounded servicemen. That was where I first met Hal.

"I was thirteen years old when my father took me there, showed me how to light a cigarette and gave me a box containing cigarettes and matches, pen, paper and stamps, the Bible and a couple of other books, chewing gum and Life Savers, a deck of cards and instructions to walk around and try to be of some help and comfort. The rooms were full, beds and stretchers were crowded in the lobby and halls. The doctors, nurses, and other staff were busy with serious needs, so any help with the little trivialities that can bring peace and comfort was welcome.

"I remembered Hal because he was measuring his arm on the radiator next to him. He still had the infection. He was scheduled for another surgery and was afraid that they would cut off more of his arm than they had told him and that it was getting closer to the elbow. The loss of a joint meant the loss of many capabilities.

"I never saw him again until he showed up in the school where I was teaching many years later.

"Hal was discharged from the hospital and from the service and returned to Westbury, painfully thin, was wondering what to do with his life, but lacking the will or the strength to do anything at all.

"Henry Hicks began writing to him as soon as his name appeared in the Westbury paper as a returned local service man hospitalized in New Jersey. He sent lists of occupations open to a person with one hand. He assured Hal that life was still very worthwhile. He kept him from self pity and supplied him with a barrage of information and names of sources of help, hope and challenge. He found a hospital near home that taught all these new amputees how to manage the details of daily life and put them in touch with one another. He told him about new careers that were opening up because of technologies developed for war purposes being now for peaceful purposes. He offered to help him start a business in his own greenhouse, raising ornamental shrubs. He also offered to help him start a number of other businesses and gave him the name of a banker who would give him start-up money.

"But most of all, he encouraged him to go on with his education and talked him into attending a meeting sponsored by New York State Colleges as part of an effort to accommodate the surge of returning veterans with special needs. Many of those men were still weak and sickly from wounds, malnutrition and tuberculosis. They were in and out of hospitals and unable to commit to a daily schedule. The plan was that they could attend and work at whatever pace they could manage. This was what Hal needed. He became a student. Some relatives had a farm near the college he attended where he could rest and recover whenever necessary. This upstate farm remained a very happy memory for him and later that memory changed the direction of our lives. Soon the tuberculosis was just a bad memory and he began to feel better.

"After graduation, he was determined to choose an occupation that would have a positive impact on society to "make up for" the negative impact of bombing civilian population centers during the war. He opted to work with troubled teenage boys and their families, and for a number of years he worked for the family court system and social services on Long Island, NY.

"Eventually, he transferred to the public school system of a smal city named Glen Cove, first as a teacher, then helping teachers, then assistant to the junior high school principal, then as assistant to the superintendent, where he acted as grantsman and initiator of new projects as education began to change with new problems, new needs, new technology.

"He was working in the same small city in an experimental alternative school. We worked together on many projects and became close friends. We were surprised to recall our first meeting and marvelled at the coincidence of our meeting again. He continued with his formal education, earning two masters degrees, a phibetakappa key, and was working on his doctorate.

"He contineud to be troubled about that final mission, and so he took a sabbatical and travelled across the country one year to find and talk with every member of the crew. After that he seemed to be at peace.

"We were married soon after he returned. We lived on Long Island. For a fun week-end project we bought a funny old house with a beautiful garden and set about "fixing up the house a bit." It grew into a bigger, larger, and more fascinating project than expected. We finally stripped the house down to a skeleton, rebuilt it, put on an addition that doubled the size of the original building and moved in. We had not done anything like that before. We learned a lot. We found the work rewarding and the result thrilling, and we continued to take on bigger and bigger building projects.

"Hal always had fond memories of the up-state farm where he had stayed while attending college and he longed to find such a place for us. He looked and looked, but nothing was "just right." Then I asked him to make a list of exactly what he was looking for. Every week I would save the Sunday paper and call each likely looking classified add number to ask questions.

"One Friday I called a number and all the answers were "yes." We drove up-state that evening: the next morning we picked up the real estate lady and found the perfect farm for us: wooded mountains, sparkling streams, field full of wild flowers. We went to see the owner and bought it that day on a handshake. We set a date to come back later and take care of the legalities and paperwork. But the whole time we were talking with the owner, he and Hal kept thinking that they had met each other and asking: "Where you ever here" and "Were you ever there?"

"The next month we drove up again to finalize the purchase, and we were again sitting in the owner's living room. Suddenly both men jumped up and ran to the middle of the room and hugged each other. "I remember where I know you." The owner was the Norwegian captain of the hospital ship that brought Hal home! Amazing?

"We did not intend to live on this acreage. It was intended just for vacations, and Hal loved planting trees and camping there on the Vermont border in the foothills of the Green Mountains. We had two children (one girl, one boy) and they loved to go upstate to explore the woods and play in the stream.

"Then for health reasons, we were told to relocate. We sold our house and car, put furniture in storage, Hal took early retirement, we took the children out of school and bought a motorhome. We travelled in our little "house-on-wheels" and by boat, plane, train and bus. When we started out, we expected to be settled within six months; however, we were on the move for several years. We zig-zagged all over the United States, eastern Canada, Mexico and Europe. Occasionally, we would visit our little "farm," and although we had thought of upstate News York as a place of rather harsh climate, we never encountered health problems while there. And so we found ourselves again building a house!

"We met someone at a dinner we attended who knew the Canadian doctor Hal had tried to find. The doctor had moved to Australia. Hal was happy to be able to contact him again. Life is so full of intriguing coincidences!

"Hal continued to have difficulties resulting from the war, but he never complained. He also continued to study the political psychology connected to war and in his own life to seek ways to (as he put it) "make up for the damage done." He died on August 4, 1989.

Right Waist-Gunner Sgt. H. Hamby.

By Bill MacCall, brother-in-law.

Right Waist-Gunner Sgt. H. Hamby

"George was born in Florida in 1924. His parents moved to Pennsylvania at an early age. After high school, he became a welder at the Sun Shipyards in Chester. They were building ships for the military. The shipyard wanted to get George a deferment to continue working at the ship yard, but George refused as he wanted to join the Air Corps.

"Subsequently, he soon found himself as a waist gunner on a B-17 in England. On April 29, 1944, they were shot down on a bombing mission over Berlin, George had a bullet go through his wrist. The wound was never treated by his captors. Parachuting out of his crippled plane, his boots flew off as the chute opened. He hid inside of Germany for seven days, straining drinking water through his handkerchief. Wounded, his wrist festering from the wound, he was discovered by some Polish farmers and turned over to the Nazis.

"The treatment for over a year was harsh and unsympathetic, and George did not adapt well to the ordeal. He had a difficult time with claustrophobia, and would spent countless hours pacing back and forth in captivity during the nights.

"His life was forever more a constant battle of doctors, as they tried to help him over what was an eternal nightmare. It was many years after his discharge from the military before any appreciable pensions came his way. Unable to travel, through whatever fears he had, he was relegated to smaller jobs close to home. He died at age 78.

***

Acknowledgements;
Judith Murphy, daughter of navigator 2Lt. William F. Murphy Jr.
Sue Eubanks, daughter of radio-operator Sgt. John R. Baas
Margaret Mason, widow of ball-turret gunner Sgt. William F. Mason
Doris Donohue, widow of waist-gunner Sgt. Harold J. Donohue
Bill MacCall, brother-in-law of waist-gunner Sgt. H. Hamby

CHAPTER 55

452ND BOMB GROUP
729TH BOMB SQUADRON

Type: B-17 • Serial: 42-39920 "Karen B."
MACR: 4449 • Air Base: Deopham Green

Aircraft B-17G, # 42-39920 was damaged by flak over the target and was last observed after the Group had left the target area, straggling behind the formation under control, along with aircraft B-17G, # 42-39981 also missing, and flying just above the undercast.

Missing Air Crew Report # 4449

Pilot: 2Lt. Hal J. Nelson, 0-689085, EVD, Iowa City, IA

Co-Pilot: 2Lt. Charles F. Ramlow, 0-818746, EVD, Shawano Lake, WI

Navigator: 2Lt. Noyes Richey, 0-708376, POW, Ragley, LA

Bombardier: 2Lt. Philip R. Cavanaugh, 0-757750, EVD, Baltimore, MD

Engineer: S/Sgt. Michael Dencavage, 36175982, EVD, Philadelphia, PA

Radio: S/Sgt. George P. Paulk, 34539372, EVD, Bartow, FL

Ball-Turret Gunner: Sgt. Robert W. Zercher, 13092429, KIA, York, PA

Left Waist-Gunner: Sgt. Don E. Jackson, 35602808, POW, Stone Creek, OH

Right Waist-Gunner: T/Sgt. Victor A. Ryczko, EVD, 6976087, Corona, NY

Tail-Gunner: Sgt. Floyd E. Ragsdale, 39649424, POW, Honea Path, SC

1 KIA, 3 POW, 6 EVD

Crash Site: Near Ruurlo, Netherlands
Time: 13.40

Pilot 2Lt. Hal J. Nelson.

Filed this report immediately after the war:

"Losing one engine over Berlin, we fell out of formation and proceeded to head for England alone. At one time it looked if as if all crew members would have to leave the plane. No. 2 engine was on fire and the gas tank to that engine was leaking. At this time I called all members of the crew on the inter-phone and told them the condition of the plane and told them if they didn't already have their parachutes on, to get them on.

Pilot 2Lt. Hal J. Nelson's photo for false ID

"Upon hearing this, Sgt. John E. Jackson, waist-gunner, immediately bailed out. It may have been he misunderstood directions. Other crew members said he was standing by the waist door and upon hearing my call, went right out. According to reports he was taken prisoner right away. He was liberated near the end of the war and is now at his home.

"Shortly after crossing the Dutch border, with three engines gone and a fire in one of the nacelles, we were forced to go down. The plane being under control, I chose to crash-land it instead of bailing out. No one was injured and after staying at the plane long enough to be sure it was going to burn up, we left it and headed for some woods to evade capture. That night we were taken in by the underground. After a few weeks we were separated in different groups.

Jelle Reitsma, Brigadier-General Royal Dutch Army (ret.) about the crew of "Karen B" and the Dutch underground.

"In the period December 1943 - January 1944 the 452nd Bomb Group moved to the United Kingdom. Deopham Green in Norfolk became their home base. The crew was assigned to the "Karen B." a B-17G Flying Fortress with the serial # 42-39920. With this aircraft they completed their first operational flight on April, 24; Braunschweig was the target and they returned unscathed.

"On the early morning of Saturday 29 April 1944 the ‹Karen B' took off from Deopham Green as one of the more than seven hundred heavy bombers that were going to bomb the Friedrichstrasse railway station in Berlin. This station was a key point in the city's passenger traffic system. By eliminating it, the Americans thought, they would deal a terrific blow to the German war industry in and around Berlin. The factory workers would no longer be able to reach their factories and as a result, production would strongly decrease.

"To protect the bombers against German fighters, the ‹Mighty Eighth brought an impressive array of more than 800 fighters, P-38 Lightnings, P-51 Mustangs and P-47 Thunderbolts, into action

"For the ‹Karen B' the outward flight was relatively uneventful but over Berlin she was hit by anti aircraft fire. That resulted in no. 2 engine burning and its fuel tank leaking. The B-17 could no longer keep up with the formation and had to continue the flight home alone. Very soon it became clear that it would be impossible to return to the home base. At a given moment it appeared that the complete crew would have to bail out. The pilot told his crew members on the intercom hours how serious the situation of the plane was and ordered them to put on their parachutes if they had not already done so. On hearing this, Sergeant Don Jackson, the left waist gunner, immediately, bailed out. It could be possible that he misunderstood the orders. Don landed in the village Ölper, approximately 3 km northwest of Braunschweig. He was given a severe beating by the local population upon landing. He spent the rest of the war as a POW.

"Shortly after passing the Dutch border, with three engines gone by now, and one burning, the plane lost more and more altitude. The plane being still under control, the pilot decided to make a crash-landing. During the landing only the pilots, the lieutenants Nelson and Ramlow, sat in the cockpit - the rest of the crew stood together in the radio room. It was 13:30 hours that the plane crash-landed in Nazi-occupied Holland at some 5 kilometers south of the city Ruurlo. Nobody was hurt. The crew tried to set fire to the plane, but to no avail; only one wing burned out. They then fled and hid themselves in the woods and in ditches to avoid capture.

"Helping downed Allied aviators was a very risky business for the members of the Dutch underground and quite a few of them ended up in front of an execution squad. Nevertheless the underground, in the person of Hendrik Wieggers picked all crew members up that night. Nine Americans found their first shelter at the house of milkman Hendrikus Lambertus Becking in Aalten. On 1 May 1944, an important football game was being played and because of the crowds in the streets it permitted a relatively safe transfer of the airmen to Zutphen. They went there by two taxis.

"By continually changing hiding places, the risk of detection could be reduced. The ultimate aim was to put the aviators on an escape-line that went all the way from Holland, through Belgium and France and into Spain from where they could return to their bases in England.

"Two crew members remained a long time in the region where they had crash-landed; pilot Hal Nelson and bombardier Philip Cavanaugh. The underground hid them in the town Nijverdal. On April 6, 1945, members of the 2nd Canadian Infantry Division liberated them.

"Two other crew members, bombardier Michael Dencavage and waist-gunner Victor Ryczko, were put on an "escape-line." On their way to Liege in Belgium they were liberated in September 1944 by units of the First American Army.

"Sooner or later, the five other crew members arrived in Apeldoorn, Holland. Around August 10, 1944, tail-gunner Floyd Ragsdale and radio-operator George Paulk were moved from Laren by members of the underground group called "Narda." They all cycled together to Apeldoorn. To avoid the German control at the birdges across the river IJssel they crossed the river in a small rowing boat. They found shelter in Apeldoorn with the Kliest family where they joined John Low and Bill Moore from the 467th Bomb Group, who had jumped from their bomber: also on Saturday, April 29, 1944.

Waist-Gunner Victor Ryczko

"Ball-turret gunner Robert "Bob" Zercher and co-pilot Charles Ramlow were also brought to Apeldoorn by bicycle. Navigator Noyes Richey could not ride a bicycle; he was picked up by car on August, 18.

***

"In June the Allied Forces Headquarters notified the underground that airmen were no longer allowed to use escape lines but had to stay put in occupied territory and await their liberation. Moreover, in the autumn of 1944, many of the Resistance, who were involved in the ‹pilot escape lines', fell into the hands of the Germans, as a result of treason.

"Losing the battle of Arnhem on 26 September 1944 was not only a heavy moral blow for occupied Holland, but also for the underground and for the airmen in hiding. Everyone had thought that the liberation was imminent, and that it would only take a couple of days before the Allies would arrive in Apeldoorn. It didn't come true.

"Saturday, 30 September turned out to be a disastrous day. Because of treason the underground group Narda group was eliminated. The SD set a trap in the house of the group's female leader, Narda van Terwisga. They arrested Narda and most of the members of her group.

"The Germans also tried to arrest another member of the group, Joop Bitter, the son of Mrs. Bitter-Van der Noordaa. They raided Joop's house and to their great surprise they also found there the Englishman Kenneth Ingram and the American Bob Zercher. In the confusion Joop was able to escape.

"Bob Zercher was a reserved, matter-of-fact kind of person, a sharp observer with a good sense of humor and a sense of self-mockery. Not exactly an Adonis, he once said: ‹Nobody loves me, I'm a monkey'. This type of humor was typical for him; he found pleasure in playing the fool at bridge or poker at the start of the game but later he showed to be an accomplished player. While awaiting the coming liberation he and Kenneth Ingram, the British flight sergeant, being in the same boat together, made drawings of the American and English flag, so that they could be reproduced rapidly after the liberation.

"Both Robert Zercher and Kenneth Ingram wore civilian clothes when they were arrested but the Germans knew they were Allied airmen. Both of them should have been treated as prisoners of war. On the contrary, they were shot the next day without trial.

"Due to these arrests, the existing secret addresses were considered compromised by the underground and so John Low, Bill Moore, David Smith, George Paulk and Floyd Ragsdale moved to a safer address in Apeldoorn: safer but not safe. Also this address was raided by the Germans and Bill Moore was arrested but they did not discover the shelter in the attic where the remaining aviators were hidden.

***

"Operation "Market-Garden," Field-Marshall Montgomery's ambitious plan to bring his Second Army over the main rivers in the Netherlands with the help of three airborne divisions came to a stop in Arnhem. South of the river Rhine was allied territory, the main part of the Netherlands, north of the Rhine was still in the hands of the Germans. Many British para's had evaded capture and were hiding north of the river. A plan was made to bring them, together with allied airmen hidden in the area, back across the river. The first crossing in the night of 22 to 23 October – code name "Pegasus I" - was a success. However, the Germans got wind of it and took the necessary measures: the area south of the highway Utrecht - Arnhem and a strip north of the highway was declared out of bounds.

"The next attempt of "Pegasus II," scheduled for November 18, 1944, started under an unlucky star. The airmen who were going to participate had to be relocated to different farms near the Rhine. Among them Charles Ramlow and Noyes Richey. Charles was able to cycle and was the first to be moved. The next day Noyes Richey went on foot to a place 5 km from Apeldoorn . He traveled from there as a passenger on the back of a bicycle to the village Barneveld. Via this village Ramlow and Richey both reached the meeting point for "Pegasus II."

"The operation failed. George Paulk and Floyd Ragsdale were captured by the Germans and Noyes Richey was shot through the lung. Ramlow however succeeded to stay out of the hands of the Germans and finally crossed the front line in March, 1945.

"Waist-gunner Don Jackson spent the rest of the war in a German POW camp and was finally liberated in May 1945. As has been described before, Michael Dencavage and Victor Ryczko finally managed to escape, as did Charles Ramlow. It lasted till March 1945 before Hal Nelson and Philip Cavanaugh were liberated in Holland. George Paulk and Floyd Ragsdale were confined to the POW

728

camp Stalag Luft 4 - at Gross-Tychow

"When the Russians approached the prisoner of war camp, the Germans cleared the camp at the beginning of February 1945 and forced the prisoners to march to camps in Germany. The circumstances were terrible, it was icy cold, the roads were covered with snow and the food supply during the march was abominable. For many prisoners, the trip lasted almost three months. The number of casualties was considerable.

"According to an interview with Floyd Ragsdale, he and George Paulk did not take part in this 'death march'. They were finally "liberated" by the Russians who only knocked down the fences but let the POWs fence for themselves. After approximately two weeks the American POWs were transported to France by B-17 bombers.

"Navigator Noyes Richey was confined in Stalag Luft 1, the only camp that the Germans did not evacuate. On 1 May 1945 the Russians liberated him.

"Only Bob Zercher, who was executed in Apeldoorn, was the only member of this crew not to survive the war. He was after the war re-interred in the American War Cemetery Neuville-Condroz (Neupré) in the Belgian Ardennes where he still rests.

"The others returned to the United States and they met once again in 1945. At that time Noyes Richey was still suffering badly, from his lung complaint. Hal Nelson remained in the service and retired eventually as a lieutenant colonel in the Air Force. Charles Ramlow was killed in an aircraft crash in Miami Beach in 1946. Michael Dencavage reenlisted in 1946 in the Air Force as Technical Sergeant. The others resumed their studies or returned to their civilian professions. George Paulk returned to the Netherlands in the 80's to meet the people who had helped him and to visit the scene of the crash-landing once again.

Navigator 2Lt. Noyes Richey.

"The plane was damaged. In fact we had lost two engines as we left the target Berlin. I plotted courses to both Sweden and England, but we 'opted for England. We were flying at about 10,000 feet because that's where the cloud cover was, and we wanted to avoid German fighters. When the cloud cover dissipated we knew that we had to go down to tree top level to avoid fighters.

"At this point the pilot said, "It looks shaky, if anyone wants to bail out go ahead." One member of the crew bailed out. The rest of us stayed with the plane. We went down to about the tree tops to avoid the fighters. We were flying on two engines. Just after we crossed into Holland the third engine went out. A B-17 won't fly on one engine! We crash-landed all of us safely.

"On hitting the ground the crew was met by the Dutch Underground who took us to a place of hiding. The nine men were hidden in barns, haystacks, cellars, attics, sewers, just anywhere that would keep the Germans from capturing them.

For me this went on from April 29, to November 19, 1944. The objective was to try to get the allied service men back to England.

Daughter Ruth Rumsey shared information that appeared in the book, *The Richeys of Ragley*, written and compiled by Noyes' sister, Carmel Richey Estaville.

"On the night of November 19, 1944 the Dutch Underground had assembled about seventy-five men whose planes had been shot down, or who had parachuted at Arnhem and had avoided capture.

Navigator 2Lt. Noyes Richey

"It was a very dark night. Shortly after midnight, before the group reached the rendezvous area they ran into a German patrol. The Germans shot them up; some were killed, some were wounded, some were captured, some escaped.

"Noyes was wounded, and taken prisoner. He was given good medical treatment at an evacuation hospital where he was held for about three days. Then he was transferred to a hospital in Apeldoorn, Holland. On recovery, about three weeks later, he was shipped to Stalag Luft 1, a Prisoner Of War camp for allied airmen in Northern Germany.

"When the train made a brief stop, Noyes looked around and realized that no German soldiers were paying any attention to him. POWs are supposed to escape their captors whenever possible. It was very cold and the ground covered in snow. He had gone quite a good distance before anyone saw him. The Germans caught him, and returned him to the train. Noyes felt that by having a German soldier stationed to guard only him, all the way to Stalug Luft 1, he was doing his part.

Noyes was a prisoner of war for five months and twenty-four days. The POWs at Stalag Luft 1 were liberated by the Russians, about the middle of May in 1945. After some delays Noyes returned to America, was honorably released from service, and returned home to Ragley, Louisiana, in late 1945. He received the Purple Heart Medal for wounds received in action while fighting an enemy of the United States.

"From April 29th to November 19, while avoiding capture by the Germans, Noyes spent some time with a family on their farm in Holland. Decades later, in the 1970s, accompanied by his wife, Dorothy, Noyes paid the family a visit. It was an emotional occasion for all of them. Dorothy was surprised as Noyes, seeing the elderly couple for the first time in so long began to speak to them in Dutch.

"Noyes' wife, Dorothy Hilliard Richey, was a Civil Air Patrol pilot during WWII, patrolling the Louisiana and Texas Gulf coasts. She, and another girl pilot spotted a German submarine entering the mouth of the Mississippi River. Upon landing, they alerted the US Coast Guard, who captured the submarine crew. The majority of this German Navy crew spent the rest of the War working for rice farmers in Louisiana and Texas.

***

"After resting a bit and enjoying a home atmosphere with Mama's cooking, Noyes returned to Lafayette and finished his degree work in chemistry. With this diploma in hand, he received a position as a chemist with Cities Service Corporation in Lake Charles. After cutting his teeth with on-the-job-experience at Cities Service, he decided to try a broader range of activity in petro-chemical work.

He associated himself with Texas Butadiene Corporation in Houston. with all this experience he thought he would try for a position as Chief Chemist. This he found with Atlantic Hichfield Corporation in 1960. Later he was promoted to the position of Manager, Quality Administration. He held this position until his retirement in January, 1982. While employed by ARCO, Noyes lived in Beaumont but commuted to the plant at Port Arthur, Texas.

Noyes married the former Dorothy Hilliard of Lake Charles, whom he had met while at L.S.I. in 1940 and again in 1945, when they returned to college. The wedding took place in Lake Charles on Saturday 12 April, l947. Their devoted, loving marriage has had an

impact on their five children and their sixteen grandchildren.

Shortly after retiring, Noyes and Dorothy sold their house in Beaumont, TX and bought a beautiful place on the outskirts of Austin, TX. Theirs is a rambling modern beautiful ranch style white rock house sitting on a one and one third acre spread. A wonderful place for retirement, away from the hustle and bustle of city life, but close enough to enjoy all the advantages of the metropolis if one has a mind to.

With all of this, one would think that Noyes would stay at home breathing the pure clean Texas air. But no, he and his one of his three attorney sons, Kenneth, organized a corporation: Quality Control Systems.

***

After living in Austin for several years, Noyes and Dorothy moved back to Beaumont, TX.

Noyes Richey, Sr. passed away in 1990 at the age of 69, after a lengthy illness, directly related to his war injuries. Dorothy Hilliard Richey passed away two years later, also at 69 years.

Ball-Turret Gunner Sgt. Robert W. Zercher.

Robert W. Zercher was born in 1907 as the son of Frank and Ella Zercher, in Hallam, York, Pennsylvania, where he grew up with his twin sister Pauline. He went to college for four years and started afterwards to work in a shop. He remained single and enlisted in the Air Corps September, 22 1942 in Harrisburg. He was trained as a ball-turret gunner, was promoted to sergeant and assigned to the crew of 2nd Lieutenant Hall J. Nelson.

After the crash-landing of his bomber he also found shelter at various addresses in the Eastern part of the Netherlands. He ended up in the house of Mrs. Bitter-Vander Noorda, whose son Joop Bitter was a member of the underground group "Narda." Joop then was the boyfriend of Els Meurs, the sister of John Meurs; the author of this book. Joop later became John's brother-in-law.

Author John Meurs wrote sixty years later in his memoirs:

"Joop Bitter, the boyfriend of my sister Els, was a member of a small group in the Dutch underground, specialised in helping allied air-crews to get back to their bases in England. They were a bunch of well-meaning, enthusiastic but hopelessly inexperienced partisans, trying to find their way in that jungle called active resistance. It was a small group; around ten people.

"In the autumn of 1944, two allied airmen were staying with Joop and his mother. The Englishman Kenneth Ingram had jumped out of a Lancaster bomber of the RAF, that crashed a few miles north of Apeldoorn. The American Robert Bob Zercher, was a ball-turret gunner with the 452nd Bomb Group of the 8th Army Air Force. On April 29, 1944, he had been on a mission to Berlin and was on the way back to England. His B-17 bomber "Karen B" had been hit by flak and with only one engine and the pilots made a successful belly-landing in the eastern part of the Netherlands.

"The whole crew had walked away from the wreck and were immediately hidden by a member of the underground. They were split up over various addresses and Bob Zercher landed with Joop Bitter and his mother. Joop and his mother lived a few houses down the street from where we lived. I then was a nine year old schoolboy.

"One night, in the end of September 1944, we were roused by loud voices and a running car engine. It was long after curfew. Looking out of our sleeping-room window, we heard men shouting in German and saw people coming out of one of the houses further up the road, entering a waiting car and driving of. When nothing further happened, we went back to our warm beds and fell asleep again.

"My elder brother Hans, who had his bedroom at the back of the house, woke up about two hours later, by a light tapping on the door leading to a small balcony. Looking out of his window he saw Joop standing in the dark. He opened the door, Joop slipped in and briefly told Hans what had happened. "We have been raided by a bunch of plain clothes men of the Sicherheits Dienst. When I woke up I saw one of the them standing next to my bed. He told me to get up and get dressed. When I had put some clothes on, the SD-man turned to look into the drawer of my nightstand. I kicked him in the bottom. He fell with his head through the mirror on the stand and I managed to run down two flights of stairs and to escape via the kitchen door, through the back garden and into the woods behind the house."

"Joop stopped talking to recover his breath and continued after a few moments; "I got away unnoticed because the SD was completely surprised by the presence of Bob and Kenneth. I heard one of them cry out; 'Komm schnell, hier sind zwei Engländer." ("Come here quickly. I've got two Englishmen"). I ran through the woods, scaled the fence of the local swimming pool and hid myself there in one of the changing-booths. I waited until I was certain that nobody had followed me, sneaked out again, climbed up the drainage pipe to get to your room and here I am."

"Hans went to my sisters' bedroom and whispered; "Joop is here." Miep, my other sister and only half awake, replied; "Oh, that's nice," and went back to sleep again. Joop said; "Not so nice, our house has been raided by the SD." John and his mother woke up and joined the whispered conversation. Joop told Els where his revolver was hidden in his room and asked her to try and fetch it the next day, when and if the coast would be clear.

"The following morning Els found Joop's house deserted when she tip-toed through the back door and up to the bedroom were the weapon was concealed. She found it and brought it home where Joop was waiting. "No trace of your mother," she told him. "And the bottle of wine she had guarded to celebrate the liberation, lies on the garden-path, empty."

My mother, Joop and the rest of the family discussed the next step to be taken. They reasoned that the Germans would quickly find out that Joop had a girlfriend and could possibly come to question Els. My mother was afraid that the Germans would arrest Els and use her as a hostage in forcing Joop to give himself up. That meant not only that Joop had to leave our house immediately, but also that Els had to move to another address. Joop left without telling where he was going. Els moved to friends a few houses further down the road.

"News reached us later that day that almost all members of this underground group and been arrested the previous night with the exception of Joop. His mother had been taken to the German headquarters, together with the two airmen she had hidden in her house.

"The following morning the people of Apeldoorn found, at various intersections in the village, the dead bodies of all male members of the group, including the two airmen. All carried a carton notice board on their chest on with the word 'terrorist'.

The underground had the strong suspicion that one of the members of this group had betrayed their names and addresses to the German Sicherheits Dienst (Gestapo) and they soon found out that a new member, Willem L'Ecluse, had been arrested together with the others but had not been executed. Interrogated after the war, l'Ecluse made the following statement:

"In September 1944 I was living in Apeldoorn and was a member of an underground group leaded by Miss Terwisga, who was known in our organisation as Miss "Jansen." My number in the underground movement was 105. In June 1944 I had contacted Miss Terwisga and became a member of her group as I thought that in doing so I was helping my country. I then was a clerk with the Arbeidsdienst (a German oriented organization – John Meurs). In September 1944 I went to a certain Hemmes, who was also in the Arbeidsdienst, and asked him if I could get a pass in which the Germans stated that I was free of pressed labour to build defences along the river IJsel. He said to me that I was a member of the underground and told me that I had to go with him to the SD (Gestapo) to give information about the group and that he then would see that would get the pass. I did not feel that I was a traitor then and went with him to the SD headquarters in Apeldoorn.

"We went directly to the room of Hauptsturmführer Filietz who spoke to me in German. Hemmes acted as interpreter. Filietz showed me a list of about fifteen names and told me that he already knew everything, that the SD was only after arms and that no harm would be done to the people involved. I then told him the names of the people in the organization. I knew Joop Bitter but did not know that an English and an American airman were living in his house. Filietz promised me money, new clothes and a job in Germany. He also told me that I had to go with a SD man in civilian clothes to point out the houses of the people of our movement."

"The next morning I had to report to SD headquarters where they told me, that I had to bring a message to the house of Miss Van Terwisga, stating that number 105 wanted to speak to her at 13:00 hours. The house was encircled by the SD and when she came home, she was arrested and I was confronted with her and told the SD that she was indeed Miss Van Terwisga. On Sunday I had to report to the SD again and saw that about twelve people were arrested among them the British and American airmen."

One of the members of the SD in Apeldoorn was the Belgian Eugeen Dirckx. After the war he gave the following statement;

"In June 1943 I started to work for the SD as a civilian police employee and interpreter. In September 1944 I was enlisted in the SS. On September 30, 1944, several persons of the underground movement in Apeldoorn were arrested. Among them two allied airmen. On the evening of September 30, 1944 I was ordered to come the next morning to our office with my truck. The following morning the prisoners were loaded in my truck and we brought them to the Apeldoornse Bosch, a SS camp not far from Apeldoorn. When we arrived there, an execution platoon of about twenty men was already drawn up. The commanding officer was already there. The prisoners were lined up with their backs to a bunker. The execution platoon stood at about seven meters.

"Filietz then told the prisoners, among them the two airmen, that they were to be executed because they were found guilty of the possession of forbidden arms and anti Nazi propaganda. Then he gave the prisoners over to the commander of the execution platoon. One of the condemned by the name of Colonel Barentz started to sing the Dutch national anthem "Wilhelmus" and opened his coat in which he was followed by some of the other prisoners. Then the order to shoot was given. The prisoners were not dead at once and several coups de grace were needed to complete the job.

"I saw that Filietz looted the bodies of the victims after they had been shot and put their valuables and identity papers in his pocket. He then gave me the order to back up my truck to where the bodies were laying, gave one of them a push with his foot and said "Weg damit!" ("Away with them!)"

"We then put the bodies on the truck and deposited them on several spots in Apeldoorn, which were pointed out by Filietz, whereupon Filietz himself put a sign on which the word "Terrorist" was written, around their necks."

Author John Meurs continues in his memoirs;

"Among the men who were executed was a young engineer, Hans Wijma, who lived with his wife and a son of four in a nice villa a few hundred meters behind our house. He was employed by his brother-in-law, Heinrich Klaproth, a German who had come to live in Holland a couple of years before the war and had founded a profitable lock-and-key factory in a village five miles north of Apeldoorn.

"Klaproth, who lived in our neighborhood, found himself in a difficult position after the German attack on the Netherlands. He was married to a Dutch girl, had lived and worked in Holland for quite some time, but was still a German and as such an enemy of the people around him. He was not a fervent Nazi, but had become friends with quite a few officers in the German army of occupation and often threw parties for them in his sprawling villa facing the municipal park. The people in the neighborhood treated him and his family politely but coolly. He was not a bad German, but still. It was one of those typical war-time ironies, that his brother-in-law was involved in the underground.

"Hans Wijma and his wife were still up and about, when the SD arresting squad started to hammer on their front door. It still amazes the author that Hans Wijma did apparently not try to escape via the back of the house, but came himself to the front door and fell thus in the waiting arms of the SD. They took him to their car and whisked him away. He also was to be found, the following day, dead, with bullet-holes through his chest, on a crossing in the village center: a young man, with a nice family and a good job: with a sound career and with a bright future in front of him

"His wife saw him disappear in the car and ran, in spite of the curfew, to her sister's house. We don't know if Klaproth tried that night to interfere on behalf of his brother-in-law, but it's obvious that whatever he did was not sufficient to save Hans Wijma from the execution squad.

"Joop's mother and Miss Terwisga were later transported to Germany and put behind barbed wire in the Ravensbrück concentration camp for women. Joop's mother died there of starvation and exhaustion few weeks before the British troops liberated the camp.

***

On October, 2 1969 a memorial stone was unveiled at the spot of the execution. The monument is in remembrance of those who did everything in their power to regain our freedom.

Tail-Gunner Sgt. Floyd E. Ragsdale.

By daughter Shirley Adams.

"My father was born on October 31, 1923, to Floyd Orr Ragsdale and Grace Mitchell (Ragsdale). Both of his parents were from the Honea Path, Belton, South Carolina area. They were quite a comfortable family, though not wealthy.

"My grandfather called on tailors with his fabric, so I suppose he was a salesman. He looked very stylish and neat in his photos. My grandmother was from a very nice family and had a lily-white reputation. Everyone loved her.

"When Daddy was around ten when his mother died from pneumonia complications, leaving three little children. Daddy had two sisters, younger by several years. The girls went to live with their maternal grandmother and an aunt who never married. Daddy remained with his father. When Daddy was around fourteen his father died.

"The Ragsdales wanted the children to go to an orphanage so they could stay together; the Mitchells wanted them to be reared in loving homes. The girls stayed where they were and Daddy went to live with a maternal aunt and her husband who had two boys.

"They loved him but could not give him what other boys had, so Daddy had to share a bike with his cousin. Being a very handsome boy, he was popular and very athletic. When he was in high school, he broke a record in track and met my mother. I asked him once what attracted him to my mama. He told me she was so neat in her clothes, always pressed, with her hair in place, and that her legs weren't bad either.

"If I must say, I had gorgeous parents. Mama was a true beauty, inside and out. They married March 12, 1942, eloped, and moved to Rock Hill, South Carolina. Very soon afterward, he was drafted, as were many young men in 1943.

"Floyd Evans Ragsdale came home from prison camp where he left his boyhood behind. He graduated from Erskine College in 1949 where he found a mentor, Professor Thomas Leslie, who encouraged him to become a land surveyor. My daddy was a quite successful registered surveyor and loved his work. He died in 2000 at the age of 75 with Mama, my sister, Sandra and our husbands by his side. I was and am so proud to be his daughter.

***

Acknowledgements;
Ruth Rumsey, daughter of Navigator 2Lt. Noyes Richey.
Shirley Adams, daughter of Tail-Gunner Sgt. Floyd E. Ragsdale.

CHAPTER 56

452ND BOMB GROUP
729TH BOMB SQUADRON

Type: B-17 • Serial: 42-31784 "Section Eight"
MACR: N/A • Air Base: Deopham Green

"We all sat on the top edge of the dinghy awaiting a rescue. It took about 45 minutes for the English boat to rescue us. The plane sank in about 57 minutes, with the help of the British and .30 caliber machine guns to sink it. None of our crew were injured....We were taken to an English hospital for two nights, then released for several days of flak leave. The "Section Eight" crew was back flying missions in eight days."

Tail-Gunner Marion D. Mason

Pilot: 1Lt. Paul E. Suckow, RTD

Co-Pilot: Kenneth Dunaway, 0-755656, RTD, Italy, TX

Navigator: John R. Jeans, RTD

Bombardier: George Le Grand, RTD

Engineer: Richard J. Walsh, 12125677, RTD, Brooklyn, NY

Radio: Joseph C. Spermbaur, 37544660, RTD, St. Paul, Minnesota

Ball-Turret Gunner: George A. Pruitt, 18191908, RTD, Graham, OK

Waist-Gunner: George Dragich, 19106367, RTD, Johnstown, PA

Waist-Gunner: Robert J. Sampson, 32381137, RTD, Dunkirk, NY

Tail-Gunner: Marion D. Mason, 39279227, RTD, Hernet, CA

10 RTD

Crash Site: North Sea

452nd Bomb Group, 729th Bomb Squadron (Suckow)

Back row (left to right):Pilot 1Lt. Paul Suckow, Navigator John Jeans, Bombardier Graham (not in final crew), Engineer Richard J. Walsh

Front row: Tail-Gunner Marion Mason, Waist-Gunner Robert Sampson, Co-Pilot Kenneth Dunaway, Waist-Gunner George Dragich, Ball-Turret Gunner George Pruitt, Radio Algren (not in final crew)

Pilot 1Lt. Paul E. Suckow

By daughter Judy Kapusta.

"My father was born on 22 December 1918 in Chicago, Illinois to Dorothy and Walter Suckow. Although the years of the Great Depression were difficult for all who lived at that time, Dad's father was a Chicago Fireman so there was always food on the table. When Dad was 17 years old, his father was hit by a truck crossing the street and died from his injuries. Dad graduated in 1936 from Steinmetz High School. He was able to acquire an apprenticeship at the global communications company, R.R. Donnelley in Chicago, the same year.

"Paul met Ginny Murray one afternoon at a bowling alley in Chicago. His brother Wally knew Ginny and told Dad that she was a real nice girl. After their courtship, they married on 4 October 1941. When the US entered the war, Dad knew he would be called and decided to enlist before he was drafted. He had always been interested in flying, riding his bike as a teenager with his brother to Palwaukee Airport on weekends. He took the required tests to become a pilot and enlisted in the Army Air Corps on 7 April 1942.

Pilot 1Lt. Paul E. Suckow

"Dad completed his Cadet Pilot Training in La Junta, Colorado on 20 May 1943, earning the rank of 2nd Lieutenant. The remainder of the year included the final phases of training on the B-17. On 2 January 1944, Dad departed from the US and flew his new plane, which the crew named "Section Eight," overseas to the United Kingdom.

"Dad's brother Wally also served in the Army Air Corp and visited Deopham Green when Dad was stationed there. I remember Dad telling me that he and his fellow officers managed to sneak Wally into the Officers' Quarters for meals and overnight stays.

"Dad flew 30 missions and was Lead Squadron on 10 missions. He earned the rank of 1st Lieutenant on 14 March 1944, before his return to the US on 2 August 1944. He earned the Air Medal with 3 Oak Leaf Clusters, the Distinguished Flying Cross, the EAME Theatre Ribbon with 2 stars, and membership in the Goldfish Club for escaping death on 29 April 1944 with a successful landing in the North Sea.

"With Dad's return to the US, he saw his first daughter, Paula, born in February 1944, for the first time. Reporting for duty after leave, he began flight instruction on B-29, and subsequently became pilot on that aircraft. On 23 October 1945, he was relieved from active duty. Dad continued his relationship with the Army Air Corps by remaining in the Officers' Reserve Corp at the Reserve Training Center at Orchard Place Airport in Park Ridge, Illinois. This airport would later become Chicago's O'Hare International Airport. Dad was instructor in pilot training in the Officers' Reserve, and earned the rank of Captain on 29 August 1947.

"Dad and his brother were very close, having lost their father when they were only teenagers. After the war, the brothers bought homes on the far northwest side of Chicago, only a couple miles from one another. Sadly, Wally died of a massive heart attack when he was a young father, leaving three pre-school aged children. Norma (his wife) and children moved to California shortly after his death to be closer to her family.

"Over the course of Dad's career with R.R. Donnelley, he was promoted to Pressroom Foreman in 1948 (the same year I was born), and continued in production for 40 of his 50 years with the company. Dad ended his career with R.R. Donnelley in 1986 as Manager of the In-House Credit Union and Savings & Loan. RRD counted the time he was away serving his country and, in fact, he drew a small paycheck during that time which helped my mother. There were only 14 people prior to Dad's retirement in 1986 who achieved the 50 year milestone with the company, which was founded in 1864.

"Dad's hobby was always photography. He had his own darkroom and developed his own film. Most of his free time was spent reading. My parents had a very good life after the war, and my sister and I enjoyed a normal, middle class upbringing. After we married and moved out of the family home, my parents began to travel abroad and continued to travel extensively until retirement, when they purchased a condo in Naples, Florida. They managed to spend winters there for 13 years before deciding to give it up. Dad passed away peacefully in his sleep on 14 November 2007 in his own home, next to his loving wife of 66 years, 5 weeks short of his 89th birthday.

"On a more personal note, I would like to say that I have never known anyone who was more self-disciplined than my father. He was a conservative man, a humble Christian, and an excellent roll model. He rarely spoke of his time overseas during the war. On the rare occasion when he did, it was only at urging, and with a heavy heart. I'm sure he saw many horrific sights during those 30 missions. I knew about the ditching in the North Sea and I pestered him to write an essay. As he grew older, I stepped up my pestering. One day when I was over at his house in 2001, he handed me a half dozen handwritten pages. I typed up his words and have his narrative of that fateful day to pass on to future generations.

Paul Suckow recalls;

"29 April 1944 started as so many others. The crews scheduled to fly were awakened at 2:00 am and then had breakfast, including fresh eggs. Having fresh eggs at an Air Corps base in England at this time was cause for suspicion. The general briefing ended with the Commanding Officer opening the curtain covering the wall map. It showed the red yarn marking our route to Berlin, which was cause for the usual groaning. After adjourning, we gathered for separate briefings for pilots, bombardiers and navigators. The gunners retrieved their gun innards and drew ammunition. The crews then completed the necessary tasks to prepare their planes.

"As the "Start Engine" time approached, the sky was starting to lighten. Taxi and then takeoff followed. Forming seven planes to a squadron, twenty-one to a group, three groups to make up a wing, and climbing to 30,000 feet before starting out over Holland took a bit of time. It was a beautiful day, clear and bright, and we had no fear of enemy fighters. The P-51 and P-47 fighter planes were protecting us. It was not that way early in the year before the 51's and 47's were shipped to England. We were over a solid cloud cover halfway to the target. Not to be concerned, the lead plane had radar to find the "Aiming Point."

We were at the IP (Initial Point), turned to the target, usually seven minutes away, when the anti-aircraft shells started exploding around us. "Hold it straight and level, close up the formation," came over the radio from the Group Commanding Officer. One crew member was shoving chaff (paper backed metallic strips) down a chute as fast as he was able. The German gunners at first aimed at the chaff, but soon learned to fire at the planes and not the decoy.

"Co-pilot Kenneth Dunaway was flying the plane, and I was counting the bombs as they left the bomb bay. A light flashed on my control panel as each dropped. Almost all were out when we took a hit, apparently in the #3 engine. The plane started to vibrate badly. The red light was on, indicating no oil pressure. I had the feather button for the #3 engine depressed with no results. The top gunner reported the right main landing gear was down and covered with gobs of oil.

"We slid out of formation and headed east and then north around Berlin to get away from the anti-aircraft shelling. Away from the flak, I headed west. About this time the vibration ceased, apparently the engine froze up and the shaft sheared, allowing the propeller to windmill. This is not a good situation as a windmilling prop is a large drag. I could not retract the gear or the bomb bay doors. Walsh, the Engineer, cranked the gear up and got the bomb bay doors closed with the emergency procedure. By this time, the crew had dumped overboard everything possible to lighten the ship. I tried to reduce power on the three engines and discovered #1 was not responding. I hit the feather switch and was afraid to look out. When I finally forced a look, the blades were just coming to a stop in the full feathered position. Things were looking better, but I was still trading altitude for air speed, and both remaining engines were nudging the head temperature red line. Unknown to me, Walsh managed to drop the ball turret with the handy tools he always carried. The plane put its nose up and started to fly.

"We were holding about 9,000 feet altitude at this time. With no armament aboard, I headed for the North Sea in order to put some space between us and any enemy fighter cruising around. That windmilling propeller seemed to be rocking back and forth, so I kept reducing air speed. Fuel was becoming a problem. We apparently lost the 400 gallons in the #3 main tank when that engine was hit, and were using a great deal of fuel with the increased power settings we had to use in order to hold our altitude. We were getting close to home, however. I was switched to the Air/Sea Rescue radio channel.

"At this time, first one of our two remaining engines quit, followed by the other. Walsh really had our fuel divided evenly between our two engines. I hit the transmit button and called May Day several times. A British voice answered immediately, "Aircraft calling May Day, hold your mike switch down, you are too low, I'm not getting a good bearing on you." I had my side window open and was trying to determine the direction the sea was running. The crew was ready for ditching, and I called for full flaps. I heard the belly of the plane slap a wave, then we ploughed into the next wave and shuddered to a stop. By the time I climbed out my window, Dunaway was standing on his window frame counting the crew members. When all were accounted for, he jumped for the wet wing, slid off, and in he went! Someone dragged him back onto the wing. Each side had a life raft slowly inflating, and all of us were able to scramble aboard and paddle around the rear of the plane and tie together.

"The radio man was working with an emergency transmitter while Walsh was checking the emergency supplies. There was quite a sea running. We would be up on the top of a wave and then down in the trough. About this time I heard the sound of powerful engines. After coming to the crest of the waves several times, I spotted a boat approaching from the northeast, but it was pointed at least 30 degrees away from us. Walsh had a flare ready and asked if I wanted it fired. Someone said, "No, no, it's a German Beatle." I had no desire to end up in a Prisoner of War camp, but if they missed us we could sit out in our rubber rafts for several days before being found. All of us were partially soaked, Dunaway was shivering and sea sick to boot. On top of the next wave, the boat was still pointed away. I called to Walsh, "Fire that flare!" Bang! Up it went. Up on the next wave the boat was turning toward us. After several more waves, I saw the bulls eye of Great Britain on the bow of a crash boat. Soon we were scrambling up a boarding net to be greeted with a mug of brandy. I estimated we were no more than 30 miles from landfall when we went down.

"When we arrived at the Royal Naval Barracks at Great Yarmouth, we were put in the care of an officer with a full beard and stripes on his sleeve up to his elbow. After being checked by a doctor, we were ushered into a kitchen and served a meal of beans, fatback and heavy bread. Not having anything to eat for 16 hours, it tasted so good! The commander then sent the enlisted men to another part of the complex and took the rest of us to the club bar room. We were celebrities! Seems the group awarded a case of Scotch to the boat crew that picked up the most live survivors for the month. The crew that rescued us was leading the pack, and we added ten to their score. Another round of drinks was in order!

"I finally had to ask the Commander if he could find us a place to sleep. We bedded down in what seemed like a large dormitory, which we had all to ourselves. I was awakened the next morning by a young lady saying, "Here is your tea, sir." She was a member of the Women's Auxiliary Air Force, British, of course. Another young lady was pulling the blackout drapes. We were then directed to breakfast, white table cloth, no less.

"In a short time a truck from our base showed up with some of our clothes, and we were able to return the ones that were loaned us. Soon we were back at our base and the next day saw our squadron Comanding Officer. He congratulated me and then said, "I must send you and your crew to a resort for a week's rest leave, but I'm really short of crews. Could you fly several more missions, and I'll get you off next week?" What could I say but, "Yes, Sir."

Radio Joseph Carl Spermbaur.

By daughter Donna Severson.

"Joseph Carl Spermbaur was born in St Paul, Minnesota to Carl and Margaret Spermbaur on January 16th, 1922. He attended St Bernard's in St Paul for elementary school. Joseph furthered his education at Mechanic Arts in St Paul. He gota job as a laborer at American Hoist and worked there until he enlisted in the US Army Air Corps on December 28, 1942.

"On October 16, 1943, Joseph married the neighbor girl, Julia Sophie Schubert. When he was discharged from the military he and his bride continued to reside on Galtier Street. He went to work as a dockworker at Witte Transportation, where he worked for the duration of his life.

Radio Joseph Carl Spermbaur

"In 1950 with the help of his friends, Joseph bought some property in White Bear Lake, Minnesota and built a three bedroom Rambler for his growing family.

"Life has a way of throwing us a curveball. In 1957 Joseph was diagnosed with Diabetes. On November 12, 1958, Joseph's wife Julia went into the hospital for Goiter surgery. She was given sodium penathol and had an allergic reaction to it. She went into cardiac arrest and the doctors were unable to revive her. She was 33 years old.

"Joseph was devastated. He was left alone to raise 6 children ranging from 2 to 13 years. He trudged on, making sure that all of the children went to a private school as he and Julia had planned. He became very quiet and to himself and lived day to day. He never remarried. He dated the same girl off and on for 10 years, but it never became permanent.

"Joseph enjoyed the outdoors. He and the neighbor created and built their own homemade tent trailers in the 60's and used them for camping and for their hunting trips. He loved hunting for deer, pheasants and ducks. He would go with his friends and his older sons.

Joseph and the boys also got into a phase of archery, practicing in the back yard. He also liked to fish, including fly fishing. For a few years he had a hobby of tying his own flies. He really enjoyed that.

"He had an acre lot, and half of that he plowed for a large garden. He was so proud of the vegetables he could grow in the rich black soil. He even tried his hand at raising chickens and rabbits for a while. Every year he would go to his parent's house and they would make blood sausage and head cheese.

"He was not afraid to try doing different things. That was his life, working, providing for his family and enjoying his hobbies whenever he had the chance.

"All too soon though, that life took a toll on Joseph. On April 7, 1972 while he was sleeping, he had a massive heart attack. He was only 50 years old when he died.

Ball-Turret George A. Pruitt.

From his personal notes.

"April 29, 1944. Hit Berlin, Germany. On the way to the target number 2 engine started acting up. Over target - number 3 engine was knocked out, loosing oil pressure and were unable to feather propeller. As a result, we had to let it wind-mill.

"As we were leaving the target area, number 1 engine was shot out, leaving us with only two engines. We were unable to stay with any of the returning formations and we were losing altitude. So, we threw out all our guns and ammunition. The ship was shot to pieces by flak. We were coming in "on a wing and a prayer," just hoping and praying we'd have enough gas to get out of enemy territory, and praying we wouldn't be intercepted by enemy fighters.

"And our prayers came true. We weren't intercepted and we got out of enemy territory. But as we were crossing the North Sea, flying at about 4,000 feet, our two faithful engines run out of gas, forcing us to dead stick land in the water. The pilot made a beautiful landing and we all got out uninjured.

We were in our dinghies 40 minutes when the air sea rescue picked us up. Our plane floated 57 minutes, which is believed to be the longest period of time any US Army Air Force plane has floated. Lt. John R. Jeans, our navigator, got a few chips of glass in his eye when the plexiglass nose was hit by flak. Thanks to Lt. Suckow's beautiful land and the wonderful work done by radio operator S/Sgt. Joe C Spermbaur in contacting Air Sea Rescue we all survived that mission.

D-Day, June 6, 1944

"Completion of my last tour of duty. Didn't get any sleep last night. Briefing at 10:30 pm. Take off at 2:10 am. Bombed beachhead 8 minutes before invasion troops landed. Never saw such perfect timing and teamwork as was displayed by our air and ground forces this morning. Everything worked perfect. We bombed at 7:22 am and troops landed at 7:30 am. We landed back at our base at 9:45 am. Every available airplane in the 8th and 9th Air Force were flying. Here 's hoping those boys over there the best of luck in seizing and establishing their stronghold. God only knows they're apt to need it.

George Pruitt's nterview with Davis W. Imman

""We flew so low over the beach that I was able to fire on the Germans below. I could see the army moving across the beaches."

"On June 1, 2008, as the summer heat pressed into the windows in Snyder, Texas, I sat interviewing George Pruitt, a former ball-turret gunner aboard a B-17 bomber who was stationed in England during his tour of duty in World War II.

"A native of Ardmore, Oklahoma, George had been working with the Civilian Conservation Corps, otherwise known as the CCC, when he heard the news about the Japanese bombing Pearl Harbour. "I had been working in Wyoming and was heading back home when our bus stopped at a hole-in-the-wall diner in Denver, Colorado for lunch. We heard the news broadcast announce the attack. The next day, I joined the Army Air Corps.

"George didn't wait to be drafted. "No, I knew what I had to do immediately. My brother joined on the same day, but neither of us knew it." I asked him if he was worried about joining the war, but he smiles and replied, "No, we knew we were going to win before we ever left."

"But leaving took awhile. First, he had to endure basic training at Randolph Field in San Antonio, Texas. From there, he attended a series of schools from South Dakota to Pyote, Texas training him how to be a gunner and how to function as a bombardier. He recalled flying over Carlsbad, New Mexico, where they dropped dummy bombs on targets carved out of the desert for just such a purpose. These targets can still be seen in Carlsbad, and an occasional dummy bomb made from concrete is occasionally unearthed on these sites.

"Once his training was complete, he was assigned to the 452nd bomb Group, 729th Bomb Squadron, and he and his combat crew flew to England and made a home at Deopham Green, just outside of Attleborough in Norfolk. Once they were settled in, the flight engineer Richard W. Walsh, suggested they name their plane "Section 8" which was heartily agreed upon. Walsh even managed to to get an eight ball painted on the plane. Of course, most Americans will recognize the military term, section 8, which means a discharge based on a assessment of being psychologically unfit for duty. They figured they were crazy to get in a plane and fly over Germany. Lt. Paul E. Suckow was the pilot over plane #42-31784. "Section 8" was now in service.

"Throughout he course of a year, the crew of the "Section 8" flew 30 missions, which was required of each crew before they could be returned stateside. They had their share of harrowing experiences during their tour of duty. George recalled one instance when a German fighter, was making a sweeping run on them from their right. He began firing at the plane and hit it when it was only 400 yards away. "He'd have gotten us if I hadn't shot him first," he recalled, with a distant glance into the past, a tribute to his memory.

"And he hadn't forgotten when the "Section 8" was shot down near the end of their tour. "We knew we were going down immediately. They hit the engine and it was all over. We had to ditch the plane in the English Channel.

"Perhaps the most interesting occurrence for George was when he was on leave and was hitchhiking back to the airfield. "We hitched a ride everywhere we went. One day, I was hitching a ride and was surprised to open the door and see Queen Elizabeth. Of course, she was still a princess then, but she was very nice and we chatted for several minutes until they dropped me off. The Queen wasn't the only high profile figure he encountered overseas. "Once, I met both Doris Day and Betty Grable when they came through doing a tour. I think meeting Doris Day was the best part of my being there.

"After his part was played, George and the crew returned stateside and cheered on the boys who continued the fight. "Those were different days. Everyone knew what their part was, and everyone did what was expected of them. None of us complained; we just did what we had to do." Once back in the States, George met Martha in Fort Worth, Texas, who was working at piecing together war planes. "She was my "Rosy Riveter" and I knew I better marry her if I knew what was good for me."

"The Pruits have been happily married for 60 years, and resided in Hamlin, Texas, for most of these years. To-day, they live in Snyder, Texas, were they are just as happy as the have ever been, being continuously surrounded by family. I count it an honor to have an opportunity to sit in the presence of such great men as George Pruitt. Without the contribution these men made, we'd be drinking French wine with German labels, and the maps would be drawn differently as the are currently.

"Thank you, George, for the sacrifice you made in order to guarantee our freedom. May God richly bless you and your family.

Tail-Gunner Marion D. Mason.

"Over Brunswick our # 1 engine was hit and knocked out. Our No. 3 engine was hit and knocked out over Berlin, Germany. We lost altitude, with flak bursting all around us, there was a huge hole in the left wing, with many other holes. We were heading back to our home base in England.

"It was a long 4 1/2 hours before we would touch down. The radio operator was sending SOS messages to the British for help and an air-rescue. To gain altitude, everything loose was thrown out. The ball turret was unbolted and dropped. We continued toward England, only two engines working. We lost altitude over

Holland and over the water. The two remaining engines quit. Our experienced pilot, with a belly flop landing, landed our damaged aircraft on the cold, choppy waters of the North Sea, between four and five in the afternoon.

"Flares were released. All of us had 40 hours of dinghy escape training. Both wing dinghys were used. Several individual dinghys were inflated and towed behind the main dinghy. We all got in one dinghy. The entire crew, before impact, was all sitting on the radio room floor sitting straddle legged one in front of each other. No.1 was Walsh and I was No. 2. I remember Walsh was short; I pushed him up and out of the top hatch after we landed in the water. The first one out pulled the next one up and out until we were all out. The pilot and co-pilot were the first ones out, as they had side windows in which to escape. We all reached the wing area, then into the dinghys.

We all sat on the top edge of the dinghy awaiting a rescue. It took about 45 minutes for the English boat to rescue us. The plane sank in about 57 minutes, with the help of the British and .30 caliber machine guns to sink it. We were 10 miles off of the British shoreline, but I could not see the shoreline. None of our crew were injured. I did have a piece of shrapnel hit me in my back. It did not penetrate my leather jacket. I still have that piece of metal. We were taken to an English hospital for two nights, then released for several days of flak leave. The "Section Eight" crew was back flying missions in eight days.

***

Acknowledgements
Judy Kapuska and Paula Panek, daughters of pilot Paul E. Suckow
Donna Severson, daughter of radio-operator Joseph Spermbaur
Will Inman, husband of granddaughter of ball-turret gunner George Spruit.

CHAPTER 57

453ᴿᴰ BOMB GROUP
732ᴺᴰ BOMB SQUADRON

Type: B-24H • Serial: 42-52301 "Ken O Kay"
MACR: 4940 • Air Base: Old Buckenham

"Gas consumption caused ditching at 15:15 hours on April 29th in the North Sea, 30 miles due east of Great Yatmounth, England."

Statement by pilot Max Davison, Missing Air Crew Report # 4940

Pilot: 1Lt. Max A. Davison, 0-729821, RTD

Co-Pilot: 2Lt. Alan W. Kingston, 0-755963, RTD, Bowler, WI

Navigator: 2Lt. Wayne M. Rose, 0-688650, RTD, Firth, ID

Bombardier: 2Lt. David Lustgarten, 0-746896, RTD, New York, NY

Engineer: T/Sgt. William C. Lake, 35664677, RTD, Berea, KY

Radio: T/Sgt. Robert L. Krentler, 16151572, RTD

Ball-Turret Gunner: S/Sgt. James C. Hetherington, 17092620, RTD

Left Waist-Gunner: S/Sgt. Floyd E. Hobart, 17175501, RTD, Welda, KS

Right Waist-Gunner: S/Sgt. William M. Heins Jr., 12204034, RTD, Phillipsburg, NJ

Tail-Gunner: S/Sgt. Harold G. Oakes, 11015918, KIA, Brattleboro, VT

1 KIA, 9 RTD

Crash Site: North Sea
Time: 15.15

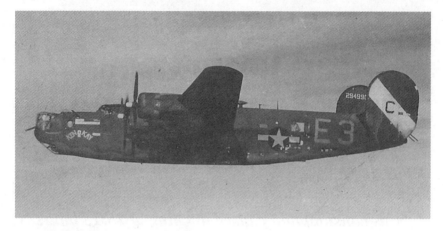

B-24, serial # 42-52301 "Ken O Kay"

Co-pilot 2Lt. Alan W. Kingston

By son Dick Kingston.

"Alan was born and raised in Gillette, a small rural town in northeastern Wisconsin. During his youth, he learned to hunt and fish, and continued to do so all of his life. In high school, he played football, basketball and baseball. After high school, he enrolled at the University of Wisconsin-Stevens Point. Before he could finish, WWII came and he enlisted in the Army Air Corp. While in the service, he met and married Hazel Phillips.

"After the war, Alan finished his teaching degree. He and a friend bought a small airplane, so he could continue his love of flying. Alan lived in Madison, but he was most happy when he was at his cottage on

Co-pilot 2Lt. Alan W. Kingston

Lake Superior. He enjoyed maintaining the house and grounds, and hunted and fished at his leisure. After he retired, he moved to the cottage on the lake. Later he and Hazel moved to Florida, to get away from the cold winters. He spent his final days there enjoying the warmth.

Engineer T/Sgt. William Coolidge Lake.

By Debbie Lake.

"William Coolidge Lake (lovingly called Booger Bill by his family) was born January 29, 1921 in Garrard County Kentucky to William Lake (Bill) and Effie Jennings. Bill acquired his pet name from a Truancy Officer named Booger Johnson. Bill was a very intelligent little boy and would finish his school work before the rest of his class mates. He would catch the teachers head turned and sneak off to the swimming hole. Of course the school would send the truancy officer to fetch him back to class. So, that's how he got his nickname Booger.

"Bill was a graduate of Berea High School and Salutatorian of his class. After high school Bill entered the service in 1942 and was discharged in 1945 after serving in the European Theatre with the U.S. Air Force during WWII. He was an engineer and turret gunner on a B-24 plane and flew a total of 27 missions.

"On his 8th mission he was wounded in the shoulder by shrapnel and on his fourteenth mission his bomber ditched in the North Sea. He received the Distinguished Flying Cross, the Bronze Star, the Purple Heart, the Good Conduct Medal, and other decorations. Though very quiet and modest regarding his combat years, Lake made a worthy and honorable contribution to his country.

"When Bill returned home from the war, he made his living driving a truck and doing other odd jobs in the community. Bill never married or had children and after a lifelong battle against alcoholism due to what is now called PTSD, Bill died of a heart attack on April 19, 1985 at his home in Berea, Madison County, Kentucky.

Radio T/Sgt. Robert L. Krentler.

"Ditching In The North Sea" by R. L. (Bob) Krentler

"According to Roger A Freeman "Ditching a B-24 was recommended only as a last resort. The flimsy bomb bay doors usually gave way on impact resulting in the aircraft being flooded in a very few seconds or breaking in two. From the very rare, partially successful B-24 ditchings in the North Sea only a few men had escaped."

"On April 29, 1944, the crew of "Ken O Kay" was to experience the reality of a crash-landing in the icy waters of the North Sea. Frankly we were not trained for this situation. Our training consisted mainly of viewing the film clip of a B-24 gliding to a perfect landing on the Potomac River. While the plane floated the crew members climbed out of the hatches, inflated the life rafts and peddled their way to safety. Well, it wasn't that easy.

"On that Saturday in April 1944, the Quonset hut door opened with the usual message, "O.K. guys, let's go, it's mission time." I thought, three o'clock in the

751

morning – it must be a long one, no milk run today. Little did I know what lay ahead. After a hearty breakfast of bacon and eggs, we assembled in the briefing room. You could sense the tension in the air as we waited for the target map to be displayed. The 453rd had been on "Maximum Effort" all during the month of April. According to Roger Freeman, "The month of April, 1944 was a month of sustained aerial combat that has no equal in the annals of Eighth Air Force history. Three hundred sixty-one heavy bombers were lost." The 453rd had suffered more than its share of losses. In addition, the long-promised replacement crews had not arrived. We all knew replacement crews were essential if we were to complete our tour of combat missions. The loss ratio for the Eighth Air Force was extremely high; without replacements your chances for survival were slim at best.

"When the curtain went up the red line stretched deep into Germany – all the way to Berlin. When the Air Exec. announced the target as the Underground Railroad station in the center of the city I was very excited. This was to be the second daylight raid on Berlin. I didn't want to finish my tour of combat missions without participating in the big one: BERLIN ! While we had been on a couple of missions to the Berlin area – mostly airfields – we had not been scheduled to fly the first daylight raid. Matter of fact, I had volunteered to go with another crew as a tail gunner. Fortunately, that mission was aborted after about two hours flying time due to weather. Flying in the tail turret was a very scary experience. I felt like I was sitting on a stepladder five miles above the ground, with wind blowing so hard I thought the turret would blow off any moment.

"Well, now I would get a second chance at Berlin with the security of being in the top turret or at the radio position in the cabin. While we were at the "hard stand" sweating out take-off, the crew was unusually quiet; none of the jokes or smart remarks that always took place as we went through our respective pre-flight check lists. The maximum effort was taking its toll. Everyone was glassy-eyed from lack of sleep and struggling to perform their duties without error. God, where are those replacements?

"Take-off and forming went without incident. I can remember sitting in the top-turret marveling at the sight of hundreds of heavy bombers flying in a formation that stretched as far as the eye could see. I felt a great sense of security seeing all of those well-armed friendly airplanes. Add to that the tremendous skill of our pilot Lt. Max Davison had displayed on our previous 18 missions and there certainly was no cause to fear this mission. (Oh, to be 20 years old again!)

"Some flak was encountered as we crossed the coast, but nothing to worry about. We had a good number of friendly fighter planes accompanying us most of the way to the target. The question was: How far into Germany would their fuel supply take them? Unfortunately, not all the way to Berlin.

"As we approached the city we were attacked by the Luftwaffe in force. ME's and FW's were all around us. Our gunners reported two kills and one probable. As we began our bomb run, flak took over and it was savage. On the bomb run it was my job to take photos of the target in order to determine how effective the bombing was. Lying prone, with my head, arms and the camera extended out over the open bomb bay taking pictures of the bombs exploding on the target as the flak was exploding almost in my face was exciting. I had the best seat in the house.

"Soon after dropping our bombs, but before we could leave the target area, we took a hit from flak, which caused us to feather two engines. With only two engines functioning, we began to lose air speed and altitude. Worse yet, we were required to operate the remaining engines at maximum RPM, thus using up our fuel supply at too fast a rate.

"As we battled loss of altitude and enemy fighter planes, it became apparent that we wouldn't make it back to the base. At this point, I began to send out distress signals. What a surprise was in store for me: all the frequencies were jammed with S.O.S. signals. By this time we were over water but down to a couple thousand feet of altitude. Now I was really sweating. I kept tuning my transmitter through the range of frequencies for air-sea rescue; still no reply.

"We were under 1500 feet when I finally got a response to my Mayday call. I locked down the transmission key and prepared to ditch. Lt. Davison told me to go to the waist to make sure all equipment had been jettisoned and that the crew was in position to ditch. By the time I got through the bomb bay and to the waist, the plane was under 500 feet.

"Hobart, the waist gunner, shouted "We are all set here, get you're a - - back up front." I ran through the bomb bay and slid into my ditch position behind the co-pilot's armored plate seat about two seconds before we hit the water.

"SWISH - - POW. That was the "Ken O Kay" hitting the water. The next thing I knew, water was flowing in from the overhead hatch like a waterfall. I can remember fighting the force of the water with all my strength and finally getting my arms on the fuselage. Then the top turret began to sink and in the process caught the sleeve of my heated suit between the ring and the gears. Using what must have been super-human strength, I was able to rip the sleeve wires free from the turret and float away from the plane.

"The thought struck me: if I had so much trouble getting out, what about the flight engineer Bill Lake, the pilot Max Davison, co-pilot Alan Kingston, navigator Lt. Rose, and bombardier Lt. Lustgarten? I looked around and, miraculously; they were all in the water. Lake came out of the hatch after me; the pilots, navigator and bombardier floated to the surface when the nose of the plane broke off. Lake apparently swallowed a lot of salt water, probably while I was trying to free my arm. Also, he couldn't swim, nor could Davison. At this point, Alan Kingston was a real hero - - holding Lake above the water line and at the same time letting Max Davison hold on to his Mae West straps in order to stay together. Meanwhile, when I pulled the cord to inflate my Mae West, nothing happened. The top had a big hole. Not to worry - - I felt very buoyant due to the air trapped in my heated flying suit.

"I remember it was a bright, sunny day, the water seemed to have swells of about 30 feet. Friendly aircraft were circling overhead. I watched as the "Ken O Kay" slowly sank below the surface. All of this seemed like an eternity but probably took only five minutes at the most. The next thing I knew, an air sea rescue boat came roaring up to us. I thought it must be the one that answered my SOS call because his signal was very strong, indicating he was nearby. Just then a very courageous British sailor threw a cork ring into the sea and jumped overboard. He got into the ring and began to paddle toward us. At that time I still had some buoyancy left in my flying suit so I told him to pick up my buddies first. I could see Alan was having a rough time holding up Max and Lake. This was rather dumb on my part because the air quickly dissipated from my suit and my body became numb. I was struggling to stay afloat when he reached me and grabbed my hands, which were then secured to the inside of the life ring. This kept my head out of the water. Good thing, because I lost consciousness at this point and didn't wake up until we were almost to Great Yarmouth.

"I was later to learn that my best buddy, tail-gunner Harold Oakes, was unable to get out. Poor Harold. Whenever I go to the American cemetery at Cambridge, I stop at Harold's name up there on the marble wall and give him my love. It's a very emotional thing for me.

"The fellows in the waist didn't fare so well. In addition to Harold being lost at sea, Hobart suffered a broken leg and a cut that ran from his mouth to his right ear. It was a terrible sight with his teeth and jawbone exposed to the salt water. Hobart  was so strong he was able to swim the mile or so to the rescue ship. Hines and Hetherington made it to ship as well as Rose and Lustgarten but they were pretty banged up. After picking me up the British sailor was able to rescue Lake, Davison and Kingston.

"When I regained consciousness, I asked the British sailor why he didn't pick up my buddies first, since they were in obvious trouble. He said they were trained to pick up the nearest survivors first. If they did it in the way I suggested they wouldn't rescue anyone. I thought that was a lesson I would never forget.

"The next day, clothed in blue jeans, T-shirts, and tennis shoes, we were invited to a celebration on board the Royal Navy rescue ship. It seems that the ship, which successfully rescues someone at sea, hosts a party for the other ships as well as the survivors. After the party we were returned to Old Buck to rejoin the group and complete our remaining missions. Ironically when I returned to the Quonset hut, all of my clothes had been stolen. I later learned this was fairly common practice when a crew was missing. I went on to complete my tour of 31 missions shortly after D-Day.

Ball-Turret Gunner S/Sgt. James C. Hetherington.

By son James.

"David Creed Hetherington, my grandfather, was a Lieutenant in the infantry in WWI. My grandmother, Amelia Hetherington, was the daughter of German immigrants from Hamberg, Germany. My grandfather spent his life farming and later building houses. He and my grandmother pushed their youngest two children to go to college to become an aeronautical engineer and a journalist. My Dad's oldest brother Orlyn Hetherington was a B-17 pilot in WWII and flew for most of the rest of his life even flying for the CIA during the Vietnam conflict. His brother Charles Hetherington spent WWII in a submarine in the Pacific.

Ball-Turret Gunner S/Sgt. James C. Hetherington

"My Dad was a farm boy born in Morrison, Oklahoma and spent his childhood there. He actually did ride a horse to school in a snow storm. He reminded me of some of the hardships he endured and of many of the good times he enjoyed while growing up with his four brothers and one sister. His family moved to Mancos, Colorado when he started high school.

"When he was a senior in high school Pearl Harbor happened. He graduated in the spring of 1942 and could hardly wait to get " in the action ". He enlisted in the U.S. Army Air Corps and went active December 8, 1942 at the ripe old age of 18. He said he regretted not becoming a pilot but was in a big hurry to get into the war so he went to gunnery school instead as well as armament school, and training in basic aircraft maintenance and hydraulics.

"The air crew consisted of only officers and sergeants because the German high command had a soft spot for airmen so they were treated a little better when captured. He was matched up with his air crew by then and spent time training in Idaho and Texas dropping bombs and shooting at flying targets towed by other aircraft. In November of 1943 his plane and crew along with some other aircraft left Texas for South America and flew across the Atlantic to Morocco, where they spent several weeks. I have a couple of very old Arab knives that he purchased for souvenirs and saved to give to me I suppose.

"His plane and crew arrived at Old Buckenham field in England February 22, !944, he turned 20 two days before. One of the things he remembered most about the winter in England was the cold. The Quonset huts they lived in were uninsulated and heated by a coal stove with little coal to be had.

"He always had high words of praise for his pilot Lt. Max Davison. He said Max was an exceptional pilot and saved their lives on many occasions especially April 29, 1944 when they were forced to ditch in the English Channel. Lt. Davison also taught every crew member how to land a B-24 in the event the pilot or co-pilot were unable to.

"After my Dad had completed his 31 missions he was sent back to the states to Denver, Colorado, where he served as a military policeman. This is where he met my mom and they were married in August of 1945. He was discharged October 24, 1945.

"My parents moved to Grand Junction, Colorado where, in the summer of 1946, they started a peach orchard. My dad also went to carpenters school on the G.I. Bill. He worked as a fruit farmer and built many houses as a general contractor. His fruit orchard is still in business today. I followed in his steps somewhat and expanded the acreage and have moved to the mountains to enjoy my senior years.

"My Dad often talked of how beautiful the clouds were when he was looking down on them while he was flying. He would also talk of the little dark puffs of clouds he would see and say how they reminded him of flak from the German guns. I think the times when he talked of flak were the only times I ever saw fear in his eyes. The last twenty years of his life he and my Mom spent the winters in Mexico deep sea fishing. He had a boat that he named " Mustang " honoring the P-51 Mustang aircraft that saved so many bomber crews lives by having the long range capability of flying cover the whole distance to and from the bombers targets.

"My Dad was awarded the Air Medal, the Distinguished Flying Cross with oak leaf clusters and two Bronze Stars. He never mentioned the Distinguished Flying Cross and the Bronze Stars. He only mentioned the Air Medal because of the man who pinned it on him, General James Stewart, better known to the world as Hollywood actor Jimmy Stewart.

***

Acknowledgements;
Dick Kingston, son of co-pilot 2Lt. Alan W. Kingston.
Debbie Lake for T/Sgt. William Coolidge Lake
James Hetherington, son of ball-turret gunner S/Sgt. James C. Hetherington.

CHAPTER 58

453ᴿᴰ BOMB GROUP
734ᵀᴴ BOMB SQUADRON

Type: B-24H • Serial: 42-50322
MACR: 4493 • Air Base: Old Buckenham

B-24 in our Group hit by enemy aircraft. Engine
number 3 smoking. ME-109 hit him from between
5 - 7 o'clock. Ship still going when last seen.
14.00 hours, 20,000 feet.

Missing Air Crew Report # 4493

Pilot: 1Lt. Francis R. Tye, 0-737902, KIA, Tujunga, CA

Co-Pilot: 2Lt. Willard R. Larson, 0-685251, KIA, Garland, UT

Navigator: 2Lt. Fred Gordon, 0-809352, KIA, Lecuinstor, MA

Bombardier: 1Lt. John W. Skidgell, 0-663672, KIA, Baltimore, MD

Engineer: S/Sgt. Mauriece P. Mackey, 18183067, KIA, Colorado City, TX

Radio: S/Sgt. Kenyon G. Hills, 11102662, KIA, Hartford, CT

Ball-Turret Gunner: Sgt. Manuel C. DeLeon, 18060438, KIA, Houston, TX

Left Waist-Gunner: Sgt. Frank J. Litton, 17089345, KIA, Colorado Springs, CO

Right Waist-Gunner: Sgt. Thomas E. Nolan, 19173010, KIA, Los Angeles, CA

Tail-Gunner: Sgt. Harold A. Leighton Jr., 32833504, KIA, Buffalo, NY

10 KIA

Crash Site: North Sea

S/Sgt. Mauriece P. Mackey, engineer

From nephew Harry Senn – July 25, 2015

"My mom, grandfather, the whole family grew up during our Great Depression Days. I learned from the "stuff" grandfather saved that he learned to make do with what he had.

Model airplane carved as a boy by Engineer S/Sgt, Mauriece P. Mackey

"Then as a preteen, staying a week at grandpa's house during one summer, I investigated the closet of the bedroom where I slept. In a wooden chest, carefully packed with silk handkerchiefs, was a wooden, hand carved airplane, painted with house paint. I later found out that was carved by Preston when he was my age. That's when I learned the process of creating for myself what I wanted and providing for myself what I needed.

"I took the wood from the apple boxes grandfather would discard and carve my own airplanes. Grandpa would intentionally ask the grocery store people in town to put his groceries in the apple boxes then he headed back to his house out in the country. Maybe grandpa suspected I was trying to carve airplanes and I needed the wood.

"I passed this heritage on to my son Jonathan. We learned to invent solutions to whatever we need. Even yesterday he came by the house. Even though we needed to visit, he really wanted to rummage in my big workshop to see what he could gather. Don't know what he got, but I saw him carry a big box packed over the top to his car. I am very proud of him. Jonathan named his second son, Preston, just to pass down the heritage of the hand carved wooden plane.

"Even though his first name was Mauriece, mom and Paul, baby sister and brother to Preston, always called him Preston. Paul also reminded me often when we talked about Preston that his first name was spelled with an "ie" in Mauriece.

***

CHAPTER 59

458ᵀᴴ BOMB GROUP
752ᴺᴰ BOMB SQUADRON

Type: B-24H • Serial: 41-28718 "BO"
MACR: 4451 • Air Base: Horsham St. Faith

North of Hannover at 11.04 hours, 8-10 FW190's and ME109's out of a formation of an estimated 30 enemy aircraft made a one pass attack from 12 o'clock high using roller coaster tactics. One of our aircraft was lost in this engagement.

After Mission Intelligence Report

Instructor Pilot: 1Lt. Edwin A. Grant, INT

Pilot: 2Lt. Dale R. Morris, 0-685167, INT

Co-Pilot: 2Lt. George A. Griffin, 0-812245, INT

Navigator: 2Lt. William C. Lane, INT

Bombardier: 2Lt. Louis S. Beckett, 0-752833, INT

Engineer: Sgt. Stonewall J. Johnson Jr., 35499061, INT

Radio: S/Sgt. Samuel Thomas C. Bell Jr., 15334764, INT

Ball-Turret Gunner: Sgt. Lynn L. Lemons, 39855467, INT

Left Waist-Gunner: Sgt. Charles A. Frazier, 37233872, INT

Right Waist-Gunner: Sgt, William E. Marr, 39192421, INT

Tail-Gunner: Sgt. Earl C. Savage, 11038039, INT

11 INT

Target: Friedrichstrasse Station in the heart of Berlin
Crash Site: Rinkaby Airfield, Sweden

From the 458th Website.

"Many stories have been told about the one crew "that did not have time to un-pack" before they were lost on a mission. Dale Morris' crew could be one of those mentioned in the 458th. This crew was assigned on Sunday, April 23, 1944. The next Saturday night, they were "guests" in Sweden, having been forced to divert to that neutral country during the day's mission. Not quite the 24-hour turn around that most of the stories are made of, but the crew's tenure with the group was certainly short lived.

"Morris and his crew flew their first mission on April 27, 1944 to the marshalling yards in the French town of Blainville. This mission by all accounts was a milk run – only a few enemy aircraft were seen in the distance, but no attacks made on the 458th formation, and none of the group sustained battle damage. Morris dropped on the primary target with the rest of the group and made a landing back at Horsham St. Faith with no trouble.

"On Saturday, April 29, the 458th headed to Berlin, the target Friedrichstrasse Station. The 458th put 29 Liberators into the air. Of these, six aircraft aborted and the remaining 23, including Morris made it to the target. For reasons unknown,

1Lt. Edwin A. Grant

Morris' crew had arrived at the 458th without a navigator, and filling in on this mission was 2Lt. William C. Lane. Lane had been the navigator on Lt. Beckley's crew #12 before Beckley became ill and the crew disbanded, spread out amongst the 752nd squadron. Also new to the crew on this mission was 1Lt. Edwin A. Grant. He was almost half way through his combat tour, having flown 13 missions with his own crew who were not flying on this date. He was flying from the co-pilot's seat, acting as an Instructor Pilot for the new crew. 2Lt. George A. Griffin, co-pilot, who did not have to fly since his seat was taken, apparently elected to stick with his crew, as squadron records note that "he flew as an observer on this trip.""

Pilot 2Lt. Dale R. Morris.

From son Dale Morris.

"Dad was born in 1920 on the family homestead in Saint John, Washington. St. John is in what is called the Palouse country – an area noted for wheat farming. At the time his parents were homesteading 330 acres of land in a remote part of Montana. When my grandmother was close to delivering my father they drove back to the family homestead in Saint John in a Model T Ford to be with family. This was quite a trip back then and took several days. After dad was born they returned to Montana but the land was so dry they eventually left the farm and moved to Chewelah, Washington where they farmed a piece of land approximately 5 miles south of the town.

"While growing up dad attended Elementary School at a one room school house that was at the end of the dirt road where their farm was located. After that he attended school in Chewelah and either walked or rode a horse the approximate five miles. He attended Jenkins High School and did chores on the farm in the early mornings

Pilot 2Lt. Dale R. Morris

and then did various jobs such as sweeping out a grocery store in town before going to school. "Somehow he found time to play football while in high school. He played right tackle and was good enough that he was offered a football scholarship at Gonzaga University in Spokane which he didn't accept because of family reasons. This was unfortunate as he wanted to be a doctor and spent the first few years after high school trying to earn money for college.

"By the time he was seventeen he had worked many jobs around the small town of Chewelah. This included working for a funeral parlor and driving a gasoline truck. One job that he took was working in a magnesite mine. Shortly after starting he was called into the office and asked why he hadn't registered for the selective service. He had to admit to them that he was only seventeen. Because of federal laws that prohibited anyone under the age of 18 of working in a mine they had to take him out. They did give him another job above ground. By the time he was 19 he had saved enough money to buy a Texaco gas station in Chewelah.

"Besides football dad loved fly fishing and pheasant hunting. He spent most of what little free time he had pursuing these activities.

"It was in Chewelah where dad had his first flying experience. A traveling carnival passed through the town and one of the attractions was an airplane. Dad paid a nickel to get a ride in the bi-plane and immediately loved flying. He tried to join the Army Air Corps when he was 19 but was turned down for flat feet. This was a bit of irony as he had excellent vision (20/15 in both eyes) and was exceptionally strong. Both very desirable attributes for pilots at that time.

"For reasons I don't know dad moved to the town of Yakima, Washington in 1941. I don't know if he was working or started college although there were no major schools there. It was there that he met my mother, the former Dorothy Smith. They began dating and were having dinner in a Chinese restaurant on December 7 when it was announced that Pearl Harbor had been attacked. Dad went down to the recruiting office and enlisted the following day.

"Pilot training was scattered all over the country. Dad took his basic training at Enid, Oklahoma, his primary training was in Vernon, Texas and his multi engine training was at Pampa, Texas. My mother drove down to Vernon, Texas and mom and dad were married there. She and dad's navigator's wife followed their husbands around the country as they trained at various fields. Dad and his navigator, Roy Devlin, were very close and they and their wives would go into town to see movies and have dinner whenever the guys could get a pass to leave the base. I know that besides Texas and Oklahoma the crew also did training in the California desert and in Kansas.

"Following training dad was assigned a new B-25 and was scheduled to go to the South Pacific. Just hours before they were to leave he and one other crew were pulled out and told they weren't going. Instead they were given orders to go to Langley AFB in Virginia. There they were instructed in the use of the H2X radar. Following training in Langley the crew left for the 8th Air Force in England. My mother was several months pregnant with my sister Marilynn when dad left.

"Upon arrival in England Roy Devlin was assigned to another squadron. I have no knowledge as to why but assume that another more experienced crew was in need of a navigator trained on the H2X. On April 29, 1944 dad's crew was part of a raid on the marshaling yards at Friedrichstrasse. As a pathfinder his B-24 was loaded with flares. My understanding is that the lead aircraft equipped with the H2X radar would lead their formation in and drop flares on the target for the rest of the group to drop their bombs on.

"Unfortunately at 11:04 hours near the town of Celle his aircraft was attacked by a FW-190. Dad said that among other damage they lost an engine to the attack. After dropping into the clouds he turned toward Sweden and was again attacked, this time by flak, near Ystad. Dad said that a second engine was destroyed by flak. After the second attack and leaving the coast the crew spotted fighters approaching their aircraft. They were relieved to see that they were Swedish fighters. (I imagine the Swedish pilots were relieved not to be fired upon as well.) It would take a lot of courage to approach a combat weary bomber crew in a small plane. I've heard it said by several of our own fighter pilots that they tried to keep some distance from the bomber formations because they had been shot at so much that the fighter pilots were afraid the gunners might mistake them for German fighters. One of the fighter pilots motioned to dad to follow them and they escorted them to Rinkaby field. So began the internment. Mom only knew that he was missing in action. A friend of dad's who knew where he was wrote her a letter from England. Because of censorship at the time he could not tell her where dad was. Instead, he just wrote something like "Dale has been busy" which indicated to her that he was alive.

"In Sweden: here things get a bit sketchy. He told me that he, another officer and a number of enlisted men were cannibalizing from aircraft that made it to Sweden to make a good airplane which he would then fly back to England. I remember him saying that they had to strip all the armament off the aircraft so as not to endanger the agreement Sweden had with Germany. He didn't talk much about his time there but indicated that there was a lot of intrigue. I remember him commenting once how strange it was standing on the beach in Sweden along with British, German and even occasional Japanese and seeing planes being shot down over Copenhagen.

***

"Dad returned to the U.S. in 1945. He was assigned somewhere in California immediately after returning from Sweden. and was still flying until his discharge from the Army Air Corps at McChord Field near Tacoma, Washington. I believe he was discharged in 1946. He was a First Lt. at the time and won the bronze star. This I only found out after his death when I read his discharge papers. He wanted to fly for an airlines but my mother was so upset at the idea that he finally agreed not to pursue a flying career.

"Dad also gave up the idea of being a doctor because he now had a wife and daughter to support. Instead he went to mortician school in San Francisco. Upon receiving his license the family moved to the little town of Wenatchee, Washington. He worked two years for a funeral home in Wenatchee and it was there that I was born. Dad then bought his own funeral home in Walla Walla, Washington. He decided he really didn't want to do that work for a career and became interested in a Dairy Queen drive-in across the street from the funeral home. After many conversations with the Dairy Queen owner he decided to sell the funeral home and buy a Dairy Queen of his own in Portland, Oregon in 1950. After owning a store in Portland and then in Seattle he became a Regional Representative for Dairy Queen International. In 1959 he and a friend formed a partnership and bought the Dairy Queen franchise for three counties in Washington. They eventually built 35 Dairy Queen Stores before retiring and selling the business in 1990. Dad was president of the business and both he and his partner were members of the Board of Directors for the parent company Dairy Queen International.

"Dad never lost his love of hunting and fishing and passed that passion on to me. Some of the very best memories of my youth were spending time with him hunting pheasants and trout and salmon fishing. Sometime while I was overseas in the Air Force (approximately 1967) dad rekindled an interest in golf. By the time I was out of the Air Force he could rightly be called a "golf nut." He belonged to three country clubs at the same time and usually played five or six days a week weather permitting.

"After retirement he and mom sold their house and moved into the beach cabin they had built on Whidbey Island in the mid sixties. Over the winter they designed a remodel of the cabin and turned it into a house. Now retired he played golf and fished for salmon in front of his house whenever he wanted. The only time he returned to Europe was in 1986 when he and mom came to visit when I was assigned to the embassy in Prague, Czechoslovakia.

"Dad passed away on Whidbey Island in February, 1998 from Parkinson's disease. Mom survived him by twelve years.

Co-Pilot 2Lt. George A. Griffin.

By his widow Helen Griffin

"George Albert Griffin was born April 24, 1922 in Concord, North Carolina. He graduated from a two-year college, then worked for a short time in shipbuilding at Wilmington, North Carolina, before enlisting in the Air Corps in September 1942. After training at various fields, he received his wings and promotion to 2nd Lieutenant in October 1943. After more advanced training, he was assigned as co-pilot of a B-24, named "Bo."

"His crew arrived in England on March 16, 1944 as member of the Second Division, 458th Bomb Group of 8th Army Air Force. They flew their second mission on April 29, 1944, target Friedrichstrasse Station in the heart of Berlin. Their plane was damaged but they were able to land in Sweden. They were interned there and returned to England on October 18, 1944. They may not have been allowed to return to combat because of agreement with Sweden so they returned to the United States. George was assigned to duty of flight instructor. He was promoted to 1st Lt. in February 1945. He separated from service in June 1946.

"He returned to college September 1946 to study architecture. I returned to graduate school the same month. We met that fall and were married in Decem-

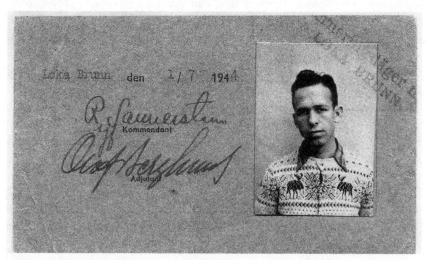

2Lt. George A. Griffin, Swedish ID Card

ber 1947. He graduated in June 1950. He opened his architectural office here in Concord in 1955.

"He designed a new Sanctuary and Educational Building for our church, our county courthouse, municipal building, schools, medical buildings, banks and other commercial buildings, a few houses.

"George died October 2005. Our son studied architecture. He worked with George and continues to carry on the business.

"George and I never attended any of the internee reunions in Sweden, but we did visit Sweden in 1988 as part of a Scandinavian tour. We spent one night in Falun where he had spent some time while interned."

***

Acknowledgements;
Dale Morris; son of pilot Dale Morris
Helen Griffin, widow of co-pilot George Griffin

CHAPTER 60

466ᵀᴴ BOMB GROUP
784ᵀᴴ BOMB SQUADRON

Type: B-24H • Serial: 41-29399 "Playboy"
MACR: 4448 • Air Base: Attlebridge

Bomber was abandoned after flak and fighters had caused considerable damage and killed the ball-turret gunner. Plane crashed near Tolplas, town of Daarle, Netherlands.

Missing Air Crew Report # 4448

Pilot: 2Lt. Franklynn V. Cotner, 0-813568, POW, Boise, ID

Co-Pilot: 2Lt. John B. Stuart, 0-751573, POW, Chicago, IL

Navigator: 2Lt. Melvin H. Everding, 0-685502, POW, St. Louis, MO

Bombardier: 2Lt. Norman H. Roth, 0-686692, POW, Atlantic City, NJ

Engineer: T/Sgt. Robert F. Pipes, 20821082, EVD, Dallas, TX

Radio: T/Sgt. Charles F. Doring, 32469409, POW, Bayonne, NJ

Ball-Turret Gunner: S/Sgt. Robert I. Falk, 32677413, KIA, Big Flats, NY

Left Waist-Gunner: S/Sgt. Edward L. Mount, 14140605, POW, Brantley, AL

Right Waist-Gunner: S/Sgt. H. L. Heafner Jr., 34472989, EVD, Greenwood, MS

Tail-Gunner: Sgt. Ralph J. Fiskow, 16046751, POW, Milwaukee, WI

1 KIA, 7 POW, 2 EVD

Crash Site: Tolplas/Daarle, Netherlands
Time: 14.40

From "Tales to Noses over Berlin" By Ray Bowden.

"The assigned target for the 466th Bomb Group and the rest of the 2 Bomb Division was the Friedrichstrasse rail station in the middle of Berlin, the centre of the main rail and underground system networks. One of the group's planes airborne that day was an ageing camouflaged B-24H named *Playboy* (41-29399) by its crew. The left nose of the ship was painted with a rendering of Donald Duck in top hat and tails.

"The enlisted men on the crew that day had not expected to be flying. They had notched up their 10th mission two days previously and anticipated a respite, freely indulging in the local brew the previous night confident that they could sleep it off in the morning. Their dreams were shattered, however, just three hours after getting to bed when they were woken and told to prepare for day's mission - to Berlin!

"Missing both breakfast and the briefing, they arrived at the hardstand to find their pilot, Lt. Franklynn Cotner, ready and waiting to start engines. All went well, as *Playboy* flew the course along with the group, until at the Initial Point a direct hit from 88mm flak smashed the No. 3 engine. Lt Cotner feathered the prop and managed to keep his place within the formation. After bombing *Playboy* headed for home.

"Without their heavy bomb load the other B-24's were able to pick up speed but *Playboy* fell further and further behind. Just as the plane filled into a vacant slot in a following B-17 group, twenty FW19Os launched an attack. Singling out their victim, five fighters streaked in from the rear to be met by a hail of tracers and armour-piercing bullets from the tail and top turret. In the ensuing seconds, fighters broke away left and right, some streaming flames, others leaving a trail of black greasy smoke. The tail turret on *Playboy* took several direct hits from incoming 20mm shells, plexiglass shattered and the turret caught fire. The tail gunner sustained injuries and burns, a waist gunner died instantly - shot through the head. The No. 2 engine shuddered and seized up as more 20mm walked across the left wing piercing the fuel cells and sending chunks of metal flying back from the cowling. The onslaught was halted only when a flight of *Thunderbolts* arrived to drive the attackers away.

"As fuel drained from holes in the tanks and pipelines, the engineer estimated just 30-40 minutes flying time left. Cotner decided to continue flying towards the coast for as long as possible.

"The B-24 Liberator was notoriously difficult to ditch into a pitching sea. If the plane did not break up on impact its high wing format meant that the bulk of the fuselage would quickly submerge making it difficult for any crew to evacuate without loss. It was therefore decided to abandon Playboy over land and not ditch into the sea.

"At 9000 ft. the fuel finally ran dry and the crew began to abandon the aircraft. In spite of his injuries the tail gunner managed to bail out, as all the surviving members of the crew. *Playboy* continued on in a shallow dive, disappeared into cloud and eventually made a soft landing at Daarleveen in Nazi-occupied Holland, narrowly missing a house. There would be no more nights at the pub for the crew for a very long time.

Pilot 2Lt. Franklynn V. Cotner.

"On April 29, 1944 we were flying a mission to Berlin, Germany. About halfway to the target we received a direct hit from anti-aircraft fire. This hit produced a three-foot hole in our right wing between the fuselage and the number three engine. We were fortunate in that we were able to feather the prop and continue the mission. We dropped our bombs and headed back to England. The damage to our number three engine did not prevent us from continuing the mission.

"On our return, suddenly the air group on our left began an "essing" maneuver, which was bringing them directly into our formation. The pilots of our group, 466th, immediately scattered and began to regroup further to the right. It was during this regrouping that the loss of power by the absence of number three engine had the most impact. Even though we could maintain our position in straight and level flight, we did not have enough power to execute the maneuvers necessary to regroup.

"While I was trying to find another formation to tack on to, the enemy hit us. Four Focke-Wulf 1905 came at us, from six o'clock, pumping 20mm cannon rounds into our plane. Robert F. Pipes, our engineer who manned the top turret guns, and Sgt. Mount, the tail gunner, were able to destroy two or three enemy fighters. I don't know what damage our other gunners caused. During this firefight, the right waist gunner, Sgt. Robert Falk, flying his first mission, was instantly killed by a shot through his head. Edward Mount, one of gunners, really took a beating. He suffered wounds and burns and, as I remember, was blown out of his turret and back into the plane.

"The fighter attack caused other extensive damage, including the knocking out of our number two engine and some damage to our number one engine. The damage to number one caused intermittent surges of power. Had I been able to depend on number one, I could have established a power glide across the English Channel and then made other decisions over England.

"It was then that I trimmed the ship for a straight glide, expecting that it would continue on into the water, and gave the order to abandon ship.

"Of the nine crewmen who jumped that afternoon, all of them eventually made it back to the United States, and as of now, 1988, most are still alive, so the decision must have been the right one. I might mention that after I bailed out, our airplane made a complete 360-degree turn to the left and came a lot closer to me than I wanted.

"Engineer Robert Pipes was sent to the rear of the ship to make sure everyone was out. Two of the crew were standing on the catwalk at the rear of the bomb bay, and one of the men could not bring himself to bail out and was helped by Pipes and H.L. Heafner. Heafner followed him out and Pipes came forward to check on me. I was on my way from the flight deck after trimming the aircraft. Pipes bailed out and linked up with Heafner and they evaded capture for the rest of the war.

"When I bailed out I could see there was a hole, approximately three feet in diameter, between our fuselage and our number three engine. There was a similar hole through the bomb bay doors. I could see that the fuselage had sustained thousands of holes and the right rudder was almost destroyed. The left rudder was severed at the middle. This damage was a result of the attacks by the Luftwaffe fighter planes.

"I later learned that the *Playboy* had made a soft belly landing at Daarle, Holland, with the body of Sgt. Falk still aboard. Sgt. Mount used Sgt. Falk's parachute because his had been destroyed by enemy fire.

"I landed in a little farming community in Holland and was almost instantly surrounded by very friendly Dutch civilians. I had injured my left side in the landing and this made walking very difficult. Some farmers brought a door and laid me on it and carried me into a large house.

"I was there only a few minutes when one of them spoke to me in English. He said that they could help me to escape, except that I was so badly hurt. Another fellow arrived and came to the center of the group. He looked down at me and said, "Hi, buddy, where are you from?" I told him I was from the United States, to which he replied, "Well, I'm from Chicago myself!" Apparently, like a lot of Americans, he was caught in Holland when war was declared.

"The villagers took me to a small hospital at Armelo. I stayed in the hospital overnight. The next morning a little chubby, rosy-cheeked nurse of about 40 somehow informed me in a mixture of English, Dutch, and "gestures" that the Germans would come soon to take me away. She said my injuries were not serious enough to prevent that. However, if it was all right with me, they could take a sledgehammer and break my leg so that I might be left in the hospital longer. I told her that anything would be okay, but before they could get the hammer, the Germans came.

"From there I was taken to a very large prison in Amsterdam and put in solitary confinement with two meals a day of sawdust-flavored bread and warm tea. I don't remember how long I was there.

"Next, I was taken to Frankfurt on the Mainz, where again I resided in a solitary cell, with the same filthy conditions. Once a day I was interrogated by a German Air Force major. The singular question asked of me was "How many bombs did you carry on your last mission?" This went on for days, while outside my window the Germans were trying to dig up and defuse an eight-thousand-pound, delay action English bomb. I didn't know whether the bomb was live or if it had been placed there for obvious reasons. I finally told the major we carried fifty

100-pound bombs on that mission. This seemed to satisfy him and he said I could go and join my friends in another part of the area. We actually carried 75 bombs.

"This other area was next to a street that hundreds of German officers took on their way to a war college. So each morning, noon, and evening as the officers walked by we would serenade them with a little song. Some of the words were "We will oompah, oompah, right in the Fuhrer's face."

"In late 1944, Stuart, Everding, Roth, and I arrived at Sagan Stalag Luft III, This prison camp was about 90 kilometers southeast of Berlin.

"On or about January 29th, 1945 we began a march from Sagan to Nuremberg. There were quite a few POWs who had previous military experience before they became air crew. I had been in the infantry for three years prior to going in the Air Force. 1 had a pretty good idea of how to take care of myself in situations like this. Before leaving Sagan I had made a ski mask from a pair of long johns. It covered my head and face, and I cut two eyeholes in it. I was in slightly better condition than some of the others who were inexperienced. After approximately 28 hours of marching, and during a regular rest stop, we found ourselves deep in a forest.

"During this stop, there was a horse-drawn wagon, which was filled with German records. These were contained in trunks with heavy metal supports on each corner. One of the horses froze to death in its traces. When the traces were cleared, it alarmed the other horse, which bolted. The metal edges on the boxes being dragged started making a noise like machine gun fire. The Germans thought the Russians were upon them and they started firing their machine guns indiscriminately.

"We jumped off to the side of the road and lay in ditches for twenty minutes. During that time our body heat melted the snow so that when we continued the march, the clothing on our front was wet. When we stopped for our five-to-ten-minute rest each hour, many of the inexperienced POWs would kneel in the middle of the road and start rocking back and forth on their hands and knees, not knowing they were freezing to death. I and some others did everything we could do to get them back on their feet. We dragged them, kicked them in the fanny, and swore at them. We did anything that would cause a spark and would get them going. Some POWs, exhausted by the day's march, crawled off the road and froze to death.

"After a miserable 24- or 36-hour march, we arrived at a town (Dresden or Chemnitz) and were billeted in a pottery plant. It was an opportunity to remove my pack and two packs that I was carrying for other marchers. There I learned my arms and legs had been mildly frostbitten and I began to have pain. From there we went by boxcar to Nuremberg - Stalag Luft VII D. This camp was located very close to railway marshalling yards, and both the RAF and our 8th Air Force flew bomb raids over it. Sometimes our barracks would be moved off the foundations by four or five inches by the concussion of the bomb blasts and the next day be moved back again. The windows were all shattered.

"The Germans said we could not seek shelter during the raids and kept us inside at gunpoint. We replied, "Up your bucket," dug trenches outside our barracks with "KLIM" cans (milk spelled backward), and jumped out of the broken windows during air raids and into the trenches. We even removed the wooden covers from the windows and used them to shield ourselves from flying debris.

"We could see all the devastation being wreaked on Nuremberg and more than once said, "Isn't it wonderful that when we get home we'll have the United States, and the German POWs all of this to come back to."

"After the end of February to mid March, Red Cross parcels began coming through. Shortly after Easter we were told we would march to Moosburg, which was about 145 kilometers distant. Colonel Alkire and the German kommandant reached an agreement that would make the march less demanding on the POWs.

"Our officers created a Commando Group, and I was selected, along with some others, to march directly behind the senior American officers and the German major in charge. Our job was to save as many POWs as we could if their lives were in danger. We also had some bed sheets to spread out in a field in the letters "P.O.W" or to wave as white flags if the American fighter planes discovered the column.

"Finally at Moosburg and Stalag VII-A we found showers and enjoyed our first in two and a half months. Red Cross food parcel delivery was very good. There was much bombing around us again.

"Suddenly on April 29th, 1945, rifle and machine gunfire began. As I was sitting peeling potatoes, a bullet went through the tent and missed my head by only a few inches. There was some commotion outside so we tumbled out to see what the problem was. There was a light aircraft flying over the camp. I believe they wanted everyone out of the tents and into slit trenches. As I looked out to the east there was a column of American tanks on a hill, moving to the south. We hit the trenches and the war began again.   The tanks started their bombardment and the Germans fired in reply. It lasted into the night.

"The next day we were told that some SS troopers had gone into the barracks and told the Wehrmacht soldiers that they should resist to the end. The Wehrmacht were a bunch of middle-aged farmers who did not care one way or the other about the outcome of the war. They made it clear to the SS that they were not going to fight it out to the end. The SS fired a bazooka into the barracks, killing quite a few of the Wehrmacht troops. Then the SS took off when the sound of the American artillery could be heard close by.

"General Patton's 14th Armored Division came into our camp, followed by GI trucks and jeeps. The American flag was raised, and I was on the beginning of my trip home.

"I was put aboard an Italian liner, the USS Monticello, and the minute I hit the gangplank I began to feel seasick. For 12 days I was in a miserable condition. I couldn't eat, I couldn't sit down or stand up. I couldn't lie down. The only relief I got was at night when the barber shop closed. I made a deal with the barber so that I could sleep in his swivel chair. I could tilt the chair in a certain way and get some rest.

"I landed at Camp Miles Standish, Massachusetts, where steak, mashed potatoes, pie, milk, anything we wanted was served to us by German POWs. Personally, I couldn't eat anything except potatoes without gravy. The German POWs ate with us, piling up their plates and sitting in their own section of the dining hall. They gobbled down everything as I sat there watching them, while I ate nothing.

Co-Pilot 2Lt. John B. Stuart.

by daughter Sheri Stuart Denk.

"Lt. John Brown Stuart was born in Chicago, Illinois, on October 17, 1917. He passed away in Bay Pines Veteran's Hospital St. Petersburg, Fla. on February, 24, 1979. His father was George Thomas Stuart, a Scottish immigrant. His mother was Lily Bell, who was born in Canada and immigrated with her family from Canada to Chicago.

"John attended Chicago schools; the Earle School and Harper Junior High. He attended Lindblom High School where he graduated in 1937. The following year he attended night school at Armour Institute of Technology from 1938 to 1939. After graduation, he was a switchman at Commonwealth Edison Compa-

Co-Pilot 2Lt. John B. Stuart, with his wife

ny from January 1936 to October 1941. He was employed after the war at Commonwealth Edison from Nov 1945 to Jan 1947 as an Electricians Apprentice.

"John and Eva Lorene Gathright were married by her father Reverend Thomas Gathright on July 20, 1945 in Garrison, Texas at the First Baptist Church. After their marriage, they traveled to Chicago for a wedding reception and settled in Chicago. Illinois. He moved to Texas in 1947 to open a photography studio called Stuart's Studio in Palestine, Texas at 205 and a half W. Main St. He operated the studio until Dec 1948 when he returned to active duty.

"During his later military career, he was assigned to the Army Security Agency beginning in 1951. His last stateside assignment was project officer and later commanding officer of Project Dimaon later changed to Carryback (410th US-ASA Co).

"On a resume when asked to define his special skills, he wrote *"ability to lead personnel, organized and commanded personnel comprising of 16 different nationalities. Last assignment in Korea, I was the Personnel Officer employing 85 Korean nationals. "*

"Major Stuart retired in Bradenton, Florida, with his wife Eva and four children. Eva's married life demonstrated the courageous life of a military wife, traveling and settling in new places, appearing to do so seamlessly. John was a story teller of funny, heroic and impossible tales that fascinated his children and grandchildren. These stories seemed possible only when he told them. His hobbies were fishing, boating and swimming. He taught his children to swim, dive and held swimming and diving competitions with the grandchildren. Photography remained a lifelong interest.

Navigator 1st Lt. Melvin H. Everding.

Dictated to daughter Barbara Poplin.

Navigator 1st Lt. Melvin H. Everding

"My name is Melving H. Everding and my rank was 1st Lt. During World War II I was a navigator on the B-24 *Play Boy* and flew 12-13 bombing missions flying out of England. Lt. Cotner was our pilot. Stuart was a fill-in for our co-pilot, Roth was the bombardier and I was the navigator. Sgt. Pipes was 1st engineer, Sgt. Charles Doring (radio), Robert Falk and H.L. Haefner were waist-gunners. Ed Mount was tail-gunner, and Ralph Fiskow was ball-turret gunner.

"On a mission on April 29, 1944 we were hit by flak over Berlin and were unable to keep up with the formation. The German planes came in to pick off the stragglers. Sgt. Falk was the first one killed on the mission. He was shot in the head. I moved him from his position and manned the gun. By the time I got into position to man the gun, fighters had already his us several times. I was able to get in-sight and range and I fired the gun three times and I felt that I had hit a plane. I didn't consider it a clear hit because the plane flew to the other side.

"It was a few minutes later that I received a call from Lt. Cotner and we discussed our future action. Sgt. Pipes had informed us that we were getting low on gas. I told Lt. Cotner that we could possibly glide into the coast of Holland but that it was swarming with anti-aircraft guns. Lt. Cotner made the decision to abandon the plane and bail.

"I told Mount to get in front of me so I could help him since he was injured. He jumped out first from the bomb-bay and I followed. I landed where a large mound of dirt and the ground met, my left leg up in the air on the mound. I was sitting on my right leg and thought I had broken it. Mount was standing by a barbed wire fence and called to me; *Hey Mel, which way to the base?* I said, *Base hell, let's get our asses out of here. We are in Holland!*

"We started down a road and went into a big forest with what looked like a passage-way. As we went further into the woods and it looked more like a drainage ditch for rainwater on the ground. We hid ourselves in a crevice which was overlapped with branches and pine needles. Germans walked right by but did not see us.

"We stayed hidden until dark and then crawled out and decided to go up to the road. That's when Baron Van Pallant and another man came by and we identified ourselves as Americans. The men identified themselves as Dutch and said, *Follow us.* As we were walking another man came toward us and I am sure he saw us. When we got to the Baron's home, the phone rang and he received word that we had been seen with him. We stayed with the Baron until the Germans came to get us. We didn't want to endanger the Baron and his family who might have been killed.

"I was taken for interrogation for three hours the first day, second day three hours and the third day for about four hours with a German major. He was very angry and red faced because I wouldn't divulge anything except my name and serial number. He said, *We will talk to-morrow, and you will tell me or else.* I became frightened upon hearing this. Lots of people asked me if I was scared in the War, but I was only scared then because I was alone, and did not know what might happen the next day. Fortunately, my visit with the major was cancelled and an hour later I was in a train station in Frankfurt. The city had been completely destroyed as was the train station, but they had been able to repair the station to work again. We were marched through the station and people were very angry and could have harmed us but for the German soldiers and their guns.

"After we boarded the train we were taken to Stalag Luft 3 where I stayed until the winter of 1944. Then we were marched to Nuremberg and then on to Moosburg. That was where General Patton's army freed us on April 29, 1945, exactly one year from the date of my capture. From there we were rounded up and sent to Camp Lucky Strike from where we boarded a ship to Port of Spain. After a short stay there we headed to the States arriving in New York. We were treated to a steak dinner but we retired early so that we could visit the family of Robert Falk who was killed on the plane. After our visit, we returned the following day to board a train to take us to our home towns.

"I had married my wife Ruth on September 5, 1942, before I was captured, and she waited patiently for me to be released. Upon my return home we had two daughters and I continued to work as a carpenter, builder and general contracter until I retired.

Engineer T/Sgt. Robert F. Pipes.

From "The Playboy Crew" by Robert F. Pipes.

"Heafner, Fiskow, and Mount, the gunners; Doring, the radio operator; Everding, the navigator; Roth, the bombardier; Stuart, the co-pilot; Corner, the pilot; and I (flight engineer and top turret gunner) jumped at about ten thousand feet. Falk, the dead gunner, was still on board.

"Mount and Everding landed in a forest near a castle that belonged to Baron Van Pallandt of Ommen. As many as one hundred airmen and others were aided by the baron or stayed at his estate during a five-year period. (We saw the baron's daughter, Mrs. Adrie De La Porte, on our later visit to Holland, who now lives in a home designed by Frank Lloyd Wright, built in 1938. The baron's castle is now an extension of the University of Cambridge, London, England.)

"Mount and Everding were hidden by the baron for several days. He had to surrender the two flyers to the Germans because Mount needed medical attention for his wounds. The Germans suspected the baron was hiding them and he had no alternative but to give them up to the Germans to protect his work of helping other Allied flyers.

"Fiskow landed in a tree and his parachute was entangled in the branches. Before he could extricate himself, the Germans captured him. He landed very near a prison camp. Cotner hurt his leg upon landing and was unable to escape the Germans. He was taken to a hospital nearby in the village of Ommen and given medical attention. Roth, Stuart, and Doring were captured by the Germans immediately upon landing. All were prisoners of war until April, 1945. Heafner and I, the two southerners, would evade capture by being hidden from the Nazis for about a year.

***

"As I descended under my parachute, I heard an aircraft approaching and feared it was German. I breathed a sigh of relief when I saw that it was an American P47. The plane circled around me until I was very near the ground. He was protecting me from being strafed by German pilots; then he waggled the aircraft's wings as a gesture of good luck and departed.

"I landed in a plowed field and was trying to decide which way to go when a man approached me and wanted to know if I was English. I told him that I was an American, and he motioned for me to follow him. I had a tough time keeping up with him, though, because both my flying boots had been pulled from my feet when I bailed out. We were met by his wife and they motioned for me to follow them into a barn. A young boy came on a bicycle and told me to get on behind him. We took off down a country dirt road. I was on the back trying to hold on to a bunched-up parachute with one hand and him with the other. The Dutchman took me to a dense pine forest, hid me in an abandoned rabbit hole, and covered me with pine needles. I peered out a short time later and saw the left waist gunner, Sgt. Heafner, riding behind a man on a bicycle. He was also hidden in a rabbit hole. Heafner and I talked about what we would do. We heard German soldiers talking. They were all around us but they didn't find us because it was getting dark. German search parties were also looking for the other crew members.

"Our airplane crash-landed at Daarle, apparently after making a 360-degree turn, in a field, making a fairly good landing with no one at the controls. The autopilot had been turned on prior to the crew bailing out. On its descent, the plane had clipped some tree tops and barely missed a house. It threw off the two outboard engines. Sgt. Falk's body was thrown out of the fuselage. He was buried in a local cemetery and later in the United States. J.H. Kamphuis of Daarle got to the crash site before the Nazis and took a radio from the plane. He still had the radio when we visited Holland in 1988. He also showed us a picture of a German soldier with a cutting torch, cutting the plane into smaller sections for salvage.

"The farmer returned to where we had been hiding. He took us to his barn, where we hid in a tunnel in the haymow (loft). He later brought us milk and food. We stayed in the haymow for a day or two without coming out because the Germans were still searching for us. Finally, the farmer came for us and took us to his house. His wife gave us tea and cookies. Two men dressed in business suits came into the room and said they would help us return to England. They asked us to give up our GI (government issue) wristwatches, .45 caliber automatic pistols, identification tags, and anything that might reveal our identity as Americans, which we did... reluctantly. One of the men was called "Colonel." It seemed to us that they were officials for the Germans, but actually they were part of the Dutch Resistance. We left in the early morning hours in a fancy Mercedes-Benz for Baron Van Pallandt's mansion, Where we were given civilian clothing, and we left for the city of Almelo, Holland.

"We stayed in a secret compartment in a house in Almelo for two or three nights; then we were given identification cards and train tickets to the city of Enschede, Holland. We were escorted to the railroad station by a member of the underground who was to show us which train to board. German soldiers were numerous in the railway station and in the streets. The underground agent motioned for us to follow him, and two German soldiers got in between us and the resistance member. It looked like the soldiers were following our guide. The guide made several detours and we finally eluded the soldiers.

"We boarded the train and were assigned a compartment. Two German soldiers in full field equipment and arms entered and were seated opposite us. Trying to act nonchalant, I rolled a cigarette from tobacco and papers given to me by a Resistance member. Immediately after I lit the cigarette, one of the Germans banged his rifle butt on the floor and pointed to the sign that read, "Verboden te Rooken," which I assumed meant "Forbidden to Smoke." Startled, I soon realized that all I had done was light a cigarette and I quickly put it out on the floor. He smiled at me as if to say, "No harm done."

"We arrived at a railroad station and a man motioned for us to follow him. A sign at the station read, Enschede, Holland. Until this time I didn't know where we were or where we had been. We followed the guide into a shop, which was a two-story building with living quarters in the back and several bedrooms upstairs.

"We were introduced to a family of eight, named Blokzijl. who lived there and operated the shop. We stayed with them for two or three weeks. We slept in a secret compartment, but we had freedom of the house until we were warned that Germans were nearby, and then it was back to the compartment. Sometimes I would look through the curtain separating the living quarters from the store and watch the German officers who had come in to make purchases. There were two Blokzijl children I remember, a daughter 14 or 15 years old and a son who was 12 or 13, with whom we played a card game called "Pang," which was similar to the card game Old Maid.

"We had been there about three weeks before we could get toothbrushes. We tried to describe to one of the Blokzijl girls what we wanted. She finally understood my Dutch with a Texas accent of "tandenbostel," which meant toothbrush, and brought us a horsehair-bristled, wooden-handled brush that was about ten inches long. As funny as the toothbrushes looked, we were sure glad to have them.

"The senior Blokzijl was a very religious man and at mealtimes would say grace, sometimes for long as 30 minutes. Heafner would nudge me as if to say "How much longer?" We would recognize the words "Jesus Christi" every once in a while during the long prayers. We were told that we would stay there until we were contacted by another agent who would take us to the North Sea to catch a submarine back to England and freedom. The man never came.

"After about two weeks, American P-51 Mustang fighters bombed and strafed a Luftwaffe airfield about four kilometers north of Enschede. Much damage was done to the airfield and aircraft on the ground, and many of the Luftwaffe personnel were killed or wounded. The Blokzijl family's fear of being taken hostage made them decide that we should be moved again.

"Heafner and I were getting very impatient to get back to England by this time. We spent the next few days following an agent on bicycles to Hengelo, and then to Almelo. Finally, after some two months of evading, D-Day,June 6th 1944 came, with the Allies coming ashore at Normandy, but it would be many more months before we would be going home.

"During this time there was much tension among the underground, and it was decided to move us to a dense forest, with practically no inhabitants, near the Zuider Zee. Our means of transportation to get to the forest were; car, horse-drawn cart, canal barge, and bicycle. Once there, we slept in a dugout, living off the land. We were later joined by two other American flyers, Martin Cech of Cleveland, Ohio, and Raymond Swick of Richmond, Indiana. (*Raymond Swick belonged to the 44th BG, 66th BS. His B-24 crashed on March 15, 1944, near Balbrug, 25 miles ene of Zwolle, Netherlands, note of John Meurs).* We were also joined by a jewish rabbi, and a young Dutchman named Jan.

"Martin Cech was an evader without an identifiable plane being downed. No one could get any information from him. It was humorously rumored that he had been thrown out of a passing plane during a fight on board because Martin liked to argue…about everything! (*Left waist-gunner S/Sgt. Martin Cech, ID-number 6927336. Was with 306th BG 423rd BS. On March 6,1944 he flew with the Albert Adams crew on B-17 #42-31025. On this mission he and 3 other crew members bailed out over Holland. Martin Cech evaded capture for one year until he was picked up by Canadian troops. (E&E Report 2934) Adams crew was not his original crew. –John Meurs)*

"We dug a hole about three feet deep and built a sort of sod house to live in. Jan would get milk and bread from a nearby farmer. We caught rabbits and birds in snares and traps for food. I remember July 31st, 1944, when a B-17 that had been shot up pretty badly came over our camp, which we had dubbed "Camp Eisenhower," and the crew started bailing out. We went to a clearing in the forest and found one of the gunners. We took him to cover. Soon we heard gunfire, so we returned to the clearing. I saw Germans chasing another crew member and motioned for him to come to me. We got back to our camp with the Germans in hot pursuit, evacuated our dugout hurriedly, and got the hell out of there!

"We followed a railroad track all night and into early the next morning until some P-5ls attacked a trainload of German V2 missiles. After the attack we continued on. We came to the station in Marienberg, a small village in the country. W/e split up again. The two B-17 gunners, Harold L. Chapman (*Harold Chapman, service number 32502903. waist-gunner belonged to the 95th BG, 336 BS, His B-17, # 42-37889 had landed near Den Ham, Netherlands.)* and Stuart Bouly, went with a underground leader. The rabbi and Jan went on their own, and Heafner and I stayed with a man named Bannock at the station for several days. We were later separated, with Martin Cech and I going to the home of Gerrit Salomons for about three weeks. I stayed at his home again later.

"Later we were sent with a member of the underground to a farm in the village of Beerzerveld, which was owned by a prominent family named De Bruin. They had built a secret compartment in the haymow. We stayed in our hiding spot during the day and came out only at night for exercise.

"A month earlier an OSS (Office of Strategic Services) team, trained in sabotage and subversive duty, was taken to the De Bruin farm. It was commanded by a Frenchman whose code name was McBeef. He was formerly a captain in the French Foreign Legion and a mercenary. The men had been trained in England and had parachuted into Holland at night. Their duties were to upset the German transportation and communications systems. They had been hiding in an old shed on the farm by day, doing their subversive work at night. We stayed with them for several weeks, helping to destroy bridges and other strategic locations. Then the Germans scattered us. Later I met other OSS teams, soldiers, and four airmen from other countries.

"Jan, a member of the team, had a radio with which he communicated with headquarters in England. (Jan still lives in the area. We were not able to see him because he was on a trip to southern France during our visit in 1988.) He could only transmit for a few minutes because the Germans could use a homing device to find the location of the transmitter. I gave Jan, the radio operator, a list including the names, rank, and serial numbers of our group of six Americans and instructed him to transmit the information to USAAF Headquarters in London, which he did. To our amazement, the reply the next night was for us to report back to our units in England!

"Jan must have transmitted too long because the Germans came that night to attack us. All escaped the raid, but McBeef was shot through his hand and another was shot in the shoulder. The de Bruin family located a doctor and the wounded were treated.

"The two B-17 gunners, Chapman and Bouly, turned up there, as well as an RAF pilot who had been shot down, a Canadian Lancaster pilot and a British captain who had escaped from the Germans after being captured at the Arnhem, Holland, parachute landing in September, 1944. He escaped the Nazis by jumping from a small bathroom window on the train that was taking him and other British paratroopers to a POW camp in Germany. He had been severely wounded at Arnhem and had tumbled down an embankment after jumping from the train. He then was found by the Resistance Force and given medical attention.

"There was always a shortage of food, although many good vegetables were raised during the summer. At this time there was now snow on the ground. Suddenly, we saw about 30 or 40 big partridges behind the barn. I could just visualize those birds cooked and steaming on a platter…enough for a feast! The De Bruins told us that those birds were not good for eating. I insisted we try to catch them, so we got a wooden frame and put a net over it. We left a trail of seed to our trap and pulled the string attached to a stick that held up the frame when the birds got under it. We showed the De Bruin girls how to prepare the birds and we ate partridge for several meals.

"When I was shot down, I had all the confidence in the world that within six weeks I would be back in England flying missions again. We frequently had briefings from people who had bailed out and had made it back. The Underground had a very good system set up. They used submarines, boats, and sometimes flew people out. Some would walk all the way to France and Spain, some into Denmark. We had maps printed on linen, a compass, and candy bars; this was part of our escape kit.

"Now, after all this time, I had become discouraged and decided to take off on my own, hoping to reach the Allied line. I picked a bad time to try it as there was snow on the ground. But with a bottle of water and two sandwiches, I began crossing the fields to evade the Germans. I came to a road and decided to travel it for a while, because it was much easier and faster traveling.

"I hadn't gone very far when I encountered a German officer and a woman riding in a fancy horse-drawn buggy. He immediately drew a pistol from his holster and ordered me to halt. About this time I decided I had made a big mistake in leaving the farm. The German asked me a number of questions, but I remained silent. We had been instructed to remain silent if confronted by the enemy, hoping that they would think we were deaf and dumb. I had no idea what he was saying. Finally, the woman said something to the German officer and he motioned for me to proceed down the road. I walked on until I thought I was out of their sight, where I crossed a field to a farmhouse. Weak with relief from feeling that any minute the German might change his mind and shoot, I hid in a shed until dark. When the farmer came out of his house I called to him and he took me inside. He fed me and put me into a secret room. It seemed that every house had secret rooms or compartments. This room's entrance was through a closet like the family of Anne Frank's hidden compartment in Amsterdam.

"The farmer, Gerrit Salomons, was afraid to keep me. The Germans were actively trying to catch him in some subversive work. I later learned that Salomons had been captured and shot to death. I was told that the Germans took two hundred hostages before a firing squad and shot them, actually murdering them. We saw the memorial where 117 Resistance Force members were shot and killed. The place is named Woeste Hoeve, which means Wild Farm. Salomons and Klaus Huibers were killed there, and Klaus Huibers' body was moved after the war to a small Catholic cemetery near the De Bruin farm. (I visited his grave site later, in 1988. We also saw Nete, Gerrit's widow, in Hardenberg during our return visit. She was very strong to remember those times that had caused her husband's death.

"I was contacted by another agent, who said that things looked grave for the Allies. During this winter of 1944, December 12th to be exact, the last German Panzer attack had broken through the lines in Ardennes in Belgium (the Battle of the Bulge), thereby threatening to capture the port of Antwerp. (In 1988 we visited the Airborne Museum near Arnhem, where the British Airborne Division was annihilated by Nazi Panzers in 1944.)

"I abandoned my plans to reach the Allies at that time. I had been on the run for about ten months. The agent who Salomons had contacted wanted to know how long I had been in Holland and where I had been hiding. I was reluctant to tell him about the De Bruins because I thought that he could be a German agent. I finally told him and was taken back to the de Bruin farm. I had been gone about a week and had only travelled about ten kilometers, or a little more than six miles.

"About this time, Martin Cech decided that he would go out on his own and try to get to Enschede. He made it to Belgium and the Underground picked him up. They had extensive records of all downed planes and could not verify Martin's origin (no identifiable plane). He was suspected of being a German spy and there was no proof that he wasn't. Finally someone thought to check his underwear, which turned out to be GI underwear stenciled with his serial number. He was saved from a possible firing squad. Martin returned to the De Bruin farm after being gone for about a week.

"Years later, around 1949, I saw Martin in the train station in Cleveland, Ohio. He was an MP and later had a junkyard in California, near Los Angeles.

"One day, while at the De Bruin farm, Martin and I decided to make some liquor to drink. We asked De Bruin for something like corn or oats for mash. He brought us some rye. We made a bin for the rye with a water tank for the water to drip onto the rye to begin fermentation. Our "distillery" consisted of black rubber hoses and we built the fire from peat. It aged from the spout to the glass, and I took one sip and tasted only the rubber hose. I wanted no more, but Martin added a bottle of beer for flavor and drank it all. It was a good thing that we had no more than a quart, because Martin had all of the hangover he could handle for the next two or three days.

"Soon afterward the English parachuted arms and ammunition, including pistols, explosives, machine guns, bazookas, and food. These were dropped in a field near our former Camp Eisenhower in the forest, and a underground group under the leadership of Marinus de Bruin received the equipment.

"While un-packaging the items from the air drop, Cornelius shot himself in the hand accidently with a nine millimeter pistol, unaware that the pistol was loaded. There wasn't any way we could treat his hand because we had no medical supplies, so he wrapped his hand with a piece of cloth and continued his chores about the farm. The wound eventually healed with no complications.

"Arie de Bruin was fascinated with a piece of instantaneous blasting fuse that we had received from the British air drop, and while fooling around with it, the fuse exploded, making a very large noise. Apparently, no one had heard the explosion, even though the enemy was close, within a quarter of a mile. But our luck didn't hold out.

"We had just received some guns and ammunition in a night drop from B-24's. We didn't get the equipment any too soon because a few nights later the German SS troops surrounded the farmhouse and began shooting into the house and attached barn. It had been a routine day, and at about 10:00 p.m., Heafner and I went to the "room" in the top of the haymow between the bales of hay. The barn was attached to the back of the house with two large doors at the end. The barn was higher and wider than the house, about 100 feet long and about 70 feet wide. Under the thatched roof was a vent-like shaft that opened through the roof. There was hay stacked to the very top in the haymow.

"We had a prearranged signal for trouble. The light inside the barn had been turned out for the night. If the light flashed three times, there was danger. We were alerted and grabbed arms. We heard a noise in the path through the hay that was the vent and saw flashes of light fall into the room. Heafner or Swick put a machine gun into the shaft opening and fired. A nine millimeter German Lugar fell out of the shaft and onto the floor. I picked up the gun and headed down from the haymow because the Germans had heard the gunfire. I later learned that the man in the shaft who was shot had died the next day in a hospital.

"The Germans were at each corner of the barn. We ran the De Bruins' two Belgian draft horses out, hoping to cause some confusion. The Germans shot at the horses. Heafner and I threw hand grenades at the men at each corner of the barn through the door and ran out into the darkness. I don't believe the Germans realized there were so many of us or that we were so well armed. We killed or wounded a number of them and we retreated into the darkness. Heafner and the others jumped onto a boat, but I was too far away and missed it. I swam across the canal and came across another canal which I also swam. I never saw Heafner in Holland again.

"I ran all night and spent the next day hiding in a pile of potato vines. I was soaked to the skin after swimming across the two canals. It was the last day of February. I stayed in this field all day and all night. The next morning a farmer came to plow his field. He plowed all day in a circle and I was afraid he was going to "plow" me up too.

"As night approached, I went to another farmhouse. I recognized it as the Smeenck farmhouse, a family with whom I had stayed briefly some months earlier: Johan, Jelle, Klara, and Greta Smeenck of Kloosterdijk, near Beerzerveld. The Smeenck family grandmother answered the door and I asked for Jelle, her grandson. About this time a big German shepherd dog came racing toward the door, but he obeyed Jelle and didn't attack me. Jelle whisked me out to their barn, and dry clothes and food were brought to me by his sister, Klara. And then I slept.

"The next day I was taken to a canal barge where we were joined by the others from the De Bruin farm raid. We had been at the De Bruin farm for about seven months. We went to the huge bunker, where some of the arms were hidden, to sleep, but it wasn't large enough for all of us. So four of us went looking for a haystack to sleep in. Finding our " Haystack Hilton," we started digging a tunnel in it only to find out it was already occupied by several men, with no vacancies. They turned out to be young Dutchmen hiding from the Germans to keep from being sent away as forced laborers in Germany or other countries.

782

"By this time we had grown in number to a small army. There were six Americans, one Canadian, two Englishmen, and several men of other nationalities. We were getting so numerous that we had to be dispersed while plans were made to retaliate against the Germans for the De Bruin farm raid. The British captain and I were put into a bunker (a hole in the ground lined with bales of hay and covered with sod and potato vines with a small trapdoor). The others were dispersed to other farms and hideouts. We stayed here several days; then someone came for the captain, leaving me alone.

"When I was in the bunker after the captain left, I heard machine gunfire and looked out of the slit hole alongside the canal. The Germans had shot the lock off the barn and gone inside. I heard no more gunfire, so I assumed no one else was endangered. After some time, a curvaceous, feminine leg appeared down on the steps through the entrance. It was Greta Smeenck calling to me, "Robert, come with me on this bicycle, we must move you." I knew I needed to keep up with Greta, but I had trouble because the wooden shoes called "klompen" kept falling off my feet as I pedaled. I followed Greta north, away from the Allied lines, most of the night.

"Klaus Huibers was captured during the De Bruin farm raid. He was a Dutch Underground railroad worker who worked for SHAEF (Supreme Headquarters for Allied Expeditionary Forces). Their plan was to paralyze the movement of trains and interrupt communications. Klaus was in his late fifties. He was later executed by the Nazis along with Gerrit Salomons. Also captured at the farm raid was Marie de Bruin. She was taken to a prison where she was interrogated and held for several weeks. She was only 18 years of age at the time. She insisted she knew nothing of the subversive work going on at the farm. The Germans finally released her to tend to her father, Mijnheer de Bruin, the family patriarch. He was a semi-invalid and had escaped the attack by crawling into the cellar to hide. He was taken prisoner but was later released because of his bad health.

"After the raid on the farm, Marinus de Bruin returned and fired several bazooka rockets into their house so it could not be used by the Germans. Marinus then went into hiding with the other underground members. From there, the braver or less cautious of the group made several forays into towns to kill German soldiers. Finally the Germans increased patrols drastically and we were dispersed into the countryside. Greta Smeenck was working with Jan Kolkman (a Dutch policeman and Resistance member) and he may have told her to take me to the Amsink family farm. I'm sure Kolkman and his new bride, Dini, helped many evaders. He and I became friends. He gave me one of their wedding pictures that was taken in August, 1943. His uniform in the photo was the dress uniform of the Dutch police.

"This farmer, Jan Hendrik Amsink, had about seven children. (We saw five surviving children and Jan in 1988.) We were in the village of Ane, near Gramsbergen. When I was there as an evader, none of the family could speak English.

783

After being in Holland for almost a year I had picked up some Dutch so we got along well. I helped them with the farm chores, milking cows, feeding chickens, pigs, and other livestock, and sorting potatoes. During my stay here I heard shrill noises that sounded like bombs, but were somehow a different sound. After I was liberated I learned that the shrill sounds were probably from German V2 missiles soaring overhead.

***

"Finally, I was rescued by Canadians when they liberated the area. The 2nd Canadian Division came across the Rhine, cut off the Germans, and drove them north to the sea near the German border. I had been living at the Amsink farm for several weeks then. We had gotten word that the Canadians had liberated a nearby small town named De Krim.

"Wearing blue denim overalls and wooden shoes, I was taken by Jan Kolkman, the policeman, to De Krim on a small motorcycle. (Jan remained on the Dutch police force until 1971, when he was 61 years old; then he retired.) On foot I approached a Canadian soldier guarding a bridge. I told him I was an American and tried to explain how I happened to be attired as a farmer. "You're about the saddest-looking American I've ever seen," the Canadian told me. He turned me over to his commander.

"They were treating me as a spy because I was out of uniform. They put me into a small cage and told me I would stay there until they sent for an intelligence officer to interrogate me. During my questioning one of the Canadians told me, "If you really are from Texas, you should be able to answer questions about the football teams in the 1938 Rose Bowl." I said that one of them was Southern Methodist University, and one of the men turned to the commander and said, "This guy is not an imposter." After a year of hiding, running, and being scared and hungry most of the time because of strict food rationing, I was finally among Allied Forces.

"After that, it was a matter of going from place to place on my trip home. I rode with a Canadian armored scout car for two days. The Canadians had liberated Cognac and Champigny, France, from the Germans. They offered a ride to me and I graciously accepted. I went by jeep to Brussels, Belgium, where I was turned over to a British unit. I was then flown to Paris, France, wearing a Canadian uniform. In Paris, two Canadian MPs stopped me and wanted to know if I was AWOL from the Canadian army because they knew that their 2nd Armored Division was currently in the Netherlands. Finally, in Paris, I was issued an American uniform. I then sent a telegram to my parents saying, "I'm alive and well, be home soon!"

"My mother had corresponded with Heafner, Doring, and Falk's families while we were missing. No family members knew about our experiences in Holland until sometime in April, 1945.

"Next, it was on to Le Havre, France, to a processing center where they loaded me onto a ship to New York. From there, I went by train to Dallas on a 30-day leave and was told that I could get out of the service. I didn't want to get out. I guess they thought that I was crazy, but I had planned to be a career man.

"I was 25 years old and married during my year in the Netherlands, and I was listed as missing in action all of that time. My family never presumed that I was dead. They learned by letter that I had been shot down and usually, after a few weeks, the Red Cross confirms that you are a prisoner of war. They had never received any word about me and didn't learn until after World War II was over what had happened to me. They got word on Friday the 13th of April, 1945 that I was all right. A day that they always remembered.

"There were times in Holland when I thought I would never see my family again, but I never lost faith that I would escape. Somehow I knew that I would survive over there. Planes were being shot down, planes were flying into each other, but I always felt that I would be okay. Of course, I used to talk to God quite a bit.

"There may have been as many as two thousand Allied flyers hidden in Holland during the war, and the Dutch people helped us just because we needed help. It didn't matter to them who you were, as long as you weren't a Nazi.

"If I had it to do over, I would do the same thing. I have no bitterness because I was young and I thought I was just doing my duty.

"The war continued in the Pacific, and I was training on the B29 Super Fortress when the war ended in August, 1945.

"Many of the people who were connected with the Resistance Movement were given a medal and a certificate signed by Gen. Dwight D. Eisenhower, Commander of SHAEF. Some received a pension for their work aiding Allied Military Personnel, from the British Commonwealth of Nations. In 1945 the United States reimbursed them for their expenses for 13 months of providing refuge to us.

***

"After the war I was stationed at various bases across the United States and Guam. The last three years and eight months of my 20-year career, I flew KC97 fueling tankers for the Strategic Air Command. I flew the same plane in the reserve after my retirement, November 30th, 1960.

"After my retirement from the military I worked 14 years as an engineer for Solar Turbines in Dallas, Texas. Another employee at Solar Turbines, Doug Hyde, left to form his own company in Durant, Oklahoma. I went to visit him and other former associates and was offered a job with his new company, Universal Parts. Doug Hyde introduced me to his secretary's sister, Betty, who after two and a half years became Mrs. Pipes. Betty and I spent two wonderful decades together camping, fishing, travelling, and enjoying our lives and our families... Betty passed away the 9th of October, 2005.

785

Left Waist-Gunner S/Sgt. Edward L. Mount.

By his daughter Sharon M. Kilcrease

"Edward was the second child of eight children born to Henry Lee Mount and Bessie Loy Lovick. He was born at home in Luverne, Al Crenshaw County. As a child he grew up poor and started working at a very young age. The family moved almost every year thus daddy attended several schools including Brundidge, Glenwood, Rutledge, Greenville, and Banks, Al. His army records shows the 8th grade was the last grade he completed.

"When they lived in Banks, Edward joined the CCC Camp lying about his age. He was about fourteen or fifteen years old. While in the CCC Camp he came home to pick cotton for his daddy. While living at home the average weeks' pay was about $35.00 his father would take all the money earned and give the boys back $15.00 each spending money but the girls got nothing back only clothing and a place to stay .

Left Waist-Gunner S/Sgt. Edward L. Mount

"In October, 1942 Dad enlisted in the Army Air Corps at Ft McPherson GA. and was trained as aircraft gunner.

"On April 29, 1944 the B-24 called *"The Playboy"* headed out on its last mission when they were attacked by enemy fighters. They came so close that daddy saw one of the enemy pilots' face and made eye contact before he shot him down and that always bothered daddy. The right waist gunner Robert Falk was shot in the head during this attack and daddy was severely injured in his back by 20 mm shell shrapnel.

Their bomber was damaged and low on fuel so over Holland the orders were given to bail out. Daddy's parachute was damaged by fire so he used S/Sgt. Robert Falks.

"Daddy and navigator Melvin Everding found shelter with Baron Van Palland but after a week Van Polland had to surrender them to the Germans as he was fearing for his own life. He also expected they would be treated rather well as POWs and my Dad urgently needed medical attention. He, together with radio operator Charles Doring and ball-turret gunner Ralph Fiskow landed together in Stalag Luft VI in East Prussia.

786

***

"On June 22, 1945 Edward Lee Mount married Mavis Folmar, she was eighteen and he was twenty two. They lived in a small house owned by my mother's father "Dude" Folmar. Daddy sharecropped with my granddad Dude and every time a plane would fly over Dude said my Dad would drop to his knees skittish and neurotic and my granddaddy Dude would tell him everything was okay.

"On July 22, 1948 due to post traumatic stress disorder from WWII my father shot himself in front of my granddaddy's house. He was twenty five and mother was twenty one with two babies less than two years old and was two months pregnant with me. was diagnosed at age 68 with Alzheimer's and died at age 75.

***

Acknowledgements:
Co-Pilot 2Lt. John B. Stuart, daughter Sheri Stuart Denk
Navigator 1st Lt. Melvin H. Everding, daughter Barbara Poplin
Waist-Gunner S/Sgt. Edward L. Mount, by his daughter Sharon Kilcrease.

CHAPTER 61

466TH BOMB GROUP 787TH BOMB SQUADRON

Type: B-24H • Serial: 41-28754 "Tell Me More"
MACR: 4447 • Air Base: Attlebridge

---

*Bomber made an emergency landing on April 29
at 15:30 hours. 4 Kilometers south of Teuge near
Apeldoorn. The who crew escaped.*

German Report. Part of Missing Air Crew Report # 4447

Pilot: 1Lt. Carl E. Hitchcock, 0-664597, POW

Co-Pilot: 2Lt. Lloyd G. Young, 0-680791, POW, Knoxville, TN

Navigator: 2Lt. Robert E. Willson, 0-698245, POW, El Paso, TX

Bombardier: 2Lt. Vito J. Bochicchio, 0-682047, POW, New York, NY

Top-Turret Gunner: Sgt. Carmine G. Dimanno, 31276739, POW, Hartford, CT

Radio: S/Sgt. Thomas J. McCue, 12188732, POW, Brooklyn, NY

Ball-Turret Gunner: S/Sgt. Charles G. Browne, 19116027, POW, Glendale, CA

Left Waist-Gunner: S/Sgt. Alex P. Lugosi Jr., 36631214, POW, Chicago, IA

Right Waist-Gunner: S/Sgt. David L. Smith, POW, 18213749, New Franklin, MO

Tail-Gunner: S/Sgt. Thomas G. Dorrian, 12121740, POW, East Helmhurst, NY

10 POW

Crash Site: Twello, Holland
Time: 15.30

Crashsite of B-24, Serial #41-28754 "Tell Me More" in Twello, Holland

Pilot 1Lt. Carl E. Hitchcock.

By daughter Polly Noel.

"Carl Edward Hitchcock was born on January 17, 1915 in Weston, Texas in Collin County to William Samuel Hitchcock and Mary Elizabeth Dunn. Carl was the 5th of 6 boys in the family. Carl's father was a farmer and the family did not have much money. Carl's father died in 1933, around the time that Carl graduated from Chambersville High School in Collin County. Soon after, Carl moved to McKinney, Texas, the county seat. Like others during the Great Depression, Carl worked in a series of odd jobs (e.g., "soda jerk" and truck driver) over the next several years. Eventually he moved to Corpus Christi, Texas in 1939 and started working for Alamo Iron Works.

"In 1942, Carl enlisted in the Army Air Corps and received his wings and commission at Foster Field in Victoria, Texas. He was an instructor at Waco Field for one year. In 1943, he was assigned as a B-24 pilot to the 466th Heavy Bombardment Group, 787th Bomb Squadron. In February 1944, his squadron was sent to Europe to join to the 8th Air Force and participated in the first daylight air raid over Berlin.

"His plane was shot down on his 10th mission on April 29th, 1944. There were no injuries to the crew and they separated in pairs. With help from the Dutch underground, Carl and his navigator eventually made their way to Antwerp, but

789

apparently they were betrayed by an informant. At a "safe house," they were introduced to a large red-haired man who spoke perfect English. After a nice dinner and conversation, the man said "I hate to have to do this to you boys" and then told them that he was with the Gestapo and that they were being taken into custody.

"Carl was imprisoned in the Stalag Luft III POW Camp near Sagan, Poland and was initially placed in solitary confinement. Carl was among the group of POWs who were evacuated by the Germans to Stalag VII-A at Moosburg, which was liberated by Patton's Third United States Army on April 29th, 1945. Carl contracted rheumatic fever while in POW camp and weighed less than 100 lbs at the

Pilot 1Lt. Carl E. Hitchcock

time he was liberated. He was hospitalized for several weeks at a VA hospital. He received the Air Medal with one Oak Leaf Cluster and was promoted to Captain.

"Following his hospitalization and separation from the service, Carl spent time in McKinney visiting his mother. While there, he met Mary Ann Nelson. Although Carl returned to his job in Corpus Christi, he corresponded with Mary Ann and they eventually became engaged. After their marriage in 1948, the couple lived in Corpus Christi, where their three children were born. In 1963, the family moved to San Antonio, Texas where Carl continued to work for Alamo Iron Works as the General Sales Manager and later as Senior Vice President. He retired from the company in 1980 after 41 years. Carl died on September 25, 1995 due to complications of a heart murmur that resulted from the rheumatic fever he contracted as a POW.

Bombardier 2Lt. Vito J. Bochicchio.

From daughter Anne:

"He was born on January 1, 1917 (at home) at 234 west 20th St. in New York, NY. His parents were Vito and Marguerite Bochicchio. He was the 2nd oldest of four children. His older brother Modesto was in the Army and on his way to the Philippines when his ship made a stop in Pearl Harbor. He was there when Pearl Harbor was bombed. He survived that, went to the Philippines and eventually went back to the U.S. to teach hand to hand combat to new recruits. After a while, he was sent back overseas and was eventually shot in both legs while fighting in

France. He later found out that the mission he was on was to liberate POWs in Germany. He was actually on his way to help liberate his brother! He was sent home and lived until the age of 90 in New Jersey.

"My father went to school at P.S. 11 Elementary School on 21st Street in New York City. He had Scarlet Fever somewhere around the age of 10 and was out of school for a month. Yet, when he went back to school, he ended up skipping a grade. He went to Commerce High School and then City College. He worked at the College while going to school. He also helped his father (who owned a local grocery store on Bleeker St.) by delivering groceries in Manhattan.

"He worked at City College as a Registrar. I believe he enlisted in the Air Corps in 1943. He trained in Midland Texas and New Mexico. He became a 2nd Lt. (he said he picked bombardier due to the higher pay grade since he was helping to support his mother – he was too short to be a pilot!). He was based in Attlebridge, England, once he went overseas.

***

April 29, 1944. Told by Vito Bochicchio.

"Flak over Berlin had damaged the fuel pump to transfer fuel into the main tank in the right wing. This prevented us from reaching England. It was decided to crash-land as our altitude at the time was too low to parachute out. Our maps showed that we landed a short distance south of a road midway between Deventer and Apeldoorn.

"Five members of the crew tried to hide in a small wood nearby and were captured on the same day. One crew member managed to stay out for one month before being captured.

"I and the co-pilot (Lloyd G. Young) paired up to try to get, eventually, to Spain. The pilot and navigator also paired up. Lloyd and I travelled by night in a southwesterly direction for 4 days and nights. Farmers fed us and let us sleep in barns and even gave us some clothing to cover our uniforms. They had to be very careful because of the severe consequences that would result if the Germans found out who helped us.

"When we got to what we believed was the Rhine we realized that it would not be possible to swim across it due to the weather and the very strong current. We saw a ferry boat and got on board. Unfortunately, German military police emerged from below and we were trapped. We did manage to secrete the civilian clothing we were wearing before we were captured.

"We were taken to a local jail for one night and taken by rail to Amsterdam to be interrogated by German Intelligence. They were satisfied we were airmen and not saboteurs and sent on to Frankfurt for processing and further interrogation.

"We were later taken to Stalag Luft III near Sagan. On January 20, 1945 the camp was evacuated as the Russian Army closed in. We went by rail to a camp outside of Nuremberg for 3 months. When the American Army advanced in Western Germany, we were evacuated, on foot, to Moosburg in Bavaria not far from Munich. This camp was liberated on april 29, 1945, exactly one year after we had landed in the Netherlands.

***

Daughter Ann continues:

"After the war, he took some time off since he had a lot of stomach issues due to the living conditions and food (and lack of food) they were given in the prison camp. He eventually went back to work at City College. That is where he met my mother. They married on November 20, 1954.

"He retired from City College in 1974 to work at John Jay College of Criminal Justice when it opened. He retired from there and worked for a few years at Stone and Webster Co. He retired for good in 1982 when he had triple bypass surgery.

Top-Turret Gunner TSgt. Carmine G. Dimanno

By daughter Dorria Dimanno;

"Dad was born in Unionville, CT on July 7, 1923. His family subsequently moved to Hartford, CT and lived on Orchard Street and then Martin Street. He was the youngest child of Peter and Maria Dimanno, from Casserta/Fondi, Italy, and the only child to be born in the US. All of his siblings were born in Italy. He attended Hartford public schools, but left high school: either to go to work or to enlist. When he was sure he would be drafted, he enlisted in the Army Air Corps.

"When his plane was shot down, they all had instructions to disperse in pairs. Dad's partner, a lieutenant, felt that he should go with the other officers, so Dad found a farmhouse and the family sheltered him for about three days until the Germans found him. Imagine being 20 years old and alone in Holland. The officers were all captured in a matter of hours after the crash-landing. We remember the big bump Dad had on his forehead from the crash. They were taken to Neuremberg, but later marched to Moosburg.

"Although he said they were not ill-treated, food was scarce. He once told us about eating peas with bugs inside and how much they learned to love potato skins. The young German guards did not fare much better and they were kindred souls. Prisoners were allowed to have a Catholic Mass each Sunday and Dad was one of the singers. We found painstakingly handwritten sheet music in the bag he brought back with him.

"Cigarettes were sent to the prisoners by the Red Cross and were a form of barter because the Germans could not easily acquire them. We have a horse-hair backpack, cutlery (emblazoned with the swastika) and hand woven cigarette cases with the cigarettes still inside. I'm guessing that making the cases was a way to pass the time. They would cut up tin cans into strips and weave them into shape. If you look on the inside, you can see the hand painted can labels. He also played solitaire – endlessly, I think – and kept a log of his winning percentages.

"We also have nearly every letter that he received from our Mom, the former Lorraine Miller, of Manchester, CT. I would imagine they'd give a different perspective of the war - and the trials of the people in the states. I've never been able to bring myself to read every one of them.

"When he was liberated, Dad spent some time with families in the area before coming home. At that time, US companies were mandated to take back their workers who were returning from service. Dad got his job back at the Allen Manufacturing Company, and married our Mom. He enrolled under the GI bill in Hillyer College, which is now the University of Hartford. He received his degree as a Drafting Engineer and continued as a draftsman at Allen Manufacturing.

"Dad, who was known as Gerry, was a marvelous singer – he performed with a barbershop quartet, in the church choir at Emanuel Lutheran Church in Manchester, and in Gilbert and Sullivan operettas for decades. One of the first songs we learned to sing as little girls was the Air Force (Army Air Corps) song. He loved to bowl, to play poker with friends, and he adored animals. He especially loved his granddaughters – the only two of his five grandchildren he lived to see. He also loved watching the American television program "Hogan's Heroes" – a comedy, strangely, about life in a German prison camp in World War II.

"Dad later partnered with pharmacist Charles Barbato, and in 1959, they opened a pharmacy in Bolton, Connecticut, which he ran until his death at age 53 from colon cancer.

Waist-Gunner S/Sgt. David L. Smith.

John Low was the top-turret gunner aboard the B-24, # 42-52506, of the 467th Bomb Group. On April 29, 1944, he and his crew had bailed out over Holland. John had found shelter with Aart Kliest in Apeldoorn Netherlands and recalls the arrival of David Smith. The "Dick" and "Mary" in his story were members of the Dutch underground.

"This new arrival came about the fifth day after Dick had made his first visit. Aart came in late that evening and looked like the cat that had been enjoying a nice canary. His mother questioned him as to why he was late, but he only abated the questioning and downed a quick meal. While Mek was clearing the table, he called me over in a corner and told me the news. It seemed that one of the fingers had scratched up something in the way of a B-24 gunner. He was shot down the same day as we were and had been living in a pig house. A farmer had been feeding him. Aart said he and Mary were going to get him now and they would be back in about an hour. He didn't want the others to know about it just yet.

"He was gone just about an hour when he and Mary came back with David Smith.

David brought with him the aroma of his last quarters and his first words were, "I'm sure glad to see Americans and can I get a bath." It all came out in one long breath. We shook hands and I told him we were certain he could and would have a bath before we went to bed. He wore civilian clothes and they were clean and in good order as the farmer had given them to him just before he left. We all went into the dining room for David to meet the family. I wondered how Mother was going to take this new addition to the family. Yap introduced him around to all and it all went off smooth as clock work. No fuss at all. It just went to prove that Mother was more than happy to do her bit and that her uprise the first night we came was due to us being the first of a new class of "underwater boys."

"I told David that we usually had coffee in about an hour and asked if he would like to bathe now or just before going to bed and he was all for a bath now because of the piggish smell and so was everyone else. Bill helped heat the water and was on hand to answer some of David's questions and Aart, Yap, and I went up to enlarge the sleeping quarters. All we did was put in another mattress and David would have te crawl in and then crawl over Bill's bed and into his own.

"When David was all through with his bath, we had our coffee. We told David about our plans to go to Spain and told him we were certain he would be helped too. This was the news he wanted to hear. We told him this man Dick would take his name, rank, serial number,etc., and these would go to England and then home. He wanted to know when he would see Dick and we said it should be in a couple of days.

"David was a different person after he heard this and he jumped with joy. He was a comical Joe and right here he put on a monkey act. He walked about the room chattering and swaying like a monkey. This went over big with the family and we all had a good laugh.

"We next asked David if he would like to hear the news and he was all for it. The poor guy had just about gone off the deep end staying in the pig pen for two weeks with no one to talk to but the pigs. He said he would talk to them by the hour but they couldn't understand a word he had to say because they were Dutch pigs.

"I said that didn't make any difference because pigs, even American pigs, couldn't understand what he had to say. David would not have it that way. He was a farmer and he knew damn well that pigs at home could understand him.

"It was a little crowded around the radio that night, but the five of us were able to wedge in and get the news. Aart and Yap left us in our hideaway and turned out the lights saying, "Sleep Well." Bill and I did, except when David would wake us coughing. He had a hard deep cough and we were worried about him for a day or so.

"The next evening, David was moved to another house. It was felt that it would be better for David to be in a bed until he was well and at this other house was a school teacher and her mother. She and mother would sleep together and if the police should come at night, David could quickly get out of bed into a similar hideaway as we had and the school teacher could say she had been sleeping in the bed David vacated.

Tail-Gunner S/Sgt. Thomas G. Dorrian.

By daughter Marie Jane Galvin.

"My Dad was born in New York City, New York on November 28 1920. His parents were James and Sarah Dorrian. They were born in Ireland but did not meet until they were in New York. My Dad had an older brother, John and a younger sister Winifred. His cousin Kitty lived with his family and he considered her a sister. My Dad was very close to his parents, especially his mom. While he was a prisoner of war she became very ill and died. He did not find this out until he returned from the war and described this as one of the hardest times of his life.

"He attended Newtown High School in New York and after graduating he worked as a typist. He was in California on vacation with a friend when Pearl Harbor was attacked and he came home immediately and enlisted.

"It was on April 29, 1944 on the return from a mission to Berlin that his plane was hit by flak. Protocol was that they parachute out but his pilot Carl Hitchcock made the decision to crash-land. They did land safely in Twello, Holland. Per the pilot's instructions the crew split up with the officers going off in one direction and the enlisted men in another. This was also against protocol and my Dad said he never quite understood what was behind that decision. In any event it was only hours later that a German soldier with a rifle came upon him and his fellow enlisted soldiers and captured them.

"They were put on a train in Amsterdam and taken to prison camps in Poland and Germany. He remained a prisoner until the liberation of Europe in 1945. His date of capture was April 29th 1944 and the liberation was exactly one year later. He was moved from prison camp to prison camp during that year and they marched from place to place with attack dogs at their sides. My Dad never could feel comfortable around dogs again. He said he was never mistreated and had books to read thanks to the Red Cross. He also used exercise to stay in shape and to maintain a positive outlook. However, food was scarce and he lost fifty pounds during his time as POW.

"After the war he joined the New York Police Department and retired after twenty years. His subsequent work was in hospital security at Columbia Presbyterian Hospital in New York City.

"He met my mother in 1945 after returning home from the war. They married on September 27, 1947, and remained together until his death on August 26, 2014. They had 11 children.

In 2002 Thomas visited the spot where 58 years earlier his bomber had landed. A local journalist wrote the following story;

"While over the target, anti-aircraft guns hit the aircraft and on its way back to Attlebridge (England) the aircraft lost continuously fuel. The crew did not succeed to pump enough fuel into the other wing and above Deventer in the Netherlands the moment came a forced landing was inescapable. The Liberator then had already lost so much height that parachuting out of the plane was too risky.

"Half past two in the afternoon the pilot made a wheels-up landing in a pasture at the corner of the Zonnenberg Street and the Leemsteeg Street. The ten crew members survived the forced landing. They jumped out of the plane and ran away. Away from the place of disaster and away from the Germans who could appear any moment. During the weeks after the landing they were all captured and became Prisoners of War.

"Also Thomas G. Dorrian, who was a tail gunner - 'the worst place in the plane' - in the Liberator. Yesterday it was for the first time he returned to the place where his aeroplane made a forced landing on 29 April 1944. He didn't recognize the surrounding area, but he felt the fear of death again. "You don't expect to survive. You never forget something like that!"

"Dorrian is very glad he can now show to his family the place where it all happened. He owed it to Wilco Gorter (25) from Twello, who tracked him down in America. The Second World War fascinates Gorter, and during the past years he is absorbed in plane-crashes in the municipality of Voorst. Via Dutch and German archives he found much information, and even the names of the crew. Almost to his own amazement he succeeded in tracking (with the help of the internet) the addresses of some of the Liberator crew who are still alive.

"The correspondence with Thomas G. Dorrian, 81 years old, resulted in an invitation to come to the Netherlands. After a short stay in France, Dorrian yesterday arrived with his wife and five of his ten children in Twello, where they had a cordial welcome by the Gorter family. The most important moment of the day was their visit to the farm of the Gorkink family at the Leemsteeg, where the mayor of Voorst, Mr J. van Blommestein, welcomed the Americans. He thanked Thomas Dorrian for the effort he and his mates had in the liberation of the Netherlands. The emotions came in the pasture behind the farm, where Wilco had marked the place of the crash with flags.

***

Acknowledgements;
Polly Noel, daughter of 1Lt. Carl E. Hitchcock, pilot.
Anne Bochicchio, daughter of 2Lt. Vito J. Bochicchio, bombardier.
Dorria DiManno, daughter of TSgt. Carmine G. Dimanno, top-turret gunner
Marie Jane Galvin, daughter of S/Sgt. Thomas G. Dorrian, tail-gunner

CHAPTER 62

467ᵀᴴ BOMB GROUP
790ᵀᴴ BOMB SQUADRON

Type: B-24H • Serial: 41-28749
MACR: 4943 • Air Base: Rackheath

"In the vicinity of Hannover, we were attacked from 12 o'clock level by three F.W. 190's. As they came thru the formation, I saw #4 engine of B-24 H-41-29749 hit and then start windmilling. At the same time the entire leading edge of the right vertical stabilizer was shot, the slipstream then ripped it right off."

Statement by 1Lt. Robert S. Seiler , Missing Air Crew Report # 4943

Pilot: 1Lt. Frank P. Prokop, 0-687345, POW, Detroit, MI

Co-Pilot: 2Lt. Robert J. Pittman, 0-699725, POW, Lockland, OH

Navigator: 2Lt. George W. Milliron, 0-698135, KIA, Dubois, PA

Bombardier: 2Lt. Edward H. Condon, 0-668899, KIA, Baltimore, MD

Top-Turret Gunner: S/Sgt. Edward J. Dreksler, 16116911, KIA, South Haven, MI

Radio: S/Sgt. James R. Boucher, 35544768, KIA, Bryan, OH

Ball-Turret Gunner: S/Sgt. Richard C. Peters, KIA, 36578724, Detroit, MI

Right Waist-Gunner: S/Sgt. John H. Burgelin, POW, 32835000, Rochester, NY

Left Waist-Gunner: S/Sgt. Floyd D. Williams, 18042480, KIA, Houston, TX

Tail-Gunner: S/Sgt. LeRoy M. Hill, 18168713, KIA, Mabelvale, AR

7 KIA, 3 POW

Crash Site: Darenhorst/Uetze, Germany.
Time: 11.15

Pilot 1Lt. Frank P. Prokop.

By Frank P. Prokop.

Pilot 1Lt. Frank P. Prokop

"I was born to Agnes Prokop and Anthony Prokop on October 4, 1921 at home, the second of two sons. My brother, Raymond, was three years older. My parents divorced soon after my birth. I grew up on the east side of Detroit. My mother married Alfred Keller when I was still very young. Alfred was a good but strict man, the only father I ever knew. I attended Holy Name Catholic elementary school. I was the dumbest kid in the class for the first 5 years. Suddenly I realized it was up to me and I excelled! When I graduated from 8th grade I was awarded the American Legion Medal of Honor for scholarship.

"I then attended Wilbur Wright, a high school/trade school, graduating as a tool and die maker. All during high school I was a model airplane buff, specializing in rubber powered models and participating in competitions. I was the National Moffet champion in 1939 for the United States and second internationally.

"I joined the Army Air Corps in 1939 - the day after my high school graduation and enrolled in the aviation mechanic school. Upon graduation I was held back as an instructor in the electrical division of mechanics. In 1942 I was accepted into the pilot training program and graduated and received my wings in July 1943. I went on to specialize in four engine bombers (B-24's) and in 4 months I was sent to England as part of the 467th Bomb Group. On April 29, 1944, I was shot down on my 6th mission near Hannover on the way to Berlin. I was captured and became a POW, transferred among several camps and was liberated exactly one year later on April 29, 1945 from a camp in Bavaria.

***

"I returned to the United States with a new goal of becoming a physician. I took specialized high school classes on my own to better prepare myself for college at the University of Detroit. After 3 years I received a degree of Bachelor of Science and was accepted at the Stritch School of Medicine at Loyola University in Chicago in 1950.

"On June 17, 1950 I married Eleanor Buslowicz and we moved to Chicago where Eleanor worked in secretarial jobs and I attended medical school. Upon graduation I was accepted at Johns Hopkins Hospital for an internship/residency in Internal Medicine with a grand salary of $20 a month, the same amount I received when I entered the service.

"After two years I was stone broke, with a pregnant wife and a toddler so we returned to Detroit, where I was accepted at the Detroit Receiving Hospital for an additional two years of training in Internal Medicine. We lived in a low income housing project on a salary of $2900 per year! After fulfilling my requirements in Internal Medicine, I joined a small group of physicians in Dearborn and moved my family to Dearborn.

"After two years, I left the group and became a solo practitioner until retirement in 1989. Along the way we welcomed 4 more children, bringing the total to 6: 1 son and 5 daughters. During this period of time we were active members of St. Alphonsus parish and our children attended the parish elementary school.

"Around 1968 it became apparent that my wife was exhibiting serious memory problems. After numerous tests and psychiatric evaluation she was diagnosed with Alzheimer's disease. A difficult period of approximately 18 years followed and ultimately she ended up dying in a nursing home.

"In 1988 I married Madeline Parks and we will celebrate 24 years of happiness in August. In 1989 I retired from active practice as a physician.

April 29, 1944 – As I remember.

"April 29, 1944, 5 am, we, the officers, were awakened with a pounding on the door of our Quonset hut. We slept in our heavy flying suits as there was no heat and April in England was still cold and damp. A visit to the local common latrine, taking care of personal toileting and then off to breakfast of powdered eggs, bacon, toast, fruit and coffee. Who is hungry at 5:30 am?

"On to briefing - officers in the front, enlisted men in the rear of the room. A hush, and the map of the day's raid is displayed. Berlin; our first visit to the large city. Details of the route, the target, anti-aircraft fire, fighter coverage and weather along the way and over the target were given.

"By jeep, the crew is driven to our plane. A general inspection is performed and all seems to be in order. At a signal flare from the tower the engines are started and checked by the pilot and co-pilot. Another tower flare and we taxi out to assume our place in take off position so as to assemble in our proper part of the formation. Takeoffs are 30 seconds apart into a usually cloud covered sky. Assembly is mostly by instrument flying, with circling at the proper altitude in good visibility above the clouds over a radio station. Note – other groups are simultaneously assembling over adjacent stations.

"At a given time, by radio, the various groups assume their position in the parade and we're off to Fortress Europa! The English channel appears and the gunners are instructed to try out their guns. Oxygen masks are donned at 10,000 feet and we set off at a steady climb to bombing altitude. Small puffs of flak begin to appear and we begin taking evasive action. Where are our escorting fighters? Some confusion exists and with the clouds we seem to be on our own. Obviously communicating our locations and altitudes to the fighters is also being communicated to the German Air Force and they sense an easy target.

"And so they appear and the fight begins. I see this FW 190 approaching at 12 o'clock. Then a sudden thud, the right inboard engine is on fire. Losing power I begin to fall back, out of formation. I jettison my load of incendiary bombs and head for the deck, using low altitude to make it harder for the German planes to shoot us down. And then another misfortune strikes. Suddenly another thud and all of my controls go limp. Time to bail out but unfortunately the plane is tumbling at a high rate and I am unable to move, plastered against the cabin walls. I now surrender to the inevitable - I'm going to die. Curiously, I mull over the idea of my death and wonder if it will be painful. It occurs to me than mankind will never know as the dead tell no tales!

"All this time the plane, on fire, is tumbling with engines roaring and suddenly all is quiet. I seem to be in a twilight state wondering - this isn't Hell - it's not bad enough. This isn't Heaven - it's not good enough. You don't suppose you're out of the plane? What do you have to lose - pull the ripcord! I pull and then the sudden realization that I did not have the leg straps fastened. A sudden jerk, a few broken ribs and my hands tangled above my head save me. My oxygen mask covers my face and my vision is limited to seeing down only.

"As I approach the ground, I flex my knees and land with a sweeping pendulum motion, tumbling to the ground. I stand and see countless people approaching - I surrender. I was captured by young farmers out feeding their cattle and they approach with pitchforks. They are laughing as they look at me because I have no shoes on. My feet were too swollen with frostbite and my shoes didn't fit. If I had reported to medical or to get bigger shoes I would not have been allowed to fly! So I flew wearing only socks. At some point the Germans gave me shoes which were huge to accommodate my swollen feet.

"I am taken to the local jail. My broken ribs are assessed and after a short time I am taken to another prison where I was placed in solitary confinement. Here I lose track of time for a day or so. Most of the time I sleep. Food is non-existent.

"I am then interrogated, many wild threats made, but they decide I can give them no more information than they already have. A day later I am transferred to the Stalag near Nuremburg, Germany. Nightly raids by the British Air Force keep us awake but after a period of days I am off to my home to be at Stalag Luft III. Here I discover my next door neighbor from Detroit, Henry (Hank) Kaczynski, a fighter pilot, shot down the same day as I was!

"We spent the next 10-11 months in boredom. Food was scarce and usually consisted of a slice of bread and hot water for breakfast and for lunch a bowl of "soup" made with water and dehydrated vegetables with assorted maggots and insects. Occasional Red Cross packages reached us to fill in the meals - instant coffee, Spam, cigarettes, and a bar of chocolate. Outside information reached us by secret radio.

"The war continues, the Russians are coming closer. We are, after all in Selasia, near Russia. The Germans decided to move us as we are bargaining chips, and so in the middle of the night with snow falling we began our march. The journey is hard on POWs as well as the guards. At times POWS were assisting the guards and vice versa, even carrying their rifles. Time began to blur and we eventually end up on a train - standing room only - with occasional stops for urination. Again time blurs, and we march, ending up in Bavaria. Here we stay - flea infested - no food - essentially until liberated by the US Army. Even then we stay put as the war was still in progress. But with food and DDT and the promise of freedom - life was good. We probably waited there about a week. A lazy boat ride back to the USA helped us both mentally and physically. We arrive in the USA and are told to "go home and let your mothers fatten you up!"

"I do believe that what has happened to me made me a different person, whether due to adversity or maturity. I went on to college and medical school, becoming a physician in private practice of Internal Medicine and after 39 years I am retired and living with no regrets. When I returned from the service I met a wonderful woman, we married and created a family of 6 children: 1 son and 5 daughters and now have 12 grandchildren. The mother of my children died after a prolonged illness with Alzheimer's disease and I remarried 24 years ago. My life has been filled with many blessings from God.

***

Acknowledgements;
Frank P. Prokop, pilot

CHAPTER 63

467ᵀᴴ BOMB GROUP
790ᵀᴴ BOMB SQUADRON

Type: B-24H • Serial: 41-28730 "Blond Bomber"
MACR: 4942 • Air Base: Rackheath

---

*Shot down by fighters. Crashed 2 miles north of Essel,
19 miles NNW of Hannover. Five survivors were
captured near the crash site, The sixth survivor, John
Angus, escaped but was captured a on May 4 by farmer
in Rosebruch, about 25 miles north of the crash site.*

Missing Air Crew Report # 4942

Pilot: 1Lt. John P. Gavin, 0-803181, POW, Memphis, TN

Co-Pilot: 2Lt. Frank L. Billiter, 0-541846, POW, Winchester, IN

Navigator: 2Lt. Linton A. Allen, 0-755209, POW, Macon, GA

Bombardier: 2Lt. Duane E. Atley, 0-541847, KIA, Cincinnati, OH

Engineer: T/Sgt. Eugene J. Kuhns, 35312341, POW, Cleveland, OH

Radio: S/Sgt. Vernon M. Baize, 16160533, POW, Detroit, MI

Ball-Turret Gunner: S/Sgt. Raymond T. Russell, 18063422, KIA, Paris, TX

Waist-Gunner: S/Sgt. Leonard G. Sager, 32225485, KIA, Newburgh, NY

Waist-Gunner: S/Sgt. Glen L. Hinkebein, 17038895, KIA, Chaffee, MO

Tail-Gunner: S/Sgt. John B. Angus, 11007263, POW, Cambridge, MA

4 KIA , 6 POW

Crash Site: Essel/Schwarmstedt, Germany
Time: 11.30

From the Missing Air Crew Report # 4942,

"Shot down by fighters. Crashed 2 miles north of Essel, 19 miles NNW of Hannover. Five survivors were captured near the crash site, The sixth survivor, John Angus, escaped but was captured a on May 4 by farmer in Rosebruch, about 25 miles north of the crash site.

"The four KIA's were initially buried in the local cemetery of Essel. Duane Atley was properly identified but the three others not. They were buried with an Unknown Airman who was later identified as Robert W. Rowlett, the TG of # 42-110062 of the 392nd BG.

**

CHAPTER 64

467ᵀᴴ BOMB GROUP
788ᵀᴴ BOMB SQUADRON

Type: B-24H • Serial: 42-52506
MACR: 4944 • Air Base: Rackheath

"You cannot shoot me. I am an American officer."

Last words of pilot Bill F. Moore before his execution

Comd. Pilot: Maj. Robert L. Salzarulo, 0-424730, POW, Richmond, IN

Pilot: 1Lt. Bill F. Moore, 0-794442, KIA, Atlanta, GA

Navigator: 1Lt. Frank D. Coslett, 0-801361, EVD, Wilkes Barre, PA

Bombardier: 2Lt. Edward Verbosky, 0-754780, POW, Smithfield, PA

Nose-Turret Gunner: 1Lt. John L. Low, 0-2043763, EVD

Top-Turret Gunner: T/Sgt. Clinton L. Watts, 18053597, POW, Sallisaw, OK

Radio: S/Sgt. James R. Anslow, 15354506, EVD, Bucyrus, OH

Ball-Turret Gunner: S/Sgt. Henry E. Allen. 14141180, POW, Vicksburg, MS

Left Waist-Gunner: S/Sgt. Werner G. Braun, EVD, Coldwater, OH

Right Waist-Gunner: S/Sgt. Walter T. Kilgore, 13014321, EVD, Dayton, OH

Tail-Gunner: 2Lt. Edgar J. Powell, 0-692814, POW, Aspinwall, PA

1 KIA, 5 POW, 5 EVD

Crash Site: Uddel near Apeldoorn, Holland
Time: 14.30

Command Pilot Maj. Robert L. Salzarulo.

From a newspaper article.

Command Pilot Maj. Robert L. Salzarulo

"Major Salzarulo said that after he had bailed out of his stricken command plane and had alighted in Holland he wandered about for about eight hours. He remembered a briefing he and his officers had received: that if it were necessary to bail out over Holland, Belgium or France and alight in open country the proper procedure was to seek cover and remain in hiding until a civilian approached, and then ask him for assistance.

"We were instructed that a native would do three things: would pass you without speaking but would not reveal your whereabouts, would take you to some "underground" place of hiding, or indicate he would help you, and then report you to the Germans," the major said. "The first man I met ignored me and walked away, the next two men would not help me but pointed to where the Germans were located. The fourth man motioned to me to follow him and he took me to his home and fed me. He left the house when I was eating and returned a little later with two German soldiers who came in with their revolvers drawn. They searched me carefully, took what they wanted, even the ripcord of my parachute, and then took me to jail."

"The major said his crew members were scattered when they parachuted but he eventually met four of them in a prison camp. They did not know the fate of their other comrades.

By son Bob Salzarulo,

"Robert Louis Salzarulo was born November 14, 1919 to Italian immigrants; Louis and Maria (Scotece) Salzarulo at their home 121 North 15th Street, Richmond Indiana. He went to high school at Richmond High and then on to college at Indiana University. While he studied at the University, he joined the civil air patrol learning to fly.

"When WWII broke out, he left Indiana University having finished his junior year and joined the Army Air Corp, teaching future pilots at an air base in Texas. He requested a transfer overseas and his new orders dated September 1943 put him as the Commanding Officer of the 788th Bomber Squadron of the 467 Bomber Group to be based in Rackheath, England by spring 1944.

"Captain Salzarulo was liberated in June 1945. The homecoming photo was of Captain Salzarulo having returned home to Richmond, Indiana, after recently being liberated as a POW. In this photo he had met his mother and father at the Railway Station in Richmond. His brother Frank is pictured with them in this photo. Frank, a military reporter, had joined the liberating troops to report on the liberation of the POWs. As Robert's older brother, Frank was tasked by their mother to bring her son Robert home, which he did.

"After the war, now Major Salzarulo remained with the USAF, career military, with stints at Wright Patterson AFB, Dayton Ohio, Wiesbaden Germany, the Pentagon and Van Nuys California Defense Contracts Office. While stationed at Van Nuys, he completed his business degree at UCLA. He retired from the military as "full bird" Colonel in 1969.

"His business career (post-military) landed him in Prattville, Alabama, as President and Chief Executive Officer at Continental Moss Gordon, a cotton gin/ corn dryer manufacturer. He medically retired from Continental.

"He died July 8, 1993 and was interred at St. Mary's Cemetery Richmond Indiana next to his wife Alma and close to his parents.

Pilot 1Lt. Bill F. Moore.

The story of Bill Moore is well described by Bombardier John Low (see below) until Bill separated himself from the group of airmen hidden in the house that was raided by the Germans. It is not clear where, when and under what circumstances he was captured. He ended up in the Willim III Barracks in Apeldoorn. On December 2, 1944, he was executed together with members of the Dutch underground.

Eugene Dircks of the SD (Gestapo) was present at the execution. Interrogated after the war he declared;

"Upon arrival at the Willem III Barracks, together with Untersturmführer Wigger, I saw Oberleutnant Adolph Gluck with his squad waiting in front of the waiting room. In the hall of the waiting room a number of prisoners, approximately twenty men, were standing ready.

"Under the direction of Guard Commander Bender the prisoners were taken, in three groups with a little time elapse between, to the sport grounds situated next to the barracks. Upon arrival there, a firing squad was ready under the command of Gluck. The prisoners were executed in groups. After the execution of the first group, the second group was led forward.

"Among the last group was a young man, dressed in civilian clothes, about thirty years old and of dark appearance, who, upon arrival at the place of execution and seeing what went on there, turned to the soldiers and shouted; "I will not," followed by some words which I didn't understand, but which apparently meant that he was an English or American soldier, and therefore a prisoner of war. He refused to go before the firing squad.

"Oberleutnant Gluck gave an order to two of his soldiers. The above-mentioned young man who had stopped as some distance from the place of execution was grabbed by these two soldiers. Under great resistance of the young man he was literally dragged to the place of execution. As he had put his heels in the loose earth, he left a deep trace in the ground. As Wigger had to justify himself toward the soldiers for having an English or American soldier shot, he called out; "Swine, we'll help you throw bombs on our women and children."

"The two soldiers dragged the man to about seven meters from the place of execution but as his resistance remained strong, Lt. Gluck went over to him, stood behind him, and shot him with his automatic gun several times in the back, at the height of his belly, whereupon the man fell down, deadly hurt. Wiggert told me not to speak about the incident with anyone.

On February 15, 1950, Adolf Gluck was sentenced to three years of prison by the Court in Arnhem, Netherlands.

Bombardier Edward Verbosky.

By daughter Judith Montavon.

"Edward Verbosky was born on December 9, 1916 in Smithfield, Pennsylvania. His parents, Andrew and Mary Verbosky had thirteen children; one died in infancy. Six sons and six daughters survived, Ed being the oldest.

"Growing up during the Great Depression, Ed, along with the older siblings, was unable to complete a formal education and began working in the coal mines to help support his family. The Great Depression was a severe worldwide economic depression, which started in most countries in 1929, and lasted through the late 1930's. It was the longest, deepest, and most widespread depression of the 20th century.

"As a young man, he worked for the Civilian Conservation Corps (CCC) for one year, prior to WWII. The CCC was formed under President Franklin D. Roosevelt's famous Congressional legislation - which was a public work relief program, as a part of President Roosevelt's famed "New Deal" program. The typical worker was an unemployed, unmarried man. The CCC planted over three billion trees, built 800 parks nationwide, updated forest fighting methods, built service buildings and roadways, and provided relief for major flooding, during the years of the depression. The CCC operated from 1933 to 1942, in the U.S. and provided work for over three million men. It provided these men with shelter, clothing and food, together with a small wage of $30 a month, of which $25 had to be sent home to their families.

"Edward then enlisted in the U.S. Army Air Corps in March 1942 (the first in his family). He became a 2nd Lieutenant and was the bombardier on a B-24 bomber, when it was hit in the skies over Germany, then downed over the Netherlands. This occurred when they were on a return trip from a bombing mission in Berlin, on April 29, 1944. That mission was his eighth, and final mission.

"I was told by my mother that Ed stayed behind with a fellow crew member who was injured while all nine other crew members were separated. 2nd Lt. Verbosky, and Sgt. Watts were both captured by the Germans, and taken as prisoners of war. Ed was taken to Stalag Luft III - which was called West Camp, Stalag Luft III, in Sagan, Germany. Edward spent one full year as a prisoner. He was honorably released from the service on October 18, 1945.

"Edward, along with two of his brothers, Eugene and Robert, all served simultaneously in WWII. Two other brothers, Thomas and Richard, also served in WWII, with some of their service time overlapping the first three brothers. His youngest brother, James, was not born as of 1940, but he too, later joined the U.S. Marine Corps. All six brothers proudly served their country during their lives. It is interesting to note that all six Verbosky brothers returned home safely from the service, and were released honorably.

***

Five Brothers In The Services---Three Back Home

EUGENE VERBOSKY   EDWARD VERBOSKY   ROBERT VERBOSKY   THOMAS VERBOSKY   RICHARD VERBOSKY

Three Of Five Brothers In The Armed Services Are Discharged

"After the war, Ed moved to Akron, Ohio, U.S.A., in search of work, which he found, first at a local dairy, then at Goodyear Aerospace. In November 1947, Ed married Olga Janosik, from Shoaf, Pennsylvania, which was a nearby "burg," or "patch," as the locals called it, to his hometown of Smithfield, which was also called a "patch."

"Eventually, Ed began his work career with the United States Postal Service, (the USPS) where he worked as a letter carrier (mailman), in Tallmadge, Ohio, a nearby town to Akron. He also worked part-time at a sheet metal shop to help support his wife, and the three children they would have (Linda, Gary, and my-self).

"Over the course of his lifetime, he also built and repaired new and used lawn-mowers, tractors, bicycles, and go-karts. He was the local "go-to" man for neighbors, who needed their lawnmowers serviced, or needed to buy one at a lower cost than the store.

"Ed continued to help people his whole life. He demonstrated this with his work - as a letter carrier, he delivered the mail up to six days a week, year-round, to every household on his route, despite the worst weather elements possible. Some of the routes were "walking" routes, meaning the carrier had to carry the mail the entire route, despite any inclement weather. He also had some "driving" routes, because the houses were in a rural area, and thus far apart. They used a special vehicle to deliver in, (and still do). This vehicle has the steering wheel on the right-hand side, like many European countries, so they could reach out and deposit the mail into the individual rural mailboxes. He had a perfect "no-accident" driving record, during his career with the USPS, which was about 30 years.

"Olga died of cancer in 1977 at 54 years old. Ed died six months later of a heart attack, during a horrific blizzard in January 1978, at the age of 61. According to neighbors, Ed was doing the kind of thing he always did, and was helping shovel snow, not just at his home, but from their driveways and sidewalks also. He had his fatal heart attack following this.

Radio S/Sgt. James R. Anslow.

James Anslow, was a son of Ben & Ethel Gainey Anslow, born in Massillon, and had three siblings. He graduated from Bucyrus High School in 1941, and enlisted on December 5, 1942. Trained as a Radio Operations/Gunner; arriving in England, early 1943, flying there via South America, and Africa. After only four missions they were "shot up" and too low on gas to make it back successfully. The pilot-less plane crashed into a farmhouse, killing a young girl.

From the Escape and Evasion Report.

"About 13:30 on April 29, 1944, the plane in which Anslow was flying crashed in a forest near Harderwijk near the Zuider Zee. After two nights on his own he found help with some farmers in Apeldoorn. The village doctor took him to the railroad station and escorted him to a house in Deventer from which he went to a school master, Jansen, who had sheltered many airmen.

"After eight days he went to Zwolle where he stayed until evening with a man who had a boarding house near the station. He bicycled to Ommen where he stayed eight days in the woods with a young man and his wife. With an escaped French POW, H.C. Ravel, he went by car to Enschede. Stayed with the owner of a woolen mill, and went to a place near Lanneke where he stayed two weks with a man called Blijdestijn.

"He moved next to a house in Enschede for a night and there met an Austra-liam called B.L. Navis and a Canadian. The next day he was taken to the rail road station and went to Tilburg. From there, about May 27, he and the French escaped POW Ravel, walked across the Belgian border, seeing Poppel in the distance. They went to Turnhout and tried three churches but could not find help. A farmer hid them in his bomb shelter after which they stayed four days with a lady in the trucking business. They then bicycled to the French border near Tournai, and stayed with a farmer North of that place who arranged things for crossing.

"On June 4, they continued their journey. A woman in a café gave them an address in Soissons but she was too afraid of the Gestapo to take them in. They stayed for about three weeks at a farm South of Soissons, the control on the road seeming too severe for them to move on. The man sheltering them had something to do with champignon mushrooms.

"About June 26 they bicycled to Montmirail, spent the night with a farmer, and the next day they went on to Courtenay, where they stayed for the night. On June 28 they stayed north-west of Sancerre at a place where three days before an American also going south per bicycle had been. They rested the next day. On June 30 they stayed in a barn between St. Aman and Montlucon. On July 1 they went to a garage man looking for a map. They were directed to Villefrance-sur-allier where they saw a Maquis chief and went to a Maquis camp where they stayed two weeks, participating in two parachutages. Two men parachuted, a radio-operator who broke his ankle and a French officer. About 14 July the Ger-man came out to investigate a sabotage. The French parachutists gave Anslow and Ravel clothes and bicycles and they started out again. At St. Angel they stopped at a garage to get maps. The garage man also was a Maquisard and told them he that he would get in touch with a British mission. He put hem up in a hotel for the night.

"Two days later they went to a Maquis camp near Meymac run by a regular cavalry captain. After one night they motored to the village of Chadbec where they met the British mission in charge of which was Major De Gatis and with him was F/Lt. André Simon, Captain Bisset, a French Major and a radio-operator. Here Anslow was assured that he would return to England by the first available Dakota. He waited three weeks staying with F/Lt. Simon and the radio-operator, helping to decode messages. Two Mustang pilots an a British Squadron Leader came in.

"About September 9, he went to Limoages. An RAF piloted Hudson came in. Seven evaders boarded. With them was Major Sorenson, an English agent who had spent a year in prison and apparently came from Toulouse.

Nose-Gunner 1Lt. John L. Low

"The Brave Dutch" by John Low.

"I have a story to tell — it is a story about the people Mr. Churchill calls "the brave Dutch." I don't know why I should try to add to these three words of Mr. Churchill, because no other three words could more appropriately be used to describe these people.

"First, before I start my story, I must clear up one particular point. I was a Bombardier on a B-24 Liberator that was forced down in Holland after bombing Berlin. Holland was occupied at the time by the Hun, as this was in April, 1944. For 296 days I hid in Holland before I successfully made it through the enemy lines and to Allied hands. But the point I want to make clear is that this story about me and my exploits, it is a story of the "Underground." I will be compelled to tell this story in the first person as that is the way I learned it and it will revolve around my day to day experiences. However, it is not my intention to blow my own horn. My escape was made good entirely through the efforts of the "Dutch Underground"— "the brave Dutch."

"While we are clearing up points, let us eliminate one or two more. I have no intention of trying to stir you up with tales of atrocities and I am not trying to breed hate for the Germans as the world is full of that. If I tell of some cases where the Dutch were captured and what kind of torture they underwent, it is only to emphasize that even this horrible retaliation by the Germans for the the unfortunate members of the underground that were caught did not frighten the Dutch. It just made them more determined to rid their land of the trespasser. I, too, learned to hate the Hun with a sinful passion, but if you will appreciate that I was there, and I saw these things that I shall write about, you may understand.

***

"It was in the early hours of the morning of April 29th that I was awakened and told to "get cracking." Take off was set for 0730 and first I had to dress, eat, attend briefing and then get out to the planes. I was the Group Bombardier but on this particular day I was flying up in the nose turret as a gunner with a more specific job of doing pinpoint pilotage navigation.

"We were what is known in the 8th Air Force as a "Lead Crew." The duty of the "Lead Crew," or lead ship, is to find the target, bomb it, and lead the other ships back to the home base. Usually there are nine to twelve ships that fly close formation just behind this lead ship and they all drop their bombs when and where the lead ship does.

"When we got to briefing and saw that we were going to Berlin, I must say that I was a bit nervous. Berlin is what we call a "long haul," a long way to fly and the anti—aircraft guns that defend the city are not there just for the German kids to play with.

"We had a rather uneventful trip into the city as our Intelligence Officers had routed us where they knew there were but few flank guns. The Luftwaffe was up in strength that day, however, and while they did not attack our group on the way in, they did go after another group that was flying just ahead of us.

"When we got over Berlin, the German flak boys opened up with I think everything they had — I'm not absolutely sure, but I thought I saw the kitchen sink thrown up at us. We got our bombs away and on the target before we were hit the first time.

"This first hit started a small electrical fire in the back part of the ship but the gunners got that out okay. The next hit was up front and it knocked out the bombardier's oxygen supply. His job was done, so he was able to leave his station and go up by the pilot where there was another oxygen outlet he could use for his oxygen mask.

"The third time we were hit, our left hand aside engine took the worst part of it and stopped almost at once. A gas line was also hit. However, the pilot, Lt. Bill F. Moore, and the command pilot Major Salzarolo, were not ready to call it quits by any means. We lost about 1000 feet right at first and had to leave our formation but the pilot stepped up the output of the other three engines and joined in the formation of another group of Liberators. We would have made it home okay had we not lost so much gas due to the cut gasline.

"Finally, we ran out of gas just before we reached the coastline of Holland. No one on board was wounded and everyone got out of the ship okay. As I was floating to earth with my parachute opened beautifully above me, I counted seven other chutes close by. There were eleven men in the plane and I worried about the other four and wondered why I didn't see them. However, I found out later that everyone did get out okay.

"Just before the pilot gave the order to abandon ship, the 1st navigator told the crew over the inter-phone system that we were over Holland and that it was one of the countries the Germans had occupied. He said that it was believed that most of the Dutch people were pro-allied and would probably help us if they could.

"We were up rather high and I tried to delay pulling my rip cord until I had fallen most of the way, but I didn't succeed. I yielded to the temptation to open my chute, as the only thought you have when falling through space like that is wondering if your chute will open when the time comes. It took me about fifteen minutes to come down. I remember one thing that impressed me as I was floating down and that was how unbelievably quiet it was. It was ghostly and remorseful. I felt empty and as I looked below I wondered what the land and people were like. I remembered from my schooldays, reading about wooden shoes, wind-mills, the tulips, and the dykes.

"I looked to the West and could see the North Sea; to the North was the Zuiderzee. I prayed that the wind would not change directions because if it did I might be blown into the water – it didn't change. When I finally did reach terra firma, I had my first lucky break of a series of lucky breaks that were to help me to go free. I came down in a small forest of fir trees. Holland has very few trees and only a very small amount of land that can be called forest.

"My parachute spread out over the tops of three trees and I was just left hang-ing. I didn't get scratched up as I had expected I would, if I landed in trees. I unbuckled my harness and dropped down to the ground. I was in Holland.

"And what was next? Scared ? Yes,I was a bit. I was alone which is what made it so bad. I looked up at my chute in the trees. I stood there for a minute, half dazed, and half happy that I was safe on the ground. Did I say safe? What am I thinking about? I have to get away from here; two facts came very clear to my mind - one was that I wouldn't be safe long if I stayed around under that chute showing in the trees and the other was that I was certain and determined that I didn't want to be captured. I'd get back, back to England somehow. But how? I'll worry about that later. Right now, I wanted to find some better spot to hide.

"I settled down to a fast walk in as straight a direction as possible. I stayed in the thick parts of the woods and off the paths. After I had made what I thought to be about four miles I came upon a deep hole in the ground in a heavily wooded area. I crawled in to rest and to think. Here I took off my heavy flying boots and put on my G.I. shoes which I had tied to my belt.

"I sat tight and just kept my eyes and ears open for about three hours. It began to get dusk and I had seen or heard no one so I decided to make my way farther and try to find some better place to sleep for the night. At first I stuck to the heavy part of the woods and then finally I ventured out on a small path. I had only been walking down this path a short distance when I heard a motor car. I knew only Germans would have a car out on a path like this so I dove head first into a cluster of bushes just by the path. And not any too soon either, for it turned out to be three Germans in an amphibious auto, about the same size as our jeep. One of them was standing up in the back with a machine gun. He was looking right and left in the woods, but, as they passed me, he didn't look right or I probably would not have been left. I guess I was well concealed in this bush and my clothes were green as were my surroundings but I sure felt as though I stood out like a spotlight in a cellar. Anyway, they went their way and didn't see me.

"Retreating back into the woods, I began to think – it didn't matter too much what part of Holland I was in, I had to go south. I would try to make my way through Holland, Belgium, France and then into Spain. Spain, being a neutral country would be compelled to return me to England, I had heard of others making their way out like that.

"It was dark now and I felt much safer. I passed several farm houses and finally picked one that looked rather run-down and had a haystack just behind it close to the woods. I crawled up in this haystack with difficulty as it was about 20 ft. high, and then more or less covered myself with the hay. It had begun to rain and I was a little damp and cold, but the hay was warm and I was out of the wind.

"I had been in the haystack about an hour when the farmer's son who looked to be about twenty years old came to get hay for the cows. He would not have seen me for I was buried deep in the hay, but I knew I was going to have help in the way of food and civilian clothing if my journey was to be a success, so I called to him rather softly, "American." At first his eyes were as large as saucers and then I remember seeing a quick change in his expression to that of fear! My first thought was he was afraid of me, so I showed both hands to let him see I had no weapons. His expression did not change. He looked like a small child that didn't know whether or not he should take a second piece of cake.

"The Dutch word for American is almost the same as the English. It is "Amerikaan," with an accent on the kaan. There is no question, but that he knew I was an American flyer. He was rather stunned at first. Just think how you would feel if you opened your garage door some night and found that you had acquired a German or a Jap.

"He looked about in all directions very carefully and then he crawled over to where I lay in the hay. I knew beyond a shadow of a doubt that he would befriend me and I gave a big sigh of relief and a big smile to my new friend. He still had signs of fear about him, but when I held out my hand, he took it and shook it vigorously and his fears were gone.

"We sat about to make a conversation with our hands and the language card I had. Repeatedly we would throw in a big handshake just for the hell of it. It seemed to make us both feel better about the whole situation. This language card had a few phrases in English and to the right of each one was the same thing in Dutch. It was through this that he finally put the idea over to me that if I were found on his farm, he and all his family would be killed.

"Once he saw that I realized the danger to him and to his family, his fears left and he relaxed. This fear did not return. Instead, he was very confident and he left me and set about his work in the yard with perfect poise and if anything an air of indifference about the whole thing. After fiddling about the yard for about ten minutes, he returned to the house by way of the big double doors in the rear. As he opened these doors, I got a quick look in and saw two large cows looking out.

"Yes, what I had read in my school books about the barn and the house being made into one was holding good. I have also neglected to say that my young friend was wearing wooden shoes! That was important to me at the time for some reason, which I have never figured out. He stayed in the house for about a half hour and then I heard the double doors rattling. As he came out, his mother and father came quickly to the doors and by light of a lantern waved a short cheery hello and then they went back in. He stood about in the yard a few minutes making certain that no one was around and then came up in the haystack.

"When he was settled, he opened up his coat and brought out a bottle of hot milk and a small package of bread. The milk, I truly went for as I was very thirsty and it warmed me all over. The bread consisted of two pieces of what they call rye bread with butter and sugar in between, and two pieces of which we could call whole wheat bread only theirs is much coarser. Between the slices of white bread was butter and raw bacon. I ate it all down to the last crumb but I can't say that I enjoyed it. Did you ever eat a piece of cold, raw bacon?

"When I had finished my bread and milk, my young friend took the milk bottle and then shook my hand and said what I think was "good-night - sleep well." As he started down out of the haystack, he handed me a hard boiled egg, smiled and then retreated through those big double barn doors. Since I was rather full up to the neck on bread, I thought I would save the egg for some other time as emergencies do come up!

"As I dug down deep into this warm hay and made myself as comfortable as possible, a feeling of loneliness began to come over me. My next thoughts were of these loved ones at home. I hadn't had much time to think of home up to now. I hadn't thought about the telegram my wife was to receive in the next few days from Washington saying,"We regret to inform you that your husband ,Lt. John Low Jr., has been reported missing in action from a combat mission in the E.T.O." These things stood out clearly now in the cold, black rainy night.

"I was more or less in a tough spot and what my future was I did not know, but at least I knew the present and that was more than my wife and family knew or would know for sometime to come. The day's experience began to tell and my eyes were heavy. I remember as I dropped off to sleep that night it was about home and my wife that I was thinking.

"The morning broke with a heavy fog and I woke about six. The house was almost obscured in the fog but I could see those big double doors and it was these that I watched and waited for my friend to come through. I knew he would.

"About six-thirty, the doors opened and as he came out I could see his mother and father had come as far as the door to wave a "good-morning." They were simple folks and not like any I had ever seen before. She wore a long dark dress and he had on a pair of brown corduroy pants with a heavy blue denim coat, high-necked so you could not tell if he had on a shirt or not. She had some sort of a cap on, but I couldn't see her very well through the fog.

"My young friend advanced to the haystack looking in all directions to make sure no one saw him. He came up and sat down by me. We shook hands again and he opened his coat and out came hot coffee and more bread just like I had had the night before.

"I slipped down from the haystack and made for the woods again. Just before I lost sight of the haystack and the house, due to the fog, I turned and we waved a very heartfelt "so long.."

"Late in the afternoon, I made my second contact with my good Dutch friends. I had walked about 15 miles south as the crow flies, and the woods were beginning to thin. This worried me as I was still in my dark green flying suit. I realized that it would be impossible to always have woods to hide and hike in so I was dead set to get some civilian clothes.

"I saw a small path that seemed to leave the woods and run by several small houses. In the front yard of the first house I could see a man working, he was raking leaves. I put on just an average air and walked past him. I wanted to see what notice he would take to the clothing I was wearing at the time. He saw me all right but he kept about his business and didn't pay any unusual attention as I walked past. Before I reached the second house, I turned around and returned. When he saw me returning he stopped raking and took a bit of notice. I had taken care to see there was no one in sight so I walked straight up to the gate, stood there a second and then softly (why softly I don't know for no one could have heard if I had shouted) I said "American." — "American."

"He stood still for a moment or two and then after looking in all directions came hurriedly to the gate and practically dragged me inside his house, shaking my hand all the time. He was a man that I would take for 35. He wore a rather unusual, all green, not too dark, corduroy suit. The pants were tight-legged and the coat was half a coat and half a jacket affair. He had on a green, high-pointed felt hat with a bright red feather in the band. As I was to learn later, he was about the same as our "forester." They called him a "keeper of the woods."

"He called his wife who was on the second floor and she came down straight way. I placed her age at about 30 and she looked just about like any housewife in the States.

"While he and she were talking I sat looking as hungry as I knew how. A child, looking about three, nosed its way into the room, but the father sent the child upstairs. He sat me down in a chair near the table in the kitchen and sat down beside me. As he drew up his chair, he said in a very businesslike manner, "I speak a little English."

"Boy, was that good sounding to me. Little did I know that he had made a gross understatement. What he should have said was, "I speak very, very little English." But before I realized it I swung into a fast conversation of which he understood about 5%. I told him that I was a Bombardier on a Liberator and that I had been forced to jump the day before. I would like to have civilian clothing if such a thing were possible as I would try to make my way to Spain. As I neared the end of the story I could see that very little had registered.

"Then I set about to tell my story again, this time using my hands, simple English words and my language card. I finally got to the part about going to Spain and that I would need civilian clothes. This was very hard for me to put across as he seemed to think I would be no better off there than I was in Holland. Finally he said in his very best broken English, "Tonight come man, good man, speak English good, you stay?" That was the best bit of news I've heard since I've been in Holland."

"He got up from the table and made motions for me to follow him after he looked out the window and front door. He and I crossed the road and into the woods we went. We walked for about ten minutes and then he seemed to be look-ing for something. Finally he came to a small clump of low fir trees. There was a sort of hut that was two-thirds underground. The top was covered over with leaves and one tree grew right through the center of it. It was only about four feet high on the inside and about ten feet square. The floor was covered in straw and once inside you were very warm and comfortable. It was about seven when he left me and as I lay back to rest a bit, before I knew it I fell asleep.

"I was awakened by someone putting in a head and calling softly, "Good-evening, friend." We seated ourselves just outside the door in the moonlight and my new friend that had awakened me was the first to speak. "Are you cold? We have brought blankets and hot coffee." It was good to hear someone speaking English properly.

"I asked the newcomer where he learned to speak English and he said he had learned in public schools but he also spent about two years at different times in England. Finally, he struck a note that was near and dear to my heart - he said, "If you will give me your wife's name and address, I think I can get word to her through the Red Cross that you are alive and well." In as polite a manner as possible, I told him that my squadron would notify my wife that I was Missing In Action. I would either be back in England soon, or I would be captured and, in the event of the latter, I would be able to write home through the Red Cross.

"We all rose and said goodnight with handshakes. The forester spoke in Dutch to his friend and then the forester said, "Your host here will come in the morning with food and he says for you to keep the thermos of coffee."

"That night I slept very little and I lay long hours just worrying and thinking what I should do. For some reason, I did not like or trust this new contact. His knowledge of just what questions to ask is what finally made me make up my mind what I was to do. Just before dawn broke, I drank the remainder of the cof-fee, it was still hot and warming, and then I left and headed south.

"As dawn broke, I seemed to be again coming into heavy woods and I was able to leave the paths. For this I was thankful, for I didn't fancy walking down these paths while I still wore my flying suit. About noon, I stopped by a brook and ate the egg that I had been saving. The cool, clear water was just what the doctor ordered. After an hour's rest, I again pointed my nose south.

"It was about three o'clock when the woods thinned to almost nothing and I began to reach open fields, meadows, and farm land. I knew I would look too conspicuous if I started marching across plowed fields and climbing fences, so I once again took to the paths.

"Keeping as alert as possible and ducking most of the passers-by, it was around four o'clock I heard someone coming behind me. I turned slowly to have a look and it was a man on a bike. As he came up beside me, he slowed his speed and gave me a thorough scrutinizing. He stopped about five paces up ahead and again I knew it was no good to run, at least not yet! I walked on and as I came up beside him he said rather softly, "Englishman?" I answered, "American - do you speak English"?

"He understood my question but shook his head in the negative. He got off his bike and with a clear cut smile on a serious face said,"Come." He lifted his bike over a fence, crawled over himself and spread the wire for me to come through. I hesitated a moment to think and again he said with a smile, "Come."

"When we had gone a safe distance into the woods he laid down his bike and we shook hands. He made motions for me to sit. He left his bike by me and went off. Some time later he returned with a young boy. He looked to be about 14 at a distance. The young boy seemed to speak English well. He had a large bundle under his arm. He said, "Shall we sit? When we were seated he asked. "Are you hungry? I have had only one egg this day and the walking had sharpened my appetite. I answered, "Yes, I am a bit."

"He pulled a small sandwich box from inside his overcoat. Yes, they were raw bacon sandwiches and sandwiches of cheese. He was almost 17, and he had learned to speak English in public schools. He said that they were members of the "Underground" and could help me and would as soon as they had asked me some questions. I asked why these questions were necessary and was told that the Germans had at times planted English-speaking Germans about, posing as Allied airmen. I told him that if he wished to ask questions about my homeland, that I would answer these but if his questions were of a military character that I would simply have to refuse to answer even if it meant refusing his help. He gave a translation to the older man and this was quite agreeable with him.

"The questions that they asked were not important but seemed to satisfy my friends. The two talked a bit and then the young lad turned to me and asked, "Do you know a Lt. Bill Moore?"

"I replied, "Do I know him, why he's my pilot, how do you know him?"

"We have found him, too, and he is close by here in these woods. We shall take you to him." The young boy handed me the bundle and I found a pair of blue coveralls.

"Moore had been only about a mile from where the forester had sat me down to wait while he went after the young lad, who at the time had been talking to "Bill.""

Now we all four sat down and the forester asked the boy in Dutch to ask us what our plans were. We told them that we would like to try to make Spain; that we need civilian clothes and we asked if it would be possible to get false papers. The forester and the boy said it was possible to get both - that we would have to go into town that night and to a home where we could stay a few days until the false papers could be prepared.

"We never saw the forester again, but about seven that evening the young lad came back with his bike. He had a civilian suit for each of us. He said a man and a girl were waiting for us at the path - he would go with us to them and then I was to take his bike, "Bill" was to take the man's bike, and the man and the girl would go on the girl's bike; that we should ride about thirty yards behind and that if they were stopped by anyone we were to turn about and come back here to the woods.

"As we walked from the woods, I shall never forget a statement he made, "I wish I were a soldier." Bill assured him that he was a soldier; that the "Underground" soldier was as much a soldier as those that wore a uniform. He said, "But I would like to be a real soldier."

"We neared the edge of the woods where the man and girl waited. Bill walked up to the man and took his bike, and the man took the girl on the other bike and started down the path. We were only about five miles outside the town of Apeldoorn and the ride did not take us long. The house that we went to was just on the outskirts of town, on the same side as we went in on. We rode through the front gate and to the rear of the house. Little did we suspect that we would remain inside for five months. One night when it was very dark I walked around in the back yard for about fifteen minutes and looked at the stars, but if my memory serves me right, Bill never set his foot out the door in these months.

"As I say, we were to stay in this house for five months, so I want to tell you something about the people who live here. This man and girl that had been our guides were two of the leaders of the underground. This man, our guide, was Aart, and the girl we called Mary. Mary didn't live at Aart's place, but she was a frequent visitor and just like one of the family. She was later captured by the German Gestapo for doing underground work and was sent to a concentration camp.

"Aart's mother, and we all called her Mother, was confined to the bed at the time. The father, Abe, was truly one fine person. He was about sixty. Aart's wife was Mek and was she was very easy on the eye. So her twin sister. One of the sons was living there too. This was Jaap. He was an intellectual sort and he spoke reasonably good English. His age, I think, was 22.

"The only other person in the house was a very unusual lady we called "Merouw." She was about 60 (for all I knew, she could have been 50 or 90) and she had lived in the Dutch East Indies for some years. She had traveled a good bit, spoke Dutch perfectly (which many of the Dutch do not do) English, French, German and Malaysian. She was a very steady person and hated the Germans with a fiery anger. She had two rooms on the second floor of the house, and we did not see her often.

***

Note from the author.

I briefly interrupt John Low's story here and insert what Aart Kliest wrote in 1945 about how he came in contact with John Low and pilot Bill Moore. The "Aart" in John's story is Aart Kliest, "The young boy" who brought John and Bill together in the woods near Apeldoorn, Netherlands, was Joop "Joke" Bitter, my late brother-in-law. "Mary" in John's story was Narda Terwisga.

Aart Kliest's story.

"Miss Narda Terwisga, Apeldoorn, Netherland, and I were both active in the Dutch resistance. Joke "Joop" Bitter, also living in Apeldoorn, informed Narda that he had made contact with two American airmen. Joke had asked Narda if she could arrange for a safe shelter for these two men. After having tried several addresses without success she came to me on May 1, 1944 at nine o'clock p.m.

"We had not much time for discussion as the Germans had ordered a curfew after 11 o'clock. We decided to go immediately to the spot where Joke Bitter and the two airmen were hiding; in the woods that belong to the Royal Palace in Apeldoorn. To reach this spot near the "Aardhuis," the hunting lodge belonging to the palace, we had to travel six miles per bicycle.

"I decided to bring these two airmen to my home. However, the big problem was who to transport these men. The road to be taken was not very secure as various German control posts were checking the traffic. We decided that the Americans would take Joke's and my bike. Joke would the walk home. While Narda and I would take her bike and travel in front of the Americans to show the way. We would enough distance between us and the Americans so that, if we were stopped, they would have enough room to go back. Without any problems we arrived at a 10:45 p.m. at my place.

"Another little problem presented itself. My wife and I lived in the house of my parents and as my mother was recovering from an eye illness, we were not sure that she would be prepared to look together with us after these two flyers. Fortunately she immediately agreed to help the airmen, regardless of the great dangers that were involved for all parties. We had a rather good place to hide as my two brothers, who had been summoned to go and work in Germany, stayed in our house. This is how the first Americans, called Bill F. Moore and John Low, came to stay in our house.

***

John Low continues;

"Bill and I stood our bikes against the side of the house and we were shown into the dining room where Aart's mother was laying on some kind of a day bed. We all sat around and talked about an hour. Of course, much translation had to be made, but it was surprising to me how well Mary, Jaap and Mevrouw spoke English. Aart could understand 90% of what we said but in speaking English he didn't do so well.

"We were asked if we would like to wash up and shave before we went to bed and we jumped at this chance. While Bill and I washed up, Art and Jaap were busy fixing a place for us to sleep. I want to go into some detail to describe our sleeping quarters for it was a very cleverly concealed hide-away.

"The house was three stories tall, the first floor was at the same level as the ground, as are most of the houses in Holland. The third floor was what you might call half an attic and half a sleeping room. This third floor was not finished with wallpaper and such. The rafters were exposed and the ceiling was the roof. As the roof slanted down from the crest to the eve of the house, it came in about four feet from the rain gutter and there we have a wall that goes up from the floor and hits the roof. The wall is only about two feet high. This two foot wall looks as if it were the main wall or side of the house when actually it leaves a compartment behind it just large enough to lay a single bed mattress. This is where we slept. We crawled in through a trap door, pulled closed the trap door in the wall and we were set.

"Bill and I didn't do any talking and we were soon dead to the world. A mattress laid on the floor in the eve of a house may not sound like heaven to some, but that is what it was to us that night. I slept for twelve straight hours and had not Mek awakened me the next day at noon, I might have been sleep yet. We got up, washed and dressed.

"About 1:30 Mary arrived and she and Aart came up and we went into the bedroom to talk. It seemed that what they took two hours to tell was nothing short of the fact that the young lad and the forester had a little over-encouraged us. It was true that Aart and Mary could get us false papers, but they had never themselves anything to do with helping airmen back to England and they didn't know anyone just at the moment who had.

"Bill and I were not so happy to get the news that our trip was not set and we would have to sit tight a day or so until Aart and Mary could find some other organization, one that had a way for us to go to Spain. Mary said that she knew a man that knew a man that had a friend that might be able to help us. Three days, the man that Mary said she knew came by to talk with us. He was a very nice person. He looked to be about 35, had on riding pants, a brown coat and, instead of riding boots, wore heavy wool socks that came up to his knees. He wore heavy black rimmed glasses and spoke English poorly. Later on he made our pictures for false papers and from this we called him Photo Joe, although his name was not Joe.

"We stayed upstairs in the attic during the day and until the black-out curtains were drawn. Then we would go down to the living room and dining room where Mother had her bed. After about a week, Aart put up curtains over the windows so we could come down during the day.

"We had been here just one week to the day when the man came that was to help us. For some reason I had expected a man around 40, but he turned out to be a young man of 23. He was a British Officer. He had been dropped in Holland by parachute to help organize a way for flyers to get back to England. He called himself "Dick" and was one of the cleverest persons I have ever known. One has to be clever to be a spy.

"One day we saw a young boy come in the gate on his bike and make for the back of the house. Up the stairs we went so as not to be seen. In a few minutes he came up with Mek were. She had told him we were "Underwater boys" but she did not tell him we were Americans. This was Joop, the youngest brother of Aart. Joop turned out to be a great friend of ours. We spent many pleasant hours together. He had been hiding on a farm. He had been called to work in Germany but they hadn't called loud enough for him to hear.

"I learned a lot about Dick in my ten months stay in Holland, but all he told us the first day was that he was dropped Allied airmen escape. That up until the last week he had two routes or ways by which we could reach Spain, but this last week one had folded up. Dick said we would leave in about eight days and go the other route.

"I would like to tell you a little more about this fellow Dick. To say he is a spy is enough to say of his bravery. How could you have a spy and not have a brave man, unless you have a damn fool, and Dick was certainly not that. He was half Dutch and half English and had lived in Holland until he was a child of about ten, when he moved to England.

"Dick stayed about two hours this first time and when we had finished with the business he asked many questions about England. Bill and I had been in England such a short time we were unable to tell him much. He was a very cheery person and he had us in good spirits before he left. Just before leaving, he talked with Aart and made arrangements with Aart to have our pictures made. This man I told you we called Photo Joe was to come by the next morning to make our pictures here at the house and Dick would be back in about a week with the papers on which these pictures would go. Then, he would take us away.

"The next morning, Photo Joe came by with his camera and made the pictures. These first pictures did not turn out good and he came back the following day to do it over. Two days later, the pictures came and they were okay this time.

"A new arrival came about the fifth day after Dick had made his first visit. Aart came in late that evening and looked like the cat that had been enjoying a nice canary. It seemed that one of the fingers had scratched up something in the way of a B-24 gunner. He was shot down the same day as we were and had been living in a pig house. A farmer had been feeding him. Aart said he and Mary were going to get him now and they would be back in about an hour. He didn't want the others to know about it just yet.

"He was gone just about an hour when he and Mary came back with David Smith. (*Sgt. David L. Smith was the right waist-gunner of the B-24, # 41-28754, Pilot Carl Hitchcock, of the 466th Bomb Group. On April 29, 1944, this aircraft was crash-landed in Twello. The whole crew of nine survided – note by John Meurs*). David brought with him the aroma of his last quarters and his first words were, "I'm sure glad to see Americans and can I get a bath." It all came out in one long breath. We shook hands and I told him we were certain he could and would have a bath before we went to bed.

"I told David that we usually had coffee in about an hour and asked if he would like to bathe now or just before going to bed and he was all for a bath now because of the piggish smell and so was everyone else. Bill helped heat the water and was on hand to answer some of David's questions and Aart, Jaap, and I went up to enlarge the sleeping quarters. All we did was put in another mattress and David would have to crawl in and then crawl over Bill's bed and into his own.

"When David was all through with his bath, we had our coffee. We told David about our plans to go to Spain and told him we were certain he would be helped too. This was the news he wanted to hear. He jumped with joy. He was a comical Joe and right here he put on a monkey act. He walked about the room chattering and swaying like a monkey. This went over big with the family and we all had a good laugh.

"We next asked David if he would like to hear the news and he was all for it. It was a little crowded around the radio that night, but the five of us were able to wedge in and get the news. Aart and Jaap left us in our hideaway and turned out the lights saying, "Sleep Well." Bill and I did, except when David would wake us coughing. He had a hard deep cough and we were worried about him for a day or so.

"The next evening, David was moved to another house. It was felt that it would be better for David to be in a bed until he was well and at this other house was a school teacher and her mother. She and mother would sleep together and if the police should come at night, David could quickly get out of bed into a similar hideaway as we had and the school teacher could say she had been sleeping in the bed David vacated.

"It was while David was at this other house and about eight days after Dick's first visit that Dick came back to see us and with bad news. He said that he would not be able to help David nor us to reach Spain at this time.

"He said that he had send our names by radio and that orders had come back for us to stay where we were and not to attempt to go to Spain or anywhere else at this time. The reason being the trains in France were being heavily attacked by our Air Force and that the invasion would come some where soon. Dick had his orders not to help any airmen to travel and he strongly advised us not to attempt to go this long journey without help. He said he could keep us supplied in ration cards and the families we stayed with would be paid enough to pay for what we ate if we took his advice and waited.

"So we took his advice and agreed to stay. Aart was told of the plans and Dick asked if it would be possible for us to stay on here with him. He told Aart if it was not agreeable with him for us to stay here, he had other addresses that the people would let us stay with them. Aart said he wanted us to stay as long as necessary but he would have to ask his mother. As I told you before, mother was all for it, so we settled down to wait, and wait, and wait.

***

"After about a week, David came back to stay with us. He was better now and he was lonesome by himself. We would read, play the radio, play cards and help Mek with the housework to pass away the hours.

"Two more Americans came to stay with us and that made us five strong, but that's only the beginning. There were two more scratched up for the school teacher, while the other members of Aart's organization opened there homes to more still. Three English airmen were with a candy manufacturer, one stayed with a doctor, and an American and an Englishman stayed with a grocer. The Organization was taking care of 13 in all.

"With five Americans in the house, you can see that the family would have to live entirely for us. They couldn't go out without making certain that at least one member of the family would be home. They couldn't have their friends in for coffee. The whole family did everything they could to make us comfortable and happy. Jaap would spend his evenings teaching Bill to speak Dutch. Aart was always busy with his work in the underground. Mother got better as the days went on and was finally able to get up. Abe was always on the go, bringing milk, going to the grocer, and going a thousand places like that. We, the five "underwater boys," pitched in and helped Mek with the housework, but there was much that we could do and a lot that they just plain wouldn't let us do.

"In reading back over what I have been writing, the last few pages, I see that I have neglected to give you the names of our two new American flyers that were living with us. One was Jim Dunham, a radio operator from a B-17 Fortress crew and the other was Charles Holmes, a tail gunner from the same crew. Both of these boys were married while Bill and David were not, so we had that in common.

"Charley was a quiet easy going guy and went the way the wind blew, but Jim was a bit more restless. It was Jim and I that finally decided that things had been going too slow to suit us and we were ready to set out to reach Allied hands. The invasion had come in June in France and now it was August and our boys were in Paris. Jim and I figured that if they continued to advance at the same rate as they had, then we would only have to make about 220 miles before we reached our troops. We would get up as close to the front lines as we could and then sit tight and let our Army advance over us.

"After we had eaten our lunch, I called Aart off to one side and we told him of our plans. At first Aart did not believe us and thought we were joking but then he saw we were serious. He said things were going too smooth just now for us to go off against orders from England and take the chance of being caught. We felt sure that by sticking to back roads and only trying to make about 20 miles a day that we would make it okay. The afternoon was spent in this discussion and around 4:30 Aart left the house and didn't say where he was going.

"That evening, after we had finished eating, members of the organization began to just casually drop in to say hello. I knew then where Aart had been when he left at 4:30. By eight o'clock the house was full it seemed. We had coffee and then it was De Vries that opened up with the more pressing business. He said,"John, I understand that you and Jim want to leave in the morning." De Fries spoke very good English. I said yes, and talked for the next 15 minutes straight trying to explain to them all how much we appreciated all they had done for us, but that we felt that we could make it through to our troops and we should try.

"De Fries said that he agreed with us up to a point. He, too, thought that our chances of getting through to our troops were percentage wise very good, but, here is what stopped us. But, if on the other hand, we were caught he felt certain that we would not be treated as POWs and that we would be handed over to the Gestapo. He said we would be given more than just the third degree and while he was certain that we would not tell anything about the Underground while we were in our right senses, anyone could crack under the type of torture they employed and we might finally talk.

"I told him that I did not think they would use strong-arm methods on American airmen who were trying to escape, as the Geneva Conference gave every soldier the right to try to escape.

"His answer to this was that had we been captured a short time after we came down we would have known nothing about the Underground Organization and there would have been no point in the Gestapo putting us through the paces. But now the Germans knew the day we came down, and that we were hidden by someone, probably an Underground Organization and as soon as we gave them our identity tags we would be turned over to the Gestapo because more than anything they wanted to get the Underground Organization.

"I asked how did they know I was in Holland and what day I came down. He said he was certain they knew - maybe a crew member had talked too much. I did not believe that any of our crewmen would talk but it was then I remembered my parachute hanging in the trees. It had my name on it.

"Mary spoke up and said if we were dead set to go they would not try to stop us but since they did not believe in it, they would not help us to even get out of town. She pointed out that since we knew so much about the organization and with whom the other airmen were staying, that if we went they would have to find other places for these men - places that would not be as comfortable, nor as safe, probably.

"She said if we truly did appreciate what they had done for us and for the other boys, we would take their advice and stay. That is what we did. One of the first laws an evader has to recognize is that he must take his orders from those that help him. After this, I never gave any argument to even a suggestion made by those that were risking their all to help me. Their slightest requests were commands to me. I backed these Underground boys to the last ditch. They made mistakes and sometimes I could see them coming, but I was riding in the boat as a passenger and not at the helm. If the boat went down, they went down with it, just as I. It was their show.

"I have said the Underground made mistakes and I want to give you information on a couple of these. Please understand that I am not saying by any means that I or someone else would not have made these same mistakes, or worse ones. I am not saying, "I told you so," nor do I offer solutions to some of the entanglements. I am only inserting them here so you may see that these mistakes only added to their difficulty in functioning. I also feel that if I do not show some of the rough spots my reader will get the idea that I think the Dutch Underground is all Holy just because I was there and they helped me. You might feel that I have a biased view when I make the statement that the Dutch Underground operated under far greater adversities than any of the underground movements while they were just as successful in doing what they were called on to do.

"One of their mistakes was brought on through jealousy. If two groups in the same area were doing the same type of work you would find more rivalry between them than you do between two colleges of the same state. This is hard for me to explain but, for example, I'll give you this case; There were two American airmen found and brought into town. Dick was in touch with this organization that found the two boys and he made frequent calls to this organization to see if he could help them in any way or if they could help him. In this particular case the two boys were upstairs on the second floor of a house when Dick was visiting downstairs. The man of the house did not even tell Dick that he had the two boys because he wanted his organization to be the one that helped the boys and not Dick. At the time all Dick could have done was send their names to England but had something big come off, as it did just a little later, these boys might have been left out. Here was Dick, the only man in Holland at the time dropped for the specific purpose of aiding evaders,'out looking for men to help, and in the same house with two of them, but he never knew it.

"Of course, as many men came out of Holland without knowing there was such a person as Dick, as Dick helped. But still he was in touch with England and knew the ropes and the rough spots. I know in many cases Dick's advice was not taken by some of the men evading but in almost every case Dick proved to be right.

"Another mistake was in the small organizations it was difficult to get the members to act under orders of one leader. When a problem came up there was too much argument among themselves. It is obvious that in every case there would be need for discussion in doing this sort of work so as to get opinions, but often you found the attitude, "if that is the way it is to be you can count me out." Remember, this was volunteer workers and a leader had no way to force a decision. This is one of the problems to which I could offer no solution.

"Very few of the organizations of one town knew that organizations in another town existed and so you can see the difficulty of grouping these into one large organization. It was absolutely impossible. The organizations sprung up by themselves and that is the way they functioned. There were areas that did group under area leaders, but here again an area leader could not force his orders and so the network was loose. The ones that most successfully licked this problem were the ration card boys. They could hold their organization in two by just cutting off a subordinate organizations supply if they did not toe the line.

"Another organization that was strong nationally was the one that was organized to fight once they had their orders from Eisenhower. Here too the top men held control because they were making distribution of the guns and ammunition, and by stopping the supply of a subordinate organization they could keep them in track.

"One thing I must not do, and that is paint this picture too black. Don't get the idea that everything was disorganized and all were pulling in different directions. Had this been true, the Germans could have cleaned up the Underground before it got started.

"It was in early August when Jim and I set up this cry to go traveling. After that, we took it easy, listened to the radio, peeled potatoes, washed dishes, read, played cards and just let the days go past as they would.

"Photo Joe came to see us often. Mary was in and out but she didn't eat with us any more after we were five strong as the table wasn't large enough. A couple of the members of the organization came once in a while and had coffee. One brought a model airplane for us to construct. Mr. De Vries was sure swell to us, too. He would come by almost every Saturday with a bottle of gin. One bottle among ten did not go far, but it sure hit the spot as a pick-me-up. He could get this gin by trading some chocolate he had saved from before the war. He always brought sugar or something to eat. On my wedding anniversary, his wife even sent me a cake and Mary and some of the others sent flowers. I almost choked up that day. My only prayer was that my wife had had as a nice day as I. She couldn't have had.

"Things rocked along like this and the news got better and better. The troops had taken Paris, now they were in Brussels, and now they had even taken part of Holland. We began to see more and more of the fighting planes as the troops came nearer and nearer. Then it happened - September 17th, paratroops were dropped in Holland and on a large scale. The battle for Arnhem opened in full swing. We were only 19 miles north of Arnhem, as the crow flies, and we saw part of the planes as they brought the gliders.

"The Arnhem show was a failure and the River Rhine was not crossed. Where did this leave the Underground? Out on a limb - way out on a limb! The organization that Aart and Mary were in was one of these organizations that went way out. They let in a new member and they didn't check on him too close. Why should they check on him - it was certain that the British would be in by tomorrow. Aart was sick at the time and he sent word to them to take it easy and go slow.

"Too late! This new member turned out to be a Gestapo man. He only worked in the organization for a few days and he knew all the members and where they lived, except Aart. As I said, Aart was sick and had been for six weeks so he had not been active in the work and because of this the Gestapo did not have a check on him.

***

"On October 1st, 1944 the Gestapo started rounding up those who they had a tab on. Mary was captured; also Photo Joe, De Vries and almost all the others. I believe they caught 27 men and Mary. De Freese talked himself free with a number of quick impressive lies and got home before they came to search his house.

"He got the Englishmen out and away. Two of the airmen staying with the grocer (*they were in fact hiding in the house of Joop Bitter – note of John Meurs*) were not so lucky. The Englishman, Kenneth Ingram and one American, Bob Zercher, were captured as the Gestapo made its roundup.

"Mary was sent to Germany to a concentration camp and the men of the Underground were killed. Ken and Bob were also killed. You might say Ken was murdered because, as I have pointed out earlier, the Geneva Conference gives a soldier the right to go into civilian clothing to try to escape. Ken was seen by neighbors as he was taken from the house where he was hiding and his face was bleeding and his clothing was torn. The Gestapo boys never heard of Geneva.

"By noon, the news was passed from mouth to mouth all over town and as soon as Aart heard it he set out to find another place for us to hide. He was afraid that some of the captured might be tortured into telling his name and address.

He knew he must find a place where no one in the house had been doing Underground work or we would be just as bad off as we would be if we had stayed on with him.

"About three, he came back with a man we had never seen. He spoke English and we went away with him. Aart said he did not know where this man would take us and that way we would be safe if he were captured. He said he too was going to leave home. Jaap and Mek also would leave and Mother was going to return to bed to pretend to be sick so she could claim ignorance of anything that had gone on in the house. Mevrouw could claim she never even came out of her room and this would only leave Abe without an alibi but he said he was old and would not leave his home and his wife and if they took him it just wouldn't matter.

"When we left it was just like saying good-bye to our own blood kin. Just think of the number of hours we had spent with these people. I have no brothers and sisters and I had learned to love these people in just that sort of light. We all did, and they loved us, too. It wasn't just Mother who cried when we left. She just cried the loudest. We all shed a tear or two as it was just like breaking up a very large family under very adverse conditions.

"We didn't think it wise for us to all leave the house at once and go marching down the street in a large group, so Charles and Jim went first. Aart's friend was back in about three minutes and Bill, David and I went along with him. We didn't go far and soon we were at our new home. As we went in through the door, I wondered if it was possible that we would stay here for five months.

"There was only one person in the house and she met us at the door. Her husband had died several years past. She was a very nice lady, and she was about the same age as Aart's mother. She was very pleasant and seemed very happy to have us.

"Our new hostess spoke English and she made us feel at ease from the first. We went into the living room where Charles and Jim were and then we had tea. She told us that she wished it were possible that we could stay on with her but she had people living with her that talked too much. These people were away for a week and the man that brought us would come for us in a day or two as soon as he found good safe places for us to stay. She told us he had said he would be back in the morning and let us know when and where we were going.

"That night we had very wonderful beds to sleep in as she did not have a place such as we had at Aart's. She did have a similar set up but it was large enough for the five of us to get in and stand up. It was even more cleverly hidden than the one at Aart's (Thank the Dear Lord, and I mean that reverently).

"It was in the back of a closet up in the attic. This closet was more of a storage room and about 10 feet wide at the rear. In the rear was a double wall arrangement, with a very well concealed trap door. It was this hiding place that saved four of us from being caught by the Gestapo.

"The next morning we were all up early and the good lady had fixed our coffee and bread when we came down. It was while we were eating that the bad news started coming in. The lady left the house about ten to go to the grocer and when she came back she was excited and very nervous. She said that the Germans were shooting men because they would not come dig trenches and they would leave their bodies in the streets with signs on them saying they were terrorists and no one could remove these bodies for three days. Among them were Photo Joe and the others.

"This was why the man that brought us had not come back that morning. We told the lady that if she should let us stay on in the house until dark, we would slip out of the house and go away. We did not want to do even this because it meant that we could not get back in touch with the man that had brought us and therefore Aart would not know where we had gone, and Dick would not know. We did not know where we would go but we would start all over getting in touch with some other organization in some other town.

"We asked the lady if she would go to the house of the man that brought us and tell him what we planned to do. She did and when she came back she had changed her mind and said it was better that we stay on at her house and not go away. The man had settled her nerves and he told her he did not think her house would be searched. Nevertheless, she said she would sleep in the house of a friend that night and we would have a window signal out in the morning if all had gone well and if it was safe for her to return. She prepared our evening meal and then she packed an overnight bag and left just in time to reach her friend's house before curfew.

"Everyone had to be off the streets by 8 o'clock at night. It was about 8:30 when there came a hard knock at the front door. Bill and I were down stairs and the other boys were up in the attic sitting by a large window. The house was blacked out and Bill and I were just sitting by the light of the fire. We cracked the curtains a little and looked out. There were two men in civilian clothes. The had pistols and were shining flash lights about. Bill and I went to the rear of the house and there, too, was a man in civies and with a pistol. We didn't have to be told that these were men of the Gestapo. I turned to Bill and said quietly, "Let's go up stairs as quickly and quietly as possible." The knocking was stronger and shouts to open up followed.

"I made my way quietly and slowly to the stairs. It was difficult as we were not familiar with the house and it was as dark as the inside of a black cow's stomach. Bill did not follow me. I believe what he did was to stay by a window and as they broke down the door, I think he went out the window. All in all, I think, too, this was the wisest thing to do because once you are caught on the 3rd floor of a house you don't stand much of a chance to make a break for it.

"But Bill's luck ran out and he was captured. I honestly don't believe Bill was caught in the house because we could hear every sound made in the house that night and at no time did these Gestapo boys sound as though they had found someone. I believe yet that he was picked up on the streets that night for being out after curfew time and the whoever picked him up discovered he was not Dutch. Or, maybe later he was captured in the home of someone who was hiding him.

"All I know is the last time I saw Dick, just before I got out of Holland, he told me that he had talked with a boy who had escaped from a prison or jail in Apeldoorn. In this jail he had talked with a boy who said his name was Bill Moore. Then two days later one of the English boys that came back through the lines with me said he had heard from an Underground worker that the Gestapo had shot and killed an American named Bill Moore who wouldn't tell them who had helped him.

"When at last I reached the attic, I found that it took me as long to find the closet and trap door as it had to climb the two flights of stairs. Going up the stairs had been tricky as they creaked something awful. I would only chance putting my weight on a new step at the same time as the Gestapo men were beating at a window or while they were knocking down the door. This way, their noise would cover the sound that I made. I realized that once any sort of noise came from upstairs the game was over, because then they would know we were here and would search until they found us, or they might burn the house down.

"I felt my way as I moved through the attic and the only noise I heard was the breathing of a mouse somewhere about. I had arrived so quietly that it gave the other three boys a bit of a start when I put my head in through the trap door and hissed. They hissed back as they were already in the hideaway and waiting only for Bill and me to arrive before closing the trap door. No one said one word.

"It had taken me right close to half an hour to make my way upstairs and into the hideaway. In this time, the Gestapo thugs had knocked down the back door and had just about completed their search of the bottom floor. I had only reached the attic when I heard the back door give way and swing open but I knew that they would search the bottom floor before the second and the second before the attic and that way I knew I had plenty of time. As a matter of fact, we did not close the trap door until we heard them start up the stairs that led to the attic as all that time we were waiting for Bill to come up.

"There was a door at the bottom of the stairs that led to the attic and this had a peculiar squeak. It was when we heard them open this door that we pulled the trap door closed and the shelf fell to cover the crack.

"It took them about twenty minutes to search the bottom floor and about the same for the second floor. We could clearly hear them as they went from room to room. They were now in the attic and what would the next twenty minutes bring? They searched the large part of the attic, shouting and turning over chairs, trunks, and chatting all the time. They came to our room and then in the closet. Four hearts stopped!

"They kicked things around in the closet and...and, at last, they started pulling out. We had won! At least we had won the first round. We heard them reach the bottom floor before a man spoke. We had a council to decide our next step. Should we come out of hiding, slip downstairs and away in the darkness, or would we wait until morning? Had they left a guard? Was the house being watched?

"We all agreed that it was best to wait where we were for two hours and then chance getting out and away from the house. We would start all over and try to contact some other organization in some other town.

"But as we arrived at this decision, we heard marching troops come to a halt outside. The three had only been gone ten minutes when they returned, this time twenty strong. We had made a wise decision by sitting tight because we would about time to have gotten downstairs and the four of us climbing the stairs would have certainly made enough noise to give us away.

"When the new search began our hearts sank as we heard the ripping up of floors and tearing down of walls on the bottom floor. We were certain we would be found. We were also certain it would not be a POW camp for us either.

"This time they worked for an hour on each floor below us. Slowly our nerves began to give way. Why the hell didn't they come on upstairs and get it over with? It was as though we were cutting the cards for life or death. When they finally opened the stair door with the loud squeak we all started praying. There is no joke about that - if ever I concentrated on a prayer in my life it was then.

"The first thing they did was to rip up most of the floor. I learned later that what they were actually looking for was not "underwater" men, but hidden weapons. The lady's daughter had been working in an organization that had been meeting planes at night that would drop guns and then she would help to distribute these pistols and machine guns. So you can see just the smallest nook or corner would serve as a hiding place for these. And here we were in a place large enough for five or six men to stand up in.

"Next, they started knocking at the walls. If a knock sounded hollow or sounded as though it was not a solid wall, in would get a pixk axe or a crowbar. If the pickaxe or crowbar struck solid they would move on the next spot. The slightest detail was not overlooked. One of the (censored) Huns at long last came in the closet and this time he really started kicking things around. And I started praying all the harder. He knocked the board down that had been the shelf and the crack to our door was exposed. He found it and called for someone to come. I guess he called for a crowbar because that's what came. I felt like just throwing in the towel and start crawling out to save them the trouble of tearing out the wall. I guess that was what I would have done but I was just too scared to move.

"We had had the whole duty bunch that night. We could tell from what they said that the dogs outside engaged in the hunt were German Gestapo, Dutch Quislings, S.S. Troops, and a general assortment of others. Then the head-knocker, who was a German, called the search to an end and they all went away.

"But again they were only gone ten minutes when they returned and they had a wagon with them. The job they had returned for was just looting.

"I had a flashlight and all along we had been keeping up with the time. A look now showed that we had been in this hideaway for six hours. Again we agreed we should stay two hours before coming out. When these two hours had passed, we crawled out as quiet we could and slipped down the stairs. Eight hours we had spent in that cramped up place but the thought furthest from our minds had been comfort.

"We had just one hill now to get over and it did not look too high. That was getting out of the house and out of town without being seen. We knew we were on the north side of town and so we headed north. It was not as easy as it sounds. It was a bright moon lit night and there were Jerries all over the place. Don't forget just 20 miles south of us the battle of Arnhem was just winding up and with the Jerries winning.

"But we stuck to the shadows, took it slow and after an hour, we had made it to pastures and clear sailing. Which do you think saw us through, Lady Luck or God? Personally, I think God had a hand in it and unquestionably Lady Luck had put in a little overtime, too!

***

"The four of us that had lucked it out together went north three miles before the sun began to rise. We found a haystack that was a little more than a hundred yards from a farm house and crawled in to wait for the morning to break through. Just before noon the farmer and a young boy that was working on his farm came for hay.

"We talked with them in our best Dutch, which was still very poor as none of us had made a real attempt to learn the language. We told him we would like very much to hide in his haystack for a few days and he was willing and happy to have us to do so. He said he had enough food and that we would not need to contact an Underground Organization for ration cards. At the time, we felt sure that it was only a matter of a few days or at the most a couple of weeks before the Allies would cross the Rhine River and we would be freed. We all talked it over and decided since the farmer had volunteered food that it was better that we not try to contact any Underground Organization, as they were having enough troubles of their own at this time.

"This was the first of October and the weather was not bad. We let the top over the haystack down until it rested on the hay. This left us in what you might call a house built of hay. The farmer brought us out blankets and the top was rain proof and 90% wind proof. Each night the farmer would slip out to the haystack with a large pan of hot potatoes and bread and milk for the next day. We stayed on here for a month before we realized that the Germans had been able to stabilize their lines and the Allies could not break through at this time. In this month, the Underground was able to smooth out of their troubles and settle down to the work they had thought was over.

"After a month had passed, we asked the farmer if he knew someone he could trust that spoke English. He brought a lovely Dutch girl who I took to be about 25. We asked her if she could get us in touch with some Underground Organization and she said she could and she did. She brought a man who told us that things were better now in the Underground Organizations and that they were trying to get all the Allied Airmen over the Rhine River into the hands of the English. This we were for.

"One by one the Underground took us away. The farmer was truly sorry to see us go. The day that each of us left, he would have us in the house and give us a little farewell drink.

"They ran like this: Why wasn't I back in the States in a nice warm, comfortable bed? Why did my folks have to suffer? Why was I in this damnable war anyway? Why? Why ? Why?

"It is very tempting here to devote the remainder of this book to just writing about Paris. All my life I have heard of what a wonderful city Paris is, but I will pass on with this remark - Paris is not a city, but an institution.

***

Here John Low's story ends abruptly. He did not talk about how he crossed the River Rhine because he was probably ordered to remain silent about this subject. These crossings were in the first place organized for the members of the First British Airborne Division who, after the Battle of Arnhem was lost, had been sheltered by the Dutch underground. Some Allied airmen, hidden in the area, were included in the crossings. Code name of these was "Pegasus," the mythical white horse with wings that appeared on the paras' uniform patches. "Pegasus I" was a big success but a liberated para told his story to a British journalist who had presented himself as a intelligence officer. The story appeared in a British newspaper and when "Pegasus II" took place the Germans were forewarned. Many paras and airmen were captured, wounded or killed.

Right Waist-Gunner S/Sgt. Walter T. Kilgore

By daughter Kathy Kilgore.

"Walter was a mountain child, born to and raised in Appalachia by a family of coal miners. His early years were spent in hours running bare foot through the mountain laurel, imagining a world outside the small hollow in which he was born. His mother, Mary Emma, was a loving, but strong mountain woman, running her household within the strict confines of Appalachian Protestantism, no dancing, no drinking, no smoking, and definitely no cursing.

835

"Walter Thomas was one of eight children born to Isaac and Mary. He was the youngest of three boys to live into adult hood. In those days, it was not uncommon for babies and toddlers to die. Times were tough for the family all the years Walter was growing up and into his teenage years. Isaac worked in the coal mines and the family moved around depending on where he could get work in the mines. For a while, before 1912, Isaac worked cutting timber for a lumber company and Mary did the cooking for the lumberjacks. During those years, they often lived in tents.

"Walter was a fun loving young boy and teenager who loved teasing and playing the jokester. He was often obstinate, and wanted to be always right and to win at all costs. His sisters adored him, but vacillated between chastising and praising him. He was Peck's bad boy with a lopsided grin. Walter Thomas' whole countenance was one that radiated mischievousness; pretty baby face, sandy blond hair, ears that stood out a little too much from his head and always that perpetual lopsided grin.

"He started smoking at age eleven or twelve. Mommie found out when he was about fourteen. She was not happy, but she sat him down and told him, "Walter, I don't like ya smoking, but worse then that, I don't like ya sneakin behind my back." So she started buying his tobacco. Smoking out in the open was a whole lot better than smoking on the sly and everybody in the hollow knowing but her. He smoked Buffalo or Golden Grain tobacco. In those days, the tobacco came in little pouches tied with a string and a tag on the end with the name of the tobacco. Walter would put the pouch in his shirt pocket with the little gold tag hanging out. Boy, did he think he was something. He would strut about and act the big man.

"When he was fourteen, Walter got drunk for the first time. They were back living in Seco and there was a dirt tennis court at the bottom of the hill. He and his buddies got hold of a jug of moonshine, which wasn't too difficult in those days, and went down to the tennis court to drink. He got so drunk, he had to be carried home. When Mommie saw her son being carried home by four friends, she dropped a pan of corn bread she was putting on the table, and ran out to meet him. Once she realized he was drunk, and not hurt, she hurried them up into the house. She was so embarrassed she couldn't say anything. To her, what Walter did was too awful to talk about and she definitely didn't want any of the neighbors to see her son in such a condition. Walter was sent to stay with his Uncle George, who lived about three miles away, for a few days until the whole incident was forgotten by the neighbors.

"Although Mary thought drinking was a sin, Walter remembers that his father kept a jar of whiskey hidden. Every morning before work, Isaac took a drink. Mary had to know about this clandestine ritual, but she never said a word. Only when Poppie made a barrel of wine and attempted to bring it inside the house, did Mary put her foot down. She then kicked over the barrel, spilling the contents onto the ground. Walter never heard of his father making any more again.

"A year before the tennis court drinking incident, Walter's father was electrocuted in Mine # 214 in McRoberts, Kentucky. Isaac was only 57 years of age and Walter was getting ready to start high school at age 13. Isaac was a man of little words, but he was kind and loved his children. He rarely fussed at them, leaving any punishment for Mary to deliver.

"The Elks Lodge took up a collection for Mary after Isaac's death. The $500 they gave her was enough to buy a lot and house in Whitaker. In Whitaker, Walter attended Fleming High School. With the loss of Isaac's wages, Mary was forced to go to work. She got a job in the elementary school in Seco fixing lunches. Fortunately, only two children, Walter and Kathryn, were still at home at this time. Charles was living in McRoberts and working in the mines at the time, so he sent Mary money every month to help supplement her meager salary.

"The High School sat on a hill in Fleming. Fleming was another mining town that abutted the town of Neon. In those years, Neon was not a mining town. In 1933, Fleming High was considered a 'modern' school since it had been built only in 1925. It had 7 or 8 classrooms, an auditorium, a library, and the principal's office.

"Once Walter got to high school, the girls flocked to him like hummingbirds to nectar because of his good looks. But as they got to know him they realized he wasn't husband material. He was a teller of tall tales. He loved to embellish the truth, often manipulating the facts to make a story better. He also loved to argue. It didn't matter about what. If someone said something was so, Walter Thomas was sure to convince you it wasn't.

"He graduated from Fleming High School in May 1937. He was named the 'class pest.'' Under his picture in the senior class book is the caption, "Just leave it to Walter to argue his way thru' and there's one thing we can say for him, he usually wins. He's a very good student in spite of arguing until his opponent is convinced he is wrong." His class quotation was, "Now, Mr. Holbrooks, that's not right"! He even willed "arguments for Max Carter" for his Class Will. Max was a junior who looked up to Walter Thomas and apparently wanted to follow in his footsteps.

"By the time Walter Thomas got out of high school, he was smoking and drinking every opportunity he could. These behaviors caused Mommie such grief. She could no longer take that switch to his backside, but she did spend a great deal of time harping at him during the day and praying for him at night. I think she was a little grateful that those were the only things he did. He didn't curse, didn't fool around with the girls, and didn't get in trouble with the law. Basically, he was an honest young man, loving and caring to family and friends. I don't remember much about my grandmother as she died when I was about nine and we always lived away from her. But I do remember that she idolized my father. He always seemed to be her favorite. Even his sisters and two brothers knew this, but didn't seem to mind. He was their favorite too. Walter Thomas had one of those charismatic personalities that caused people to overlook his shortcomings and instead make excuses for his carousing and story telling.

"Once out of high school, Walter Thomas was expected to get a job, and that meant going to work in the coal mines. There weren't any other options if he wanted to stay in the hollow. So he followed his father and two older brothers down into the mines.

"I can't imagine what affect this had on a young, vibrant, fun loving, worry free eighteen year old. The mines were hellholes in those days. Truly, if you worked in the mines, you 'owed your soul to the company store'. I came across one of my father's pay envelopes from June 15, 1939, and his take home pay for the month was $12.10. The rest was applied to such things as rent, garbage processing, company doctor checkups, and purchases at the company store.

"He didn't talk much about his feelings during that time of his life. Oh, he was quick to tell you what the mines looked like, about the soot and the quality of air, but not what he was feeling while down in the those dark dungeons.

"That time in his life he felt he was suffocating, both literally and figuratively. Eventually, the mines would take one of his brothers, Charles, who would die of the 'black lung'. Stanley was able to escape by taking a job on the railroads. Hanging on the wall in my house is the original miner's cap Stanley wore when he worked in the mines. On the front is a place for a light, first a candle, then later a flashlight. Once, when I asked Uncle Stanley what he remembered most about the mines he told me, "the darkness and the putrid smell of damp, decaying earth." I don't think my father ever could tolerate closed in spaces, whether they were physical, emotional or mental.

"There were some good times during those years, though. They were a large family and found ways to entertain themselves. On long summer evenings they stayed outside until late, trying to catch any hint of a breeze. They would sit on their front porch and watch the sunset, listening to the sounds of the birds and mountain critters settle in for the night. In those moments, however, he often felt restless. A feeling of urgency would come on so quickly that his heart would beat fast and he could barely catch breath. When he couldn't stand it any longer, he would jump down from the porch and walk quickly half way down the path towards town just so that he could run back up the hill and have an excuse for being out of breath.

"Of course, the winters were hard. They got a lot of snow, and some days it was so cold that it was hard to breathe if you sat on the porch after the sun went down. They would all stay huddled inside after dinner around the coal stove that heated the large main room.

"People in the hollow would take any opportunity to celebrate, which wasn't too often. Most of the social life of these mountain people centered on church activities, which of course seemed really boring to the young folk. A really big,

big time was when there was a tent revival. Then you would see and hear such hooping and hollering as to make the recent dead rise up from their graves and forget for a moment they were dead.

"Walter was just shy of twenty-one when a United States Air Force (then the Army Air Corps) recruiter visited the hollow. With promises of vast opportunities and magnificent places to see, Walter signed up. It was 1940 and Walter felt that his whole life up until that point had been spent in slow motion, moving through a suffocating atmosphere. He loved his family, and in a deep part of his core, he even loved his small isolated hollow, but he was on a dead end street that led to nowhere. Military service gave him his ticket to freedom from the strict confines and constraints of his hillbilly existence.

"In November, 1940, Walter and a friend heard that an Army Air Corps recruiter was in Norton, Virginia signing up recruits. He was just four days shy of being 21. Mommie gave him permission to enlist and his friend's Daddy drove them there. The two young men just left with the clothes on their backs; no suitcases, no notice to the mining company.

"My father never went back to visit those mining towns once he left home except for one brief visit in 1942 after basic training. He always told us, "I didn't leave anything behind, so why would I go back there?" Fortunately, during the war years his mother, three sisters, and one remaining brother moved to larger towns and cities.

"In Norton, Virginia, after a physical and a written test, Walter signed on the dotted line and became a military man. They took the young recruits to a restaurant and fed them a nice meal and put them up for the night in a hotel. The next day, they were on the train to Richmond, Virginia to the main recruiting office where they took a sworn oath. From there, they went to Langley Field in Virginia for training. They were given uniforms, towels, a toothbrush, a razor, a comb, and a gas mask. After a year and ½ of training at Langley Air Field, Daddy was given a short leave of three days to visit his family in McRoberts, Kentucky.

"In 1942, once finished with basis training, Walter put in for gunnery school, cadets training and OCS at the same time. Gunnery school came through first, so he went to Panama City, Florida, for classroom study and then to Apalachicola, Florida, for air to air gunnery training. When he graduated in 1943, he was sent to Keesler Air Base in Biloxi, Mississippi, to attend air craft maintenance (A & M) school. He was in school for about six months when a buddy, Harry McDonald, set him up on blind date with a girl from New Orleans, LA. Harry had met Pauline Prestia, his date's girlfriend, at a dance at St. Joseph's Church. That girl, Pauline Prestia, later married Walter and became my mother. After that first date, Walter visited New Orleans once a week over several months to see Pauline. In fact, he actually went AWOL one time to spend more time with her. He was put in the military jail for a month because he was three days late getting back from a weekend pass.

Right Waist-Gunner S/Sgt. Walter T. Kilgore in New Orleans

"Soon after that, he was sent to Salt Lake City. All of the enlisted men were told to report to a big hangar so they could be assigned to a crew. Each man's name was called and they were told to which crew they were assigned. Walter was assigned to crew 69 with whom he stayed throughout the war. All of his training was with crew 69 in Salt Lake City. He was assigned the position of engineer gunner.

"Salt Lake, they went to Mountain Home, Idaho and his crew was placed in a Group, the 467th. This Group was made up of 4 squadrons with 15 to 20 crews in each squadron. The group left Idaho for Windover Field in Utah where they finished training. From there, they went to Harrington, Kansas.

"During the time, he was in Harrington, my mother visited him. She traveled by train and stayed one week. That was a pretty risqué thing in the 1940s. But daddy was quick to point out that "nothing happened" and by that time, they were engaged.

"From Harrington, the crew flew to West Palm Beach, Florida. One evening, his plane took off and after one hour in the air, they opened their orders. They were to fly to Greenwich, Scotland but first they landed in Trinidad staying over night before flying to Fortalazio, South America (not sure of spelling). They stayed one night there and then flew to Belem, South America, then Dakar, Africa and then to Marakesh. Once in Marasksh, their orders changed. They flew to Valley, Wales and then to Norwich, England which became their home base. From there, they flew about 19 missions over about a two month period.

***

"On April 29, 1944, their plane took off for Germany but was hit multiple times in route. They were losing gas and the engine was stalling. The crew parachuted from the plane before it crashed. Walter's parachute caught in a tree and helped ease his fall. He and one other crew member, Robert Braun, landed near each other. They had no guns and not knowing exactly where they were, they started waking in the direction of the English Channel. They saw a turn in the road and attempted to run across to get to the other side. Just then, three boys on bikes came around the bend. They were not sure if they were Germans. Walter and Robert briefly spoke to each other reassuring themselves they could physically over take the boys if needed. Just then, however, the boys saw them and motioned for them to remain hidden. Once the boys saw the two men understood them, they took off on their bikes riding quickly back the way they came.

"In about 30 minutes, the boys returned with a forest ranger who turned out to be one of the boy's fathers. He too motioned for them to remain hidden and that he would be back soon. In about another 30 minutes, the ranger came back. He unrolled his sock to reveal a piece of paper on which a message was written in English, "You are in the underground and will be picked up tonight."

"Right around that time, the navigator from the plane, Frank Cosslett, joined Walter and Robert. He told them that one crew member was captured by the Germans and another broke his leg and was taken prisoner. During the twelve to thirteen months Walter was missing in action and hiding with the Dutch underground, he was moved to many safe houses. In at least two places, he actually lived in an underground dwelling. I have one or two pictures from that time that show Daddy standing as part of a crowd while German soldiers are marching by.

***

"In early May of 1944, my grandmother received a letter from the Assistant Chief of Air Staff, that her son, Walter, was reported as missing in action over Germany since April 29th. Details were sketchy at the time, but the official report indicated that the plane sustained damage from enemy antiaircraft fire while returning home. The last radio message from Walter's plane indicated the crew was bailing out. This occurred at about 2:05 p.m. in the vicinity of Zutphen, Netherlands. Attached to my grandmother's letter, was a list of the names of the other ten crew members with addresses of their next of kin. The Assistant Chief assured by grandmother that a continuing search was being made to locate the missing personnel.

"Of course, my grandmother, aunts and uncles launched a writing campaign so they would be kept up to date on the search progress. They received at least two correspondences between April and November 1944 that indicated there was no change in Walter Thomas' status.

"On November 7, 1944, a Red Cross telegram from a Walter Zeilmaker of the Netherlands was delivered to my grandmother in McRoberts, Kentucky. Although the telegram was typed in Dutch, at the very bottom there was a handwritten signature, Walter, very clearly written in my father's handwriting. A second message was received on January 10, 1945.

***

"In early May, 1945, Walter heard rumors that the war was over. He and two other Americans left the last safe house in hopes of reaching the Allies. On May 8, 1945, they located the 1st Canadian Army and were officially rejoined the occupation forces. They were flown to a British airbase the next morning and from there to Brussels and finally to Paris a few days later. From Paris, they went to Le Havre, France and from there they were shipped home.

"Walter landed in New York and immediately went to Camp Shanks, Mississippi where he was given a 90 days leave to go to New Orleans. On June 29, 1945, he married Pauline Prestia. Although his family knew he was back in the states, he did not go to see his mother or siblings until after he married. Once he and Pauline were married, they went to Dayton, Ohio to visit Walter's family.

"My father was a recovered alcoholic and when he died at age of 87 years from a heart condition he had been sober for over 37 years. However, there were a few years in the mid 1960s and early 1970s when my parents were separated. During that time, he stayed with his sisters in Ohio and Michigan. He returned to New Orleans, stopped drinking and he and my mother were reconciled.

"He was a maintenance supervisor at several elite hotels in the French Quarter in downtown New Orleans. When he retired from that job sometime in the early 1980s, he and my mother moved to Biloxi, Mississippi which is the home of my older sister, Paula April. They lived a happy life there until his death February 20, 2006.

"The week leading up to his death, my mother was in the hospital with pneumonia. I spent a week with him until February 17th so that I could visit with my mother. While I was there, we visited my mother in the hospital, when out to eat, and just had a chance to visit with each other. My younger sister, Valerie, relieved me on the 17th. The night before he died (February 20th), he ate one of his favorite meals - red beans with rice and ham and cornbread. Valerie left after dinner to stay the night with my mother in the hospital. After she left, he did the dishes, took a bath, put on his P.J.s and went to bed. He didn't wake up.

"My sister, Paula, found him the next morning still in bed. He was on his side and looked like he was just sleeping. Although Daddy had begun to have some heart trouble, he was robust until the end. Most people who met him thought he was still in his 70's and not a man of 87. His passing was peaceful.

"My father was not one of those men who shared 'war time' stories. In fact, I had to coax him to answer questions. I actually interviewed him on several occasions to get as much information as I could. I will tell you, however, that he always spoke highly of the Dutch people. He said they were courageous and he owed his life to them.

Tail-Gunner 2nd Lt. Edgar J. Powell.

"On April 29, 1944, we were selected to lead the Wing of 104 planes and the target was Berlin. Our crew was increased with a group navigator, a group bombardier and our squadron commander who was to fly in my co-pilot's seat.

"I was formation control officer, whose duty was to aid the leader in efficiently assembling the formation to conserve fuel and aid to maintain the proper formation during the flight. My position was in the tail-turret. I was issued an Aldis spot light for signaling as radio silence was to be maintained. We were escorted by our fighters, all equipped with external gas tanks to permit range sufficient to see us as near the target as possible. These tanks would be dropped when the P-47's and P-51's were engaged by German fighters.

"The Luftwaffe was waiting for us and soon every fighter was in a "Dog Fight." I had the best view as our fighters and their wing men tried to get on the tail of German fighters. The external tanks were dropped and we knew we wouldn't have their protection for long.

"Flak near Berlin was heavy and while on the bomb run, we received a direct hit to our number 2 engine and gas tank. The prop would not feather, causing maximum power and fuel consumption necessary with the other three engines at least until we had completed the bomb run.

"After dropping our bombs on the railroad yard, we left our formation in search of other damaged planes who would be limping back home at slower speed. Fortunately we located several B-17's who normally flew about twenty miles per hour slower than our B-24's, and we formed a formation to provide better fire power against the fighters which we knew loved to pick on wounded planes. We were harassed constantly, and many of the planes in our formation were shot down.

""My turret suddenly went dead and I called one of our waist gunners for help. He took one look and said: "No wonder it's dead. A shell has penetrated the oil tank and all the oil is gone. You're lucky the shell didn't explode or you'd be dead." I suddenly realized a guy could get killed up here.

"Soon a second engine quit and we began to worry about remaining fuel to make it back. We were ordered to throw everything overboard which wasn't nailed down, and this included the .50 calibre waist guns and most of our belts of ammunition. When the third engine stopped, we began discussing the best plan for when the last engine would quit. We were still 175 miles from England and if we tried to glide across the coast for ditching in the North Sea, we would probably be shot out of the sky by German coastal batteries. Besides, ditching is a matter of last resort in a B-24 which wouldn't float even if successfully ditched, which was unlikely with four engines out. We elected to turn south towards Spain and the Pyrenees—the recommended escape route.

"We were now all lone in the sky and six German fighters were attacking. When the last engine stopped, the pilot pushed the bail-out alarm. The plane was flying level at 17,000 feet and we were between cloud layers. The lower layer was estimated at 3,000 feet. I was determined not to open my chute until I had fallen through the lower clouds to avoid being shot at by the fighters, or worse have them fly close enough to cause the air to spill from the chute.

"A minute and a half after leaving the plane I fell through the clouds to find the earth quite near and approaching at 120 miles per hour. I pulled the ripcord and a second or two later hit a grove of pine trees. These trees saved my life as the chute caught in the tops, breaking my fall. I climbed down and started running only to discover I was in my bare feet. The sudden change of speed when my chute opened, from 120 to 12 miles per hour, removed my flying boots, shoes and socks. Since we carried a spare pair of shoes for just such an emergency, I ran back to the trees and retrieved my shoes. Running a distance again, I stopped, put on my shoes and opened my escape kit. I found sign posts at an intersection and copied the sign information in a small note book I carried. This almost cost me my life as the Germans later claimed these notes branded me as a spy. My ears were still ringing from the fast descend, but I could hear dogs of a search party in the woods on both sides of the road. I decided the safest route was down the road and away from this area as quickly as possible.

"I might have made it except one of the German soldiers decided to cross the road to the woods on the other side. He pulled his Luger and shouted, "Halt halten," and I became a prisoner of war. Enroute to the local jail in the town of Apeldoorn, I saw the remains of my plane which must have been crippled and knocked down seconds after we jumped.

"The next day, I was taken to a jail in Amsterdam where I met several others of my crew. Three days later we were on a train to Frankfurt and a German interrogation center. I was placed in solitary confinement for eight days, being questioned each day. The officer had a list of our crew on that fateful day, something he could only have obtained directly from England. His concern was six officers on board, and he was sure we were using a new technique, possibly radar, for bombing through cloud cover. He had my notebook and accused me of being a spy, threatening to have me shot every day. He finally realized we were not using radar and gave up on me. I was soon on a train along with about a hundred others and moved to Stalag Luft III at Sagan, about a hundred miles southeast of Berlin.

***

Acknowledgements:
Bob Salzarulo, son of Major Robert L. Salzarulo, command pilot,
Kythy Kilgore, daughter of S/Sgt. Walter T. Kilgore, right waist-gunner
Judith, Linda and Gary, children of 2Lt. Edward Verbosky, bombardier
Ward Powell, son of 2nd Lt. Edgar J. Powell, tail-gunner

ABOUT THE AUTHOR

John Meurs was born in Nijmegen in the Netherlands in 1935. When he was a nine-year-old
schoolboy living in the Nazi-occupied village
of Apeldoorn, a B-17 crashed behind his house.
The date was November 26, 1944. He never
forgot it.

After primary and secondary school Meurs
attended the State College of Tropical Agriculture in Deventer (Holland). Why "tropical?"
Because his parents had spent a long time in
the Dutch East Indies, what is now called Indonesia, and had planted a desire to go and live
in the tropics.

Instead of becoming a planter on one of
the big plantations in Indonesia after having
finished his studies, Meurs went to Cameroun
in West Africa to work for a Dutch internation-

John Meurs

al trading house with subsidiaries all over the African west coast. There he had
all the things he could not get at that time in Holland: a large apartment, an interesting job, and quite a bit of money in his pocket. He witnessed the transition of
the French colony Cameroun into the independent République du Cameroun—a
very interesting period.

After four years in Cameroun, Meurs spent another five years in Zaire, also
in West Africa, and also in the importing-exporting business. Then he left Africa
to settle again in Europe. There he joined the giant electronic company Philips
in 1967 and worked at their headquarters in Eindhoven (Holland). He had some
trouble, after his wild African years, adapting himself to the regular life in Holland.

In 1968 Meurs met his future wife Carien, who had grown up about ten miles
from his hometown. She's the sister of one of his Dutch colleagues in Zaire.

Early 1970 Meurs joined the American GTE and worked in the export department of their European HQ in Geneva, Switzerland. He and Carien married
on May 5, 1970—Liberation Day in Holland. It is celebrated each year to mark
the end of the Nazi occupation during World War II.

In 1979 the Meurs left Geneva and moved to Rüti, a small town in the Ger-
man-speaking part of the country where they live today.

Both John and Carien are now retired.

Note: Meurs uses both terms Holland and Netherlands in his book. This is because
the country is officially called the Kingdom of the Netherlands of which the provinces
of North and South Holland are only a small part, but as they were historically very
important. Foreigners (and almost all the Dutch) call the whole country Holland.

Ordering Information

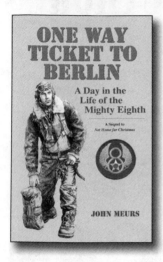

ONE WAY TICKET TO BERLIN

A Day in the Life of the Mighty Eighth

A Sequel to *Not Home for Christmas*

by John Meurs

Paperback • 848 pages • $25.00

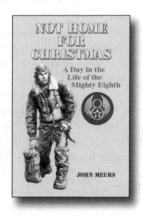
